Street by Street

WEST YORKSHIRE

PLUS BARNSLEY, LITTLEBOROUGH, MILNROW, PENISTONE, SHAW, SKIPTON, TADCASTER

Enlarged Areas Bradford, Halifax, Huddersfield, Keighley, Leeds, Wakefield

2nd edition January 2003

© Automobile Association Developments Limited 2003

Ordnance Survey® This product includes map data licensed from Ordnance Survey® with the permission of the Controller of Her Majesty's Stationery Office. © Crown copyright 2003. All rights reserved. Licence No: 399221.

Published by AA Publishing (a trading name of Automobile Association Developments Limited, whose registered office is Millstream, Maidenhead Road, Windsor, Berkshire SL4 5GD. Registered number 1878835).

The Post Office is a registered trademark of Post Office Ltd. in the UK and other countries.

Schools address data provided by Education Direct.

One-way street data provided by:

Tele Atlas © Tele Atlas N.V.

Mapping produced by the Cartographic Department of The Automobile Association. A01539

A CIP Catalogue record for this book is available from the British Library.

Printed by G. Canale & C. S.P.A., Torino, Italy.

Ref: MX016z

Key to map pages	ii-iii
Key to map symbols	iv-1
Enlarged scale pages	2-15
Street by Street	16-271
Index – towns & villages	272-273
Index – streets	274-339
Index – featured places	339-347

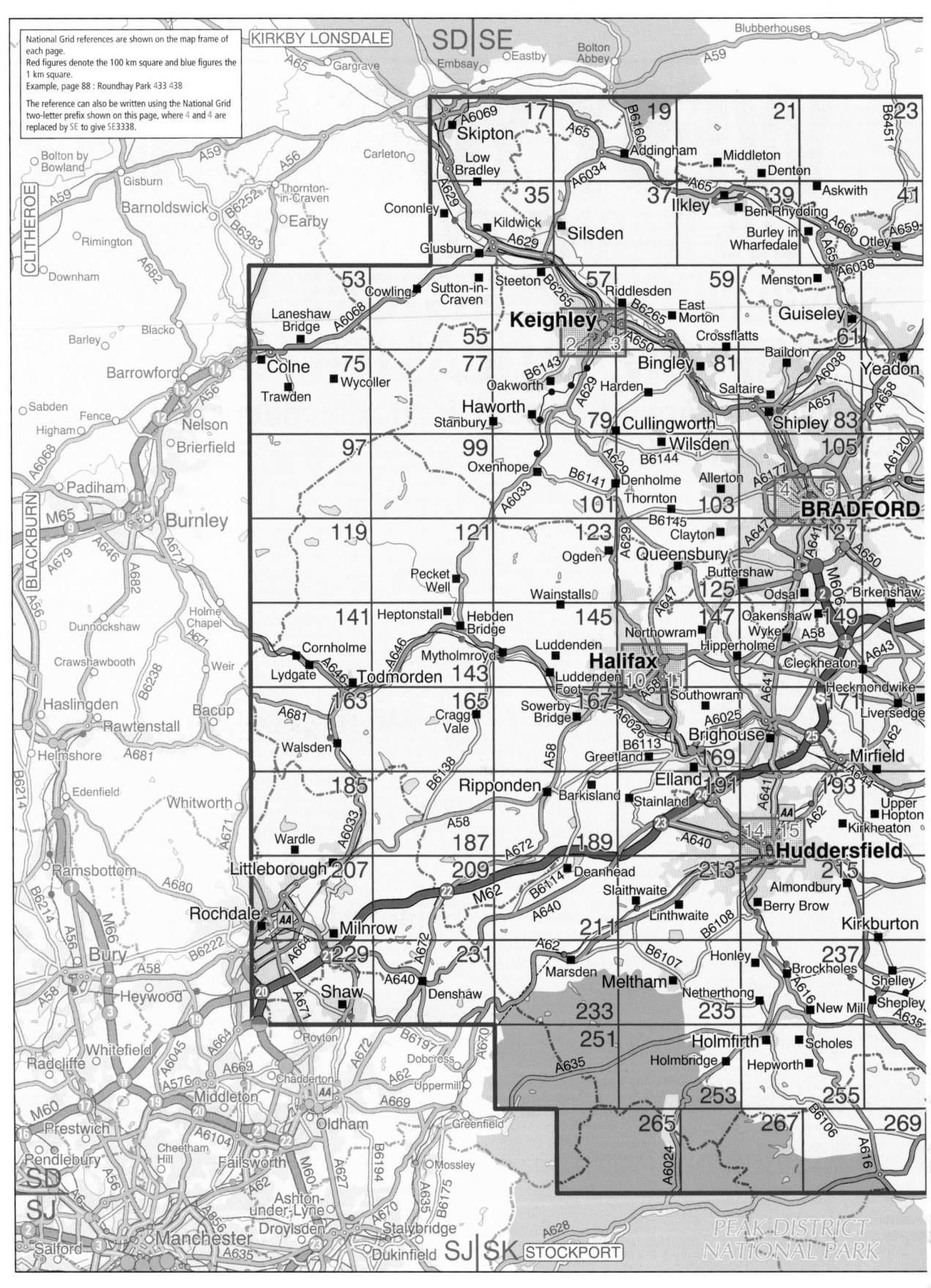

ii

National Grid references are shown on the map frame of each page.
Red figures denote the 100 km square and blue figures the 1 km square.
Example, page 88 : Roundhay Park 433 438

The reference can also be written using the National Grid two-letter prefix shown on this page, where 4 and 4 are replaced by SE to give SE3338.

KIRKBY LONSDALE

SD | SE

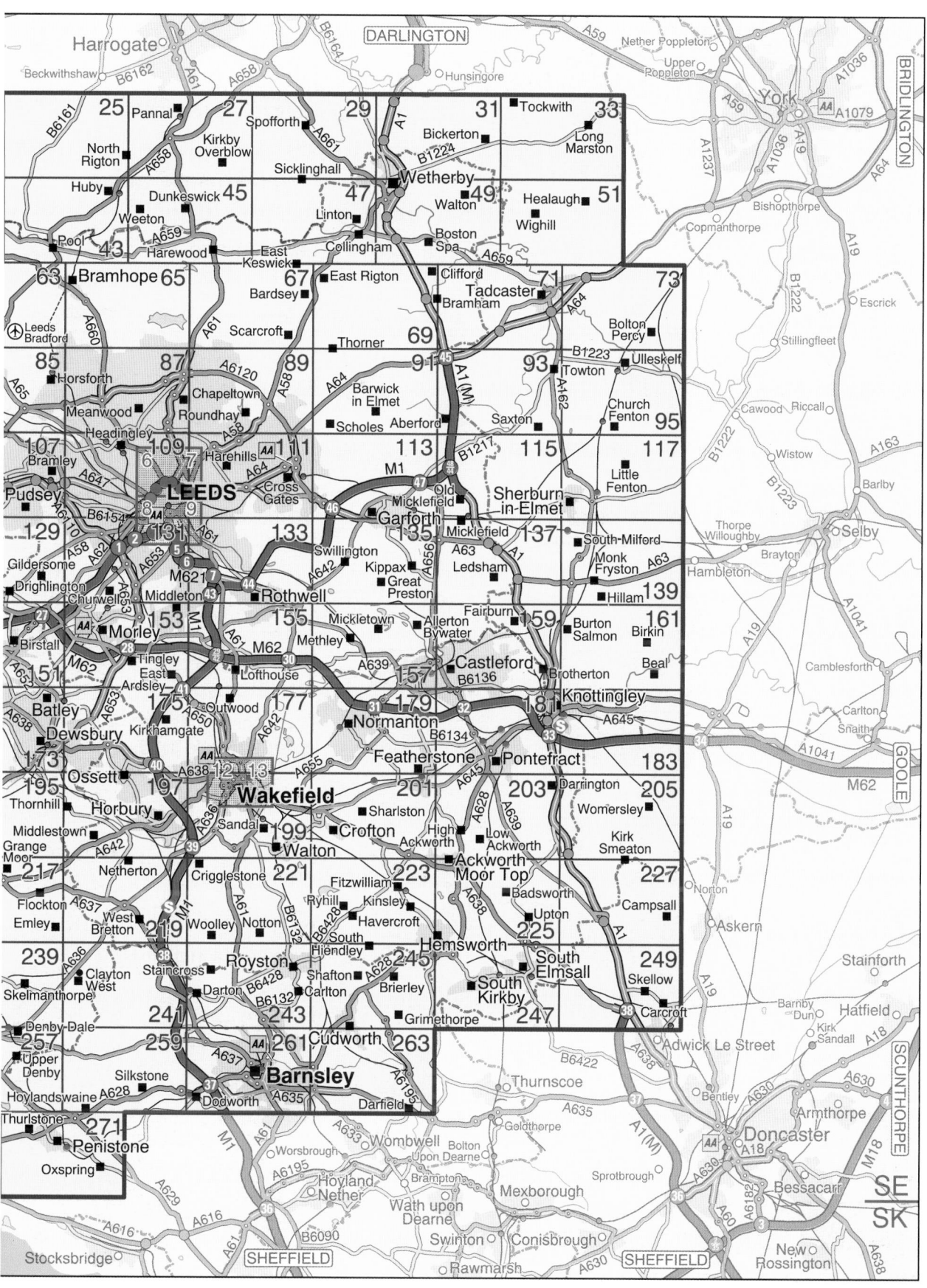

3.6 inches to 1 mile

iv

Junction 9	Motorway & junction		⊖	Underground station
Services	Motorway service area		⊖	Light railway & station
	Primary road single/dual carriageway		++++++++	Preserved private railway
Services	Primary road service area		LC	Level crossing
	A road single/dual carriageway		•—•—•—•	Tramway
	B road single/dual carriageway		---------	Ferry route
	Other road single/dual carriageway		....	Airport runway
	Minor/private road, access may be restricted		-·-·-·-	County administrative boundary
←— ←—	One-way street		▾▾▾▾▾▾	Mounds
	Pedestrian area		93	Page continuation 1:17,500
	Track or footpath		7	Page continuation to enlarged scale 1:10,000
	Road under construction			River/canal, lake, pier
	Road tunnel			Aqueduct, lock, weir
AA	AA Service Centre		465 ▲ Winter Hill	Peak (with height in metres)
P	Parking			Beach
P+	Park & Ride			Woodland
	Bus/coach station			Park
	Railway & main railway station			Cemetery
	Railway & minor railway station			Built-up area

	Featured building			Abbey, cathedral or priory
	City wall			Castle
A&E	Hospital with 24-hour A&E department			Historic house or building
PO	Post Office		Wakehurst Place NT	National Trust property
	Public library			Museum or art gallery
i	Tourist Information Centre			Roman antiquity
	Petrol station Major suppliers only			Ancient site, battlefield or monument
†	Church/chapel			Industrial interest
	Public toilets			Garden
	Toilet with disabled facilities			Arboretum
PH	Public house AA recommended			Farm or animal centre
	Restaurant AA inspected			Zoological or wildlife collection
	Theatre or performing arts centre			Bird collection
	Cinema			Nature reserve
	Golf course			Visitor or heritage centre
▲	Camping AA inspected			Country park
	Caravan site AA inspected			Cave
	Camping & caravan site AA inspected			Windmill
	Theme park			Distillery, brewery or vineyard

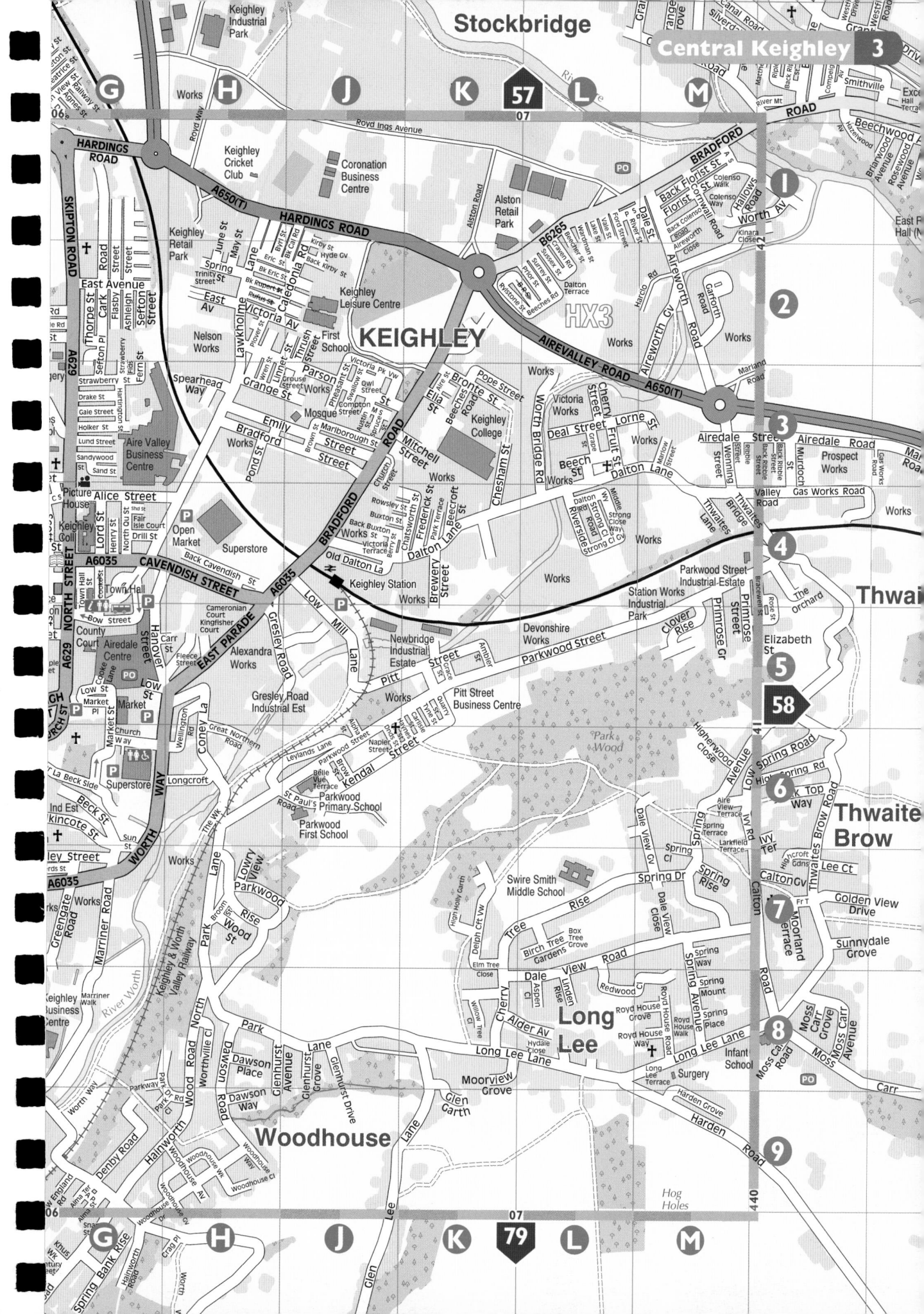

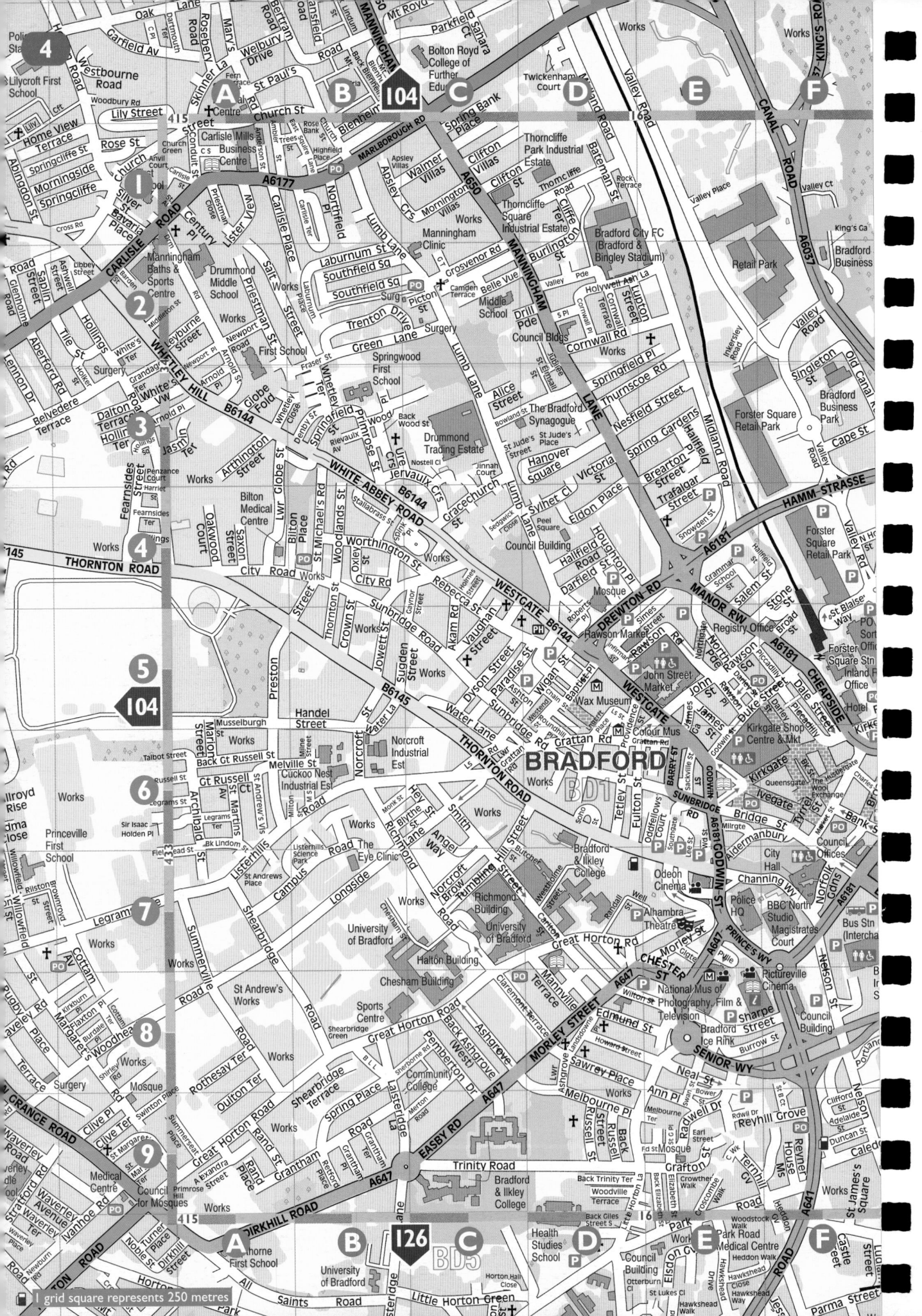

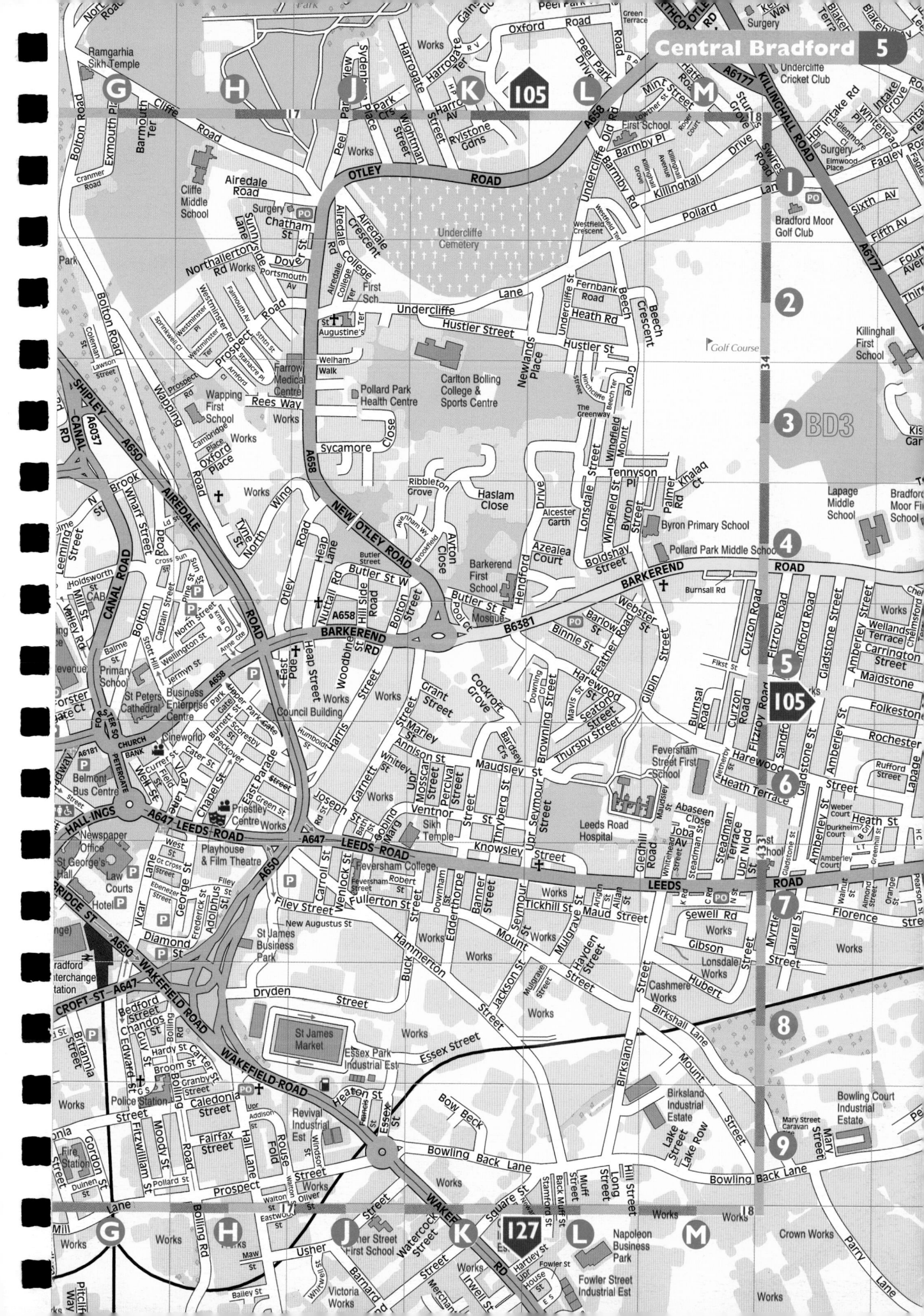

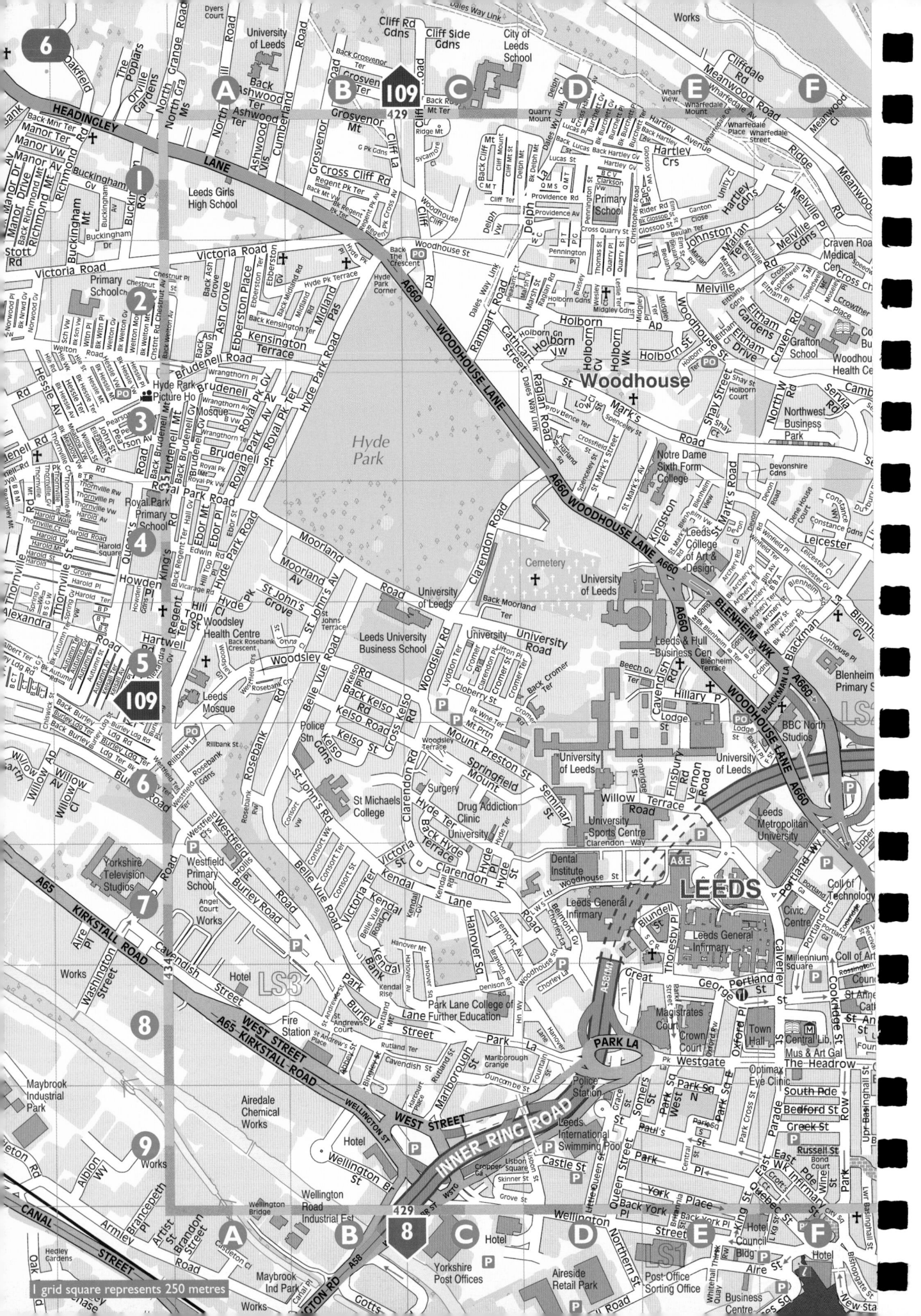

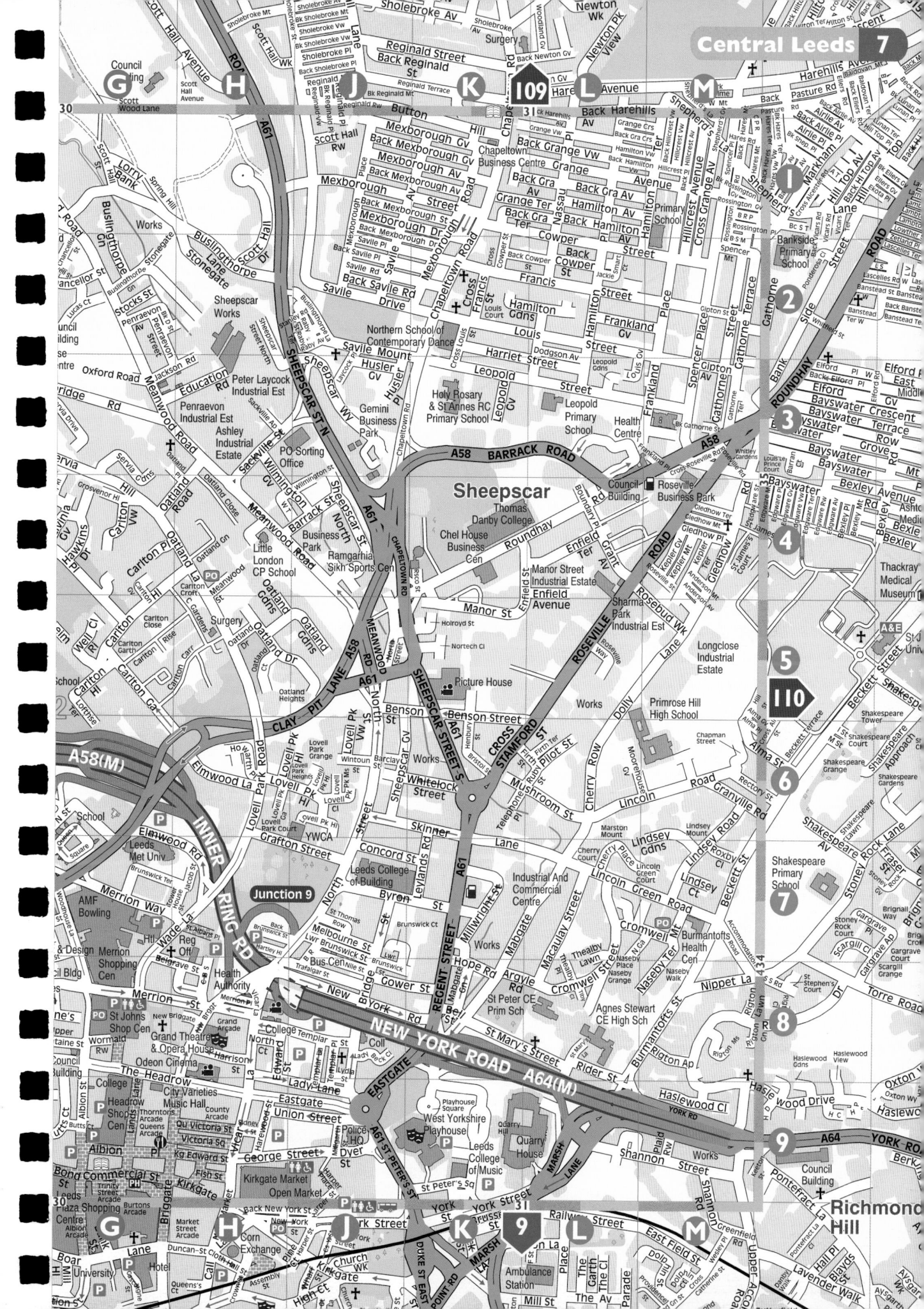

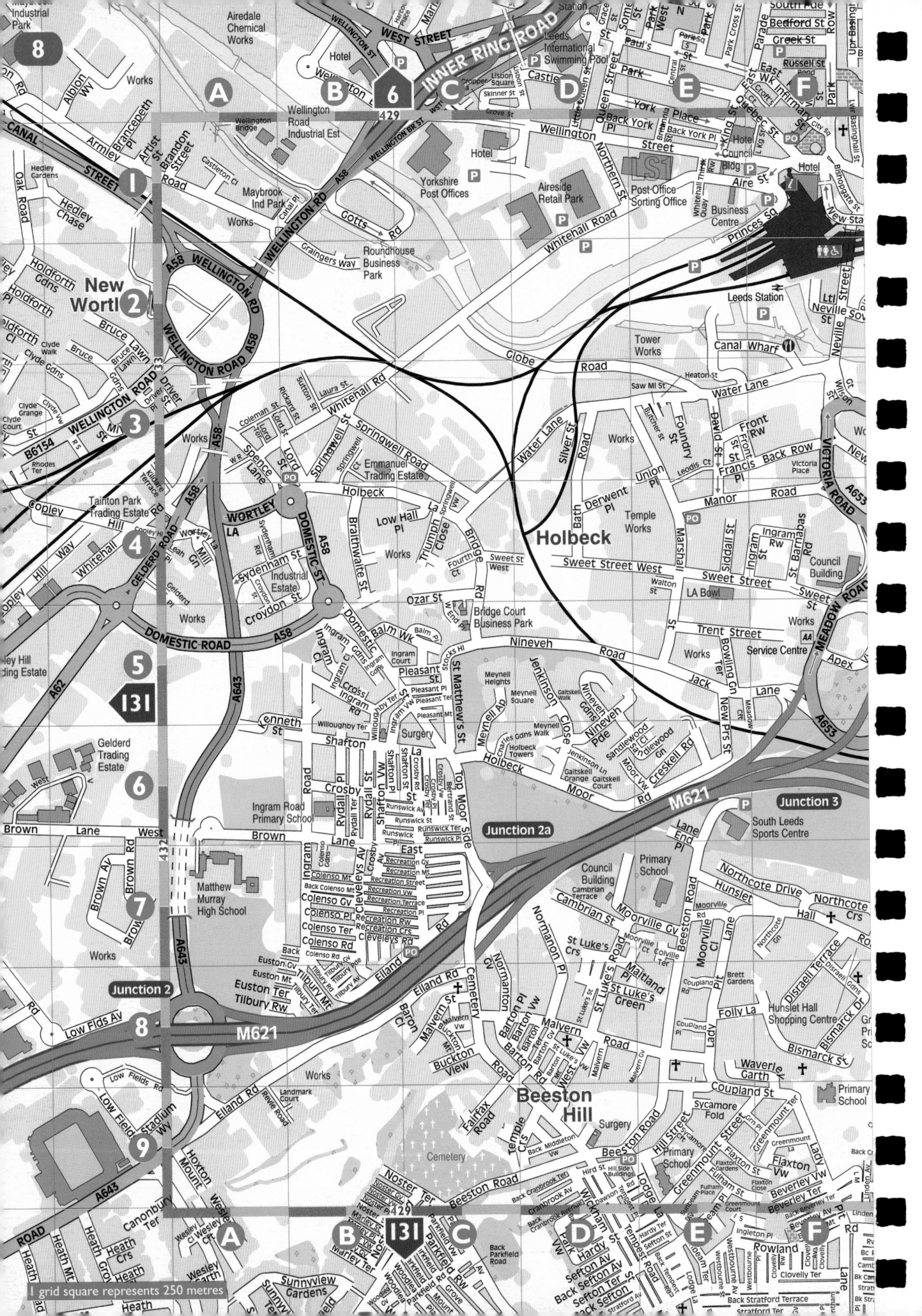

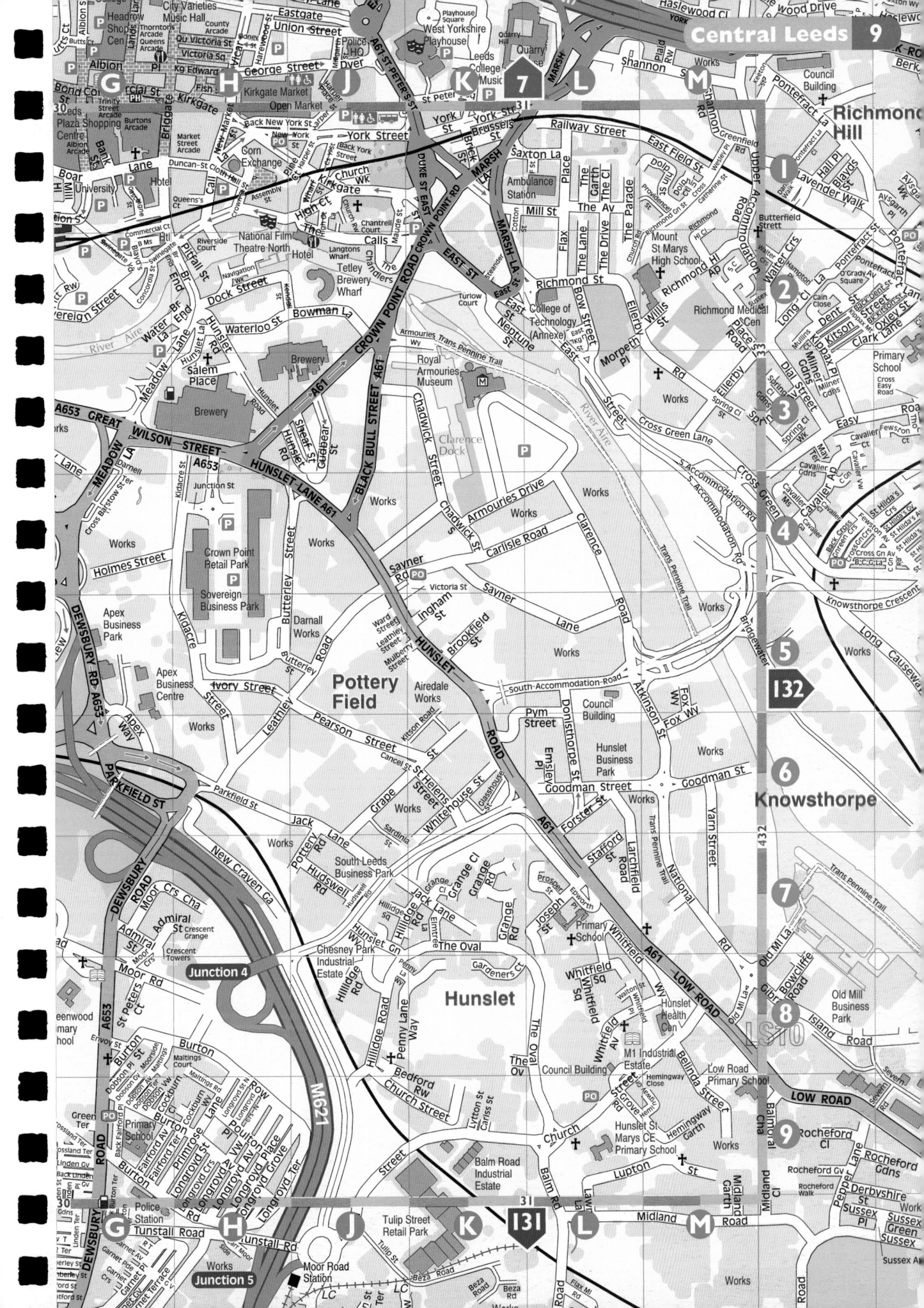

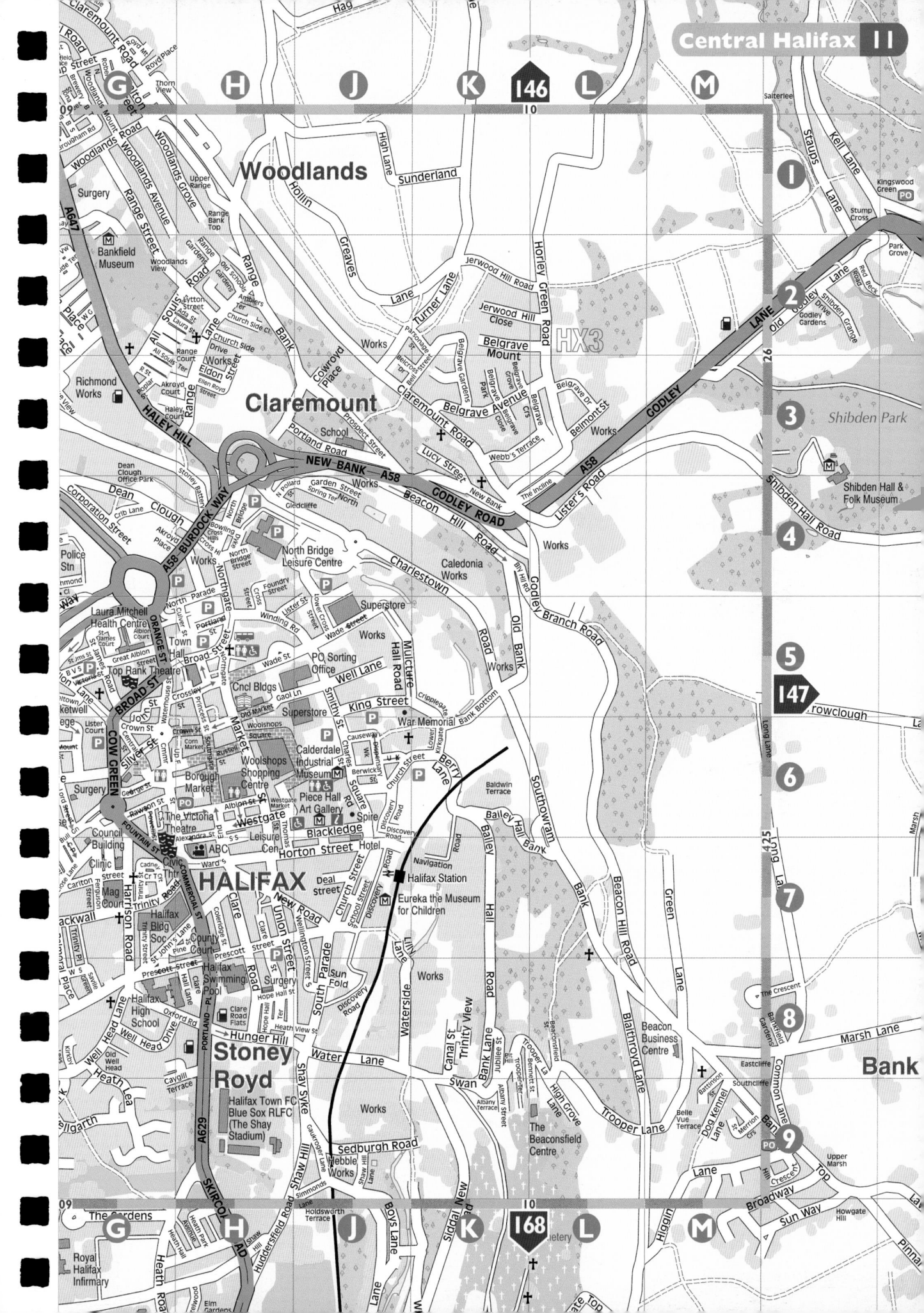

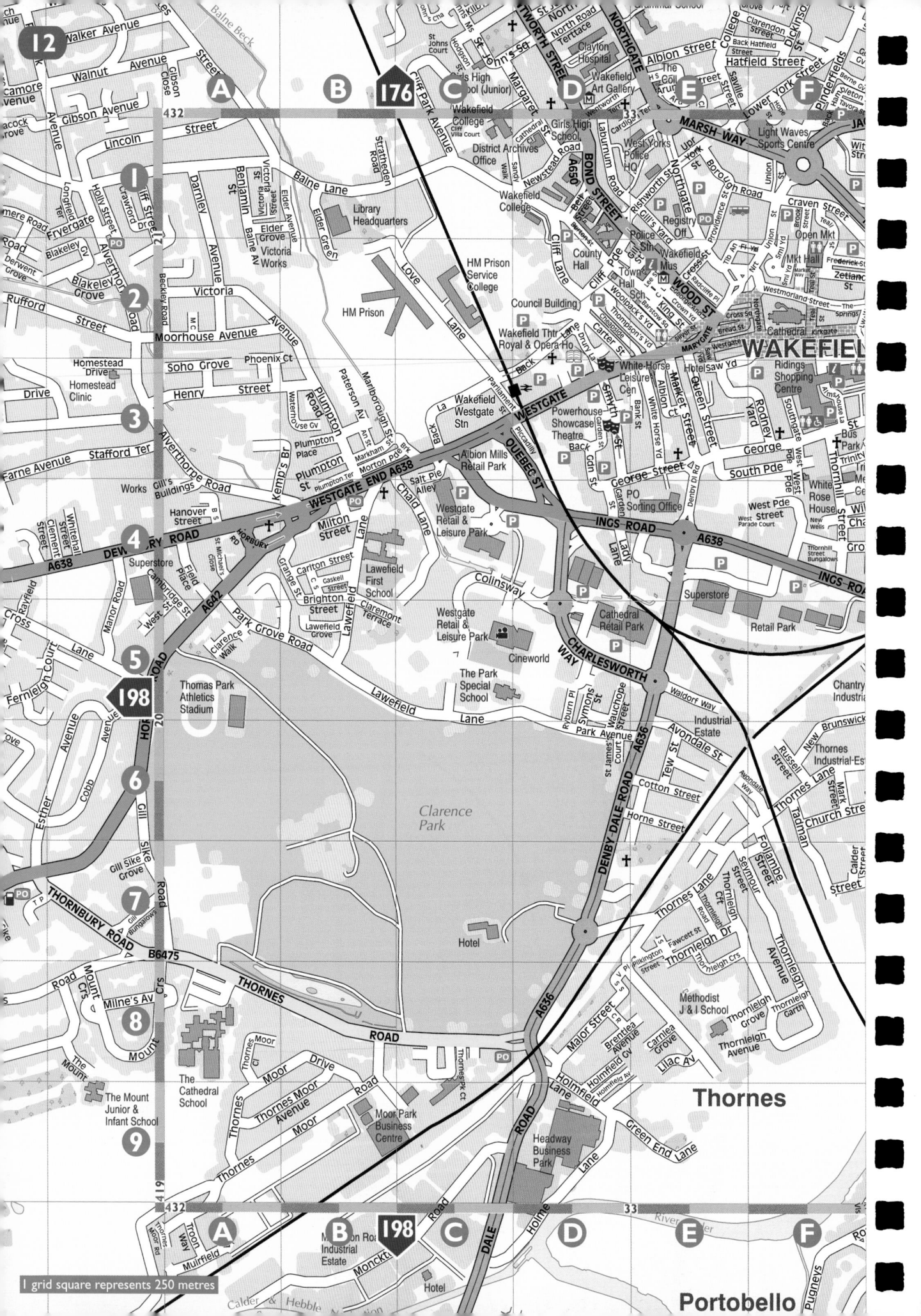

I grid square represents 250 metres

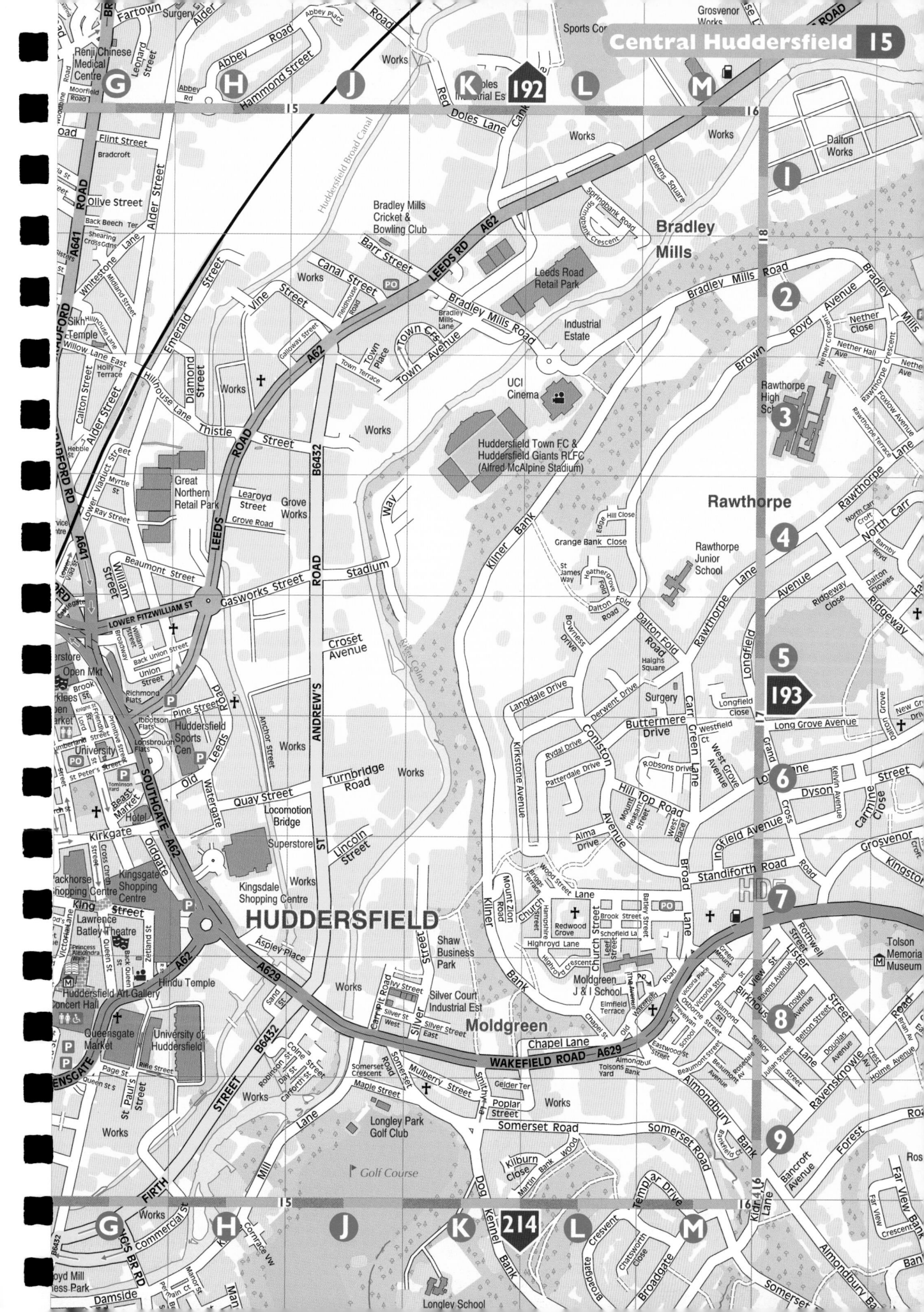

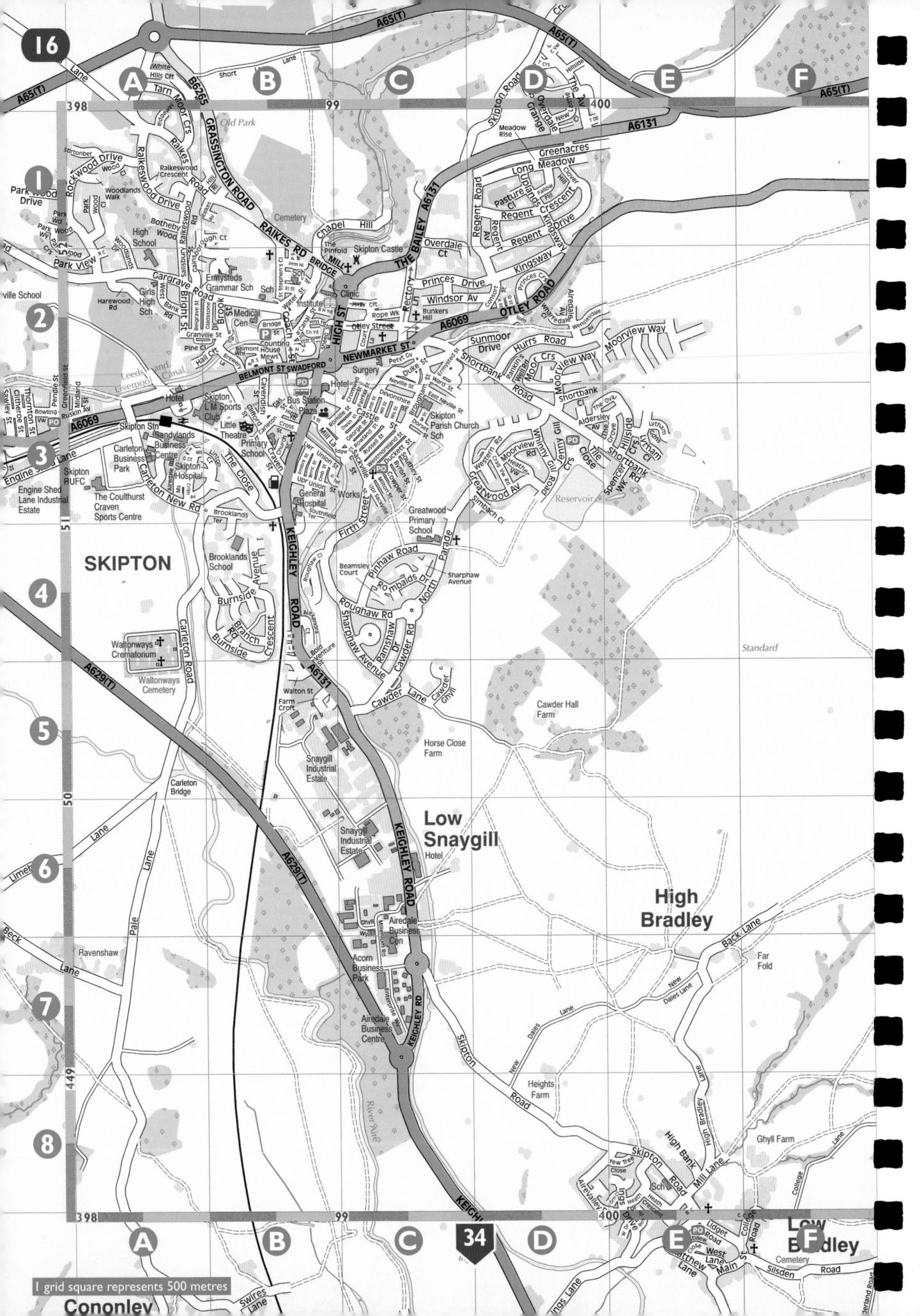

SKIPTON

Low
Snaygill

High
Bradley

1 grid square represents 500 metres

Cononley

Low
Bradley

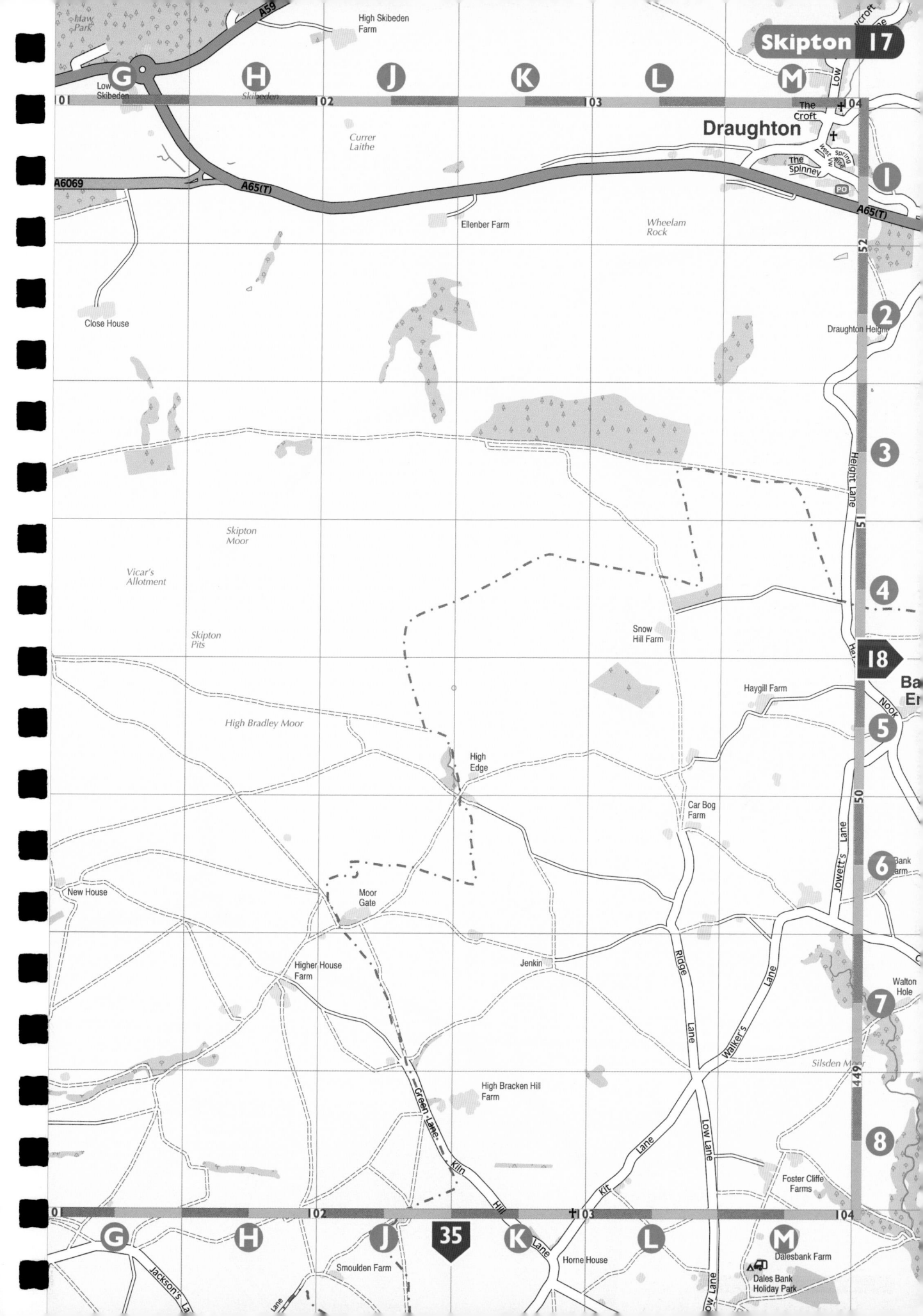

Haw Park

High Skibeden Farm

A59

G
H
J
K
L
M

Low Skibeden
01
Skibeden
02
03
04

Draughton

The Croft

Currer Laithe

A6069
A65(T)
A65(T)

The Spinney

PO

1

Ellenber Farm

Wheelam Rock

Close House

Draughton Height

2

52

3

Height Lane

51

Skipton Moor

Vicar's Allotment

4

Snow Hill Farm

18

Skipton Pits

Haygill Farm

Ba En

High Bradley Moor

5

High Edge

Car Bog Farm

Noo

6

Bank arm

50

New House

Moor Gate

Jenkin

Jowett's Lane

Walton Hole

7

Higher House Farm

Ridge Lane

Walker's Lane

Silsden Moor

4449

High Bracken Hill Farm

Low Lane

8

Green Lane

Kiln Hill Lane

Kit Lane

Foster Cliffe Farms

0
01
02
35
03
04

G
H
J
K
L
M

Jackson's La
Smoulden Farm
Horne House
Dales Bank Holiday Park
Dalesbank Farm
Low Lane

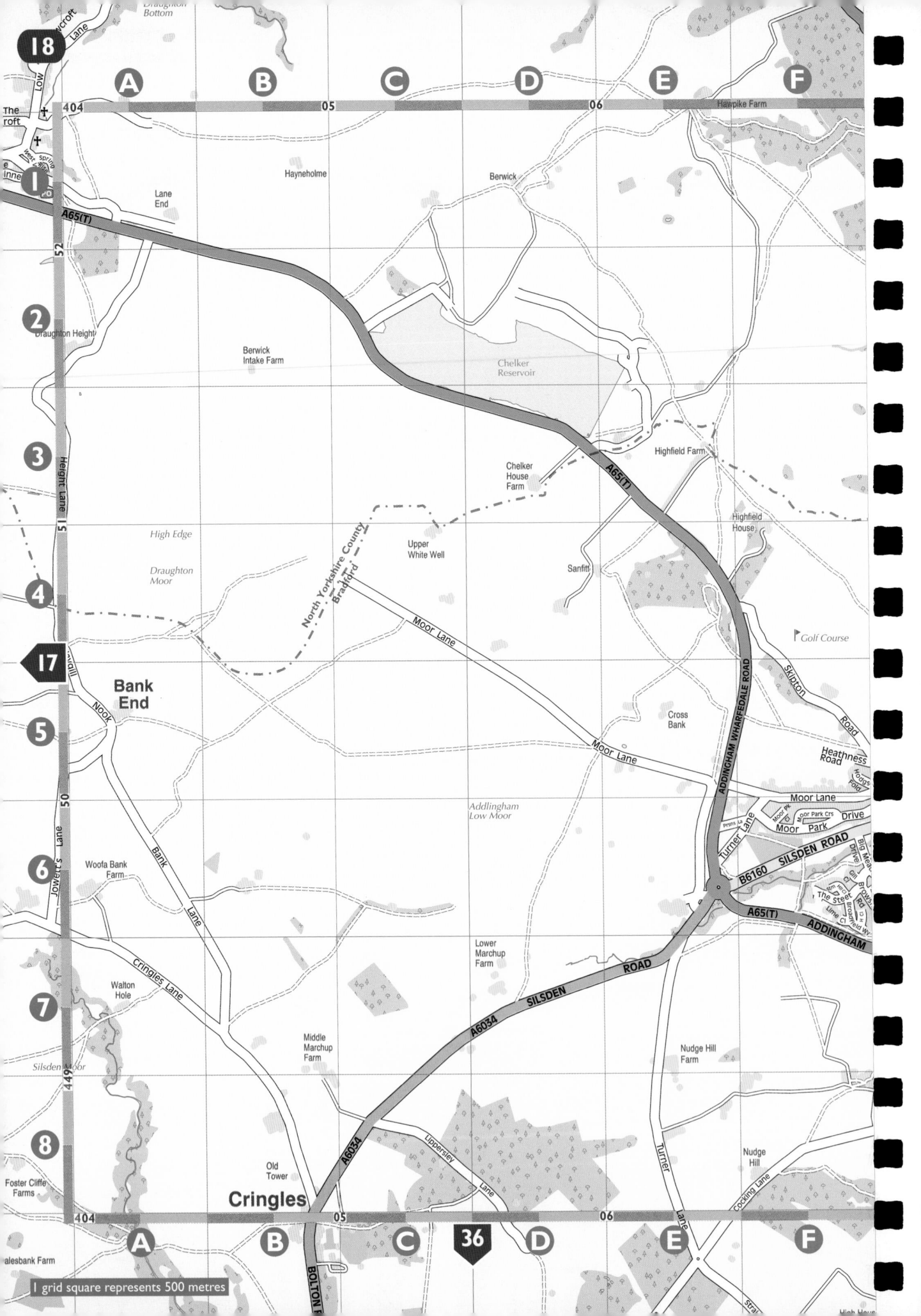

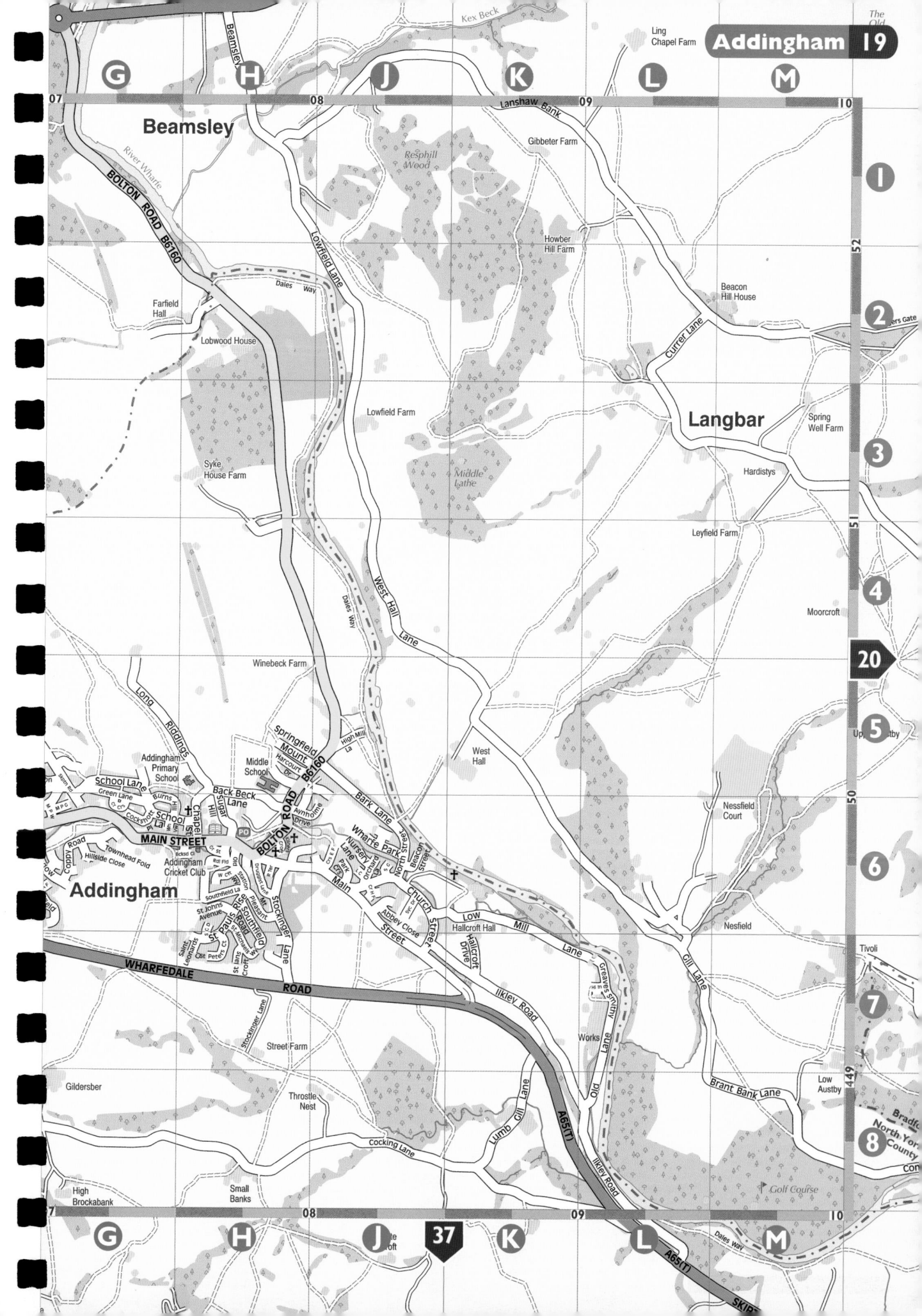

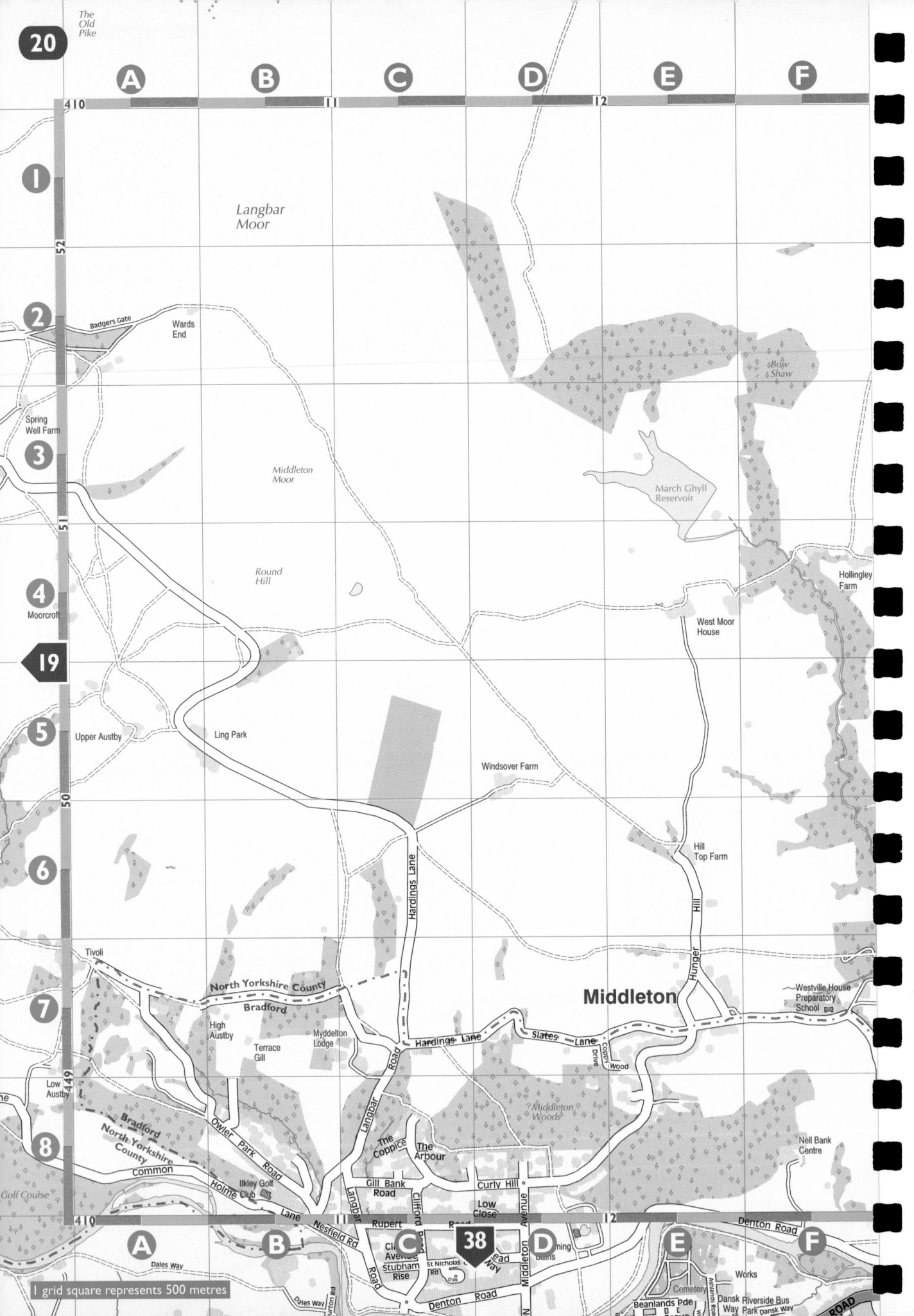

410   11   12

A   B   C   D   E   F

I

52

2   Badgers Gate   Wards End

Langbar Moor

Bow Shaw

Spring Well Farm

3   Middleton Moor

March Ghyll Reservoir

51

Round Hill

4   Moorcroft

West Moor House   Hollingley Farm

19

5   Upper Austby   Ling Park

50   Windsover Farm

6   Hill Top Farm

Tivoli

North Yorkshire County
Bradford

7   High Austby   Myddelton Lodge   Hardings Lane   Slates Lane   Middleton   Westville House Preparatory School

Terrace Gill   Copse Wood

449   Low Austby   Middleton Woods   Nell Bank Centre

Bradford North Yorkshire County Common

8   Owler Park Road   The Coppice   The Arbour

Holme Lane   Ilkley Golf Club   Gill Bank Road   Curly Hill   Low Close

Golf Course

410   11   12

A   B   C   38   D   E   F

Langbar Road   Nesfield Rd   Rupert   Clifford Road   Middleton Avenue   Denton Road

Stubham Rise   St Nicholas Rd   Head Way   Denton Road

Dales Way   Burton Rd   Dales Way   Beanlands Pde   Cemetery   Works   Dansk Way   Riverside Bus Park   Dansk Way   ROAD

G　H　J　K　L　M

13　14　15　16

I

52

2

3

51

4

22

5

50

6

7

449

8

Denton
Moor

Hollingley
Intake

High Denton
Farm

Moorside Farm

Yarnett House
Farm

Smithy
Lane

Dunkirk

Hathenshaw
Farm

Carrow
Bank

Willow
Hill Farm

Stubbs
Wood

Bow Beck

Denton Road

Hole House
Beck

Smithy Lane

Hundwith Beck

Quarry
House Farm

West
Park
Wood

Beck
Foot Farm

Carter's Lane

Denton

†

Denton Park

Whitbeck
Manor

13　14　15　16

G　H　J　K　L　M

Wharfedale

39

West Lane

Denton Road

Low Park Road

Carr

22

416   17   18

Timble

A   B   C   D   E   F

1

52

2

3

51

4

21

5

50

6

7

449

8

416   17   40   18

A   B   C   D   E   F

Timble Gill Beck

Shaw Hall

Low Snowden

Askwith Moor Road

Snowden Crags

Carr Farm

Askwith
Moor

Snowden
Carr

Snowden Carr Road

Dob
Park

Weston Moor Road

Weston
Moor

Brick
House
Farm

Moor Lane

Quarry
House Farm

Moorside Lane

Hobb Nook Lane

Scales
House Farm

Moorside Farm

Moor
Plantation

Whin
Castle Farm

Hall Lane

East Beck

Askwith Lane

Town
Head

Grassgarth Farm

Lane Head
Farm

Whitbeck
Manor

West Lane

Askwith CP
School

E Beck Court

Covey Hall
Farm

Askwith

1 grid square represents 500 metres

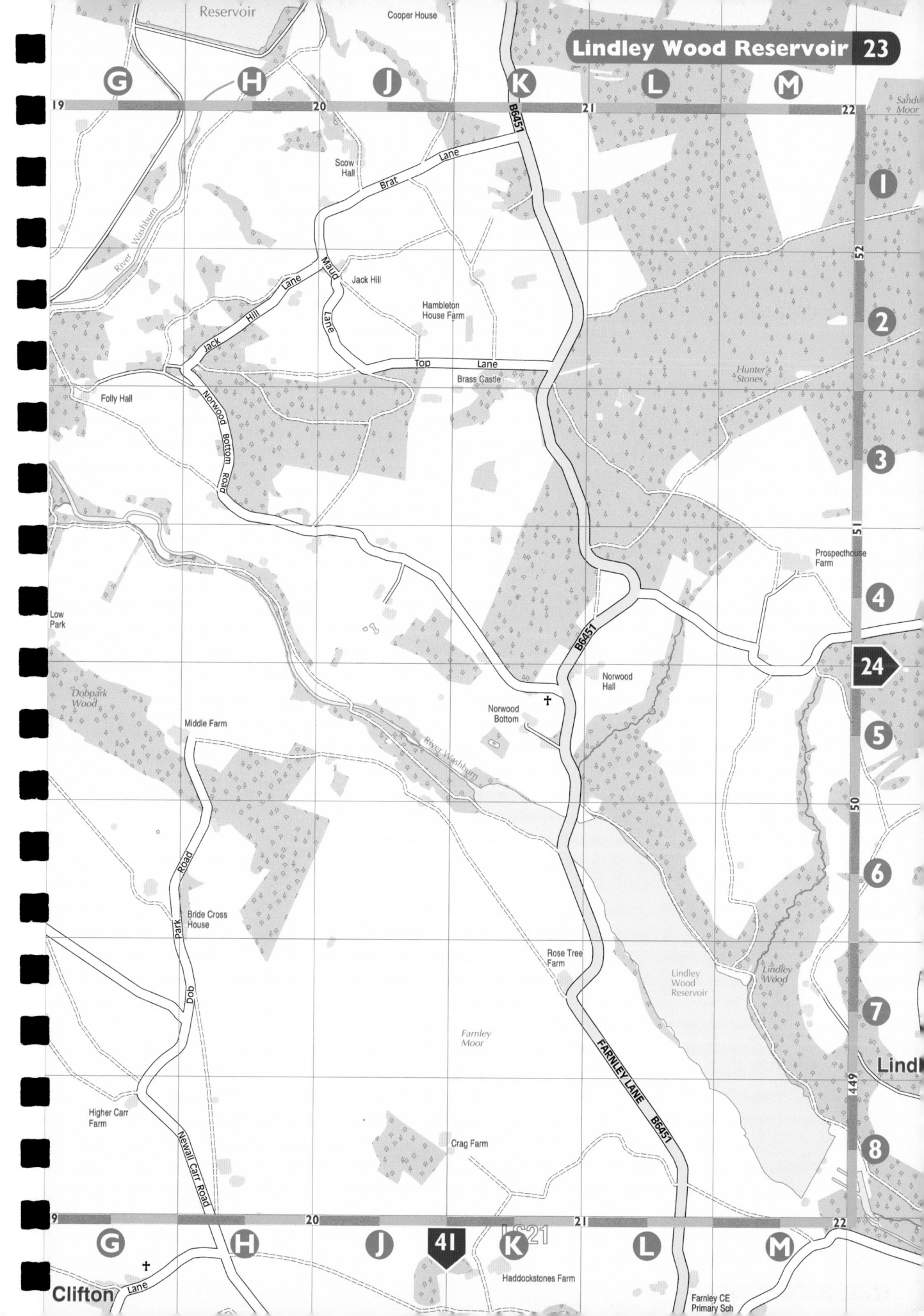

G H J K L M

19 20 21 22

I

2

3

4

24

5

6

7

8

52

51

50

449

Reservoir

Cooper House

B6451

Scow Hall

Brat Lane

Jack Hill

Maud Lane

Jack Hill Lane

Hambleton House Farm

Top Lane

Brass Castle

Hunter's Stones

Folly Hall

Norwood Bottom Road

Low Park

Prospecthouse Farm

Norwood Hall

Norwood Bottom

River Washburn

River Washburn

Dobpark Wood

Middle Farm

Park Road

Bride Cross House

Dob

Rose Tree Farm

Lindley Wood Reservoir

Lindley Wood

Lind

Farnley Moor

FARNLEY LANE B6451

Higher Carr Farm

Newall Carr Road

Crag Farm

Haddockstones Farm

Clifton

Lane

LS21

Farnley CE Primary Sch

G H J 41 K L M

9 20 21 22

Sandy Moor

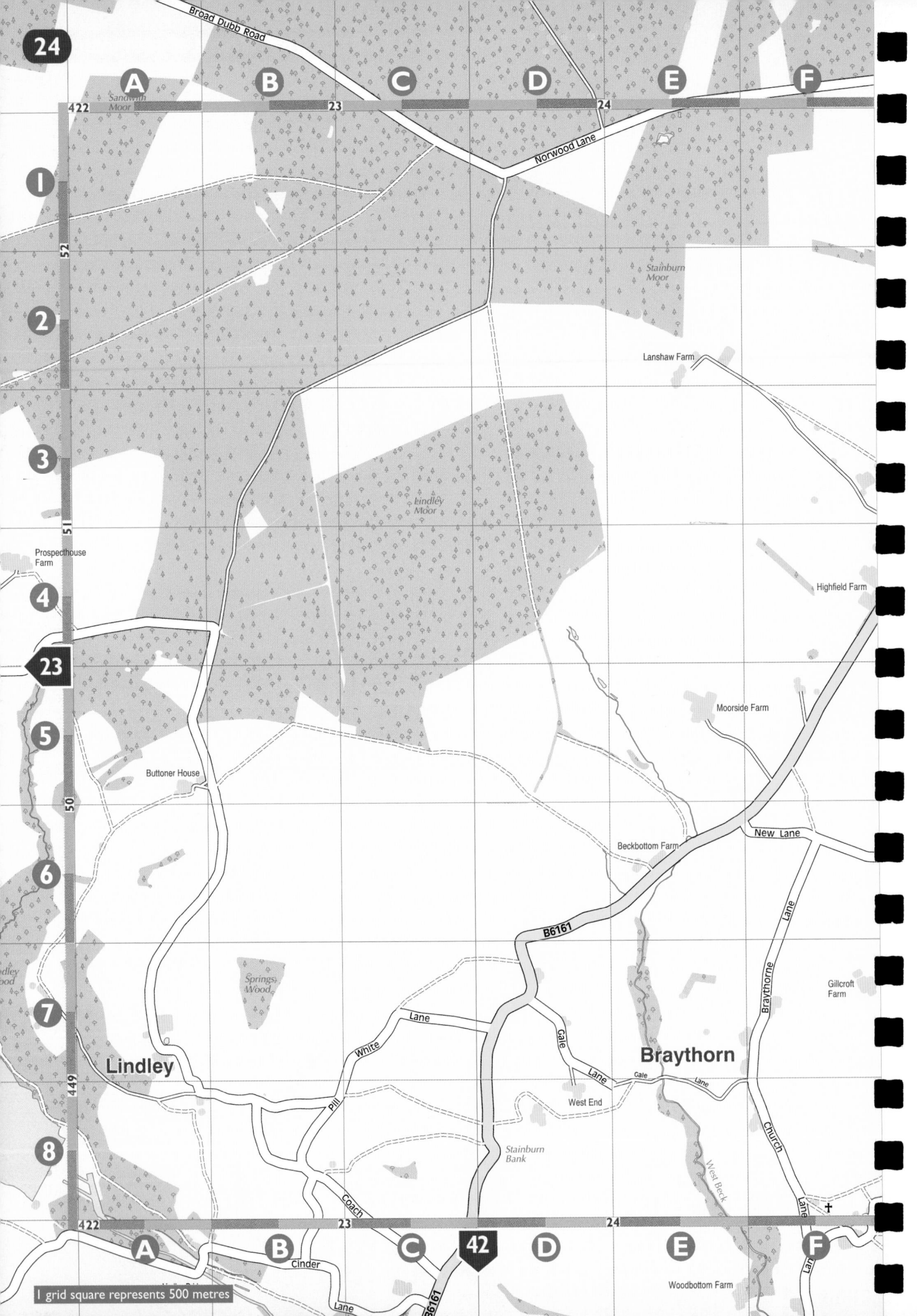

A   B   C   D   E   F

422
Broad Dubb Road
23
24

Sandwith Moor

Norwood Lane

I
52

2

Stainburn Moor

Lanshaw Farm

3
51

Prospecthouse Farm

Lindley Moor

Highfield Farm

4

23

Moorside Farm

5
50

Buttoner House

Beckbottom Farm   New Lane

6

Braythorne Lane

dley Wood

Springs Wood

B6161

Gillcroft Farm

7
449

White   Lane

Lindley

Gale   Lane

Braythorn

Gale   Lane

Pill

West End

Church Lane

8

Stainburn Bank

West Beck

422
Coach
23
24
†

A   B   C   42   D   E   F

Cinder   Lane

B6161

Woodbottom Farm

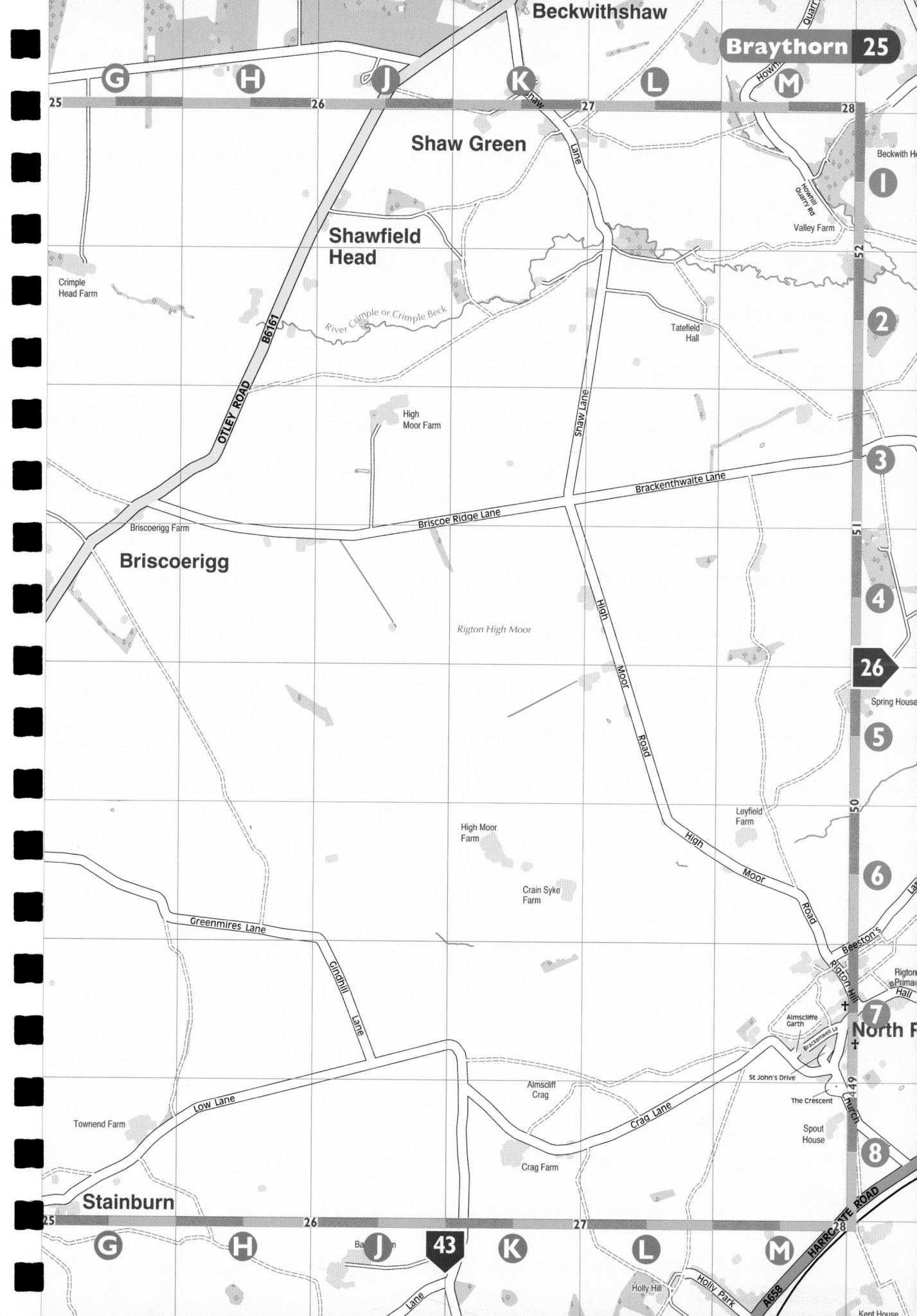

Beckwithshaw

Shaw Green

Shawfield
Head

Crimple
Head Farm

River Crimple or Crimple Beck

High
Moor Farm

Briscoerigg Farm

Briscoerigg

Briscoe Ridge Lane

Brackenthwaite Lane

Tatefield
Hall

Rigton High Moor

High Moor
Farm

Crain Syke
Farm

Greenmires Lane

Leyfield
Farm

Townend Farm

Low Lane

Almscliff
Crag

Crag Lane

Crag Farm

Stainburn

Holly Hill

Holly Park

Beckwith He

Valley Farm

Spring House

Rigton
Prima
Hall

Almscliffe
Garth

North F

St John's Drive

The Crescent

Spout
House

Kent House

OTLEY ROAD

B6161

Shaw Lane

High Moor Road

Gindhill Lane

Rigton Hill

Beeston's

Brackenwell La

Church

HARROGATE ROAD

A658

G H J K L M

I

26

25 26 27 28

52

51

50

49

1 2 3 4 5 6 7 8

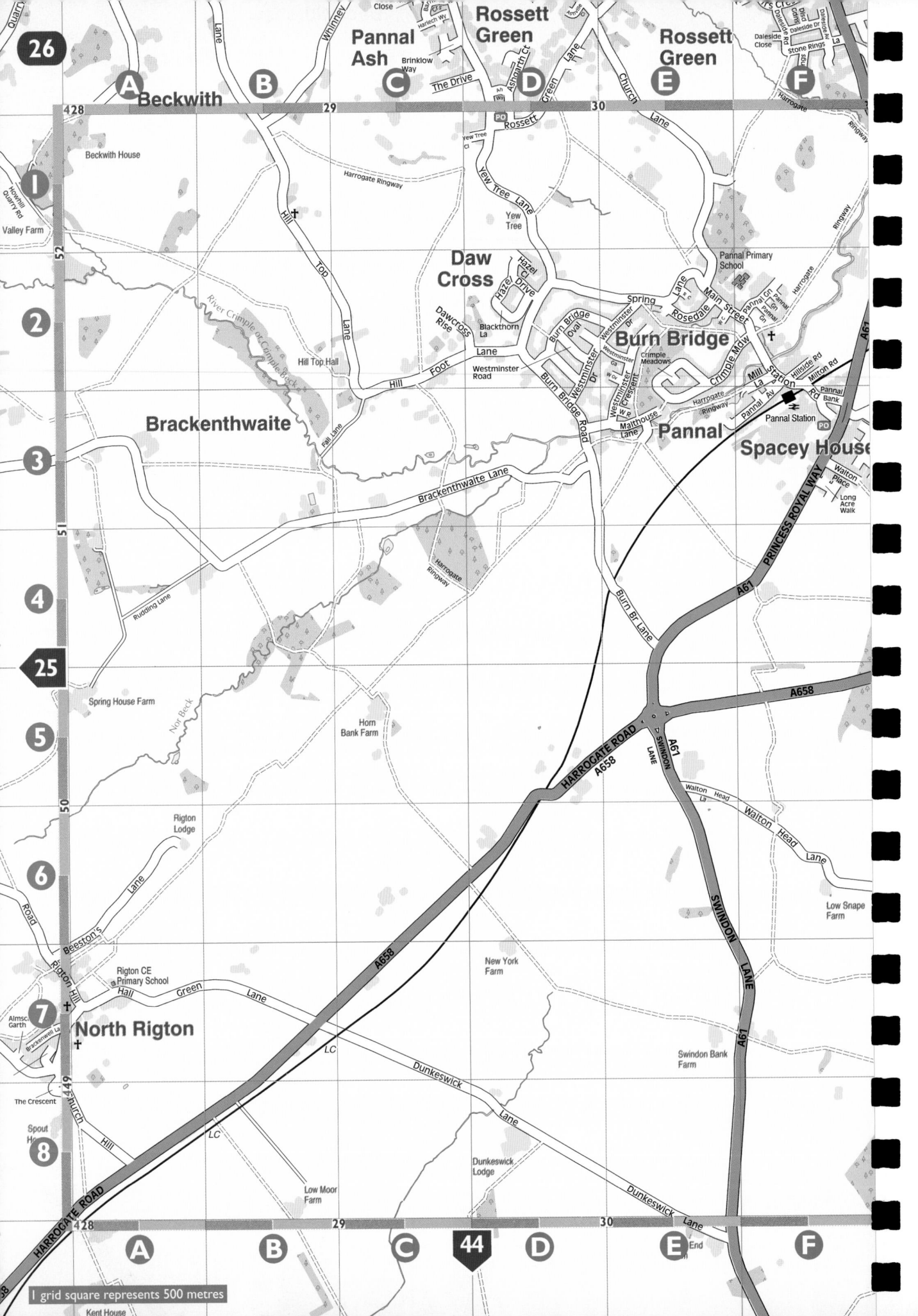

A Beckwith **B** **C** Pannal Ash **D** Rossett Green **E** Rossett Green **F**

428

Whinney Lane

Close

Hartech Wy

Ashgarth Ct

Green

Church Lane

Harrogate

Quarry Rd

Daleside Close
Daleside
Stone Rings

29 30

Brinklow Way

The Drive

Rossett

PO

Yew Tree Cl

Harrogate Ringway

Ringway

1
Howhill Quarry Rd
Beckwith House

Valley Farm

52

Yew Tree Lane

Yew Tree

Pannal Primary School

Harrogate

Ringway

2
River Crimple or Crimple Beck

Hill Top Lane

Daw Cross

Hazel Ct Drive

Hazel

Spring Lane

Main Street

Pannal
Pannal Ch

†

Hill Top Hall

Dawcross Rise

Blackthorn La

Rosedale

J C W

Burn Bridge

3
Brackenthwaite

Hill Foot Lane

Westminster Road

Lane

Burn Bridge Oval

Burn Bridge Road

Westminster Dr

Westminster Cres

Crimple Meadows

Crimple Mdw

Mill La

Pannal Av

Station

Hillside Rd

Milton Rd

Pannal Bank

†

A61

Fall Lane

Westminster W R

Malthouse Lane

Harrogate Ringway

Pannal

Pannal Station

PO

Spacey House

51

Brackenthwaite Lane

Harrogate Ringway

Walton Place

Long Acre Walk

PRINCESS ROYAL WAY

4
Rudding Lane

Burn Br Lane

A61

25

A658

5
Spring House Farm

Nor Beck

Horn Bank Farm

Harrogate Road A658

SWINDON LANE

Walton Head La

Walton Head Lane

50

6
Rigton Lodge

Beeston's

Road

Lane

New York Farm

SWINDON LANE

Low Snape Farm

7
Rigton Hill

Rigton CE Primary School

Hall Green Lane

Almscliff Garth

Brackenwell La

North Rigton

†

†

LC

Dunkeswick

A61

Swindon Bank Farm

449

The Crescent

Spout Ho

8
Church Hill

LC

Low Moor Farm

Lane

Dunkeswick Lodge

Dunkeswick Lane

End

HARROGATE ROAD

428 29 **44** 30

A **B** **C** **D** **E** **F**

Kent House

1 grid square represents 500 metres

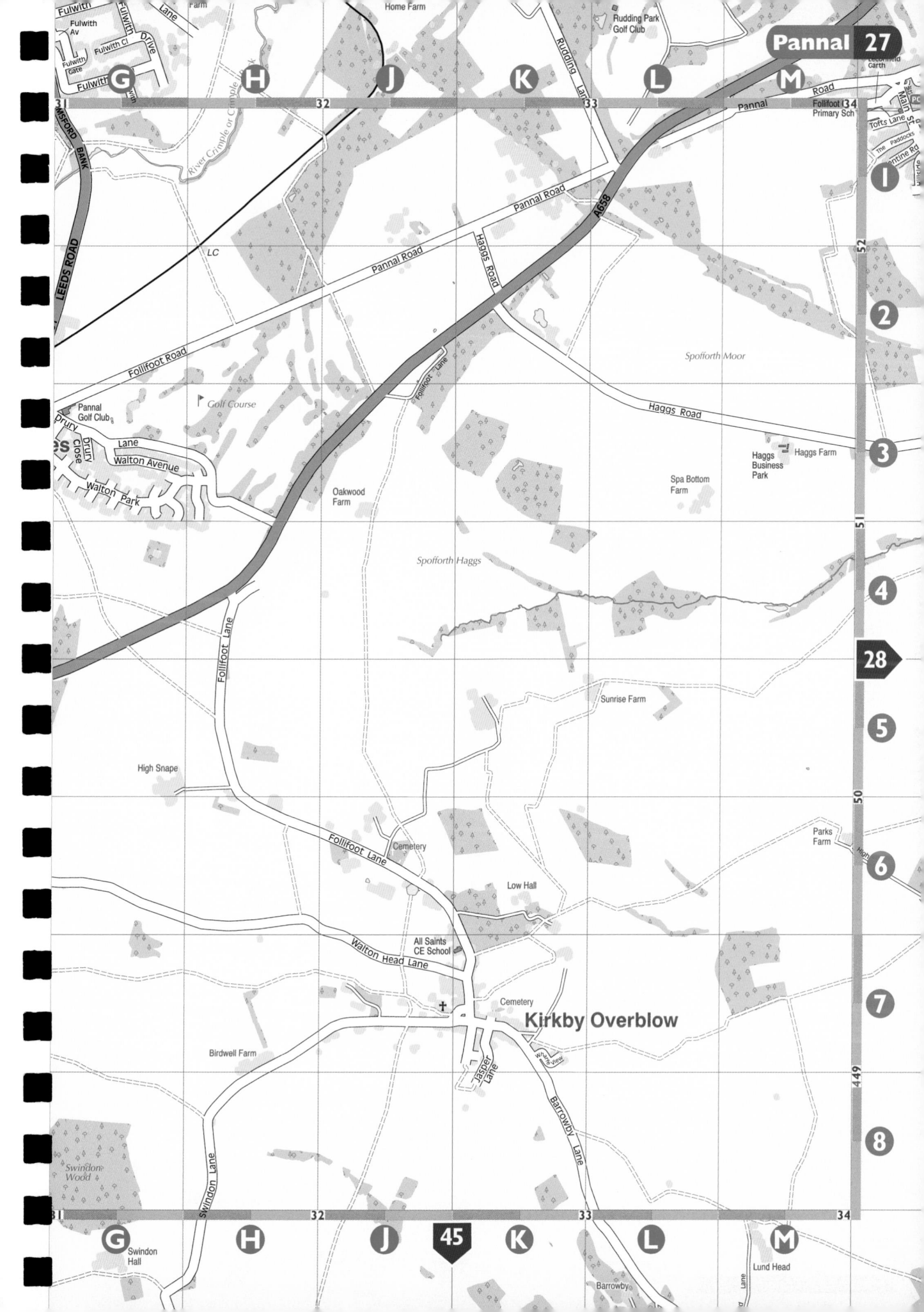

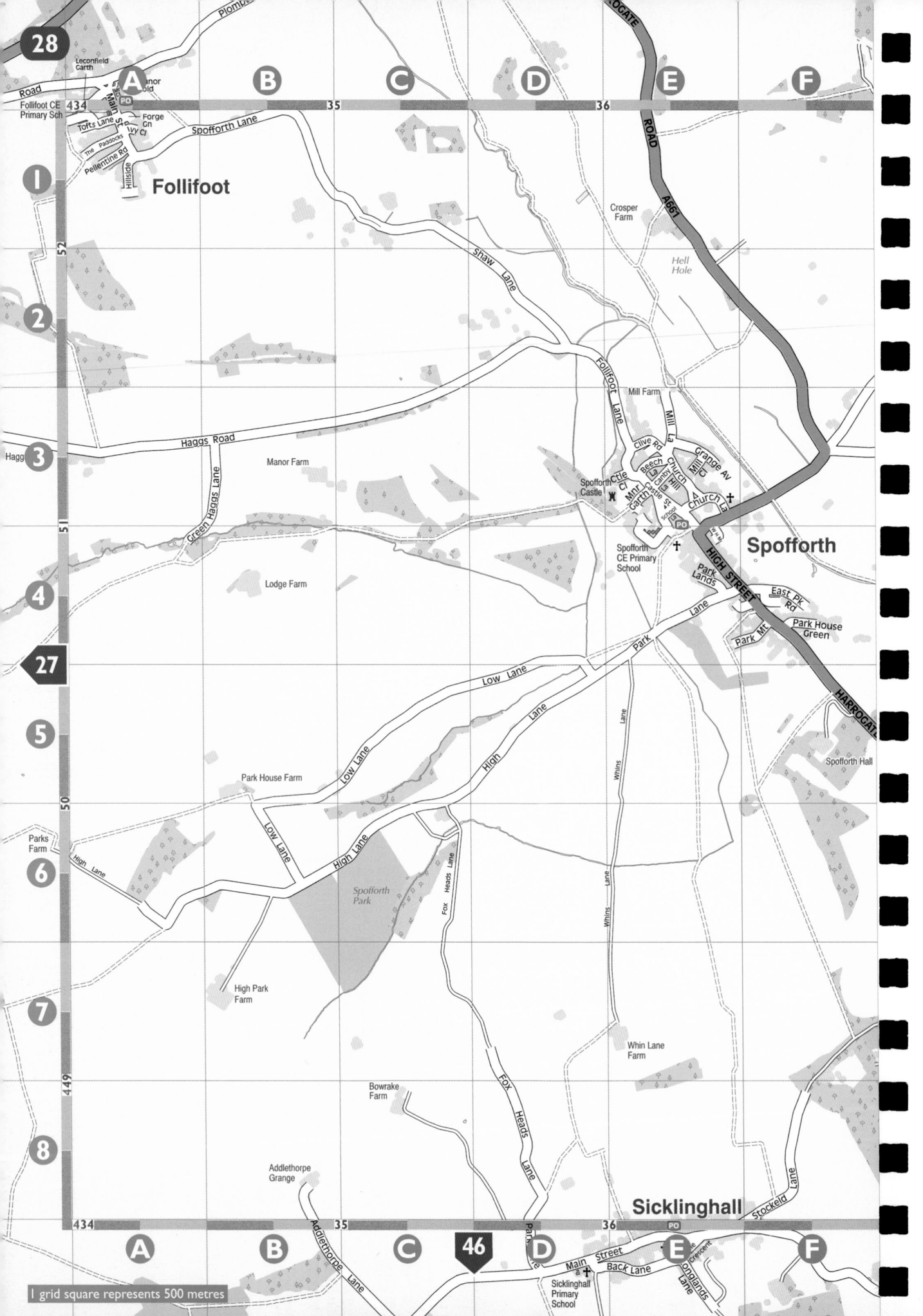

28

A B C D E F

Leconfield
Garth
Road
Follifoot CE 434 Main St
Primary Sch
Tofts Lane   Forge
Ivy Cl   Gn
The Paddocks
Pellentine Rd
Hillside

Follifoot

Plomb

TOGATE

ROAD A661

Crosper
Farm

Hell
Hole

Spofforth Lane

35   36

Shaw Lane

1

52

2

Haggs Road

Hagg

Manor Farm

Green Haggs Lane

Mill Farm

Follifoot Lane

Mill La

Clive Rd
Beech Candy
La   Hill
Ctle   Church
Cl   Castle St
Mnr   School
Garth PO

Grange Av
Mill
Cl
Church La

3

51

Spofforth
Castle

Lodge Farm

Spofforth
CE Primary
School

†

Spofforth

4

27

Park House Farm

Low Lane

Low Lane

Park Lane

Low Lane

Lane

High Lane

HIGH STREET

Park
Lands

East Pk
Rd

Park Mt

Park House
Green

HARROGATE

Spofforth Hall

5

50

Parks
Farm

High Lane

6

Spofforth
Park

Fox Heads Lane

High Lane

Whins Lane

Whins Lane

7

High Park
Farm

449

Bowrake
Farm

Fox Heads Lane

Whin Lane
Farm

8

Addlethorpe
Grange

Addlethorpe Lane

Sicklinghall

434   35   46   36   Main Street PO

Back Lane

Stockeld Lane

Sicklinghall
Primary
School

onglands
Lane

A B C 46 D E F

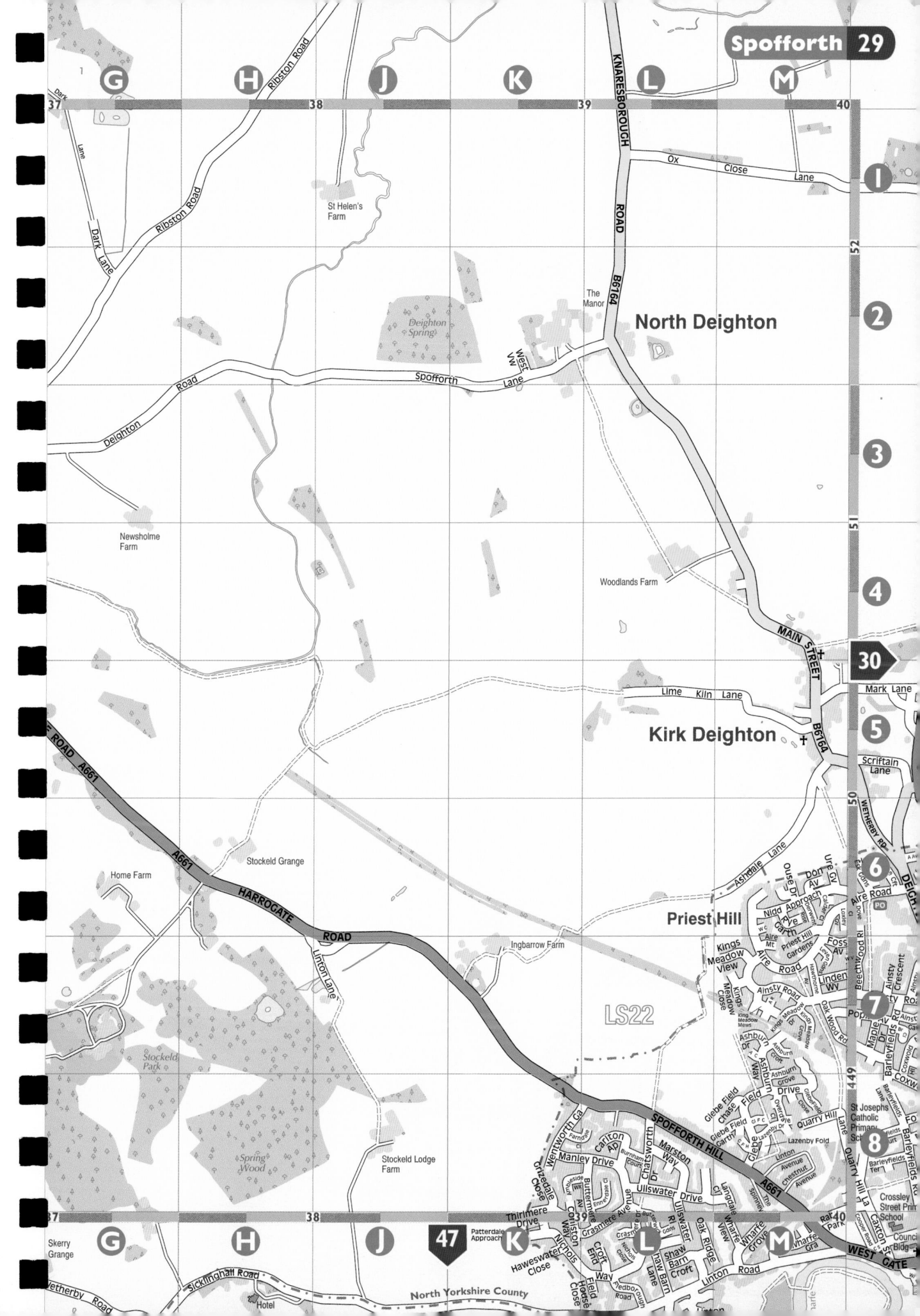

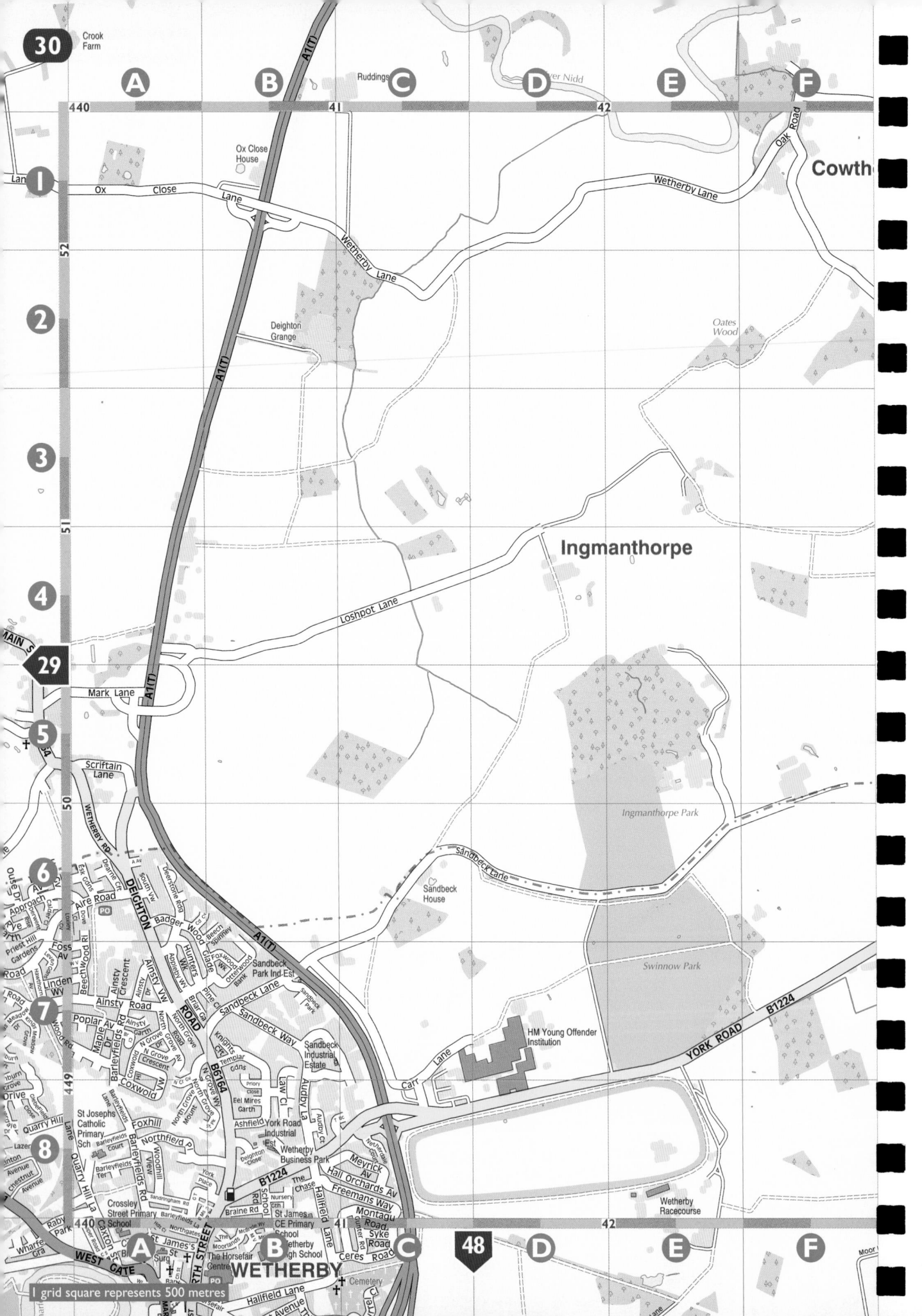

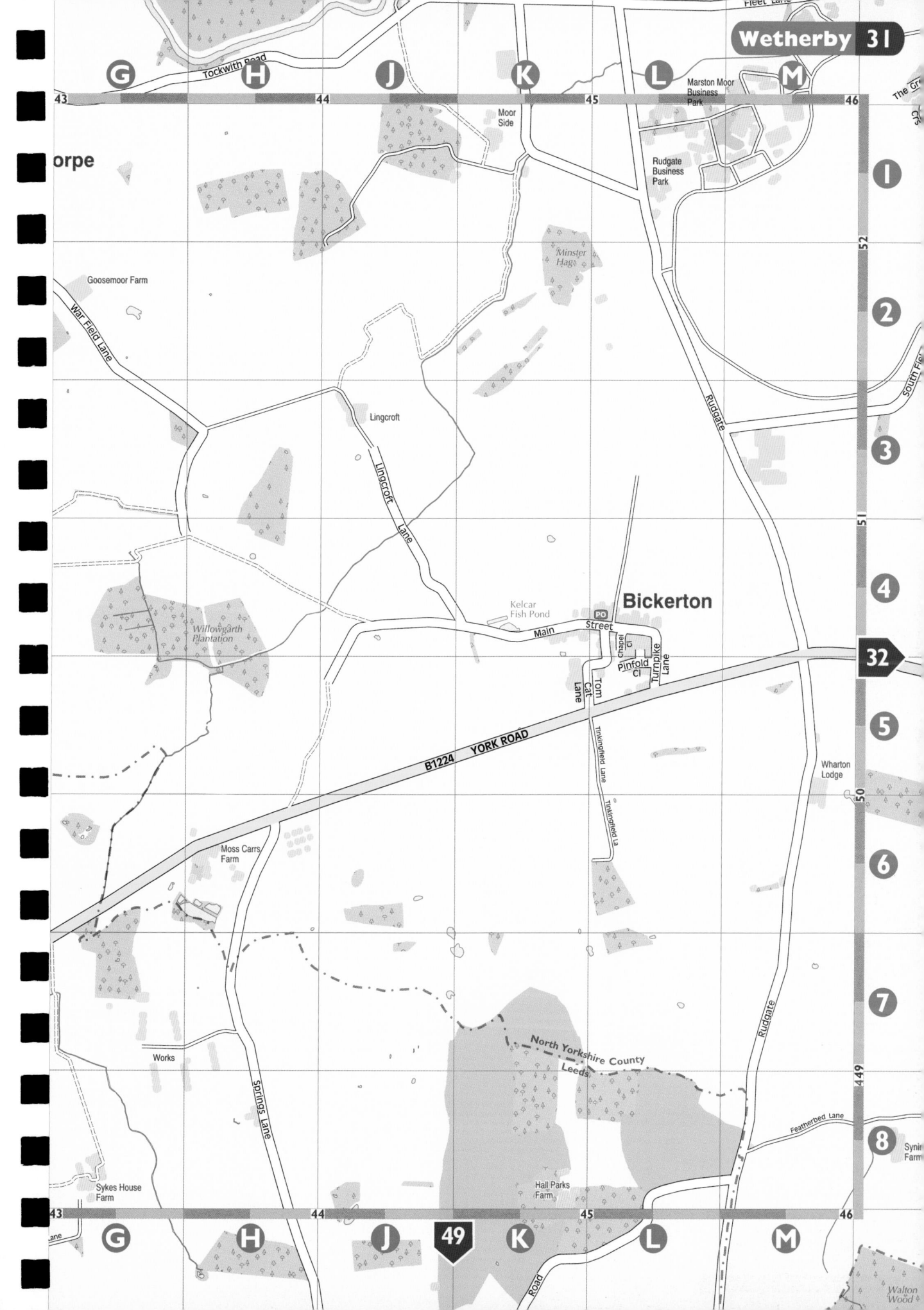

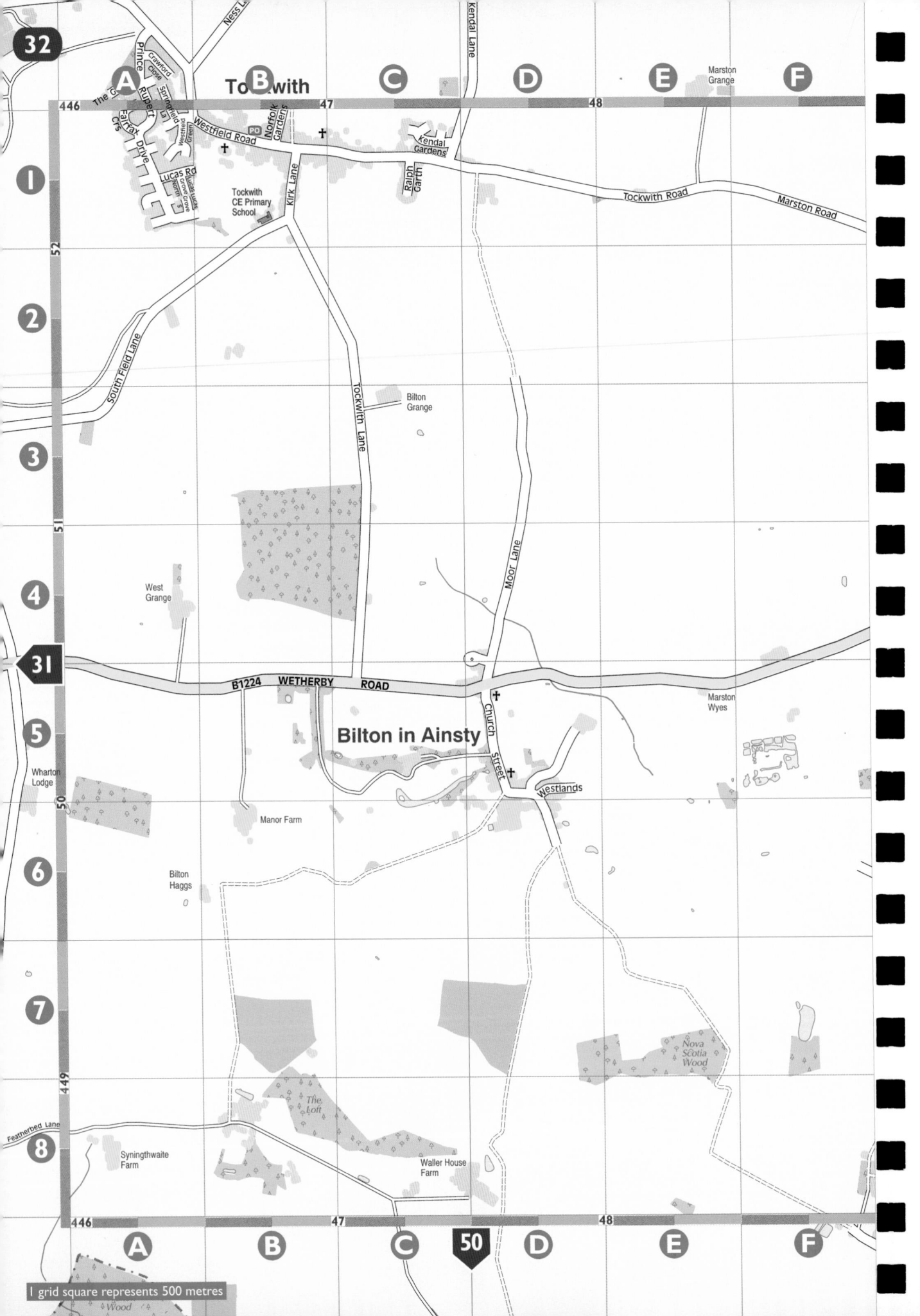

A   B   C   D   E   F

Tockwith

446   47   48

Ness La.

Kendal Lane

Marston Grange

Crawford Close

The Green

Prince

Rupert

Springfield La.

Westfield Road

Westfield Gardens

Fairfax Crs

Drive

Lucas Rd

North Grove

Lucas Grove S

PO

Norfolk Gardens

Kirk Lane

Kendal Gardens

Ralph Garth

Tockwith CE Primary School

52   1

2

South Field Lane

Tockwith Lane

Bilton Grange

51   3

4

West Grange

Bilton Grange

Tockwith Road

Marston Road

Moor Lane

31   B1224   WETHERBY   ROAD

Marston Wyes

Church Street

Bilton in Ainsty

5

Wharton Lodge

50

Manor Farm

Westlands

6

Bilton Haggs

449   7

Nova Scotia Wood

Featherbed Lane

8

Syningthwaite Farm

The Loft

Waller House Farm

446   47   50   48

A   B   C   D   E   F

1 grid square represents 500 metres

Wood

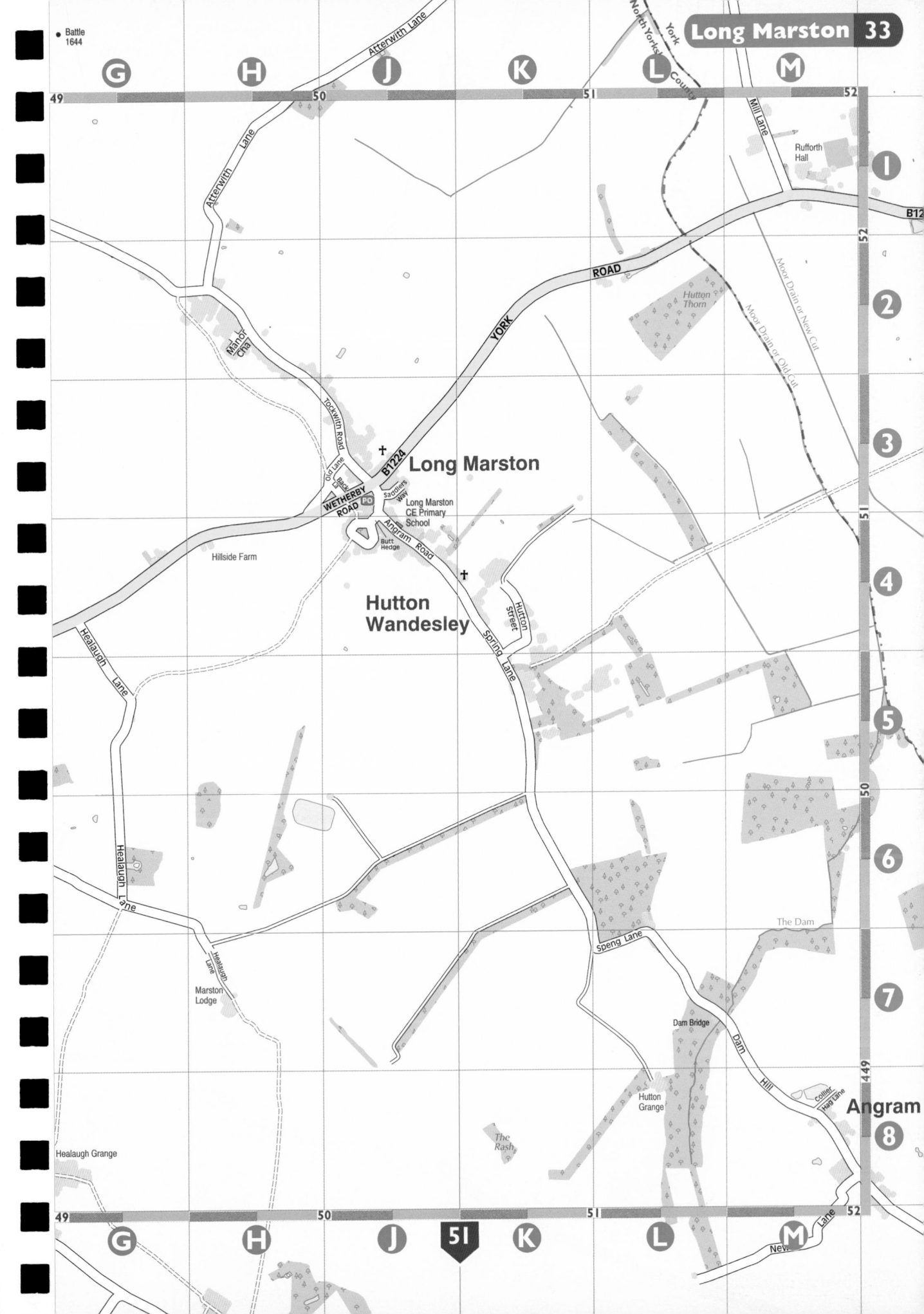

• Battle
1644

G   H   J   K   L   M

Afterwith Lane

North Yorks/

York County

Mill Lane

Rufforth
Hall

I

B12

Moor Drain or New Cut

Moor Drain or Old Cut

52

2

YORK   ROAD

Hutton
Thorn

Afterwith Lane

Manor
Cha

Tockwith Road

3

† B1224   **Long Marston**

51

Old Lane

Back

Saddlers
Way

Long Marston
CE Primary
School

WETHERBY
ROAD   PO

Angram   Road

Butt
Hedge

†

4

**Hutton
Wandesley**

Hutton
Street

Spring Lane

Hillside Farm

Healaugh   Lane

5

50

6

The Dam

Healaugh
Lane

Speng Lane

7

Marston
Lodge

Dam Bridge

Dam   Hill

Collier
Hag Line

449

Angram

8

Healaugh Grange

Hutton
Grange

The
Rash

G   H   J   51   K   L   M

New   Lane

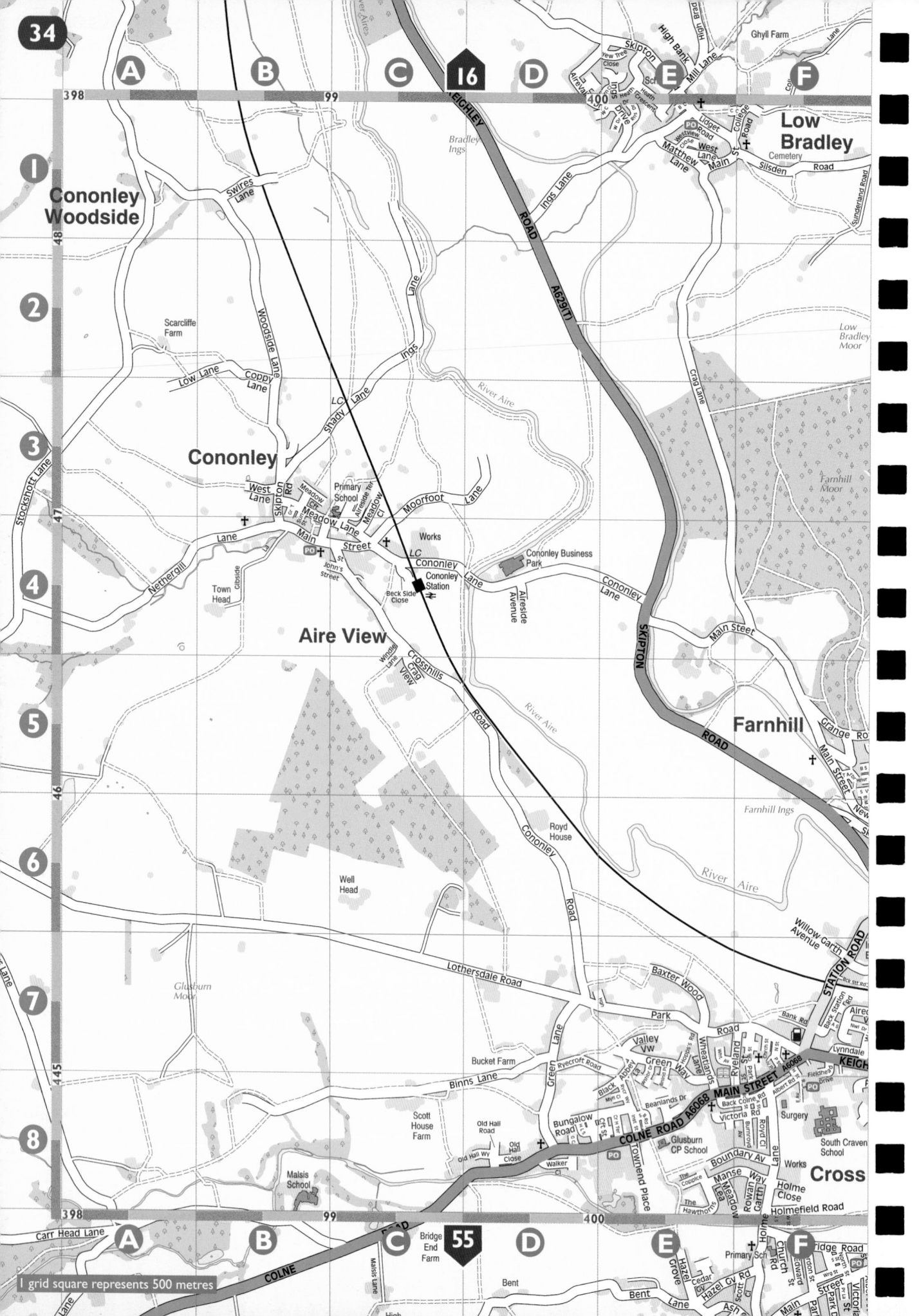

A B C **16** D E F

398 99 400

1 Cononley
Woodside

48

2 Scarcliffe
Farm

47

3 Cononley

4 Aire View

46

5 Farnhill

6

445

7

8

398 99 400

55

A B C D E F

Swires Lane
Woodside Lane
Low Lane
Coppy Lane
Shady Lane
Ings
Ings Lane
Bradley Ings
KEIGHLEY ROAD A629(T)
High Bank
High Bank
Mill Lane
Ghyll Farm
Skipton
Yew Tree Close
Ings
Heath
Crescent
Alreva Drive
Sch
College
Low
Bradley
Cemetery
Silsden Road
Sunderland Road
Ligget Road
Westview
West Lane
Matthew Lane
Main
Crag Lane
Low Bradley Moor
Farnhill Moor
River Aire

Stockshott Lane
West Lane
Skipton Rd
Meadow CR
Meadow Lane
Meadow Ter
Meadow Cl
Primary School
Alreside Ter
Moorfoot
Lane
Works
Conholey Business Park
Main Street
St John's Street
LC
Cononley Station
Beck Side Close
Aireside Avenue
Cononley Lane
Skipton Road
Farnhill
Netherfill Lane
Town Head
Gibside
PO
Winding Lane
Crosshills View
Craig View
Road
River Aire
Conholey Road
Royd House
Farnhill Ings
Main Steet
Grange Road
Main Street
Newby

Well Head

Glusburn Moor

Lothersdale Road
Baxter Wood
Park
Bank Rd
Willow Garth Avenue
STATION ROAD
River Aire

Binns Lane
Bucket Farm
Green Lane
Ryecroft Road
Valley Vw
Green Way
Wheatlands Lane
Abbey Road
Victoria
KEIGH
Lynndale
PO

Scott House Farm
Old Hall Road
Old Hall Wy
Old Hall Close
Walker Cl
Bungalow Road
Glusburn CP School
COLNE ROAD A6068 MAIN STREET A6068
Back Colne Rd
Townend Place
Boundary Av
Surgery
South Craven School
The Coppice
Manse Lane
Rowan Garth
Holme Close
Works
Cross

Carr Head Lane
Bridge End Farm
Bent
COLNE ROAD
Malsis School
Malsis Lane
Bent Lane
Primary Sch
Hazel Grove
Cedar
Ash
PO
Bridge Road

I grid square represents 500 metres

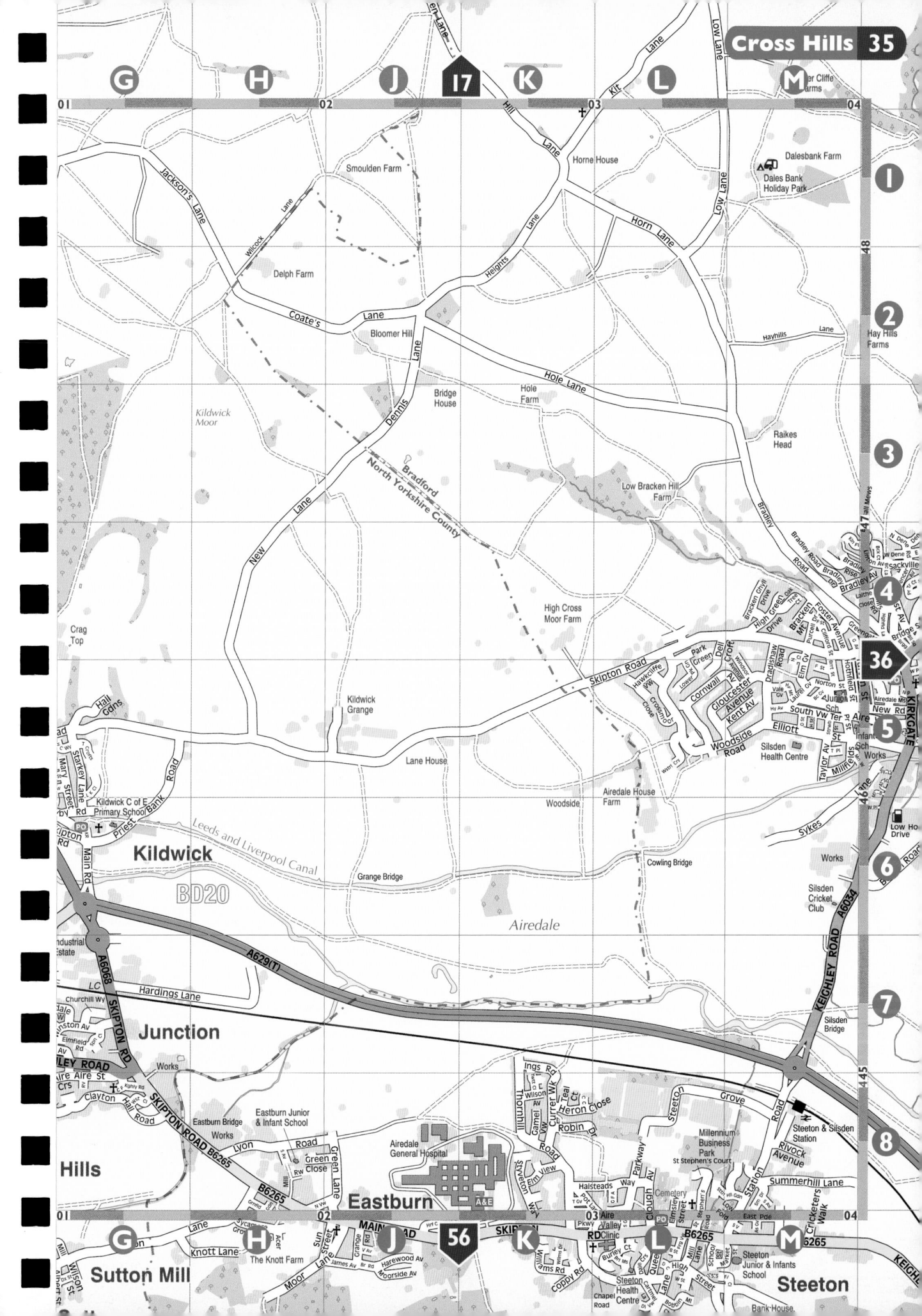

Cringles

18

I

bank Farm

Bank Farm

Hay Hills
Farms

2

Silsden
Reservoir

Fishbeck

Fishbeck

Lane

Sea Moor
Farm

Lane

Lane

Uppersley

Crag House

Lippersley
Lane

Brown Bank Lane

Hang Goose
Farm

Light Bank Lane

Nudge
Hill

Straight

Lane

High House

Hodson's Farm

Cocking Lane

Turner

Lane

3

Nab
View

Works

Brown Bank Lane

Swartha Lane

Nab
End

White
Crag
Plantation

Town Head

Swartha

Raikes House
Farm

Brunthwaite
Crag

Light Bank Lane

4

SILSDEN

North

A6034

Dale

Bolton Ter

Hamber Cote Lane

Hawber Lane

35

KIRKGATE

PO

New Rd

Bradley Av

Foster

Hillcrest Av

Bridge St

Oak View

Banklands

La

Banklands

Brunthwaite

5

Aire View

Infant
Sch

Works

Middleway

Craven

Drive

Craven Av

Daisy

Aireville

Aireville Mount

Jacques Gv

Aire
Vale

Cemetery

Silsden
Golf Club

Brunthwaite Lane

6

Silsden
Cricket
Club

Bolton Road

A6034

Low House Drive

Howden
Road

Claymore Ri

Charlton Gv

Ings

Telford

Jennings
Close

Waterside

Lowfield
Crescent

Rombalds

Golf Course

Lane

Tomling
Cote

Ghyll Grange

7

ILEY ROAD

A6034

445

Silsden
Bridge

Hen Holme Lane

Hainsworth
Road

Low Lane

Brunthwaite Br Lane

Brunthwaite Bridge

Tomling

Cote

Holden Lane

Canal Lane

Howden Park

Rough
Holden

8

Steeton
ation

erhill Lane

A629(T)

Howden House

Spring
Crag
Wood

Cricketers
Walk

36265

KEIGH

404

05

Low Lane

06

57

Alder
Carr
Wood

Lower
Holden

Holden
Gate

Nest

Cocking Lane

Lumb Cliff

A65(T)

Ilkley Road

G H J **19** K L M

07 08 09 10

High
Brockabank

High
Banks

Gate
Croft

Netherwood
House

Course

I

Dales Way

SKIPTON ROAD

48

Moorside Lane

Curlew
Close

Beverley

Briery
Close

2

Addingham Moorside

Briery Wood
Farm

Heber's
Grove

Heber's Cr

3

Windgate
Nick

Noon
Stone

Heber's
Ghyll

47

Addingham
High Moor

Doubler Stones
Allotment

Black
Beck Hole

4

Doubler
Stones

Long
Ridge End

38

Crawshaw
Moss

Jerry Lane

Black
Pots

Heber
Moss

5

46

Rombalds Moor

6

Buck
Stones

Cowper's
Cross

High Moor

Whetstone
Allotment

7

445

Ilkley Road

Rivock Oven

8

High
Bradup

Low
Bradup

07 08 09 10 Morton
Moor

G H J **58** K L M

Brass Castle

I grid square represents 500 metres

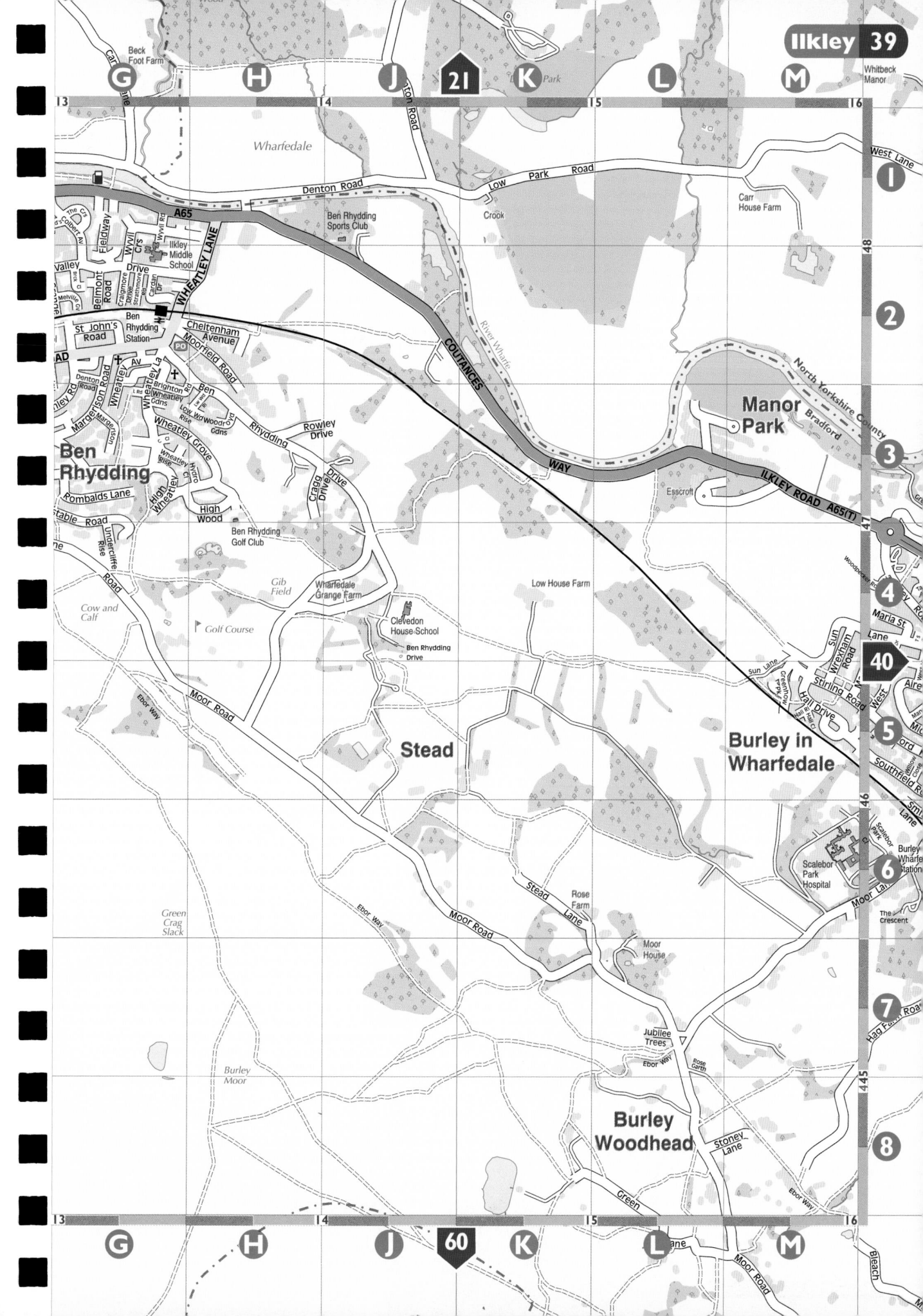

40

A B C **22** D E F

Whitbeck Manor

West Lane

Askwith CP School

Askwith

1

48

West Beck

2

North Yorkshire County
Bradford

3

ROAD A65(T)

Greenholme Farm

Leather Bank

Green La

Great Pasture

Covey Hall Farm

Hallam Lane

Moor Lane

Weston Manor

East Wood

Weston

Weston Park

Church Lane

Meagill
Weston Drive
Weston Park Vw
Weston Lane

Ash Holme

4

39

Ilkley Road
Maria St
Lane
Rushfield Road
Stirling Road
Hall Drive

West View
Main St
Long Mdw

School
Aireville Terrace
Manse Road
Midgley Road

Grange Road
Main Street
Surgery

Iron Row
Yorkroad
Mill Lane

River Wharfe

5

Langford Road
Southfield Road

Beckside Close
Langford
Hanover Wy

Burley Middle School

St Philip's Vw
St Philip's

Otley   Road

6

Scalebor Park Hospital

Moor Lane

Smithy Lane
The Copse

Burley in Wharfedale Station

The Drive

The Crescent

Rose Bank
Elm
Heather

Prospect Road
St Michael's Way

Burley Woodhead C of E Sch

Laund House Farm

Maple Grange

7

Hag Farm Road

445

Sandholme
Greenfields Wy
Holme Pk
Hill Crs
Holme Gv

BRADFORD

ROAD

Endor Crs

Moss Brook

Golf Course

Otley Golf Club

8

Ebor Way

Menston

Clarence Drive

A65

Windermere Avenue

Cemetery

Busk
West
Fawkes Drive
Duncan Avenue
Maylea Drive
Sunnydale Ridge

BRADFORD ROAD

416

A B **61** C D E F

Halstead Drive

BURLEY RD
Halstead Drive

Westbourne
St John's Park
Victoria Avenue

Bridgland Avenue
Brooklands

ROAD
A6038
BRADFORD

Imperial Works

Oaks Farm

St Chevin Road

Chevin

I grid square represents 500 metres

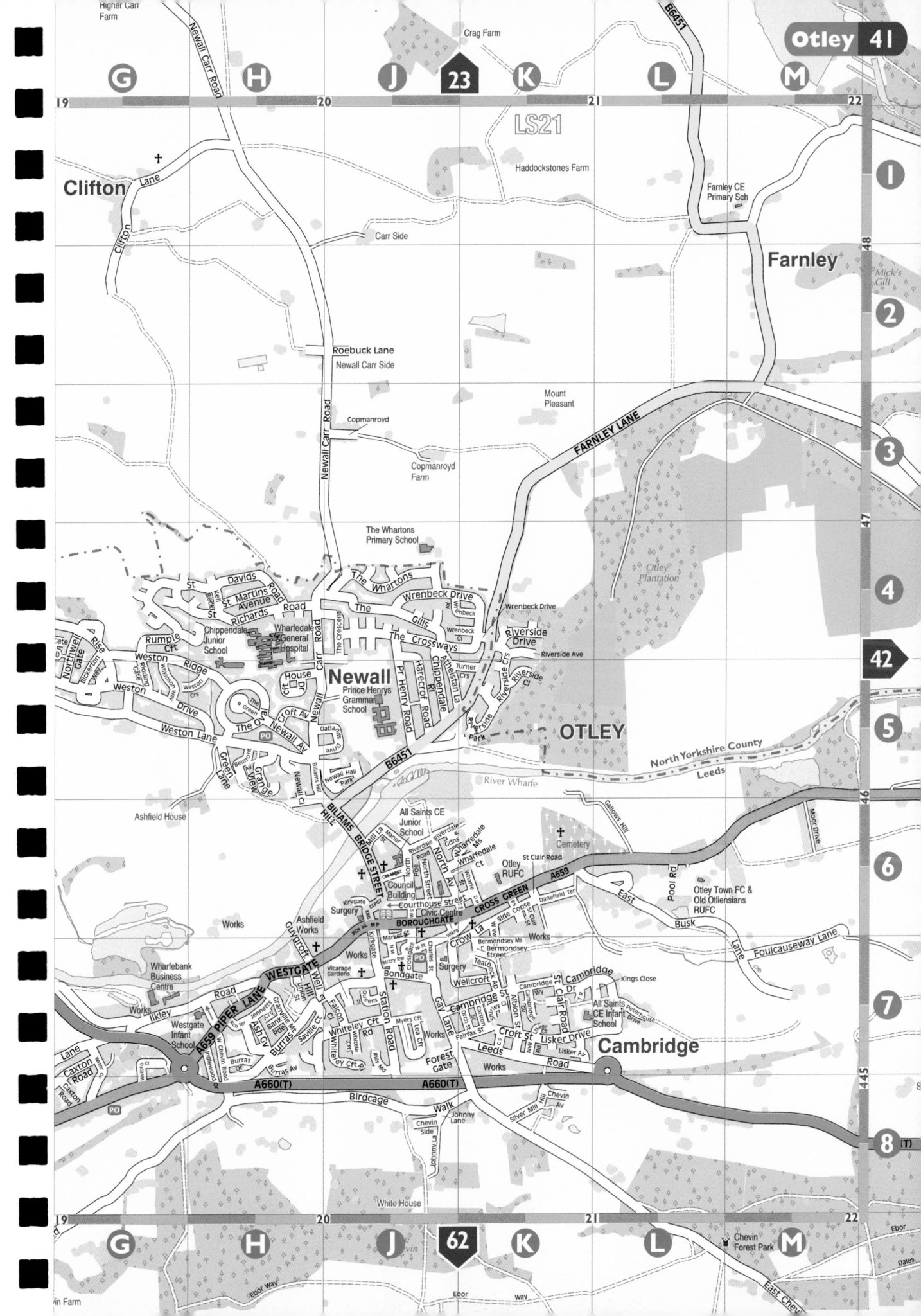

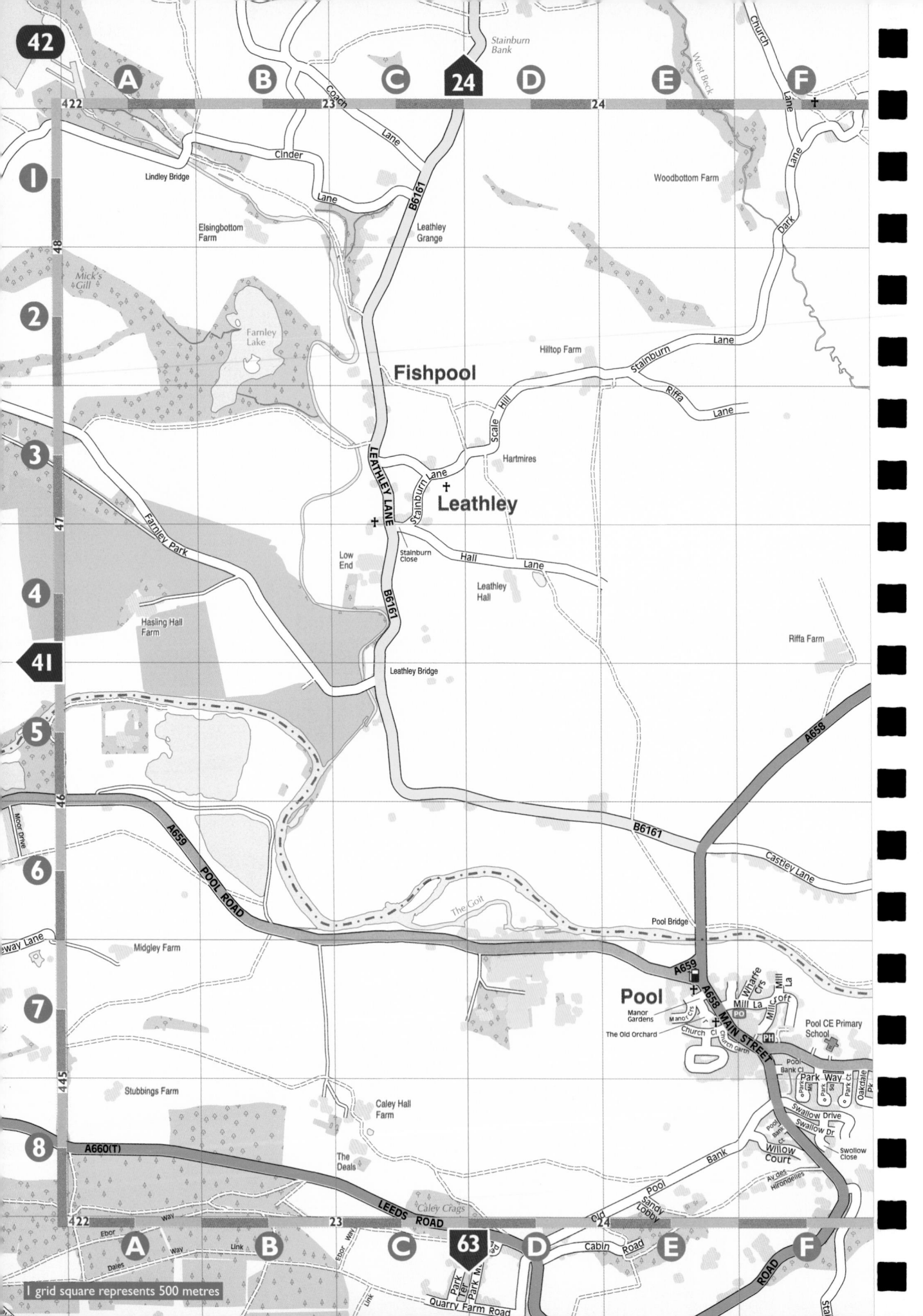

42

A   B   C   **24**   D   E   F

422   23   24

1

Lindley Bridge

Coach Lane

Cinder Lane

Elsingbottom Farm

Church Lane

Woodbottom Farm

West Beck

48

2

Mick's Gill

Farnley Lake

Leathley Grange

Fishpool

Hilltop Farm

Stainburn Lane

Riffa Lane

Dark Lane

3

47

Farnley Park

Scale Hill

Hartmires

Stainburn Lane

†

Leathley

†

4

Hasling Hall Farm

Low End

Stainburn Close

B6161

Hall Lane

Leathley Hall

Riffa Farm

41

Leathley Bridge

5

46

A659

POOL ROAD

6

Moor Drive

The Goit

B6161

Castley Lane

A658

Pool Bridge

7

445

Midgley Farm

Manor Gardens

The Old Orchard

Pool

Manor Crs

Church Cl

A659

A658 MAIN STREET

PO

Wharfe Crs

Mill La

Millcroft

Mill La

PH

Pool Bank Cl

Pool Bank

Park Way

Park Sq

Oakdale Pk

Pool CE Primary School

Church Garth

8

A660(T)

Stubbings Farm

Caley Hall Farm

The Deals

LEEDS ROAD

Caley Crags

Pool Bank

Sandy Lobby

Old Cabin Road

Willow Court

Swallow Drive

Swallow Dr

Av des Hirondelles

Swallow Close

ROAD

Ebor Way

Dales Way

Link

Ebor Way

Park Ter

Park M

Quarry Farm Road

422   23   24

A   B   C   **63**   D   E   F

Stainburn Bank

I grid square represents 500 metres

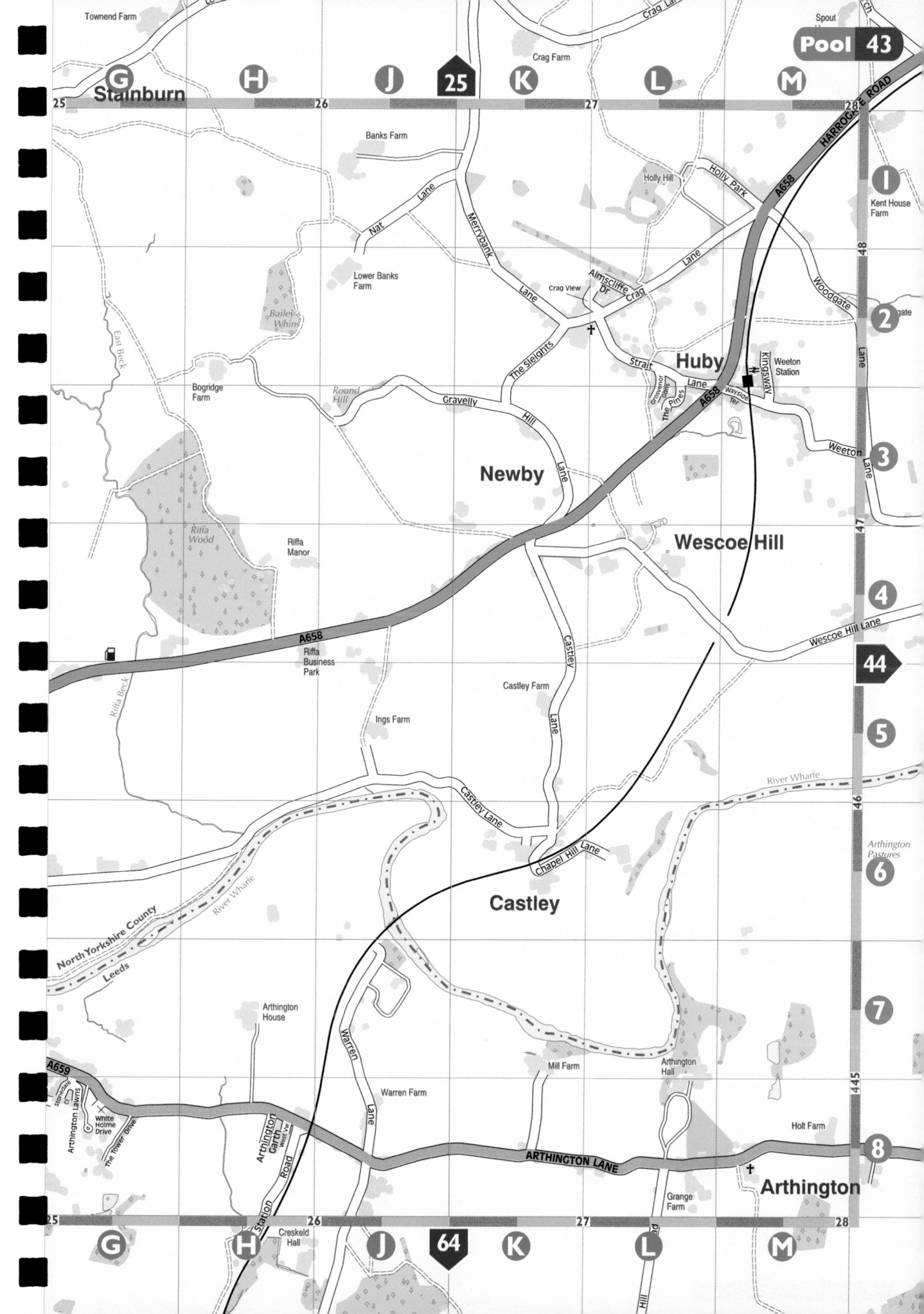

G Stainburn H J 25 K L M

Townend Farm

Crag La

Spout

Crag Farm

HARROGATE ROAD

Banks Farm

Holly Hill

Holly Park

A658

Kent House Farm

I

Nat Lane

Merrybank Lane

Lower Banks Farm

Bailey's Whins

East Beck

Crag View

Almscliffe Crag

Crag

Lane

Woodgate

gate

2

Bogridge Farm

Round Hill

The Sleights

Gravelly

Hill

Strait

Huby

Grosvenor Gdns
The Pikes

A658

Weeton Station

Kingsway

Wayside Ter

Weeton Lane

48

Newby

Lane

Wescoe Hill

3

Riffa Wood

Riffa Manor

A658

Riffa Business Park

Castley Lane

Castley Farm

Wescoe Hill Lane

47

4

44

Ings Farm

Riffa Beck

Castley Lane

River Wharfe

5

Arthington Pastures

46

Chapel Hill Lane

Castley

North Yorkshire County

River Wharfe

Leeds

River Wharfe

6

Arthington House

Warren Lane

Mill Farm

Arthington Hall

7

A659

Stonecliffe Ct

Arthington Lawns

White Holme Drive

The Tower Drive

Arthington Garth

Station Road

West Vw

Warren Farm

Holt Farm

445

ARTHINGTON LANE

Grange Farm

Arthington

8

Creskeld Hall

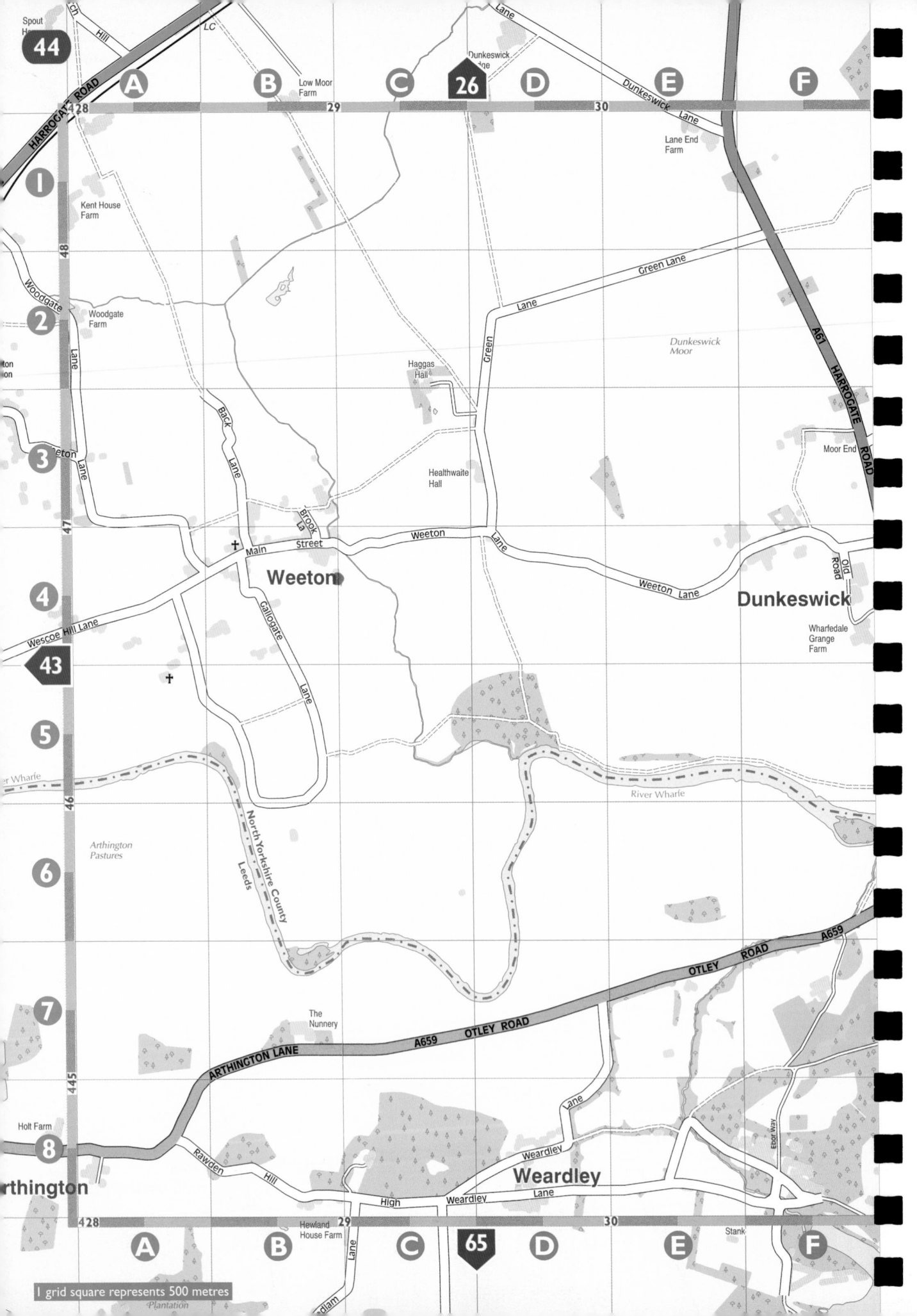

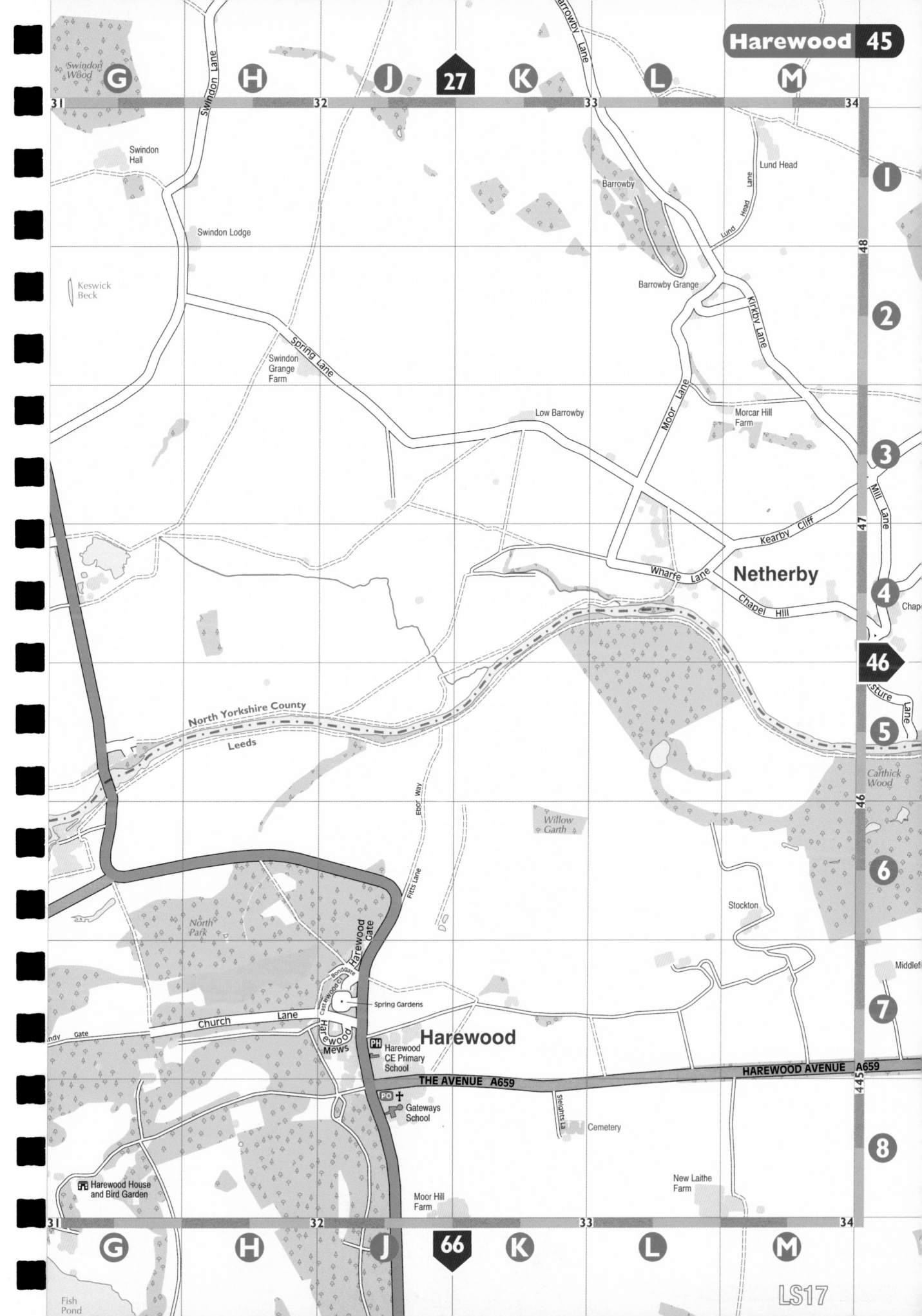

LS17

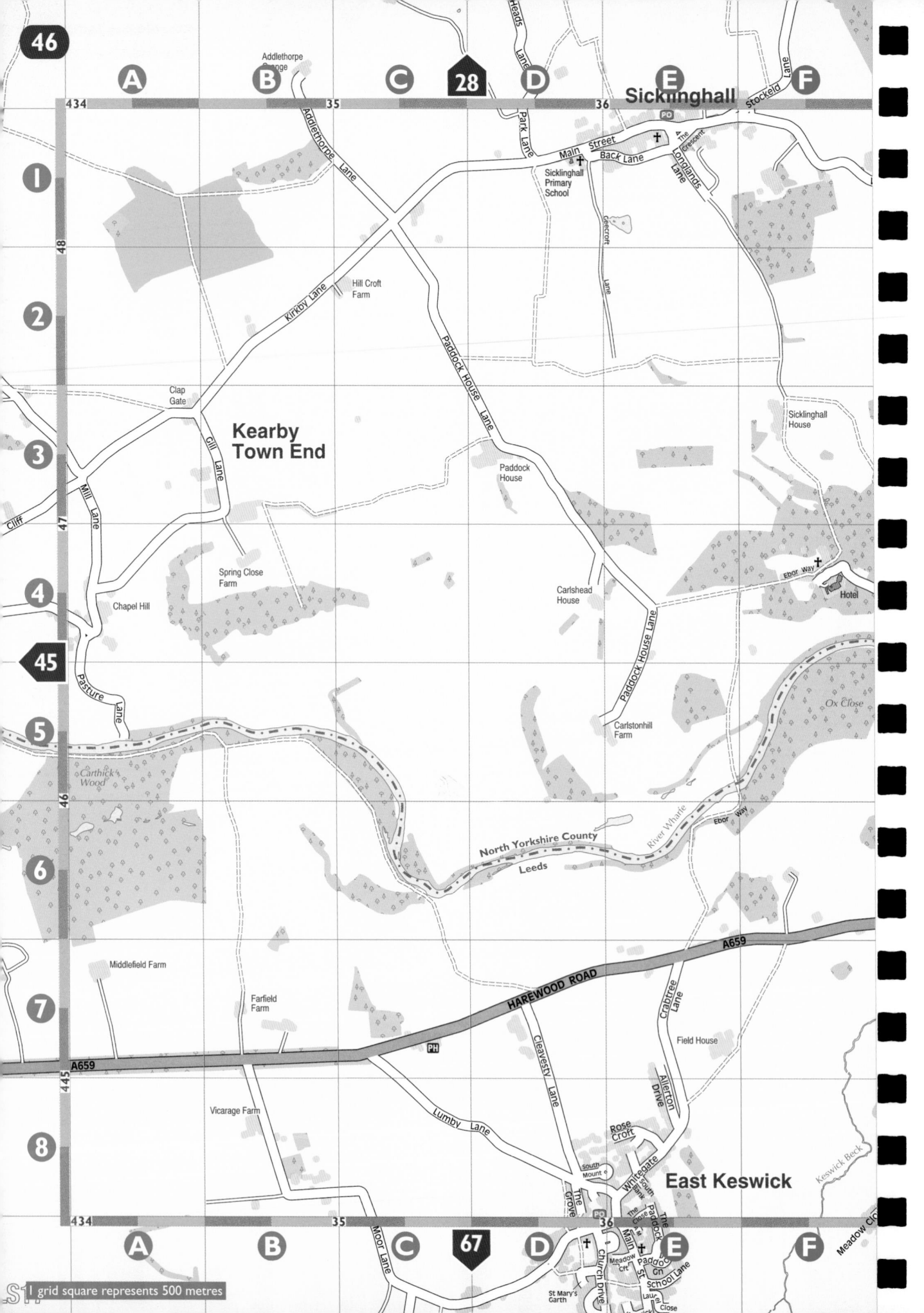

A   B   C   **28**   D   E   Sicklinghall   F

434   35   36

48

Addlethorpe Grange

Addlethorpe Lane

Park Lane

Main Street

Back Lane

Sicklinghall Primary School

Longlands Lane

The Crescent

Greecroft Lane

1

Kirkby Lane

Hill Croft Farm

Paddock House Lane

Sicklinghall House

2

47

Clap Gate

Kearby Town End

Gill Lane

Paddock House

3

Cliff

Mill Lane

Spring Close Farm

Carlshead House

Ebor Way

Hotel

4

Chapel Hill

45

Pasture Lane

Carlstonhill Farm

Ox Close

5

46

Carthick's Wood

River Wharfe

Ebor Way

6

North Yorkshire County

Leeds

Middlefield Farm

A659

HAREWOOD ROAD

Crabtree Lane

Field House

Allerton Drive

7

445

Farfield Farm

A659

PH

Cleavesty Lane

Lumby Lane

Vicarage Farm

Rose Croft

Whingate

South Mount

Meadow Crt

8

The Grove

South Bank

East Keswick

PO

The Paddock

Keswick Beck

Meadow Clo

434   35   **67**   36

A   B   C   D   Church Drive   E   F

School Lane

St Mary's Garth

Paddock Gn

Close

1 grid square represents 500 metres

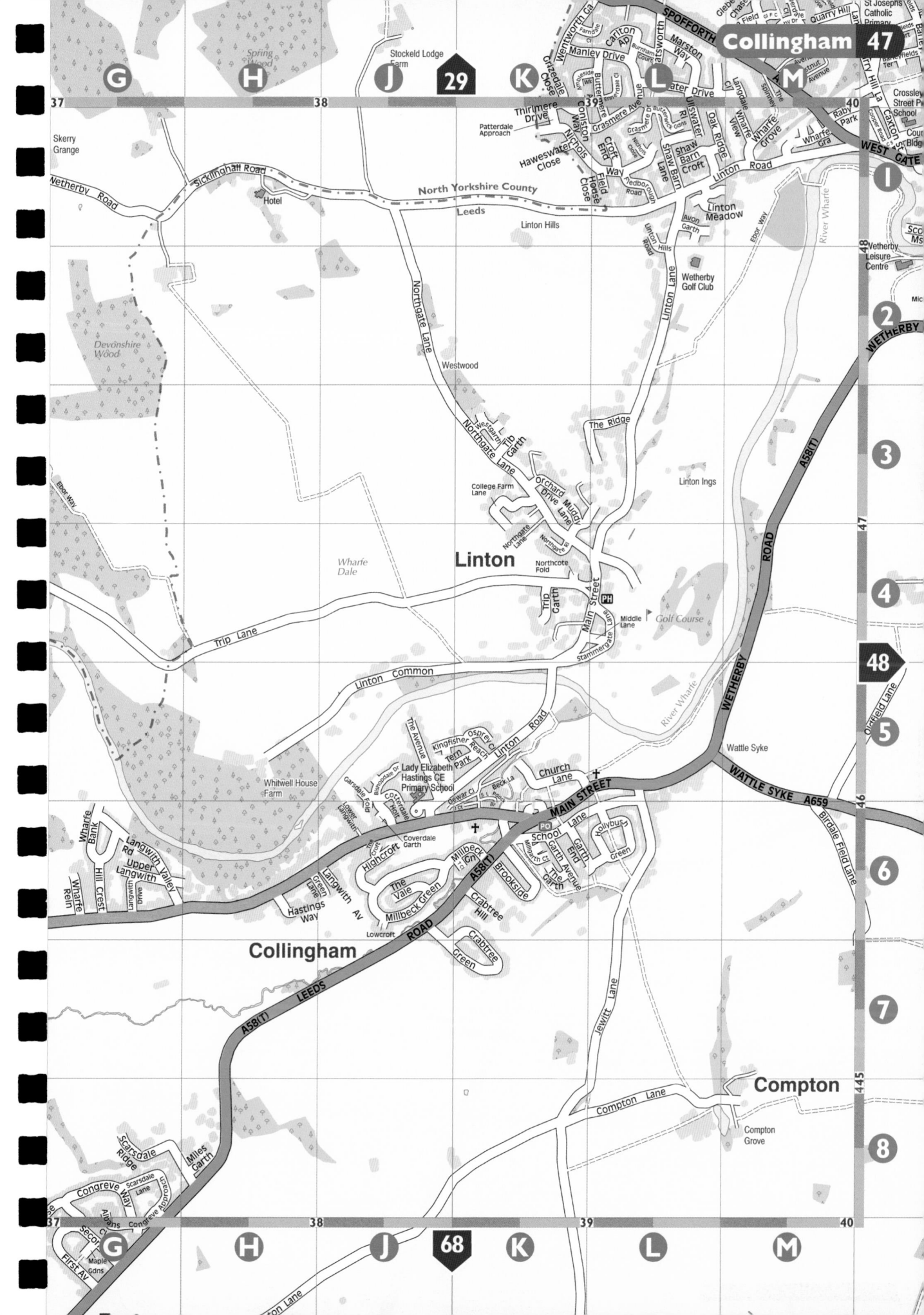

I grid square represents 500 metres

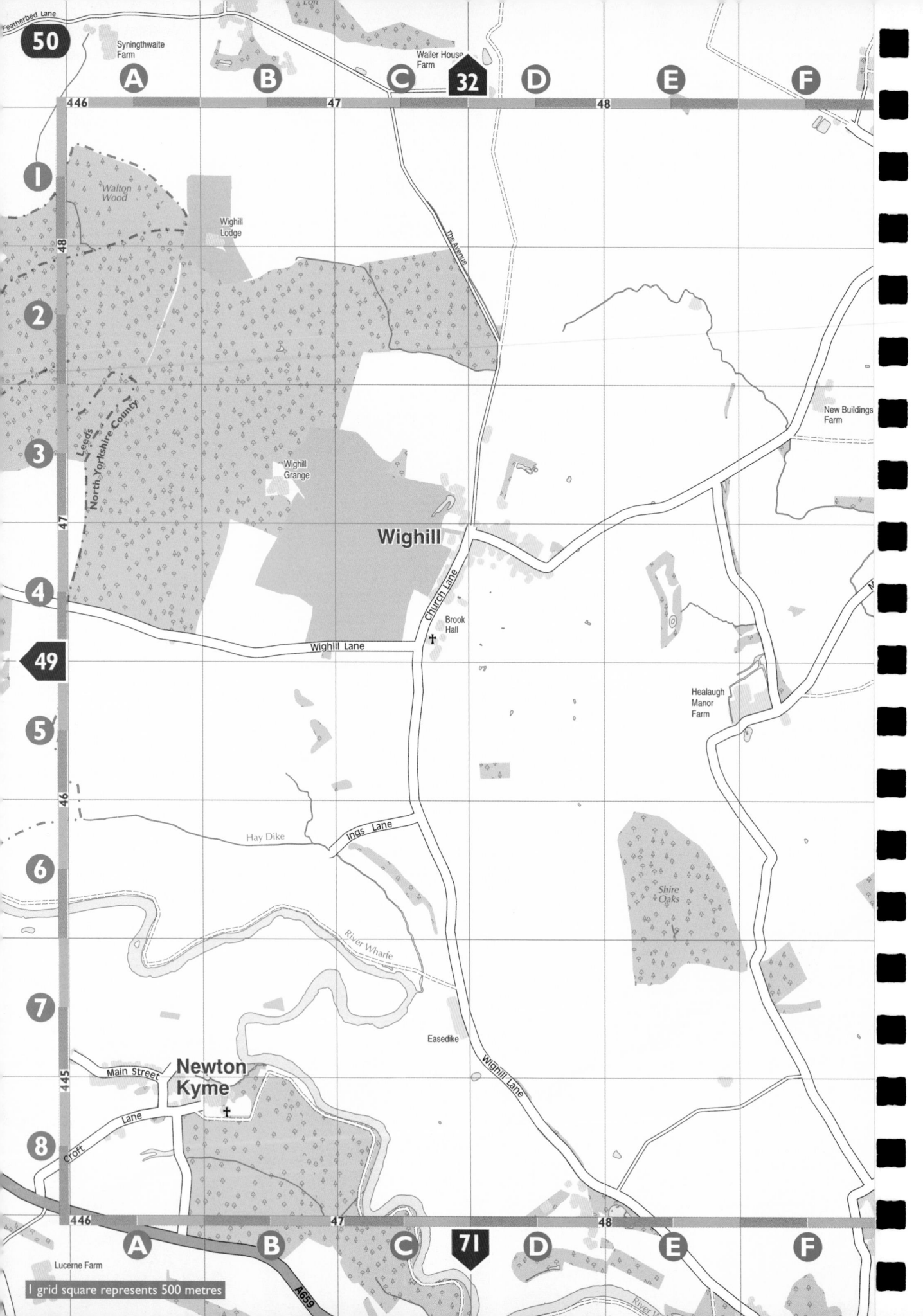

50

A B C 32 D E F

446 47 48

Featherbed Lane
Syningthwaite Farm
Waller House Farm

1

Walton Wood

48

Wighill Lodge

2

Leeds North Yorkshire County

3

Wighill Grange

The Avenue

New Buildings Farm

47

Wighill

4

Church Lane

Brook Hall

Wighill Lane

49

Healaugh Manor Farm

5

46

Hay Dike

Ings Lane

6

Shire Oaks

River Wharfe

7

Easedike

Wighill Lane

445

Main Street

Newton Kyme

8

Croft Lane

A B C 71 D E F

Lucerne Farm

446 47 48

A659

1 grid square represents 500 metres

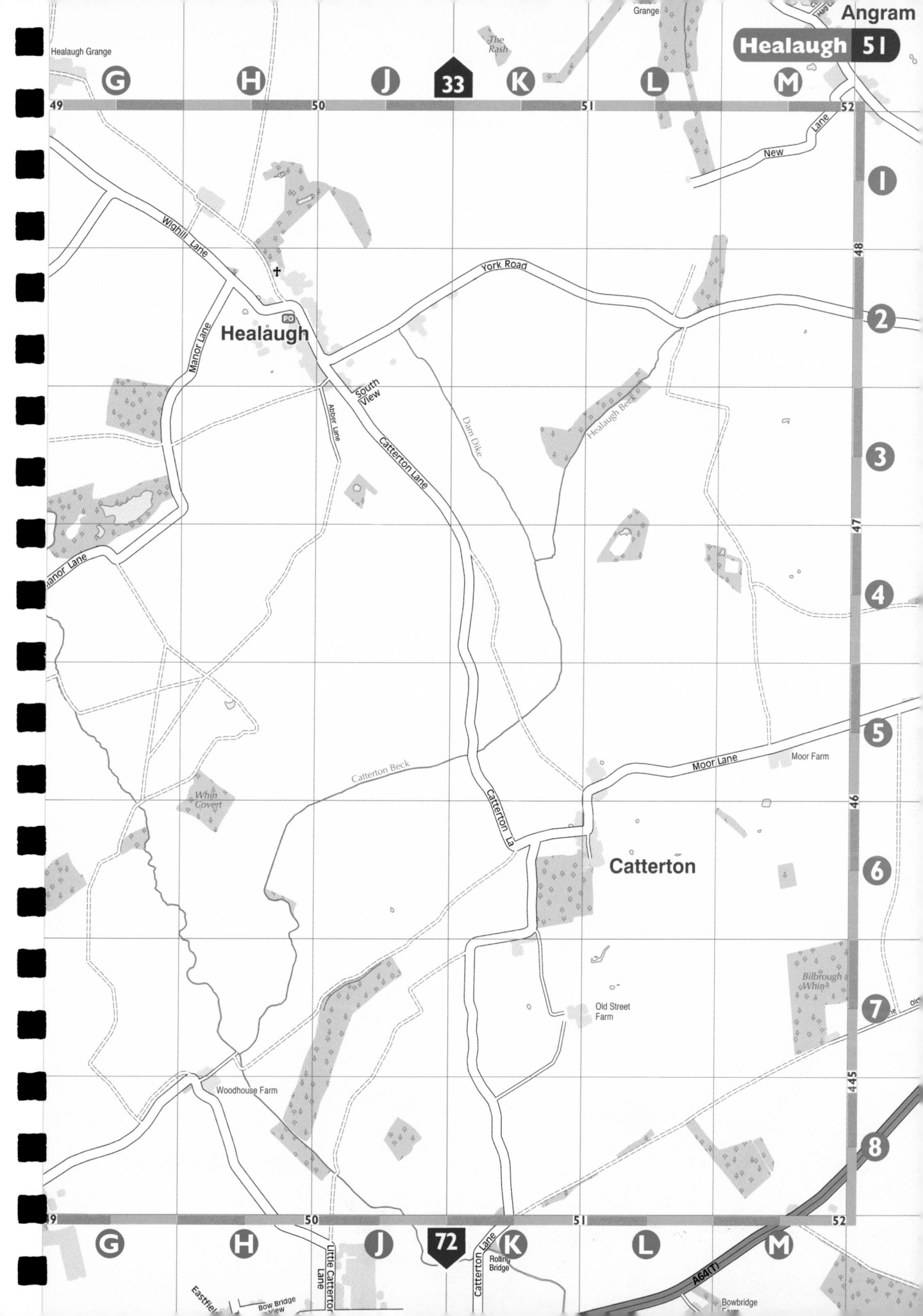

G   H   J   33   K   L   M

49   50   51   52

Healaugh Grange

Wighill Lane

PO   Healaugh

Manor Lane

Atber Lane

South View

Catterton Lane

York Road

Dam Dike

Healaugh Beck

The Rash

Grange

New Lane

❶

❷

❸

48

❹

47

Manor Lane

Catterton Beck

Whin Covert

Catterton La

Moor Lane   Moor Farm

Catterton

❺

46

❻

445

Bilbrough Whin

Old Street Farm

❼

Woodhouse Farm

❽

G   H   J   72   K   L   M

49   50   51   52

Little Catterton Lane

Catterton Lane

Rolling Bridge

A64(T)

Eastfield

Bow Bridge View

Bowbridge

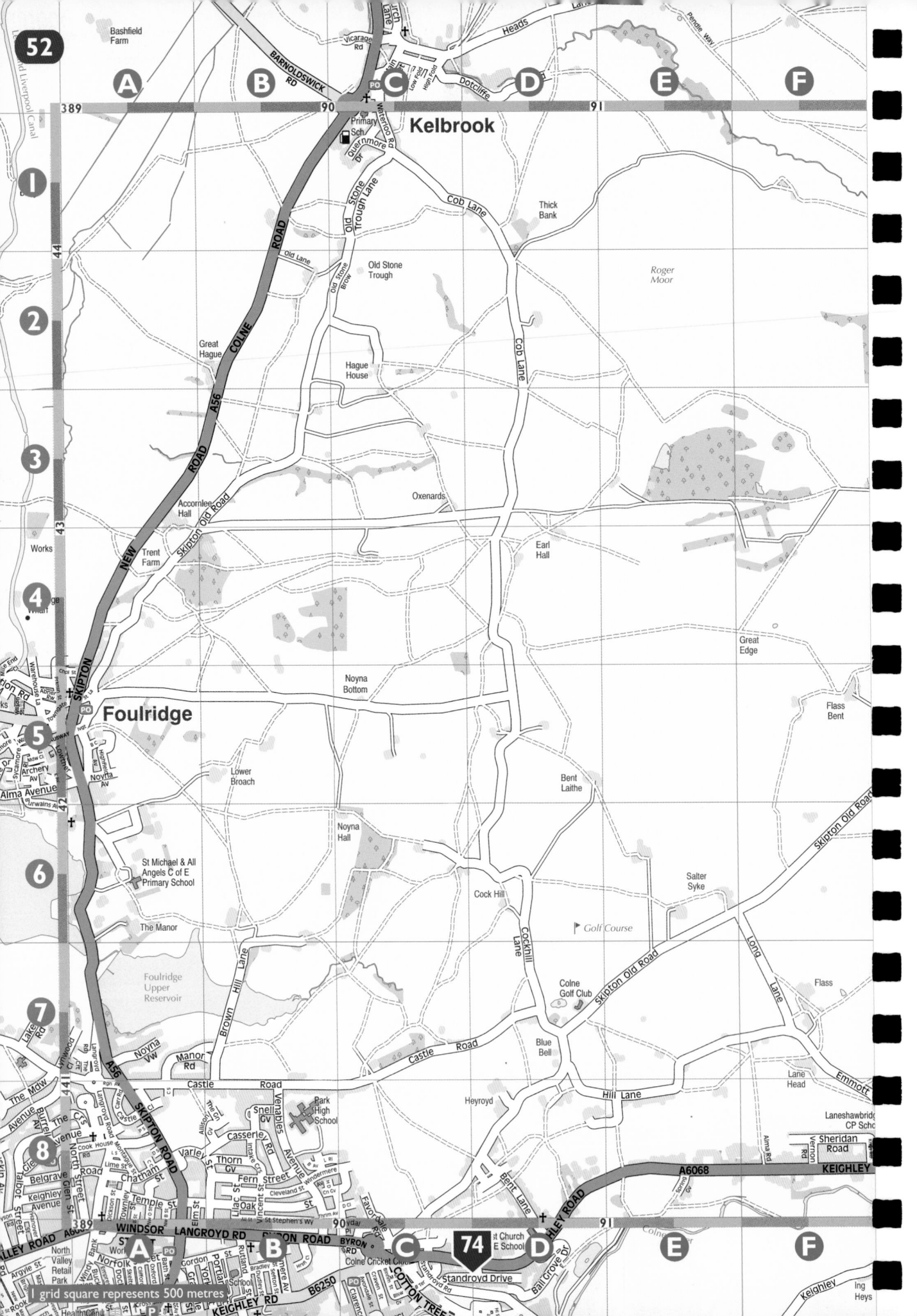

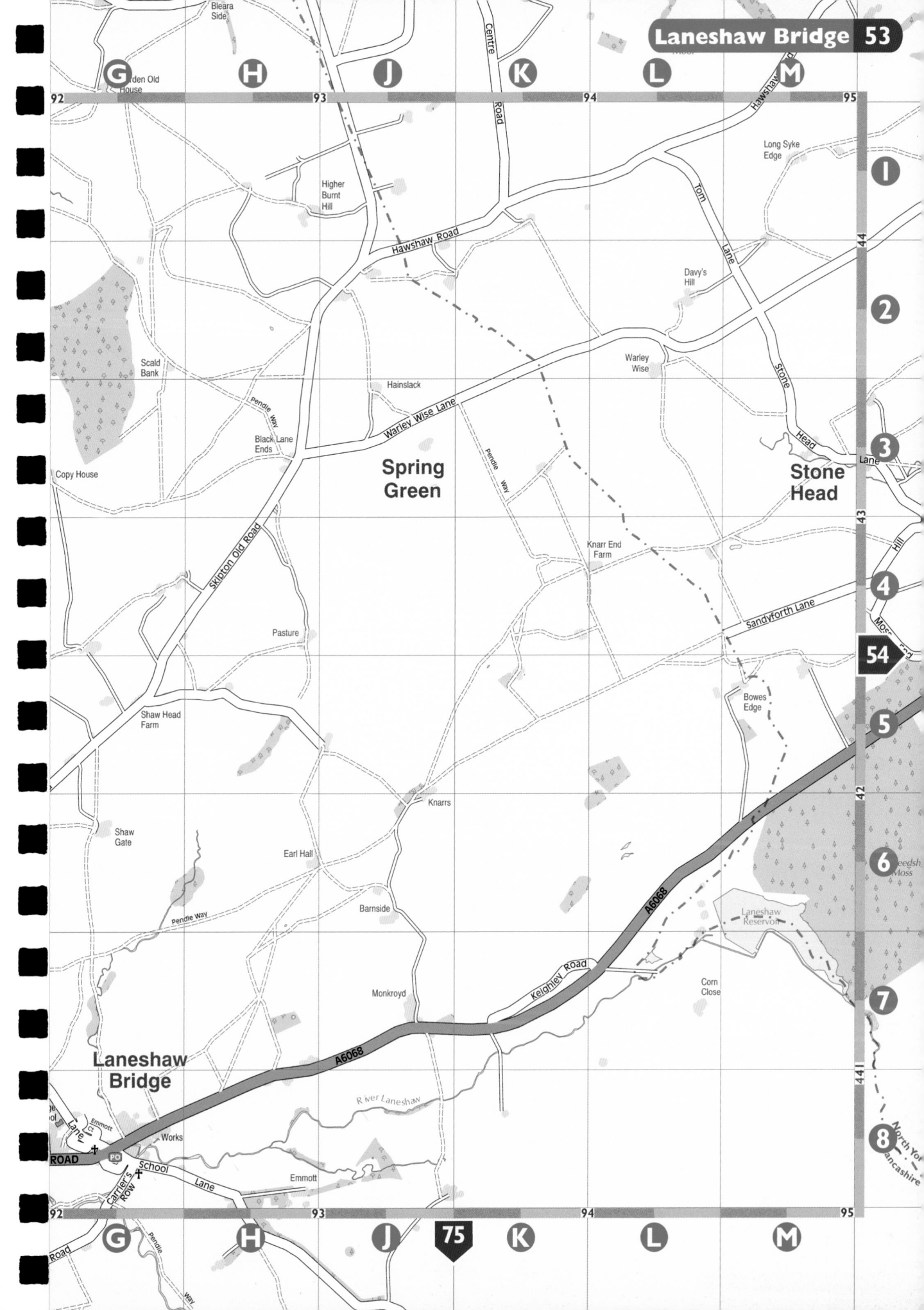

G H J K L M

92 93 94 95

Bleara Side

Garden Old House

Higher Burnt Hill

Long Syke Edge

I

Hawshaw Road

Davy's Hill

2

Scald Bank

Warley Wise

Hainslack

Warley Wise Lane

Black Lane Ends

Pendle Way

Spring Green

Pendle Way

Stone Head

3

Copy House

Knarr End Farm

Sandyforth Lane

4

Skipton Old Road

54

Pasture

Bowes Edge

5

Shaw Head Farm

6

Reedsh Moss

Knarrs

Shaw Gate

Earl Hall

Pendle Way

A6068

Laneshaw Reservoir

Barnside

Keighley Road

Corn Close

7

Monkroyd

A6068

Laneshaw Bridge

River Laneshaw

Works

8

Emmott

ROAD

PO

School Lane

Carrier's Row

Emmott

North Yor Lancashire

92 93 94 95

G H J **75** K L M

Road

Pendle Way

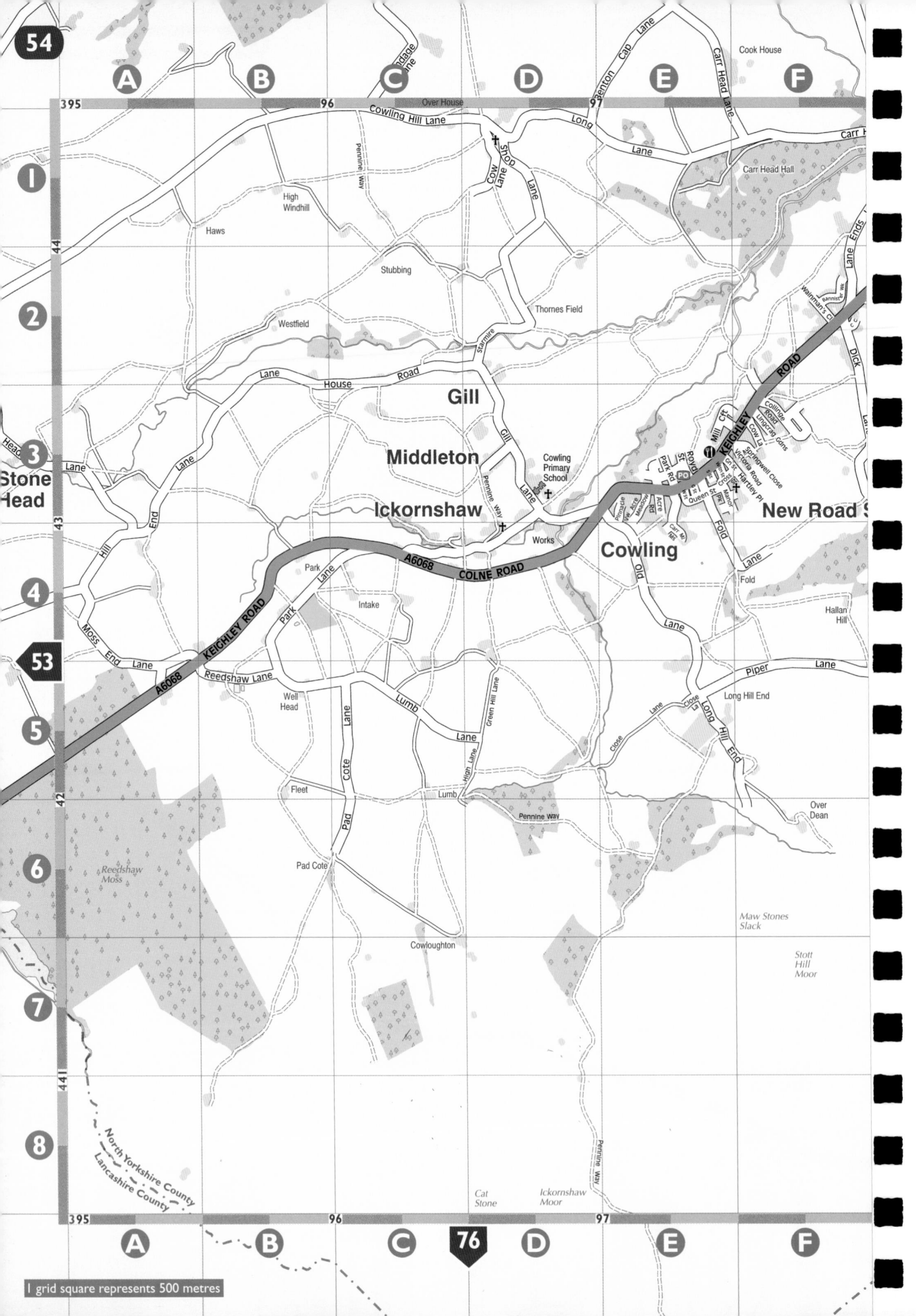

A B C D E F

395 96 97

I

High
Windhill

Haws

Stubbing

Over House

Cowling Hill Lane

Long
Lane

Cook House

Carr Head Hall

Carr H

Lane Ends

2

Westfield

House

Lane

Road

Thornes Field

Stanmire

Gill

Collinge
Road

Ungood Gdns

Victoria Road

3

Stone
Head

Lane

Lane

End

Hill

Lane

Middleton

Ickornshaw

Gill

Lane

Pennine Way

Cowling
Primary
School

Works

KEIGHLEY

Royd

St

PO

Park Rd

Queen St

Mill Cft

Fold

New Road S

ROAD

KEIGHLEY

4

Park Lane

Park

Lane

Intake

A6068 COLNE ROAD

Cowling

Acre

Meadow

Old

Lane

Fold

Lane

Hallan
Hill

53

KEIGHLEY ROAD

A6068 Reedshaw Lane

Well
Head

Lane

Cote

Lumb

Lane

Green Hill Lane

High Lane

Close

Lane

Lane

Close Ct

Long Hill End

Piper Lane

Long Hill End

5

Fleet

Pad

Lumb

Pennine Way

Over
Dean

6

Reedshaw
Moss

Pad Cote

Cowloughton

Maw Stones
Slack

Stott
Hill
Moor

7

441

8

North Yorkshire County

Lancashire County

Cat
Stone

Ickornshaw
Moor

Pennine Way

395 96 97

A B C D E F

I grid square represents 500 metres

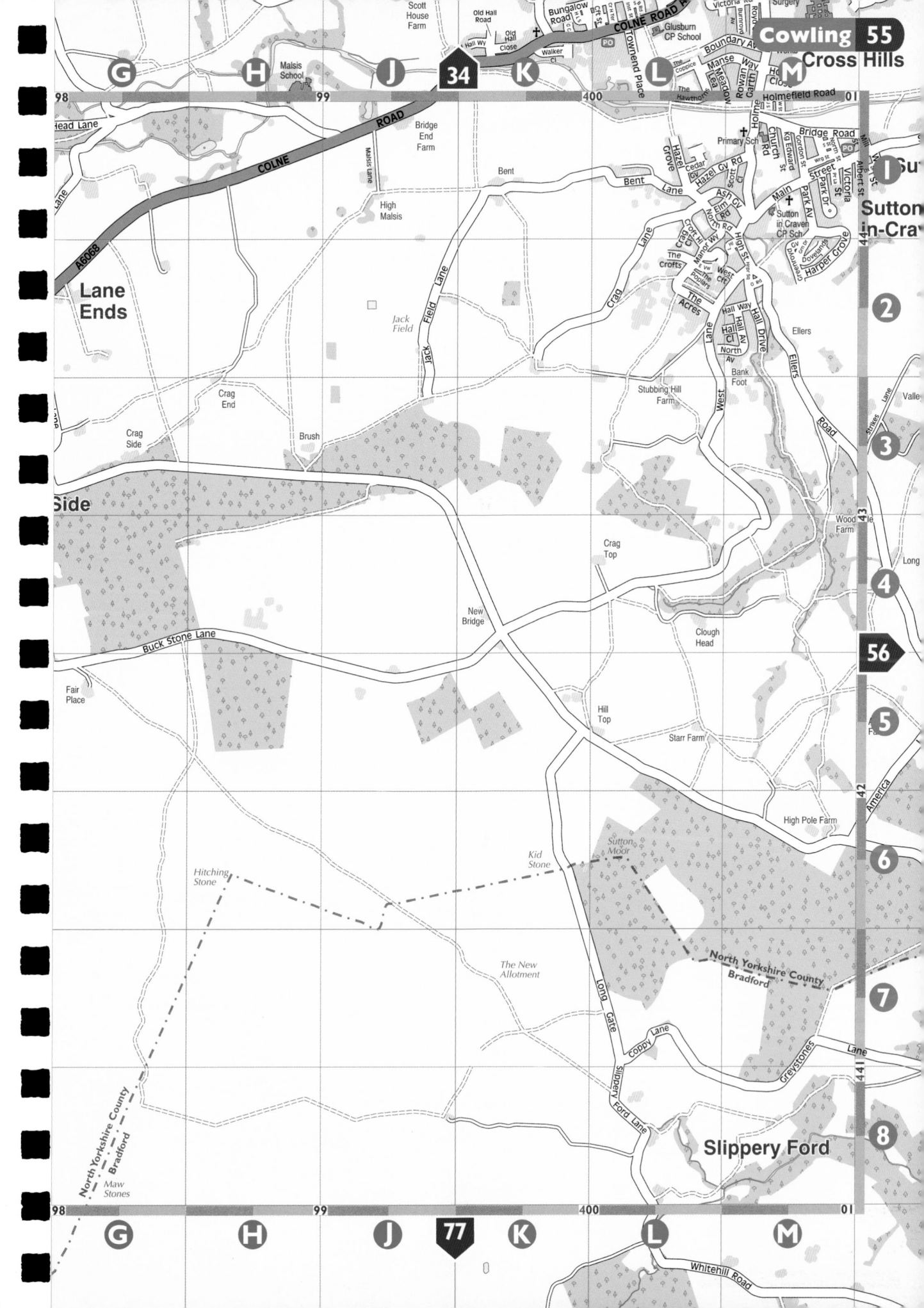

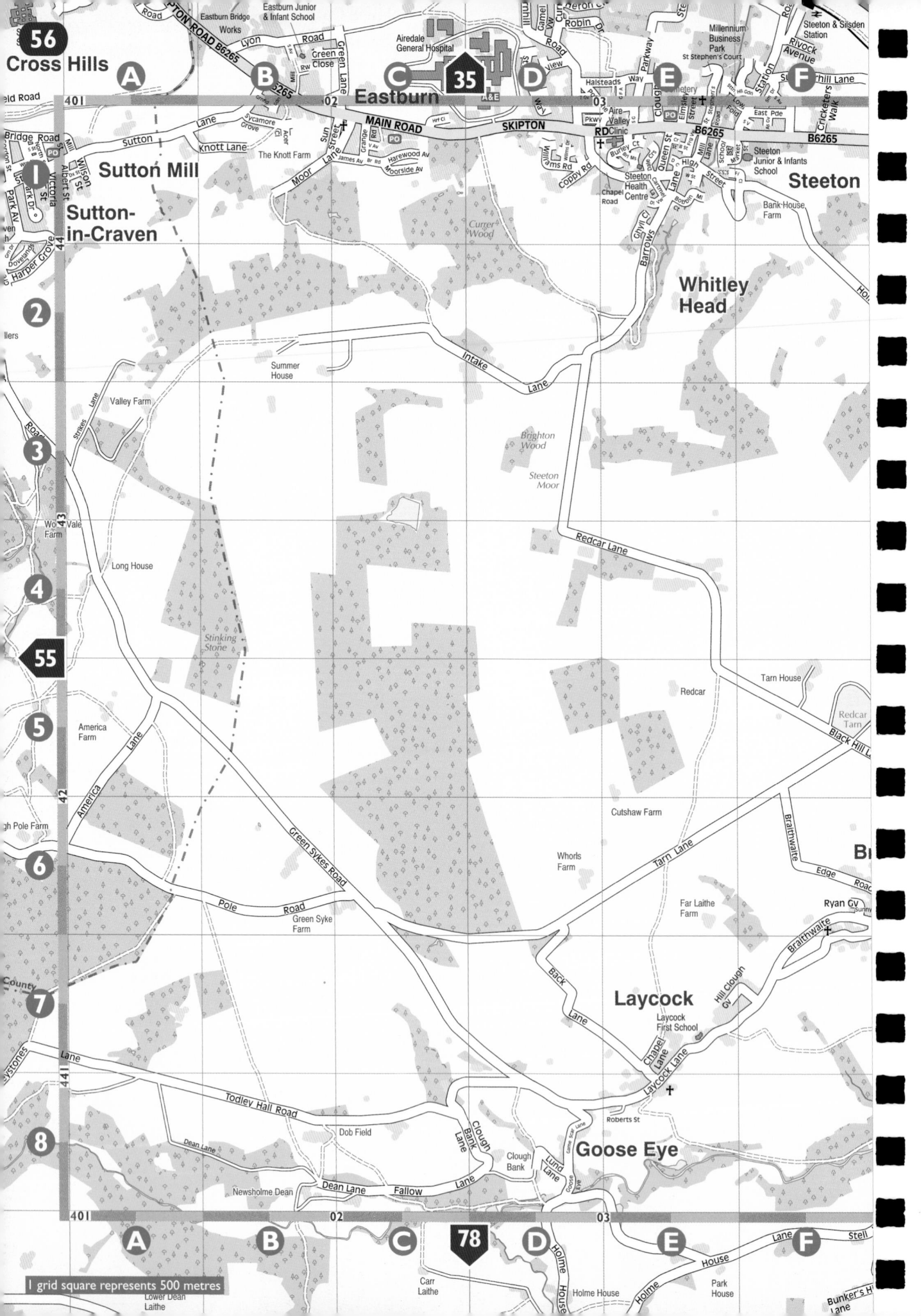

56 Cross Hills

A B C **35 Eastburn** D E F

I 2 3 4 **55** 5 6 7 8

A B **78** C D E F

Sutton Mill
Sutton-in-Craven
Airedale General Hospital
Eastburn Bridge Works
Eastburn Junior & Infant School
SKIPTON
Steeton
Steeton & Silsden Station
Rivock Avenue
Millennium Business Park
St Stephen's Court
Whitley Head
Steeton Junior & Infants School
Bank House Farm
Steeton Health Centre
Summer House
Brighton Wood
Steeton Moor
Redcar Lane
Redcar
Tarn House
Redcar Tarn
Black Hill Lane
Valley Farm
Long House
Stinking Stone
America Farm
America Lane
Green Sykes Road
Pole Road
Green Syke Farm
Cutshaw Farm
Whorls Farm
Tarn Lane
Braithwaite
Edge Road
Ryan Gv
Far Laithe Farm
Back Lane
Laycock
Laycock First School
Hill Clough Gv
Todley Hall Road
Dean Lane
Dob Field
Clough Bank Lane
Clough Bank
Lund Lane
Chapel Lane
Laycock Lane
Goose Eye
Newsholme Dean
Dean Lane
Fallow Lane
Carr Laithe
Holme House
Park House
The Knott Farm
Knott Lane
Main Road
Moor Lane
Intake Lane
Harewood Road
Moorside Av
Sycamore Grove
Lower Dean Laithe

I grid square represents 500 metres

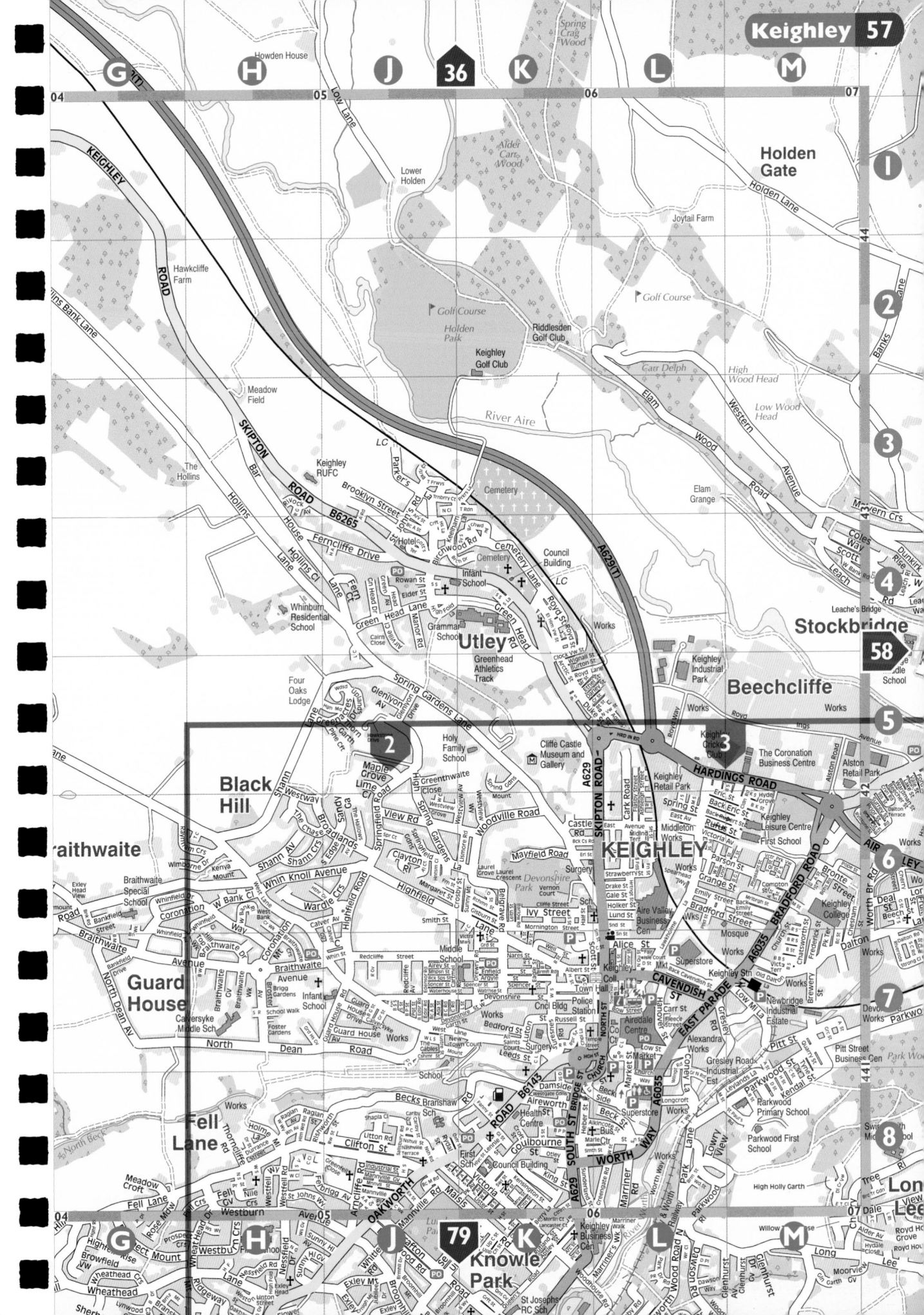

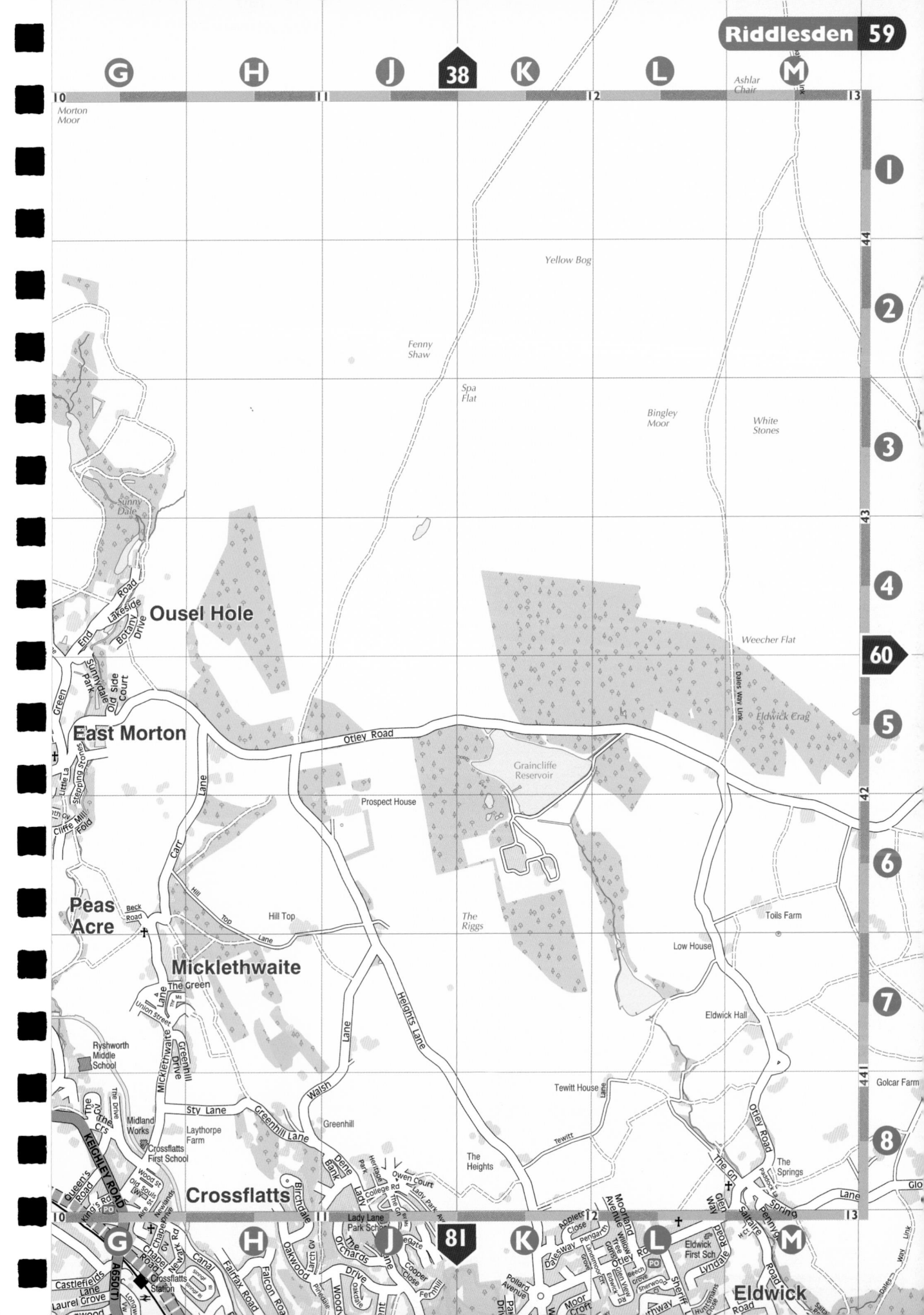

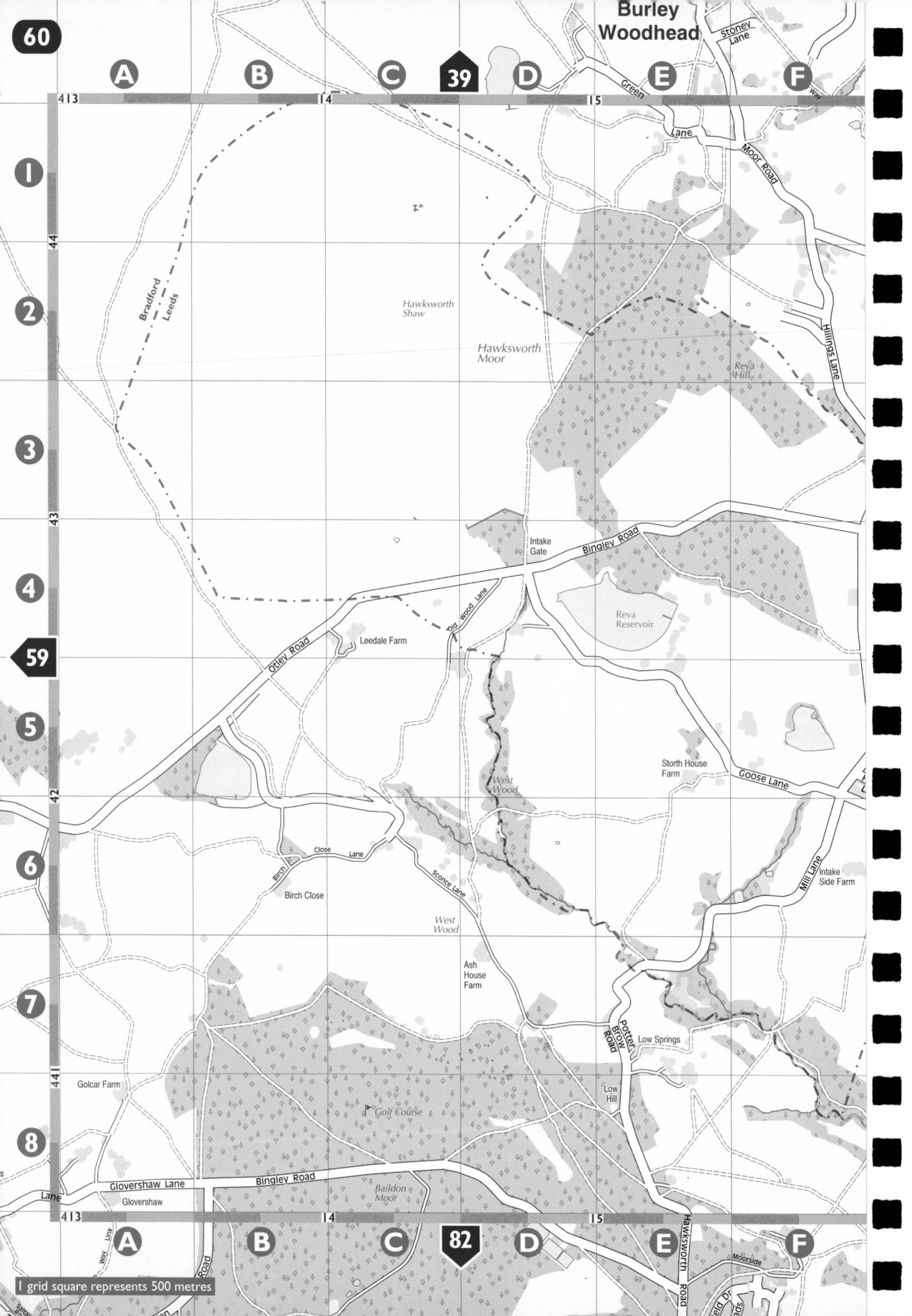

Burley Woodhead

A B C 39 D E F

413 14 15

I
44
2
3
43
4
59
5
42
6
7
441
8

Bradford
Leeds

Hawksworth Shaw

Hawksworth Moor

Reva Hill

Intake Gate

Bingley Road

Reva Reservoir

Old Wood Lane

Otley Road

Leedale Farm

West Wood

Storth House Farm

Goose Lane

Close Lane

Birch Close

Sconce Lane

West Wood

Ash House Farm

Potter Brow Road

Low Springs

Low Hill

Mill Lane

Intake Side Farm

Golcar Farm

Golf Course

Glovershaw Lane

Bingley Road

Baildon Moor

Glovershaw

Way Link

Lane

413 14 15

A B C 82 D E F

Stoney Lane

Green Lane

Moor Road

Hillings Lane

Way

Hawksworth Road

Moorside

1 grid square represents 500 metres

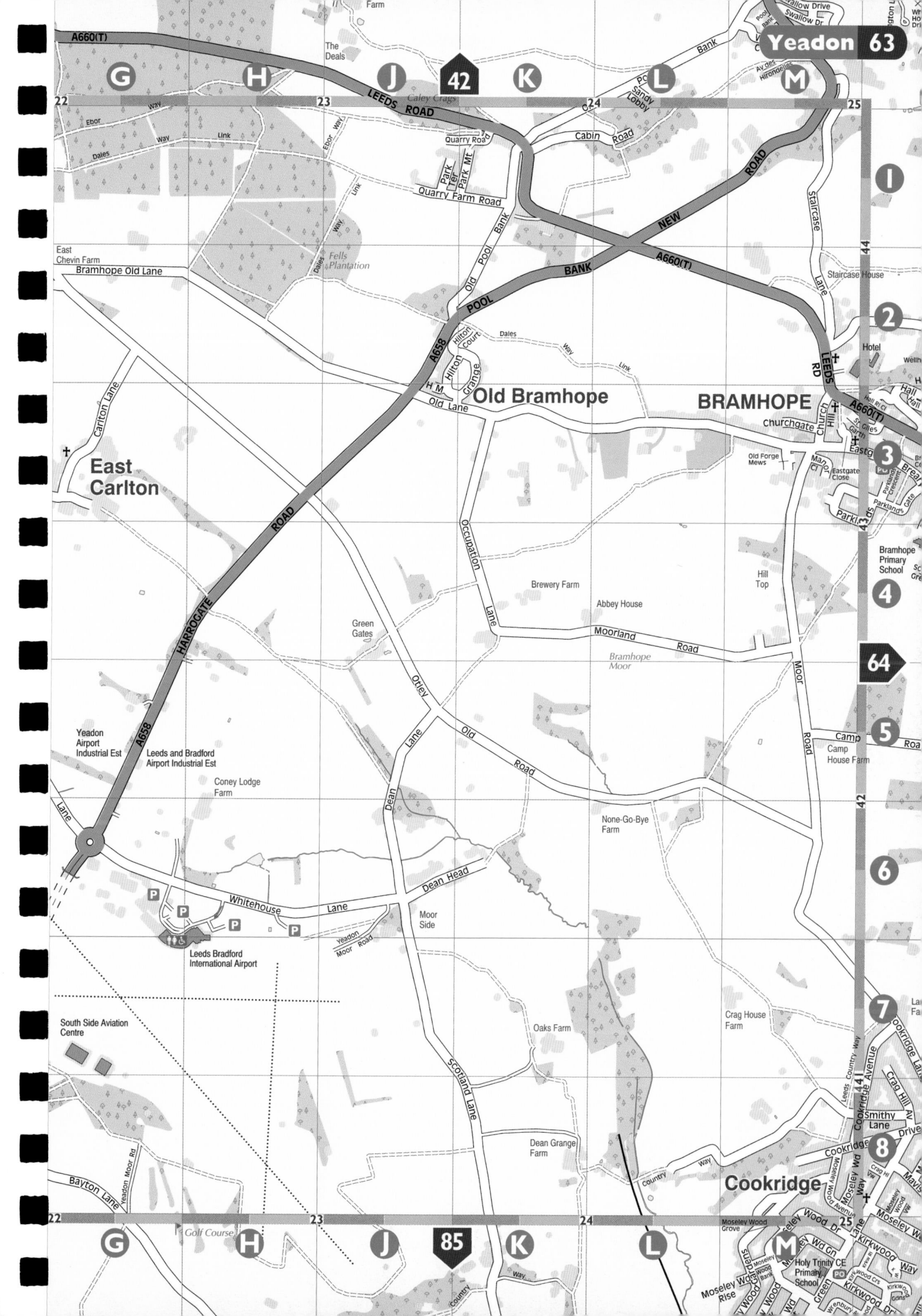

64

A   B   C   43   D   E   A F hingto

425   26   27

I

Staircase Lane

Staircase House

2

Hall Drive

Hotel

Wellhead Close

LEEDS RD

A660(T)

Church Hill

St. Giles' Garth

Eastgate

3

Eastgate Close

PO

Glenmore Court

Breary Court

Creskeld Gdns

Creskeld Dr

Creskeld Garth

Creskeld Park

Breary Crescent

Breary Lane

Creskeld Lane

Breary Lane East

Dales Way

Link

Dales

Bank Top

East Breary

Bank Foot Farm

Bank Side

Bank Hill

Black Hill Road

Arthington Garth West

Station Road

Creskeld Hall

Wood Top Farm

Creskeld Lane

ARTHINGTON LANE

Holt Farm

Grange Farm

43

Parkland's Gate

Tredgold Crs

Tredgold Garth

Tredgold Avenue

Bramhope Primary School

School Green

Breary Rise

High Rdg Way

Spring Wood

Breary Grange

4

Long Meadows

South Mead

North Mead

Sandy Wk

Wynmore End

Meadow End

Wynmore Drive

Wynmore Crescent

Wynmore Avenue

Southfield

Meadow Garth

The Poplars

The Rowans

The Cedars

Birches

63

Moor Road

5

Camp Road

Camp House Farm

The Sycamore Close

The Sycamores

West Park Bramhope RUFC

Bramhope Grove Farm

Breary Marsh

Kings Road

Kings Road

A660(T)

LEEDS ROAD

Arthington Road

Black Hill

Blackhill Farm

6

42

Country Way

Leeds

Golden Acre Park and Gardens

Leeds Country Way

FIV

7

Lane End Farm

Rushes Farm

Lane

Cocker Hill Farm

Adel Dam

Eccup Lane

Cookridge Lane

Cragg Hill Av

Golf Course

Pinfold

LS16

OTLEY ROAD

Adel Mi

Golf

8

Cookridge Avenue

Smithy Lane

Crag Hill Drive

Mavis Av

Cookridge Gv

Cookridge Lane

Hall La

Cookridge Hall Golf & Country Club

Cookridge Hall

Manor Farm

A660(T)

Kingsley Dr

Headingley Golf Club

Stairfoot Close

Stair

Moseley Wood Dr

Moseley Wd Gn

Kirkwood Way

Holy Trinity CE Primary School

PO

Moseley Way

425   26   Holt   27

A   B   86   C   D   E   F

Holtdale Avenue

Holtdale Approach

Holt Pk Close

Holt Farm Rd

Holt Pk Road

Gainsbro Avenue

Gainsbro Drive

Kingsley Dr

Kingsley Drive

Chestnut Court

Beechwood Court

Back Church Lane

Church

1 grid square represents 500 metres

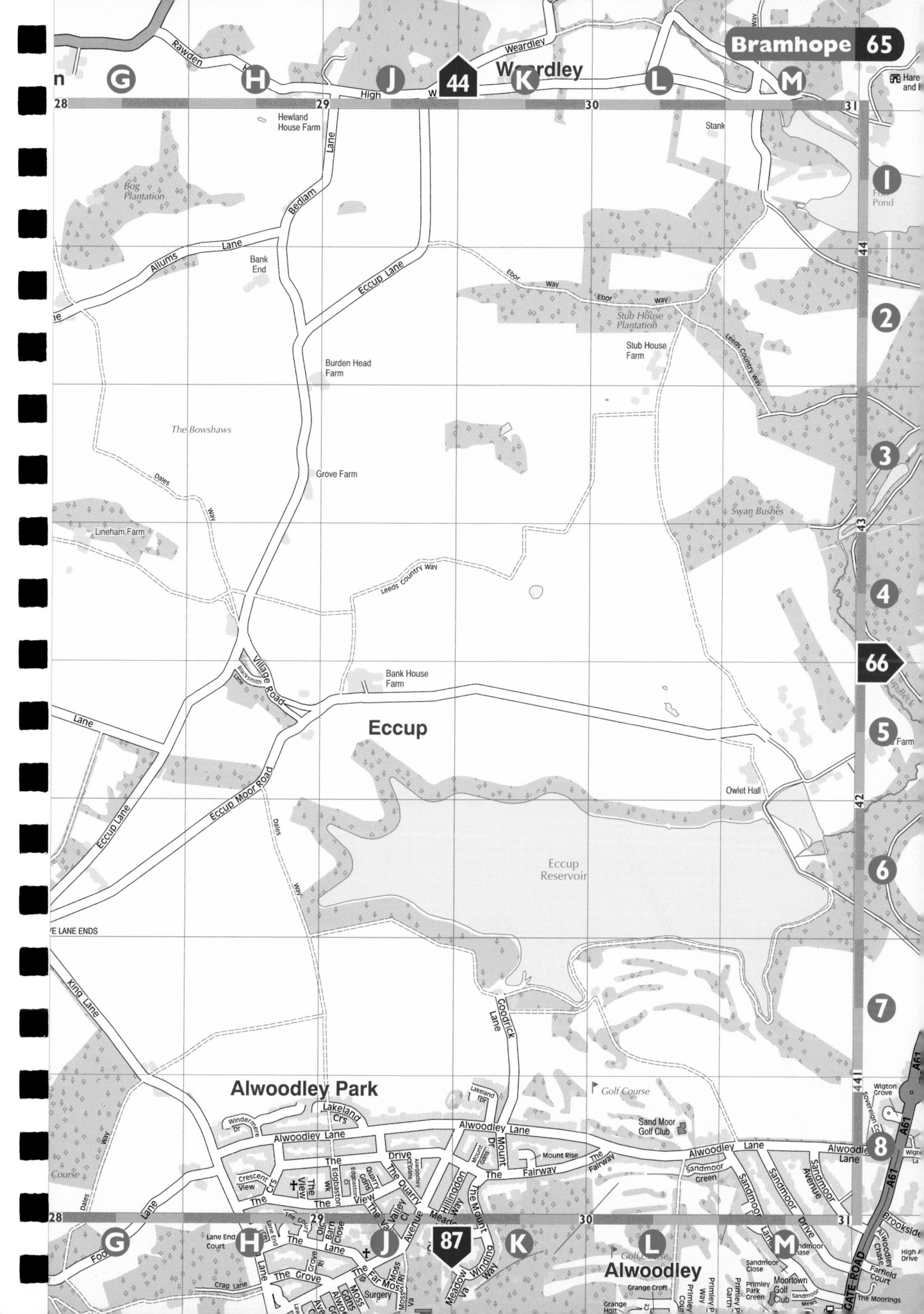

G H J 44 K L M

28 29 30 31

Rawden
Weardley
Weardley
High
Lane
W

Hewland
House Farm

Bog
Plantation

Bedlam

Allums

Lane

Bank
End

Eccup Lane

Ebor Way

Way

Ebor Way

*Stub House
Plantation*

Stub House
Farm

Stank

Fish
Pond

I

2

Leeds Country Way

43

3

Swan Bushes

Burden Head
Farm

The Bowshaws

Dales

Way

Grove Farm

Lineham Farm

Leeds Country Way

4

66

ub Beck

Village Road

Blacksmith Lane

Bank House
Farm

Lane

Eccup

Eccup Lane

Eccup Moor Road

Dales

Way

Owlet Hall

5 Farm

42

6

*Eccup
Reservoir*

VE LANE ENDS

King Lane

Lane

Goodrick

7

441

Wigton
Grove

sovereign cr

A61

A61

Alwoodley Park

Windermere
Dr

Lakeland
Crs

Alwoodley Lane

Lakeland
Dr

Golf Course

Sand Moor
Golf Club

Alwoodley Lane

8 Wigto

Crescent
View

The
View

Wk

Drive

Edgbaston

The Quarry

Quarry
Gdns

Junctions

Alwoodley Lane

Mount
Dr side

The
Fairway

Mount Rise

The
Fairway

Sandmoor
Green

Sandmoor

Drive

Sandmoor
Avenue

Alwoodley
Lane

Sandmoor

Brookside

High
Drive

Farfield
Court

Course

Way

Dales

Lane

The
Crs

The

The Cot

The
Grove

Lane End

Barn
Close

Far Moss

Moss
Rd

St Valley Cl

Hillingdon

The
Lane

Meadow

Winding Way

The Mount

Way

GATE ROAD

The Moorings

Mews

G H J 87 K L M

28 29 30 31

Foo Lane Court Lane End The 87 Winding **Alwoodley**

Crag Lane

The Grove

Moss

Surgery

Golf

Grange Croft

Primley
Park Green

Primley
Way

Primley
Court

Moortown
Golf Club

Sandmoor
Chase

Grange
Holt

Sandmoor
Close

Primley P
Garth

45

88

65

LS17

A   B   C   D   E   F

1

2

3

4

5

6

7

8

Fish Pond

Grey Stone

Lofthouse Grange

Hollin Hall

HARROGATE ROAD

A61

Wike Lane

Lofthouse Farm

New Laithe Farm

Cemetery

Low Green Farm

Fortshot House

Fortshot Lane

Forge Lane

Wike

Manor Farm

Leeds Golf Centre

Wikefield Farm

Herd Farm

Eccup beck

School Lane

Golf Course

Brandon Lane

Millfield Farm

Wike Ridge

Manor House

HARROGATE ROAD

Manor House Lane

Leeds Grammar Junior School

Leeds Grammar School

Wigton Moor

Tarn Lane

Brandon Hall

Alwoodley Gates

A61

Wigton Grove

Wigton Gate

Alwoodley Golf Club

Wigton

Sovereign Court

Woodley Lane

Sandmoor Avenue

Golf Course

Wike Ridge Avenue

Wike Ridge Chase

Wigton Green

Wigton Park Close

Wigton Lane

West Dene

High Ash

High Ash Mt

Wigton Moor Primary Avenue

Carlton Garth

Wike Ridge Fold

Wike Ridge Ct

Wike Ridge Ms

Wike Ridge Lunt

Harrogate View

Emville Av

Brandon Ct

Silverdale

Newby Garth

Raygill Cl

Plantation Av

Brandon Golf Club

Back Holywell Lane

Golf Course

431

441

44

43

42

32

33

Sandmoor Chase

Gateways School

Moor Farm

1 grid square represents 500 metres

G 34 H 35 J ◆46 K L East Keswick M

Vicarage Farm
Lumby Lane
Rose Croft
South Mount
Whitegate
Meadow Cft
Paddock Gn
The Paddock
Main St
The Grove
P 36
Meadow Crse
Congre
Second
Maple
First Av

St Mary's Garth
Church Drive
School Lane
Keswick Gra
Laur
Close
I

Burn's Farm

The Drive

Keswick View
Wetherby Road
44
E R

Keswick Lane
Woodacre Green
Bankfield
Undel Close
Rigton Bank
Rigton Grn
Rigt
Greg
2

Gateon House Farm
Gateon House Lane
Rigton Grange
Woodacre Crescent
Bardsey Primary School
Woodacre Lane
Cornmill Close
Castle Cl
C L
Castle La
Grange Close
Margaret Av
Mill Lane
Wood Lane
Bardsey

Rigton Carr Farm
Leeds Country Way
Castle Gv
The Dell
†
A58(T)
43
3

Biggin Farm
Hetchell View
Bingle
Pump
4

Smithy Lane
Tithe Barn Lane
The Ginnel
Leeds Country Way
Wayside Crescent
Wayside Mount
LEEDS
A58(T)
ROAD
42
◆68

Wike Whin
Gill Beck
Spear Fir
Blackmoor Lane
Wayside Av
Leeds Country Way
5

Gill Lane
ckstone
Sheepcote Farm
Glenfield Caravan Park
Moor Lodge Park
Wayside Gardens

The Village Golf Course
Moss Syke
Malthouse Close
Green VW
Green Vw
PO
North Hill
The Croft
Scarcroft Court
Scarcroft

Golf Course
Scarcroft Golf Club
Green Wl
Thorner Lane
6

Coal Road
Golf Course
Moor Allerton Golf Club
Syke Lane
Bracken Park
Woodlands Park
Woodlands Close
Syke Gn
Stonefield
Larch Wood
7

Bracken Park
Fern Way
Fern Chase
Fern Croft
The Glade
Heather Vale
The Firs
Ling Lane
Heather Gardens
Manor Pk
Hellwood Lane
Manor
441

Ling Lane
Tarn Lane
Brandon Lane
Bay Horse Lane
Brandon Crescent
Brandon Lodge
Brandon Crescent
Manor Cottage Mews
8

The Path Road
G 34 H 35 J ◆89 K A58(T) ROAD 36 L M 37
Stoney Lane
LEEDS ROAD
Beech Grove
Carr Lane
Eltofts

LS23

West Woods

West Woods Farm

Clifford Moor Farm

Rhodes Lane

Clifford

Bramham Primary School

Bramham

Lyndon Road
Lyndon Avenue
Wetherby Road
Croft Drive
Clifford Road
Firbeck Road
Back Lane
New Rd
Town Hl
High St
Vicarage
Folly Lane
Orchard Ct
Bowcliffe Road
Freely Lane
Aberford Road
Prospect Bank

Minthorpe Lane

Hope Hall

Thorner Lane

Thorner Road

Tenter Hill

Bramham Biggin

Bramham Lodge

Bowcliffe Hall

Wellhill Farm

Terry Lug

Thorner Road

Dalton Lane

South Approach

Bramham Park

Rakes Wood

Paradise Farm

Black Fen

New Black Fen

Whittle Car

Margill Lane

South Approach

Windsor Farm

48

91

70

A1(T)

A1(M)

A   B   C   **51**   D   E   F

449   50   51

I

Hudson Way
Eastfield Close
Little Catterton Lane
Catterton Lane
Rolling Bridge
A64(T)
Bowbridge Farm
Auster Bank Vw
Field Drive
Toll Bar Way
Bow Bridge View
Turnpike Rd
A659
Ingleby
Prospect Court
Parkland Dr
Astr Bnk Crscnt
PO
Old Brewery Gdns
The Foss

2
COMMERCIAL STREET
YORK ROAD A659
Surg
Grange Crs
Grange Av
Tadcaster East Primary School
A64(T)
Oxton Hall
LS24

3
ster FC
Beech Close
Ouston Lane
Oxton Lane
Oxton Drive
Ouston Lane
Oxton Lane
Slice Lane

Oxton

4
Pallathorpe Farm

71

5
Kettleman Bridge
Ouston Farm

42

6
Grimston Grange
Limekiln Wood
Hornington Manor

7
Grimston Park

441

Kirkby Wharfe

8
River Wharfe

449   50   51

A   B   C   **94**   D   E   **F** est End

B1223

West End Approach   Mai

LANE

I grid square represents 500 metres

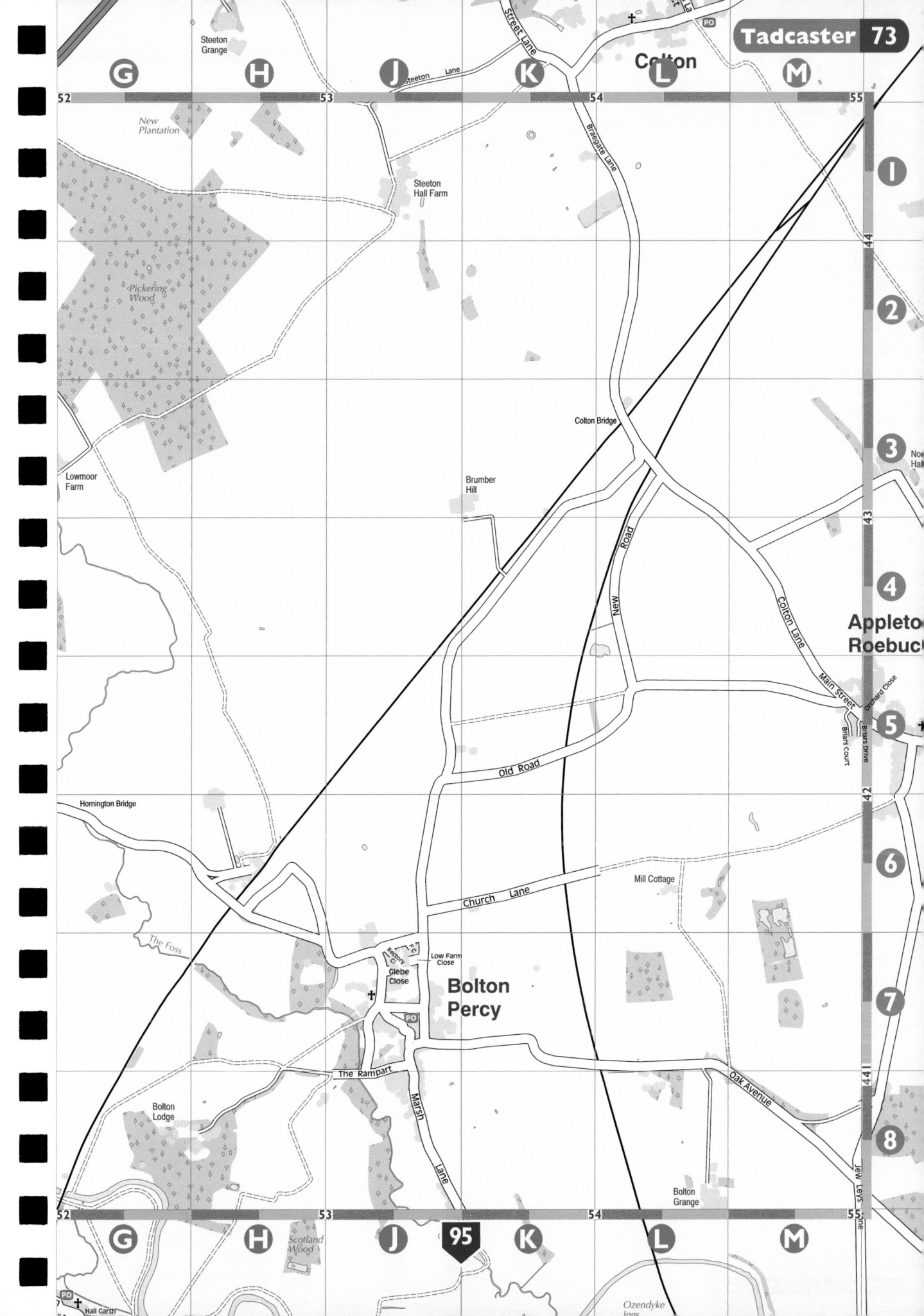

G H J K L M

52 53 54 55

I
2
3
4
5
6
7
8

Steeton
Grange

Colton

New
Plantation

Steeton Lane

Street Lane

Braegate Lane

PO

Steeton
Hall Farm

Pickering
Wood

Colton Bridge

Nor
Hal

Lowmoor
Farm

Brumber
Hill

New Road

Appleto
Roebuc

Colton Lane

Main Street

Orchard Close

Briars Drive

Briars Court

Hornington Bridge

Old Road

Church Lane

Mill Cottage

The Foss

Rectory

Low Farm
Close

Glebe
Close

**Bolton
Percy**

PO

The Rampart

Marsh Lane

Oak Avenue

Bolton
Lodge

Bolton
Grange

Jew Leys Lane

44

43

42

441

Scotland
Wood

PO

Hall Garth

Ozendyke
Ings

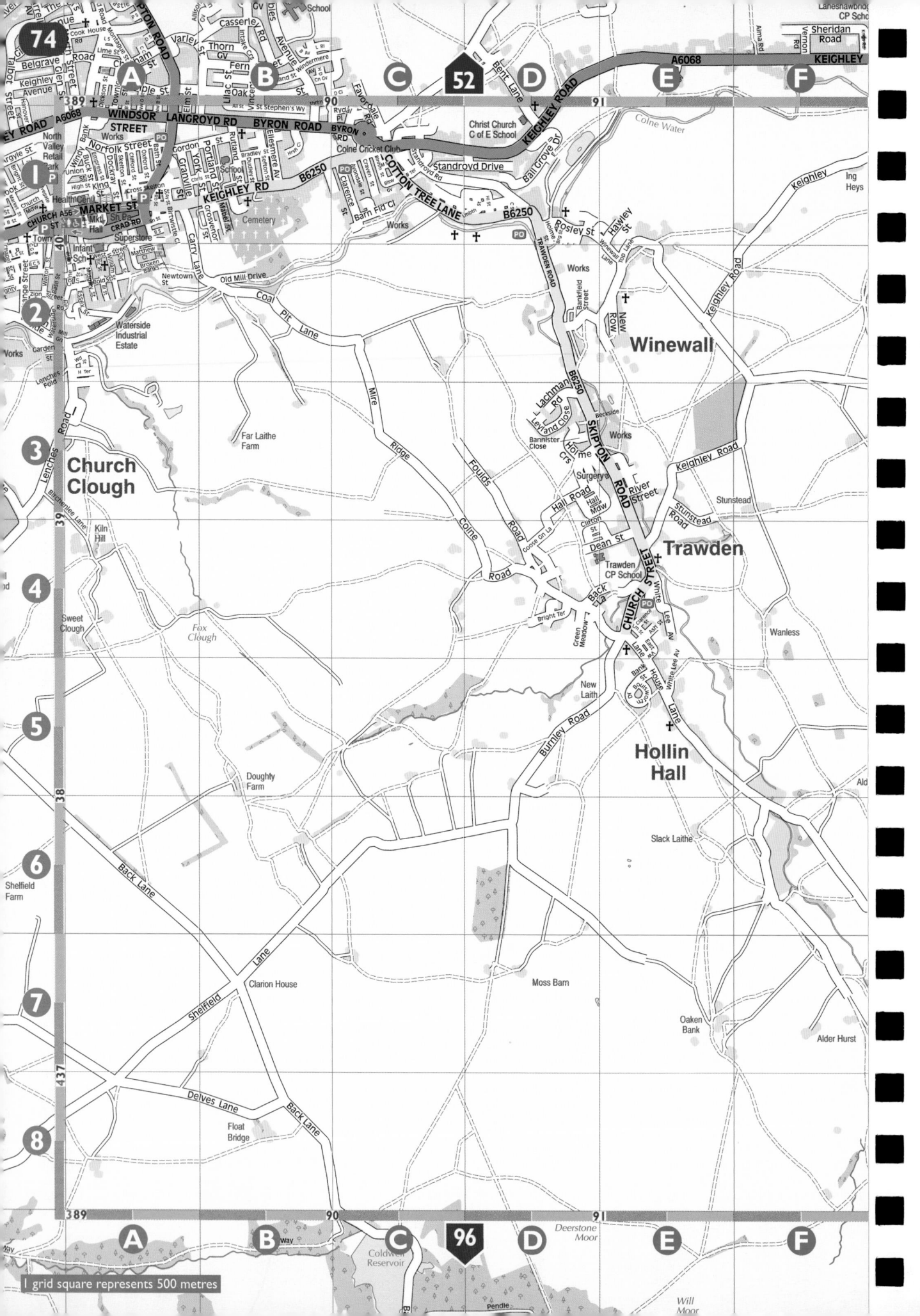

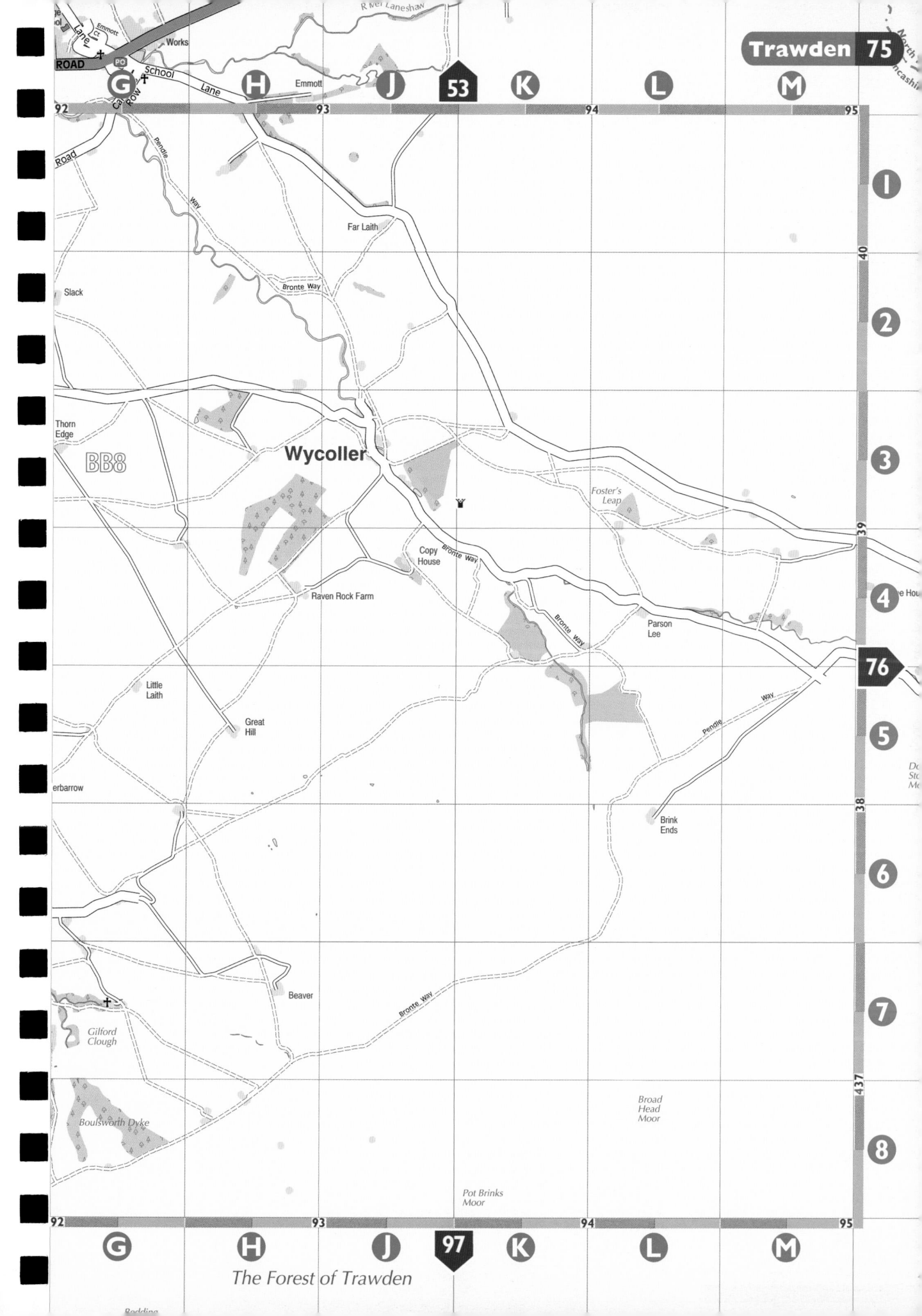

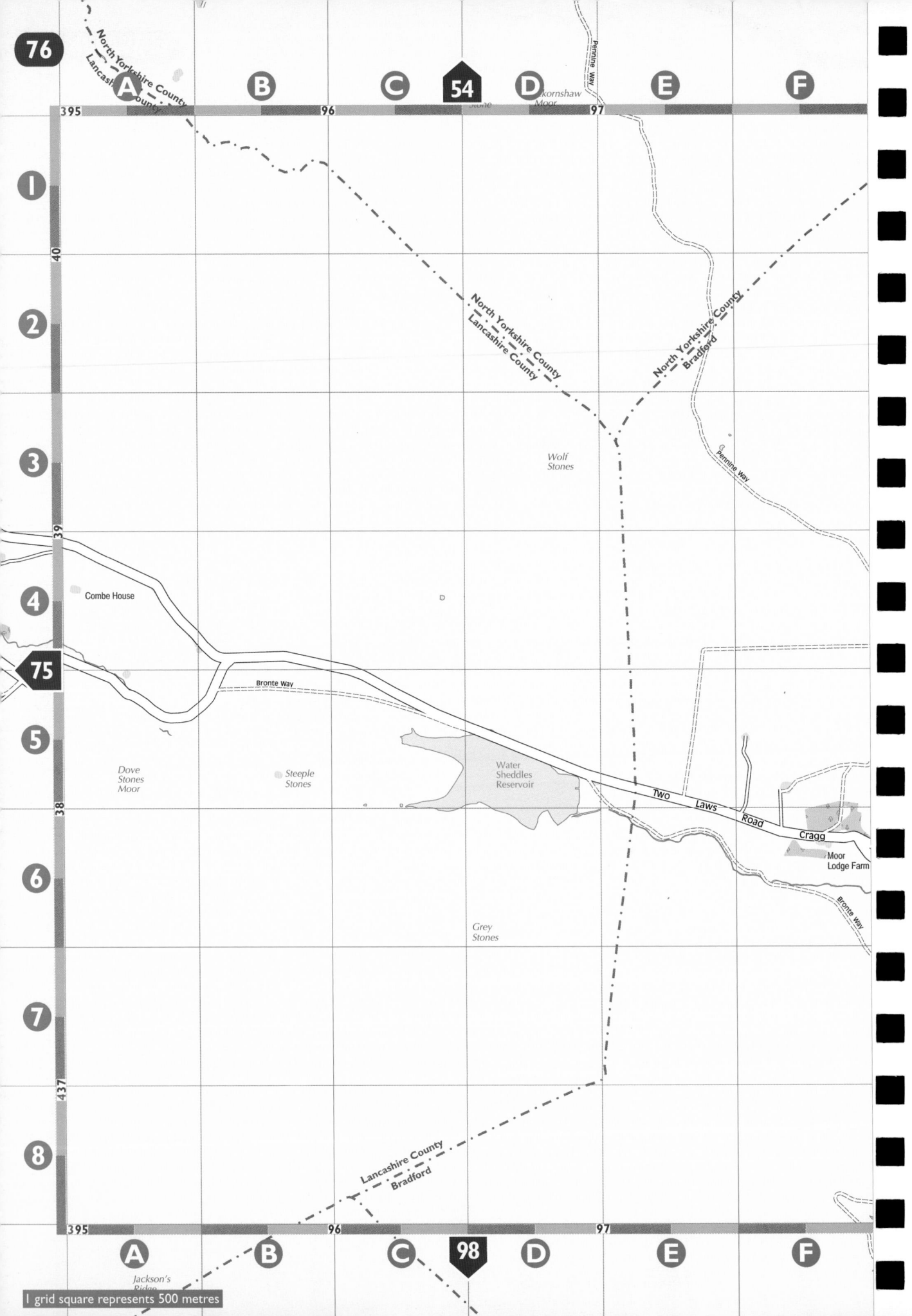

A **B** **C** 54 **D** **E** **F**

395 96 97

North Yorkshire County
Lancashire County

Pennine Way

1

40

North Yorkshire County
Lancashire County

North Yorkshire County
Bradford

2

3

39

Wolf
Stones

Pennine Way

Combe House

4

75

Bronte Way

5

38

Dove
Stones
Moor

Steeple
Stones

Water
Sheddles
Reservoir

Two Laws Road

Cragg

Moor
Lodge Farm

Bronte Way

6

Grey
Stones

7

437

8

395 96 97

Lancashire County
Bradford

A **B** **C** 98 **D** **E** **F**

Jackson's
Ridge

Lancashire County
Bradford

1 grid square represents 500 metres

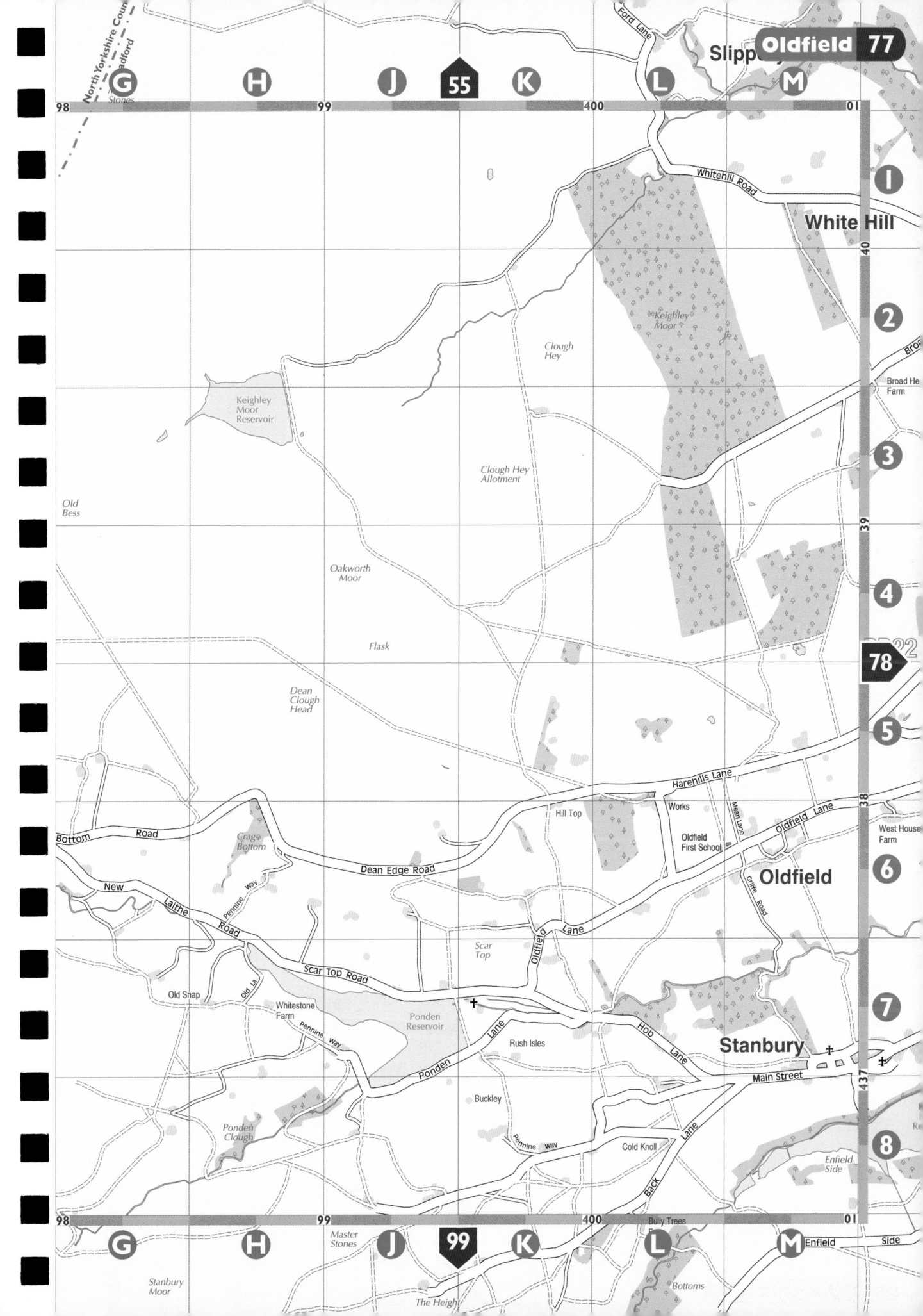

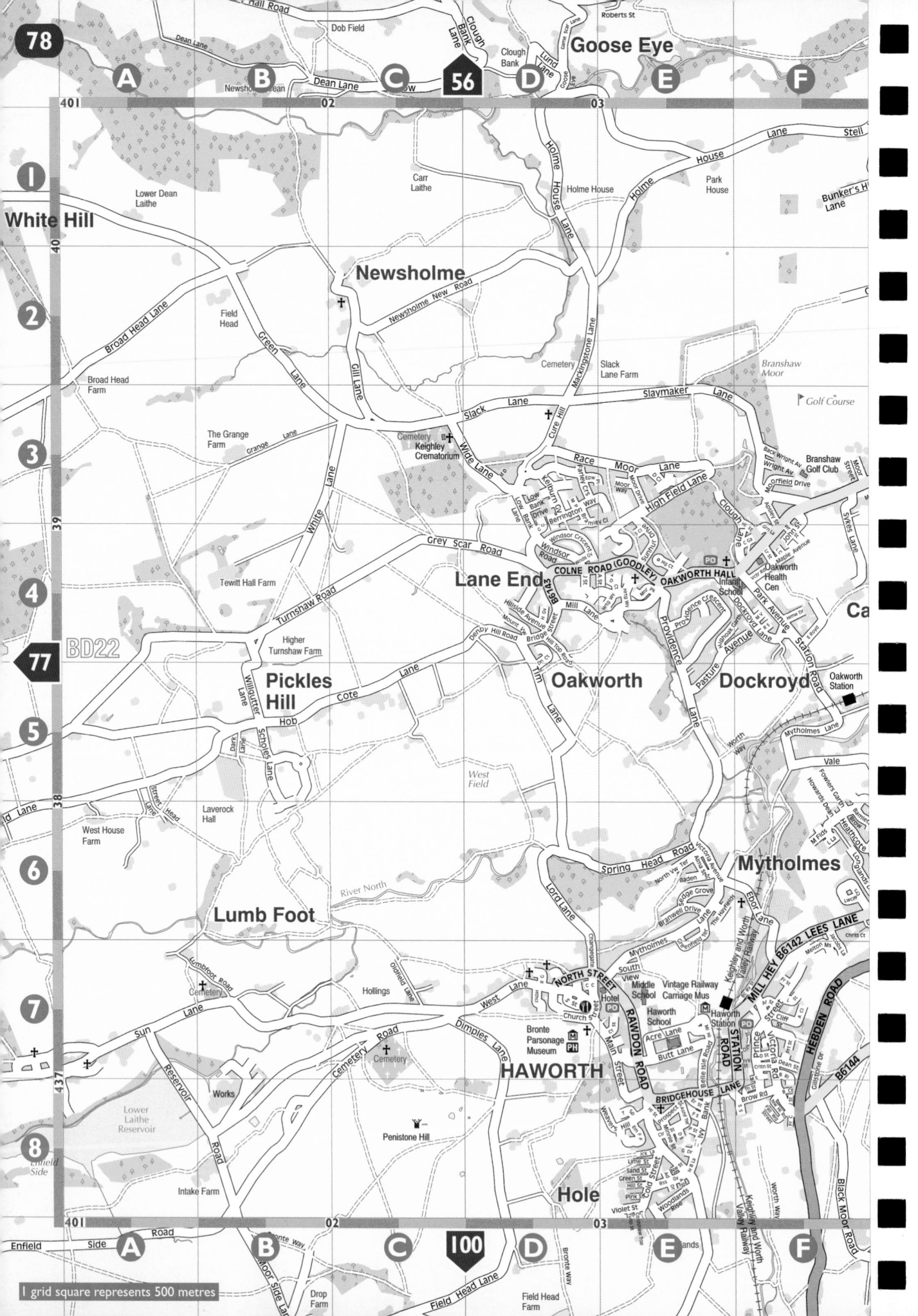

Goose Eye

White Hill

Newsholme

Lane End

Oakworth

Dockroyd

Mytholmes

Pickles Hill

Lumb Foot

HAWORTH

Hole

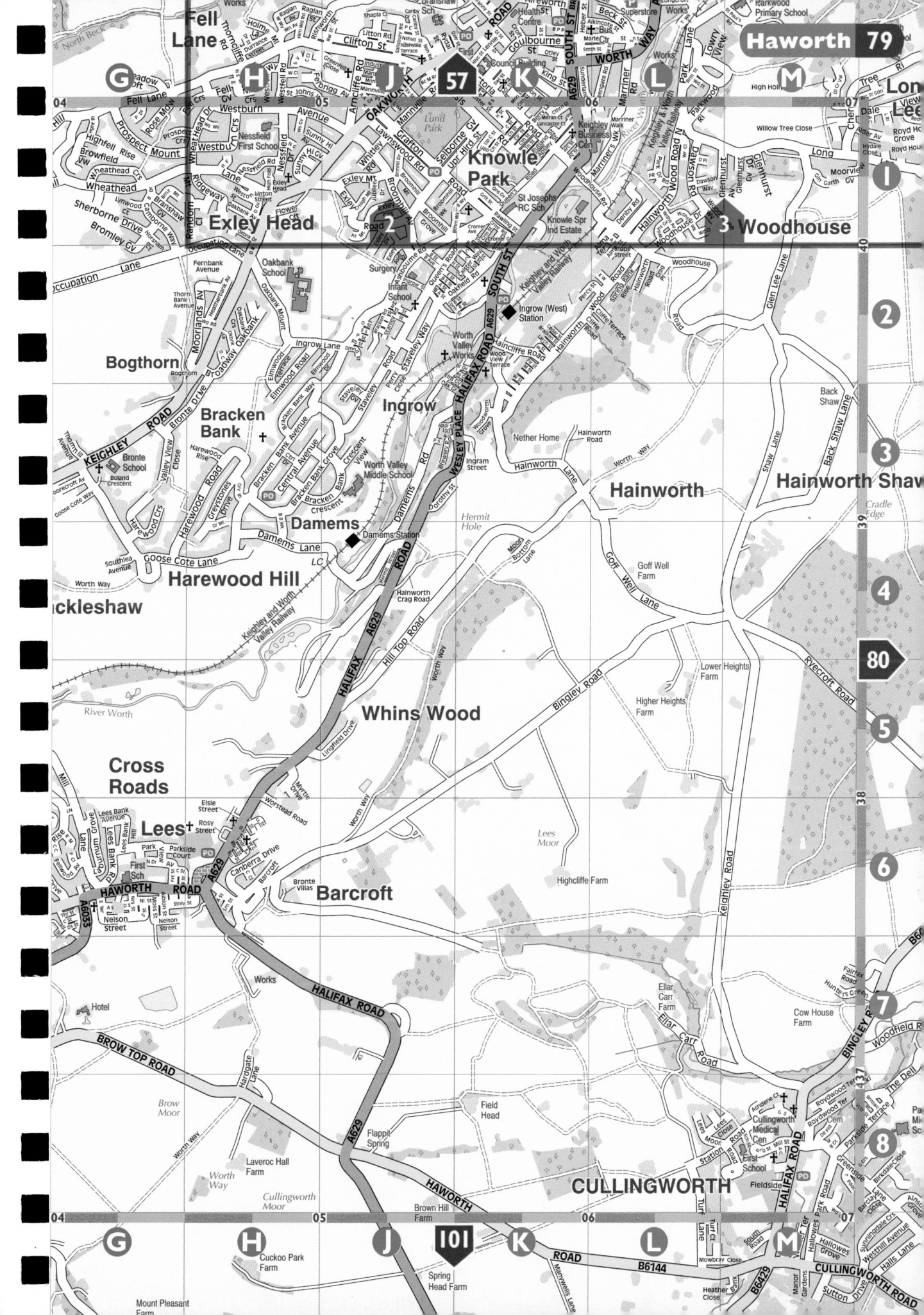

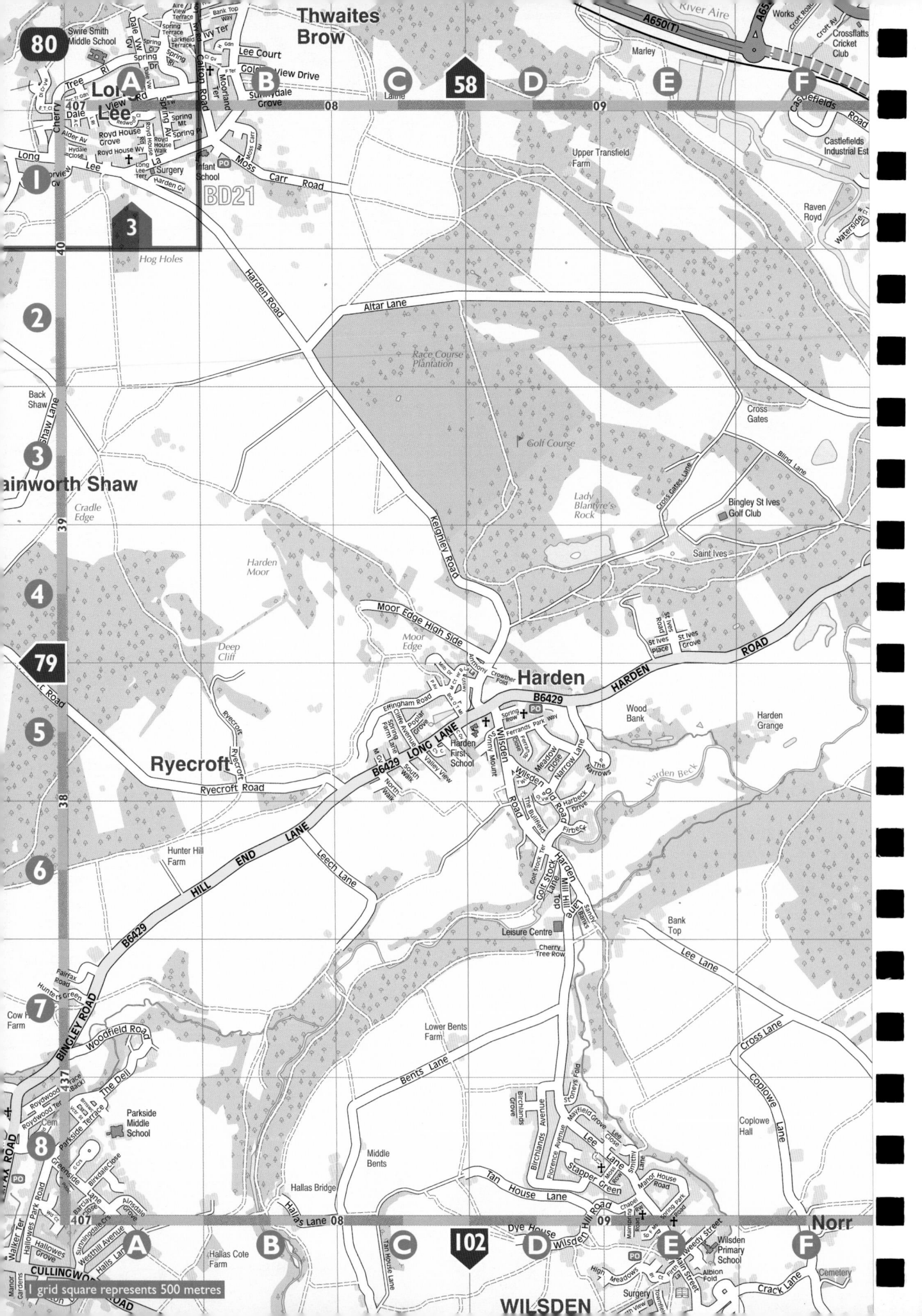

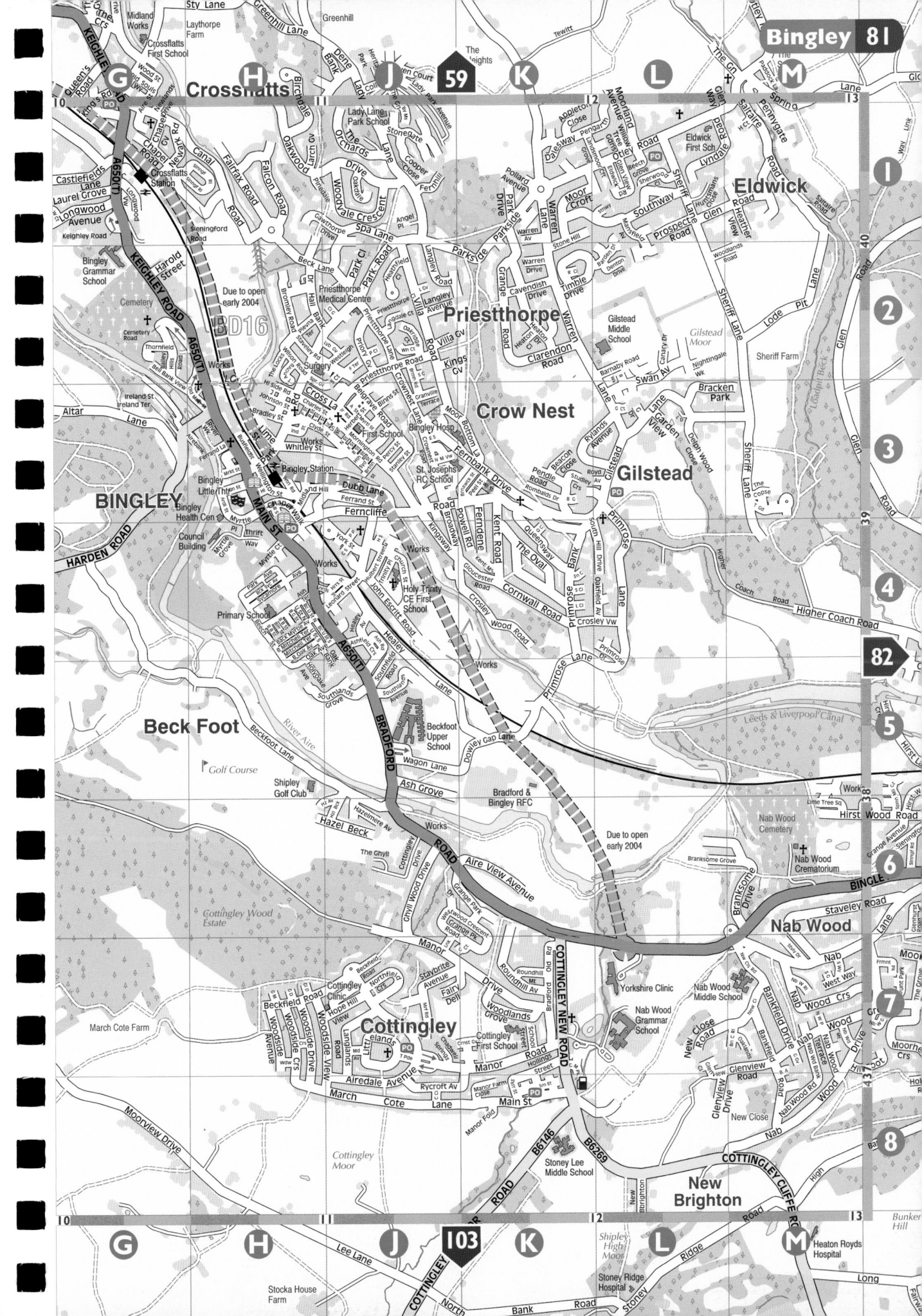

1 grid square represents 500 metres

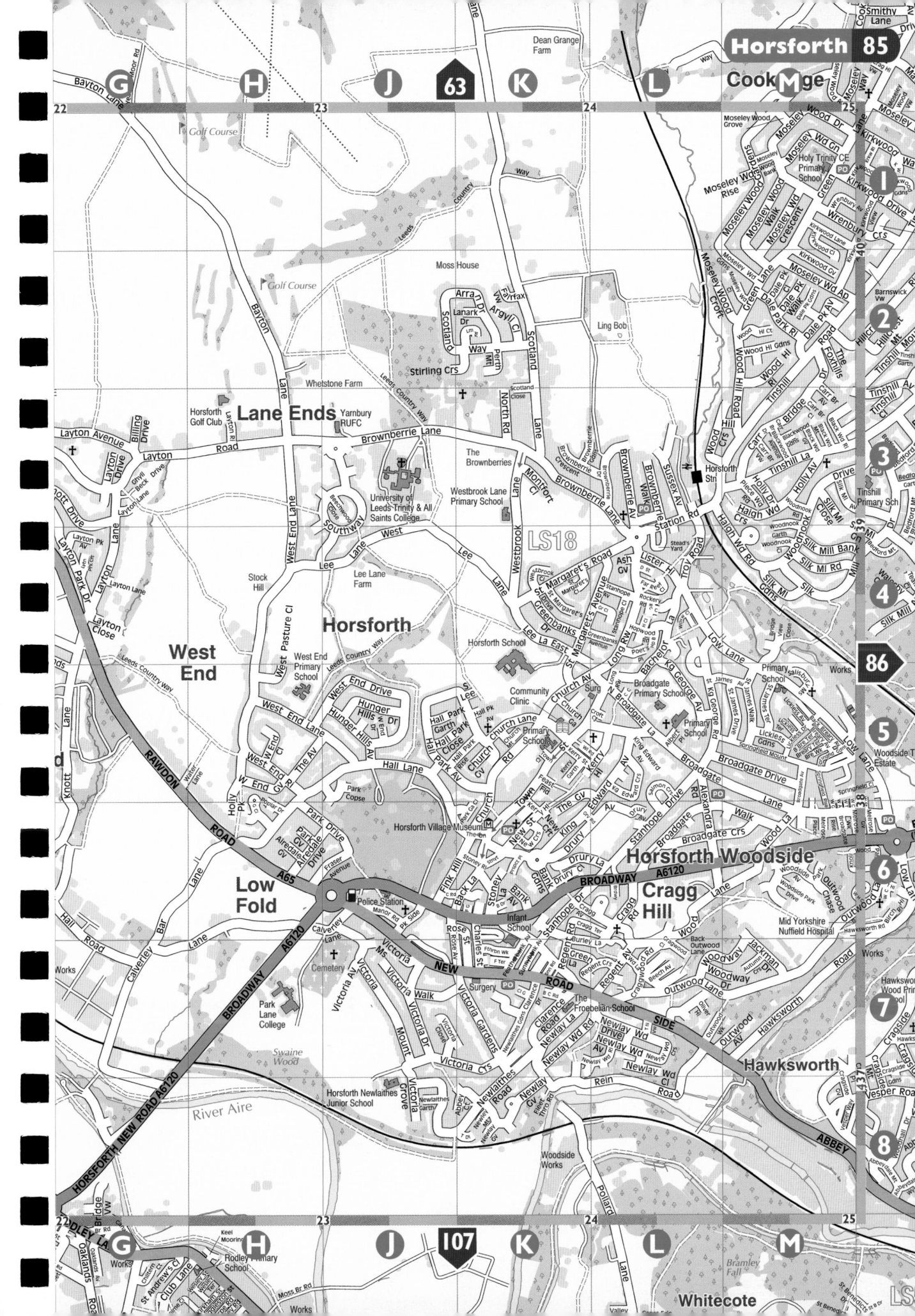

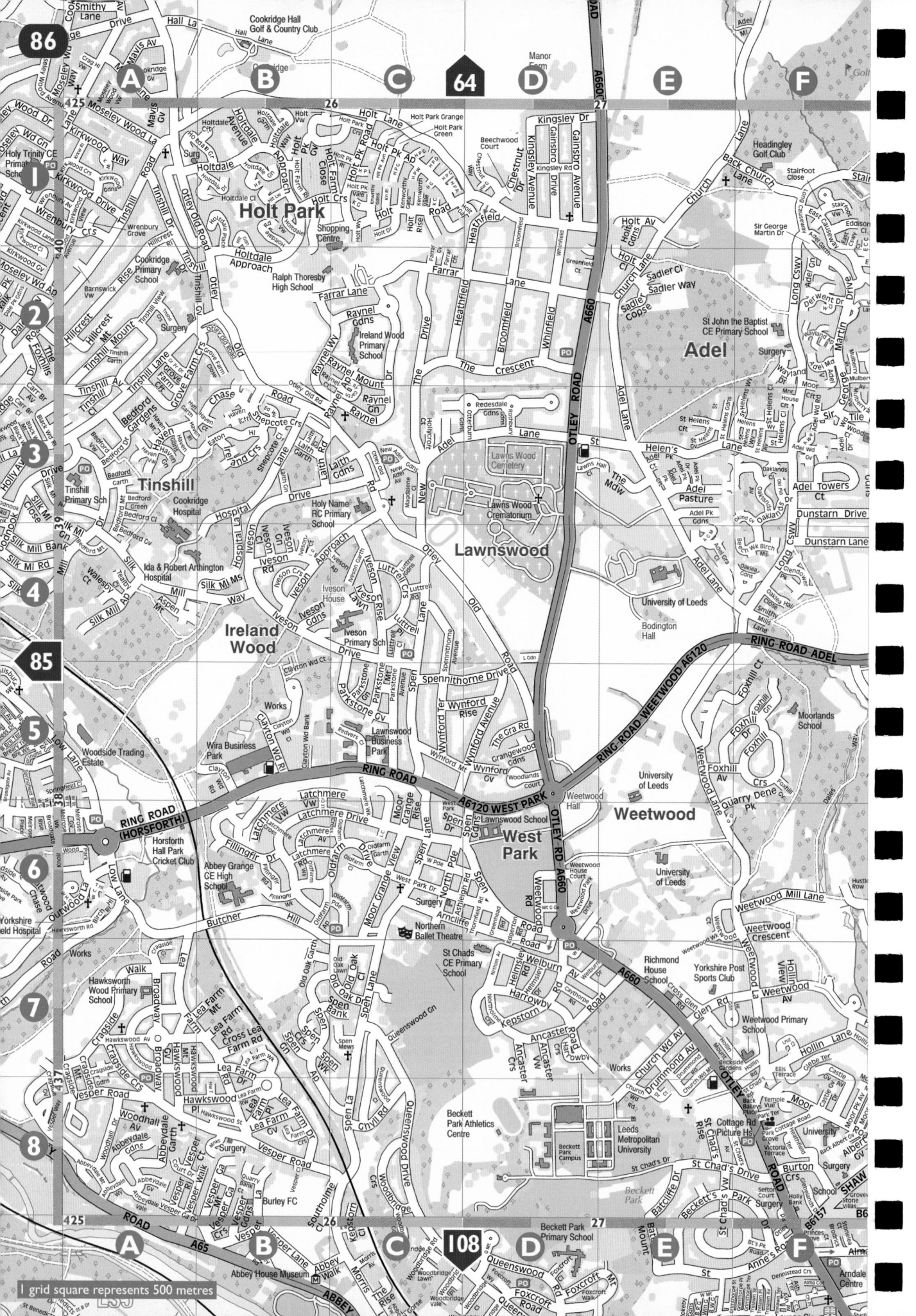

I grid square represents 500 metres

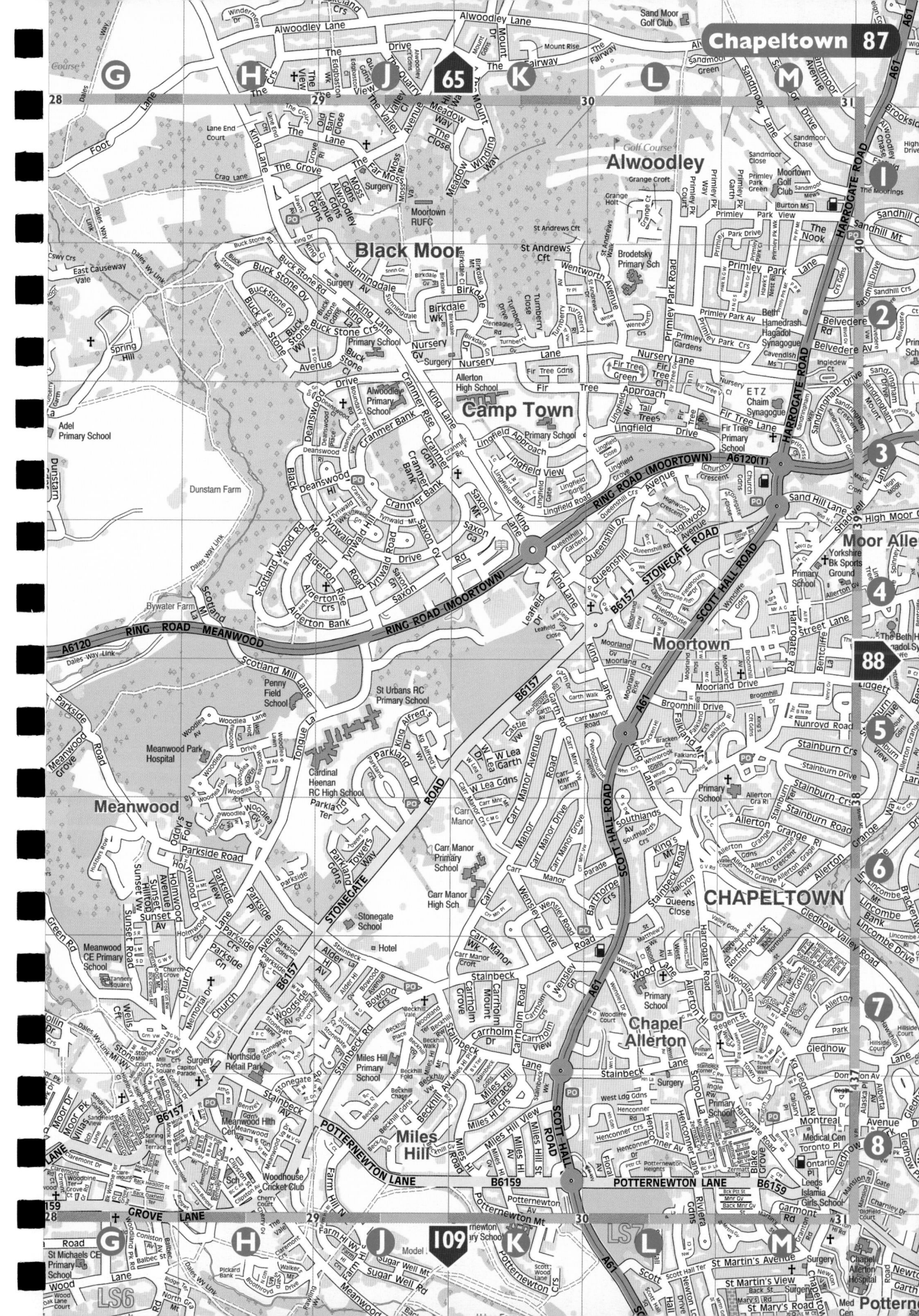

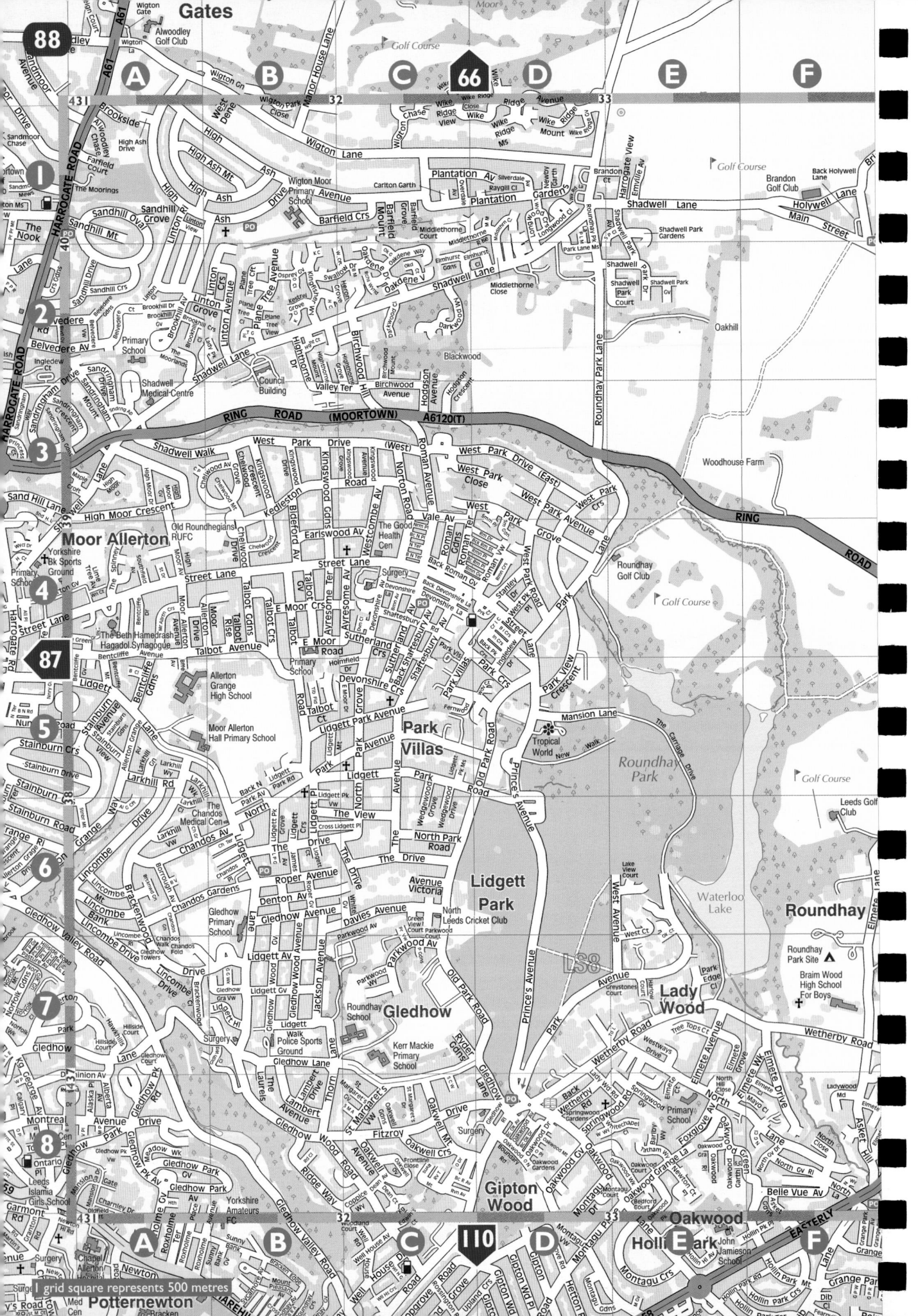

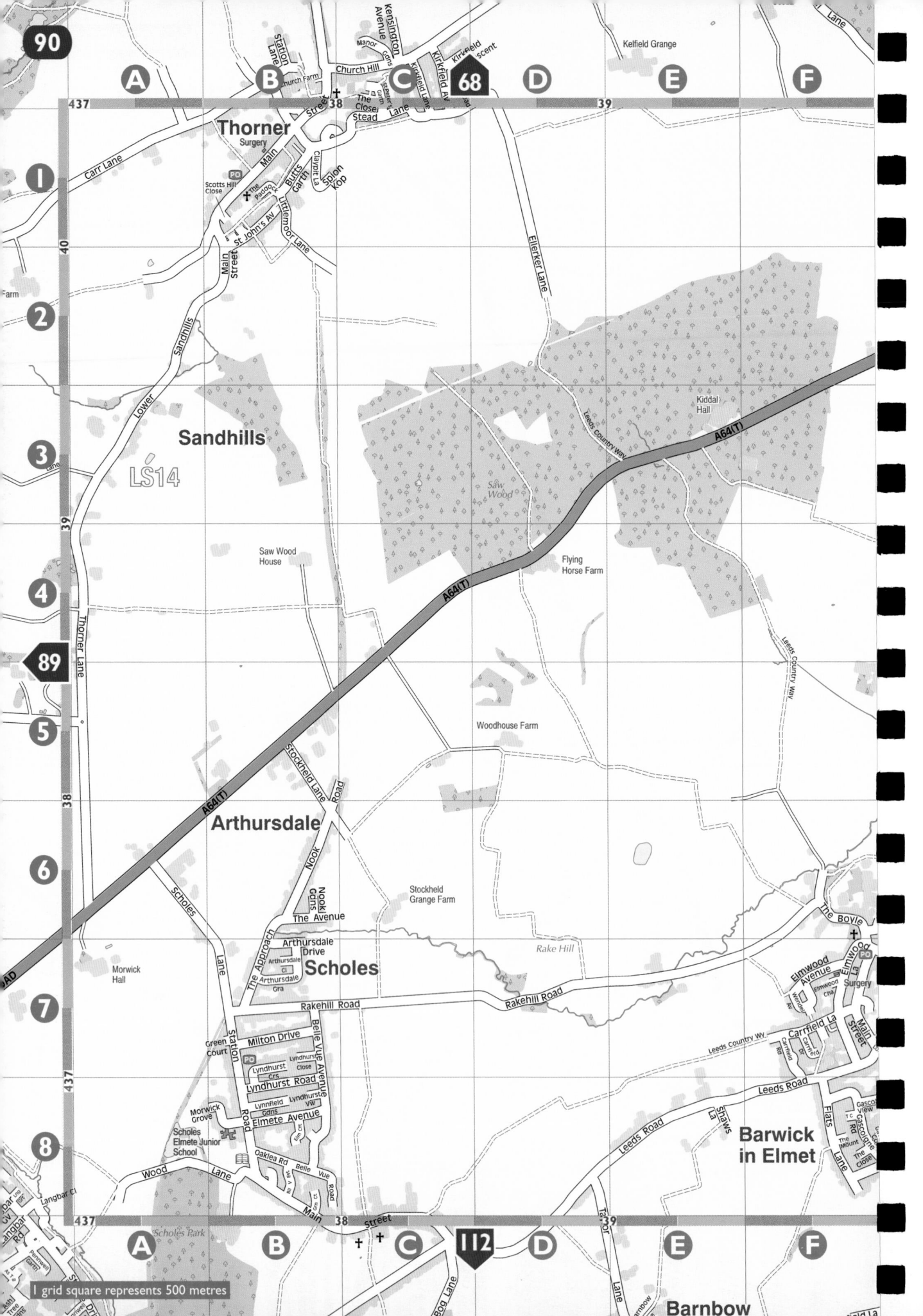

Ⓐ Ⓑ Ⓒ **68** Ⓓ Ⓔ Ⓕ

437 438 39

Ⅰ

Carr Lane

Church Farm

Kelfield Grange

Manor Gdns

Kensington Avenue

Church Hill

Kirkfield Av

Kirkfield Cscent

Station Lane

Thorner

Surgery

The Closed Stead

Kirkfield Lane

Garth

PO

Scotts Hill Close

The Paddock

Spion Kop

Butts Garth

Clayplt La

Littlemoor Lane

Main Street

St. John's Av

Ellerker Lane

Ⓘ

2

Sandhills

Lower Lane

Line 39

Sandhills

LS14

Kiddal Hall

Leeds Country Way

A64(T)

3

Saw Wood

Saw Wood House

Flying Horse Farm

Leeds Country Way

4

Thorner Lane

89

5

Woodhouse Farm

38

437

Stockheld Lane

Arthursdale

A64(T)

6

Nook Lane

Nook Gdns

The Avenue

Stockheld Grange Farm

Rake Hill

The Boyle

Elmwood Avenue

Elmwood La

PO

Surgery

Morwick Hall

The Approach

Arthursdale Drive

Arthursdale Cl

Arthursdale Gra

Scholes

Rakehill Road

Rakehill Road

Carrfield La

Main Street

Carrfield Rd

Leeds Country Wy

Shaws La

Elmwood Cha

Webster Row

7

Scholes Lane

Station Road

Green Court

Milton Drive

Belle Vue Avenue

PO

Lyndhurst Crs

Lyndhurst Close

Lyndhurst Road

Lyndhurste VW

Lynnfield Gdns

Morwick Grove

Elmete Avenue

Leeds Road

Leeds Road

Gascoigne View

Gascoigne Rd

Flats

The Mount

The Close

Barwick in Elmet

8

Scholes Elmete Junior School

Oaklea Rd

Belle Vue Road

Rim Crt

Wood Lane

Main Street

Bog Lane

Taylor Lane

Langbar Cl

Langbar Rd

Scholes Park

437 438 39

Ⓐ Ⓑ Ⓒ **112** Ⓓ Ⓔ Ⓕ

Barnbow

1 grid square represents 500 metres

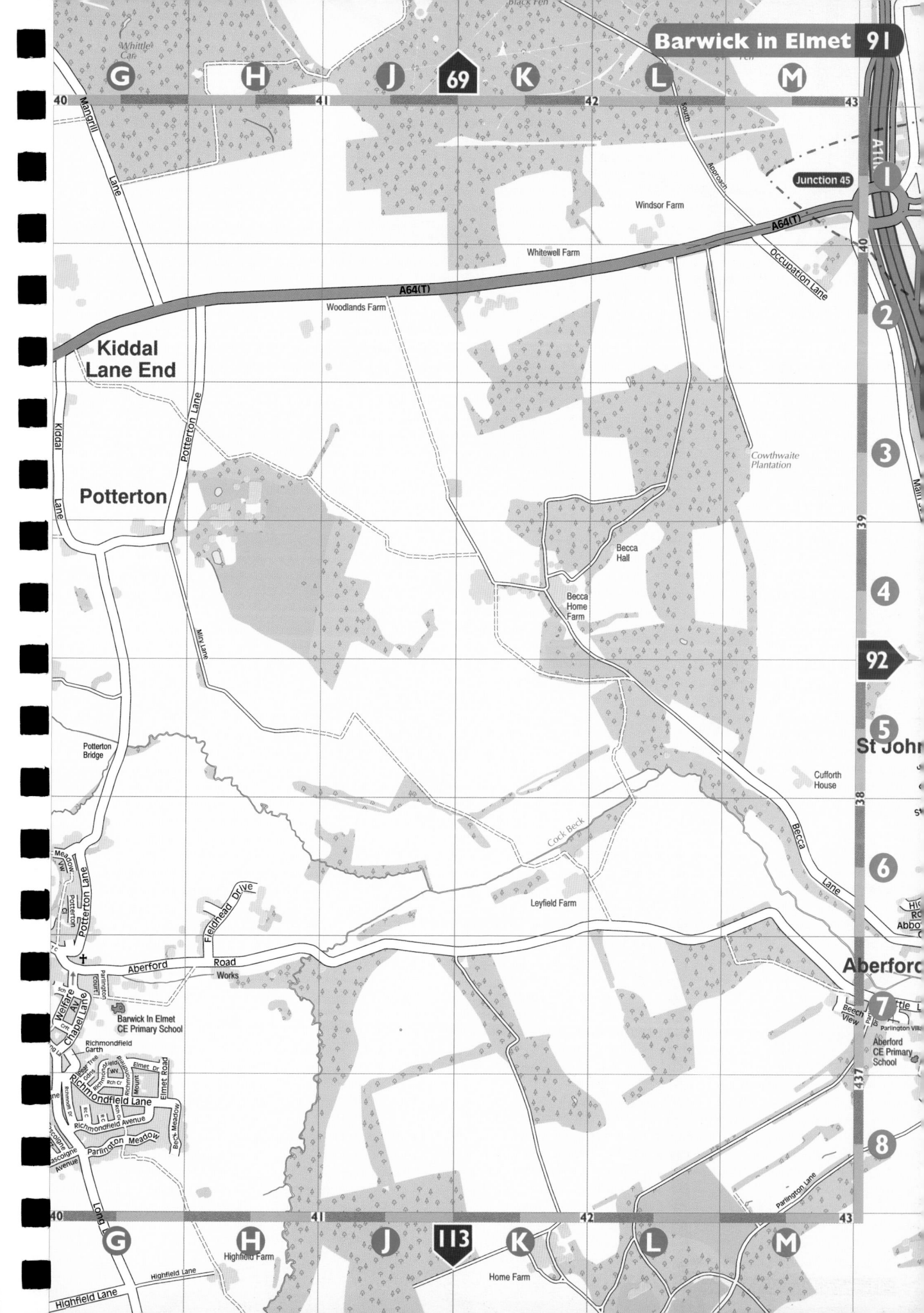

G H J 69 K L M

40 41 42 43

Whittle Carr

Black Fen

I

Junction 45

A64(T)

Windsor Farm

Occupation Lane

Approach

South

2

Whitewell Farm

A64(T)

Woodlands Farm

Kiddal
Lane End

Potterton Lane

Cowthwaite
Plantation

3

Potterton

Kiddal Lane

Becca Hall

4

Becca
Home
Farm

92

Miry Lane

5

St John

Cufforth
House

Potterton
Bridge

Becca Lane

6

Cock Beck

Meadow VW

Potterton Lane

Potterton
Cl

Fieldhead Drive

Leyfield Farm

Aberford Road

Aberford

Works

7

Beech
View

Little L

Parlington Villa

Parlington Court

Barwick In Elmet
CE Primary School

Aberford
CE Primary
School

A1237

Richmondfield
Garth

Rose Tree

Elmet Dr

Welfare Ave

Chapel Lane

Richmondfield Lane

Elmet Road
Elmet Mount

Beck Meadow

Gascoigne
Avenue

Richmondfield Avenue

Parlington Meadow

Long Ln

8

Parlington Lane

40 41 42 43

G H J 113 K L M

Highfield Farm

Home Farm

Highfield Lane

Highfield Lane

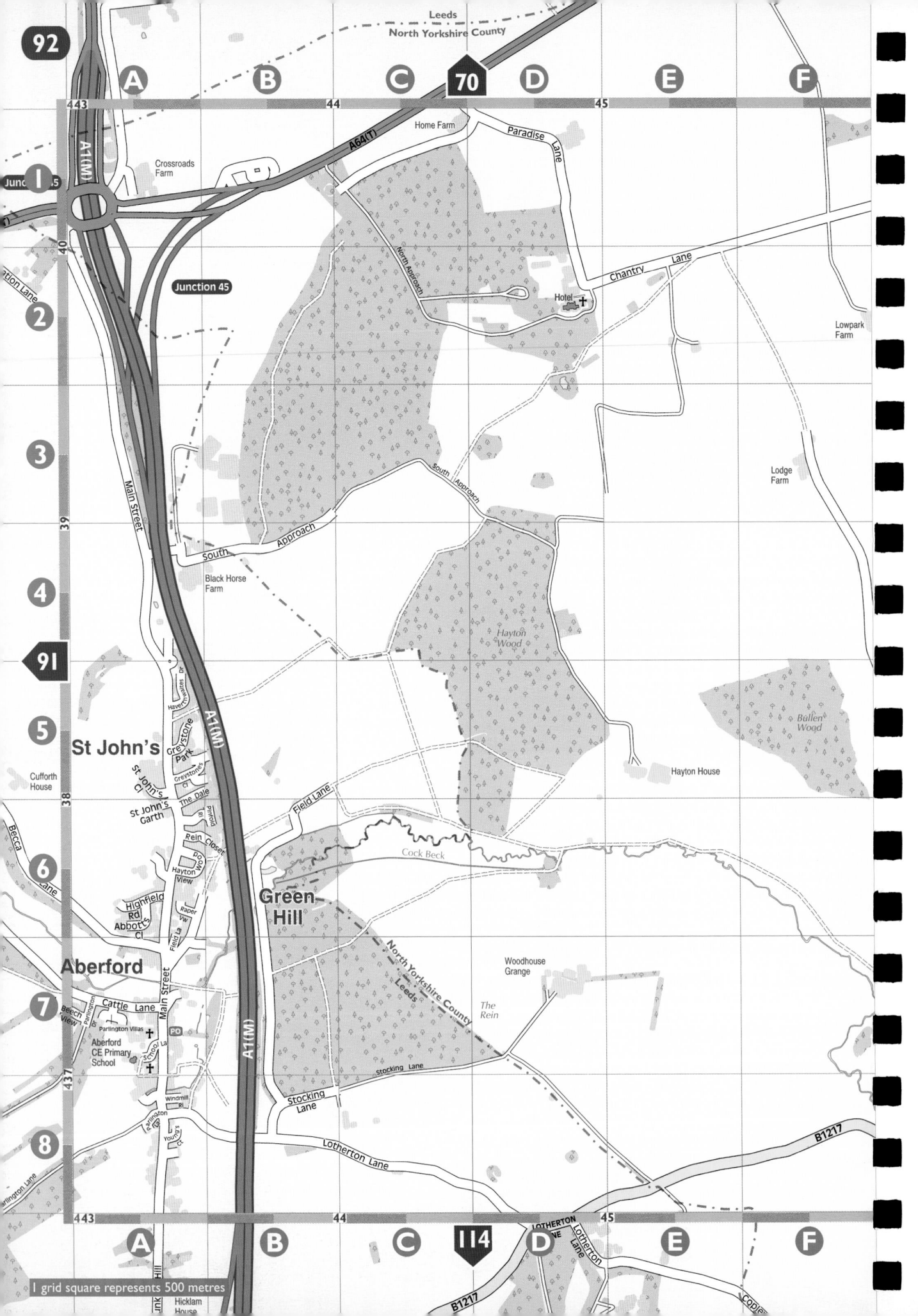

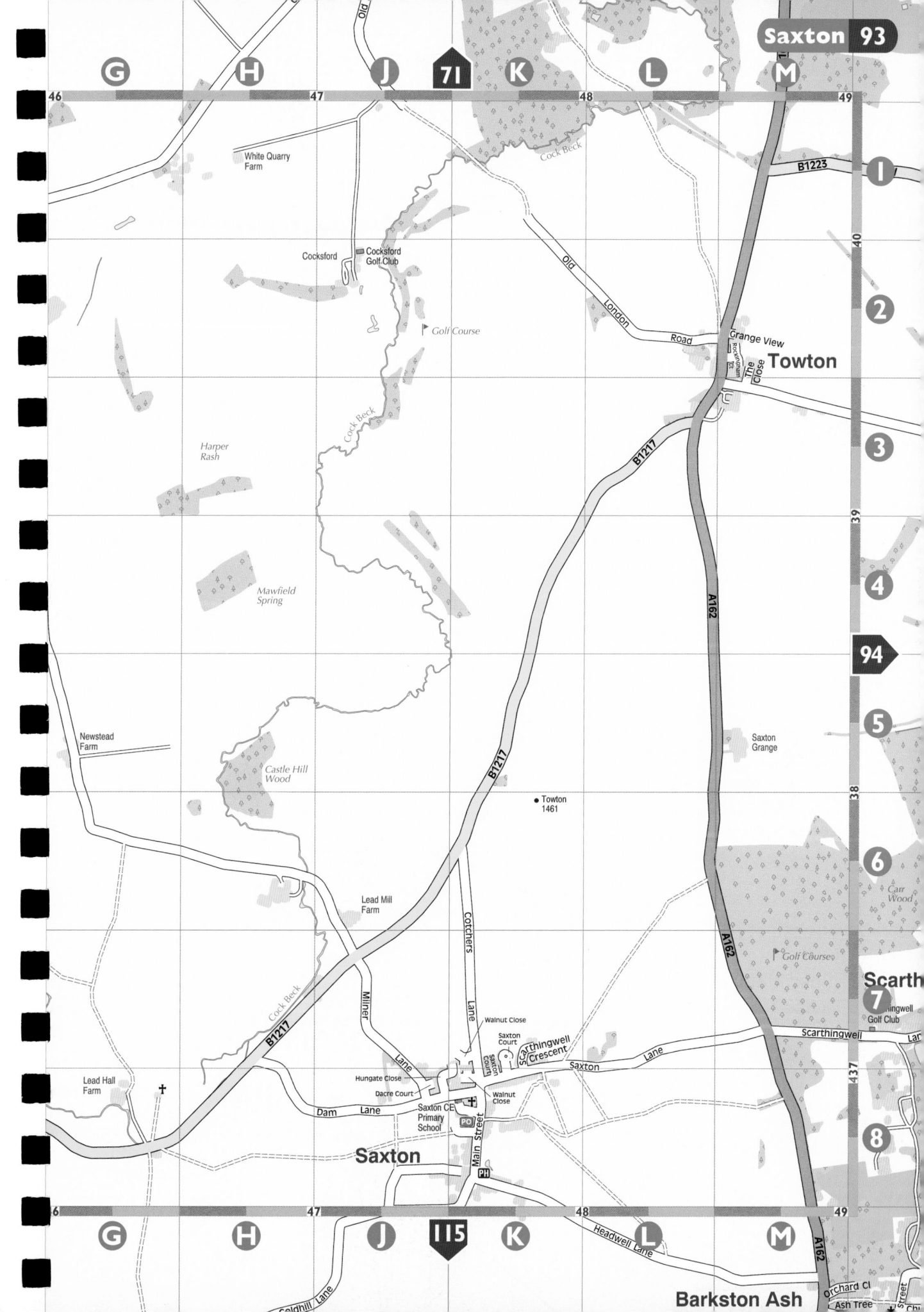

G H J **71** K L M

46 47 48 49

White Quarry Farm

Cock Beck

B1223

I

Cocksford

Cocksford Golf Club

Old London Road

Grange View

Rockingham Ct

The Close

Towton

Golf Course

2

Harper Rash

B1217

3

A162

94

Mawfield Spring

Saxton Grange

5

Newstead Farm

Castle Hill Wood

● Towton 1461

B1217

6

Carr Wood

Lead Mill Farm

Golf Course

Scarth

Cock Beck

Milner Lane

Cotchers Lane

Walnut Close

Saxton Court

Scarthingwell Crescent

Saxton Court

Scarthingwell Golf Club

Scarthingwell

7

Saxton Lane

B1217

Lead Hall Farm

✝

Hungate Close

Dacre Court

Dam Lane

Saxton CE Primary School

PO

Walnut Close

✝

Main Street

Saxton

PH

8

40

2

39

38

437

6 47 48 49

G H J **115** K L M

A162

Headwell Lane

Orchard Cl

Coldhill Lane

Ash Tree

Barkston Ash

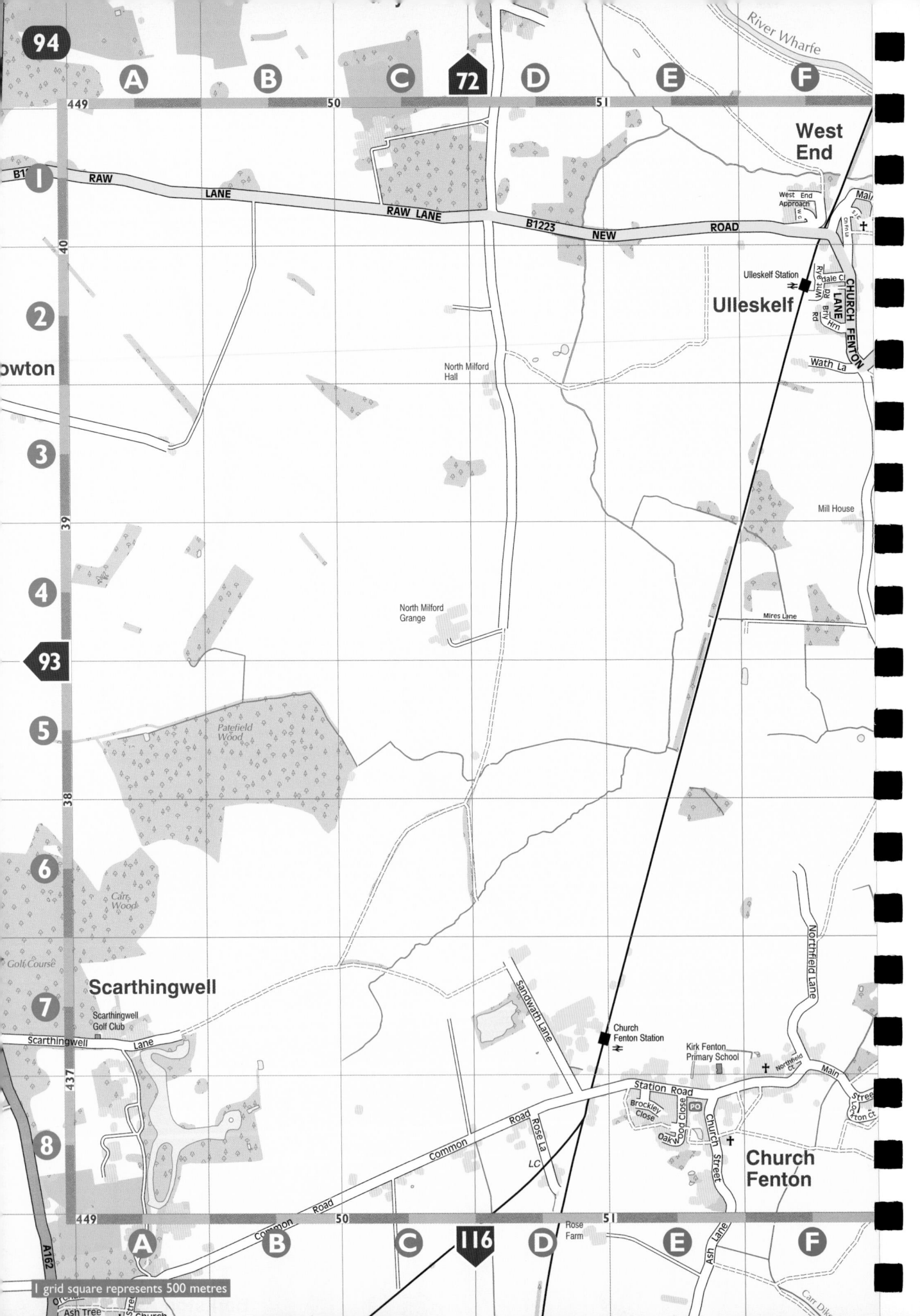

94

A   B   C   **72**   D   E   F

449   50   51

River Wharfe

West End

B1...   1   RAW   LANE

RAW LANE   B1223   NEW   ROAD

West End Approach

40

Ulleskelf Station

Ulleskelf

CHURCH FENTON LANE

Wath La

2

owton

North Milford Hall

3

39

Mill House

4

Mires Lane

93

5

38

Patefield Wood

North Milford Grange

6

Carr Wood

Golf Course

Scarthingwell

Northfield Lane

7

Scarthingwell Golf Club

437

Scarthingwell Lane

Sandwath Lane

Church Fenton Station

Kirk Fenton Primary School

Station Road

Northfield Ct

Main Street

Brockley Close

PO

Rose La

Oakw...

Church Street

8

A162

Common Road

Common Road

LC

Rose Farm

Church Fenton

Ash Lane

449   50   51

A   B   C   **116**   D   E   F

Ash Tree ... Church ...

Carr Dike

I grid square represents 500 metres

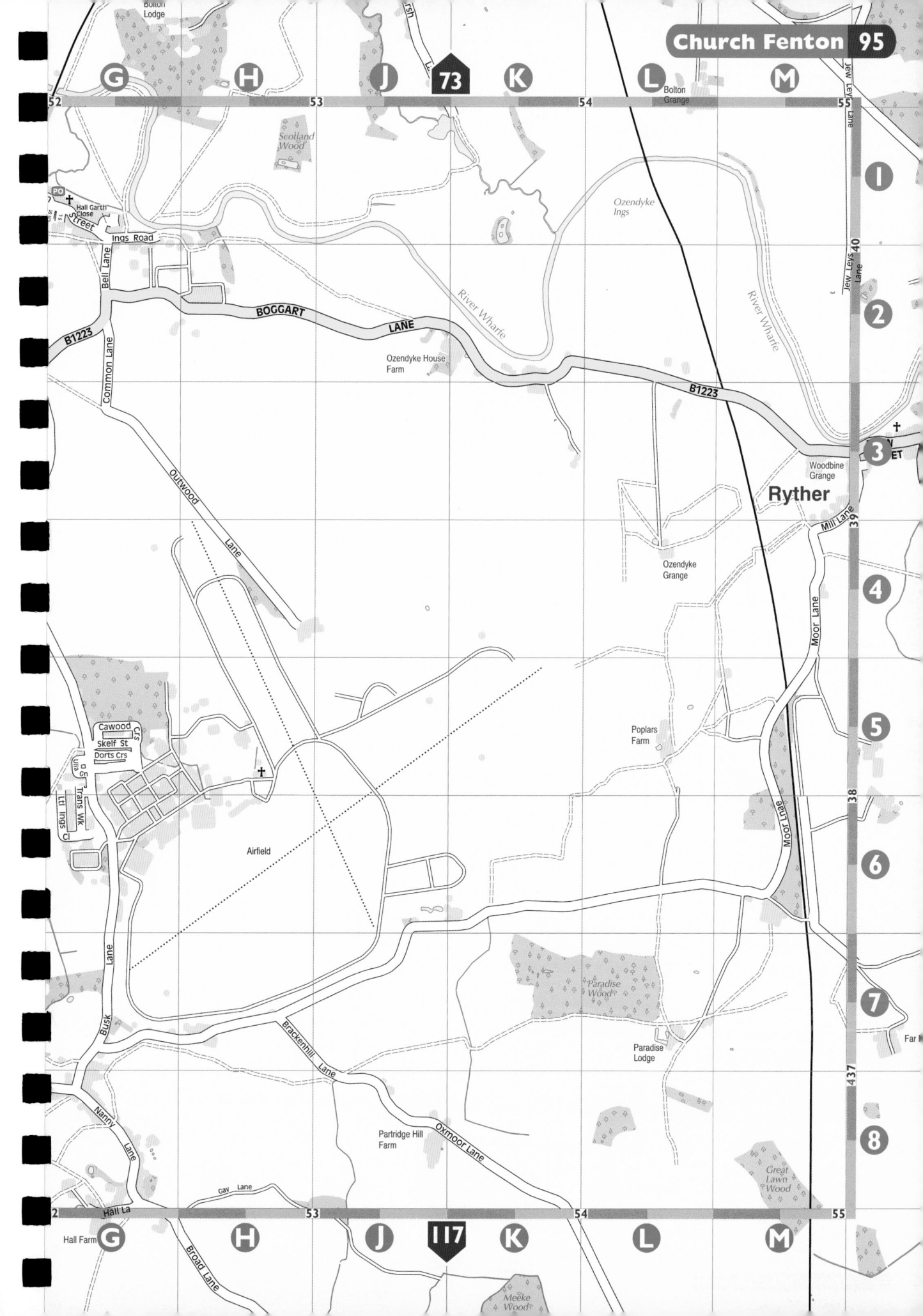

G   H   J   **73**   K   L   M

52   53   54   Bolton Grange   55

Scotland Wood

I

PO
Hall Garth Close
Street
Ings Road
Bell Lane

Ozendyke Ings

River Wharfe

River Wharfe

2

BOGGART   LANE

B1223

Common Lane

Ozendyke House Farm

B1223

Woodbine Grange

3
ET

Ryther

Outwood Lane

Ozendyke Grange

Mill Lane

4

Moor Lane

Poplars Farm

5

Cawood Crs
Skelf St
Dorts Crs

Julia Gdns
Trans Wk
Ltt Ings
Cl

6

Airfield

Moor Lane

Paradise Wood

7

Busk Lane

Brackenhill Lane

Paradise Lodge

Far

8

Nanny Lane

Partridge Hill Farm

Oxmoor Lane

437

Great Lawn Wood

Gay Lane

2   Hall La   53   54   55

Hall Farm   **G**   **H**   **J**   **117**   **K**   **L**   **M**

Broad Lane

Meeke Wood

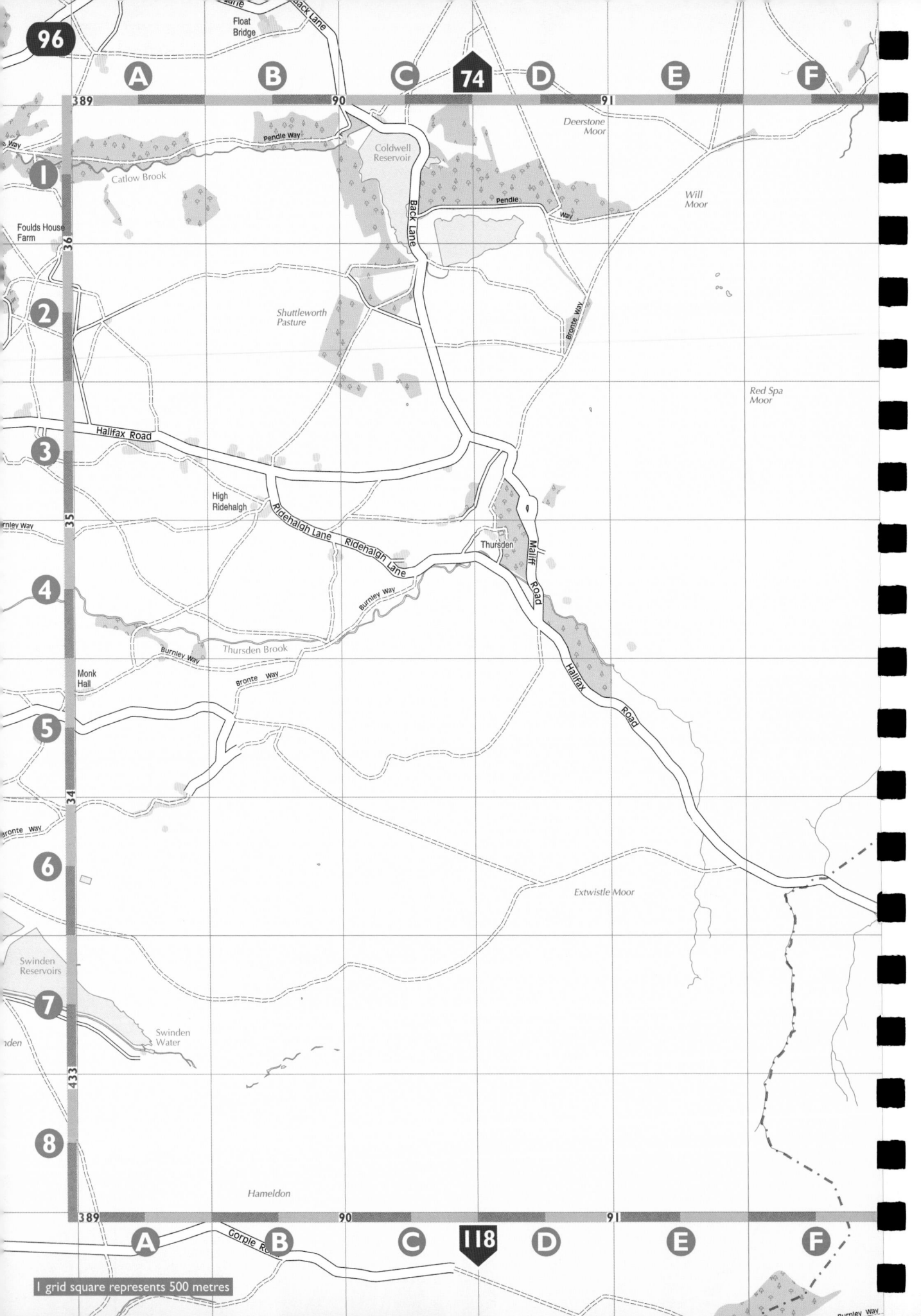

74

1 grid square represents 500 metres

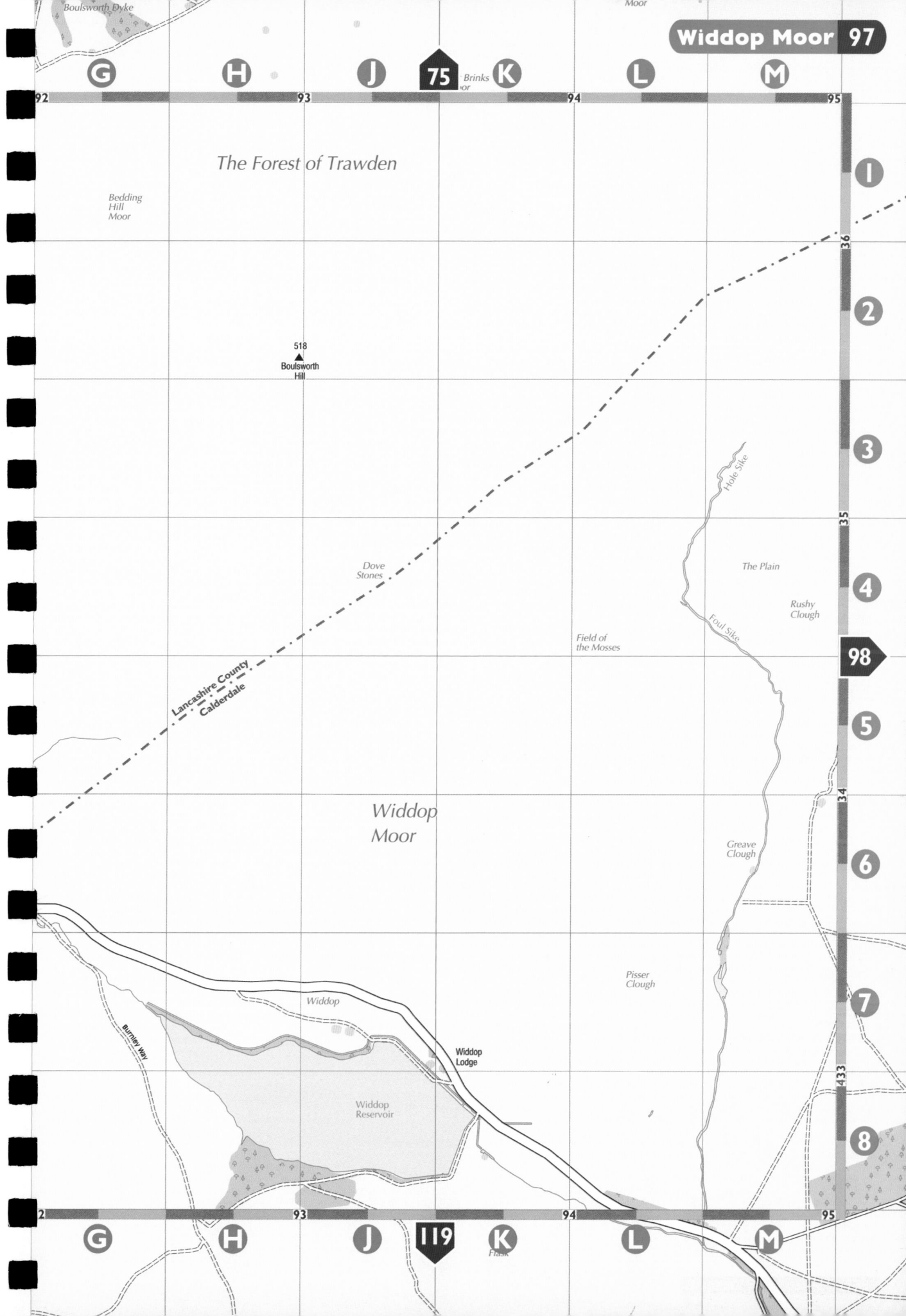

The Forest of Trawden

Boulsworth Dyke

Bedding Hill Moor

518
▲
Boulsworth Hill

Dove Stones

Lancashire County
Calderdale

Widdop Moor

Brinks or

Hole Sike

The Plain

Rushy Clough

Foul Sike

Field of the Mosses

Greave Clough

Pisser Clough

Widdop

Widdop Lodge

Burnley Way

Widdop Reservoir

98

G   H   J   **75**   K   L   M

92   93   94   95

Flick

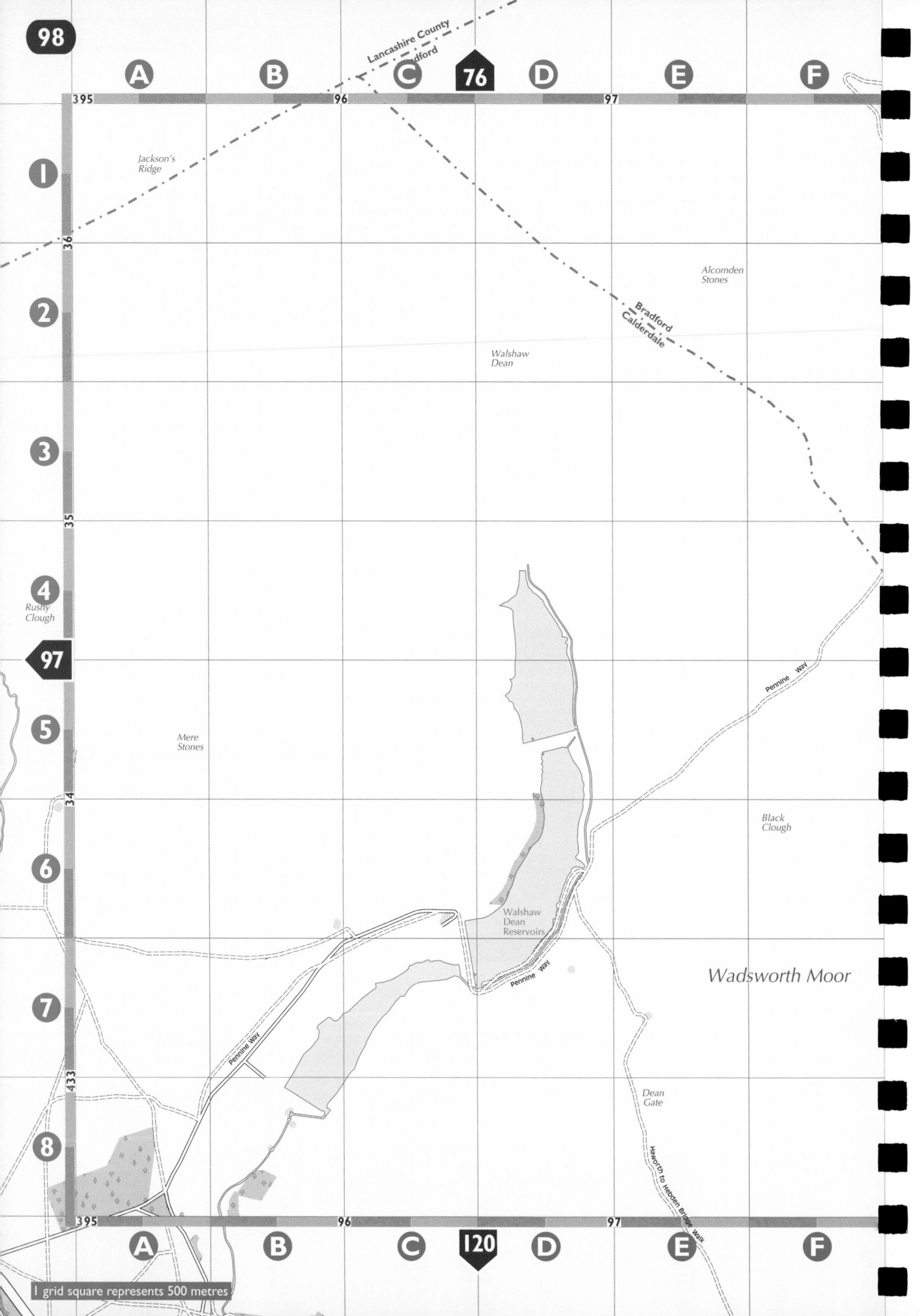

A   B   C   76   D   E   F

395   96   97

1   36

Jackson's
Ridge

Lancashire County
dford

2

Walshaw
Dean

Alcomden
Stones

Bradford
Calderdale

3

35

4
Rushy
Clough

97

5

Mere
Stones

34

Pennine Way

Black
Clough

6

7

Pennine Way

Walshaw
Dean
Reservoirs

Pennine Way

Wadsworth Moor

Pennine Way

Dean
Gate

433

8

Haworth to Hebden Bridge Walk

395   96   97

A   B   C   120   D   E   F

1 grid square represents 500 metres

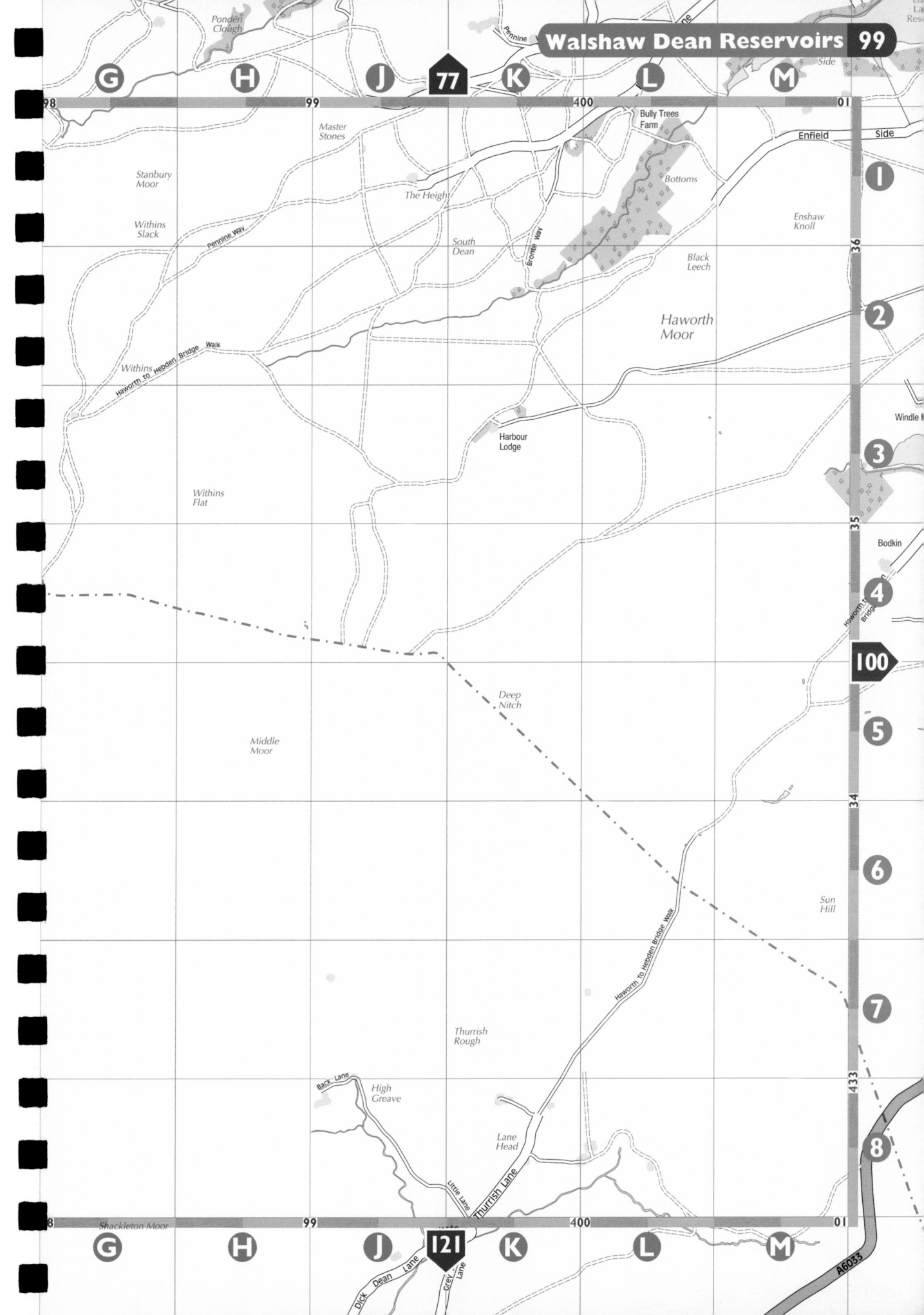

G H J **77** K L M

98 99 400 01

I

2

3

4

100

5

6

7

8

36

35

34

433

G H J **121** K L M

98 Shackleton Moor 99 400 01

Ponden Clough

Master Stones

Stanbury Moor

The Height

Withins Slack

Pennine Way

South Dean

Withins Hebden Bridge Walk

Haworth to

Bronte Way

Harbour Lodge

Withins Flat

Deep Nitch

Middle Moor

Thurrish Rough

Haworth to Hebden Bridge Walk

Back Lane

High Greave

Lane Head

Little Lane

Thurrish Lane

Dick Dean Lane

Grey Lane

Bully Trees Farm

Bottoms

Enshaw Knoll

Black Leech

Haworth Moor

Windle

Bodkin

Haworth to Bridge

Sun Hill

Enfield Side

Side

Pennine

A6033

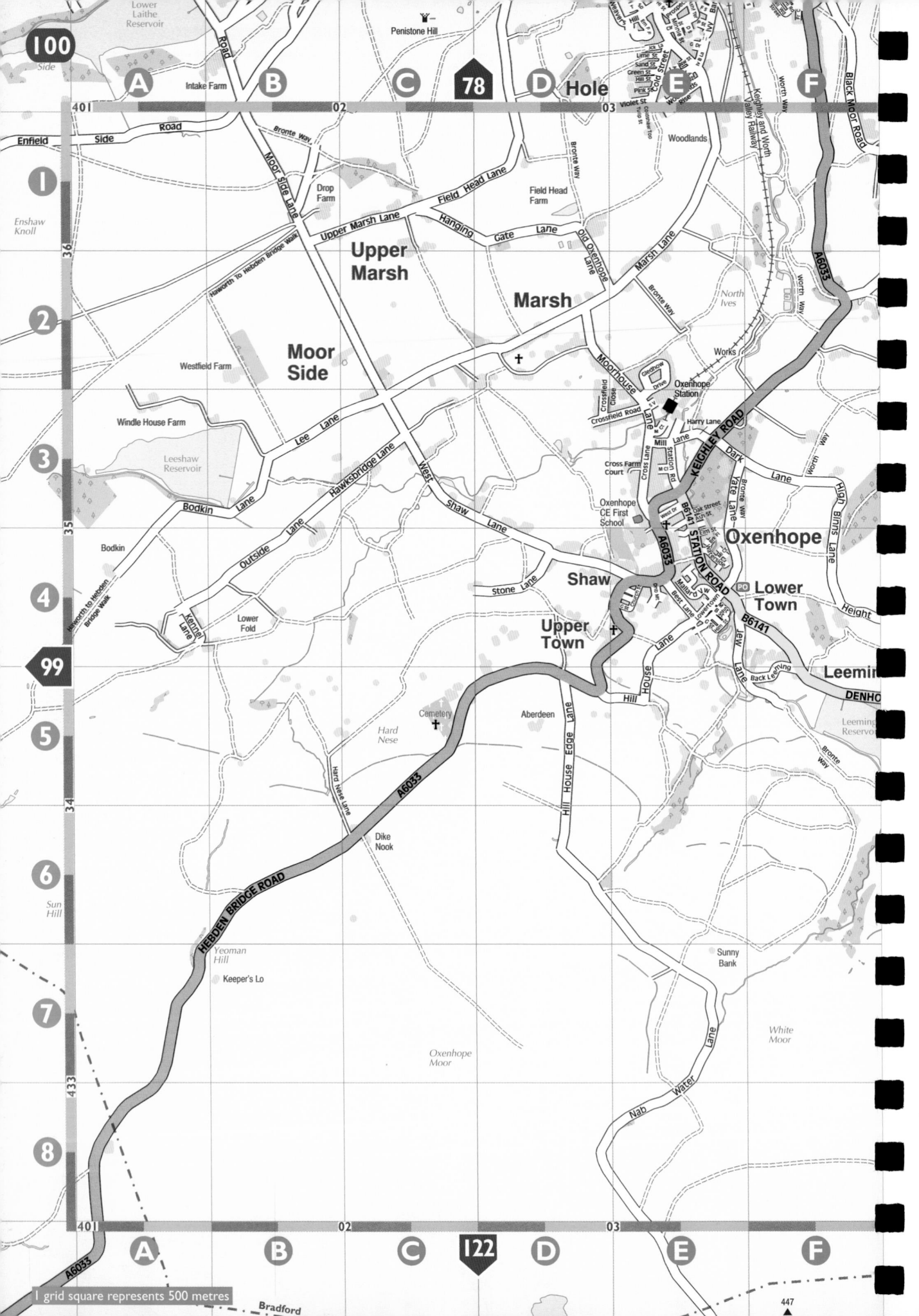

A B C **78** D Hole E F

I

2

3

4

99

5

6

7

8

A B C **122** D E F

Lower Laithe Reservoir

Side

Penistone Hill

Woodlands

Enfield Side Road

Bronte Way

Moor Side Lane

Drop Farm

Field Head Lane

Field Head Farm

Enshaw Knoll

Upper Marsh Lane

Ranging Gate Lane

Old Oxenhope Lane

Bronte Way

Marsh Lane

North Ives

Keighley and Worth Valley Railway

Worth Way

Upper Marsh

Marsh

36

Moor Side

Westfield Farm

Moorhouse Lane

Gledhow Drive

Oxenhope Station

Works

Haworth To Hebden Bridge Walk

Crossfield Close

A6033

2

Windle House Farm

Lee Lane

Hawksbridge Lane

West Shaw Lane

Crossfield Road

Cross Farm Court

Station Rd

Harry Lane

Mill Lane

Keighley Road

Dark Lane

Worth Way

High Binns Lane

Leeshaw Reservoir

Bodkin Lane

Oxenhope CE First School

B6141

Oxenhope

3

35

Bodkin

Outside Lane

Stone Lane

Shaw

STATION ROAD

A6033

PO

Lower Town

B6141

Height

Haworth to Hebden Bridge Walk

Kennel Lane

Lower Fold

Upper Town

Hill House Lane

Back Leeming

Lane

Leemin

DENHO

4

433

Cemetery

Aberdeen

Sunny Bank

Leeming Reservoir

Hard Nese

Hard Nese Lane

A6033

Hill House Edge Lane

White Moor

Sun Hill

HEBDEN BRIDGE ROAD

Dike Nook

Oxenhope Moor

Nab Water Lane

Bronte Way

34

Yeoman Hill

Keeper's Lo

A6033

Bradford

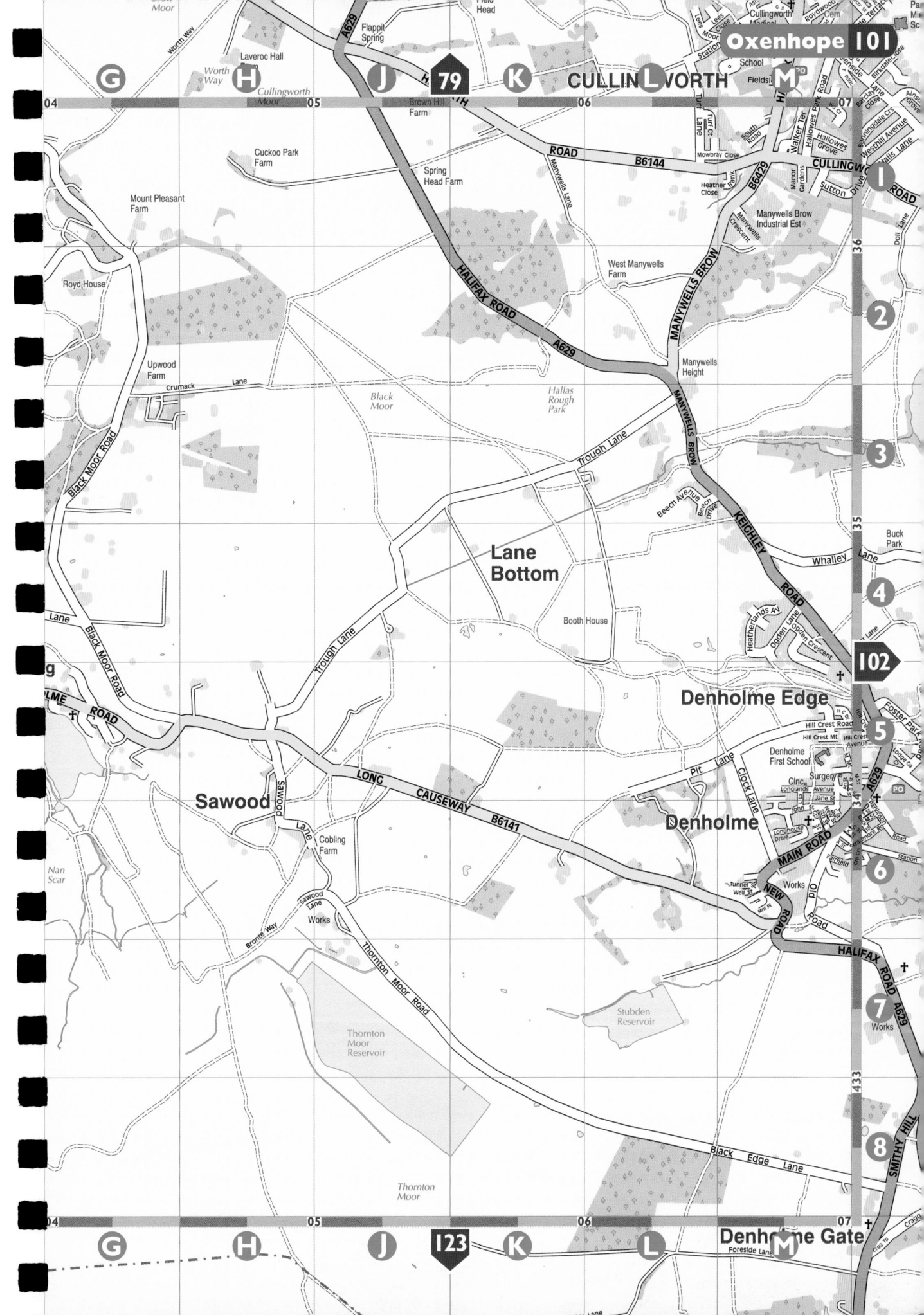

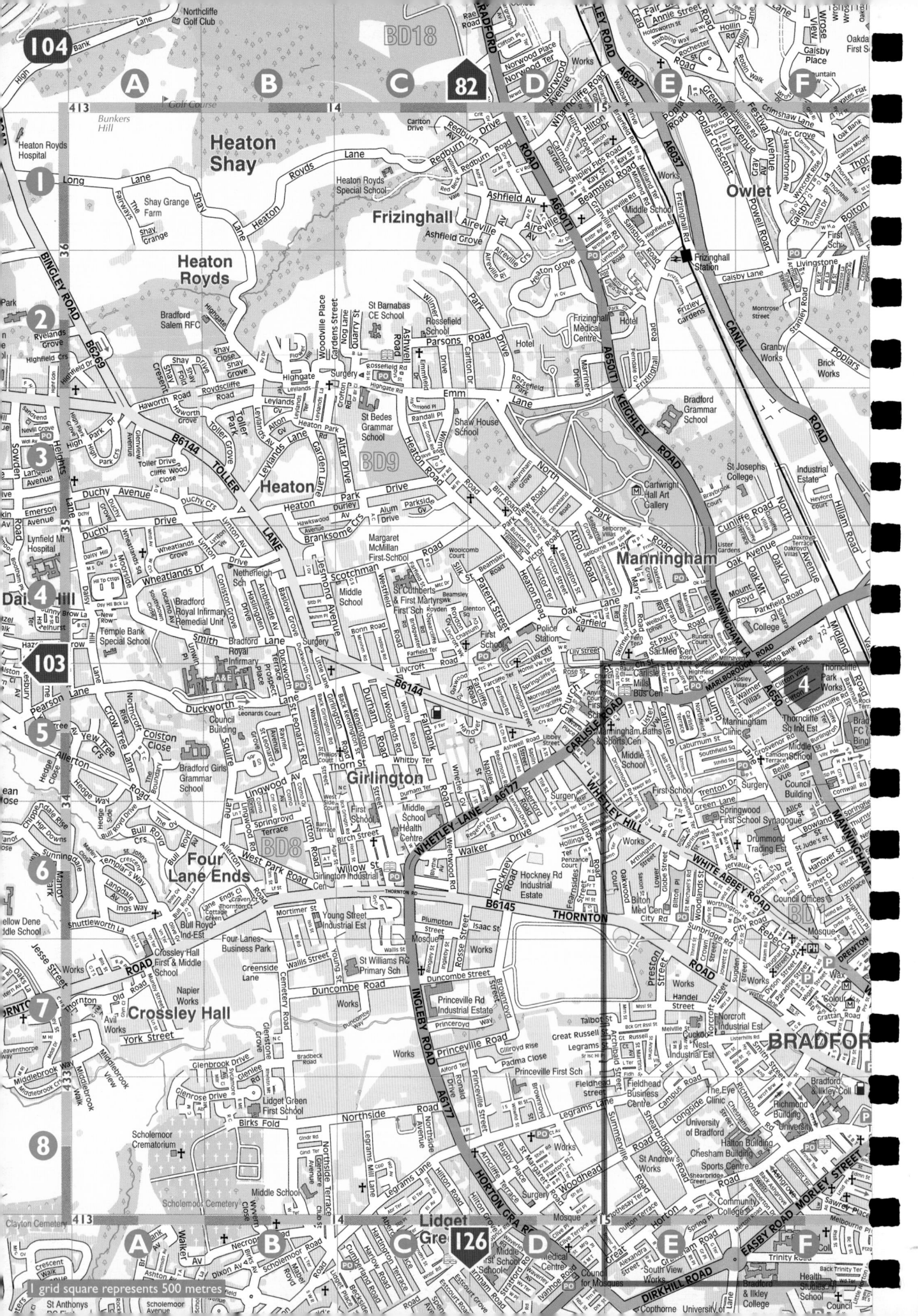

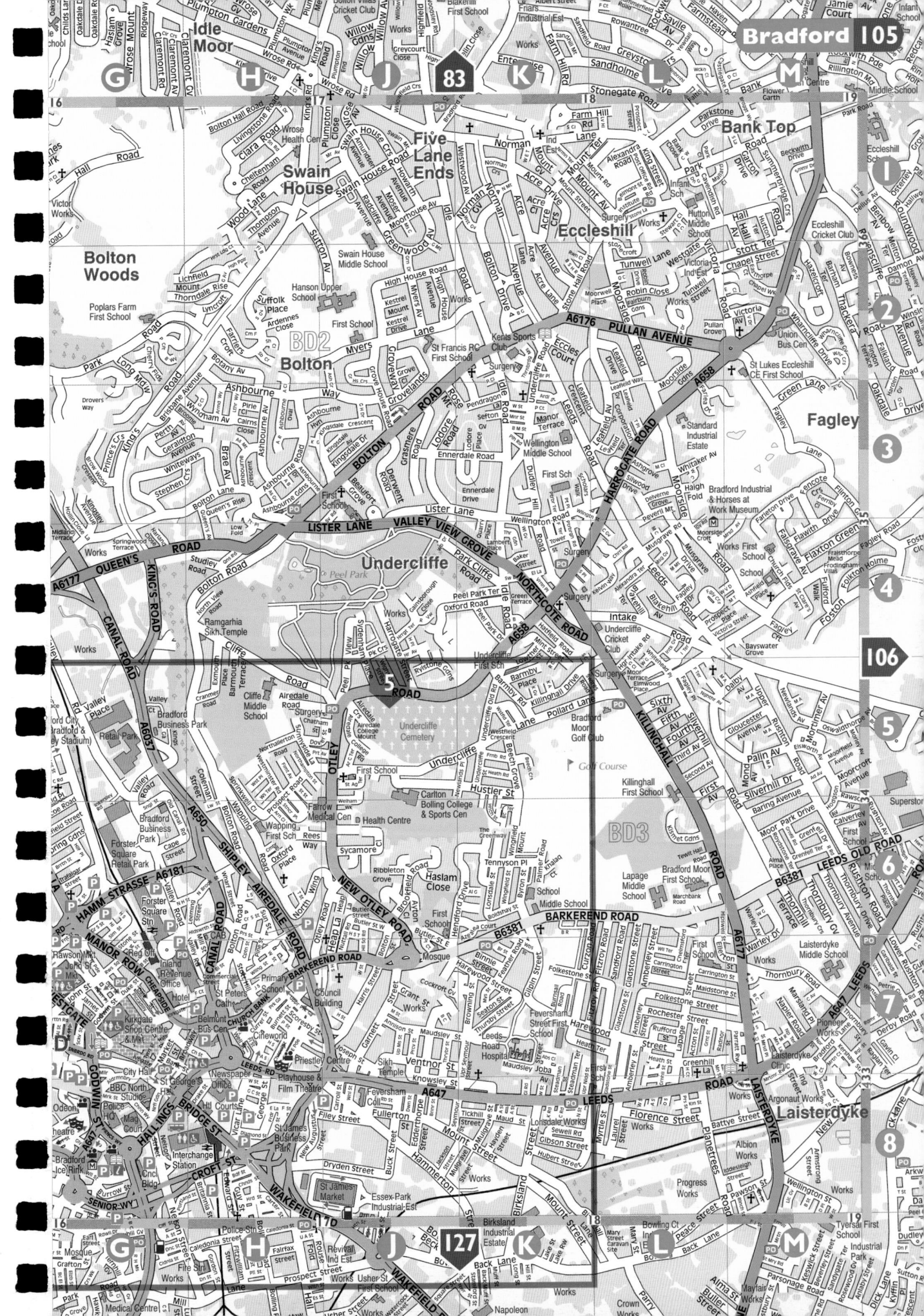

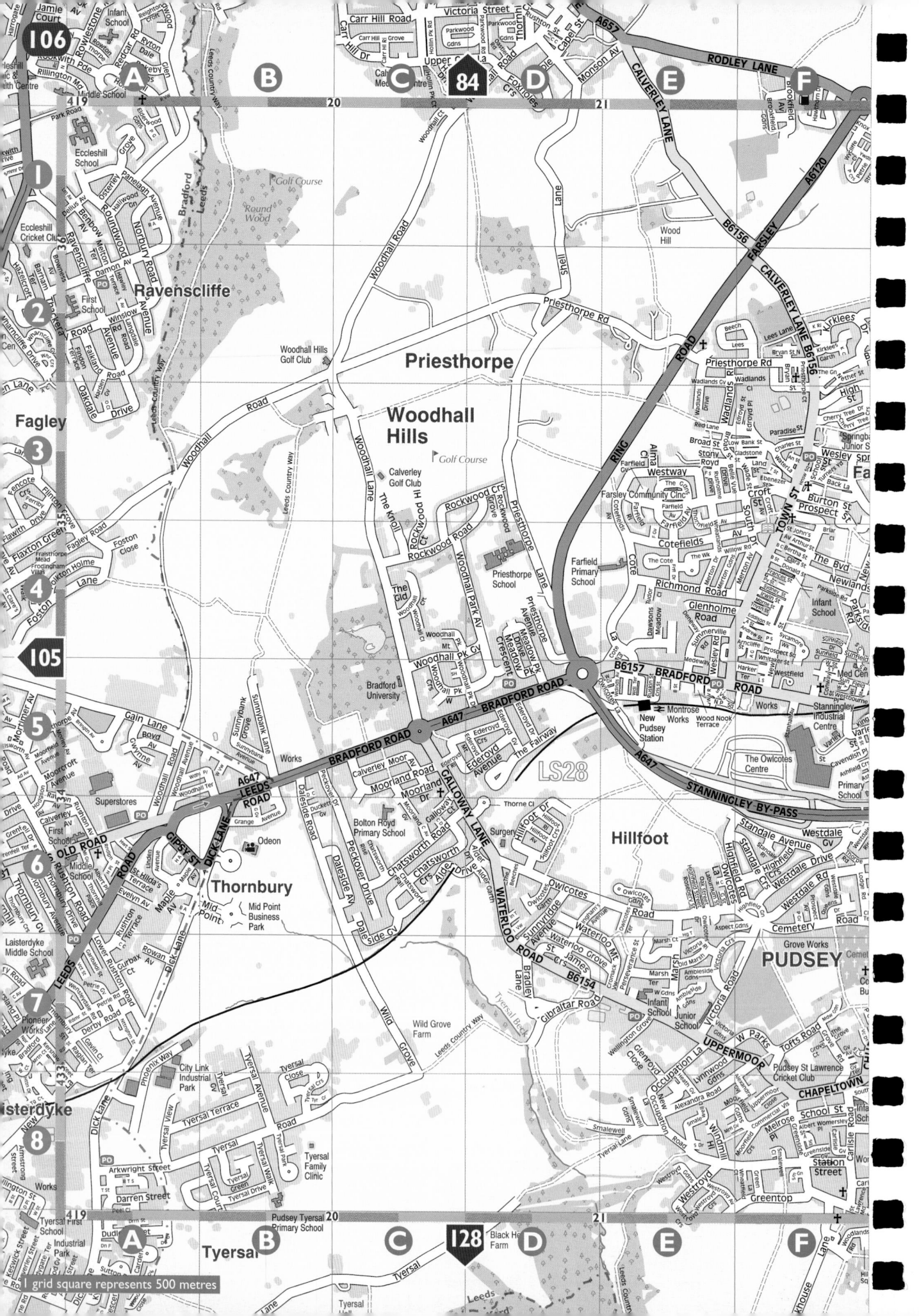

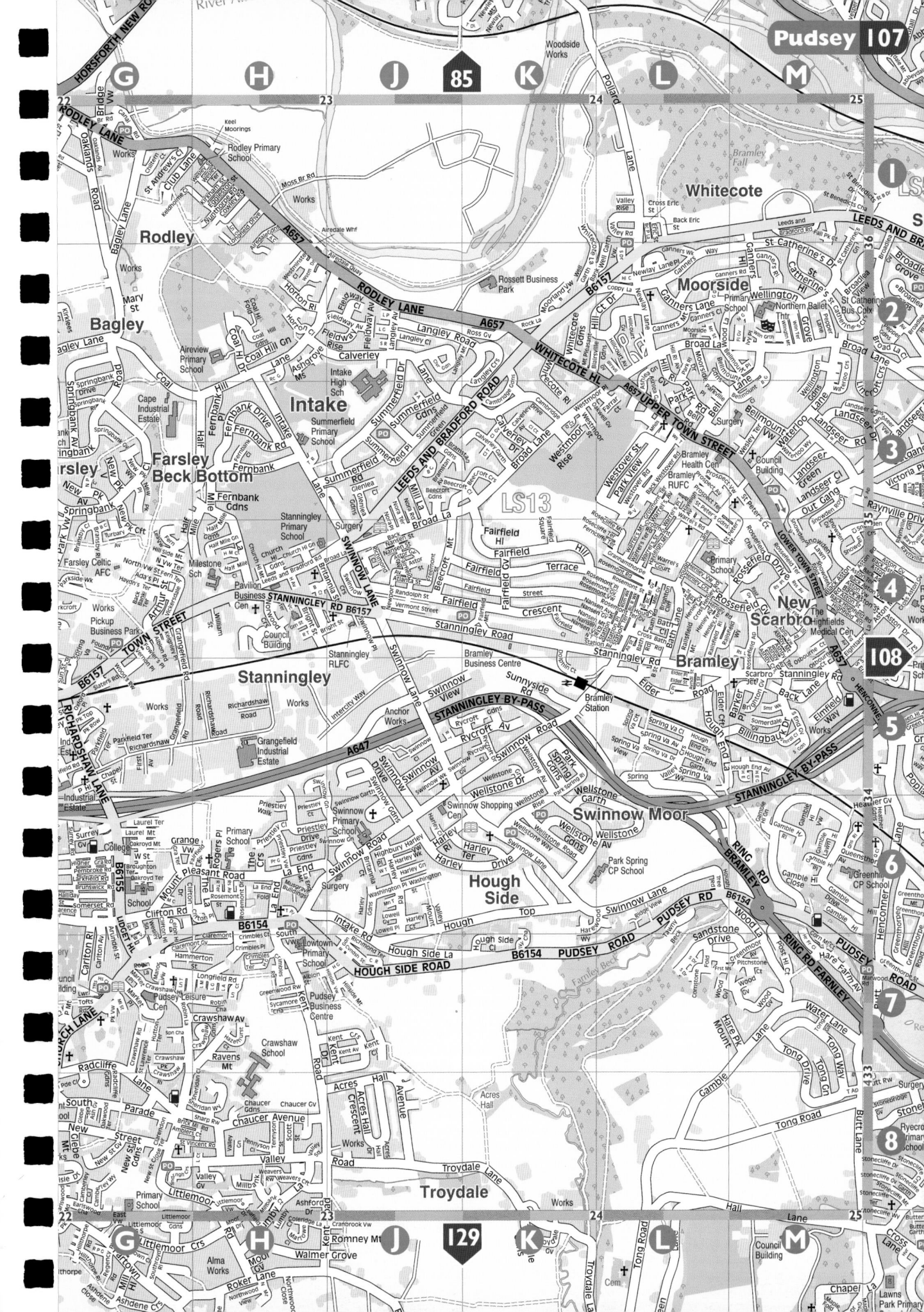

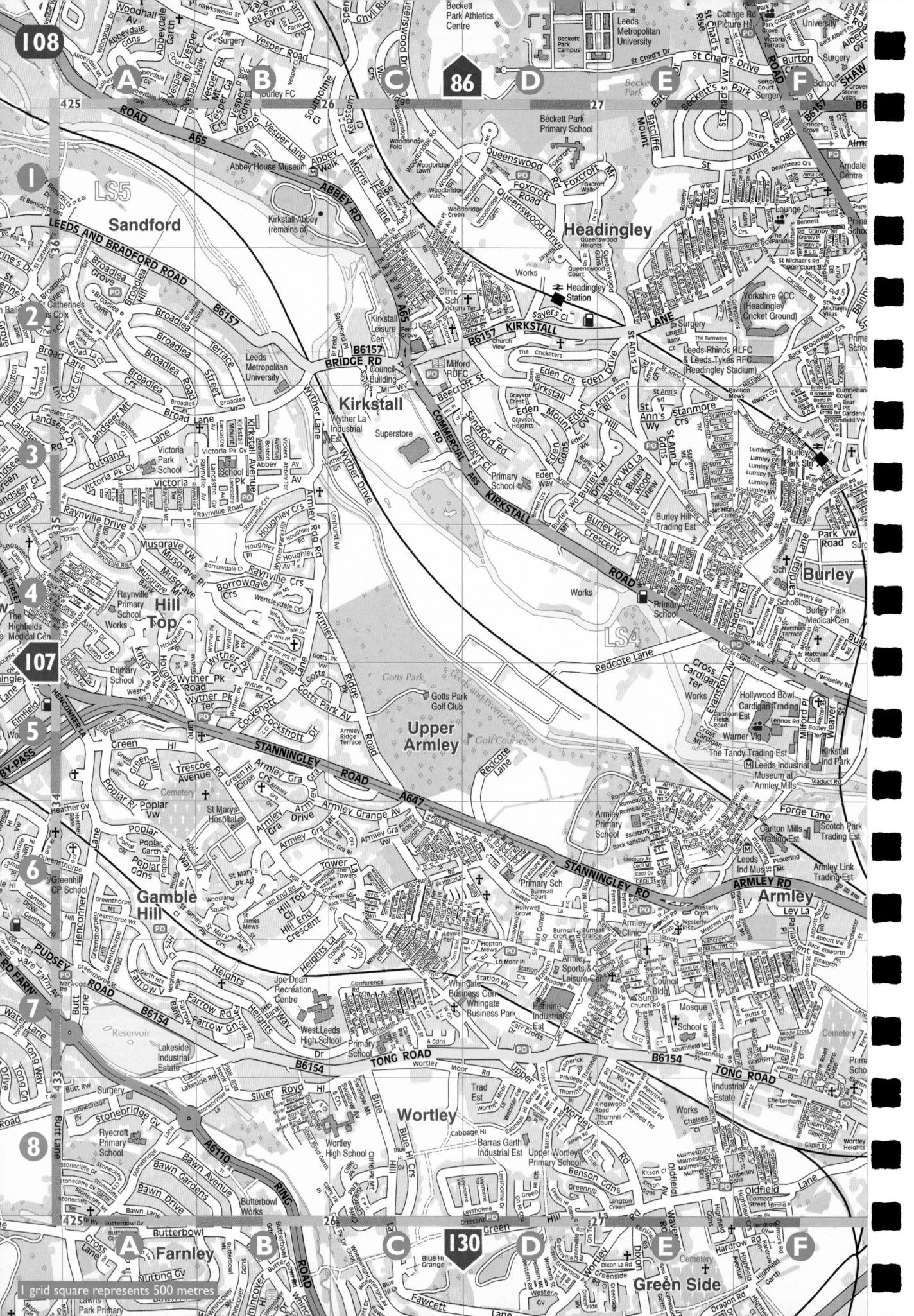

I grid square represents 500 metres

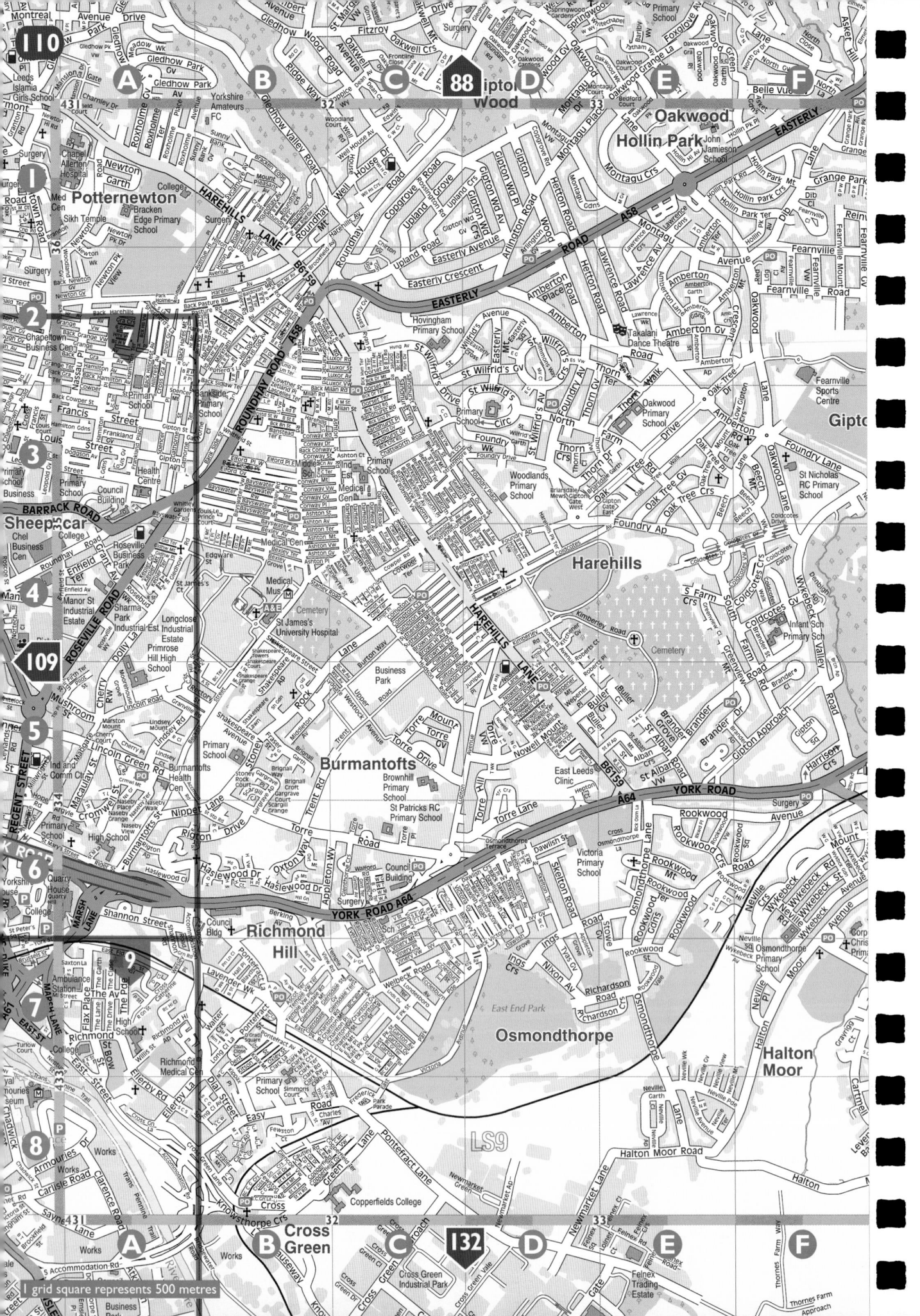

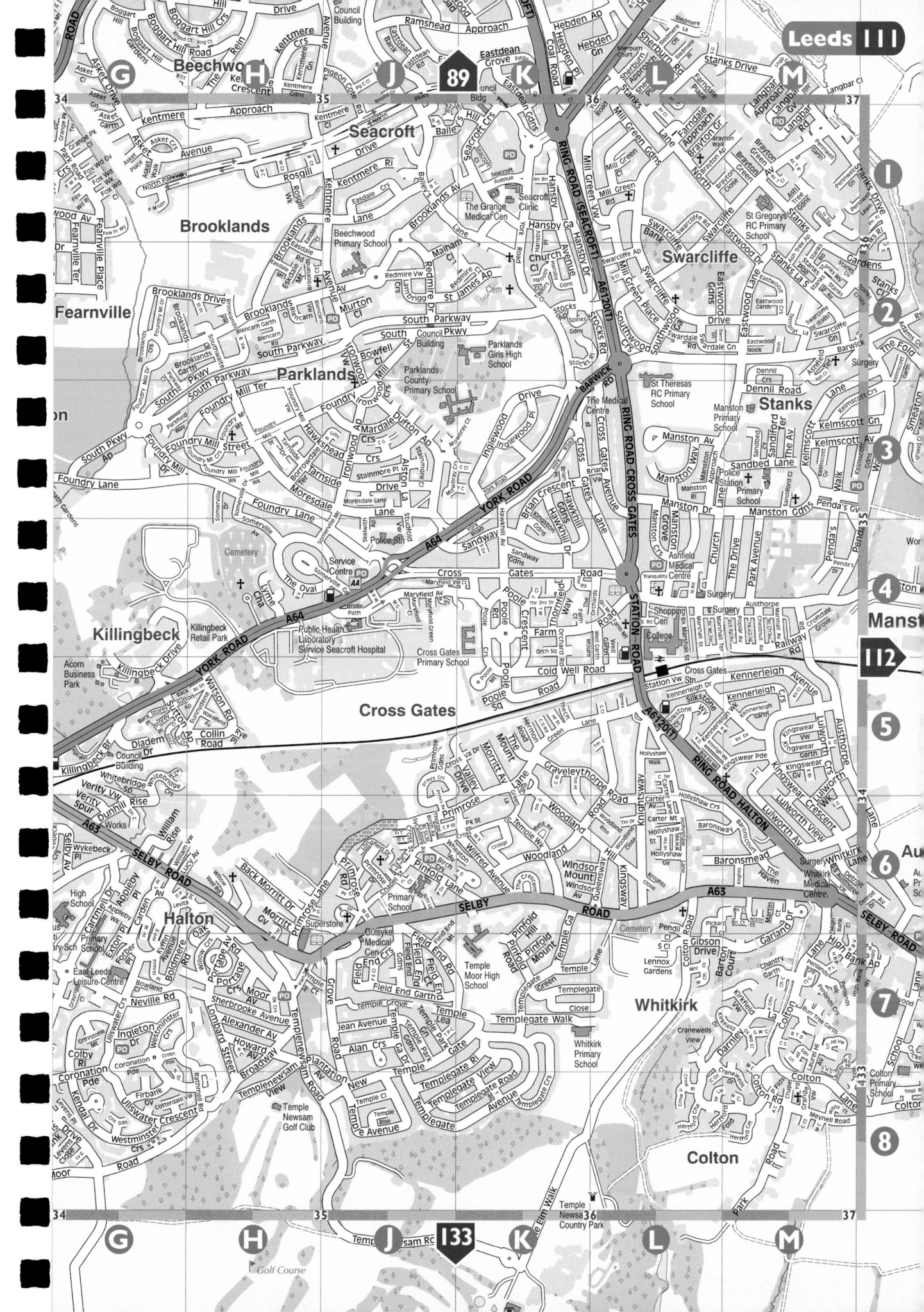

Barwick in Elmet

A **B** **C** 90 **D** **E** **F**

437 38 39

Leeds Road

Scholes Elmete Junior School

Scholes Park

Main Street

Barnbow Carr

Highfield La

I

Stanks Drive

Langbar Cl

Barwick Lane

Upper Barnbow Farm

Bog Lane

Barnbow Lane

Leeds Road

2

The Fold

Swarcliffe

Adams Gv

Surgery

Leeds Road

Barnbow Lane

Carr Beck

3

Kelmscott Gn

Kelmscott

Smeaton Approach

John Smeaton Sports Centre

John Smeaton High School

Pendas Fields

Mercia

Smeaton

Chelsfield Way

Biddenden Road

Badgers Mt

Barnbow Wood

4

Penda's

Manston Lane

Sandleas Way

Barnbow Lane

III

Croftdale Grove

Manston House

Works

Manston

LS15

Lazencroft Farm

Manston Lane

Barnbow Common

5

Thorpe

Crescent

Leeds Country W

M1

6

Austhorpe Primary School

Austhorpe

Barrowby Crs

Barrowby Lane

Barrowby Lane

Barrowby Hall

White Medical Centre

Lane

Barrowby

Austhorpe Gardens

Bradbury Grange

7

High Bank Ap

Austhorpe Grove

Austhorpe Av

Barrowby Av

Century Way

Brown Moor

SELBY ROAD

A63(T)

WAKEF

Queensway

Alandale Road

Colton Retail Park

A63(T)

Alandale Drive

Kingsway

8

Colton Primary School

Colton Road East

Junction 46

Cross Row

SELBY

Westbourne Terrace

Springbank

Ringway

Westway

A642

Meynell Road

Mead Gv

Swillington Common

ROAD

A63(T)

SELBY ROAD

Westbourne

West Garforth

437 38 39 A63(T)

A **B** **C** 134 **D** **E** **F**

Works

1 grid square represents 500 metres

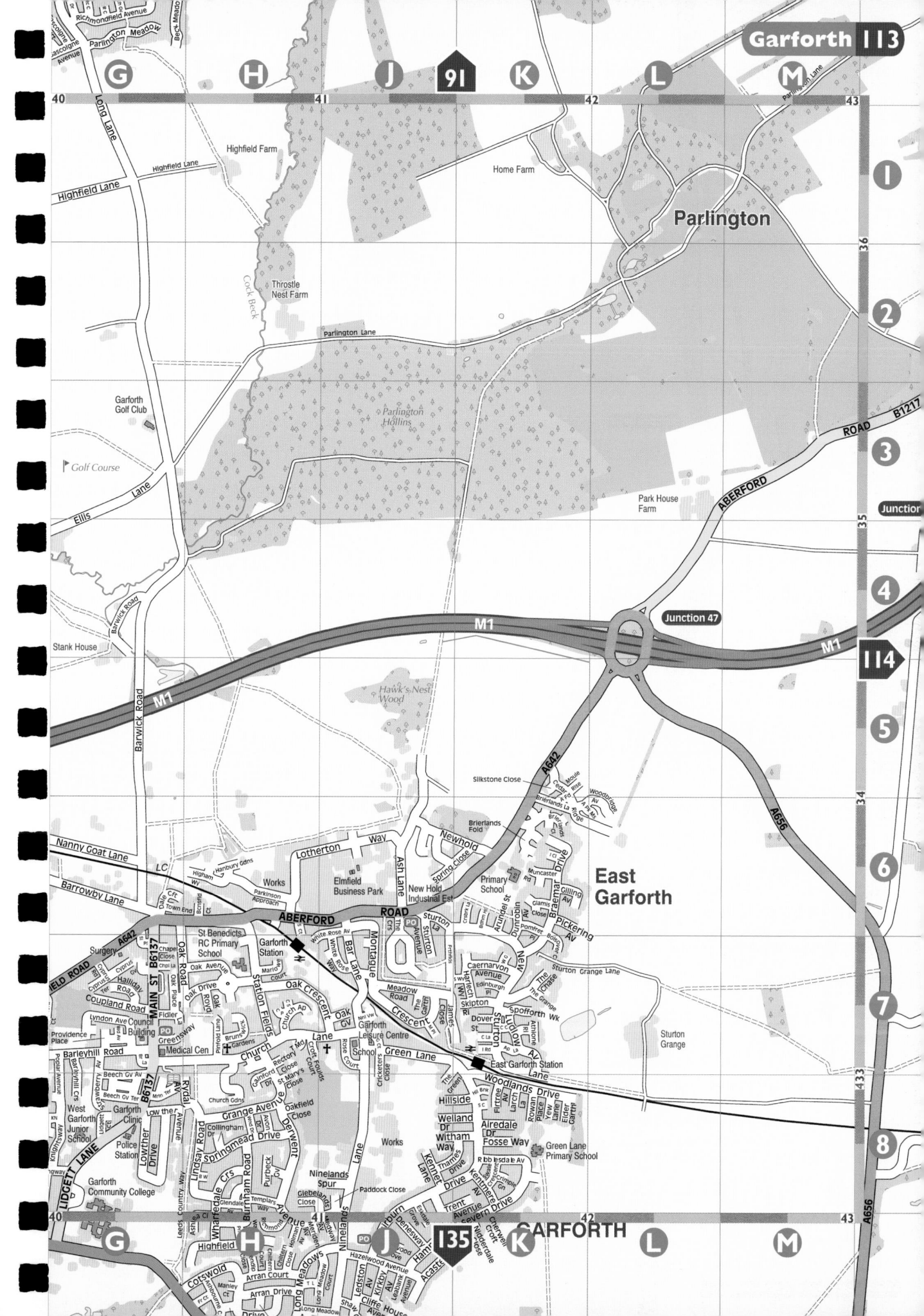

G   H   J   **91**   K   L   M

40   41   42   43

1

Parlington

Highfield Farm

Home Farm

Highfield Lane

Highfield Lane

2

Cock Beck

Throstle
Nest Farm

Parlington Lane

Parlington
Hollins

ROAD B1217

3

Garforth
Golf Club

ABERFORD

Golf Course

Park House
Farm

35   Junction

Ellis   Lane

Barwick Road

4

Stank House

Junction 47

M1

M1

114

M1

5

A642

Silkstone Close

Maule
Rise

Woodbridge

Hawk's Nest
Wood

Cedar
Av

Brierlands La Ridge

34

A656

Brierlands
Fold

6

Nanny Goat Lane

LC

Higham
Wy

Hanbury Gdns

Lotherton   Way

Ash Lane

Newhold

Spring Close

Muncaster
Rd

Primary
School

Glamis
Close

Gilling
Av

East
Garforth

Barrowby Lane

Works

Parkinson
Approach

Elmfield
Business Park

New Hold
Industrial Est

Sturton
St

Arundel St

Dunrobin

Pomfret St

Braemar   Drive

Pickering
Av

ABERFORD   ROAD

St Benedicts
RC Primary
School

Garforth
Station

White Rose Av

Bar Lane

Montague

PO

Sturton
Avenue

Caernarvon
Avenue

Sturton Grange Lane

FIELD ROAD

A642

Surgery

Chapel
Close

Chpl La

Oak   Road

Oak Avenue

Oak
Place

White Rose
Way

Marton
Court

Meadow
Road

Harrech

James
Close

Edinburgh
Dr

The
Chase

MAIN ST

B6137

Cyprus

Cyprus

Halliday
Road

Oak Drive

Oak
Rd

Church Ap

Crescent

Skipton

Dover
St

Spofforth
Wk

Athlone
Av

Sturton
Grange

Coupland Road

Fidler

Oak
GV

Oak
Lane

Garforth
Leisure Centre

Ludlow

Lyndon Ave

Council
Building

PO

Pinfold Lane

Bruns

Gardens

Rectory
Rd

Calnford

St Mary's
Close

The
I Rd

East Garforth Station
Lane

Providence
Place

Greensway

Medical Cen

Church

School

Croft Foulds

Green Lane

The
Green

Barleyhill Road

Barleyhill
Av

Beech Gv Av

Mrtn Ter

Church
Lane

Cricketers
Close

Rose Court

Woodlands Drive

Hillside

Rowan
Place

Yew
Lane

Elder
Garth

Green Lane

B6137

Beech Gv Ter

Church Gdns

Oakfield
Close

Welland
Dr

Aireдale
Dr

Fosse Way

Green Lane
Primary School

West
Garforth
Junior
School

KN

Garforth
Clinic

Low ther

Grange Avenue

Collingham
Dr

Avon

Witham
Way

Ribblesdale Av

Knightsway

Police
Station

Lowther
Drive

Lindsay Road

Springmead

Derwent

Purbeck
Dr

Works

Kennet
Lane

Thames
Dr

Crimple

Nideerdale
Croft

Kenmere
Av

LIDGETT LANE

Garforth
Community College

Burnham Road

Ninelands
Spur

Paddock Close

Trent
Drive

Cherwell
Av

Severn Drive

40   41   Leeds Country Way   Ash   Cl   Glendale

Wharfedale   Crs

Templars
Way

Glebeland
Close

Litbourn
Dr

Deneway

PO

Hampd

Acaste

42   43

135

GARFORTH

A656

G   H   J   K   L   M

Highfield

Cotswold

Manley
Cl

Arran Court

Arran Drive

Long Meadows

Chiltern
Av

Kirkby
Av

Ledston

Cliffe House

Hazelwood Avenue

Shaw

7

8

33

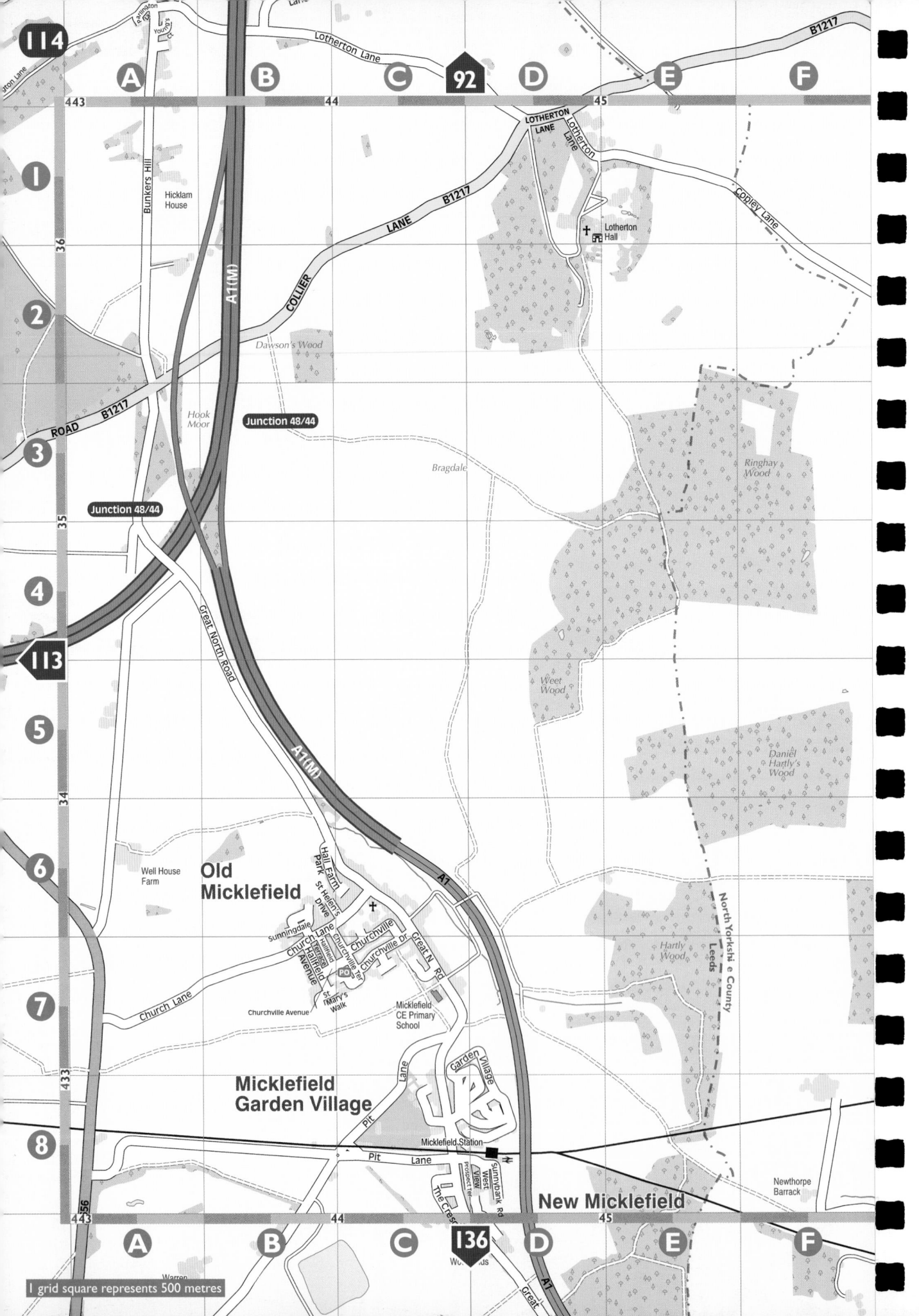

A B C **92** D E F

443   44   45

1

Bunkers Hill

Hicklam House

Lotherton Lane

LOTHERTON LANE

Lotherton Lane

Copley Lane

B1217

36

COLLIER LANE B1217

Lotherton Hall

2

A1(M)

Dawson's Wood

35

Hook Moor

ROAD B1217

3

Junction 48/44

Bragdale

Ringhay Wood

Junction 48/44

4

Great North Road

◄ **113**

Weet Wood

5

34

Daniel Hartly's Wood

A1(M)

6

Well House Farm

Old Micklefield

Hall Farm Park

St Helen's Drive

Church Lane

Churchville

Hatfield

Sunningdale

Churchville Ter

Churchville Dr

Hartly Wood

North Yorkshire County Leeds

A1

Great N. Rd

PO

7

Church Lane

Hatfield Avenue

St Mary's Walk

Churchville Avenue

Micklefield CE Primary School

Micklefield Garden Village

Pit Lane

Garden Village

8

Pit Lane

Micklefield Station

Sunnybank Rd

West View

Prospect Ter

Newthorpe Barrack

The Crest

New Micklefield

433

456

443   44   45

A B C **136** D E F

Woodlands

A1

Great

Warren

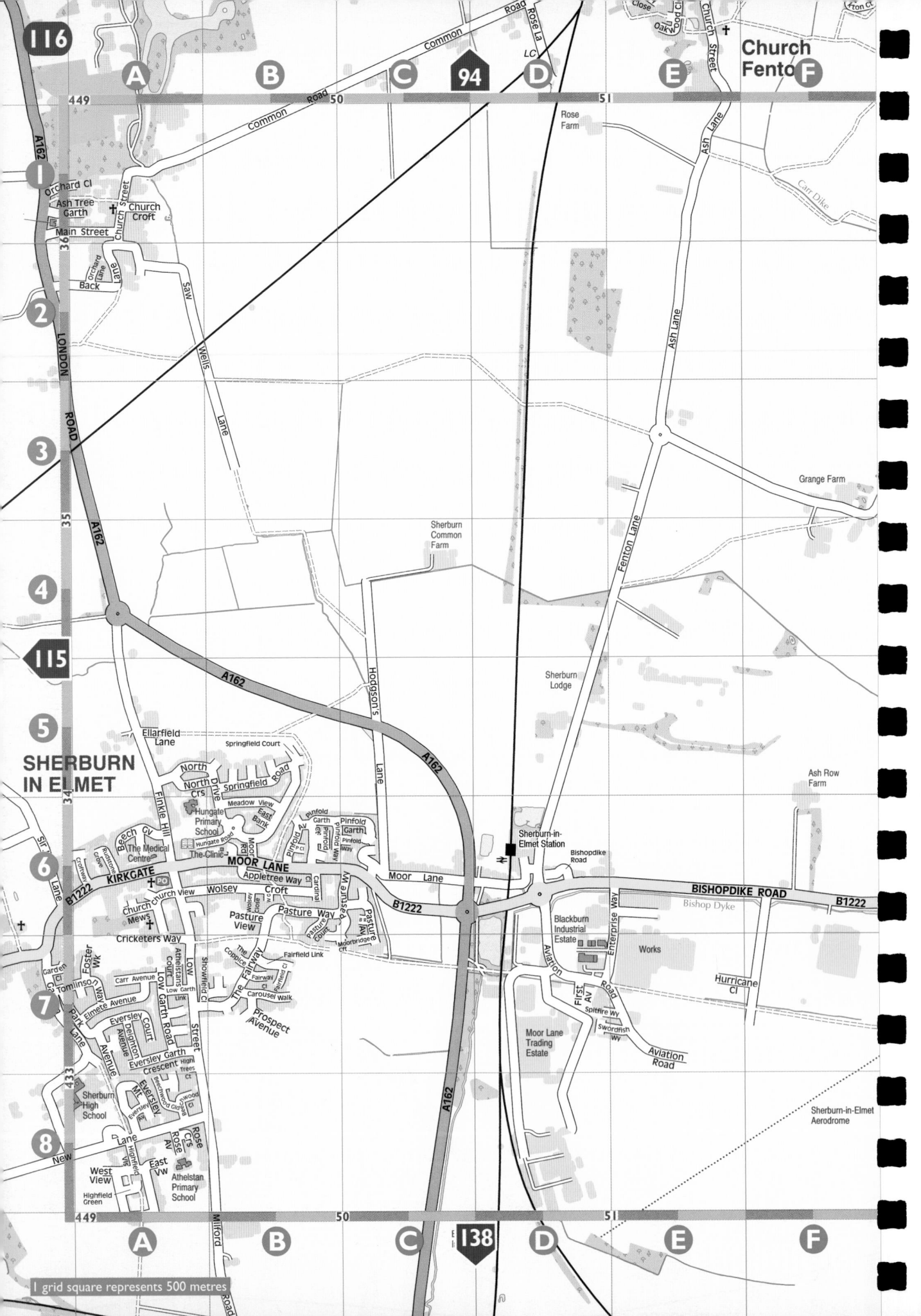

116

A B C **94** D E **Church Fento** F

1 449 Common Road 50 51

A162

Orchard Cl

Ash Tree Garth

Church Croft

Main Street

Orchard Lane

Back

Saw Wells Lane

LONDON ROAD

35

2

3

A162

4

115

A162

5

SHERBURN IN ELMET

Ellarfield Lane

Springfield Court

North Drive

North Crs

Springfield Road

Meadow View

East Bank

Hungate Primary School

Hungate Road

Finkle Hill

Beech Cv

Rustson Close

Crowtree Close

The Medical Centre

The Clinic

KIRKGATE

PO

Church View

Wolsey

Croft

Church Mews

Cricketers Way

Foster Wk

Garden Cl

Tomlinson

Carr Avenue

Elmete Avenue

Eversley Court

Deighton Avenue

Eversley Garth Crescent

Beechwood Glade

Rose Crs

Rose Av

Park Lane

New Lane

433

Sherburn High School

Eversley Av

High Trees Cl

Y Wood Cl

West View

East Vw

Highfield Green

Athelstan Primary School

6 MOOR LANE

Appletree Way

Cardinal

Pinfold Av

Pinfold Garth

Pinfold Lee

Pinfold Cl

Pinfold Way

Pinfold Garth

Low Garth

Low Garth Link

Showfield Cl

The Fairway

Fairway

Carousel Walk

The Coppice

Coppice Walk

Prospect Avenue

Pasture Way

Pasture View

Pasture Cl

Pasture Court

Moorbridge

Fairfield Link

The Wynd

Moor Rd

Hodgson's Lane

B1222

Moor Lane

MOOR LANE

Sherburn Common Farm

Sherburn Lodge

Sherburn-in-Elmet Station

Bishopdike Road

Blackburn Industrial Estate

Aviation Road

First Av

Spitfire Wy

Swordfish Wy

Moor Lane Trading Estate

Aviation Road

Enterprise Way

Works

BISHOPDIKE ROAD B1222

Bishop Dyke

Ash Row Farm

Hurricane Cl

Sherburn-in-Elmet Aerodrome

Rose Farm

Rose La

LC

Common Road

Church Street

Ash Lane

Carr Dike

Fenton Lane

Grange Farm

Close

Oakw

Wood Cl

Ft on Ct

Church Street

7

8 New 449 Milford Road 50 **138** 51

A B C **138** D E F

1 grid square represents 500 metres

G H J 95 K L M

52 53 54 55

G H J 139 K L M

I
2
3
4
5
6
7
8

36
35
34
433

Hall La
Hall Farm
Nanny Lane
Gay
Broad Lane
Partridge Hill Farm
Oxmoor Lane
Meeke Wood
Broad Lane
Lodge Farm
Pickrowfield
Lane
Little Fenton Lodge
Biggin Lane
Little Fenton
Biggin Lane
Spring Well House
Oxmoor Lane
Biggin
Ash La
Sweeming Lane
BISHO
B1222
Mattram Hall
North Sweeming
B1222
Rest Park
Low Hall Farm
Lennerton Lane
New Lennerton Lane
Lennerton Farm
Low Rest Park Farm
Melton Leys
Milford Hagg Farm
Habholme

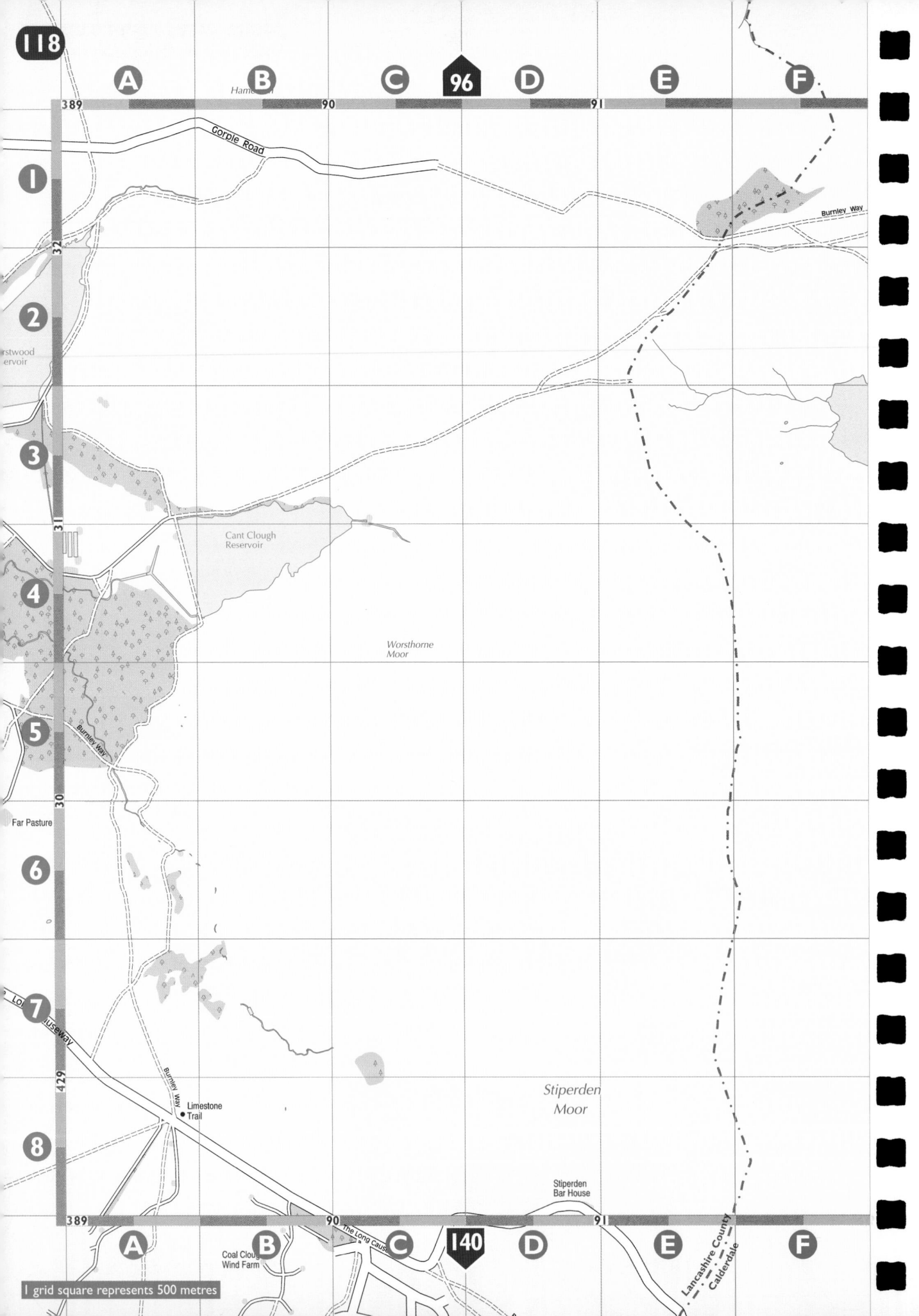

A   B   C   96   D   E   F

389   Hameldon   90   91

Corple Road

Burnley Way

1

32

2

rstwood
ervoir

3

31

Cant Clough
Reservoir

4

Worsthorne
Moor

5

Burnley Way

30

Far Pasture

6

Lo...
useway

7

429

Burnley Way

Limestone
Trail

Stiperden
Moor

8

Stiperden
Bar House

389   90   The Long Caus...   91

A   B   C   140   D   E   F

Coal Clough
Wind Farm

Lancashire County
Calderdale

1 grid square represents 500 metres

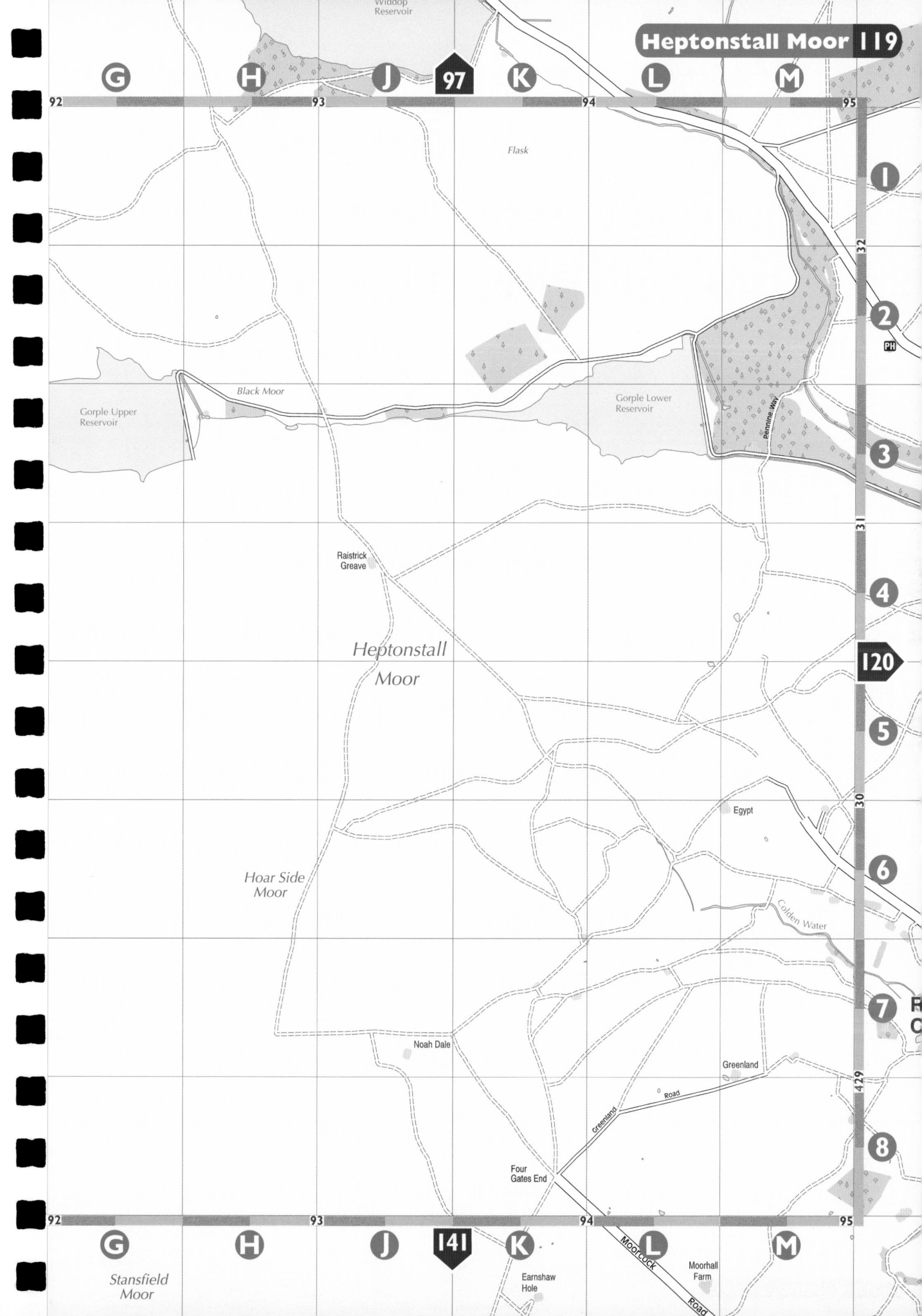

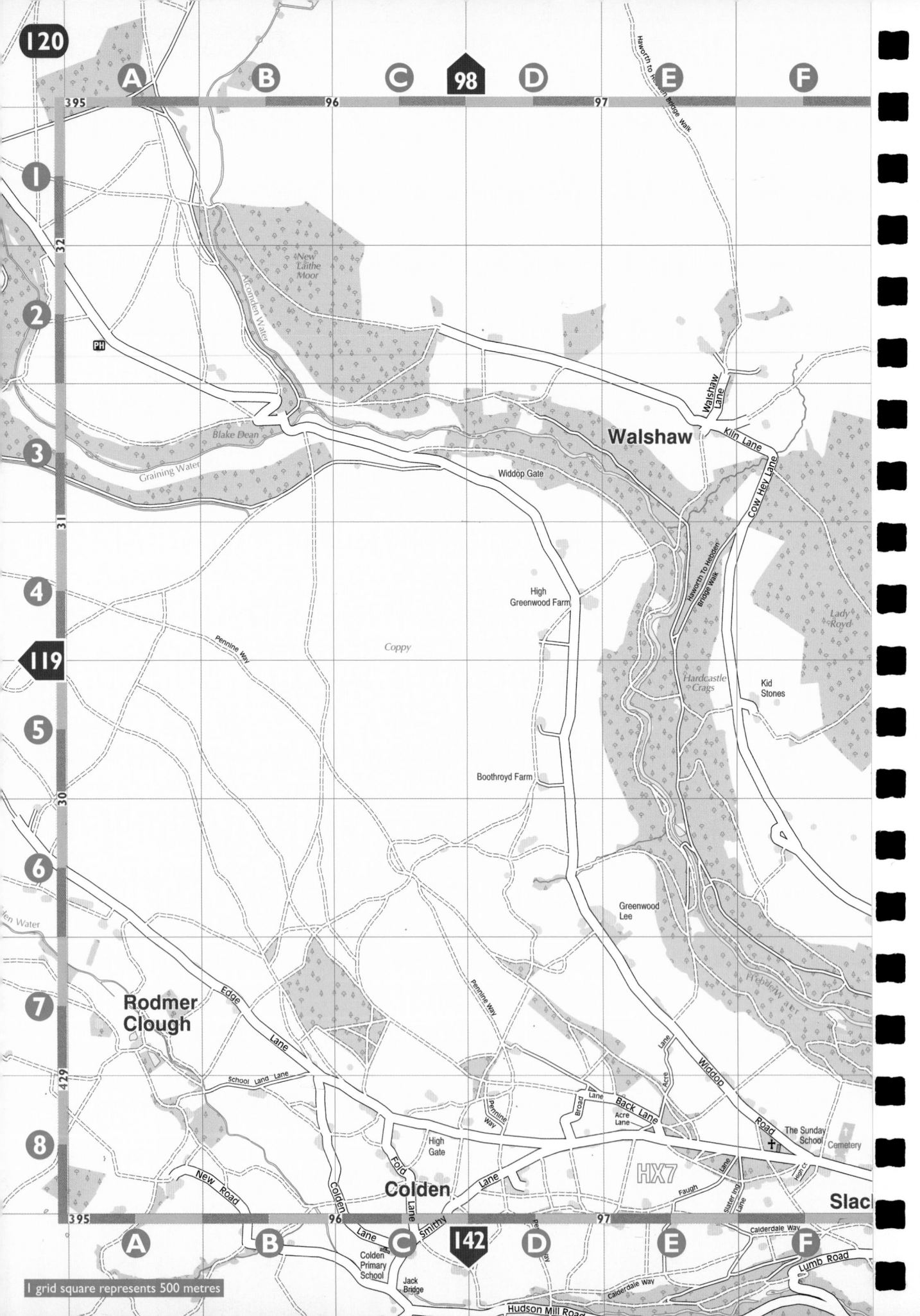

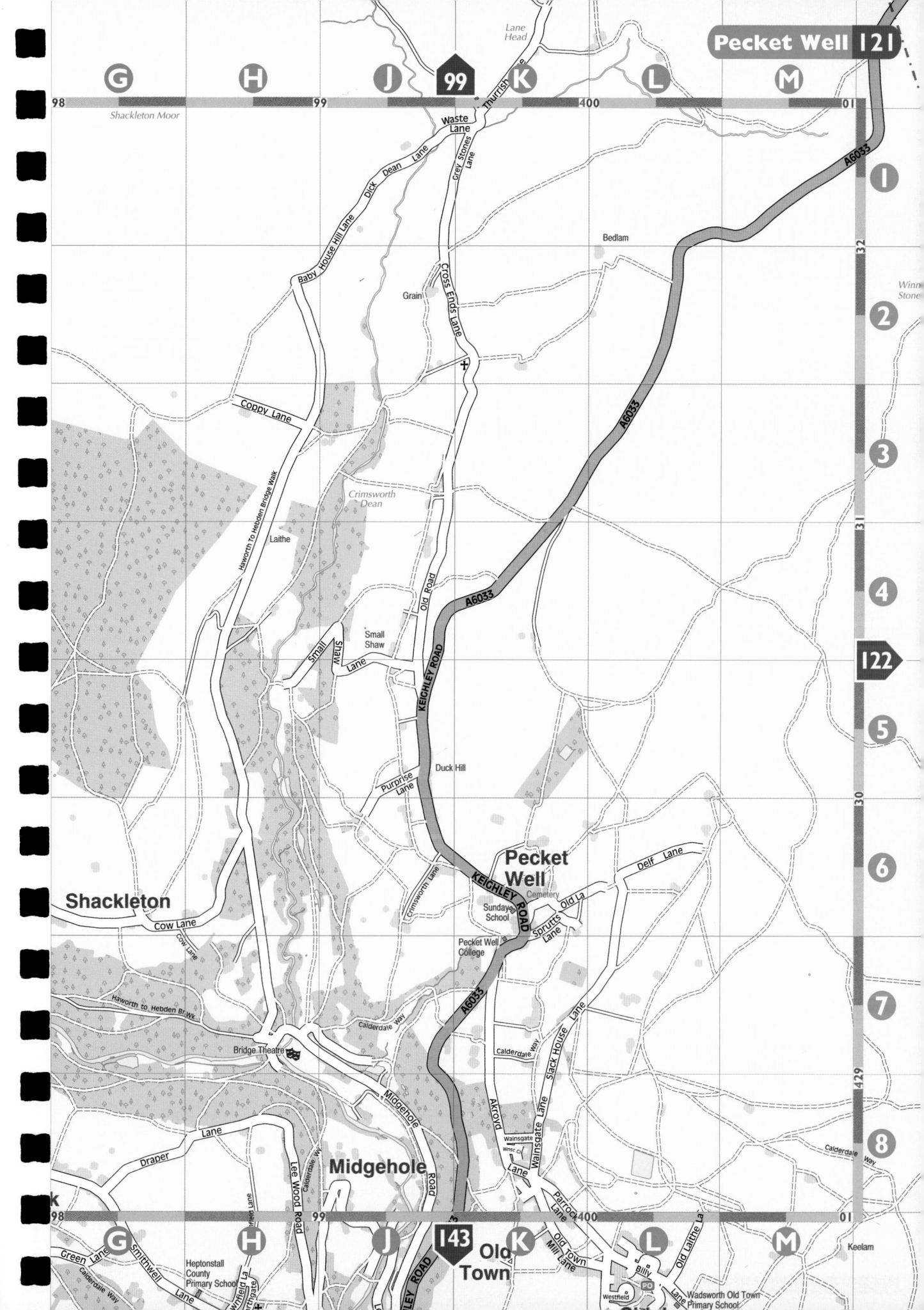

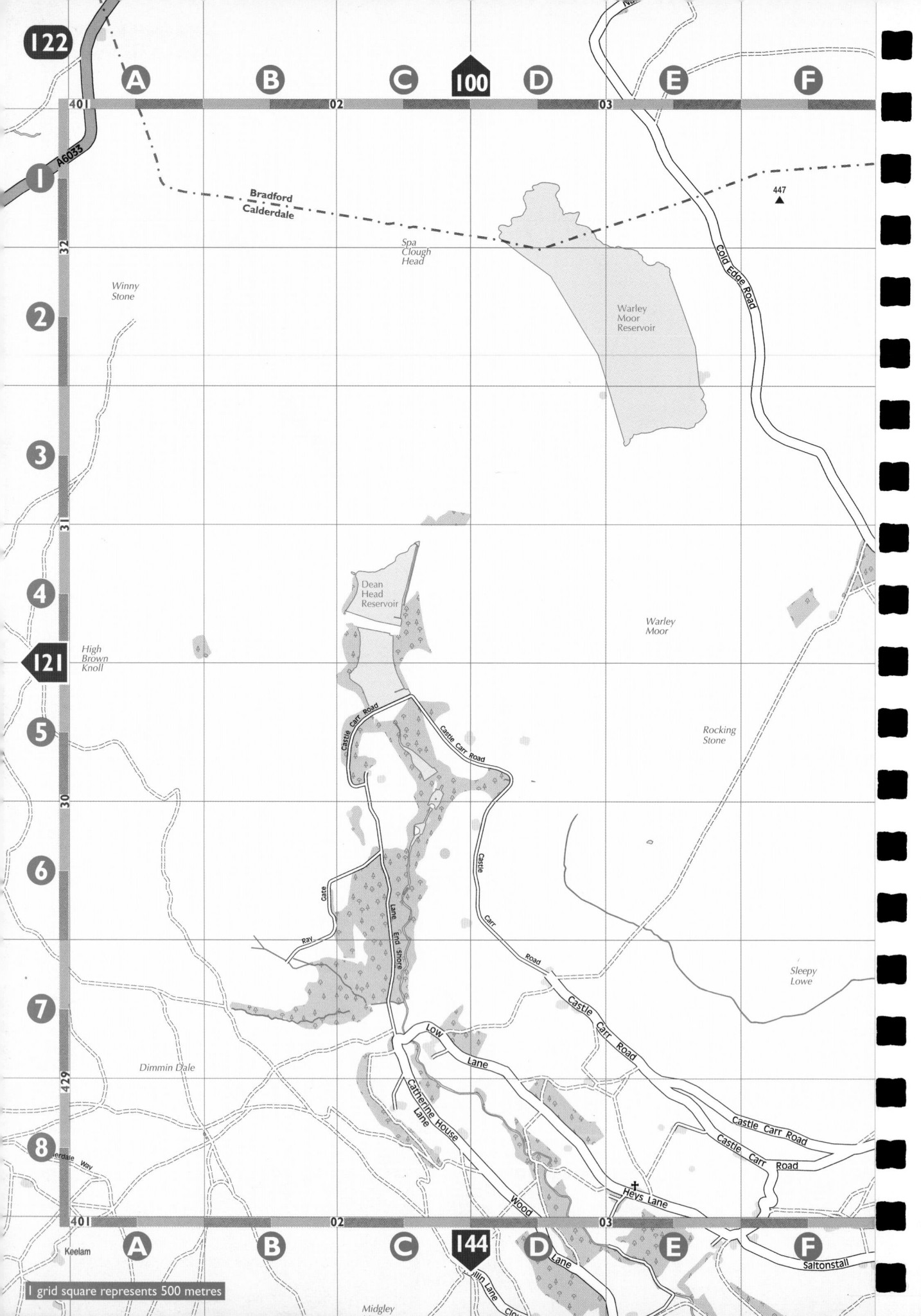

A B C ◆ 100 D E F

401 02 03

A6033

1

32

Winny
Stone

2

3

31

4

High
Brown
Knoll

121

30

5

6

429

7

Dimmin Dale

8

derdale Way

401 02 03

A B C ◆ 144 D E F

Keelam

Bradford
Calderdale

Spa
Clough
Head

447
▲

Warley
Moor
Reservoir

Cold Edge Road

Dean
Head
Reservoir

Warley
Moor

Rocking
Stone

Castle Carr Road

Castle Carr Road

Castle

Carr

Road

Castle Carr Road

Gate

Lane

End Shore

Ray

Low

Lane

Catherine House

Lane

Wood Lane

Sleepy
Lowe

Castle Carr Road

Castle Carr Road

Heys Lane

✝

Saltonstall

Midgley

Jilin Lane Clo

1 grid square represents 500 metres

G H J 101 K L M

Thornton Moor

04 05 06 07

Denholme Gate

Foreside Lane

I

Foreside Lane

Foreside

Bradford
Calderdale

2

Coal Lane

Causew
F t

3

Ovenden
Moor

Ogden
Plantation

Ogden Lane

Syke

Ogden
Reservoir

Ogden

4

Cold
Edge

Withens New Road

124

Withens Road

5

Golf Course

Union Lane

Rocks Lane

30

Halifax
Golf Club

A629

Cow Hill Gate Lane

Calderdale

6

Lane Lane

Stod Fold

Head Lane

Brookhouse

Rocks Lane

Upper
Brockholes

Calderdale Way

Per Lane

Pavemen

Cold Edge Dams

Field

Head Lane

Bolton

KEIGHLEY

Lumb

Calderdale Way

Ogden View
West Botton

7

Hays Lane

White Gate

ROAD

The Willow

Castle Carr Road

Lumb Lane

Rope Walk

Lumb Lane

Edge Road

Calderdale Way

Hebble Brook
Business Park

Mixenden Reservoir

Mill Lane

Long House Road

Mixenden Lane

Spring Hill

Cemetery
Keighley

Natt

Illing

8

Abbey Park
School

Heathmoor Park Rd

IGLEY HILL

Kell Lane

Wainstalls Log La

Rough Hall

Tree

Wainstalls School

Brow Bottom Lane

Ivy Lane

Mixenden County
Primary School

Heathmoor

Clough Lane

Wainstalls

G H J 145 K L Mixenden M

PO

Hambleton

Stanningley Drive

Woodbrook Av

Raw Lane

Turner Av N

Church

Hunter
Hill Road

Clough
Place

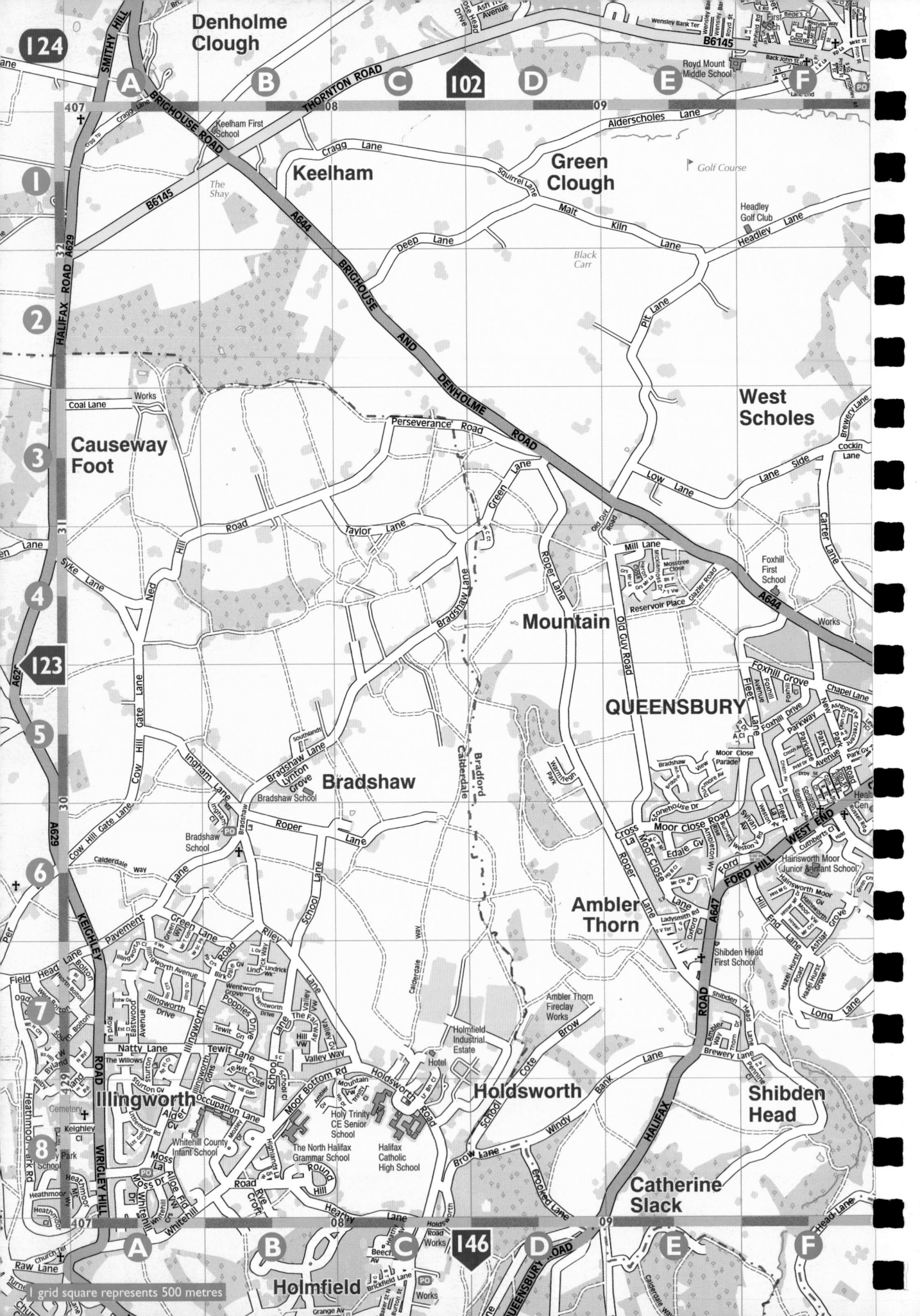

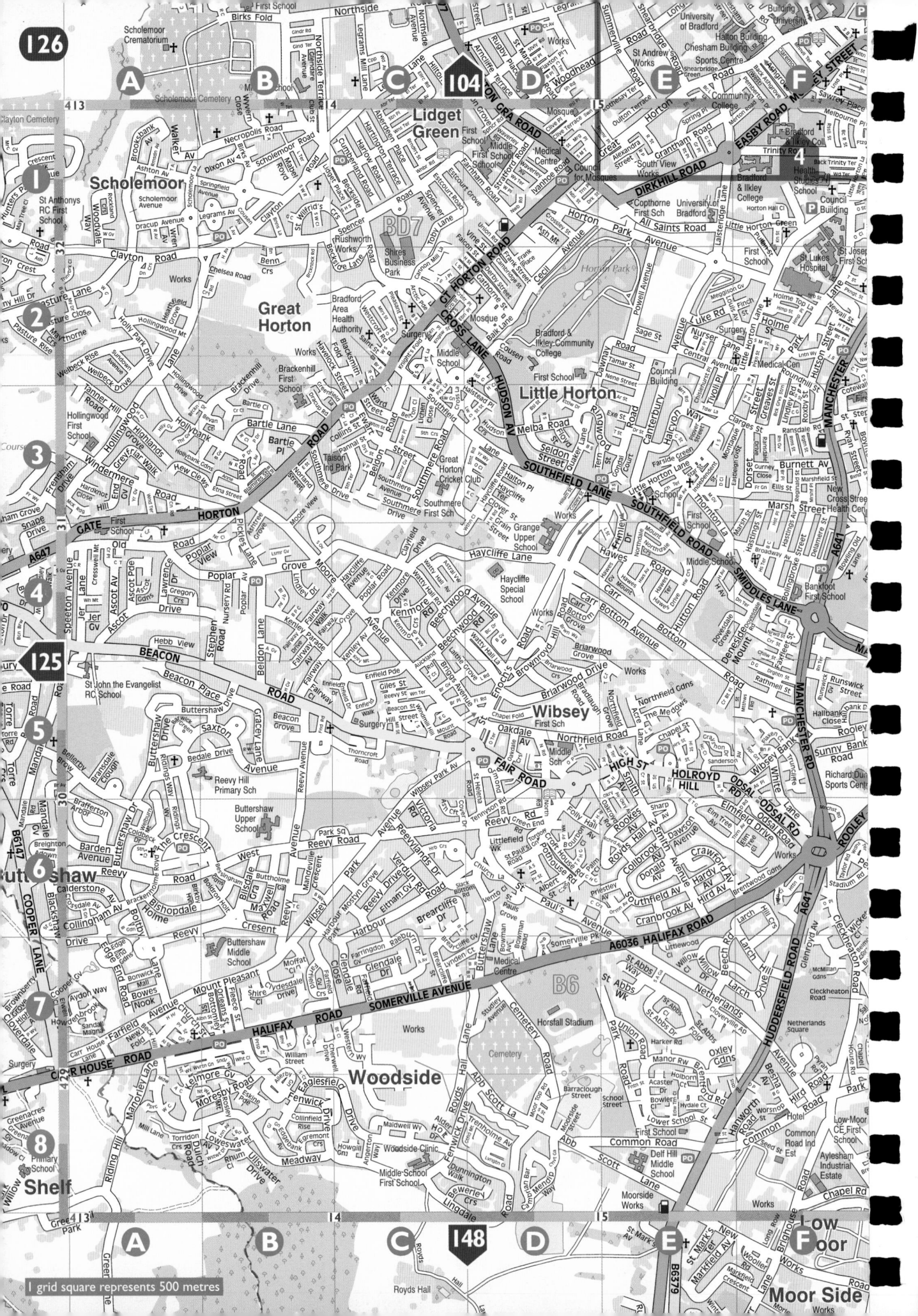

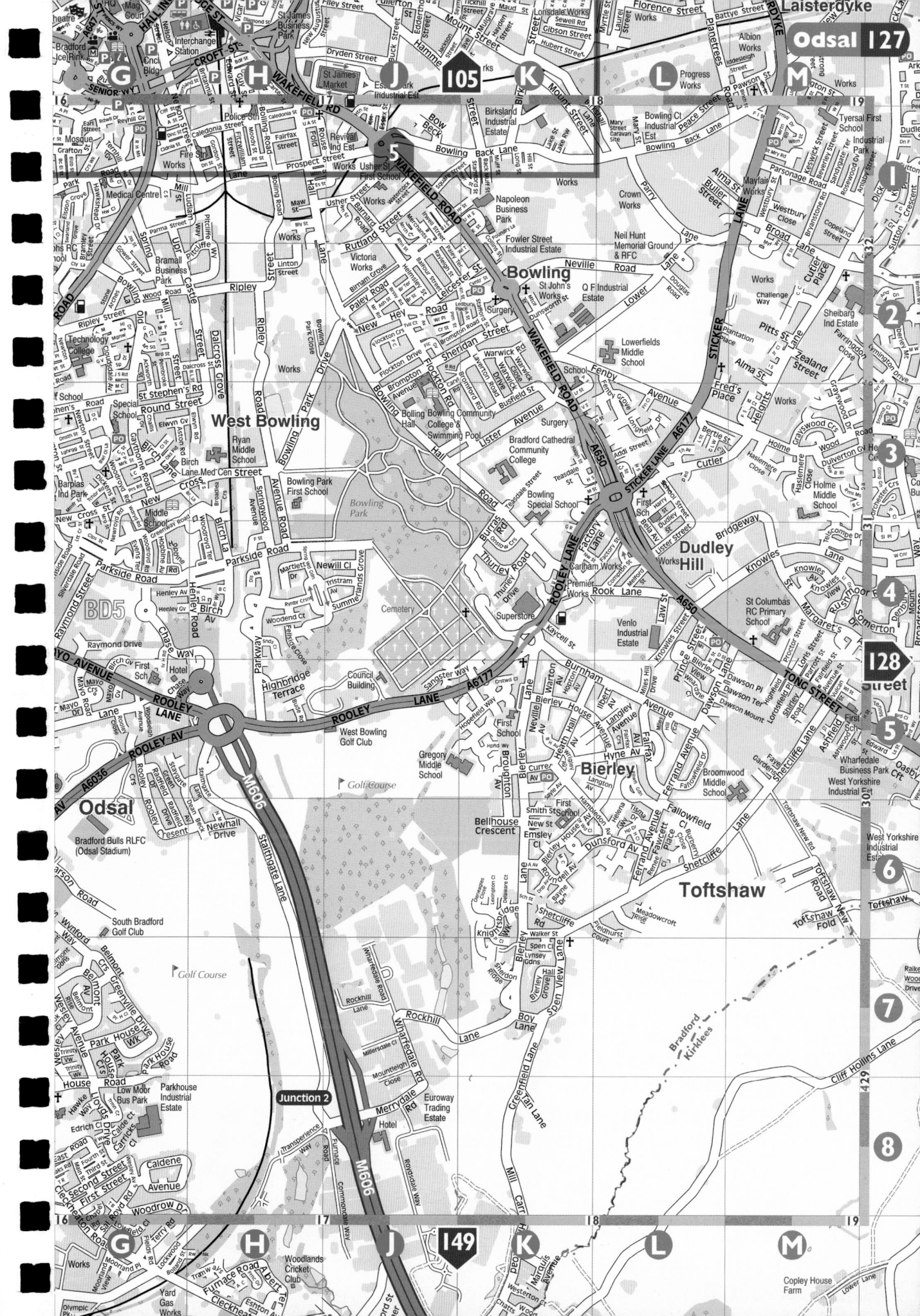

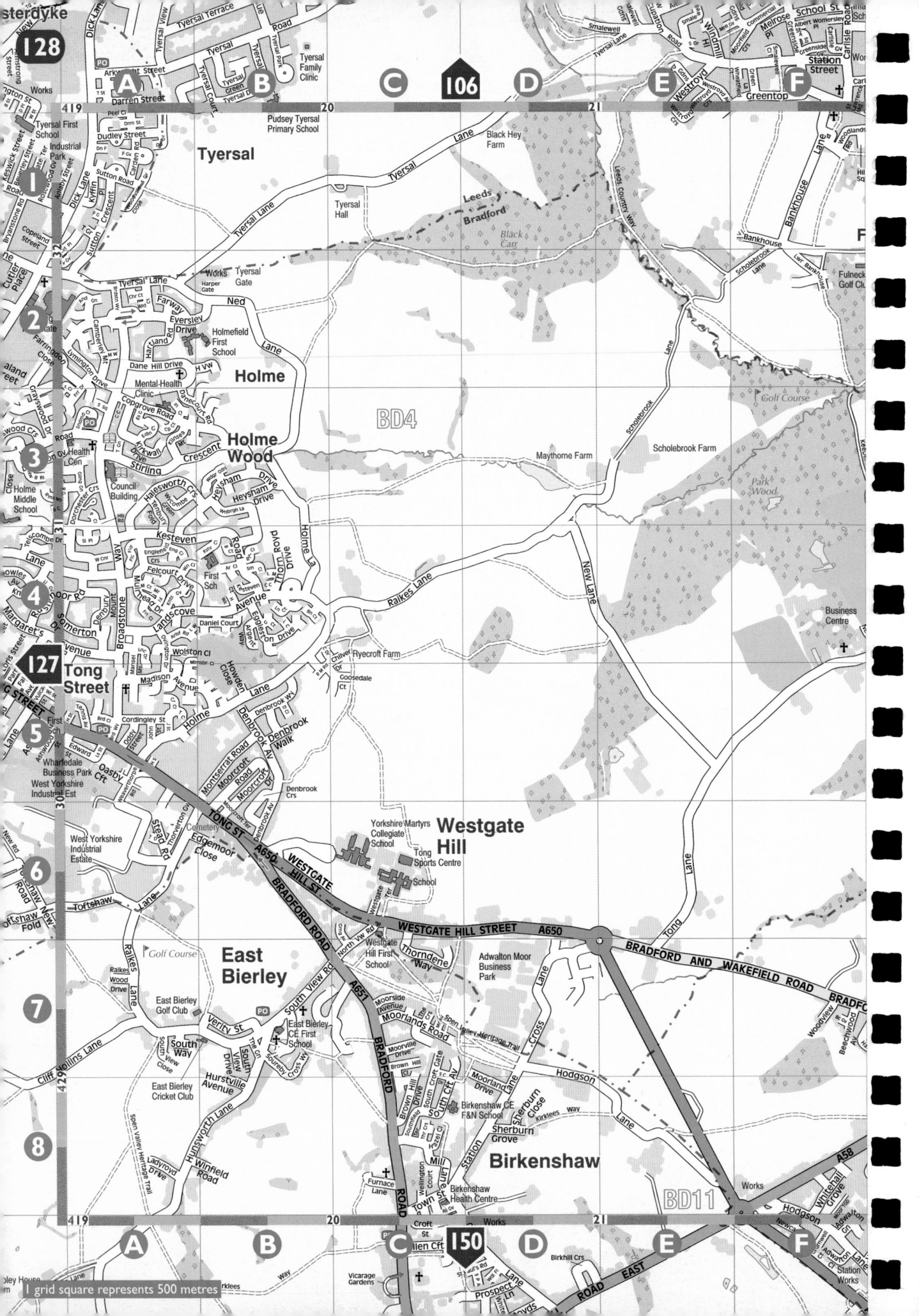

sterdyke

128

419

A Darren Street B 20 C **106** D 21 E Westroyd F Station Street

Greentop

Tyersal First School

Tyersal

Pudsey Tyersal Primary School

Tyersal Hall

Leeds Bradford

Black Hey Farm

Black Carr

Leeds Country Way

Bankhouse

Fulneck Golf Club

Works

Tyersal Lane

Tyersal Gate

Harper Gate

Ned Lane

Holmefield First School

Holme

BD4

Eversley Drive

Dane Hill Drive

Mental Health Clinic

Holme Wood

Maythorne Farm

Scholebrook Farm

Golf Course

Park Wood

Council Building

Kesteven

Scholebrook Lane

New Lane

First Sch

Landscove Avenue

Daniel Court

Raikes Lane

Business Centre

127 Tong Street

Wolston Cl

Howden Lane

Ryecroft Farm

Goosedale Ct

5

First Sch

Denbrook Walk

Denbrook Av

Wharfedale Business Park

West Yorkshire Industrial Est

Montserrat Road

Moorcroft Road

Denbrook Crs

6

West Yorkshire Industrial Estate

Toftshaw Lane

Eggemoor Close

Cemetery

Tong St

A650

Bradford Road

Westgate Hill St

A651

Yorkshire Martyrs Collegiate School

Tong Sports Centre

School

Westgate Hill

7

Golf Course

East Bierley

Raikes Wood Drive

East Bierley Golf Club

Verity St

South View Rd

Westgate Hill First School

North Vw Rd

Thorndene Way

Westgate Hill Street A650

Adwalton Moor Business Park

Lane

Cross Lane

BRADFORD AND WAKEFIELD ROAD

BRADF

East Bierley CE First School

Moorside Avenue

Moorlands Road

Spen Valley Heritage Trail

Hodgson

South Way

South View Close

South View Drive

Sourbeby Cross Wy

Moorside

Moorville Drive

Brown Hill

Moorland Drive

Sherburn Close

8

Hurstville Avenue

East Bierley Cricket Club

Huntsworth Lane

Winfield Road

Ladyroyd Drive

Spen Valley Heritage Trail

Birkenshaw CE F&N School

Southmere

Brown Drive

South Croft Gate

Kirklees Way

Sherburn Grove

Hodgson Lane

Birkenshaw

Works

A58

BD11

Furnace Lane

Wellington Court

Mill

Town Street

Station Road

Birkenshaw Health Centre

Works

Whitehall Grove

419

A 20 B C **150** D 21 E **ROAD EAST** F

Croft St

llen Crt

Birkhill Crs

St Paul's Rd

Vicarage Gardens

Prospect Ln

Adwalton

Station Works

1 grid square represents 500 metres

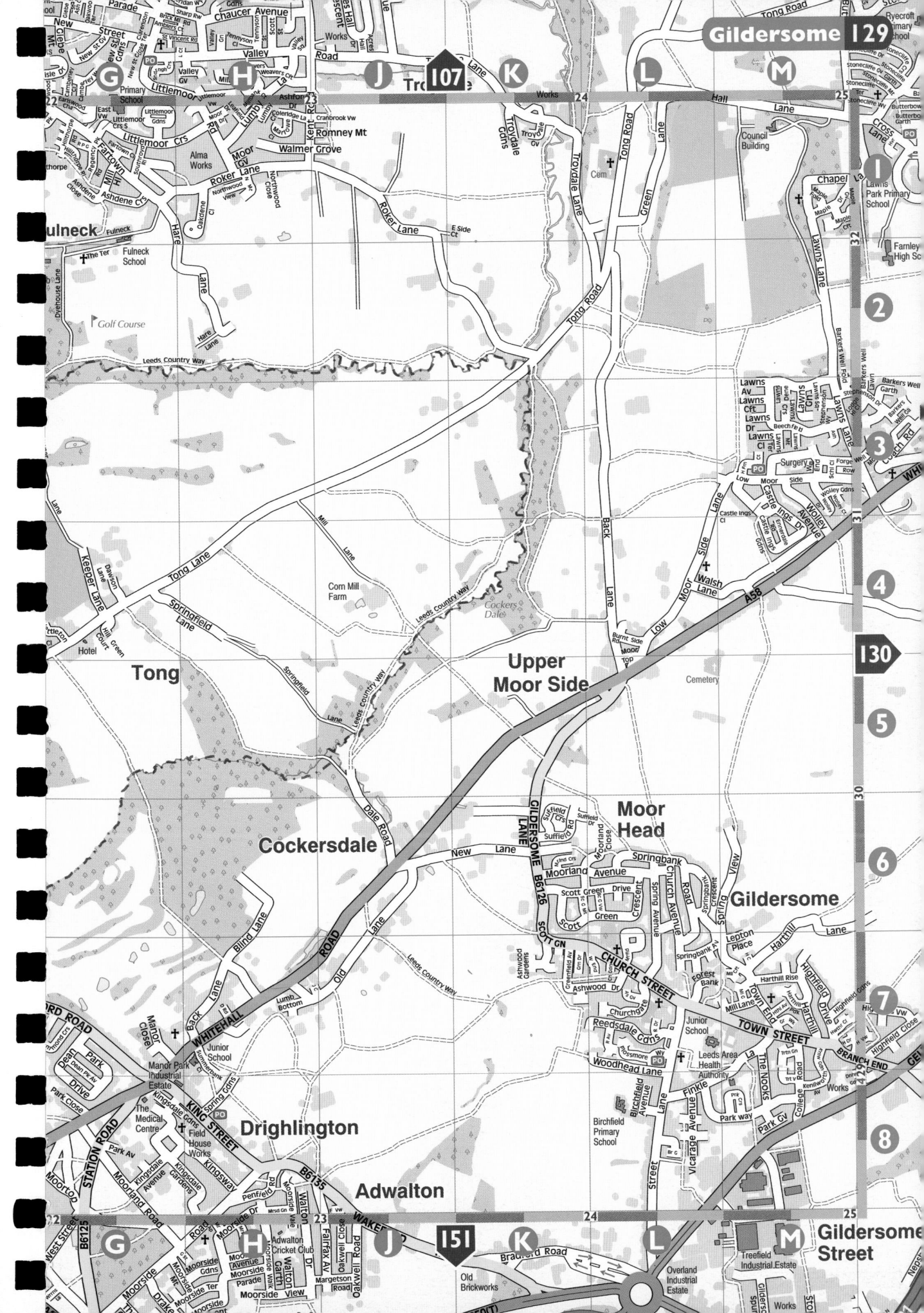

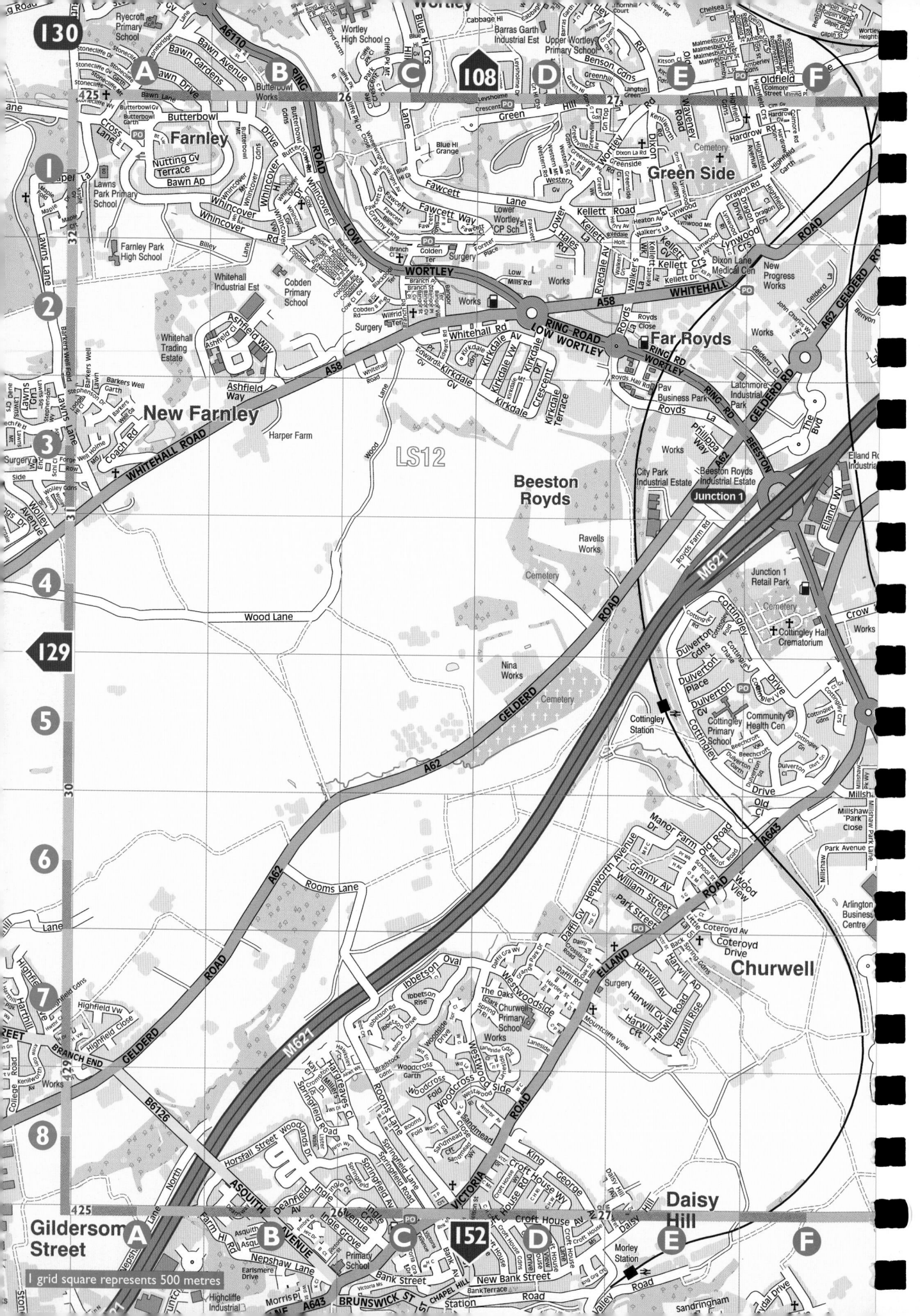

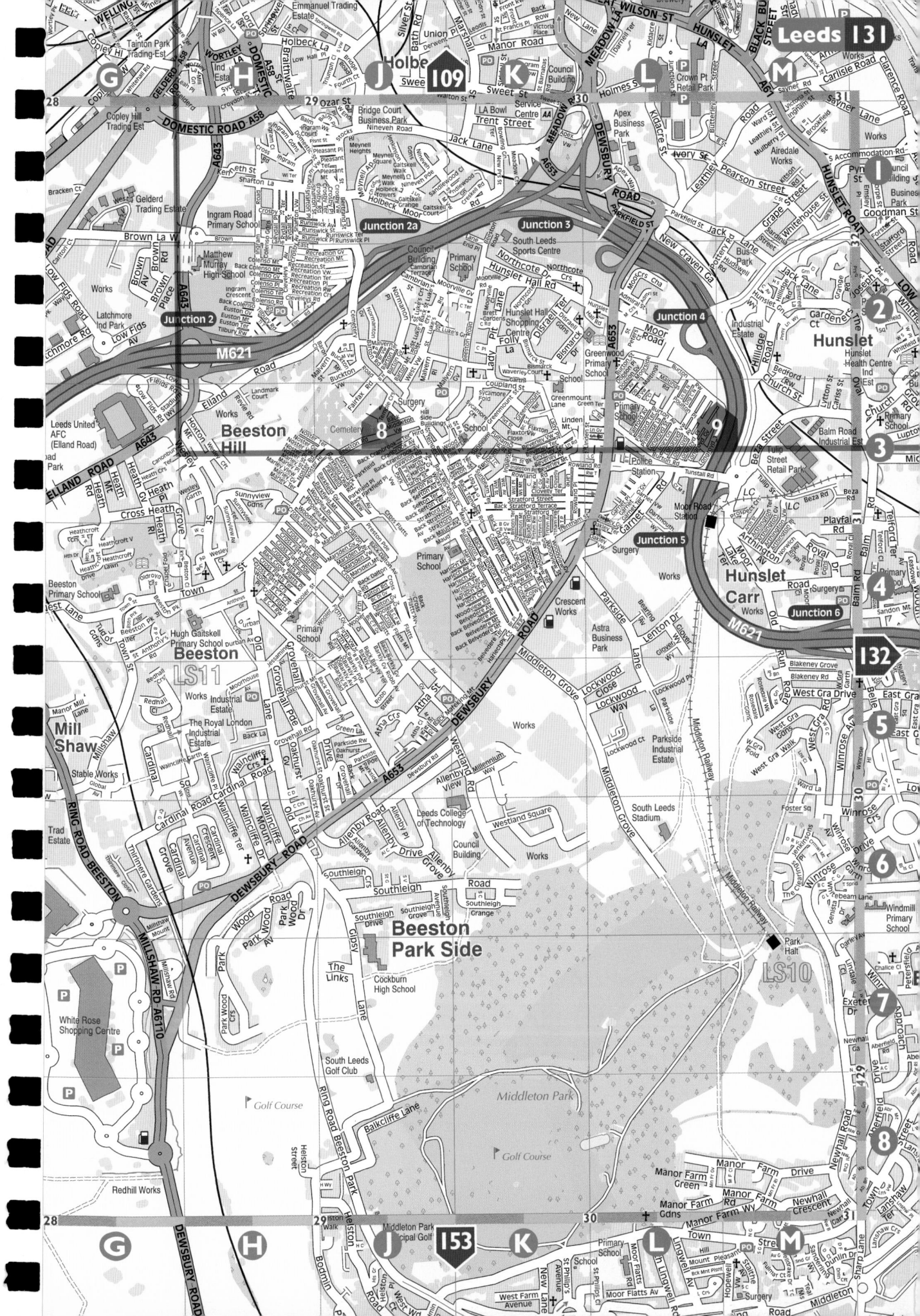

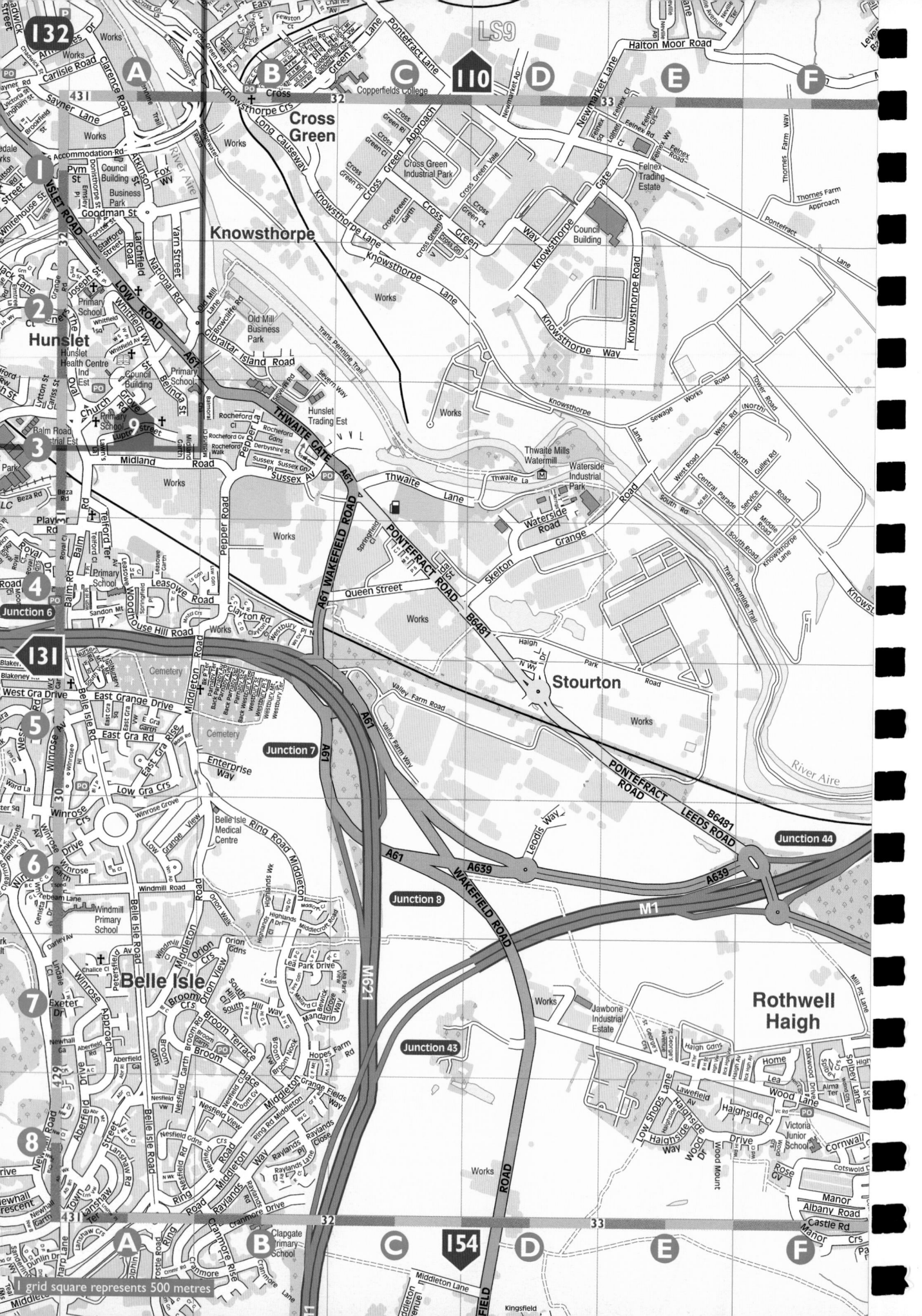

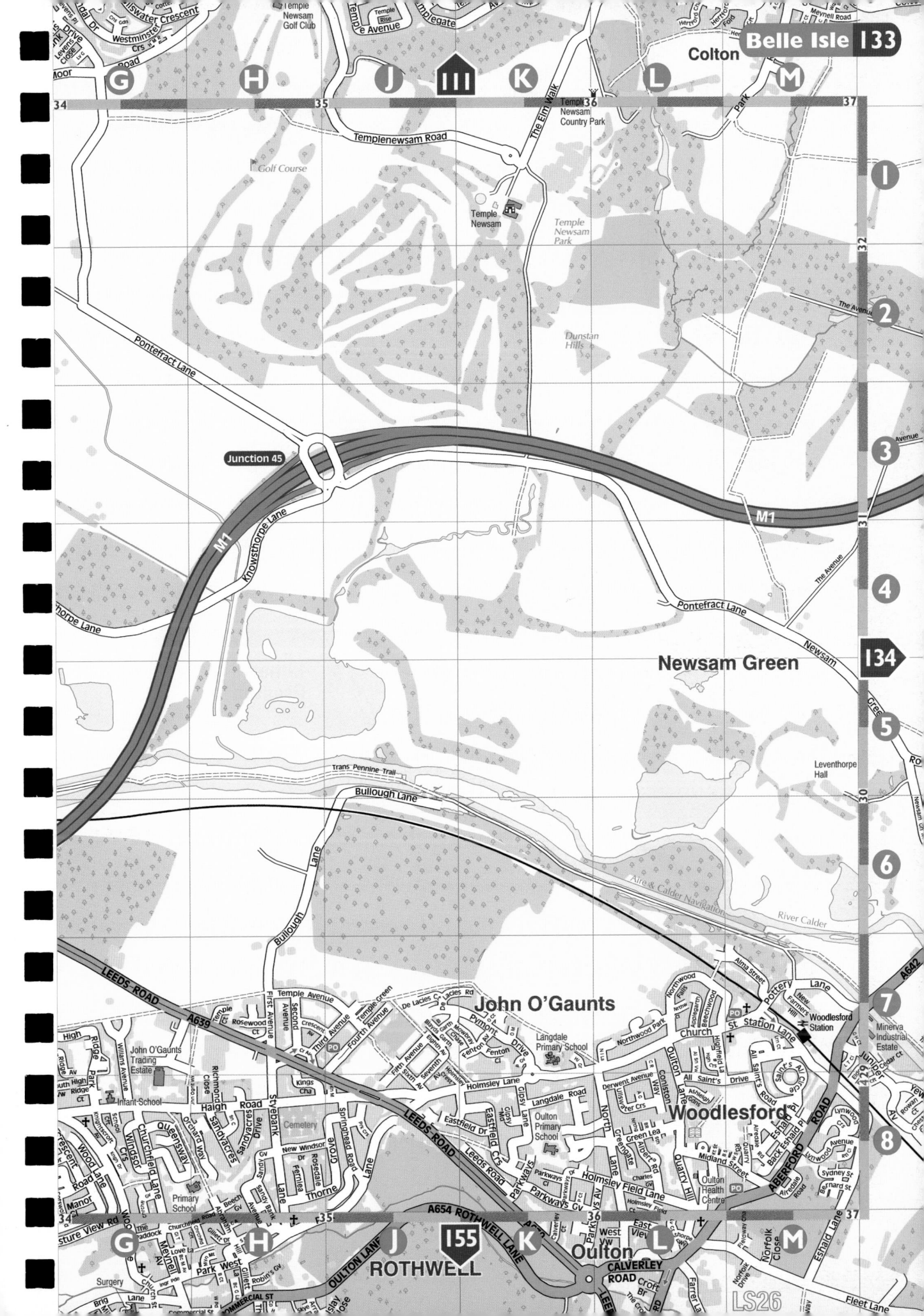

A   B   C   112   D   E   F

SELBY ROAD

Swillington
Common

West
Garforth

I

2   The Avenue
Avenue
Wood

Hollinthorpe

3   The Avenue

4   The Avenue

133

Swillington

Swillington
Primary
School

Works

Goody
Cross

Little
Preston

Church
Lane

The
Crest

5   Leventhorpe
Hall

St Mary's
Surgery

Park
AV

Astley Lane
Industrial
Estate

6   Jinny
Moor
Lane

Leeds Country Way

7   Woodlesford
Station

Minerva
Industrial
Estate

Trans Pennine Trail

Leeds Country Way

8   Yew Tree Dr

A   B   C   156   D   E   F

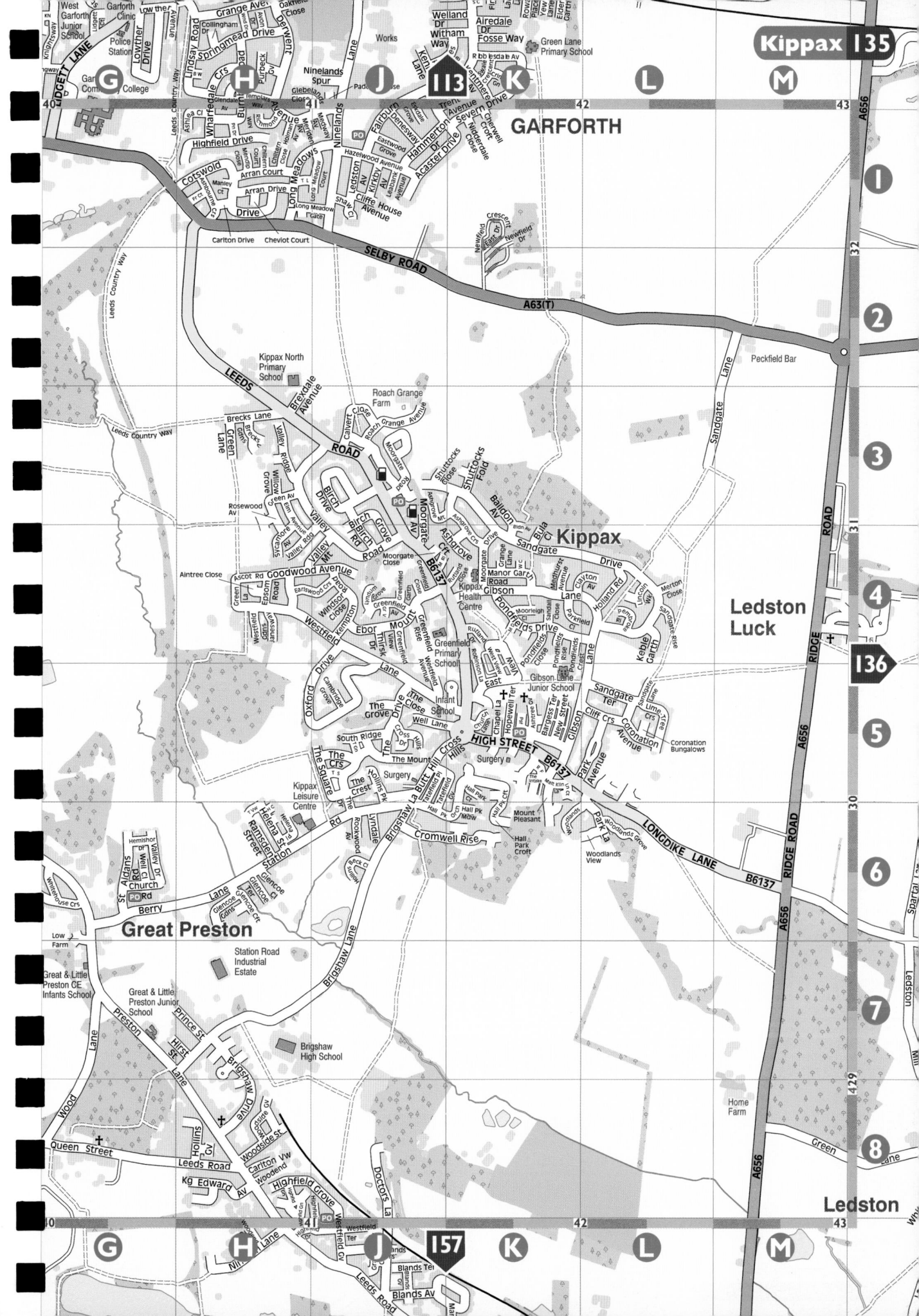

Garden Village

136

Micklefield Station

Pit Lane

Pit Lane

A
B
C
114
D
New Micklefield
E
F

443
44
45

Newth Barrac

1

Warren Farm

Woodlands

32

Great North Road

A1

Highfield Lane

2

A63(T)
SELBY ROAD
A63(T)

Hotel

Beacon Plantation

ROAD

3

31

Ledston Park

New Road

4

Church View

135

+

5

A656

New Road

Park Lane

Park Lane

RIDGE ROAD

30

6

Spartal Lane

Park House Farm

Lane

PH

Manor Garth

Newfield La

Ledsh

A656

Ledston

Mill

Claypit Lane

7

429

Back Newton Lane

8

Manor Pk

Dovecote Hall Dr

Lane

Newfield Farm

Leeds

North Yorkshire County

Ledston

White Horse Fold Street

Main

A
443
B
44
C
158
D
45
E
F

I grid square represents 500 metres

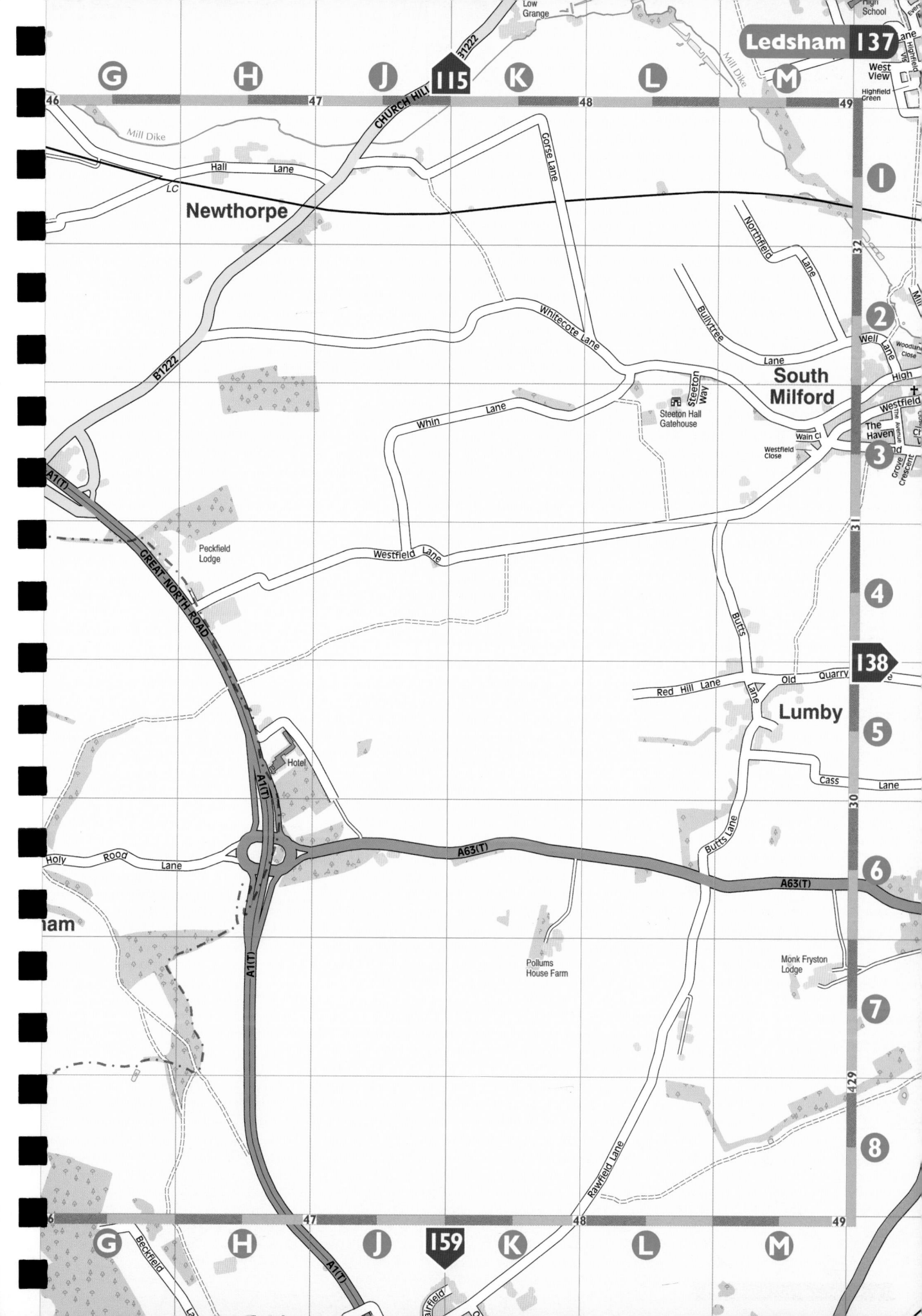

138

High School
Eversley Av
Old Glebe

Rose
CFs
East Vw
Rose Av
Rose Vlg

West View

A

B

C

116

D

E

F

Milford Road

Athelstan Primary School

Highfield Green

449

50

51

Bond Ings

Sherburn-in-Elmet Aerodrome

1

South Milford Station

2

32

Surgery

Bridge Garth

Mill Lane

Mill Lane

A162

Woodlands Close

Well Lane

PO

High Street

Common Lane

Cawdel Way

Burley Close

Common Lane

Milford Lodge

South Milford

Westfield Lane

School Lane

Primary School

Maple Close

Low Street

Turpin Lane

Beech Dr

The Avenue

Nook

Orchard Close

Church View

Stemcroft Road

Southlea Close

Wain Cl

3

The Haven

Sand

Grove

Legion Street

The Meadow

Grove Crescent

Lund Sike La

Lund Sike Lane

A162

31

Turpin Lane

4

137

Lumby Lane

Ingthorns Lane

Ingthorns Lane

Ingthorns Lane

Fryston Common Lane

Old

Lane

Lumby

5

30

Lumby Lane

Long Heads Lane

Ingthorpe Way

Cass

Lane

Ingthorpe Lane

Lumby Lane

Deer Park Ct

Fryston Common Lane

Priory Park Grove

6

A63(T)

A63(T)

MAIN STREET

A63(T)

A162

Hotel

PO

The Meadows

A63(T)

Church Lane

Old Vicarage Lane

Water Lane

Orchard Cl

Cemetery

Primary School

7

Monk Fryston Lodge

LC

Hillcrest

Monk Fryston

Chestnut Cn

Hillcrest

Mill Close

Lumby Hill

Dunce Mire Road

Austfield Lane

429

Betteras Hill Road

LC

Hillside Cl

Bedfords Fold

Hillam

Hillam Common Lane

Chapel Street

8

A162

Lilac Oval

Pine Tree Lane

Rose Lea Close

Hillam Hall Lane

HHW

Hillam Hall Close

Stocking Lane

449

50

51

A

B

C

160

D

Lane

E

F

Hillam Lane

Woodlands Lane

1 grid square represents 500 metres

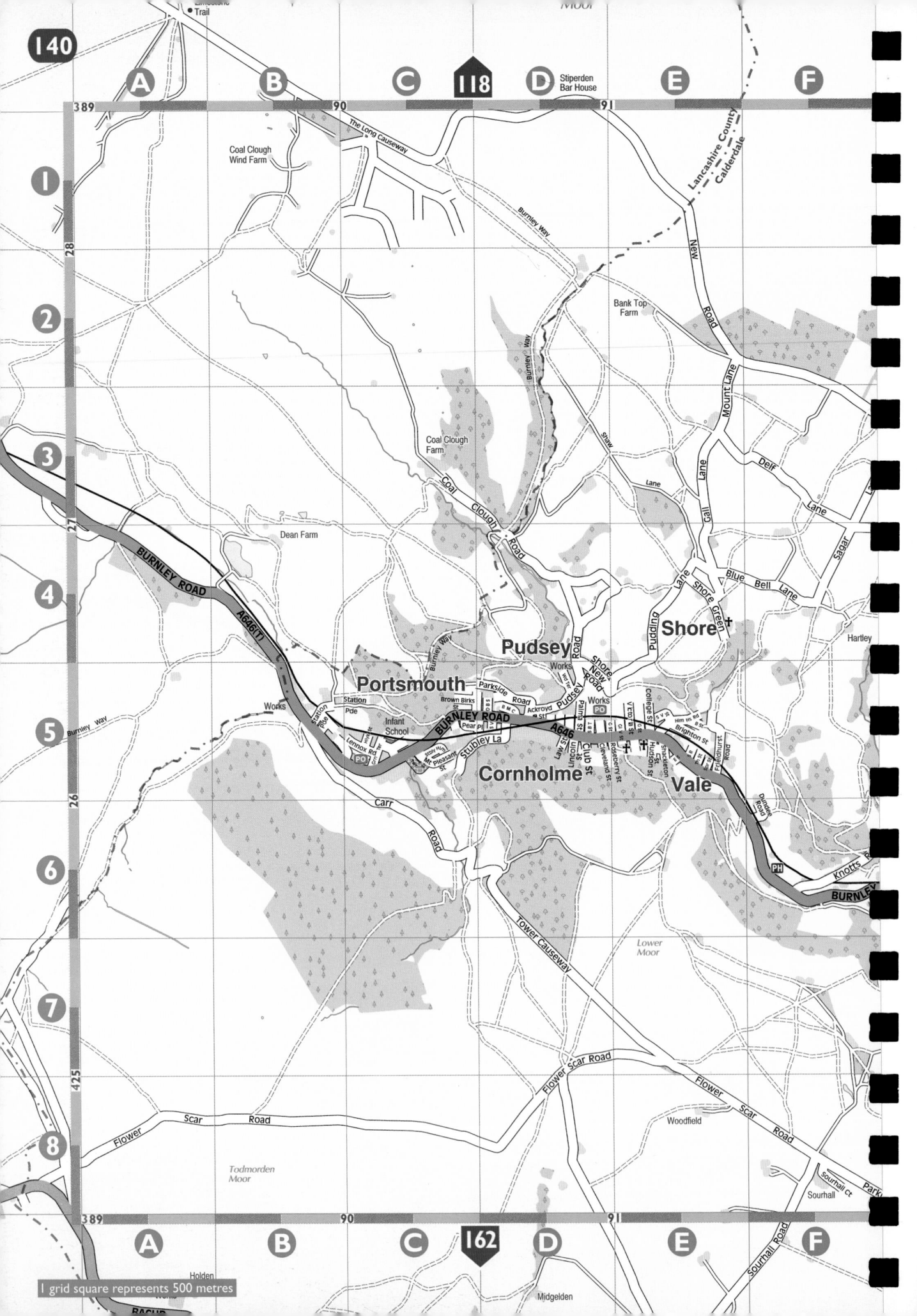

A   B   C   **118**   D   E   F

Stiperden
Bar House

389   90   91

Limestone
Trail

The Long causeway

Coal Clough
Wind Farm

Burnley Way

Lancashire County
Calderdale

New

Road

Bank Top
Farm

Mount Lane

Burnley Way

Coal Clough
Farm

Shaw

Lane

Lane

Call

Lane

Delf

Lane

Dean Farm

Coal

Clough

Road

Blue Bell Lane

Lane Shore Green

Pudding

Hartley

BURNLEY ROAD

A646(T)

Shore

Burnley Way

Burnley Way

Works

Road

Pudsey
New
Road

Shore

Pudsey

Parkside   Road

Works

Works
PO

Burnley Way

Brown Birks

Ackroyd   Pudsey

Portsmouth

Station
Pde

Station

Pde

BMC

Works

College St

Brighton St

Works

Infant
School

BURNLEY ROAD

Pear Pl

A646

Lennox Rd

Mt Pleasant

Stubley La

Palma St

Law St

Lincoln St

Club St

Roseberry St

Hudson St

Shackleton St

Cleveland St

V St

Friddlhurst

Road

Dudder

Vale

PO

Cornholme

Carr

Road

Knotts

PH

BURNLEY

Tower Causeway

Lower
Moor

Flower   Scar   Road

Flower Scar Road

Woodfield

Flower   Scar   Road

425

Flower   Scar   Road

Park

Todmorden
Moor

Sourhall ct

Sourhall Road

Sourhall

A   B   C   **162**   D   E   F

Holden

BACUP

Midgelden

1 grid square represents 500 metres

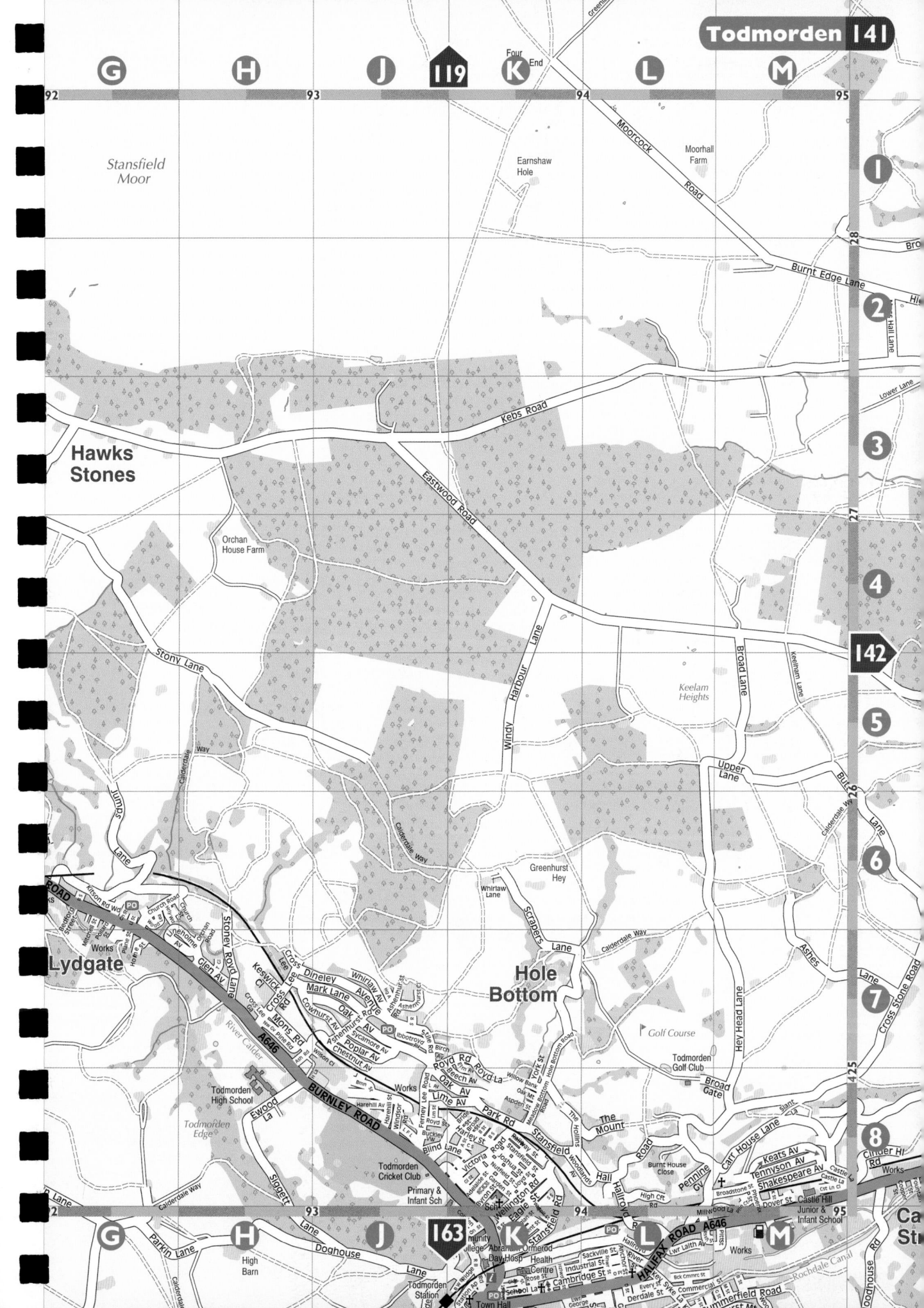

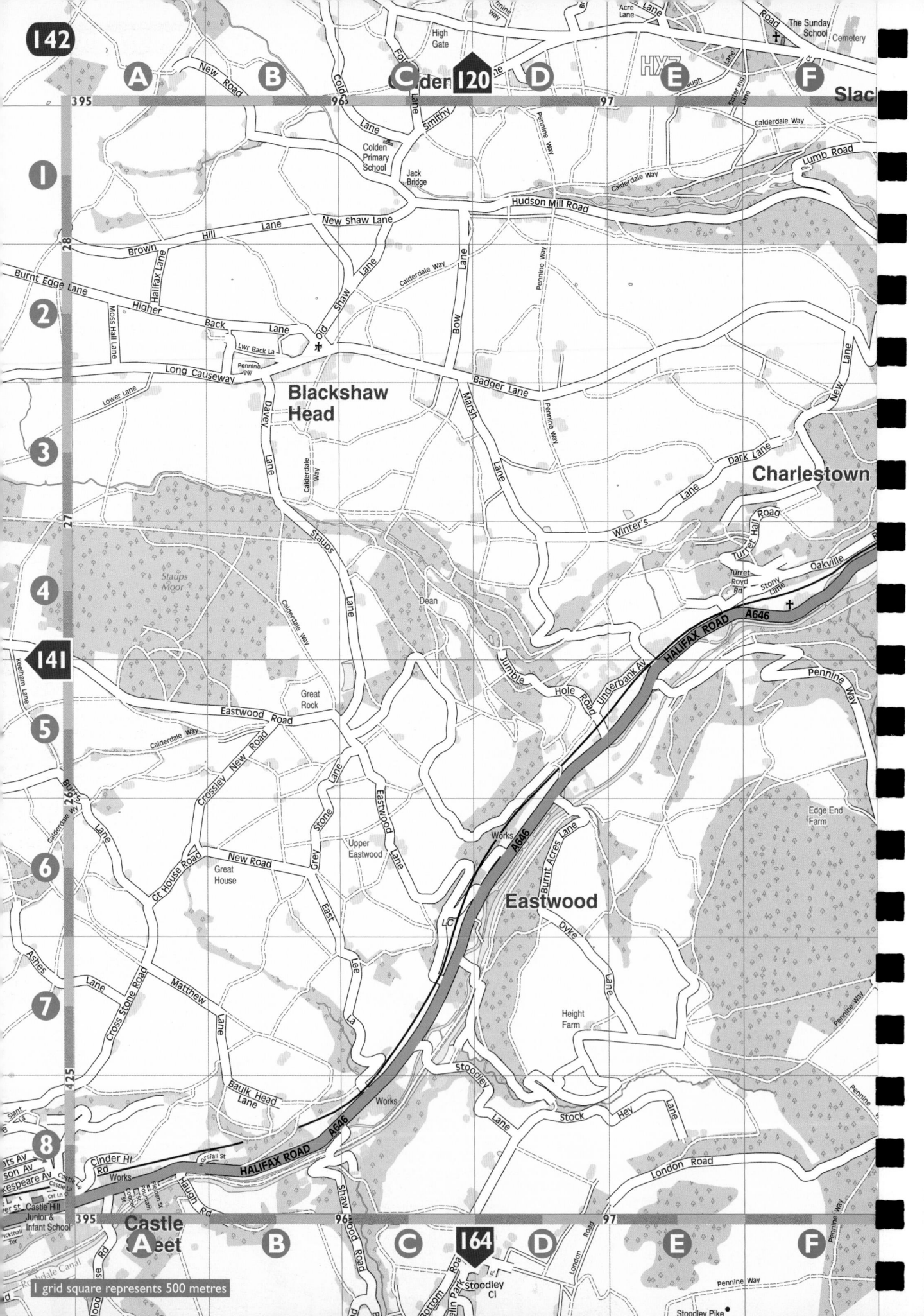

A   **B**   **C** Colden **120**   **D**   **E** HX7   **F** Slac

395   963   97

HX7

The Sunday School
Cemetery
Acre Lane
Calderdale Way
Lumb Road

I

28

New Road
Colden Lane
Smithy Lane
Colden Primary School
Jack Bridge
High Gate
Fore... Lane
Hudson Mill Road
Calderdale Way
Pennine Way
Sister In... Lane

New Shaw Lane

Hill Lane
Brown
Burnt Edge Lane
Halifax Lane
Higher Back Lane
Moss Hall Lane

2

Old Shaw Lane
Bow Lane
Calderdale Way
Pennine Way

Lwr Back La
Long Causeway
Pennine Wy
Lower Lane

Blackshaw Head

Badger Lane
Marsh Lane
Pennine Way

3

27

Davey Lane
Calderdale Way
Staups Lane
Calderdale Way

Charlestown

Dark Lane
Winter's Lane
Turret Hall Road
Oakville
Stony Lane
Turret Royd Rd

4

Staups Moor
Dean
Lane

HALIFAX ROAD A646

I41

Keeham Lane
Eastwood Road
Great Rock
Calderdale Way
Crossley New Road
Stone Lane
Eastwood Lane
Jumble Hole Road
Underbank Av
Pennine Way

5

Calderdale Way
Calderdale Wy
Lane
26...

6

Gt House Road
New Road
Great House
Upper Eastwood
Grey
Stone
East
Lee
Works
A646
Burnt Acres Lane
Edge End Farm

Eastwood

Dyke Lane

Ashes Lane
Cross Stone Road
Matthew Lane

7

425

Bauk Head Lane
La
Lee
LC
Height Farm
Pennine Way

8

Cinder Hl Rd
Horsfall St
Works
Castle...
Castle Hill
Junior & Infant School
HALIFAX ROAD A646
Haugh Rd
Shaw Wood Road
Works
Stoodley Lane
Stock Lane
Hey Lane
London Road
Pennine Way

395   963   97

Castle... eet

A   **B**   **C**   **164**   **D**   **E**   **F**

Stoodley Cl
London Road
Pennine Way
Stoodley Pike

1 grid square represents 500 metres

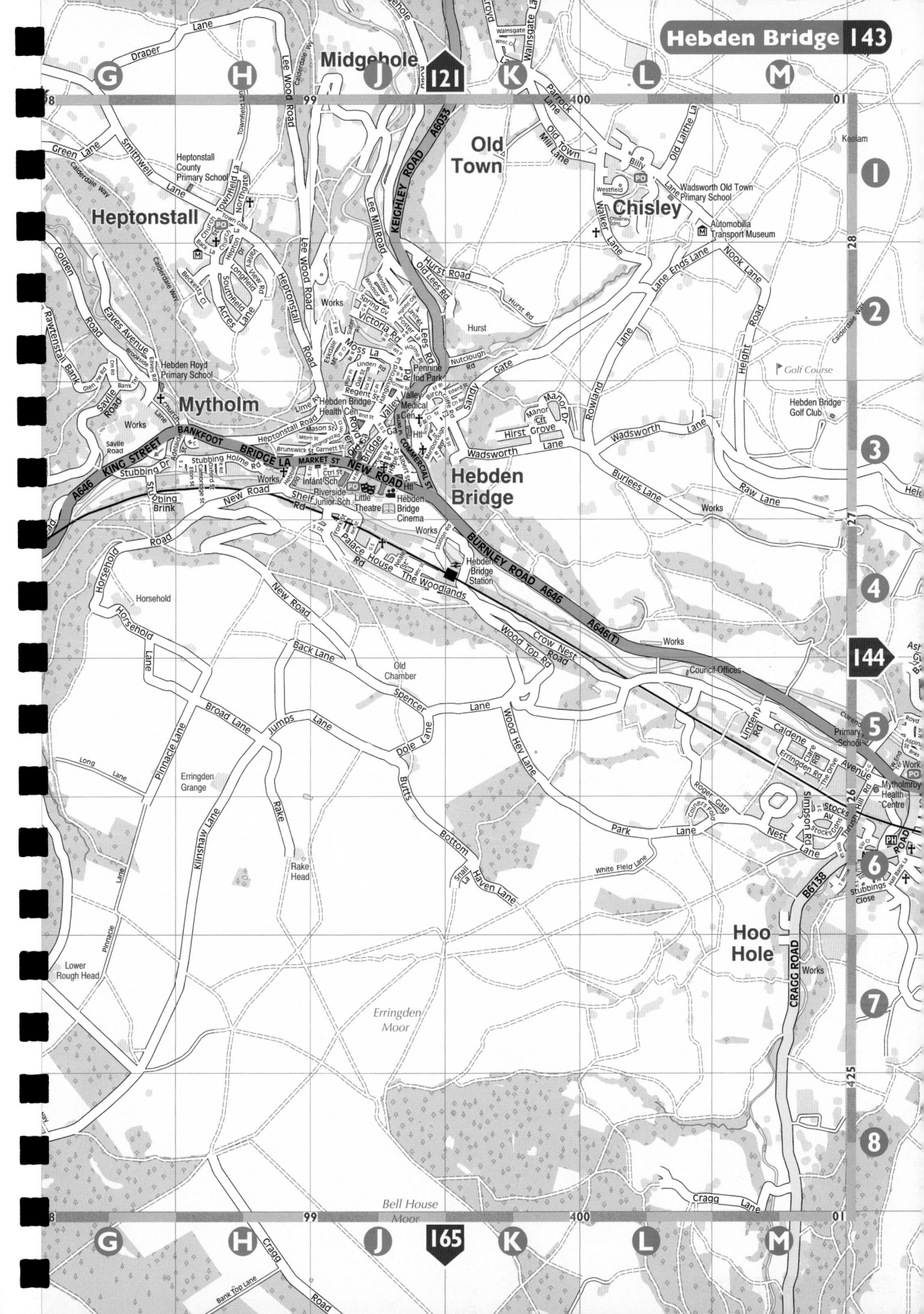

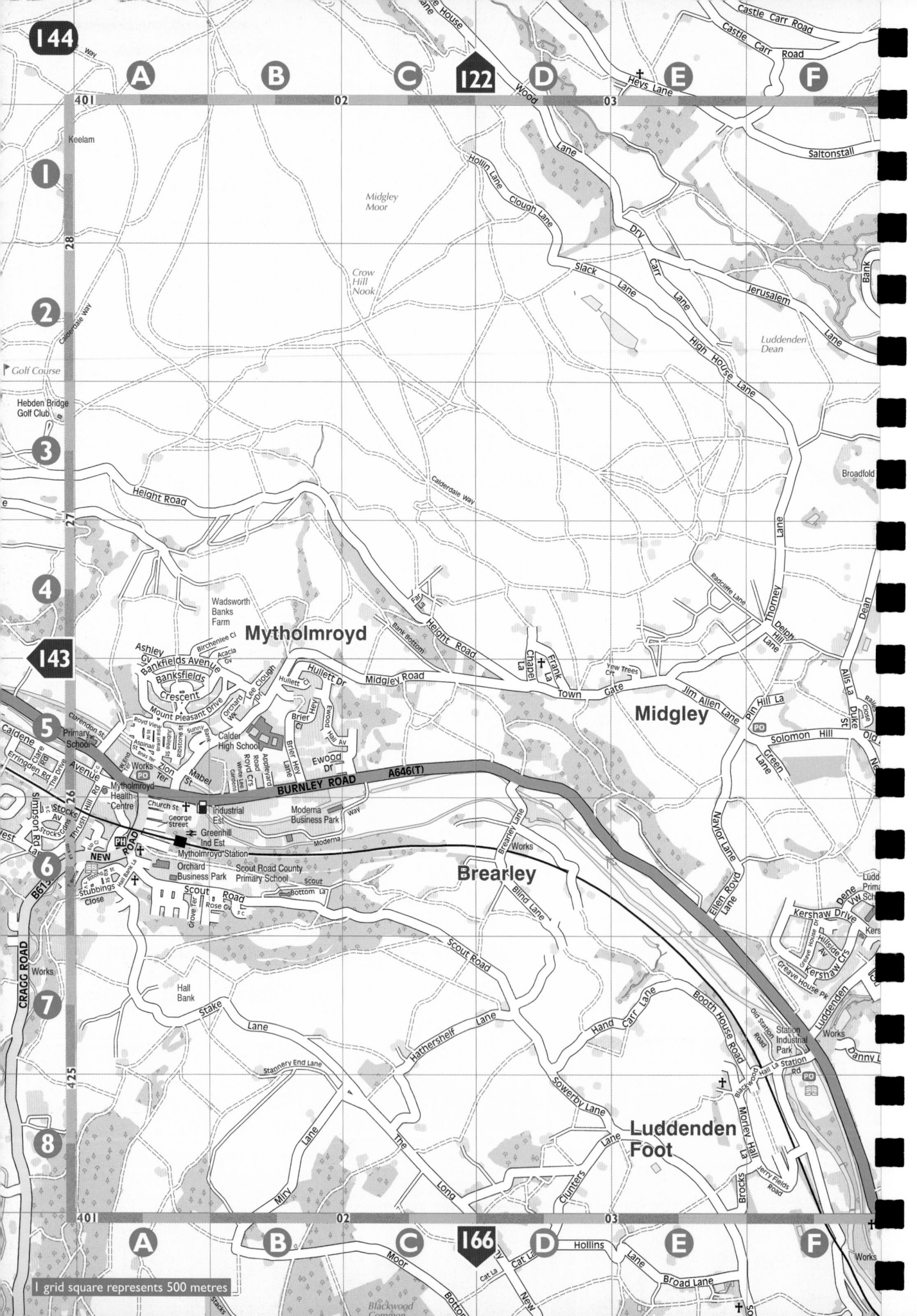

A   B   C   122   D   E   F

401   02   03

Way

Keelam

I   **2**   **3**

Midgley
Moor

Crow
Hill
Nook

Hollin Lane

Clough Lane

Dry

slack

Carr

Lane

Lane

High House Lane

Jerusalem

Lane

Bank

Luddenden
Dean

Broadfold

Golf Course

Hebden Bridge
Golf Club

Cinderdale Way

28

27

Height Road

Calderdale Way

Radcliffe Lane

Thorney Lane

Delph Hill Lane

Alis La

Duke St

Dean

4

143

Wadsworth
Banks
Farm

Mytholmroyd

Bank Bottom

Fall

Height Road

Chapel La

Frank La

Town Gate

Jim Allen Lane

Yew Trees Cft

Pin Hill La

Midgley

Green Lane

Naylor Lane

Old

Solomon Hill

PO

Ashley Gv
Bankfields Avenue
Bankfields
Crescent

Birchenlee Cl

Acacia Gv

Mount Pleasant Drive

Orchard Way

Lee Clough
Dr

Hullett Cl

Hullett Dr

Midgley Road

Clarendon St

Royd View

Primary
School

Aspinall St

Sunny Bank

Zion Ter

Mabel St

Calder High School

Brier Hey

Brier Hey
Cl

Ewood Dr

Royd Cts

White Lee

Appleyard

Brier Lane

Ewood Dr

Hall Av

Gardens

5

26

Caldene Av

Clare Rd

Errington Rd

The Drive

Avenue

Stocks Av

Thrush Hill Rd

Works

PO

Mytholmroyd
Health
Centre

BURNLEY ROAD   **A646(T)**

Church St

Industrial
Est

George
Street

Greenhill
Ind Est

Moderna
Business Park

Way

Moderna

Brearley Lane

Works

Simpson Rd

Stocks La

Big Cl

PH

NEW

ROAD

Hill Bank La

Mytholmroyd Station

Orchard
Business Park

Scout Road County
Primary School

Scout
Bottom La

Brearley

Blind Lane

Ellen Royd Lane

Ludd
Primary
VW Sch

Kershaw Drive

Kers

Hillside Av

Creave House Pk

Luddenden

6

B613

Stubbings
Close

Grove Ter

Scout   Road

Rose Gv

S C

CRAGG ROAD

Works

425

Hall
Bank

Stake

Lane

Hathershelf

Lane

Hand Carr Lane

Booth House Road

Old Station Road

Hall La

Station
Industrial
Park

Station

Works

Danny La

PO

7

Stannery End Lane

The Long

Lane

Miry

Lane

Sowerby Lane

Clunters Lane

Lane

Morley Hall La

Blackwood

Brooks

Berry Fields Road

**Luddenden
Foot**

PO

Rd

8

401   02   03

A   B   C   166   D   Hollins   E   F

Moor

Cat La

Cat La

New

Lane

Broad Lane

So

Works

Blackwood
Common

Bottom

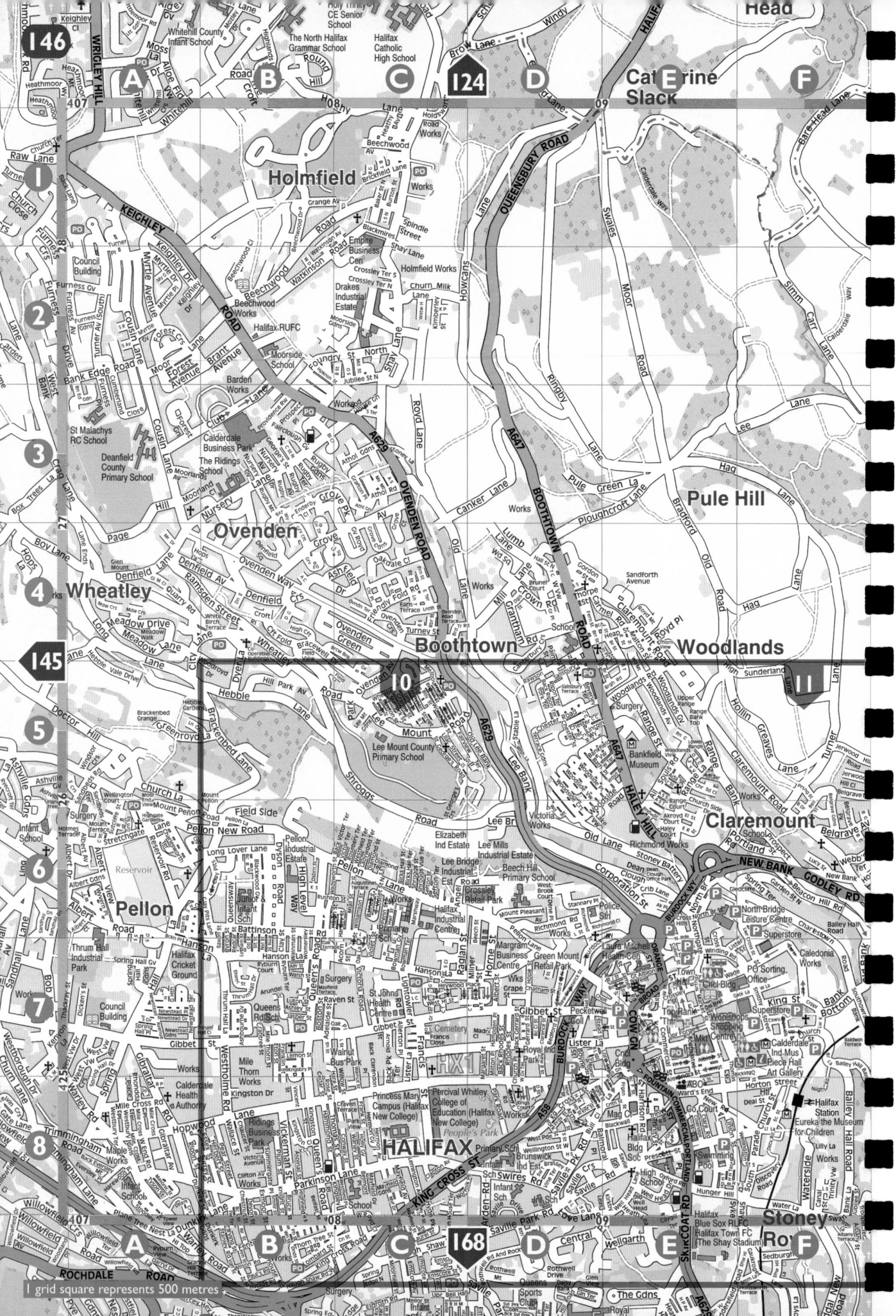

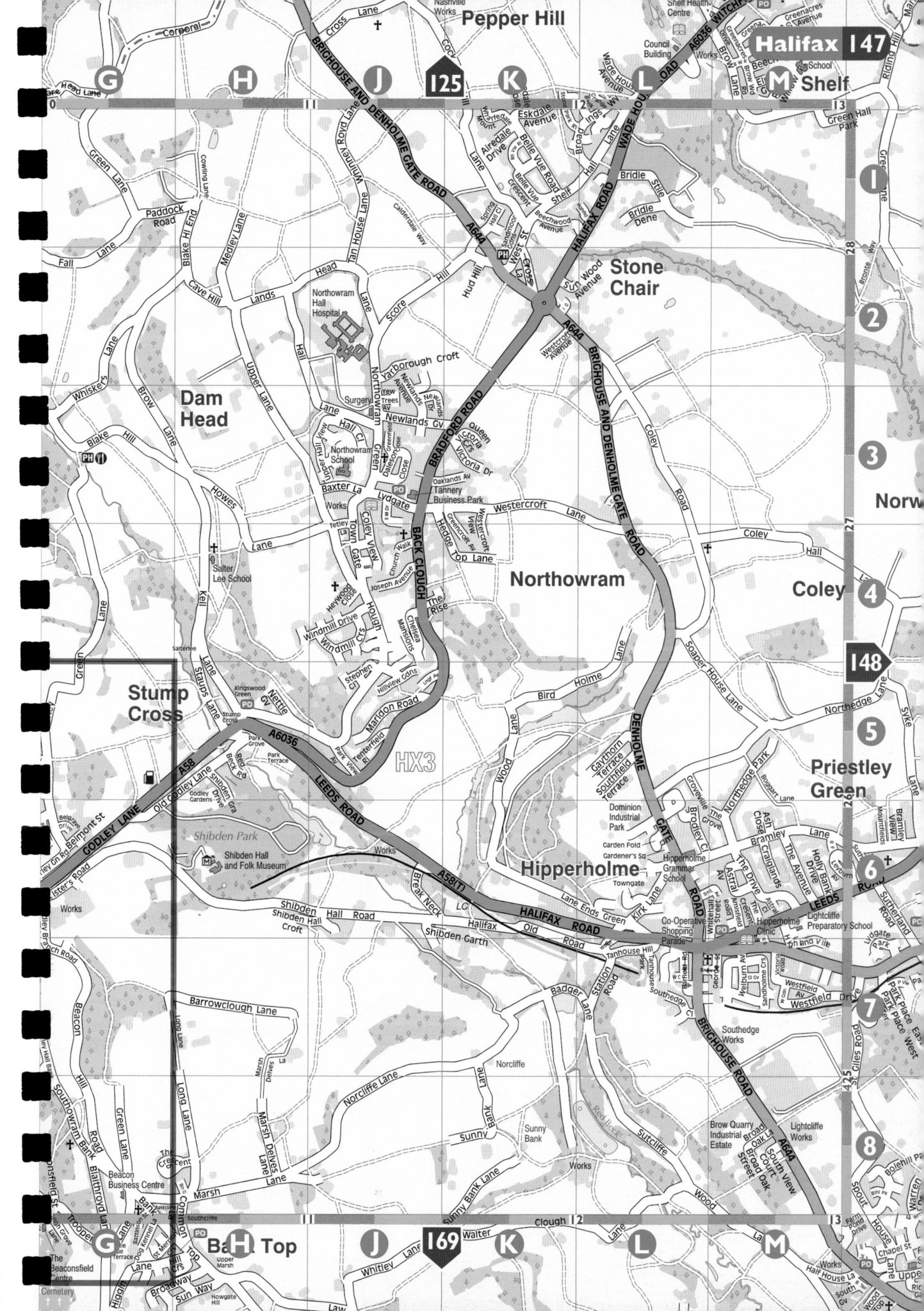

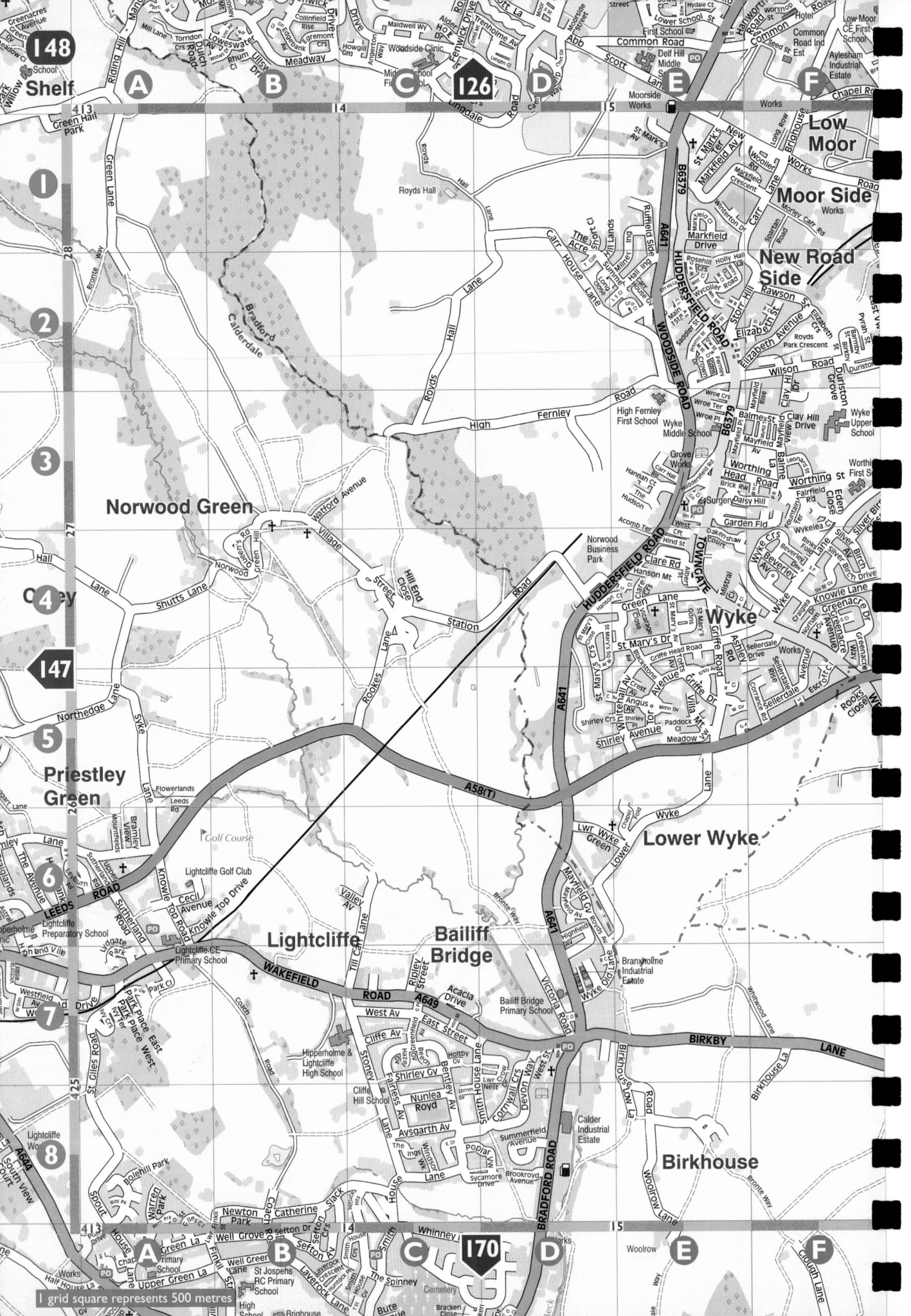

Shelf

126

Low Moor

Moor Side

New Road Side

Royds Hall

Norwood Green

147

Priestley Green

Wyke

Lower Wyke

Lightcliffe

Bailiff Bridge

Birkhouse

170

1 grid square represents 500 metres

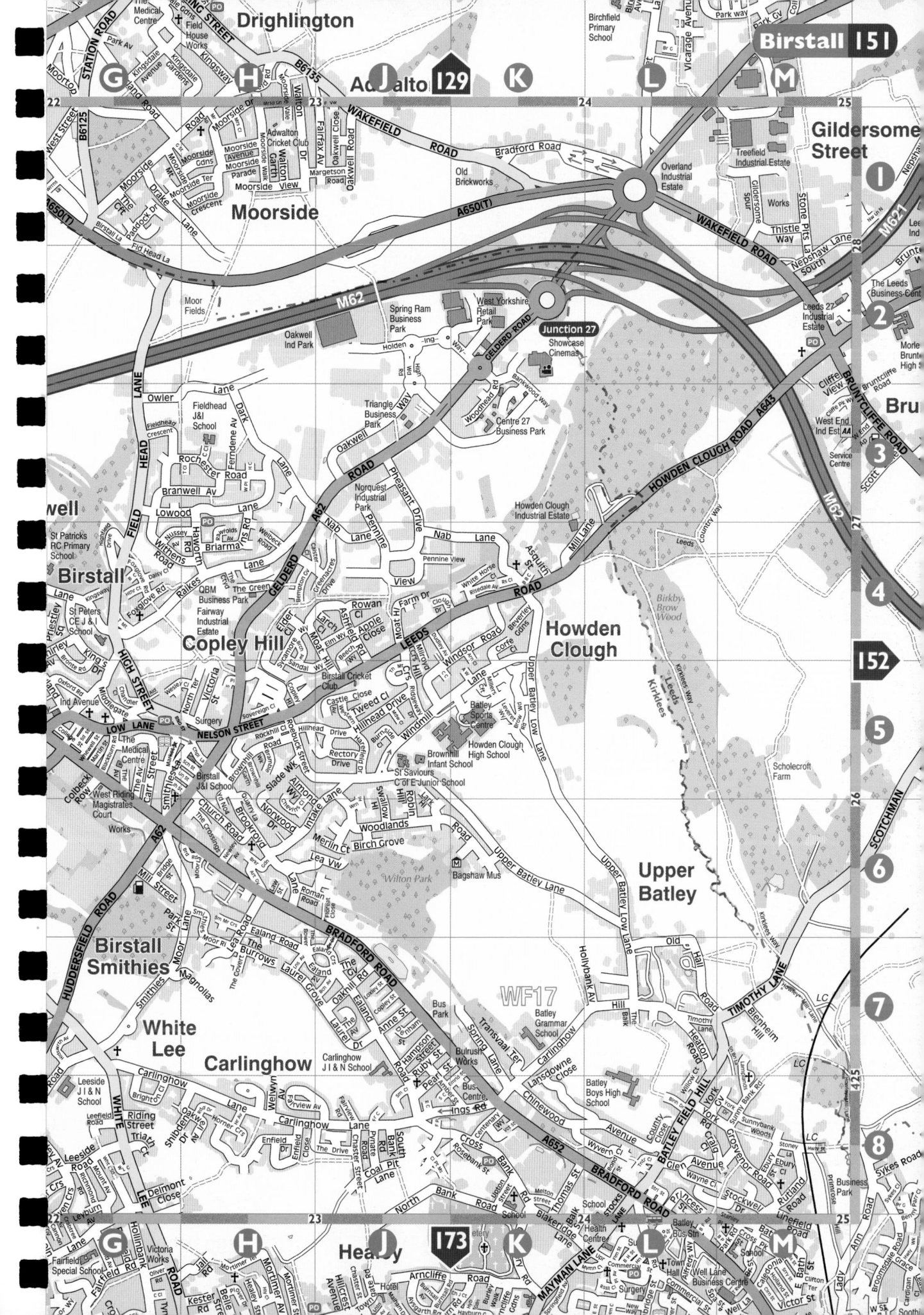

152

130

A **B** **C** **D** **E** **F**

Gildersome
Street

1

Daisy
Hill

Morley Station

2

New Brighton

Bruntcliffe

LS27

Morley

3

4

Birks

151

Junction 28

5

M62

6

Works

Woodkirk
High School

Brick
Works

7

Howley Hall
Golf Club

Golf Course

Leeds Country Way

Woodkirk

8

Leeds Country Way

West
Ardsley

Lower
Soothill

A **B** **C** **174** **D** **E** Eggarington **F**
Hill

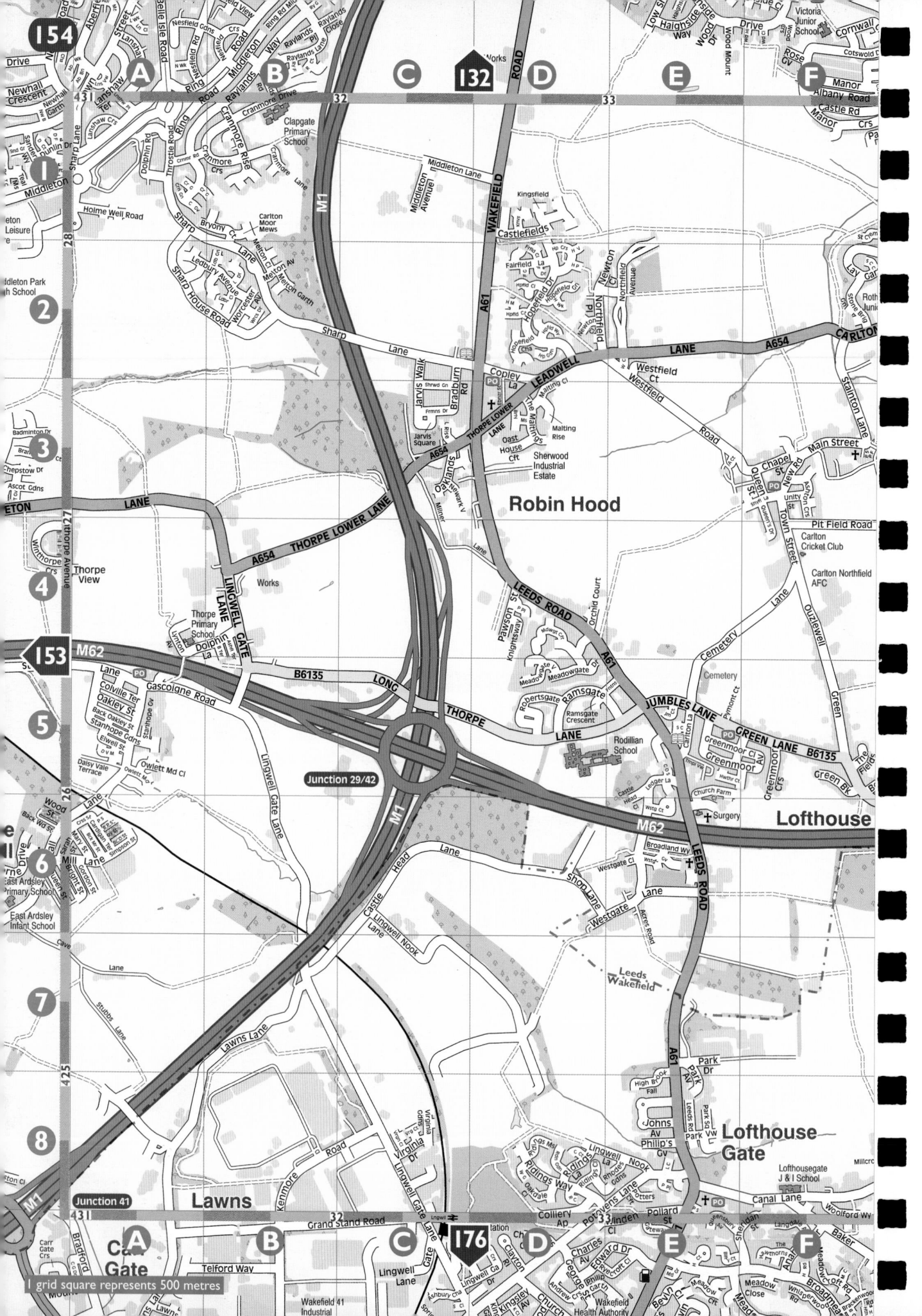

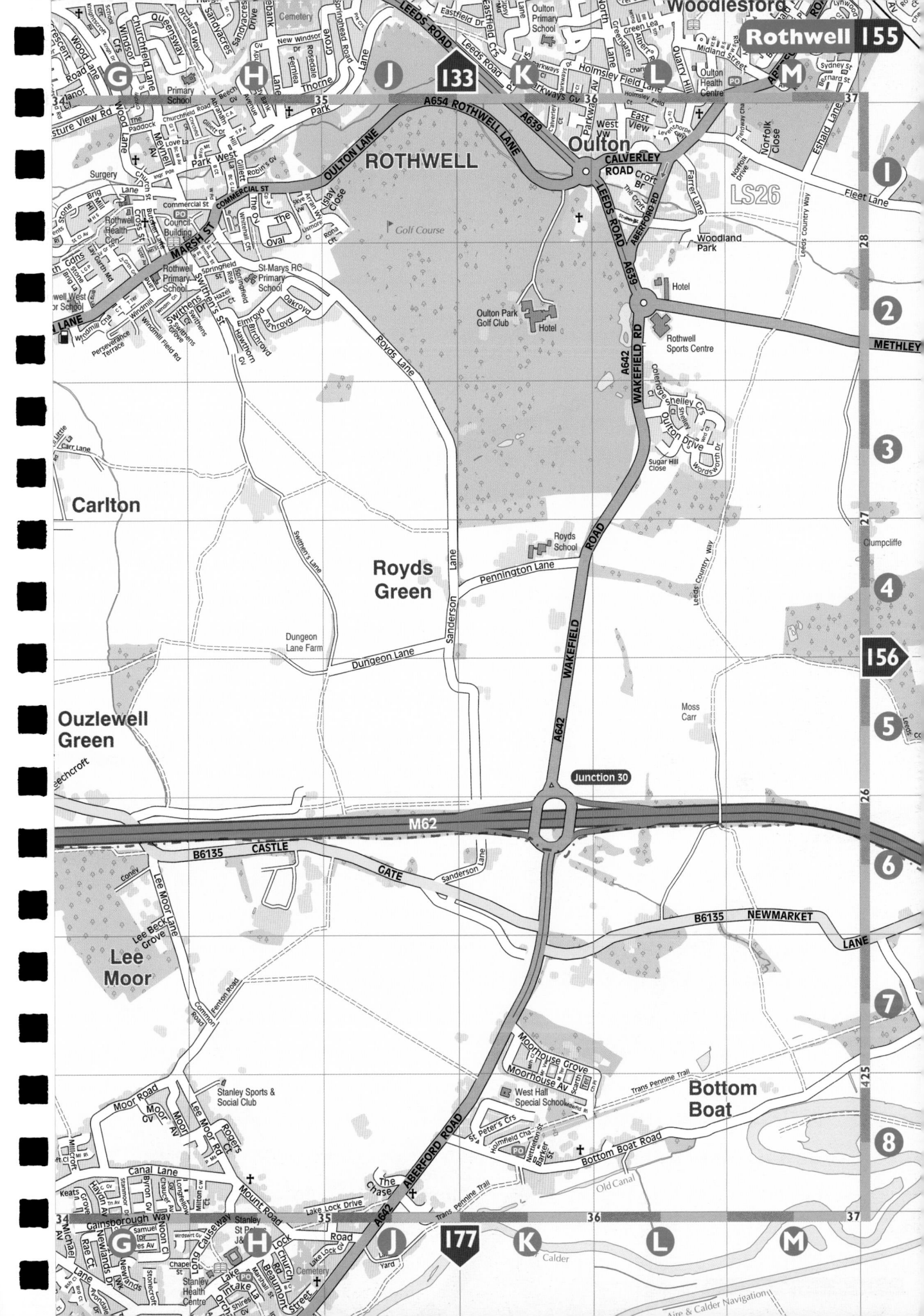

Woodlesford

Oulton Primary School

ROTHWELL

Oulton

CALVERLEY ROAD

LS26

Golf Course

Oulton Park Golf Club

Hotel

Woodland Park

Hotel

Rothwell Sports Centre

Carlton

Royds Green

Royds School

Pennington Lane

Clumpcliffe

156

Dungeon Lane Farm

Dungeon Lane

Moss Carr

Ouzlewell Green

Junction 30

M62

B6135 CASTLE GATE

Sanderson Lane

B6135 NEWMARKET LANE

Lee Moor

Stanley Sports & Social Club

Moorhouse Grove

Moorhouse Av

West Hall Special School

Trans Pennine Trail

Bottom Boat

Bottom Boat Road

Old Canal

133

177

Aire & Calder Navigation

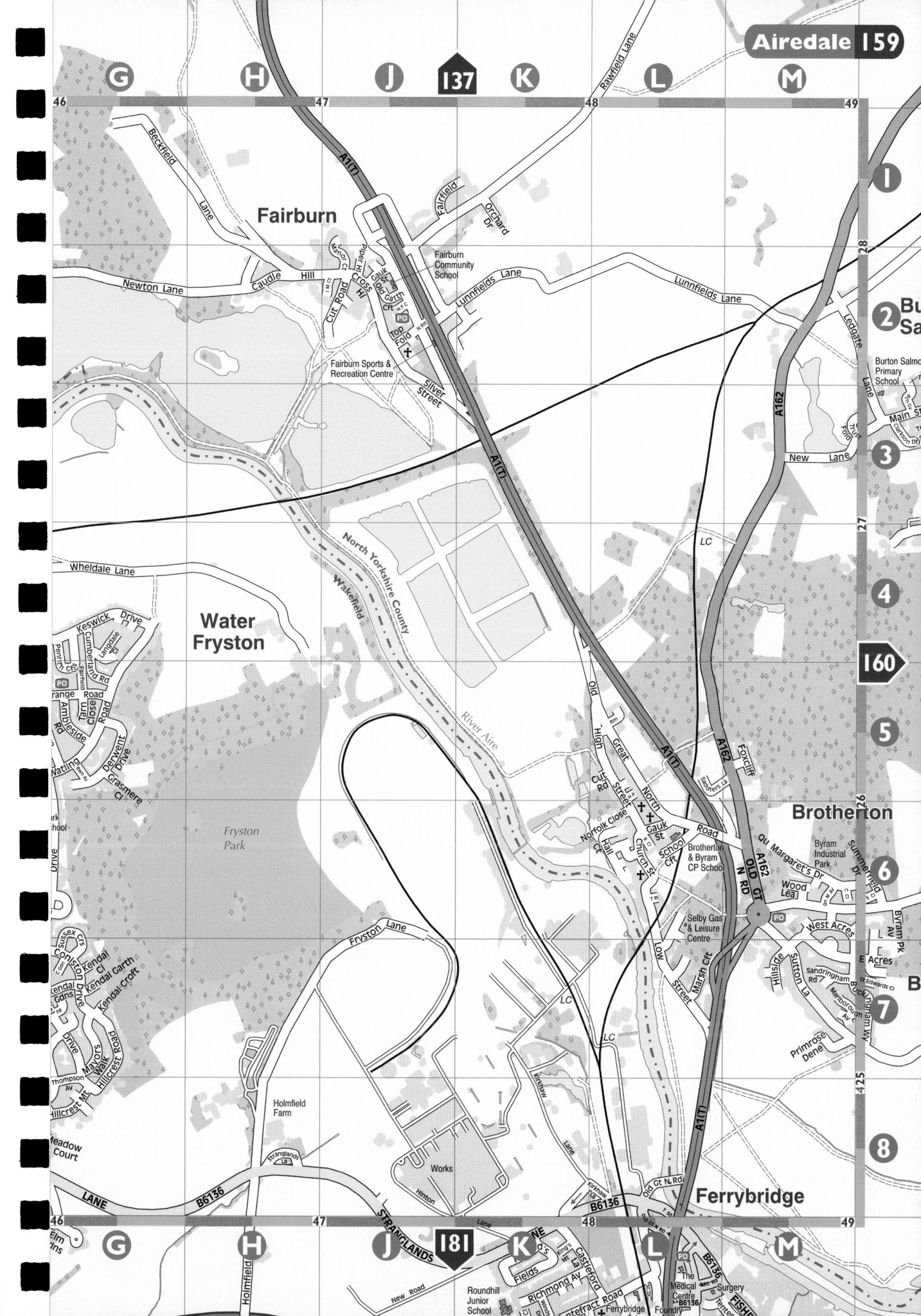

138

A B C D E F

449 50 51

I

Hillam Lane

Woodlands Lane

Fairfield Lane

Pine Tree Lane
Rose Lea Close
Chapel Street
Hillam Hall Lane
Hillam Hall Close
Stocking Lane

28

2

Burton
Salmon

Burton Salmon Primary School
The Paddock

Burton Common Lane

Burton Common Farm

Main St
Top Stone
Clarkson Dri Cl
ew

27

3

Poole Lane

Tledgate Lane

4

159

5

Byram
Hall

Byram Farm

Brotherton

26

Byram Industrial

Summerfield Dri

Byram Pk Av

6

Byram Park Road

Byram Park Road

Sutton Lane

Birkin Lane

West Acres

E Acres

Sutton Lane

Tipsity Lane

Byram

Sutton

Smeathalls Farm

Sutton La
Sandringham Rd
St Edwards Cl
Buckingham Wy
Marlborough Av

7

425

Primrose Dene

8

Marsh La

River Aire

A B C D E F

449 50 51

182

West Ings Crescent
West Ings Lane
West Ings Way
West Ings Mews
Croftlands
Aire Street
St

River Aire

1 grid square represents 500 metres

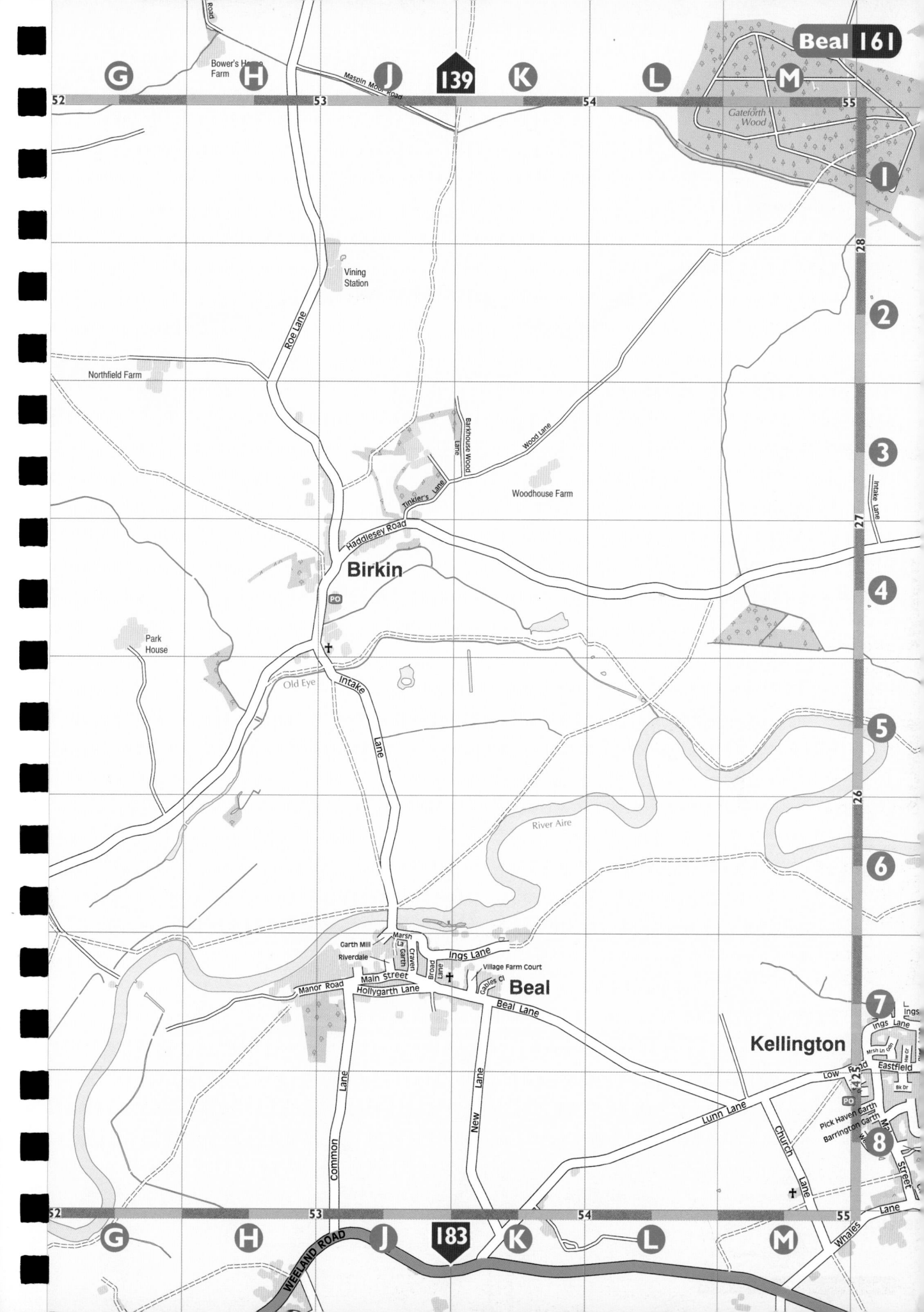

G   H   J **139** K   L   M   **I**

52   53   54   55

Bower's House
Farm

Maspin Moor Road

Gateforth
Wood

2

Vining
Station

Roe Lane

Northfield Farm

Barkhouse Wood
Lane

Wood Lane

Intake Lane

27

3

Tinkler's Lane

Woodhouse Farm

Haddlesey Road

4

Birkin

PO

Park
House

Old Eye

Intake Lane

5

River Aire

26

6

Garth MIll
Riverdale

Marsh
La Garth

Ings Lane

Broad Lane

Craven Lane

Village Farm Court

Main Street

Gables Cl

Beal

Manor Road

Hollygarth Lane

7

Beal Lane

Kellington

Ings Lane

Marsh Ln Cth

Eastfield

Common Lane

New Lane

Low Road

A425

Bk Dr

PO

Pick Haven Garth

Barrington Garth

8

Lunn Lane

Church Lane

Main Street

Whales Lane

52   53   54   55

G   H   J **183** K   L   M

WEELAND ROAD

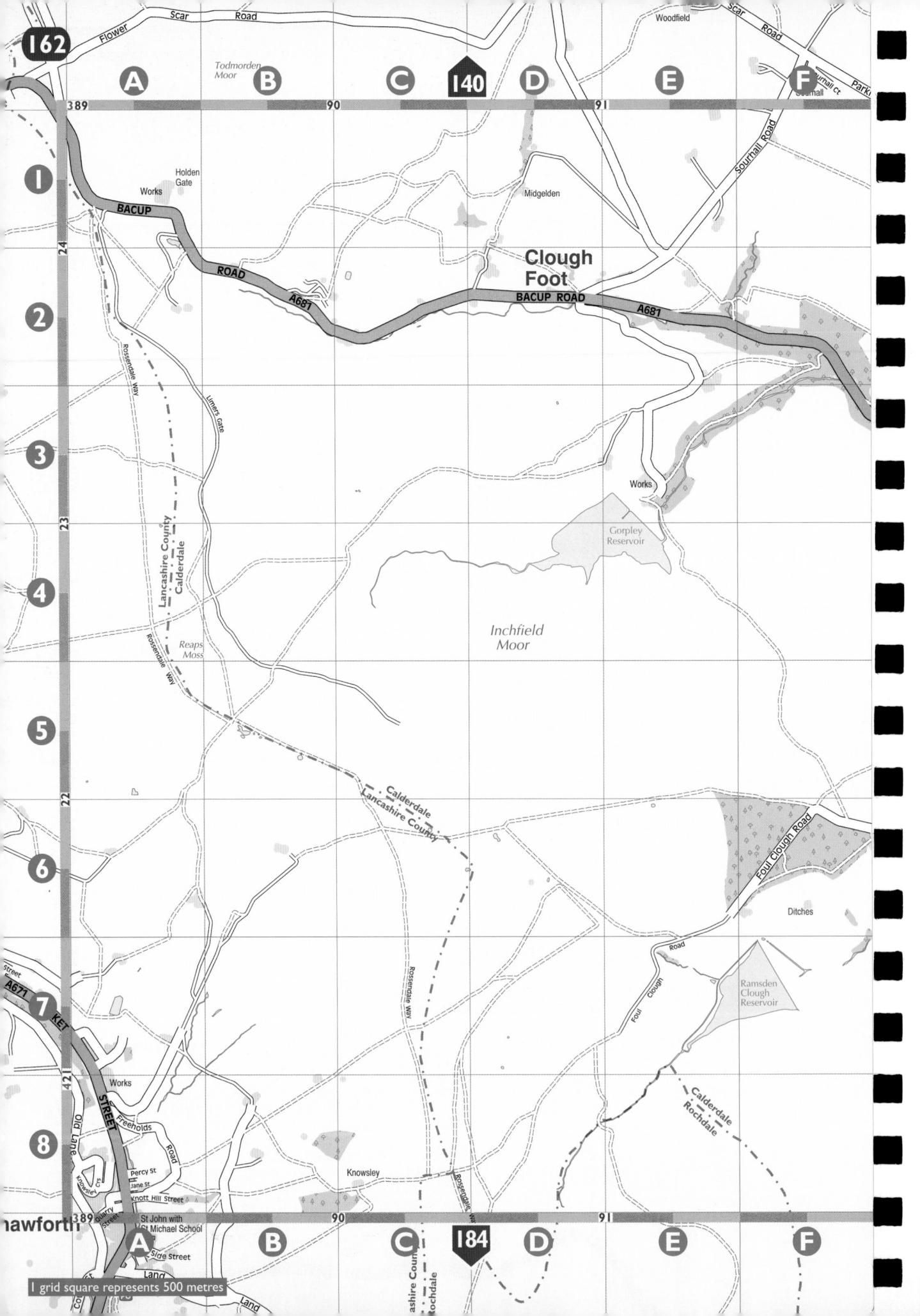

140

184

A B C D E F

Scar Road

Woodfield

Flower

Todmorden Moor

Holden Gate

Works

BACUP

ROAD

A681

Midgelden

Clough Foot

BACUP ROAD A681

Sournall Road

Sournail Ct

Sournall

Parkin

389

90

91

24

1

Rossendale Way

Liners Gate

Works

Gorpley Reservoir

2

3

23

Lancashire County
Calderdale

Inchfield Moor

4

Rossendale Way

Reaps Moss

5

22

Calderdale
Lancashire County

Foul Clough Road

6

Ditches

Road

Foul Clough

Ramsden Clough Reservoir

Street

A671

7

KET

421

Works

Freeholds

Rossendale Way

Calderdale
Rochdale

STREET

DIO Lane

Knowsle

8

Percy St

Jane St

Knott Hill Street

Knowsley

hawforth

389

St John with
St Michael School

Side Street

Co Land

Land

Quarry Street

90

91

A B C D E F

184

1 grid square represents 500 metres

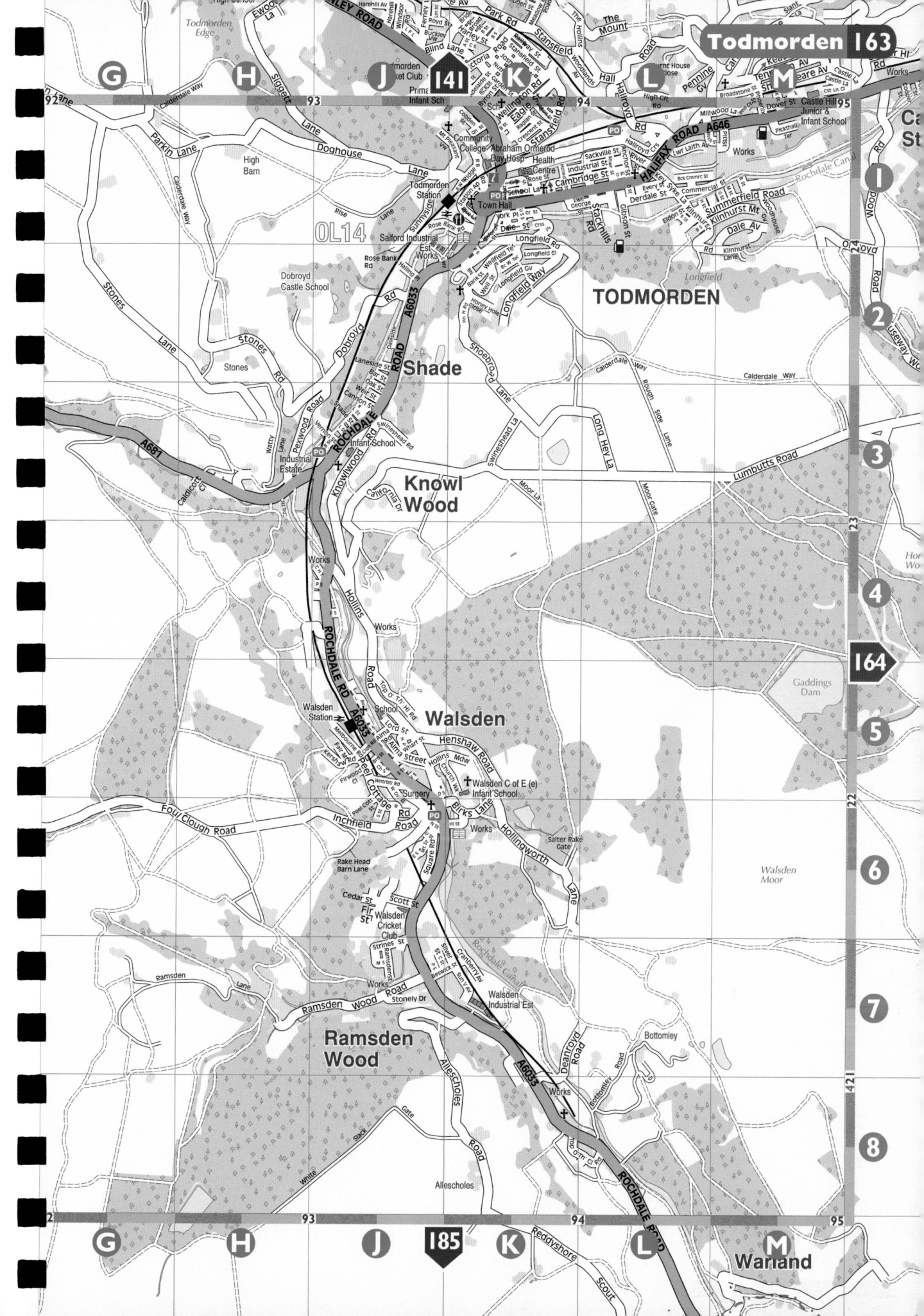

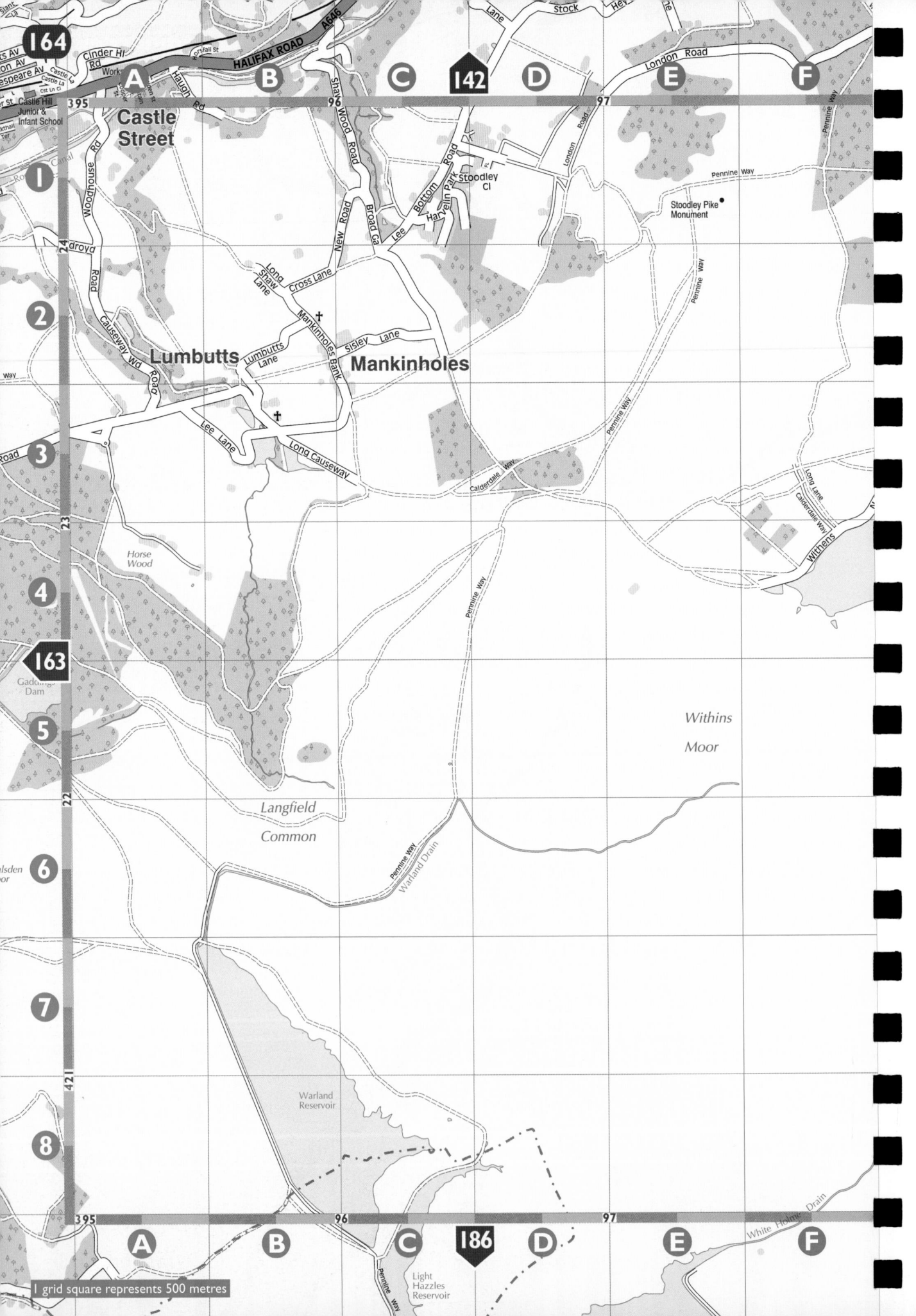

A646 Halifax Road

HALIFAX ROAD

A · · · · B · · · · C · · · · 142 · · · · D · · · · E · · · · F

London Road

395 · · · 96 · · · 97

Castle
Street

Pennine Way

Shaw Wood Road

London Road

Stoodley
Cl

Harvelin Park

Bottom

Lee

Broad Ga

New Road

1

Canal

Woodhouse Rd

droyd Road

Stoodley Pike
Monument

Pennine Way

Pennine Way

2

Causeway Wd

Lumbutts

Lumbutts Bank

Lumbutts Lane

Mankinholes

Mankinholes Bank

Sisley Lane

Cross Lane

Long Shaw Lane

†

Way

23

†

3

Lee Lane

Long Causeway

Calderdale Way

Long Lane

Calderdale Way

Withens

Road

Horse
Wood

Pennine Way

4

163

Gaddings
Dam

Withins

Moor

5

22

Langfield

Common

Pennine Way

Warland Drain

Isden oor

6

421

7

Warland Reservoir

8

White Holme Drain

395 · · · 96 · · · 97

A · · · · B · · · · C · · · · 186 · · · · D · · · · E · · · · F

Pennine Way

Light
Hazzles
Reservoir

1 grid square represents 500 metres

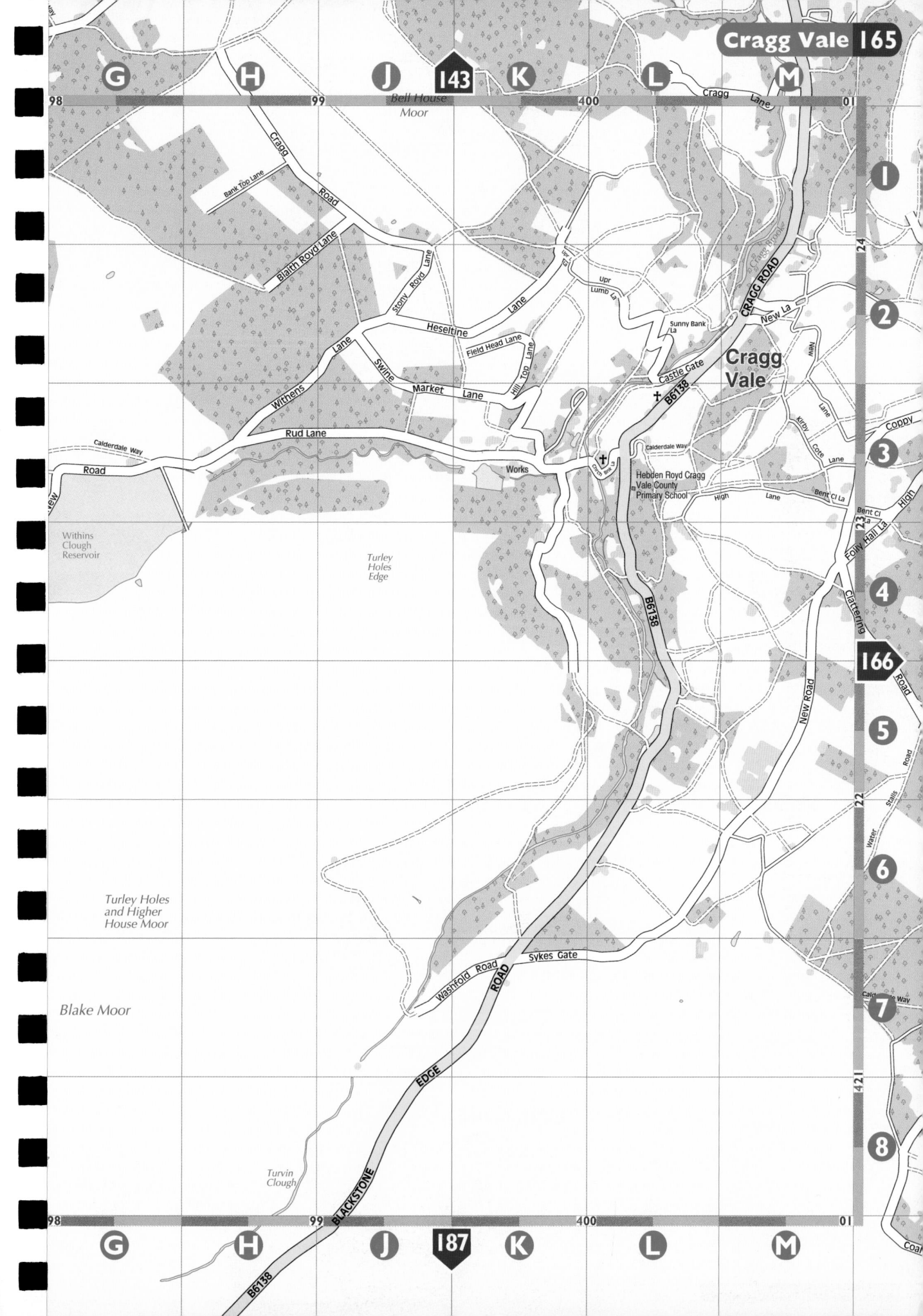

G H J **143** K L M

98 99 400 01

Bell House
Moor

Cragg Lane

I

24

2

Cragg
Road

Bank Top Lane

Blaith Royd Lane

Stony Royd Lane

Heseltine Lane

Field Head Lane

Hill Top Lane

Swine

Market Lane

Lane

Withens

Rud Lane

Upr Lumb La

Sunny Bank La

Castle Gate

CRAGG ROAD

New La

New Lane

Cragg
Vale

Kirby Cote Lane

Coppy

3

Calderdale Way

Road

New

Withins
Clough
Reservoir

Works

Church Bnk La

Calderdale Way

Hebden Royd Cragg
Vale County
Primary School

High Lane

Bent Cl La

Bent Cl La

High

23

Folly Hall La

Turley
Holes
Edge

B6138

Clattering

4

166

Road

5

22

Stalls Road

Water

6

Turley Holes
and Higher
House Moor

New Road

7

Calderdale Way

Blake Moor

Washfold Road

ROAD

Sykes Gate

421

EDGE

8

Turvin
Clough

BLACKSTONE

98 99 400 01

G H J **187** K L M

B6138

Coal

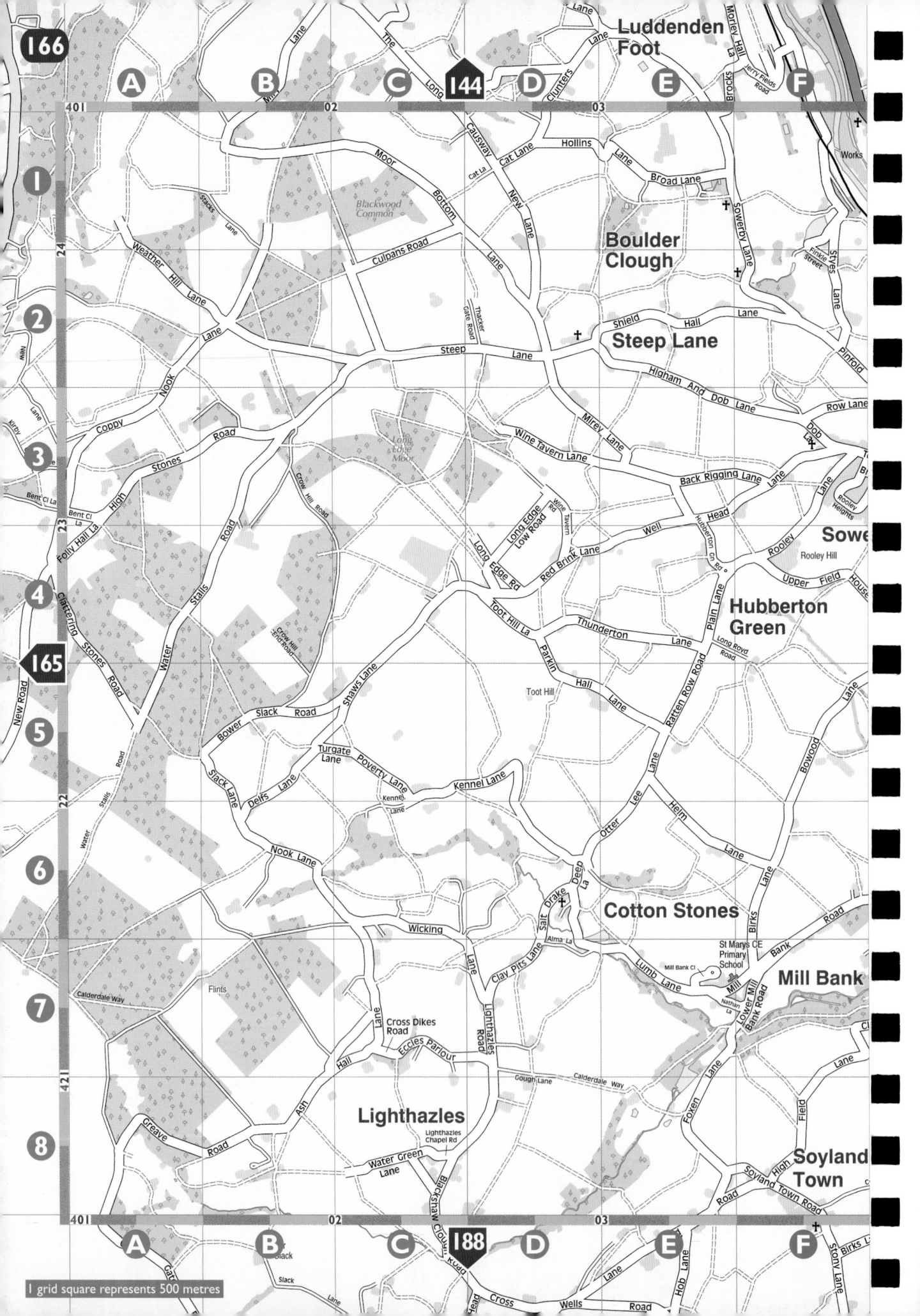

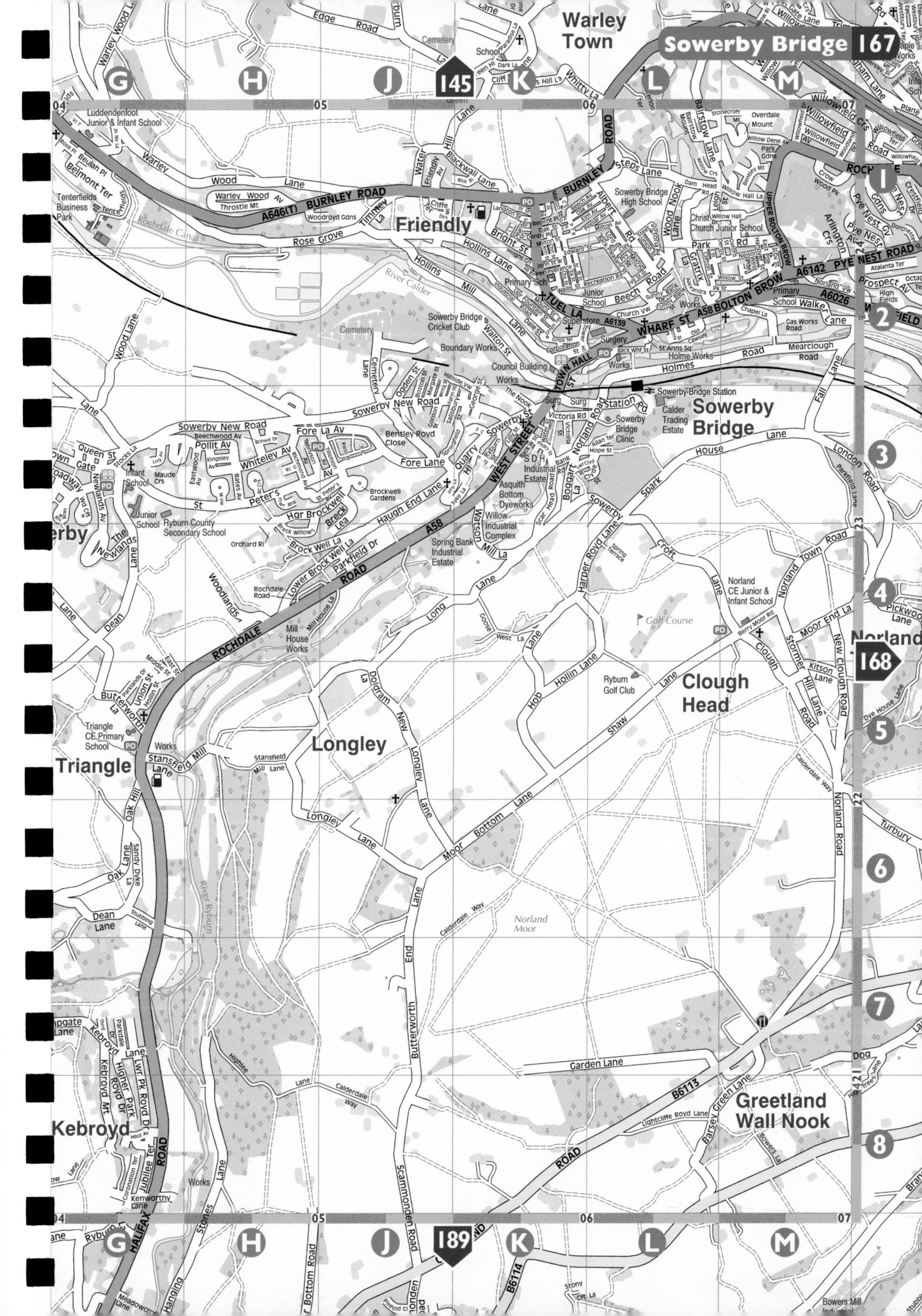

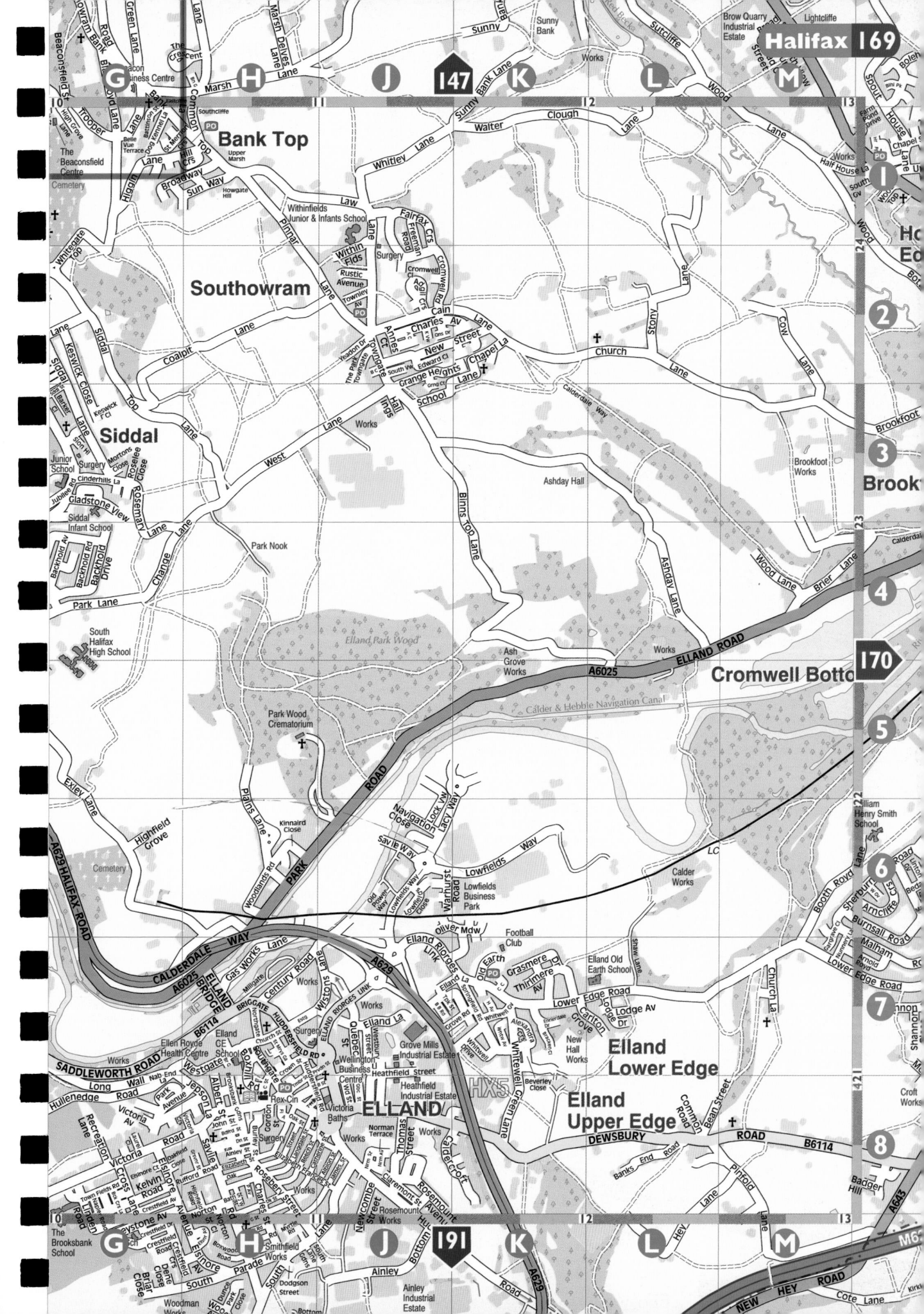

G
H
J
147
K
L
M

Sunny Bank
Sunny Bank
Works
Brow Quarry Industrial Estate
Lightcliffe
Red Beck
Sutcliffe

10

Beaconsfield St
High Grove
Cowram Road
Green Lane
Marsh Delves Lane
Marsh Lane
Marsh
Southcliffe
PO
Bank Top
Upper Marsh
Sunny
Clough
Walter
Lane
Wood
Lane
Spout
Boley Hill

I
PO
Half House La
South
Gv
Chapel La
Farm Pond Drive
Ho Ed

Beacon Business Centre
The Crescent
Common
St Henry
Whitley Lane
Broadway
Sun Way
Howgate Hill
Law
Lane
Withinfields Junior & Infants School

2
24
Cow Lane
Stony Lane

The Beaconsfield Centre
Cemetery
Whitegate Top
Belle Vue Terrace
Kennel La
Higgin Lane
Southowram
Fairfax Crs
Freeman Road
Pinnar Lane
Within Flds
Rustic Avenue
Townley Av PO
Surgery
Cromwell
Agr
Cromwell Road

Church

Keswick Close
Siddal Top Lane
Coalpit Lane
Lane
Charles Av
Annies Ct
Cain Lane
Yeadon Dr
Towngate
South Vw
New
Chapel La
Grange He/ghts
Edward Cl
School
Calderdale Way
Brookfoot Works

3
23
Brook

Siddal
Junior School
Surgery
Mortons La
Roseacre Close
Rosemary
Cinderhills La
Gladstone View
West Lane
Hays Ings
Works
Ashday Hall
Brookfoot Works

Jubilee St
Siddal Infant School
Rosemary Lane
Park Nook
Binns Top Lane
Ashday Lane
Wood Lane
Brier Lane

4
Calderdale

Backhold Av
Backhold Rd
Backhold Drive
Change Lane
South Halifax High School
Elland Park Wood
Ash Grove Works
Works
ELLAND ROAD
A6025
170

Park Lane
Park Wood Crematorium
A6025
ELLAND ROAD
Cromwell Botto

5
22

Exley Lane
Plains Lane
PARK ROAD
Calder & Hebble Navigation Canal
William Henry Smith School

A629 HALIFAX ROAD
Highfield Grove
Cemetery
Kinnaird Close
Woodlands Rd
Navigation Close
Lacy Way
Lock Vw
Savile Way
Warhurst
Lowfields Way
Lowfields Close
Lowfields Way
Lowfields Business Park
Calder Works
LC

6
Booth Royd Lane
Sherburn Crs
Arncliffe
Burnsall Road
Malham

Oliver Mdw
Football Club
Shaw Lane
Lower Edge Road

7
421
Church La

CALDERDALE WAY
A6025
ELLAND BRIDGE
Gas Works Lane
Century Road
Works
A629
Elland Riorges Link
Earth PO
Grasmere
Thirmere Av
Grasmere
Elland Old Earth School
Lodge Av Dr

B6114
Millgate
Briggate
Elland CE School
Foxhill Rd
HUDDERSFIELD RD
Quebec St
Westgate St
Wiston's Lane
Elland La
Springfield
Grove Rd
Whitwell
Alexandra
Carlton Grove
New Hall Works
Elland Lower Edge
Common Road
Bean Street
Croft Works

SADDLEWORTH ROAD
Ellen Royde Health Centre
Westgate
Nab End
Crown St
PO
Elland La
Wellington Business Centre
Grove Mills Industrial Estate
Heathfield Street
Whitwell Green Lane
Beverley Close
Elland Upper Edge
DEWSBURY ROAD B6114

8
A63

Works
Long Wall
Hullenedge Road
Park Avenue
Victoria Av
Albert St
John St
Gordon St
Rex-Cin
Victoria Baths
PO
Norman Terrace
Thomas Street
Works
HX5
Heathfield Industrial Estate
ELLAND
Banks End Road
Pinfold
Badger Hill

10
The Brooksbank School
Recreation Lane
Victoria Road
Kelvin Road
Saville St
Burley St
Elizabeth St
Oak
Claremont St
Rosemount
New Combe Street
Rosemount Avenue
M6

11
12
13

G
H
J
191
K
L
M

Greystone Av
Briar Close
Woodman Works
Woodman
Crestfield Rd
Smithfield
Dodgson Street
Ainley Road
A629
Hey Lane
New Hey Road
Cote Lane
M62

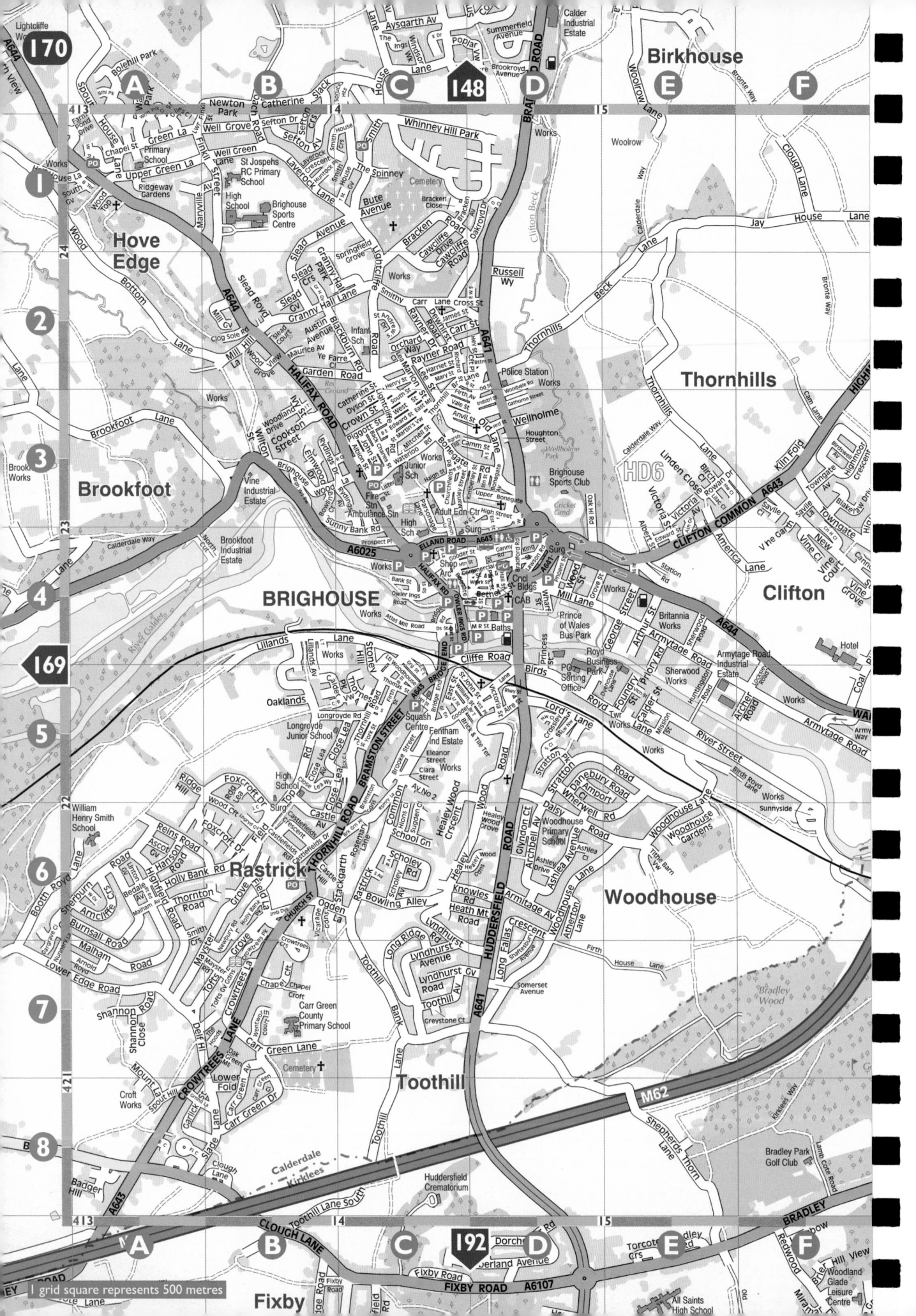

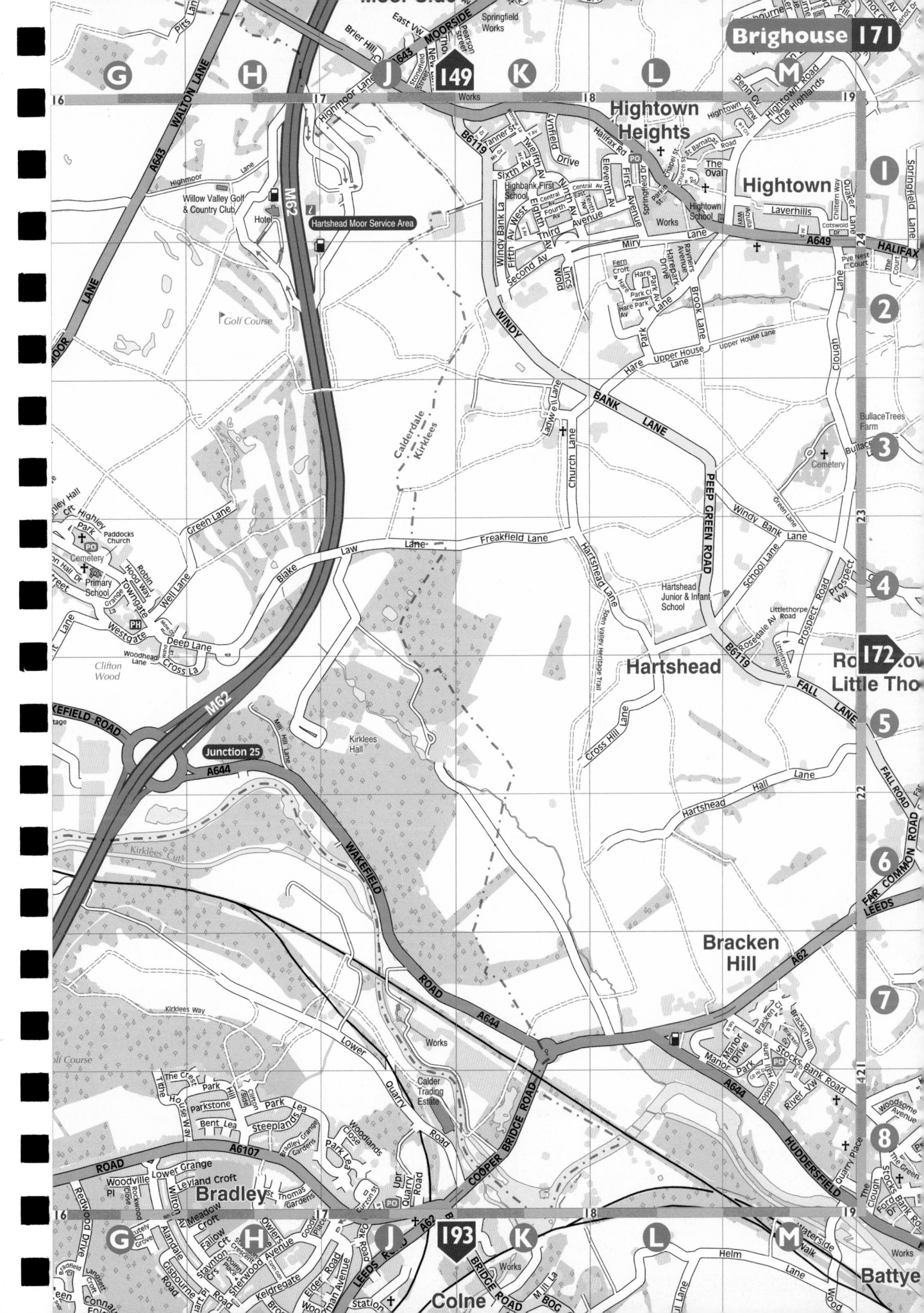

Rawfolds

Spen Valley Industrial Park

Rawfolds Industrial Estate

A638

Cartwright

New Street

Princess Mary Stadium

Littletown J&I School

Castle Hill

COMERSAL ROAD

Stubley Farm Road

LEEDS Old Rd

Littletown

Firthcliffe Parade

Berwick AV

Scott AV

Hadfield Rd

Lonsbrough AV

Briar

ROAD

Westfield

Cemetery

Hec

Heckmondwike Sports Club

A649

HALIFAX ROAD

Elizabeth Street

Gray Street

Victoria Spring Bus Park

Fair View

Stanley Lane

Carr Street

BRADFORD ROAD

Listing Dr

Hotel

County Works

Millbridge J&I School

Vernon Road

New North Road

Mosque

Heckmondwike School

Mosque

HALIFAX ROAD

Low House Fold

Cross Lane Business Park

Bus Park

Holme

Healds AV

FROST HL FLUSH

WESTGATE

Market PL

Church

Claremont

Hec Gra

Milton Sq

Liversedge

Crosslane Industrial Estate

Spen Valley High School

Works

Union Street

Smith Street

BMK Industrial Estate

Boundary Street

Wormald Street

Spenborough Industrial Estate

Superstore

Council Bldgs

MARKET STREET

Thomas St

Artillery Street

WF15

Bullace Trees Farm

Bullace Trees Lane

Cemetery

Spen Valley High School

HUDDERSFIELD ROAD

Hindley Road

Victoria Road

Headlands Ct

Dymond Road

Union Lane

Parker Street

Beck Lane

Cornmill

Cornmill Drive

Forge Lane

Milton Avenue

Milton Dr

Station Rd

Works

Railway

Orchard Works

Sycamore Industrial Estate

Spen Vale Street

Norristhorpe

Hall Pk Av

Park Avenue

Hall Dr

Millstone Ri

Spring House Works

Kings Lea

Church

Roberttown Lane

Liversedge Cricket Club

Sunnyside Av

Lumb Lane

Norristhorpe Lane

Norristhorpe Primary School

Spring House Works

Elm Tree

Lodge Lane

Roberttown

Little Thorpe

FALL LANE

Church Road

Commonside

Robertown

Meadow Cl

Meadow Drive

Fountain Close

Fountain Dr

Fountain St

John Booth Cl

Aston

Lincoln

Lincoln Gv

Wendron

Balmfield Crs

Balmfield

Rydal

Owlet Hurst Lane

Owlet Hurst

Park Farm

FALL ROAD

Far Common Road

HUDDERSFIELD ROAD

A62

Sunny Bank

Moor VW

Moor Top

Taylor

Hall Lane

Works

FAR COMMON ROAD

LEEDS

A62

Sunny Bank Dr

Sunny Bank Pde

Portal Crs

Dyke Close

Portal

Linnet

Crossley Lane

Crossley Cl

Robin Royd

Robin Royd La

Crossley

Cv

Jill

Cyprus Crs

Bright St

Sunny Bank

Wellhouse Av

Lockwood Av

Wellhouse Ct

Wellhouse Middle School

Woodward Court

Crossley Lane

Jill Lane

Northorpe

Northway Gardens

Taylor Hall Gdns

Orlando

Oliver Hall Gdns

Chestnut Mdw

Old Bank J I & N School

Eastway

Bank Road

Greenside

Works

Hepworth Lane

Hedworth

Northorpe Lane

Mirfield Moor

Northway

Westway

Southway

Hill

Road

Kitson HI Cl

Fox Royd La

Fox Royd

Savile Place

Savile Pl

Green

Mirfield Parish Cricket Club

Shillbank View

Eastfield Road

Bank Lane

Northstead

Bracken Hill

Bank Road

Woodsome Avenue

Kitson

Lady Heton Cl

Lady Heton Drive

Farral Hall Lane

Kitson HI Cl

Water Royd

Water Royd Lane

Lee

Flash Lane

Mary's Walk

Mary's Avenue

Shillbank Avenue

Shill Bank Avenue

Works

North Road

Surgery

HUDDERSFIELD

A619

Priory Walk

Priory Close

Battyeford CE (c) Junior & Infant School

Farrar Av

Kenilworth Cl

Norman Drive

Norman Rd

Heathfield

Fox Royd Av

Kings Head Rd

Uplands Drive

MIRFIELD

Over Hall Rd

Fernhurst Rd

Towngate

Dunbottle Way

Dunbottle Lane

Camm La

Nevins

Infant School

Quarryside Road

The Nab

Meadow Bank Crs

Field Ct

Brickyard

Wilson Avenue

Wilson Ter

Council Building

Pinfold La

Vicarage Meadow

Junior School

Crowlees

Crowless Rd

Lee Rd

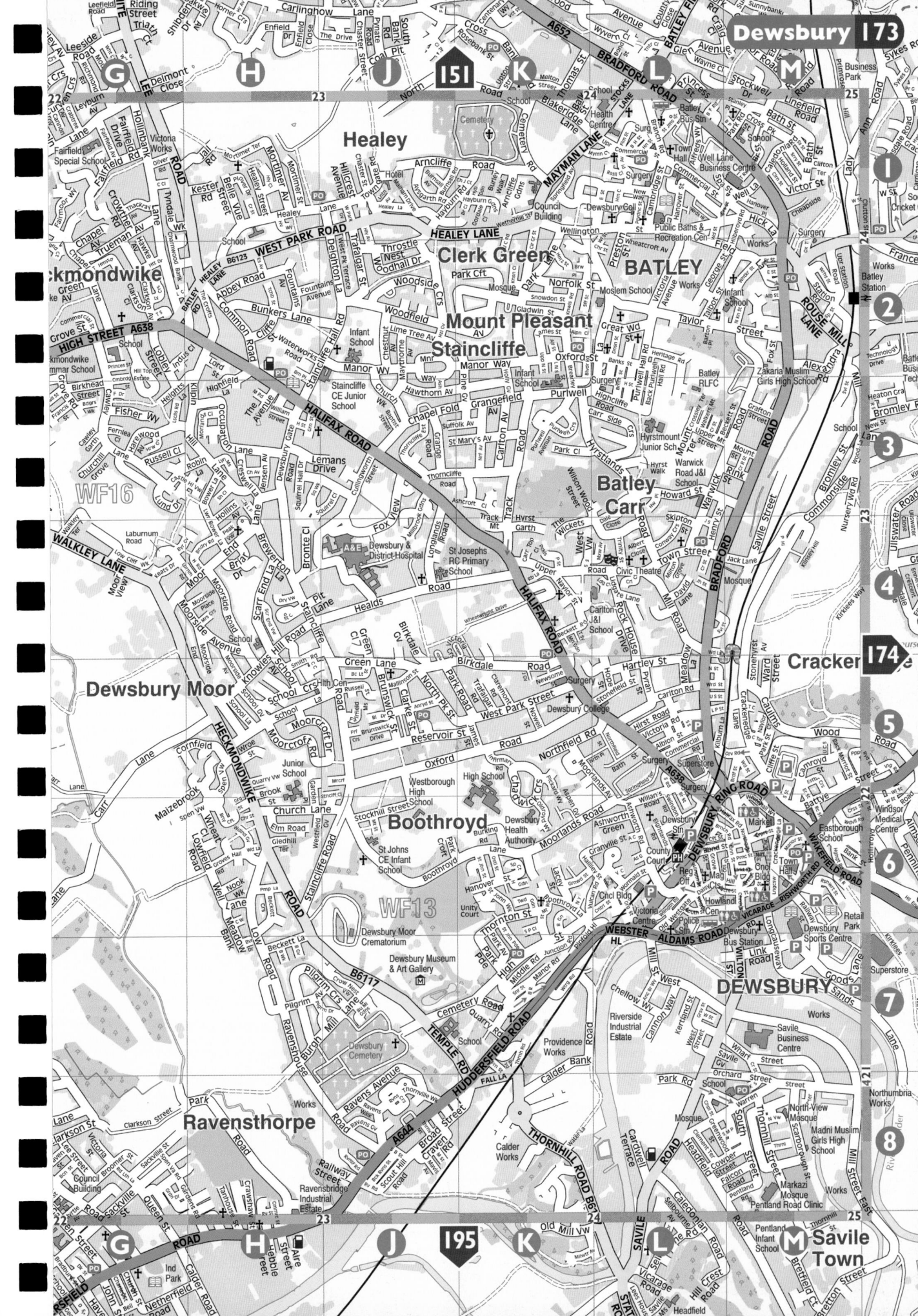

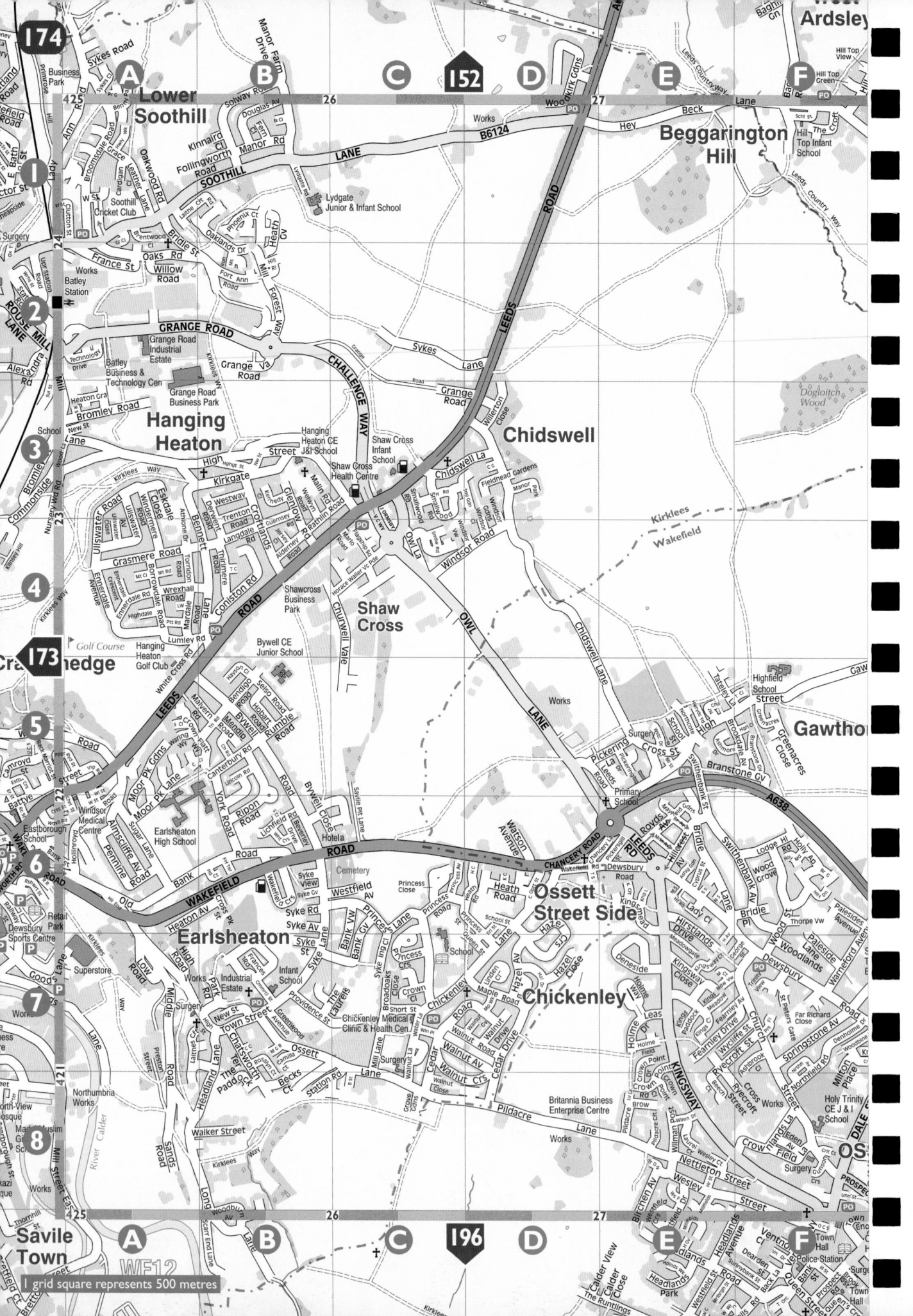

A Lower Soothill B C 152 D E F

Ardsley

Hill Top View

Hill Top Green

PO

Beggarington Hill

Hill Top Infant School

Leeds Country Way

Leeds Country Way

Dogloitch Wood

Kirklees
Wakefield

Chidswell

Shaw Cross Health Centre

Chidswell La

Fieldhead Gardens

Windsor Road

Owl La

Hanging Heaton CE J&I School

Shaw Cross Infant School

Kirkgate

Westway

Shaw Cross

Owl Lane

Shawcross Business Park

Bywell CE Junior School

Hanging Heaton Golf Club

Gawtho

Highfield School Street

Greenacres Close

Pickering La

Primary School

Cross St

Branstone Gv

A638

Earlsheaton High School

Wakefield Road

Hotel a

Chancery Road

Ossett Street Side

Dewsbury Road

Hirstlands Drive

Bridle Pl

Thorpe Vw

Palesides Avenue

WAKEFIELD ROAD

Earlsheaton

Cemetery

Westfield Av

Princess Close

Heath Road

Hazel Close

Kingsway Close

Deneside

Dewsbury Woodlands

Chickenley

Chickenley Medical Clinic & Health Cen.

Britannia Business Enterprise Centre

Pildacre Lane

Works

Holly Trinity CE J & I School

Savile Town A WF12 B C 196 D E F Town Hall Police Station

OS

1 grid square represents 500 metres

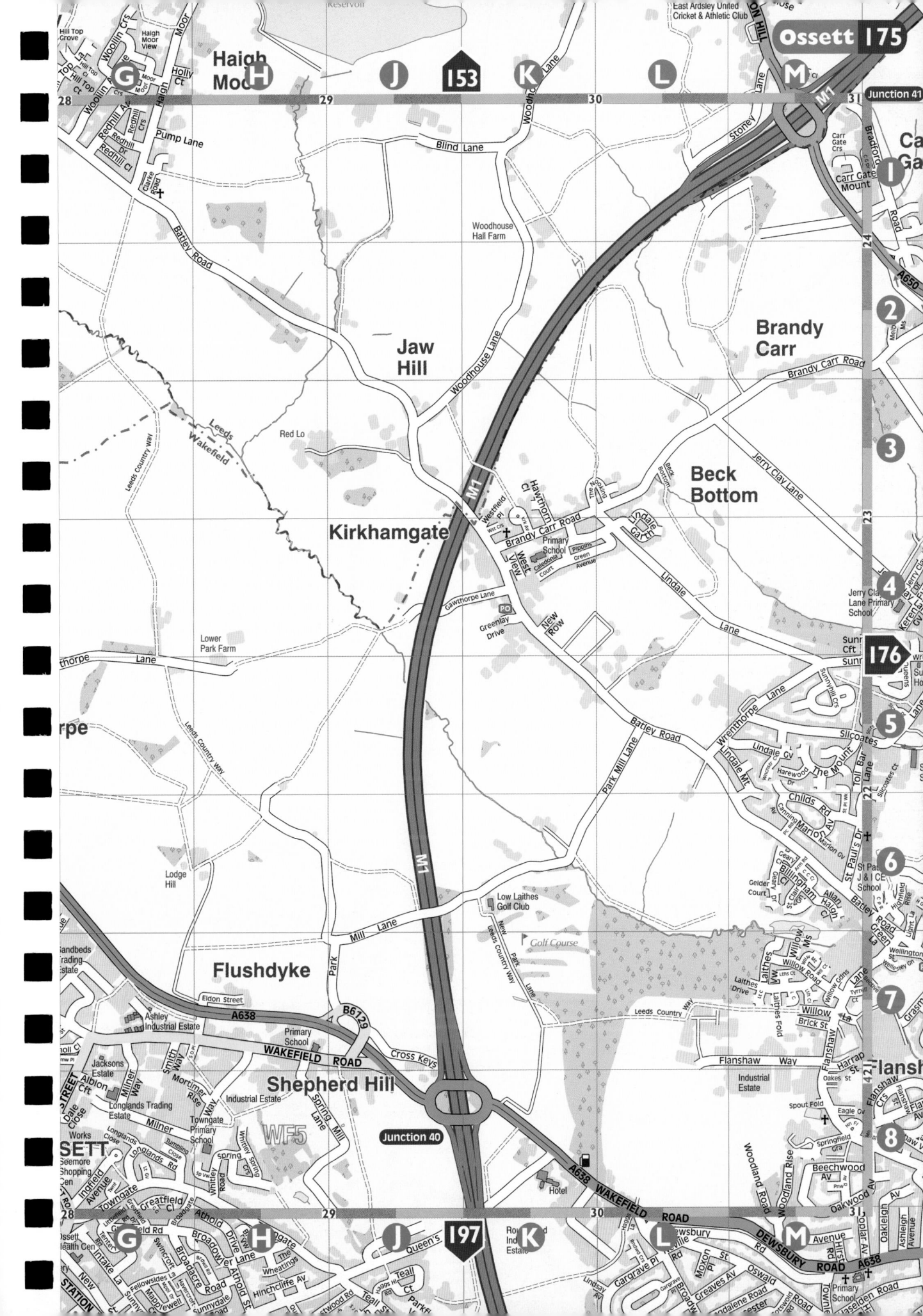

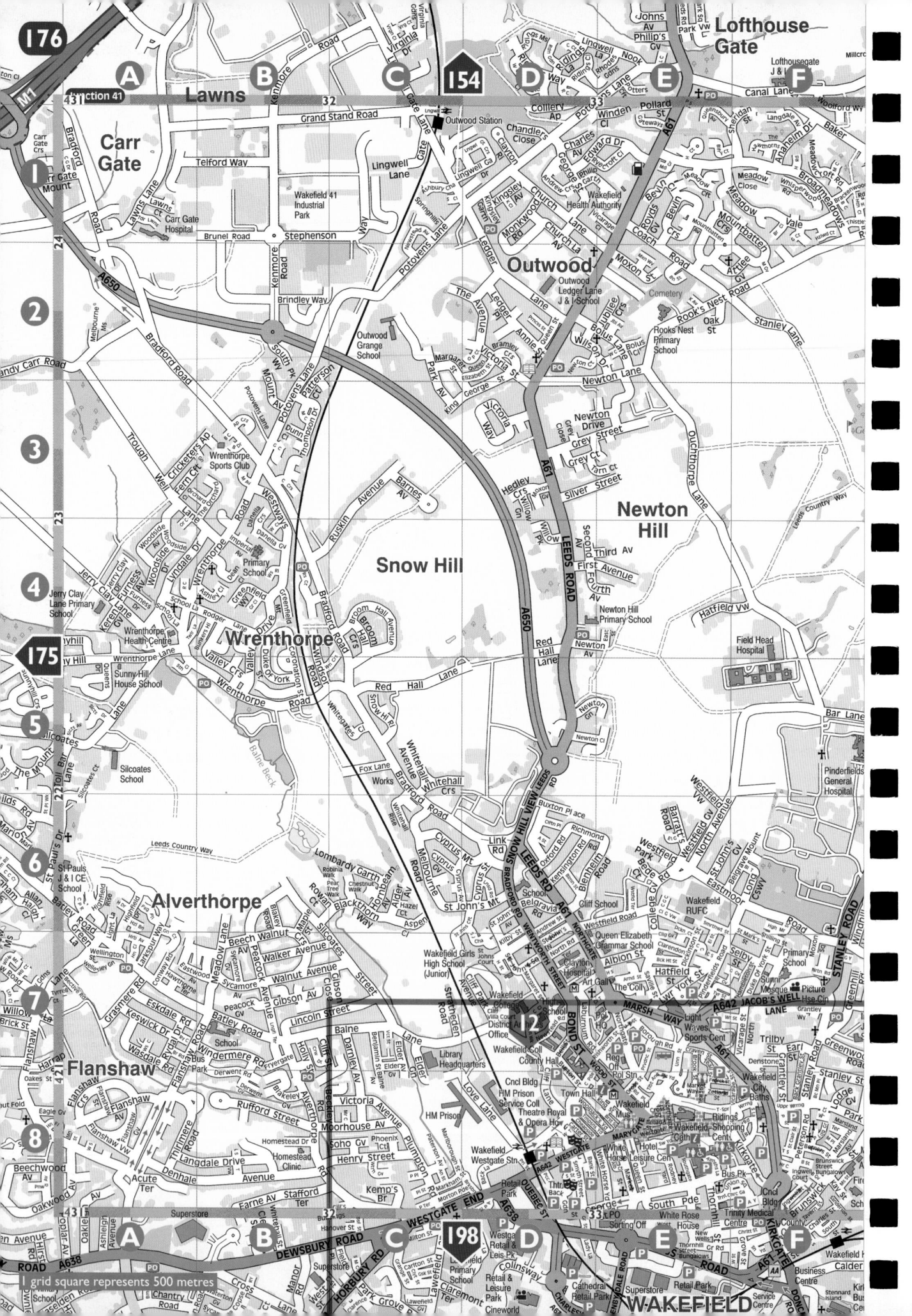

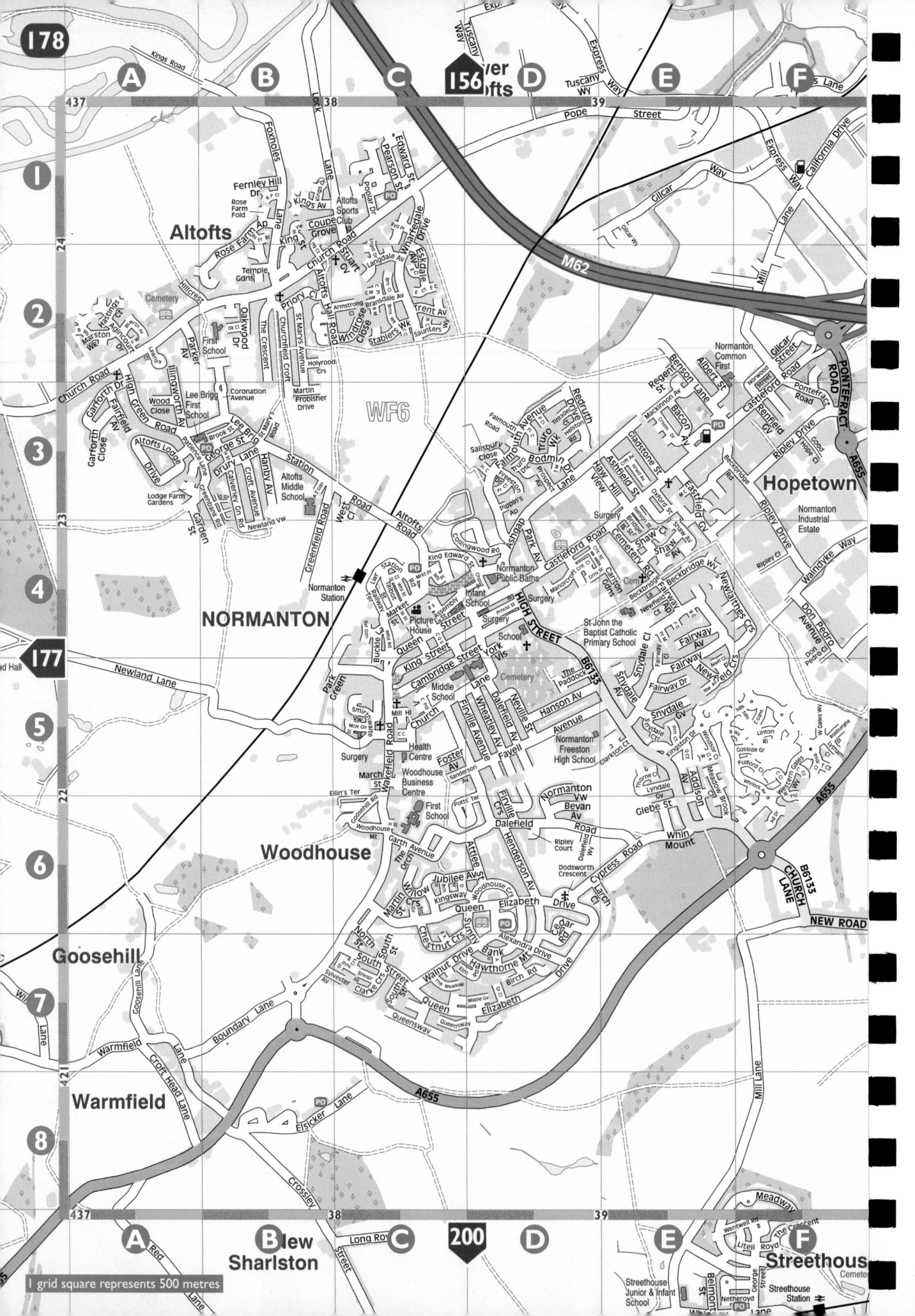

1 grid square represents 500 metres

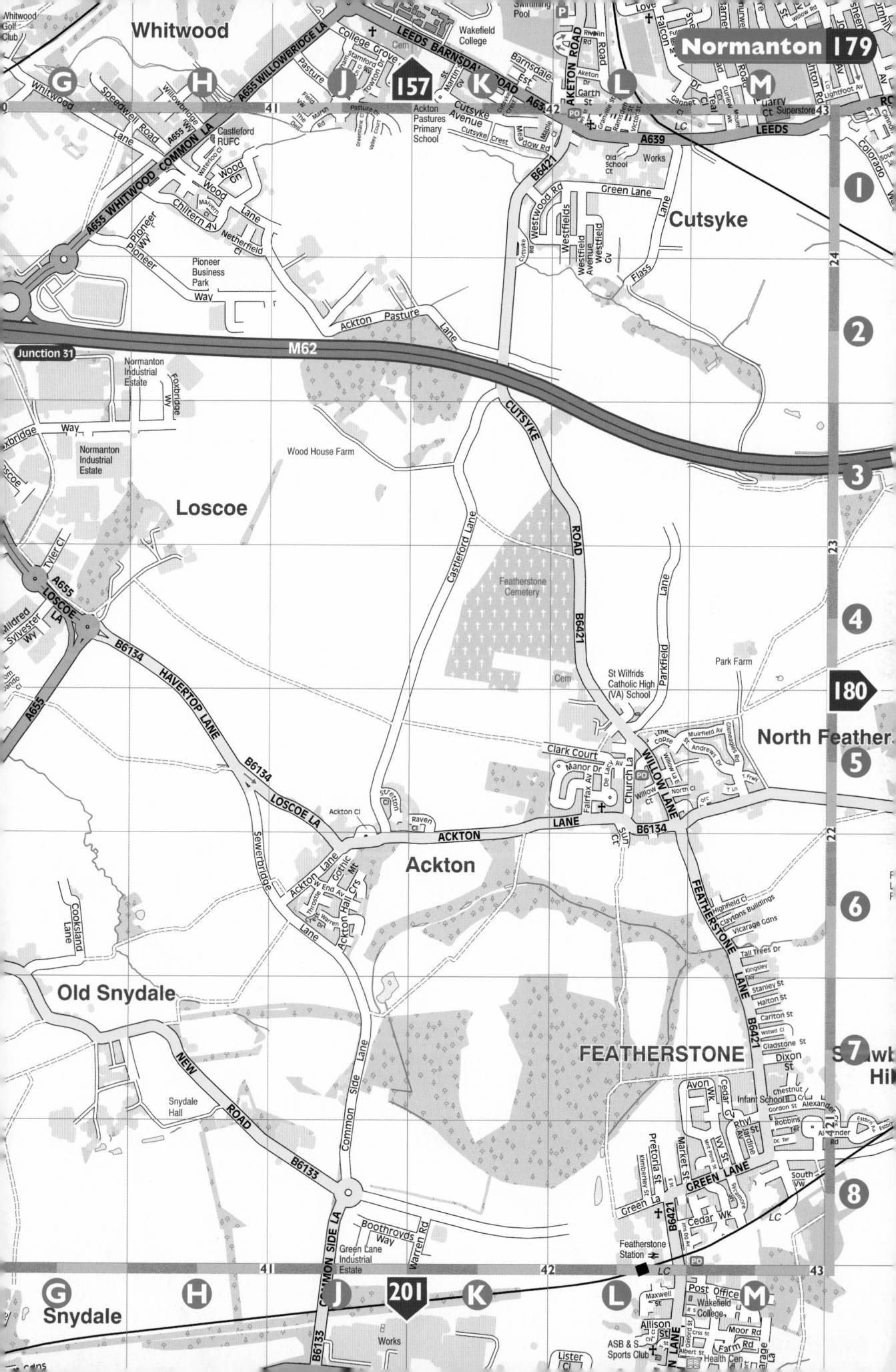

182

A   B   160   C   D   E   F

449   50   51

I

Works

Pottery
Grange
North Vw
RIBBRIDGE RD
B6136
Clifton Forge
Business Park
Knottingley
Vale J&I
Schol

2

PONTEFRACT RD
Knottingley Station
KNOTTINGLEY

River Aire

Holderness Av
Saltersgate
Forge Hill
Fisher
Belvoir Av
Middleton Wy
Bridge La
Grafton St
Hill Top
A645
Rope Walk
Knottingley
CE (C) J&I
School

Malvern Rd
Chiltern Av
Pentland
Marine Vila
Grove La
Cleveland Av
Cheviot Pl
Superstore
Glebe La
Banks La
Middle Lane
LC

Air St
Croftlands
Garden Lane
Aire Street
The Croft
Sunny Bank

West Ings
Crescent
West Ings
Lane
West Ings
Way
West Ings
Mews
West Ings Court

Marsh End
Marsh Lane

Fernley Green
Close
Fernley Green Rd

Stocking Lane

3

PO
Sycamore
23

Spawd
Bone
Hazel Rd
Cherry
Tree Av
Elm Pl
Poplar Gv
Ryedale Av

Hilgarth
Kershaw La
Health
Centre
Works

Elmhurst
Oakfield
The Ridgeway
Eastfield
Cr

Northfield Rd
Westfield Av
Westfield Rd
PO

Headlands La
Bone La
Northfield La
Englands La

The Paddock
LC

England
Lane J&I
School

Middle Lane
Quarry
Avenue

Womersley Road
Springfields
LC
Springfields Av
Harker Street
Gillann Street

Broomhill
Grove
Broomhill Avenue
Broomhill Cl
Broomhill Crescent
Cemetery
Broomhill Drive

Racca Avenue
Lamb La
Surgery
Low Green
Works
Fernley Green
Industrial Estate
Surgery

Common Lane
LC
LC

Blackburn Lane
Southmoor Lane

4

Avenue
Sycamore Cl
Hazel
Carsdale Walk
Garsdale Walk
Windermere
Road
Throstle Farm
J&I School

Leys Lane

The Poplars
Downland Crescent

181

5

M62
M62
M62
Cridling
Park
22

6

Grove
Farpark
Farm

Leys

7

Hodgewood
Farm

Stubbs Lane
North Yorkshire County
Wakefield

Wrights

North

8

A1(T)
Havercroft
Golf Course
Leys Road

449   50   51

A   B   204   C   D   E   F

Wake
Wood

Scrombeck
Farm

I grid square represents 500 metres

Cft Cl

awforth

A **B** Knowsley **C** 162 **D** **E** **F**

90 91

Knott Hill Street

St John with
St Michael School

I

Moss Side Street

Land Gate

Land Gate

Lancashire County
Rochdale

MARKET STREET

2

Rossendale Way

3

Cemetery

Facit

Rossendale Way

A671

4

Long Acres

Council
Building

Street

Lancashire County
Rochdale

5

Watergove
Reservoir

6

WHITWORTH

Rake

Slack Gate

Hard

Lane

Ramsden

Lobden
Golf Club

Barn Field Lane

Lower House Lane

Alderbank

Wardle Fold

Bank Lane

7

Golf Course

Bent La

Old Hey Bottom Lane

Knowl Syke St

Wardle Fold

Bank Barn Lane

Primary School

Alpine Drive

Pennine

Crossfield Road

Woodend Lar

8

Clough House Lane

Fern

Clough Street

East St

Birch

Hill

Wardle

Dirty Leach L

Hey Bottom Lane

Rydings

Wardle Road

Grove

389 90 91

A **B** **C** 206 **D** **E** **F**

G H Turvin Clough J 165 K 400 L M

Blackstone

99

B6138

BLACKSTONE EDGE ROAD

B6138

I

20

2

HX6

Manshead End

Baitings Pasture

Soyland Moor

3

Blue L

Blue Ball Road

ROCHDALE ROAD

A58

Baitings Reservoir

19

4

Back O' Th' Height

188

ROCHDALE ROAD

A58

5

18

6

Rishworth Drain

Cat Stones

Rishworth Moor

7

Rishworth Moor

417

8

Joiner Stones

G H Green Withens Reservoir 99 J 209 K 400 L M 01

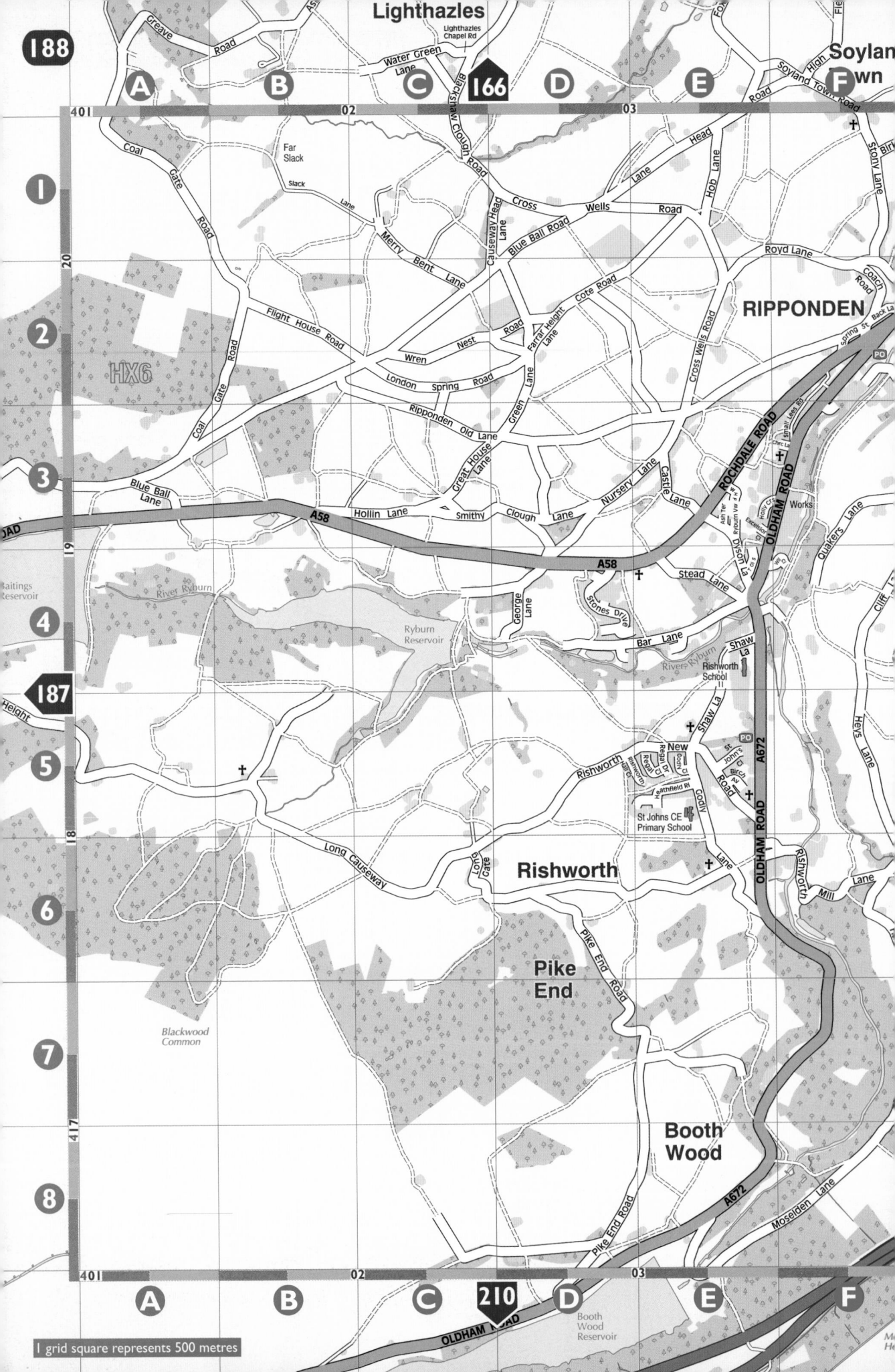

G

H

J

167

K

L

M

05

06

07

GREETLAND ROAD

HALIFAX ROAD

A58

Jubilee Ter

Kenworthy Lane

Works

Stones Lane

Hanging

Moor Bottom Road

Scammonden Road

Jackson La

Jackson Mdw

Lightcliffe Royd Lane

Barsey Gr

Stony

Stony Crft La

Stony Crft La

Field Hurst

Upr Hil Fd

M Gr

Sand Foot

Bowers Mill Industrial Estate

St

Meadowcroft Lane

Ripponden Junior & Infant School

ELLAND ROAD

ELLAND ROAD

RIPPONDEN NEW BANK

Ripponden Old Bank

West Lane

PH

School Close

Way

Stainland Road

Pinfold Cl

Stonelea

Infant School

PO

Barkisland Cricket Club

RISHWORTH ROAD

Fiddle Lane

Fiddle Lane

SADDLEWORTH ROAD

Slack

Lane

Howroyd Lane

Barkisland

B6114

Beestonley Lane

I

20

2

Bank Hey Lane

Bank Bottom

Gosling Lane

B6114

CAUSEWAY

Clough House Lane

Bottomley

Bottomley Lane

Pitt Hill Lane

Crow Wood Lane

Steel Lane Head

Black Brook

HX4

Cray Lane

Dog

19

3

4

Krumlin

Bank Royd Lane

Steele Lane

Penny Hill

Stainland Dean

Forest Hill Road

190

Ringstone Edge Moor

Ringstone Edge Reservoir

Green Lane

SADDLEWORTH ROAD

Moor Field Road

Scammonden Road

Firth House Lane

Hey Lane

Berry Mill Lane

Dean House Lane

Broom Hill

18

5

6

Pit Lane

Withens Lane

B6114

Withens End Lane

Pike Law

417

7

Lower Road

8

M62

Rye Field Lane West

Rye Fld Lane

Road

Chapel Hill Lane

Croft House Rd

M62

Ryburn Cl

G

H

J

211

K

L

M

05

06

07

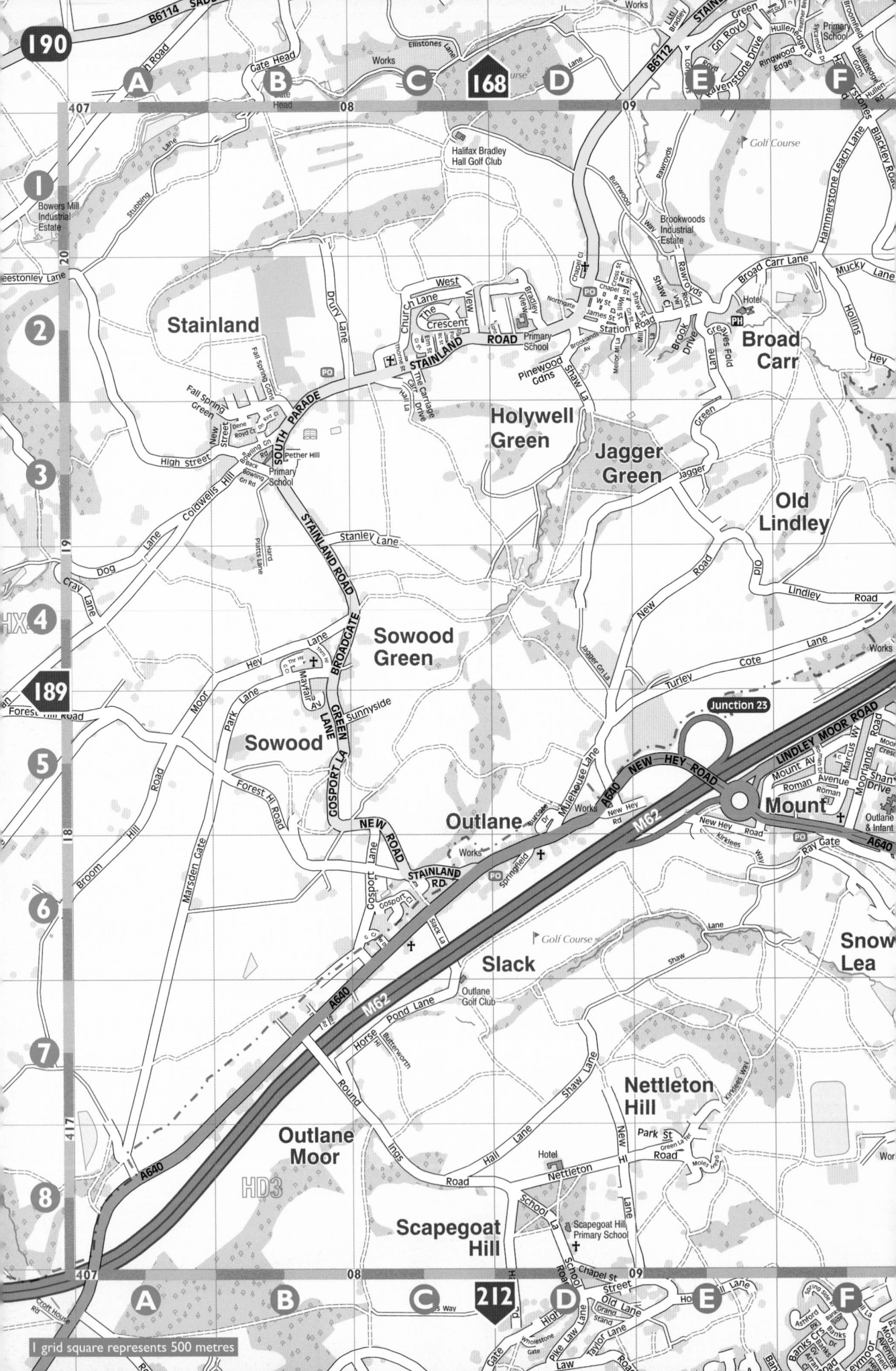

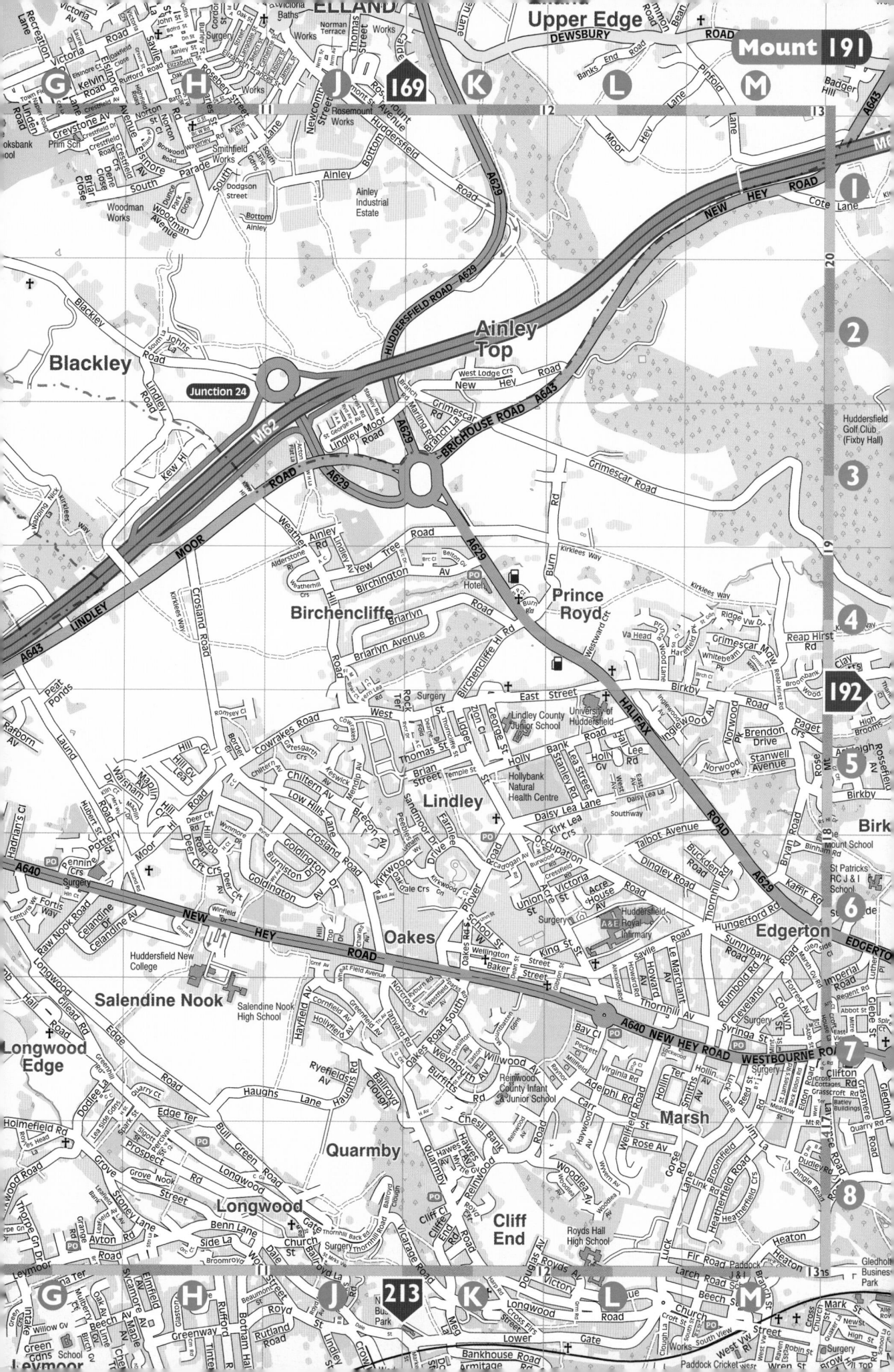

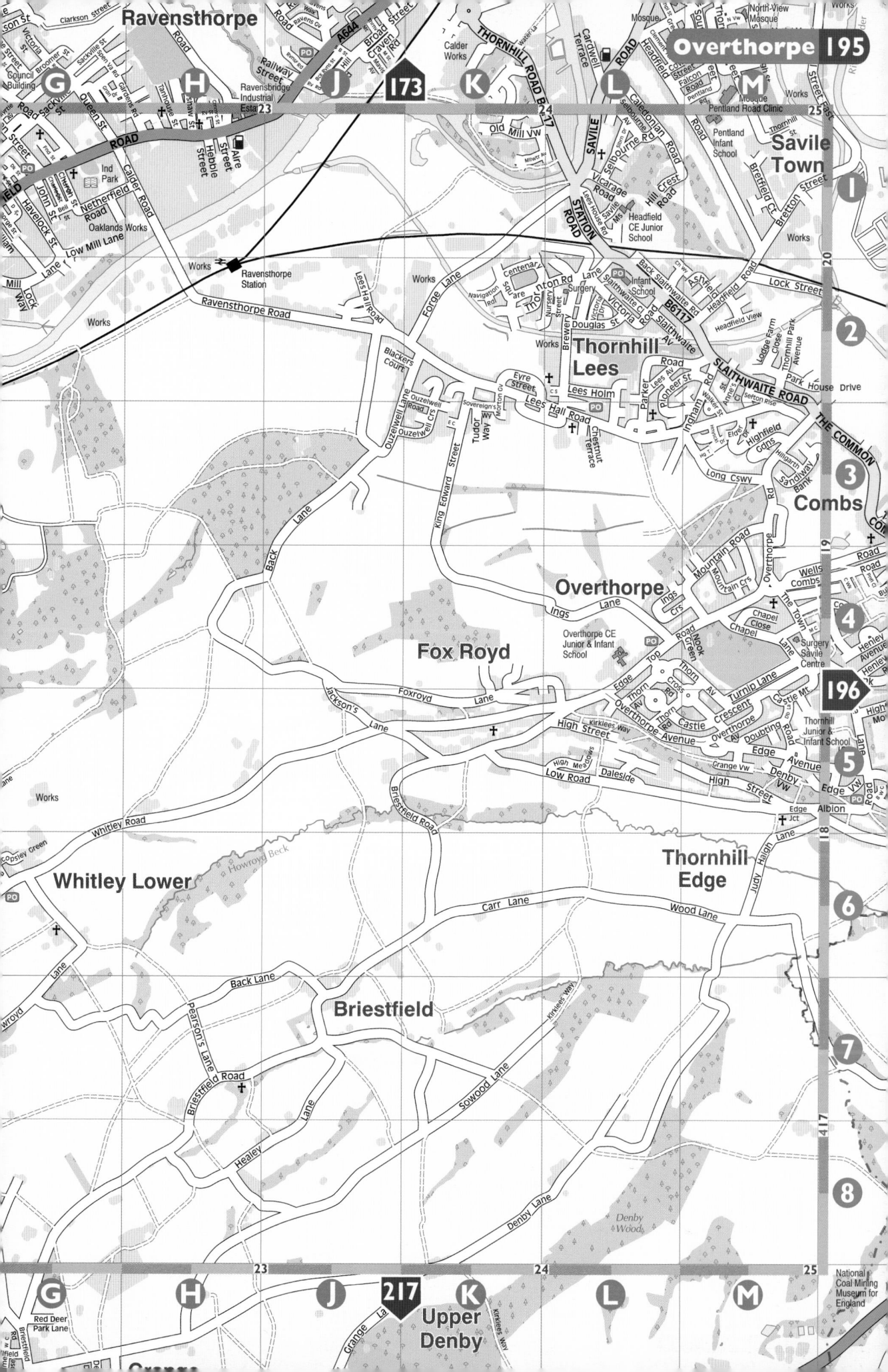

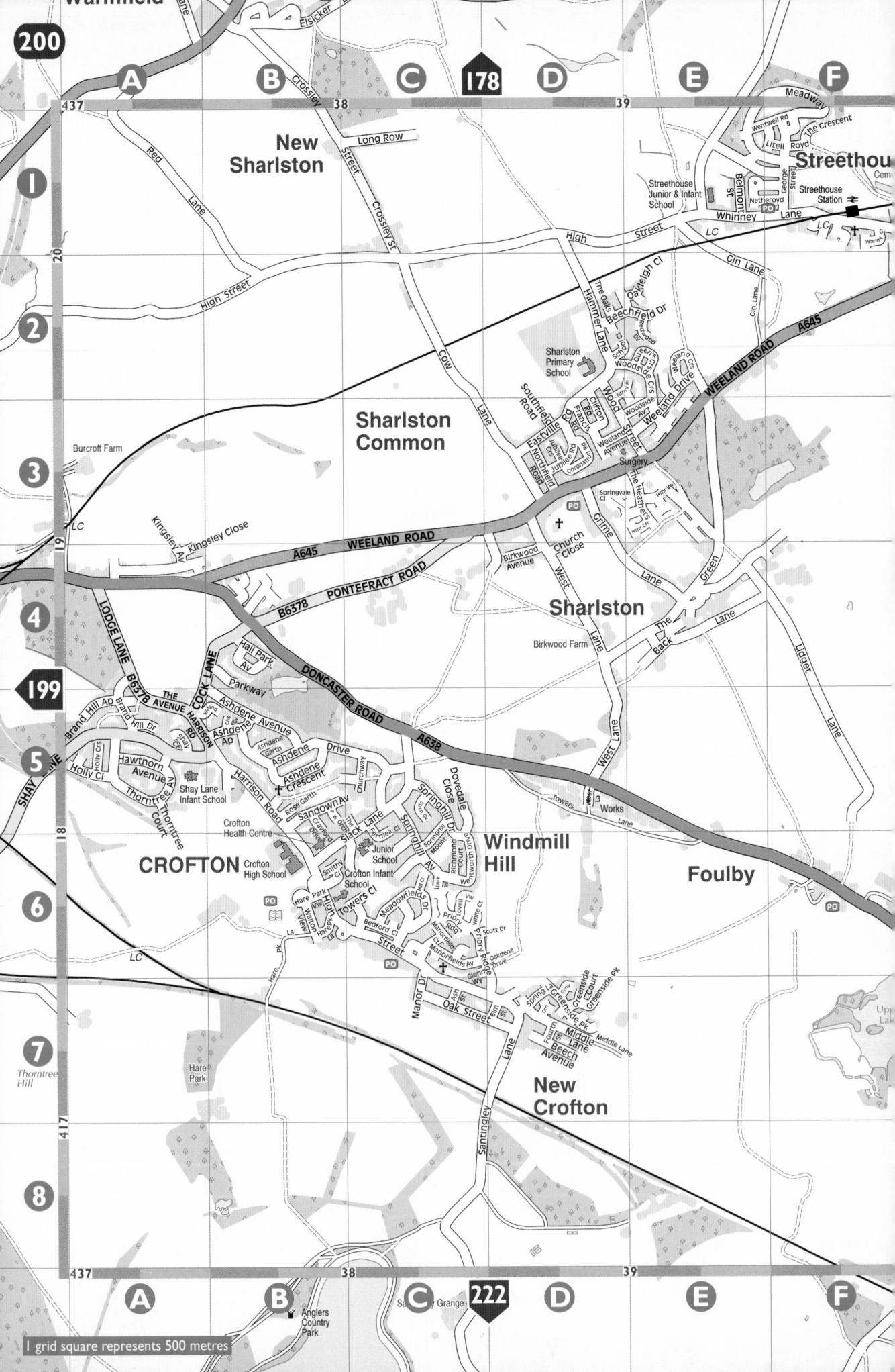

G H J **179** K L M

41 42 43

Snydale

Green Lane
Booth
W
Bootl
St Green Lane
Common
Industrial
Estate

Leatherstone
Station

B6133

B6421

B6421

Maxwell
St

Post Office Road

Wakefield
College

Moor Rd

Allison
St

ASB & S
Sports Club

St Thomas
CE Junior
School

Lister
Cl

Lister Rd

Health Cen

Victoria St

Vicarage

Victoria St

Surgery

Mews Ct

A645 WAKEFIELD ROAD

Farm Gdns

ney La

Lynwood Cl

Huntwick Lane

Huntwick Lane

Wentworth
Rd

Hillcrest Av

Southfield
Av

Wentworth
Av

Priory Road

Priory Rd

Priory Road

St Martins

St Andrew St

St Thms
Rd

PONTEFRACT ROAD

STATION LANE

HALL ST

A645

Lea La

Wentb

Wellgarth

A645

2

Priordale
Rd

Priory Rd

Hardwick Road

Infant School

Girnhill Lane

Nunn's
La

Nunn's
La

Bedford Cl

Nunn's
Gn

Katrina Grove

B6421

Huntwick
Av

Southfield
Dr

Huntwick
Dr

Ashcroft
Cl

Ashcroft Av

Went
Av

Verner St

Nunn's
Cl

Nunn's
Cr

Bedford Cl

Henley

Katrina
Grove

Briggs
Rw

Katrina Grove

Went Av

WF7

ACKWORTH

3

4

202

Huntwick
Grange Farm

Hardwick Lane

Hardwick Lane

NEW ROAD

Hill Top

WENT LANE

Owlet
Hall

5

West
Hardwick

WENT

Hessle

18

6

Nostell Park

Wakefield
Independent
School

Nostell Priory
(NT)

Engine Ln

B6428

Hessle Common

Hessle
Lane

417

7

A638

DONCASTER ROAD

Chapel
Cl

Wragby

Went
Lane

CROSS HANDS LANE

DONCASTER ROAD

A638

King Royd
Lane

Green
Lane

Brackenhill

8

Wakefield
Independent
Junior School

Brickworks

Long
Row

Swine
Lane

OFFLEY LANE

WAKEFIELD

Bracken Hill

Green
St

Sykes
Lane

Leigh St

West View

Francis
St

Industrial
Estate

G H J **223** K L M

41 42 43

GARMIL

COMMON LANE

B273

A   Course   B   C   182 Wake Wood   D   E   F

1 449   Havercroft   50   51

Mid Yorkshire Golf Club

Scrombeck Farm

20

Valley Gdns   Valley   Road   Bank Wood Road   North Lodge Lane   Works   Bank Wo

2

Court Road
Hotel

Stapleton Park Farm

3

19

4

203

Stapleton Park

New Road

Castle

5

North Yorkshire County
Wakefield

18

6

A1(T)

Hotel

Jackson's   Lane   Leys   Lane

7

River Went

417

WEST EDGE ROAD   B6474   West   Edge   Road   West   Edge   Road

8

A1(T)

449   50   51   **Kirk Smeaton**

Pinfold Lane   Main   Street   PO   Kirk CE Sch   Manor Close

A   B   C   226   D   E   F   Nor   ld Lane

Spring Lodge

G H J 183 K L M

53 54 55

LC

Grange Farm

1

Bon

Northfield Lane

20

2

Woodhall Lane

Road

3

Northfield Close

Womersley CE Primary School

Cow Lane

Fulham Lane

19

Womersley

Cemetery

Main Street

Park Lane

Station Road

Highfield Lane

LC

Stocking Green Farm

4

Wormesley Park

Churchfield Lane

18

5

417

6

Smeatley's Lane

Churchfield Lane

7

Little Lane

Willowbridge Road

LC

LC

8

Little Smeaton

Wentdale Lane

stan Valley

Springfield Crs

Water Lane

Cem

el

dge

LC

Wentbank House

Tall Lane

53 54 55

Works

G H J 227 K L M

Stubbs Road

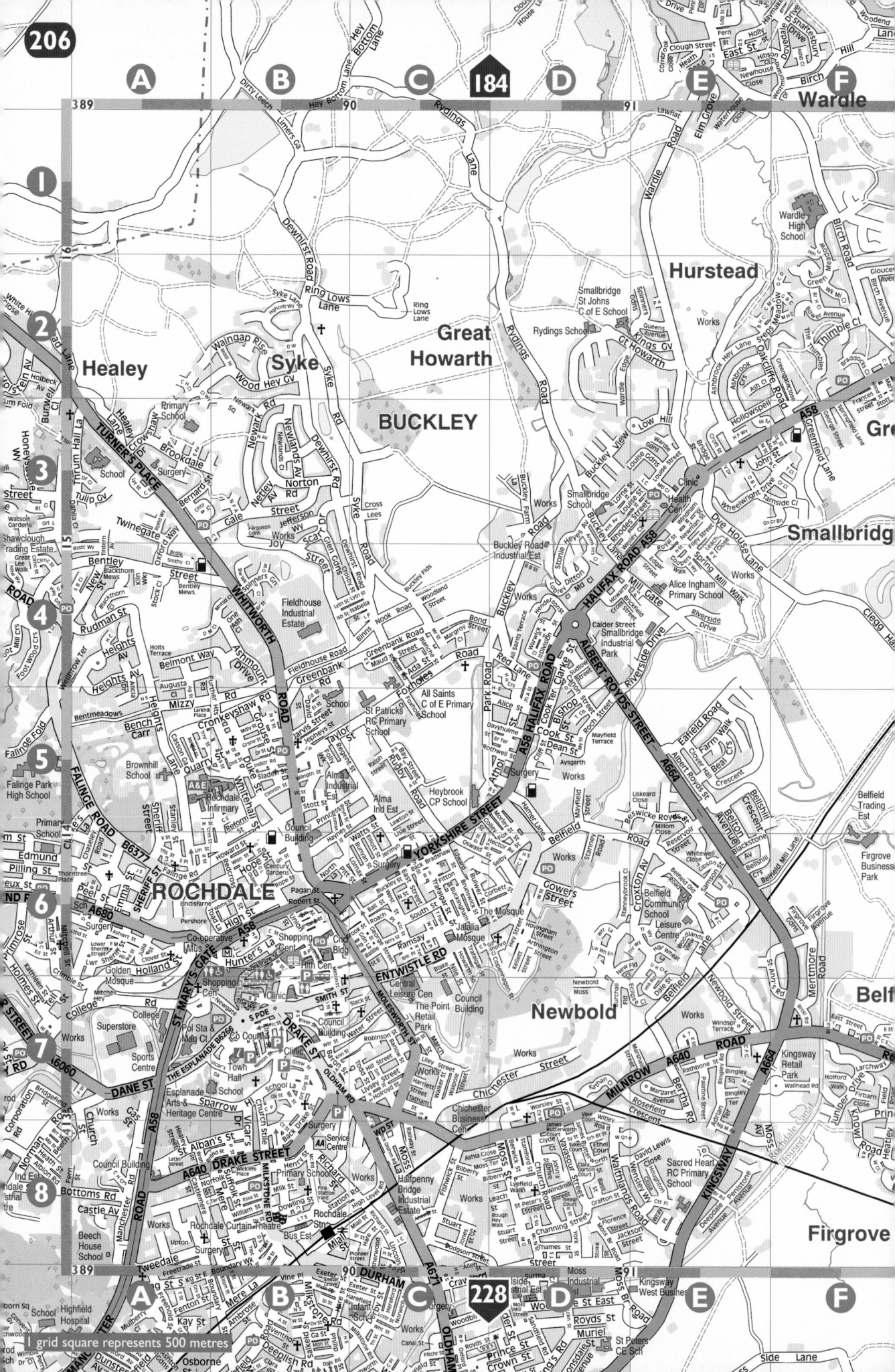

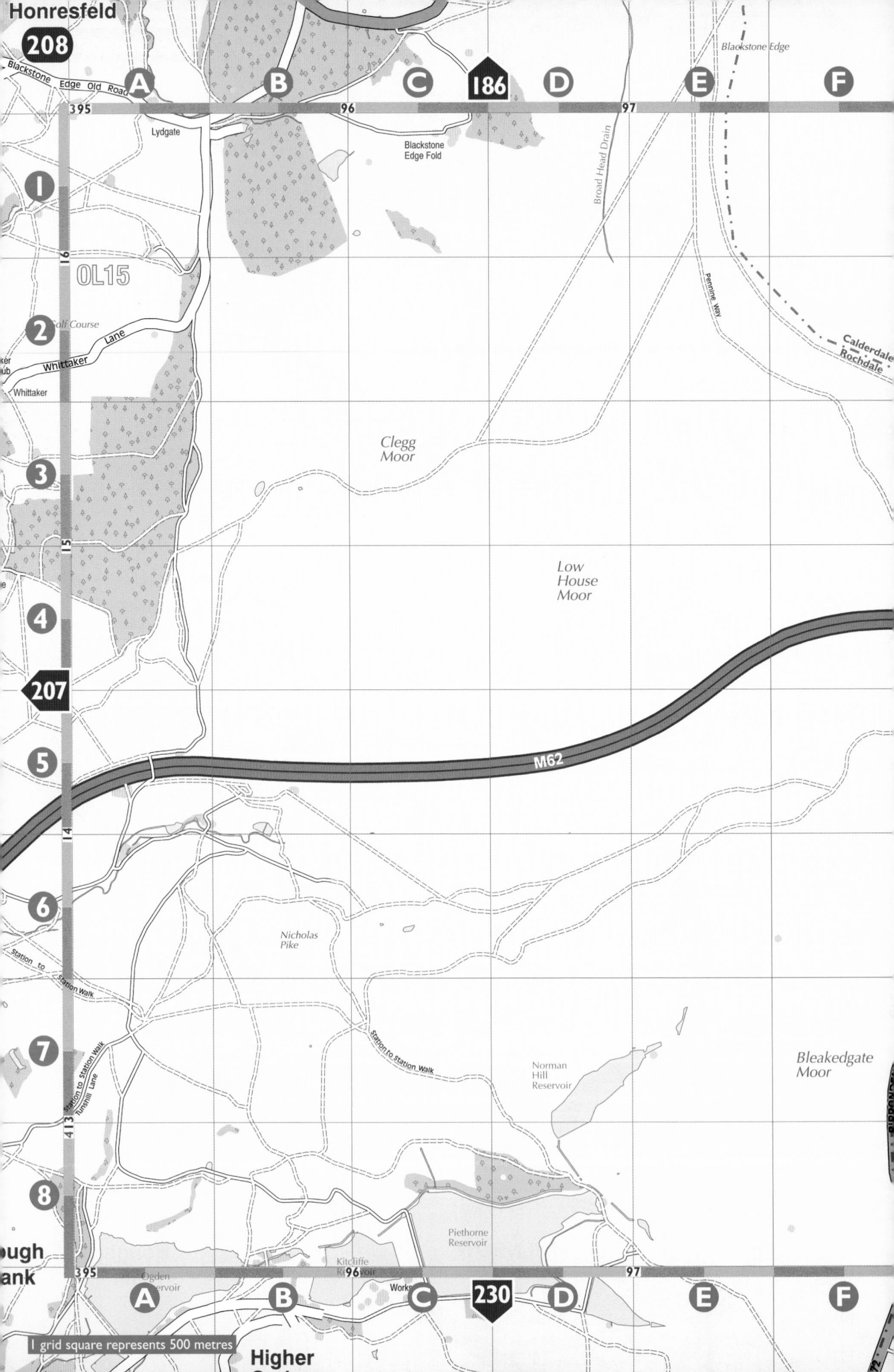

Honresfeld

208

Blackstone Edge Old Road

A   B   C   **186**   D   E   F

395   96   97

Lydgate

Blackstone Edge Fold

Blackstone Edge

Broad Head Drain

Pennine Way

1

16

OL15

Calderdale
Rochdale

2

Golf Course

Whittaker Lane

ker
ub

Whittaker

Clegg
Moor

3

15

Low
House
Moor

4

207

M62

5

14

6

Station to Station Walk

Nicholas
Pike

Station to Station Walk

7

413

Station to Station Walk

Tunshill Lane

Norman
Hill
Reservoir

Bleakedgate
Moor

8

ough
ank

395

Ogden
Reservoir

96

Kitcliffe
Reservoir

Works

Piethorne
Reservoir

97

A   B   C   **230**   D   E   F

1 grid square represents 500 metres

Higher

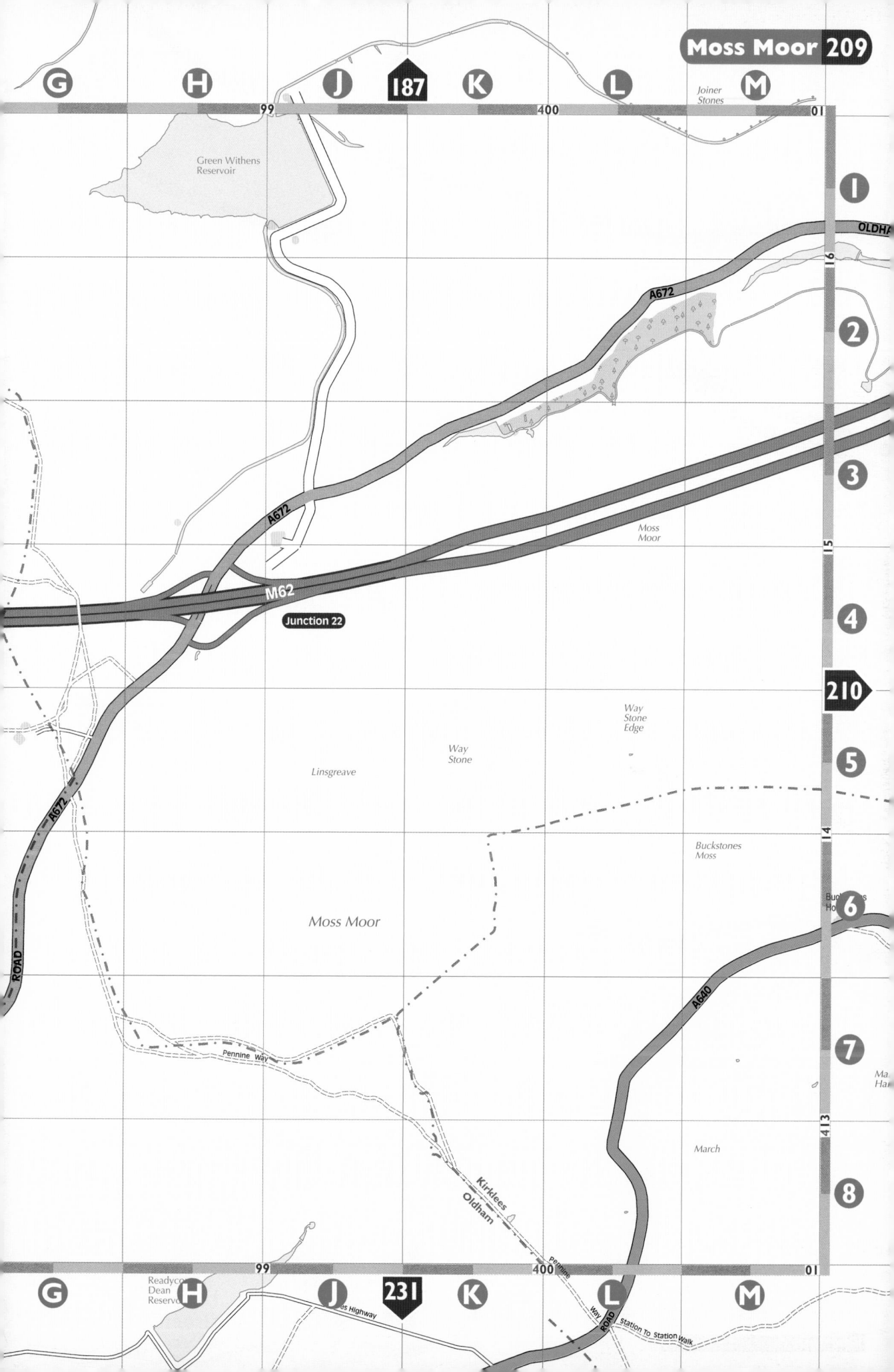

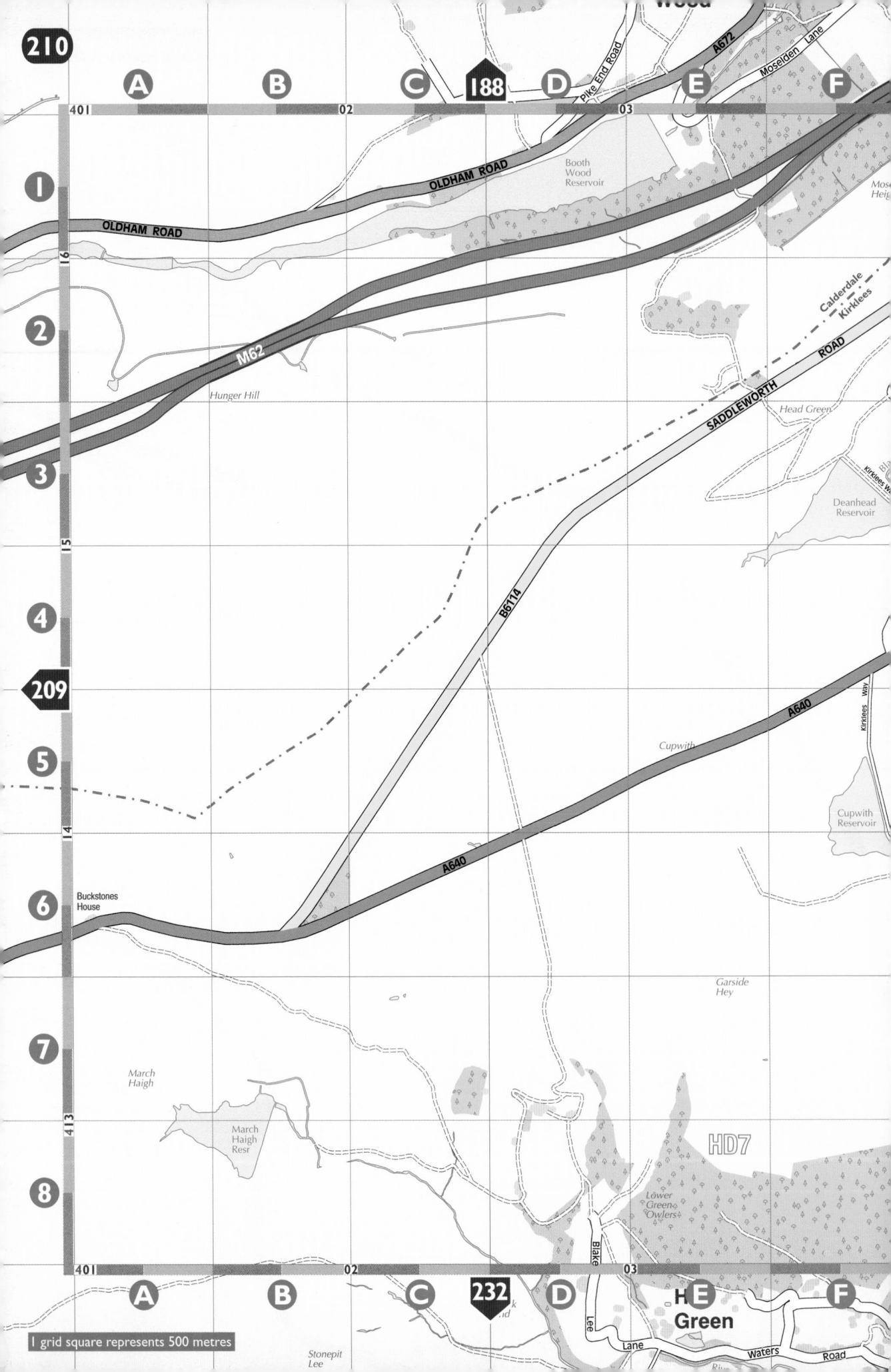

A   B   C **188** D   E   F

401   02   03

16

I

OLDHAM ROAD

OLDHAM ROAD

Booth
Wood
Reservoir

Wood

A672

Moselden Lane

Mose
Heig

2

M62

Calderdale
Kirklees

Hunger Hill

SADDLEWORTH ROAD

Head Green

15

3

Kirklees W

Deanhead
Reservoir

B6114

4

◀ **209**

A640

Kirklees Way

Cupwith

5

Cupwith
Reservoir

14

6

Buckstones
House

A640

Garside
Hey

413

7

March
Haigh

HD7

8

March
Haigh
Resr

Lower
Green
Owlers

401   02   03

A   B   C **232** D   E   F

Blake

H Green

Lee
Lane

Waters   Road

Stonepit
Lee

M62

G H J **189** K L M

Chapel

M62

I

Croft House Rd

Church Lane

Rye Field Lane West

Rye Field Lane

Lower

Hill Lane

Pinfold Lane

Hey Lane

Scammonden Water

6

B6114

Deanhead

Cemetery

Pole Gate Branch

Pole Gate

2

Pole Moor

A640 NEW HEY ROAD

Worts Hill Side

Sledge Gate

Scammonden Sailing Club

Worts Hi Lane

Worts Hill Lane

Kirklees Way

Crimea Lane

Pole Road

3

Moor Side

Tiding Field Lane

5

A640

Back

O'wait

Laund Road

Burnt Plats Lane

Goat Hill

Laund Road

Intake Road

Heys

Wilberlee

4

Wilberlee Junior & Infant School

Lane

Bradshaw Lane

Colne Valley Circular Wk

Tyas Lane

Clough House Lane

Head

Longl

Longla

212

Coal Gate

Bradshaw

Scout Lane

North Lane

Follingworth Lane

5

Slaithwaite Moor

New Cl Lane

Slaithw CE Prim School

4

Colne Valley Circular Walk

Old Ground

Slack La

Cop Hill Side

Scout Lane

Row La

Holme Lane

6

Shaw Lane

Cop Hill Lane

Marsden Lane

Shaw Fields Lane

Booth Bank

MANCHESTER ROAD

7

Drop Clough

Green Lane

White Hill

Old Lane

413

Lane

W. Slaithwaite Road

Crow Trees Road

School Lane

Hollins

Lingards Ro

Lingards Wood

8

Marsden Lane

Kertle Lane

Park Gate Road

A62

Colne Va. Circular Wk

River Colne

G H J **233** K L M

ER ROAD (MAR

B6107

Plains Ro

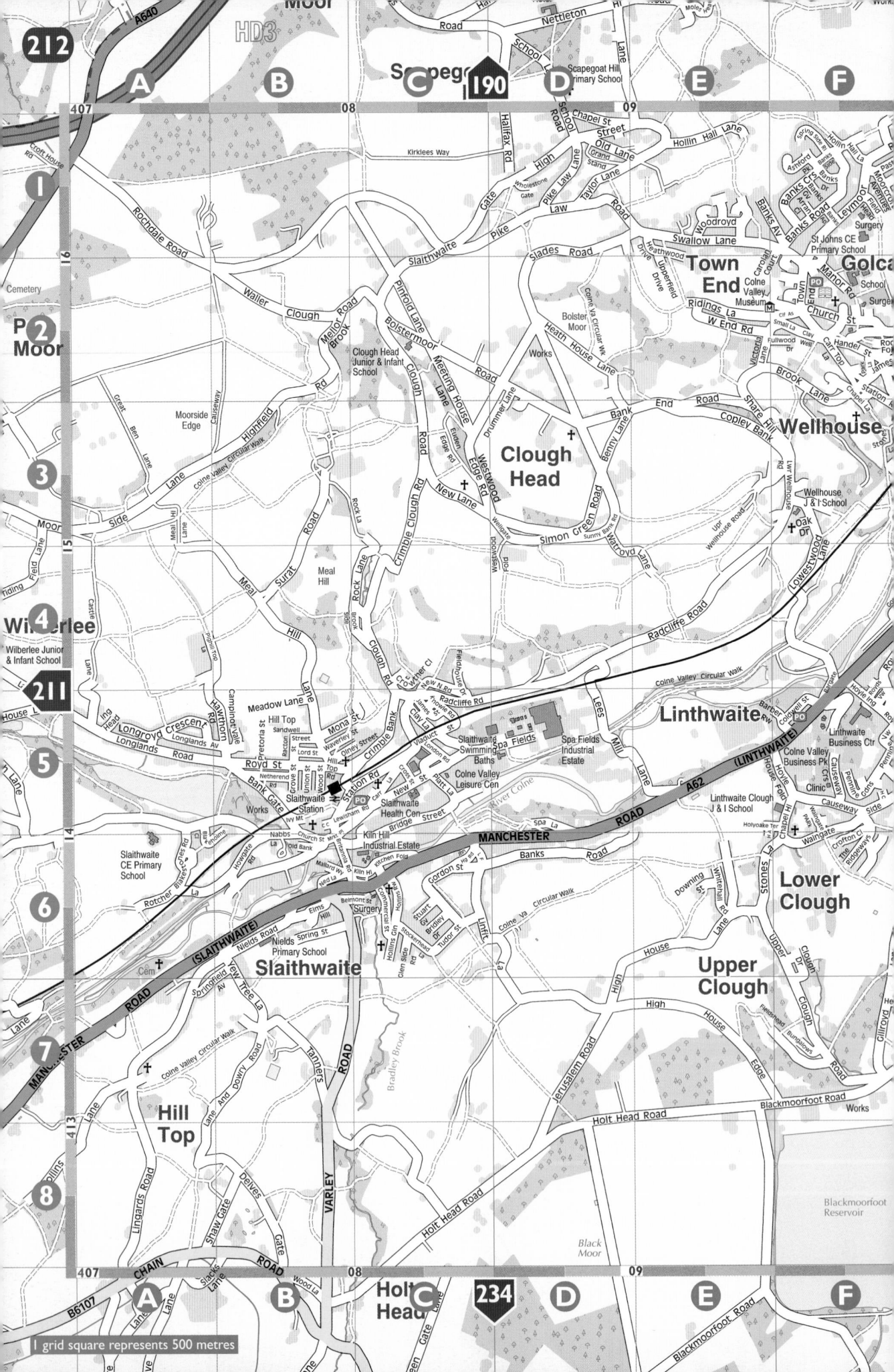

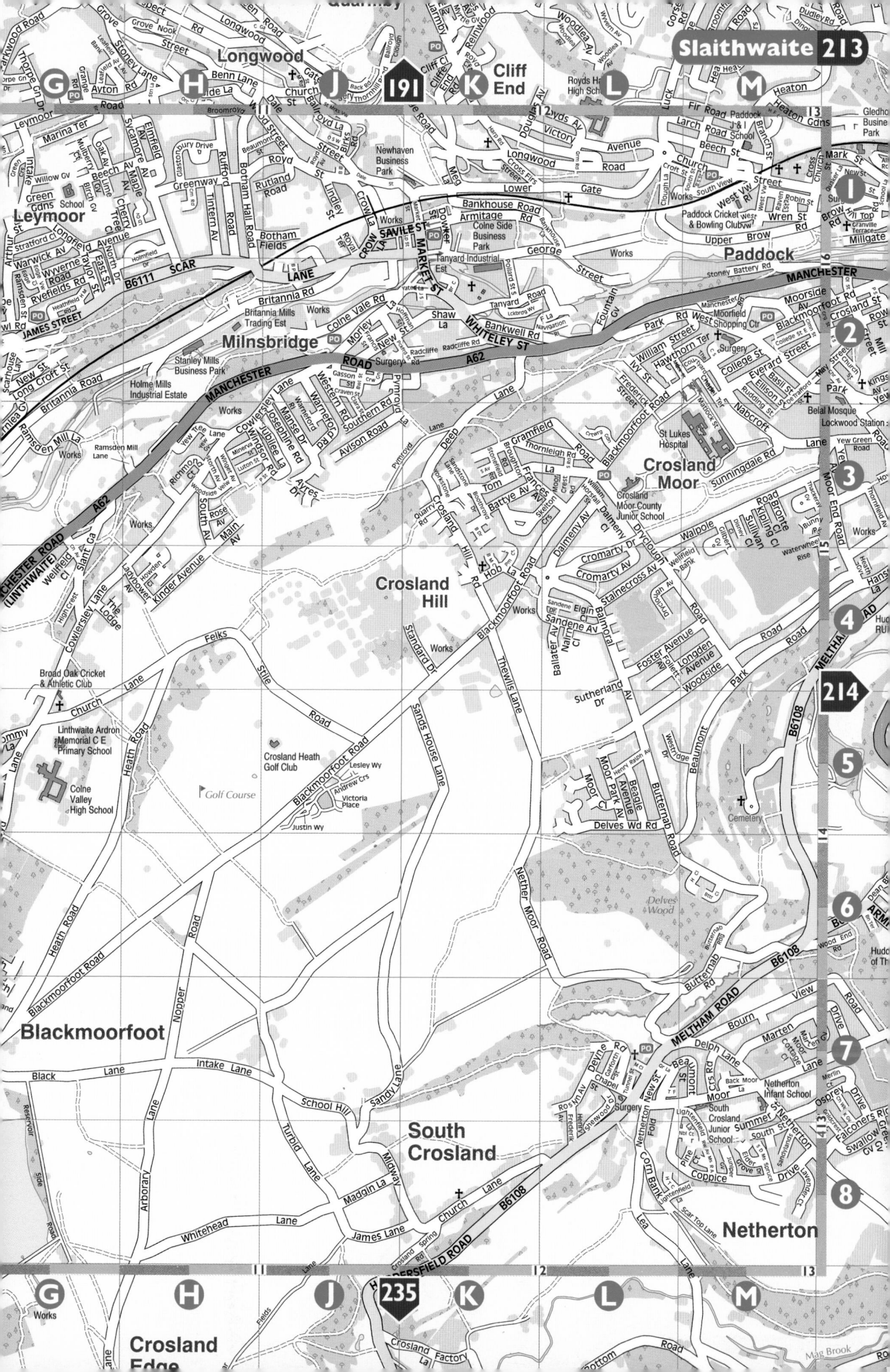

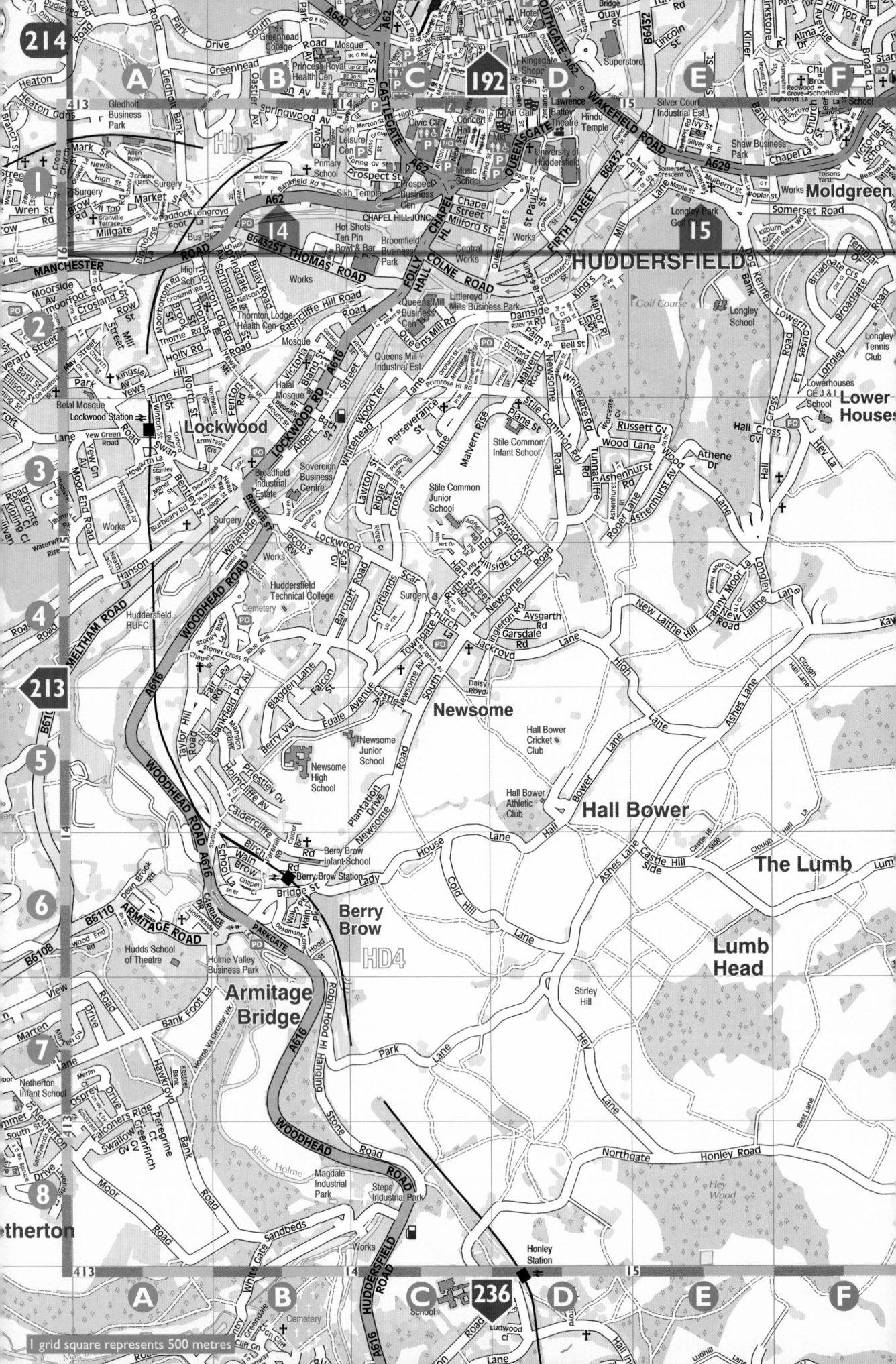

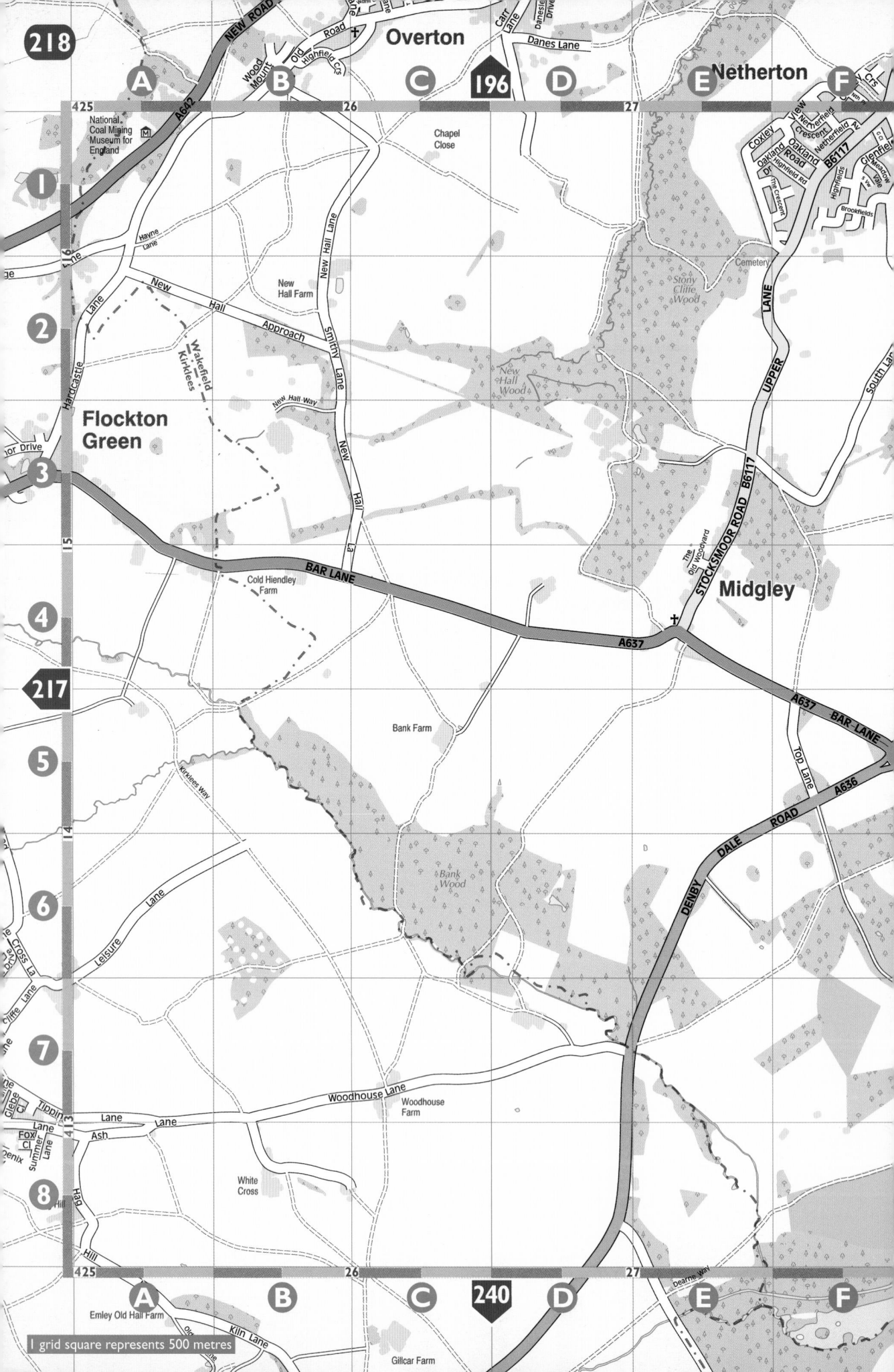

A   B   C   204   D   E   F

449   50   51

Kirk Smeaton

West Edge Road

Main Street

Manor Close

Pinfold Lane

Kirk CE Sch

Nor

PO

1

16

Middlefield Lane

Middle Field

Long Lane

2

3

A659

DONCASTER ROAD

A1(T)

Coal Pit Lane

Harewood La

Crab Tree Lane

4

Walton Wood House

Barnsdale Bar Service Area

225

A659 DONCASTER

5

North Yorkshire County
Doncaster

Long Lane

Warren House Farm

Road

Shirley Dr

School Street

WOODFIELD ROAD

A1(T)

6

Malton Road

Clayton Avenue

Bell St

Dorman Av

McLaren Av

Stricklan...

...nam Av

Sheepwalk Lane

Sheepwalk Lane

Wood

Ash

Askham

Lane

Smeaton

Tom

Saxon Cl

Barnsdale Way

Lings Lane

Wrangbrook Lane

7

Wrangbrook

Wrangbrook Lane

Sleep

Hill

Lane

8

Hollins Farm

Sleep Hill Lane

Lane

Bannister

413   449   50   51

A   B   C   248   D   E   F

1 grid square represents 500 metres

Skelbrooke

Little
Smeaton

G   H   J   205   K   L   M

I

2

Smeaton
Industrial
Park

North Yorkshire County
Doncaster

Norton
Priory

Norton Mill Lane

Walden Stubbs Road

Stubbs Road

Works

Stubbs Road

Wentbank House

Tanpit Lane

Lane

Springfield Crs

Water

nd Kirk Smeaton Road

River Went

Spittlerush Lane

Norton And Kirk Smeaton Road

Westfield   Lane

Greengate   Road

Back   Lane

West   End   Road

Cliff Hill Road

Cliff
Hill

Rvecroft Av

Barnsdale Av

Broc-O-Bank

Newthorpe Rd

Forester's Close

Trafford Rd

Adelaide
Rd

Arundel
Orch'd

Headingley
Rd

The
Close

PO

Priory Road Or Hall Lane

Street

High

Lyndhurst Dr

Lyndhurst
Close

Den

Lynhurst Close

Pinfold
Lane

Lyn
Rise

3

Norton

Manor
Close

Fir Tree
Drive

Norton County
Junior &
Infant School

Common

Lne

Ryecroft

Balk

Windmill Lane

Stygate Lane

Campsall   Road

4

Fox Covert Road
Or Whin Covert La

White   Ley   Road

Campsmount
School

Campsmount
Home Farm

Shakespeare
Av

Tennyson   Av

Wordsworth

The Avenue

Wellingtone
Drive

Church

Park

Glebe Road

East
View

Grange
Road

Field

Drive

Willow Road

Beech   Road

5

Cemetery

Woodlands
Rise

Loxley Mount

Campsall park   Road

Campsall Hall   Road

Vaughan
Road

Campsall

Askern
Swimming
Pool

Road

6

Woodfield Road

New   Road

Brayton
Gdns

Cedar
Walk

High
Street

Back   Lane

Church View

PO

Barnsdale Lane

The
Orchard

Mews

Cherry Garth

Bone Lane

Sutton   Ct

Burghwallis Road

Woodgarth
Road

7

Woodfield Farm

New Close Lane

8

Sutton

G   H   J   249   K   L   M

53   54   55

Burghwallis   Road

Lane
Gap

The Abbe's
Close

Lady

Sixrood

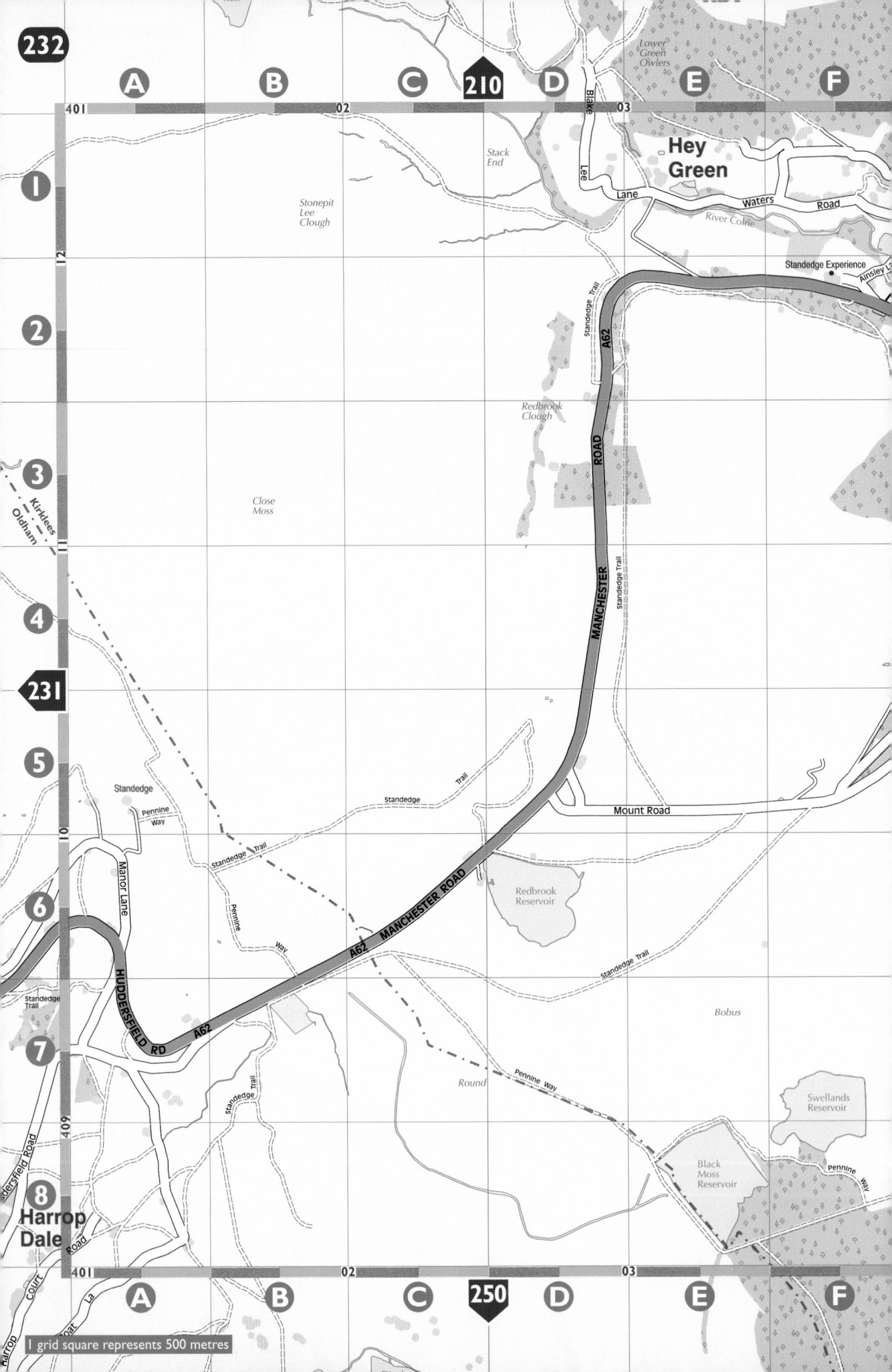

A   B   C   210   D   E   F

401   02   03

1

12

2

3

Kirklees
Oldham

4

231

5

10

6

7

409

8

401   02   03

A   B   C   250   D   E   F

Stonepit
Lee
Clough

Stack
End

Lower Green
Owlers

Hey
Green

Blake Lee Lane

Waters Road

River Colne

Standedge Experience

Ainsley L

Standedge Trail

A62

MANCHESTER ROAD

Redbrook
Clough

Close
Moss

Standedge Trail

Standedge Trail

Mount Road

Redbrook
Reservoir

Standedge
Pennine
Way

Standedge Trail

Pennine Way

MANCHESTER ROAD

A62

Manor Lane

HUDDERSFIELD RD   A62

Standedge
Trail

Standedge Trail

Round

Pennine Way

Bobus

Swellands
Reservoir

Black
Moss
Reservoir

Pennine Way

Harrop
Dale

dersfield Road

Court La

Harrop

I grid square represents 500 metres

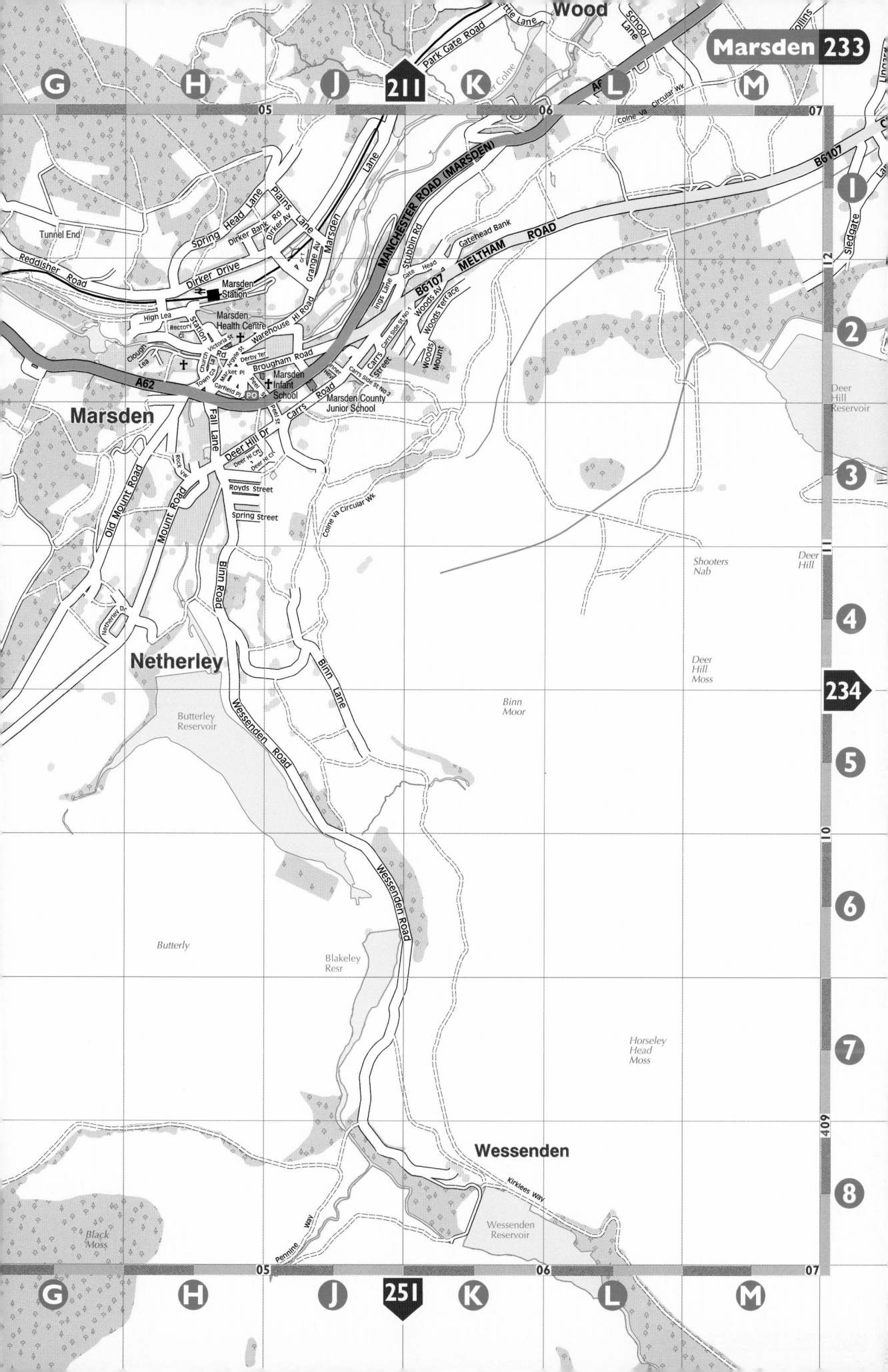

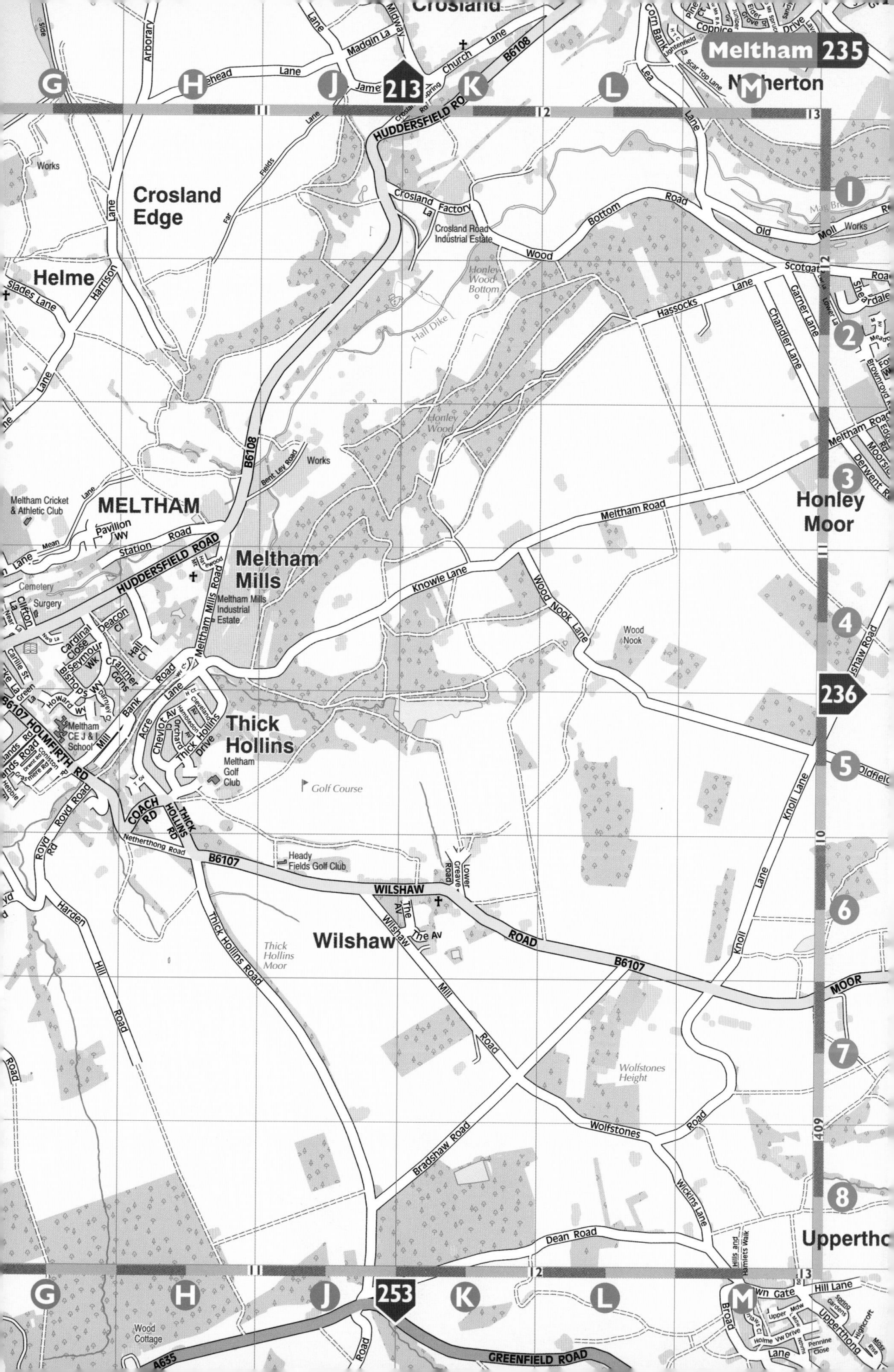

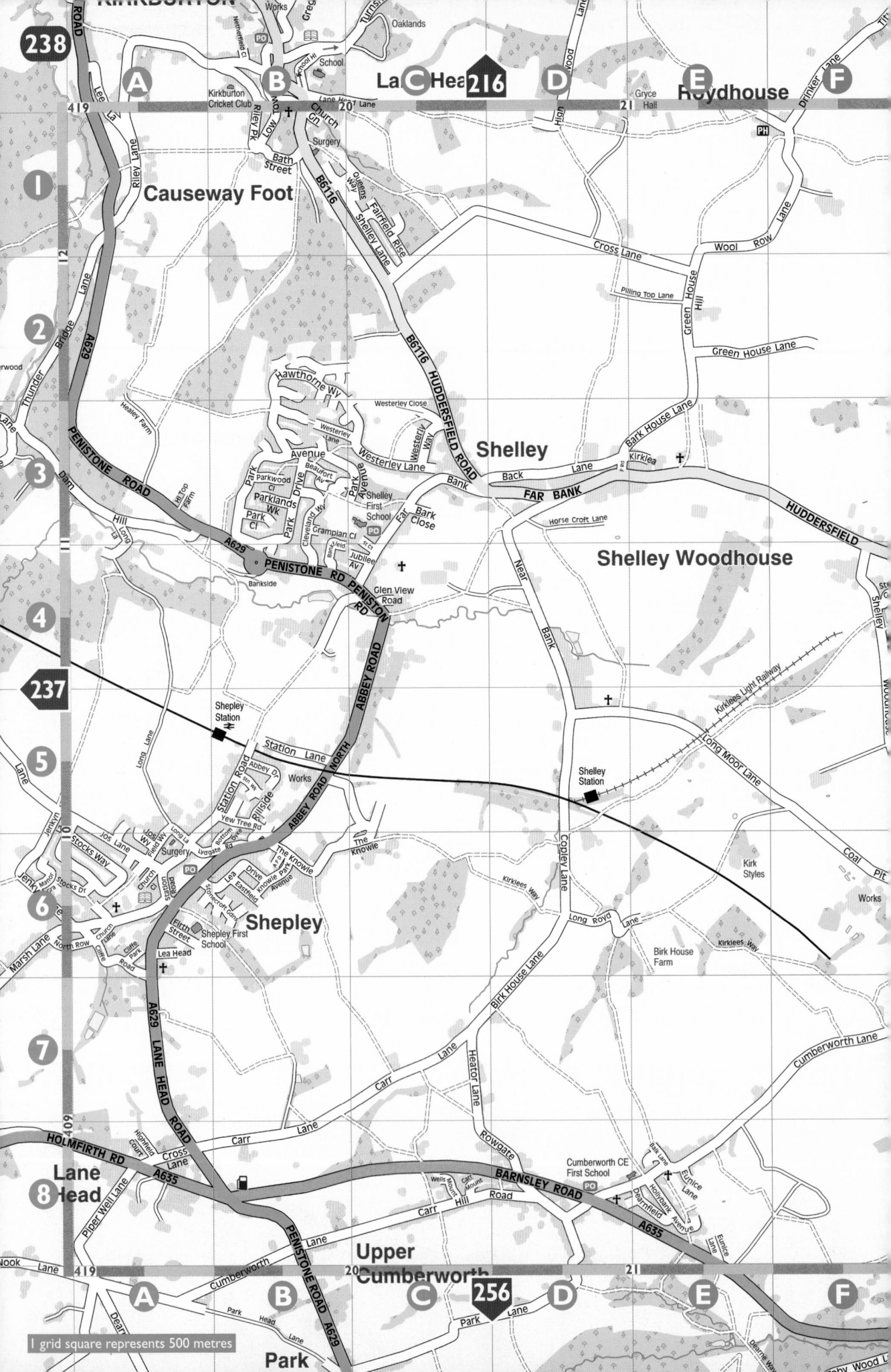

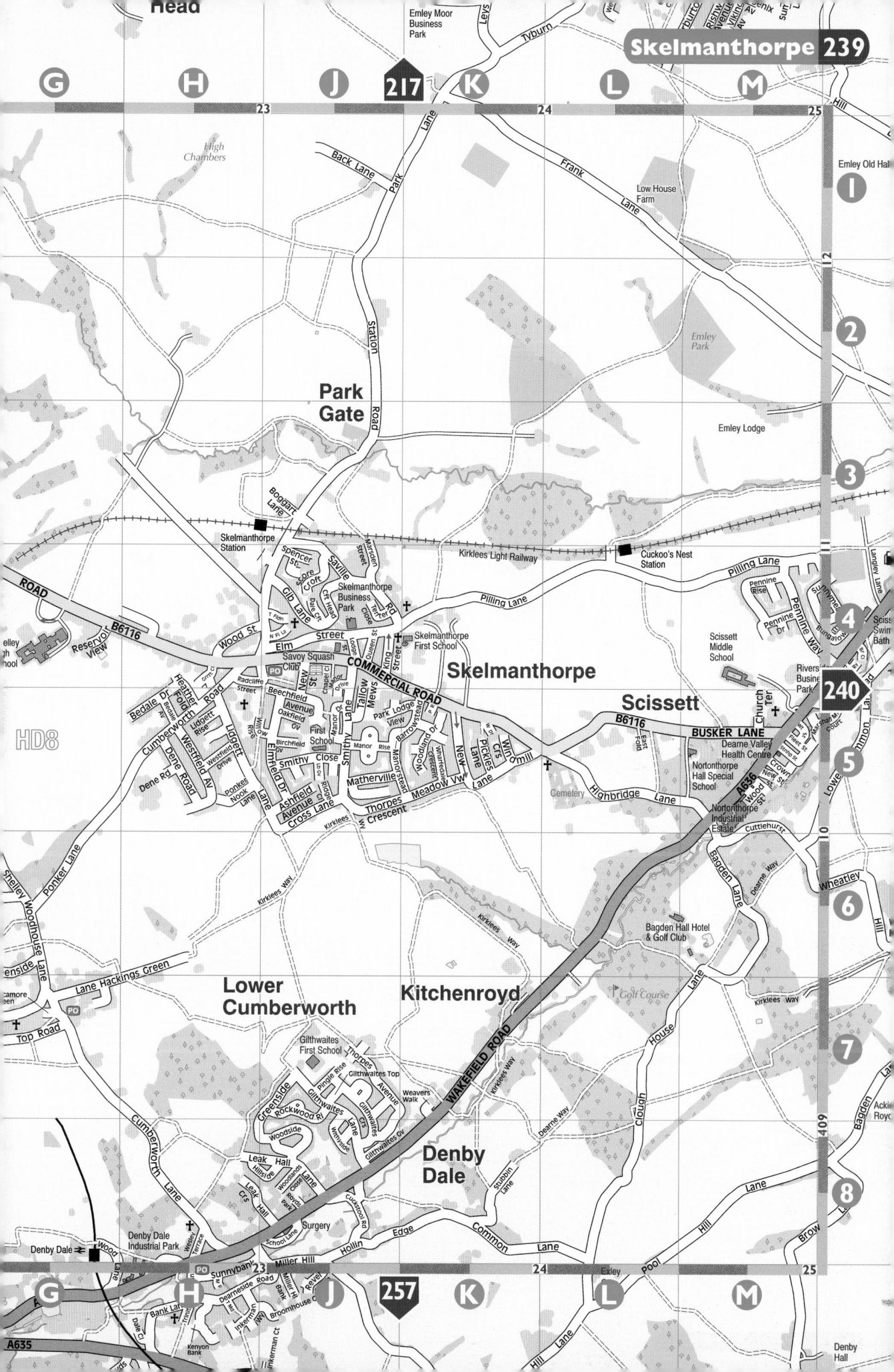

Head

Emley Moor Business Park

Tyburn

G   H   J   **217**   K   L   M

23   24   25

High Chambers

Back Lane

Frank Lane

Low House Farm

Emley Old Hall

I

2

Emley Park

Station Road

Park Gate

Emley Lodge

3

Boggart Lane

Skelmanthorpe Station

Kirklees Light Railway

Cuckoo's Nest Station

Pilling Lane

Pennine Rise

Langley Lane

ROAD

B6116

Reservoir View

Spencer St
Score Croft
Saville Street
Marsden Street

Pilling Lane

Pennine Dr

Scissett Swim Bath

Scissett Middle School

4

Wood St

Elm Street

Skelmanthorpe Business Park

Skelmanthorpe First School

Skelmanthorpe

Rivers Business Park

240

HD8

Bedale Dr
Heather
Fourth
Cumberworth Road
Westfield Av
Dene Road
Dene Rd
Lidgett Rise
Westfield Drive
Ponker Nook

Radcliffe Street
Beechfield Avenue
Oakfield Gv
Birchfield Gv
First School
Smithy Close
Elmfield Dr
Ashfield Avenue
Cross Lane
Matherville
Thorpes Crescent

New
Chapel St
Tallow Mews

COMMERCIAL ROAD

Park Lodge View
Barrowstead
Woodland Dr
Meadow Vw

Pickles Lane
New
Windmill

Scissett

B6116

East Fold

BUSKER LANE

Dearne Valley Health Centre

Nortonthorpe Hall Special School

Church Ter
Crown

New St
Wood St

Marsh Ms
Court

5

Savoy Squash Club

Manor Rise
Manor Road

Highbridge Lane

Cemetery

Nortonthorpe Industrial Estate

Cuttlehurst

A636

Lower Common

Wheatley

10

Kirklees

Ponker Lane

Shelley Woodhouse Lane

Kirklees Way

Kirklees Way

Bagden Lane

Dearne Way

6

Lane Hackings Green

Lower Cumberworth

Kitchenroyd

Bagden Hall Hotel & Golf Club

Golf Course

Kirklees Way

Bagden

Top Road

Glilthwaites First School

Thorpes

Pingle Rise

Avenue

WAKEFIELD ROAD

Kirklees Way

Clough House Lane

Kirklees Way

Acklam Royd

7

Cumberworth Lane

Greenside
Rockwood Rd
Woodside
Glilthwaites
Glilthwaites Top
Weavers Walk
Glilthwaites Lane
Wayside
Glilthwaites Gv

Leak Hall
Hillside
Leak Crs
Hall

Woodlands
Close
Lane

Denby Dale

Stubbin Lane

Pool Hill Lane

Brow

8

Denby Dale ≠

Wood Lane

Denby Dale Industrial Park

Wesley Terrace

PO

Sunnybank

23

Dearneside Road

Miller Hill Bank

Broomhouse Ct
Inkerman

Surgery

School Lane

Miller Hill

Revel

Hollin Edge

Common Lane

Exley

Pool Hill

A635

Dale Cl

Bank Lane

Kenyon Bank

Inkerman ct

Denby Hall

G   H   J   **257**   K   L   M

23   24   25

218

Park Mill

Clayton West

High Hoyland

239

258

1 grid square represents 500 metres

G H J **219** K L M

G H J **259** K L M

1
2
3
4
242
5
6
7
8

M1

A637

Beaumont Drive

Bretton
Country Park

Barnsley Boundary

29

Wakefield
Barnsley

Lower
Lake

Haigh

Junction 38

Jebb Lane

Longsides

High
Wood

Huddersfield Road

Haigh Lane

Moorhouse La

Near
Moon Farm

Barnsley Boundary Walk

River Dearne

Dearne Way

WALK ROYD HILL

PARK HILL

SMITHIES HILL

M1

Spring Ram
Business
Park

Birthwaite
Hall

Dearne Way

A637

HUDDERSFIELD ROAD

Ballfield
Lane

Darton Station

Lane

Upper Field Lane

Upper Field Lane

Cawthorne
Park

Darton
High School

Brookhill Rd

Holme Road

Walk Royd

Highfields

Birthwaite Rd

Ballfield Lane

Priestley
Av

Cooper Rd

Windsor
Avenue

Bretton
Close

Bretton
Road

Airedale Rd

Allendale Road

Lynton

Swallow Cl

Strafford
St

Wentworth
Road

Churchfield

Kexbrough

Primary
School

Infant
School

Uplands Av

Churchfield Lane

Churchfield Close

Hawthorne Ct

Kibroyd Dr

Bence Lane

Beaumont Rd

Kexbrough Dr

Roman Rd

Lansdowne Crs

Hedge Lane

Council
Offices

Alan
Rd

Agnes

Richard Rd

CHURCH ST

Church Close

Mill Lane

BARNSLEY

Meyrick
Dr

Thurdale

Bence

Meadow

Chedworth
Close

M1

Barnsley Boundary Walk

Cinder
Hill

Cawthorne Lane

29
30
31

Barugh

Baruch Lane

BARUCH LANE

CLIFF HILL

Five
Acres

Barnby

Da

Darton

409

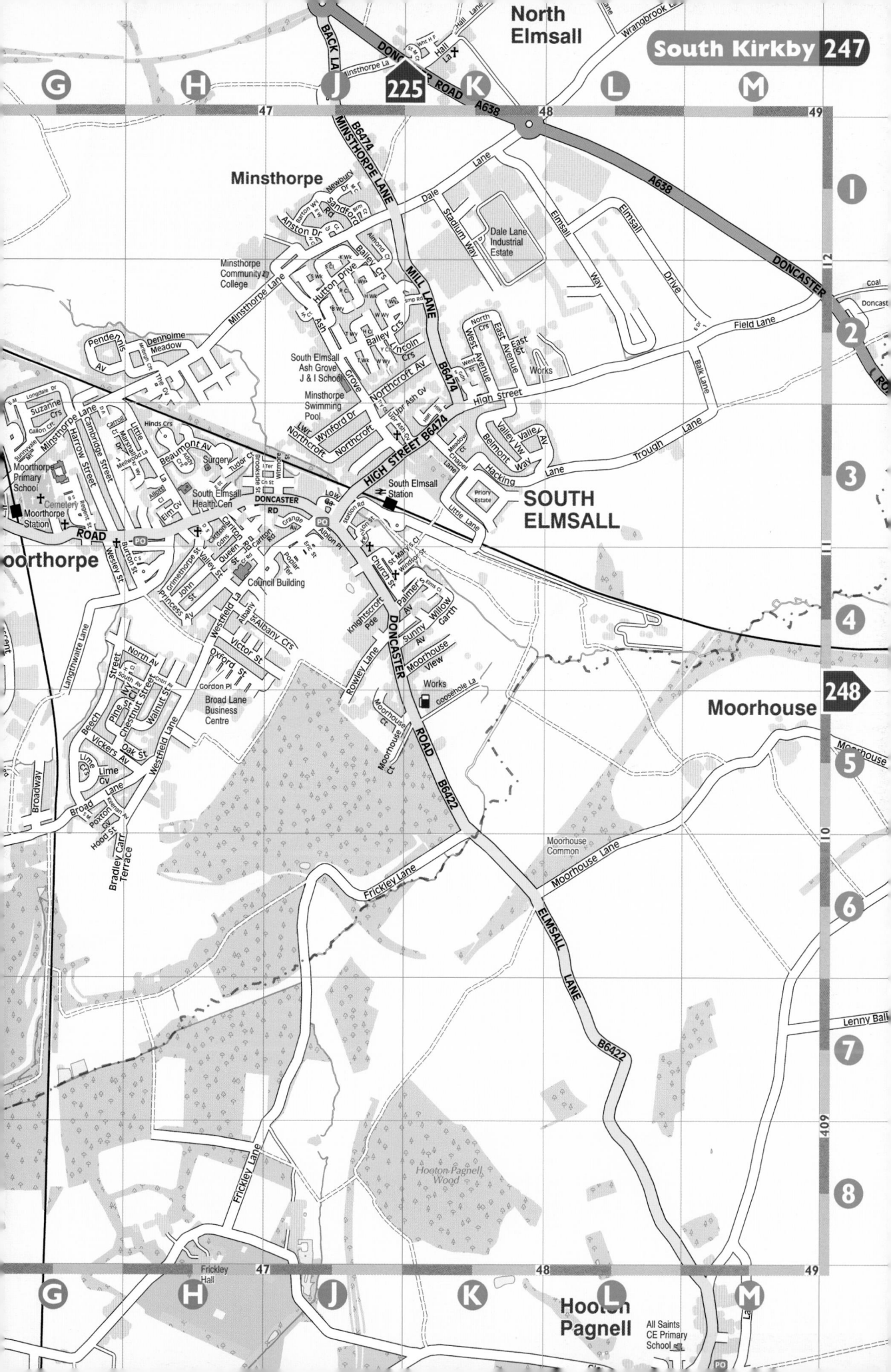

A   B   C   D   E   F

449   50   51

226

Sleep Hill Lane

Skelbrooke

Bannister Lane

A1(T)

1

DONCASTER

Coal   Pit

Lane

Doncaster Road

Straight Lane

Doncaster Lane

2

LANE

ROAD

A638

Wakefield
Doncaster

Stubbs
Hall

Hazel Lane

Stubbs Bridge

Leys Lane

3

4

Moorhouse Lane

Hampole Field Lane

North Fld Rd. Moorhouse Gap

Old street

Hazel La

A638

Main Street

Hampole

5

Old Street

6

Lenny Balk

Hampole Grange

Junction 38

7

409

Hampole Wood

8

449   50   51

A   B   C   D   E   F

Ling   Field   Road

A1(M)

Windy Mount

Lound Hill

Lound Hill

G H J **227** K L M **Sutton**

53 54 55

1

Burghwallis Lane

Lady Gap Lane

Sim

Scorcher Hills Lane

Stony Lane

Grange Lane

The Abbe's Close

Burghwallis

The Abbe's Walk **2**

Squirrel Wood

Burghwallis Grange

Stony Croft Lane

Ows

North Pa **3**

St

Robin Hood Golf Club

Green Lane

North Park Lane

Golf Course **4**

Mill Lane

Strawthorne

Finghall Rd

Bellerby Road

Willowbrook

Fullerton Close

Owston Skellow First School

Carcroft

Owston Lane

Crabgate Lane

Newlands Av

Harmby Cl

Bellerby Pl

Cranfield Dr

Acacia Road

Crossfield Road

Ash Rd

Lane

Road

Lodge Road

Skellow

Owston Park Golf Club

Owston Lane

Crabgate Drive

Sherwood

Leyburn Road

Amberley Close

Lavenham Pl

Waltham Cl

Hauxwell

Wrigley Place

Apperley Place

Lawndale

Cross Hl

Cranfield Dr

Crossfield Dr

Crossfield Dr

Elm Road

Mansfield Crs

George St

Edward Road

Rydal Rd

Markham Avenue

Owston Road

Paxton Avenue

New Street

A(T)

Hampole Balk

HAMPOLE BALK B1220

Cross HI

Wri

Bridge

South Dr

Skellow Farm

Skellow Fairs Gdns

SKELLOW ROAD

Laurel

Briar Road

Birch Av

Beech Av

Poplar Terrace

Charles Street

Chestnut Avenue

Milton Rd

Crasmere Rd

Borrowdale Cl

Grisdale Gdns

Glenwood Rd

5

Howden Avenue

Ings Lane

Humber Rd

Humber Av

Ridgill Av

B1220

PO

Willington Rd

Brenton Rd

Sandyfields Vw

Dalcroft Rd

Victor St

Langdale Road

Bullcroft Cl

Trafalgar Rd

Crossdale Gdns

Butlermere Rd

Owston Road

ASKERN R

6

Repton Road

Roberton Rd

Chapel Street

X

Carcroft Health Centre

Park Avenue

High Street

Queen's Road

PO

SKELLOW ROAD B1220

Works

Station Road

7

Red House

Cemetery

Red House Lane

Planet Road

Carcroft Industrial Estate

Wellsyke Road

Works

Brooklands Rd

Bentle

Hangthwaite Road

Holmeroyd Road

A638

A638

Roman Ridge

Kingfisher Rd

Kingfisher Road

Kestrel Dr

Ogley Cl

Falcon Cl

Mill Lane

Fern Bank

Fernbank School

Planet Road

Church Lane B1220

James Road

Victoria Road

Edward Road

Alexandra Road

8

Elmwood Avenue

St Vincent Av

Lawn Avenue

Beaumont Av

Great North Rd

Bosworth Road

Ashburton Close

Cambourne Cl

Whinfell Close

Park Way

Village Council Bldg

PO

John Street

Adwick Station

Adwick Lar

Kennington Av

The Circuit

Shaftsbury Avenue

Harwood Av

Lutterworth

Cherton Avenue

Swinbourne Avenue

Lawn Avenue

A638

GREAT

53

ADWICK LE STREET

54

Town Hall

Park View

55

G H J K L M

Adwick School

Tenter Balk Lane

Ridge Balk Lane

Works

Fair Vw Av

B1220

232

A B C D E F

401 02 03

1

Black
Moss
Reservoir

Pennine
Way

Diggle
Resr

Works

Green

2

Ravenstone
Rocks

Kirklees
Oldham

3

Running
Hill Head

South
Clough

Oldham
Way

Hill

Lane
Gate

4

Broadstone

Hill

Hollin
Brown
Knoll

Oldham Way

5

Pobgreen
Lane

Stones La

Pobgreen

Upperwood
House

6

Oldham
Way

Saddlewor

Greenfield
Reservoir

Dick

7

405

Oldham Way

Yeoman
Hey
Resr

Ashway
Hey

Ashway
Rocks

Brook Lane

8

Alderman's

Oldham Way

Ashway
Stone

401 02 03

A B C D E F

Raven
Stones
Brow

1 grid square represents 500 metres

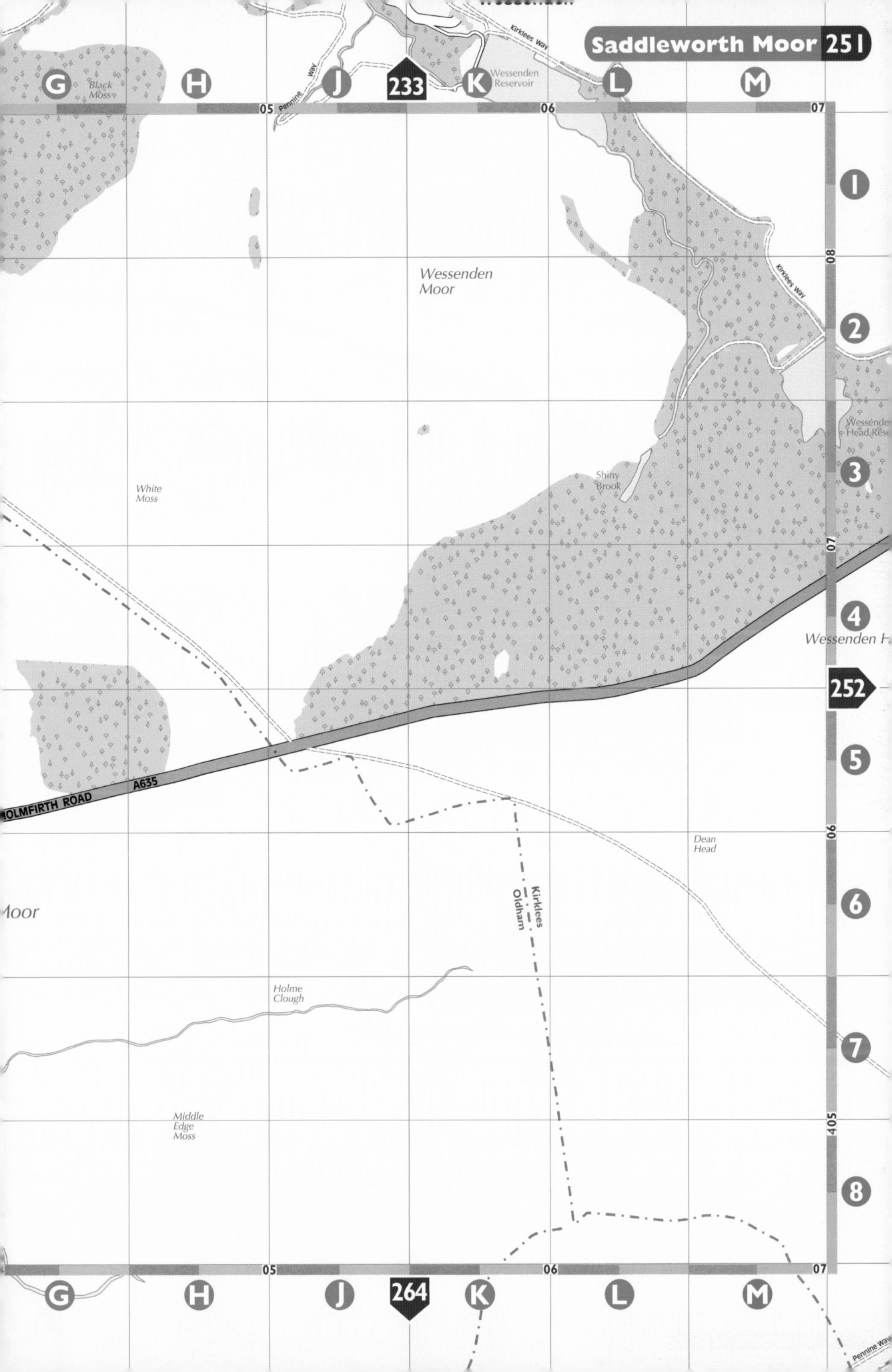

G   H   J   **233**   K   L   M

Kirklees Way

05   06   07

Wessenden Reservoir

1

Kirklees Way

2

Wessenden Moor

Wessenden Head Resr

3

White Moss

Shiny Brook

07

4

Wessenden H

252

5

06

Dean Head

Moor

6

Kirklees Oldham

HOLMFIRTH ROAD   A635

Holme Clough

7

4·05

Middle Edge Moss

8

05   06   07

G   H   J   **264**   K   L   M

Pennine Way

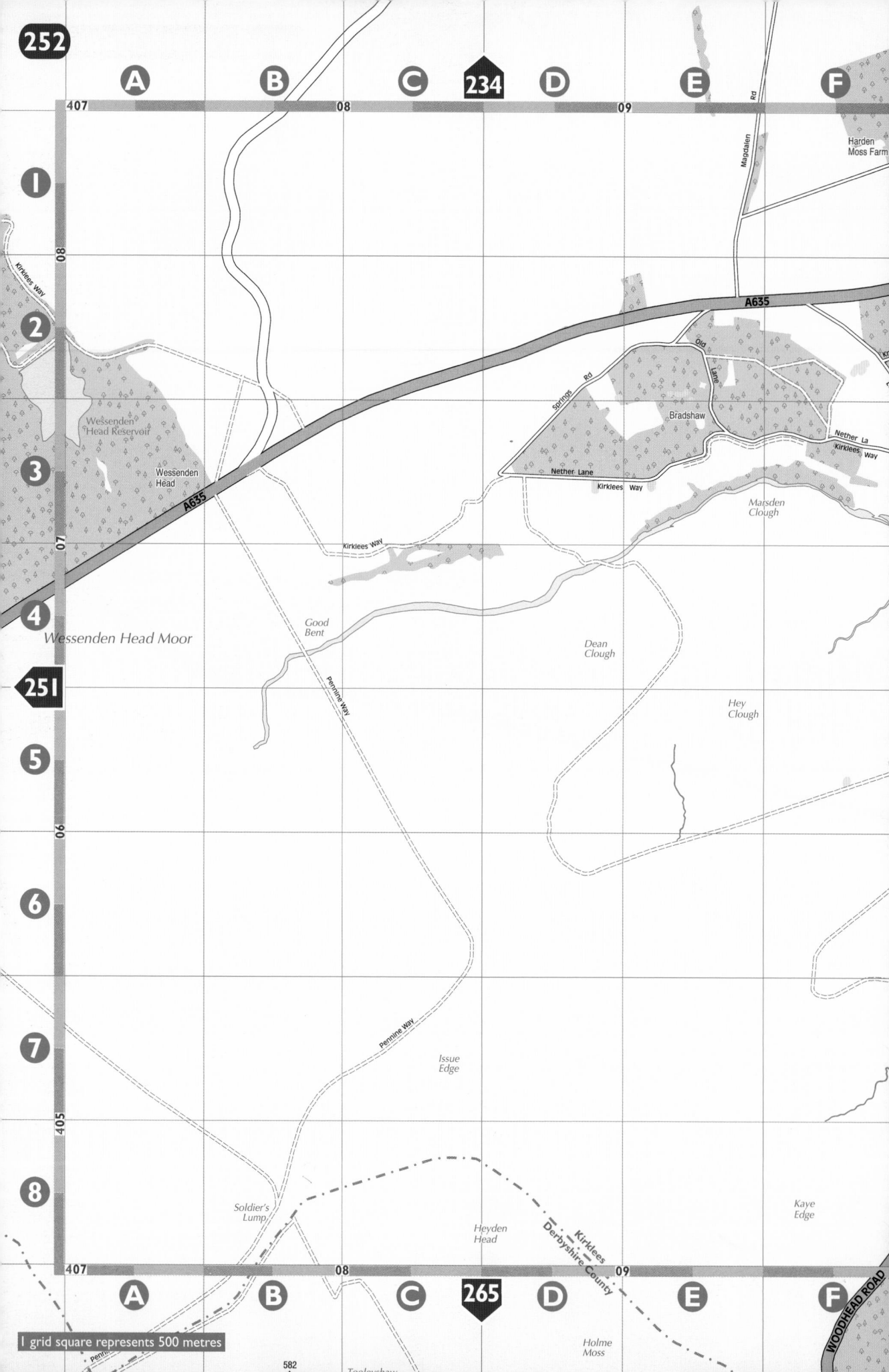

Ⓐ   Ⓑ   Ⓒ   **234**   Ⓓ   Ⓔ   Ⓕ

407   08   09

Magdalen Rd

Harden Moss Farm

Ⓘ

Kirklees Way

A635

2

Springs Rd

Old Lane

Bradshaw

Nether La

3

A635

Nether Lane

Kirklees Way

Kirklees Way

Marsden Clough

Wessenden Head Reservoir

Wessenden Head

07

Kirklees Way

4

Good Bent

Dean Clough

Wessenden Head Moor

◄ **251**

Pennine Way

Hey Clough

5

06

6

Pennine Way

7

Issue Edge

405

8

Soldier's Lump

Kaye Edge

Heyden Head

Kirklees Derbyshire County

Holme Moss

Woodhead Road

407   08   09

Ⓐ   Ⓑ   Ⓒ   **265**   Ⓓ   Ⓔ   Ⓕ

582

Tooleyshaw

I grid square represents 500 metres

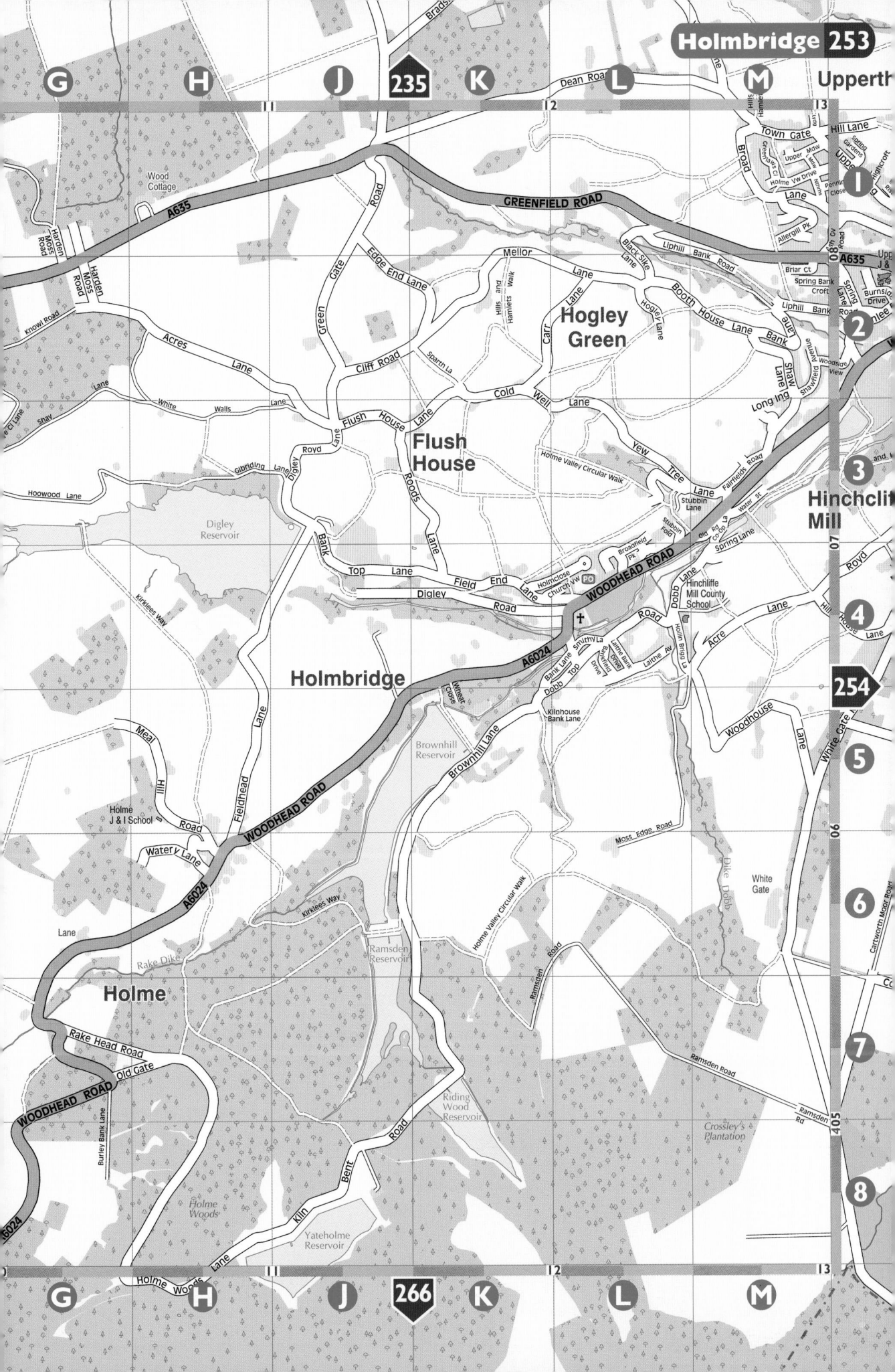

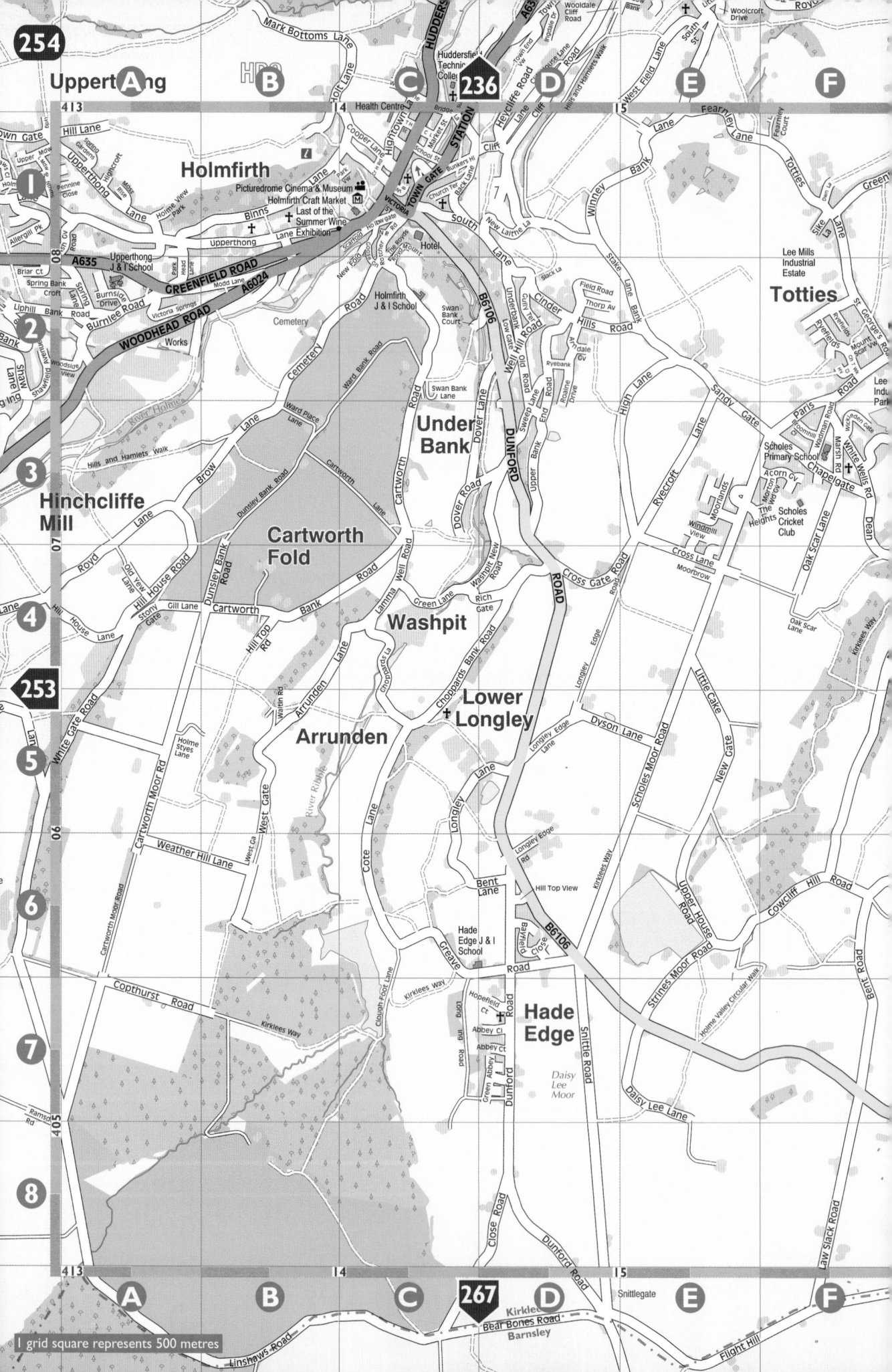

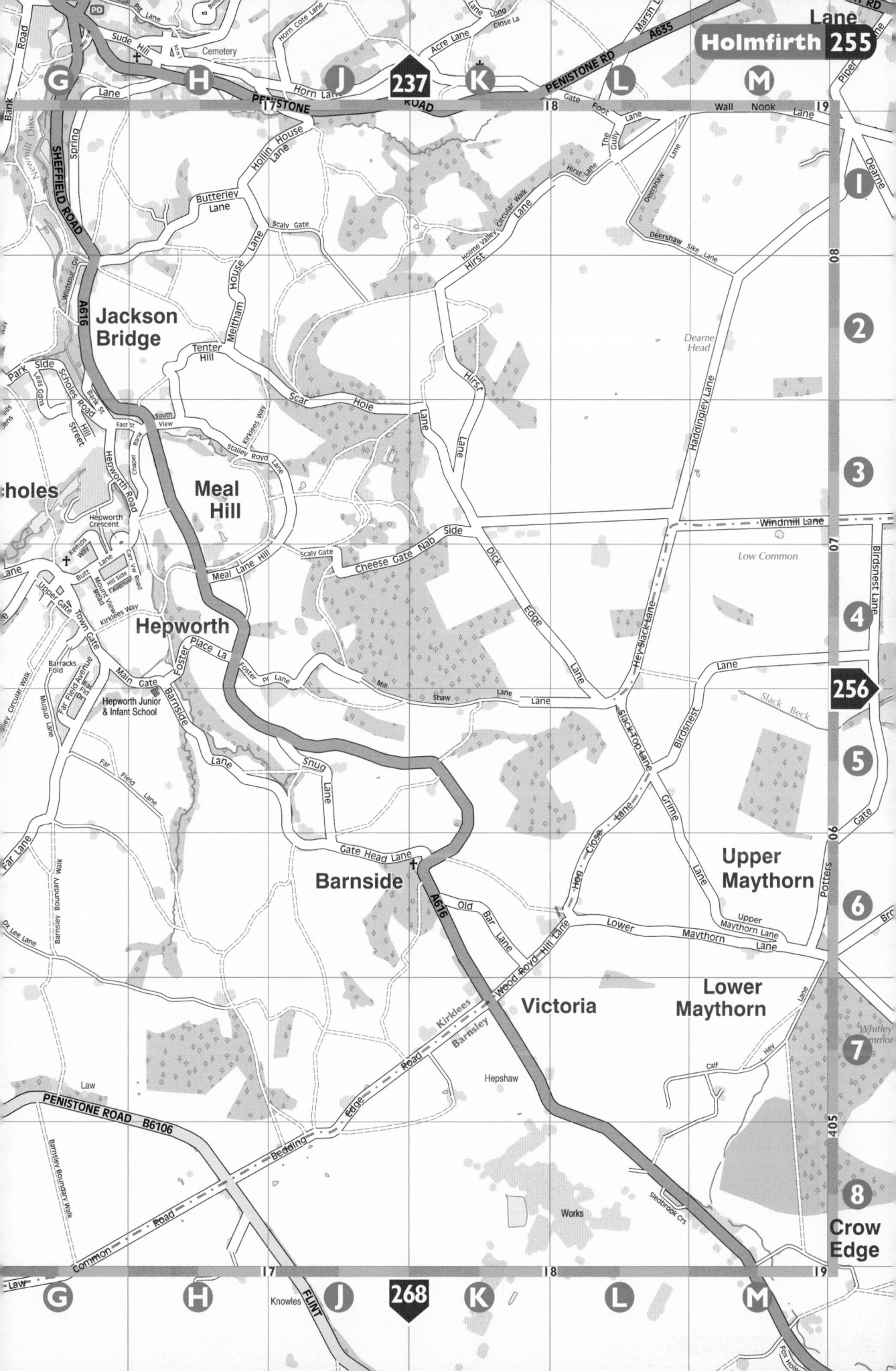

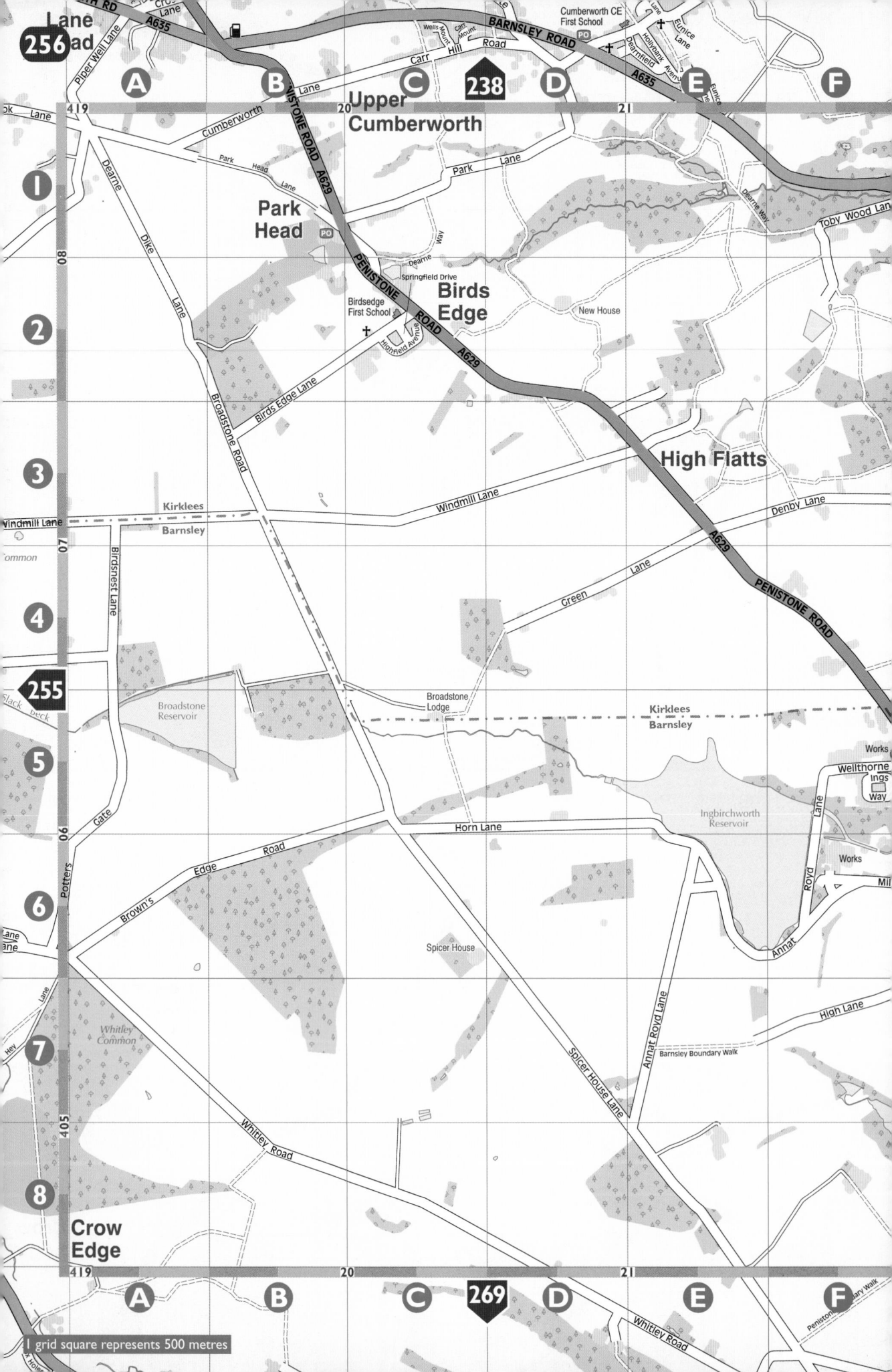

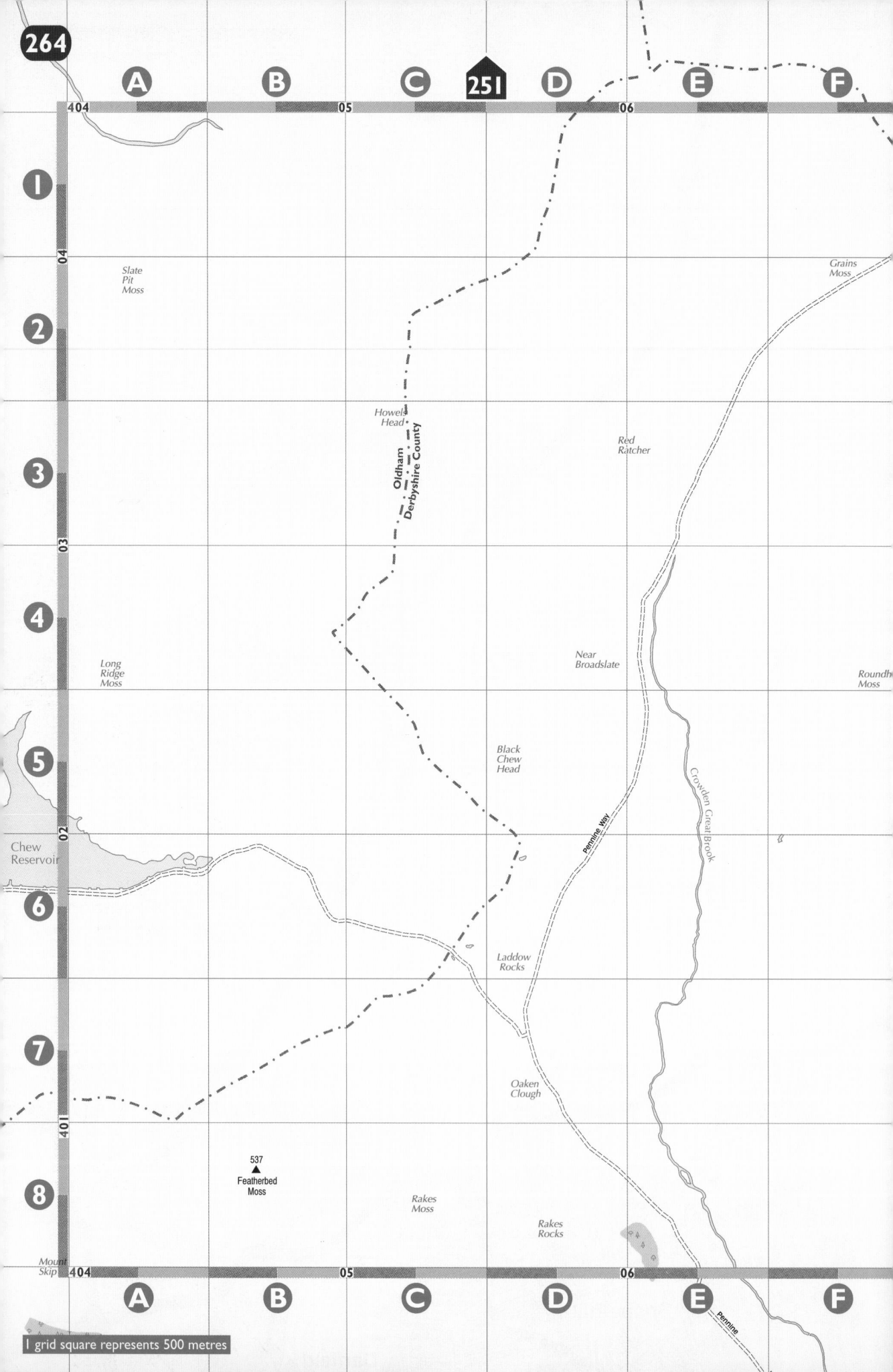

251

A   B   C   D   E   F

404   05   06

1

04

2

Slate
Pit
Moss

3

03

Howels
Head

Oldham
Derbyshire County

4

Red
Ratcher

Long
Ridge
Moss

Near
Broadslate

Roundh
Moss

5

Black
Chew
Head

02

Crowden Great Brook

Chew
Reservoir

6

Laddow
Rocks

Pennine Way

7

Oaken
Clough

401

8

537
▲
Featherbed
Moss

Rakes
Moss

Rakes
Rocks

Grains
Moss

Mount
Skip   404   05   06

A   B   C   D   E   F

Pennine

1 grid square represents 500 metres

G
H
J
252
K
L
M
A6024

7
08
09
10

Soldier's
Lump

Pennine Way

Holme
Moss

WOODHEAD ROAD

1

582
Black Hill

Tooleyshaw
Moss

Kirklees
shire County

04

2

Upper
Heyden

A6024

Sliddens
Moss

Tooleyshaw
Moor

3
-bysr

03

Stable
Clough

Crowden
Meadows

White
Low

4

266

Crowden Little Brook

Heyden
Moor

Binns

5

A6024

Binns
Moss

Heyden Brook

02

Crowden
Little
Moor

Black
Hill
End

Tup
Stones

6

Grea
Intak

7

Hey
Moss

Butterley
Moss

401

Hey
Clough

Oaksike
Clough

Heyden
Bridge

8

7
08
09
10

G
H
J
K
L
M
A6024

Hey
Edge

Woodhead

266

266

A6024

HEAD ROAD

410

A

Holme Woods Lane

Holme
Woods

Bent

Kiln

B

Yateh
Reserv

C

253

D

E

F

11

12

1

04

I

2

Ramsden
Clough

Twizle
Head
Moss

3

Kirklees
Derbyshire County

Kirklees
Barnsley

03

able
ough

4

265

265

024

02

West
Withens
Clough

Great
Grains
Clough

Grains
Moss

5

Withens
Edge

Withens
Moor

Dewhill
Naze

Barnsley
Derbyshire County

6

Great
Intake

Cat
Clough

7

Little
Intake

401

Stone
Low

Pikenaze
Moor

8

en
e

410

A

11

B

C

12

D

E

F

1 grid square represents 500 metres

Hawthorn
Clough

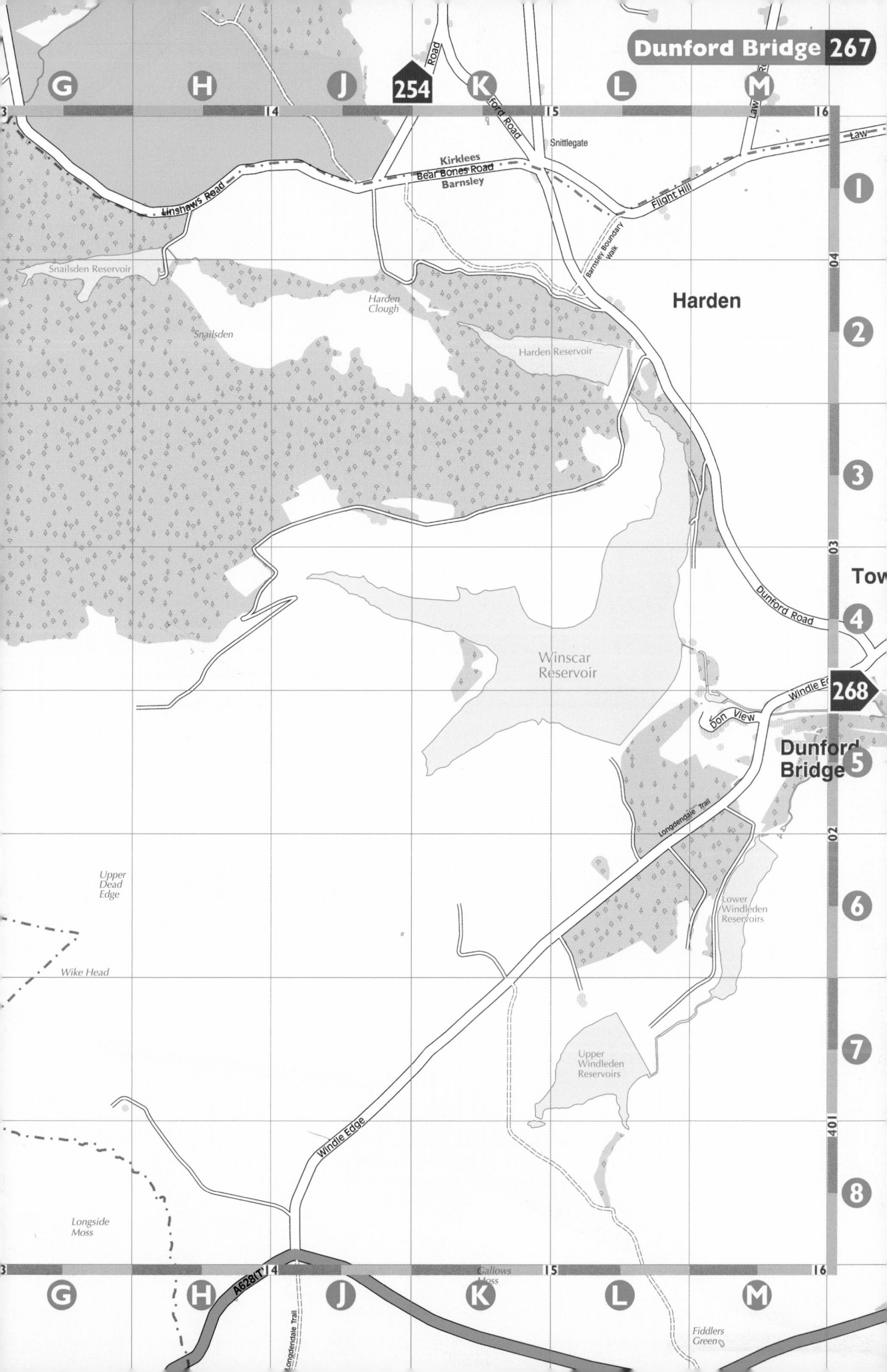

G   H   J   **254**   K   L   M

Road
Kirklees
Bear Bones Road
Barnsley
Snittlegate
Linshaws Road
Flight Hill
Barnsley Boundary Walk
Law

I

Harden

Snailsden Reservoir
Harden Clough
Harden Reservoir

2

Snailsden

3

Dunford Road

Tow

4

Winscar Reservoir

Windle E
268
Don View

Dunford Bridge

5

Upper Dead Edge
Longdendale Trail
Lower Windleden Reservoirs

6

Wike Head

Upper Windleden Reservoirs

7

401

Windle Edge

8

Longside Moss

Longdendale Trail
A628(T)
Gallows Moss
Fiddlers Green

G   H   J   K   L   M

A B C D E F

255

416   17   18

1

04

2

3

03

Carlecotes

Townhead

02

River Don

4

267

Dunford
Lodge

5

Thurlstone
Moors

Wogden
Clough

6

401

7

8

A628(T)

416   17   18

A B C D E F

Barmings

Long
Moor
Clough

Knowles

FLINT LANE B6106

BENTS ROAD

Town Brook

Brook Hill Lane

Soug

Works

Sledbrook Crs

Fox Holes Cv

Eltock Farm

Middlecliffe
Drive

Common   Road

Law

Horsley Boundary Walk

Hordron Road

1 grid square represents 500 metres

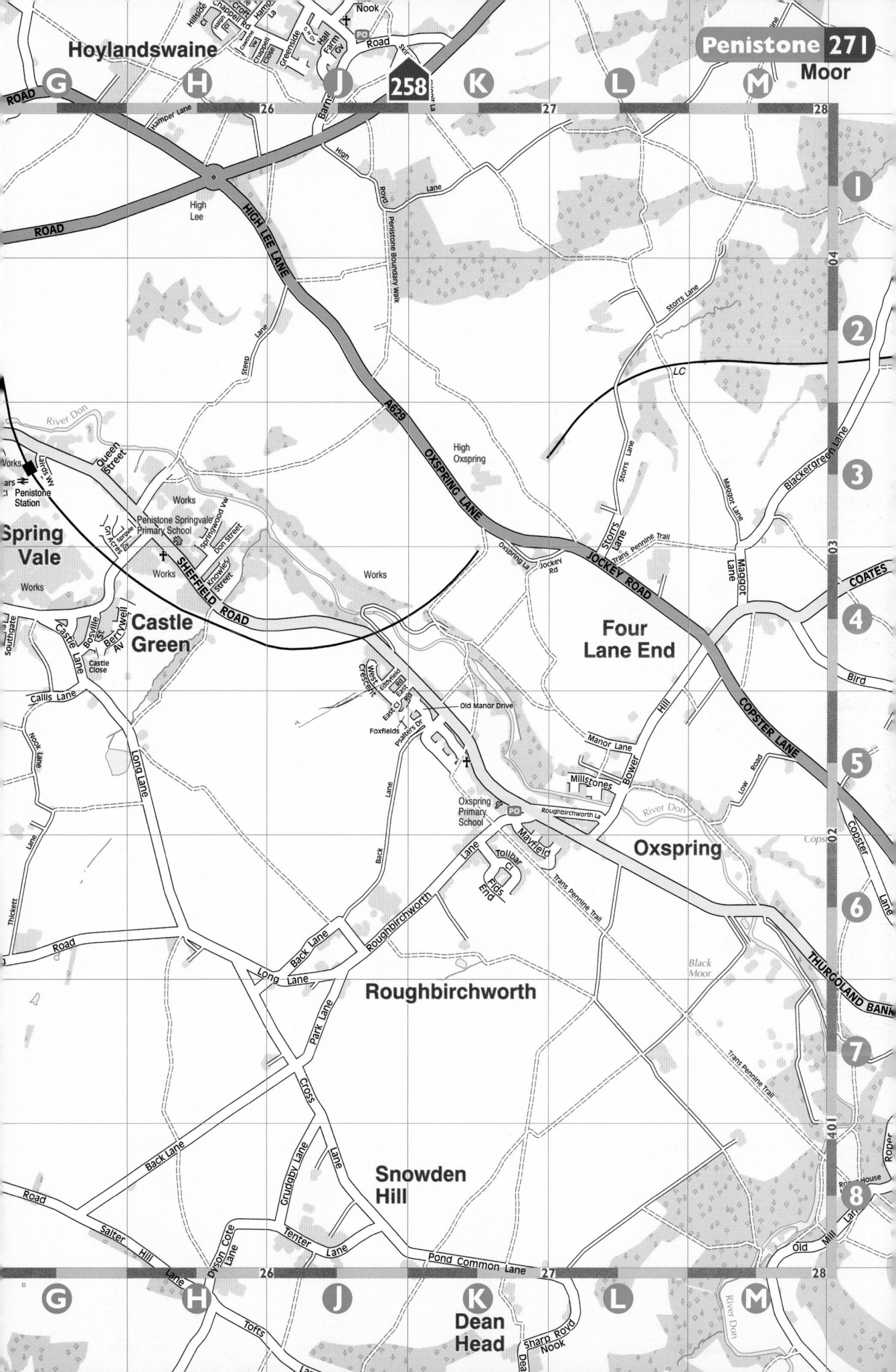

Hoylandswaine

Moor

Spring Vale

Castle Green

Four Lane End

Oxspring

Roughbirchworth

Snowden Hill

Dean Head

258

COATES

River Don

Aberford 91 M7
Ackton 179 J6
Ackworth Moor Top 224 A1
Addingham 19 G6
Addingham Moorside 36 F2
Adel 86 E2
Adwalton 129 J8
Agbrigg 13 J9
Ainley Top 191 K2
Airedale 158 D7
Aire View 34 B4
Allerton 103 L6
Allerton Bywater 157 L2
Almondbury 215 H2
Altofts 178 A1
Alverthorpe 176 A6
Alwoodley 87 L1
Alwoodley Gates 66 A8
Alwoodley Park 65 H8
Ambler Thorn 124 D6
Angram 33 M8
Apperley Bridge 84 A3
Appleton Roebuck 73 M4
Ardsley 262 B7
Armitage Bridge 214 B7
Armley 108 F6
Arrunden 254 B5
Arthington 43 M8
Arthursdale 90 B6
Askwith 40 B1
Athersley North 243 H6
Athersley South 243 J7
Austhorpe 112 A6
Badsworth 224 F4
Bagley 107 G2
Baildon 82 F3
Baildon Green 82 C4
Bailiff Bridge 148 C6
Balderstone 228 D4
Bank End 18 A5
Bank Top 105 L1
Bank Top 169 H1
Bantam Grove 152 F2
Barcroft 79 H6
Bardsey 67 L2
Barkisland 189 K2
Barkston Ash 115 L1
Barnbow Carr 112 E1
Barnside 255 J6
Barnsley 261 J7
Barugh 242 A8
Barugh Green 260 A2
Barwick in Elmet 90 E8
Batley 173 L1
Batley Carr 173 L3
Battyeford 194 A1
Beal 161 K7
Beamsley 19 G1
Beck Bottom 175 L3
Beck Foot 81 G5
Beechcliffe 57 M5
Beechwood 89 G8
Beeston 131 G4
Beeston Hill 8 C9
Beeston Park Side 131 J6
Beeston Royds 130 D3
Beggarington Hill 174 E1
Belfield 206 F7
Belle Green 244 E7
Belle Isle 132 A7
Belle Vue 13 K7
Ben Rhydding 39 G3
Bentgate 229 J2
Berry Brow 214 B6
Bickerton 31 L4
Bierley 127 K5
Biggin 117 M4
Bilton in Ainsty 32 C5
Bingley 81 G3
Birchencliffe 191 J4
Birds Edge 256 C2
Birkby 14 A1
Birkenshaw 128 D8
Birkenshaw Bottoms 150 E2
Birkhouse 148 E8
Birkin 161 J4
Birks 152 C4
Birstall 151 G4
Birstall Smithies 151 G7
Blacker 242 E7
Black Hill 2 A2
Blackley 191 L6
Black Moor 87 J2
Blackmoorfoot 213 G7
Blackshaw Head 142 B3
Bleak Hey Nook 231 L7
Bogthorn 79 G2
Bolton 105 H2
Bolton Percy 73 J7
Bolton Woods 105 G2
Booth 145 G3
Boothroyd 173 J6
Boothtown 146 C4
Booth Wood 188 E8
Boston Spa 48 E3
Bottom Boat 155 L8
Bottomley 189 M3
Boulder Clough 166 E1
Bowling 127 K2
Bracken Bank 79 H3
Brackenhall 192 D2
Bracken Hill 171 L7
Bracken Park 67 H7
Brackenthwaite 26 A3
Bradford 4 D6
Bradley 171 H8
Bradley Mills 15 M1
Bradshaw 124 B5
Bradshaw 211 J5
Bradup 58 D1
Braithwaite 56 F6
Brakenhill 201 L8
Bramham 69 M3
Bramhope 63 L3
Bramley 107 L5
Brandy Carr 175 M2
Braython 24 E7
Brearley 144 C6

Brierley 245 H3
Briestfield 195 J7
Brighouse 170 B4
Briscoerigg 25 G4
Broad Carr 190 E2
Brockholes 236 F4
Brookfoot 170 A3
Brookhouse 123 K6
Brooklands 111 G1
Brotherton 159 M6
Brown Moor 112 B7
Bruntcliffe 152 A3
Brunthwaite 36 C5
Buckley 206 C3
Buersil Head 228 E5
Burghwallis 249 K2
Burley 108 F4
Burley in Wharfedale 39 M5
Burley Woodhead 39 L8
Burmantofts 110 B5
Burn Bridge 26 E2
Burnedge 229 G5
Burton Salmon 160 A2
Buttershaw 125 M6
Byram 160 A7
Cackleshaw 78 F4
Calderbrook 185 M5
Calder Grove 197 L8
Caldermoor 185 J8
Calverley 84 E8
Cambridge 41 L7
Campall 227 M6
Camp Town 87 K3
Carcroft 249 L4
Carlecotes 268 C3
Carleton 203 H1
Carlinghow 151 H7
Carlton 155 G3
Carlton 243 M5
Carr Gate 176 A1
Cartworth Fold 254 B3
Castleford 157 K7
Castleford Ings 158 A5
Castle Green 271 H4
Castle Street 164 A1
Castley 43 K6
Catherine Slack 124 E8
Cat Hill 257 M7
Catshaw 269 K3
Catterton 51 L6
Causeway Foot 124 A3
Causeway Foot 238 A1
Cawthorne 258 F2
Chapel Allerton 220 C2
Chapel Fenton 94 F8
Chapeltown 87 L6
Charlestown 83 G4
Charlestown 142 F3
Chat Hill 125 J1
Chequerfield 181 H8
Chevin End 61 M1
Chickenley 174 D7
Chidswell 174 D3
Chiserley 143 L1
Church Clough 74 A3
Church Fenton 94 F8
Churwell 130 E7
Claremount 11 H3
Clayton 125 L2
Clayton Heights 125 L4
Clayton West 240 C4
Cleckheaton 150 A6
Clerk Green 173 J2
Cliff End 191 K8
Clifford 69 M1
Clifton 41 G1
Clifton 170 F4
Clough 185 J7
Clough 229 M8
Clough Foot 162 D2
Clough Head 167 L5
Clough Head 212 D3
Cockersdale 129 H6
Cockley Hill 193 M6
Colden 120 C8
Cold Hiendley 221 M5
Coley 147 M4
Collingham 47 H7
Colne Bridge 193 J1
Colton 111 L8
Combs 195 M3
Compton 47 M8
Cononley 34 A3
Cookridge 63 M8
Copley 168 C4
Copley Hill 151 H4
Cornholme 140 D5
Cottingley 81 J7
Cotton Stones 166 E6
Cowcliffe 192 B3
Cowling 54 E4
Cowmes 215 L1
Cowthorpe 30 F1
Coxley 196 F7
Crackenedge 173 M5
Cragg Hill 85 L6
Cragg Vale 165 M2
Crawshaw 217 J6
Cridling Stubbs 183 G7
Crigglestone 198 B8
Cringles 18 B8
Crofton 200 A6
Crompton Fold 229 L5
Cromwell Bottom 169 L5
Crosland Edge 235 H1
Crosland Hill 213 J4
Crosland Moor 213 L3
Crossflatts 59 H8
Cross Gates 111 J5
Cross Green 132 B1
Cross Hills 34 F8
Crossley 172 C6
Crossley Hall 104 A7
Cross Roads 79 G5
Crow Edge 256 A8
Crow Nest 81 K3
Cubley 270 E6
Cudworth 244 E8

Cudworth Common 262 F2
Cullingworth 79 K8
Cundy Cross 261 M5
Cutsyke 179 L1
Daisy Hill 103 M4
Daisy Hill 130 E8
Dalton 193 H8
Damems 79 H4
Dam Head 147 H3
Darrington 203 L1
Darton 242 A6
Daw Cross 26 C2
Dearnley 207 H2
Deighton 193 H2
Denholme 101 L6
Denholme Clough 102 A8
Denholme Edge 101 L5
Denholme Gate 123 M1
Denshaw 230 F4
Denton 21 J8
Dewsbury 173 L7
Dewsbury Moor 173 G5
Dockroyd 78 E5
Dodworth 260 B7
Dodworth Bottom 260 A8
Dodworth Green 259 M8
Dog Hill 230 A7
Dogley Lane 215 L5
Draughton 17 L1
Drighlington 129 H8
Drub 150 B4
Dudley Hill 127 L4
Dunford Bridge 267 M5
Dunkeswick 44 E4
Durkar 198 C7
Durn 207 L1
Earlsheaton 174 A7
East Ardsley 153 J7
East Bierley 128 B7
Eastburn 35 J8
East Carlton 63 G3
East Garforth 113 L6
East Hardwick 203 H4
East Keswick 46 E8
East Moor 177 H1
East Morton 59 C5
East Rigton 68 A1
Eastwood 142 D6
Eccleshill 105 K1
Eccup 65 J5
Ecklands 269 M4
Edgerton 191 M6
Egypt 102 D6
Eldwick 81 M1
Elland 169 J8
Elland Lower Edge 169 L7
Elland Upper Edge 169 K8
Emley 217 L7
Esholt 83 L1
Exley 168 E4
Facit 184 A4
Fagley 105 M3
Fairburn 159 H1
The Fall 153 M6
Farnhill 34 E5
Farnley 41 M2
Farnley 130 A1
Farnley Bank 215 G6
Farnley Tyas 215 H8
Far Royds 130 E2
Farsley 106 F3
Farsley Beck Bottom 107 G3
Fartown 192 C4
Fearnville 111 G2
Featherstone 179 L7
Felkirk 222 C8
Fell Lane 2 A6
Fenay Bridge 215 L2
Ferrybridge 159 L8
Firgrove 206 F8
Fishpool 42 F2
Fitzwilliam 223 J2
Five Lane Ends 105 J1
Fixby 192 B1
Flanshaw 176 A8
Flockton 217 L3
Flockton Green 218 A3
Flushdyke 175 H7
Flush House 253 K3
Follifoot 28 A1
Foulby 200 E6
Foulridge 52 A5
Four Lane End 271 L4
Four Lane Ends 104 A6
Fox Royd 195 K4
Friendly 167 J1
Frizinghall 104 C1
Fullshaw 269 K7
Fulneck 128 F1
Fulstone 237 K2
Gale 185 L7
Gamble Hill 108 A6
Garden Village 114 B8
Garforth 135 K1
Gawber 260 C3
Gawthorpe 174 F5
Gawthorpe 193 M8
Gildersome 129 M6
Gildersome Street 151 M1
Gill 54 C3
Gilstead 81 L3
Gipton 110 F3
Gipton Wood 88 D8
Girlington 104 C5
Glass Houghton 180 C1
Gledhow 88 C7
Golcar 212 F2
Gomersal 150 E6
Goose Eye 56 D8
Goosehill 177 M7
Grange Moor 217 H1
Gravel Hole 228 F7
Great Cliff 219 L2
Great Horton 126 B2
Great Howarth 206 C2
Great Preston 135 G6

Green Clough 124 D1
Greengate 206 F3
Greengates 83 M8
Green Hill 92 B6
Green Side 130 E1
Green Side 237 G2
Greenside 215 H1
The Green 270 F5
Greetland 168 C2
Greetland Wall Nook 167 M8
Grimethorpe 245 J7
Grove Town 181 G7
Guard House 57 G7
Guiseley 61 L6
Hade Edge 254 D7
Haigh 241 J2
Haigh Moor 153 H8
Hainworth 79 L3
Hainworth Shaw 79 M3
Halifax 11 H7
Hall Bower 214 D5
Hall Green 220 B3
Halton 111 G6
Halton Moor 110 F7
Hambleton 139 M5
Hampole 248 D5
Hanging Heaton 174 A3
Harden 80 D5
Harden 267 L2
Hare Croft 102 B2
Harehills 110 D4
Harewood 45 J7
Harewood Hill 79 G4
Harrop Dale 231 M3
Hartshead 171 L5
Hartshead Moor Side 149 J8
Hartshead Moor Top 149 G7
Haugh 229 L3
Havercroft 222 D5
Hawks Stones 141 G3
Hawksworth 61 H6
Hawksworth 85 M7
Haworth 78 D7
Hazlehead 269 G4
Headingley 108 D1
Healaugh 51 H2
Healey 173 J1
Healey 196 E3
Healey 206 A2
Heath Common 199 K2
Heaton 104 B3
Heaton Royds 104 A2
Heaton Shay 104 A1
Hebden Bridge 143 K3
Heckmondwike 172 F2
Helme 235 G2
Hemsworth 223 K7
Henshaw 84 C1
Heptonstall 143 G1
Hepworth 255 H4
Hessle 202 A7
Hey Green 232 E1
High Ackworth 202 C6
Higham 260 A3
Higham Common 260 A4
High Bradley 16 E6
Highburton 216 B6
High Crompton 229 C7
Higher Ogden 230 B1
High Flatts 256 E3
High Green 216 B4
High Hoyland 240 F5
Highroad Well Moor 145 K3
Hightown 171 M1
Hightown Heights 171 L1
Hillam 138 E8
Hillfoot 106 E6
Hill Side 193 L7
Hill Side 270 B4
Hill Top 102 E7
Hill Top 108 A4
Hill Top 212 A7
Hill Top 258 D6
Hinchliffe Mill 253 M3
Hipperholme 147 K6
Hogley Green 253 L2
Holbeck 8 D4
Holden Gate 57 M1
Holdsworth 124 D8
Hole 78 D8
Hole Bottom 141 K7
Hollingthorpe 219 M3
Hollin Hall 74 E5
Hollin Park 110 E1
Hollinthorpe 134 C2
Holmbridge 253 J4
Holme 128 B2
Holme 128 B3
Holme Wood 128 B3
Holmfield 146 B1
Holmfirth 254 A1
Holt Head 234 C1
Holt Park 86 B1
Holywell Green 190 D3
Honley 236 A2
Honley Moor 235 M3
Honresfeld 185 M8
Hoo Hole 143 M7
Hopetown 178 F3
Horbury 197 H6
Horbury Bridge 196 F5
Horbury Junction 197 G5
Horsforth 85 H4
Horsforth Woodside 85 L6
Hough Side 107 K6
Houses Hill 194 B8
Hove Edge 170 A1
Howden Clough 151 K4
Hoylandswaine 258 A8
Hoyle Mill 261 L5
Hubberton Green 166 E4
Huby 43 L2
Huddersfield 15 H7
Hungate 156 B6
Hunslet 9 K8
Hunslet Carr 131 M4
Hunsworth 150 A3

Hurstead 206 E2
Hutton Wandesley 33 L4
Ickornshaw 54 C3
Idle 83 K6
Idle Moor 83 H8
Ilkley 38 C2
Illingworth 124 A8
Ingbirchworth 257 G5
Ingmanthorpe 30 D4
Ingrow 79 J2
Intake 107 H3
Ireland Wood 86 B4
Jackson Bridge 255 G6
Jagger Green 190 D3
Jaw Hill 175 J2
John O'Gaunts 133 K7
Jubilee 229 K4
Junction 35 G7
Kearby Town End 46 B3
Kebroyd 166 F3
Keelham 124 B1
Keighley 3 J2
Kelbrook 52 C1
Keicliffe 61 M4
Kellingley 182 F2
Kellington 161 M7
Kendray 261 K8
Keresforth Hill 260 E8
Kettlethorpe 198 C8
Kexbrough 241 L6
Kiddal Lane End 91 G2
Kildwick 35 G5
Killingbeck 111 G4
Kine Moor 258 F8
Kingstone 260 F7
Kinsley 223 J4
Kippax 135 K2
Kirkburton 216 A8
Kirkby Overblow 27 K7
Kirkby Wharfe 72 C8
Kirk Deighton 29 L5
Kirkhamgate 175 J4
Kirkheaton 193 L6
Kirkholt 228 A3
Kirk Smeaton 226 C1
Kirkstall 108 C3
Kirkthorpe 177 M3
Kitchenroyd 239 J7
Knottingley 182 A2
Knowle Park 2 D8
Knowl Wood 163 J3
Knowsthorpe 9 M6
Krumlin 189 J5
Lady House 229 G2
Lady Wood 88 E7
Laisterdyke 105 M8
Lane Bottom 101 K4
Lane End 78 C4
Lane Ends 55 G2
Lane Ends 85 H7
Lane Head 216 C8
Lane Head 237 H7
Laneshaw Bridge 53 C7
Langbar 19 L3
Langsett 269 L4
Larkfield 84 F2
Lawns 154 A4
Lawnswood 86 C4
Laycock 56 E7
Leathley 42 C3
Ledsham 136 F6
Ledston 135 M8
Ledston Luck 135 K4
Leeds 6 C7
Leeming 100 F5
Lee Moor 155 G7
Lees 79 G6
Lepton Edge 216 E3
Leventhorpe 103 L8
Leymoor 213 G1
Lidget Green 126 C1
Lidgett Park 88 C6
Lightcliffe 148 B7
Lighthazles 166 C8
Lindley 24 A7
Lindley 191 K5
Lindwell 168 E6
Lingards Wood 211 L8
Lingbob 102 F2
Linthwaite 212 C5
Linton 47 J4
Littleborough 207 K1
Little Clegg 207 G4
Little Fenton 117 G3
Little Horton 126 D3
Little Houghton 263 M6
Little Lepton 216 C4
Little London 84 C3
Little Preston 134 E5
Little Smeaton 205 H8
Little Thorpe 171 M5
Littletown 172 C1
Liversedge 172 C2
Lockwood 214 A3
Lofthouse 154 F6
Lofthouse Gate 154 E8
Long Lee 3 L8
Longley 167 H5
Long Marston 33 J3
Longwood 191 H8
Longwood Edge 191 G7
Loscoe 179 G3
Low Ackworth 202 E7
Low Barugh 242 B8
Low Bradley 34 F1
Low Compton 229 G8
Lower Altofts 156 C8
Lower Clough 212 F6
Lower Cumberworth 239 H7
Lower Grange 103 L7
Lower Hopton 194 A3
Lower Houses 214 F3
Lower Longley 254 C5
Lower Maythorn 255 M7
Lower Mickletown 157 H4
Lower Place 228 C2
Lower Soothill 152 A8

Lower Town 100 F4
Lower Wyke 148 E6
Low Fold 85 H6
Low Green 84 E3
Low Laithes 262 D7
Low Moor 148 F1
Low Snaygill 16 C6
Luddenden 145 G5
Luddenden Foot 144 E8
Lumb Foot 78 B6
Lumb Head 214 E6
The Lumb 214 E6
Lumbutts 164 A2
Lumby 137 M5
Lundwood 262 A3
Lupset 198 A2
Lydgate 141 G7
Mankinholes 164 C2
Manningham 104 E4
Manor Park 39 M3
Manston 112 A4
Mapplewell 242 E5
Marsden 233 G3
Marsh 100 D2
Marsh 191 L8
Meal Hill 255 H3
Meanwood 87 G6
Measborough Dike 261 K6
Meltham 235 C3
Meltham Mills 235 H4
Menston 61 H3
Merchant Fields 150 A5
Methley 156 E4
Methley Junction 156 F6
Methley Lanes 156 A7
Micklefield 114 B8
Micklethwaite 59 C7
Middlecliffe 263 L7
Middlestown 196 D7
Middleton 20 D7
Middleton 54 C3
Middleton 153 M2
Midgehole 121 J8
Midgley 144 E5
Midgley 218 E4
Miles Hill 87 J8
Mill Bank 166 F7
Millhouse Green 269 L3
Mill Shaw 131 C5
Milnrow 207 J8
Milnsbridge 213 H2
Milnthorpe 198 E7
Minsthorpe 247 H1
Mirfield 172 C8
Mixenden 145 L1
Moldgreen 15 K8
Monk Bretton 261 K2
Monk Fryston 138 C7
Monkhill 180 F4
Monkswood 89 H7
Moor Allerton 87 M4
Moor End 48 D6
Moor End 145 J2
Moorhead 82 A7
Moor Head 129 L6
Moor Head 217 H8
Moorhouse 247 M5
Moor Side 100 B2
Moor Side 148 F1
Moorside 107 L2
Moorside 151 H1
Moorthorpe 246 F4
Moor Top 172 A6
Moortown 87 L4
Morley 152 D3
Mount 190 E5
Mountain 124 D4
Mount Pleasant 173 J2
Mount Tabor 145 J3
Mytholm 143 H3
Mytholmes 78 F6
Mytholmroyd 144 B4
Nab Hill 193 J5
Nab Wood 81 M6
Netherby 45 M4
Nether End 257 M1
Netherley 233 H4
Netheroyd Hill 192 C7
Netherthong 236 C6
Netherton 196 E8
Netherton 213 M8
Nether Yeadon 84 C1
Nettleton Hill 190 D7
Newall 41 J5
Newbold 206 D7
New Brighton 81 L8
New Brighton 152 B2
Newby 43 K3
New Crofton 200 D7
New Farnley 130 A3
New Fryston 158 F3
Newhey 229 H3
New Holland 102 C9
New Lodge 242 F7
New Micklefield 114 D8
New Mill 237 G7
Newmillerdam 220 E2

New Road Side 54 F3
New Road Side 148 F2
Newsam Green 133 L5
New Scarbro 107 M4
New Sharlston 200 B1
Newsholme 78 C2
Newsome 214 C5
Newstead 222 E4
Newthorpe 137 H1
Newton Hill 176 E3
Newton Kyme 50 A7
New Town 180 F2
New Wortley 109 G7
Noblethorpe 259 G7
Noon Nick 103 K2
Norland Town 167 M4
Normanton 178 B4
Norr 102 F1
Norristhorpe 172 D4
North Deighton 29 L2
North Elmsall 225 K8
North Featherstone 179 M5
Northorpe 172 F7
Northowram 147 K4
North Rigton 26 A7
Norton 227 L3
Norwood Green 148 A3
Notton 221 H8
Oakenshaw 149 G2
Oakes 191 J6
Oakwell 150 F3
Oakwood 110 E1
Oakworth 78 D5
Odsal 127 G6
Ogden 123 M4
Old Bramhope 63 K3
Old Dolphin 125 J4
Oldfield 77 M6
Oldfield 236 B5
Old Lindley 190 F3
Old Micklefield 114 A6
Old Snydale 179 C7
Old Tame 230 D6
Old Town 143 K1
Osmondthorpe 110 D7
Ossett 174 F8
Ossett Spa 197 J3
Ossett Street Side 174 D6
Otley 41 K5
Oulton 155 K1
Ousel Hole 59 G4
Outlane 190 C5
Outlane Moor 190 B8
Outwood 176 D2
Ouzlewell Green 155 G5
Ovenden 146 B4
Overthorpe 195 L4
Overton 196 C8
Overtown 221 J1
Owlet 104 E1
Oxenhope 100 E4
Oxspring 271 L6
Oxton 72 C3
Paddock 213 M1
Painthorpe 220 A3
Pannal 26 E3
Pannal Ash 26 C1
Park Gate 239 J2
Park Head 256 B1
Parklands 111 H2
Park Mill 240 C2
Park Villas 88 C5
Parlington 113 L1
Peas Acre 59 G6
Pecket Well 121 K6
Pellon 146 A6
Pendas Fields 112 B3
Penistone 270 D3
Penny Hill 189 L5
Pepper Hill 125 K8
Pickles Hill 78 B5
Pickwood Scar 168 A5
Pike End 188 D6
Pike Law 189 H7
Pledwick 220 F1
Pogmoor 260 C4
Pole Moor 211 M2
Pontefract 180 E6
Pool 42 E7
Portobello 198 D4
Portsmouth 140 C5
Potternewton 110 A1
Potterton 91 G3
Pottery Field 9 J5
Priest Hill 29 L6
Priesthorpe 106 C2
Priestley Green 147 M5
Priestthorpe 81 J2
Prince Royd 191 L4
Pudsey 106 F7
Pudsey 140 D4
Pule Hill 146 E3
Purston Jaglin 202 A2
Quarmby 191 J8
Queensbury 124 E5
Rakewood 207 L5
Ramsden Wood 163 J7

Rastrick 170 B6
Ravenscliffe 106 A2
Ravensthorpe 173 G8
Rawdon 84 E3
Rawdon Carrs 84 F4
Rawfolds 172 A1
Raw Green 258 E2
Rawthorpe 15 M4
Red Hill 158 C7
Richmond Hill 110 B6
Riddlesden 58 C5
Ripponden 188 E2
Rishworth 188 D6
Roberttown 171 M5
Robin Hood 154 D3
Rochdale 206 A6
Rodley 107 G1
Rodmer Clough 120 A7
Rothwell 155 J1
Rothwell Haigh 132 F7
Rough Bank 207 M8
Roughbirchworth 271 J7
Roundhay 88 F6
Rowley Hill 216 A4
Royd 269 M2
Roydhouse 216 E8
Royd Moor 224 D6
Royd Moor 270 A1
Royds Green 155 J4
Royston 243 J4
Running Hill Head 250 A3
Ryecroft 80 A5
Ryhill 222 D5
Ryther 95 M3
St Helen's 261 L1
St John's 92 A5
Salendine Nook 191 G7
Saltaire 82 C5
Sandal 198 F5
Sandal Magna 199 H5
Sandford 108 A1
Sandhill 263 M5
Sandhills 90 A3
Sandy Lane 103 H3
Savile Town 195 M1
Sawood 101 H6
Saxton 93 J8
Scapegoat Hill 190 C8
Scarcroft 67 L5
Scarthingwell 94 A7
Scholemoor 126 A1
Scholes 90 B7
Scholes 149 H6
Scholes 254 F3
Scholey Hill 156 C6
School Green 103 J8
Scissett 239 L5
Scout Dike 257 K8
Seacroft 111 J1
Shackleton 121 G6
Shade 163 J2
Shadwell 89 H2
Shafton 244 C3
Shafton Two Gates 244 C4
Sharlston 200 D4
Sharlston Common 200 C3
Shaw 100 D4
Shaw 229 J6
Shaw Cross 174 C4
Shawfield Head 25 J1
Shaw Green 25 J1
Shaw Lands 260 E5
Shay Gate 103 G2
Sheepridge 192 D3
Sheepscar 7 K4
Shelf 125 M8
Shelley 238 C3
Shelley Woodhouse 238 D4
Shepherd Hill 175 H8
Shepley 238 B6
Sherburn in Elmet 115 M5
Shibden Head 124 F8
Shipley 82 C7
Shore 140 E4
Shore 185 H8
Sicklinghall 28 E8
Siddal 169 G3
Silkstone 259 G6
Silsden 36 A5
Skelbrooke 248 E1
Skellow 249 J4
Skelmanthorpe 239 K4
Skipton 16 A4
Slack 120 F8
Slack 190 C6
Slackcote 230 D7
Slaithwaite 212 B6
Slippery Ford 55 L8
Smallbridge 206 F3
Smithies 261 H1
Smithy Bridge 207 J3
Snowden Hill 271 J8
Snow Hill 176 C4
Snow Lea 190 F6
Snydale 201 G1
Soughley 268 F4
South Crosland 213 K8

South Elmsall 247 K3
South Hiendley 222 E8
South Kirkby 246 E5
South Lane 258 D5
South Milford 137 M2
South Ossett 197 G2
Southowram 169 H2
Sowerby 166 F4
Sowerby Bridge 167 L3
Sowood 190 B5
Sowood Green 190 C4
Soyland Town 166 F8
Spacey Houses 26 F3
Spofforth 28 F4
Spring Green 53 J3
Spring Vale 271 G3
Stainburn 25 G8
Staincliffe 173 J2
Staincross 242 D4
Stainland 190 A2
Stairfoot 262 A7
Stanbury 77 L7
Stanks 111 M3
Stanley 177 G2
Stanley Ferry 177 K3
Stanningley 107 H5
Stead 39 J5
Steep Lane 166 E2
Steeton 56 F1
Stockbridge 57 M4
Stone Chair 147 L2
Stone Head 53 M3
Stoneyfield 228 B2
Stoney Royd 11 H8
Stourton 132 D5
Strawberry Hill 180 A7
Streethouse 200 F1
Stutton 71 L7
Summit 185 K5
Summit 228 D7
Sutton 160 B7
Sutton 227 M8
Sutton-in-Craven 56 A1
Sutton Mill 56 A1
Swain House 105 H1
Swallow Hill 242 C7
Swarcliffe 111 L2
Swartha 36 B4
Swillington 134 C4
Swillington Common 112 B8
Swincliffe 150 C2
Swinnow Moor 107 K6
Syke 206 B2
Sympson Green 83 L5
Tadcaster 71 L2
Tandem 215 K1
Tarn 83 G2
Thackley 83 J5
Thackley End 83 H4
Thick Hollins 235 H5
Thongsbridge 236 E6
Thornbury 106 B6
Thorncliff 216 E7
Thorner 90 B1
Thornes 12 E9
Thornham Fold 228 C7
Thornhill 196 B4
Thornhill Edge 195 L6
Thornhill Lees 195 L2
Thornhills 170 E2
Thornton 103 G8
Thorp Arch 49 G6
Thorpe Audlin 225 J1
Thorpe Edge 83 K8
Thorpe on The Hill 153 L4
Thunder Bridge 237 L3
Thurlstone 270 B2
Thurstonland 237 H5
Thwaites 58 B7
Thwaites Brow 58 B8
Tingley 153 G5
Tinshill 86 A3
Tivy Dale 258 F2
Todmorden 163 L2
Toftshaw 127 L6
Tong 129 G5
Tong Park 83 H2
Tong Street 127 M5
Toothill 170 C8
Totties 254 F2
Toulston 70 E1
Town End 212 E2
Town Head 36 B4
Townhead 268 A4
Towton 93 M2
Trawden 74 A2
Triangle 167 G5
Troydale 107 J8
Tunshill 207 L7
Turf Hill 228 F2
Tyersal 128 B1
Tyersal 94 E2
Ulleskelf 94 E2
Under Bank 254 C3
Undercliffe 105 J4
Upper Armley 108 C5
Upper Batley 151 L6
Upper Brockholes 123 L6

Upper Clough 212 E6
Upper Cudworth 244 E6
Upper Cumberworth 238 C8
Upper Denby 217 K1
Upper Denby 257 G3
Upper Green 153 G5
Upper Heaton 193 J3
Upper Hopton 194 A4
Upper Marsh 100 C2
Upper Maythorn 255 M6
Upper Moor Side 129 K5
Upperthong 235 M8
Upper Town 100 D4
Upton 225 L7
Upwood 58 E2
Utley 57 K4
Vale 140 E5
Victoria 255 K7
Wainstalls 145 G1
Wakefield 12 E2
Walsden 163 J5
Walshaw 120 E3
Walton 49 J2
Walton 199 K8
Wardle 184 F8
Warland 185 M1
Warley Town 145 K8
Warmfield 178 A8
Washpit 254 C4
Water Fryston 159 H4
Wayside Gardens 67 L5
Weardley 44 D8
Weeton 44 B4
Weetwood 86 E6
Well Heads 102 C7
Wellhouse 212 F3
Wellington Hill 89 G5
Wellroyd 84 F5
Wentbridge 203 L7
Wescoe Hill 43 L4
Wessenden 233 K8
West Ardsley 152 F8
West Bowling 127 H3
West Bretton 219 H6
West Carlton 62 D3
West End 85 G4
West End 94 F1
West End 149 K7
Westfield 84 A1
Westfield 172 F1
West Garforth 134 C7
Westgate Hill 128 C6
West Green 244 B8
West Hardwick 201 K5
West Morton 58 C4
Weston 40 D3
West Park 86 D6
West Royd 82 F6
West Scholes 124 F3
West Vale 168 F8
Wetherby 48 B1
Wheatley 145 M4
Wheldale 158 D5
Whinmoor 89 L6
Whins Wood 79 J5
Whitecote 107 L1
White Hill 77 M1
White Lee 151 G7
Whitkirk 111 L7
Whitley Head 56 E2
Whitley Lower 195 G6
Whitwood 157 G8
Wibsey 126 D5
Wighill 50 C4
Wike 66 F5
Wilberlee 211 M4
Wilsden 102 D1
Wilshaw 235 J6
Wilthorpe 260 E2
Windhill 82 F7
Windmill Hill 200 C3
Winewall 74 E2
Wintersett 222 C2
Womersley 205 J3
Woodhall Hills 106 C3
Woodhouse 3 H9
Woodhouse 6 D3
Woodhouse 170 E6
Woodhouse 178 B6
Woodkirk 152 E7
Woodlands 11 H1
Woodlands 146 E4
Woodlesford 133 L8
Wood Row 156 D3
Woodside 126 C8
Woolgreaves 198 F8
Woolley 220 C8
Worsbrough Common 261 G8
Wortley 108 C8
Wragby 201 J7
Wrangbrook 226 B7
Wrenthorpe 176 B4
Wrose 83 G8
Wycoller 75 H3
Wyke 148 E4
Yeadon 84 D1

USING THE STREET INDEX

Street names are listed alphabetically. Each street name is followed by its postal town or area locality, the Postcode District, the page number, and the reference to the square in which the name is found.

Standard index entries are shown as follows:

Aachen Wy *HFAX* HX1 ....**10** C9

Street names and selected addresses not shown on the map due to scale restrictions are shown in the index with an asterisk:

Abbeydale *WHIT* * OL12 ....**206** A6

GENERAL ABBREVIATIONS

ACC	ACCESS
ALY	ALLEY
AP	APPROACH
AR	ARCADE
ASS	ASSOCIATION
AV	AVENUE
BCH	BEACH
BLDS	BUILDINGS
BND	BEND
BNK	BANK
BR	BRIDGE
BRK	BROOK
BTM	BOTTOM
BUS	BUSINESS
BVD	BOULEVARD
BY	BYPASS
CATH	CATHEDRAL
CEM	CEMETERY
CEN	CENTRE
CFT	CROFT
CH	CHURCH
CHA	CHASE
CHYD	CHURCHYARD
CIR	CIRCLE
CIRC	CIRCUS
CL	CLOSE
CLFS	CLIFFS
CMP	CAMP
CNR	CORNER
CO	COUNTY
COLL	COLLEGE
COM	COMMON
COMM	COMMISSION
CON	CONVENT
COT	COTTAGE
COTS	COTTAGES
CP	CAPE
CPS	COPSE
CR	CREEK
CREM	CREMATORIUM
CRS	CRESCENT
CSWY	CAUSEWAY
CT	COURT
CTRL	CENTRAL
CTS	COURTS
CTYD	COURTYARD
CUTT	CUTTINGS
CV	COVE
CYN	CANYON
DEPT	DEPARTMENT
DL	DALE
DM	DAM
DR	DRIVE
DRO	DROVE
DRY	DRIVEWAY
DWGS	DWELLINGS
E	EAST
EMB	EMBANKMENT
EMBY	EMBASSY
ESP	ESPLANADE
EST	ESTATE
EX	EXCHANGE
EXPY	EXPRESSWAY
EXT	EXTENSION
F/O	FLYOVER
FC	FOOTBALL CLUB
FK	FORK
FLD	FIELD
FLDS	FIELDS
FLS	FALLS
FLS	FLATS
FM	FARM
FT	FORT
FWY	FREEWAY
FY	FERRY
GA	GATE
GAL	GALLERY
GDN	GARDEN
GDNS	GARDENS
GLD	GLADE
GLN	GLEN
GN	GREEN
GND	GROUND
GRA	GRANGE
GRG	GARAGE
GT	GREAT
GTWY	GATEWAY
GV	GROVE
HGR	HIGHER
HL	HILL
HLS	HILLS
HO	HOUSE
HOL	HOLLOW
HOSP	HOSPITAL
HRB	HARBOUR
HTH	HEATH
HTS	HEIGHTS
HVN	HAVEN
HWY	HIGHWAY
IMP	IMPERIAL
IN	INLET
IND EST	INDUSTRIAL ESTATE
INF	INFIRMARY
INFO	INFORMATION
INT	INTERCHANGE
IS	ISLAND
JCT	JUNCTION
JTY	JETTY
KG	KING
KNL	KNOLL
L	LAKE
LA	LANE
LDG	LODGE
LGT	LIGHT
LK	LOCK
LKS	LAKES
LNDG	LANDING
LTL	LITTLE
LWR	LOWER
MAG	MAGISTRATE
MAN	MANSIONS
MD	MEAD
MDW	MEADOWS
MEM	MEMORIAL
MKT	MARKET
MKTS	MARKETS
ML	MALL
ML	MILL
MNR	MANOR
MS	MEWS
MSN	MISSION
MT	MOUNT
MTN	MOUNTAIN
MTS	MOUNTAINS
MUS	MUSEUM
MWY	MOTORWAY
N	NORTH
NE	NORTH EAST
NW	NORTH WEST
O/P	OVERPASS
OFF	OFFICE
ORCH	ORCHARD
OV	OVAL
PAL	PALACE
PAS	PASSAGE
PAV	PAVILION
PDE	PARADE
PH	PUBLIC HOUSE
PK	PARK
PKWY	PARKWAY
PL	PLACE
PLN	PLAIN
PLNS	PLAINS
PLZ	PLAZA
POL	POLICE STATION
PR	PRINCE
PREC	PRECINCT
PREP	PREPARATORY
PRIM	PRIMARY
PROM	PROMENADE
PRS	PRINCESS
PRT	PORT
PT	POINT
PTH	PATH
PZ	PIAZZA
QD	QUADRANT
QU	QUEEN
QY	QUAY
R	RIVER
RBT	ROUNDABOUT
RD	ROAD
RDG	RIDGE
REP	REPUBLIC
RES	RESERVOIR
RFC	RUGBY FOOTBALL CLUB
RI	RISE
RP	RAMP
RW	ROW
S	SOUTH
SCH	SCHOOL
SE	SOUTH EAST
SER	SERVICE AREA
SH	SHORE
SHOP	SHOPPING
SKWY	SKYWAY
SMT	SUMMIT
SOC	SOCIETY
SP	SPUR
SPR	SPRING
SQ	SQUARE
ST	STREET
STN	STATION
STR	STREAM
STRD	STRAND
SW	SOUTH WEST
TDG	TRADING
TER	TERRACE
THWY	THROUGHWAY
TNL	TUNNEL
TOLL	TOLLWAY
TPK	TURNPIKE
TR	TRACK
TRL	TRAIL
TWR	TOWER
U/P	UNDERPASS
UNI	UNIVERSITY
UPR	UPPER
V	VALE
VA	VALLEY
VIAD	VIADUCT
VIL	VILLA
VIS	VISTA
VLG	VILLAGE
VLS	VILLAS
VW	VIEW
W	WEST
WD	WOOD
WHF	WHARF
WK	WALK
WKS	WALKS
WLS	WELLS
WY	WAY
YD	YARD
YHA	YOUTH HOSTEL

POSTCODE TOWNS AND AREA ABBREVIATIONS

AIRE	Airedale
AL/HA/HU	Alwoodley/Harewood/Huby
AWLS/ASK	Adwick le Street/Askern
BAIL	Baildon
BCUP	Bacup
BEE/HOL	Beeston/Holbeck
BFD	Bradford
BFDE	Bradford east
BGLY	Bingley
BHP/TINH	Bramhope/Tinshill
BIRK/DRI	Birkenshaw/Drighlington
BOW	Bowling
BRAM	Bramley
BRFD/BLYE	Brierfield/Burnley east
BRIG	Brighouse
BSLY	Barnsley
BSLYN/ROY	Barnsley north/Royston
BTLY	Bentley
BULY	Burley
BVRD	Belle Vue Road
BWCK/EAR	Barnoldswick/Earby
CAS	Castleford
CHAL	Chapel Allerton
CLAY	Clayton
CLECK	Cleckheaton
COL	Colne
COP/BISH	Copmanthorpe/Bishopthorpe
CUD/GR	Cudworth/Grimethorpe
CUL/QBY	Cullingworth/Queensbury
DEWS	Dewsbury
DOD/DAR	Dodworth/Darton
EARD/LOFT	East Ardley/Lofthouse
EARL	Earlsheaton
ECHL	Eccleshill
ELL	Elland
FEA/AMT	Featherstone/Ackworth Moor Top
GFTH/SHER	Garforth/Sherburn in Elmet
GIR	Girlington
GLE	Goole
GLSP	Glossop
GSLY	Guiseley
GTHN	Great Horton
GTL/HWG	Greetland/Holywell Green
HARS	Harrogate south
HBR	Hebden Bridge
HDGY	Headingley
HECK	Heckmondwike
HEM/SK/SE	Hemsworth/South Kirby/South Elmsall
HFAX	Halifax
HIPP	Hipperholme
HOLM/MEL	Holmfirth/Meltham
HOR/CROF	Horbury/Crofton
HORS	Horsforth
HTON	Heaton
HUD	Huddersfield
HUDE	Huddersfield east
HUDN	Huddersfield north
HUDS	Huddersfield south
HUDW	Huddersfield west
HWTH	Haworth
IDLE	Idle
ILK	Ilkley
KBTN	Kirkburton
KGHY	Keighley
KNA	Knaresborough
KNOT	Knottingley
KSTL	Kirkstall
LDS	Leeds
LDSU	Leeds University
LIT	Littleborough
LM/WK	Low Moor/Wyke
LUD/ILL	Luddenden/Illingworth
LVSG	Liversedge
MDTN	Middleton (Gtr.Man)
MID	Middleton (W.Yorks)
MILN	Milnrow
MIRF	Mirfield
MOR	Morley
MSTN/BAR	Manston/Barwick in Elmet
NORM	Normanton
OLD	Oldham
OSM	Osmandthorpe
OSS	Ossett
OT	Otley
PBR	Pateley Bridge
PDSY/CALV	Pudsey/Calverley
PONT	Pontefract
RHAY	Roundhay
ROCH	Rochdale
ROY/SHW	Royton/Shaw
RPDN/SBR	Ripponden/Sowerby Bridge
RTHW	Rothwell
RYKW	Rural York west
SCFT	Seacroft
SEL	Selby
SHPY	Shipley
SKP/WHF	Skipton/Wharfedale
STKB/PEN	Stocksbridge/Penistone
TAD	Tadcaster
TOD	Todmorden
UPML	Uppermill
WBOW	West Bowling
WBSY	Wibsey
WBY	Wetherby
WHIT	Whitworth
WIL/AL	Wilsden/Allerton
WKFDE	Wakefield east
WKFDW/WTN	Wakefield west/Walton
WMB/DAR	Wombwell/Darfield
WOR/ARM	Wortley/Armley
YEA	Yeadon

A

Aachen Wy *HFAX* HX1 **10** C9
Aaron Wilkinson Ct
HEM/SK/SE WF9 **246** C4
Abaseen Cl *BFDE* BD3 **5** M6
Abber La *TAD* LS24 **51** J3
The Abbe's Cl *AWLS/ASK* DN6 **249** K1
The Abbe's Wk *AWLS/ASK* DN6 **249** M2
Abbey Av *KSTL* LS5 **108** B3
Abbey Cl *HOLM/MEL* HD9 **254** C7
ILK LS29 **19** J6
Abbey Ct *HOLM/MEL* HD9 **254** C7
HORS LS18 **85** K8
Abbeydale *WHIT* * OL12 **206** A6
Abbeydale Gdns *KSTL* LS5 **86** A8
Abbeydale Garth *KSTL* LS5 **86** A8
Abbeydale Gv *KSTL* LS5 **86** A8
Abbeydale Mt *KSTL* LS5 **86** A8
Abbeydale V *KSTL* LS5 **86** A8
Abbeydale Wy *KSTL* LS5 **86** A8
Abbey Dr *KBTN* HD8 **238** B5
LIT OL15 **207** H3
Abbey Farm Dr *KBTN* HD8 **238** B6
Abbey Farm Vw *CUD/GR* S72 **262** D1
Abbey Gdns *PONT* WF8 **181** G3
Abbey Gorse *KSTL* LS5 **108** C1
Abbey Gv *BSLYN/ROY* S71 **262** A2
Abbey La *BSLYN/ROY* S71 **262** A5
LUD/ILL HX2 **145** H7
Abbey Lea *WIL/AL* BD15 **103** L6
Abbey Ms *PONT* WF8 **180** F2
Abbey Pl *HUDN* HD2 **192** E5
Abbey Rd *BTLY* WF17 **173** H2
HUDN HD2 **192** D5
KBTN HD8 **238** C5
KSTL LS5 **85** M8
Abbey Rd North *KBTN* HD8 **238** B5
Abbey Sq *BSLYN/ROY* S71 **262** A2
Abbey St *BVRD* LS3 **6** B8
Abbey Ter *KSTL* LS5 **108** B3
Abbey Vw *KSTL* LS5 **108** C1
Abbey Wk *HIPP* HX3 **168** E2
KSTL LS5 **108** B1
PONT WF8 **180** F2
Abbey Wk South *HIPP* HX3 **168** E2
Abbot La *HOR/CROF* WF4 **220** D8
Abbotside Cl *IDLE* * BD10 **83** L8
Abbots Rd *BSLYN/ROY* S71 **262** B3
Abbot St *HUDW* HD3 **14** A4
Abbotsway *GFTH/SHER* LS25 **112** F8
Abbott Ct *WOR/ARM* LS12 **108** F6
Abbott Rd *WOR/ARM* LS12 **108** F6
Abbotts Cl *GFTH/SHER* LS25 **92** A6
Abbotts Ter *HFAX* HX1 **10** C6
Abbott Ter *WKFDE* WF1 **13** H8
Abbott Vw *WOR/ARM* LS12 **108** F6
Abb Scott La *LM/WK* BD12 **126** D8
Abb St *HUDW* HD3 **191** M7
Abelia Mt *GTHN* BD7 **104** A8
Abel St *LM/WK* BD12 **148** E2
Aberdeen Dr *WOR/ARM* LS12 **108** C7
Aberdeen Gv *WOR/ARM* LS12 **108** C7
Aberdeen Pl *GTHN* BD7 **126** C1
Aberdeen Rd *WOR/ARM* LS12 **108** C7
Aberdeen Ter *CLAY* BD14 **125** M2
GTHN BD7 **104** C8
Aberdeen Wk *WOR/ARM* LS12 **108** C7
Aberfield Bank *MID* LS10 **132** A8
Aberfield Cl *MID* LS10 **132** A7
Aberfield Crest *MID* LS10 **132** A8
Aberfield Dr *HOR/CROF* WF4 **220** A2
MID LS10 **132** A8
Aberfield Ga *MID* LS10 **132** A7
Aberfield Mt *MID* LS10 **132** A8
Aberfield Ri *MID* LS10 **132** A8
Aberfield Rd *MID* LS10 **132** A7
Aberfield Wk *MID* LS10 **131** M8
Aberford Rd *BSPA/BRAM* LS23 **69** M5
GFTH/SHER LS25 **113** H6
GIR BD8 **104** D5
MSTN/BAR LS15 **91** G7
RTHW LS26 **155** L2
WKFDE WF1 **177** G6
Aberley Fold *LIT* OL15 **185** H7
Abingdon Cl *ROCH* OL11 **228** A2
Abingdon St *GIR* BD8 **104** D5
HUDN HD2 **192** C5
Aboukir St *MILN* OL16 **206** D6
Abraham Hl *RTHW* LS26 **133** H8
Acacia Cl *CAS* WF10 **158** F8
Acacia Dr *BRIG* HD6 **148** C7
CAS WF10 **158** E8
WIL/AL BD15 **103** J2
Acacia Gv *CUD/GR* S72 **244** E4
HBR HX7 **144** B4
Acacia Park Crs *IDLE* BD10 **84** B4
Acacia Park Dr *IDLE* BD10 **84** B4
Acacia Park Ter *IDLE* BD10 **84** B4
Acacia Rd *AWLS/ASK* DN6 **249** J4
Acaster Dr *GFTH/SHER* LS25 **135** J1
LM/WK BD12 **126** E8
Accommodation Rd *OSM* LS9 **7** M7
Acer Cl *AIRE* BD20 **56** B1
Acer Wy *CLECK* BD19 **149** H6
Ackroyd Ct *CUL/QBY* * BD13 **102** F8
Ackroyd St *MOR* LS27 **152** D2
TOD OL14 **140** D5
Ackton Cl *FEA/AMT* WF7 **179** J5
Ackton Hall Crs *FEA/AMT* WF7 **179** J6
Ackton La *FEA/AMT* WF7 **179** J6
Ackton Pasture La *CAS* WF10 **179** J2
Ackworth Av *YEA* LS19 **62** E8
Ackworth Bridle Rd
PONT WF8 **203** C7
Ackworth Crs *YEA* LS19 **62** E8
Ackworth Dr *YEA* LS19 **62** E8
Ackworth House Cl
FEA/AMT WF7 **202** C6
Ackworth Rd *FEA/AMT* WF7 **201** M3
PONT WF8 **202** D2
Ackworth St *WBOW* BD5 **127** G2
Acme Ter *WKFDE* WF1 **13** H8
Acomb Ter *LM/WK* BD12 **148** E3
Acorn Cl *WBSY* BD6 **126** A8
Acorn Dr *SCFT* LS14 **89** L6
Acorn Gv *HOLM/MEL* HD9 **254** F3
Acorn Pk *BAIL* BD17 **83** G4
Acorn St *HFAX* HX1 **10** C5
Acre Av *ECHL* BD2 **105** K1
Acre Barn *ROY/SHW* OL2 **229** G6
Acre Cl *ECHL* BD2 **105** K1
Acre Crs *ECHL* BD2 **105** K1
MID LS10 **153** L2
Acre Dr *ECHL* BD2 **105** K1
Acre Fold *ILK* LS29 **18** F6
Acre Gv *ECHL* * BD2 **105** K1
MID LS10 **153** L2
Acre House Av *HUDW* HD3 **191** L6
Acrehowe Ri *BAIL* BD17 **82** F2
The Acre *LM/WK* BD12 **148** D1
Acre La *ECHL* BD2 **105** K2
HBR HX7 **120** E8
HOLM/MEL HD9 **235** H5
HOLM/MEL HD9 **237** K8
HOLM/MEL HD9 **253** M4
HWTH BD22 **78** E7
STKB/PEN S36 **257** M8
WBSY BD6 **126** E5
Acre Meadow *HWTH* BD22 **54** E3
Acre Mt *MID* LS10 **153** L2
Acre Pl *MID* LS10 **153** L2
Acre Ri *BAIL* BD17 **82** E2
Acre Rd *CUD/GR* S72 **262** E2
HWTH BD22 **54** E3
MID LS10 **153** L2
Acresfield *COL* * BB8 **74** C1
Acres Hall Av *PDSY/CALV* LS28 **107** J8
Acres Hall Crs *PDSY/CALV* LS28 **107** J8
Acres Hall Dr *PDSY/CALV* LS28 **107** J8
Acres La *HBR* HX7 **143** H2
HOLM/MEL HD9 **253** H2
Acre Sq *MID* LS10 **153** L2
The Acres *AIRE* BD20 **55** L2
ILK LS29 **19** H5
Acres Rd *EARD/LOFT* WF3 **154** E6
Acres St *KGHY* BD21 **2** E7
Acre St *HUDW* HD3 **191** K6
MID LS10 **153** L2
Acre Ter *MID* LS10 **153** M2
Acton Flat La *HUDW* HD3 **191** J3
Acton St *BFDE* BD3 **105** L7
WHIT OL12 **206** C5
Acute Ter *WKFDW/WTN* WF2 **176** A8
Adam Ct *HUDW* HD3 **191** K5
Adam Cft *CUL/QBY* BD13 **79** M8
Adam La *DOD/DAR* S75 **259** J4
Adams Gv *MSTN/BAR* LS15 **112** A2
Adam St *TOD* OL14 **141** K8
WBSY BD6 **126** D5
Ada's Pl *PDSY/CALV* LS28 **107** G4
Ada St *BAIL* BD17 **83** G4
CUL/QBY BD13 **124** F5
HIPP HX3 **11** H2
KGHY BD21 **2** D5
SHPY BD18 **82** B6
WHIT OL12 **206** C4
Addingford Cl
HOR/CROF WF4 **197** J6
Addingford Dr
HOR/CROF WF4 **197** J6
Addingford La
HOR/CROF WF4 **197** J6
Addingham Gdns
WOR/ARM LS12 **108** C7
Addingham Wharfedale Rd
ILK LS29 **18** E5
Addison Av *BFDE* BD3 **105** M5
NORM WF6 **178** E5
Addison Ct *HOR/CROF* WF4 **197** L4
MSTN/BAR LS15 **111** M8
Addison Dr *HWTH* BD22 **78** E8
Addi St *BOW* BD4 **127** L3
Addle Croft La *HUDE* HD5 **216** A1
Addlethorpe La *WBY* LS22 **46** B1
Addy Crs *HEM/SK/SE* WF9 **247** H3
Adelaide Rd *AWLS/ASK* DN6 **227** M3
Adelaide St *HBR* HX7 **143** G3
HFAX HX1 **10** B6
TOD OL14 **141** K8
WBOW BD5 **4** F9
Adel Garth *BHP/TINH* LS16 **86** F1
Adel Grange Cl *BHP/TINH* LS16 **86** E4
Adel Grange Cft
BHP/TINH * LS16 **86** E4
Adel Grange Ms *BHP/TINH* LS16 **86** E4
Adel Gn *BHP/TINH* LS16 **86** F2
Adel La *BHP/TINH* LS16 **86** E2
Adel Md *BHP/TINH* LS16 **86** F2
Adel Ml *BHP/TINH* LS16 **64** F8
Adel Park Cl *BHP/TINH* LS16 **86** E3
Adel Park Ct *BHP/TINH* LS16 **86** E3
Adel Park Cft *BHP/TINH* LS16 **86** E3
Adel Park Dr *BHP/TINH* LS16 **86** E3
Adel Park Gdns *BHP/TINH* LS16 **86** E3
Adel Pasture *BHP/TINH* LS16 **86** E3
Adelphi Rd *HUDW* HD3 **191** L7
Adel Towers Ct *BHP/TINH* LS16 **86** F3
Adel V *BHP/TINH* LS16 **86** F2
Adel Wood Dr *BHP/TINH* LS16 **86** F3
Adel Wood Gv *BHP/TINH* LS16 **86** F3
Adel Wood Pl *BHP/TINH* LS16 **86** F3
Adel Wood Rd *BHP/TINH* LS16 **86** F3

Aden St WHIT OL12 206 C5
Adgil Crs HIPP HX3 169 J2
Adkin Royd DOD/DAR S75 259 H6
Administration Rd OSM LS9 132 E3
Admiral St BEE/HOL LS11 9 G7
Adolphus St BFD BD1 5 H7
Adowsley Cl FEA/AMT WF7 202 A8
Adrian Ter MILN OL16 206 E8
Adwalton Cl BIRK/DRI BD11 150 F1
Adwalton Gn BIRK/DRI BD11 150 E1
Adwalton Gv CUL/QBY BD13 125 H5
Adwick Gv WKFDW/WTN WF2 220 D1
Adwick Pl BULY LS4 108 E4
Agar St GIR BD8 104 B6
Agar Ter GIR BD8 104 B6
Agbrigg Gv WKFDW/WTN WF2 199 G4
Agbrigg Rd WKFDE WF1 13 L9
Agincourt Dr NORM WF6 178 A2
Agnes Rd BSLY S70 261 G6
DOD/DAR S75 241 M6
Agnes St KGHY BD21 57 L5
Agnes Ter BSLY S70 261 G6
Ails La LUD/ILL HX2 144 F5
Aimbry Ct HUDE HD5 215 H4
Ainley Bottom ELL HX5 191 H1
Ainley Cl HUDW HD3 191 J4
Ainley Pk MAR/SLWT HD7 213 G2
Ainley Rd HUDW HD3 191 J3
Ainley St ELL HX5 169 H8
Ainsbury Av IDLE BD10 83 K3
Ainsdale Ct BSLYN/ROY S71 261 M1
Ainsdale Gv CUL/QBY BD13 80 A8
Ainsdale Rd BSLYN/ROY S71 243 K1
Ainsley La MAR/SLWT HD7 232 F2
Ainsty Crs WBY LS22 30 A7
Ainsty Dr WBY LS22 30 A7
Ainsty Garth WBY LS22 30 A7
Ainsty Rd WBY LS22 29 M7
Ainsty Vw WBY LS22 30 A7
Ainsworth St MILN OL16 206 C8
Aintree Cl GFTH/SHER LS25 135 H4
Airebank BGLY BD16 81 H3
Aire Cl BAIL BD17 82 D5
Aire Crs AIRE BD20 34 F8
Airedale Av BGLY BD16 81 J8
SKP/WHF BD23 16 D2
Airedale College Mt BFDE * BD3 5 J1
Airedale College Rd BFDE BD3 5 J1
Airedale College Ter BFDE BD3 5 J2
Airedale Ct SCFT LS14 111 H1
Airedale Crs BFDE BD3 5 J1
Airedale Cft BRAM LS13 107 H2
Airedale Dr CAS WF10 158 E4
GFTH/SHER LS25 113 K8
HIPP HX3 147 K1
HORS LS18 85 H6
Airedale Gdns BRAM LS13 107 H2
Airedale Gv HORS LS18 85 H6
RTHW * LS26 133 M8
Airedale Hts
WKFDW/WTN WF2 197 L2
Airedale Ms AIRE BD20 36 A5
SKP/WHF BD23 16 A3
Airedale Mt AIRE BD20 58 E6
Airedale Pl BAIL BD17 83 G4
Airedale Quay BRAM LS13 107 J2
Airedale Rd BFDE BD3 5 H1
CAS WF10 158 D7
DOD/DAR S75 241 L6
KGHY BD21 58 B6
RTHW LS26 133 M8
Airedale St BGLY BD16 81 H3
ECHL BD2 105 K3
KGHY BD21 3 M3
Airedale Ter MOR LS27 152 D2
RTHW * LS26 133 M8
Airedale Vw AIRE BD20 34 F7
RTHW * LS26 133 M8
Airedale Whf BRAM LS13 107 H1
Aire Gv YEA LS19 62 E8
Aire Mt WBY LS22 29 M7
Aire Pl BVRD LS3 109 G5
Aire Rd WBY LS22 29 M7
Aireside Av AIRE BD20 34 D4
Aireside Ter AIRE BD20 34 C3
Aire St AIRE BD20 35 G8
BGLY BD16 81 G1
BRIG HD6 170 D5
CAS WF10 157 M6
DEWS WF13 195 H1
HWTH BD22 78 F7
IDLE BD10 83 J5
KGHY BD21 3 K3
KNOT WF11 182 C1
LDS LS1 8 E1
Aire Ter CAS WF10 157 M6
Aireton Rd BSLY S70 260 F4
Aire Valley Dr AIRE BD20 16 D8
Airevalley Rd KGHY BD21 3 L2
Aire Vw AIRE BD20 35 M5
AIRE BD20 58 B4
YEA LS19 62 E8
Aire View Av BGLY BD16 81 K6
SHPY BD18 82 C6
Aireview Crs BAIL BD17 82 C5
Aire View Dr AIRE BD20 58 E7
Aire View Ter KGHY BD21 3 M6
Aireview Ter SKP/WHF * BD23 16 A3
Aireville Av SHPY BD18 104 D1
Aireville Cl AIRE BD20 57 J4
SHPY BD18 104 D1
Aireville Crs AIRE BD20 36 B5
HTON BD9 104 D1
Aireville Dr AIRE BD20 36 B5
HTON BD9 104 D1
Aireville Gra SHPY BD18 104 D1
Aireville Gv HTON BD9 104 D1
Aireville Mt AIRE BD20 58 E7
Aireville Mouny AIRE BD20 36 B5
Aireville Ri HTON BD9 104 D2
Aireville Rd HTON BD9 104 E1
Aireville St AIRE BD20 57 J4
Aireville Ter ILK LS29 40 A5
Aire Wy BAIL BD17 82 C5
Aireworth Cl KGHY BD21 3 M2
Aireworth Gv KGHY BD21 3 M3
Aireworth Rd KGHY BD21 3 M2
Aireworth St KGHY BD21 2 F6
Airey St KGHY BD21 2 D4
Airlie Av RHAY LS8 110 B2
Airlie Pl RHAY LS8 110 B2
Akam Rd BFD BD1 4 C5
Aked's Rd HFAX HX1 10 E7
Aked St BFD * BD1 5 H6
Aketon Dr CAS WF10 157 L8
Aketon Rd CAS WF10 157 L8
Akroyd Ct HIPP HX3 11 G3
Akroyd La HBR HX7 121 K8
Akroyd Pl HFAX HX1 11 G4
Akroyd Ter LUD/ILL HX2 168 B1
Alabama St HFAX HX1 10 B5
Alan Crs MSTN/BAR LS15 111 J7
Alandale Crs GFTH/SHER LS25 112 F8
Alandale Dr GFTH/SHER LS25 112 F8
Alandale Gv GFTH/SHER LS25 112 F8
Alandale Rd GFTH/SHER LS25 112 F7
HUDN HD2 193 G1
Alan Rd DOD/DAR S75 241 M6
Alaska Pl CHAL LS7 88 A8
Alba Cl WMB/DAR S73 263 G8
Albans Cl AL/HA/HU LS17 47 G8
Alban St BOW BD4 127 K2
Albany Cl WMB/DAR S73 262 C8
Albany Ct KGHY BD21 2 D3
PONT WF8 180 F7
Albany Crs HEM/SK/SE WF9 247 H4
Albany Dr HUDE HD5 193 J8
Albany Rd HUDE HD5 193 J8
RTHW LS26 132 F8
Albany Rw ILK * LS29 61 H2
Albany St HEM/SK/SE WF9 247 H4
HIPP HX3 11 K9
HUD HD1 214 B3
ROCH OL11 228 C1
WBOW * BD5 127 G2
WBSY BD6 126 E5
WOR/ARM LS12 108 C7
Albany Ter HIPP HX3 11 K9
WOR/ARM * LS12 108 C7
Alberta Av CHAL LS7 88 A8
Albert Av IDLE BD10 83 L6
LUD/ILL HX2 146 A6
SHPY BD18 82 A5
Albert Cl BTLY WF17 173 L4
Albert Ct LUD/ILL HX2 146 A6
Albert Crs BIRK/DRI BD11 150 D2
CUL/QBY BD13 125 G5
Albert Dr LUD/ILL HX2 145 M6
MOR LS27 152 F1
Albert Gdns LUD/ILL HX2 146 A6
Albert Gv HDGY LS6 86 F8
Albert Pl BFDE BD3 106 A6
HORS LS18 85 L5
Albert Prom HIPP HX3 168 C2
Albert Rd AIRE BD20 34 F8
CUL/QBY BD13 124 F4
KBTN HD8 240 A3
LUD/ILL HX2 146 A6
MOR LS27 152 D1
RPDN/SBR HX6 167 L1
RTHW LS26 133 L8
SHPY BD18 82 B6
Albert Royds St MILN OL16 206 D4
Albert Sq AIRE BD20 36 A5
Albert St AIRE BD20 55 M1
BAIL BD17 82 E5
BRIG HD6 170 E3
BSLY S70 261 H5
CAS WF10 157 M6
CLECK * BD19 149 M6
CUD/GR S72 244 E5
CUL/QBY BD13 102 F8
CUL/QBY BD13 125 H5
ELL HX5 169 H8
FEA/AMT WF7 201 M1
HBR HX7 143 J3
HBR HX7 144 A5
HFAX HX1 10 E5
HUD HD1 214 B3
HWTH BD22 79 H6
IDLE BD10 83 K8
KGHY BD21 2 F4
LIT OL15 207 J1
LM/WK BD12 148 E4
LVSG WF15 172 E3
MILN OL16 229 H1
NORM WF6 178 E2
PDSY/CALV LS28 106 E4
ROY/SHW OL2 229 J7
WBSY BD6 126 D6
WIL/AL BD15 102 E2
Albert Ter LM/WK BD12 149 H1
SHPY BD18 82 B5
SKP/WHF BD23 16 B2
Albert Vw LUD/ILL HX2 146 A6
Albert Wk SHPY BD18 82 A6
Albert Wy BIRK/DRI BD11 150 D2
Albert Yd HUD HD1 14 F8
Albion Ar LDS LS1 9 G1
Albion Av WOR/ARM LS12 108 F7
Albion Cl BSPA/BRAM LS23 69 M1
Albion Ct HFAX HX1 11 G5
WKFDE WF1 12 E3
Albion Cft OSS WF5 175 G8
Albion Fold WIL/AL BD15 102 E1
Albion Pl HEM/SK/SE WF9 247 J3
LDS LS1 7 G9
Albion Rd BSLYN/ROY S71 243 L7
EARL WF12 195 M5
IDLE BD10 83 L6
PDSY/CALV LS28 107 G4
Albion St BRIG HD6 170 C3
BSPA/BRAM LS23 69 M1
BTLY WF17 173 M2
CAS WF10 157 L6
CLECK BD19 150 A7
CUL/QBY BD13 102 A6
CUL/QBY BD13 124 F5
DEWS WF13 173 L5
DEWS * WF13 195 H1
EARD/LOFT WF3 154 F3
ELL HX5 169 J8
HECK WF16 172 E2
HEM/SK/SE WF9 223 H3
HFAX HX1 11 H6
HUD HD1 14 F8
HWTH BD22 79 G6
LDS LS1 7 G9
LIT OL15 207 J1
LVSG WF15 172 C2
MOR * LS27 152 C2
OT LS21 41 K7
PDSY/CALV LS28 107 H7
WBSY BD6 126 A7
WKFDE WF1 176 E7
Albion Ter BSLY S70 261 J6
BSPA/BRAM LS23 48 F8
Albion Wy WOR/ARM LS12 109 G6
Albion Yd SKP/WHF * BD23 16 C2
Alcester Garth BFDE BD3 5 L4
Alcester Pl RHAY * LS8 110 B2
Alcester Rd RHAY LS8 110 B2
Alcester St RHAY * LS8 110 B2
Alcester Ter RHAY LS8 110 B2
Aldams Rd EARL WF12 173 L7
Aldbury Cl BSLYN/ROY S71 243 K8
Alden Av MOR LS27 152 C4
Alden Cl MOR LS27 152 C4
Alden Ct MOR LS27 152 C4
Alden Crs PONT WF8 180 D7
Alden Fold MOR * LS27 152 C4
Alder Av HOLM/MEL HD9 236 E6
KGHY BD21 3 K8
WKFDW/WTN WF2 176 C6
Alderbank WHIT OL12 184 E7
Alder Carr BAIL BD17 82 D3
Alder Cl DOD/DAR S75 242 C5
Alder Dr PDSY/CALV LS28 106 C6
Alder Garth PDSY/CALV LS28 106 D6
Alder Gv LUD/ILL HX2 124 A8
NORM WF6 178 D7
Alder Hill Av CHAL LS7 87 J7
Alder Hill Gv CHAL LS7 87 J7
Alder Holt Dr WBSY BD6 126 C8
Aldermanbury BFD BD1 4 E7
Alderney Rd EARL WF12 174 B4
Alderscholes Cl CUL/QBY BD13 102 F8
Alderscholes La CUL/QBY BD13 124 E1
Aldersley Av SKP/WHF BD23 16 D3
Alderson Dr BSLYN/ROY S71 243 J8
Alderson St WBSY BD6 126 A7
Alderstone Ri HUDW HD3 191 J4
Alder St HUD HD1 15 G3
Aldersyde BTLY WF17 151 G5
Alderton Bank AL/HA/HU LS17 87 H4
Alderton Crs AL/HA/HU LS17 87 H4
Alderton Mt AL/HA/HU LS17 87 H4
Alderton Pl AL/HA/HU LS17 87 H4
Alderton Ri AL/HA/HU LS17 87 H4
Aldham Crs WMB/DAR S73 262 C8
Aldonley HUDE HD5 215 J2
Aldwych ROCH OL11 228 B3
Alegar St BRIG HD6 170 E4
Alexander Av MSTN/BAR LS15 111 H7
Alexander Crs FEA/AMT WF7 179 M7
Alexander Dr MILN OL16 207 G8
Alexander Rd FEA/AMT WF7 179 M8
Alexander Sq CLAY BD14 125 K2
Alexander St LDS * LS1 6 F8
WBSY BD6 126 D6
Alexander Ter HFAX HX1 10 B5
Alexandra Cl RPDN/SBR HX6 167 L2
Alexandra Ct SKP/WHF BD23 16 B4
Alexandra Crs ELL HX5 169 K7
ILK LS29 38 C2
Alexandra Dr NORM WF6 178 D7
Alexandra Gv HDGY LS6 109 G4
PDSY/CALV LS28 106 E7
Alexandra Rd AWLS/ASK DN6 249 M8
BTLY WF17 173 M2
ECHL BD2 105 L1
HBR * HX7 143 J3
HDGY * LS6 109 G4
HORS LS18 85 L5
HUDW HD3 191 L6
PDSY/CALV LS28 106 E8
SHPY * BD18 82 C7
Alexandra St CUL/QBY * BD13 125 G5
GTHN BD7 4 A9
HFAX HX1 11 G7
LVSG WF15 172 C2
Alexandra Ter BSLYN/ROY S71 262 B6
ECHL BD2 105 L4
YEA LS19 62 E7
Alford Cl DOD/DAR S75 260 D2
Alford Ter GTHN BD7 104 C7
Alfred St East HFAX * HX1 11 J6
Alfred St BRIG HD6 170 D3
BSLYN/ROY S71 244 A2
BTLY WF17 173 K2
EARL * WF12 174 A5
GTL/HWG HX4 168 F7
HECK * WF16 172 F3
HFAX HX1 10 B5
HUD HD1 14 F9
LIT OL15 185 L3
LVSG WF15 172 D2
MOR * LS27 130 E6
ROY/SHW OL2 229 J7
Alfreds Wy BTLY WF17 173 L1
Alice St CLECK BD19 149 M6
GIR BD8 4 C3
HWTH BD22 78 E8
KGHY BD21 3 G4
WHIT OL12 206 D5
Alicia Dr WHIT OL12 206 A4
Alison St ROY/SHW OL2 229 J6
Alkincote St KGHY BD21 2 F7
All Alone Rd IDLE BD10 83 H7
Allanbridge Cl IDLE BD10 83 L7
Allandale Av WBSY BD6 126 C7
Allandale Rd WBSY BD6 126 C7
Allan Haigh Cl
WKFDW/WTN WF2 175 M6
Allan St BFDE BD3 5 L7
Allan Ter RPDN/SBR HX6 167 L3
Allatt Cl BSLY S70 261 H6
Allenby Crs BEE/HOL LS11 131 J6
Allenby Dr BEE/HOL LS11 131 J6
Allenby Gdns BEE/HOL LS11 131 J6
Allenby Gv BEE/HOL LS11 131 J6
Allenby Pl BEE/HOL LS11 131 J6
Allenby Rd BEE/HOL LS11 131 J6
Allenby St ROY/SHW OL2 229 J7
Allenby Vw BEE/HOL LS11 131 J5
Allen Cl ROY/SHW OL2 229 J8
Allen Cft BIRK/DRI BD11 150 C1
Allendale Rd DOD/DAR S75 241 M6
DOD/DAR S75 261 G2
Allendale St COL BB8 74 B1
Allen Rw HUD HD1 14 A8
Allen St MILN OL16 228 C1
Allerby Gn WBSY BD6 126 B8
Allergill Pk HOLM/MEL HD9 253 M1
Allerton Cl WIL/AL BD15 103 K5
Allerton Dr AL/HA/HU LS17 46 E8
Allerton Grange Av
AL/HA/HU LS17 88 A5
Allerton Grange Cl
AL/HA/HU LS17 87 L6
Allerton Grange Crs
AL/HA/HU LS17 87 M6
Allerton Grange Cft RHAY LS8 88 A6
Allerton Grange Dr
AL/HA/HU LS17 87 M6
WIL/AL BD15 103 K5
Allerton Grange Gdns
AL/HA/HU LS17 87 M6
Allerton Grange Ri
AL/HA/HU LS17 87 M6
Allerton Grange V
AL/HA/HU LS17 87 M6
Allerton Grange Wk
AL/HA/HU LS17 87 M6
Allerton Grange Wy RHAY LS8 87 M6
Allerton Gv AL/HA/HU LS17 87 M4
Allerton Hl CHAL LS7 87 L7
Allerton La WIL/AL BD15 103 J7
Allerton Pk CHAL LS7 87 M7
Allerton Pl AL/HA/HU LS17 87 M4
HFAX HX1 10 C6
Allerton Rd WIL/AL BD15 102 F5
WIL/AL BD15 103 K5
Allerton St BULY LS4 108 F5
Allescholes Rd TOD OL14 163 J7
Alliance St WOR/ARM LS12 108 C7
Allington ROCH * OL11 206 A8
Allinson St WOR/ARM LS12 109 G8
Allison Dr HUDN HD2 192 C3
Allison Gv COL BB8 52 A8
Allison La ECHL BD2 104 F2
Allison St FEA/AMT WF7 201 L1
Alloe Field Vw LUD/ILL HX2 124 A8
Allott Cl HEM/SK/SE WF9 247 H3
All Saint's Cir RTHW LS26 133 M7
All Saints Cl DOD/DAR S75 259 J6
KBTN HD8 240 B4
All Saints Ct KGHY BD21 2 E5
All Saint's Dr RTHW LS26 133 L8
All Saints Rd GTHN BD7 126 E1
RTHW LS26 133 M7
All Saints Ter KGHY BD21 2 E4
WHIT OL12 206 D4
All Saint's Vw RTHW LS26 133 L7
All Souls' Rd HIPP HX3 11 G2
All Souls' St HIPP * HX3 11 G2
All Souls St HIPP HX3 11 G2
Allums La OT LS21 65 G2
Alma Cl PDSY/CALV LS28 106 E3
Alma Cottages HDGY LS6 108 F1
Alma Dr HUDE HD5 15 L7
Alma Gv OSM LS9 7 M5
Alma La HECK WF16 150 F8
RPDN/SBR HX6 166 D7
Alma Pl BFDE BD3 105 M6
KGHY BD21 3 G9
OSM LS9 7 M5
Alma Rd COL BB8 52 F8
HDGY LS6 108 F1
TOD OL14 163 J5
Alma St BOW BD4 127 L1
BSLY S70 260 F5
CUL/QBY BD13 124 F5
HWTH BD22 78 E6
KGHY BD21 79 L2
OSM LS9 7 M6
RTHW LS26 133 M7
SHPY BD18 82 F6
TOD OL14 163 J5
WHIT * OL12 206 B5
YEA LS19 62 E7
Alma Ter KGHY BD21 79 L2
RTHW LS26 132 F8
Almond Av CUD/GR S72 244 D7
Almondbury Bank HUDE HD5 15 L8
Almondbury Cl HUDE HD5 215 J3
Almondbury Common
HUDS HD4 215 H5
Almond Cl HEM/SK/SE WF9 247 J1
LIT OL15 185 H8
Almondroyd HECK WF16 172 E2
Almond St BFDE BD3 105 L8
Almond Wy BTLY WF17 151 H5
Almscliffe Av EARL WF12 174 A6
Almscliffe Dr AL/HA/HU LS17 43 K2
Almscliffe Garth AL/HA/HU LS17 25 M7
Almshouse Hl BSPA/BRAM LS23 69 M4
Almshouse La WKFDE WF1 12 F3
WKFDW/WTN WF2 220 D3
Alperton Cl BSLYN/ROY S71 262 B1
Alpha St KGHY BD21 3 J5
Alpine Cl BTLY WF17 173 K2
Alpine Dr MILN OL16 207 J7
WHIT OL12 184 E8
Alpine Ri CUL/QBY BD13 102 F7
Alric Dr BSLYN/ROY S71 262 A5
Alston Av ROY/SHW OL2 229 K6
Alston Cl DOD/DAR S75 259 H6
HTON BD9 103 M5
Alston La SCFT LS14 111 J3
Alston Rd KGHY BD21 3 K1
Altar Dr AIRE BD20 58 C5
HTON BD9 104 C3
Altar La BGLY BD16 80 C2
Althorpe Gv IDLE BD10 83 J8
Altinkool St WKFDE WF1 199 G4
Altofts Hall Rd NORM WF6 178 B2
Altofts La CAS WF10 156 F8
Altofts Lodge Dr NORM WF6 178 B2
Altofts Rd NORM WF6 178 C3
Alton Av HUDE HD5 193 H7
Alton Gv HTON BD9 104 B3
SHPY BD18 104 D1
Alton Wy DOD/DAR S75 242 C5
Alum Ct HTON BD9 104 C3
Alum Dr HTON BD9 104 C3
Alvanley Ct GIR BD8 103 M6
Alverthorpe Rd
WKFDW/WTN WF2 176 B8
Alwen Av HUDN HD2 192 B4
Alwin Rd ROY/SHW OL2 229 J6
Alwoodley Cha AL/HA/HU LS17 88 A1
Alwoodley Court Gdns
AL/HA/HU LS17 65 J8
Alwoodley Gdns AL/HA/HU LS17 87 J1
Alwoodley La AL/HA/HU LS17 65 H8
Amberley Ct BFDE * BD3 105 L7
Amberley Gdns
WOR/ARM LS12 108 E8
Amberley Ri AWLS/ASK DN6 249 H4
Amberley Rd WOR/ARM LS12 108 E8
Amberley St BFDE BD3 105 L8
WOR/ARM LS12 108 E8
Amber St BTLY WF17 151 J8
Amberton Ap RHAY LS8 110 E2
Amberton Cl RHAY LS8 110 E1
Amberton Crs RHAY LS8 110 E2
Amberton Gdns RHAY LS8 110 E2
Amberton Garth RHAY LS8 110 E2
Amberton Gv RHAY LS8 110 E2
Amberton La RHAY LS8 110 E2
Amberton Mt RHAY LS8 110 E2
Amberton Pl RHAY LS8 110 D2
Amberton Rd RHAY LS8 110 D2
Amberton St RHAY LS8 110 E2
Amberton Ter RHAY LS8 110 E2
Ambler Gv LUD/ILL HX2 124 B8
Amblers Ct PDSY/CALV LS28 107 G8
Amblers Cft IDLE BD10 83 K4
Amblers Ter HIPP HX3 11 H2
Ambler St CAS WF10 157 M7
GIR BD8 104 E4
KGHY BD21 3 K5
Ambler Wy CUL/QBY BD13 124 E7
Ambleside Av HTON BD9 104 B4
Ambleside Dr
WKFDW/WTN WF2 199 J8
Ambleside Gdns
PDSY/CALV LS28 106 E7
Ambleside Gv BSLYN/ROY S71 262 C6
RTHW LS26 133 L8
Ambleside Rd CAS WF10 159 G5
Ambleside Wk WBY LS22 29 K8
Ambleton Wy CUL/QBY BD13 124 E6
Ambrose St ROCH OL11 228 B1
Amelia St SHPY BD18 82 B6
America La AIRE BD20 56 A6
BRIG HD6 170 E4
America Moor La MOR LS27 152 C4
Amisfield Rd HIPP HX3 147 M6
Amos St HFAX HX1 10 B5
Amport Cl BRIG HD6 170 D5
Amspool Ct EARD/LOFT WF3 154 E3
Amundsen Av ECHL BD2 105 J1
Amyroyce Dr SHPY BD18 83 G7
Amy St BGLY BD16 81 J3
HIPP HX3 146 C4
Anaheim Dr WKFDE WF1 176 F1
Ancaster Crs BHP/TINH LS16 86 D7
Ancaster Rd BHP/TINH LS16 86 D7
Ancaster Vw BHP/TINH LS16 86 D7
The Anchorage BGLY BD16 81 H2
Anchor Bridge Wy EARL WF12 173 L7
Anchor St HUD HD1 15 H6
TOD OL14 163 L1
Ancote Cl DOD/DAR S75 260 C5
Andersen Ct CAS WF10 180 E1
Anderson Av RHAY LS8 7 M4
Anderson Mt RHAY LS8 7 M4
Anderson St GIR BD8 4 A1
PONT WF8 180 E5
WKFDW/WTN WF2 12 B3
Anderton St AIRE BD20 34 F7
WKFDE WF1 13 K8
Andover Gn BOW BD4 128 A2
Andrew Cl HIPP HX3 169 J2
Andrew Crs HUDS HD4 213 J5
WKFDE WF1 176 D1
Andrews Gv FEA/AMT WF7 202 B8
Andrew St FEA/AMT WF7 201 L2
PDSY/CALV LS28 106 F4
WKFDE WF1 176 D7
Angel Ct BVRD LS3 6 A7
Angel Pl BGLY BD16 81 J1
Angel Rd HFAX HX1 10 D4
Angel St BAIL BD17 82 F2
Angel Wy BFD BD1 4 C6
Angerton Wy WBSY BD6 126 C8
Angram Rd RYKW YO26 33 J4
Angus Av LM/WK BD12 148 E5
Anlaby St BOW BD4 127 M1
Annan Cl DOD/DAR S75 260 A1
Annat Royd La STKB/PEN S36 256 E7
Anne Crs CUD/GR S72 245 G1
Anne Ga BFDE BD3 5 H5
Annersley Av ROY/SHW OL2 229 J8
Annes Ct HIPP HX3 169 J2
Anne St BTLY WF17 151 J7
GTHN BD7 126 B3
Annie St HEM/SK/SE WF9 223 J2
KGHY * BD21 3 G1
MOR LS27 152 D2
RPDN/SBR HX6 167 K1
SHPY BD18 82 E8
WKFDE WF1 176 D2
Anning Fold GFTH/SHER LS25 113 K6
Annison St BFDE BD3 5 J6
Annottes Cft HUDE HD5 193 H7
Ann Pl WBOW BD5 4 E9
Ann St CUL/QBY BD13 101 M5
KGHY BD21 2 E6
ROCH * OL11 206 B8
Anroyd St DEWS WF13 173 J5
Ansdell Rd MILN OL16 228 D2
Anson Cft SEL YO8 139 M5
Anson Gv GTHN BD7 126 B4
Anston Dr HEM/SK/SE WF9 247 J1
Anthony La BGLY BD16 80 D4
Antony Cl HUDW HD3 190 F5
Anvil Ct GIR BD8 104 D5

Anvil St BRIG HD6 ....170 C3
GIR BD8 ....104 D5
Apex Vw BEE/HOL LS11 ....8 F5
Apex Wy BEE/HOL LS11 ....9 G6
Apperley Gdns IDLE BD10 ....84 A6
Apperley La IDLE BD10 ....84 A6
YEA LS19 ....84 C3
Apperley Rd IDLE BD10 ....83 M6
Appleby Cl CUL/QBY BD13 ....124 E5
DOD/DAR S75 ....242 B5
Appleby La GFTH/SHER LS25 ....113 K7
Appleby Pl AWLS/ASK DN6 ....249 H4
MSTN/BAR LS15 ....111 G6
Appleby Wk MSTN/BAR LS15 ....111 G6
Appleby Wy MOR LS27 ....152 D1
WBY LS22 ....30 A7
Apple Cl BTLY WF17 ....151 J4
Applegarth RTHW LS26 ....133 L7
WKFDW/WTN WF2 ....199 G7
Applehaigh Gv BSLYN/ROY S71 ....243 J2
Applehaigh La HOR/CROF WF4 ....221 J8
Applehaigh Vw
BSLYN/ROY S71 ....243 J2
Applehurst Bank BSLY * S70 ....261 K6
Appleshaw Crs
WKFDW/WTN WF2 ....176 B3
Apple St HWTH BD22 ....79 J3
HWTH * BD22 ....100 E4
Appleton Cl BGLY BD16 ....81 K1
LM/WK BD12 ....149 H1
Appleton Gv OSM LS9 ....110 D6
Appleton Wy OSM LS9 ....110 B6
Appletree Cl BSPA/BRAM LS23 ....48 F7
Apple Tree Cl EARD/LOFT WF3 ....153 L6
PONT WF8 ....180 D8
Apple Tree Ct
EARD/LOFT * WF3 ....153 L7
Appletree Dr SEL YO8 ....139 M4
Apple Tree Gdns ILK LS29 ....38 B2
Apple Tree Rd FEA/AMT WF7 ....202 A2
Appletree Wy GFTH/SHER LS25 ....116 B6
Appleyard Rd HBR HX7 ....144 B5
The Approach MSTN/BAR LS15 ....90 B7
April Cl BSLYN/ROY S71 ....261 L2
April Ct LVSG WF15 ....172 C4
April Dr BSLYN/ROY S71 ....261 M2
Apsley Crs GIR BD8 ....4 B1
Apsley St HWTH BD22 ....78 F3
KGHY BD21 ....2 F8
Apsley Vls GIR BD8 ....4 B1
Aquamarine Dr HUDN HD2 ....192 E4
Aqueduct St BSLYN/ROY S71 ....261 H3
Aquila Wy LVSG WF15 ....171 M1
Arborary La HOLM/MEL HD9 ....213 H8
The Arbour AIRE BD20 ....34 F5
ILK LS29 ....20 C8
The Arcade BSLY * S70 ....261 G5
Arcadia St KGHY BD21 ....2 F8
Archbell Av BRIG HD6 ....170 D6
Archer Rd BRIG HD6 ....170 F5
Archer St CAS WF10 ....157 L8
Archery Pl LDSU LS2 ....6 E5
Archery Rd LDSU LS2 ....6 E4
Archery St LDSU LS2 ....6 F5
Archery Ter LDSU LS2 ....6 E5
The Arches HIPP * HX3 ....11 H1
Arches St HFAX HX1 ....10 F7
Archibald St GTHN BD7 ....4 A6
Arcon Cl MILN OL16 ....207 G8
Arctic Pde GTHN BD7 ....126 C2
Arctic St HWTH BD22 ....79 G6
KGHY BD21 ....57 K5
Arden Ct HOR/CROF WF4 ....197 J6
HUDE HD5 ....193 L7
Ardennes Cl ECHL BD2 ....105 H2
Arden Rd GIR BD8 ....103 L7
HFAX HX1 ....10 E9
Ardsley Cl BOW BD4 ....128 B4
Argent Wy BOW BD4 ....128 B4
Argie Av BULY LS4 ....108 D3
Argie Gdns BULY LS4 ....108 E4
Argie Rd BULY LS4 ....108 E4
Argie Ter BULY LS4 ....108 E4
Argyle Ms AL/HA/HU LS17 ....67 L1
Argyle Rd KNOT WF11 ....181 L1
OSM LS9 ....7 K8
Argyle St BOW BD4 ....127 K2
KGHY BD21 ....2 E4
MAR/SLWT HD7 ....233 H2
ROCH OL11 ....228 C2
SHPY BD18 ....82 D8
WKFDE WF1 ....13 J7
Argyll Av PONT WF8 ....180 D6
Argyll Cl BAIL BD17 ....83 G4
HORS LS18 ....85 K2
Arkendale Ms GTHN * BD7 ....126 A3
Arkenley La HUDS HD4 ....215 H5
Arkenmore HUDE HD5 ....193 H7
Arksey Pl WOR/ARM * LS12 ....108 E6
Arksey Ter WOR/ARM LS12 ....108 E6
Arkwright St BOW BD4 ....106 A8
CLAY BD14 ....125 K2
Arkwright Wk MOR LS27 ....130 C8
Arlesford Rd BOW BD4 ....128 A4
Arley Cl HOLM/MEL HD9 ....236 B6
Arley Dr ROY/SHW OL2 ....229 L6
Arley Gv WOR/ARM LS12 ....108 E6
Arley Pl WOR/ARM LS12 ....108 E6
Arley St WOR/ARM LS12 ....108 E6
Arley Ter WOR/ARM LS12 ....108 E6
Arlington Crs LUD/ILL HX2 ....167 M1
Arlington Gv CAS * WF10 ....158 B7
RHAY LS8 ....110 D2
Arlington Rd RHAY LS8 ....110 D2
Arlington St BFDE BD3 ....5 L7
WKFDE WF1 ....176 D6
Arlington Wy HUDE HD5 ....193 J7
Armadale Av BOW BD4 ....127 K6
Armgill La SHPY BD18 ....104 F2
Armidale Wy ECHL BD2 ....105 H3
Armitage Av BRIG HD6 ....170 D6
Armitage Rd HFAX HX1 ....10 A9
HUDN HD2 ....192 B5
HUDS HD4 ....214 A6
HUDW HD3 ....213 K1
LM/WK BD12 ....149 H2
WKFDW/WTN WF2 ....175 M6
Armitage Sq PDSY/CALV LS28 ....106 F8
Armitage St CAS WF10 ....157 L6
DEWS WF13 ....194 F1
HUDS HD4 ....214 C2
RTHW * LS26 ....155 G2
Armley Gra WOR/ARM LS12 ....108 B6
Armley Grange Av
WOR/ARM LS12 ....108 B6
Armley Grange Crs
WOR/ARM LS12 ....108 B5
Armley Grange Dr
WOR/ARM LS12 ....108 B6
Armley Grange Mt
WOR/ARM LS12 ....108 B6
Armley Grange Ov
WOR/ARM LS12 ....108 B5
Armley Grange Ri
WOR/ARM LS12 ....108 B6
Armley Grange Vw
WOR/ARM LS12 ....108 C6
Armley Grange Wk
WOR/ARM LS12 ....108 C6
Armley Grove Pl
WOR/ARM LS12 ....108 F7
Armley Lodge Rd
WOR/ARM LS12 ....108 E5
Armley Park Rd
WOR/ARM LS12 ....108 E5
Armley Ridge Cl
WOR/ARM LS12 ....108 C6
Armley Ridge Rd
WOR/ARM LS12 ....108 B4
Armley Ridge Ter
WOR/ARM LS12 ....108 C5
Armley Rd WOR/ARM LS12 ....108 F6
Armouries Dr MID LS10 ....9 K4
Armouries Wy MID LS10 ....9 J2
Armoury Av MIRF WF14 ....194 C1
Arm Rd WHIT OL12 ....207 G1
Armstrong Cl NORM WF6 ....178 C2
Armstrong Hurst Cl WHIT OL12 ....206 D3
Armstrong St BOW BD4 ....105 M8
PDSY/CALV LS28 ....106 F4
Armstrong Ter PONT WF8 ....180 D7
Armyne Gv BSLYN/ROY S71 ....262 A5
Armytage Crs HUD HD1 ....214 A3
Armytage Rd BRIG HD6 ....170 E4
Armytage Wy BRIG HD6 ....170 F5
Arncliffe Av HWTH * BD22 ....2 C7
Arncliffe Ct HUDW HD3 ....14 A4
Arncliffe Crs BRIG HD6 ....170 A6
MOR LS27 ....152 E4
Arncliffe Dr BSLY S70 ....260 D5
KNOT WF11 ....181 K2
Arncliffe Gdns BTLY WF17 ....173 K1
Arncliffe Garth
PDSY/CALV LS28 ....106 F4
Arncliffe Gra AL/HA/HU LS17 ....87 M4
Arncliffe Gv HWTH BD22 ....2 C8
Arncliffe Pl HWTH BD22 ....2 C7
Arncliffe Rd BHP/TINH LS16 ....86 C6
BTLY WF17 ....173 J1
HWTH BD22 ....2 C8
WKFDE WF1 ....177 H6
Arncliffe St PDSY/CALV LS28 ....106 F4
Arncliffe Ter GTHN BD7 ....104 D8
Arndale Gv HOLM/MEL HD9 ....254 D1
Arnford Cl BFDE BD3 ....5 H3
Arnold Av BSLYN/ROY S71 ....243 H6
HUDN HD2 ....192 B5
Arnold Pl GIR BD8 ....104 D6
Arnold Royd BRIG HD6 ....170 A7
Arnold St GIR BD8 ....4 A2
HFAX HX1 ....10 C6
HUDN HD2 ....14 D1
LVSG WF15 ....172 C2
RPDN/SBR * HX6 ....167 K2
Arnside Av AIRE BD20 ....58 A5
Arnside Cl CAS WF10 ....158 F6
ROY/SHW OL2 ....229 M7
Arnside Crs CAS WF10 ....158 F6
Arnside Rd WBOW BD5 ....126 F4
Arran Cl MAR/SLWT HD7 ....212 F1
Arran Ct GFTH/SHER LS25 ....135 H1
Arran Dr GFTH/SHER LS25 ....135 H1
HORS LS18 ....85 K2
Arran Wy RTHW LS26 ....155 H1
Arrunden La HOLM/MEL HD9 ....254 B5
Arthington Av MID LS10 ....131 M4
Arthington Cl EARD/LOFT WF3 ....152 F7
Arthington Garth OT LS21 ....43 H8
Arthington Gv MID LS10 ....131 M4
Arthington La OT LS21 ....43 G7
Arthington Lawns OT LS21 ....43 G8
Arthington Pl MID LS10 ....131 M4
Arthington Rd BHP/TINH LS16 ....64 E5
Arthington St GIR BD8 ....4 A3
MID LS10 ....131 M4
MILN OL16 ....206 D6
Arthington Ter MID LS10 ....131 M4
Arthington Vw MID LS10 ....131 M4
Arthur Av GIR BD8 ....103 M7
Arthur Gv BTLY WF17 ....151 H6
Arthursdale Cl MSTN/BAR LS15 ....90 B7
Arthursdale Dr MSTN/BAR LS15 ....90 B7
Arthursdale Gra
MSTN/BAR LS15 ....90 B7
Arthur St BGLY * BD16 ....81 H3
BRIG HD6 ....170 E4
HWTH BD22 ....78 D4
IDLE BD10 ....83 K8
MAR/SLWT HD7 ....213 G2
PDSY/CALV LS28 ....106 F4
ROY/SHW OL2 ....229 J7
WKFDE WF1 ....13 K8
Artillery St HECK WF16 ....172 F3
Artist St WOR/ARM LS12 ....109 G7
Arum St WBOW BD5 ....126 E3
Arundel Av ROCH OL11 ....228 A2
Arundel Cl BTLY WF17 ....151 K4
Arundell Dr BSLYN/ROY S71 ....262 B2
Arundel Rd AWLS/ASK DN6 ....227 M3
Arundel St GFTH/SHER LS25 ....113 K6
HFAX HX1 ....10 B5
PDSY/CALV LS28 ....107 G6
ROCH OL11 ....228 A2
WKFDE WF1 ....176 E7
Arundel Wk BTLY WF17 ....151 K5
Ascot Av GTHN BD7 ....126 A4
Ascot Dr WBSY BD6 ....126 A4
Ascot Gdns EARD/LOFT WF3 ....153 M3
GTHN BD7 ....126 A4
Ascot Gv BRIG HD6 ....170 A6
Ascot Pde GTHN BD7 ....126 A4
Ascot Rd GFTH/SHER LS25 ....135 H4
Ascot Ter OSM LS9 ....110 B7
Asdale Rd HOR/CROF WF4 ....198 C7
Ash Av HDGY LS6 ....108 F1
Ashbourne Av CLECK BD19 ....149 M8
ECHL BD2 ....105 H3
Ashbourne Bank ECHL BD2 ....105 H3
Ashbourne Cl ECHL BD2 ....105 H3
WHIT OL12 ....184 F8
Ashbourne Crs CUL/QBY BD13 ....124 F5
ECHL BD2 ....105 H3
GFTH/SHER LS25 ....135 H1
Ashbourne Cft CLECK BD19 ....149 M8
Ashbourne Dr CLECK BD19 ....149 M8
ECHL BD2 ....105 H3
PONT WF8 ....202 F1
Ashbourne Gdns CLECK BD19 ....149 M8
ECHL BD2 ....105 H3
Ashbourne Garth ECHL BD2 ....105 J2
Ashbourne Gv ECHL BD2 ....105 H3
HFAX HX1 ....10 A6
Ashbourne Hvn ECHL BD2 ....105 H3
Ashbourne Mt ECHL BD2 ....105 H3
Ashbourne Ov ECHL BD2 ....105 H3
Ashbourne Ri ECHL BD2 ....105 H3
Ashbourne Rd BSLYN/ROY S71 ....243 J7
ECHL BD2 ....105 H3
HWTH BD22 ....79 J2
Ashbourne Vw CLECK BD19 ....149 M8
Ashbourne Wy CLECK BD19 ....149 M8
ECHL BD2 ....105 H3
Ashbrook Cl OSS WF5 ....174 F8
Ashbrook Crs WHIT OL12 ....206 E2
Ashbrook Pk BEE/HOL * LS11 ....131 L4
Ashbrook Hey La WHIT OL12 ....206 E2
Ash Brow HOR/CROF WF4 ....217 L3
Ash Brow Rd HUDN HD2 ....192 D3
Ashburn Cl WBY LS22 ....29 M7
Ashburn Cft WBY LS22 ....29 M7
Ashburn Dr WBY LS22 ....29 M7
Ashburn Gv BAIL BD17 ....82 E2
WBY LS22 ....29 M8
Ashburnham Gv HTON BD9 ....104 D3
Ashburn Pl ILK LS29 ....38 C3
Ashburn Wy WBY LS22 ....29 M7
Ashburton Cl AWLS/ASK DN6 ....249 J8
Ashbury Cha WKFDE WF1 ....176 C1
Ashby Av BRAM LS13 ....107 M4
Ashby Cl LVSG WF15 ....172 B5
Ashby Ct BSLY S70 ....260 F6
Ashby Crs BRAM LS13 ....107 M4
Ashby Mt BRAM LS13 ....107 M4
Ashby Sq BRAM LS13 ....107 M4
Ashby St BOW BD4 ....127 J2
Ashby Ter BRAM LS13 ....107 M4
Ashby Vw BRAM LS13 ....107 M4
Ash Cl HIPP HX3 ....147 M6
ILK LS29 ....38 A2
WHIT OL12 ....206 E2
Ashcombe Dr KNOT WF11 ....182 B3
Ash Ct CLECK BD19 ....149 H6
Ash Crs EARD/LOFT WF3 ....177 H2
HDGY LS6 ....108 E1
Ash Cft WBSY BD6 ....126 C6
Ashcroft Av FEA/AMT WF7 ....201 L2
Ashcroft Cl BTLY WF17 ....173 J3
Ashcroft Rd FEA/AMT WF7 ....201 L3
Ashdale WKFDW/WTN WF2 ....199 G6
Ashdale La WBY LS22 ....29 M6
Ashday La HIPP HX3 ....169 L4
Ashdene WOR/ARM LS12 ....129 M3
Ashdene Ap HOR/CROF WF4 ....200 B5
Ashdene Av HOR/CROF WF4 ....200 B5
Ashdene Cl PDSY/CALV LS28 ....129 G1
Ashdene Ct CUL/QBY BD13 ....79 M8
Ashdene Crs HOR/CROF WF4 ....200 B5
PDSY/CALV LS28 ....129 G1
Ashdene Dr HOR/CROF WF4 ....200 B5
Ashdene Garth
HOR/CROF WF4 ....200 B5
Ashdene Gv PONT WF8 ....181 H2
Ashdown St BRAM LS13 ....107 L4
Ashdown Wy ROY/SHW OL2 ....229 G6
Ash Dyke Cl DOD/DAR S75 ....241 M7
Ashenhurst Av HUDS HD4 ....214 E3
Ashenhurst Cl HUDS HD4 ....214 D3
TOD OL14 ....141 J7
Ashenhurst Ri HUDS HD4 ....214 D3
Ashenhurst Rd HUDS HD4 ....214 D3
TOD OL14 ....141 H7
Ashes La HUDS HD4 ....214 D6
MILN OL16 ....207 G7
TOD OL14 ....141 M7
Ashfield BOW BD4 ....127 M5
EARL WF12 ....195 M2
WBY LS22 ....30 B8
Ashfield Av KBTN HD8 ....239 J5
MOR LS27 ....152 B4
ROCH OL11 ....228 B1
SHPY BD18 ....104 D1
Ashfield Cl DOD/DAR S75 ....260 E3
HIPP HX3 ....146 B4
MSTN/BAR LS15 ....111 M3
WOR/ARM LS12 ....130 A2
Ashfield Ct BSLY * S70 ....261 M6
Ashfield Crs BGLY BD16 ....81 J4
PDSY/CALV LS28 ....106 F5
Ashfield Dr BAIL BD17 ....82 F2
HIPP HX3 ....146 C4
SHPY BD18 ....104 D1
Ashfield Gv PDSY/CALV * LS28 ....107 G5
SHPY BD18 ....104 C1
Ashfield La MILN OL16 ....229 H2
Ashfield Pk HDGY LS6 ....109 G1
Ashfield Pl ECHL BD2 ....105 M4
OT * LS21 ....41 H7
Ashfield Rd BTLY WF17 ....151 J4
CUL/QBY BD13 ....102 F8
GTL/HWG HX4 ....168 D7
HEM/SK/SE WF9 ....245 M1
HUDN HD2 ....14 B1
IDLE BD10 ....83 L5
MOR LS27 ....152 B4
PDSY/CALV LS28 ....106 F5
ROCH OL11 ....228 B1
SHPY BD18 ....82 A7
Ashfield St HUDN HD2 ....192 D4
NORM WF6 ....178 E3
Ashfield Ter EARD/LOFT WF3 ....154 B4
GTL/HWG HX4 ....168 D6
HWTH BD22 ....78 E8
MSTN/BAR LS15 ....111 M2
Ashfield Wy WOR/ARM LS12 ....130 B3
Ashford Ct BSLYN/ROY * S71 ....243 K1
KBTN HD8 ....216 B7
Ashford Dr PDSY/CALV LS28 ....107 H8
Ash Ford Gn WBSY * BD6 ....126 B5
Ashford Mnr KBTN HD8 ....215 M5
Ashford Pk MAR/SLWT HD7 ....212 F1
Ashgap La NORM WF6 ....178 D4
Ash Gdns HDGY LS6 ....108 F1
Ash Ghyll Gdns BGLY * BD16 ....81 H2
Ash Gv AIRE BD20 ....55 L1
AIRE BD20 ....56 F1
BGLY BD16 ....81 J5
BIRK/DRI BD11 ....128 C8
BRIG HD6 ....170 E4
BSLY S70 ....261 M7
CLECK BD19 ....150 C5
COL * BB8 ....53 G8
EARD/LOFT WF3 ....177 H4
HDGY LS6 ....6 A2
HEM/SK/SE WF9 ....247 J2
HORS LS18 ....85 L4
HWTH BD22 ....79 J2
ILK LS29 ....38 E1
LIT OL15 ....207 H1
MILN OL16 ....229 J3
OT LS21 ....41 H7
PDSY/CALV LS28 ....107 G8
PONT WF8 ....203 L1
ROY/SHW OL2 ....228 F8
Ashgrove ECHL BD2 ....105 L3
GTHN BD7 ....4 C8
IDLE BD10 ....84 A7
MILN OL16 ....228 D5
Ashgrove Av HIPP * HX3 ....169 G3
Ashgrove Crs GFTH/SHER LS25 ....135 K3
Ashgrove Cft GFTH/SHER LS25 ....135 J4
GFTH/SHER * LS25 ....135 K4
Ashgrove Ms BRAM LS13 ....107 H2
Ashgrove Mt GFTH/SHER LS25 ....135 J3
Ash Grove Rd HOLM/MEL HD9 ....254 A1
Ashgrove Rd AIRE BD20 ....57 J4
HUDE HD5 ....193 H4
Ash Hall La RPDN/SBR HX6 ....166 B8
Ash Hill Dr AL/HA/HU LS17 ....89 H2
Ash Hill Gdns AL/HA/HU LS17 ....89 H2
Ash Hill La AL/HA/HU LS17 ....89 H2
Ashia Cl MILN OL16 ....206 C8
Ashington Cl ECHL BD2 ....105 M3
Ashlands Rd ILK LS29 ....38 E1
Ash La GFTH/SHER LS25 ....113 J6
GFTH/SHER LS25 ....117 G4
KBTN HD8 ....218 A8
TAD LS24 ....116 E1
Ashlar Cl HWTH BD22 ....78 F7
Ashlar Gv CAS WF10 ....158 B8
CUL/QBY BD13 ....124 F7
Ash Lea EARD/LOFT WF3 ....177 H4
Ashlea Av BRIG HD6 ....170 D6
Ashlea Cl BRIG HD6 ....170 D6
GFTH/SHER LS25 ....135 H1
Ashlea Dr BRIG HD6 ....170 D6
Ashlea Ga BRAM LS13 ....107 L2
Ashlea Gn BRAM LS13 ....107 L3
Ashleigh CUD/GR S72 ....245 J3
Ashleigh Av PONT WF8 ....180 F7
WKFDW/WTN WF2 ....198 A1
Ashleigh Cl KBTN * HD8 ....238 B4
Ashleigh Dl HUDN HD2 ....192 A5
Ashleigh Gdns OSS WF5 ....174 E6
RTHW LS26 ....133 L8
Ashleigh Rd BHP/TINH LS16 ....86 C6
Ashleigh St KGHY BD21 ....3 G2
Ashley Av OSM LS9 ....110 C4
Ashley Cl CLECK BD19 ....150 C4
WKFDW/WTN WF2 ....176 B4
Ashley Ct HEM/SK/SE WF9 ....246 B5
Ashley Cft BSLYN/ROY S71 ....243 K2
Ashley Gv HBR HX7 ....144 A4
Ashley La BAIL BD17 ....82 C6
Ashley Park Ms
GFTH/SHER LS25 ....113 K6
Ashley Rd BGLY BD16 ....81 J4
LM/WK BD12 ....148 E4
OSM LS9 ....110 C4
WOR/ARM LS12 ....108 D8
Ashley St HFAX HX1 ....10 B6
SHPY BD18 ....82 D6
Ashley Ter OSM LS9 ....110 C4
Ashmead BSPA/BRAM LS23 ....69 M1
BTLY WF17 ....173 J3
Ash Meadow Cl HUDN HD2 ....192 E3
Ashmere Gv HUDN HD2 ....192 D4
Ashmews IDLE * BD10 ....84 A7
Ashmore Dr OSS WF5 ....174 E5
Ashmore Gdns BOW * BD4 ....127 K6
Ashmount CLAY BD14 ....125 M2
Ash Mt GTHN BD7 ....126 D1
KGHY BD21 ....2 C9
Ashmount Dr WHIT OL12 ....206 B4
Ash Rd AWLS/ASK DN6 ....249 K4
CUD/GR S72 ....244 F4
HDGY LS6 ....108 E1
Ashroyd RTHW LS26 ....155 H2
Ash St AIRE BD20 ....34 F8
CLECK BD19 ....149 L7
COL BB8 ....74 E4
EARD/LOFT WF3 ....177 H4
HOR/CROF WF4 ....200 C7
HUD HD1 ....14 F2
HWTH BD22 ....100 E3
WMB/DAR S73 ....262 C8
Ash Ter BGLY BD16 ....81 H4
HDGY LS6 ....108 F1
RPDN/SBR HX6 ....188 E3
Ashtofts Mt GSLY LS20 ....62 A5
Ashton Av GTHN BD7 ....126 A1
RHAY LS8 ....110 B4
Ashton Clough Rd LVSG WF15 ....172 C2
Ashton Ct RHAY LS8 ....110 C3
Ashton Crs EARD/LOFT WF3 ....154 F3
Ashton Gdns ROCH OL11 ....228 A1
Ashton Gv OSM LS9 ....110 B4
Ashton Mt OSM LS9 ....110 B4
Ashton Pl OSM LS9 ....110 B4
Ashton Rd CAS WF10 ....157 M8
RHAY LS8 ....110 C3
Ashton St BFD BD1 ....4 C5
CAS WF10 ....157 M7
RHAY LS8 ....110 B3
ROCH OL11 ....228 A1
Ashton Ter RHAY LS8 ....110 B4
Ashton Vw OSM LS9 ....110 B4
Ashton Wk IDLE BD10 ....83 J7
Ash Tree Ap SCFT LS14 ....111 M2
Ash Tree Av CUL/QBY BD13 ....102 D8
Ash Tree Bank SCFT LS14 ....111 M1
Ash Tree Cl SCFT LS14 ....111 M2
Ash Tree Gdns LUD/ILL HX2 ....145 L1
NORM WF6 ....178 B3
SCFT LS14 ....111 M1
Ash Tree Garth TAD LS24 ....115 M1
Ashtree Gv GFTH/SHER LS25 ....135 K5
GTHN BD7 ....126 B4
Ash Tree Gv SCFT LS14 ....111 M1
Ash Tree Pk GFTH/SHER * LS25 ....135 K5
Ash Tree Rd LUD/ILL HX2 ....145 L1
Ash Tree Wk ILK LS29 ....40 A5
Ash Vw EARD/LOFT WF3 ....153 L7
Ashville Av HDGY LS6 ....108 F3
Ashville Cft LUD/ILL HX2 ....145 M5
Ashville Gdns LUD/ILL HX2 ....145 M5
Ashville Gv HDGY LS6 ....108 F3
LUD/ILL HX2 ....145 M5
Ashville Rd HDGY LS6 ....108 F3
Ashville St HIPP * HX3 ....10 D1
Ashville Ter HDGY LS6 ....108 F3
Ashville Vw HDGY LS6 ....109 G4
Ashwell Cl CUD/GR S72 ....244 E3
Ashwell Rd GIR BD8 ....104 D5
HTON BD9 ....104 C2
Ashwell St GIR BD8 ....104 D5
Ashwood SCFT LS14 ....89 K5
Ashwood Cl HUDN HD2 ....192 E3
Ashwood Dr AIRE BD20 ....58 C5
LIT OL15 ....207 H1
MOR LS27 ....129 K7
Ashwood Gdns MOR LS27 ....129 K7
Ashwood Gra HOR/CROF WF4 ....198 A8
Ashwood Gv CUD/GR S72 ....263 M3
HOR/CROF WF4 ....197 L4
MOR LS27 ....129 L7
Ashwood St BOW BD4 ....127 M5
Ashwood Ter HDGY LS6 ....109 H2
Ashwood Vls HDGY LS6 ....6 A1
Ashworth Cl DEWS WF13 ....173 L6
LIT OL15 ....185 J7
Ashworth Gdns DEWS WF13 ....173 L6
Ashworth Gn DEWS WF13 ....173 L6
Ashworth Pl WBSY BD6 ....126 F5
Ashworth Rd DEWS WF13 ....173 L6
PONT WF8 ....181 G3
Ashworth St WHIT OL12 ....206 A6
Askam Av PONT WF8 ....181 H2
Asket Av SCFT LS14 ....111 G1
Asket Cl SCFT LS14 ....89 G8
Asket Crs SCFT LS14 ....111 G1
Asket Dr SCFT LS14 ....89 G8
Asket Gdns RHAY LS8 ....88 F8
Asket Garth SCFT LS14 ....111 G1
Asket Gn SCFT LS14 ....89 G8
Asket Hl RHAY LS8 ....88 F8
Asket Pl SCFT LS14 ....111 G1
Asket Wk SCFT LS14 ....111 G1
Askey Av MOR LS27 ....152 D4
Askey Crs MOR LS27 ....152 D4
Askham Gv HEM/SK/SE WF9 ....226 A6
Askham Rd CAS WF10 ....158 F5
Askwith La OT LS21 ....22 C8
Askwith Moor Rd OT LS21 ....22 B1
Aspden St TOD OL14 ....141 K8
Aspect Gdns PDSY/CALV LS28 ....106 E6
Aspen Cl KGHY BD21 ....3 L8
WKFDW/WTN WF2 ....176 C6
Aspen Ct EARD/LOFT WF3 ....152 E5
KBTN HD8 ....217 L7
Aspen Gv DEWS WF13 ....173 K5
Aspen Mt BHP/TINH LS16 ....86 A4
Aspen Ri WIL/AL BD15 ....103 H2
Aspen Wy TAD LS24 ....71 K3
Aspinall St HBR HX7 ....144 A5
HFAX HX1 ....10 B8
Aspley Pl HUD HD1 ....15 H7
Asprey Dr WIL/AL BD15 ....103 K6
Asquith Av MOR LS27 ....130 B8
Asquith Cl MOR LS27 ....152 B1
Asquith Ct LUD/ILL * HX2 ....145 M7
Asquith Dr MOR LS27 ....152 B1
Asquith St BTLY WF17 ....151 K4
Assembly St LDSU LS2 ....9 H1
NORM WF6 ....178 C4
Assheton Rd ROY/SHW OL2 ....229 H7
Astley Av RTHW LS26 ....134 C5
Astley Cl ROY/SHW OL2 ....229 H7
Astley La RTHW LS26 ....134 D6
Astley Wy RTHW LS26 ....134 D6
Aston Av BRAM * LS13 ....107 M4
Aston Cl LVSG WF15 ....172 B4
Aston Crs BRAM LS13 ....108 A4
Aston Dr BRAM LS13 ....108 A4
BSLYN/ROY S71 ....243 J8
Aston Gv BRAM LS13 ....108 A4
Aston Mt BRAM LS13 ....108 A4
Aston Pl BRAM LS13 ....108 A4
Aston Rd BRAM LS13 ....107 M4
WBOW BD5 ....127 G3
Aston St BRAM LS13 ....107 M4
Aston Ter BRAM LS13 ....107 M4
Aston Vw BRAM LS13 ....107 M4
Astor Gv BRAM LS13 ....107 J4
Astor St BRAM LS13 ....107 J4
Astral Av HIPP HX3 ....147 M6
Astral Cl HIPP HX3 ....147 M6
Astral Vw WBSY BD6 ....126 C4
Astra Pk BEE/HOL * LS11 ....131 L4
Atalanta Ter LUD/ILL HX2 ....168 A2
Atha Cl BEE/HOL LS11 ....131 J5

Atha Crs BEE/HOL LS11 131 J5
Atha St BEE/HOL LS11 131 J5
Athelstan La OT LS21 41 J4
Athelstans Ct GFTH/SHER LS25 116 A7
Athene Dr HUDS HD4 214 E3
Athersley Crs BSLYN/ROY S71 243 J8
Athersley Rd BSLYN/ROY S71 243 J8
Atherstone WHIT * OL12 206 B6
Atherstone Rd WIL/AL BD15 103 K6
Atherton La BRIG HD6 170 D6
Athlone Dr EARL WF12 174 A3
Athlone Gv WOR/ARM LS12 108 E7
Athlone Ri GFTH/SHER LS25 113 K7
Athlone St WOR/ARM LS12 108 E7
Athlone Ter WOR/ARM LS12 108 E7
Athold Dr OSS WF5 197 H1
Athold St OSS WF5 197 H1
Athol Gdns HIPP HX3 146 C3
Athol Gn HIPP HX3 146 C3
Athol Rd HIPP HX3 146 C3
HTON BD9 104 D4
Athol St HIPP HX3 146 C3
KGHY BD21 3 M1
WHIT OL12 206 D5
Atkinson Ct NORM * WF6 178 C5
Atkinson La PONT WF8 181 H4
Atkinson St MID LS10 9 L5
SHPY BD18 82 D6
Atlanta St BRAM LS13 107 J4
Atlas Mill Rd BRIG HD6 170 C4
Atlas St GIR BD8 104 D5
Atterwith La RYKW YO26 33 H1
Attlee Av HOR/CROF WF4 222 E5
Attlee Crs WKFDW/WTN WF2 199 G7
Attlee Gv WKFDE WF1 176 E2
Attlee St NORM WF6 178 D6
Aubrey St ROCH OL11 228 B1
Auckland Rd WBSY BD6 126 C5
Audby Ct WBY LS22 30 B8
Audby La WBY LS22 30 B7
Audrey St OSS WF5 197 G2
Audsley's Yd HOR/CROF WF4 197 G5
Augusta Cl WHIT OL12 206 A5
Augusta Dr NORM WF6 178 F6
Augusta St WHIT OL12 206 A4
Auster Bank Av TAD LS24 72 A2
Auster Bank Crs TAD LS24 72 A2
Auster Bank Rd TAD LS24 72 A1
Auster Bank Vw TAD LS24 72 A1
Austfield La GFTH/SHER LS25 138 E7
Austhorpe Av MSTN/BAR LS15 112 A7
Austhorpe Ct MSTN/BAR LS15 112 A7
Austhorpe Dr MSTN/BAR LS15 112 A7
Austhorpe Gdns
MSTN/BAR LS15 112 B6
Austhorpe Gv MSTN/BAR LS15 112 A7
Austhorpe La MSTN/BAR LS15 111 M5
Austhorpe Rd MSTN/BAR LS15 111 M4
Austhorpe Vw MSTN/BAR LS15 111 M6
Austin Av BRIG HD6 170 B2
Austin Rd CAS WF10 158 F6
Austin St KGHY BD21 3 J3
Austwick Cl DOD/DAR S75 242 C4
Austwick Wk BSLY * S70 260 F4
Authorpe Rd CHAL LS7 87 H8
Autumn Av HDGY LS6 109 G4
WBY LS22 30 A6
Autumn Crs HORS LS18 85 M7
Autumn Gv HDGY LS6 109 G4
Autumn Pl HDGY LS6 109 G4
Autumn St HDGY LS6 109 G4
HFAX * HX1 10 B9
Autumn Ter HDGY LS6 109 G4
Auty Crs EARD/LOFT WF3 177 H1
Auty Sq MOR LS27 152 D3
Avenel Rd WIL/AL BD15 103 K6
Avenel Ter WIL/AL BD15 103 K6
Avenham Wy BFDE BD3 5 J4
Avens Cl PONT WF8 180 F7
The Avenue AL/HA/HU LS17 45 J8
AL/HA/HU LS17 87 J1
AWLS/ASK DN6 227 L5
BGLY * BD16 81 K6
BSLYN/ROY S71 244 A2
BTLY WF17 151 G5
BTLY WF17 151 J7
CLAY BD14 125 K2
DEWS WF13 173 H3
EARD/LOFT WF3 153 J6
GFTH/SHER LS25 138 A3
HIPP HX3 147 M6
HOLM/MEL HD9 235 K6
HOR/CROF WF4 200 A5
HORS LS18 85 H5
HUDE HD5 15 L8
IDLE BD10 84 A3
MSTN/BAR LS15 90 B6
MSTN/BAR LS15 111 M3
MSTN/BAR LS15 133 M4
OSM LS9 9 L1
RHAY LS8 88 C6
ROY/SHW OL2 229 J8
TAD LS24 50 C1
WBY LS22 47 J5
WKFDE WF1 176 C2
Avenue A BSPA/BRAM LS23 49 K3
Avenue B BSPA/BRAM LS23 49 J5
Avenue C East BSPA/BRAM LS23 49 L4
Avenue Crs RHAY LS8 110 B2
Avenue C West
BSPA/BRAM LS23 49 K5
Avenue D BSPA/BRAM LS23 49 K6
Avenue Des Hirondelles
OT LS21 42 F8
Avenue E East BSPA/BRAM LS23 49 L5
Avenue E West
BSPA/BRAM LS23 49 K6
Avenue F BSPA/BRAM LS23 49 L5
Avenue G BSPA/BRAM LS23 49 M4
Avenue Gdns AL/HA/HU LS17 87 H1
Avenue Hl RHAY LS8 110 B2
Avenue No 2 BRIG HD6 170 C5
Avenue Rd WBOW BD5 127 H3
WKFDW/WTN WF2 199 G5
Avenue St BOW BD4 127 M5
Avenue Victoria RHAY LS8 88 C6
Averingcliffe Rd IDLE BD10 83 M8
Aviary Gv WOR/ARM LS12 108 E6
Aviary Mt WOR/ARM LS12 108 E6
Aviary Pl WOR/ARM LS12 108 E6
Aviary Rd WOR/ARM * LS12 108 E5
Aviary Rw WOR/ARM LS12 108 E6
Aviary St WOR/ARM LS12 108 E6
Aviary Ter WOR/ARM LS12 108 E6
Aviary Vw WOR/ARM LS12 108 E6
Aviation Rd GFTH/SHER LS25 116 E7
Avison Rd HUDS HD4 213 J3
Avison Yd WKFDE WF1 13 G3
Avis St ROY/SHW OL2 229 J7
Avocet Garth MID LS10 153 M1
Avon Cl AL/HA/HU LS17 89 H2
DOD/DAR S75 260 A3
MILN OL16 207 J8
Avon Ct AL/HA/HU LS17 89 G1
Avondale KGHY BD21 2 C3
Avondale Crs SHPY BD18 82 C7
Avondale Dr BSLYN/ROY S71 243 L5
EARD/LOFT WF3 177 G1
Avondale Gv SHPY BD18 82 C7
Avondale Mt SHPY BD18 82 C7
Avondale Pl HIPP HX3 168 D2
Avondale Rd SHPY BD18 82 B7
Avondale St BRAM LS13 107 L5
COL BB8 74 C1
WKFDW/WTN WF2 12 E6
Avondale Wy WKFDW/WTN WF2 12 E6
Avon Dr GFTH/SHER LS25 113 H8
Avon Garth WBY LS22 47 L1
Avon Rd ROY/SHW OL2 229 K6
Avon St BSLYN/ROY S71 261 J5
Avon Wk FEA/AMT WF7 179 M7
Axis Ct MOR * LS27 152 A1
Aydon Wy WBSY BD6 126 A7
Aygill Av HTON BD9 103 M3
Aylesbury St HWTH BD22 79 J2
Aylesford Cl BSLYN/ROY S71 261 H3
Aylesford Mt MSTN/BAR LS15 112 B3
Aynholme Dr ILK LS29 19 H6
Aynsley Gv WIL/AL BD15 103 K5
Ayres Dr HUDS HD4 213 J3
Ayresome Av RHAY LS8 88 C4
Ayresome Ov WIL/AL BD15 103 J7
Ayresome Ter RHAY LS8 88 B4
Ayrton St COL BB8 74 A1
Aysgarth MILN OL16 206 D5
Aysgarth Av BRIG HD6 148 C8
BSLYN/ROY S71 262 D6
Aysgarth Cl LM/WK BD12 148 E4
OSM LS9 110 B7
WKFDW/WTN WF2 197 M3
Aysgarth Crs LUD/ILL HX2 145 J3
Aysgarth Dr OSM LS9 110 B7
WKFDW/WTN WF2 197 M3
Aysgarth Fold MID LS10 153 L2
Aysgarth Pl OSM LS9 110 B7
Aysgarth Rd BTLY WF17 173 J1
HUDS HD4 214 D4
Aysgarth Wk OSM LS9 110 B7
Ayton Cl BFDE BD3 5 K4
Ayton Rd HUDW HD3 191 G8
Azealea Ct BFDE BD3 5 L4

B

Baby House Hill La HBR HX7 121 H2
Bachelor La HORS * LS18 85 L4
Back Ada St KGHY BD21 2 D5
Back Aireview Ter KGHY * BD21 3 M6
Back Aireville St AIRE BD20 57 J4
Back Airlie Av RHAY * LS8 110 B2
Back Airlie Pl RHAY LS8 110 B2
Back Albert Gv HDGY LS6 86 F8
Back Albert Ter HDGY * LS6 109 G4
Back Alcester Pl RHAY * LS8 110 B2
Back Alcester Rd RHAY * LS8 110 B2
Back Alcester Ter RHAY * LS8 110 B2
Back Anderton St WKFDE * WF1 13 K8
Back Ann St CUL/QBY * BD13 101 M5
Back Archery Pl LDSU LS2 6 E4
Back Archery Rd LDSU LS2 6 F5
Back Archery St LDSU LS2 6 F5
Back Archery Ter LDSU LS2 6 E5
Back Ash Gv HDGY LS6 6 A2
Back Ashgrove West GTHN BD7 4 C8
Back Ashley Av OSM * LS9 110 C4
Back Ashley St OSM LS9 110 C4
Back Ashville Av HDGY LS6 108 F4
Back Ashville Gv HDGY LS6 108 F3
Back Ashville Rd HDGY LS6 108 F3
Back Ashville Ter HDGY LS6 108 F3
Back Ashwood Ter HDGY LS6 109 H2
Back Aston Pl BRAM LS13 108 A4
Back Aston St BRAM LS13 107 M4
Back Aston Ter BRAM LS13 107 M4
Back Aston Vw BRAM LS13 107 M4
Back Athlone Av
WOR/ARM * LS12 108 E7
Back Athlone Gv
WOR/ARM LS12 108 E7
Back Athlone Ter
WOR/ARM * LS12 108 E7
Back Atlanta St BRAM * LS13 107 J4
Back Austhorpe Rd
MSTN/BAR * LS15 111 M4
Back Autumn Rd HDGY * LS6 109 G4
Back Aylesbury St HWTH * BD22 79 J2
Back Baileys Pl HDGY LS6 86 F8
Back Baker St SHPY * BD18 82 C6
Back Baldovan Ter RHAY LS8 110 B2
Back Balfour St BGLY BD16 81 H4
KGHY * BD21 2 E7
Back Bank St CAS WF10 157 M6
Back Bank Ter PDSY/CALV LS28 107 G4
Back Banstead St RHAY LS8 110 B3
Back Barden Pl
WOR/ARM LS12 108 C7
Back Barkly Gv BEE/HOL LS11 131 J4
Back Barkly Pde
BEE/HOL LS11 131 J4
Back Barkly Ter BEE/HOL LS11 131 J4
Back Barrowby Vw
MSTN/BAR LS15 112 A7
Back Bath Rd BRAM * LS13 107 L4
Back Beamsley Gv HDGY * LS6 109 G4
Back Beamsley Mt HDGY LS6 109 G3
Back Beamsley Ter HDGY * LS6 109 G4
Back Beaumont St
BTLY * WF17 173 L3
Back Beck La ILK LS29 19 H5
Back Beech St BGLY BD16 81 H4
Back Beech Ter HUD HD1 15 G1
Back Beechwood Gv BULY LS4 108 F3
Back Beechwood Rd
BULY * LS4 108 F3
Back Bellbrooke Gv OSM LS9 110 D4
Back Bellbrooke Pl OSM LS9 110 D4
Back Bellbrooke Ter OSM LS9 110 C4
Back Belvedere Av
BEE/HOL LS11 131 K4
Back Belvedere Mt
BEE/HOL LS11 131 K4
Back Bentley Av HDGY LS6 87 H8
Back Bentley Gv HDGY LS6 87 H8
Back Berkeley Av RHAY LS8 110 C3
Back Berkeley Ter RHAY LS8 110 C3
Back Beverley Ter
BEE/HOL LS11 131 K3
Back Blackwood Gv HFAX HX1 10 A3
Back Blenheim Av LDSU LS2 6 F4
Back Blenheim Mt GIR * BD8 104 E4
Back Blenheim Ter LDSU LS2 6 E5
Back Boundary Ter BVRD * LS3 109 G5
Back Bower Rd ELL HX5 169 J7
Back Bowling Green Rd
GTL/HWG HX4 190 B3
Back Bowman St WKFDE WF1 13 L9
Back Bradshaw Rd
HOLM/MEL HD9 236 B3
Back Bradshaw St MILN OL16 206 C6
Back Breary Av HORS LS18 85 M5
Back Breary Ter HORS LS18 85 M5
Back Bridge St SKP/WHF BD23 16 B2
Back Briggate AIRE BD20 36 A4
Back Broad La BRAM * LS13 107 M2
Back Broomfield Crs HDGY LS6 108 F2
Back Broomfield Pl HDGY LS6 108 F3
Back Broomfield Rd HDGY LS6 108 F3
KGHY BD21 2 F4
Back Broomfield St KGHY * BD21 2 F4
Back Broughton Av OSM LS9 110 C4
Back Broughton Ter OSM LS9 110 C4
Back Brudenell Gv HDGY LS6 6 A4
Back Brudenell Mt HDGY LS6 109 G4
Back Brudenell Rd HDGY LS6 109 G4
Back Brunswick St
DEWS * WF13 173 J5
LDSU LS2 7 H7
Back Burchett Gv HDGY LS6 6 D1
Back Burchett Pl HDGY LS6 6 D1
Back Burley Hl BULY LS4 108 E4
Back Burley Lodge Rd
HDGY LS6 109 G4
Back Burley Lodge Ter
HDGY LS6 109 G5
Back Burley St BVRD * LS3 6 C8
Back Burlington Pl
BEE/HOL LS11 131 K4
Back Burlington Rd
BEE/HOL LS11 131 K4
Back Burton Crs HDGY * LS6 86 F8
Back Burton Ter
BEE/HOL * LS11 131 L3
Back Buxton St KGHY BD21 3 J4
Back Byrl St KGHY * BD21 3 H1
Back Byrom St TOD OL14 141 K8
Back Caister St KGHY * BD21 79 J2
Back Caledonia Rd KGHY BD21 3 J2
Back Camberley St
BEE/HOL * LS11 131 L3
Back Carberry Pl HDGY LS6 109 G4
Back Carberry Rd HDGY LS6 109 G4
Back Carberry Ter HDGY LS6 109 G4
Back Carter Ter
MSTN/BAR * LS15 111 L5
Back Cartmel Rd KGHY BD21 2 D5
Back Castle Rd KGHY BD21 2 F2
Back Cavendish Rd IDLE BD10 83 K7
Back Cavendish St KGHY BD21 3 H4
Back Cavendish Ter HFAX HX1 10 D5
Back Cecil St HUD HD1 14 D7
Back Chapel La HDGY LS6 108 F2
Back Chapel St WHIT * OL12 184 E7
Back Charles St BRIG HD6 170 C3
Back Charlton Rd OSM LS9 110 C7
Back Chatsworth Rd RHAY LS8 110 C3
Back Chestnut Av HDGY LS6 109 G3
MSTN/BAR LS15 111 M4
Back Chiswick Ter HDGY * LS6 109 G4
Back Christ Church Vw
WOR/ARM * LS12 108 D6
Back Church La BHP/TINH LS16 86 E1
KSTL LS5 108 C2
Back Church Vw WKFDE WF1 199 G4
Back Claremont Av BVRD * LS3 6 C7
Back Clarence Rd HORS LS18 85 K7
Back Clarence St HFAX HX1 10 E6
Back Clarendon Pl HFAX HX1 10 C6
Back Clarkson Vw HDGY LS6 6 D1
Back Clayton St RTHW LS26 155 H1
Back Cliff Mt HDGY LS6 6 C1
Back Clifton Rd HUD HD1 14 A5
Back Clifton Ter OSM LS9 110 C7
Back Clipston Av HDGY LS6 87 H8
Back Clock View St
KGHY * BD21 57 K4
Back Close Lea BRIG HD6 170 C5
Back Close Lea Dr BRIG * HD6 170 C5
Back Clough HIPP HX3 147 J4
Back Coldcotes Av OSM LS9 110 D4
Back Colenso Mt BEE/HOL LS11 8 B7
Back Colenso Rd BEE/HOL LS11 8 A7
KGHY BD21 3 M1
Back Colne Rd AIRE BD20 34 E8
Back Colton Rd
WOR/ARM LS12 108 E7
Back Colwyn Pl
BEE/HOL * LS11 131 K4
Back Colwyn Vw
BEE/HOL * LS11 131 K4
Back Commerical St TOD OL14 163 L1
Back Compton St KGHY * BD21 3 J3
Back Conway St RHAY LS8 110 B3
Back Cowper Gv RHAY * LS8 110 C3
Back Cowper St CHAL LS7 7 K2
Back Cranbrook Av
BEE/HOL LS11 131 J3
Back Cranbrook Ter
BEE/HOL LS11 8 C9
Back Croft House La
AIRE * BD20 57 J4
Back Cromer Av KGHY * BD21 79 K2
Back Cromer Ter LDSU LS2 6 D5
Back Cromwell Ter HFAX HX1 10 E5
Back Cross Flatts Av
BEE/HOL LS11 131 J4
Back Cross Flatts Crs
BEE/HOL LS11 131 H4
Back Cross Flatts Gv
BEE/HOL LS11 131 J4
Back Cross Flatts Mt
BEE/HOL LS11 131 J4
Back Cross Flatts Pl
BEE/HOL LS11 131 H4
Back Cross Flatts Rw
BEE/HOL LS11 131 H4
Back Cross Green Crs OSM LS9 110 B8
Back Cross Green La OSM LS9 110 B8
Back Crossland Ter
BEE/HOL LS11 8 F9
Back Cross La ELL HX5 169 G8
Back Dalton Av BEE/HOL LS11 131 J4
Back Dalton Gv BEE/HOL LS11 131 J4
Back Dalton Rd BEE/HOL LS11 131 J4
Back Dargai St CHAL LS7 7 G2
Back Dawlish Mt OSM LS9 110 D6
Back De Lacy Mt KSTL LS5 108 C1
Back Delph Mt HDGY LS6 6 D1
Back Dent St OSM * LS9 110 B7
Back Der St TOD * OL14 163 L1
Back Devonshire La RHAY LS8 88 C4
Back Dorset Mt RHAY LS8 110 C2
Back Dorset Rd RHAY LS8 110 C2
Back Dorset Ter RHAY LS8 110 C3
Back Drake St MILN OL16 206 B8
Back Dudley Hill Rd
ECHL * BD2 105 K4
Back Duke of York St
WKFDE * WF1 176 F7
Back Duke St FEA/AMT * WF7 179 L8
Back Dunbar St WKFDE WF1 13 L7
Back Durham St ROCH OL11 228 C1
Back East Park Rd OSM * LS9 110 C7
Back Eaton St HWTH BD22 79 J2
Back Ecclesburn Gv OSM * LS9 110 D7
Back Ecclesburn St OSM LS9 110 C7
Back Edensor Rd KGHY BD21 2 D5
Back Eldon Rd HUD HD1 191 M7
Back Elford Pl RHAY LS8 110 B3
Back Elizabeth St WBOW BD5 4 E9
Back Ellers Gv RHAY LS8 110 B2
Back Ellers Rd RHAY LS8 110 B2
Back Elmfield Ter HFAX HX1 168 C1
Back Elsworth St
WOR/ARM LS12 108 F7
Back Emily St KGHY * BD21 3 J3
Back Eric St BRAM LS13 107 L1
KGHY BD21 3 H2
Back Eshald Pl RTHW LS26 133 M8
Back Esmond Ter
WOR/ARM LS12 108 D7
Back Estcourt Av HDGY LS6 108 E1
Back Eversley Mt LUD/ILL HX2 146 A8
Back Fairford Pl BEE/HOL LS11 9 G9
Back Ferguson St HFAX * HX1 11 G7
Back Field Ct CUL/QBY * BD13 102 F8
Back Fitzwilliam St HUD HD1 14 D6
Back Florist St KGHY BD21 3 M1
Back Fold CLAY BD14 125 K1
Back Foster Rd KGHY BD21 2 E9
Back Garden St WKFDE WF1 12 D3
Back Garton Rd OSM LS9 110 C7
Back Garton Ter OSM LS9 110 C7
Back Gathorne St RHAY LS8 7 M3
Back Gerrard St HFAX HX1 10 E6
Back Giles Street Sout
WBOW BD5 126 F1
Back Giles St South
WBOW * BD5 126 F1
Back Gillett La RTHW LS26 155 H1
Back Girlington Rd GIR BD8 104 C5
Back Gladstone St BGLY BD16 81 H4
Back Glenthorpe Ter OSM LS9 110 C6
Back Glossop St HDGY LS6 6 E1
Back Gooder La BRIG * HD6 170 D5
Back Gordon St WKFDE WF1 13 L9
Back Gordon Ter HDGY LS6 87 H8
Back Graham Gv BULY LS4 108 F3
Back Granby Gv HDGY LS6 108 F2
Back Grange Av CHAL LS7 7 L1
Back Grange Crs CHAL LS7 7 L1
Back Grange Ter CHAL LS7 7 K1
Back Grange Vw CHAL LS7 7 K1
Back Grantley St WKFDE WF1 13 G2
Back Grant St HWTH BD22 2 C5
Back Graveley St
MSTN/BAR LS15 111 J6
Back Great Russell St GTHN BD7 4 A6
Back Greaves Streen
WBOW BD5 126 F3
Back Gn MOR LS27 130 E7
Back Greenhead Rd HUD HD1 14 D7
Back Greenmount Ter
BEE/HOL * LS11 8 F9
Back Greenwood Mt HDGY LS6 87 G7
Back Grosvenor Ter HDGY LS6 109 H2
HFAX HX1 10 D6
Back Grouse St KGHY * BD21 3 J3
Back Grovehall Av
BEE/HOL LS11 131 J5
Back Grovehall Dr
BEE/HOL LS11 131 J5
Back Grove Rd ILK LS29 38 D2
Back Haigh Av RTHW LS26 132 F7
Back Haigh St RTHW LS26 132 E7
Back Haigh Vw RTHW LS26 132 E7
Back Halliday Gv
WOR/ARM LS12 108 C6
Back Halliday Pl
WOR/ARM LS12 108 C6
Back Hambleton St
WKFDE WF1 12 F1
Back Hamilton Av CHAL LS7 7 L1
Back Hamilton Vw CHAL LS7 7 L1
Back Harehills Av CHAL LS7 109 M2
Back Harehills Park Vw
OSM LS9 110 D4
Back Harehills Pl RHAY * LS8 110 B3
Back Harehills Rd RHAY * LS8 110 B3
Back Hares Av RHAY LS8 110 B2
Back Hares Mt RHAY LS8 7 M1
Back Hares Ter RHAY LS8 110 B2
Back Hares Vw RHAY LS8 110 B2
Back Harold Gv HDGY LS6 109 G4
Back Hartley Av HDGY LS6 6 E1
Back Hartley Gv HDGY LS6 6 D1
Back Hartley St MOR LS27 152 D3
Back Hatfeild St WKFDE WF1 176 E7
Back Headingley Av HDGY LS6 108 E1
Back Headingley Mt HDGY LS6 108 E1
Back Heddon St HDGY LS6 87 G8
Back Heights Rd
CUL/QBY BD13 102 D7
Back Henrietta St BTLY WF17 173 L1
Back Hessle Av HDGY LS6 109 G3
Back Hessle Mt HDGY * LS6 109 G3
Back Hessle Ter HDGY * LS6 109 G3
Back Hessle Vw HDGY * LS6 109 G3
Back Highbury Ter HDGY LS6 87 G8
Back Highfield Rd BRAM LS13 107 M4
Back High St CUL/QBY BD13 102 F8
Back Highthorne Gv
WOR/ARM * LS12 108 C6
Back Highthorne St
WOR/ARM LS12 108 C6
Back Hillcrest Av CHAL LS7 7 M1
Back Hillcrest Vw CHAL LS7 7 M1
Back Hill Top Av RHAY LS8 110 B2
Back Hill Top Mt RHAY LS8 110 B2
Back Hilton Gv RHAY * LS8 110 B2
Back Hilton Pl RHAY LS8 110 B2
Back Hilton Rd RHAY LS8 110 B2
Back Hird St KGHY * BD21 2 E7
Backhold Av HIPP HX3 169 G4
Backhold Dr HIPP HX3 168 F4
Backhold La HIPP HX3 168 F4
Backhold Rd HIPP HX3 169 G4
Back Hollyshaw Ter
MSTN/BAR LS15 111 L6
Back Holywell La
AL/HA/HU LS17 88 F1
Back Honoria St HUDN HD2 14 F1
Backhouse La HOR/CROF WF4 220 B7
Back Hovingham Gv RHAY LS8 110 C2
Back Hovingham Mt RHAY LS8 110 C2
Back Hovingham Ter RHAY LS8 110 C3
Back Hyde Ter LDSU LS2 6 C6
Back Ibbetson Pl LDSU LS2 6 E6
Back Ingledew Crs RHAY LS8 88 D4
Back Irwell St BOW BD4 127 J1
Back Ivy Av OSM LS9 110 C6
Back Ivy Gv OSM * LS9 110 D7
Back Ivy Mt OSM LS9 110 C6
Back Ivy St OSM LS9 110 C6
Back John St CUL/QBY BD13 102 F8
Back Karnac Rd RHAY LS8 110 B2
Back Kelso Rd LDSU LS2 6 B5
Back Kendal La BVRD * LS3 6 C7
Back Kennerleigh Wk
MSTN/BAR LS15 111 L5
Back Kensington St GIR BD8 104 C5
Back Kensington Ter HDGY LS6 6 A2
Back Kirby St KGHY BD21 3 J2
Back Kirkgate SHPY * BD18 82 C7
Back Kitson St OSM * LS9 110 B7
Back Knowl Rd MIRF WF14 172 B8
Back Laisteridge La GTHN BD7 4 B8
Back Lambton Gv RHAY * LS8 110 B2
Back Landseer Av BRAM LS13 108 A3
Back Landseer Gv BRAM LS13 108 A3
Back Landseer Ter
BRAM * LS13 108 A3
Back La AIRE BD20 16 E7
AIRE BD20 36 A4
AIRE BD20 58 F5
AL/HA/HU LS17 44 B3
AWLS/ASK DN6 227 L6
AWLS/ASK DN6 227 L2
BEE/HOL LS11 131 H5
BIRK/DRI BD11 129 H7
BRAM LS13 107 M5
BRFD/BLYE BB10 74 A6
BRFD/BLYE BB10 96 C1
BSLYN/ROY S71 261 L2
BSPA/BRAM LS23 69 M3
CAS WF10 157 K3
COL BB8 74 D4
CUL/QBY BD13 102 F7
CUL/QBY BD13 103 G7
CUL/QBY BD13 125 K4
EARL WF12 195 G5
EARL WF12 195 J4
GSLY LS20 61 M5
HBR HX7 99 J8
HBR HX7 120 E8
HBR HX7 143 H1
HBR HX7 143 H4
HECK WF16 172 F2
HEM/SK/SE WF9 225 G4
HEM/SK/SE WF9 225 J8
HOLM/MEL HD9 254 C1
HOR/CROF WF4 200 E4
HOR/CROF WF4 216 F1
HOR/CROF WF4 220 C8
HOR/CROF WF4 222 D2
HORS LS18 85 K6
HTON BD9 104 C2
HWTH BD22 56 D7
HWTH BD22 77 L8
IDLE BD10 83 J6
ILK LS29 40 B5
KBTN HD8 238 D3
KBTN HD8 239 J1
KBTN HD8 240 C3
LUD/ILL HX2 145 M1
MIRF WF14 194 A1
MIRF WF14 194 D7
OSS WF5 196 F1

PDSY/CALV LS28 ....106 F3
RPDN/SBR HX6 ....188 F2
RYKW YO26 ....33 J3
STKB/PEN S36 ....270 F3
STKB/PEN S36 ....271 H8
TAD LS24 ....116 A2
WBY LS22 ....46 D1
WIL/AL BD15 ....103 G2
WKFDE WF1 ....12 D3
WOR/ARM LS12 ....129 L3
YEA LS19 ....84 C1
Back La West BSLYN/ROY S71 ....243 J2
Back Langdale Gdns HDGY LS6 ....108 E2
Back Langdale Ter HDGY LS6 ....108 E2
Back Leatham St DEWS WF13 ....173 J5
Back Leeming HWTH BD22 ....100 F5
Back Lime St KGHY * BD21 ....79 K3
Back Linden Gv BEE/HOL LS11 ....8 F9
Back Lindom St GTHN BD7 ....4 A6
Back Lindum St GIR BD8 ....104 E4
Back Lodge La BEE/HOL LS11 ....131 K3
Back Lombard St YEA LS19 ....84 C2
Back Longroyd Ter
BEE/HOL * LS11 ....131 L3
Back Lord St HFAX * HX1 ....10 F6
Back Lucas St HDGY LS6 ....6 D1
Back Lunan Pl RHAY * LS8 ....110 B2
Back Lune St COL * BB8 ....74 A2
Back Lyon St CUL/QBY BD13 ....125 H5
Back Mafeking Av
BEE/HOL * LS11 ....131 J5
Back Mafeking Mt
BEE/HOL LS11 ....131 J5
Back Malt St HWTH * BD22 ....79 J2
Back Mannville Rd KGHY BD21 ....2 D7
Back Manor Dr HDGY LS6 ....109 G3
Back Manor Gv CHAL LS7 ....87 M8
Back Manor St ECHL BD2 ....105 K3
Back Manor Ter HDGY LS6 ....109 G2
Back Market St WBSY * BD6 ....126 E5
Back Markham Av RHAY LS8 ....110 B2
Back Marriot St DEWS WF13 ....173 M5
Back Marshall St
MSTN/BAR LS15 ....111 L4
Back Marshall Ter
MSTN/BAR LS15 ....111 L4
Back Mary St AIRE BD20 ....34 F5
EARD/LOFT WF3 ....154 A6
Back Masham St
WOR/ARM * LS12 ....108 F7
Back Maud Av BEE/HOL LS11 ....131 J4
Back Mayville Av HDGY LS6 ....109 G3
Back Mayville Pl HDGY LS6 ....109 G3
Back Mayville St HDGY LS6 ....109 G3
Back Mayville Ter HDGY LS6 ....109 G3
Back Meadow Vw HDGY LS6 ....109 G3
Back Melbourne Gv
BRAM LS13 ....107 L4
Back Methley Dr CHAL LS7 ....87 M8
Back Mexborough Av CHAL LS7 ....7 J1
Back Mexborough Dr CHAL LS7 ....7 J1
Back Mexborough Gv CHAL LS7 ....7 J1
Back Mexborough St CHAL LS7 ....7 J1
Back Meynell Av RTHW LS26 ....155 G1
Back Middle Cross St
WOR/ARM * LS12 ....108 F7
Back Middleton Vw
BEE/HOL LS11 ....8 D9
Back Midland Rd HDGY LS6 ....6 A2
Back Milan Av RHAY LS8 ....110 B3
Back Milan Rd RHAY LS8 ....110 B3
Back Milan St RHAY LS8 ....110 C3
Back Minnie St KGHY * BD21 ....2 E7
Back Mitchell Ter BGLY BD16 ....81 H4
Back Mitford Rd
WOR/ARM LS12 ....108 F7
Back Model Rd
WOR/ARM LS12 ....108 F7
Back Model Ter
WOR/ARM LS12 ....108 E7
Back Model Vw
WOR/ARM LS12 ....108 F7
Back Monk Bridge Dr HDGY LS6 ....87 H8
Back Montague St WKFDE WF1 ....13 L9
Back Moorfield St HFAX HX1 ....10 C9
Back Moorfield Ter
WOR/ARM LS12 ....108 C6
Back Moorland Ter LDSU LS2 ....6 C4
Back Moor La HUDS HD4 ....213 M7
Back Morning St KGHY * BD21 ....79 K2
Back Morritt Dr
MSTN/BAR LS15 ....111 H6
Back Mount Pleasant
MID LS10 ....153 L1
WKFDE WF1 ....13 H2
Back Mount Vw HDGY LS6 ....6 B1
Back Muff St BOW BD4 ....5 L9
Back Myrtle Av BGLY BD16 ....81 H4
Back Nansen St BRAM LS13 ....107 J4
Back Newport Gdns HDGY LS6 ....108 F3
Back Newport Mt HDGY LS6 ....108 F3
Back Newport Pl HDGY LS6 ....108 F3
Back Newton Gv CHAL LS7 ....109 M2
Back Newton La CAS WF10 ....136 C7
Back New York St LDS LS1 ....9 H1
Back Nice Vw RHAY * LS8 ....110 B2
Back Norman Mt KSTL LS5 ....108 C2
Back Norman Pl RHAY LS8 ....88 C4
Back Norman Ter RHAY LS8 ....88 C4
Back Northbrook St CHAL LS7 ....87 M7
Back Northfield Pl GIR * BD8 ....4 B1
Back Northgate PONT WF8 ....180 F5
Back North Park Av RHAY LS8 ....88 B5
Back North St LM/WK * BD12 ....149 J2
Back Norwood Gv HDGY LS6 ....109 G3
Back Norwood Pl HDGY LS6 ....109 G3
Back Norwood Rd HDGY LS6 ....109 G3
Back Nowell Crs OSM LS9 ....110 D5
Back Nowell Mt OSM LS9 ....110 D5
Back Nowell Pl OSM LS9 ....110 D5
Back Nowell Ter OSM LS9 ....110 D5
Back Nunington St
WOR/ARM LS12 ....108 F6
Back Nunington Vw
WOR/ARM LS12 ....108 E5
Back Nunroyd Rd
AL/HA/HU LS17 ....87 M5
Back Nursery Mt MID * LS10 ....132 A5
Back Oak Av BGLY BD16 ....81 H5
Back Oakfield Ter HDGY LS6 ....87 G8
Back Oakley St
EARD/LOFT WF3 ....154 A5
Back Oakley Ter
BEE/HOL * LS11 ....131 L4
Back Oak Rd CHAL * LS7 ....109 M1
Back Oakwood Av RHAY LS8 ....88 D8
Back Oakwood Dr RHAY LS8 ....88 D8
Back O' Dam MAR/SLWT * HD7 ....212 C6
Back of the Beck
SKP/WHF * BD23 ....16 B2
Back Oldham Rd MILN OL16 ....206 C8
Back Osmondthorpe La
OSM LS9 ....110 E6
Back O' the Ml BGLY BD16 ....80 C5
Back O' th' Height
RPDN/SBR HX6 ....187 L4
Back Otterburn St KGHY * BD21 ....3 G2
Back Outwood La HORS LS18 ....85 L7
Back Overdale Ter
MSTN/BAR * LS15 ....111 J6
Back O'wall HUDW HD3 ....211 K3
Back Oxford St
EARD/LOFT WF3 ....154 A6
Back Paget St KGHY BD21 ....2 D5
Back Parish Ghyll Rd ILK LS29 ....38 D3
Back Park Crs RHAY LS8 ....88 D4
Back Parkfield Pl
BEE/HOL LS11 ....131 J3
Back Parkfield Rd
BEE/HOL LS11 ....131 J3
Back Park Ter HFAX HX1 ....10 C6
Back Park Vw BEE/HOL LS11 ....131 J3
Back Park View Av BULY LS4 ....108 F3
Back Parkville Rd BRAM * LS13 ....107 L3
Back Parnaby Av MID LS10 ....132 B5
Back Parnaby St MID LS10 ....132 B5
Back Parnaby Ter MID LS10 ....132 B5
Back Pasture Gv CHAL LS7 ....87 M7
Back Pasture Rd RHAY LS8 ....110 A2
Back Pawson St
EARD/LOFT WF3 ....154 A6
Back Pleasant St
RPDN/SBR HX6 ....167 L1
Back Pollard La BRAM LS13 ....107 L1
Back Pollard St HUDN HD2 ....192 D4
Back Poplar Av
MSTN/BAR LS15 ....111 M4
Back Potternewton La
CHAL LS7 ....87 L8
Back Potters St CHAL LS7 ....87 M8
Back Prospect Pl KGHY BD21 ....2 F6
Back Prospect Ter OSM * LS9 ....110 B7
Back Providence Av HDGY * LS6 ....6 D1
Back Providence St
BTLY * WF17 ....173 L1
Back Purlwell Hall Rd
BTLY WF17 ....173 L3
Back Quarry Mount Ter
HDGY * LS6 ....6 D1
Back Queen St GTL/HWG HX4 ....168 E8
HUD HD1 ....15 G7
Back Ravenscar Av RHAY LS8 ....88 C8
Back Ravens St DEWS WF13 ....173 J8
Back Raynville Mt BRAM LS13 ....108 A3
Back Regent Park Ter HDGY LS6 ....6 B1
Back Regent St WKFDE WF1 ....13 K8
Back Regent Ter HDGY LS6 ....6 A4
Back Reginald Mt CHAL * LS7 ....109 M2
Back Reginald Pl CHAL * LS7 ....109 M2
Back Reginald St CHAL LS7 ....109 M2
Back Rhodes St HFAX HX1 ....10 E6
Back Ribble St KGHY BD21 ....58 B6
Back Richardson St
LM/WK BD12 ....149 J2
Back Richmond Mt HDGY LS6 ....109 G3
Back Ridge Mount Ter
HDGY LS6 ....109 J2
Back Ridge St TOD * OL14 ....163 K1
Back Ridge Vw CHAL LS7 ....109 J1
Back Rigging La
RPDN/SBR HX6 ....166 E3
Back Ripley St AIRE BD20 ....58 B5
Back Ripon Ter HIPP HX3 ....10 F1
Back River St HWTH BD22 ....78 F7
Back Rd LM/WK BD12 ....148 E2
Back Roberts St RTHW * LS26 ....133 L8
Back Rochester Ter HDGY LS6 ....108 F2
Back Rokeby Gdns HDGY LS6 ....108 E1
Back Roman Gv RHAY LS8 ....88 C4
Back Roman Pl RHAY LS8 ....88 C4
Back Roman St RHAY LS8 ....88 C4
Back Rosebank Crs HDGY LS6 ....6 A5
Back Rosemont Wk
BRAM LS13 ....107 L4
Back Rossall Rd RHAY * LS8 ....110 C2
Back Rossington Gv RHAY LS8 ....7 M1
Back Rossington Pl RHAY LS8 ....7 M1
Back Rossington Rd RHAY LS8 ....7 M2
Back Roundhay Av RHAY LS8 ....110 B1
Back Roundhay Crs RHAY LS8 ....110 B1
Back Roundhay Gv RHAY LS8 ....110 B1
Back Roundhay Pl RHAY * LS8 ....110 B1
Back Roundhay Vw
RHAY * LS8 ....110 B1
Back Rw BEE/HOL LS11 ....8 F3
Back Rowland Ter
BEE/HOL * LS11 ....131 L3
Back Royds St MILN OL16 ....228 C1
Back Rupert St KGHY BD21 ....3 H2
Back Russell St WBOW BD5 ....4 D9
Back Ruthven Vw RHAY LS8 ....110 C3
Back Rydal St HWTH BD22 ....2 D6
Back Rylstone St KGHY BD21 ....3 K2
Back St Alban Crs OSM LS9 ....110 E5
Back St Elmo Gv OSM * LS9 ....110 C6
Back Saint Ives Mt
WOR/ARM LS12 ....108 C6
Back St Luke's Crs
BEE/HOL * LS11 ....8 D8
Back St Mary's Rd CHAL LS7 ....109 M1
Back St Paul's Rd SHPY * BD18 ....82 C7
Back Salisbury Gv
WOR/ARM LS12 ....108 E6
Back Salisbury Ter
WOR/ARM LS12 ....108 E6
Back Salisbury Vw
WOR/ARM LS12 ....108 E6
Back Saltaire Rd North
SHPY BD18 ....82 C6
Back Sandhurst Gv RHAY LS8 ....110 C3
Back Sandhurst Pl RHAY LS8 ....110 C3
Back Sandhurst Rd RHAY LS8 ....110 C3
Back Savile Pde HFAX HX1 ....168 D1
Back Savile Pl CHAL LS7 ....7 J2
Back Savile Rd CHAL LS7 ....7 J2
Back School Vw HDGY LS6 ....109 G3
Back Seaforth Av OSM LS9 ....110 D4
Back Seaforth Ter OSM * LS9 ....110 C3
Back Sefton Av BEE/HOL LS11 ....131 J3
Back Sefton Ter BEE/HOL LS11 ....131 J4
Back Shaftesbury Av RHAY LS8 ....88 C5
Back Shaw La KGHY BD21 ....79 M3
Back Shepherd's La CHAL LS7 ....110 A2
Back Shepherd's Pl RHAY LS8 ....110 B2
Back Sholebroke Av CHAL LS7 ....109 M1
Back Sholebroke Mt CHAL LS7 ....109 M2
Back Sholebroke Pl CHAL LS7 ....109 M2
Back Sholebroke Rw CHAL LS7 ....109 L2
Back Sholebroke Ter CHAL LS7 ....109 L1
Back Sholebroke Vw CHAL LS7 ....109 M2
Back Sidlaw Ter RHAY LS8 ....110 B2
Back Simpson St KGHY BD21 ....2 D4
Back Sladen St KGHY BD21 ....2 D5
Back Slaithwaite Rd
EARL WF12 ....195 L2
Back Smith Rw WBOW * BD5 ....126 E3
Back South End Gv BRAM LS13 ....108 A4
Back South St HUD HD1 ....213 M1
Back Spencer Mt RHAY LS8 ....7 M2
Back Springfield Mt
WOR/ARM LS12 ....108 C7
Back Springfield Rd ELL * HX5 ....169 K7
Back Spring Grove Wk
HDGY LS6 ....109 G4
Back Spring St HUD HD1 ....14 D7
Back Stanley St OSM * LS9 ....110 B4
Back Stanmore Pl BULY LS4 ....108 E3
Back Stanmore St BULY LS4 ....108 E3
Back Station Rd AIRE BD20 ....34 F7
BTLY * WF17 ....173 M2
MIRF WF14 ....194 C2
Backstone Gill La
AL/HA/HU LS17 ....66 F5
Back Stone Hall Rd ECHL BD2 ....105 K2
Backstone La ILK LS29 ....38 E3
Backstone Wy ILK LS29 ....38 F2
Back Storey Pl SCFT LS14 ....111 G5
Back Stratford Av
BEE/HOL LS11 ....131 J4
Back Stratford St
BEE/HOL * LS11 ....131 L3
Back Stratford Ter
BEE/HOL LS11 ....131 K3
Back St BSPA/BRAM LS23 ....69 L3
PONT WF8 ....180 E6
Back Sunnydene SCFT LS14 ....111 H5
Back Sutton Ap SCFT LS14 ....111 G5
Back Swinton St HFAX HX1 ....10 A8
Back Sycamore Av BGLY BD16 ....81 H4
Back Tamworth St BOW BD4 ....106 A8
Back Tempest Rd
BEE/HOL LS11 ....131 K3
Back Temple Vw BEE/HOL * LS11 ....8 D9
Back the Crs HDGY LS6 ....6 B2
Back Thornhill St
PDSY/CALV * LS28 ....84 D8
Back Thornville Rw HDGY LS6 ....109 G4
Back Tower Gv WOR/ARM LS12 ....108 B6
Back Trafford Av OSM LS9 ....110 D4
Back Trentham Pl
BEE/HOL LS11 ....131 K4
Back Trinity Ter WBOW BD5 ....4 D9
Back Union St HUD HD1 ....15 G5
Back Unity St North BGLY BD16 ....81 H4
Back Unity St South BGLY BD16 ....81 H4
Back Vicars Rd RHAY * LS8 ....110 B2
Back Victoria Gv OSM LS9 ....110 D6
Back Victoria St HFAX HX1 ....11 G5
Back Victor Ter HFAX HX1 ....10 C3
Back Walmsley Rd HDGY LS6 ....109 G3
Back Walnut St KGHY * BD21 ....79 K3
Back Waverley Rd ELL HX5 ....191 H1
Back Webster St DEWS * WF13 ....173 L6
Back Wellfield Ter TOD OL14 ....163 K2
Back Welton Av HDGY LS6 ....109 G3
Back Welton Gv HDGY LS6 ....109 G3
Back Welton Mt HDGY LS6 ....109 G3
Back Welton Pl HDGY LS6 ....109 G3
Back Wentworth St HUD HD1 ....14 D6
Back Wesley St CAS WF10 ....157 M6
Back Westbourne Ter LDSU LS2 ....6 C5
Back Westbury St MID LS10 ....132 B5
Back Westlock Av OSM LS9 ....110 C5
Back Westover Rd BRAM LS13 ....107 L3
Back West St RPDN/SBR HX6 ....167 K3
Back Wetherby Gv BULY LS4 ....108 E4
Back Wetherby Rd RHAY LS8 ....88 D8
Back Wharf St RPDN/SBR HX6 ....167 L2
Back Wickham St
BEE/HOL LS11 ....131 J3
Back William Av
MSTN/BAR * LS15 ....111 G6
Back Wilton Gv HDGY * LS6 ....87 G8
Back Winfield Gv LDSU * LS2 ....6 F4
Back Winston Gdns HDGY LS6 ....108 E1
Back Winterburn St KGHY * BD21 ....3 G2
Back Woodbine Ter HDGY LS6 ....87 G8
Back Woodland Park Rd
HDGY * LS6 ....109 G1
Back Wood St EARD/LOFT WF3 ....153 M6
GIR BD8 ....4 B3
Back Wright Av HWTH BD22 ....78 F3
Back York Pl LDS LS1 ....8 E1
Back York St LDSU LS2 ....9 J1
Bacon Av NORM WF6 ....178 E3
Bacon St GSLY LS20 ....62 B6
Bacup Rd TOD OL14 ....162 A1
Baddeley Gdns IDLE BD10 ....83 J5
Baden Powell Crs PONT WF8 ....180 F7
Baden St HWTH BD22 ....78 E6
Badger Brow HOLM/MEL HD9 ....234 F4
Badger Cl HOR/CROF WF4 ....198 B7
MILN OL16 ....228 E3
Badger Ga HOLM/MEL HD9 ....234 F4
Badgergate Av WIL/AL BD15 ....102 E2
Badger Hl BRIG HD6 ....169 M8
Badger La HBR HX7 ....142 C2
HIPP HX3 ....147 K7
MILN OL16 ....228 D4
STKB/PEN S36 ....269 G8
Badgers Ga ILK LS29 ....20 A2
Badgers Mt MSTN/BAR LS15 ....112 B4
Badgers Wk HECK WF16 ....173 G3
Badgers Wy ECHL BD2 ....105 G2
Badger Wood Gld WBY LS22 ....30 A6
Badminton Dr EARD/LOFT WF3 ....153 M3
Badsworth Ct HEM/SK/SE WF9 ....225 G3
Badsworth Vw
HEM/SK/SE WF9 ....225 J6
Bagden La KBTN HD8 ....240 A8
Baghill Ct PONT WF8 ....181 H6
Baghill Gn EARD/LOFT WF3 ....152 F8
Baghill La PONT WF8 ....181 G5
Baghill Rd EARD/LOFT WF3 ....152 F8
Bagley La PDSY/CALV LS28 ....106 F2
Bagnall Ter WBSY BD6 ....126 D5
Baildon Av GFTH/SHER LS25 ....135 K4
Baildon Cl SCFT LS14 ....89 L8
Baildon Dr SCFT LS14 ....89 L8
Baildon Gn SCFT LS14 ....89 L8
Baildon Holmes BAIL BD17 ....82 E5
Baildon Pl SCFT LS14 ....89 L8
Baildon Rd BAIL BD17 ....82 E4
SCFT LS14 ....89 L7
Baildon Wood Ct BAIL BD17 ....82 E4
The Bailey SKP/WHF BD23 ....16 C2
Bailey Crs HEM/SK/SE WF9 ....247 J2
Bailey Hall Bank HIPP HX3 ....11 K6
Bailey Hall Rd HIPP HX3 ....11 K6
Bailey Hills Rd BGLY BD16 ....81 G2
Bailey's Ct SCFT LS14 ....111 J1
Bailey's Hl SCFT LS14 ....111 J1
Bailey's La SCFT LS14 ....111 J1
Baileys Lawn SCFT LS14 ....111 J1
Bailey St BOW BD4 ....127 H1
Bailey Wk HOR/CROF WF4 ....220 B3
Bailey Wells Av WBOW BD5 ....126 E3
Baillie St MILN * OL16 ....206 B7
Baillie St East MILN OL16 ....206 C6
Bainbrigge Rd HDGY LS6 ....108 F2
Baines St HFAX HX1 ....10 C4
RTHW * LS26 ....155 G1
Bainton Dr BSLY S70 ....260 F7
Baird St WBOW BD5 ....127 G2
Bairstow Ct LUD/ILL HX2 ....145 L8
Bairstow La LUD/ILL HX2 ....145 L8
Bairstow Mt LUD/ILL HX2 ....167 L1
Bairstow St WIL/AL BD15 ....103 J3
Bakehouse La DOD/DAR S75 ....260 C3
Baker Crs MOR LS27 ....152 C3
Baker Fold HFAX HX1 ....10 D5
Baker La EARD/LOFT WF3 ....176 F1
Baker Rd MOR LS27 ....152 C3
Baker's St HBR HX7 ....143 J2
Baker St ECHL BD2 ....105 K4
HUDW HD3 ....191 K6
MOR LS27 ....152 C3
SHPY BD18 ....82 C6
Baker St North LUD/ILL HX2 ....146 C1
Bakes St GTHN BD7 ....126 C2
Bakewell Rd BSLYN/ROY S71 ....243 J8
Bakston Cl HUDE HD5 ....215 G3
Bala St BSLYN/ROY S71 ....261 H5
Balbec Av HDGY LS6 ....109 G1
Balbec St HDGY LS6 ....109 G1
Balderstone Hall La
MIRF WF14 ....172 E8
Balderstone Rd ROCH OL11 ....228 C4
Baldovan Mt RHAY LS8 ....110 B2
Baldovan Pl RHAY LS8 ....110 B2
Baldovan Ter RHAY LS8 ....110 B2
Baldwin La CLAY BD14 ....125 J3
Baldwin Ter HIPP HX3 ....11 K6
Balfour St BGLY BD16 ....81 H4
BOW BD4 ....127 J2
KGHY BD21 ....2 E7
ROY/SHW OL2 ....229 K6
The Balk BTLY WF17 ....151 L7
DOD/DAR S75 ....242 E4
WKFDW/WTN WF2 ....199 K8
Balk Av EARD/LOFT WF3 ....177 J4
Balkcliffe La MID LS10 ....131 J8
Balk Crs EARD/LOFT WF3 ....177 H4
Balk La EARD/LOFT WF3 ....177 J4
GTHN BD7 ....126 D2
HEM/SK/SE WF9 ....247 M2
HOR/CROF WF4 ....197 H7
HUDE HD5 ....193 K7
KBTN HD8 ....238 E8
Balkram Dr LUD/ILL HX2 ....145 J1
Balkram Edge LUD/ILL HX2 ....145 H1
Balkram Rd LUD/ILL HX2 ....145 K1
Balks LVSG WF15 ....172 B2
Balk St BTLY WF17 ....173 K1
Ballantyne Rd IDLE BD10 ....83 J4
Ballard Cl LIT OL15 ....185 K7
Ballard Wy ROY/SHW OL2 ....229 L7
Ballater Av HUDS HD4 ....213 L4
Ballfield La DOD/DAR S75 ....241 K5
Ball Grove Dr COL BB8 ....74 D1
Ballroyd Clough HUDW HD3 ....191 J8
Ballroyd La HUDW HD3 ....191 J8
Ball Royd Rd HUDN HD2 ....192 D4
Ball St CUL/QBY BD13 ....103 G8
MILN OL16 ....206 C6
Balme La LM/WK BD12 ....148 F3
Balme Rd CLECK BD19 ....149 M6
Balme St BFD BD1 ....5 G5
LM/WK BD12 ....148 E3
Balme Ter HWTH * BD22 ....78 E8
Balmfield LVSG WF15 ....172 C4
Balmfield Crs LVSG WF15 ....172 C4
Balmoral Av HUDS HD4 ....213 L4
Balmoral Cha MID LS10 ....132 B3
Balmoral Cl MILN OL16 ....207 J8
PONT WF8 ....202 D1
STKB/PEN S36 ....270 C2
Balmoral Dr KNOT WF11 ....181 K2
Balmoral Pl HFAX HX1 ....10 F7
Balmoral St HBR HX7 ....143 J3
Balmoral Wy YEA LS19 ....62 F8
Balm Pl BEE/HOL LS11 ....8 C5
Balm Rd MID LS10 ....132 A4
Balm Wk BEE/HOL LS11 ....8 B5
Balne Av WKFDW/WTN WF2 ....12 A1
Balne La WKFDW/WTN WF2 ....12 B1
Bamborough St WKFDE WF1 ....13 M8
Bamburgh Rd MSTN/BAR LS15 ....112 A3
Bamford Av BSLYN/ROY S71 ....243 J8
Bamford Cl DOD/DAR S75 ....260 A7
Bamford St LIT OL15 ....207 H1
Bamlett Brow HWTH BD22 ....78 F6
Banbury Rd PONT WF8 ....181 G3
Bancroft Av HUDE HD5 ....215 G1
Bangor Gv WOR/ARM LS12 ....130 C2
Bangor Pl WOR/ARM LS12 ....130 C2
Bangor St MILN * OL16 ....206 D8
WOR/ARM LS12 ....130 C2
Bangor Ter WOR/ARM LS12 ....130 C2
Bangor Vw WOR/ARM LS12 ....130 C2
Bank IDLE BD10 ....83 M8
Bank Av HORS LS18 ....85 K6
MOR LS27 ....152 C1
Bank Barn La WHIT OL12 ....184 F7
Bank Bottom HBR HX7 ....144 C4
HFAX HX1 ....11 K6
Bank Bottom La LUD/ILL HX2 ....145 G5
Bank Cl IDLE BD10 ....105 L1
LIT OL15 ....207 J3
Bank Crest BAIL BD17 ....82 E3
Bank Crest Ri SHPY BD18 ....81 M7
Bank Dr WBSY BD6 ....126 F6
Bank Edge Gdns LUD/ILL HX2 ....146 A3
Bank Edge Rd LUD/ILL HX2 ....145 M3
Bank End Knoll
HOLM/MEL HD9 ....236 F5
Bank End La HUDE HD5 ....215 G2
KBTN HD8 ....240 C5
Bank End Rd MAR/SLWT HD7 ....212 D3
Banker St BULY LS4 ....108 F5
Bankfield AL/HA/HU LS17 ....67 M2
KBTN HD8 ....238 B4
MAR/SLWT * HD7 ....233 J2
Bankfield Av HUDE HD5 ....193 K6
SHPY BD18 ....81 M8
Bankfield Cl OSS WF5 ....197 H2
Bankfield Ct HUDE HD5 ....15 M9
MIRF WF14 ....194 B1
WKFDW/WTN WF2 ....176 B3
Bankfield Dr HOLM/MEL HD9 ....253 L4
HWTH BD22 ....57 G7
SHPY BD18 ....81 M7
WKFDW/WTN WF2 ....176 B3
Bankfield Flats HWTH * BD22 ....78 D4
Bankfield Gdns BULY LS4 ....108 E4
HIPP HX3 ....147 H8
Bank Field Gra GTL/HWG HX4 ....168 E7
Bankfield Gv BULY LS4 ....108 E3
Bankfield La HUDE HD5 ....193 K6
Bankfield Mt HWTH BD22 ....57 G7
Bankfield Park Av HUDS HD4 ....214 B5
Bank Field Rd BTLY WF17 ....173 L1
Bankfield Rd BULY * LS4 ....108 E4
HUD HD1 ....14 D9
HWTH BD22 ....57 G6
SHPY BD18 ....81 M7
Bankfields Av HBR HX7 ....144 A5
Bankfield St COL BB8 ....74 D2
HWTH BD22 ....57 G6
Bankfield Ter BAIL BD17 ....82 F4
BULY LS4 ....108 E4
HUDS HD4 ....214 A6
Bankfield Vw HIPP HX3 ....10 F2
Bankfield Wk HWTH BD22 ....57 G7
Bankfield Yd HIPP * HX3 ....10 F1
Bankfoot HBR HX7 ....143 H3
Bank Foot La HUDS HD4 ....214 A7
Bank Foot Pl BTLY * WF17 ....173 L1
Bank Foot Rd HUDS HD4 ....215 H6
Bank Foot St BTLY * WF17 ....173 L1
Bank Gdns HORS LS18 ....85 K6
Bank Ga MAR/SLWT HD7 ....212 B5
Bank Gv EARL WF12 ....174 C7
Bank Hey Bottom La
RPDN/SBR HX6 ....189 G3
Bankholme Ct BOW BD4 ....128 B4
Bankhouse PDSY/CALV LS28 ....128 F1
Bank House Cl MOR LS27 ....152 C1
Bank House La LUD/ILL HX2 ....144 F2
Bankhouse La HIPP HX3 ....168 F4
HUDW HD3 ....213 K1
PDSY/CALV LS28 ....128 F1
Bankhouse Rd HUDW HD3 ....213 K1
Banklands AIRE BD20 ....36 A4
Banklands Av AIRE BD20 ....36 B4
Banklands La AIRE BD20 ....36 B4
Bank La AIRE BD20 ....18 A6
HOLM/MEL HD9 ....236 D7
HOLM/MEL HD9 ....253 K4
HOLM/MEL HD9 ....253 M2
KBTN HD8 ....257 H2
WHIT OL12 ....184 E7
Bank Pde OT LS21 ....41 H7
Bank Rd AIRE BD20 ....34 F7
RPDN/SBR HX6 ....167 K3
Bank Royd La GTL/HWG HX4 ....189 K5
Banks Ap MAR/SLWT HD7 ....212 F1
Banks Av FEA/AMT WF7 ....224 A1
MAR/SLWT HD7 ....212 E1
PONT * WF8 ....180 E6
Banks Buildings
FEA/AMT * WF7 ....201 M2
Banks Crs MAR/SLWT HD7 ....212 F1
Banks Dr MAR/SLWT HD7 ....212 F1
Banks End Rd ELL HX5 ....169 L8
Banksfield Av YEA LS19 ....62 D6
Banksfield Cl YEA LS19 ....62 D6
Banksfield Crs YEA LS19 ....62 D6
Banksfield Gv YEA LS19 ....62 D6
Banksfield Mt YEA LS19 ....62 D6
Banksfield Ri YEA LS19 ....62 D6
Banksfield Rd HBR HX7 ....144 A5
Banksfields Crs HBR HX7 ....144 A5
Banksfield Ter HBR HX7 ....144 A5
Banks Gv MAR/SLWT HD7 ....212 F1
Bankside KBTN HD8 ....238 B4
TOD OL14 ....163 K2
Bank Side St RHAY LS8 ....110 B3
Banks La AIRE BD20 ....58 A2
KNOT WF11 ....182 B2

Banks Mt PONT WF8 180 E6
Bank Sq MOR LS27 152 C1
Banks Rd HOLM/MEL HD9 236 D3
MAR/SLWT HD7 212 D6
MAR/SLWT HD7 212 F1
Banks Side MAR/SLWT HD7 212 F1
Banks St BTLY WF17 173 L2
Bank St BFD BD1 4 F6
BRIG HD6 170 C4
BSLY S70 261 H7
BSLYN/ROY S71 262 A6
CAS WF10 157 M6
CLECK BD19 149 L7
COL BB8 74 E5
CUD/GR S72 244 D7
EARL WF12 173 M6
HOLM/MEL HD9 255 G2
HOR/CROF WF4 197 J5
LDS LS1 9 G1
MIRF WF14 194 A1
MOR LS27 152 C1
OSS WF5 196 F1
ROCH OL11 228 C2
SHPY BD18 82 D6
TOD OL14 163 K2
WBSY * BD6 126 E5
WBY LS22 48 A1
WKFDE WF1 12 E3
Bank Ter HBR HX7 143 G3
MOR LS27 152 C1
Bank Top HIPP HX3 11 M9
Bank Top Dr AIRE BD20 58 B4
Bank Top La HBR HX7 165 H1
HOLM/MEL HD9 253 J3
OT LS21 64 F3
Bank Top Wy KGHY BD21 58 B8
Bank Vw BAIL BD17 82 D4
EARL WF12 174 C7
HOLM/MEL HD9 236 E4
STKB/PEN * S36 271 L5
Bank View Ter CHAL LS7 87 K7
Bank Wk BAIL BD17 82 E3
Bankwell Fold WBSY BD6 126 F5
Bankwell Rd HUDS HD4 213 K2
Bankwood BTLY * WF17 151 K2
Bank Wood Rd PONT WF8 204 B2
Bankwood Wy BTLY WF17 151 K2
Bannerman St LM/WK BD12 149 J1
Banner St BFDE BD3 5 K7
Bannister Cl COL BB8 74 D3
Bannister La AWLS/ASK DN6 248 E1
Bannister Wk HWTH BD22 54 F2
Bannockburn Ct BOW * BD4 127 J5
Bannockburn Wy NORM WF6 178 A2
Banstead St East RHAY LS8 110 B3
Banstead St West RHAY LS8 110 B3
Banstead Ter East RHAY LS8 110 B3
Banstead Ter West RHAY * LS8 110 B3
Bantam Cl MOR LS27 152 F2
Bantam Grove La MOR LS27 152 F2
Bantam Grove Vw MOR LS27 152 F2
Bantree Ct IDLE BD10 83 J5
Baptist Fold CUL/QBY BD13 125 G5
Baptist La OSS WF5 197 K2
Baptist Pl BFD BD1 4 D5
Baptist St BTLY WF17 173 J3
Bar Av DOD/DAR S75 242 F6
Barber Rw MAR/SLWT HD7 212 E5
Barberry Av BFDE BD3 106 A6
Barber Sq HECK WF16 172 E2
Barber St BRIG HD6 170 C2
Barclay Cl CUL/QBY BD13 102 A1
Barclay St CHAL LS7 7 J6
Barclyde St ROCH OL11 228 A1
Bar Cft HUDE HD5 193 K5
Barcroft DOD/DAR S75 260 C2
HWTH BD22 79 H6
Barcroft Gv YEA LS19 62 C8
Barcroft Rd HUDS HD4 214 B4
Barden Av WBSY BD6 125 M5
Barden Cl BTLY WF17 173 K1
WOR/ARM LS12 108 C7
Barden Dr BGLY BD16 81 L2
DOD/DAR S75 260 D3
Barden Gn WOR/ARM LS12 108 C7
Barden Gv WOR/ARM * LS12 108 C7
Barden Mt WOR/ARM LS12 108 C7
Barden Pl WOR/ARM LS12 108 C7
Barden Rd WKFDE WF1 13 M2
Barden St GIR BD8 104 D5
Barden Ter WOR/ARM LS12 108 C7
Bardon Hall Ms
BHP/TINH * LS16 86 F7
Bardsey Crs BFDE BD3 5 K6
Bardwell Ct EARD/LOFT WF3 177 G1
Bare Head La HIPP HX3 124 F8
Barehill St LIT OL15 185 K8
Barfield Av YEA LS19 62 C8
Barfield Crs AL/HA/HU LS17 88 B1
Barfield Dr YEA LS19 62 C8
Barfield Gv AL/HA/HU LS17 88 C1
Barfield Mt AL/HA/HU LS17 88 C1
Barfield Rd HIPP HX3 147 L7
Bargate MAR/SLWT HD7 212 F5
Bargess Ter GFTH/SHER LS25 135 K5
Barge St HUD HD1 214 B2
Bargrange Av SHPY BD18 82 D8
Bargreen HUDE HD5 193 K5
Barham Ter IDLE BD10 105 M2
Bar House La AIRE BD20 57 H3
Bari Cl WMB/DAR S73 263 G8
Baring Av BFDE BD3 105 M6
Bark Cl KBTN HD8 238 C3
Barker Cl HIPP HX3 169 G3
Barker Ct HUDN HD2 192 A5
Barkerend Rd BFDE BD3 5 H5
Barker Pl BRAM LS13 107 M5
Barker Rd HOR/CROF WF4 197 H4
Barker's Rd HOR/CROF WF4 198 A8
Barker St EARD/LOFT WF3 155 K8
LVSG WF15 172 D2
TOD OL14 141 K8
Barkers Well Fold
WOR/ARM LS12 129 M2
Barkers Well Garth
WOR/ARM LS12 130 A3
Barkers Well Ga
WOR/ARM LS12 130 A3
Barkers Well Lawn
WOR/ARM LS12 130 A3
Barke St MILN OL16 207 G3
Bark House La DOD/DAR S75 258 E2
KBTN HD8 238 D3
Barkhouse Wood La
KNOT WF11 161 K3
Bark La ILK LS29 19 J6
Barkly Av BEE/HOL LS11 131 J5
Barkly Dr BEE/HOL * LS11 131 J5
Barkly Gv BEE/HOL LS11 131 J4
Barkly Pde BEE/HOL LS11 131 J4
Barkly Pl BEE/HOL LS11 131 J5
Barkly Rd BEE/HOL LS11 131 H4
Barkly St BEE/HOL LS11 131 J5
Barkly Ter BEE/HOL LS11 131 J4
Bark Mdw DOD/DAR S75 260 C7
Barkston Rd BSLYN/ROY S71 243 L8
Bar La AIRE BD20 58 B5
BSPA/BRAM LS23 49 J8
DOD/DAR S75 242 F6
GFTH/SHER LS25 113 J7
HOR/CROF WF4 218 B4
HORS LS18 85 G6
RPDN/SBR HX6 188 E4
SEL YO8 139 M5
WKFDE WF1 176 F5
Barlbro' Pl HUDW HD3 213 J2
Barlby Wy RHAY LS8 88 E8
Barleycorn Cl WKFDE WF1 177 G5
Barley Cote Av AIRE BD20 58 B4
Barley Cote Gv AIRE BD20 58 C4
Barley Cote Rd AIRE BD20 58 B4
Barley Cft DEWS WF13 173 H6
Barleyfield Cl WKFDE WF1 177 G6
Barley Field Ct
MSTN/BAR * LS15 111 J6
Barleyfields Cl WBY LS22 30 A7
Barleyfields Ct WBY LS22 30 A8
Barleyfields La WBY LS22 30 A8
Barleyfields Ms WBY LS22 48 A1
Barleyfields Rd WBY LS22 30 A8
Barleyfields Ter WBY LS22 30 A8
Barleyhill Crs GFTH/SHER LS25 113 G7
Barleyhill La GFTH/SHER LS25 113 G7
Barleyhill Rd GFTH/SHER LS25 113 G7
Barley Horn Rd TAD LS24 94 F2
Barley Ms EARD/LOFT WF3 154 D3
Barley St HWTH BD22 79 J2
Barlow Rd KGHY BD21 2 E3
Barlow St BFDE BD3 5 L5
MILN OL16 206 C7
Barmby Cl OSS WF5 197 H2
Barmby Crs OSS WF5 197 J2
Barmby Fold OSS WF5 197 H2
Barmby Pl ECHL BD2 5 L1
Barmby Rd ECHL BD2 5 L1
Barmby St LM/WK BD12 148 F2
Bar Mt GFTH/SHER * LS25 113 J7
Barmouth Ter BFDE BD3 5 G1
Barnabas Wk BSLYN/ROY S71 261 H3
Barnaby Rd BGLY BD16 81 L2
Barnard Cl MSTN/BAR LS15 112 A3
Barnard Rd BOW BD4 127 J1
Barnard Wy MSTN/BAR LS15 112 A3
Barnbow La MSTN/BAR LS15 112 D2
MSTN/BAR LS15 112 E1
Barnbrough St BULY LS4 108 E4
Barnby Av GIR BD8 103 L7
Barnby Royd HUDE HD5 193 G7
Barncroft Cl SCFT LS14 89 H7
Barncroft Dr SCFT LS14 89 G8
Barncroft Gdns SCFT LS14 89 H8
Barncroft Mt SCFT LS14 89 G8
Barncroft Ri SCFT LS14 89 H8
Barncroft Rd SCFT LS14 89 H8
Barnes Av WKFDE WF1 176 C3
Barnes Mdw LIT OL15 185 L5
Barnes Rd CAS WF10 157 M8
GIR BD8 104 B6
Barnes St TOD OL14 163 J5
Barnet Gv MOR LS27 152 C4
Barnet Rd WOR/ARM LS12 108 F7
Barn Field Cl COL BB8 74 C1
Barn Field La WHIT OL12 184 C7
Barnfield Ri ROY/SHW OL2 229 J5
Barnfield St WHIT OL12 206 B4
Barnsdale Est CAS WF10 157 K8
Barnsdale Ms AWLS/ASK DN6 227 L6
Barnsdale Rd CAS WF10 135 M8
RTHW LS26 156 E5
Barnsdale Vw AWLS/ASK DN6 227 K2
Barnsdale Wy HEM/SK/SE WF9 226 A7
Barnside Cl STKB/PEN * S36 270 F4
Barnside La HOLM/MEL HD9 255 H5
Barnsley Beck Gv BAIL BD17 82 A3
Barnsley Boundary Wk
DOD/DAR S75 241 G8
DOD/DAR S75 241 M1
DOD/DAR S75 258 E2
HOLM/MEL HD9 255 G8
HOLM/MEL HD9 267 L2
HOR/CROF WF4 222 D6
KBTN HD8 257 K3
STKB/PEN S36 256 E7
Barnsley Rd CUD/GR S72 244 C8
CUD/GR S72 245 H3
DOD/DAR S75 259 K2
DOD/DAR S75 259 J6
DOD/DAR S75 260 A7
FEA/AMT WF7 224 C2
HEM/SK/SE WF9 246 F3
HOR/CROF WF4 217 L8
KBTN HD8 238 E8
KBTN HD8 240 A5
STKB/PEN S36 270 F2
WKFDE WF1 13 H7
WMB/DAR S73 263 H7
Barnstone V WKFDE WF1 177 G6
The Barn LM/WK BD12 127 G8
Barn St HWTH BD22 100 E2
Barnswick Cl PONT WF8 180 F8
Barnswick Vw BHP/TINH LS16 86 A2
Baron Cl BEE/HOL LS11 8 B8
Baronscourt MSTN/BAR LS15 111 M6
Baronsmead MSTN/BAR LS15 111 L6
Baron St MILN OL16 206 B7
Baronsway MSTN/BAR LS15 111 L6
Barrack Rd CHAL LS7 7 K3
Barracks Fold HOLM/MEL HD9 255 G4
Barracks St HECK WF16 172 E2
Barrack St CHAL LS7 7 J4
Barraclough Sq LM/WK BD12 148 E2
Barraclough St LM/WK BD12 126 D8
Barran St BGLY BD16 81 J3
Barras Garth Pl
WOR/ARM LS12 108 D8
Barras Garth Rd
WOR/ARM LS12 108 D8
Barras Pl WOR/ARM LS12 108 D8
Barras St WOR/ARM LS12 108 D8
Barras Ter WOR/ARM LS12 108 D8
Barratt's Rd WKFDE WF1 176 E6
Barrett St AIRE BD20 35 M5
Barrington Cl HIPP HX3 169 J2
Barrington Garth GLE DN14 161 M8
Barrington Pde CLECK BD19 150 C6
Barrowby Av MSTN/BAR LS15 112 A7
Barrowby Crs MSTN/BAR LS15 112 A6
Barrowby La MSTN/BAR LS15 112 B6
PBR HG3 27 K8
Barrowby Rd MSTN/BAR LS15 112 B7
Barrowclough La HIPP HX3 147 H7
Barrows La AIRE BD20 56 E2
Barrowstead KBTN HD8 239 J5
Barr St HUD HD1 15 J2
Barr Ter GIR BD8 104 B6
Barry St BFD BD1 4 E6
Barsey Green La GTL/HWG HX4 167 L8
Barstow Fall PONT WF8 181 G3
Barstow Sq WKFDE WF1 12 E2
Bar St BTLY WF17 173 M2
TOD OL14 163 J2
Barthorpe Cl BOW BD4 128 B4
Barthorpe Crs CHAL LS7 87 L6
Bartle Cl GTHN BD7 126 B3
Bartle Fold GTHN BD7 126 C2
Bartle Gill Dr BAIL BD17 83 G2
Bartle Gill Ri BAIL BD17 83 G2
Bartle Gill Vw BAIL * BD17 83 G2
Bartle Gv GTHN BD7 126 B3
Bartle La GTHN BD7 126 B3
Bartle Pl GTHN BD7 126 B3
Bartle Sq GTHN BD7 126 C2
Bartlett Rd ROY/SHW OL2 229 J8
Barton Ct MSTN/BAR LS15 111 L7
Barton Gv BEE/HOL LS11 8 D8
Barton Hl BEE/HOL * LS11 8 C8
Barton Manor Cl HUDS HD4 213 K4
Barton Mt BEE/HOL LS11 8 D8
Barton Pl BEE/HOL LS11 8 C8
BTLY WF17 173 L2
Barton Rd BEE/HOL LS11 8 C8
Barton St BRIG * HD6 170 C3
WBOW BD5 126 D3
Barton Ter BEE/HOL LS11 8 D8
Barton Vw BEE/HOL LS11 8 C8
Barton Wy HEM/SK/SE WF9 247 J1
Barugh Green Rd
DOD/DAR S75 260 A2
Barugh La DOD/DAR S75 260 A1
Barwick Gn WBSY BD6 126 A5
Barwick Rd GFTH/SHER LS25 113 G5
SCFT LS14 111 K3
Basford Ct WKFDW/WTN * WF2 12 A4
Basford St WKFDW/WTN WF2 12 A4
Basil Ct MILN * OL16 206 D8
Basil St HUDS HD4 213 M2
MILN OL16 206 D8
WBOW BD5 126 D3
Baslow Crs DOD/DAR S75 260 A7
Baslow Gv HTON BD9 104 B4
Baslow Rd BSLYN/ROY S71 243 K7
Bassett Wy WHIT OL12 206 A4
Batcliffe Dr HDGY LS6 86 E8
Batcliffe Mt HDGY LS6 108 E1
Bateman Cl CUD/GR S72 244 C4
Bateman St GIR BD8 4 D1
Bates Av RPDN/SBR HX6 167 H3
Bates La PONT WF8 203 H1
Bateson St IDLE BD10 84 A7
Bath Cl BRAM LS13 107 L4
Bath Gv BRAM * LS13 107 L4
Bath La BRAM LS13 107 L4
Bath Pl CLECK BD19 149 M7
HIPP HX3 10 F2
Bath Rd BEE/HOL LS11 8 D4
BRAM LS13 107 L4
CLECK BD19 149 M7
HECK WF16 172 F2
HIPP HX3 168 E2
Bath St BFDE BD3 5 J6
BTLY WF17 173 M1
COL BB8 74 A1
DEWS WF13 173 L5
ELL HX5 169 H8
HFAX * HX1 11 J7
HUD HD1 14 E5
ILK LS29 38 E1
KBTN HD8 238 B1
KGHY BD21 2 F4
TOD OL14 163 K1
WHIT OL12 206 C5
Batley Av HUD HD1 191 M8
Batley Buildings HUD HD1 14 A5
Batley Ct BAIL BD17 82 F2
Batley Field Hl BTLY WF17 151 L8
Batley Rd EARD/LOFT WF3 175 G1
HECK WF16 173 H2
WKFDW/WTN WF2 175 L5
Batley St HIPP HX3 10 D1
HUDE HD5 15 M7
Batter La YEA LS19 84 E2
Battinson Rd HFAX HX1 10 A4
Battinson St HIPP HX3 11 M9
Batty Av CUD/GR S72 244 C8
Battye Av HUDS HD4 213 K3
Battye St BOW BD4 105 L8
EARL WF12 173 M6
Baulk Head La TOD OL14 142 B8
Bavaria Pl GIR BD8 104 D5
Bawn Ap WOR/ARM LS12 130 A1
Bawn Av WOR/ARM LS12 108 A8
Bawn Dr WOR/ARM LS12 108 A8
Bawn Gdns WOR/ARM LS12 108 A8
Bawn La WOR/ARM LS12 108 A8
Bawson Ct CLECK BD19 150 C5
Baxandall St WBOW BD5 126 F3
Baxtergate PONT WF8 180 F6
Baxter La HIPP HX3 147 J3
Baxter Wd AIRE BD20 34 E7
Baycliff Cl BSLYN/ROY S71 243 M7
Bay Cl HUDW HD3 191 L7
Bayfield Cl HOLM/MEL HD9 254 D6
Bay Hall Common Rd
HUDN HD2 14 E1
Bay Horse La AL/HA/HU LS17 67 J7
Bay Horse Yd SKP/WHF BD23 16 B2
Bayldons Pl BTLY * WF17 173 L1
Baylee St HEM/SK/SE WF9 224 A8
Bayne Dr BOW BD4 127 K6
Bay of Biscay WIL/AL BD15 103 K2
Bay St WHIT OL12 206 C5
Bayswater Crs RHAY LS8 110 B3
Bayswater Gv ECHL BD2 105 M4
RHAY LS8 110 B3
Bayswater Mt RHAY LS8 110 B3
Bayswater Pl RHAY LS8 110 B3
Bayswater Rw RHAY LS8 110 B3
Bayswater Ter HIPP HX3 168 E3
RHAY LS8 110 B3
Bayswater Vw RHAY LS8 110 B3
Bayton La YEA LS19 63 G8
Beacon Av MOR LS27 152 D4
Beacon Brow WBSY BD6 125 M4
Beacon Cl BGLY BD16 81 K3
DOD/DAR S75 259 J8
Beacon Ct DOD/DAR S75 259 J8
Beacon Dr HEM/SK/SE WF9 225 J6
Beaconfield Rd
HEM/SK/SE WF9 225 H5
Beacon Gv MOR LS27 152 D4
WBSY BD6 126 B5
Beacon Hl DOD/DAR S75 259 J8
HEM/SK/SE WF9 225 J6
Beacon Hill Rd HIPP HX3 11 J4
Beacon Pl WBSY BD6 126 A5
Beacon Ri ILK LS29 38 A2
Beacon Rd WBSY BD6 126 A4
Beaconsfield Ct
GFTH/SHER LS25 113 H6
Beaconsfield Rd CLAY BD14 125 L2
Beaconsfield St BSLY S70 261 G6
HIPP HX3 11 L8
TOD OL14 163 L1
Beacon St DEWS WF13 173 G8
GTHN * BD7 126 A4
HUDN HD2 14 E1
ILK LS29 19 J6
WBSY BD6 126 C5
Beacon Vw HEM/SK/SE WF9 246 E3
Beaden Dr KBTN HD8 216 A4
Beadon Av HUDE HD5 215 K1
Beagle Av HUDS HD4 213 L5
Bealbank Cl MILN OL16 229 J3
Beal Crs MILN OL16 206 E5
Bealcroft Cl MILN OL16 207 G7
Beal La GLE DN14 161 K7
KNOT WF11 183 H4
ROY/SHW OL2 229 L8
Beamshaw HEM/SK/SE WF9 246 D5
Beamsley Ct SKP/WHF BD23 16 C4
Beamsley Gv BGLY BD16 81 K3
HDGY LS6 109 G4
Beamsley Mt HDGY * LS6 109 G4
Beamsley Pl HDGY LS6 109 G4
Beamsley Rd HTON BD9 104 D4
HTON BD9 104 D1
Beamsley Ter HDGY * LS6 109 G4
Beamsley Vw ILK LS29 38 A2
Beamsley Wk HTON BD9 104 C4
Beancroft Rd CAS WF10 157 M7
Beancroft St CAS WF10 157 L8
Beanlands Dr AIRE BD20 34 E8
Beanlands Pde ILK LS29 38 E1
Beanlands Pl AIRE BD20 34 E8
Bean St ELL HX5 169 L8
Bear Bones Rd
HOLM/MEL HD9 267 K1
Bearing Av BEE/HOL LS11 131 L4
Bear Pit Gdns HDGY LS6 108 F3
Beastfair PONT WF8 180 E6
Beast Market HUD HD1 15 G6
Beatrice St CLECK BD19 149 M6
HWTH BD22 100 E4
KGHY BD21 57 L5
Beaufort Av KBTN HD8 238 B3
Beaufort Gv ECHL BD2 105 J3
Beaulieu Cl DOD/DAR S75 242 E6
Beaulieu Vw DOD/DAR S75 242 E6
Beaumont Av AWLS/ASK DN6 249 H8
BSLY S70 260 D5
HEM/SK/SE WF9 247 H3
HUDE HD5 15 M8
RHAY LS8 88 C4
Beaumont Cl EARD/LOFT WF3 177 H1
LIT OL15 207 H1
Beaumont Dr HOR/CROF WF4 219 H8
Beaumont Park Rd HUDS HD4 213 M5
Beaumont Pl BTLY WF17 173 H2
Beaumont Rd DOD/DAR S75 241 L7
GIR BD8 104 D5
Beaumont St BTLY WF17 173 L3
EARD/LOFT WF3 177 H1
HUD HD1 15 G4
HUDE HD5 15 M8
HUDS HD4 213 L7
HUDW HD3 213 H1
KBTN HD8 217 L7
TOD OL14 141 J8
Beaver Dr DEWS WF13 173 H7
Becca La GFTH/SHER LS25 91 M6
Beck Bottom PDSY/CALV LS28 84 A8
WKFDW/WTN WF2 175 L3
Beckbridge La NORM WF6 178 E4
Beckbridge Rd NORM WF6 178 E3
Beckbridge Wy NORM WF6 178 E4
Beckbury Cl PDSY/CALV LS28 106 F4
Beckbury St PDSY/CALV LS28 106 F4
Beckenham Pl HFAX HX1 146 A6
Beckers Av BTLY * WF17 151 K4
Beckett Cl HOR/CROF WF4 197 L4
Beckett Crs DEWS WF13 173 H6
Beckett Gv DEWS WF13 173 H7
Beckett Hospital Ter
BSLY * S70 261 H6
Beckett La DEWS WF13 173 H7
Beckett Park Campus
HDGY LS6 86 D8
Beckett Rd DEWS WF13 173 K4
Becketts Cl HBR HX7 143 H2
Beckett's Park Dr HDGY LS6 108 E1
Beckett's Park Rd HDGY LS6 108 F1
Beckett St BSLYN/ROY S71 261 H4
BTLY WF17 173 L3
OSM LS9 7 M7
Beckett Ter OSM LS9 110 B5
Beckett Wk DEWS WF13 173 H7
Beckfield La KNOT WF11 159 G1
Beckfield Rd BGLY BD16 81 H7
Beckfoot La BGLY BD16 81 H5
Beck Gv ROY/SHW OL2 229 M6
Beck Hl WBSY BD6 126 A7
Beckhill Ap CHAL LS7 87 J8
Beckhill Av CHAL LS7 87 J8
Beckhill Cha CHAL LS7 87 J8
Beckhill Cl CHAL * LS7 87 J8
Beckhill Dr CHAL LS7 87 J7
Beckhill Fold CHAL LS7 87 J7
Beckhill Gdns CHAL LS7 87 J8
Beckhill Garth CHAL LS7 87 J8
Beckhill Ga CHAL LS7 87 J8
Beckhill Gn CHAL LS7 87 J8
Beckhill Gv CHAL LS7 87 J8
Beckhill Lawn CHAL * LS7 87 J8
Beckhill Pl CHAL LS7 87 J7
Beckhill Rw CHAL LS7 87 J8
Beckhill V CHAL LS7 87 J7
Beckhill Vw CHAL LS7 87 J8
Beckhill Wk CHAL LS7 87 J7
Beck La BGLY BD16 81 H2
LVSG WF15 172 E3
WBY LS22 47 K5
Beckley Rd WKFDW/WTN WF2 176 B8
Beck Meadow MSTN/BAR LS15 91 G8
Beck Ri HEM/SK/SE WF9 223 M7
Beck Rd BGLY BD16 59 G6
HUD HD1 14 F4
RHAY LS8 110 B2
Becks Ct EARL WF12 174 B8
Beckside COL BB8 74 D3
Beck Side KGHY BD21 3 G6
Beck Side Cl AIRE BD20 34 C4
Beckside Cl ILK LS29 19 G6
ILK LS29 40 B5
Beckside Gdns BHP/TINH LS16 86 E7
HUDE HD5 215 L2
Beckside La GTHN BD7 126 B1
Beckside Rd GTHN BD7 126 C1
Beckside Vw MOR LS27 152 E2
Becks Rd HWTH BD22 2 C6
Beck St KGHY BD21 3 G6
Beck Vw HOR/CROF WF4 221 J8
Beckwith Dr IDLE BD10 105 M1
Bective Rd WKFDW/WTN WF2 176 A7
Bedale EARD/LOFT WF3 152 F6
Bedale Av BRIG HD6 170 A6
KBTN HD8 239 H5
Bedale Dr KBTN HD8 239 H5
WBSY BD6 126 A5
Bedding Edge Rd
HOLM/MEL HD9 255 J8
Bede Ct WKFDE WF1 176 E6
Bede's Cl CUL/QBY BD13 102 F8
Bedford Av HOR/CROF WF4 217 G1
ROY/SHW OL2 229 H7
Bedford Cl BHP/TINH LS16 86 A3
FEA/AMT WF7 201 M3
HOR/CROF WF4 200 C6
KBTN HD8 216 A3
Bedford Ct RHAY LS8 88 E8
Bedford Dr BHP/TINH LS16 86 A3
Bedford Fld HDGY * LS6 109 J2
Bedford Gdns BHP/TINH LS16 86 A3
Bedford Garth BHP/TINH LS16 86 A3
Bedford Gn BHP/TINH LS16 86 A3
Bedford Gv BHP/TINH LS16 86 A4
Bedford Mt BHP/TINH LS16 86 A4
Bedfords Rw MID LS10 9 J8
Bedfords Fold
GFTH/SHER LS25 138 D8
Bedford St BOW BD4 5 G8
BSLY S70 261 H7
CUD/GR S72 263 J1
ELL HX5 169 H8
HFAX HX1 10 F6
KGHY BD21 2 E5
LDS LS1 6 F9
TOD OL14 141 G7
Bedford St North HFAX HX1 10 F5
Bedford Ter BSLYN/ROY S71 261 J1
Bedford Vw BHP/TINH LS16 86 A3
Bedivere Rd GIR BD8 103 M7
Bedlam La OT LS21 65 H1
Beech Av CUD/GR S72 244 D6
CUL/QBY BD13 101 L3
EARD/LOFT WF3 177 H2
HOLM/MEL HD9 236 E5
HOR/CROF WF4 200 D7
HORS LS18 85 L7
HUDE HD5 215 H1
MAR/SLWT HD7 213 G1
RPDN/SBR HX6 167 K1
TOD OL14 141 J8
WKFDW/WTN WF2 176 B7
Beech Cl CUD/GR S72 245 J3
GFTH/SHER LS25 138 B2
HEM/SK/SE WF9 246 D4
HIPP HX3 125 M8
IDLE BD10 83 K4
ILK LS29 40 C8
OSM LS9 110 F3
PONT WF8 181 G8
TAD LS24 72 A3
Beech Ct OSS WF5 174 E8
Beech Crs BAIL BD17 82 B5
BFDE BD3 5 M2
CAS WF10 158 F8
PONT WF8 203 L1
Beechcroft EARD/LOFT WF3 154 F5
Beech Cft PONT WF8 181 G3
WKFDW/WTN WF2 199 J7

Beechcroft Cl BEE/HOL LS11 130 E5
Beechcroft Md AL/HA/HU LS17 88 C2
Beechcroft Vw BEE/HOL LS11 130 E5
Beechdale Av BTLY WF17 151 J7
Beech Dr CUL/QBY BD13 101 L3
FEA/AMT WF7 202 C5
GFTH/SHER LS25 138 B2
WOR/ARM LS12 108 E6
Beecher St HIPP HX3 146 D4
KGHY BD21 3 L1
The Beeches BAIL BD17 82 F2
GSLY LS20 62 A4
PDSY/CALV LS28 106 D6
WBY LS22 30 B8
Beeches End BSPA/BRAM LS23 49 G7
Beeches Rd KGHY BD21 3 K3
Beechfield WKFDW/WTN WF2 199 G5
WOR/ARM LS12 129 M3
Beechfield Av KBTN HD8 239 J5
Beechfield Dr HOR/CROF WF4 200 D2
Beechfield Rd MILN OL16 229 G1
Beech Gdns CAS WF10 158 F8
Beech Gv AIRE BD20 35 M5
BFDE BD3 5 L2
BGLY BD16 81 L1
BSLY S70 260 F7
CLAY BD14 125 L2
CLECK BD19 150 C5
GFTH/SHER LS25 116 A6
GFTH/SHER LS25 160 A3
HEM/SK/SE WF9 223 J4
HIPP HX3 148 C7
NORM WF6 178 C6
RTHW LS26 133 H8
Beech Grove Av
GFTH/SHER LS25 113 G8
Beech Grove Ter
GFTH/SHER LS25 113 G8
LDSU LS2 6 D5
Beech Hl OT LS21 41 J6
PONT WF8 181 G5
Beech La OSM LS9 110 E3
PBR HG3 28 E3
Beech Lees PDSY/CALV LS28 106 E2
Beech Mt OSM LS9 110 F3
Beechmount Cl BAIL BD17 82 F2
Beechnut La PONT WF8 180 E5
Beech Rd AWLS/ASK DN6 227 M5
AWLS/ASK DN6 249 J5
BSPA/BRAM LS23 48 E6
CUD/GR S72 244 F4
HEM/SK/SE WF9 225 K7
RPDN/SBR HX6 167 L2
WBSY BD6 126 E7
Beech Spinney WBY LS22 30 B6
Beech Sq CLAY BD14 125 L2
Beech St AIRE BD20 34 F8
AIRE BD20 56 E1
BGLY BD16 81 H4
BSLY S70 261 H6
EARD/LOFT WF3 153 G5
ELL HX5 169 H8
GTL/HWG HX4 190 C2
HEM/SK/SE WF9 247 G5
HFAX HX1 10 E5
HOLM/MEL * HD9 254 C1
HUD HD1 213 M1
KGHY BD21 3 L3
MILN OL16 229 J2
MIRF WF14 194 C1
PONT WF8 180 F7
Beech Ter BFDE BD3 5 L3
Beechtree Ct BAIL BD17 82 C4
Beech Tree Rd FEA/AMT WF7 202 A2
Beechtree Rd TAD LS24 71 K4
Beech Vw GFTH/SHER LS25 91 M7
HOR/CROF WF4 220 B3
RPDN/SBR * HX6 167 K1
Beech Wk BHP/TINH LS16 86 F4
CLECK BD19 150 D2
OSM LS9 110 F3
TAD LS24 71 K3
Beech Wy BTLY WF17 151 J5
Beechwood PONT WF8 180 D7
ROY/SHW OL2 229 M6
RTHW LS26 133 L7
Beechwood Av AIRE BD20 58 B5
BIRK/DRI BD11 128 F7
HIPP HX3 147 K1
LIT OL15 207 J3
LUD/ILL HX2 146 C1
MIRF WF14 194 C1
PONT WF8 180 D6
RPDN/SBR HX6 167 H3
SHPY BD18 82 A7
WBSY BD6 126 C4
WKFDW/WTN WF2 175 M8
Beechwood Cl
GFTH/SHER LS25 116 A8
HORS LS18 85 J3
LUD/ILL HX2 146 B2
Beechwood Ct BHP/TINH LS16 86 D1
SCFT LS14 89 G8
Beechwood Crs BULY LS4 108 F3
HEM/SK/SE WF9 223 L8
PONT WF8 180 D7
RPDN/SBR HX6 167 H3
Beechwood Cft
GFTH/SHER * LS25 116 A8
Beechwood Dl FEA/AMT WF7 202 D7
Beechwood Dr LUD/ILL HX2 146 B2
ROY/SHW OL2 228 E8
RPDN/SBR HX6 167 H3
WBSY BD6 126 D4
Beechwood Gld
GFTH/SHER LS25 116 A8
Beechwood Gv BIRK/DRI BD11 128 F7
BULY LS4 108 F3
HOR/CROF WF4 197 L5
HUDN HD2 192 C1
ILK LS29 38 B2
LUD/ILL * HX2 146 B2
SHPY BD18 82 A7
WBSY BD6 126 D4
Beechwood Mt BULY LS4 108 F3
HEM/SK/SE WF9 223 M8
Beechwood Pl BULY * LS4 108 F3
Beechwood Ri WBY LS22 30 A7
Beechwood Rd BULY LS4 108 F3
LUD/ILL HX2 146 B2
MIRF WF14 172 C8
WBSY BD6 126 C4
Beechwood Rw BULY LS4 108 F3
Beechwood St HDGY LS6 108 F3
PDSY/CALV LS28 106 E5
Beechwood Ter BULY LS4 108 F3
Beechwood Vw BULY LS4 108 F3
Beecroft Cl BRAM LS13 107 J3
Beecroft Crs BRAM LS13 107 K3
Beecroft Gdns BRAM LS13 107 J3
Beecroft Mt BRAM LS13 107 J4
Beecroft St KGHY BD21 3 K4
KSTL LS5 108 C3
Beehive St WBSY * BD6 126 B7
Beehive Yd WBSY * BD6 126 B7
Beestonley La GTL/HWG HX4 189 M2
Beeston Park Cft
BEE/HOL LS11 131 G4
Beeston Park Garth
BEE/HOL * LS11 131 G4
Beeston Park Pl BEE/HOL LS11 131 G4
Beeston Park Ter
BEE/HOL LS11 131 G4
Beeston Rd BEE/HOL LS11 131 J3
Beeston's La AL/HA/HU LS17 25 M7
Beeston Sq BSLYN/ROY S71 243 H6
Beever La DOD/DAR S75 260 C3
Beevor Ct BSLYN/ROY S71 261 J5
Beevor St BSLYN/ROY S71 261 K5
Bela Av BOW BD4 127 L3
Belcross Dr HIPP HX3 11 J3
Beldon Brook Gn KBTN HD8 215 M5
Beldon La WBSY BD6 126 B5
Beldon Park Av GTHN BD7 126 B4
Beldon Park Cl GTHN BD7 126 B4
Beldon Pl ECHL BD2 105 K4
Beldon Rd GTHN BD7 126 C3
Belfast St HFAX HX1 10 B8
Belfield Cl MILN OL16 206 E6
Belfield La MILN OL16 206 F7
Belfield Mill La MILN OL16 206 E6
Belfield Old Rd MILN OL16 206 E6
Belfield Rd MILN OL16 206 D6
The Belfry YEA LS19 62 E8
Belfry Ct WKFDE WF1 176 E1
Belfry Wy NORM WF6 178 E5
Belgrave Av HIPP HX3 11 K3
OSS WF5 197 G2
Belgrave Cl HIPP HX3 11 K3
Belgrave Crs HIPP HX3 11 L3
Belgrave Dr HIPP HX3 11 L3
Belgrave Gdns HIPP HX3 11 K2
Belgrave Gv HIPP HX3 11 K3
Belgrave Ms YEA * LS19 84 C2
Belgrave Mt HIPP HX3 11 K2
WKFDE WF1 176 F6
Belgrave Pk HIPP HX3 11 K3
Belgrave Rd BGLY BD16 81 J3
BSLYN/ROY S71 261 J5
KGHY BD21 2 E3
Belgrave St LDSU LS2 7 G8
OSS WF5 197 G2
RPDN/SBR HX6 167 K2
SKP/WHF BD23 16 A2
Belgrave Ter HUD HD1 14 D5
WKFDE WF1 176 F6
Belgravia Gdns RHAY * LS8 110 C2
Belgravia Ms ROY/SHW OL2 229 L7
Belgravia Rd WKFDE WF1 176 D6
Belinda St MID LS10 9 M8
Bell Bank Vw BGLY BD16 81 G2
Bellbrooke Av OSM LS9 110 D4
WMB/DAR S73 263 H7
Bellbrooke Gv OSM LS9 110 D4
Bellbrooke Pl OSM LS9 110 D4
Bellbrooke St OSM LS9 110 C4
Bell Dean Rd WIL/AL BD15 103 K6
Belle Green Cl CUD/GR S72 244 E7
Belle Green Gdns CUD/GR S72 244 E7
Belle Green La CUD/GR S72 244 E7
Belle Isle Av WKFDE WF1 13 H7
Belle Isle Cl MID LS10 132 A6
Belle Isle Crs WKFDE WF1 13 H7
Belle Isle Dr WKFDE WF1 13 H7
Belle Isle Pde MID LS10 132 A6
Belle Isle Rd HWTH BD22 78 E8
MID LS10 132 A6
Bellerby Brow WBSY BD6 125 M5
Bellerby Pl AWLS/ASK DN6 249 H4
Bellerby Rd AWLS/ASK DN6 249 H4
Belle View Ri HIPP HX3 147 K1
Belle Vue CUL/QBY BD13 125 G7
GIR BD8 4 C2
ILK LS29 38 E3
Belle Vue Av MSTN/BAR LS15 90 B7
RHAY LS8 88 F8
Belle Vue Ct BVRD * LS3 6 B7
Belle Vue Crs HIPP HX3 147 K1
HUDN HD2 192 E3
Belle Vue Dr PDSY/CALV LS28 106 E3
Belle Vue Est MSTN/BAR LS15 90 B8
Belle Vue Pk HFAX * HX1 10 D6
Belle Vue Rd HIPP HX3 147 K1
LDSU LS2 6 B5
MSTN/BAR LS15 90 B8
WKFDE WF1 13 K9
Belle Vue St BTLY WF17 173 H1
Belle Vue Ter HIPP HX3 11 M9
KGHY BD21 3 J6
Bellgreave Av HOLM/MEL HD9 237 H8
Bell Hall Mt HFAX HX1 168 C1
Bell Hall Ter HFAX HX1 168 C1
Bell House Av BOW BD4 127 K5
Bellhouse Crs BOW BD4 127 K6
Bellingham Cl ROY/SHW OL2 229 K6
Bell La BRAM LS13 107 L3
FEA/AMT WF7 224 B1
MILN OL16 207 K7
TAD LS24 95 G2
Bellmont Crs HEM/SK/SE WF9 224 A8
Bellmount Cl BRAM LS13 107 M3
Bellmount Gdns BRAM LS13 107 L2
Bellmount Gn BRAM LS13 107 M3
Bellmount Pl BRAM LS13 107 L2
Bellmount Vw BRAM LS13 107 M3
Belloe St WBOW BD5 126 F2
Bell Rd BRAM LS13 107 L3
Bellshaw St GIR BD8 104 A7
Bellshill Crs MILN OL16 206 E6
Bell Sq AIRE BD20 36 A4
Bell St DEWS WF13 195 G1
HEM/SK/SE WF9 226 A6
HIPP HX3 11 J3
HUDS HD4 214 D2
LM/WK BD12 148 E2
MILN OL16 206 B6
OSM LS9 7 K8
WKFDE WF1 12 D1
Bellstring La HUDE HD5 194 A5
Bellwood Av BSPA/BRAM LS23 48 F8
Belmont CUD/GR * S72 262 E2
KNOT WF11 159 L5
Belmont Av BAIL BD17 82 D3
BSLYN/ROY S71 261 K1
LM/WK BD12 127 G7
OT LS21 41 H5
Belmont Cl BAIL BD17 82 D3
HUD HD1 14 E5
Belmont Crs LM/WK BD12 127 G7
SHPY * BD18 82 C6
Belmont Gdns WBSY BD6 126 F7
Belmont Gv LDSU LS2 6 D7
WBSY BD6 126 F7
YEA LS19 84 E1
Belmont Pl HFAX HX1 10 C8
Belmont Ri BAIL BD17 82 D3
LM/WK BD12 127 G7
Belmont Rd ILK LS29 39 G2
Belmont St ECHL BD2 105 L1
FEA/AMT WF7 200 E1
HIPP HX3 11 L3
HUD HD1 14 D5
MAR/SLWT HD7 212 B6
RPDN/SBR * HX6 167 L2
SKP/WHF BD23 16 B2
WKFDE WF1 176 D6
Belmont Ter EARD/LOFT WF3 154 B4
LUD/ILL HX2 167 G1
SHPY * BD18 82 C6
Belmont Wy HEM/SK/SE WF9 247 K3
WHIT OL12 206 A4
Belmont Whf SKP/WHF BD23 16 B2
Belridge Cl DOD/DAR S75 260 D2
Belton Av MILN OL16 206 E5
Belton Cl GTHN BD7 126 C3
Belton Gv HUDW HD3 191 K4
Belton Rd AIRE BD20 36 A6
Belton St HUDE HD5 215 G1
Belvedere Av AL/HA/HU LS17 87 M2
BEE/HOL LS11 131 K4
Belvedere Cl CUD/GR S72 244 E4
Belvedere Ct AL/HA/HU LS17 88 A2
Belvedere Dr WMB/DAR S73 263 G7
Belvedere Gv AL/HA/HU LS17 87 M2
Belvedere Mt BEE/HOL LS11 131 K4
Belvedere Rd AL/HA/HU LS17 87 M2
BTLY WF17 173 K2
Belvedere Ter BEE/HOL LS11 131 K5
GIR BD8 104 D6
Belvedere Vw AL/HA/HU LS17 88 A2
Belvoir Dr KNOT WF11 182 A2
Belvoir Gdns HIPP HX3 168 E3
Belvoir Mdw MILN OL16 207 G2
Bembridge Ct
WKFDW/WTN WF2 198 A1
Bempton Ct GTHN * BD7 126 D2
Bempton Gv BTLY WF17 151 H4
Bempton Pl GTHN * BD7 126 D2
Ben Bank Rd DOD/DAR S75 259 J8
Ben Booth La HOR/CROF WF4 217 G1
Benbow Av IDLE BD10 106 A1
Bence Cl DOD/DAR S75 242 A7
Bence La DOD/DAR S75 241 L7
Bence St COL BB8 74 A1
Bench Carr WHIT OL12 206 A5
Bendigo Rd EARL WF12 174 B5
Benjamin St LVSG WF15 172 D3
WKFDW/WTN WF2 12 A1
Benjamin Sykes Wy
WKFDW/WTN WF2 197 L2
Benn Av GTHN BD7 126 B2
Benn Crs GTHN BD7 126 B2
Bennet Ct MSTN/BAR LS15 111 M6
Bennett Av HOR/CROF WF4 197 L4
Bennett La EARL WF12 174 A3
Bennett Rd HDGY LS6 108 F1
Bennett St HIPP HX3 11 K8
LVSG WF15 172 D2
SKP/WHF BD23 16 B3
Benn La HUDW HD3 191 H8
Benns La LUD/ILL HX2 145 H4
Benny La MAR/SLWT HD7 212 D3
Benny Parr Cl BTLY WF17 174 A1
Benomley Crs HUDE HD5 215 G3
Benomley Dr HUDE HD5 215 G3
Benomley Rd HUDE HD5 215 G3
Ben Rhydding Dr ILK LS29 39 H3
Ben Rhydding Rd ILK LS29 38 E3
Benson Gdns WOR/ARM LS12 108 D8
Benson La NORM WF6 178 E2
Benson St CHAL LS7 7 K5
Bentcliffe Av AL/HA/HU LS17 88 A4
Bentcliffe Cl AL/HA/HU LS17 88 A5
Bentcliffe Dr AL/HA/HU LS17 88 A4
Bentcliffe Gdns AL/HA/HU LS17 88 A5
Bentcliffe Gv AL/HA/HU LS17 88 A5
Bentcliffe La AL/HA/HU LS17 87 M5
Bentcliffe Mt AL/HA/HU LS17 88 A5
Bent Close La HBR HX7 165 M3
Bentfield Cottages CLAY BD14 125 L1
Bentfield Crs MILN OL16 229 J2
Bentgate Cl MILN OL16 229 J2
Bentgate St MILN OL16 229 J3
Bentham Dr BSLYN/ROY S71 261 M2
Bentham Wy DOD/DAR S75 242 C4
Bent La AIRE BD20 55 L1
COL BB8 52 D8
HOLM/MEL HD9 254 C6
Bent Lea HUDN HD2 171 H8
Bentley Av BRIG HD6 148 C7
Bentley Cl BAIL BD17 82 D2
BSLYN/ROY S71 262 A1
Bentley Gdns CHAL LS7 87 H8
Bentley Gv HDGY LS6 87 H8
Bentley La HDGY LS6 87 H8
Bentley Ms WHIT OL12 206 A4
Bentley Moor La
AWLS/ASK DN6 249 M7
Bentley Mt HDGY LS6 87 H8
RPDN/SBR HX6 167 M1
Bentley Pde HDGY LS6 87 H8
Bent Ley Rd HOLM/MEL HD9 235 J3
Bentley Rd WKFDW/WTN WF2 198 A2
Bentley Royd Cl
RPDN/SBR HX6 167 J3
Bentley St HUDS HD4 214 A3
LM/WK * BD12 148 F3
WHIT OL12 206 A4
Bentmeadows WHIT OL12 206 A5
Benton Crs HOR/CROF WF4 197 L4
Benton Park Av YEA LS19 84 E1
Benton Park Crs YEA LS19 84 E1
Benton Park Dr YEA LS19 84 E1
Benton Park Rd YEA LS19 84 E1
Bent Rd HOLM/MEL HD9 254 F7
Bents COL * BB8 52 D8
Bents Farm Cl LIT * OL15 207 H1
Bents La MAR/SLWT HD7 211 K7
WIL/AL BD15 80 C8
Bents Rd STKB/PEN S36 268 E2
Bent St HUDS HD4 214 D2
STKB/PEN S36 270 E2
Benyon Park Wy
WOR/ARM LS12 130 F2
Beresford Rd WBSY BD6 126 D7
Beresford St LM/WK BD12 149 J1
MILN OL16 229 K2
Berkeley Av RHAY LS8 110 C3
Berkeley Crs RHAY LS8 110 C3
Berkeley Cft BSLYN/ROY S71 243 K2
Berkeley Dr MILN OL16 228 D2
Berkeley Gv RHAY LS8 110 C3
Berkeley Mt RHAY LS8 110 C3
Berkeley St RHAY LS8 110 C3
Berkeley Ter RHAY LS8 110 C3
Berkeley Vw RHAY LS8 110 C3
Berking Av OSM LS9 110 B6
Berkley Wk LIT OL15 207 H1
Bermondsey Ms OT LS21 41 K7
Bermondsey St OT LS21 41 K7
Bernard St HUDN HD2 193 G3
RTHW LS26 133 M8
WHIT OL12 206 A3
Berne Gv WKFDE WF1 176 E7
Berners St WKFDE WF1 13 H3
Berneslai Cl BSLY S70 261 G4
Berrington Wy HWTH BD22 78 D3
Berry Bank La HOLM/MEL HD9 236 D6
Berry Cft HOLM/MEL HD9 236 B2
Berryfield Garth OSS WF5 174 F6
Berry La HFAX HX1 11 K6
HOR/CROF WF4 197 K5
KGHY BD21 2 F8
RTHW LS26 135 G6
Berry Moor Rd RPDN/SBR HX6 167 M4
Berry Rd HOLM/MEL HD9 234 E3
Berry St KGHY BD21 3 J4
Berry's Yd HOR/CROF WF4 197 J4
Berry Vw HUDS HD4 214 B5
Berrywell Av STKB/PEN S36 271 G4
Bertha Rd MILN OL16 206 E7
Bertha St PDSY/CALV LS28 106 F4
Bertie St BOW BD4 127 L3
Bertram Dr BAIL BD17 82 D4
Bertram Rd GIR BD8 104 E4
Bertrand St BEE/HOL LS11 8 C6
Berwick Av HECK WF16 150 F8
Berwick St HFAX HX1 11 J6
MILN OL16 206 D8
Bescaby Gv BAIL * BD17 83 G3
Besha Av LM/WK BD12 126 F7
Besha Gv LM/WK BD12 126 F8
Bessingham Gdns WBSY BD6 126 B6
Best La HUDS HD4 214 F8
HWTH BD22 100 E4
Beswick Cl BFDE BD3 105 M7
Beswicke Royds St MILN OL16 206 D5
Beswicke St LIT OL15 207 L1
WHIT OL12 206 A6
Beswick St TOD OL14 163 J7
Bethany La MILN OL16 229 L2
Bethel Gn LIT * OL15 185 L5
Bethel Rd SHPY BD18 82 F6
Bethel St AIRE BD20 58 F6
BRIG HD6 170 D4
HIPP HX3 146 C4
Betjeman Pl ROY/SHW OL2 229 M7
Betteras Hill Rd
GFTH/SHER LS25 138 A7
Betula Wy KBTN HD8 216 A4
Beulah Gv HDGY LS6 6 E2
Beulah Mt HDGY * LS6 6 E2
Beulah Pl LUD/ILL HX2 167 G1
Beulah St HDGY LS6 6 E2
Beulah Ter HDGY LS6 6 E1
Beulah Vw HDGY * LS6 6 E2
Bevan Av NORM WF6 178 D6
Bevan Ct GTHN BD7 126 B3
Bevan Pl WKFDW/WTN WF2 197 L2
Bevedere Gdns AL/HA/HU LS17 88 A2
Beverley Av BEE/HOL LS11 131 K3
BSLY S70 261 H8
LM/WK BD12 148 F4
Beverley Cl BSLYN/ROY S71 243 G7
ELL HX5 169 K8
Beverley Dr EARL WF12 174 B6
LM/WK BD12 148 F4
Beverley Gdns BTLY WF17 151 K4
Beverley Garth FEA/AMT WF7 224 C1
Beverley Mt BEE/HOL LS11 131 K3
Beverley Pl HIPP HX3 10 F1
MILN OL16 206 C6
Beverley Ri ILK LS29 38 A2
Beverley St BOW BD4 127 M1
Beverley Ter BEE/HOL LS11 131 K3
HIPP HX3 10 F1
Beverley Vw BEE/HOL LS11 8 F9
Beverley Wk GFTH/SHER LS25 113 H8
Beverston ROCH * OL11 206 A8
Bevin Cl WKFDE WF1 176 E1
Bevin Crs WKFDE WF1 176 E1
Bevor Crs HECK WF16 172 F1
Bewerley Crs LM/WK BD12 126 C
Bewick Ct CUL/QBY BD13 125 K
Bewick Gv RTHW LS26 132 B
Bexhill Cl PONT WF8 181 H
Bexley Av RHAY LS8 110 B
Bexley Gv OSM LS9 110 B
Bexley Mt RHAY LS8 110 B
Bexley Pl RHAY LS8 110 B
Bexley Rd RHAY LS8 110 B
Bexley Ter OSM LS9 110 B
Bexley Vw OSM LS9 110 B
Beza Rd MID LS10 131 M
Beza St MID LS10 131 M
Bickerton Wy OT LS21 41 G
Biddenden Rd MSTN/BAR LS15 112 B
Bidder Dr EARD/LOFT WF3 153 L
Bideford Av RHAY LS8 88 B
Bidston Cl ROY/SHW OL2 229 M
Bierley Hall Gv BOW BD4 127 K
Bierley House Av BOW BD4 127 K
Bierley La BOW BD4 127 K
Bierley Vw BOW BD4 127 L
Biggin La GFTH/SHER LS25 117 H
Big Meadow Dr ILK LS29 18 F
Bilberry Cl CLAY BD14 125 L
Bilberry Ri HWTH BD22 78 F
Bilberry St MILN OL16 206 C
Bilham Rd KBTN HD8 240 C
Billams Hl OT LS21 41 H
Billey La WOR/ARM LS12 130 A
Billingbauk Dr BRAM LS13 107 M
Billing Ct YEA LS19 84 F
Billing Dr YEA LS19 85 G
Billingham Cl
WKFDW/WTN WF2 175 M
Billing Vw IDLE BD10 83 L
YEA LS19 84 F
Billingwood Dr YEA LS19 84 F
Bill La HOLM/MEL HD9 236 E
Billy La HBR HX7 143 L
Bilsdale Gra WBSY BD6 126 B
Bilsdale Wy BAIL BD17 82 B
Bilton Pl GIR BD8 4 B
Binbrook Vw WIL/AL * BD15 103 K
Bingley Bank AL/HA/HU LS17 67 L
Bingley Ct DOD/DAR * S75 260 F
Bingley Rd BAIL BD17 60 B
CUL/QBY BD13 79 M
HTON BD9 103 M
ILK LS29 60 D
KGHY BD21 79 K
MILN OL16 206 E
SHPY BD18 81 M
Bingley Sq MILN OL16 206 E
Bingley St BVRD LS3 6 B
DOD/DAR S75 260 F
GIR BD8 104 C
Bingley Ter MILN OL16 206 E
Binham Rd HUDW HD3 191 M
Binks Fold LM/WK BD12 148 F
Binks St WKFDE WF1 176 E
Binks Yd OSS * WF5 174 F
Binnie St BFDE BD3 5 L
Binn La MAR/SLWT HD7 233 J
Binn Rd MAR/SLWT HD7 233 H
Binns Hill La LUD/ILL HX2 145 K
Binns La AIRE BD20 34 C
GTHN BD7 126 B
HOLM/MEL HD9 254 B
Binns Nook Rd WHIT OL12 206 C
Binns St BGLY BD16 81 J
Binns Top La HIPP HX3 169 K
Birch Av AWLS/ASK DN6 249 J
KBTN HD8 216 A
MSTN/BAR LS15 111 J
RPDN/SBR HX6 188 E
TOD OL14 141 J
WBOW BD5 127 H
WHIT OL12 206 F
Birch Cliff BAIL BD17 82 D
Birchcliffe Rd HBR HX7 143 J
Birch Cl BRIG HD6 170 E
WBOW BD5 127 H
Birch Close La BGLY BD16 60 B
Birch Crs MILN OL16 229 J
MSTN/BAR LS15 111 J
Birchdale BGLY BD16 59 H
Birch Dr GFTH/SHER LS25 135 J
Birchen Av OSS WF5 196 E
Birchencliffe Hill Rd
HUDW HD3 191 K
Birchenlee Cl HBR HX7 144 A
The Birches BHP/TINH LS16 64 B
GSLY LS20 62 A
Birchfield Av MOR LS27 129 L
Birchfield Crs DOD/DAR S75 260 C
Birchfield Garth SCFT LS14 89 L
Birchfield Gv KBTN HD8 239 J
Birchfields Av SCFT LS14 89 L
Birchfields Cl SCFT LS14 89 L
Birchfields Ct SCFT LS14 89 L
Birchfields Crs SCFT LS14 89 L
Birchfields Ri SCFT LS14 89 L
Birchfield Wk DOD/DAR S75 260 D
Birch Gv BTLY WF17 151 J
CAS WF10 158 E
GFTH/SHER LS25 135 J
HWTH BD22 79 J
MAR/SLWT HD7 213 G
WBOW BD5 127 G
Birch Hey Cl WHIT OL12 206 E
Birch Hill Crs WHIT OL12 207 G
Birch Hill La WHIT OL12 184 F
Birch Hill Ri HORS LS18 86 A
Birchington Av HUDW HD3 191 J
Birchington Cl HUDW HD3 191 K
Birchington Dr HUDW HD3 191 J
Birchlands Av WIL/AL BD15 80 D
Birchlands Gv WIL/AL BD15 80 D
Birch La LUD/ILL HX2 145 H
WBOW BD5 127 G
Birch Ms BHP/TINH LS16 86 F
Birch Mt WHIT OL12 207 G
Birch Pk HOLM/MEL HD9 236 F
Birch Pl HBR * HX7 143 J
Birch Rd BSLY S70 261 M
GFTH/SHER LS25 135 J
HUDS HD4 214 B

NORM WF6 178 D7
WHIT OL12 206 F1
Birchroyd RTHW LS26 155 H2
Birchroyd Cl HUDN HD2 191 M4
Birch St GIR BD8 104 C6
MOR LS27 152 D4
WHIT OL12 184 E8
WKFDE WF1 13 K7
Birchtree Cl WKFDE WF1 177 H6
Birch Tree Gdns KGHY BD21 3 L7
Birchtree Wy BHP/TINH * LS16 86 A4
Birch Wk TOD * OL14 141 K8
Birch Wy WBOW BD5 127 H4
Birchwood Av AIRE BD20 57 K4
AL/HA/HU LS17 88 C3
BTLY WF17 151 H4
Birchwood Ct ILK LS29 38 C2
LVSG WF15 172 D3
Birchwood Dr AIRE BD20 57 J4
Birchwood Hl AL/HA/HU LS17 88 C2
Birchwood Mt AL/HA/HU LS17 88 C2
Birchwood Pk HOLM/MEL HD9 237 G8
Birchwood Rd AIRE BD20 57 J4
Birdale Field La WBY LS22 47 M6
Birdcage Hl HIPP HX3 168 C3
Birdcage La HIPP HX3 168 C3
Birdcage Wk OT LS21 41 J8
Bird Holme La HIPP HX3 147 K5
Birds Edge La KBTN HD8 256 B3
Birdsnest La HOLM/MEL HD9 255 L5
KBTN HD8 256 A4
Birds Royd La BRIG HD6 170 E5
Birdswell Av BRIG HD6 170 F3
The Birdwalk CUL/QBY BD13 125 L4
Birdwell Rd DOD/DAR S75 260 C8
Birfed Crs BULY LS4 108 D3
Birk Av BSLY S70 261 L7
Birkby Brow Crs BTLY WF17 151 K4
Birkby Fold HUDN HD2 14 B2
Birkby Hall Rd HUDN HD2 14 A1
Birkby Hvn WBSY BD6 126 A6
Birkby La BRIG HD6 148 E7
Birkby Lodge Rd HUDN HD2 14 B1
Birkby Rd HUDW HD3 191 L4
Birkby St LM/WK BD12 148 F2
Birk Crs BSLY S70 261 L7
Birkdale Av HUDW HD3 191 J6
Birkdale Cl AL/HA/HU LS17 87 K2
CUD/GR S72 244 E6
CUL/QBY BD13 80 A8
Birkdale Ct AIRE BD20 57 J3
Birkdale Dr AL/HA/HU LS17 87 K2
Birkdale Gn AL/HA/HU LS17 87 K2
Birkdale Gv AL/HA/HU LS17 87 J2
DEWS WF13 173 J4
LUD/ILL HX2 124 B7
Birkdale Mt AL/HA/HU LS17 87 K2
Birkdale Pl AL/HA/HU LS17 87 J2
Birkdale Ri AL/HA/HU LS17 87 J2
Birkdale Rd BSLYN/ROY S71 243 K1
DEWS WF13 173 K5
MILN OL16 228 E2
Birkdale Wk AL/HA/HU LS17 87 J2
Birkenshaw La BIRK/DRI BD11 150 D1
Birkett St CLECK BD19 149 M6
Birk Gn BSLY S70 261 M7
Birkhead St HECK WF16 173 G3
Birkhill CAS WF10 158 E6
Birkhill Crs BIRK/DRI BD11 150 D1
Birk House La BSLY S70 261 M7
KBTN HD8 238 D7
Birkhouse La BRIG HD6 148 F8
HUDE HD5 15 M8
HUDS HD4 14 B9
Birkhouse Rd BRIG HD6 148 E7
Birkin La KNOT WF11 160 F6
Birklands Moor CLECK BD19 150 D3
Birklands Rd HUDN HD2 192 B4
SHPY BD18 82 C7
Birklands Ter SHPY BD18 82 D7
Birk La MOR LS27 152 A2
Birk Lea St WBOW BD5 127 G2
Birk Rd BSLY S70 261 L7
Birks Av GTHN BD7 126 B1
STKB/PEN S36 270 A3
Birks Fold GTHN BD7 104 B8
Birkshall La BFDE BD3 5 M8
Birks Hall St HFAX HX1 10 D4
Birks Hall Ter HFAX HX1 10 D4
Birksland St BOW BD4 5 L9
Birks La HUDE HD5 215 J3
KBTN HD8 237 M3
RPDN/SBR HX6 166 F6
STKB/PEN S36 270 A4
TOD OL14 163 K6
Birks Rd HUDW HD3 213 J1
Birk Ter BSLY S70 261 L7
Birkwith Cl SCFT LS14 89 K6
Birkwood Av CUD/GR S72 262 E2
HOR/CROF WF4 200 D4
Birkwood Rd NORM WF6 177 K3
Birley St WHIT OL12 206 C5
Birmingham La
HOLM/MEL HD9 234 E3
Birnam Gv BOW BD4 127 J2
Birr Rd HTON BD9 104 D3
Birstall La BIRK/DRI BD11 151 G1
Birthwaite Rd DOD/DAR S75 241 K6
Birtwistle Cl COL BB8 74 A1
Bishopdale Dr WBY LS22 47 J5
Bishopdale Holme WBSY BD6 126 A6
Bishopdike Rd
GFTH/SHER LS25 116 E6
Bishopgate St LDS LS1 8 F1
Bishopsgate Wk MILN OL16 228 E2
Bishop St HTON BD9 104 D3
MILN OL16 206 D5
Bishops Wy BSLYN/ROY S71 261 L3
HOLM/MEL HD9 235 G4
MIRF WF14 171 M7
Bishop Wy EARD/LOFT WF3 153 H6
Bisley Cl BSLYN/ROY S71 244 A3
Bismarck Ct BEE/HOL * LS11 8 F8
Bismarck Dr BEE/HOL LS11 8 F8
Bismarck St BEE/HOL LS11 8 F8
BSLY S70 261 H7
Bitterne Ct CUL/QBY BD13 125 L4
Bittern Ri MOR LS27 152 E3
Black Abbey La AIRE BD20 34 E8
Black Aston Rd BRAM LS13 107 M4
Blackberry Wy CLAY BD14 125 K3
Blackbird Gdns GIR BD8 103 K7
Black Brook Wy GTL/HWG HX4 168 E8
Black Bull St MID LS10 9 J4
Blackburn Cl GIR BD8 103 M7
HIPP HX3 146 B3
Blackburn Ct RTHW LS26 155 H1
Blackburn La DOD/DAR S75 260 F4
KNOT WF11 182 E3
Blackburn Pl BTLY WF17 173 M1
Blackburn Rd BRIG HD6 170 B2
BTLY WF17 151 G5
Blackchapel Dr MILN OL16 228 D3
Black Dyke TOD * OL14 164 B3
Black Dyke La CUL/QBY BD13 102 D5
Black Edge La CUL/QBY BD13 101 L8
Blacker Crs HOR/CROF WF4 197 G8
Blackergreen La
STKB/PEN S36 271 M3
Blacker La CUD/GR S72 244 E3
HOR/CROF WF4 197 J8
Blacker Rd DOD/DAR S75 242 E6
HUDW HD3 14 C3
Blacker Rd North HUDN * HD2 14 D2
Blackers Ct EARL WF12 195 J2
Blackett St PDSY/CALV LS28 84 D7
Black Gates Ct
EARD/LOFT WF3 153 H6
Blackgates Crs
EARD/LOFT WF3 153 G6
Blackgates Dr EARD/LOFT WF3 153 H6
Blackgates Fold
EARD/LOFT WF3 153 H6
Black Gates Ri
EARD/LOFT * WF3 153 H6
Blackheath Cl BSLYN/ROY S71 243 K7
Blackheath Rd BSLYN/ROY S71 243 K7
Blackheath Wk
BSLYN/ROY S71 243 K7
Black Hill La AIRE BD20 56 F5
BHP/TINH LS16 64 F5
Black Hill Rd OT LS21 64 E1
Blackhouse Rd HUDN HD2 192 D4
Black La MAR/SLWT HD7 213 G7
Blackledge HFAX HX1 11 J7
Blackley Rd ELL HX5 190 F1
Blackman La LDSU LS2 6 F5
Blackmires LUD/ILL HX2 146 C1
Blackmoorfoot Rd
HOLM/MEL HD9 234 E1
MAR/SLWT HD7 213 G7
Blackmoor La AL/HA/HU LS17 67 K4
Black Moor Rd AL/HA/HU LS17 87 H3
HWTH BD22 78 F8
Blackpool Gv WOR/ARM LS12 130 C2
Blackpool Pl WOR/ARM LS12 130 C2
Blackpool Ter WOR/ARM LS12 130 C2
Blackpool Vw WOR/ARM LS12 130 C2
Black Rd WKFDE WF1 199 K3
Blackshaw Beck La HIPP HX3 125 J7
Blackshaw Clough Rd
RPDN/SBR HX6 166 C8
Blackshaw Dr WBSY BD6 125 M6
Blackshaw St TOD OL14 163 M1
Black Sike La HOLM/MEL HD9 253 L1
Blacksmith GTHN BD7 126 C2
Blacksmith Fold GTHN BD7 126 C2
Blacksmith La BHP/TINH LS16 65 H5
Blacksmiths Fold HUDE HD5 215 H3
Blackstone Av LM/WK BD12 148 E4
MILN OL16 206 E6
Blackstone Edge Old Rd
LIT OL15 185 M8
Blackstone Edge Rd HBR HX7 165 H8
RPDN/SBR HX6 187 G2
Blackthorn Cl WHIT OL12 206 A4
Blackthorn Ct MID LS10 9 K9
Blackthorn La PBR HG3 26 D2
Blackthorn Ms WHIT OL12 206 A4
Blackthorn Wy
WKFDW/WTN WF2 176 C6
Black Wk PONT WF8 181 G4
Blackwall HFAX HX1 10 F7
Blackwall La RPDN/SBR HX6 167 J1
Blackwall Ri RPDN/SBR HX6 167 K1
Blackwood Av BHP/TINH LS16 85 M3
Blackwood Gdns
BHP/TINH LS16 85 M3
Black Wood Gv BHP/TINH LS16 85 M3
Blackwood Gv HFAX HX1 10 A4
Blackwood Hall La
LUD/ILL HX2 144 E8
Black Wood Mt BHP/TINH LS16 85 M3
Black Wood Ri BHP/TINH LS16 85 M3
Blacup Moor Vw CLECK BD19 149 M7
Blagden La HUDS HD4 214 B5
Blair Cl ROY/SHW OL2 229 K7
Blairsville Gdns BRAM LS13 107 K2
Blairsville Gv BRAM LS13 107 L2
Blaith Royd La HBR HX7 165 H2
Blaithroyd La HIPP HX3 11 L8
Blake Crs GSLY LS20 62 B6
Blake Gv CHAL LS7 87 M8
Blake Hall Dr MIRF WF14 194 D2
Blake Hall Rd MIRF WF14 194 D2
Blake Hl HIPP HX3 147 G3
Blakehill Av ECHL BD2 105 L4
Blake Hill End HIPP HX3 147 H2
Blakehill Ter ECHL BD2 105 M4
Blakeholme Cl MAR/SLWT HD7 212 A5
Blakelaw Dr BRIG HD6 170 F3
Blake Law La BRIG HD6 171 H4
Blake Lee La MAR/SLWT HD7 210 B4
Blakeley Cl BSLYN/ROY S71 243 K7
Blakeley Gv WKFDW/WTN WF2 176 B8
Blakelock St ROY/SHW OL2 229 J7
Blakeney Gv MID LS10 131 M5
Blakeney Rd MID LS10 131 M5
Blakeridge La BTLY WF17 173 K1
Blakestones Rd
MAR/SLWT HD7 212 A6
Blake St MILN OL16 206 C6
Blakey Rd WKFDW/WTN WF2 176 B6
Blamires Pl GTHN BD7 126 B3
Blamires St GTHN BD7 126 B3
Blanche St BOW BD4 105 M8
WHIT OL12 206 C4
Blandford Gdns LDSU LS2 6 E5
Blandford Gv LDSU LS2 6 E5
Blands Av CAS WF10 157 J1
Bland's Cl CAS WF10 157 M7
Blands Crs CAS WF10 157 J1
Blands Gv CAS WF10 157 J1
Blands Ter CAS WF10 157 J1
Bland St HFAX * HX1 10 F6
HUD HD1 214 B2
Blantyre Ct CUL/QBY BD13 79 M8
Blayds Garth RTHW LS26 133 J7
Blayds Ms LDS LS1 9 G2
LDS * LS1 9 G2
Blayds St OSM LS9 110 B7
Blayd's Yd LDS LS1 9 G2
Bleachcroft Wy BSLY S70 262 A7
Bleach Mill La ILK LS29 61 G1
Bleak Av CUD/GR S72 244 E4
Bleak Hey Nook La UPML OL3 231 L6
Bleakley Av HOR/CROF WF4 221 K8
Bleakley Cl CUD/GR S72 244 E4
Bleakley La BSLYN/ROY S71 243 K1
Bleakley Ter HOR/CROF WF4 221 K8
Bleak St CLECK BD19 150 E6
Bleak St Lower CLECK BD19 150 E6
Bleasdale Av HUDN HD2 192 B5
KNOT WF11 182 A1
Bleasdale Gv BSLYN/ROY S71 261 J2
Blencarn Cl SCFT LS14 111 H2
Blencarn Garth SCFT LS14 111 H2
Blencarn Rd SCFT LS14 111 H2
Blencarn Vw SCFT LS14 111 H2
Blenheim Av BSLY S70 261 G6
LDSU LS2 6 F4
Blenheim Cl KNOT WF11 181 L2
Blenheim Ct HFAX * HX1 10 F4
LDSU * LS2 6 E5
Blenheim Dr BTLY WF17 151 L8
DEWS WF13 173 J5
Blenheim Gv BSLY S70 260 F6
LDSU LS2 6 F5
Blenheim Hl BTLY WF17 151 M7
Blenheim Mt GIR BD8 104 E4
Blenheim Pl IDLE BD10 83 K5
Blenheim Rd BSLY S70 260 F7
GIR BD8 4 B1
WKFDE WF1 176 D6
Blenheim Sq LDSU LS2 6 F4
Blenheim St COL BB8 74 C1
HBR HX7 143 J3
Blenheim Ter LDSU LS2 6 E5
Blenheim Vw LDSU LS2 6 E4
Blenheim Wk LDSU LS2 6 E5
Blind La AL/HA/HU LS17 89 G2
BGLY BD16 80 F3
BIRK/DRI BD11 129 H7
EARD/LOFT WF3 175 J1
LUD/ILL HX2 144 D6
TOD OL14 141 J8
Bloemfontein St CUD/GR S72 244 C8
Bloomfield Ri DOD/DAR S75 242 B5
Bloomfield Rd DOD/DAR S75 242 B5
Bloomhouse La DOD/DAR S75 242 A4
Blossom Pl MILN OL16 206 B6
Blucher St BOW BD4 105 M8
BSLY S70 261 G5
COL BB8 74 A2
Blue Ball La RPDN/SBR HX6 188 A3
Blue Ball Rd RPDN/SBR HX6 187 L4
RPDN/SBR HX6 188 D1
Bluebell Av STKB/PEN S36 270 E3
Bluebell Cl PONT WF8 180 F7
SHPY BD18 104 F1
WIL/AL * BD15 103 K6
Bluebell Ct BTLY WF17 151 G4
Blue Bell Hl HUDS HD4 214 B4
Blue Bell La TOD OL14 140 E4
Bluebell Rd DOD/DAR S75 242 A3
Bluebell Wk LUD/ILL HX2 145 G6
Bluebell Wy HEM/SK/SE WF9 225 H7
Blueberry Dr ROY/SHW OL2 229 M7
Bluebird Wk BGLY BD16 81 L2
Blue Butts OSS WF5 196 F1
Bluefields ROY/SHW OL2 229 M6
Blue Hill Crs WOR/ARM LS12 108 C8
Blue Hill Gra WOR/ARM LS12 130 C1
Blue Hill Gv WOR/ARM LS12 108 C8
Blue Hill La WOR/ARM LS12 108 C8
Blundell Ct BSLYN/ROY S71 261 M1
Blundell St HEM/SK/SE WF9 247 G3
LDS LS1 6 E7
Bly Rd WMB/DAR S73 263 H8
Blyth Av LIT * OL15 207 H3
Blythe Av GIR BD8 104 C6
Blythe St GTHN BD7 4 B6
Boardman St TOD OL14 141 K8
Boar La LDS LS1 9 G1
Boathouse La MIRF WF14 194 E4
Boat La RTHW LS26 157 J4
Bobbin Mill Cl TOD OL14 140 D5
Bobbin Mill Ct AIRE BD20 55 E1
Bob La LUD/ILL HX2 145 M7
Bodiham Hl GFTH/SHER LS25 113 K6
Bodkin La HWTH BD22 100 A3
Bodley Ter BULY LS4 108 F5
Bodmin Ap MID LS10 153 J1
Bodmin Av SHPY BD18 83 G7
Bodmin Ct BSLYN/ROY S71 261 K3
Bodmin Crs MID LS10 153 J1
Bodmin Cft MID LS10 153 K2
Bodmin Dr NORM WF6 178 D3
Bodmin Gdns MID LS10 153 J2
Bodmin Garth MID LS10 153 J2
Bodmin Pl MID LS10 153 J2
Bodmin Rd MID LS10 153 H1
Bodmin St MID LS10 153 J1
Boggard La STKB/PEN S36 270 E4
Boggart Hl SCFT LS14 89 G8
Boggart Hill Crs SCFT LS14 89 G8
Boggart Hill Dr SCFT LS14 89 G8
Boggart Hill Gdns SCFT LS14 89 G8
Boggart Hill Rd SCFT LS14 89 G8
Boggart La HIPP HX3 147 M5
KBTN HD8 239 J3
RPDN/SBR HX6 167 K3
TAD LS24 95 H2
Bog Green La HUDE HD5 193 K1
Bog La MSTN/BAR LS15 112 C1
Bogthorn HWTH BD22 79 G2
Boland Crs HWTH BD22 79 G3
Boldgrove St EARL WF12 174 C8
Boldmere Rd MSTN/BAR LS15 111 G7
Boldron Holt WBSY BD6 126 B6
Boldshay St BFDE BD3 5 L4
Bold St COL BB8 74 A2
Bold Venture St SKP/WHF BD23 16 B4
Bolehill Pk BRIG HD6 148 A8
Bolingbroke St WBOW BD5 126 F4
Bolland St LM/WK BD12 149 G1
Bolling Rd BOW BD4 5 H8
ILK LS29 38 F2
Bolsover Cl GFTH/SHER LS25 113 K7
Bolstermoor Rd
MAR/SLWT HD7 212 C2
Boltby La WBSY BD6 126 A6
Bolton LUD/ILL HX2 124 A7
Bolton Brow RPDN/SBR HX6 167 L2
Bolton Dr ECHL BD2 105 K2
Bolton Gra YEA LS19 62 E8
Bolton Gv ECHL BD2 105 K2
Bolton Hall Rd SHPY BD18 104 F1
Bolton La ECHL BD2 105 H3
Bolton Rd AIRE BD20 36 A4
BFDE BD3 5 G1
ECHL BD2 105 J3
ILK LS29 19 H6
SKP/WHF BD23 19 G1
YEA LS19 62 E8
Bolton St BFDE BD3 5 J5
LM/WK BD12 126 E8
Bolton Ter AIRE BD20 36 A4
Bolton Wy BSPA/BRAM LS23 48 E7
Bolton Wife Hl HOR/CROF WF4 220 B5
Bolus Cl WKFDE WF1 176 E2
Bolus La WKFDE WF1 176 D2
Bond Ct LDS LS1 6 F9
Bondgate AL/HA/HU LS17 45 J7
OT LS21 41 J7
PONT WF8 181 H4
Bondings Ri GFTH/SHER LS25 116 C6
Bond Rd DOD/DAR S75 260 F3
Bond St BRIG HD6 170 C3
BTLY WF17 151 G5
BTLY WF17 151 L8
DEWS WF13 173 L6
HBR HX7 143 J3
HFAX * HX1 10 F7
LDS LS1 7 G9
PONT WF8 181 G4
TOD * OL14 163 K1
WHIT OL12 206 C4
WKFDE WF1 12 D1
Bonegate Av BRIG HD6 170 D3
Bonegate Rd BRIG HD6 170 C3
Bone La AWLS/ASK DN6 227 K6
Bonnaccord Ter BTLY * WF17 173 L2
Bonn Rd HTON BD9 104 C4
Bonwick Ml WBSY BD6 126 A7
Boocock St PDSY/CALV * LS28 107 G5
Bookers Fld CLECK BD19 150 E7
Bootham Pk HTON BD9 103 M4
Booth House La
HOLM/MEL HD9 253 L2
Booth House Rd LUD/ILL HX2 144 E7
Boothman Wk KGHY BD21 2 D9
Booth Royd IDLE BD10 83 K5
Boothroyd Dr HDGY LS6 109 H1
HUDS HD4 213 K3
Booth Royd Dr IDLE BD10 83 K5
Boothroyd Gn DEWS WF13 173 K6
Booth Royd La BRIG HD6 169 M6
Boothroyd La DEWS WF13 173 K6
Boothroyds Wy FEA/AMT WF7 179 J8
Booth St CAS WF10 157 M6
CLECK BD19 149 M6
IDLE BD10 83 K7
ILK LS29 40 A4
SHPY BD18 82 F7
Boothtown Rd HIPP HX3 146 D3
Border Cl HUDW HD3 191 H5
Boroughgate OT LS21 41 J6
Borough Market HFAX * HX1 11 H6
Borough Rd WKFDE WF1 12 E1
Borrins Wy BAIL BD17 82 F3
Borrough Av RHAY LS8 88 A6
Borrough Vw RHAY LS8 88 A6
Borrowdale Cl AWLS/ASK DN6 249 L5
BSLYN/ROY S71 262 C6
ROY/SHW OL2 228 F8
WOR/ARM LS12 108 B4
Borrowdale Crs
WOR/ARM LS12 108 B4
Borrowdale Cft YEA LS19 62 C7
Borrowdale Dr CAS WF10 158 F5
Borrowdale Rd EARL WF12 174 A4
WKFDW/WTN WF2 176 A7
Borrowdale Ter SCFT LS14 111 H3
Boston Av KSTL LS5 108 B3
Boston Rd WBY LS22 48 A2
Boston St CAS WF10 158 A6
HFAX HX1 10 B6
RPDN/SBR HX6 167 J3
Boston Wk WBSY BD6 126 B6
Bosville St STKB/PEN S36 271 G4
Boswell Cl BSLYN/ROY * S71 243 K2
Bosworth Av NORM WF6 178 A2
Bosworth Cl WIL/AL BD15 103 K5
Bosworth Rd AWLS/ASK DN6 249 J8
Botany Av ECHL BD2 105 H2
Botany Dr AIRE BD20 59 G4
Botany La KBTN HD8 216 B1
Botesworth Gn MILN OL16 229 J1
Botham Flds MAR/SLWT HD7 213 H1
Botham Hall Rd HUDW HD3 213 H1
Botheby Wd SKP/WHF BD23 16 A1
Bottom Boat Rd
EARD/LOFT WF3 155 K8
Bottom Dyke KBTN HD8 238 B6
Bottom La HOLM/MEL HD9 236 E7
Bottomley La GTL/HWG HX4 189 L4
Bottomley Rd TOD OL14 163 L8
Bottomley St BRIG HD6 170 D2
WBOW BD5 126 F2
WBSY BD6 126 B7
Bottoms HIPP HX3 168 F3
Bottoms La BIRK/DRI BD11 150 D2
Boulder Bridge La CUD/GR S72 244 B4
The Boulevard BEE/HOL LS11 130 F3
PDSY/CALV LS28 106 F4
Boulsworth Dr COL BB8 74 E5
Boulsworth Gv COL BB8 74 C1
Boulview Ter COL BB8 74 C1
The Boundary GIR BD8 104 A5
Boundary Av AIRE BD20 34 E8
Boundary Cl BAIL BD17 82 F2
MSTN/BAR LS15 112 A7
Boundary Dr CUD/GR S72 245 J3
Boundary Farm Rd
AL/HA/HU LS17 87 J3
Boundary La WKFDE WF1 178 B7
Boundary Pl CHAL LS7 7 L4
Boundary Rd DEWS WF13 173 H4
Boundary St BSLY S70 261 K6
CHAL * LS7 7 L4
LIT OL15 185 J8
LVSG WF15 172 E3
ROCH OL11 228 A1
Boundary Ter DEWS * WF13 173 K4
Boundary Wk ROCH OL11 228 B1
Bourbon Cl WBSY BD6 126 D6
Bourne Ct DOD/DAR S75 242 E4
Bourne Rd ROY/SHW OL2 229 J6
Bourne St IDLE BD10 83 K4
Bourne Wk DOD/DAR S75 242 D4
Bourn View Rd HUDS HD4 213 M7
The Bourse LDS * LS1 9 G1
Bowater Ct BOW BD4 128 B4
Bow Beck BOW BD4 5 K9
Bowbridge Rd WBOW * BD5 127 G3
Bow Bridge Vw TAD LS24 72 B1
Bowcliffe Rd BSPA/BRAM LS23 69 L4
MID LS10 132 B2
Bowden Gv DOD/DAR S75 260 B7
The Bower BTLY WF17 151 H6
Bower Av WHIT OL12 206 F2
Bower Gn BFDE * BD3 105 L7
Bower Hl STKB/PEN S36 271 L5
Bower La DEWS WF13 173 H3
Bower Rd MSTN/BAR LS15 112 A3
Bower Slack Rd
RPDN/SBR HX6 166 B5
Bowers La GTL/HWG HX4 167 M8
Bower St WBOW BD5 4 E9
Bowes Nook WBSY BD6 126 A7
Bowfell Cl SCFT LS14 111 J2
Bowfell Vw BSLYN/ROY S71 261 J2
Bow Gn CLAY BD14 125 M2
Bowland Cl MSTN/BAR LS15 111 G7
ROY/SHW OL2 229 G7
Bowland Gv MILN OL16 229 H2
Bowland St GIR BD8 4 C3
Bow La HBR HX7 142 C2
Bowler Cl LM/WK BD12 126 E8
Bowler St ROY/SHW OL2 229 K7
Bowlers Wk WHIT OL12 206 B4
Bowling Aly BRIG HD6 170 C6
Bowling Av WKFDE * WF1 176 B4
Bowling Back La BOW BD4 5 K9
Bowling Ct BRIG HD6 170 B3
Bowling Dyke HFAX HX1 11 H4
Bowling Green Ct HUDW HD3 191 G7
Bowling Green Rd
GTL/HWG HX4 190 B3
Bowling Green Ter
BEE/HOL LS11 8 E5
Bowling Hall Rd BOW BD4 127 J3
Bowling Old La WBOW BD5 126 F4
WBOW BD5 127 G2
Bowling Park Cl BOW BD4 127 H2
Bowling Park Dr WBOW BD5 127 H3
Bowling St HUDS HD4 213 J2
Bowman Av WBSY BD6 126 D7
Bowman Gv HFAX HX1 10 C5
Bowman La MID LS10 9 J2
Bowman Pl HFAX * HX1 10 C5
Bowman Rd WBSY BD6 126 D7
Bowman St HFAX * HX1 10 C5
WKFDE WF1 13 L9
Bowman Ter HFAX HX1 10 D5
Bownas Rd BSPA/BRAM LS23 48 E6
Bowness Av CAS WF10 159 G5
IDLE BD10 105 M2
Bowness Dr HUDE HD5 15 L5
Bowood Av CHAL LS7 87 J7
Bowood Crs CHAL LS7 87 J7
Bowood Gv CHAL LS7 87 J7
Bowood La RPDN/SBR HX6 166 F5
Bow St CUD/GR S72 244 D7
HUD HD1 14 D8
KGHY BD21 3 G5
OSM LS9 9 L2
Bowwood Dr AIRE BD20 58 D6
Boxhill Rd ELL HX5 169 H7
Box La PONT WF8 181 G4
Box St LIT OL15 207 J1
Box Tree Cl GIR BD8 104 A5
Box Tree Gv KGHY BD21 3 L7
Box Trees La LUD/ILL HX2 145 M3
Boxwood Rd ELL HX5 191 H1
Boycott Dr FEA/AMT WF7 224 C1
Boyd Av BFDE BD3 106 A5
Boy La BOW BD4 127 K7
HIPP HX3 145 M4
The Boyle MSTN/BAR LS15 90 F6
Boyne Dr WKFDW/WTN WF2 220 C1
Boyne Hl HOR/CROF WF4 220 C2
Boyne St HFAX HX1 10 F6
Boynton St WBOW BD5 126 F3
Boynton Ter WBOW BD5 127 G3
Boys La HIPP HX3 168 F1
Bracewell Av WIL/AL BD15 103 J6
Bracewell Bank HIPP HX3 146 B4
Bracewell Dr HIPP HX3 146 B4
Bracewell Gv HIPP HX3 10 C1
Bracewell Rd HOLM/MEL HD9 234 E5
Bracken Av BRIG HD6 170 C1
Bracken Bank Av HWTH BD22 79 H3
Bracken Bank Crs HWTH BD22 79 H3
Bracken Bank Gv HWTH BD22 79 H3
Bracken Bank Wy HWTH BD22 79 H3
Brackenbeck Rd GTHN BD7 126 B2
Brackenbed Gra LUD/ILL HX2 146 A5

Brackenbed La HFAX HX1 10 A1
Bracken Cl BRIG HD6 170 C1
ELL HX5 169 K7
MIRF WF14 171 M7
Bracken Ct AL/HA/HU LS17 87 L5
WOR/ARM LS12 131 G1
Brackendale IDLE BD10 83 H4
Brackendale Av IDLE BD10 83 J4
Brackendale Dr IDLE BD10 83 H4
Brackendale Gv IDLE BD10 83 H4
Brackendale Pde IDLE BD10 83 H4
Bracken Edge IDLE BD10 83 L7
RHAY LS8 110 B1
Bracken Ghyll Dr AIRE BD20 35 M4
Bracken Gv HUDN HD2 192 D2
MIRF WF14 171 M7
Bracken Hall Rd HUDN HD2 192 E3
Bracken Hl AL/HA/HU LS17 87 L5
FEA/AMT WF7 223 M1
HEM/SK/SE WF9 246 F2
MIRF WF14 171 M7
Brackenhill Dr GTHN BD7 126 B3
Brackenhill La TAD LS24 95 H7
Brackenholme Royd
WBSY BD6 126 A6
Bracken Mt AIRE BD20 35 M4
Bracken Pk BGLY BD16 81 L3
SCFT LS14 67 J6
Bracken Rd AIRE BD20 56 C1
BRIG HD6 170 C1
HWTH BD22 79 J2
Brackens La HIPP HX3 125 K7
Bracken Sq HUDN * HD2 192 E2
Bracken St KGHY BD21 79 K2
Brackenthwaite La PBR HG3 25 L3
Brackenwell La AL/HA/HU LS17 25 M7
Brackenwood Cl ILK LS29 39 G2
RHAY LS8 88 A7
Brackenwood Ct WKFDE WF1 176 F1
Brackenwood Dr RHAY LS8 88 A6
Brackenwood Gn RHAY LS8 88 A6
Brackenwood Rd WKFDE WF1 176 F1
Bradbeck Rd GTHN BD7 104 B7
Bradburn Rd EARD/LOFT WF3 154 C3
Bradbury St BSLY S70 260 F5
DEWS WF13 195 G1
Bradcroft HUDN HD2 15 G1
Bradd Cl LVSG * WF15 172 D1
Braddocks Cl WHIT OL12 206 F2
Bradfield Cl HUDN HD2 193 G1
Bradford & Wakefield Rd
BOW BD4 128 E7
Bradford La BFDE BD3 105 M7
Bradford Old Rd BGLY BD16 81 K7
HIPP HX3 146 E3
Bradford Rd BGLY BD16 81 J5
BIRK/DRI BD11 150 C2
BIRK/DRI BD11 151 K1
BRIG HD6 170 D2
BTLY WF17 150 F5
CLAY BD14 125 M1
CLECK BD19 149 K3
CLECK BD19 149 L5
DEWS WF13 173 L4
EARD/LOFT WF3 153 G5
EARD/LOFT WF3 153 L7
GSLY LS20 61 L5
HIPP HX3 147 H5
HUD HD1 15 G3
HUDN HD2 192 D2
IDLE BD10 105 J1
ILK LS29 40 B6
KGHY BD21 3 J4
OT LS21 40 E8
PDSY/CALV LS28 106 B5
SHPY BD18 82 C6
WKFDW/WTN WF2 176 A2
Bradfords Cl BSPA/BRAM LS23 69 L3
Bradford St DEWS WF13 173 M5
KGHY BD21 3 H3
Bradlaugh Rd WBSY BD6 126 D5
Bradlaugh Ter WBSY BD6 126 E5
Bradley Av AIRE BD20 35 M4
CAS WF10 157 L6
Bradley Bvd HUDN HD2 192 E3
Bradley Carr Ter
HEM/SK/SE WF9 247 G6
Bradley Dr AIRE BD20 35 M4
Bradley Grange Gdns
HUDN HD2 171 H8
Bradley La GTL/HWG HX4 168 D8
MILN OL16 229 K2
PDSY/CALV LS28 106 D7
Bradley Mills La HUD HD1 15 K2
Bradley Mills Rd HUD HD1 15 K2
Bradley Quarry Cl HUDN * HD2 171 J8
Bradley Ri AIRE BD20 35 M4
Bradley Rd AIRE BD20 35 M4
HUDN HD2 192 E1
Bradley Smithy Cl WHIT OL12 206 A4
Bradley St BGLY BD16 81 H3
CAS WF10 157 M6
COL BB8 74 B1
HTON BD9 104 E2
MILN OL16 229 K2
Bradley Vw GTL/HWG HX4 190 D2
Bradshaw Av HOLM/MEL HD9 236 A3
Bradshaw Cl DOD/DAR S75 260 C4
HOLM/MEL HD9 236 A3
Bradshaw Crs
HOLM/MEL * HD9 236 A3
Bradshaw La LUD/ILL HX2 124 B6
MAR/SLWT HD7 211 J5
Bradshaw Rd HOLM/MEL HD9 235 K8
HOLM/MEL HD9 236 A4
Bradshaw St MILN OL16 206 C6
Bradshaw Vw CUL/QBY BD13 124 E5
Bradstock Gdns MOR LS27 130 C8
Brae Av ECHL BD2 105 H3
Braegate La TAD LS24 73 K1
Braemar Cft CUD/GR S72 222 F7
Braemar Dr GFTH/SHER LS25 113 K6
Braemar Ri CUD/GR S72 222 F7
Braemore Cl ROY/SHW OL2 229 G6
Brafferton Arbor WBSY BD6 126 A6
Braine Rd WBY LS22 30 B8
Braithwaite Av HWTH BD22 57 G7
Braithwaite Crs HWTH BD22 2 B4
Braithwaite Dr HWTH BD22 2 A4
Braithwaite Edge Rd
HWTH BD22 56 F6
Braithwaite Gv HWTH BD22 2 A4
Braithwaite Rd HWTH BD22 56 F7
Braithwaite Rw MID * LS10 132 A4
Braithwaite St BEE/HOL LS11 8 B4
Braithwaite Wk HWTH BD22 2 A4
Braithwaite Wy HWTH BD22 2 A4
Brakehouse Cl MILN OL16 207 G8
Bramah St BSLYN/ROY S71 243 L5
The Brambles ILK LS29 38 B2
Bramble Av BSPA/BRAM LS23 48 D7
Bramble Cl CLAY BD14 125 K3
LIT OL15 207 H1
PONT WF8 180 D8
Bramble Ct HWTH BD22 78 F8
Bramble Wk BTLY WF17 151 H5
Brambling Dr CUL/QBY BD13 125 L4
Brambling Ms MOR LS27 152 E2
Bramcote Av BSLYN/ROY S71 243 G6
Bramhall Cl MILN OL16 207 G8
Bramham Dr BAIL BD17 82 F2
Bramham La BSPA/BRAM LS23 68 C2
Bramham Park Ct
EARD/LOFT WF3 153 M3
Bramham Rd BGLY BD16 81 J2
BSPA/BRAM LS23 69 M1
CAS WF10 157 J8
SCFT LS14 68 D8
Bramhope Old La OT LS21 63 G2
Bramhope Rd CLECK BD19 149 L6
Bramleigh Dr MOR LS27 130 C8
Bramleigh Gv MOR LS27 130 C8
Bramley Cl HOLM/MEL HD9 236 F7
HWTH BD22 78 D3
Bramley Crs WKFDE WF1 176 D2
Bramley Fold HIPP HX3 147 M6
Bramley La HIPP HX3 147 M6
HOR/CROF WF4 219 J6
Bramley St BRAM LS13 107 L5
WBOW BD5 127 G2
Bramley Vw HIPP HX3 148 A6
Brampton Ct HEM/SK/SE WF9 247 J1
Bramstan Av BRAM LS13 107 J3
Bramstan Cl BRAM LS13 107 J3
Bramstan Gdns BRAM LS13 107 J3
Bramston Gdns BRIG HD6 170 C6
Bramston St BRIG HD6 170 C5
Brancepeth Pl WOR/ARM LS12 109 G7
Branch Cl WOR/ARM LS12 130 C2
Branch End MOR LS27 129 M7
Branch La HUDW HD3 191 K3
Branch Pl WOR/ARM LS12 130 C2
Branch Rd BTLY WF17 173 L1
CLECK BD19 149 H5
DEWS WF13 173 L6
GTL/HWG HX4 168 A8
HOR/CROF WF4 219 L2
HUDW HD3 191 J2
LIT OL15 207 G5
SKP/WHF BD23 16 B4
WOR/ARM LS12 108 E6
WOR/ARM LS12 130 C2
Branch St HUD HD1 213 M1
WOR/ARM LS12 130 C2
Brander Ap OSM LS9 110 F5
Brander Cl OSM LS9 110 E5
Brander Dr OSM LS9 110 E5
Brander Gv OSM LS9 110 E5
Brander Rd OSM LS9 110 E5
Brander St OSM LS9 110 F4
Brandfort St GTHN BD7 126 C1
Brand Hill Ap HOR/CROF WF4 200 A5
Brand Hill Dr HOR/CROF WF4 200 A5
Brandon Ct AL/HA/HU LS17 88 D1
Brandon Crs AL/HA/HU LS17 67 H8
ROY/SHW OL2 229 J6
Brandon La AL/HA/HU LS17 67 H7
Brandon Rd BVRD LS3 6 C7
Brandon St MILN OL16 207 G8
WOR/ARM LS12 8 A1
Brandon Wy CHAL LS7 109 M1
Brandy Carr Rd
WKFDW/WTN WF2 175 K4
Branksome Av BSLY S70 260 E5
Branksome Ct HTON * BD9 104 B4
Branksome Crs HTON BD9 104 B4
Branksome Dr SHPY BD18 81 M6
Branksome Gv BGLY BD16 81 L6
Branksome Pl HDGY LS6 109 G4
Branksome St HDGY * LS6 109 G4
Branksome Ter HDGY * LS6 109 G4
Bransby Cl PDSY/CALV LS28 107 G4
Bransby Ct PDSY/CALV LS28 107 G4
Bransby Ri PDSY/CALV LS28 107 G4
Bransdale Av GSLY LS20 62 A6
NORM WF6 178 C2
Bransdale Cl BAIL BD17 82 C4
GSLY LS20 62 A6
NORM WF6 178 C2
Bransdale Clough WBSY BD6 126 A5
Bransdale Garth GSLY LS20 62 A6
Bransdale Ms NORM WF6 178 C2
Bransdale Wk NORM WF6 178 C2
Branshaw Dr HWTH BD22 79 G1
Branshaw Gv HWTH BD22 79 G1
Branshaw Mt HWTH BD22 79 G1
Branstone Gv OSS WF5 174 F5
Bran St HWTH BD22 79 J2
Brant Av LUD/ILL HX2 146 B2
Brant Bank La ILK LS29 19 L8
Brantcliffe Dr BAIL BD17 82 D2
Brantdale Cl HTON BD9 103 L2
Brantdale Rd HTON BD9 103 L2
Brantford St CHAL LS7 87 M8
Brant La TAD LS24 71 J7
Brantwood Av HTON BD9 103 L2
Brantwood Cl HTON BD9 103 L2
Brantwood Crs HTON BD9 103 K2
Brantwood Dr HTON BD9 103 L2
Brantwood Gv HTON BD9 103 K2
Brantwood Ov HTON BD9 103 L2
Brantwood Rd HTON BD9 103 K2
Brantwood Vls HTON BD9 103 L2
Branwell Av BTLY WF17 151 G3
Branwell Ct HTON BD9 104 A4
Branwell Dr HWTH BD22 78 E6
Brassey Rd BOW BD4 127 J2
Brassey St HFAX HX1 10 F8
Brassey Ter BOW BD4 127 J2
Brathay Gdns SCFT LS14 111 J3
Brat La OT LS21 23 J1
Braybrook Ct GIR BD8 104 E3
Bray Cl WBSY * BD6 125 M4
Brayshaw Dr GTHN BD7 125 M4
Brayshaw Rd EARD/LOFT WF3 153 L7
Brayside Av HUDN HD2 192 B4
Braythorne La OT LS21 24 F7
Brayton Ap SCFT LS14 111 L1
Brayton Cl SCFT LS14 111 L1
Brayton Gdns AWLS/ASK DN6 227 L5
Brayton Gn SCFT LS14 111 M1
Brayton Gv SCFT LS14 111 L1
Brayton Wk SCFT LS14 111 L1
Brazil St CAS WF10 158 A6
Bread St WKFDE WF1 12 E2
Breakmoor Av AIRE BD20 36 A4
Break Neck HIPP HX3 147 J6
Breaks Rd LM/WK BD12 126 F8
Brearcliffe Cl WBSY BD6 126 C6
Brearcliffe Dr WBSY BD6 126 C6
Brearcliffe Gv WBSY BD6 126 C7
Brearcliffe Rd WBSY BD6 126 D7
Brearcliffe St WBSY BD6 126 C7
Brearley Gdns LVSG WF15 172 C3
Brearley La LUD/ILL HX2 144 D6
Brearley St BTLY WF17 173 K2
Brearton St BFD BD1 4 E3
Breary Av HORS LS18 85 M5
Breary Ct BHP/TINH LS16 64 A3
Breary La BHP/TINH LS16 64 A3
Breary La East BHP/TINH LS16 64 B3
Breary Ri BHP/TINH LS16 64 A4
Breary Ter HORS LS18 85 M5
Breary Wk HORS LS18 85 M5
Breck Lea RPDN/SBR HX6 167 J4
Brecks Gdns GFTH/SHER LS25 135 H3
Brecks La GFTH/SHER LS25 135 H3
RTHW LS26 134 E2
Brecks Rd CLAY BD14 125 M1
Breck Willows RPDN/SBR HX6 167 H4
Brecon Ap OSM LS9 110 F4
Brecon Av HUDW HD3 191 J5
Brecon Cl IDLE BD10 83 K7
ROY/SHW OL2 228 E8
Bredon Av SHPY BD18 83 H7
Bredon Cl HEM/SK/SE WF9 224 A7
Breeze Cl COL BB8 52 A5
Breighton Adown WBSY BD6 125 M6
Brellafield Dr ROY/SHW OL2 229 H5
Bremner St OT LS21 41 K6
Brendon Ct BOW BD4 127 M3
MIRF WF14 194 B4
Brendon Dr HUDN HD2 191 M5
Brendon Wk BOW * BD4 127 M4
Brentford Gv WOR/ARM * LS12 108 E7
Brentford Rd WBSY BD6 126 E7
Brentlea Av WKFDW/WTN WF2 12 D8
Brentwood Cl BTLY WF17 174 A1
LIT OL15 207 H3
PONT WF8 225 J1
Brentwood Gdns WBSY BD6 126 E6
Brentwood St
WOR/ARM * LS12 108 E7
Brentwood Ter
WOR/ARM LS12 108 E7
Bretfield Ct EARL WF12 195 M1
Brettegate HEM/SK/SE WF9 223 J7
Brett Gdns BEE/HOL LS11 8 E8
Bretton Cl DOD/DAR S75 241 L6
Bretton Ct WBSY * BD6 126 B6
Bretton La HOR/CROF WF4 219 K5
Bretton Rd DOD/DAR S75 241 M6
Bretton St EARL WF12 195 M1
Bretton Vw CUD/GR S72 262 C1
Brevitt St WKFDE WF1 13 J8
Brewerton La DEWS WF13 173 H4
Brewery Ct HUDW HD3 191 J4
Brewery La CUL/QBY BD13 124 E7
CUL/QBY BD13 124 F3
EARL WF12 195 L2
SKP/WHF BD23 16 B2
Brewery Rd HWTH BD22 79 J3
ILK LS29 38 E2
Brewery St HECK * WF16 172 F3
HIPP HX3 146 E4
KGHY BD21 3 K4
TOD OL14 141 G6
Brewery Whf MIRF WF14 194 C2
Brexdale Av GFTH/SHER LS25 135 H3
Brian Crs MSTN/BAR LS15 111 K4
Brian Pl MSTN/BAR LS15 111 K3
Brian Royd La GTL/HWG HX4 168 B7
Brian St HUDW HD3 191 K5
Brian Vw MSTN/BAR LS15 111 K3
Briar Av HOLM/MEL HD9 234 E3
Briar Bank HEM/SK/SE WF9 223 J4
Briar Cl ELL HX5 191 G1
HECK WF16 172 F1
PDSY/CALV LS28 106 F4
Briar Ct HOLM/MEL HD9 253 M2
Briardale Rd HTON BD9 103 K2
Briardene RTHW * LS26 155 L1
Briar Dr DEWS WF13 173 H4
Briarfield Av IDLE BD10 83 J7
Briarfield Cl IDLE BD10 83 J7
ILK LS29 38 F3
Briarfield Gdns SHPY BD18 82 D8
Briarfield Gv IDLE BD10 83 J7
Briarfield Rd HOLM/MEL HD9 236 E7
SHPY BD18 82 E8
Briar Ga WBY LS22 30 A7
Briar Gv CUD/GR S72 245 J3
STKB/PEN S36 270 F4
WKFDE WF1 13 K9
Briarlea Cl YEA LS19 62 B8
Briarlyn Av HUDW HD3 191 J4
Briarlyn Rd HUDW HD3 191 J4
Briarmains Rd BTLY WF17 151 H4
Briar Rhydding BAIL BD17 83 G4
Briar Rd AWLS/ASK DN6 249 J5
Briars Ct COP/BISH YO23 73 M5
Briarsdale Ct RHAY * LS8 110 E3
Briarsdale Cft RHAY * LS8 110 E3
Briarsdale Garth RHAY LS8 110 D3
Briarsdale Hts OSM * LS9 110 E3
Briarsdale Ms OSM LS9 110 D3
Briars Dr COP/BISH YO23 73 M5
Briar Wd SHPY BD18 83 G7
Briarwood Av KGHY BD21 58 B5
Briarwood Cl WKFDE WF1 176 F1
Briarwood Crs WBSY BD6 126 D5
Briarwood Dr WBSY BD6 126 D5
Briarwood Gv WBSY BD6 126 D4
Briary Cl WKFDE WF1 199 H4
Brick & Tile Ter BRIG HD6 170 C5
Brickbank HUDE * HD5 215 H3
Brickfield Gv LUD/ILL HX2 146 C1
Brickfield La LUD/ILL HX2 146 C1
Brickfield St MILN OL16 206 D4
Brickfield Ter LUD/ILL HX2 146 C1
Brick Mill Rd PDSY/CALV LS28 107 G8
Brick Rw LM/WK BD12 148 E3
Brick St CLECK BD19 149 L7
OSM LS9 9 K1
WKFDW/WTN WF2 175 M7
Brick Ter BRIG HD6 170 D5
Brickyard MIRF WF14 194 B1
Bride St TOD OL14 141 K8
Bridge Bank Rd LIT OL15 207 H3
Bridge Cl BSPA/BRAM LS23 49 G6
HOR/CROF WF4 196 F5
KBTN HD8 240 A4
Bridge Ct HEM/SK/SE WF9 223 J3
MOR LS27 152 D3
Bridge Cft HUDS HD4 213 K2
Bridge End BRIG HD6 170 C5
LDS LS1 9 H2
Bridge End St TOD * OL14 140 E5
Bridge Fold KSTL LS5 108 C2
Bridge Foot BSPA/BRAM LS23 49 G6
Bridge Gdns BSLYN/ROY S71 261 H3
Bridge Garth BSPA/BRAM LS23 48 F8
GFTH/SHER LS25 138 B2
Bridge Ga HBR HX7 143 J3
Bridgegate Wy IDLE BD10 83 M8
Bridgehouse La HWTH BD22 78 E8
Bridge La HIPP HX3 125 K7
HOLM/MEL HD9 236 C8
ILK LS29 38 C1
KNOT WF11 182 B1
PONT WF8 225 J2
HBR HX7 143 H3
Bridgenorth Dr LIT OL15 207 H3
Bridge Rd AIRE BD20 55 M1
BEE/HOL LS11 8 C4
BRAM LS13 107 G1
BRIG HD6 170 C4
BSPA/BRAM LS23 49 G6
HOR/CROF WF4 197 G5
HUDN HD2 193 K1
KSTL LS5 108 B2
Bridge St AIRE BD20 36 A4
BFD BD1 4 E6
BSLYN/ROY S71 261 H4
BSLYN/ROY * S71 262 A6
BTLY WF17 151 G6
BTLY WF17 173 M1
CAS WF10 158 A6
DOD/DAR S75 242 A5
HECK WF16 172 E2
HUD HD1 214 B3
HUDS HD4 214 B6
HWTH BD22 78 D4
KGHY BD21 2 F6
LDSU LS2 9 H3
MAR/SLWT HD7 212 C5
MILN OL16 207 H8
MOR LS27 152 D4
NORM WF6 178 E4
OT LS21 41 J6
PONT * WF8 180 F6
ROY/SHW * OL2 229 L6
SKP/WHF BD23 16 B2
STKB/PEN S36 270 E2
TAD LS24 71 M3
TOD OL14 163 K1
WHIT OL12 206 E3
WKFDE WF1 13 H6
Bridge Vw BRAM LS13 107 G1
Bridge View Cl HORS LS18 85 M4
Bridgewater HDGY LS6 87 G8
Bridgewater Park Dr
AWLS/ASK DN6 249 H4
Bridgewater Rd OSM LS9 9 M5
Bridgeway BOW BD4 127 L4
Bridgland Av ILK LS29 61 J1
Bridgwater Rd HTON BD9 104 C4
Bridle Av OSS WF5 174 E6
Bridle Cl HOR/CROF WF4 197 G7
Bridle Dene HIPP HX3 147 L1
Bridle La HOR/CROF WF4 197 G7
OSS WF5 174 E6
Bridle Pth MSTN/BAR LS15 111 J4
Bridle Path Rd AL/HA/HU LS17 88 F1
Bridle Path Wk
MSTN/BAR LS15 111 J4
Bridle Pl OSS WF5 174 F6
Bridle Stile HIPP HX3 147 L1
Bridle Stile La CUL/QBY BD13 125 G4
Bridle St BTLY WF17 174 A1
Bridley Dr MAR/SLWT HD7 212 C6
Brierdene AIRE BD20 36 A4
Brierey Cl DOD/DAR S75 242 C6
Brierfield Cl DOD/DAR S75 260 E4
Brierfield Gdns MOR LS27 129 L8
Brier Hey Cl HBR HX7 144 B5
Brier Hey La HBR HX7 144 B5
Brier Hill Cl CLECK BD19 149 J8
Brier Hill Vw HUDN HD2 192 F1
Brierlands Cl GFTH/SHER LS25 113 K6
Brierlands Fold
GFTH/SHER LS25 113 K6
Brierlands La GFTH/SHER LS25 113 K6
Brier La ELL HX5 169 M4
HOR/CROF WF4 222 D6
Brierley Cl SHPY BD18 82 E8
Brierley Crs HEM/SK/SE WF9 246 E3
Brierley Rd CUD/GR S72 244 F4
CUD/GR S72 245 J6
CUD/GR S72 245 G1
Brier St HIPP HX3 146 D4
KGHY BD21 79 K2
Briery Cl ILK LS29 38 A2
Briery Fld SHPY BD18 104 D1
Briery Gv MIRF WF14 194 C3
Briestfield Rd EARL WF12 195 H7
HOR/CROF WF4 217 G1
Briggate AIRE BD20 36 A4
BAIL BD17 82 D6
BRIG HD6 170 C4
ELL HX5 169 H7
LDS LS1 9 G1
Brigg Gdns HWTH BD22 2 B4
Briggland Ct WIL/AL BD15 102 E1
Brigglands WIL/AL * BD15 102 E1
Brigg's Av CAS WF10 157 M8
WBSY BD6 126 C5
Briggs Gv WBSY BD6 126 C5
Briggs Pl WBSY BD6 126 C5
Briggs Rd BSLYN/ROY S71 243 L5
Briggs Rw FEA/AMT WF7 201 M2
Briggs St CUL/QBY * BD13 125 G5
Briggs Ter HUDE HD5 15 L7
Briggs Yd OSS * WF5 196 E1
Brighouse & Denholme Gate Rd
HIPP HX3 125 J8
Brighouse & Denholme Rd
CUL/QBY BD13 124 C2
Brighouse Rd CUL/QBY BD13 102 A8
CUL/QBY BD13 125 G5
HIPP HX3 147 L7
HUDW HD3 191 K3
LM/WK BD12 148 F1
Brighouse Wood La BRIG HD6 170 B3
Brighouse Wood Rw BRIG HD6 170 B3
Brighton Av MOR LS27 152 B1
Brighton Cliff BRAM LS13 107 L4
Brighton Cl BTLY WF17 151 G8
Brighton Gv BRAM LS13 107 M5
HFAX HX1 10 C4
Brighton Rd ILK LS29 39 G3
Brighton St BAIL BD17 82 D6
CUD/GR S72 245 J7
HECK WF16 172 F1
HIPP HX3 10 D1
IDLE BD10 83 J5
TOD OL14 140 E5
WKFDW/WTN WF2 12 B5
Brighton Ter CLECK BD19 149 H6
Bright St AIRE BD20 34 F5
CLAY * BD14 125 K2
COL BB8 74 D1
CUL/QBY BD13 125 H5
DEWS * WF13 173 L5
EARD/LOFT WF3 153 M6
MILN OL16 228 C1
MIRF WF14 172 B6
MOR LS27 152 C2
PDSY/CALV LS28 107 H4
RPDN/SBR HX6 167 K1
SKP/WHF BD23 16 A2
TOD OL14 163 J3
WIL/AL BD15 103 K5
Bright Ter COL BB8 74 D4
Brignall Cft OSM LS9 110 B5
Brignall Garth OSM LS9 110 B5
Brignall Wy OSM LS9 110 B5
Brigshaw Dr CAS WF10 135 H7
Brigshaw La CAS WF10 135 J7
Brimmy Croft La UPML OL3 230 E3
Brinckman St BSLY S70 261 H6
Brindle Park Dr CAS WF10 158 C8
Brindley Gv GIR BD8 103 L7
Brindley Rd AIRE BD20 36 B6
Brindley Wy
WKFDW/WTN WF2 176 B2
Brisbane Av ECHL BD2 105 G3
Briscoe La GTL/HWG HX4 168 D7
Briscoe Ridge La PBR HG3 25 J4
Bristol Av AIRE BD20 58 D6
Bristol St CHAL LS7 7 K6
COL BB8 74 A1
HIPP HX3 168 F3
Britannia Av ROY/SHW OL2 229 L8
Britannia Cl BSLY S70 261 H6
PDSY/CALV LS28 107 H4
Britannia Ct BRAM LS13 107 J6
Britannia Rd MAR/SLWT HD7 212 B6
MAR/SLWT HD7 213 G3
MOR LS27 152 B4
Britannia St BGLY BD16 81 J3
LDS LS1 8 E1
PDSY/CALV LS28 107 H4
WBOW BD5 5 G8
Britannia Ter CLECK BD19 149 M6
Britton Cl DOD/DAR S75 260 C5
Britton St MILN OL16 206 C6
Broadacre Rd OSS WF5 197 G1
Broad Acres HOR/CROF WF4 198 C7
Broadbent Cft HOLM/MEL HD9 236 C2
Broad Carr La GTL/HWG HX4 190 E2
Broadcroft Cha
EARD/LOFT WF3 153 G6
Broadcroft Dr EARD/LOFT WF3 153 G6
Broadcroft Gv
EARD/LOFT WF3 153 G6
Broadcroft Wy
EARD/LOFT WF3 153 G6
Broad Cut Rd HOR/CROF WF4 197 M8
Broadfield Cl BOW BD4 128 A5
Broadfield Dr LIT OL15 207 H3
Broadfield Pk HOLM/MEL HD9 253 L4
Broadfield Stile MILN OL16 206 A8
Broadfield St MILN OL16 206 A8
Broadfield Wy ILK LS29 18 F6
Broadfolds CLAY BD14 125 L2
Broadgate GTL/HWG HX4 190 B4
HUDE HD5 214 F2
OSS WF5 197 G1
Broad Ga TOD OL14 141 L8
TOD OL14 164 C1
Broadgate Av HORS LS18 85 M5
Broadgate Crs HORS LS18 85 L6
HUDE HD5 214 F2
Broadgate Dr HORS LS18 85 L5
Broadgate La HORS LS18 85 L5
Broadgate Ri HORS LS18 85 M6
Broad Gates DOD/DAR S75 259 H6
Broadgate Wk HORS LS18 85 L6
Broad Head La HWTH BD22 78 A2

Broad Ings Wy *HIPP* HX3 .....147 L1
Broadlands *KGHY* BD21 .....2 C2
Broadlands Rd
 HOLM/MEL HD9 .....234 F3
Broadlands St *BOW* BD4 .....127 M2
Broadland Wy
 EARD/LOFT WF3 .....154 E6
Broad La *BOW* BD4 .....127 M1
 GLE DN14 .....161 J7
 HBR HX7 .....120 D8
 HBR HX7 .....143 H5
 HEM/SK/SE WF9 .....246 C5
 HOLM/MEL HD9 .....253 M1
 HUDE HD5 .....15 M7
 LUD/ILL HX2 .....166 E1
 MILN OL16 .....228 E3
 PDSY/CALV LS28 .....107 H4
 TAD LS24 .....117 H1
 TOD OL14 .....141 M4
 UPML OL3 .....231 G7
Broad Lane Cl *BRAM* LS13 .....108 A2
Broadlea Av *BRAM* LS13 .....108 A2
Broadlea Cl *BRAM* LS13 .....108 A2
Broadlea Crs *BRAM* LS13 .....108 A2
 WBOW BD5 .....127 H3
Broadlea Gdns *BRAM* LS13 .....108 A2
Broadlea Gv *BRAM* LS13 .....108 A2
Broadlea HI *BRAM* LS13 .....108 A2
Broadlea Mt *BRAM* LS13 .....108 A3
Broadlea PI *BRAM* LS13 .....108 A3
Broadlea St *BRAM* LS13 .....108 A2
Broadlea Ter *BRAM* LS13 .....108 A2
Broadlea Vw *BRAM* LS13 .....107 M2
Broadley Av *LUD/ILL* HX2 .....145 K5
Broadley Cl *LUD/ILL* HX2 .....145 L5
Broadley Gv *LUD/ILL* HX2 .....145 L5
Broadley La *LUD/ILL* HX2 .....145 K5
Broadmead *CAS* WF10 .....158 B6
Broadmeadows *WKFDE* WF1 .....176 F1
Broad Oak La *HIPP* HX3 .....147 M8
 STKB/PEN S36 .....257 M5
Broadoaks La *EARL* WF12 .....174 C7
Broad Oak St *HIPP* HX3 .....147 M8
Broadowler La *OSS* WF5 .....197 G1
Broad Shaw La *MILN* OL16 .....228 E4
Broadstone Rd *KBTN* HD8 .....256 B2
Broadstones Pk *BGLY* BD16 .....81 M3
Broadstone St *TOD* OL14 .....141 M8
Broadstone Wy *BOW* BD4 .....128 A4
Broad St *BFD* BD1 .....4 F5
 DEWS WF13 .....173 J8
 HFAX HX1 .....11 H5
 PDSY/CALV LS28 .....106 E3
 TOD OL14 .....141 K8
Broad Tree Rd *HIPP* HX3 .....146 C4
Broad Vw *OSS* WF5 .....197 H1
Broadway *BFD* BD1 .....4 F6
 BCLY BD16 .....81 J3
 BSLY S70 .....260 D6
 DOD/DAR S75 .....242 D5
 GSLY LS20 .....61 L6
 HEM/SK/SE WF9 .....247 G5
 HIPP HX3 .....169 G1
 HORS LS18 .....85 H7
 HUD HD1 .....15 G5
 KSTL LS5 .....86 A7
 MSTN/BAR LS15 .....111 H8
 PONT WF8 .....181 G7
 RPDN/SBR HX6 .....166 F3
 WKFDW/WTN WF2 .....197 L1
Broadway Av *WBOW* BD5 .....126 F4
Broadway Cl *WBOW* BD5 .....126 F4
Broad Way Ct *EARL* WF12 .....196 A5
Broadway Dr *HORS* LS18 .....85 K6
Broadwell Rd *OSS* WF5 .....197 H1
Broadwood Av *LUD/ILL* HX2 .....145 L5
Brockadale Av *PONT* WF8 .....202 F1
Brock Bank *HUDE* HD5 .....193 H7
Brockholes La *HOLM/MEL* HD9 .....236 C4
 STKB/PEN S36 .....270 C7
Brockholes Rd
 HOLM/MEL HD9 .....236 F2
Brocklebank Rd *MILN* OL16 .....206 F7
Brocklehurst Av *BSLY* S70 .....261 M8
Brocklesby Dr *WIL/AL* BD15 .....103 K5
Brockley Cl *TAD* LS24 .....94 E8
Brocks *LUD/ILL* HX2 .....144 E8
Brockstones *GTL/HWG* HX4 .....168 B7
Brockswood Ct
 WKFDW/WTN WF2 .....221 L1
Brockway *MILN* OL16 .....228 E7
Brockwell Ct
 RPDN/SBR HX6 .....167 J3
Broc Well La *RPDN/SBR* HX6 .....167 H4
Broc-o-Bank *AWLS/ASK* DN6 .....227 L3
Brodley Cl *HIPP* HX3 .....147 L6
Brodrick Ct *HDGY* LS6 .....108 F1
Broken Banks *COL* BB8 .....74 A2
Broken Cross *HUDE* HD5 .....215 G4
Broken Wy *WBOW* * BD5 .....126 F4
Bromcliffe Pk *BSLYN/ROY* S71 .....262 A1
Bromet PI *ECHL* BD2 .....105 K2
Bromfield *WHIT* * OL12 .....206 B6
Bromford Rd *BOW* BD4 .....127 J2
 ROY/SHW OL2 .....228 D8
Bromley Gv *HUDE* HD5 .....79 G1
Bromley Mt *WKFDE* WF1 .....13 H7
Bromley Rd *BGLY* BD16 .....81 H2
 BTLY WF17 .....174 A3
 HUDN HD2 .....192 B5
 SHPY BD18 .....82 A6
Bromley St *BTLY* WF17 .....173 M3
Brompton Av *BOW* BD4 .....127 J3
Brompton Gv *BEE/HOL* LS11 .....131 K4
Brompton Mt *BEE/HOL* LS11 .....131 K4
Brompton Rd *BOW* BD4 .....127 J2
Brompton Rw *BEE/HOL* LS11 .....131 K4
Brompton Ter *BEE/HOL* LS11 .....131 K4
Brompton Vw *BEE/HOL* LS11 .....131 K4
Bronshill Gv *WIL/AL* BD15 .....103 L5
Bronte Av *KNOT* WF11 .....181 K2
Bronte Cl *BSLYN/ROY* S71 .....261 K3
 CLECK BD19 .....150 D5
 DEWS WF13 .....173 H4
 HTON BD9 .....104 A4
 HUD HD4 .....213 M3

Bronte Ct *PONT* WF8 .....180 F4
Bronte Dr *HWTH* BD22 .....79 G3
Bronte Gv *HEM/SK/SE* WF9 .....223 L8
 MIRF WF14 .....194 E2
Bronte PI *CUL/QBY* BD13 .....103 G8
Bronte Ri *CAS* WF10 .....180 F1
Bronte Rd *BTLY* WF17 .....151 G4
 KGHY BD21 .....3 K3
Bronte Vls *HWTH* BD22 .....79 H6
Bronte Wy *BRFD/BLYE* BD10 .....96 C2
 BRIG HD6 .....148 D8
 BRIG HD6 .....170 F2
 COL BB8 .....75 H2
 CUL/QBY BD13 .....103 H8
 CUL/QBY BD13 .....125 K5
 HWTH BD22 .....99 K2
 HWTH BD22 .....100 B1
 MIRF WF14 .....194 E2
The Brook *HBR* HX7 .....143 M6
 LIT OL15 .....185 L5
Brook Av *ROY/SHW* OL2 .....229 K6
Brook Cl *OSS* WF5 .....197 H3
Brookdale *WHIT* OL12 .....206 A3
Brookdale Av *OSS* WF5 .....174 K5
Brookdale Bank *HUDW* HD3 .....213 J1
Brook Dr *GTL/HWG* HX4 .....190 D5
Brooke Ct *PONT* WF8 .....202 E1
Brooke Fold *HOLM/MEL* HD9 .....236 M5
Brooke St *BRIG* HD6 .....170 C5
 CLECK BD19 .....150 A7
 HECK * WF16 .....172 F3
Brookeville Av *HIPP* HX3 .....147 L7
Brook Fld *MIRF* WF14 .....194 B4
Brookfield *KBTN* HD8 .....215 M8
 ROY/SHW OL2 .....229 J5
Brookfield Av *BRAM* LS13 .....84 F8
 CAS WF10 .....158 B7
 CLECK BD19 .....149 M5
 RHAY LS8 .....110 B2
 SHPY BD18 .....82 F6
Brookfield Ct *NORM* WF6 .....178 E4
Brookfield Dr *FEA/AMT* WF7 .....202 E6
 LIT OL15 .....185 G8
Brookfield Gdns *BRAM* LS13 .....84 F8
Brookfield PI *BFDE* BD3 .....5 K4
 HDGY LS6 .....87 G8
 SHPY BD18 .....82 F6
Brookfields *HOR/CROF* WF4 .....218 F1
Brookfields Av *CLECK* BD19 .....149 G6
Brookfields Rd *LM/WK* BD12 .....148 F5
Brookfield St *MID* LS10 .....9 K5
 TOD OL14 .....140 E5
Brookfield Ter *CLECK* BD19 .....149 M8
 MID * LS10 .....9 K5
Brookfield Vw *CLECK* BD19 .....150 A5
Brookfoot Av *BIRK/DRI* BD11 .....150 C1
Brookfoot La *HIPP* HX3 .....170 A3
Brook Gdns *HOLM/MEL* HD9 .....234 F3
Brook Grain HI *BRIG* HD6 .....170 C6
Brook Hey Cl *WHIT* OL12 .....206 A3
Brookhill Av *AL/HA/HU* LS17 .....88 A2
Brookhill Cl *AL/HA/HU* LS17 .....88 A2
Brookhill Crs *AL/HA/HU* LS17 .....88 A2
Brookhill Dr *AL/HA/HU* LS17 .....88 A2
Brookhill Gv *AL/HA/HU* LS17 .....88 A2
Brook Hill La *STKB/PEN* S36 .....268 B3
Brookhill Rd *DOD/DAR* S75 .....241 K6
Brookhouse Gdns *IDLE* BD10 .....84 B6
Brook House La *STKB/PEN* S36 .....269 H8
Brooklands *HUDN* HD2 .....193 H1
Brooklands Av *GTL/HWG* HX4 .....190 D6
 SCFT LS14 .....111 H2
 WKFDW/WTN WF2 .....199 K7
Brooklands Cl *SCFT* LS14 .....111 G2
Brooklands Ct *OSS* WF5 .....197 H2
 SCFT LS14 .....111 H2
Brooklands Crs
 HOR/CROF WF4 .....222 F5
 SCFT LS14 .....111 G2
 YEA LS19 .....62 D8
Brooklands Dr *SCFT* LS14 .....111 G2
 YEA LS19 .....62 D8
Brooklands Garth *SCFT* LS14 .....111 G2
Brooklands La *ILK* LS29 .....61 J1
 SCFT LS14 .....111 H2
Brooklands Rd *AWLS/ASK* DN6 .....249 L7
 WKFDW/WTN WF2 .....199 K7
Brooklands Ter *SKP/WHF* * OL16 .....16 B3
Brookland St *WHIT* * OL16 .....228 D3
Brooklands Vw *SCFT* LS14 .....111 H2
Brooklands Wk *ILK* LS29 .....61 K1
Brooklands Wy *ILK* LS29 .....61 J1
Brook La *AL/HA/HU* LS17 .....44 B3
 LVSG WF15 .....171 L2
 MAR/SLWT HD7 .....212 F2
 MILN OL16 .....228 B3
Brooklyn Av *HUDE* HD5 .....193 H8
 LIT OL15 .....185 J7
 MILN OL16 .....206 F2
 WOR/ARM LS12 .....108 E7
Brooklyn Ct *CLECK* BD19 .....149 M6
Brooklyn Dr *CLECK* BD19 .....149 M6
Brooklyn PI *WOR/ARM* LS12 .....108 E7
Brooklyn Rd *CLECK* BD19 .....150 A6
Brooklyn St *AIRE* BD20 .....57 J3
 WOR/ARM LS12 .....108 E7
Brooklyn Ter *BRIG* HD6 .....170 A1
 WOR/ARM LS12 .....108 E7
Brook Rd *DEWS* WF13 .....173 K7
Brook Rw *GTL/HWG* * HX4 .....168 B7
Brookroyd Av *BRIG* HD6 .....148 D8
Brookroyd Gdns *BTLY* WF17 .....151 H6
Brookroyd La *BTLY* WF17 .....151 H6
Brooksbank *WKFDW/WTN* WF2 .....12 C3
Brooksbank Av *GTHN* BD7 .....126 A1
Brooksbank Dr
 MSTN/BAR LS15 .....111 J6
Brooksfield *HUDE* HD5 .....215 J7
Brookside *MAR/SLWT* HD7 .....212 C4
Brookside *AL/HA/HU* LS17 .....88 A1
 HBR HX7 .....143 G2
 HEM/SK/SE WF9 .....224 A7
 WBY S22 .....47 K6
Brookside Dr *BSLY* S70 .....261 M8
Brookside Fold *HWTH* BD22 .....100 E4

Brookside St *HEM/SK/SE* WF9 .....247 H3
Brooks Ter *CUL/QBY* BD13 .....125 K4
Brook St *CAS* WF10 .....158 E3
 DEWS WF13 .....173 H6
 ELL HX5 .....169 J8
 HBR HX7 .....143 J2
 HUD HD1 .....14 F5
 HUD HD1 .....214 D4
 HUDE HD5 .....15 L7
 ILK LS29 .....38 D3
 KGHY BD21 .....2 F8
 LIT OL15 .....207 L1
 LM/WK BD12 .....149 K2
 NORM WF6 .....178 B3
 OSS WF5 .....196 F1
 SKP/WHF BD23 .....16 E2
 WKFDE WF1 .....12 F1
Brooks Yd *DEWS* WF13 .....173 K7
 HUD HD1 .....14 F7
 HUDN HD2 .....171 J8
Brookvale *BSLYN/ROY* S71 .....261 M3
Brookway *FEA/AMT* * WF7 .....201 M3
Broombank *HUDN* HD2 .....191 M4
 KBTN HD8 .....257 H7
Broom Cl *BSLY* S70 .....261 M8
 DOD/DAR S75 .....242 C5
Broom Crs *MID* LS10 .....132 A7
Broomcroft *CLAY* BD14 .....125 K2
Broomcroft Rd *OSS* WF5 .....196 F2
Broom Cross *MID* LS10 .....132 A7
Broome Av *ECHL* BD2 .....105 G3
Broome Cl *NORM* WF6 .....178 C3
Broomer St *DEWS* WF13 .....173 G8
Broomfield *BHP/TINH* LS16 .....86 D2
 CLAY BD14 .....125 J3
 GTL/HWG HX4 .....168 F4
Broomfield Av *HIPP* HX3 .....168 D3
Broomfield Cl *BSLY* S70 .....260 D6
 KBTN HD8 .....217 L7
Broomfield Crs *HDGY* LS6 .....108 F2
Broom Field La *KBTN* HD8 .....217 K6
Broomfield PI *CLAY* BD13 .....125 J3
 HDGY LS6 .....108 F3
Broomfield Rd *HDGY* LS6 .....108 F3
 HUD HD1 .....191 M8
 HUDN HD2 .....192 C1
Broomfield Sq *ROCH* * OL11 .....228 B1
Broomfield St *CUL/QBY* BD13 .....125 J3
 HDGY * LS6 .....108 F3
 KGHY BD21 .....2 F4
Broomfield Ter *CLECK* BD19 .....149 K8
 HDGY LS6 .....108 F3
 HUD HD1 .....191 M7
 MILN OL16 .....229 K2
Broomfield Vw *HDGY* LS6 .....108 F3
Broom Gdns *MID* LS10 .....132 B7
Broom Garth *MID* LS10 .....132 B7
Broom Gv *MID* LS10 .....132 B8
Broom Hall Av *WKFDE* WF1 .....176 C4
Broom Hall Crs *WKFDE* WF1 .....176 C4
Broomhead St *DOD/DAR* S75 .....242 D6
Broomhey Av *KBTN* HD8 .....217 M8
Broomhill *CAS* WF10 .....158 C8
Broomhill Av *AL/HA/HU* LS17 .....87 M4
 KGHY BD21 .....2 C8
 KNOT WF11 .....182 D3
Broomhill Cl *HOLM/MEL* HD9 .....254 F5
 KNOT WF11 .....182 D3
Broomhill Crs *AL/HA/HU* LS17 .....87 M4
 KNOT WF11 .....182 D3
Broomhill Dr *AL/HA/HU* LS17 .....87 L5
 KNOT WF11 .....182 D3
Broomhill Gv *KGHY* BD21 .....2 D9
 KNOT WF11 .....182 D3
Broomhill PI *KNOT* WF11 .....182 D3
Broomhill Sq *KNOT* WF11 .....182 D3
Broomhill St *KGHY* * BD21 .....79 J2
Broomhill Wk *KGHY* BD21 .....2 D9
 KNOT WF11 .....182 D3
Broomhouse Cl *KBTN* HD8 .....257 J1
Broom Nook *MID* LS10 .....132 B7
Broom PI *MID* LS10 .....132 A7
Broomroyd *HUDN* HD3 .....191 H8
Broomsdale Rd *BTLY* WF17 .....174 A1
Broom St *BOW* BD4 .....128 A1
 CLECK BD19 .....149 K8
 KGHY BD21 .....3 H7
 MILN OL16 .....229 K2
Broom Ter *MID* LS10 .....132 B7
Broom Vw *MID* LS10 .....132 B7
Broomy Lea La
 HOLM/MEL HD9 .....236 D7
Broster Av *HWTH* BD22 .....2 B4
Brotherton Av *WKFDE* WF1 .....13 J1
Brougham Rd *HIPP* HX3 .....10 F1
 MAR/SLWT HD7 .....233 H2
Brougham St *HIPP* HX3 .....11 G1
 SKP/WHF BD23 .....16 C3
Broughton Av *BOW* BD4 .....127 K5
 OSM LS9 .....110 C4
Broughton Rd *HUDS* HD4 .....213 K3
 SKP/WHF BD23 .....16 A3
Broughton Ter
 PDSY/CALV LS28 .....107 G6
Brow Bottom La *LUD/ILL* HX2 .....123 K8
Browcliff *AIRE* BD20 .....36 A4
Brow Cl *BSLY* S70 .....261 H8
Browfield Vw *HWTH* BD22 .....79 G3
Browfoot *WHIT* BD18 .....82 F7
Browfoot Dr *LUD/ILL* HX2 .....145 M7
Brow Foot Gate La
 LUD/ILL HX2 .....145 M8
Browgate *BAIL* BD17 .....82 B2
Brow Grains Rd
 HOLM/MEL HD9 .....234 C5
Brow La *CLAY* BD14 .....125 H3
 HIPP HX3 .....125 M8
 HIPP HX3 .....147 G5

 HOLM/MEL HD9 .....254 F4
 KBTN HD8 .....239 M8
 LUD/ILL HX2 .....145 J4
Brown Av *BEE/HOL* LS11 .....131 G2
Brown Bank La *ILK* BD20 .....36 B3
Brown Bank Rd *LIT* OL15 .....207 H3
Brownberrie Av *HORS* LS18 .....85 L3
Brownberrie Crs *HORS* LS18 .....85 K3
Brownberrie Dr *HORS* LS18 .....85 K3
Brownberrie Gdns *HORS* LS18 .....85 K3
Brownberrie La *HORS* LS18 .....85 K3
Brownberrie Wk *HORS* LS18 .....85 L3
Brownberry Gv *HIPP* HX3 .....125 M7
Brown Birks St *TOD* OL14 .....140 C5
Brown Hill Av *OSM* LS9 .....110 C4
Brown Hill Cl *BIRK/DRI* BD11 .....128 C7
Brownhill Garth *BTLY* WF17 .....151 H5
Brown Hill La *COL* BB8 .....52 B7
 HBR HX7 .....142 A2
Brownhill La *HOLM/MEL* HD9 .....253 K5
Brownhill Rd *BTLY* WF17 .....151 H5
Brownhill Ter *OSM* LS9 .....110 C4
Browning Av *HIPP* * HX3 .....168 F3
Browning Cl *BSLYN/ROY* S71 .....261 K1
Browning Rd *HUDN* HD2 .....192 F3
Browning St *BFDE* BD3 .....5 L6
Brown La East *BEE/HOL* LS11 .....8 A6
Brown La West
 WOR/ARM LS12 .....131 G1
Brown Lee La *WIL/AL* BD15 .....102 C3
Brown Lodge St *LIT* OL15 .....207 H3
Brown PI *BEE/HOL* LS11 .....131 G2
Brown Rd *BEE/HOL* LS11 .....131 G2
Brownroyd Av *BSLYN/ROY* S71 .....243 L4
Brownroyd Hill Rd *WBSY* BD6 .....126 D5
Brownroyd Rd
 HOLM/MEL HD9 .....236 A2
Brownroyd St *GIR* BD8 .....104 D7
Brownroyd Wk *WBSY* BD6 .....126 E4
Browns Ct *AIRE* BD20 .....34 E1
Brown's Edge La
 STKB/PEN S36 .....269 J8
Brown's Edge Rd
 STKB/PEN S36 .....256 A6
Brownside Cl *MILN* OL16 .....206 E3
Brown's Knoll Rd *HUDS* HD4 .....237 H3
Brown's PI *BTLY* WF17 .....173 K2
Brown St *BTLY* WF17 .....173 K2
Brown St *KGHY* BD21 .....3 J3
 LIT OL15 .....207 J1
 MIRF WF14 .....194 B1
Brow Rd *HWTH* BD22 .....78 E8
Browsfield Rd *ILK* LS29 .....18 F6
Browsholme St *KGHY* * BD21 .....2 F7
Brow St *KGHY* BD21 .....3 J6
 ROCH 228 C2
Brow Top Rd *HWTH* BD22 .....79 G7
Brow Wood Crs *ECHL* BD2 .....105 G3
Brow Wood Ri *HIPP* HX3 .....125 M8
Brow Wood Rd *BTLY* WF17 .....151 K5
 HIPP HX3 .....125 M8
Browwood Ter *WBSY* BD6 .....126 B7
Bruce Av *BSLY* S70 .....261 H8
Bruce Gdns *WOR/ARM* LS12 .....109 G7
Bruce Lawn *WOR/ARM* LS12 .....109 G7
Bruce St *HFAX* HX1 .....10 B8
Brudenell Gv *HDGY* LS6 .....6 A3
Brudenell Mt *HDGY* LS6 .....6 A3
Brudenell Rd *HDGY* LS6 .....109 G3
Brudenell St *HDGY* LS6 .....6 A3
Brudenell Vw *HDGY* LS6 .....6 A3
Brunel Cl *HTON* BD9 .....104 C4
Brunel Ct *HIPP* HX3 .....146 D4
Brunel Rd *WKFDW/WTN* WF2 .....176 B1
Brunswick *HOR/CROF* WF4 .....218 A2
Brunswick Cl *BSLYN/ROY* S71 .....261 L3
Brunswick Ct *LDSU* LS2 .....7 J7
Brunswick Dr *DEWS* WF13 .....173 J5
Brunswick Gdns
 GFTH/SHER LS25 .....113 H7
 HFAX HX1 .....10 F6
Brunswick Gv *WKFDE* WF1 .....13 H3
Brunswick PI *IDLE* BD10 .....83 M7
Brunswick Rd *IDLE* BD10 .....83 M7
 PDSY/CALV LS28 .....107 G6
Brunswick Rw *LDSU* LS2 .....7 H4
Brunswick St *BGLY* BD16 .....81 K3
 BTLY * WF17 .....173 L1
 CUL/QBY BD13 .....80 A8
 CUL/QBY BD13 .....125 H5
 DEWS WF13 .....173 J5
 HBR HX7 .....143 H5
 HECK * WF16 .....172 F3
 HUD HD1 .....14 E6
 MILN OL16 .....206 C6
 MOR LS27 .....152 C1
 ROY/SHW OL2 .....229 K7
 WKFDE WF1 .....13 G4
Brunswick St Bungalows
 WKFDE WF1 .....13 H3
Brunswick Ter *LDSU* LS2 .....7 J7
Bruntcliffe Av *MOR* LS27 .....152 A1
Bruntcliffe Cl *MOR* LS27 .....152 B2
Bruntcliffe Dr *MOR* LS27 .....152 A1
Bruntcliffe La *MOR* LS27 .....152 A2
Bruntcliffe Rd *MOR* LS27 .....151 M2
Bruntcliffe Wy *MOR* LS27 .....152 A2
Brunthwaite Br *AIRE* BD20 .....36 C7
Brunthwaite Bridge La
 AIRE BD20 .....36 B7
Brunthwaite La *AIRE* BD20 .....36 C5
Brussels St *OSM* LS9 .....9 K1
Bryan Cl *CAS* WF10 .....157 J6
Bryan Rd *GTL/HWG* HX4 .....168 F8
 HUDW HD3 .....191 M6
Bryanstone Rd *BOW* BD4 .....127 M1
Bryan St *BRIG* HD6 .....170 C2
 PDSY/CALV LS28 .....106 F2
Bryan St North
 PDSY/CALV LS28 .....106 F2
Bryan Ter *HUDW* HD3 .....191 G8
Bryer St *DEWS* WF13 .....173 L5
Bryngate *RTHW* LS26 .....133 L8

Bryony Ct *EARD/LOFT* WF3 .....154 A1
Bubwith Gv *LUD/ILL* * HX2 .....146 A8
Buckden Ct *AIRE* BD20 .....36 A4
Buckden Rd *BSLY* S70 .....260 F4
 HUDW HD3 .....191 M6
Buckfast Ct *BOW* BD4 .....83 K7
Buckingham Av *HDGY* LS6 .....109 G2
Buckingham Ct
 BSLYN/ROY S71 .....243 K2
 WKFDE WF1 .....13 L7
Buckingham Crs *CLAY* BD14 .....125 M1
Buckingham Dr *HDGY* LS6 .....109 G3
 WKFDE WF1 .....13 L8
Buckingham Gv *HDGY* LS6 .....109 G2
Buckingham Mt *HDGY* LS6 .....109 G3
Buckingham Park Cl
 ROY/SHW OL2 .....229 K6
Buckingham Rd *HDGY* LS6 .....109 G3
Buckingham St *MILN* OL16 .....206 C6
Buckingham Wy
 BSLYN/ROY S71 .....243 K2
 KNOT WF11 .....159 M7
Buckland PI *HFAX* HX1 .....146 A8
Buck La *BAIL* BD17 .....83 H3
Buckle La *ILK* LS29 .....61 L2
 NORM WF6 .....178 C5
Buckley Brook St *WHIT* OL12 .....206 D4
Buckley Cha *MILN* OL16 .....229 L5
Buckley Cl *BSLY* S70 .....261 H6
Buckley Dr *UPML* OL3 .....230 E5
Buckley Farm La *WHIT* OL12 .....206 D3
Buckley Flds *WHIT* OL12 .....206 D4
Buckley Hill La *WHIT* OL16 .....229 G1
 WHIT OL12 .....206 D3
Buckley La *LUD/ILL* HX2 .....145 L4
 WHIT OL12 .....206 D3
Buckley Rd *WHIT* OL12 .....206 D4
Buckley St *MILN* OL16 .....206 C6
 ROY/SHW OL2 .....229 L7
Buckley Vw *TOD* OL14 .....141 J8
 WHIT OL12 .....206 D3
Buckley Wood Bottom
 TOD OL14 .....163 K1
Buck Mill La *IDLE* BD10 .....83 J3
Buck Pk *CUL/QBY* * BD13 .....102 A4
Buckrose St *HUD* HD1 .....14 F1
Buckrose Ter *HUDN* HD2 .....14 E1
Buck Stone Av *AL/HA/HU* LS17 .....87 H2
Buck Stone Cl *AL/HA/HU* LS17 .....87 J2
Buck Stone Crs *AL/HA/HU* LS17 .....87 H2
Buckstone Dr *YEA* LS19 .....84 C3
Buck Stone Gdns
 AL/HA/HU LS17 .....87 J2
Buckstone Garth *AIRE* BD20 .....58 F5
Buck Stone Gn *AL/HA/HU* LS17 .....87 H2
Buck Stone Gv *AL/HA/HU* LS17 .....87 H2
Buck Stone La *HWTH* BD22 .....55 G4
Buck Stone Mt *AL/HA/HU* LS17 .....87 J2
Buck Stone Ri *AL/HA/HU* LS17 .....87 H2
Buck Stone Rd *AL/HA/HU* LS17 .....87 H2
Buckstones Rd *OLD* OL1 .....230 A8
 ROY/SHW OL2 .....229 L5
Buck Stone Vw
 AL/HA/HU LS17 .....87 H2
Buck Stone Wy *AL/HA/HU* LS17 .....87 H2
Buck St *BFDE* BD3 .....5 K8
 COL BB8 .....74 A2
 CUL/QBY BD13 .....102 A6
Buckthorne Cl
 EARD/LOFT WF3 .....153 M6
Buckthorne Ct
 EARD/LOFT WF3 .....153 M6
Buckthorne Dr
 EARD/LOFT WF3 .....153 M6
Buckthorne Fold
 EARD/LOFT * WF3 .....153 M6
Buckton Cl *BEE/HOL* * LS11 .....8 C8
Buckton Mt *BEE/HOL* LS11 .....8 C8
Buckton Vw *BEE/HOL* LS11 .....8 C8
Bude Ct *BSLYN/ROY* S71 .....261 L3
Bude Rd *BEE/HOL* LS11 .....131 K4
 WBOW BD5 .....127 H5
Buersil Av *MILN* OL16 .....228 D2
Buersil St *MILN* OL16 .....228 D3
Bula Cl *GFTH/SHER* LS25 .....135 K4
Bulay Rd *HUD* HD1 .....214 B2
Bullace Trees La *LVSG* WF15 .....171 M3
Bull Close La *HFAX* HX1 .....10 F7
Bullcroft Cl *AWLS/ASK* DN6 .....249 L5
Bullenshaw Rd
 HEM/SK/SE WF9 .....223 M8
Bullenshaw Vls
 HEM/SK/SE * WF9 .....224 C8
Buller Cl *OSM* LS9 .....110 D5
Buller Ct *OSM* LS9 .....110 E5
Buller Gv *OSM* LS9 .....110 D5
Buller St *BOW* BD4 .....127 L1
 RTHW LS26 .....133 L8
Bullerthorpe La *RTHW* LS26 .....134 A6
The Bullfield *BGLY* BD16 .....80 D5
Bullfields Cl *EARL* WF12 .....196 A4
Bull Gn *HFAX* HX1 .....11 G7
Bull Green Rd *HUDW* HD3 .....191 H8
Bull Haw La *DOD/DAR* S75 .....259 H6
Bullhouse La *STKB/PEN* S36 .....269 L4
Bulla La *HEM/SK/SE* WF9 .....246 A4
 HOR/CROF 220 B1
Bullough La *RTHW* LS26 .....133 H7
Bull Ring *WKFDE* * WF1 .....12 E2
Bull Royd Av *GIR* BD8 .....104 A6
Bull Royd Crs *GIR* BD8 .....104 A6
Bull Royd Dr *GIR* BD8 .....104 A6
Bull Royd La *GIR* BD8 .....104 A6
Bullstyle Rd *PONT* WF8 .....180 E8
Bullytree La *GFTH/SHER* LS25 .....137 L2
Bulwer St *MILN* OL16 .....206 C6
Bundria Ct *AIRE* BD20 .....104 E4
The Bungalows
 FEA/AMT * WF7 .....201 M2
 FEA/AMT * WF7 .....202 A8
 HIPP * HX3 .....169 G4
 KBTN HD8 .....240 D7
 LUD/ILL * HX2 .....145 M5
 NORM WF6 .....178 C1
 OSS * WF5 .....174 E8
 RPDN/SBR * HX6 .....167 J3
Bungalow Rd *AIRE* BD20 .....34 D8
Bunkers HI *GFTH/SHER* LS25 .....114 A1

HOLM/MEL HD9 254 C1
SKP/WHF BD23 16 C2
WKFDW/WTN WF2 176 B4
Bunker's Hill La HWTH BD22 78 F1
Bunkers La BTLY WF17 173 H2
Bunny Pk HUDS HD4 213 M3
Bunting Dr CUL/QBY BD13 125 L4
Bunyan St WHIT OL12 206 B5
Burbeary Rd HUDS HD4 214 A3
Burberry Cl BOW BD4 127 L6
Burchall Fld MILN OL16 206 D7
Burchett Gv HDGY LS6 6 D1
Burchett Pl HDGY LS6 6 D1
Burchett Ter HDGY LS6 6 D1
Burcote Dr HUDW HD3 190 D5
Burdale Pl GTHN BD7 104 D8
Burdett Ter BULY LS4 108 E4
Burdock Wy HFAX HX1 10 F6
Burfitts Rd HUDW HD3 191 K7
Burghley Ms EARD/LOFT WF3 153 M3
Burgh Mill Gdns DEWS WF13 173 J7
Burgh Mill La DEWS WF13 173 H7
Burghwallis La AWLS/ASK DN6 249 L1
Burghwallis Rd AWLS/ASK DN6 227 L7
Burkill St WKFDE WF1 198 F4
Burking Rd DEWS WF13 173 K6
Burlees La HBR HX7 143 L3
Burleigh Ct BSLY S70 261 H5
Burleigh St BSLY S70 261 H5
HFAX HX1 10 B9
Burley Bank La
HOLM/MEL HD9 253 G8
Burley Cl GFTH/SHER LS25 138 B2
Burley Ct AIRE BD20 56 E1
Burley Hill Crs BULY LS4 108 D3
Burley Hill Dr BULY LS4 108 D3
Burley La HORS LS18 85 K7
ILK LS29 61 H1
Burley Lodge Pl HDGY * LS6 109 G5
Burley Lodge Rd HDGY LS6 109 G4
Burley Lodge Ter HDGY LS6 109 G4
Burley Ms AIRE BD20 56 E1
Burley Rd BULY LS4 108 E3
ILK LS29 40 C8
Burley St BVRD LS3 6 B8
ECHL BD2 104 F2
ELL HX5 169 H8
Burley Wk BTLY WF17 173 K1
Burley Wood Crs BULY LS4 108 D3
Burley Wood La BULY LS4 108 E3
Burley Wood Mt BULY LS4 108 D4
Burley Wood Vw BULY LS4 108 E3
Burlington Ar BSLY S70 261 H5
Burlington Av BFDE BD3 106 A5
Burlington Pl BEE/HOL LS11 131 K4
Burlington Rd BEE/HOL LS11 131 K4
Burlington St GIR BD8 4 D2
HFAX HX1 10 B5
ROCH OL11 228 C2
Burmantofts St OSM LS9 7 L8
Burn Bridge La PBR HG3 26 E4
Burn Bridge Ov PBR HG3 26 D2
Burn Bridge Rd PBR HG3 26 D2
Burned Gv HIPP HX3 125 L7
Burned Rd HIPP HX3 125 M7
Burneston Gdns WBSY BD6 126 A6
Burnet Cl MILN OL16 206 E7
Burnett Av WBOW BD5 126 F3
Burnett Pl WBOW BD5 126 F3
Burnett Ri CUL/QBY BD13 124 E6
Burnett St BFD BD1 5 H6
Burnham Av BOW BD4 127 K5
DOD/DAR S75 242 D5
Burnham Ct WBY LS22 29 L8
Burnham Rd GFTH/SHER LS25 135 H1
Burnhill La HEM/SK/SE WF9 225 H1
Burniston Cl WIL/AL BD15 102 E2
Burniston Dr HUDW HD3 191 J6
Burnlee Rd HOLM/MEL HD9 254 A2
Burnley Rd COL BB8 74 D5
HBR HX7 143 K4
RPDN/SBR HX6 167 K1
TOD OL14 140 A4
Burnleys Ct RTHW LS26 156 F5
Burnleys Dr RTHW LS26 156 F5
Burnleys Ms RTHW LS26 156 F6
Burnleys Vw RTHW LS26 156 F5
Burnleyville CLECK BD19 150 D5
Burnley Wy BRFD/BLYE BB10 118 A7
HBR HX7 118 F1
TOD OL14 140 D1
Burn Pl BSLYN/ROY S71 243 G7
Burn Rd HUDW HD3 191 L4
Burnroyd Av AIRE BD20 34 F8
Burnsall Av BTLY WF17 173 J1
Burnsall Ct WOR/ARM LS12 108 D6
Burnsall Cft WOR/ARM LS12 108 D6
Burnsall Gdns WOR/ARM LS12 108 D6
Burnsall Gra WOR/ARM LS12 108 D6
Burnsall Gv BSLY S70 261 M8
Burnsall Ms AIRE BD20 36 A4
Burnsall Rd BFDE BD3 5 M4
BRIG HD6 169 M6
BTLY WF17 173 J1
LVSG WF15 172 B2
Burns Av HEM/SK/SE WF9 246 B5
Burns Ct BTLY WF17 150 F4
Burnsdale WIL/AL BD15 103 J3
Burnshaw Ms EARD/LOFT WF3 153 L3
Burns Hl ILK LS29 19 G6
Burnside ROY/SHW OL2 229 M6
Burnside Av SKP/WHF BD23 16 B4
Burnside Cl BTLY WF17 151 J5
Burnside Crs SKP/WHF BD23 16 B4
Burnside Dr HOLM/MEL HD9 254 A2
Burnside Rd MILN OL16 206 E8
Burns St HIPP HX3 146 C2
Burns Wy BSPA/BRAM LS23 48 F8
Burnt Acres La TOD OL14 142 D6
Burnt Edge La HBR HX7 141 M2
Burnt House Cl TOD OL14 141 L8
Burnt Plats La MAR/SLWT HD7 211 J4
Burnt Side Rd WOR/ARM LS12 129 L4
Burntwood Av
HEM/SK/SE WF9 246 E4
Burntwood Bank
HEM/SK/SE WF9 245 M1
Burnt Wood Crs
HEM/SK/SE WF9 246 E5
Burntwood Dr
HEM/SK/SE WF9 246 D4
Burntwood Gv
HEM/SK/SE WF9 246 E5
Burnt Wood La CUD/GR S72 246 A5
Burntwood Rd CUD/GR S72 245 K8
Burnup Gv CLECK BD19 149 L7
Burnwells Av IDLE BD10 83 J4
Burrage St BGLY BD16 81 H3
Burras Av OT LS21 41 H7
Burras Dr OT LS21 41 H7
Burras La OT LS21 41 H7
Burras Rd BOW BD4 127 K4
Burrel Cl WBY LS22 48 C1
Burrell St WKFDE WF1 13 H3
The Burrows BTLY WF17 151 H7
Burrow St WBOW BD5 4 E8
Burr Tree Dr MSTN/BAR LS15 111 M7
Burr Tree Garth
MSTN/BAR LS15 111 M7
Burr Tree V MSTN/BAR * LS15 111 M7
Burrwood Wy GTL/HWG HX4 190 D1
Burton Acres La KBTN HD8 216 A7
Burton Acres Ms KBTN HD8 216 A6
Burton Acres Wy KBTN HD8 216 A7
Burton Av BEE/HOL LS11 9 G9
BSLYN/ROY S71 261 M2
Burton Bank Rd
BSLYN/ROY S71 261 J3
Burton Common La
GFTH/SHER LS25 160 C2
Burton Crs BSLYN/ROY S71 262 A1
HDGY LS6 86 F8
Burton Ms AL/HA/HU LS17 87 M1
Burton Rd BEE/HOL LS11 9 G9
BSLYN/ROY S71 261 J3
Burton Rw BEE/HOL LS11 9 H8
Burton Royd La KBTN HD8 216 D7
Burtons Ar LDS LS1 9 G1
Burton St BEE/HOL LS11 9 G8
BOW BD4 127 J2
BSLYN/ROY S71 261 G3
HEM/SK/SE WF9 247 G3
KGHY BD21 57 K5
LUD/ILL HX2 146 C1
PDSY/CALV LS28 106 F3
WKFDE WF1 12 D1
Burton Ter BEE/HOL LS11 131 L3
BSLY S70 261 K6
Burton Wy OSM LS9 110 C5
Burwood Rd HUDW HD3 191 K6
Busely Ct MOR LS27 152 B1
Busfield St BGLY BD16 81 H3
BOW BD4 127 K3
Bushill Fold CUL/QBY BD13 124 E4
Bush St HEM/SK/SE WF9 223 M8
Busker La KBTN HD8 239 M5
Busk La TAD LS24 95 G7
Buslingthorpe Gn CHAL LS7 7 G2
Buslingthorpe La CHAL LS7 7 H2
Bussey Ct HDGY LS6 6 D2
Busy La SHPY BD18 83 G5
Butcher Hl BHP/TINH LS16 86 B6
Butcher Hill Station Rd
HEM/SK/SE WF9 224 A6
Butcher La RTHW LS26 155 G1
Butcher St BEE/HOL LS11 8 E3
BFD BD1 4 C7
Bute Av BRIG HD6 170 C1
Bute St SHPY BD18 104 F2
Butler La BAIL BD17 82 F2
Butler St BFDE BD3 5 J4
Butler St East BFDE BD3 5 K4
Butler St West BFDE BD3 5 J4
Butterbowl Dr WOR/ARM LS12 130 A1
Butterbowl Gdns
WOR/ARM LS12 130 B1
Butterbowl Garth
WOR/ARM LS12 130 A1
Butterbowl Gv WOR/ARM LS12 130 A1
Butterbowl Lawn
WOR/ARM LS12 130 A1
Butterbowl Mt WOR/ARM LS12 130 B1
Butterbowl Rd WOR/ARM LS12 130 B1
Buttercross AWLS/ASK DN6 249 J5
Buttercross Cl AWLS/ASK DN6 249 J4
Buttercross Dr CUD/GR S72 263 L6
Buttercup Cl HEM/SK/SE WF9 225 H7
Butterfield Homes BAIL * BD17 82 E2
BGLY * BD16 81 K8
Butterfield St OSM LS9 110 B7
Butterley Dr BSLY * S70 261 M8
Butterley La HOLM/MEL HD9 255 H1
Butterleys DOD/DAR S75 260 C7
Butterley St MID LS10 9 H5
Buttermeade Cl WBSY BD6 126 C7
Buttermere Av COL BB8 52 B8
WBY LS22 29 L8
Buttermere Cl AWLS/ASK DN6 249 K5
Buttermere Cft
WKFDW/WTN WF2 199 J8
Buttermere Dr HUDE HD5 15 L6
Buttermere Gv ROY/SHW OL2 228 F7
Buttermere Wy
BSLYN/ROY * S71 262 D6
Butternab Rdg HUDS HD4 213 M6
Butternab Rd HUDS HD4 213 L5
Buttershaw Dr WBSY BD6 126 A6
Buttershaw La LVSG WF15 171 K1
WBSY BD6 126 D7
Butterton Cl DOD/DAR S75 242 E5
Butterwick Gdns WBY LS22 47 L1
Butterwood Cl HUDS HD4 213 M6
Butterworth End La
RPDN/SBR HX6 167 J7
Butterworth Hall MILN OL16 229 J1
Butterworth Hl HUDW HD3 190 C7
Butterworth La
RPDN/SBR HX6 167 G5
Butterworth St LIT OL15 207 J1
Butt Hedge RYKW YO26 33 M4
Butt Hl GFTH/SHER LS25 135 J5
Buttholme Ga WBSY BD6 126 B6
Butt La HOLM/MEL HD9 255 G4
HWTH BD22 78 E7
IDLE BD10 83 K6
WOR/ARM LS12 107 M8
Button Hole ROY/SHW OL2 229 M7
Button Pk PONT WF8 180 E7
Buttress La LUD/ILL HX2 145 G5
Butt Rw WOR/ARM LS12 108 A8
The Butts PONT WF8 180 F5
The Butts Av MILN * OL16 206 B7
Butts Bottom HBR HX7 143 J5
Butts Cl HUDS HD4 237 G1
Butts Ct LDS LS1 7 G9
Butts Garth SCFT LS14 90 B1
Butts Green La LUD/ILL HX2 145 H7
Butts Green Rd LUD/ILL HX2 145 H7
Butts Hl CLECK BD19 150 C6
Butts La GFTH/SHER LS25 137 L6
HOR/CROF WF4 196 D7
TOD OL14 141 M5
Butts Mt WOR/ARM LS12 108 F7
Butts Rd HUDS HD4 215 G8
Butts Wy HUDS HD4 215 G8
Butts Yd CLECK BD19 149 M7
Buxton Av HTON * BD9 104 E2
Buxton Crs MILN OL16 228 D2
Buxton La HTON BD9 104 E2
Buxton Pl WKFDE WF1 176 D6
Buxton Rd BSLYN/ROY S71 243 J7
Buxton St HIPP HX3 10 C1
HTON BD9 104 D4
KGHY BD21 3 J4
Buxton Wy HIPP HX3 146 B3
HUD * HD1 14 F8
Byeway GSLY LS20 61 L5
Byland LUD/ILL HX2 123 M8
Byland Cl BSPA/BRAM LS23 48 E7
Byland Gv WIL/AL BD15 103 H4
Byland Wy BSLYN/ROY S71 261 L4
Byram Ar HUD * HD1 14 F6
Byram Park Av KNOT WF11 160 A6
Byram Park Rd KNOT WF11 160 A6
Byram St HUD HD1 14 F6
Byrl St KGHY BD21 3 H2
Byrne Cl DOD/DAR S75 260 A2
Byron Av AWLS/ASK DN6 227 L5
RPDN/SBR * HX6 167 K1
Byron Dr BSLYN/ROY S71 261 K2
Byron Gv DEWS WF13 173 G4
EARD/LOFT WF3 155 G8
Byron Ms BGLY BD16 81 J1
Byron Rd COL BB8 74 C1
Byron St BFDE BD3 5 L4
HFAX HX1 10 A5
LDSU LS2 7 J7
RPDN/SBR HX6 167 K1
SKP/WHF BD23 16 C3
TOD OL14 163 K1
The Byways PONT WF8 180 F8
Bywell Cl EARL WF12 174 B5
Bywell Rd EARL WF12 174 B5

C

Cabbage Hl WOR/ARM LS12 108 C8
Cabin Rd OT LS21 63 K1
Cad Beeston Ms BEE/HOL * LS11 8 C9
Cadney Cft HFAX HX1 11 G7
Cadogan Av HUDW HD3 191 K6
Cadwell Cl CUD/GR S72 244 E6
Caenarvon Cl BTLY WF17 151 J5
Caernarvon Av
GFTH/SHER LS25 113 K7
Caesar St ROCH OL11 228 C4
Cain Cl OSM LS9 110 B7
Cain La HIPP HX3 169 J2
Cairn Cl AIRE BD20 36 A4
Cairns Cl ECHL BD2 105 H3
Caister Cl BTLY WF17 151 H4
Caister Gv KGHY * BD21 79 J2
Caister St KGHY BD21 79 K2
Caister Wy KGHY BD21 79 K2
Caistor Av BSLY S70 260 E7
Calcaria Crs TAD LS24 71 K4
Calcaria Rd TAD LS24 71 K4
Calde Ct LM/WK BD12 127 G8
Caldene Av HBR HX7 143 M5
LM/WK BD12 127 G8
Calder Av BSLYN/ROY S71 244 A3
LIT OL15 185 J7
LUD/ILL HX2 168 B1
Calder Bank Rd EARL WF12 173 K8
Calder Banks CUL/QBY BD13 125 J5
Calderbrook Rd LIT OL15 185 K6
Caldercliffe Rd HUDS HD4 214 B5
Calder Cl OSS WF5 196 E1
Calder Crs BSLY S70 261 M7
Caldercroft ELL HX5 169 J8
Calderdale Wy BRIG HD6 170 E1
ELL HX5 169 G7
ELL HX5 191 K2
GTL/HWG HX4 168 C6
HBR HX7 164 F3
HBR HX7 165 G3
HBR HX7 165 L3
HIPP HX3 147 J1
Calder Dr HUDS HD4 214 B6
Calder Edge TOD * OL14 142 C7
Calder Gv HBR HX7 144 A5
ROY/SHW OL2 229 J6
Calder Island Wy
WKFDW/WTN WF2 198 D4
Calder Rd DEWS WF13 195 G1
MIRF WF14 194 C3
Calderstone Av WBSY BD6 125 M6
Calderstone Ct
HOR/CROF WF4 196 C7
Calder St BRIG HD6 170 E5
CAS WF10 157 K6
GTL/HWG HX4 168 F7
MILN OL16 206 D4
TOD OL14 163 K1
WKFDE WF1 12 F7
Calder Ter HBR * HX7 143 H3
HIPP HX3 168 C5
Caldervale BSLYN/ROY S71 244 A2
Calder Vale Rd HOR/CROF WF4 197 L6
WKFDE WF1 13 H4
Calder Vw BRIG HD6 170 B5
HOR/CROF WF4 220 A1
OSS WF5 196 D1
Calder Wy AIRE BD20 36 A6
Caldicott Cl TOD OL14 163 H3
Caledonia Ct
WKFDW/WTN WF2 175 K4
Caledonian Rd EARL WF12 173 L8
Caledonia Rd BTLY WF17 173 M1
KGHY BD21 3 H2
Caledonia St WBOW BD5 4 F9
Calf Hey LIT OL15 185 H8
Calf Hey La STKB/PEN S36 255 M7
Calf Hey North ROCH OL11 228 C2
Calf Hey Rd ROY/SHW OL2 229 M6
Calf Hey South ROCH OL11 228 C2
Calf Hill Rd HOLM/MEL HD9 236 D6
Calgary Crs EARD/LOFT WF3 153 H7
Calgary Pl CHAL LS7 87 M8
California Crs BSLY S70 261 G7
California Dr CAS WF10 178 F1
HOR/CROF WF4 197 L5
TOD OL14 163 J3
California Gdns BSLY S70 261 H6
California La CLECK BD19 150 D7
California Ms MOR LS27 130 D8
California St BSLY S70 261 G7
MOR * LS27 152 D2
California Ter BSLY S70 261 G7
Calliards Rd MILN OL16 207 G2
Callis La STKB/PEN S36 271 G5
Callis Wy STKB/PEN S36 270 F4
Call La LDS LS1 9 H1
The Calls LDSU LS2 9 J1
Calmlands Rd HOLM/MEL HD9 234 F5
Calpin Cl IDLE * BD10 83 K6
Calton Gv KGHY BD21 58 B8
Calton St HUD HD1 15 G3
KGHY BD21 2 E8
Calver Av HWTH BD22 2 B3
Calver Gv KGHY BD21 2 B3
Calverley Av BFDE BD3 105 M6
BRAM LS13 107 K3
Calverley Ct BRAM LS13 107 K3
RTHW LS26 155 K1
Calverley Cutting IDLE BD10 84 B6
Calverley Dr BRAM LS13 107 K3
Calverley Gdns BRAM LS13 107 J2
Calverley Garth BRAM LS13 107 K3
Calverley Green Rd
NORM WF6 178 B3
Calverley Gv BRAM LS13 107 K3
Calverley La BRAM LS13 107 J3
HORS LS18 85 G7
PDSY/CALV LS28 84 E8
Calverley Moor Av
PDSY/CALV LS28 106 C5
Calverley Rd RTHW LS26 155 L1
Calverley St LDS LS1 6 F7
Calverley Ter BRAM LS13 107 K3
Calverley Wy WHIT OL12 206 A2
Calver Rd HWTH BD22 2 B4
Calversyke St HWTH BD22 2 C5
Calvert Cl GFTH/SHER LS25 135 J3
Calverts Wk OSS WF5 197 H2
Calvey Orch CUD/GR S72 244 E7
Camargue Fold ECHL BD2 105 H2
Camberley Cl PDSY/CALV LS28 107 G8
Camberley Mt BOW BD4 128 A2
Camberley St BEE/HOL * LS11 131 L3
Camberley Wy
PDSY/CALV LS28 107 G8
Camborne Dr HUDN HD2 192 B3
Camborne Rd HUDN HD2 192 B3
Camborne Wy BSLYN/ROY S71 261 K3
HWTH BD22 79 G1
Cambourne Cl AWLS/ASK DN6 249 K8
Cambrian Bar LM/WK BD12 126 D8
Cambrian Dr MILN OL16 207 J8
Cambrian St BEE/HOL LS11 8 D7
Cambrian Ter BEE/HOL LS11 8 D7
Cambridge Cl MOR LS27 152 D1
Cambridge Ct MOR LS27 152 D1
Cambridge Crs HOR/CROF WF4 199 L4
Cambridge Dr BRAM LS13 107 K3
OT LS21 41 K7
Cambridge Gdns BRAM LS13 107 K3
Cambridge Gv
GFTH/SHER LS25 135 J5
OT LS21 41 K7
Cambridge Pl BFDE BD3 5 H3
CUL/QBY BD13 125 G5
Cambridge Rd BTLY WF17 150 F5
CHAL LS7 6 F3
HUD HD1 14 E4
Cambridge St BTLY WF17 173 L1
CAS WF10 157 M7
CLAY * BD14 125 K2
CUL/QBY BD13 125 H5
GTHN BD7 126 D2
HBR HX7 143 H3
HECK WF16 173 G3
HEM/SK/SE WF9 247 G3
NORM WF6 178 C5
OT LS21 41 J7
TOD OL14 163 K1
WKFDW/WTN WF2 198 B1
Cambridge Wy OT LS21 41 K7
Camden Rd CAS WF10 158 F6
Camden Ter GIR BD8 4 C2
Camellia Cl WKFDW/WTN WF2 197 M3
Camellia Ct SHPY BD18 104 F1
Camellia Mt GTHN BD7 104 A8
Cameron Av LM/WK BD12 148 D5
Cameron Ct ROY/SHW OL2 228 F8
Cameronian Ct KGHY BD21 3 H5
Camilla Ct EARL WF12 174 B7
Cam La BRIG HD6 170 F3
Camm La MIRF WF14 172 D8
Camm St BRIG HD6 170 C3
Campbell St AIRE BD20 34 F7
CUL/QBY BD13 125 H5
KGHY BD21 3 G4
WHIT * OL12 206 A4
Campden Rd HBR HX7 143 G2
Campinot V MAR/SLWT HD7 212 B4
Campion Cl PONT WF8 180 F7
Camp Mt PONT WF8 180 D6
Camp Ri PONT WF8 180 D6
Camp Rd BHP/TINH LS16 63 M5
HEM/SK/SE WF9 246 B5
Campsall Balk AWLS/ASK DN6 227 M4
Campsall Hall Rd
AWLS/ASK DN6 227 M5
Campsall Park Rd
AWLS/ASK DN6 227 M5
Campsall Vw AWLS/ASK * DN6 227 L3
Campsmount AWLS/ASK DN6 227 L6
Campus Rd GTHN BD7 4 A7
Camroyd St DEWS WF13 173 M5
Canada Crs YEA LS19 84 E2
Canada Dr YEA LS19 84 E1
Canada Rd YEA LS19 84 E1
Canada St BSLY S70 261 G7
Canada Ter YEA LS19 84 E2
Canal Ct EARD/LOFT * WF3 154 F8
Canal La AIRE BD20 36 C7
EARD/LOFT WF3 154 F8
Canal Pl WOR/ARM LS12 8 B1
Canal Rd AIRE BD20 58 A4
BFDE BD3 5 G3
BGLY BD16 81 H1
BRAM LS13 107 G1
ECHL BD2 104 E2
RPDN/SBR HX6 168 A2
WOR/ARM LS12 108 F6
Canal St BRIG HD6 170 D4
BSLYN/ROY S71 261 H3
HIPP HX3 11 K8
HUD HD1 15 J2
LIT OL15 207 K1
ROCH OL11 228 C1
SKP/WHF BD23 16 B2
WOR/ARM LS12 109 G6
Canal Wk EARD/LOFT WF3 155 H8
Canal Whf BEE/HOL LS11 8 E2
Canal Yd SKP/WHF BD23 16 B2
Canary Dr BGLY BD16 81 L2
Canary St CLECK BD19 149 M6
Canberra Cl HWTH BD22 79 H6
Canberra Dr HWTH BD22 79 H6
Canby Gv HUDE HD5 215 K1
Canby La PBR HG3 28 E3
Cancel St MID LS10 9 J6
Canford Dr WIL/AL BD15 103 K5
Canford Gv WIL/AL BD15 103 L5
Canford Rd WIL/AL BD15 103 K5
Canker La HIPP HX3 146 C3
HUD HD1 15 K1
Canning Av WKFDW/WTN WF2 175 M6
Cannon Gv HECK WF16 173 G1
Cannon Hall Cl BRIG HD6 170 F4
Cannon Hall Dr BRIG HD6 170 F4
Cannon Mill La GTHN BD7 126 C2
Cannon St BGLY BD16 81 J4
CAS WF10 158 A8
HFAX * HX1 10 B9
TOD OL14 163 J3
Cannon Wy DOD/DAR S75 260 B1
EARL WF12 173 L7
Canonbury Ter BEE/HOL LS11 131 G3
Canon Flynn Ct MILN OL16 206 E7
Canon St MILN OL16 206 D4
Canons Wy BSLYN/ROY S71 261 L3
Canterbury Av WBOW BD5 126 E3
Canterbury Ct PONT WF8 181 G3
Canterbury Crs HIPP HX3 10 E1
Canterbury Dr HDGY LS6 108 E2
Canterbury Rd EARL WF12 174 B5
HDGY LS6 108 E2
The Canter MID LS10 153 M3
Capel Ct PDSY/CALV LS28 84 D8
Capel St BRIG HD6 170 C5
PDSY/CALV LS28 84 D8
Capesthorne Dr ROY/SHW OL2 229 H7
Cape St BFD BD1 4 F3
Capitol Pde HDGY LS6 87 G7
Capri Ct WMB/DAR S73 263 G8
Caprington Ct NORM WF6 178 F5
Captain St BFD BD1 5 G5
Carberry Pl HDGY LS6 109 G4
Carberry Rd HDGY LS6 109 G4
Carberry Ter HDGY LS6 109 G4
Carbis Cl BSLYN/ROY S71 261 K3
Cardan Dr ILK LS29 39 G2
Carden Av MSTN/BAR LS15 111 G6
Carden Rd BOW BD4 128 A1
Cardigan Av MOR LS27 152 C4
Cardigan Cl BTLY WF17 174 A1
Cardigan Ct HDGY LS6 109 G2
Cardigan Fields Rd BULY LS4 108 E5
Cardigan La BULY LS4 108 F4
OSS WF5 197 H3
Cardigan St CUL/QBY BD13 125 G5
WHIT OL12 206 A3
Cardigan Ter EARD/LOFT WF3 154 A6
WKFDE WF1 12 D1
Cardinal Av BEE/HOL LS11 131 H6
Cardinal Cl GFTH/SHER LS25 116 B6
HOLM/MEL HD9 235 G4
Cardinal Crs BEE/HOL LS11 131 H6
Cardinal Gdns BEE/HOL LS11 131 G6
Cardinal Gv BEE/HOL LS11 131 G6
Cardinal Rd BEE/HOL LS11 131 H6
Cardinal Sq BEE/HOL LS11 131 G5
Cardinal Wk BEE/HOL LS11 131 G5
Cardwell Ter EARL WF12 173 L8
Carey Av BSLYN/ROY S71 261 J5
Carforth St HUD HD1 15 H9
Carisbrooke Crs WBSY BD6 126 D6
Carisbrooke La
GFTH/SHER LS25 113 K6
Cariss St MID LS10 9 K9
Cark Rd KGHY BD21 3 G2
Carlby Gv HWTH BD22 2 D6
Carlby St HWTH BD22 2 D6
Carleton Av SKP/WHF BD23 16 A3
Carleton Br SKP/WHF BD23 16 A5
Carleton Cl BSPA/BRAM LS23 48 D6
PONT WF8 180 F7
Carleton Crest PONT WF8 181 G8
Carleton Dr BSPA/BRAM LS23 48 D7
Carleton Ga PONT WF8 180 E8
Carleton Gln PONT WF8 180 F7
Carleton Green Cl PONT WF8 181 G8
Carleton New Rd
SKP/WHF BD23 16 A3

Carleton Park Av *PONT* WF8 ....180 F7
Carleton Park Rd *PONT* WF8 ...180 F8
Carleton Rd *PONT* WF8 ....180 F7
PONT WF8 ....203 J2
SKP/WHF BD23 ....16 A4
Carleton St *KGHY* BD21 ....57 L5
SKP/WHF BD23 ....16 B3
Carleton Vw *PONT* WF8 ....180 F8
Carlile St *HOLM/MEL* HD4 ....235 G4
Carling Cl *GTHN* BD7 ....126 A4
Carlinghow Hi *BTLY* WF17 ......151 K7
Carlinghow La *BTLY* WF17 ....151 K7
Carlisle Av *YEA* LS19 ....62 E8
Carlisle Cl *DEWS* WF13 ....173 L4
Carlisle Dr *PDSY/CALV* LS28 ...106 F8
Carlisle Gv *PDSY/CALV* LS28 ...106 F8
Carlisle Pl *GIR* BD8 ....4 A1
Carlisle Rd *GIR* BD8 ....104 D5
MID LS10 ....9 K4
PDSY/CALV LS28 ....106 F8
Carlisle St *GIR* BD8 ....4 A1
KGHY BD21 ....3 K5
LUD/ILL HX2 ....146 A6
PDSY/CALV LS28 ....106 A5
WHIT OL12 ....206 A3
Carlisle Ter *GIR* BD8 ....4 B1
Carlton Ap *WBY* LS22 ....29 L8
Carlton Av *BTLY* WF17 ....173 K3
CAS WF10 ....158 B7
PDSY/CALV LS28 ....107 G7
SHPY BD18 ....82 B6
Carlton Carr *CHAL* LS7 ....7 G5
Carlton Cl *CHAL* LS7 ....7 G5
HEM/SK/SE WF9 ....223 H5
NORM WF6 ....178 D4
Carlton Ct *OSS* WF5 ....174 F8
WOR/ARM LS12 ....131 G2
Carlton Cft *CHAL* LS7 ....7 H4
WKFDW/WTN WF2 ....198 F8
Carlton Dr *BAIL* BD17 ....82 E2
GFTH/SHER LS25 ....135 H1
GSLY LS20 ....62 B4
HTON BD9 ....104 C2
Carlton Gdns *CHAL* LS7 ....7 H5
HEM/SK/SE WF9 ....247 H5
NORM WF6 ....178 E4
Carlton Garth *AL/HA/HU* LS17 ...88 C1
CHAL LS7 ....7 G5
Carlton Ga *CHAL* LS7 ....7 G5
Carlton Gv *CHAL* LS7 ....7 G5
ELL HX5 ....169 K7
SHPY BD18 ....104 D1
WBOW BD5 ....126 F3
Carlton Hi *CHAL* LS7 ....7 G5
Carlton House Ter *HFAX* HX1 ....10 D9
Carlton La *EARD/LOFT* WF3 ....154 E5
GSLY LS20 ....62 B4
Carlton Moor Ms
   EARD/LOFT WF3 ....154 B1
Carlton Mt *YEA* LS19 ....62 E6
Carlton Pl *CHAL* LS7 ....7 G7
HFAX HX1 ....11 G7
PDSY/CALV LS28 ....107 G7
Carlton Ri *CHAL* LS7 ....7 G5
PDSY/CALV LS28 ....107 G7
Carlton Rd *BSLYN/ROY* S71 ....243 K8
DEWS WF13 ....173 L5
HEM/SK/SE WF9 ....247 H4
LVSG WF15 ....172 C3
SHPY BD18 ....82 A6
Carlton Rw *WOR/ARM* LS12 ...108 C7
Carlton St *BSLYN/ROY* S71 .....261 G2
CAS WF10 ....157 M6
CUD/GR S72 ....244 D7
CUD/GR S72 ....245 J8
FEA/AMT WF7 ....179 M7
GTHN BD7 ....4 D7
HBR * HX7 ....143 J3
HFAX HX1 ....11 G7
HOR/CROF WF4 ....197 J5
HWTH BD22 ....78 F7
NORM WF6 ....178 D4
OT LS21 ....41 K7
WKFDW/WTN WF2 ....12 B4
Carlton Ter *HFAX* HX1 ....11 G7
Carlton Vw *CAS* WF10 ....135 H8
CHAL LS7 ....7 G4
Carlton Wk *SHPY* BD18 ....82 B6
Carlyle Crs *CAS* WF10 ....158 C7
Carlyle Rd *CAS* WF10 ....158 C7
Carmel Rd *HIPP* HX3 ....146 D4
Carmine Cl *HUDE* HD5 ....193 G8
Carmona Av *SHPY* BD18 ....104 D1
Carmona Gdns *SHPY* BD18 ....104 D1
Carnaby Rd *GTHN* BD7 ....126 A4
Carnegie Dr *SHPY* BD18 ....82 E6
Carnforth Rd *BSLYN/ROY* S71 .261 M1
Carnlea Gv *WKFDW/WTN* WF2 ...12 B8
Carnoustie Gdns *NORM* WF6 ...178 D5
Carnoustie Gv *BGLY* BD16 ....81 J7
Carolan Ct *MAR/SLWT* HD7 ....212 E2
Caroline St *CLECK* BD19 ....149 M6
SHPY BD18 ....82 B6
Carousel Wk *GFTH/SHER* LS25 .116 B7
Carpenters Wy *MILN* OL16 ......206 F3
Carperley Crs *CUL/QBY* BD13 ..102 A6
Carr Av *GFTH/SHER* LS25 ....116 A7
Carr Bank *AIRE* BD20 ....58 D5
Carr Bottom Av *WBOW* BD5 ....126 D4
Carr Bottom Fold *WBSY* BD6 ..126 D4
Carr Bottom Rd *IDLE* BD10 ....84 A8
WBOW BD5 ....126 E4
Carr Bridge Av *BHP/TINH* LS16 .85 M3
Carr Bridge Cl *BHP/TINH* LS16 ..85 M3
Carr Bridge Dr *BHP/TINH* LS16 .85 M3
Carr Bridge Vw *BHP/TINH* LS16 .85 M3
Carr Cl *YEA* LS19 ....84 A7
Carr Crofts *WOR/ARM* LS12 ....108 D7
Carr Crofts Dr *WOR/ARM* LS12 .108 D7
Carrfield Cl *DOD/DAR* S75 ....241 M7
Carrfield Dr *LUD/ILL* HX2 ....145 G6
Carrfield La *MSTN/BAR* LS15 .....90 F7
Carrfield Rd *MSTN/BAR* LS15 ....90 F7
Carr Furlong *BSLYN/ROY* S71 ..243 H5
Cargate *HEM/SK/SE* WF9 ....223 K4
Carr Gate Crs
   WKFDW/WTN WF2 ....175 M1

Carr Gate Dr
   WKFDW/WTN WF2 ....176 A1
Carr Gate Mt
   WKFDW/WTN WF2 ....175 M1
Carr Green Av *BRIG* HD6 ....170 B8
Carr Green Cl *BRIG* HD6 ....170 B8
Carr Green Dr *BRIG* HD6 ....170 B8
Carr Green La *BRIG* HD6 ....170 B7
DOD/DAR S75 ....242 E7
HUDE HD5 ....15 M5
Carr Hall La *GTL/HWG* HX4 ....190 C2
Carr Hall Rd *LM/WK* BD12 ....148 E3
Carr Hill Dr *PDSY/CALV* LS28 .....84 C8
Carr Hill Gv *PDSY/CALV* LS28 ....84 C8
Carr Hill Nook *PDSY/CALV* * LS28 .84 C8
Carr Hill Ri *PDSY/CALV* LS28 .....84 C8
Carr Hill Rd *KBTN* HD8 ....238 C5
PDSY/CALV LS28 ....84 C8
Carrholm Crs *CHAL* LS7 ....87 K7
Carrholm Dr *CHAL* LS7 ....87 K7
Carrholm Gv *CHAL* LS7 ....87 K7
Carrholm Mt *CHAL* LS7 ....87 K7
Carrholm Rd *CHAL* LS7 ....87 K7
Carrholm Vw *CHAL* LS7 ....87 K7
Carr House La *LM/WK* BD12 .....148 E2
Carr House La *HIPP* HX3 ....126 A7
LM/WK BD12 ....148 D1
TOD OL14 ....141 M8
Carr House Mt *LM/WK* * BD12 .148 E2
Carr House Rd *HIPP* HX3 ....125 M8
HOLM/MEL HD9 ....254 C1
Carriage Dr *GTL/HWG* HX4 ....168 A7
GTL/HWG HX4 ....190 C2
RHAY LS8 ....88 E5
The Carriage Dr *GTL/HWG* HX4 .168 A7
Carriage Dr *CLECK* BD19 ....150 D4
HUDS HD4 ....214 A4
LIT OL15 ....185 K7
Carricks Cl *LM/WK* BD12 ....127 G8
Carrier's Rw *COL* BB8 ....53 G8
Carrington Av *DOD/DAR* S75 ...261 G2
Carrington Cl *MILN* OL16 ....206 F3
Carrington St *BFDE* BD3 ....105 L7
DOD/DAR S75 ....260 F3
Carrington Ter *GSLY* LS20 ....61 M6
Carr La *AIRE* BD20 ....58 C5
AL/HA/HU LS17 ....89 J2
CAS WF10 ....180 B1
CUL/QBY BD13 ....102 A4
EARD/LOFT WF3 ....155 G3
EARL WF12 ....195 K6
HECK WF16 ....172 F5
HEM/SK/SE WF9 ....223 H3
HEM/SK/SE WF9 ....246 E2
HOLM/MEL HD9 ....253 K2
HOR/CROF WF4 ....196 D8
KBTN HD8 ....238 B7
LM/WK BD12 ....148 F1
MAR/SLWT HD7 ....212 C5
MILN OL16 ....207 L8
SHPY BD18 ....82 F7
STKB/PEN S36 ....257 K7
WBY LS22 ....30 C8
WKFDW/WTN WF2 ....198 F7
YEA LS19 ....84 F3
Carr Lane Av *CAS* WF10 ....180 A1
Carr Manor Av *AL/HA/HU* LS17 .87 K6
Carr Manor Crs *AL/HA/HU* LS17 .87 K5
Carr Manor Cft *AL/HA/HU* LS17 .87 K7
Carr Manor Dr *AL/HA/HU* LS17 .87 K6
Carr Manor Gdns
   AL/HA/HU LS17 ....87 K6
Carr Manor Garth
   AL/HA/HU LS17 ....87 K5
Carr Manor Gv *AL/HA/HU* LS17 .87 K6
Carr Manor Mt *AL/HA/HU* LS17 .87 K6
Carr Manor Pde *AL/HA/HU* LS17 .87 L6
Carr Manor Pl *AL/HA/HU* LS17 ..87 K6
Carr Manor Rd *AL/HA/HU* LS17 .87 K6
Carr Manor Vw *AL/HA/HU* LS17 .87 K6
Carr Manor Wk *CHAL* LS7 ....87 K6
Carr Mill Ms *HWTH* BD22 ....54 E4
Carr Moor Side *BEE/HOL* LS11 .131 L3
Carr Mt *KBTN* HD8 ....238 C8
Carroll Ct *HEM/SK/SE* WF9 ......247 G3
Carroll St *BFD* * BD1 ....5 J7
Carron Dr *DOD/DAR* S75 ....242 A6
Carr Pit Rd *HUD* HD1 ....15 J8
Carr Rd *COL* BB8 ....52 A8
LM/WK * BD12 ....148 E3
PDSY/CALV LS28 ....84 B8
TOD OL14 ....140 C6
Carr Side Crs *BTLY* WF17 ....173 K3
Carrs La *CUD/GR* S72 ....262 D1
Carrs Rd *MAR/SLWT* HD7 ....233 J3
Carrs Side Street No 2
   MAR/SLWT HD7 ....233 J2
Carrs St *MAR/SLWT* HD7 ....233 J2
Carr St *BRIG* HD6 ....170 C2
BSLYN/ROY S71 ....261 M1
BTLY WF17 ....151 G6
CLECK BD19 ....149 M7
DEWS WF13 ....173 L4
HUDW HD3 ....191 K7
KGHY BD21 ....3 G5
LVSG WF15 ....172 C1
WBOW BD5 ....126 F4
Carr Top Cl *DEWS* WF13 ....173 K4
Carr Top La *MAR/SLWT* HD7 ....212 F2
Carr Vw *HEM/SK/SE* WF9 ....246 E2
Carr View Rd *HOLM/MEL* HD9 ..255 G4
Carr Wood Gdns
   PDSY/CALV LS28 ....84 C8
Carrwood Rd *BSLY* S70 ....262 A5
Carr Wood Rd *CAS* WF10 ....180 B1
Carry La *COL* BB8 ....74 A1
Carter Av *MSTN/BAR* LS15 ....111 L6
Carter La *CUL/QBY* BD13 ....124 F3
MSTN/BAR LS15 ....111 L6
Carter Mt *MSTN/BAR* LS15 ......111 L6
Carter's La *ILK* LS29 ....21 G8
Carter St *BFD* BD1 ....5 H8
WKFDE WF1 ....12 D1
Carter Ter *MSTN/BAR* LS15 ......111 L5
Cartmel *WHIT* * OL12 ....206 B6
Cartmel Av *MILN* OL16 ....229 H2
Cartmel Ct *BSLYN/ROY* S71 .....243 M7

Cartmel Dr *MSTN/BAR* LS15 ....110 F8
Cartmell Rd *KGHY* BD21 ....2 D5
Cartworth Bank Rd
   HOLM/MEL HD9 ....254 B4
Cartworth La *HOLM/MEL* HD9 ..254 B5
Cartworth Moor Rd
   HOLM/MEL HD9 ....254 A6
Cartworth Rd *HOLM/MEL* HD9 .254 C3
Cartwright Gdns *HUDS* HD4 .....213 L3
Cartwright St *CLECK* BD19 ....150 B3
Carver St *CLECK* BD19 ....149 M6
Caryl Rd *BOW* BD4 ....127 J3
Cashmere St *HWTH* BD22 ....2 D5
Casson Av *EARD/LOFT* WF3 .....153 K5
Casson Dr *EARD/LOFT* WF3 .....153 K5
Casson Ga *WHIT* OL12 ....206 A5
Casson Gv *EARD/LOFT* WF3 .....153 K5
Cass La *GFTH/SHER* LS25 ....137 M5
Casserley Rd *COL* BB8 ....52 B8
Casterton Gdns *SCFT* LS14 ....111 J3
Castle Av *BRIG* HD6 ....170 B6
HUDS HD4 ....214 C5
ROCH OL11 ....206 A8
WKFDW/WTN WF2 ....198 F4
Castle Carr Rd *LUD/ILL* HX2 .....122 C8
Castle Cl *AL/HA/HU* LS17 ....67 M3
BSLYN/ROY S71 ....261 K3
BTLY WF17 ....151 J5
COL BB8 ....52 A8
PBR HG3 ....28 E3
STKB/PEN S36 ....271 G4
Castle Crs *EARL* WF12 ....195 K5
Castle Cft *BGLY* BD16 ....80 C5
Castlefield Ct *CAS* * WF10 ....157 M6
Castlefields *RTHW* LS26 ....154 D1
Castlefields Dr *BRIG* HD6 ....170 B6
Castlefields La *BGLY* BD16 ....81 G1
Castlefields Rd *BGLY* BD16 ....80 F1
BRIG HD6 ....170 B6
Castleford Br *CAS* WF10 ....158 A5
Castleford La *FEA/AMT* WF7 ....179 K4
KNOT WF11 ....181 K1
Castleford Rd *NORM* WF6 ....178 D4
Castlegate *HUD* HD1 ....14 E8
Castlegate Dr *IDLE* BD10 ....83 L8
PONT WF8 ....202 D1
Castlegate Slip *HUD* HD1 ....14 E5
Castle Gra *YEA* * LS19 ....62 F8
Castle Gv *AL/HA/HU* LS17 ....67 M3
BGLY BD16 ....80 C5
HOR/CROF WF4 ....197 K6
Castle Grove Av *HDGY* LS6 ....86 F7
Castle Grove Dr *HDGY* LS6 ....86 F8
Castle Head Cl
   EARD/LOFT WF3 ....154 E5
Castle Head La
   EARD/LOFT WF3 ....154 C6
Castle Hi *BRIG* HD6 ....170 B6
HWTH BD22 ....2 A1
PONT WF8 ....197 L2
Castle Hill Ct *HWTH* * BD22 ....2 A1
Castle Hill Crs *ROCH* OL11 ....206 A8
Castle Hill Dr *BRIG* HD6 ....150 D8
Castle Hill Side *HUDS* HD4 ....214 C6
Castle Hill Vw *HECK* WF16 ....173 G3
Castle Ings Cl *WOR/ARM* LS12 .129 M3
Castle Ings Dr *WOR/ARM* LS12 .129 M3
Castle Ings Gdns
   WOR/ARM LS12 ....129 M4
Castle La *MAR/SLWT* HD7 ....212 A4
RPDN/SBR HX6 ....188 E3
STKB/PEN S36 ....271 G4
TOD OL14 ....141 M8
Castle Lane Cl *TOD* OL14 ....141 M8
Castle Mdw *HOR/CROF* WF4 ....220 B3
Castlemere St *ROCH* OL11 ....206 A8
Castlemore Rd *BAIL* BD17 ....82 F4
Castle Mt *EARL* WF12 ....195 M5
Castle Pde *CAS* WF10 ....158 B8
Castlereagh St *BSLY* S70 ....261 G5
Castlerigg Dr *ROY/SHW* OL2 ....228 E8
Castle Rd *COL* BB8 ....52 A8
ILK LS29 ....38 D2
KGHY BD21 ....2 F2
RTHW LS26 ....154 F1
SHPY BD18 ....82 C7
WKFDW/WTN WF2 ....198 F5
Castle Rd West
   WKFDW/WTN WF2 ....198 F4
Castle St *BSLY* S70 ....261 G6
LDS LS1 ....6 D9
PBR HG3 ....28 E3
SKP/WHF BD23 ....16 C3
WBOW BD5 ....127 G1
Castle Syke Hi *FEA/AMT* WF7 ...202 D3
Castle Syke Vw *PONT* WF8 ....180 E8
Castle Ter *WKFDW/WTN* WF2 ..198 F6
Castleton Cl *WOR/ARM* LS12 ....8 A1
Castleton Rd *ROY/SHW* OL2 .....228 E6
WOR/ARM LS12 ....109 G6
Castle Vw *AL/HA/HU* LS17 ....87 K5
HOLM/MEL HD9 ....236 B5
HOR/CROF WF4 ....197 L6
MIRF WF14 ....194 D1
WKFDW/WTN WF2 ....198 F6
Castle View Ter
   SKP/WHF * BD23 ....16 B1
Castle Wood Cl *AL/HA/HU* LS17 ..43 J7
Castley La *AL/HA/HU* LS17 ....43 L4
OT LS21 ....42 F6
Catania Ri *WMB/DAR* S73 ....263 G8
Cater St *BFD* BD1 ....5 H6
Cathcart St *HDGY* LS6 ....6 C2
HIPP HX3 ....146 D4
Cathedral Cl *WKFDE* WF1 ....12 D1
Catherine Av *BEE/HOL* * LS11 ...131 K3
Catherine House La *HBR* HX7 ....122 C8
Catherine Rd *HUDN* HD2 ....192 D2

Catherine Slack *BRIG* HD6 ....148 B8
Catherine St *BRIG* HD6 ....170 C3
ELL HX5 ....169 H8
HEM/SK/SE WF9 ....223 J2
KGHY BD21 ....2 F8
Cat Hill La *STKB/PEN* S36 ....257 M6
Cat La *GTL/HWG* HX4 ....168 A7
LUD/ILL HX2 ....166 D1
Catlow St *CAS* WF10 ....157 L7
Caton St *MILN* OL16 ....206 B8
Catshaw La *STKB/PEN* S36 ....269 K3
Catterton La *TAD* LS24 ....51 J3
Cattlelaith La *KNOT* WF11 ....181 L3
Cattle La *GFTH/SHER* LS25 ....92 A7
Cattle Market St *OT* LS21 ....41 J6
Caudle Hi *KNOT* WF11 ....159 H2
Cauldwell Gdns *WBOW* * BD5 ...127 G2
Caulms Wood Rd *DEWS* WF13 ..173 M5
Causeway *GTL/HWG* HX4 ....189 J7
HFAX HX1 ....11 J6
MAR/SLWT HD7 ....212 B3
Causeway Crs *MAR/SLWT* HD7 .212 F5
Causeway Garth La
   PONT WF8 ....225 L2
Causeway Head
   RPDN/SBR * HX6 ....188 D1
Causeway Head La
   RPDN/SBR HX6 ....188 D2
Causeway Side
   MAR/SLWT HD7 ....212 F5
TOD * OL14 ....164 A2
Causeway Wood Rd *TOD* OL14 .164 A2
Cautley Rd *OSM* LS9 ....110 B8
Cavalier Ap *OSM* LS9 ....110 B8
Cavalier Cl *OSM* * LS9 ....110 B8
Cavalier Ct *OSM* LS9 ....110 B8
Cavalier Dr *IDLE* BD10 ....83 M7
Cavalier Gdns *OSM* LS9 ....110 B8
Cavalier Ga *OSM* LS9 ....110 B8
Cavalier Gn *OSM* LS9 ....110 B8
Cavalier Ms *OSM* LS9 ....110 B8
Cavalier Vw *OSM* LS9 ....110 B8
Cave Crs *WKFDW/WTN* WF2 ....198 A2
Cave La *EARD/LOFT* WF3 ....153 M7
Cavendish Av *WOR/ARM* LS12 .108 E6
Cavendish Ct *KGHY* * BD21 ....3 G4
GSLY LS20 ....61 M6
Cavendish Dr *BGLY* BD16 ....81 K2
GSLY LS20 ....61 M6
Cavendish Gv *GSLY* LS20 ....61 M6
Cavendish Ms *AL/HA/HU* LS17 ...87 M2
Cavendish Pl *PDSY/CALV* LS28 ...106 F5
Cavendish Rd *DOD/DAR* S75 ....260 F3
GSLY LS20 ....61 M6
IDLE BD10 ....83 K7
LDS LS1 ....6 A7
ROCH OL11 ....228 A3
Cavendish St *HFAX* HX1 ....10 D5
KGHY BD21 ....3 G4
PDSY/CALV LS28 ....107 J7
YEA LS19 ....62 E8
Cavendish Ter *HFAX* * HX1 ....10 D6
Cavewell Cl *OSS* WF5 ....197 H3
Cavewell Gdns *OSS* WF5 ....197 H3
Cawcliffe Dr *BRIG* HD6 ....170 C2
Cawcliffe Rd *BRIG* HD6 ....170 C2
Cawdel Cl *GFTH/SHER* LS25 .....138 B2
Cawdel Wy *GFTH/SHER* LS25 ...138 B2
Cawder Ghyll *SKP/WHF* BD23 ....16 C5
Cawder La *SKP/WHF* BD23 ....16 C5
Cawder Rd *SKP/WHF* BD23 ....16 C5
Cawley Garth *HECK* WF16 ....173 G3
Cawley La *HECK* WF16 ....173 G3
Cawley Rd *BSLYN/ROY* S71 ......261 J2
Cawood Crs *TAD* LS24 ....95 G5
Cawood Hvn *WBSY* * BD6 ....126 A6
Cawthorne Av *HUDN* HD2 ....192 C4
Cawthorne La *DOD/DAR* S75 ....259 J1
Cawthorne Rd *DOD/DAR* S75 ...259 M2
WKFDW/WTN WF2 ....198 D8
Cawthorne Vw *STKB/PEN* S36 ..258 F8
Caxton Gdns *PONT* WF8 ....180 F3
Caxton Rd *OT* LS21 ....41 G8
Caxton St *BSLY* S70 ....261 G3
WBY LS22 ....48 A1
Caygill Ter *HFAX* HX1 ....11 G9
Cayley St *MILN* OL16 ....206 D7
Caythorne Wk *IDLE* BD10 ....105 L1
Caythorpe Cl *BSLYN/ROY* S71 ..262 C1
Caythorpe Rd *BHP/TINH* LS16 ...86 D7
Cayton Cl *BSLYN/ROY* S71 ....243 G7
Cecil Av *BAIL* BD17 ....82 E2
GTHN BD7 ....148 A6
HIPP HX3 ....148 A6
Cecil Gv *WOR/ARM* LS12 ....108 E6
Cecil Mt *WOR/ARM* LS12 ....108 E6
Cecil Rd *WOR/ARM* LS12 ....108 E6
Cecil St *HUD* HD1 ....14 D7
HWTH BD22 ....79 G6
LIT OL15 ....207 H1
ROCH OL11 ....228 B5
WOR/ARM LS12 ....108 E6
The Cedars *BHP/TINH* LS16 ....64 B5
Cedar Av *HUD* HD1 ....14 C4
OSS WF5 ....197 G3
Cedar Cl *BSLYN/ROY* S71 ....243 J2
PONT WF8 ....202 E1
WOR/ARM LS12 ....108 E7
Cedar Covert *WBY* LS22 ....30 A6
Cedar Ct *RTHW* LS26 ....134 A7
Cedar Dr *EARL* WF12 ....174 D8
LM/WK BD12 ....149 G2
TAD LS24 ....71 K3
Cedar Gv *AIRE* BD20 ....55 L1
FEA/AMT WF7 ....179 M5
GTL/HWG HX4 ....168 D7
ROY/SHW OL2 ....228 D7
Cedar La *MILN* OL16 ....229 J3
WOR/ARM LS12 ....108 D7
Cedar Pl *WOR/ARM* LS12 ....108 D7
Cedar Rdg *GFTH/SHER* LS25 .....113 K5
Cedar Rd *EARL* WF12 ....174 D8
NORM WF6 ....178 D7

Cedar St *HFAX* HX1 ....10 B6
HUD HD1 ....14 B5
KGHY BD21 ....79 K2
TOD OL14 ....163 J6
WHIT OL12 ....206 B5
WOR/ARM LS12 ....108 D7
Cedar Ter *WOR/ARM* LS12 ....108 D7
Cedar Wk *CLECK* BD19 ....150 C6
Cedar Wy *AWLS/ASK* DN6 ....227 L6
FEA/AMT WF7 ....179 M8
Celandine Av *HUDW* HD3 ....191 G6
Celandine Cl *LIT* OL15 ....185 H8
PONT WF8 ....180 F7
Celandine Dr *HUDW* HD3 ....191 G6
Cemetery La *AIRE* BD20 ....57 K4
EARD/LOFT WF3 ....154 C5
RPDN/SBR HX6 ....167 J2
Cemetery Rd *BEE/HOL* LS11 ....8 C8
BGLY BD16 ....81 G2
BSLY S70 ....261 H6
BTLY WF17 ....173 K1
CUD/GR S72 ....245 J7
DEWS WF13 ....173 J7
GIR BD8 ....104 B7
HECK WF16 ....172 F2
HEM/SK/SE WF9 ....223 L7
HOLM/MEL HD9 ....254 B2
HOR/CROF WF4 ....222 D5
HUD HD1 ....14 C4
HWTH BD22 ....78 C7
NORM WF6 ....178 E4
PDSY/CALV LS28 ....106 F6
WBSY BD6 ....126 D7
YEA LS19 ....62 E7
Centenary Rd *BAIL* BD17 ....82 D4
CUD/GR S72 ....245 J7
HEM/SK/SE WF9 ....223 J2
HEM/SK/SE WF9 ....247 H4
HUDN HD2 ....192 D4
HWTH BD22 ....79 J3
LIT OL15 ....185 K8
LVSG WF15 ....171 K1
SHPY BD18 ....82 D7
WBOW BD5 ....126 E2
Centenary Sq *EARL* WF12 ....195 K2
Centenary Wy *BTLY* WF17 ....151 K8
Central Av *BAIL* BD17 ....82 D4
CUD/GR S72 ....245 J4
HEM/SK/SE WF9 ....223 J2
HEM/SK/SE WF9 ....247 H4
HUDN HD2 ....192 D4
HWTH BD22 ....79 J3
LIT OL15 ....185 K8
LVSG WF15 ....171 K1
SHPY BD18 ....82 D7
WBOW BD5 ....126 E3
Central Av East *LVSG* WF15 ......171 K1
Central Cl *HUDN* HD2 ....192 H7
Central Dr *BSLYN/ROY* S71 ....243 J3
CAS WF10 ....157 H7
HUDN HD2 ....192 H7
HWTH BD22 ....79 H3
Central Pde *OSM* LS9 ....132 C3
Central Pk *HFAX* HX1 ....10 F9
Central Rd *HUDN* HD2 ....192 D7
Central St *DEWS* WF13 ....173 L6
HBR HX7 ....143 J3
HFAX HX1 ....11 G6
LDS LS1 ....6 E9
Centre La *TAD* LS24 ....71 M3
Centre St *HECK* * WF16 ....172 E2
HEM/SK/SE WF9 ....223 M7
HEM/SK/SE WF9 ....247 H4
WBOW * BD5 ....126 E3
Centre Vale Cl *LIT* OL15 ....185 L7
Centuria Wk *HUDW* HD3 ....191 G6
Century Gdns *WHIT* OL12 ....206 B6
Century Pl *GIR* BD8 ....4 A1
Century Rd *ELL* HX5 ....169 H7
Century St *KGHY* * BD21 ....79 K2
Century Wy *MSTN/BAR* LS15 ....112 B7
Ceres Rd *WBY* LS22 ....48 A1
Chaddlewood Cl *HORS* LS18 ......85 L5
Chadwell Springs *BGLY* BD16 .....81 J7
Chadwick Cl *MILN* OL16 ....229 J1
Chadwick Rd *DEWS* WF13 ....173 K5
Chadwick Fold La *MIRF* WF14 ...194 C2
Chadwick Hall Gdns
   MIRF WF14 ....194 B2
Chadwick La *MILN* OL16 ....228 A1
MIRF WF14 ....194 B3
Chadwick St *MID* LS10 ....9 K5
MILN OL16 ....207 G2
Chadwick St South *MID* LS10 ......9 K5
Chaffinch Dr *GIR* BD8 ....103 L7
Chaffinch Wk *HUDS* HD4 ....214 A7
Chain Rd *MAR/SLWT* HD7 ....234 A1
Chain St *BFD* BD1 ....4 D5
CAS WF10 ....157 L7
Chalcroft Cl *HECK* WF16 ....173 G1
Chald La *WKFDW/WTN* WF2 ......12 C4
Chalfont Rd *BHP/TINH* * LS16 .....86 D7
Chalice Cl *MID* LS10 ....132 A7
Challenge Wy *BOW* BD4 ....127 M2
BTLY WF17 ....174 B2
Challis Gv *WBOW* BD5 ....127 G3
Chalner Av *MOR* LS27 ....152 B4
Chalner Cl *MOR* LS27 ....152 B4
Chalwood *HUDN* HD2 ....193 G2
Champion Av *CAS* WF10 ....180 A1
Champness Hall *MILN* * OL16 ...206 B7
Chancellor St *HDGY* LS6 ....7 G2
Chancel Pl *MILN* OL16 ....206 B7
Chancel Wy *BSLYN/ROY* S71 ....261 L3
Chancery Cl *HUD* * HD1 ....14 F7
Chancery La *HUD* HD1 ....14 F7
OSS WF5 ....197 G3
ROY/SHW * OL2 ....229 L7
WKFDE WF1 ....12 E2
Chancery Rd *EARL* WF12 ....174 D6
The Chandlers *MID* LS10 ....9 J2
Chandler Cl *BTLY* WF17 ....151 G5
Chandler La *HOLM/MEL* HD9 ....235 M2
Chandlers Cl *WKFDE* WF1 ....176 D1
Chandos Av *RHAY* LS8 ....88 A4
Chandos Fold *RHAY* LS8 ....88 A7
Chandos Gdns *RHAY* LS8 ....88 A6
Chandos Garth *RHAY* LS8 ....88 A6
Chandos Gn *RHAY* LS8 ....88 A6
Chandos Pl *RHAY* LS8 ....88 A7
Chandos St *BOW* BD4 ....5 G8
KGHY BD21 ....2 F8
ROY/SHW OL2 ....229 L7
Chandos Ter *RHAY* LS8 ....88 B6
Chandos Wk *RHAY* LS8 ....88 A7
Changegate *HWTH* BD22 ....78 D6

Changegate Ct *HWTH* BD22 ....**78** D7
Change La *HIPP* HX3 ....**169** G4
Channing Ct *MILN* * OL16 ....**206** D8
Channing Sq *MILN* OL16 ....**206** D8
Channing Wy *MILN* OL16 ....**206** D8
Channing St *MILN* OL16 ....**206** D8
Chantrell Ct *LDSU* LS2 ....**9** J1
Chantry Cl *PONT* WF8 ....**180** D7
Chantry Cft *MSTN/BAR* LS15 ...**111** M7
Chantry Garth *MSTN/BAR* LS15 ...**111** M7
Chantry Gv *BSLYN/ROY* S71 ....**243** L3
Chantry La *TAD* LS24 ....**71** H8
TAD LS24 ....**92** E2
Chantry Rd *WKFDW/WTN* WF2 ...**198** A2
Chapel Av *BSLYN/ROY* S71 ....**243** L5
HBR HX7 ....**143** K3
HECK WF16 ....**173** G2
Chapel Bank *HOLM/MEL* HD9 ....**255** H3
Chapel Cl *CUD/GR* S72 ....**244** E8
EARL WF12 ....**195** M4
GFTH/SHER LS25 ....**113** G7
GTL/HWG HX4 ....**190** D2
HOR/CROF WF4 ....**201** H7
HUDS HD4 ....**214** B6
KBTN HD8 ....**239** J3
WBY LS22 ....**31** L5
Chapel Ct *MSTN/BAR* LS15 ....**111** J6
Chapel Cft *BRIG* HD6 ....**170** B7
Chapel Field La *STKB/PEN* S36 ..**270** E4
Chapelfields *HEM/SK/SE* WF9 ...**246** D4
Chapel Fold *BEE/HOL* LS11 .....**131** G4
BTLY WF17 ....**173** J3
LM/WK BD12 ....**148** E6
MSTN/BAR LS15 ....**111** J6
PDSY/CALV * LS28 ....**107** G8
WBSY BD6 ....**126** D5
Chapel Garth *FEA/AMT* WF7 .....**202** C8
Chapelgate *HOLM/MEL* HD9 ......**254** F5
Chapel Ga *MILN* OL16 ....**207** H8
Chapel Gv *BGLY* BD16 ....**81** G1
Chapel Hl *KBTN* HD8 ....**240** F7
LIT OL15 ....**185** K8
MAR/SLWT HD7 ....**212** F6
MIRF WF14 ....**194** C5
MOR LS27 ....**152** C1
SKP/WHF BD23 ....**16** B1
WBY LS22 ....**45** M4
YEA LS19 ....**62** D7
Chapel Hill Jct *HUD* HD1 ....**14** E9
Chapel Hill La *HUDW* HD3 ....**189** K8
OT LS21 ....**43** K6
Chapel House Rd *LM/WK* BD12 ..**126** F7
Chapel La *BAIL* BD17 ....**83** K1
BSLYN/ROY S71 ....**243** L6
BSPA/BRAM LS23 ....**48** F8
BTLY WF17 ....**151** M4
CUD/GR S72 ....**263** L6
CUL/QBY BD13 ....**124** F5
CUL/QBY BD13 ....**125** K4
EARL WF12 ....**195** M4
GFTH/SHER LS25 ....**113** G4
GFTH/SHER LS25 ....**135** K7
HBR HX7 ....**144** D4
HDGY LS6 ....**108** F2
HECK WF16 ....**173** G2
HEM/SK/SE WF9 ....**225** G4
HEM/SK/SE WF9 ....**247** K3
HIPP HX3 ....**168** F4
HIPP HX3 ....**169** K2
HUDE HD5 ....**15** L8
HWTH BD22 ....**56** E7
KBTN HD8 ....**217** K7
KGHY BD21 ....**2** F5
MAR/SLWT HD7 ....**212** F2
MSTN/BAR LS15 ....**91** G7
PONT WF8 ....**204** F8
RPDN/SBR HX6 ....**167** M2
STKB/PEN S36 ....**270** E4
WIL/AL BD15 ....**103** L6
WOR/ARM LS12 ....**108** G3
WOR/ARM LS12 ....**129** M1
YEA LS19 ....**62** D7
Chapel Ms *GIR* * BD8 ....**103** L6
HDGY LS6 ....**108** F1
Chapel Pl *BSLYN/ROY* S71 ....**262** B6
HDGY LS6 ....**108** F1
Chapel Rd *AIRE* BD20 ....**56** E1
BGLY BD16 ....**81** G1
CHAL LS7 ....**109** M1
LM/WK BD12 ....**126** F8
Chapel Rw *WIL/AL* BD15 ....**80** E8
Chapel St South *TOD* OL14 ....**163** J5
Chapel St *AIRE* BD20 ....**36** A4
AWLS/ASK DN6 ....**249** K6
BFD BD1 ....**5** H6
BRIG HD6 ....**170** A1
BSLYN/ROY S71 ....**262** B6
CLECK BD19 ....**150** A6
CUD/GR S72 ....**244** E3
CUD/GR S72 ....**245** J8
CUL/QBY BD13 ....**101** M6
CUL/QBY BD13 ....**102** J3
CUL/QBY BD13 ....**124** F5
EARD/LOFT WF3 ....**153** H5
EARD/LOFT WF3 ....**153** L7
EARD/LOFT WF3 ....**154** J1
EARD/LOFT WF3 ....**177** G1
EARL WF12 ....**173** L8
ECHL BD2 ....**105** M2
GFTH/SHER LS25 ....**138** E8
GTL/HWG HX4 ....**190** D2
HDGY * LS6 ....**108** F1
HOR/CROF WF4 ....**222** C5
HUDE HD5 ....**15** L8
HUDS HD4 ....**213** L7
HUDS HD4 ....**214** A4
ILK LS29 ....**19** H6
LIT OL15 ....**185** M4
LUD/ILL * HX2 ....**146** A6
LVSG WF15 ....**171** L9
LVSG WF15 ....**172** B3
MAR/SLWT HD7 ....**212** D1
MIRF WF14 ....**194** C1
MSTN/BAR LS15 ....**111** J6
OSS WF5 ....**197** J2
PDSY/CALV LS28 ....**84** D7
PDSY/CALV LS28 ....**107** G5
ROCH OL11 ....**228** C2
ROY/SHW * OL2 ....**229** K7

TAD LS24 ....**71** L3
WBOW * BD5 ....**126** F2
WBSY BD6 ....**126** E5
WHIT OL12 ....**184** E4
YEA * LS19 ....**84** D2
Chapel Ter North *LUD/ILL* HX2 ..**146** B3
HOLM/MEL HD9 ....**236** B2
HUDS HD4 ....**213** M2
WIL/AL * BD15 ....**103** K5
Chapeltown *HFAX* HX1 ....**10** F5
PDSY/CALV LS28 ....**106** F8
Chapeltown Rd *CHAL* LS7 ....**7** J4
Chapel Wk *BGLY* BD16 ....**81** H3
ECHL BD2 ....**105** M2
Chapelway Gdns
ROY/SHW OL2 ....**228** F8
Chapel Yd *MSTN/BAR* LS15 .....**111** M8
Chapman St *BOW* BD4 ....**105** M8
OSM LS9 ....**7** M6
Chappell Cl *STKB/PEN* S36 ....**258** B8
Chappell Rd *STKB/PEN* S36 ......**258** B8
Chapter Wy *BSLYN/ROY* S71 ....**261** L3
DOD/DAR S75 ....**259** J5
Chariot Wy *PONT* WF8 ....**225** J2
Charity Rd *BSLYN/ROY* S71 .....**244** B8
Charles Av *BFDE* BD3 ....**105** M7
HIPP HX3 ....**169** J2
HUDW HD3 ....**191** J6
OSM LS9 ....**110** B8
WKFDE WF1 ....**13** M9
WKFDE WF1 ....**176** D1
Charles Cotton Cl
WKFDW/WTN WF2 ....**175** M6
Charles Ct *HWTH* * BD22 ....**100** E4
Charles Gdns *BEE/HOL* LS11 ....**8** C7
Charles Gv *RTHW* LS26 ....**133** L8
Charles Jones Ct *BTLY* WF17 ...**173** K1
Charles La *MILN* OL16 ....**229** J1
Charles Ms *MILN* OL16 ....**229** J1
Charles St *AWLS/ASK* DN6 ......**249** K4
BAIL BD17 ....**83** K1
BFD BD1 ....**4** F6
BGLY BD16 ....**81** H3
BSLY S70 ....**261** G6
BTLY WF17 ....**173** L2
CAS WF10 ....**158** A7
CLECK BD19 ....**150** D6
COL BB8 ....**74** A1
CUD/GR S72 ....**244** E6
CUD/GR S72 ....**245** J8
CUD/GR S72 ....**245** G1
CUD/GR S72 ....**263** M7
WOR/ARM LS12 ....**108** E8
DEWS WF13 ....**173** H6
DEWS WF13 ....**195** G1
EARL WF12 ....**174** A6
ELL HX5 ....**169** H8
HFAX HX1 ....**11** J6
HOR/CROF WF4 ....**197** L7
HOR/CROF WF4 ....**222** C5
HORS LS18 ....**85** K6
HUDS HD4 ....**213** M2
LIT OL15 ....**207** J1
OSS WF5 ....**197** H2
OT LS21 ....**41** J7
PDSY/CALV LS28 ....**106** F3
RPDN/SBR HX6 ....**167** K1
WKFDE WF1 ....**13** H4
Charlestown Est
FEA/AMT WF7 ....**224** C2
Charlestown Rd *HIPP* HX3 ....**11** J4
Charlesworth Ct *EARL* * WF12 ..**195** M4
Charlesworth Gv *LUD/ILL* HX2 ..**146** A6
Charlesworth Pl
EARD/LOFT WF3 ....**155** K8
Charlesworth Sq *CLECK* BD19 ..**150** C6
Charlesworth St *EARL* WF12 ....**195** M4
Charlesworth Ter *LUD/ILL* HX2 ..**146** A6
Charlesworth Wy
WKFDW/WTN WF2 ....**12** D5
Charlotte Cl *BTLY* WF17 ....**151** H1
Charlotte Ct *HWTH* BD22 ....**78** F6
Charlotte Gv *OSS* * WF5 ....**197** H2
Charlotte St *ROCH* OL11 ....**228** C2
WKFDE WF1 ....**12** F4
Charlotte Yd *WKFDE* * WF1 ....**13** G4
Charlton Gv *AIRE* BD20 ....**36** B6
OSM LS9 ....**110** B7
Charlton Mt *OSM* LS9 ....**110** B7
Charlton Pl *OSM* LS9 ....**110** B7
Charlton Rd *OSM* LS9 ....**110** B7
Charlton St *OSM* LS9 ....**110** C7
Charnley Dr *CHAL* LS7 ....**88** A8
Charnwood Bank *HECK* WF16 ...**173** G1
Charnwood Cl *ECHL* * BD2 ......**105** L4
ROY/SHW OL2 ....**229** G6
Charnwood Gv *ECHL* BD2 ....**105** L4
Charnwood Rd *ECHL* BD2 ....**105** L4
Charterhouse Rd *IDLE* BD10 .....**83** K5
Charteris Rd *GIR* BD8 ....**103** M7
Charter St *MILN* OL16 ....**228** D2
Chartists Wy *MOR* LS27 ....**152** C3
Charville Gdns *AL/HA/HU* LS17 ..**89** H2
Chaseley Rd *WHIT* OL12 ....**206** A6
The Chase *EARD/LOFT* WF3 ....**155** J8
GFTH/SHER LS25 ....**113** K7
KGHY BD21 ....**2** B2
WBY LS22 ....**30** B8
YEA LS19 ....**84** D2
Chase Wy *WBOW* BD5 ....**127** C5
Chassum Gv *HTON* BD9 ....**104** C4
Chaster St *BFDE* BD3 ....**5** H1
COL BB8 ....**52** A8
HFAX HX1 ....**10** E5
RPDN/SBR HX6 ....**167** K1
Chat Hill Rd *CUL/QBY* BD13 ....**125** H1
Chatswood Av *BEE/HOL* LS11 ..**131** H6
Chatswood Crs *BEE/HOL* LS11 ..**131** H6
Chatswood Dr *BEE/HOL* LS11 ..**131** H5
Chatsworth Av
PDSY/CALV LS28 ....**106** F3
PONT WF8 ....**181** G3
Chatsworth Cl *HUDE* HD5 ....**214** F2
RHAY LS8 ....**110** C3
ROY/SHW OL2 ....**229** L6
Chatsworth Ct *EARL* WF12 ....**174** B7

Chatsworth Crs
PDSY/CALV LS28 ....**106** C6
Chatsworth Dr
PDSY/CALV LS28 ....**106** C6
WBY LS22 ....**29** L8
Chatsworth Fall
PDSY/CALV LS28 ....**106** C6
Chatsworth Ms *MOR* LS27 ....**152** E3
Chatsworth Pl *GIR* BD8 ....**104** C4
Chatsworth Ri *DOD/DAR* S75 ...**260** B8
Chatsworth Rd
BSLYN/ROY S71 ....**243** J8
PDSY/CALV LS28 ....**106** C6
RHAY LS8 ....**110** C3
WHIT OL12 ....**206** K3
Chatsworth Ter *EARL* WF12 .....**174** B7
Chatts Wood Fold
LM/WK BD12 ....**149** K1
Chaucer Av *EARD/LOFT* WF3 ...**155** L8
PDSY/CALV LS28 ....**107** H8
Chaucer Cl *HOLM/MEL* HD9 ....**236** B3
Chaucer Gdns *PDSY/CALV* LS28 ..**107** H8
Chaucer Gv *PDSY/CALV* LS28 ..**107** H8
Chaucer St *HFAX* HX1 ....**10** A7
Cheapside *BFD* BD1 ....**4** F5
BSLY * S70 ....**261** H5
BTLY WF17 ....**173** M1
CLECK BD19 ....**150** A7
HFAX * HX1 ....**11** H6
HIPP HX3 ....**125** L8
NORM WF6 ....**178** D4
WKFDE WF1 ....**12** D1
Cheddington Gv *WIL/AL* BD15 ..**103** K6
Chedworth Cl *DOD/DAR* S75 ....**242** A7
Cheese Gate Nab Side
HOLM/MEL HD9 ....**255** J4
Cheetham Hl *ROY/SHW* OL2 ....**229** K8
Cheetham St *HBR* HX7 ....**143** J3
MILN OL16 ....**206** B6
ROY/SHW OL2 ....**229** L8
Chelburn Vw *LIT* OL15 ....**185** L5
Chellow Gdns *WIL/AL* * BD15 ..**103** J4
Chellow Grange Rd *HTON* BD9 ..**103** J4
Chellow La *HTON* BD9 ....**103** L4
Chellow St *WBOW* BD5 ....**126** A4
Chellow Wy *WIL/AL* WF12 ....**173** L7
Chelmsford Rd *BFDE* * BD3 ....**105** L6
Chelmsford Ter *BFDE* BD3 ....**105** L6
Chelsea Cl *ROY/SHW* OL2 ....**229** K7
WOR/ARM LS12 ....**108** E8
Chelsea Man *HIPP* HX3 ....**147** J4
Chelsea Rd *GTHN* BD7 ....**126** B2
Chelsea St *KGHY* BD21 ....**2** E8
Chelsfield Wy *MSTN/BAR* LS15 ..**112** B3
Cheltenham Av *ILK* LS29 ....**39** C2
Cheltenham Gdns *HIPP* HX3 ....**168** F2
Cheltenham Pl *HIPP* HX3 ....**168** F2
Cheltenham Rd *ECHL* BD2 ......**105** H1
Cheltenham St *WOR/ARM* LS12 ..**108** F8
Chelwood Av *BHP/TINH* LS16 ....**88** A4
Chelwood Crs *RHAY* LS8 ....**88** B4
Chelwood Dr *RHAY* LS8 ....**88** B4
WIL/AL BD15 ....**103** K7
Chelwood Gv *RHAY* LS8 ....**88** B3
Chelwood Mt *RHAY* LS8 ....**88** B3
Chelwood Pl *RHAY* LS8 ....**88** A3
Chenies Cl *SCFT* LS14 ....**111** G5
Chepstow Cl *GFTH/SHER* LS25 ..**113** K7
Chepstow Dr *EARD/LOFT* WF3 ..**153** M3
Chequerfield Av *PONT* WF8 .....**181** G1
Chequerfield Crs *CAS* WF10 .....**157** J8
Chequerfield Dr *PONT* WF8 .....**181** G2
Chequerfield La *PONT* WF8 ......**181** H6
Chequerfield Mt *PONT* WF8 .....**181** H6
Chequerfield Rd *PONT* WF8 .....**181** G7
Chequers Cl *PONT* WF8 ....**181** H6
Chequers Ct *PONT* WF8 ....**181** H6
Cheriton Av *AWLS/ASK* DN6 ....**249** J8
Cheriton Dr *CUL/QBY* BD13 ....**125** H5
Cherry Cl *BSLYN/ROY* S71 ....**243** J2
CUD/GR S72 ....**244** D6
Cherry Ct *HDGY* LS6 ....**87** H8
HFAX * HX1 ....**10** D7
OSM LS9 ....**7** L7
Cherry Flds *ECHL* BD2 ....**105** G2
Cherry Garth *AWLS/ASK* DN6 ..**227** L6
HEM/SK/SE WF9 ....**223** L8
Cherry Gv *HDGY* LS6 ....**87** H8
ILK LS29 ....**38** G3
ROY/SHW OL2 ....**228** E8
Cherry Hall Dr *ROY/SHW* * OL2 ..**229** J8
Cherry Hills *DOD/DAR* S75 ....**242** C5
Cherry La *KBTN* HD8 ....**240** H8
LIT OL15 ....**230** D3
Cherry Lea Ct *YEA* LS19 ....**84** D2
Cherry Nook Rd *HUDN* HD2 ....**193** G3
Cherry Pl *OSM* LS9 ....**7** L7
Cherry Ri *SCFT* LS14 ....**89** L6
Cherry Rw *OSM* LS9 ....**7** L6
Cherrys Rd *BSLYN/ROY* S71 ....**261** G6
Cherry St *HWTH* BD22 ....**79** G6
KGHY BD21 ....**3** L3
Cherry Tree Av *IDLE* * BD10 ......**83** M8
KNOT WF11 ....**182** A2
Cherry Tree Cl *DOD/DAR* * S75 ..**242** E5
MAR/SLWT HD7 ....**213** G1
Cherry Tree Ct
EARD/LOFT WF3 ....**153** L7
Cherry Tree Crs
PDSY/CALV LS28 ....**106** F3
WKFDW/WTN WF2 ....**199** M3
Cherry Tree Dr *GTL/HWG* HX4 ..**168** D2
PDSY/CALV LS28 ....**106** F3
WKFDW/WTN WF2 ....**199** M3
Cherry Tree Gdns *SHPY* BD18 ....**83** H8
Cherry Tree Ri *KGHY* BD21 ....**3** K4
Cherry Tree Rd
WKFDW/WTN WF2 ....**199** M2
Cherry Tree Rw *BGLY* BD16 ....**80** D7
Cherry Tree Wk
EARD/LOFT WF3 ....**153** L7
HOLM/MEL HD9 ....**254** F2
LDS * LS1 ....**9** L1
Cherrywood Cl *SCFT* LS14 ....**89** K5
Cherrywood Gdns *SCFT* LS14 ....**89** K5

Chertsey Cl *ROY/SHW* OL2 ......**229** K6
Chervana Ct *BOW* BD4 ....**128** A2
Cherwell Cft *GFTH/SHER* LS25 ..**135** K1
SEL YO8 ....**139** M5
Cherwell Dr *WBSY* BD6 ....**126** E5
Chesham Rd *BSLY* S70 ....**260** F5
Chesham St *GTHN* BD7 ....**4** B7
KGHY BD21 ....**3** K4
Chesil Bank *HUDW* HD3 ....**191** K8
Chesilton Av *HUDW* HD3 ....**191** K7
Chesney Av *MID* * LS10 ....**9** J7
Chesnut End *BSPA/BRAM* LS23 ..**49** G7
Chessington Dr
HOR/CROF WF4 ....**217** M3
Chester Cl *HIPP* HX3 ....**10** F1
Chester Gv *HIPP* * HX3 ....**10** F1
Chester Pl *HIPP* HX3 ....**10** F1
Chester Rd *HIPP* HX3 ....**10** F1
Chester St *GTHN* BD7 ....**4** D7
HIPP HX3 ....**10** F1
RPDN/SBR * HX6 ....**167** K2
WOR/ARM LS12 ....**108** E6
Chester Ter *HIPP* HX3 ....**10** F1
Chesterton Ct *HOR/CROF* WF4 ..**197** L4
MSTN/BAR LS15 ....**111** M8
Chesterton Dr *HOLM/MEL* HD9 ..**236** B3
Christopher Rd *HDGY* LS6 ....**6** D2
The Chestnuts *PONT* WF8 ....**181** H2
Chestnut Av *AWLS/ASK* DN6 ...**249** K5
BSPA/BRAM LS23 ....**48** E6
BTLY WF17 ....**173** J2
CUD/GR S72 ....**245** H3
HDGY LS6 ....**109** G3
MSTN/BAR LS15 ....**111** M4
TOD OL14 ....**141** J7
WBY LS22 ....**29** M8
WKFDW/WTN WF2 ....**199** J3
Chestnut Cl *FEA/AMT* WF7 ....**179** M7
GTL/HWG HX4 ....**168** D6
HUDS HD4 ....**214** C4
HWTH * BD22 ....**2** B7
ILK LS29 ....**39** G3
Chestnut Ct *BSLY* S70 ....**261** H7
SHPY BD18 ....**82** A7
Chestnut Crs *BSLY* S70 ....**261** K7
NORM WF6 ....**178** C6
Chestnut Dr *BHP/TINH* LS16 .....**86** D7
CUD/GR S72 ....**244** F1
Chestnut Garth *HUDW* * HD3 ..**191** K7
Chestnut Gn *GFTH/SHER* LS25 ..**138** D7
Chestnut Gv *BSPA/BRAM* LS23 ..**48** E6
ECHL BD2 ....**105** G2
HDGY * LS6 ....**109** G3
HEM/SK/SE WF9 ....**247** H5
HFAX HX1 ....**10** A8
HUDN HD2 ....**192** F3
Chestnut Ter *EARL* WF12 ....**195** L3
Chestnut Wk
WKFDW/WTN WF2 ....**176** C6
Chestnut Wy *BHP/TINH* LS16 ....**86** D1
LIT OL15 ....**207** L3
Chevet Cft *WKFDW/WTN* WF2 ..**199** G6
Chevet Gv *WKFDW/WTN* WF2 ..**199** G5
Chevet La *HOR/CROF* WF4 ......**221** K6
WKFDW/WTN WF2 ....**199** G5
Chevet Mt *WIL/AL* BD15 ....**103** J3
Chevet Park Ct
WKFDW/WTN WF2 ....**221** G3
Chevet Ri *BSLYN/ROY* S71 ....**243** J3
Chevet Vw *BSLYN/ROY* S71 .....**243** J2
Chevin Av *ILK* LS29 ....**61** J1
OT LS21 ....**41** K8
Chevin End Rd *ILK* LS29 ....**61** L2
Chevington Ct *YEA* * LS19 ....**84** D7
Chevins Cl *BTLY* WF17 ....**151** K6
Chevin Side *OT* LS21 ....**41** J8
Cheviot Av *HOLM/MEL* HD9 .....**235** H5
Cheviot Cl *HEM/SK/SE* WF9 ....**224** B7
MILN OL16 ....**207** J7
Cheviot Ct *GFTH/SHER* LS25 ...**135** H1
Cheviot Ga *LM/WK* BD12 ....**126** D8
Cheviot Pl *KNOT* WF11 ....**182** A2
Cheviots Rd *ROY/SHW* OL2 ....**229** J6
Cheviot Wy *MIRF* WF14 ....**194** B4
Cheyne Wk *KGHY* BD21 ....**2** D7
Chichester Cl *LIT* OL15 ....**207** H3
Chichester St *MILN* OL16 ....**206** C7
WOR/ARM * LS12 ....**108** E6
Chickenley La *EARL* WF12 ....**174** D3
Chidswell Gdns *EARL* WF12 .....**174** D3
Chidswell La *EARL* WF12 ....**174** C3
Child La *LVSG* WF15 ....**172** B4
Childs La *SHPY* BD18 ....**83** G8
Childs Rd *WKFDW/WTN* WF2 ..**175** M6
Chiltern Av *CAS* WF10 ....**179** M1
HUDW HD3 ....**191** H5
KNOT WF11 ....**182** A2
Chiltern Cl *GFTH/SHER* LS25 ...**135** H1
ROY/SHW OL2 ....**229** H6
Chiltern Ct *BRAM* LS13 ....**107** G1
GFTH/SHER LS25 ....**135** H1
HEM/SK/SE WF9 ....**224** B7
Chiltern Dr *FEA/AMT* WF7 ....**224** B1
MIRF WF14 ....**194** B4
Chiltern Rd *EARL* WF12 ....**174** B5
Chiltern Wy *LVSG* WF15 ....**171** M1
Chilton St *BSLY* S70 ....**261** J6
Chilver Dr *BOW* BD4 ....**128** C4
Chilwell Cl *BSLYN/ROY* S71 .....**243** H5
Chilwell Gdns *BSLYN/ROY* S71 ..**243** H5
Chimney La *KBTN* HD8 ....**215** M2
Chinewood Av *BTLY* WF17 ....**151** K8
Chippendale Ri *GIR* BD8 ....**103** M6
OT LS21 ....**41** J4
Chipping Fold *MILN* OL16 ....**229** H1
Chirton Gv *RHAY* LS8 ....**110** C1
Chiserley Gdns *HBR* HX7 ....**143** L1
Chislehurst Pl *WBOW* BD5 ......**126** E3

Chiswick St *HDGY* LS6 ....**109** G5
Chiswick Ter *HDGY* LS6 ....**109** G4
Choppards Bank Rd
HOLM/MEL HD9 ....**254** C6
Choppards La *HOLM/MEL* HD9 ..**254** C5
Chorley La *BVRD* LS3 ....**6** D9
Chrisharben Pk *CLAY* BD14 .....**125** L2
Chrismoor *IDLE* BD10 ....**83** J7
Christ Church Av
WOR/ARM LS12 ....**108** D6
Christ Church Mt
WOR/ARM LS12 ....**108** D6
Christ Church Pde
WOR/ARM LS12 ....**108** D6
Christ Church Pl
WOR/ARM LS12 ....**108** D6
Christ Church Rd
WOR/ARM LS12 ....**108** D6
Christ Church Ter
WOR/ARM LS12 ....**108** D6
Christ Church Vw
WOR/ARM LS12 ....**108** D6
Christine St *ROY/SHW* OL2 .....**229** K7
Christopher Rd *HDGY* LS6 ....**6** D2
Christopher St *WBOW* BD5 .....**126** E3
Christopher Ter *WBOW* BD5 ....**126** E3
Church Ap *GFTH/SHER* LS25 ...**113** H7
Church Av *HDGY* LS6 ....**87** H7
HEM/SK/SE WF9 ....**246** E4
HORS LS18 ....**85** K5
HUDS HD4 ....**214** A2
MAR/SLWT HD7 ....**213** G4
MOR LS27 ....**129** L6
RTHW LS26 ....**134** C4
WKFDE WF1 ....**177** L1
Churchbalk Dr *PONT* WF8 ....**181** G8
Churchbalk La *PONT* WF8 ....**181** G7
Church Bank *BFD* BD1 ....**5** G6
LUD/ILL HX2 ....**145** M8
RPDN/SBR * HX6 ....**167** L2
Church Bank La *HBR* HX7 ....**165** L3
Churchbank Wy *EARL* WF12 ....**195** L2
Church Cswy *BSPA/BRAM* LS23 ..**49** H5
Church Cl *DOD/DAR* S75 ....**242** A6
HECK * WF16 ....**172** F2
HOR/CROF WF4 ....**200** D4
KBTN HD8 ....**238** A6
LUD/ILL HX2 ....**145** M1
OT LS21 ....**42** E1
RTHW LS26 ....**134** C4
SCFT LS14 ....**111** K2
Church Ct *GTHN* * BD7 ....**126** B1
NORM WF6 ....**178** B1
YEA LS19 ....**62** D8
Church Crs *AL/HA/HU* LS17 ....**87** L2
HOR/CROF WF4 ....**197** G8
RTHW LS26 ....**134** C5
TAD LS24 ....**71** K7
YEA LS19 ....**62** C8
Church Cft *TAD* LS24 ....**116** A1
Church Dr *AL/HA/HU* LS17 ....**67** K1
HEM/SK/SE WF9 ....**246** E4
Church Farm Cl
EARD/LOFT WF3 ....**154** E5
NORM * WF6 ....**178** B2
Churchfarm Garth
AL/HA/HU LS17 ....**89** H2
Church Farm Vw
MSTN/BAR * LS15 ....**91** G7
Church Fenton La *TAD* LS24 ......**94** F2
Churchfield Av *CUD/GR* S72 ....**244** D8
DOD/DAR S75 ....**241** L8
Churchfield Cl *DOD/DAR* S75 ..**241** K6
LVSG WF15 ....**172** C2
Churchfield Ct *BSLY* S70 ....**261** G4
Churchfield Crs *CUD/GR* S72 ...**244** D8
Churchfield Cft *NORM* WF6 .....**178** B2
RTHW LS26 ....**155** H1
Churchfield Gv *RTHW* LS26 .....**155** G1
Churchfield La *AWLS/ASK* DN6 ..**205** K4
CAS WF10 ....**158** B8
DOD/DAR S75 ....**241** L6
RTHW LS26 ....**133** G8
Church Field Rd
AWLS/ASK DN6 ....**227** M5
Churchfield Rd *RTHW* LS26 .....**155** G1
Church Flds *ECHL* BD2 ....**105** M4
NORM WF6 ....**178** B1
Churchfields Cl *BSLY* * S70 .....**261** G4
Churchfields Rd *BRIG* HD6 ......**170** C3
Churchfield St *BTLY* * WF17 ....**173** L1
Churchfield Ter *CUD/GR* S72 ...**244** D8
Church Gdns *AL/HA/HU* LS17 ....**87** M3
GFTH/SHER LS25 ....**113** H6
MOR LS27 ....**129** L2
Church Garth *CAS* WF10 ....**158** B4
OT LS21 ....**42** E2
Churchgate *BHP/TINH* LS16 ......**63** M1
Church Ga *HORS* LS18 ....**85** K5
Churchgate *MOR* LS27 ....**129** L2
Church Gn *GIR* BD8 ....**104** D2
KBTN HD8 ....**216** B8
LUD/ILL * HX2 ....**146** A2
Church Gv *BSLYN/ROY* S71 .....**261** L2
HDGY LS6 ....**87** G2
HEM/SK/SE WF9 ....**246** E4
HORS LS18 ....**85** K5
Church Hts *STKB/PEN* S36 ....**258** B7
Church Hl *AL/HA/HU* LS17 ....**87** L2
BAIL BD17 ....**82** F7
BHP/TINH LS16 ....**63** M1
BSLYN/ROY S71 ....**243** J8
BSPA/BRAM LS23 ....**69** M4
GFTH/SHER LS25 ....**137** J2
PBR HG3 ....**28** E2
SCFT LS14 ....**68** C4
Church Hill Gdns
PDSY/CALV LS28 ....**107** H5
Church Hill Gn
PDSY/CALV LS28 ....**107** H4
Church Hill Mt
PDSY/CALV LS28 ....**107** H4
Churchill Gdns *LDSU* LS2 ....**9** K9

Churchill Gv HECK WF16 ....173 G3
  WKFDW/WTN WF2 ....199 G6
Churchill Rd CUL/QBY BD13 ...103 H8
Churchill St TOD OL14 ....141 G6
Churchill Wy AIRE BD20 ....35 G7
Church La AL/HA/HU LS17 ....45 H7
  AWLS/ASK DN6 ....249 L8
  BAIL BD17 ....83 L1
  BHP/TINH LS16 ....86 E2
  BRIG HD6 ....170 C3
  BSLY S70 ....261 G4
  CHAL LS7 ....87 M8
  CLECK BD19 ....150 E6
  COP/BISH YO23 ....73 K6
  CUD/GR S72 ....222 C8
  DEWS WF13 ....173 H6
  DOD/DAR S75 ....240 F3
  DOD/DAR S75 ....259 H2
  EARD/LOFT WF3 ....152 F7
  EARD/LOFT WF3 ....153 L7
  EARL WF12 ....196 A4
  ELL HX5 ....169 M7
  FEA/AMT WF7 ....178 F6
  FEA/AMT WF7 ....179 L5
  GFTH/SHER LS25 ....113 H7
  GFTH/SHER LS25 ....114 A7
  GFTH/SHER LS25 ....135 K5
  GFTH/SHER LS25 ....138 D6
  GLE DN14 ....161 M8
  GTL/HWG HX4 ....190 C2
  HBR HX7 ....143 G3
  HDGY LS6 ....87 H7
  HECK WF16 ....172 F2
  HIPP HX3 ....169 L2
  HOR/CROF WF4 ....197 G7
  HOR/CROF WF4 ....220 C2
  HOR/CROF WF4 ....222 A7
  HORS LS18 ....85 K5
  HUDE HD5 ....15 K7
  HUDE HD5 ....193 K7
  HUDS HD4 ....213 K8
  HUDS HD4 ....214 C4
  HUDW HD3 ....211 H1
  KBTN HD8 ....238 A6
  KBTN HD8 ....240 B4
  LUD/ILL HX2 ....146 A5
  LVSG WF15 ....171 K3
  LVSG WF15 ....172 C1
  MAR/SLWT HD7 ....213 L6
  MAR/SLWT HD7 ....233 H2
  MILN * OL16 ....206 B7
  MIRF WF14 ....194 E2
  MSTN/BAR LS15 ....111 L4
  NORM WF6 ....178 C5
  OT LS21 ....24 F8
  OT LS21 ....40 D4
  PBR HG3 ....28 E3
  PDSY/CALV LS28 ....107 G7
  PONT WF8 ....180 F6
  PONT WF8 ....203 M1
  RPDN/SBR HX6 ....188 F3
  RTHW LS26 ....134 C5
  RTHW LS26 ....156 E4
  STKB/PEN S36 ....258 B7
  TAD LS24 ....50 C4
  TAD LS24 ....71 K6
  WBSY BD6 ....126 D6
  WBY LS22 ....47 K5
  WKFDE WF1 ....176 D1
Church Lane Av WKFDE WF1 ...176 D1
Church Mdw BSPA/BRAM LS23...69 M3
  BTLY WF17 ....150 F5
Church Ms BSPA/BRAM LS23 ...48 E8
  GFTH/SHER LS25 ....116 A6
Church Mt HEM/SK/SE WF9 ...246 E4
  HORS LS18 ....85 K5
Church Pk LVSG WF15 ....172 A4
Church Pl GFTH/SHER LS25 ...113 H7
  HFAX HX1 ....10 E7
Church Rd AIRE BD20 ....55 M1
  BTLY WF17 ....151 H6
  DOD/DAR S75 ....259 G2
  EARD/LOFT WF3 ....177 H1
  HORS LS18 ....85 K6
  LVSG WF15 ....172 A4
  MILN OL16 ....206 D8
  NORM WF6 ....177 M3
  OSM LS9 ....9 L2
  ROY/SHW OL2 ....229 K8
  RTHW LS26 ....135 G6
  TOD OL14 ....141 G6
  WBSY BD6 ....126 D6
  WOR/ARM LS12 ....108 C7
Church Rw LDSU LS2 ....9 J1
Church Side RTHW LS26 ....156 E4
Church Side Cl HIPP HX3 ....11 H2
Church Side Dr HIPP HX3 ....11 H2
Churchside Vis RTHW LS26 ...156 E4
Church Sq GFTH/SHER LS25 ...113 H7
Church Stile MILN OL16 ....206 B7
Church St AIRE BD20 ....34 F7
  BGLY BD16 ....81 J4
  BRIC HD6 ....170 B6
  BSLY S70 ....261 G4
  BSLYN/ROY S71 ....243 L3
  BSLYN/ROY S71 ....243 M5
  BSPA/BRAM LS23 ....48 F7
  CAS WF10 ....157 M6
  CLECK BD19 ....150 A7
  COL BB8 ....74 E4
  CUD/GR S72 ....244 D8
  CUD/GR S72 ....245 H3
  CUL/QBY * BD13 ....79 M8
  DEWS WF13 ....195 C1
  DOD/DAR S75 ....242 A6
  DOD/DAR S75 ....242 E5
  DOD/DAR S75 ....259 G1
  DOD/DAR S75 ....260 C3
  EARL WF12 ....173 M6
  ELL HX5 ....169 H7
  GIR BD8 ....104 D5
  GSLY LS20 ....62 A5
  GTL/HWG HX4 ....168 F7
  HBR HX7 ....143 H1
  HBR HX7 ....144 A6
  HECK WF16 ....172 F3
  HEM/SK/SE WF9 ....247 J4
  HFAX HX1 ....11 J7
  HOLM/MEL * HD9 ....237 H8
  HOR/CROF WF4 ....220 B7
  HUD HD1 ....14 F6
  HUDE HD5 ....15 L1
  HUDS HD4 ....214 A2
  HUDW HD3 ....191 J8
  HUDW HD3 ....213 L1
  HWTH BD22 ....78 D7
  HWTH BD22 ....100 E4
  ILK LS29 ....19 J6
  KBTN HD8 ....217 L7
  KGHY BD21 ....2 F6
  KGHY BD21 ....3 J4
  KNOT WF11 ....159 L6
  KSTL LS5 ....108 C2
  LIT OL15 ....207 K1
  LVSG WF15 ....171 L1
  LVSG WF15 ....172 C1
  MAR/SLWT HD7 ....212 B6
  MAR/SLWT HD7 ....212 F2
  MID LS10 ....9 L9
  MILN OL16 ....206 E3
  MILN OL16 ....229 K2
  MOR LS27 ....129 L7
  MOR LS27 ....152 C1
  OSS WF5 ....174 F7
  ROCH OL11 ....206 A7
  RTHW LS26 ....133 C7
  RTHW LS26 ....155 G1
  RYKW YO26 ....32 D5
  SHPY BD18 ....82 F6
  SKP/WHF BD23 ....16 B3
  STKB/PEN S36 ....270 F3
  TAD LS24 ....94 E8
  TAD LS24 ....95 C1
  TAD LS24 ....116 A1
  TOD OL14 ....141 H6
  WBSY BD6 ....126 A7
  WBY LS22 ....48 A1
  WKFDE WF1 ....12 F6
  YEA LS19 ....62 C3
Church Ter HOLM/MEL HD9 ...254 C1
  KBTN HD8 ....239 M5
  LUD/ILL HX2 ....145 M1
  MILN OL16 ....229 H1
Church Top HEM/SK/SE WF9 ...246 E4
  CLECK BD19 ....149 K6
  CUD/GR S72 ....244 D8
  DOD/DAR S75 ....260 C3
  GFTH/SHER LS25 ....116 A6
  GFTH/SHER LS25 ....136 A4
  GFTH/SHER LS25 ....138 A3
  HEM/SK/SE WF9 ....246 E4
  HOLM/MEL HD9 ....253 K4
  HOR/CROF WF4 ....220 A4
  KSTL LS5 ....108 C2
  RPDN/SBR HX6 ....167 L2
  WKFDE WF1 ....199 G4
Church View Cl
  HOR/CROF WF4 ....222 E5
Church View Crs
  STKB/PEN S36 ....270 F3
Church View Ms
  BSPA/BRAM LS23 ....69 M1
Church View Rd
  STKB/PEN S36 ....270 F3
Church Vis HEM/SK/SE WF9 ...246 E4
Churchway HOR/CROF WF4 ...200 C5
Church Wy KGHY BD21 ....3 G6
  MOR * LS27 ....152 C1
Church Wood Av
  BHP/TINH LS16 ....86 E8
Churchwood Cl
  MAR/SLWT HD7 ....212 B5
Church Wood Mt
  BHP/TINH LS16 ....86 E8
Church Wood Rd
  BHP/TINH LS16 ....86 E8
Churcroft DOD/DAR S75 ....260 C2
Churn La LUD/ILL HX2 ....145 M7
Churn Milk La HIPP HX3 ....146 C2
Churwell Av DEWS WF13 ....173 H5
Churwell Cl CAS WF10 ....157 M8
Churwell V EARL WF12 ....174 C4
Cinder Hill Rd TOD OL14 ....142 A8
Cinderhills La HIPP HX3 ....169 G3
Cinder Hills Rd
  HOLM/MEL HD9 ....254 D2
Cinder Hills Wy DOD/DAR S75 ...260 C2
Cinder La BSPA/BRAM LS23 ...49 G8
  CAS WF10 ....157 L6
  OT LS21 ....42 B1
The Circle PONT WF8 ....181 G7
The Circuit AWLS/ASK DN6 ...249 H8
Cirrus Wy FEA/AMT WF7 ....224 B1
City La HIPP HX3 ....146 A5
City Rd GIR BD8 ....4 B7
City Sq LDS LS1 ....8 F1
Clanricarde St BSLYN/ROY S71 ...261 J5
Clapgate OT LS21 ....41 J6
Clapgate La RPDN/SBR HX6 ...166 F7
Clapham Dene Rd
  MSTN/BAR LS15 ....111 K5
Clapham St CUL/QBY BD13 ...102 A8
Clapton Av HFAX HX1 ....10 D8
Clara Dr PDSY/CALV LS28 ....84 C7
Clara Rd ECHL BD2 ....105 H1
Clara Gorton La MILN OL16 ...206 D8
Clara St BRIC HD6 ....170 C5
  HUD HD1 ....14 F2
  HUDS HD4 ....213 J2
  PDSY/CALV LS28 ....106 F4
  ROCH OL11 ....228 D1
Clare Crs LM/WK BD12 ....148 E4
Clare Hall La HFAX HX1 ....11 H8
Clare Hl HUD HD1 ....14 E3

Clarehurst Rd WMB/DAR S73 ...263 J8
Clarel Cl STKB/PEN S36 ....270 E4
Clarel St STKB/PEN S36 ....270 E4
Claremont HECK WF16 ....172 F2
  PDSY/CALV LS28 ....107 H7
Claremont Av BVRD LS3 ....6 C7
  SHPY BD18 ....83 G8
Claremont Ct HDGY LS6 ....87 G8
  SHPY BD18 ....83 G8
Claremont Crs HDGY LS6 ....109 H1
  SHPY BD18 ....83 G8
Claremont Dr HDGY LS6 ....87 G8
Claremont Gdns BGLY BD16...87 G8
Claremont Gv BVRD * LS3 ....6 C7
  PDSY/CALV LS28 ....107 G7
  SHPY BD18 ....83 G8
Claremont Pl WOR/ARM LS12 ...108 C7
Claremont Rd DEWS WF13 ...173 K5
  HDGY LS6 ....87 G8
  MILN OL16 ....229 G1
  SHPY BD18 ....83 G8
Claremont St CLECK BD19 ...149 M6
  ELL HX5 ....169 J8
  HUD HD1 ....14 E4
  RPDN/SBR * HX6 ....167 L1
  RTHW * LS26 ....133 L8
  WKFDE WF1 ....13 K7
  WOR/ARM LS12 ....108 C7
Claremont Ter GTHN BD7 ....4 C8
  WKFDW/WTN WF2 ....12 B5
  WOR/ARM LS12 ....108 C7
Claremont Vw BVRD * LS3 ....6 C7
  WKFDW/WTN WF2 ....12 B5
Claremont Vls BVRD * LS3 ....6 C7
Claremount HDGY LS6 ....87 G8
Claremount Rd HIPP HX3 ....146 E4
Claremount Ter HIPP HX3 ....146 E4
  ILK LS29 ....40 B8
Clarence Dr HORS LS18 ....85 K7
Clarence Gdns HORS LS18 ...85 K7
Clarence Pl BSLYN/ROY S71 ...261 K2
  HORS LS18 ....85 K7
  MID LS10 ....9 L4
Clarence Rd BRAM LS13 ....107 L5
  BTLY WF17 ....173 M1
  CLECK BD19 ....149 M7
  COL BB8 ....74 C1
  HFAX HX1 ....10 F6
Clarence St BRAM LS13 ....107 L5
  BSLY S70 ....260 F5
  COL BB8 ....74 D1
  HBR HX7 ....143 M5
  HWTH BD22 ....78 E8
  KGHY BD21 ....2 E8
  MILN OL16 ....228 D2
  WKFDE WF1 ....176 E7
Clarence Ter PDSY/CALV LS28 ...107 G8
Clarendon Ct WKFDE WF1 ....176 E7
Clarendon Pl CUL/QBY BD13 ...124 E6
  HFAX * HX1 ....10 E7
  LDSU LS2 ....6 C5
Clarendon Rd BGLY BD16 ....81 K2
  BSPA/BRAM LS23 ....48 E6
  LDSU LS2 ....6 C4
Clarendon St BSLY S70 ....260 F5
  COL BB8 ....74 D1
  HBR HX7 ....143 M5
  HWTH BD22 ....78 E8
  KGHY BD21 ....2 E8
  MILN OL16 ....228 D2
  WKFDE WF1 ....176 E7
Clarendon Ter PDSY/CALV LS28 ...107 G8
Clarendon Wy LDSU LS2 ....6 D7
Clare Rd CLECK BD19 ....149 L7
  HBR HX7 ....143 M5
  HFAX HX1 ....11 H7
  LM/WK BD12 ....148 A3
Clare Rd Flats HFAX HX1 ....11 H8
Clare St HFAX HX1 ....11 H7
Clarges St WBOW BD5 ....126 E3
Clarion St WKFDE WF1 ....13 K7
Clark Av OSM LS9 ....110 B7
Clark Ct FEA/AMT WF7 ....179 K5
Clark Crs OSM LS9 ....110 B7
Clarke Crs NORM WF6 ....178 C7
Clarke Gv WKFDE WF1 ....177 C5
Clarke Hall Rd EARD/LOFT WF3 ...177 G4
Clarke La HOLM/MEL HD9 ...235 C4
Clarke Rd EARD/LOFT WF3 ...175 C1
Clarke St DEWS WF13 ....173 H5
  DOD/DAR S75 ....260 F3
  MILN OL16 ....206 D4
  PDSY/CALV LS28 ....84 D8
Clark Gv OSM LS9 ....110 B7
Clark La OSM LS9 ....110 B7
Clark Mt OSM LS9 ....110 B7
Clark Rw OSM LS9 ....110 B7
Clarks Ct AWLS/ASK DN6 ....249 K8
Clarkson Av HECK WF16 ....173 C2
Clarkson Cl HECK WF16 ....173 C2
Clarkson Ct NORM WF6 ....178 E5
Clarkson Dr GFTH/SHER LS25...160 A3
Clarkson St DEWS WF13 ....172 F8
  DEWS WF13 ....173 G8
Clarkson Vw HDGY LS6 ....6 C1
Clark Spring Ri MOR LS27 ....130 D7
Clark Vw OSM * LS9 ....110 B7
Clarney Av WMB/DAR S73 ....263 H8
Clarney Pl WMB/DAR S73 ....263 H8
Clattering Stones Rd HBR HX7 ...165 M4
Clayborn Vw CLECK BD19 ....149 M8
Clay Butts HUD HD1 ....192 A4
Claycliffe Av DOD/DAR S75 ....260 E5
Claycliffe Rd DOD/DAR S75 ...260 E5
Claycliffe Ter BSLY * S70 ....260 F6
Clayfield Dr GTHN BD7 ....126 C4
Clay Hill Dr LM/WK BD12 ....148 F3
Clay House La GTL/HWG HX4 ...168 F7
Clay La MAR/SLWT HD7 ....212 C5
Claymore Ri AIRE BD20 ....36 B8
Claypit La CAS WF10 ....136 D7
Claypit La SCFT LS14 ....90 B1
Clay Pits La HFAX HX1 ....10 A7
  RPDN/SBR HX6 ....166 D7
Clay St HFAX HX1 ....10 E7
  LIT OL15 ....207 H1
  RPDN/SBR HX6 ....167 L2
Clayton Av GFTH/SHER LS25 ...135 K4
  HEM/SK/SE WF9 ....226 A4
Clayton Cl MID LS10 ....132 B4
Clayton Ct FEA/AMT WF7 ....201 L4

  MID LS10 ....132 B4
Clayton Dr MID LS10 ....132 B4
Clayton Flds HUDN HD2 ....14 C2
Clayton Fold AIRE BD20 ....35 C2
Clayton Gv YEA LS19 ....62 D7
Clayton Hall Rd AIRE BD20 ....35 C8
Clayton Holt HEM/SK/SE WF9 ...246 D5
Clayton La CLAY BD14 ....125 K3
  WBOW BD5 ....127 G2
Clayton Ms NORM WF6 ....178 C7
Clayton Pl NORM WF6 ....178 C2
Clayton Ri KGHY BD21 ....176 D1
Clayton Rd GTHN BD7 ....126 A2
  MID LS10 ....132 B4
Claytons Buildings
  FEA/AMT WF7 ....179 M6
Clayton St COL BB8 ....74 A2
  RTHW * LS26 ....155 L1
  WHIT OL12 ....206 D4
  WKFDW/WTN WF2 ....12 B4
Clayton Vw HEM/SK/SE WF9 ...246 D5
Clayton Wy MID LS10 ....132 B4
Clayton Wood Bank
  BHP/TINH LS16 ....86 B5
Clayton Wood Cl
  BHP/TINH LS16 ....86 B5
Clayton Wood Ct
  BHP/TINH LS16 ....86 B5
Clayton Wood Ri
  BHP/TINH LS16 ....86 B5
Clayton Wood Rd
  BHP/TINH LS16 ....86 B5
Clay Well MAR/SLWT HD7 ....212 F2
The Clearings MID LS10 ....131 M6
Clear Vw CUD/GR S72 ....245 J6
Cleasby Rd ILK LS29 ....61 J3
Cleavesty La AL/HA/HU LS17 ...46 D7
Cleckheaton Rd WBSY BD6 ...126 F7
Cleeve Hl YEA LS19 ....84 D2
Cleevethorpe Gv
  WKFDW/WTN WF2 ....199 G6
Clegg Hall Rd MILN OL16 ....206 F4
Clegg La GTL/HWG HX4 ....168 B7
Clegg St LIT OL15 ....185 H7
  MILN OL16 ....229 J1
Cleggswood Av LIT OL15 ....207 J3
Clement Cl NORM WF6 ....178 F5
Clement St MILN * OL16 ....206 D8
Clementina St WHIT OL12 ....206 A6
Clement Royds St WHIT * OL12 ...206 A6
Clement St GIR BD8 ....104 B6
  HUD HD1 ....14 D3
  HUDS HD4 ....213 M2
  RPDN/SBR * HX6 ....167 K2
  WKFDW/WTN WF2 ....198 B1
Clement Ter EARL WF12 ....173 L8
  RTHW LS26 ....155 G2
Cleopatra Pl BRAM LS13 ....107 L5
Clerk Green St BTLY WF17 ....173 K2
Clevedon Pl HIPP HX3 ....146 C4
Clevedon Wy BSLYN/ROY S71 ...243 K2
Cleveland Av HIPP * HX3 ....169 G2
  HOLM/MEL HD9 ....235 H5
  KNOT WF11 ....182 A2
  WKFDW/WTN WF2 ....197 M4
Cleveland Dr MILN OL16 ....207 K8
Cleveland Garth
  WKFDW/WTN WF2 ....197 M4
Cleveland Gv
  WKFDW/WTN WF2 ....197 M4
Cleveland Rd HIPP HX3 ....143 J3
  HUDW HD3 ....191 M7
Cleveland St COL BB8 ....52 B8
  TOD OL14 ....140 D5
Cleveland Wy KBTN HD8 ....238 E4
Cleveleys Av BEE/HOL LS11 ...8 B8
  MILN OL16 ....228 D3
Cleveleys Ct BEE/HOL * LS11 ...8 B7
Cleveleys Mt BEE/HOL * LS11 ...8 B7
Cleveleys Rd BEE/HOL LS11 ...8 B7
Cleveleys St BEE/HOL * LS11 ...8 B7
Cleveleys Ter BEE/HOL * LS11 ...8 B7
Clevlands Cl ROY/SHW OL2 ....229 J6
Cliff Cl CUD/GR S72 ....245 H3
  HUDW HD3 ....191 K8
Cliff Ct HOR/CROF * WF4 ....219 M2
  LVSG WF15 ....172 C3
Cliff Crs GFTH/SHER LS25 ....135 L5
  LUD/ILL HX2 ....168 A1
Cliffdale Rd CHAL LS7 ....109 K2
Cliff Dr HOR/CROF WF4 ....219 M1
Cliffe Ash MAR/SLWT HD7 ....212 F2
Cliffe Av BAIL BD17 ....82 E3
  BGLY BD16 ....80 C5
  HIPP HX3 ....148 C7
Cliffe Crs AIRE BD20 ....58 D6
  DOD/DAR S75 ....260 A7
Cliffe Dr YEA LS19 ....84 C3
Cliffe End HUDW HD3 ....191 K8
Cliffe House Av
  GFTH/SHER LS25 ....135 J1
Cliffe La BAIL BD17 ....82 E5
  BSLYN/ROY S71 ....261 L3
  CLECK BD19 ....150 A5
  CUL/QBY BD13 ....103 G7
  YEA LS19 ....84 C3
Cliffe La South BAIL BD17 ....82 E5
Cliffe La West BAIL BD17 ....82 E4
Cliffe Mill Fold AIRE BD20 ....59 G6
Cliffe Mt CLECK BD19 ....150 C5
Cliffe Pk KBTN HD8 ....238 A6
  MOR * LS27 ....151 M3
Cliffe Park Cha WOR/ARM LS12 ...108 C7
Cliffe Park Crs WOR/ARM LS12 ...130 C1
Cliffe Park Dr WOR/ARM LS12 ...108 C7
Cliffe Park Mt WOR/ARM LS12 ...108 C7
Cliffe Park Wy MOR LS27 ....151 M3
Cliffe Rd BFDE BD3 ....105 H4
  BRIC HD6 ....170 C4
  KBTN HD8 ....238 A6
  KGHY BD21 ....79 L2

Cliffestone Dr AIRE BD20 ....58 F6
Cliffe St BTLY WF17 ....173 H2
  CUL/QBY BD13 ....102 E7
  DEWS WF13 ....173 M5
  HBR HX7 ....143 J3
  KBTN HD8 ....240 B4
  KGHY BD21 ....2 F1
  LIT OL15 ....185 M4
Cliffe Ter BAIL BD17 ....82 E5
  GIR BD8 ....4 D1
  KGHY BD21 ....79 L2
  RPDN/SBR HX6 ....167 J1
Cliffe Vw KBTN HD8 ....240 B4
  MOR LS27 ....151 M3
  WIL/AL BD15 ....103 H4
Cliffe Wood Cl HTON BD9 ....104 A3
Cliffewood Ri KBTN HD8 ....240 A4
Cliff Gdns LUD/ILL HX2 ....168 A1
Cliff Gv HOR/CROF WF4 ....219 L2
Cliff Hl DOD/DAR S75 ....259 G1
Cliff Hill La LUD/ILL HX2 ....145 K8
Cliff Hill Rd AWLS/ASK DN6 ....227 K3
  ROY/SHW OL2 ....229 L5
Cliff Hollins La LM/WK BD12 ....127 M8
Cliff House La HOLM/MEL HD9 ...236 D8
Cliff La CUD/GR S72 ....245 G4
  HDGY LS6 ....6 D1
  HOLM/MEL HD9 ....254 D1
  RPDN/SBR HX6 ....188 F4
  WKFDE WF1 ....12 D1
Cliff Mt HDGY LS6 ....6 C1
Cliff Mount St HDGY LS6 ....6 C1
Cliff Mount Ter HDGY LS6 ....6 C1
Clifford Av ILK LS29 ....38 C1
  WKFDW/WTN WF2 ....198 F4
Clifford Ct BSPA/BRAM * LS23 ...70 C1
Clifford Hodgson Pl
  MOR * LS27 ....130 D7
Clifford Moor Rd
  BSPA/BRAM LS23 ....48 D7
Clifford Rd BAIL BD17 ....82 E4
  BSPA/BRAM LS23 ....49 G7
  BSPA/BRAM LS23 ....69 M3
  HEM/SK/SE WF9 ....246 D4
  ILK LS29 ....20 C8
Clifford St AIRE BD20 ....35 M4
  COL BB8 ....74 A1
  CUD/GR S72 ....244 E5
  HEM/SK/SE WF9 ....247 H4
  ROCH OL11 ....228 B1
  SKP/WHF BD23 ....16 B3
  WBOW BD5 ....4 F7
Clifford Vw WKFDW/WTN WF2 ...198 F4
Cliff Pde WKFDE WF1 ....12 D1
Cliff Park Av WKFDE WF1 ....176 D7
Cliff Rd HDGY LS6 ....6 C1
  HOLM/MEL HD9 ....253 J2
  HOLM/MEL HD9 ....254 D1
  HOR/CROF WF4 ....219 L3
Cliff Side Gdns HDGY LS6 ....109 J2
Cliff St HWTH BD22 ....78 F7
  MILN OL16 ....206 D5
  PONT WF8 ....180 G6
  WKFDW/WTN WF2 ....176 D7
Cliff Ter BSLYN/ROY S71 ....261 J5
  HDGY LS6 ....6 C1
Cliff Vale Rd SHPY BD18 ....104 C3
Cliff Villa Ct WKFDE WF1 ....12 C1
Cliff Wood Av SHPY BD18 ....82 D8
Clifton Av BSLYN/ROY S71 ....243 G6
  EARD/LOFT WF3 ....177 G1
  HFAX HX1 ....10 A8
  HOLM/MEL HD9 ....236 D8
  HOR/CROF WF4 ....197 J4
  OSM LS9 ....110 C5
  PONT WF8 ....180 D6
Clifton Cl BSLYN/ROY S71 ....243 G6
  HOR/CROF WF4 ....197 M4
Clifton Common BRIG HD6 ....170 E4
Clifton Ct DEWS WF13 ....173 H5
Clifton Crs BSLYN/ROY S71 ....243 H5
  HOR/CROF WF4 ....197 J4
Clifton Dr HOR/CROF WF4 ....197 J4
  PDSY/CALV LS28 ....107 G5
Clifton Gdns CUD/GR S72 ....245 G3
Clifton Gv OSM LS9 ....110 C5
Clifton Hl PDSY/CALV LS28 ....107 G6
Clifton La HOLM/MEL HD9 ....235 G4
  OT LS21 ....41 G2
Clifton Mt OSM LS9 ....110 C5
Clifton Pl PDSY/CALV LS28 ....107 G6
  SHPY BD18 ....82 D7
  WKFDE WF1 ....176 D6
Clifton Rd CUD/GR S72 ....245 J7
  HIPP HX3 ....168 C2
  HOR/CROF WF4 ....197 J5
  HOR/CROF WF4 ....200 J3
  HUD HD1 ....14 A5
  ILK LS29 ....38 F3
  PDSY/CALV LS28 ....107 G6
Clifton Side HUDN HD2 ....171 H4
Clifton St BSLY S70 ....261 J6
  COL BB8 ....74 D4
  GIR BD8 ....4 C1
  HEM/SK/SE WF9 ....223 G6
  HIPP HX3 ....10 C1
  HWTH BD22 ....2 C7
  MILN OL16 ....207 H8
  ROCH * OL11 ....228 C6
  RPDN/SBR HX6 ....167 L2
Clifton Ter BTLY WF17 ....173 M1
  OSM LS9 ....110 C5
Clifton Vw HOLM/MEL HD9 ....236 D8
Clifton Vls GIR BD8 ....4 C1
Cliftonville Rd MILN OL16 ....228 E6
Clipston Av HDGY LS6 ....87 H3
Clipstone Av BSLYN/ROY S71 ...243 H6
Clipstone St WBOW BD5 ....127 G4
Clipston St HDGY LS6 ....87 H3
Clipston Ter HDGY * LS6 ....87 H3
Clive Dr GTHN BD7 ....126 D1
Clive Rd PBR HG3 ....28 E3
Clive Ter GTHN BD7 ....126 D1
Cloberry St LDSU LS2 ....6 C3
Clock La CUL/QBY BD13 ....101 M5
Clock Row Av HEM/SK/SE WF9 ...246 F3
Clock Row Gv HEM/SK/SE WF9 ...246 F3
Clock Row Mt HEM/SK/SE WF9 ...246 F3

Clock View St KGHY BD21 ...57 K5
Clog Br AIRE BD20 ...36 A5
Clog Sole Rd BRIG ...170 B2
The Cloisters HFAX HX1 ...10 C9
  MILN OL16 ...206 D5
Cloisters Wy BSLYN/ROY S71 ...261 M4
The Close AL/HA/HU LS17 ...67 L1
  AL/HA/HU LS17 ...87 J1
  AWLS/ASK DN6 ...227 M3
  BSLYN/ROY S71 ...243 L5
  BSLYN/ROY S71 ...262 A3
  BSPA/BRAM LS23 ...48 F6
  EARD/LOFT WF3 ...153 M7
  GFTH/SHER LS25 ...135 J5
  GSLY LS20 ...61 L6
  HOR/CROF WF4 ...198 A7
  KBTN HD8 ...240 A4
  MSTN/BAR LS15 ...90 F8
  OSM LS9 ...9 L1
  PONT WF8 ...181 H7
  SCFT LS14 ...68 C8
  SKP/WHF BD23 ...16 B3
  TAD LS24 ...93 M3
  WBY LS22 ...47 K6
Close Cl WBY LS22 ...29 M6
Close Head Dr CUL/QBY BD13 ...102 C7
Close Head La CUL/QBY BD13 ...102 D7
Close La HWTH ...54 C5
Close Lea BRIG HD6 ...170 B5
Close Lea Av BRIG HD6 ...170 B5
Close Lea Ga BRIG HD6 ...170 B6
Close Lea Dr BRIG HD6 ...170 B6
Close Lea Wy BRIG HD6 ...170 B5
Close Rd CAS WF10 ...158 B7
Closes Rd BRIG HD6 ...170 B5
Close St HEM/SK/SE WF9 ...223 L7
Cloth Hall St DEWS * WF13 ...173 M6
  HUD HD1 ...14 F7
  LDS LS1 ...9 H1
Cloudberry Wy DOD/DAR S75 ...242 F6
Cloudsdale Av WBOW BD5 ...127 G2
The Clough KBTN HD8 ...215 M3
  MIRF WF14 ...172 A8
Clough Av AIRE BD20 ...56 E1
Clough Bank LUD/ILL HX2 ...145 K1
Clough Bank La HWTH BD22 ...56 D8
Clough Dr BTLY WF17 ...151 J4
  KBTN HD8 ...215 M4
  MAR/SLWT HD7 ...212 F6
Clough Foot La
  HOLM/MEL HD9 ...254 C7
Clough Ga HOR/CROF WF4 ...216 F1
  HWTH BD22 ...78 F4
Clough Gate Dr
  HOR/CROF WF4 ...216 F1
Clough Gn DOD/DAR * S75 ...258 E3
Clough Hall La HUDS HD4 ...214 E6
Clough Head STKB/PEN S36 ...270 F5
Clough Hey MAR/SLWT * HD7 ...233 H2
Clough House La
  GTL/HWG HX4 ...189 K3
  KBTN HD8 ...239 L4
  MAR/SLWT HD7 ...211 M5
  WHIT OL12 ...184 D8
Clough La BRIC HD6 ...170 B8
  BRIG HD6 ...170 F1
  HBR HX7 ...144 F1
  HUDW HD3 ...213 L1
  HWTH BD22 ...78 E3
  LUD/ILL HX2 ...123 L8
  LVSG WF15 ...171 M2
Clough Lea MAR/SLWT HD7 ...233 H2
Clough Ml TOD * OL14 ...163 J5
Clough Pk KBTN HD8 ...215 M4
Clough Pl LUD/ILL HX2 ...145 K1
Clough Rd HOR/CROF WF4 ...217 M5
  HUDN HD2 ...192 C4
  LIT OL15 ...185 J6
  MAR/SLWT HD7 ...212 C2
  ROY/SHW OL2 ...229 M8
  RPDN/SBR HX6 ...167 M4
  TOD OL14 ...163 J5
Clough St MOR LS27 ...152 D2
  WBOW BD5 ...127 G3
  WHIT OL12 ...184 E8
Clough Ter LIT * OL15 ...185 J7
Clough Wy KBTN HD8 ...215 M4
Clovelly Av BEE/HOL LS11 ...131 K3
Clovelly Gv BEE/HOL LS11 ...131 K3
Clovelly Pl BEE/HOL LS11 ...131 K3
Clovelly Rw BEE/HOL LS11 ...131 K3
Clovelly Ter BEE/HOL LS11 ...131 K3
Clover Ct PDSY/CALV LS28 ...84 C8
Clover Crs PDSY/CALV LS28 ...84 C7
Cloverdale HIPP HX3 ...125 M7
Clover Hall Crs MILN OL16 ...206 E5
Clover Hl LVSG WF15 ...171 M1
  SKP/WHF BD23 ...16 D1
Clover Hill Cl HFAX HX1 ...10 F8
Clover Hill Rd HFAX HX1 ...168 D1
Clover Hill Ter HFAX HX1 ...168 D1
Clover Hill Vw HFAX * HX1 ...168 D1
Cloverlands DOD/DAR S75 ...242 E6
Clover Rl KGHY BD21 ...3 M5
Clover St GTHN BD7 ...126 D3
  WHIT OL12 ...206 A6
Clover Vw MILN * OL16 ...206 E7
Cloverville Ap WBSY BD6 ...126 E7
Clover Wk HEM/SK/SE WF9 ...225 H7
Clubhouses Cft
  HOR/CROF WF4 ...197 J5
Club La BRAM LS13 ...107 J1
  LUD/ILL HX2 ...146 B3
Club Rw CHAL LS7 ...87 L7
  YEA LS19 ...62 F6
Club St BSLYN/ROY S71 ...261 L2
  GTHN BD7 ...104 B8
  TOD OL14 ...140 D5
Clumber Dr CLECK BD19 ...150 D7
Clumber St DOD/DAR S75 ...260 F4
Cluntergate HOR/CROF WF4 ...197 K5
Clunters La LUD/ILL HX2 ...144 D8
Clutton St BTLY WF17 ...174 A1
Clyde Ap WOR/ARM * LS12 ...109 G8
Clyde Cha WOR/ARM LS12 ...109 G8
Clyde Ct MILN OL16 ...206 D8
  WOR/ARM LS12 ...109 G8
Clyde Gdns WOR/ARM LS12 ...109 G8
Clyde Gra WOR/ARM LS12 ...109 G8

Clydesdale Dr WBSY BD6 ...126 B7
Clyde St BGLY BD16 ...81 H3
  BSLYN/ROY S71 ...261 H5
  RPDN/SBR HX6 ...167 K3
  WKFDE WF1 ...13 K7
Clyde Vw WOR/ARM * LS12 ...109 G8
Clyde Vw WOR/ARM LS12 ...109 G7
Coach Gate La STKB/PEN S36 ...257 M4
Coach House Dr HUDE HD5 ...215 H1
Coach House La BSLY S70 ...261 H8
Coach La CLECK * BD19 ...150 A6
  CUL/QBY BD13 ...103 H8
  OT LS21 ...24 B8
Coach Rd GSLY LS20 ...61 M7
  HIPP HX3 ...148 B7
  HUD/MEL HD9 ...235 H5
  HUDN HD2 ...192 B4
  RPDN/SBR HX6 ...188 F2
  WKFDE WF1 ...176 E1
  WOR/ARM LS12 ...130 A3
Coach St SKP/WHF BD23 ...16 B2
Coach Street Yd
  SKP/WHF * BD23 ...16 B2
Coalby Wk BSLY * S70 ...261 G4
Coal Clough Rd TOD OL14 ...140 C3
Coal Ga MAR/SLWT HD7 ...211 H5
Coal Gate Rd RPDN/SBR HX6 ...188 A1
Coal Hill Dr BRAM LS13 ...107 H2
Coal Hill Fold BRAM LS13 ...107 H2
Coal Hill Gdns BRAM LS13 ...107 H2
Coal Hill Gn BRAM LS13 ...107 H2
Coal Hill La PDSY/CALV LS28 ...107 G2
Coal La LUD/ILL HX2 ...124 A3
Coal Pit La BRIG HD6 ...170 F5
  BTLY WF17 ...151 J8
  COL BB8 ...74 B2
  CUD/GR S72 ...262 L1
  HOLM/MEL HD9 ...237 C8
  KBTN HD8 ...238 F6
  PONT WF8 ...226 B3
  HEM/SK/SE WF9 ...248 A2
Coalpit La HIPP HX3 ...169 G2
  BTLY WF17 ...257 H3
Coal Rd AL/HA/HU LS17 ...89 J2
  SCFT LS14 ...89 K8
Coates Cl EARL WF12 ...174 A3
Coate's La HUDE HD5 ...35 H2
Coates St WBOW BD5 ...126 F2
Coates Ter WBOW BD5 ...126 F2
Cobb Av WKFDW/WTN WF2 ...198 B2
Cobbler Hall HOR/CROF WF4 ...219 H6
Cobblers La PONT WF8 ...181 H4
  PONT WF8 ...181 H5
Cobcroft La KNOT WF11 ...182 F7
  KNOT WF11 ...183 K5
Cobcroft Rd HUDN HD2 ...14 F1
Cobden Ct HFAX HX1 ...10 F4
Cobden Gv WOR/ARM LS12 ...130 B2
Cobden Ms MOR LS27 ...152 C2
Cobden Pl WOR/ARM LS12 ...130 B2
Cobden Rd WOR/ARM LS12 ...130 B2
Cobden St CLAY BD14 ...125 K2
  CUL/QBY BD13 ...125 H5
  IDLE BD10 ...83 K7
  TOD OL14 ...163 K1
  WIL/AL BD15 ...103 K5
  WOR/ARM LS12 ...130 B2
Cobden Ter ELL * HX5 ...191 H1
  WOR/ARM LS12 ...130 B2
Cobham Pde WKFDE * WF1 ...176 D2
Cobham St MSTN/BAR LS15 ...112 B4
Cob La BWCK/EAR BB18 ...52 C1
Cockburn Cl BEE/HOL LS11 ...9 G9
Cockburn Wy BEE/HOL LS11 ...9 H9
Cockerham Av DOD/DAR S75 ...261 G3
Cockerham La DOD/DAR S75 ...261 G3
Cockermouth La
  HOR/CROF WF4 ...216 E4
Cockhill La COL BB8 ...52 D6
Cock Hill La HIPP HX3 ...125 J8
Cocking La ILK LS29 ...36 E1
Cockin La CUL/QBY BD13 ...124 F3
Cockley Hill La HUDE HD5 ...193 L5
Cockley Mdw HUDE HD5 ...193 L5
Cockroft Gv BFDE BD3 ...5 K5
Cockshott Cl WOR/ARM LS12 ...108 B5
Cockshott Dr WOR/ARM LS12 ...108 B5
Cockshott La IDLE BD10 ...83 J6
  WOR/ARM LS12 ...108 B5
Cockshott Pl ILK LS29 ...19 G6
Coggil St MILN OL16 ...132 C4
Coiners Fold HBR HX7 ...143 L6
Colbeck Rw BTLY WF17 ...151 G6
Colbert Av ILK LS29 ...39 G1
Colby Ri MSTN/BAR LS15 ...111 G7
Coldbeck Dr WBSY BD6 ...126 A6
Coldcotes Av OSM LS9 ...110 D4
Coldcotes Crs OSM LS9 ...110 F4
Coldcotes Dr OSM LS9 ...110 E4
Coldcotes Garth OSM LS9 ...110 F4
Coldcotes Gv OSM LS9 ...110 F4
Coldcotes Wk OSM LS9 ...110 F4
Cold Edge Rd LUD/ILL HX2 ...122 E1
  LUD/ILL HX2 ...145 H1
Colden Cl HBR * HX7 ...143 H3
Colden La HBR HX7 ...120 B8
Colden Rd HBR HX7 ...143 G2
Colders Dr HOLM/MEL HD9 ...234 F5
Colders Gn HOLM/MEL HD9 ...244 F4
Cold Greave St MILN OL16 ...229 L2
  LUD/ILL HX2 ...145 H1
Coldhill La GFTH/SHER LS25 ...115 H1
  GFTH/SHER LS25 ...115 J3
Cold Hill La HOLM/MEL HD9 ...237 G7
  HUDS HD4 ...214 C6
Cold Royd La HUDE HD5 ...193 J7
Coldshaw Top HWTH BD22 ...100 D1
Cold St HWTH BD22 ...78 E8
Cold Well La MSTN/BAR LS15 ...111 K5
Cold Well Rd MSTN/BAR LS15 ...111 K5
Coldwells Hl GTL/HWG HX4 ...190 A3
Cold Well Sq MSTN/BAR * LS15 ...111 K5

Coldwell St MAR/SLWT HD7 ...212 F5
  WOR/ARM LS12 ...8 A3
Coleman St BFDE BD3 ...5 G2
Colenso Gdns BEE/HOL LS11 ...8 B7
Colenso Gv BEE/HOL LS11 ...8 B7
  KGHY * BD21 ...3 M1
Colenso Mt BEE/HOL LS11 ...8 B7
Colenso Pl BEE/HOL LS11 ...8 B7
Colenso Rd BEE/HOL LS11 ...8 B7
Colenso Ter BEE/HOL LS11 ...8 B7
Colenso Wk KGHY BD21 ...3 M1
Coleridge Av BSLYN/ROY S71 ...261 K2
Coleridge Cl RTHW LS26 ...155 L2
Coleridge Crs
  WKFDW/WTN WF2 ...176 B3
Coleridge Gdns IDLE BD10 ...83 L6
Coleridge La PDSY/CALV LS28 ...99 J7
Coleridge Rd LIT OL15 ...207 H4
Coleridge St HFAX HX1 ...11 H7
Coleridge Wy PONT WF8 ...180 F4
Coles Wy AIRE BD20 ...57 M4
Coley Hall La HIPP HX3 ...147 M4
Coley Rd HIPP HX3 ...147 L3
Coley Vw HIPP HX3 ...147 L3
Colinsway WKFDW/WTN WF2 ...12 C4
Collbrook Av WBSY BD6 ...126 A7
Colleen Rd HOR/CROF WF4 ...220 A1
College Av BSLY S70 ...261 L8
College Farm La WBY LS22 ...47 K3
College Gv CAS WF10 ...157 J8
  WKFDE WF1 ...176 E7
College Grove Cl WKFDE WF1 ...176 E6
College Grove Rd WKFDE WF1 ...176 E6
College Grove Vw WKFDE WF1 ...176 E6
College La AIRE BD20 ...16 F8
College Lawns WOR/ARM LS12 ...108 C6
College Rd BTLY WF17 ...151 G5
  HUDS HD4 ...213 M2
  TOD OL14 ...140 E5
College St East HUDS HD4 ...213 M2
College Ter HFAX * HX1 ...168 B1
College Vw WOR/ARM LS12 ...108 C7
Colley Av BSLY S70 ...261 L8
Colley Crs BSLY S70 ...261 L8
Colley St MILN OL16 ...206 C5
Collier Av MILN OL16 ...207 H7
Collier Hag La COP/BISH YO23 ...33 M8
Collier La BAIL BD17 ...82 D2
  GFTH/SHER LS25 ...
Colliers Cl SHPY BD18 ...82 A7
Colliers La AL/HA/HU LS17 ...89 G2
Colliers Wy KBTN HD8 ...240 B2
Collindale Cl IDLE BD10 ...84 A8
Collinfield Ri WBSY BD6 ...126 B8
Collinge Rd HWTH BD22 ...54 F3
Collinge St ROY/SHW * OL2 ...229 K7
Collingham Av WBSY BD6 ...125 M6
Collingham Dr
  GFTH/SHER LS25 ...113 H8
Collingwood Rd NORM WF6 ...178 C4
Collin Moor La GTL/HWG HX4 ...168 E6
Collin Rd SCFT LS14 ...111 H5
Collins Cl DOD/DAR S75 ...260 A7
  HWTH BD22 ...79 G6
Collinson St CLECK BD19 ...149 M6
Collins St BOW BD4 ...127 K1
  GTHN BD7 ...126 C3
Colmore Gv WOR/ARM LS12 ...130 F1
Colmore Rd WOR/ARM LS12 ...130 F1
Colmore St WOR/ARM LS12 ...108 F8
Colne Hurst HUDN HD2 ...193 G2
Colne La COL BB8 ...74 A2
Colne Rd AIRE BD20 ...55 H1
  BWCK/EAR BB18 ...52 B2
  COL BB8 ...74 C4
  HUD HD1 ...214 C2
  HWTH BD22 ...54 C4
Colne Rd Goodley HWTH BD22 ...78 D4
Colne St HUD HD1 ...14 B9
  HUD HD1 ...15 J8
Colne Vale Rd HUDS HD4 ...213 J2
Colne Valley Circular Wk
  MAR/SLWT HD7 ...211 H6
  MAR/SLWT HD7 ...212 D2
  MAR/SLWT HD7 ...233 J3
Colonel's Wk PONT WF8 ...180 E5
Colorado Wy CAS WF10 ...180 A2
Colster Cl DOD/DAR S75 ...260 C4
Colston Cl GIR BD8 ...104 A5
Colton Br TAD LS24 ...73 K3
Colton Ct MSTN/BAR LS15 ...111 M7
Colton Crt MSTN/BAR LS15 ...111 M4
Colton Garth MSTN/BAR LS15 ...111 M7
Colton Rd MSTN/BAR LS15 ...111 L7
  WOR/ARM LS12 ...108 E7
Colton Rd East
  MSTN/BAR LS15 ...112 A8
Colton St WOR/ARM * LS12 ...108 E7
Coltsfoot Cl PONT WF8 ...180 F7
Columbia St BSLY S70 ...261 G7
Columbus St HIPP * HX3 ...10 D1
Colville Ter BEE/HOL LS11 ...8 E7
  EARD/LOFT WF3 ...154 A5
Colwyn Av BEE/HOL LS11 ...131 K4
Colwyn Mt BEE/HOL LS11 ...131 K4
Colwyn Pl BEE/HOL LS11 ...131 K4
Colwyn Rd BEE/HOL LS11 ...131 K4
Colwyn St HUDW HD3 ...191 M7
Colwyn Ter BEE/HOL LS11 ...131 K4
Colwyn Vw BEE/HOL LS11 ...131 K4
Colyton Mt WIL/AL BD15 ...103 J5
The Combs EARL WF12 ...196 A3
Combs Rd EARL WF12 ...195 M4
Commerce Ct BOW BD4 ...127 M2
Commercial Buildings
  LM/WK BD12 ...149 K2
Commercial Ct LDS LS1 ...9 G7
Commercial Rd DEWS WF13 ...173 L5
  KBTN HD8 ...239 J4

  KSTL LS5 ...108 C3
Commercial St BFD * BD1 ...5 G5
  BRIG HD6 ...170 C4
  BSLY S70 ...261 J6
  BTLY WF17 ...173 L1
  CAS WF10 ...157 M6
  CLECK BD19 ...150 A7
  CUL/QBY BD13 ...101 M5
  CUL/QBY * BD13 ...103 G8
  DEWS WF13 ...173 H8
  EARL WF12 ...174 B7
  HBR HX7 ...143 J3
  HUD HD1 ...214 D2
  LDS LS1 ...7 C9
  MAR/SLWT HD7 ...212 C6
  MOR LS27 ...152 C2
  RTHW LS26 ...155 G1
  SHPY BD18 ...82 B5
  TAD LS24 ...71 M3
  TOD OL14 ...163 L1
  WKFDE WF1 ...13 G6
Commercial Vls
  PDSY/CALV LS28 ...106 F8
Commondale Wy BOW BD4 ...127 J8
The Common EARL WF12 ...195 M3
Common End La KBTN HD8 ...215 M4
Common Holme La ILK LS29 ...20 A8
Common Ing La
  HOR/CROF WF4 ...222 D4
Common La AWLS/ASK DN6 ...227 M3
  BSLYN/ROY S71 ...243 L2
  BTLY DN5 ...246 D8
  EARD/LOFT WF3 ...153 L5
  GFTH/SHER LS25 ...138 B2
  GLE DN14 ...161 J8
  HEM/SK/SE WF9 ...225 H7
  HIPP HX3 ...147 H8
  HOR/CROF WF4 ...217 J5
  HOR/CROF WF4 ...219 M6
  KBTN HD8 ...217 G7
  KBTN HD8 ...239 K8
  KNOT WF11 ...182 F3
  PONT WF8 ...225 K2
  SEL YO8 ...139 K4
  TAD LS24 ...95 G3
  WKFDW/WTN WF2 ...221 H1
Common Rd BTLY WF17 ...173 H2
  CUD/GR S72 ...245 J3
  CUD/GR S72 ...246 A5
  EARD/LOFT WF3 ...155 H7
  ELL HX5 ...169 L8
  HEM/SK/SE WF9 ...223 J4
  HUD HD1 ...14 E2
  LM/WK BD12 ...126 E8
  TAD LS24 ...116 B1
Common Road Av
  HEM/SK/SE WF9 ...246 C5
Commonside BTLY WF17 ...173 M4
  LVSG WF15 ...172 A4
Common Side La
  FEA/AMT WF7 ...179 J7
Como Av GIR BD8 ...104 B5
Como Dr GIR BD8 ...104 B5
Como Gdns GIR BD8 ...104 B5
Como Gv GIR BD8 ...104 B5
Compeigne Av AIRE BD20 ...58 B5
Compton Av OSM LS9 ...110 C4
Compton Crs OSM LS9 ...110 C4
Compton Gv OSM LS9 ...110 C4
Compton La AL/HA/HU LS17 ...68 B1
Compton Mt OSM LS9 ...110 C4
Compton Pl OSM LS9 ...110 C4
Compton Rd OSM LS9 ...110 C4
Compton Rw OSM LS9 ...110 C4
Compton St BOW BD4 ...127 L4
  KGHY BD21 ...3 J5
  OSM LS9 ...110 C4
Compton Ter OSM LS9 ...110 C4
Compton Vw OSM LS9 ...110 C4
Compton Wy ROY/SHW OL2 ...229 K8
Concordia St LDS LS1 ...9 G2
Concord St HOLM/MEL HD9 ...236 B2
  LDSU LS2 ...7 J7
Concrete St HIPP HX3 ...10 D1
Condor Cl WBSY BD6 ...125 L5
Conduit St GIR BD8 ...4 A1
Cone La DOD/DAR S75 ...259 J7
Coney La KGHY BD21 ...3 H6
Coney Moor Gv RTHW LS26 ...157 H3
Coney Wk DEWS WF13 ...173 H6
Coney Warren La
  EARD/LOFT WF3 ...155 G6
Conference Pl WOR/ARM LS12 ...108 C3
Conference Rd
  WOR/ARM LS12 ...108 C3
Conference Ter
  WOR/ARM LS12 ...108 C3
Congress Mt WOR/ARM LS12 ...108 C3
Congress St WOR/ARM LS12 ...108 C3
Congreve Ap AL/HA/HU LS17 ...68 A1
Congreve Wy AL/HA/HU LS17 ...47 G8
Conisborough ROCH * OL11 ...206 A8
Conisborough La
  GFTH/SHER LS25 ...113 K7
Coniston Av CUL/QBY BD13 ...124 F5
  DOD/DAR S75 ...242 C4
  HDGY LS6 ...109 G1
  HUDE HD5 ...15 L6
Coniston Cl CUL/QBY BD13 ...124 F5
  ELL HX5 ...169 K7
  STKB/PEN S36 ...270 F2
Coniston Ct EARD/LOFT WF3 ...154 E5
Coniston Dr CAS WF10 ...159 G7
Conistone Crs WKFDE WF1 ...177 G5
Coniston Gdns CAS WF10 ...159 G7
  MSTN/BAR LS15 ...111 G8
Coniston Gv COL BB8 ...52 B9
  HTON BD9 ...104 B4
  ROY/SHW OL2 ...228 D2
Coniston Rd BSLYN/ROY S71 ...261 J5
  EARL WF12 ...174 B4
  GTHN BD7 ...126 D4
  HOLM/MEL HD9 ...235 D2
  RTHW LS26 ...133 L7
Coniston Wy RTHW LS26 ...133 L7
  WBY LS22 ...29 K8
Connaught Av ROCH OL11 ...228 D3

Connaught Fold HUDN HD2 ...193 G2
Cononley La AIRE BD20 ...34 C4
Cononley Rd AIRE BD20 ...34 C6
Consort Av ROY/SHW OL2 ...228 C8
Consort St WHF BD23 ...16 D2
  SKP/WHF BD23 ...16 D2
Consort Ter BVRD LS3 ...6 B7
Consort Vw BVRD LS3 ...6 B7
Consort Wk BVRD LS3 ...6 B7
Constable Gv WKFDW/WTN WF3 ...155 G8
Constable Rd EARD/LOFT WF3 ...153 H6
  ILK LS29 ...38 F3
Constance Gdns CHAL LS7 ...6 F4
Constance St SHPY * BD18 ...82 B6
Constance Wy CHAL LS7 ...6 F4
Constantine Rd MILN * OL16 ...206 D4
Constitutional St HFAX HX1 ...10 B9
Conway Av RHAY LS8 ...110 B3
  HOLM/MEL HD9 ...234 F5
Conway Dr RHAY LS8 ...110 B3
Conway Gv RHAY LS8 ...110 B3
Conway Mt RHAY LS8 ...110 B3
Conway Pl RHAY LS8 ...110 B3
Conway Rd RHAY LS8 ...110 B3
  WKFDW/WTN WF2 ...176 A7
Conway St BSLY S70 ...261 M6
  HFAX HX1 ...10 C7
  PDSY/CALV LS28 ...106 F5
  RHAY LS8 ...110 B3
Conway Ter RHAY LS8 ...110 B3
Conway Vw RHAY LS8 ...110 B3
Conyers Yd OSS * WF5 ...175 G7
Cooke Crs CLECK BD19 ...150 C6
Cooke La KGHY BD21 ...3 G4
Cooke St KGHY BD21 ...3 G5
Cook House Rd COL BB8 ...52 A8
Cook La HECK WF16 ...172 E2
Cookridge Av BHP/TINH LS16 ...64 A8
Cookridge Dr BHP/TINH LS16 ...63 M8
Cookridge Gv BHP/TINH LS16 ...64 A8
Cookridge La BHP/TINH LS16 ...64 A8
Cookridge St LDSU LS2 ...6 F3
Cooksland La FEA/AMT WF7 ...179 G6
Cookson Cl CAS WF10 ...180 F1
Cookson St BRIG HD6 ...170 B3
Cook St MILN OL16 ...206 D5
Cook Ter MILN OL16 ...206 D5
Coombe Hl CUL/QBY BD13 ...125 K4
Coombe Rd MAR/SLWT HD7 ...213 H1
Co-operative Buildings
  BRIG HD6 ...148 D7
  HIPP HX3 ...146 B4
Co-operative St CUD/GR S72 ...244 D8
  EARD/LOFT WF3 ...154 E5
  EARL WF12 ...174 D4
  HOR/CROF WF4 ...197 J5
  MIRF WF14 ...194 C3
  MOR LS27 ...152 C2
  ROY/SHW * OL2 ...229 K7
  TOD OL14 ...163 J7
  WKFDW/WTN * WF2 ...12 A4
Co-operative Ter
  HOLM/MEL HD9 ...236 B7
Cooper Bridge Rd HUDN HD2 ...171 K8
Cooper Cl BGLY BD16 ...81 J1
Cooperfields LUD/ILL HX2 ...167 G1
Cooper Gv WBSY BD6 ...125 M7
Cooper La HOLM/MEL HD9 ...254 C1
  STKB/PEN S36 ...258 D7
  WBSY BD6 ...125 M5
Cooper Rd DOD/DAR S75 ...241 L6
  WBY LS22 ...48 A1
Cooper St TOD OL14 ...142 A8
  WHIT OL12 ...206 F2
Coopers Wk MILN OL16 ...206 E4
Cooper Ter MILN OL16 ...206 D5
Co-op La HOLM/MEL HD9 ...253 M3
Copeland St BOW BD4 ...127 M1
Copenhagen Sq MILN OL16 ...206 C6
Copenhagen St MILN OL16 ...206 D6
Cope St BSLY S70 ...261 H7
Copeworth Dr HOR/CROF WF4 ...220 B4
Copgrove Cl BOW BD4 ...128 A3
Copgrove Ct BOW BD4 ...128 A3
Copgrove Rd BOW BD4 ...128 A3
  RHAY LS8 ...110 C1
Cop Hill La MAR/SLWT HD7 ...211 K6
Cop Hill Side MAR/SLWT HD7 ...211 K6
Copley Av HOLM/MEL HD9 ...234 E4
  LUD/ILL HX2 ...168 A1
Copley Bank Rd
  MAR/SLWT HD7 ...212 E3
Copley Gln HIPP HX3 ...168 D4
Copley Gv HIPP HX3 ...168 D4
Copley Hall St HIPP HX3 ...168 D4
Copley Hl BTLY WF17 ...151 H5
  WOR/ARM LS12 ...109 G8
Copley Hill Wy WOR/ARM LS12 ...131 G1
Copley La EARD/LOFT WF3 ...154 D2
  GFTH/SHER LS25 ...114 E1
  HIPP HX3 ...168 D4
  KBTN HD8 ...238 D6
Copley Mt HIPP HX3 ...168 D4
Copley St BTLY WF17 ...151 J7
  ROY/SHW * OL2 ...229 K6
  WBOW BD5 ...126 D3
  WOR/ARM * LS12 ...109 G8
Copley Ter HIPP HX3 ...168 D4
Copley Yd WOR/ARM LS12 ...109 G8
Coplowe La WIL/AL BD15 ...80 F7
Copmanroyd OT LS21 ...41 J3
Copperas St STKB/PEN S36 ...270 A3
Copperas House Ter TOD OL14 ...163 J4
Copperas Rw GTL/HWG * HX4 ...168 A1
Copper Beech Ct
  WKFDW/WTN WF2 ...199 J3
Copper Cl BSLY S70 ...261 G4
Copperfield Av OSM LS9 ...110 D8
Copperfield Crs OSM LS9 ...110 D8
Copperfield Dr OSM LS9 ...110 D8
Copperfield Gv OSM LS9 ...110 D8
Copperfield Mt OSM LS9 ...110 D8
Copperfield Pl OSM LS9 ...110 D8
Copperfield Rw OSM LS9 ...110 D8
Copperfield Ter OSM LS9 ...110 D8
Copperfield Vw OSM LS9 ...110 D8
Copperfield Wk OSM LS9 ...110 D8

Coppertop Ms PONT WF8 ....181 G3
The Coppice AIRE BD20 ....34 E8
GFTH/SHER LS25 ....116 B7
HFAX * HX1 ....10 E9
HUDN HD2 ....192 D2
ILK LS29 ....20 C8
MIRF * WF14 ....172 B6
MSTN/BAR LS15 ....90 F8
YEA LS19 ....84 B1
Coppice Av DOD/DAR S75 ....260 D2
Coppice CI WKFDE WF1 ....177 C6
Coppice Dr HUDS HD4 ....213 M8
Coppice Gra YEA LS19 ....62 C6
Coppice Head RTHW LS26 ....155 H1
Coppice Vw IDLE BD10 ....83 J6
Coppice Wy RHAY LS8 ....88 C8
Coppice Wood Av GSLY LS20 ....62 C5
GTHN BD7 ....104 C8
Coppice Wood CI GSLY LS20 ....62 C5
Coppice Wood Crs YEA LS19 ....62 C6
Coppice Wood Gv GSLY LS20 ....62 C6
GTHN * BD7 ....104 C8
The Coppies LM/WK BD12 ....148 D2
Coppin Hall Gv MIRF WF14 ....171 M8
Coppin Hall La MIRF WF14 ....171 M8
Coppy CI BGLY BD16 ....81 J8
Coppy La AIRE BD20 ....34 B2
BRAM LS13 ....107 L2
HBR HX7 ....121 H3
HWTH BD22 ....55 L7
Coppy Nook La HBR HX7 ....166 A3
Coppy Rd AIRE BD20 ....56 D1
ILK LS29 ....19 G6
Coppy Wood Dr ILK LS29 ....20 D7
The Copse BGLY BD16 ....81 M3
CLECK BD19 ....149 H7
FEA/AMT WF7 ....179 L5
ILK LS29 ....40 A6
Copster La STKB/PEN S36 ....271 M5
Copthorne Gdns HUDN HD2 ....193 H1
Copthurst Rd HOLM/MEL HD9 ....254 A7
Coptrod Head WHIT OL12 ....206 A2
Copt Royd Gv YEA LS19 ....62 C7
Corban St BOW BD4 ....127 L3
Corbett St MILN OL16 ....206 C6
Corby St HUDN HD2 ....192 D5
Cordingley CI BOW BD4 ....128 A5
Cordingley St BOW BD4 ....128 A5
Corfe CI BTLY WF17 ....151 K4
Corn Bank HUDS HD4 ....213 L8
Cornbrook CI WHIT OL12 ....184 E8
Corn Ex LDS * LS1 ....9 H1
Cornfield DEWS WF13 ....173 G5
Cornfield Av HUDW HD3 ....191 J7
Cornfield St MILN OL16 ....229 H1
TOD * OL14 ....141 M8
Corn Market HFAX HX1 ....11 H6
Cornmarket PONT WF8 ....180 E6
Corn MI ILK LS29 ....61 K2
Cornmill CI AL/HA/HU LS17 ....67 M3
Corn Mill Ct WOR/ARM LS12 ....107 M7
Corn Mill CI WHIT OL12 ....206 E2
Cornmill Crs LVSG WF15 ....172 D3
Cornmill Dr LVSG WF15 ....172 D3
Cornmill La AL/HA/HU LS17 ....67 M3
Corn Mill La CLAY BD14 ....125 H1
ILK LS29 ....40 C5
Cornmill La LVSG WF15 ....172 D3
Cornrace Vw HUD HD1 ....214 D2
Cornstone Fold
WOR/ARM LS12 ....107 L7
Corn St HWTH BD22 ....79 J2
Cornus Gdns MID LS10 ....131 M6
Cornwall Av AIRE BD20 ....35 C5
Cornwall CI BSLYN/ROY S71 ....261 K2
RTHW * LS26 ....132 F8
Cornwall Crs BAIL BD17 ....82 D2
BRIG HD6 ....148 D8
RTHW LS26 ....132 F8
Cornwall PI GIR BD8 ....4 D2
GIR BD8 ....4 D2
KGHY BD21 ....3 M1
Cornwall Ter GIR BD8 ....4 D2
Coronation Av CUD/GR S72 ....244 D3
CUD/GR S72 ....245 J8
GFTH/SHER LS25 ....135 L5
IDLE BD10 ....83 M2
NORM WF6 ....178 B3
Coronation Bungalows
GFTH/SHER LS25 ....135 L5
Coronation Mt HWTH BD22 ....2 B4
Coronation Pde
MSTN/BAR LS15 ....111 J8
Coronation Rd DOD/DAR S75 ....259 M2
HIPP HX3 ....168 E2
HOR/CROF WF4 ....200 D3
Coronation St BSLYN/ROY S71 ....261 L2
CAS WF10 ....158 B5
CAS WF10 ....158 C8
EARD/LOFT * WF3 ....154 F3
ELL HX5 ....169 H8
GTL/HWG HX4 ....150 D6
LM/WK BD12 ....149 J1
WKFDW/WTN WF2 ....176 B4
WMB/DAR S73 ....263 K8
Coronation Ter
BSLYN/ROY S71 ....262 B6
CAS WF10 ....158 C8
RPDN/SBR HX6 ....167 G3
Coronation Wk HWTH BD22 ....2 B3
Coronation Wy HWTH BD22 ....57 G6
Corporal La CUL/QBY BD13 ....125 C8
Corporation St BSLY S70 ....261 J7
DEWS WF13 ....173 M6
ECHL BD2 ....105 L3
HFAX HX1 ....11 G4
MOR LS27 ....152 B1
RPDN/SBR HX6 ....167 K2
Corporation Yd BTLY * WF17 ....173 K1
Corrance Rd LM/WK BD12 ....148 F5
Corrie St CUL/QBY BD13 ....103 G8
Cortina Ri WMB/DAR * S73 ....263 C8
Cotchers La TAD LS24 ....93 H6
Cote Farm La SHPY BD18 ....83 H6

Cote Gap CUL/QBY BD13 ....102 F7
Cote La HOLM/MEL HD9 ....254 C6
HUDN HD2 ....191 M1
LIT OL15 ....185 H8
PDSY/CALV LS28 ....106 E4
UPML OL3 ....231 K7
WIL/AL BD15 ....103 J5
Coteroyd Av MOR LS27 ....130 E6
Coteroyd Dr MOR LS27 ....130 E7
The Cote PDSY/CALV LS28 ....106 E4
Cote Wall Ms MIRF WF14 ....194 F3
Cotewall Rd WBOW BD5 ....126 F3
Cotswold Av ROY/SHW OL2 ....229 H6
SHPY BD18 ....83 G7
Cotswold CI DOD/DAR S75 ....260 D4
HEM/SK/SE WF9 ....224 D7
Cotswold Crs MILN OL16 ....207 J7
Cotswold Dr GFTH/SHER LS25 ....135 H1
KNOT * WF11 ....182 A2
LVSG WF15 ....171 M1
RTHW LS26 ....132 F8
Cotswold Ms KBTN HD8 ....216 B7
Cotswold Rd RTHW LS26 ....132 F8
WKFDW/WTN WF2 ....197 M1
Cottage Gn GIR BD8 ....104 B6
Cottage Ms HWTH * BD22 ....78 D7
Cottage Rd HDGY LS6 ....86 F8
IDLE BD10 ....83 M7
Cottam Av GTHN BD7 ....104 C8
Cottam Cft HEM/SK/SE WF9 ....224 A7
Cottam Ter GTHN BD7 ....104 C8
Cotterdale WIL/AL BD15 ....103 J3
Cotterdale Holt WBY LS22 ....47 J7
Cotterdale Vw MSTN/BAR LS15 ....111 J8
Cotterill Rd KNOT WF11 ....181 M3
Cottesmore CI DOD/DAR S75 ....260 E3
Cottingley Cha BEE/HOL LS11 ....130 C6
Cottingley Cliffe Rd BGLY BD16 ....81 L8
BGLY BD16 ....81 L8
Cottingley Crs BEE/HOL LS11 ....130 C5
Cottingley Dr BEE/HOL LS11 ....130 C5
BGLY BD16 ....81 L8
Cottingley Fold BEE/HOL LS11 ....130 C4
Cottingley Gdns BEE/HOL LS11 ....130 C5
Cottingley Gn BEE/HOL LS11 ....130 C5
Cottingley Gv BEE/HOL LS11 ....130 C5
Cottingley Manor Pk
BGLY BD16 ....81 K7
Cottingley Moor Rd
BGLY BD16 ....103 J1
Cottingley New Rd BGLY BD16 ....81 K7
Cottingley Rd BEE/HOL LS11 ....130 C4
WIL/AL BD15 ....103 J3
Cottingley Ter GIR * BD8 ....4 D1
Cottingley V BEE/HOL LS11 ....130 F5
Cotton Fold MILN OL16 ....206 E8
Cotton St OSM LS9 ....9 K2
WKFDW/WTN WF2 ....12 E6
Cotton Tree La COL BB8 ....74 C1
Couford Gv HUDN HD2 ....193 H2
Coule Royd HUDE HD5 ....193 G7
Coultas CI ILK LS29 ....61 K2
Counting House Ms
SKP/WHF BD23 ....16 B2
Count St MILN OL16 ....228 C2
County Ar LDS LS1 ....7 H9
County CI BTLY WF17 ....151 L8
County Wy BSLY S70 ....261 H4
Coupe Gv NORM WF6 ....178 B1
Coupland PI BEE/HOL LS11 ....8 E7
Coupland Rd BEE/HOL LS11 ....8 E7
GFTH/SHER LS25 ....113 G7
Coupland St BEE/HOL LS11 ....8 E7
The Court AL/HA/HU LS17 ....87 H1
LVSG WF15 ....172 A2
SHPY * BD18 ....82 A7
The Court Wy FEA/AMT WF7 ....202 D6
The Courtyards SCFT * LS14 ....89 K7
The Courtyard BTLY WF17 ....151 H4
The Court Yd HOR/CROF WF4 ....220 C7
The Courtyard HUDS HD4 ....213 M2
PONT WF8 ....181 G3
Court Dr BTLY WF17 ....151 H4
Courtenay CI BFDE BD3 ....106 A7
Courtenays SCFT * LS14 ....111 K2
Courthouse St OT LS21 ....41 J6
Court La LUD/ILL HX2 ....145 M7
SKP/WHF BD23 ....16 C2
Courts Leet LM/WK BD12 ....148 E2
Cousen Av GTHN BD7 ....126 C1
Cousen Rd GTHN BD7 ....126 D2
Cousin La LUD/ILL HX2 ....146 A2
Coutances Wy ILK LS29 ....39 J2
Coventry St BOW BD4 ....127 K2
HFAX * HX1 ....146 A7
ROCH OL11 ....206 B8
Coverdale Garth WBY LS22 ....47 J6
Coverdale Wy BAIL BD17 ....83 G2
Cover Dr WBSY BD6 ....126 C6
WMB/DAR S73 ....263 K8
Coverley Ri YEA LS19 ....62 B7
The Covert BTLY WF17 ....151 H7
The Covet IDLE BD10 ....83 M6
Covey Clough Ct MIRF * WF14 ....194 B5
Cowcliffe Hill Rd HUDN HD2 ....192 B4
Cowcliff Hill Rd
HOLM/MEL HD9 ....254 F6
Cow Close Gv WOR/ARM LS12 ....130 C2
Cow Close La LM/WK BD12 ....149 G4
Cow Close Rd WOR/ARM LS12 ....130 B1
Cowdray Dr CLECK BD19 ....149 H6
Cowdry CI EARL WF12 ....196 A4
Cowfold St TOD OL14 ....141 K8
Cow Ga HUDW HD3 ....191 H6
Cowgill St GIR BD8 ....4 A1
Cow Gn HFAX HX1 ....11 G6
Cow Hey La HBR HX7 ....120 F3
Cow Heys HUDE HD5 ....193 G7
Cow Hill Gate La LUD/ILL HX2 ....124 A6
Cowhurst Av TOD OL14 ....141 H7
Cowie St ROY/SHW OL2 ....229 K6
Cow La AWLS/ASK DN6 ....205 J3
HBR HX7 ....121 G7
HIPP HX3 ....168 E4
HIPP HX3 ....169 M2
HOR/CROF WF4 ....200 C2
HOR/CROF WF4 ....222 E5
HWTH BD22 ....54 D1

HWTH BD22 ....54 F3
RPDN/SBR HX6 ....166 F8
Cowlersley La MAR/SLWT HD7 ....213 G4
Cowley Crs HTON BD9 ....103 L2
Cowley Rd BRAM LS13 ....107 H1
Cowling Br AIRE BD20 ....35 L6
Cowling Hill La HWTH BD22 ....54 C1
Cowling Rd HIPP HX3 ....147 H1
Cowm St WHIT OL12 ....184 A1
Cowm Top La ROCH OL11 ....206 A4
Cowpasture Rd ILK LS29 ....38 E3
Cowper Av OSM LS9 ....110 C4
Cowper Crs OSM LS9 ....110 C4
Cowper Gv RHAY LS8 ....110 C3
Cowper Mt OSM LS9 ....110 C4
Cowper Rd OSM LS9 ....110 C4
Cowper St CHAL LS7 ....7 L2
EARL WF12 ....173 L8
SKP/WHF BD23 ....16 C3
Cowper Ter OSM LS9 ....110 C4
Cowrakes CI HUDW HD3 ....191 J5
Cowrakes Rd HUDW HD3 ....191 H5
Cowroyd PI HIPP HX3 ....11 J3
Cowslip St HUD * HD1 ....213 M1
Coxley Crs HOR/CROF WF4 ....196 F8
Coxley Rd HOR/CROF WF4 ....196 F7
Coxley Vw HOR/CROF WF4 ....218 E1
Coxwold HI WBY LS22 ....30 A7
Coxwold Vw WBY LS22 ....30 A8
Crabgate Dr AWLS/ASK DN6 ....249 G4
Crabgate La AWLS/ASK DN6 ....249 G4
Crab HI PONT WF8 ....180 E6
Crab La WKFDW/WTN WF2 ....220 D2
WOR/ARM LS12 ....108 E6
Crabtree Av HECK WF16 ....173 G1
Crabtree Gn WBY LS22 ....47 J7
Crabtree HI WBY LS22 ....47 K6
Crab Tree La PONT WF8 ....226 D4
Crabtree PI GTHN BD7 ....126 C2
Crabtree St GTHN BD7 ....126 C3
HFAX HX1 ....10 A6
Crabtree Wy EARD/LOFT * WF3 ....155 H7
Crackendale La DEWS WF13 ....173 M5
Crackendale Ter DEWS WF13 ....173 M5
Crack La WIL/AL BD15 ....102 F1
Cracoe Rd BFDE BD3 ....5 M7
Craddock St COL BB8 ....74 A1
Crag Av AIRE BD20 ....55 L2
LUD/ILL HX2 ....145 M2
Crag Gdns BSPA/BRAM LS23 ....69 M4
Cragg Av HORS LS18 ....85 K6
Cragg Bottom Rd HWTH BD22 ....76 F6
Cragg Dr ILK LS29 ....39 H3
Cragg La CUL/QBY BD13 ....124 A1
GTHN BD7 ....126 C3
HBR HX7 ....143 L8
Cragg Rd HBR HX7 ....165 H1
HBR HX7 ....165 M2
HORS LS18 ....85 L6
Cragg Ter GTHN BD7 ....126 C3
HORS LS18 ....85 K6
Cragg Top CUL/QBY BD13 ....124 A1
Cragg Vw AIRE BD20 ....36 A4
Cragg Wood Dr YEA LS19 ....84 C3
Craggwood Rd HORS LS18 ....85 L7
The Crag BSPA/BRAM LS23 ....69 M4
Crag Hill Av BHP/TINH LS16 ....64 B3
Crag Hill Rd IDLE BD10 ....64 A8
Crag Hill Vw BHP/TINH LS16 ....64 A8
Crag La AIRE BD20 ....34 E2
AIRE BD20 ....55 L2
AL/HA/HU LS17 ....25 L8
AL/HA/HU LS17 ....43 L2
AL/HA/HU LS17 ....87 H1
LUD/ILL HX2 ....145 M2
Crag Mt PONT WF8 ....180 E6
Crag PI KGHY BD21 ....79 L2
Crag Rd SHPY BD18 ....82 E8
Cragside CI KSTL LS5 ....86 A7
Cragside Crs KSTL LS5 ....86 A7
Cragside Gdns KSTL LS5 ....86 A7
Cragside Gv KSTL LS5 ....85 M7
Cragside Mt KSTL LS5 ....86 A7
Cragside PI KSTL LS5 ....85 M7
Cragside Wk KSTL LS5 ....85 M7
Crag Vw AIRE BD20 ....34 C5
AL/HA/HU LS17 ....43 K2
IDLE BD10 ....83 L7
Crag View Rd SKP/WHF BD23 ....16 F3
Craig CI BTLY WF17 ....151 L3
Craiglands HIPP HX3 ....147 M6
MILN OL16 ....228 D4
Craiglands Pk ILK LS29 ....38 E3
Craiglea Dr LM/WK BD12 ....148 F4
Craigmore Ct BOW BD4 ....128 B4
Craigmore Dr ILK LS29 ....39 G2
Cramlands DOD/DAR S75 ....260 C7
Cranberry Av TOD OL14 ....163 K7
Cranberry Rd TOD OL14 ....163 J6
Cranborne Dr DOD/DAR S75 ....242 B5
Cranborne Rd HTON BD9 ....103 M4
Cranbourne St COL BB8 ....52 A8
Cranbrook Av BEE/HOL LS11 ....131 J3
WBSY BD6 ....126 E6
Cranbrook PI WBOW BD5 ....127 G3
Cranbrook Rd BSLY S70 ....260 F6
CLAY BD14 ....125 K2
DEWS WF13 ....127 G3
Cranbrook Vw
PDSY/CALV LS28 ....129 J1
Cranewells Dr MSTN/BAR LS15 ....111 L7
Cranewells Gn MSTN/BAR LS15 ....111 L8
Cranewells Ri MSTN/BAR LS15 ....111 L8
Cranewells V MSTN/BAR LS15 ....111 L8
Cranewells Vw
MSTN/BAR LS15 ....111 L8
Cranfield Dr AWLS/ASK DN6 ....249 H4
Cranford PI WIL/AL BD15 ....102 E1
Cranleigh Mt KGHY BD21 ....2 C9
Crange Flds HUDS HD4 ....213 K6
Cranmer Bank AL/HA/HU LS17 ....87 J3
Cranmer Gdns AL/HA/HU LS17 ....87 J3
HOLM/MEL HD9 ....235 G4

Cranmer Ri AL/HA/HU LS17 ....87 J2
Cranmer Rd AL/HA/HU LS17 ....87 J3
BFDE BD3 ....5 G1
Cranmore Crs MID LS10 ....154 A1
Cranmore Dr MID LS10 ....154 A1
Cranmore Gdns MID LS10 ....154 A1
Cranmore Garth MID LS10 ....154 A1
Cranmore Gn EARD/LOFT WF3 ....154 A1
Cranmore Gv MID LS10 ....154 A1
Cranmore La MID LS10 ....154 A1
Cranmore Ri MID LS10 ....154 A1
Cranmore Rd MID LS10 ....154 A1
Cranston CI BSLYN/ROY S71 ....261 M2
Cranwood Dr HUDE HD5 ....193 J8
Craven Av AIRE BD20 ....36 A5
CUL/QBY BD13 ....103 G8
Craven CI AIRE BD20 ....36 B5
CLECK BD19 ....150 E6
GIR BD8 ....104 B6
HFAX HX1 ....10 C6
HWTH BD22 ....54 F2
SKP/WHF BD23 ....16 C2
Craven Crs ILK LS29 ....19 G6
Cravendale Rd DEWS WF13 ....172 F8
Craven Dr AIRE BD20 ....36 A5
CLECK BD19 ....150 E6
Craven Edge HFAX HX1 ....10 C7
Craven Gdns ROCH * OL11 ....228 A1
Craven Garth GLE DN14 ....161 J7
Craven Gv AIRE BD20 ....36 B5
Craven La CLECK BD19 ....150 E6
Craven Pk ILK LS29 ....61 H9
Craven Rd DEWS WF13 ....173 J8
HDGY LS6 ....6 C1
HEM/SK/SE WF9 ....223 M8
KGHY BD21 ....3 J2
Craven St BFDE * BD3 ....5 H4
COL BB8 ....74 C1
DEWS WF13 ....172 F8
HUDS HD4 ....213 J2
OT LS21 ....41 K7
SKP/WHF BD23 ....16 B3
WKFDE WF1 ....12 F1
Craven Ter HFAX HX1 ....10 C7
Craven Wood CI DOD/DAR S75 ....260 C3
Crawford Av WBSY BD6 ....126 E6
Crawford Dr
WKFDW/WTN WF2 ....176 B7
Crawford St BOW BD4 ....127 J4
MILN OL16 ....228 C1
Crawley Av HEM/SK/SE WF9 ....246 F5
Crawshaw Av PDSY/CALV LS28 ....107 H7
Crawshaw Gdns
PDSY/CALV LS28 ....107 G7
Crawshaw HI PDSY/CALV LS28 ....107 G7
Crawshaw La HOR/CROF WF4 ....217 J5
Crawshaw Pk PDSY/CALV LS28 ....107 G7
Crawshaw Ri PDSY/CALV LS28 ....107 G8
Crawshaw Rd PDSY/CALV LS28 ....107 G7
Crawshaw St DEWS WF13 ....173 H8
Crawthorne Crs HUDN HD2 ....193 G2
Crayford Dr HOR/CROF WF4 ....200 B5
The Cray MILN OL16 ....207 G8
Cray La GTL/HWG HX4 ....150 A6
Crediton Av WIL/AL BD15 ....103 K6
The Crescent AL/HA/HU LS17 ....25 M8
AL/HA/HU LS17 ....65 H8
BAIL BD17 ....82 E4
BGLY BD16 ....59 G8
BHP/TINH LS16 ....86 C2
BIRK/DRI BD11 ....128 C7
CAS WF10 ....158 B8
CUD/GR * S72 ....244 D7
DEWS WF13 ....194 F1
DOD/DAR S75 ....260 D2
EARD/LOFT WF3 ....153 M7
FEA/AMT WF7 ....200 F1
GFTH/SHER LS25 ....113 J6
GFTH/SHER LS25 ....114 C8
GFTH/SHER LS25 ....135 J5
GSLY LS20 ....61 G6
GTL/HWG HX4 ....190 C2
HOLM/MEL HD9 ....236 A2
ILK LS29 ....61 J2
KBTN HD8 ....216 C7
LVSG WF15 ....171 M1
MSTN/BAR LS15 ....111 K6
NORM WF6 ....178 B2
OT LS21 ....41 J6
PDSY/CALV LS28 ....107 H6
ROY/SHW OL2 ....228 A6
WBSY BD6 ....126 A6
WBY LS22 ....46 E1
Crescent Av DEWS WF13 ....194 F1
RTHW LS26 ....133 H7
Crescent Gdns AL/HA/HU LS17 ....87 M2
Crescent Gra BEE/HOL LS11 ....9 H7
Crescent Rd HOR/CROF WF4 ....222 E5
HUDN HD2 ....14 D1
HUDS HD4 ....213 M7
Crescent Royd HUDE HD5 ....215 J1
Crescent St TOD OL14 ....163 K1
Crescent Towers BEE/HOL LS11 ....9 G7
Crescent Vw AL/HA/HU LS17 ....65 H8
HWTH BD22 ....79 J3
Crescent Vls HEM/SK/SE * WF9 ....223 K4
Crescent Wk CLAY BD14 ....125 M1
DEWS WF13 ....194 F1
The Cresent HIPP HX3 ....147 M6
Creskeld Crs BHP/TINH LS16 ....64 B3
Creskeld Dr BHP/TINH LS16 ....64 A3
Creskeld Gdns BHP/TINH LS16 ....64 A3
Creskeld Garth BHP/TINH LS16 ....64 A3
Creskeld La BHP/TINH LS16 ....64 A3
Creskeld Pk BHP/TINH LS16 ....64 A3
Creskeld Wy WIL/AL BD15 ....103 H4
Creskell Rd BEE/HOL LS11 ....8 E6
Cressfield Rd HUDW HD3 ....191 L6
Cresswell Mt GTHN BD7 ....126 A4
Cresswell PI GTHN BD7 ....126 A4
Cresswell St DOD/DAR S75 ....260 E4
Cresswell Ter GTHN BD7 ....126 A4
Crest Av HUDE * HD5 ....215 G1
LM/WK BD12 ....148 E5
Crest Dr PONT WF8 ....181 G8

Crestfield Av ELL HX5 ....169 G8
Crestfield Crs ELL HX5 ....191 G1
Crestfield Dr ELL HX5 ....191 G1
LUD/ILL HX2 ....168 A1
Crestfield Rd ELL HX5 ....191 G1
The Crest GFTH/SHER LS25 ....135 J5
HUDN HD2 ....171 G8
RTHW LS26 ....134 C5
Crest HI RTHW LS26 ....134 C5
Crest Hill Rd HUDN HD2 ....192 D3
Crest Mt PONT WF8 ....181 G8
Crest Rd HUDN HD2 ....191 J2
Crestville CI CLAY BD14 ....125 M1
Crestville Rd CLAY BD14 ....125 L1
Crestville Ter CLAY BD14 ....125 M1
Crestwood CI BOW BD4 ....127 K5
Crewe Av KNOT WF11 ....181 H2
Crewe Rd CAS WF10 ....158 E7
Crib La HFAX HX1 ....11 G4
Crich Av BSLYN/ROY S71 ....243 J7
The Cricketers BULY LS4 ....108 C2
Cricketers Ap
WKFDW/WTN WF2 ....176 A3
Cricketers CI FEA/AMT WF7 ....224 C1
GFTH/SHER LS25 ....113 J8
Cricketers Fold AL/HA/HU LS17 ....89 G2
Cricketers Gn YEA LS19 ....62 D8
Cricketers Ter WOR/ARM LS12 ....108 E7
Cricketers Vw AL/HA/HU LS17 ....89 G2
Cricketers Wk AIRE BD20 ....56 F1
MSTN/BAR LS15 ....112 A7
Cricketers Wy
GFTH/SHER LS25 ....116 A7
Cricket Vw MILN OL16 ....229 H1
Cricklegate MSTN/BAR LS15 ....111 K6
Crimble Bank MAR/SLWT HD7 ....212 C5
Crimble Clough Rd
MAR/SLWT HD7 ....212 C4
Crimbles Ct PDSY/CALV LS28 ....107 H7
Crimbles PI PDSY/CALV LS28 ....107 H7
Crimbles Rd PDSY/CALV LS28 ....107 H7
Crimbles Ter PDSY/CALV LS28 ....107 H7
Crimea La HUDW HD3 ....211 M3
Crimple Gn GFTH/SHER LS25 ....113 K8
Crimple Mdw PBR HG3 ....26 E2
Crimshaw La SHPY BD18 ....82 F8
Crimsworth La HBR HX7 ....121 J6
Crinan Ct NORM WF6 ....178 C2
Cringles La AIRE BD20 ....18 A7
Cripplegate HFAX HX1 ....11 K5
Cripple Gate La ROCH OL11 ....228 A1
Croasdale Gdns
AWLS/ASK DN6 ....249 L6
Crodingley HOLM/MEL HD9 ....236 D6
Crodingley Farm Ct
HOLM/MEL HD9 ....236 D6
Croft Av BGLY BD16 ....58 F8
BSLYN/ROY S71 ....243 K3
EARD/LOFT WF3 ....153 M7
KNOT WF11 ....182 C1
NORM WF6 ....178 B3
NORM WF6 ....178 C4
OT LS21 ....41 H5
PDSY/CALV LS28 ....106 F3
Croft Br RTHW LS26 ....155 L1
Croft Chantry HEM/SK/SE WF9 ....223 J4
Croft CI DOD/DAR S75 ....242 C5
ILK LS29 ....61 J2
Croft Ct HOLM/MEL HD9 ....236 B3
HORS LS18 ....85 K5
ILK * LS29 ....61 H2
Croftdale Gv MSTN/BAR LS15 ....111 M4
Croft Dr BSLYN/ROY S71 ....243 H7
BSPA/BRAM LS23 ....69 M3
DOD/DAR S75 ....242 D5
HOLM/MEL HD9 ....236 A2
ILK LS29 ....61 J2
STKB/PEN S36 ....270 A3
Croft End WBY LS22 ....47 L1
Crofters Gn IDLE BD10 ....83 J6
Crofters Lea YEA LS19 ....62 B7
Croft Fld AIRE BD20 ....36 A6
Croft Fold HIPP HX3 ....146 B4
Croft Foulds Ct
GFTH/SHER LS25 ....113 H7
Croft Gdns HUDN HD2 ....192 A5
Croft Head KBTN HD8 ....239 L4
Croft Head Dr WKFDE WF1 ....178 M2
Croft Head Ter AIRE BD20 ....34 E8
Croft HI AIRE BD20 ....55 L1
Croft House Av MOR LS27 ....152 D1
Croft House CI MOR LS27 ....130 D8
WBSY BD6 ....126 D6
Croft House Ct
PDSY/CALV * LS28 ....107 G6
Croft House Dr MOR LS27 ....152 D1
OT LS21 ....41 H5
Croft House Gdns MOR LS27 ....152 D1
Croft House Gv MOR LS27 ....152 D1
Croft House La AIRE BD20 ....57 J4
MOR LS27 ....152 D1
Croft House Ms MOR LS27 ....152 D1
Croft House Mt MOR * LS27 ....130 D8
Croft House Rd HUDW HD3 ....211 M1
MOR LS27 ....152 D1
WBSY BD6 ....126 D6
Croft House Vw MOR LS27 ....152 D1
Croft House Wk MOR LS27 ....130 D8
Croftlands BTLY WF17 ....174 B3
HUDS HD4 ....214 C4
IDLE BD10 ....83 J6
KNOT WF11 ....182 C1
Croft La BSPA/BRAM LS23 ....49 J3
TAD LS24 ....49 M8
Crofton CI MAR/SLWT HD7 ....212 C6
Crofton Ri AL/HA/HU LS17 ....89 J2
Crofton Rd HTON BD9 ....104 C3
Crofton Ter AL/HA/HU LS17 ....89 J2
Croft Pk ILK LS29 ....61 H2
Croft PI BRIG HD6 ....170 D2
Croft Ri HIPP HX3 ....146 B4
ILK LS29 ....61 J2
Croft Rd AIRE BD20 ....58 F6

BSLY S70 ....261 L7
BSPA/BRAM LS23 ....69 L3
Croft's Ct LDS LS1 ....6 F9
Croftside Cl SCFT LS14 ....111 K3
The Crofts AIRE BD20 ....35 G5
  AIRE BD20 ....55 L2
  BTLY WF17 ....173 H2
  KBTN HD8 ....217 L7
The Croft BIRK/DRI BD11 ......151 G1
  CAS WF10 ....158 B9
  COL BB8 ....52 A7
  DOD/DAR S75 ....260 A1
  EARD/LOFT WF3 ....174 F1
  HEM/SK/SE WF9 ....224 F3
  HOR/CROF WF4 ....219 H6
  KNOT WF11 ....182 C1
  MSTN/BAR LS15 ....111 K5
  RTHW LS26 ....155 L1
  SCFT LS14 ....67 M6
  SKP/WHF BD23 ....17 M1
  STKB/PEN S36 ....258 B8
  WBY LS22 ....47 J6
Croft St AIRE BD20 ....34 E8
  AIRE BD20 ....56 E1
  BIRK/DRI BD11 ....150 C1
  BRIG HD6 ....170 C4
  DEWS WF13 ....173 L6
  HBR * HX7 ....143 J3
  HECK WF16 ....172 F3
  HUDW HD3 ....213 L1
  HWTH BD22 ....78 C7
  IDLE BD10 ....83 L6
  KGHY BD21 ....2 E6
  OT LS21 ....41 K7
  PDSY/CALV LS28 ....106 F3
  RPDN/SBR * HX6 ....167 L2
  SHPY BD18 ....82 D7
  WBOW BD5 ....4 E8
  WBSY BD6 ....126 E5
  WHIT OL12 ....206 B3
Croft Wy ILK LS29 ....61 J2
Croftway PDSY/CALV LS28 ...106 E7
Croisdale Vw WFSL ....
Cromack Vw PDSY/CALV LS28 ..106 E7
Cromarty Av HUDS HD4 ....213 L4
Cromarty Dr HUDS HD4 ....213 L4
Cromer Av KGHY BD21 ....2 E9
Cromer Gv KGHY * BD21 ....2 E9
Cromer Pl LDSU LS2 ....6 C5
Cromer Rd KGHY BD21 ....125 H5
  LDSU LS2 ....6 C5
Cromer Ter CUD/GR S72 ....245 J7
  HFAX HX1 ....10 A9
  LDSU LS2 ....6 C5
  ROY/SHW * OL2 ....229 K7
  WHIT OL12 ....206 A5
Cromer Ter LDSU LS2 ....6 C5
Cromford St CUD/GR S72 ....245 J7
Crompton Av BSLY S70 ....260 F6
  ROCH OL11 ....228 D3
Crompton Circuit
  ROY/SHW OL2 ....230 C4
Crompton Dr MOR LS27 ....130 D8
Crompton St ROY/SHW OL2 ..229 K7
Cromwell Bottom Dr
  BRIG * HD6 ....170 C2
Cromwell Cl HIPP HX3 ....169 J2
  KNOT WF11 ....159 M6
Cromwell Crs AWLS/ASK DN6 .249 H5
  BGLY BD16 ....103 K2
  BIRK/DRI BD11 ....150 F1
Cromwell Crs PONT WF8 ....181 C6
Cromwell Gv AWLS/ASK DN6 .249 J4
Cromwell Mt BSLY S70 ....261 G8
  MID LS10 ....131 M6
  OSM LS9 ....7 L7
Cromwell Pl OSS WF5 ....174 F7
Cromwell Ri CAS WF10 ....158 E7
Cromwell Rd CAS WF10 ....158 E7
  HIPP HX3 ....169 J2
  ROY/SHW OL2 ....228 E8
Cromwell St OSM LS9 ....7 L8
  SKP/WHF BD23 ....16 C3
Cromwell Ter HFAX * HX1 ....10 E6
Cronkeyshaw Rd WHIT OL12 .206 A0
Cronkhill La BSLYN/ROY S71 .243 M5
Crooked La HIPP HX3 ....124 D1
  IDLE BD10 ....83 M7
Crooke House La
  BSLYN/ROY S71 ....263 H5
Crooke La WIL/AL BD15 ....102 E2
Crookes La BSLYN/ROY S71 ...243 L5
Crookes St BSLY S70 ....260 F5
Crook St BSLY S70 ....260 B6
Cropper Ga LDS LS1 ....6 C9
Cropredy Cl CUL/QBY BD13 ...125 K5
Cropstones BSPA/BRAM LS23 .69 M4
Cropton Rd BSLYN/ROY S71 ..243 K3
Crosby Av BEE/HOL LS11 ....8 B7
Crosby Pl BSLYN/ROY S71 .....261 M1
Crosby Pl BEE/HOL LS11 ....8 C6
Crosby Rd BEE/HOL LS11 ....8 C6
Crosby St BEE/HOL LS11 ....8 B6
  CUD/GR S72 ....244 D6
  KGHY BD21 ....2 E3
  WHIT OL12 ....206 B4
Crosby Ter BEE/HOL LS11 ....8 C6
Crosby Vw BEE/HOL LS11 ....8 C6
Croscombe Wk WBOW BD5 ....4 E9
Croset Av HUDE HD5 ....15 J5
Crosland Ct HUDW HD3 ....191 H5
Crosland Factory La
  HUDS HD4 ....235 J1
Crosland Hill Rd HUDS HD4 ...213 H4
Crosland Rd HUD HD1 ....214 A2
  HUDW HD3 ....191 H4
Crosland Spring Rd HUDS HD4 .214 B3
Crosland St HUDS HD4 ....214 A3
Crosley Vw BGLY BD16 ....81 K4
Crosley Wood Rd BGLY BD16 ..81 K4
The Cross MSTN/BAR LS15 .....91 G7
Cross Albert Pl WOR/ARM LS12 .108 F8
Cross Alcester Rd RHAY LS8 ..110 B2
Cross Ar LDS * LS1 ....7 H9
Cross Aston Gv BRAM LS13 ...108 A4
Cross Av RTHW LS26 ....133 H7

Cross Bank Rd BTLY WF17 ......151 K8
Cross Banks SHPY BD18 ....82 D7
Cross Bank St MIRF WF14 ......194 C3
Cross Banstead St RHAY * LS8 .110 B3
Cross Barstow St BEE/HOL LS11 ..9 G4
Cross Bath Rd BRAM LS13 .....107 L4
Crossbeck Cl ILK LS29 ....38 D3
Crossbeck Rd ILK LS29 ....38 D3
Cross Beck Rd RHAY * LS8 .....110 B2
Cross Belgrave St LDSU LS2 .....7 H8
Cross Bellbrooke Av OSM LS9 .110 D4
Cross Bell St OSM * LS9 ....7 K8
Cross Bentley La HDGY LS6 .....87 H8
Cross Burley Lodge Rd
  HDGY LS6 ....109 G4
Cross Cardigan Mt BULY LS4 ..108 A8
Cross Cardigan Ter BULY LS4 ..108 E4
Cross Catherine St OSM LS9 ....9 M1
Cross Chancellor St HDGY LS6 ...6 F2
Cross Chapel St HDGY LS6 ......108 F1
Cross Church St HUD HD1 ....15 G1
  HUD HD1 ....213 M1
Cross Cliff Rd HDGY LS6 ....6 B1
Cross Cottages HUD HD1 ....191 M7
Cross Cowper St CHAL * LS7 ......7 K2
Cross Crown St CLECK BD19 ...149 M7
Crossdale Av WBSY BD6 ....125 M6
Cross Dawlish Gv OSM LS9 .....110 D6
Cross Dikes Rd RPDN/SBR HX6 .166 C7
Cross Easy Rd OSM * LS9 ....110 B8
Cross Elford St RHAY * LS8 .....110 B3
Cross Emily St KGHY * BD21 ......3 H3
Cross End Fold ILK LS29 ....19 J6
Cross Ends La HBR * HX7 ....121 J2
Cross Eric St BRAM LS13 ....107 L1
Cross Evanston Av BULY LS4 ...108 E4
Cross Farm Ct HWTH BD22 .....100 D3
Cross Fld GTL/HWG HX4 ....190 C2
Cross Field Cl HWTH BD22 ......100 D3
Crossfield Ct WHIT OL12 ....184 E7
Crossfield Ct HOR/CROF WF4 .196 B8
Crossfield Dr AWLS/ASK DN6 .249 J4
Crossfield House Cl
  AWLS/ASK DN6 ....249 J4
Crossfield La AWLS/ASK DN6 .249 J4
Crossfield Pl WHIT OL12 ....228 C1
Crossfield Rd HWTH BD22 ......100 D3
  WHIT OL12 ....184 E8
Crossfields HOR/CROF WF4 ...196 C8
Cross Flds HUDE HD5 ....193 G7
Crossfield St LDSU LS2 ....6 D3
Cross Firs St HUDW HD3 ....213 K1
Cross Flatts BEE/HOL LS11 ....131 J3
Cross Flatts Av BEE/HOL LS11 .131 J4
Cross Flatts Crs BEE/HOL LS11 .131 H4
Cross Flatts Dr BEE/HOL LS11 .131 H3
Cross Flatts Gv BEE/HOL LS11 .131 H4
Cross Flatts Mt BEE/HOL LS11 .131 H4
Cross Flatts Pde BEE/HOL LS11 .131 H4
Cross Flatts Pl BEE/HOL LS11 .131 H4
Cross Flatts Rd BEE/HOL LS11 .131 H4
Cross Flatts Rw BEE/HOL LS11 .131 H4
Cross Flatts St BEE/HOL LS11 .131 H4
Cross Flatts Ter BEE/HOL LS11 .131 H4
Cross Foundry St
  DEWS * WF13 ....195 G1
Cross Fountaine St LDS * LS1 ....6 F9
Cross Francis St CHAL * LS7 ......7 K2
Crossgate DOD/DAR S75 ....242 D5
  OT LS21 ....41 J7
Cross Gate Rd HOLM/MEL HD9 .254 D4
Cross Gates Av
  MSTN/BAR LS15 ....111 J3
Cross Gates La BGLY BD16 ......80 E3
  MSTN/BAR LS15 ....111 K3
Crossgates Rd MILN OL16 ......207 H7
Cross Gates Rd
  MSTN/BAR LS15 ....111 J4
Cross Glen Rd BHP/TINH LS16 .86 E7
Cross Granby Ter HDGY * LS6 .108 F1
Cross Grange Av RHAY LS8 ......7 M2
Cross Grasmere St
  WOR/ARM LS12 ....108 F7
Cross Gn OT LS21 ....41 K6
Cross Green Ap OSM LS9 ....132 C1
Cross Green Av OSM * LS9 ......110 B8
Cross Green Cl OSM LS9 ....132 C1
Cross Green Ct OSM LS9 ....132 D1
Cross Green Crs OSM LS9 ....110 B8
Cross Green Dr OSM LS9 ....132 C1
Cross Green Garth OSM LS9 ...132 C1
Cross Green Gv OSM LS9 ....110 B8
Cross Green La
  MSTN/BAR LS15 ....111 K6
  OSM LS9 ....9 M3
  OSM LS9 ....110 B8
Cross Green Ri OSM LS9 ....132 C1
Cross Green Rd HUDE HD5 .....193 J8
  OSM LS9 ....110 B8
Cross Green Rw HDGY LS6 ....87 G7
Cross Green V OSM LS9 ....132 C2
Cross Green Wy OSM LS9 ....132 C1
Cross Grove St HUD HD1 ....14 E8
Cross Hands La
  HOR/CROF WF4 ....201 K8
Cross Hartley Av HDGY LS6 ......6 D1
Cross Heath Gv BEE/HOL LS11 .131 G3
Cross Henley Rd BRAM LS13 ..107 L4
Cross Hi CUD/GR S72 ....245 H3
  GTL/HWG HX4 ....168 E7
  HEM/SK/SE WF9 ....223 M7
  HFAX HX1 ....11 H4
  KNOT WF11 ....159 J2
Cross Hill AWLS/ASK DN6 ......249 H4
Cross Hill La LVSG WF15 ....171 K5
Cross Hills GFTH/SHER LS25 ..135 J5
  HFAX HX1 ....11 H4
Cross Hills Dr GFTH/SHER LS25 ..135 J5
Crosshills Mt GTL/HWG HX4 ..168 E7
Crosshills St BRAM LS13 ....34 C4
Cross Hilton Gv RHAY LS8 ......110 B2
Cross House Ct LM/WK * BD12 .149 J2
Cross Ingledew Crs RHAY LS8 .88 D4
Cross Ingram Rd BEE/HOL LS11 .8 B5
The Crossings BTLY WF17 ......151 K6
Cross Ivy Mt OSM LS9 ....110 C6
Cross Kelso Rd LDSU LS2 ....6 B6

Cross Keys OSS WF5 ....175 J7
Cross Keys Ct HOR/CROF WF4 .197 K5
Crossland Ct BEE/HOL * LS11 ....8 C5
Crossland Rd MOR LS27 ....130 D7
Crossland Ter BEE/HOL LS11 .....8 F9
Cross La BGLY BD16 ....81 H3
  BIRK/DRI BD11 ....128 D7
  BRIG HD6 ....171 G5
  BSLYN/ROY S71 ....244 A3
  CUL/QBY BD13 ....124 E6
  ELL HX5 ....169 G8
  GSLY LS20 ....62 B3
  GTHN BD7 ....126 C3
  HIPP HX3 ....125 J8
  HIPP HX3 ....147 K2
  HOLM/MEL HD9 ....236 A4
  HOLM/MEL HD9 ....254 E4
  HUDS HD4 ....214 C3
  HUDS HD4 ....237 L4
  HWTH BD22 ....100 E3
  KBTN HD8 ....217 M6
  KBTN HD8 ....238 A8
  KBTN HD8 ....238 D1
  KBTN HD8 ....239 J5
  STKB/PEN S36 ....258 J6
  STKB/PEN S36 ....271 J7
  TOD OL14 ....164 B2
  WIL/AL BD15 ....80 F7
  WKFDW/WTN WF2 ....198 B1
  WOR/ARM LS12 ....108 D7
  WOR/ARM LS12 ....130 A1
Cross Lea Farm Rd KSTL LS5 ...86 B7
Cross Lee Rd TOD OL14 ....141 H7
Cross Leeds St KGHY * BD21 .....2 F5
Cross Lee Ga TOD OL14 ....141 H7
Cross Lee Rd TOD OL14 ....141 H7
Cross Lees WHIT OL12 ....206 C3
Crossley Cl MIRF WF14 ....172 C6
Crossley Gdns HFAX HX1 ....10 D4
Crossley Gv MIRF WF14 ....172 C6
Crossley Hall Ms GIR BD8 ....104 A7
Crossley Hall St GIR BD8 ....103 M7
Crossley HI HIPP HX3 ....168 F3
Crossley La HUDE HD5 ....193 J7
  MIRF WF14 ....172 C6
Crossley New Rd TOD OL14 ....142 A6
Crossley Pl SKP/WHF BD23 ......16 B2
Crossley St BRIG HD6 ....170 D5
  CUL/QBY BD13 ....147 J2
  FEA/AMT WF7 ....201 M1
  GTHN BD7 ....126 D1
  HFAX HX1 ....11 G5
  MILN OL16 ....207 G8
  ROY/SHW OL2 ....229 L7
  TOD OL14 ....163 K1
  WBY LS22 ....48 A1
  WKFDE WF1 ....178 B8
Crossley Ter BTLY WF17 ....173 L3
Crossley Ter North
  LUD/ILL HX2 ....146 C2
Crossley Ter South
  LUD/ILL HX2 ....146 C2
Crossley Vw MIRF WF14 ....172 D6
Cross Lidgett Pl RHAY LS8 ....88 B6
Cross Louis St CHAL LS7 ....7 K3
Crossman Dr NORM WF6 ....178 C3
Cross Maude St LDSU * LS2 ....9 J1
Cross Milan Rd RHAY LS8 ....110 C3
Crossmoor Cl AIRE BD20 ....35 L5
Crossmount St BTLY WF17 ......173 L3
Cross Park Av CAS WF10 ....158 B7
Cross Park St BTLY WF17 ....173 M1
  EARL WF12 ....174 B6
  HOR/CROF WF4 ....197 J5
  MSTN/BAR LS15 ....111 J4
Cross Peel St MOR LS27 ....152 D2
Cross Pipes Rd
  WKFDW/WTN WF2 ....176 A6
Cross Quarry St HDGY LS6 ....6 D1
Cross Queen St NORM WF6 ....178 C4
Cross Reginald Mt CHAL * LS7 ...7 J1
Cross Rink St BTLY WF17 ....173 M3
Cross River St KGHY * BD21 ....3 L1
Cross Rd EARL WF12 ....195 L4
  GIR BD8 ....104 D5
  HOR/CROF WF4 ....196 D8
  HOR/CROF WF4 ....220 B3
  HORS LS18 ....85 H3
  IDLE BD10 ....83 L6
  LM/WK BD12 ....149 H1
Cross Roseville Rd RHAY LS8 ....7 M3
Cross Rosse St SHPY * BD18 ...82 B3
Cross Roundhay Av RHAY LS8 .110 B1
Cross Rw MSTN/BAR LS15 .....112 C8
Cross Ryecroft St OSS WF5 ....174 F8
Cross St Michael's La
  HDGY * LS6 ....108 F2
Cross Skelton St COL BB8 ....74 A1
Cross Speedwell St HDGY LS6 ...6 F1
Cross Sq WKFDE WF1 ....12 E2
Cross Stamford St CHAL LS7 ....7 K6
Cross Stone Rd TOD * OL14 ....163 L1
Cross St BRIG HD6 ....170 C4
  BSLYN/ROY S71 ....261 L2
  BTLY WF17 ....173 L1
  CAS WF10 ....157 L6
  CLAY BD14 ....125 L2
  CUD/GR S72 ....245 K8
  DOD/DAR S75 ....259 M2
  DOD/DAR S75 ....260 F3
  EARD/LOFT WF3 ....154 A6
  EARL WF12 ....173 M7
  GTL/HWG HX4 ....168 F7
  GTL/HWG HX4 ....190 D2
  HEM/SK/SE WF9 ....223 L7
  HEM/SK/SE WF9 ....225 M6
  HFAX HX1 ....11 H4
  HFAX HX1 ....11 J1
  HOLM/MEL HD9 ....236 B2
  HOR/CROF WF4 ....197 K5
  HWTH BD22 ....54 E3
  LM/WK BD12 ....149 J2
  LVSG WF15 ....172 C4
  MAR/SLWT HD7 ....212 C5
  MILN OL16 ....206 F7
  MSTN/BAR LS15 ....111 J6
  OSS WF5 ....174 E5
  PONT * WF8 ....180 F6

  RTHW LS26 ....155 G1
  SKP/WHF BD23 ....16 B3
  WBSY * BD6 ....126 B7
  WBY LS22 ....48 A1
  WKFDE WF1 ....12 E2
Cross St West LUD/ILL * HX2 ..146 A6
Cross Sun St BFD BD1 ....5 G4
Cross Valley Dr
  MSTN/BAR LS15 ....111 J5
The Crossways OT LS21 ....41 J4
Crossway BGLY BD16 ....81 H7
Cross Wells Rd RPDN/SBR HX6 .188 D1
Cross Westfield Rd BVRD * LS3 ..6 B7
Cross Wingham St CHAL * LS7 ...7 K4
Cross Woodstock St LDSU * LS2 ..6 E4
Cross York St LDSU LS2 ....9 J1
Crowden Wk DOD/DAR S75 ....260 C5
Crowgill Rd SHPY BD18 ....82 D6
Crow Hill End Rd
  RPDN/SBR HX6 ....166 B4
Crow Hill Rd HBR * HX7 ....166 B3
Crow La HUDW HD3 ....213 J2
  OT LS21 ....41 J7
Crowlees Cl MIRF WF14 ....194 D1
Crowlees Gdns MIRF WF14 .....194 D1
Crowlees Rd MIRF WF14 ....194 C1
Crown & Anchor Yd
  PONT * WF8 ....180 E6
Crown Av BSLY S70 ....261 J7
  CUD/GR S72 ....262 E2
Crown Cl BSLY S70 ....261 H7
  EARL WF12 ....174 C7
Crown Dr LM/WK BD12 ....148 E2
Crow Nest La BEE/HOL LS11 ...130 F4
  BGLY BD16 ....81 J2
Crownest La BGLY BD16 ....81 J2
Crow Nest Pk DEWS * WF13 ...173 J7
Crow Nest Rd HBR * HX7 ....143 K4
Crown Flatt Wy EARL WF12 ....174 A5
Crown Gdns MILN OL16 ....228 D1
Crown Gn HUDS HD4 ....213 J2
Crown Hill La DOD/DAR S75 ...260 C5
Crownlands La OSS WF5 ....174 F8
Crown La HOLM/MEL HD9 ....254 C5
Crown Point Cl OSS WF5 ....174 E8
Crown Point Dr OSS WF5 ....174 E8
Crown Point Rd MID LS10 ....9 J3
  OSS WF5 ....174 E8
Crown Rd HIPP HX3 ....146 D4
Crown St BFD BD1 ....4 B5
  BRIG HD6 ....170 C3
  BSLY S70 ....261 J7
  CLECK BD19 ....149 M7
  ELL HX5 ....169 H8
  HBR HX7 ....143 J3
  HFAX HX1 ....11 G6
  HOLM/MEL HD9 ....236 B1
  ILK LS29 ....40 B5
  KBTN HD8 ....239 M5
  LDS LS1 ....9 H1
  LM/WK BD12 ....148 E2
  LVSG WF15 ....172 D2
  MILN OL16 ....228 C1
  OSS WF5 ....197 G3
  ROY/SHW * OL2 ....229 K7
Crown Well Hi BSLYN/ROY S71 .262 B6
Crown Yd MSTN/SE WF9 ....246 F3
Crowshaw Dr WHIT OL12 ....206 A3
Crowther Av MAR/SLWT HD7 .211 K8
Crowther Cl MAR/SLWT HD7 ..212 C4
Crowther Fold BGLY BD16 ....80 D5
Crowther Pl CAS WF10 ....157 M7
  HDGY LS6 ....6 F2
Crowther Rd HECK WF16 ....173 L1
  MIRF WF14 ....194 C1
Crowther St BTLY WF17 ....173 L1
  CAS WF10 ....157 L7
  CLECK BD19 ....149 M6
  HUD * HD1 ....15 H8
  HUD * HD1 ....214 B3
  IDLE BD10 ....83 M7
  LIT * OL15 ....207 G2
  LM/WK BD12 ....148 E2
  MILN OL16 ....228 C2
Crowther Wk WBOW BD5 ....4 E9
Crow Tree Cl BAIL BD17 ....82 F3
Crow Tree La GIR BD8 ....104 A3
Crowtrees Ct YEA LS19 ....84 D3
Crowtrees La BRIG HD6 ....170 A8
Crowtrees Pk BRIG HD6 ....170 A8
Crow Trees Pk YEA LS19 ....84 D2
Crow Trees Rd MAR/SLWT HD7 .211 K8
Crow Wood La HWTH BD22 .....100 D1
Crow Wood Pk LUD/ILL HX2 ...167 M1
Croxall Dr EARD/LOFT WF3 ....177 G1
Croxton Av MILN OL16 ....206 E6
Croydon Av ROY/SHW OL2 .....228 B3
Croydon Rd GTHN BD7 ....126 B2
Croydon St BEE/HOL LS11 ....8 A5
  CUL/QBY BD13 ....101 J3
Crumack La HWTH BD22 ....101 G3
Crummock Wy BSLYN/ROY S71 .262 D6
Crystal Ct HFAX HX1 ....10 D5
Crystal Pl WKFDE * WF1 ....13 H3
Crystal Ter BOW BD4 ....127 L3
Cubley Av WKFDW/WTN WF2 .198 D3
Cubley Rise Rd STKB/PEN S36 .270 E5
Cuckoo La HOLM/MEL HD9 .....236 B2
Cuckstool Rd KBTN HD8 ....239 J8
Cudbear St MID LS10 ....9 J3
Cudworth Vw CUD/GR S72 ......245 J8
Cullingworth Rd
  CUL/QBY BD13 ....101 M1
Cullingworth St DEWS WF13 ...173 J3
Culpans Rd HBR HX7 ....166 C2
Culver St HFAX HX1 ....11 G5
Culvert St MILN OL16 ....228 D4
Cumberland Av HUDN HD2 .....192 C1
Cumberland Cl LUD/ILL HX2 ...146 A2
Cumberland Ct HDGY LS6 ....108 F3
Cumberland Dr
  BSLYN/ROY S71 ....262 C6
Cumberland Rd CAS WF10 ......159 K1
  GTHN BD7 ....126 C1
  HDGY LS6 ....6 A1
  ROCH OL11 ....228 B3
Cumberland St SKP/WHF BD23 .16 B3

Cumberworth La KBTN HD8 .....238 F7
  KBTN HD8 ....256 A1
Cumberworth Rd KBTN HD8 ....239 H5
Cumbrian Cl ROY/SHW OL2 ....229 H6
Cumbrian Wy
  WKFDW/WTN WF2 ....197 M4
Cuncliffe Dr ROY/SHW OL2 ....229 M7
Cunliffe Rd GIR BD8 ....104 F4
  ILK LS29 ....38 D2
Cunliffe Ter GIR BD8 ....104 F3
Cunliffe Vls HTON BD9 ....104 F3
Cure HI HWTH BD22 ....78 D3
Curlew Cl CAS WF10 ....157 M8
  ILK LS29 ....38 A2
Curlew Cl AIRE BD20 ....35 K8
Curlew Ri MOR LS27 ....152 F3
Curlew St WBOW BD5 ....126 E3
Curly HI ILK LS29 ....20 D8
Currer Av BOW BD4 ....127 K5
Currer La ILK LS29 ....19 L2
Currer St BFD BD1 ....5 G2
Currer Wk AIRE BD20 ....35 K8
Curtis Ct CUL/QBY * BD13 ....79 M8
Curwen Crs HECK WF16 ....172 F1
Curzon Rd BFDE BD3 ....5 M6
  ROCH OL11 ....228 B4
Curzon St HUDN HD2 ....193 J1
Cuthberts Cl CUL/QBY BD13 ...124 F6
Cutland Wy LIT OL15 ....207 J2
Cutler Heights La BOW BD4 ....127 L3
Cutler La RTHW LS26 ....157 G3
Cutler Pl BOW BD4 ....127 M2
Cutlers Av BSLY S70 ....260 F6
Cut Rd KNOT WF11 ....159 J2
  KNOT WF11 ....159 L5
Cutsyke Av CAS WF10 ....157 K8
Cutsyke Crest CAS WF10 ....157 K8
Cutsyke Rd CAS WF10 ....179 K2
Cuttlehurst KBTN HD8 ....239 M5
Cutts Field Vw
  BSLYN/ROY * S71 ....243 K1
Cutty La DOD/DAR S75 ....260 C3
Cypress Fold KBTN HD8 ....216 A3
Cypress Rd BSLY S70 ....261 K7
  NORM WF6 ....178 D6
Cyprus Av IDLE BD10 ....83 H5
  WKFDE WF1 ....176 C6
Cyprus Crs MIRF WF14 ....172 F7
Cyprus Dr IDLE BD10 ....83 H5
Cyprus Gv GFTH/SHER LS25 ..113 G7
  WKFDE WF1 ....176 C6
Cyprus Mt WKFDE WF1 ....176 C6
Cyprus Rd GFTH/SHER LS25 ..113 G7
Cyprus St OSS WF5 ....174 E6
  WKFDE WF1 ....176 D6
Cyprus Ter GFTH/SHER LS25 ..113 G7
Cyril St ROY/SHW OL2 ....229 L7
Czar St BEE/HOL * LS11 ....8 C5

D

Dacre Av WKFDW/WTN WF2 ...197 L2
Dacre Cl LVSG WF15 ....172 B2
Dacre Ct TAD LS24 ....93 J7
Dacre Rd ROCH OL11 ....228 B2
Daffels Wood Cl BOW BD4 ......127 K6
Daffil Av MOR LS27 ....130 D7
Daffil Grange Ms MOR * LS27 .130 D7
Daffil Grange Wy MOR LS27 ...130 D7
Daffil Gv MOR LS27 ....130 D7
Daffil Rd MOR LS27 ....130 D7
Daffodil Cl WHIT OL12 ....206 A3
Daffodil Ct WIL/AL BD15 ....103 K6
Dagenham Rd BOW BD4 ....127 L3
The Dairies NORM * WF6 ....178 E3
Daisy Bank HFAX HX1 ....10 F9
Daisy Bank St TOD OL14 ....140 D5
Daisy Cl BTLY WF17 ....151 G4
Daisy Cft AIRE BD20 ....36 B5
Daisyfield Rd BRAM * LS13 .....107 M5
Daisy Hi AIRE BD20 ....36 B5
  EARL WF12 ....173 L6
  LM/WK BD12 ....148 E3
  MOR LS27 ....152 E1
Daisy Hill Av MOR LS27 ....130 D8
Daisy Hill Back La HTON BD9 ..104 A4
Daisy Hill Cl MOR * LS27 ....130 E8
Daisy Hill Gv HTON BD9 ....104 A4
Daisy Hill La HTON BD9 ....104 A4
Daisy Lea La HUDW HD3 ....191 L5
Daisy Lee La HOLM/MEL HD9 .254 E7
Daisy Mt RPDN/SBR HX6 ....167 J1
Daisy Rd BRIG HD6 ....170 D6
Daisy Royd HUDS HD4 ....214 C4
Daisy St BRIG HD6 ....170 C4
  GTHN BD7 ....126 C3
  HFAX HX1 ....10 E7
  HWTH BD22 ....79 G7
  WHIT OL12 ....206 A6
Daisy Vale Ms EARD/LOFT WF3 .154 A5
Daisy Vale Ter EARD/LOFT WF3 .154 A5
Dalby Av BFDE BD3 ....105 M5
Dalby St BFDE * BD3 ....105 L6
Dalcross Gv WBOW BD5 ....127 H2
Dalcross St WBOW BD5 ....127 G2
The Dale GFTH/SHER LS25 ....92 A6
  TAD LS24 ....163 M1
Dale Cl BSLYN/ROY S71 ....243 J7
  BTLY WF17 ....173 L6
  GSLY LS20 ....61 G9
  KBTN HD8 ....257 H1
  OSS WF5 ....175 G8
Dale Ct HOLM/MEL HD9 ....236 D1
Dale Cft OSS * WF5 ....174 F8
  PONT WF8 ....202 F1
Dalecourt ILK * LS29 ....39 G1
Dale Cft GFTH/SHER LS25 ......113 G6
  ILK LS29 ....38 A2
  KBTN HD8 ....239 J4
Dale Croft Ri WIL/AL BD15 .....103 J4
Dalecroft Rd AWLS/ASK DN6 ..249 K6
Dalefield Av NORM WF6 ....178 D5
Dalefield Rd NORM WF6 ....178 D5

Dalefield Wy NORM WF6 ......178 D6
Dale Garth BAIL BD17 ......82 D3
Dale Gv SHPY BD18 ......83 C5
Dalehead Dr ROY/SHW OL2 ......229 M7
Dale La HECK WF16 ......172 F1
  HEM/SK/SE WF9 ......247 K1
Dale Ms PONT WF8 ......202 F1
Dale Park Av BHP/TINH LS16 ......85 M2
Dale Park Cl BHP/TINH LS16 ......85 M2
Dale Park Gdns BHP/TINH LS16 ......85 M2
Dale Park Ri BHP/TINH LS16 ......85 M2
Dale Park Wk BHP/TINH LS16 ......85 M2
Dale Rd BIRK/DRI BD11 ......129 J6
Dales Dr GSLY LS20 ......61 K6
Daleside EARL WF12 ......195 L5
  GTL/HWG HX4 ......168 C7
  TOD OL14 ......163 J2
Daleside Av HOLM/MEL HD9 ......236 E7
  PDSY/CALV LS28 ......106 C6
Daleside Cl PDSY/CALV LS28 ......106 B5
Daleside Gv LM/WK BD12 ......149 H2
  PDSY/CALV LS28 ......106 C6
Daleside Rd AIRE BD20 ......58 C5
  BFDE BD3 ......106 B5
  SHPY BD18 ......83 C5
Daleside Wk WBOW BD5 ......127 H4
Daleson Cl HIPP HX3 ......147 J3
Dale Stone Cl KNOT * WF11 ......159 L5
Dale St BFD BD1 ......4 F5
  HUDW HD3 ......191 J8
  HUDW HD3 ......213 J1
  KGHY BD21 ......3 L1
  MILN OL16 ......206 E7
  MILN OL16 ......207 H8
  OSS WF5 ......174 F8
  ROY/SHW OL2 ......229 K8
  RPDN/SBR HX6 ......167 K2
  SHPY BD18 ......82 D7
  TOD OL14 ......163 K1
Dalesway BGLY BD16 ......81 K1
Dales Wy BHP/TINH LS16 ......65 G3
  BHP/TINH LS16 ......86 F6
  GSLY LS20 ......61 K6
  ILK LS29 ......37 M1
Dales Way Link BAIL BD17 ......82 A1
  BHP/TINH LS16 ......64 C3
  BHP/TINH LS16 ......87 C1
  HDGY LS6 ......87 C7
  OT LS21 ......63 H2
Daleswood Av BSLY S70 ......260 D5
Dale Vw AIRE BD20 ......36 A4
  AIRE BD20 ......56 E1
  HEM/SK/SE WF9 ......224 B8
  ILK LS29 ......38 A2
  LIT OL15 ......207 H4
  PONT WF8 ......202 F1
Dale View Cl KGHY BD21 ......3 M7
Daleview Ct BAIL BD17 ......82 C4
Dale View Rd KGHY BD21 ......3 M6
Dale View Rd KGHY BD21 ......3 L8
Dallam Av SHPY BD18 ......82 A6
Dallam Rd SHPY BD18 ......82 A6
Dallam Wk SHPY BD18 ......82 B6
Dalmeny Av HUDS HD4 ......213 L4
Dalmeny Cl HUDS HD4 ......213 L3
Dalmeny Ter BRAM * LS13 ......107 G1
  ROCH OL11 ......228 B2
Dalton Av BEE/HOL LS11 ......131 J4
  MILN OL16 ......206 F7
Dalton Bank Rd HUDE HD5 ......193 J3
Dalton Cl MILN OL16 ......206 F7
Dalton Clowes HUDE HD5 ......193 G7
Dalton Fold Rd HUDE HD5 ......15 L5
Dalton Green La HUDE HD5 ......193 H8
Dalton Gv BEE/HOL LS11 ......131 J4
  HUDE HD5 ......193 G7
Dalton La BSPA/BRAM LS23 ......69 G4
  KGHY BD21 ......3 K4
Dalton Rd BEE/HOL LS11 ......131 J4
  KGHY BD21 ......3 L4
Dalton Ter BSLY S70 ......261 J6
  CAS WF10 ......157 M7
  GIR BD8 ......104 D6
  KGHY BD21 ......3 L2
Damask St HFAX * HX1 ......10 F4
Dam Br COP/BISH YO23 ......33 L7
Demems La HWTH BD22 ......79 H3
Damems Rd HWTH BD22 ......79 J3
Dames La HWTH BD22 ......79 J4
Dam Head La HUDE HD5 ......194 B8
Dam Head Rd RPDN/SBR HX6 ......167 L1
Dam Hl COP/BISH YO23 ......33 M7
  KBTN HD8 ......237 M3
Dam La TAD LS24 ......93 J8
  YEA LS19 ......62 E7
Damon Av IDLE BD10 ......106 A2
Dampier St TOD OL14 ......163 J5
Damside KGHY BD21 ......2 F6
Damside Rd HUDS HD4 ......214 D2
Damson Ct CLAY BD14 ......125 L3
Damsteads DOD/DAR S75 ......260 C7
Danby Av BOW BD4 ......127 K6
Danby La WKFDW/WTN WF2 ......220 E2
Danby Wk OSM LS9 ......110 B7
Dandy Mill Av PONT WF8 ......181 H4
Dandy Mill Cft PONT WF8 ......181 H4
Dandy Mill Vw PONT WF8 ......181 H4
Danebury Rd BRIG HD6 ......170 D5
Danecourt Rd BOW BD4 ......128 A3
Danefield Ter OT LS21 ......41 K6
Dane Hill Dr BOW BD4 ......128 A2
Danella Crs WKFDW/WTN WF2 ......176 B4
Danella Gv WKFDW/WTN WF2 ......176 B4
Danes Av HOLM/MEL HD9 ......196 D8
Danesleigh Dr HOR/CROF WF4 ......196 D8
Dane St ROCH OL11 ......206 A7
Daniel Ct BOW BD4 ......128 B4
Dan La CUL/QBY BD13 ......125 L5
Danny La LUD/ILL HX2 ......144 F7
Dansk Wy ILK LS29 ......38 C1
Danum Dr BAIL BD17 ......82 E4
Darcey Hey La LUD/ILL HX2 ......168 A1
Darfield Av RHAY LS8 ......110 C3
Darfield Crs RHAY LS8 ......110 D3
Darfield Gv RHAY LS8 ......110 D3
Darfield Pl RHAY LS8 ......110 C3
Darfield Rd CUD/GR S72 ......262 F2

RHAY LS8 ......110 C3
Darfield St GIR BD8 ......4 D4
  RHAY LS8 ......110 C3
Darkfield La PONT WF8 ......181 H7
Dark La BSLY S70 ......260 D7
  BTLY WF17 ......151 H3
  BTLY WF17 ......173 K2
  HBR HX7 ......142 E3
  HUDE HD5 ......215 J3
  HWTH BD22 ......78 B5
  HWTH BD22 ......100 E3
  LUD/ILL HX2 ......145 K8
  OT LS21 ......42 F1
  PBR HG3 ......29 G1
  PONT WF8 ......180 E7
  UPML OL3 ......231 G8
Darkwood Cl AL/HA/HU LS17 ......88 C2
Darkwood Wy AL/HA/HU LS17 ......88 C2
Darley Av BSLY S70 ......261 H8
  BSLYN/ROY S71 ......243 J8
  MID LS10 ......131 M7
Darley Cl BSLYN/ROY S71 ......243 J8
Darley Rd WKFDW/WTN WF2 ......172 B1
  ROCH OL11 ......228 B2
Darley St BFD BD1 ......4 F5
  HECK WF16 ......172 F2
  KGHY BD21 ......57 K5
Darley Ter DOD/DAR S75 ......260 F4
Darlington Rd ROCH OL11 ......228 B3
Darnell Ter BEE/HOL LS11 ......9 C7
Darnes Av LUD/ILL HX2 ......168 A1
Darning La HWTH BD22 ......225 K1
Darnley Av WKFDW/WTN WF2 ......12 A1
Darnley Cl HOLM/MEL HD9 ......235 C5
Darnley La MSTN/BAR LS15 ......111 L7
Darren St BOW BD4 ......106 A8
Darrington Pl BSLYN/ROY S71 ......262 A3
Darrington Rd PONT WF8 ......203 G4
Darryl Dr LUD/ILL HX2 ......168 A1
Dartmouth Av HUDE HD5 ......215 J3
  MOR LS27 ......152 C4
Dartmouth Ms MOR LS27 ......152 B3
Dartmouth Ter GIR BD8 ......104 C4
Dartmouth Wy BEE/HOL LS11 ......131 L3
Darton Hall Cl DOD/DAR S75 ......242 B5
Darton La DOD/DAR S75 ......242 C6
Darton Rd DOD/DAR S75 ......259 H1
Darton St BSLY S70 ......261 M6
Dartree Cl WMB/DAR S73 ......263 H8
Dartree Wk WMB/DAR S73 ......263 H8
Darwin St WBOW BD5 ......126 E3
Datchett Ter ROCH OL11 ......228 B3
Daventry Rd HX7 ......228 B3
Davey La HBR HX7 ......142 E3
David La DEWS WF13 ......173 L4
David Lewis Cl MILN OL16 ......206 E8
David St BEE/HOL LS11 ......8 E5
  CAS WF10 ......157 K7
  WHIT OL12 ......206 B5
  WKFDE * WF1 ......13 K7
David St North WHIT * OL12 ......206 B5
Davies Av RHAY LS8 ......88 C4
Davis Av CAS WF10 ......158 F4
Davyhulme St WHIT OL12 ......206 C5
Dawcross Ri PBR HG3 ......26 C2
Dawes Av CAS WF10 ......158 B8
Daw Green Av HOR/CROF WF4 ......220 A2
Daw La HOR/CROF WF4 ......197 L6
  HOR/CROF WF4 ......219 M3
Dawlish Av OSM LS9 ......110 D6
Dawlish Crs OSM LS9 ......110 C6
Dawlish Gv OSM LS9 ......110 D7
Dawlish Mt OSM LS9 ......110 D6
Dawlish Pl OSM LS9 ......110 D6
Dawlish Rd OSM LS9 ......110 D6
Dawlish Rw OSM LS9 ......110 D6
Dawlish St OSM LS9 ......110 D6
Dawlish Ter OSM LS9 ......110 D6
Dawnay Rd WBOW BD5 ......126 E2
Dawn St ROY/SHW * OL2 ......229 K8
Daw Royds HUDE HD5 ......215 J1
Dawson Av BOW BD4 ......127 L5
Dawson Hl MOR LS27 ......152 C1
Dawson La BOW BD4 ......127 L5
  BOW BD4 ......129 G4
Dawson Mt BOW BD4 ......127 L5
Dawson Pl BOW BD4 ......127 L5
  KGHY BD21 ......3 H8
Dawson Rd BEE/HOL LS11 ......131 J3
  HUDS HD4 ......214 D3
  KGHY BD21 ......3 H8
Dawsons Meadow
  PDSY/CALV LS28 ......106 E4
Dawson St BOW BD4 ......127 L4
  EARD/LOFT WF3 ......152 F5
  IDLE BD10 ......83 K4
  PDSY/CALV * LS28 ......106 F5
  SKP/WHF BD23 ......16 C3
Dawson Ter BOW BD4 ......127 L5
Dawson Wy KGHY BD21 ......3 H9
Dawtrie Cl CAS WF10 ......158 F7
Dawtrie St CAS WF10 ......158 F6
Dayhouse Wy DOD/DAR S75 ......260 D5
Daykin Cl DOD/DAR S75 ......241 M6
Day St BSLY S70 ......261 G6
  DEWS WF13 ......195 G1
  HUD HD1 ......15 H9
Deacon Cl BFDE * BD3 ......105 M4
  HOLM/MEL HD9 ......235 G4
Deacon St MILN OL16 ......206 D5
Deacons Wy BSLYN/ROY S71 ......261 L3
Deadmanstone HUDS HD4 ......214 B6
Dealburn Rd LM/WK BD12 ......148 F1
Deal St HFAX HX1 ......11 J7
  KGHY BD21 ......3 L3
Dean Av HOLM/MEL HD9 ......236 B6
  RHAY LS8 ......88 C4
Dean Bank Dr MILN OL16 ......228 B3
Dean Beck Av WBSY BD6 ......127 G6
Dean Beck Ct WBSY * BD6 ......127 H6
Dean Bridge La
  HOLM/MEL HD9 ......254 F3
Dean Brook Rd
  HOLM/MEL HD9 ......236 B6
  HUDS HD4 ......214 A6
Dean Cl GIR BD8 ......103 M5
  WKFDW/WTN WF2 ......176 B4
Dean Clough HFAX HX1 ......11 G4

Dean Ct HIPP HX3 ......168 C4
  RHAY LS8 ......88 C8
Deancourt ROCH OL11 ......228 A2
Dean Edge Rd HWTH BD22 ......77 J6
Dean End GTL/HWG HX4 ......168 F6
Deanery Gdns IDLE BD10 ......105 L1
Deanfield Av MOR LS27 ......152 B1
Dean Fold KBTN HD8 ......215 M6
Dean Hall Cl MOR * LS27 ......152 B2
Dean Head HORS LS18 ......63 J6
Dean House La GTL/HWG HX4 ......189 M6
  LUD/ILL HX2 ......144 A3
Deanhouse La HOLM/MEL HD9 ......236 B6
Deanhurst Gdns MOR LS27 ......129 M8
Dean La CUL/QBY BD13 ......102 E5
  GSLY LS20 ......61 H6
  HOLM/MEL HD9 ......254 F4
  HORS LS18 ......63 J6
  HWTH BD22 ......56 B8
  RPDN/SBR HX6 ......167 G4
  RPDN/SBR HX6 ......167 G4
Dean Lane Head
  CUL/QBY * BD13 ......102 F5
Dean Park Av BIRK/DRI BD11 ......129 G7
Dean Park Dr BIRK/DRI BD11 ......129 G7
Dean Rd HOLM/MEL HD9 ......235 L8
  WBSY BD6 ......126 F6
Deanroyd Rd TOD OL14 ......163 K7
Deanstones Crs CUL/QBY BD13 ......125 G7
Deanstones La CUL/QBY BD13 ......125 G6
Dean St BSLY S70 ......260 F5
  COL BB8 ......74 D4
  GTL/HWG HX4 ......168 F7
  HUDW HD3 ......191 K7
  HWTH BD22 ......78 F7
  ILK LS29 ......38 E1
  MILN OL16 ......206 D5
Deans Wy BSLYN/ROY S71 ......261 L2
Deansway MOR LS27 ......152 B1
Deanswood Cl AL/HA/HU LS17 ......87 J3
Deanswood Dr AL/HA/HU LS17 ......87 H3
Deanswood Gn AL/HA/HU LS17 ......87 H3
Deanswood Hl AL/HA/HU LS17 ......87 J3
Deanswood Pl AL/HA/HU LS17 ......87 J3
Deanswood Ri AL/HA/HU LS17 ......87 H3
Deanwood Av WIL/AL BD15 ......103 J4
Deanwood Crs WIL/AL BD15 ......103 J4
Deanwood Wk WIL/AL BD15 ......103 J4
Dearden St LIT OL15 ......185 K8
  OSS WF5 ......196 F1
  RPDN/SBR HX6 ......167 K1
Dearne Cft WBY LS22 ......30 A6
Dearne Dike La KBTN HD8 ......256 A1
Dearne Fold HUDW HD3 ......191 K5
Dearne Hall Fold
  DOD/DAR S75 ......242 B8
Dearne Hall Rd DOD/DAR S75 ......242 B8
Dearne Pk KBTN HD8 ......240 A4
Dearneside Rd KBTN HD8 ......257 H1
Dearne St DOD/DAR S75 ......242 A5
  HEM/SK/SE WF9 ......247 H3
Dearne Wy DOD/DAR S75 ......241 L3
  DOD/DAR S75 ......242 D7
  KBTN HD8 ......239 L8
  KBTN HD8 ......240 A3
  KBTN HD8 ......256 C2
Dearnfield KBTN HD8 ......238 E8
Dearnley Cl LIT OL15 ......207 H2
Dearnley St DEWS * WF13 ......173 G8
Dearnley Vw DOD/DAR S75 ......260 F2
Dee Ct HWTH BD22 ......78 E4
Deepcar La CUD/GR S72 ......263 G3
Deep Dl BSPA/BRAM LS23 ......48 E5
Deepdale Av HOLM/MEL HD9 ......206 E8
  ROY/SHW OL2 ......228 E6
Deepdale Cl BAIL BD17 ......82 C2
Deepdale La BSPA/BRAM LS23 ......48 D5
Deep La BRIG HD6 ......171 G4
  CLAY BD14 ......125 L1
  CUL/QBY BD13 ......124 C2
  HUDS HD4 ......213 K3
  LIT OL15 ......207 K6
  LUD/ILL HX2 ......145 H7
  RPDN/SBR HX6 ......166 D6
Deeplish Rd ROCH OL11 ......228 B1
Deeplish St ROCH OL11 ......228 B1
Deer Croft Av HUDW HD3 ......191 H6
Deer Croft Crs HUDW HD3 ......191 H6
Deer Croft Dr HUDW HD3 ......191 H5
Deer Croft Rd HUDW HD3 ......191 H5
Deer Hill Cl MAR/SLWT HD7 ......233 H3
Deer Hill Ct HOLM/MEL HD9 ......234 E4
Deer Hill Cft MAR/SLWT HD7 ......233 H3
Deer Hill Dr MAR/SLWT HD7 ......233 H3
Deer Hill End Rd
  HOLM/MEL HD9 ......234 B3
Deer Park Ct GFTH/SHER LS25 ......138 C3
Deershaw La KBTN HD8 ......255 L1
Deershaw Sike La KBTN HD8 ......255 L1
Deerstone Rdg WBY LS22 ......30 A6
Defarge Ct WBOW BD5 ......127 G3
Deffer Rd WKFDW/WTN WF2 ......198 D8
Deganwy Dr HUDE HD5 ......193 L4
Deighton Av GFTH/SHER LS25 ......116 A7
Deighton Cl WBY LS22 ......30 B8
Deighton La BTLY WF17 ......173 J1
Deighton Rd HUDN HD2 ......192 F3
  PBR HG3 ......29 G3
  WBY LS22 ......30 A6
De Lacey Ms BOW BD4 ......127 L4
De Lacies Ct RTHW LS26 ......133 J7
De Lacies Rd RTHW LS26 ......133 J7
De Lacy Av BOW * BD4 ......127 K6
  FEA/AMT WF7 ......179 G1
  HUDE HD5 ......215 H4
Delacy Crs CAS WF10 ......158 F5
De Lacy Mt KSTL LS5 ......108 C2
De Lacy Ter PONT WF8 ......181 G6
Delamere Rd ROY/SHW OL2 ......229 M6
Delamere St WBOW BD5 ......126 F4
Delf Hl BRIG HD6 ......170 D4
  HBR HX7 ......121 L6
  TOD OL14 ......140 F3
Delfs La RPDN/SBR HX6 ......166 B6

Delius Av IDLE BD10 ......105 M1
Della Av BSLY S70 ......260 F6
The Dell AL/HA/HU LS17 ......67 M7
  CAS WF10 ......179 J1
  CUL/QBY BD13 ......80 A7
  MOR LS27 ......192 D2
Dell Av CUD/GR S72 ......245 J6
Dell Cft AIRE BD20 ......35 L4
Dellside Fold CUL/QBY BD13 ......79 M8
Delmont Cl BTLY WF17 ......151 G8
The Delph FEA/AMT WF7 ......202 B1
Delph Ct DOD/DAR S75 ......259 J5
Delph Crs CLAY BD14 ......125 K2
Delph Croft Vw KGHY BD21 ......3 K7
Delph Dr CLAY BD14 ......125 J2
Delph Gv CLAY BD14 ......125 K2
Delph Hl BAIL BD17 ......82 E2
  PDSY/CALV LS28 ......107 G6
Delph Hill La LUD/ILL HX2 ......144 F1
Delph Hill Rd LUD/ILL HX2 ......168 B2
Delph Hill Ter LUD/ILL HX2 ......168 B2
Delph La HDGY LS6 ......6 C1
  HUDS HD4 ......213 M7
Delph Mt HDGY LS6 ......6 C1
Delph Rd UPML OL3 ......230 E7
Delph St HFAX HX1 ......10 F7
  MILN OL16 ......207 H8
Delph Ter CLAY BD14 ......125 K2
Delph Vw HDGY LS6 ......6 C1
Delph Wood Cl BGLY BD16 ......81 L3
Delverne Gv ECHL BD2 ......105 L3
Delves Ga MAR/SLWT HD7 ......212 D8
Delves Wood Rd HUDS HD4 ......213 L5
Denbigh Ap OSM LS9 ......110 F4
Denbrook Av BOW BD4 ......128 B6
Denbrook Cl BOW BD4 ......128 B5
Denbrook Crs BOW BD4 ......128 B5
Denbrook Wk BOW BD4 ......128 B5
Denbrook Wy BOW BD4 ......128 B5
Denbury Mt BOW BD4 ......128 A4
Denby Cl BTLY WF17 ......150 F5
  LVSG WF15 ......172 B1
Denby Crest PONT WF8 ......203 L1
Denby Dale Rd
  HOR/CROF WF4 ......218 E6
  WKFDW/WTN WF2 ......12 D7
Denby Dale Rd East
  HOR/CROF WF4 ......198 A7
Denby Dale Rd West
  HOR/CROF WF4 ......197 M8
Denby Dr BAIL BD17 ......82 D5
Denby Grange La
  HOR/CROF WF4 ......217 J1
Denby Hall La KBTN HD8 ......257 M1
Denby Hill Rd HWTH BD22 ......78 D4
Denby La HOR/CROF WF4 ......195 K8
  KBTN HD8 ......256 F3
  WIL/AL BD15 ......103 K5
Denby Mt HWTH BD22 ......100 E4
Denby Park Dr HOR/CROF WF4 ......217 G1
Denby Pl RPDN/SBR HX6 ......167 K1
Denby Rd BSLYN/ROY S71 ......243 H7
  KGHY BD21 ......3 G9
  PONT WF8 ......203 L1
Denby St GIR BD8 ......4 B3
Denby Vw EARL WF12 ......195 M5
Dence Gn BOW * BD4 ......128 A1
Dence Pl MSTN/BAR LS15 ......111 G6
Dendrum Cl HWTH BD22 ......78 B3
Dene Bank BGLY BD16 ......59 J8
Dene Cl ELL HX5 ......191 C1
Dene Crs GTHN BD7 ......126 A2
Dene Gv AIRE BD20 ......36 A4
Dene Hl BAIL BD17 ......82 B3
Denehill HTON BD9 ......103 M4
Dene House Ct LDSU LS2 ......6 F4
Dene Mt WIL/AL BD15 ......103 L5
Dene Pk KBTN HD8 ......216 B7
Dene Pl HFAX HX1 ......10 F4
Dene Rd KBTN HD8 ......239 H5
  WBSY BD6 ......125 M5
Dene Royd Cl GTL/HWG HX4 ......190 B3
Dene Royd Ct GTL/HWG HX4 ......190 B3
Deneside OSS WF5 ......174 E7
Deneside Mt WBOW BD5 ......126 E5
Deneside Ter WBOW BD5 ......126 F4
Denesway GFTH/SHER LS25 ......135 J1
Dene Vw LUD/ILL HX2 ......144 F6
Deneway PDSY/CALV LS28 ......106 E4
Denfield Av HIPP HX3 ......146 A4
Denfield Crs HIPP HX3 ......146 A4
Denfield Edge HIPP HX3 ......146 A4
Denfield Gdns HIPP HX3 ......146 A4
Denfield La HIPP HX3 ......146 A4
Denfield Sq HIPP HX3 ......146 A4
Denhale Av WKFDW/WTN WF2 ......176 A4
Denham Dr MSTN/BAR LS15 ......112 A6
Denham St BRIG HD6 ......170 C5
  BTLY WF17 ......151 J7
Denholme Dr OSS WF5 ......174 F7
Denholme Gate Rd HIPP HX3 ......147 L5
Denholme Meadow
  HEM/SK/SE WF9 ......247 H2
Denholme Mow HWTH BD22 ......100 F5
  ROCH OL11 ......228 B2
Denhurst Rd LIT OL15 ......185 J8
Denison Ct BSLY S70 ......261 H6
Denison Rd BVRD LS3 ......5 C8
Denison St BTLY WF17 ......173 L2
  YEA LS19 ......62 D7
Denmark St MILN OL16 ......206 D4
  WKFDE WF1 ......13 C4
Dennil Crs MSTN/BAR LS15 ......111 M2
Dennil Rd MSTN/BAR LS15 ......111 M3
Dennington La
  HOR/CROF WF4 ......219 L3
Dennis La AIRE BD20 ......35 J3
Dennison Fold BOW BD4 ......128 A1
Dennison Hl OT LS21 ......41 K6
Dennistead Crs HDGY LS6 ......108 F1
Denshaw Dr MOR LS27 ......152 E2
Denshaw Gv MOR LS27 ......152 E2
Denshaw La EARD/LOFT WF3 ......153 G3

Denstone St WKFDE WF1 ......13 G1
Dent Dr WKFDE WF1 ......177 H6
Denton Av RHAY LS8 ......88 B6
Denton Dr BGLY BD16 ......81 L2
Denton Gdns FEA/AMT WF7 ......224 C5
Denton Gv RHAY * LS8 ......88 B6
  WHIT OL12 ......206 B5
Denton Ter CAS WF10 ......158 A6
Dent St OSM LS9 ......110 B7
Denver Rd ROCH OL11 ......228 B2
Denwell Ter PONT WF8 ......180 F5
Derby Av BFDE * BD3 ......105 M7
Derby Rd BFDE BD3 ......106 A7
  YEA LS19 ......84 D2
Derbyshire St MID LS10 ......132 B3
Derby St BSLY S70 ......260 F5
  CLAY * BD14 ......125 K2
  CUL/QBY BD13 ......124 F5
  GTHN BD7 ......126 D2
  ROCH OL11 ......228 C1
  RPDN/SBR HX6 ......167 L1
Derby Ter MAR/SLWT HD7 ......233 H2
Derdale St TOD OL14 ......163 L1
Derry Hl ILK LS29 ......61 H3
Derry Hill Gdns ILK LS29 ......61 H2
Derry La ILK LS29 ......61 H2
Der St TOD OL14 ......163 L1
Derwent Av GFTH/SHER LS25 ......113 H8
  MILN OL16 ......207 K8
  RTHW LS26 ......133 L8
  WIL/AL BD15 ......102 E2
Derwent Cl BSLYN/ROY S71 ......243 K7
  COL BB8 ......52 C8
  HBR HX7 ......143 J2
Derwent Crs BSLYN/ROY S71 ......243 K7
Derwent Dr BHP/TINH LS16 ......86 F2
  CAS WF10 ......159 G5
  HUDE HD5 ......15 L6
  LIT OL15 ......207 H4
  ROY/SHW OL2 ......229 J6
Derwent Gv WKFDW/WTN WF2 ......176 B8
Derwent Pl BEE/HOL LS11 ......8 D4
  KNOT WF11 ......182 A4
Derwent Ri EARL WF12 ......174 B3
  ECHL BD2 ......105 J3
  HOLM/MEL HD9 ......235 L6
  HOLM/MEL HD9 ......236 A3
  WKFDW/WTN WF2 ......176 B8
Derwent St KGHY * BD21 ......3 M3
  WHIT OL12 ......206 B5
Derwentwater Ter HDGY LS6 ......108 F1
Derwin Av HUDS HD4 ......237 L4
De Trafford St HUDS HD4 ......213 M3
Detroit Av MSTN/BAR LS15 ......111 M6
Detroit Dr MSTN/BAR LS15 ......112 A6
Deveron Gv HUDW HD3 ......14 B3
Devine Cl ROY/SHW OL2 ......228 F8
Devon Cl LDSU LS2 ......6 E4
  ROY/SHW OL2 ......229 H7
Devon Rd CHAL LS7 ......6 E4
Devonshire Av RHAY LS8 ......88 C4
Devonshire Crs RHAY LS8 ......88 B5
Devonshire Dr DOD/DAR S75 ......260 F2
Devonshire Gdns CHAL LS7 ......6 F3
Devonshire La RHAY LS8 ......88 C4
Devonshire Pl SKP/WHF BD23 ......16 B2
Devonshire Rd ROCH OL11 ......228 B4
Devonshire St HUDS HD4 ......214 A3
  KGHY BD21 ......2 E1
  SKP/WHF BD23 ......16 C3
Devonshire St West KGHY BD21 ......2 D5
Devonshire Ter GIR BD8 ......104 C4
Devon St HFAX HX1 ......10 A8
  ROCH OL11 ......206 B8
Devon Wy BRIG HD6 ......148 D8
Dewar Cl WBY LS22 ......47 J3
Dewhirst Cl BAIL BD17 ......82 F4
Dewhirst Pl BOW BD4 ......105 M4
Dewhirst Rd BAIL BD17 ......82 F4
  BRIG HD6 ......170 C2
  WHIT OL12 ......206 B1
Dewhurst Rd HUDN HD2 ......192 D4
Dew Meadow Cl WHIT OL12 ......206 A4
Dewsbury Gate Rd
  DEWS WF13 ......173 H3
Dewsbury Ring Rd
  DEWS WF13 ......173 L6
Dewsbury Rd BEE/HOL LS11 ......9 G7
  CLECK BD19 ......150 A5
  CLECK BD19 ......150 D4
  EARD/LOFT WF3 ......152 E3
  ELL HX5 ......169 L8
  OSS WF5 ......174 F6
  WKFDW/WTN WF2 ......197 L1
Deyne Rd HUDS HD4 ......213 L7
Diadem Dr SCFT LS14 ......111 C5
Dial St OSM LS9 ......110 B8
Diamond Av HEM/SK/SE WF9 ......247 G3
Diamond St BFD BD1 ......5 G7
  BTLY * WF17 ......151 K4
  HFAX HX1 ......10 C4
  HUD HD1 ......15 H7
  HUDE HD5 ......15 M8
  HWTH BD22 ......79 J1
Diamond Ter HFAX HX1 ......10 C3
Dibb La YEA LS19 ......62 B7
Dib Cl RHAY LS8 ......110 F1
Dib La RHAY LS8 ......110 F1
Dick Dean La HBR HX7 ......121 J1
Dicken Ct BOW BD4 ......128 A1
Dicken Gn ROCH OL11 ......228 B2
Dicken Green La ROCH OL11 ......228 B2
Dickens Dr CAS WF10 ......180 F1
Dicken's St LUD/ILL HX2 ......146 A7
  WBOW BD5 ......127 G3
Dickin Ct RPDN/SBR HX6 ......189 C2
Dickinson Ct WKFDE WF1 ......176 E6
Dickinson Pl BSLY S70 ......261 H7
Dickinson Rd BSLY S70 ......261 H7
Dickinson St HORS LS18 ......85 L4

WKFDE WF1 ....176 E7
Dickinson Ter *FEA/AMT* WF7 ...179 M8
Dick La *BFDE* BD3 ....106 B6
BOW BD4 ....128 A1
HWTH BD22 ....54 F2
Dick's Garth Rd *ILK* LS29 .....61 H2
Dickson St *COL* BB8 ....74 A1
Dicky Sykes La *FEA/AMT* WF7 ...223 M1
Digby Rd *ILK* LS29 ....61 J2
ROCH OL11 ....228 B2
Diggle St *ROY/SHW* OL2 ....229 K8
Digley Rd *HOLM/MEL* HD9 ....253 K4
Digley Royd La
HOLM/MEL HD9 ....253 J3
Dillington Rd *BSLY* S70 ....261 H7
Dillington Sq *BSLY* S70 ....261 H7
Dillington Ter *BSLY* * S70 ....261 H7
Dimple Gdns *OSS* WF5 ....196 F2
Dimples La *AIRE* BD20 ....58 F6
HWTH BD22 ....78 C7
Dimple Wells Cl *OSS* WF5 ......196 F2
Dimple Wells La *OSS* WF5 ......196 F2
Dimple Wells Rd *OSS* WF5 ......196 F2
Dineley Av *ROY/SHW* OL2 ....229 L5
Dingle Av *ROY/SHW* OL2 ....229 L5
Dingle Rd *HUD1* HD1 ....191 M8
Dingley Rd *HUDW* HD3 ....191 M8
Dirker Av *MAR/SLWT* HD7 ....233 J1
Dirker Bank Rd
MAR/SLWT HD7 ....233 H1
Dirker Dr *MAR/SLWT* HD7 ....233 H2
Dirkhill Rd *GTHN* BD7 ....126 E1
Dirkhill St *GTHN* BD7 ....126 D1
Dirty La *UPML* OL3 ....231 K6
Dirty Leech *WHIT* OL12 ....184 B8
Discovery Rd *HFAX* HX1 ....11 J7
Disney Cl *HUDS* HD4 ....213 M3
Dispensary Wk *HFAX* HX1 ....11 H1
Disraeli Gdns *BEE/HOL* LS11 ...8 F8
Disraeli Ter *BEE/HOL* LS11 ....8 F8
Ditton Mead Cl *WHIT* OL12 .....206 D4
Division St *WHIT* OL12 ....206 D4
Dixon Rd *GTHN* BD7 ....126 E1
Dixon Cl *AIRE* BD20 ....56 E1
GTL/HWG HX4 ....168 C6
Dixon Lane Rd *WOR/ARM* LS12 ...130 E1
Dixon Lane Rd *WOR/ARM* LS12 ...130 E1
Dixon St *AIRE* BD20 ....56 A1
FEA/AMT WF7 ....179 M7
Dixon's Yd *WKFDE* * WF1 ....13 G3
Dobbin Dr *ROCH* OL11 ....228 B3
Dobb La *HOLM/MEL* HD9 ....253 L4
Dobb Top Rd *HOLM/MEL* HD9 .....253 K5
Dobie St *BSLY* S70 ....261 H6
Dob Park Rd *OT* LS21 ....23 H7
Dob Royd *KBTN* HD8 ....237 M7
Dobroyd Rd *TOD* OL14 ....163 J2
Dobson Av *BEE/HOL* LS11 ......9 C9
Dobson Gv *BEE/HOL* LS11 ......9 C9
Dobson Pl *BEE/HOL* LS11 ......9 C9
Dobson Ter *BEE/HOL* LS11 .....9 C9
Dobson Vw *BEE/HOL* LS11 ......9 C9
Dockery *HUD* HD1 ....214 B3
Dockfield Pl *BAIL* BD17 ....82 E5
Dockfield Rd *BAIL* BD17 ....82 E5
Dockfield Ter *BAIL* BD17 ......82 E5
Dockray St *COL* BB8 ....74 A1
Dockroyd La *HWTH* BD22 ....78 E4
Dock St *MID* LS10 ....9 H2
Doctor Fold *HOLM/MEL* HD9 .....236 E3
Doctor Hl *IDLE* BD10 ....83 J8
LUD/ILL HX2 ....145 M5
Doctor La *HOR/CROF* WF4 ....217 K4
IDLE BD10 ....83 K5
Doctors La *CAS* WF10 ....135 J8
Dodd Cft *MILN* OL16 ....228 D4
Dodgeholme Cl *LUD/ILL* HX2 ....145 M2
Dodgson Av *CHAL* LS7 ....7 L2
MILN OL16 ....206 C8
Dodlee La *HUDW* HD3 ....191 H1
Dodsworth Crs *NORM* WF6 ....178 D6
Dodsworth Dr
WKFDE/WTN WF2 ....220 D1
Dodworth Green Rd
DOD/DAR S75 ....259 M8
Dodworth Rd *BSLY* S70 ....260 E5
Dog Hl *CUD/QBY* S72 ....244 D3
Dog Hill Dr *CUD/QBY* S72 ......244 E3
Doghouse La *TOD* OL14 ....163 J4
Dog Kennel Bank *HUDE* HD5 .....15 K9
Dog Kennel Hl *DOD/DAR* S75 ....259 G3
Dog Kennel La *HIPP* HX3 ....11 M9
Dog La *GTL/HWG* HX4 ....168 A3
GTL/HWG HX4 ....190 A4
Dogley Villa Ct *KBTN* HD8 .....215 M4
Doldram La *STKB/PEN* S36 ......270 F4
Dole La *HBR* HX7 ....143 J5
Doles Av *BSLYN/ROY* S71 ....243 K3
Doles Crs *BSLYN/ROY* S71 ......243 K3
Dole St *CUL/QBY* BD13 ....103 C8
Dolfin Pl *HUDN* HD2 ....193 H1
Doll La *CUL/QBY* BD13 ....102 A1
Dolly La *OSM* LS9 ....7 L6
Dolphin Ct *OSM* LS9 ....9 M1
Dolphin La *EARD/LOFT* WF3 .....154 A4
Dolphin Rd *MID* LS10 ....154 A1
Dolphin St *OSM* LS9 ....9 M1
Dolphin Ct *BRAM* LS13 ....107 A5
Dombey St *HFAX* HX1 ....10 D6
Domestic Rd *BEE/HOL* LS11 .....131 C1
Domestic St *BEE/HOL* LS11 .....8 B5
Dominion Av *CHAL* LS7 ....87 M8
Dominion Cl *CHAL* * LS7 ....87 M8
Donald Av *WBSY* BD6 ....126 E6
Donald St *PDSY/CALV* LS28 ....106 F4
Don Av *WBY* LS22 ....29 M6
Doncaster La *AWLS/ASK* DN6 ....248 E2
Doncaster Rd *BSLY* S70 ....261 H5
FEA/AMT WF7 ....224 C1
HEM/SK/SE WF9 ....247 H3

HEM/SK/SE WF9 ....247 J4
HOR/CROF WF4 ....199 L4
KNOT WF11 ....181 L2
PONT WF8 ....226 C5
WMB/DAR S73 ....263 K8

Doncaster Road Est
FEA/AMT WF7 ....224 C1
Doncaster St *HIPP* HX3 ....168 F3
Don Ct *AIRE* BD20 ....36 A5
Don Dr *BSLY* S70 ....261 M7
Donisthorpe St *MID* LS10 .....9 L5
Donkey Rd *NORM* WF6 ....178 F4
Don Pedro Av *NORM* WF6 ....178 F4
Don Pedro Cl *NORM* WF6 ....178 F4
Don St *KGHY* BD21 ....2 E3
STKB/PEN S36 ....271 H4
Don Vw *STKB/PEN* S36 ....267 M5
Dorchester Ct *BOW* * BD4 .....128 A3
Dorchester Crs *BAIL* BD17 .....83 H7
BOW BD4 ....128 A3
Dorchester Dr *LUD/ILL* HX2 ....168 A1
YEA LS19 ....62 E8
Dorchester Rd *HUDN* HD2 ....192 D1
TAD LS24 ....71 K4
Dorian Cl *IDLE* BD10 ....83 M8
Dorman Av *HEM/SK/SE* WF9 .....225 M6
Dorothy St *KGHY* BD21 ....79 J3
Dorset Av *ROY/SHW* OL2 ....229 H7
Dorset Ct *HEM/SK/SE* WF9 .....223 M6
WBOW BD5 ....126 E3
Dorset Gv *PDSY/CALV* * LS28 ..107 G6
Dorset Mt *RHAY* LS8 ....110 C3
Dorset Rd *RHAY* LS8 ....110 C2
Dorset St *HUD* HD1 ....14 D2
RHAY * LS8 ....110 C2
ROCH OL11 ....206 B8
SKP/WHF BD23 ....16 C3
WBOW BD5 ....126 F3
Dorset Ter *RHAY* LS8 ....110 C3
Dorts Crs *TAD* LS24 ....95 C5
Dotterel Gln *MOR* LS27 ....152 E3
Doubting La *EARL* WF12 ....195 M5
STKB/PEN S36 ....270 D7
Doubting Rd *EARL* WF12 ....195 M5
Douglas Av *BTLY* WF17 ....174 B1
HUDE HD5 ....215 C1
HUDW HD3 ....213 K1
Douglas Dr *BOW* * BD4 ....127 L2
Douglas Rd *BOW* BD4 ....127 L2
Douglas St *COL* BB8 ....52 A8
EARL WF12 ....195 L2
HIPP HX3 ....146 D4
HWTH BD22 ....79 G6
Dovebush Wy *DOD/DAR* S75 .....260 A1
Dove Cl *WBY* LS22 ....30 A6
Dovecote Dr *CAS* WF10 ....136 A3
Dovecote La *HOR/CROF* WF4 ....197 K6
Dovedale Cl *HIPP* HX3 ....125 K8
HOR/CROF WF4 ....200 C5
Dovedale Gdns
MSTN/BAR LS15 ....112 B3
Dovedale Garth
MSTN/BAR LS15 ....112 B3
Dovelands *AIRE* BD20 ....55 M2
Dover La *HOLM/MEL* HD9 ....254 D3
Dover Rd *HOLM/MEL* HD9 ....254 C3
Dover St *BFDE* BD3 ....5 H2
GFTH/SHER LS25 ....113 K7
MILN * OL16 ....206 D4
TOD OL14 ....163 M1
Dovesdale Gv *WBOW* BD5 ....126 E4
Dovesdale Rd *WBOW* BD5 ....126 F4
Dove St *SHPY* BD18 ....82 B6
Dowkell La *BSPA/BRAM* LS23 ...49 C5
Dowker St *HFAX* HX1 ....10 B9
HUDW HD3 ....213 K1
Dowley Gap La *BGLY* BD16 .....81 K5
Dowling St *ROCH* OL11 ....206 B8
Downes Crs *DOD/DAR* S75 ......260 D3
Downham St *BFDE* BD3 ....5 K7
Downing Cl *BFDE* BD3 ....5 L5
Downing Sq *STKB/PEN* S36 .....270 F4
Downing St *MAR/SLWT* HD7 .....212 E6
Downland Crs *KNOT* WF11 ......182 D4
Downshutts La
HOLM/MEL HD9 ....254 F1
Downside Crs *WIL/AL* BD15 ....103 J5
Dracup Av *GTHN* BD7 ....126 A1
Dracup Rd *GTHN* BD7 ....126 B3
Dradishaw Rd *AIRE* BD20 ......35 M5
Dragon Ct *WOR/ARM* * LS12 ....8 B3
Dragon Dr *WOR/ARM* LS12 ......130 E1
Dragon Rd *WOR/ARM* LS12 ......130 E1
Drake La *BIRK/DRI* BD11 ......151 L1
Drake Rd *LIT* OL15 ....185 L1
Drake St *KGHY* BD21 ....3 G3
MILN OL16 ....206 D4
Dransfield Av *STKB/PEN* S36 ..270 F4
Draper La *HBR* HX7 ....121 G8
Draughton Gv *WBOW* BD5 ....126 F5
Draughton St *WBOW* BD5 ....126 F5
Drayton Manor Yd
BEE/HOL * LS11 ....9 G7
Dray Vw *DEWS* WF13 ....173 H4
Drewry Rd *KGHY* BD21 ....2 B1
Drewton Rd *BFD* BD1 ....4 D5
Driftholme Rd *BIRK/DRI* BD11 .129 H7
Drill Pde *GIR* BD8 ....4 C2
Drill St *HWTH* BD22 ....78 E8
KGHY BD21 ....3 G4
Drinker La *KBTN* HD8 ....216 F8
The Drive *AL/HA/HU* LS17 .....65 J8
AL/HA/HU LS17 ....67 M1
BGLY BD16 ....59 G8
BHP/TINH LS16 ....86 C2
BTLY WF17 ....151 J8
GFTH/SHER LS25 ....135 J5
HBR HX7 ....143 H5
HIPP HX3 ....147 M6
IDLE BD10 ....83 M8
ILK LS29 ....40 A6
MSTN/BAR LS15 ....111 M4

OSM LS9 ....9 L2
RHAY LS8 ....88 C6
RTHW LS26 ....134 C5
SKP/WHF BD23 ....16 D1
WKFDE WF1 ....12 D2
Driver Pl *WOR/ARM* LS12 ......109 G8
Drivers Rw *PONT* WF8 ....180 D7
Driver St *AIRE* BD20 ....36 B4
WOR/ARM LS12 ....109 G8
Drovers Wy *ECHL* BD2 ....105 G3
Drub La *CLECK* BD19 ....150 A4
Druggist La *ILK* LS29 ....19 H6
Druids St *CLAY* BD14 ....125 K2
Drummer La *MAR/SLWT* HD7 .....212 C3
Drummond Av *HDGY* LS6 ....86 B8
Drummond Cl *BHP/TINH* LS16 ...86 E8
Drummond Rd *BHP/TINH* LS16 ...86 E7
Drury Av *HORS* LS18 ....85 K6
Drury Cl *HORS* LS18 ....85 K6
PBR HC3 ....27 C3
Dry Carr La *LUD/ILL* HX2 .....144 E5
Dryclough Av *HUDS* HD4 ....213 L4
Dryclough Cl *HIPP* HX3 ....168 E3
Dryclough La *HIPP* HX3 ....168 E3
Dryclough Rd *HUDS* HD4 ....213 L3
Dryden Rd *BSLYN/ROY* S71 .....261 J4
Dryden St *BFD* BD1 ....5 H3
BGLY * BD16 ....81 H3
Dry Hill La *KBTN* HD8 ....257 K1
Dubb La *BGLY* BD16 ....81 J3
Duchess Park Cl *ROY/SHW* OL2 .229 K6
Duchess St *ROY/SHW* OL2 ......229 L6
Duchy Av *HTON* BD9 ....104 A3
Duchy Crs *HTON* BD9 ....104 A3
Duchy Dr *HTON* BD9 ....104 A4
Duchy Gv *HTON* BD9 ....104 A4
Duchy Vls *HTON* BD9 ....104 A3
Duchywood *HTON* BD9 ....104 A3
Ducie St *IDLE* BD10 ....83 K5
Duckett Gv *PDSY/CALV* LS28 ...106 B6
Duckett St *SKP/WHF* BD23 .....16 C3
Duckworth Gv *HTON* BD9 ....104 B4
Duckworth La *HTON* BD9 ....104 A5
Duckworth St *ROY/SHW* OL2 ....229 L7
Duckworth Ter *HTON* BD9 ......104 B4
Dudfleet La *HOR/CROF* WF4 ....197 K6
Dudley Av *BTLY* WF17 ....151 J4
HUD HD1 ....191 M8
Dudley Crs *LUD/ILL* HX2 ......145 M1
Dudley Gv *BOW* BD4 ....128 A1
Dudley Hill Rd *ECHL* BD2 .....105 K3
Dudley Rd *HUD* HD1 ....191 L8
Dudley St *BOW* BD4 ....127 L3
COL BB8 ....74 B1
Dudwell Av *HIPP* * HX3 ....168 F4
Dudwell Gv *HIPP* HX3 ....168 F4
Dudwell La *HIPP* HX3 ....168 F4
Duffield Crs *GFTH/SHER* LS25 .116 B6
Dufton Ap *SCFT* LS14 ....111 J3
Duich Rd *WBSY* BD6 ....126 A8
Duinen St *WBOW* BD5 ....9 K9
Duke Crs *BSLY* S70 ....261 H6
Duke of York Av
WKFDW/WTN WF2 ....198 E5
Duke of York St *WKFDE* WF1 ...176 F7
WKFDW/WTN WF2 ....176 B4
Dukes Hl *ILK* * LS29 ....20 C8
Duke St *BFD* BD1 ....4 E5
BSLY S70 ....261 H6
CAS WF10 ....157 K6
CUD/QR S72 ....245 J8
DEWS WF13 ....195 C1
ELL HX5 ....169 H8
HEM/SK/SE WF9 ....223 J3
HWTH BD22 ....78 F7
KGHY BD21 ....2 F1
LIT OL15 ....207 J1
LUD/ILL HX2 ....144 F5
OSM LS9 ....9 K1
ROY/SHW OL2 ....229 L8
SKP/WHF BD23 ....16 C2
WHIT OL12 ....206 B5
Duke Wood Rd *KBTN* HD8 ....240 A4
Dulverton Cl *BEE/HOL* LS11 ...130 F5
PONT WF8 ....181 J1
Dulverton Gdns *BEE/HOL* LS11 .130 E4
Dulverton Garth
BEE/HOL LS11 ....130 E5
Dulverton Gn *BEE/HOL* LS11 ...130 F5
Dulverton Gv *BEE/HOL* LS11 ...130 F5
BOW BD4 ....127 M3
Dulverton Pl *BEE/HOL* LS11 ...130 F5
Dulverton Sq *BEE/HOL* LS11 ...130 F5
Dulverton Wy *PONT* WF8 ....181 J1
Dumfries Cl *UPML* OL3 ....230 E4
Dumfries Dr *UPML* OL3 ....230 E4
Dunbar Cft *CUL/QBY* BD13 .....125 H5
Dunbar St *WKFDE* WF1 ....13 L7
Dunbottle La *MIRF* WF14 ......194 D1
Dunbottle Ter *MIRF* WF14 .....172 D8
Dunbottle Wy *MIRF* WF14 ......172 E8
Duncan Av *OT* LS21 ....40 F8
Duncan St *LDS* LS1 ....9 G1
WBOW BD5 ....4 F9
Dunce Mire Rd
GFTH/SHER LS25 ....138 D7
Dunce Park Cl *ELL* HX5 ....191 H1
Dunford Rd *HOLM/MEL* HD9 .....254 D3
Dungeon La *RTHW* LS26 ....155 L5
Dunhill Crs *OSM* LS9 ....111 C6
Dunhill Ri *OSM* LS9 ....111 C6
Dunkeswick La *AL/HA/HU* LS17 .26 C7

Dunkhill Cft *IDLE* * BD10 ....83 K7
Dunkirk Crs *HFAX* HX1 ....146 A8
Dunkirk La *HFAX* HX1 ....168 A1
Dunkirk Ri *BD20* BD20 ....58 A4
WHIT * OL12 ....206 A7
Dunkirk St *HFAX* HX1 ....146 A8
Dunkirk Ter *HFAX* HX1 ....10 A8
Dunlin Cl *MOR* LS27 ....152 F3
Dunlin Ct *MID* LS10 ....153 M1
Dunlin Cft *MID* LS10 ....153 M1
Dunlin Dr *MID* LS10 ....153 M1
Dunlin Fold *MID* LS10 ....153 M1
Dunlin Wy *GIR* BD8 ....103 L7
Dunlop Av *ROCH* OL11 ....228 A3
Dunmere Cl *BSLYN/ROY* S71 ....261 J1
Dunmore Av *CUL/QBY* BD13 .....124 E5
Dunn Cl *WKFDW/WTN* WF2 ....176 B3
Dunningley La
EARD/LOFT WF3 ....153 H4
Dunnington Dr *SEL* YO8 ....139 M5
Dunnington Wk *LM/WK* BD12 ....126 A1
Dunnock Cft *MOR* LS27 ....152 E3
Dunrobin Av *GFTH/SHER* LS25 ..113 K7
Dunsford Av *BOW* BD4 ....127 K6
Dunsley Bank Rd
HOLM/MEL HD9 ....254 B4
Dunsley Ter *HEM/SK/SE* WF9 ...246 A4
Dunsmore Dr *HUDW* HD3 ....191 H6
Dunstable Cl *WHIT* * OL12 ....206 B6
Dunstan Cl *OSS* WF5 ....197 G2
Dunstan Gdns *BHP/TINH* LS16 ..87 G3
Dunstarn Dr *BHP/TINH* LS16 ...86 F3
Dunstarn Gdns *BHP/TINH* LS16 .87 G3
Dunstarn La *BHP/TINH* LS16 ...86 F4
Dunster Av *ROCH* OL11 ....228 A1
Dunsterville Ter *ROCH* OL11 ..228 A1
Dunwood Av *ROY/SHW* OL2 ......229 L6
Dunwood Park Cts
ROY/SHW * OL2 ....229 L6
Dunwoods Park Cts
ROY/SHW OL2 ....229 L5
Durban Av *BEE/HOL* LS11 ......131 H4
Durban Cl *ROY/SHW* OL2 ....229 M8
Durban Crs *BEE/HOL* LS11 .....131 H4
Durden Ms *ROY/SHW* OL2 ....229 K8
Durham Rd *GIR* BD8 ....104 C5
Durham St *CAS* WF10 ....158 A8
LUD/ILL HX2 ....146 A4
ROCH OL11 ....228 C1
Durham Ter *GIR* BD8 ....104 C5
Durkar Flds *HOR/CROF* WF4 ....198 B3
Durkar La *HOR/CROF* WF4 ......198 A3
Durkar Low La *HOR/CROF* WF4 ..198 C7
Durkar Ri *HOR/CROF* WF4 ......198 B3
Durkheim Ct *BFDE* * BD3 ......105 L7
Durley Av *HTON* BD9 ....104 B3
Durling Dr *SHPY* BD18 ....83 G7
Durlston Gv *LM/WK* BD12 ......148 F2
Durlston Ter *LM/WK* BD12 .....148 F2
Durnlaw Cl *LIT* OL15 ....207 L1
Durn St *LIT* OL15 ....185 L8
Durrance St *HWTH* BD22 ....2 A7
Durrant Cl *WBY* LS22 ....48 B1
Dutton Gn *SCFT* LS14 ....89 J6
Dutton Wy *SCFT* LS14 ....89 J7
Duxbury Ri *CHAL* LS7 ....6 F4
Dyehouse Dr *CLECK* BD19 ......149 L4
Dye House La *BRIG* HD6 ....170 E5
Dyehouse La *PDSY/CALV* LS28 ..129 G2
Dye House La *RPDN/SBR* HX6 ...168 A5
WIL/AL BD15 ....102 C1
Dyehouse Rd *LM/WK* BD12 ......149 H1
Dyer La *HIPP* HX3 ....10 A1
Dyers Ct *HDGY* LS6 ....109 H2
LIT * OL15 ....185 J8
Dyer St *LDSU* LS2 ....7 J9
Dyke Cl *MIRF* WF14 ....172 C6
Dyke La *TOD* OL14 ....142 D6
Dymond Gv *LVSG* * WF15 ....172 C3
Dymond Rd *LVSG* WF15 ....172 C3
Dymond Vw *LVSG* WF15 ....172 C3
Dyson Cl *HOLM/MEL* HD9 ....254 D5
RPDN/SBR HX6 ....188 C3
Dyson Pl *HIPP* * HX3 ....168 F3
Dyson Rd *HFAX* HX1 ....10 B4
Dyson's Hl *HOLM/MEL* HD9 .....236 B1
Dyson St *BFD* BD1 ....4 C5
BRIG HD6 ....170 C3
BSLY S70 ....260 F7
HTON BD9 ....104 C2
HUDE HD5 ....193 G8

E

Eafield Av *MILN* OL16 ....207 H7
Eafield Cl *MILN* OL16 ....207 H7
Eafield Rd *MILN* OL16 ....206 E5
Eagle Gv *WKFDW/WTN* WF2 ......175 M8
Eaglesfield Dr *WBSY* BD6 ....126 B8
Eagle St *HWTH* BD22 ....79 G7
KGHY BD21 ....2 F4
TOD OL14 ....163 K1
Ealand Av *BTLY* WF17 ....151 H7
Ealand Crs *BTLY* WF17 ....151 H7
Ealand Rd *BTLY* WF17 ....151 H6
Ealees Rd *LIT* OL15 ....207 L1
Ealing Ct *BTLY* WF17 ....151 J8
Eaming Vw *BSLYN/ROY* S71 ....261 J3
Earles Av *HUDE* HD5 ....215 G1
Earle St *FEA/AMT* WF7 ....179 L8
Earlsmere Dr *BSLYN/ROY* S71 .262 A1
MOR LS27 ....152 B1
Earls Ter *HIPP* HX3 ....146 C4
Earl St *EARL* WF12 ....174 D7
HEM/SK/SE WF9 ....223 J4
HWTH BD22 ....78 E8
KGHY BD21 ....2 F1
WBOW BD5 ....5 G8
WKFDE WF1 ....13 G1
Earls Vw *AIRE* BD20 ....55 L2
Earlswood Av *RHAY* LS8 ....88 B4
Earlswood Cha
PDSY/CALV LS28 ....107 G2

Earlswood Crs
GFTH/SHER LS25 ....135 H4
Earlswood Md
PDSY/CALV LS28 ....129 G5
Earl Ter *HIPP* HX3 ....146 C4
Earnshaw Av *WHIT* OL12 ....206 A3
Earnshaw Ter *DOD/DAR* S75 ....260 F3
Easby Av *BTLY* WF17 ....173 H2
Easby Cl *ILK* LS29 ....38 B2
Easby Dr *ILK* LS29 ....38 B2
Easby Rd *WBOW* BD5 ....4 C9
Easdale Cl *SCFT* LS14 ....111 H2
Easdale Crs *SCFT* LS14 ....111 J1
Easdale Mt *SCFT* LS14 ....111 H2
Easdale Rd *SCFT* LS14 ....111 H2
Easingwood Dr *HUDE* HD5 ......193 K5
East Acres *KNOT* WF11 ....160 A7
East Av *AIRE* BD20 ....34 F3
HEM/SK/SE WF9 ....225 J7
HOR/CROF WF4 ....197 L5
HUDW HD3 ....191 L5
KGHY BD21 ....3 J7
PONT WF8 ....180 D7
East Bank *GFTH/SHER* LS25 ....116 B6
East Bath St *BTLY* WF17 .....173 M1
East Beck Ct *OT* LS21 ....40 F1
East Bolton *LUD/ILL* HX2 .....123 M7
Eastborough Crs *DEWS* WF13 ...173 M5
Eastbourne Av *FEA/AMT* WF7 ...180 A7
Eastbourne Cl *PONT* WF8 .....181 J6
Eastbourne Crs *PONT* WF8 ....181 J6
Eastbourne Dr *PONT* WF8 .....181 J6
Eastbourne Rd *HTON* BD9 .....104 C3
Eastbourne St *ROCH* OL11 ....228 B1
Eastbourne Ter *PONT* WF8 ....181 H6
Eastbourne Vw *PONT* WF8 .....181 J6
Eastbrook Ct
BSPA/BRAM * LS23 ....69 M4
Eastburn Br *AIRE* BD20 ......35 K3
Eastbury Av *WBSY* BD6 ....125 M5
East Busk La *OT* LS21 ....41 L6
East Byland *LUD/ILL* HX2 ....124 A8
East Cswy *BHP/TINH* LS16 ....86 F1
East Causeway Cl
BHP/TINH LS16 ....86 F1
East Causeway Crs
BHP/TINH LS16 ....86 F2
East Causeway V
BHP/TINH LS16 ....87 C2
East Chevin Rd *OT* LS21 .....62 F1
Eastcliffe *HIPP* HX3 ....11 M8
East Cl *PONT* WF8 ....203 C1
STKB/PEN S36 ....271 J3
East Dale Cl *HEM/SK/SE* WF9 .224 B7
Eastdean Bank *SCFT* LS14 ....89 J8
Eastdean Dr *SCFT* LS14 ......89 J8
Eastdean Gdns *SCFT* LS14 ....89 K8
Eastdean Ga *SCFT* LS14 ......89 K8
Eastdean Gv *SCFT* LS14 ......89 K8
Eastdean Ri *SCFT* LS14 ......89 K8
Eastdean Rd *SCFT* LS14 ......89 J8
East Dene *AIRE* BD20 ....36 A4
East Down *CAS* WF10 ....158 C6
East Dr *GFTH/SHER* LS25 .....135 K1
PONT WF8 ....181 K6
East End Crs *BSLYN/ROY* S71 .244 A7
East End Vls *AWLS/ASK* DN6 ..227 M3
Easterly Av *RHAY* LS8 ....110 C2
Easterly Cl *RHAY* LS8 ....110 D3
Easterly Crs *RHAY* LS8 ......110 D3
Easterly Cross *RHAY* LS8 ....110 D3
Easterly Garth *RHAY* LS8 ....110 D3
Easterly Gv *RHAY* LS8 ....110 C2
Easterly Mt *RHAY* LS8 ....110 D3
Easterly Rd *RHAY* LS8 ....110 F1
Easterly Sq *RHAY* LS8 ....110 D3
Easterly Vw *RHAY* LS8 ....110 D3
Eastfield *KBTN* HD8 ....238 D6
Eastfield Av *KNOT* WF11 .....182 B3
STKB/PEN S36 ....270 F4
Eastfield Cl *DOD/DAR* S75 ...242 F6
TAD LS24 ....72 B1
Eastfield Crs *DOD/DAR* S75 ..242 F6
RTHW LS26 ....133 J8
Eastfield Dr *KBTN* HD8 ......216 A7
PONT WF8 ....181 H6
RTHW LS26 ....133 J8
Eastfield Gdns *BOW* BD4 .....128 A3
Eastfield Gv *NORM* WF6 ......178 E3
Eastfield La *CAS* WF10 ......158 A4
Eastfield Rd *KNOT* WF11 .....182 B3
MIRF WF14 ....172 F8
East Field St *OSM* LS9 ......9 M1
East Fold *KBTN* HD8 ....239 L5
Eastgate *BHP/TINH* LS16 .....63 M3
BSLY S70 ....261 G4
ELL HX5 ....169 H7
HOLM/MEL HD9 ....236 C2
OSM LS9 ....7 J9
Eastgate Cl *BHP/TINH* LS16 ..63 M3
East Ga *MILN* OL16 ....206 B6
East Grange Cl *MID* * LS10 ..132 A5
East Grange Dr *MID* LS10 ....132 A5
East Grange Garth *MID* LS10 .132 A5
East Grange Ri *MID* LS10 ....132 A5
East Grange Rd *MID* LS10 ....132 A5
East Grange Sq *MID* LS10 ....132 A5
East Grange Vw *MID* LS10 ....132 A5
Eastlthorpe Ct *ECHL* BD2 ....105 M2
East King St *OSM* LS9 ....9 L2
East Lands *HUDE* HD5 ....215 J2
Eastland Wk *BRAM* LS13 ......108 A5
East Lee La *TOD* OL14 ....142 F4
Eastleigh Ct *EARD/LOFT* WF3 .153 J6
Eastleigh Dr *EARD/LOFT* WF3 .153 J6
Eastleigh Gv *WBOW* BD5 ......126 F3
East Moor Crs *RHAY* LS8 .....88 B4
East Moor Gv *BSLYN/ROY* S71 .243 L4
East Moor La *BHP/TINH* LS16 .88 B4
East Moor Rd *RHAY* LS8 ......88 B4
Eastmoor Rd *WKFDE* WF1 .....176 E6
Easton Pl *HUDW* HD3 ....191 K7
East Pde *AIRE* BD20 ....56 F1
BAIL BD17 ....82 F2

BFDE BD3 .....5 H5
ILK LS29 .....38 E2
KGHY BD21 .....3 H5
LDS LS1 .....6 F9
RPDN/SBR HX6 .....167 M1
East Parade Wk *LDS* LS1 .....6 F9
East Park Dr *OSM* LS9 * 110 C7
East Park Gv *OSM* LS9 .....110 C7
East Park Mt *OSM* LS9 .....110 C7
East Park Pde *OSM* LS9 .....110 C7
East Park Pl *OSM* LS9 .....110 C7
East Park Rd *HIPP* HX3 .....10 C1
OSM LS9 .....110 B7
PBR HX3 .....28 F4
East Park St *MOR* LS27 .....152 B3
OSM LS9 .....110 C7
East Park Ter *OSM* LS9 .....110 C7
East Park Vw *OSM* LS9 .....110 C7
East Pinfold *BSLYN/ROY* S71 .....243 L3
East Rd *LM/WK* BD12 .....126 F8
STKB/PEN S36 .....271 J5
East Royd *HWTH* BD22 .....78 F4
East Side Ct *PDSY/CALV* LS28 .....129 K1
East Squire La *GIR* BD8 .....104 E4
East St *BRIG* HD6 .....170 C5
BTLY WF17 .....173 L1
CUD S72 .....245 G1
HEM/SK/SE WF9 .....247 K2
HIPP HX3 .....148 C7
HOLM/MEL HD9 .....255 G3
HOR/CROF WF4 .....222 F5
HUDW HD3 .....191 K5
LIT OL15 .....207 L1
MAR/SLWT HD7 .....213 G4
MILN OL16 .....206 C6
MILN OL16 .....206 F7
OSM LS9 .....9 K2
RPDN/SBR HX6 .....167 G4
WHIT OL12 .....184 B8
WKFDE WF1 .....176 E4
WMB/DAR S73 .....263 J8
East Ter *HWTH* BD22 .....79 G6
East Vw *AIRE* BD20 .....36 A4
AWLS/ASK DN6 .....227 M5
CAS WF10 .....157 J7
CLECK BD19 .....149 J8
COL BB8 .....74 C4
CUD/GR S72 .....244 D7
GFTH/SHER LS25 .....116 A8
GFTH/SHER LS25 .....135 K5
HUDW HD3 .....14 A4
KNOT WF11 .....182 C2
LUD/ILL * HX2 .....145 G1
MIRF WF14 .....172 B8
MSTN/BAR * LS15 .....111 L4
OSS WF5 .....197 G3
PDSY/CALV LS28 .....129 C1
RTHW LS26 .....155 L1
WBSY BD6 .....125 L4
YEA LS19 .....62 E8
East View Rd *YEA* LS19 .....62 E8
East View Ter *LM/WK* BD12 .....148 F1
Eastville Rd *HOR/CROF* WF4 .....200 D3
Eastway *MIRF* WF14 .....172 B7
ROY/SHW OL2 .....229 K8
Eastway Pk *MIRF* WF14 .....172 C7
Eastwick Vw *WIL/AL* * BD15 .....103 K5
Eastwood Av *LUD/ILL* HX2 .....124 A7
RPDN/SBR HX6 .....167 K3
WKFDW/WTN WF2 .....176 A4
Eastwood Cl *HOR/CROF* WF4 .....198 B7
LUD/ILL HX2 .....124 A7
Eastwood Crs *SCFT* LS14 .....111 M1
Eastwood Dr *SCFT* LS14 .....111 L1
Eastwood Gdns *SCFT* LS14 .....111 L2
Eastwood Garth *SCFT* LS14 .....111 M2
Eastwood Gv *GFTH/SHER* LS25 .....135 J1
LUD/ILL HX2 .....124 A7
Eastwood La *SCFT* LS14 .....111 M2
TOD OL14 .....142 C5
Eastwood Nook *SCFT* LS14 .....111 M2
Eastwood Rd *TOD* OL14 .....141 J3
Eastwood St *BOW* BD4 .....127 H1
BRIG HD6 .....170 D3
HIPP HX3 .....146 C4
HUDE HD5 .....15 M8
LIT OL15 .....207 K1
Easy Rd *OSM* LS9 .....110 B8
Eaton Hl *BHP/TINH* LS16 .....86 B3
Eaton Ms *MID* LS10 .....153 L1
Eaton Pl *HEM/SK/SE* WF9 .....224 A7
Eaton Rd *ILK* LS29 .....38 C3
Eaton Sq *MID* LS10 .....153 L2
Eaton St *KGHY* BD21 .....79 G1
Eaton Wk *HEM/SK/SE* WF9 .....247 J1
Eaves Av *HBR* HX7 .....143 C2
Eaves Rd *HBR* HX7 .....143 G2
Ebberston Gv *HDGY* LS6 .....6 A2
Ebberston Pl *HDGY* LS6 .....6 A2
Ebberston Ter *HDGY* LS6 .....6 A2
Ebenezer Pl *GTHN* BD7 .....126 C2
Ebenezer St *BFD* BD1 .....5 G7
EARD/LOFT WF3 .....154 D3
PDSY/CALV LS28 .....106 C4
Ebor Gdns *MIRF* WF14 .....194 A1
Ebor La *HWTH* BD22 .....78 F6
Ebor Mt *GFTH/SHER* LS25 .....135 J4
HDGY LS6 .....6 A4
Ebor Pl *HDGY* LS6 .....6 A4
Ebor St *HDGY* LS6 .....6 A4
Ebor Wy *AL/HA/HU* LS17 .....45 J6
AL/HA/HU LS17 .....46 E2
AL/HA/HU LS17 .....65 L2
ILK LS29 .....39 M1
ILK LS29 .....61 K2
OT LS21 .....62 C1
OT LS21 .....63 G1
Ebson House La
HOLM/MEL HD9 .....237 K8
Ebury Cl *BTLY* WF17 .....151 M8
Ebury St *BTLY* WF17 .....151 M8
Ecclesburn Av *OSM* LS9 .....110 C7
Ecclesburn Rd *OSM* LS9 .....110 C7
Ecclesburn St *OSM* LS9 .....110 C7
Ecclesburn Ter *OSM* LS9 .....110 C7

Eccles Ct *ECHL* BD2 .....105 K2
Eccles Parlour *RPDN/SBR* HX6 .....166 C7
Eccup La *BHP/TINH* LS16 .....64 E7
OT LS21 .....65 H3
Eccup Moor Rd *BHP/TINH* LS16 .....65 H6
Echo St *LVSG* WF15 .....172 B4
Ecklands Long La
STKB/PEN S36 .....269 M6
Eclipse Cl *MILN* OL16 .....206 D7
Edale Av *HUD* HD4 .....214 B5
Edale Cl *HUDE* HD5 .....193 M6
Edale Gv *CUL/QBY* BD13 .....124 E6
Edale Ri *DOD/DAR* S75 .....260 A7
Edale Wy *BHP/TINH* LS16 .....86 B3
Eddercliff Crs *CLECK* BD19 .....150 C8
Edderthorpe St *BFDE* BD3 .....5 K7
Edderthorpe La *WMB/DAR* S73 .....263 J6
Eddison Cl *BHP/TINH* LS16 .....86 F1
Eddison St *PDSY/CALV* LS28 .....106 F4
Eddyfield Rd *KNOT* WF11 .....181 M2
Edelshain Gv
WKFDW/WTN WF2 .....199 H6
WKFDW/WTN WF2 .....197 M1
Eden Av *OSS* WF5 .....174 F8
WKFDW/WTN WF2 .....197 M1
Eden Cl *DOD/DAR* S75 .....260 A1
LM/WK BD12 .....148 F3
Eden Crs *BULY* LS4 .....108 D2
Edendale *CAS* WF10 .....158 B6
Eden Dr *BULY* LS4 .....108 D2
Edenfield Cl *BSLYN/ROY* S71 .....243 M8
Eden Gdns *BULY* LS4 .....108 D3
Eden Mt *BULY* LS4 .....108 D2
Eden Rd *BULY* LS4 .....108 D2
Edensor Rd *KGHY* BD21 .....2 D5
Eden Wk *BULY* LS4 .....108 D3
Eden Wy *BULY* LS4 .....108 D3
ROY/SHW OL2 .....229 M5
Ederoyd Av *PDSY/CALV* LS28 .....106 C6
Ederoyd Crs *PDSY/CALV* LS28 .....106 C5
Ederoyd Dr *PDSY/CALV* LS28 .....106 C5
Ederoyd Gv *PDSY/CALV* LS28 .....106 C5
Ederoyd Mt *PDSY/CALV* LS28 .....106 C5
Ederoyd Ri *PDSY/CALV* LS28 .....106 C5
Edgar St *CLAY* BD14 .....125 M2
MILN OL16 .....206 E4
Edgbaston Cl *AL/HA/HU* LS17 .....65 J8
Edgbaston Wk *AL/HA/HU* LS17 .....65 J8
Edge Av *EARL* WF12 .....195 M5
Edgebank Av *WBSY* BD6 .....126 B8
Edgecliffe Pl *BSLYN/ROY* S71 .....261 J1
Edge Cl *EARL* WF12 .....196 A5
MAR/SLWT HD7 .....213 G2
Edge End Gdns *WBSY* BD6 .....126 A7
Edge End La *HOLM/MEL* HD9 .....253 J1
Edge End Rd *WBSY* BD6 .....126 A7
Edgehill Cl *CUL/QBY* BD13 .....125 H5
Edge Hill Cl *HUDE* HD5 .....15 L8
Edgehill Rd *DOD/DAR* S75 .....242 C4
Edgeholme La *LUD/ILL* HX2 .....145 K7
Edge Jct *EARL* WF12 .....195 M5
Edgelands Ri *CUD/GR* S72 .....262 D1
HBR HX7 .....120 B7
Edgemoor Cl *BOW* BD4 .....128 A6
HOR/CROF WF4 .....220 B3
HIPP HX3 .....168 D2
Edgemoor Rd *HOLM/MEL* HD9 .....236 A3
HOR/CROF WF4 .....220 B3
Edge Rd *EARL* WF12 .....196 A6
Edgerton Cl *TAD* LS24 .....71 L3
Edgerton Ct *TAD* LS24 .....71 L3
Edgerton Dr *TAD* LS24 .....71 K3
Edgerton Garth *TAD* LS24 .....71 K3
Edgerton Gn *HUDW* HD3 .....14 B4
Edgerton Grove Rd *HUD* HD1 .....14 B5
Edgerton La *HUDW* HD3 .....14 A4
Edgerton Rd *BHP/TINH* LS16 .....86 D7
HUDW HD3 .....14 A3
Edge Ter *HUDW* HD3 .....191 M7
Edge Top Rd *EARL* WF12 .....195 L5
Edge Vw *EARL* WF12 .....196 A5
MAR/SLWT HD7 .....213 G2
Edgeware Rd *HUDE* HD5 .....193 J8
Edgware Av *RHAY* LS8 .....110 B4
Edgware Gv *RHAY* LS8 .....110 B4
Edgware Mt *RHAY* LS8 .....110 B4
Edgware Pl *RHAY* LS8 .....110 B4
Edgware Rw *RHAY* * LS8 .....110 B4
Edgware St *RHAY* LS8 .....110 B4
Edgware Ter *RHAY* LS8 .....110 B4
Edgware Vw *RHAY* LS8 .....7 M4
Edinburgh Av *WOR/ARM* LS12 .....108 C6
Edinburgh Cl *BSLYN/ROY* S71 .....261 K2
Edinburgh Gv *WOR/ARM* LS12 .....108 C6
Edinburgh Pl *GFTH/SHER* LS25 .....113 K7
WOR/ARM LS12 .....108 C6
Edinburgh Rd *WOR/ARM* LS12 .....108 C6
Edinburgh Ter *WOR/ARM* LS12 .....108 C6
Edington *WHIT* * OL12 .....206 B6
Edlingham Cl *ROCH* OL11 .....206 A8
Edlington Cl *BOW* BD4 .....128 A3
Edmonton Cl *DOD/DAR* * S75 .....260 D4
Edmonton Pl *CHAL* LS7 .....87 M8
Edmunds Fold *LIT* OL15 .....185 H8
Edmund St *GTHN* BD7 .....4 B3
ROY/SHW OL2 .....229 L7
TOD OL14 .....163 J4
Edrich Cl *LM/WK* BD12 .....127 G8
Edroyd Pl *PDSY/CALV* LS28 .....106 F3
Edroyd St *PDSY/CALV* LS28 .....106 F3
Education Rd *CHAL* LS7 .....7 H3
Edward Av *LIT* OL15 .....207 H3
Edward Cl *BSLY* S70 .....261 L1
EARL WF12 .....195 K3
HIPP HX3 .....169 J2
Edward Dr *WKFDE* WF1 .....176 D1
Edward Rd *AWLS/ASK* DN6 .....249 M8
AWLS/ASK DN6 .....249 K5
MIRF WF14 .....194 B1
ROY/SHW OL2 .....229 J8
Edwards Rd *LUD/ILL* HX2 .....168 A1
Edward St *BOW* BD4 .....5 G8
BOW BD4 .....128 A5
BRIG HD6 .....170 C3
CLECK BD19 .....172 C1
DOD/DAR S75 .....242 B6
HBR HX7 .....143 K3

LDSU LS2 .....7 H9
MILN OL16 .....206 C6
NORM WF6 .....178 C1
RPDN/SBR HX6 .....167 K2
SHPY BD18 .....82 B6
WHIT OL12 .....206 F2
WKFDE * WF1 .....176 F7
Edward Turner Cl
LM/WK BD12 .....126 E8
Edwin Rd *HDGY* LS6 .....6 A4
Eel Holme View St *AIRE* BD20 .....57 K4
Eel Mires Garth *WBY* LS22 .....30 B8
Effingham Rd *BGLY* BD16 .....80 C5
Egerton Gv *WIL/AL* * BD15 .....103 H5
Egerton Pl *ROY/SHW* OL2 .....229 J8
Egerton St *LIT* OL15 .....207 L1
RPDN/SBR HX6 .....167 K2
Eggleston Dr *BOW* BD4 .....128 B4
Eggleston Sq *BSPA/BRAM* LS23 .....48 E7
Eggleston St *BRAM* LS13 .....107 H1
Egmanton Rd *BSLYN/ROY* S71 .....243 H5
Egremont Crs *WBSY* BD6 .....126 B8
Egremont Rd *MILN* OL16 .....229 G2
Egremont St *RPDN/SBR* HX6 .....167 J3
Egypt Rd *CUL/QBY* BD13 .....102 E6
Eighth Av *LVSG* WF15 .....171 K1
RTHW LS26 .....133 J7
WOR/ARM LS12 .....108 F8
Eightlands Av *BRAM* LS13 .....107 M4
Eightlands La *BRAM* LS13 .....107 M4
Eightlands Rd *DEWS* WF13 .....173 L6
Ekota Pl *RHAY* LS8 .....110 B2
Elam Wood Rd *AIRE* BD20 .....57 L3
Elbow La *ECHL* BD2 .....105 K4
LUD/ILL HX2 .....145 G6
Elder Av *HEM/SK/SE* WF9 .....225 L6
WKFDW/WTN WF2 .....12 B1
Elder Cl *BTLY* WF17 .....151 H4
Elder Cft *BRAM* LS13 .....107 L5
Elder Dr *EARL* WF12 .....195 M3
HEM/SK/SE WF9 .....225 L6
Elder Garth *GFTH/SHER* LS25 .....113 K8
Elder Gn *WKFDW/WTN* WF2 .....12 B1
Elder Gv *HUDS* HD4 .....213 M8
WKFDW/WTN WF2 .....12 A1
Elder Grove Ms *HUDS* * HD4 .....213 M8
Elder La *HUDN* * HD2 .....193 J1
Elder Lea *OSS* * WF5 .....197 G2
Elder Mt *BRAM* LS13 .....107 L5
Elder Pl *BRAM* LS13 .....107 L5
Elder Ri *RTHW* LS26 .....133 M8
Elder Rd *BRAM* LS13 .....107 L5
HUDN HD2 .....193 H1
Elder St *AIRE* BD20 .....57 J4
BRAM LS13 .....107 L5
IDLE BD10 .....84 A7
MILN OL16 .....228 D7
Elderwood Gdns *IDLE* BD10 .....106 A1
Eldon Ar *BSLY* * S70 .....261 H5
CLECK BD19 .....150 A7
Eldon Pl *BFD* BD1 .....4 D4
CLECK BD19 .....150 A7
Eldon Rd *HUD* HD1 .....191 M7
Eldon St *BSLY* S70 .....261 G5
HECK WF16 .....172 E2
HIPP HX3 .....11 H3
OSS WF5 .....175 H7
TOD OL14 .....163 L1
Eldon St North *BSLYN/ROY* S71 .....261 H4
Eldroth Mt *HFAX* HX1 .....168 C1
Eldroth Rd *HFAX* HX1 .....168 C1
Eldwick Cft *BGLY* BD16 .....81 L1
Eleanor Pl *PDSY/CALV* LS28 .....88 A7
Eleanor St *BRIG* HD6 .....170 C5
HUD HD1 .....14 F2
Eleventh Av *LVSG* WF15 .....171 K1
Elford Gv *RHAY* LS8 .....110 B3
Elford Pl East *RHAY* LS8 .....110 B3
Elford Pl West *RHAY* LS8 .....110 B3
Elford Rd *RHAY* * LS8 .....110 B3
Elgin Cl *HUDS* HD4 .....213 L4
Elia St *KGHY* BD21 .....3 K3
Elim St *LIT* OL15 .....185 L7
Eliot Gv *GSLY* LS20 .....62 B6
Eliots Cl *CAS* WF10 .....180 E1
Elil St *WBOW* BD5 .....127 H3
Elizabethan Ct *WKFDE* WF8 .....148 F1
Elizabethan Wy *MILN* OL16 .....207 G8
Elizabeth Av *CAS* WF10 .....158 E6
LM/WK BD12 .....148 E2
Elizabeth Cl *LM/WK* BD12 .....148 F2
Elizabeth Cft *CAS* WF10 .....158 E6
Elizabeth Crs *LM/WK* BD12 .....148 F2
Elizabeth Dr *CAS* WF10 .....158 E5
Elizabeth Frances St *ELL* HX5 .....169 H8
Elizabeth Gdns *WKFDE* WF1 .....176 E6
Elizabeth Pl *SCFT* LS14 .....111 J1
Elizabeth St *BGLY* * BD16 .....81 J3
CUD/GR S72 .....245 J4
ELL HX5 .....169 L6
GTL/HWG HX4 .....168 F7
HDGY LS6 .....109 G3
HUDS HD4 .....214 C3
KGHY BD21 .....58 B7
LM/WK BD12 .....148 E2
LVSG WF15 .....172 A2
WBOW BD5 .....4 E9
WKFDE WF1 .....199 G4

GTL/HWG HX4 .....190 C2
HDGY LS6 .....6 E1
HOR/CROF WF4 .....200 D7
HUDS HD4 .....214 D2
HWTH BD22 .....100 A4
KBTN HD8 .....239 J4
WHIT OL12 .....206 B5
Elm Ter *PONT* WF8 .....180 E6
Elm Tree Cl *WBSY* BD6 .....126 E6
Elm Tree Cl *KGHY* BD21 .....3 K8
LVSG WF15 .....172 A4
MSTN/BAR LS15 .....112 A7
WBSY BD6 .....126 F6
Elm Tree Gdns *WBSY* BD6 .....126 E6
Elmtree La *MID* LS10 .....9 K7
Elm Tree St *WKFDE* WF1 .....13 K7
Elm Vw *AIRE* BD20 .....35 K8
HIPP HX3 .....168 A2
The Elm *MSTN/BAR* LS15 .....133 K1
Elm Wy *BTLY* WF17 .....151 J4
Elmwood Av *AWLS/ASK* DN6 .....249 H8
HUD HD1 .....14 E5
MSTN/BAR LS15 .....90 F7
WKFDW/WTN WF2 .....199 K7
Elmwood Cha *MSTN/BAR* LS15 .....90 F7
Elmwood Cl *HUD* HD1 .....14 E5
MIRF WF14 .....194 B5
WKFDW/WTN WF2 .....199 K7
Elmwood Dr *BRIG* HD6 .....170 B3
HWTH BD22 .....79 H2
WKFDW/WTN WF2 .....199 K7
Elmwood Garth
WKFDW/WTN WF2 .....199 K7
Elmwood Gv *HOR/CROF* WF4 .....197 L5
Elmwood La *LDSU* LS2 .....7 H6
MSTN/BAR LS15 .....90 F7
Elmwood Pl *BFDE* BD3 .....105 L5
Elmwood Rd *HWTH* BD22 .....79 H3
LDSU LS2 .....7 G6
Elm Wood St *BRIG* HD6 .....170 D2
Elmwood St *HFAX* HX1 .....168 C1
Elmwood Ter *HWTH* BD22 .....79 H2
Elphaborough Cl *HBR* HX7 .....144 A6
Elsdon Gv *WBOW* BD5 .....127 G1
Elsham Ter *BULY* LS4 .....108 E4
Elsicker La *WKFDE* WF1 .....178 B8
Elsie St *HWTH* BD22 .....79 H6
KGHY BD21 .....57 K4
Elsinore Av *ELL* HX5 .....169 G8
Elsinore Ct *ELL* HX5 .....169 G8
Elstead Cl *DOD/DAR* S75 .....260 A1
Elsworth Av *BFDE* BD3 .....105 K5
Elsworth St *WOR/ARM* LS12 .....108 F7
Eltham Cl *HDGY* LS6 .....6 E2
Eltham Dr *HDGY* LS6 .....6 E2
Eltham Gdns *HDGY* LS6 .....6 E2
Eltham Gv *WBSY* BD6 .....126 C6
Eltham Ri *HDGY* LS6 .....6 E2
Elvaston Rd *MOR* LS27 .....152 C4
Elvey Cl *ECHL* BD2 .....105 M2
Elvey St *WKFDE* WF1 .....176 E7
Elwell Cl *WBSY* BD6 .....125 M7
Elwell St *EARD/LOFT* WF3 .....154 A5
Elwyn Gv *WBOW* BD5 .....127 G3
Elwyn Rd *WBOW* BD5 .....127 H3
Ely St *GTL/HWG* HX4 .....168 F8
The Embankment *MIRF* WF14 .....194 C1
Emblem Ter *WKFDE* WF1 .....13 G9
Embleton Rd *RTHW* LS26 .....156 E5
Emerald St *BTLY* WF17 .....151 J8
HUD HD1 .....15 G3
HWTH BD22 .....79 J2
Emerson Av *HTON* BD9 .....103 M3
Emily Cl *BSLYN/ROY* S71 .....261 M4
Emily Hall Gdns *WIL/AL* BD15 .....102 C1
Emily St *KGHY* BD21 .....3 H3
Emmanuel Ter *HUDS* HD4 .....214 B4
Emma St *WHIT* OL12 .....206 A6
Emmeline Cl *IDLE* * BD10 .....83 K6
Emmfield Dr *HTON* BD9 .....104 C3
Emm La *HTON* BD9 .....104 C3
Emmott Ct *COL* BB8 .....53 G8
Emmott Dr *YEA* LS19 .....84 F3
Emmott Farm Fold *HWTH* BD22 .....78 E8
Emmott La *COL* BB8 .....52 F7
Empress St *COL* BB8 .....74 A1
Emscote Av *HFAX* HX1 .....10 D9
Emscote Gdns *HFAX* HX1 .....10 D9
Emscote Gv *HFAX* HX1 .....10 D9
Emscote Pl *HFAX* HX1 .....10 D9
Emscote St South *HFAX* HX1 .....10 D9
Emsley Av *CUD/GR* S72 .....262 C2
Emsley Cl *BOW* BD4 .....127 K6
Emsley Pl *MID* LS10 .....10 C8
Emville Av *AL/HA/HU* LS17 .....88 E1
Enderby Cl *HIPP* HX3 .....146 B3
Enderley Rd *CUL/QBY* BD13 .....102 F2
Endor Crs *ILK* LS29 .....40 B7
Endor Gv *ILK* LS29 .....40 B7
Endsleigh Pl *CLAY* * BD14 .....125 K2
Enfield *YEA* LS19 .....62 D8
Enfield Av *CHAL* LS7 .....7 L4
Enfield Cl *BTLY* WF17 .....151 H8
Enfield Dr *BTLY* WF17 .....151 H8
GTHN BD7 .....126 B5
Enfield Pde *WBSY* BD6 .....126 C5
Enfield Rd *BAIL* BD17 .....82 E4
Enfield Side Rd *HWTH* BD22 .....99 M1
KGHY BD21 .....2 E6
Enfield St *CHAL* LS7 .....7 L4
Enfield Ter *CHAL* LS7 .....7 L4
Enfield Wk *WBSY* BD6 .....126 C5
Engine La *CUD/GR* S72 .....244 F5
HOR/CROF WF4 .....197 H5
WKFDW/WTN WF2 .....201 J7
England La *KNOT* WF11 .....182 B3
Englefield Crs *BOW* BD4 .....128 A4
ROY/SHW OL2 .....228 D3
Englefield Dr *BOW* BD4 .....128 A4
Ennerdale Av *EARL* WF12 .....174 A4
ROY/SHW OL2 .....228 D3
Ennerdale Cl *WBY* LS22 .....29 L8
Ennerdale Crs *EARL* WF12 .....174 A4
Ennerdale Dr *ECHL* BD2 .....105 K3
ELL HX5 .....169 K7
Ennerdale Rd *BSLYN/ROY* S71 .....262 C6
EARL WF12 .....174 A4
ECHL BD2 .....105 J3
WKFDW/WTN * WF2 .....176 B8

EARD/LOFT WF3 .....177 H2
GFTH/SHER LS25 .....135 H3
HOLM/MEL HD9 .....236 E6
RPDN/SBR HX6 .....167 K5
TOD OL14 .....141 K7
Elmbridge Cl *BSLYN/ROY* S71 .....244 A3
Elm Cl *OSS* WF5 .....197 G3
PONT WF8 .....181 G4
PONT WF8 .....203 L1
Elm Ct *CLECK* BD19 .....150 D2
KBTN HD8 .....216 B7
Elm Crs *AIRE* BD20 .....58 F6
Elm Cft *SCFT* LS14 .....89 L6
Elmet Dr *MSTN/BAR* LS15 .....91 G7
Elmete Av *GFTH/SHER* LS25 .....116 A7
MSTN/BAR LS15 .....90 B8
RHAY LS8 .....88 E8
Elmete Cl *RHAY* LS8 .....88 E8
Elmete Ct *RHAY* LS8 .....88 E8
Elmete Cft *MSTN/BAR* LS15 .....90 B8
Elmete Dr *RHAY* LS8 .....88 F7
Elmete Gv *RHAY* LS8 .....88 E8
Elmete Hl *RHAY* LS8 .....88 E7
Elmete La *RHAY* LS8 .....88 F6
Elmete Mt *RHAY* LS8 .....88 F8
Elmete Rd *CAS* WF10 .....158 F5
Elmete Wk *RHAY* LS8 .....88 E8
Elmete Wy *RHAY* LS8 .....89 G8
Elmet Rd *MSTN/BAR* LS15 .....91 G8
Elmfield *BAIL* BD17 .....82 F2
Elmfield Av *HUDW* HD3 .....213 H1
Elmfield Ct *BIRK/DRI* BD11 .....150 C2
MOR LS27 .....152 C3
Elmfield Dr *KBTN* HD8 .....239 J5
WBSY BD6 .....126 E6
Elmfield Gv *WOR/ARM* * LS12 .....108 D7
Elmfield Pl *WOR/ARM* LS12 .....108 F8
Elmfield Rd *AIRE* BD20 .....35 G7
HUDN HD2 .....192 A5
MOR LS27 .....152 D4
Elmfield Ter *HFAX* HX1 .....168 D1
HUDE HD5 .....15 L8
Elmfield Wy *BRAM* LS13 .....107 M5
Elm Gdns *CAS* WF10 .....180 E1
HFAX HX1 .....168 E1
Elm Gv *AIRE* BD20 .....35 L6
AIRE BD20 .....58 F6
CLECK BD19 .....150 C6
HECK WF16 .....172 E1
HEM/SK/SE WF9 .....247 H5
HIPP HX3 .....125 M3
HOR/CROF WF4 .....197 K5
HWTH BD22 .....79 J2
ILK LS29 .....40 B6
MILN OL16 .....229 J3
SHPY BD18 .....83 G7
WHIT OL12 .....206 E1
Elmhirst La *DOD/DAR* S75 .....259 M6
Elmhurst Cl *AL/HA/HU* LS17 .....88 C2
Elmhurst Gdns *AL/HA/HU* LS17 .....88 C2
Elmhurst Gv *KNOT* WF11 .....182 A3
Elmore Wd *LIT* OL15 .....185 G6
Elm Pk *PONT* WF8 .....180 E6
Elm Pl *BSLYN/ROY* S71 .....261 M1
KNOT WF11 .....182 A3
RPDN/SBR HX6 .....167 K1
Elm Rd *AIRE* BD20 .....55 L1
AWLS/ASK DN6 .....249 J4
DEWS WF13 .....173 H6
HEM/SK/SE WF9 .....224 A7
NORM WF6 .....178 C1
SHPY BD18 .....82 F7
Elm Rw *BSLYN/ROY* S71 .....261 K5
Elmroyd *RTHW* LS26 .....155 H2
The Elms *FEA/AMT* WF7 .....224 B1
GSLY LS20 .....62 A5
LIT OL15 .....207 G2
Elmsall Dr *HEM/SK/SE* WF9 .....247 L1
Elmsall La *AWLS/ASK* DN6 .....247 K6
Elmsall St *GIR* BD8 .....4 D3
Elmsall Wy *HEM/SK/SE* WF9 .....247 L1
Elms Hl *MAR/SLWT* HD7 .....212 B6
Elmsley St *AIRE* BD20 .....56 E1
Elm St *COL* BB8 .....74 A1

HEM/SK/SE WF9 .....247 L1
HUD HD1 .....14 E5
MSTN/BAR LS15 .....90 F7
WKFDW/WTN WF2 .....199 K7

WOR/ARM LS12....................129 M4
Ennerdale Wy
  WOR/ARM * LS12....................129 M4
Enoch La HUDS HD4....................214 B3
Enterprise Wy AIRE BD20....................16 C7
  CAS WF10....................157 L7
  GFTH/SHER LS25....................116 E7
  IDLE BD10....................83 K8
  MID LS10....................132 B5
Entwisle St MILN OL16....................207 G8
Entwistle Rd MILN OL16....................206 C7
Envoy St BEE/HOL LS11....................9 G8
Epsom Rd GFTH/SHER LS25....................135 H4
Epsom Wy HUDE HD5....................193 L5
Epworth Pl HWTH BD22....................78 D3
  MID LS10....................9 L7
Equitable St MILN OL16....................229 H1
Eric St BRAM LS13....................107 L1
  HEM/SK/SE WF9....................247 J3
  KGHY BD21....................3 H2
  LIT OL15....................185 J8
Ermysted St SKP/WHF BD23....................16 C2
Ernest St DEWS WF13....................173 M5
  TOD OL14....................140 E5
Ernest Ter WOR/ARM LS12....................206 D5
Erringden Rd HBR HX7....................143 M5
Erringden St TOD OL14....................163 L1
Escroft Cl LM/WK BD12....................148 C5
Eshald La RTHW LS26....................155 M1
Eshald Pl RTHW LS26....................133 M8
Esholt Av GSLY LS20....................61 M7
Esholt La BAIL BD17....................83 J2
Eshton Av LM/WK BD12....................149 H1
Eshton Ct DOD/DAR S75....................242 C4
Eshton Wk BSLY S70....................260 F5
Eskdale Av HIPP HX3....................147 K1
  NORM WF6....................178 C4
  ROY/SHW OL2....................228 F7
Eskdale Cl EARL WF12....................174 A3
  NORM WF6....................178 C2
Eskdale Ct NORM WF6....................178 C2
Eskdale Cft NORM WF6....................178 C2
Eskdale Gv GFTH/SHER LS25....................113 J8
Eskdale Mt HBR HX7....................143 J2
  SCFT LS14....................111 H2
Eskdale Ri WIL/AL BD15....................103 K6
Eskdale Rd BSLYN/ROY S71....................262 C6
  WKFDW/WTN WF2....................176 A7
Esk Gdns WBY LS22....................30 A6
Eskine Pde WBSY BD6....................126 B8
Esmond St GTHN BD7....................126 B3
  WOR/ARM LS12....................108 C7
Esmond Ter WOR/ARM LS12....................108 D7
The Esplanade MILN OL16....................206 H7
Essex Av ROY/SHW OL2....................229 H7
Essex Rd BSLY * S70....................261 J7
Essex St BFDE BD3....................5 K8
  COL BB8....................74 A2
  HFAX HX1....................10 A7
  ROCH OL11....................206 B8
Estcourt Av HDGY LS6....................108 E1
Estcourt Dr PONT WF8....................203 M2
Estcourt Gv GTHN BD7....................126 C1
Estcourt Rd GTHN BD7....................126 C1
  PONT WF8....................203 L1
Estcourt Ter HDGY LS6....................108 E1
Esther Av WKFDW/WTN WF2....................198 B2
Esther Gv WKFDW/WTN WF2....................198 A2
Esthwaite Gdns
  MSTN/BAR LS15....................111 G8
Ethel Ct MILN OL16....................206 H8
Ethel St KGHY BD21....................57 K5
Etna St GTHN BD7....................126 B3
Eton Av HUDE HD5....................193 L6
Eton St HBR HX7....................143 H3
  HFAX HX1....................10 B6
Euden Edge Rd
  MAR/SLWT HD7....................212 D1
Eunice La KBTN HD8....................238 E8
Euston Gv BEE/HOL LS11....................8 A7
Euston Mt BEE/HOL LS11....................8 A8
Euston Ter BEE/HOL LS11....................8 A8
Evanston Av BULY LS4....................108 E5
Eva St WHIT OL12....................206 C4
Eveline Av IDLE BD10....................83 K7
Evelyn Av BFDE BD3....................106 A6
Evelyn Pl WOR/ARM LS12....................108 E8
Evelyn Ter BSLY * S70....................261 J6
Evens Ter WBOW BD5....................127 C4
Everard St HUDS HD4....................213 M2
Everdale Mt HEM/SK/SE WF9....................223 K8
  HEM/SK/SE WF9....................247 G3
Everest Av SHPY BD18....................83 G7
Everest St ROCH OL11....................228 C4
Everleigh St OSM LS9....................110 C6
Eversley Av GFTH/SHER LS25....................116 A8
Eversley Ct GFTH/SHER LS25....................116 A7
Eversley Dr BOW BD4....................128 A2
Eversley Garth Crs
  GFTH/SHER LS25....................116 A7
Eversley Ldg LUD/ILL * HX2....................146 A8
Eversley Mt GFTH/SHER LS25....................116 A8
  LUD/ILL * HX2....................146 A8
Eversley Pl LUD/ILL HX2....................146 A8
Eversley Rd HBR HX7....................143 J2
Every St TOD OL14....................163 L1
Evesham Gv IDLE BD10....................83 K7
Ewart Pl GTHN BD7....................126 D5
Ewart St CUL/QBY * BD13....................125 C5
  GTHN BD7....................126 C5
Ewden Wy DOD/DAR S75....................260 C5
Ewood Dr HBR HX7....................144 B5
Ewood Hall Av HBR HX7....................144 B5
Ewood La TOD OL14....................141 H8
Exbury Wy WHIT * OL12....................206 A6
Excelsior Cl RPDN/SBR HX6....................188 C3
Excelsior Ter MILN OL16....................207 H3
Exchange HOLM/MEL HD9....................236 D2
Exchange Buildings
  SKP/WHF BD23....................16 C1
Exchange Sq BFD * BD1....................5 G7
Exchange St CLECK BD19....................149 M5
  GTL/HWG HX4....................168 F8
  HEM/SK/SE WF9....................247 H3
  NORM WF6....................178 C4
Exe St WBOW BD5....................126 E3
Exeter Dr MID LS10....................131 M7
Exeter Gv ROCH OL11....................228 B1

Exeter St HIPP HX3....................168 F3
  ROCH OL11....................228 B1
RPDN/SBR HX6....................167 L2
Exhibition Rd SHPY BD18....................82 B6
Exley Av KGHY BD21....................79 G3
Exley Bank HIPP HX3....................168 F4
Exley Bank Top HIPP HX3....................168 F4
Exley Crs KGHY BD21....................2 C9
Exley Dr KGHY BD21....................2 C9
Exley Gdns ELL HX5....................168 F5
Exley Head HWTH BD22....................2 B9
Exley Head Vw HWTH BD22....................57 C6
Exley La ELL HX5....................169 G5
Exley Mt GTHN BD7....................104 B8
  KGHY BD21....................2 C9
Exley Rd KGHY BD21....................2 D7
Exley St KGHY BD21....................2 C9
Exley Wy KGHY * BD21....................79 J2
Exmoor St HFAX HX1....................10 A8
Exmouth Pl BFDE BD3....................5 G1
Exmouth Sq ROCH * OL11....................228 C2
Exmouth St ROCH OL11....................228 C3
Express Wy NORM WF6....................156 D8
Eyam Ct MSTN/BAR LS15....................111 G7
Eyam Dl DOD/DAR S75....................260 A7
Eyres Av WOR/ARM LS12....................108 E6
Eyres Gv WOR/ARM LS12....................108 E6
Eyres Mill Side WOR/ARM LS12....................108 D6
Eyres St WOR/ARM LS12....................108 E6
Eyres Ter WOR/ARM LS12....................108 E6
Eyre St BTLY WF17....................173 M2
Eyrie Ap MOR LS27....................152 E3

F

Factory La BOW BD4....................127 K4
  HUDS HD4....................213 K2
Factory St BOW BD4....................127 L4
Fagley Crs ECHL BD2....................105 L4
Fagley Cft ECHL BD2....................105 M4
Fagley Dr ECHL BD2....................105 L4
Fagley La ECHL BD2....................105 M3
Fagley Pl ECHL BD2....................105 L5
Fagley Rd ECHL BD2....................106 A4
Fagley Ter ECHL BD2....................105 L5
Fair Bank SHPY BD18....................82 E8
Fairbank Rd GIR BD8....................104 C5
Fairbank Ter GIR BD8....................104 C5
Fairbrook Rd HOR/CROF WF4....................220 C2
Fairburn Ct HIPP * HX3....................169 J2
Fairburn Dr GFTH/SHER LS25....................135 J1
Fairburn Gdns ECHL BD2....................105 L2
Fairclough Gv LUD/ILL HX2....................146 B3
Fairfax Av BIRK/DRI BD11....................151 J1
  BOW BD4....................127 L5
  FEA/AMT WF7....................179 L5
  KNOT WF11....................181 M3
Fairfax Cl COP/BISH YO23....................73 J7
  SCFT LS14....................111 K5
Fairfax Crs BOW BD4....................127 L5
  HIPP HX3....................169 J1
Fairfax Dr LIT OL15....................207 H3
Fairfax Flats OT * LS21....................41 K7
Fairfax Gdns ILK LS29....................61 H1
Fairfax Gv YEA LS19....................62 B7
Fairfax Rd BEE/HOL LS11....................8 C9
  BGLY BD16....................81 H1
  CUL/QBY BD13....................79 M7
  ILK LS29....................61 H1
  PONT WF8....................181 G6
Fairfax St AIRE BD20....................35 M5
  BOW BD4....................5 H9
  HWTH BD22....................78 F7
  OT LS21....................41 J7
  SKP/WHF BD23....................16 C3
Fairfax Vw HORS LS18....................85 K2
Fairfield Av HECK WF16....................173 G1
  NORM WF6....................178 A3
  OSS WF5....................197 H2
  PDSY/CALV LS28....................107 H9
  PONT WF8....................180 D6
Fairfield Cl BRAM LS13....................107 K4
  CAS WF10....................159 G5
  GFTH/SHER LS25....................116 B7
  OSS WF5....................197 H2
  RTHW LS26....................154 D2
Fairfield Ct CAS WF10....................158 C7
  LVSG WF15....................172 B2
Fairfield Crs BRAM LS13....................107 J4
  DEWS WF13....................173 J5
Fairfield Dr BAIL BD17....................83 G2
  HECK WF16....................173 G1
  OSS WF5....................197 H2
  RTHW LS26....................154 D2
Fairfield Gdns OSS WF5....................197 H2
  RTHW LS26....................154 D2
Fairfield Gv BRAM LS13....................107 K4
  RTHW * LS26....................154 D2
Fairfield Hl BRAM LS13....................107 K4
Fairfield La GFTH/SHER LS25....................160 D2
  RTHW LS26....................154 D2
Fairfield Link GFTH/SHER LS25....................116 B7
Fairfield Ms DEWS WF13....................173 J5
Fairfield Mt BRAM LS13....................107 K4
  OSS WF5....................197 H2
Fairfield Ri KBTN HD8....................238 C1
Fairfield Rd BRAM LS13....................107 K4
  GIR BD8....................104 D5
  HECK WF16....................173 G1
  LM/WK BD12....................148 F3
  OSS WF5....................197 G2
  TAD LS24....................71 L3
Fairfields CAS WF10....................159 G7
  KBTN HD8....................257 H2
Fairfield Sq BRAM LS13....................107 K3
Fairfields Rd HOLM/MEL HD9....................255 M3
Fairfield St BOW BD4....................127 M5
  BRAM LS13....................107 K4
Fairfield Ter BRAM LS13....................107 K4
  EARL WF12....................174 B6

  OSS WF5....................197 G2
Fairfield Wk OSS WF5....................197 H2
Fairfield Wy TAD LS24....................71 L3
Fairford Av BEE/HOL LS11....................9 G9
Fairford Ter BEE/HOL LS11....................9 G9
Fairhaven Gn IDLE BD10....................83 L7
Fair Isle Ct KGHY BD21....................3 G4
Fairlands St ROCH OL11....................228 D4
Fair Lea Rd HUDS HD4....................214 A5
Fairleigh Crs EARD/LOFT WF3....................153 J6
Fairleigh Rd EARD/LOFT WF3....................153 H6
Fairless Av HIPP HX3....................148 C7
Fairmoor Wy HECK WF16....................173 G1
Fairmount HTON BD9....................104 E4
Fair Mt TOD OL14....................163 J5
Fairmount Pk SHPY BD18....................82 A7
Fairmount Ter KGHY BD21....................58 B8
Fair Rd WBSY BD6....................126 D5
Fair Vw WF15....................172 B1
  PONT WF8....................203 G1
Fairview Av BTLY WF17....................151 H8
Fairview Cl BAIL BD17....................82 D5
Fairview Crs BTLY WF17....................151 J8
Fairview Rd BTLY WF17....................151 J8
Fairview Ter HIPP * HX3....................10 D1
The Fairway AL/HA/HU LS17....................65 L8
  FEA/AMT WF7....................179 M5
  GFTH/SHER LS25....................116 B7
  HUDN HD2....................192 C2
  LUD/ILL HX2....................124 D7
  PDSY/CALV LS28....................106 D5
  TAD LS24....................71 L5
Fairway DOD/DAR S75....................260 C8
  GSLY LS20....................61 L5
  IDLE BD10....................84 B5
  SHPY BD18....................82 B7
  WBSY BD6....................126 B5
Fairway Ap NORM WF6....................178 E4
Fairway Av DOD/DAR S75....................242 E4
  GTHN BD7....................126 B5
  NORM WF6....................178 E4
Fairway Cl GFTH/SHER LS25....................116 B7
  GSLY LS20....................61 L6
  NORM WF6....................178 E5
  WBSY BD6....................126 B5
Fairway Crs HWTH BD22....................78 D3
  ROY/SHW OL2....................228 F8
Fairway Dr GTHN BD7....................126 B5
  NORM WF6....................178 E5
Fairway Gdns NORM WF6....................178 E4
Fairway Gv GTHN BD7....................126 B4
Fairway Mdw NORM WF6....................178 E4
The Fairways AIRE BD20....................57 J3
  HTON BD9....................104 A1
Fair Ways MIRF WF14....................194 B4
Fairway Wk GTHN BD7....................126 B5
Fairweather Ms GIR * BD8....................104 A7
Fairy Dell BGLY BD16....................81 J7
Fairy Hill La CAS WF10....................180 F1
Faith St BSLYN/ROY S71....................244 B8
  HEM/SK/SE WF9....................246 F2
Falcon Cliffe AIRE BD20....................56 E1
Falcon Cl AWLS/ASK DN6....................249 K8
  OT LS21....................41 J7
Falcon Dr CAS WF10....................157 L8
Falconers Ride HUDS HD4....................214 A8
Falcon Ms GIR * BD8....................103 L6
  MOR LS27....................152 E3
Falcon Rd BGLY BD16....................81 H1
Falcon St BSLY S70....................261 G4
  GTHN BD7....................126 C1
  HIPP HX3....................168 F3
  HUDS HD4....................214 B5
Falhouse La EARL WF12....................194 F7
Falinge Ms WHIT OL12....................206 A6
Falinge Rd WHIT OL12....................206 A6
Falkland Crs AL/HA/HU LS17....................87 L5
Falkland Gv AL/HA/HU LS17....................87 L5
Falkland Mt AL/HA/HU LS17....................87 L5
Falkland Ri AL/HA/HU LS17....................87 L5
  IDLE BD10....................106 A2
Fall Bank Crs DOD/DAR S75....................259 M6
Fall Brow Cl CLAY BD14....................125 J3
Falledge La STKB/PEN S36....................257 G4
Fall Head La DOD/DAR S75....................259 K5
Fall Ings Rd WKFDE WF1....................13 J7
Fall La DEWS WF13....................173 K8
  EARD/LOFT WF3....................153 M6
  HIPP HX3....................147 G2
  LVSG WF15....................171 M5
  MAR/SLWT HD7....................233 H3
  PBR HG3....................26 B3
  RPDN/SBR HX6....................167 M3
Fallow Cft HUDN HD2....................193 H1
Fallow Fld SKP/WHF BD23....................16 F5
Fallowfield Cl BOW BD4....................127 L6
Fallowfield Dr BOW BD4....................127 L5
Fallowfield Gdns BOW BD4....................127 L5
Fallow La HWTH BD22....................56 C8
Fall Park Ct BRAM LS13....................107 M1
Fall Rd LVSG WF15....................172 A5
Fall Spring Gdns GTL/HWG HX4....................190 B2
Fall Spring Gn GTL/HWG HX4....................190 A2
Fallswood Gv BRAM LS13....................107 M2
Fall Vw DOD/DAR S75....................259 J6
Fall Wood St HWTH BD22....................78 E8
Falmers Cottages HDGY * LS6....................6 B1
Falmouth Av BFDE BD3....................5 H2
  NORM WF6....................178 D3
Falmouth Cl BSLYN/ROY S71....................261 K4
Falmouth Crs NORM WF6....................178 D3
Falmouth Rd NORM WF6....................178 D3
Falmouth St ROCH OL11....................228 C1
Falstar Av ECHL BD2....................105 L4
Faltis IDLE BD10....................105 L1
Fanny La TAD LS24....................71 K7
Fanny Moor Crs HUDE HD5....................214 E4
Fanny Moor La HUDE HD5....................214 E4
Fanny St KGHY BD21....................2 E6
  SHPY BD18....................82 B6
Farcliffe Pl GIR BD8....................104 D5
Farcliffe Rd GIR BD8....................104 D5
Farcliffe Ter GIR BD8....................104 D5
Far Common Rd MIRF WF14....................172 A6

Far Cft KBTN HD8....................216 C4
Far Crook IDLE BD10....................83 H5
Fardale ROY/SHW OL2....................229 K8
Far Dene SCFT LS14....................215 M6
Farehill Rd HUDS HD4....................214 B6
Farfield Av BTLY * WF17....................151 H8
  PDSY/CALV LS28....................106 E3
  WBSY BD6....................126 A7
Farfield Ct AL/HA/HU LS17....................88 A1
  GFTH/SHER LS25....................112 F7
Farfield Crs WBSY BD6....................126 A6
Far Field Dr HOLM/MEL HD9....................255 G6
Farfield Dr PDSY/CALV LS28....................106 E4
Farfield Gv PDSY/CALV LS28....................106 E3
  WBSY BD6....................126 A7
Far Field La BSLYN/ROY S71....................244 A8
  HOLM/MEL HD9....................255 G5
Farfield Ri PDSY/CALV LS28....................106 E3
Farfield Rd BAIL BD17....................82 F5
  HUDE HD5....................215 H3
  SHPY BD18....................82 C7
  WBSY BD6....................126 C7
Far Fields La HOLM/MEL HD9....................235 H1
Farfield St CLECK BD19....................149 M5
  HTON BD9....................104 C4
Farfield Ter HTON BD9....................104 C4
Faringdon ROCH * OL11....................206 A8
Farlands Ri MILN OL16....................228 E3
Far La HBR HX7....................144 C4
  HOLM/MEL HD9....................255 G6
Far Lawns BSLYN/ROY S71....................243 M5
Farlea Dr ECHL BD2....................105 L3
Farleton Dr ECHL BD2....................105 M4
Farley Crs HWTH BD22....................78 D3
Farm Cl BSLYN/ROY S71....................261 L2
Farm Ct AWLS/ASK DN6....................249 L8
  MSTN/BAR LS15....................111 K4
Farm Cft FEA/AMT WF7....................201 G1
  SKP/WHF BD23....................16 B5
Far Mead Cft ILK LS29....................40 A4
Farmfield Dr HEM/SK/SE WF9....................223 J3
Farm Gdns FEA/AMT WF7....................201 G1
Farm Hill Crs CHAL LS7....................109 J1
Farm Hl North CHAL LS7....................87 J8
Farm Hill Rd IDLE BD10....................105 K1
Farm Hl Ri CHAL LS7....................109 J1
  MOR LS27....................152 A1
Farm Hl South CHAL LS7....................109 J1
Farm Hill Wy CHAL LS7....................109 J1
Farm House La DOD/DAR S75....................260 C4
Farm La HEM/SK/SE WF9....................223 J4
Farm Mt HOR/CROF WF4....................197 C8
  MSTN/BAR LS15....................111 L4
Far Moss AL/HA/HU LS17....................87 J1
Farm Pond Dr HDGY HD6....................170 A1
Farm Rd BSLY S70....................261 L8
  FEA/AMT WF7....................201 M1
  MSTN/BAR LS15....................111 K4
Farmstead Rd IDLE BD10....................83 L8
Farm Wk LIT OL15....................207 H1
  MILN OL16....................206 E5
Farm Wy WMB/DAR S73....................263 J8
Farnboro St TOD OL14....................163 J4
Farndale Ap SCFT LS14....................111 L1
Farndale Cl SCFT LS14....................111 L1
  WBY LS22....................29 K8
Farndale Ct GFTH/SHER LS25....................135 H4
Farndale Garth SCFT LS14....................89 L8
Farndale Pl SCFT LS14....................89 L8
Farndale Rd BAIL BD17....................82 C4
  WIL/AL BD15....................102 A3
Farne Av WKFDW/WTN WF2....................198 A1
Farnham Cl BAIL BD17....................82 F5
  SCFT LS14....................89 K5
Farnham Cft SCFT LS14....................89 K5
Farnham Rd GTHN BD7....................126 C1
Farnham Wy HOR/CROF WF4....................200 B5
Farnlee HUDW HD3....................191 K5
Farnley Cl ILK LS29....................61 J2
Farnley La OT LS21....................23 L8
Farnley Pk OT LS21....................42 A3
Farnley Rd HUDS HD4....................215 H6
  ILK LS29....................61 K2
Farnley Vw BIRK/DRI BD11....................129 J8
Farrar Av MIRF WF14....................172 B8
Farrar Ct BRAM LS13....................107 J3
Farrar Cft BHP/TINH LS16....................86 C2
Farrar Dr MIRF WF14....................172 A7
Farrar Gv BHP/TINH LS16....................86 C2
Farrar Height La
  RPDN/SBR HX6....................188 D2
Farrar La BHP/TINH LS16....................86 C2
Farrar Mill La HIPP HX3....................168 D3
Farrar St BSLY S70....................260 F5
Far Reef Cl HORS LS18....................85 L4
Farrer La RTHW LS26....................155 L1
Farriers Cft ECHL BD2....................105 H2
Farriers Pl CAS WF10....................158 D3
Farringdon Cl BOW BD4....................127 M2
Farringdon Dr BOW BD4....................128 A3
Farringdon Gv WBSY BD6....................126 C7
Farrow Bank WOR/ARM LS12....................108 A7
Farrow Cl DOD/DAR S75....................260 C7
Farrowdale Av ROY/SHW OL2....................229 K8
Farrow Gn WOR/ARM LS12....................108 A7
Farrow Hl WOR/ARM LS12....................108 A7
Farrow Rd WOR/ARM LS12....................108 A7
Farrow St ROY/SHW OL2....................229 K8
Farrow St East ROY/SHW OL2....................229 K8
Farrow V WOR/ARM LS12....................108 A7
Farside Gn WBOW BD5....................126 C5
Fartown PDSY/CALV LS28....................129 G1
Fartown Cl PDSY/CALV LS28....................129 G1
Far Townend DOD/DAR * S75....................260 B7
Fartown Green Rd HUDN HD2....................192 D5
Far View Bank HUDE HD5....................215 G1
Farway BOW BD4....................128 A2
Far Well Fold YEA * LS19....................84 F3
Far Well La HOLM/MEL HD9....................237 K6
Faugh La HBR HX7....................120 E8
Faulkner St KBTN HD8....................206 B7
Favell Av NORM WF6....................178 D4
Faversham Wk BOW * BD4....................128 A2
Favordale Rd COL BB8....................52 C5
Fawcett Av WOR/ARM LS12....................130 D1

Fawcett Bank WOR/ARM LS12....................130 C1
Fawcett Cl WOR/ARM LS12....................130 C1
Fawcett Dr WOR/ARM LS12....................130 C1
Fawcett Gdns WOR/ARM LS12....................130 C1
Fawcett La WOR/ARM LS12....................130 C1
Fawcett Pl BOW BD4....................127 L6
Fawcett St WKFDW/WTN WF2....................12 C1
Fawcett V WOR/ARM LS12....................130 C1
Fawcett Vw WOR/ARM LS12....................130 C1
Fawkes Dr OT LS21....................40 F8
Faxfleet St WBOW BD5....................126 F5
Faye Gdns BOW BD4....................127 M5
Fearnley Av OSS WF5....................174 E7
Fearnley Cl WOR/ARM LS12....................108 F7
Fearnley Ct HOLM/MEL HD9....................254 F1
Fearnley Dr OSS WF5....................174 E7
Fearnley La HOLM/MEL HD9....................254 E1
Fearnley Pl WOR/ARM LS12....................108 F7
Fearnley St DEWS WF13....................173 K7
  FEA/AMT WF7....................201 L1
Fearnside Fold
  HOR/CROF * WF4....................197 K4
Fearnside's Cl HOR/CROF WF4....................197 J5
Fearnsides St GIR BD8....................104 C6
Fearnsides Ter GIR BD8....................104 D6
Fearnville Av RHAY LS8....................110 F2
Fearnville Cl RHAY LS8....................110 F1
  RHAY LS8....................110 F2
Fearnville Gv BSLYN/ROY S71....................243 J5
  RHAY LS8....................110 F2
Fearnville Mt RHAY LS8....................110 F1
Fearnville Pl RHAY * LS8....................110 F1
Fearnville Rd RHAY LS8....................110 F2
Fearnville Ter RHAY LS8....................111 G1
Fearnville Vw RHAY LS8....................110 F2
Feast Fld HORS LS18....................85 K5
Featherbank Av HORS LS18....................85 K5
Featherbank Gv HORS LS18....................85 K5
Featherbank La HORS LS18....................85 K5
Featherbank Ter HORS LS18....................85 K5
Featherbank Wk HORS LS18....................85 K5
Featherbed Cl GTL/HWG HX4....................168 E2
Feather Bed La ELL HX5....................168 F8
Featherbed La TAD LS24....................31 M8
Feather Rd BFDE BD3....................5 L5
Featherstall Brook Vie
  LIT OL15....................207 J1
Featherstall Rd LIT OL15....................207 J1
Featherstone La
  FEA/AMT WF7....................179 M6
Federation St WBOW BD5....................127 H4
Felbrigg Av HWTH BD22....................2 C7
Felcote Av HUDE HD5....................215 G1
Felcourt Dr BOW BD4....................128 A4
Felcourt Fold BOW BD4....................128 A4
Felkirk Dr HOR/CROF WF4....................222 C5
Felkirk Vw CUD/GR S72....................244 D5
Felks Stile Rd HUDS HD4....................213 H4
Fell Crs HWTH BD22....................2 A8
Fell Greave Crs HUDN HD2....................192 D1
Fell Greave Rd HUDN HD2....................192 D1
Fell Gv HUDN HD2....................192 D2
  HWTH BD22....................2 B7
Fell La HWTH BD22....................2 B7
Fellowsides La OSS WF5....................197 G1
The Fellows HUDS HD4....................213 L7
Fellside TOD OL14....................164 D1
Fellside Cl WBOW BD5....................127 H4
Fellside Gdns LIT OL15....................185 H7
Fellwood Av HWTH BD22....................79 G6
Fellwood Cl HWTH BD22....................79 G6
Felnex Cl OSM LS9....................132 E1
Felnex Crs OSM LS9....................132 E1
Felnex Rd OSM LS9....................132 E1
Felnex Sq OSM LS9....................132 D1
Felnex Wy OSM LS9....................132 E1
Fenay Bankside KBTN HD8....................215 M3
Fenay Bridge Rd HUDE HD5....................215 L2
Fenay Crs HUDE HD5....................215 J3
Fenay Dr KBTN HD8....................215 J3
Fenay La HUDE HD5....................215 J3
Fenay Lea Dr HUDE HD5....................215 J3
Fenby Av BOW BD4....................127 K2
Fenby Cl BOW BD4....................127 K2
Fenby Gdns BOW BD4....................127 L2
Fencote Crs ECHL BD2....................105 M3
Fender Rd WBSY BD6....................126 B5
Fennec Rd BAIL BD17....................83 G2
Fennell Ct WKFDW/WTN WF2....................198 F1
Fensome Wy WMB/DAR S73....................263 H8
Fenton Av RTHW LS26....................133 K7
Fenton Cl HEM/SK/SE WF9....................246 D5
  RTHW LS26....................133 K7
Fenton La GFTH/SHER LS25....................116 E4
Fenton Ms ROCH * OL11....................228 A1
Fenton Rd EARD/LOFT WF3....................155 H7
  HFAX HX1....................10 A9
  HUD HD1....................214 B3
Fentonsgate EARD/LOFT WF3....................154 E5
Fenton Sq HUD HD1....................14 C9
Fenton St BSLY * S70....................261 G5
  EARD/LOFT WF3....................153 H5
  ILK LS29....................40 B5
  LDSU LS2....................6 F6
  MIRF WF14....................194 C2
  ROCH OL11....................228 A1
Fenwick Dr WBSY BD6....................126 B8
Fenwick St ROCH OL11....................206 A7
Ferguson Gdns WHIT OL12....................206 B3
Ferguson St HFAX HX1....................10 D9
Fern Av HOLM/MEL HD9....................234 E3
Fern Bank AWLS/ASK DN6....................249 K8
Fernbank Av BRAM LS13....................107 H3
Fernbank Av HWTH BD22....................79 H2
Fernbank Cl BRAM LS13....................107 H3
  BSLY * LS13....................261 G2
Fernbank Dr BAIL BD17....................82 C5
  BGLY BD16....................80 D3
  BRAM LS13....................107 H3
Fernbank Gdns BRAM LS13....................107 H3
Fernbank Pl BRAM LS13....................107 H3
Fernbank Rd BFDE BD3....................5 L2
  BRAM LS13....................107 H3
Fern Cha SCFT LS14....................67 J7
Ferncliffe Dr AIRE BD20....................82 D3
  BAIL BD17....................82 D3
Ferncliffe Rd BGLY BD16....................81 J3

SHPY * BD18 82 B6
Ferncliffe Ter BRAM LS13 107 K4
Fern Cl BTLY WF17 174 B1
Fern Ct AIRE BD20 57 J4
Fern Cft LVSG WF15 171 L2
SCFT LS14 67 J7
WKFDW/WTN WF2 176 A3
Ferndale Av CLAY BD14 125 J3
MILN OL16 228 E5
Ferndale Gv HTON BD9 104 E2
Ferndale Pl HEM/SK/SE WF9 223 L8
Ferndene BGLY BD16 81 K3
Ferndene Av BTLY WF17 151 H3
Ferndown Gn WBOW BD5 126 F3
Ferney Lee Rd TOD OL14 141 J8
Fernfield Ter HIPP * HX3 146 D4
Fern Gv KSTL LS5 108 C2
Fernhill BGLY BD16 81 J1
Fern Hill Av SHPY BD18 82 B7
Fern Hill Gv SHPY BD18 82 B7
Fern Hill Mt SHPY BD18 82 B7
Fern Hill Rd SHPY BD18 82 B7
Fernhurst Cl MIRF WF14 172 C8
Fernhurst Crs MIRF WF14 172 D8
Fernhurst Lea MIRF WF14 172 D8
Fernhurst Rd MIRF WF14 172 C8
Fernhurst Wy MIRF WF14 172 C8
Fernlea RTHW LS26 133 H8
Fernlea Cl HECK WF16 173 G3
HOR/CROF WF4 200 C5
Fernlea Gv MAR/SLWT HD7 213 G3
Fern Lea Rd HUDW HD3 191 J5
Fern Lea St RPDN/SBR HX6 167 K1
Fern Lea Vw PDSY/CALV LS28 107 G4
Fernleigh Ct
WKFDW/WTN WF2 198 B1
Fernley Gdns LM/WK BD12 148 E2
Fernley Green Cl KNOT WF11 182 D2
Fernley Green Rd KNOT WF11 182 D2
Fernley Hill Dr NORM WF6 178 B1
Fernside Av HUDE HD5 215 H2
Fernside Cl HUDE HD5 215 J1
Fernside Crs HUDE HD5 215 H1
Fern St BOW BD4 127 M3
COL BB8 52 B8
HIPP HX3 146 D4
HUDN HD2 14 E2
KGHY BD21 3 G3
WHIT OL12 184 E8
Fern Ter AIRE BD20 58 B5
GIR BD8 104 E4
PDSY/CALV LS28 107 G4
Fern Wy SCFT LS14 67 J7
Fernwood RHAY LS8 88 C5
Ferrand Av BOW BD4 127 L6
Ferrand La BGLY BD16 81 H3
CLECK BD19 150 C5
Ferrand Ldg LIT OL15 185 L7
Ferrand Rd LIT OL15 185 K8
Ferrands Cl BGLY BD16 80 D5
Ferrands Park Wy BGLY BD16 80 D5
Ferrand St BGLY BD16 81 J3
Ferrara Cl WMB/DAR S73 263 G8
Ferriby Cl ECHL BD2 105 M3
Ferrybridge By-pass
KNOT WF11 159 L8
Ferrybridge Rd CAS WF10 158 A6
KNOT WF11 181 M2
PONT WF8 181 G4
Ferry La EARD/LOFT WF3 177 H4
Ferry Moor La CUD/GR S72 244 F8
Ferry Top La HOR/CROF WF4 222 C3
Festival Av SHPY BD18 82 F8
Feversham St BFDE BD3 5 J7
Fewston Av OSM LS9 110 B8
WKFDE WF1 177 H6
Fewston Ct OSM LS9 110 B8
Fiddle La RPDN/SBR HX6 189 H2
Fidler La GFTH/SHER LS25 113 G7
Field Cl HECK WF16 150 F8
HIPP HX3 10 B1
WMB/DAR S73 263 J8
Fieldcroft Ct MIRF WF14 194 B1
Field Dr CUD/GR S72 262 D1
TAD LS24 72 B1
Fieldedge La AIRE BD20 58 C4
Field End MSTN/BAR LS15 111 J7
Field End Cl MSTN/BAR LS15 111 J7
Field End Ct MSTN/BAR LS15 111 J7
Field End Crs MSTN/BAR LS15 111 J7
Field End Gdns
MSTN/BAR LS15 111 J7
Field End Garth
MSTN/BAR LS15 111 J7
Field End Gn MSTN/BAR * LS15 111 J7
Field End Gv MSTN/BAR * LS15 111 K6
Field End La HOLM/MEL HD9 236 C2
HOLM/MEL HD9 253 K4
Field End Mt MSTN/BAR LS15 111 J7
Field End Rd MSTN/BAR LS15 111 J7
Fieldens Pl BTLY WF17 151 J8
Fielden Sq TOD OL14 163 K2
Fielden St TOD OL14 142 A8
Fieldgate Rd IDLE BD10 83 M7
Field Head MAR/SLWT HD7 212 F1
Fieldhead Cl PONT WF8 181 H5
Fieldhead Ct BSPA/BRAM LS23 48 E7
Fieldhead Crs BTLY WF17 151 G3
Fieldhead Dr AIRE BD20 34 F8
GSLY LS20 61 M6
MSTN/BAR LS15 91 H7
Fieldhead Gdns EARL WF12 174 D3
Field Head La BTLY WF17 151 G4
HBR HX7 165 K2
HWTH BD22 100 C1
LUD/ILL HX2 123 M7
Fieldhead La HOLM/MEL HD9 253 H5
Fieldhead Paddock
BSPA/BRAM LS23 48 E6
Fieldhead Rd GSLY LS20 61 L6
Fieldhead St GTHN BD7 104 D8
Fieldhead Wy LVSG WF15 172 E1
Fieldhouse Cl AL/HA/HU LS17 87 L4
Field House Cl WBY LS22 47 L1
Fieldhouse Dr AL/HA/HU LS17 87 L4
MAR/SLWT HD7 212 C4
Fieldhouse Gv PDSY/CALV LS28 106 E4
Fieldhouse Lawn
AL/HA/HU LS17 87 L4
Fieldhouse Rd HUD HD1 15 J2
WHIT OL12 206 B4
Fieldhouse St WKFDE WF1 13 L9
Fieldhouse Wk AL/HA/HU LS17 87 L4
Field Hurst CLECK BD19 149 H7
GTL/HWG HX4 189 K1
Fieldhurst Ct BOW BD4 127 K6
Fielding Ga WOR/ARM LS12 108 F6
Fielding Gate Ms
WOR/ARM LS12 108 F6
Field La BRIG HD6 170 B6
BSLY S70 262 A7
BTLY WF17 173 L2
DEWS WF13 172 F8
GFTH/SHER LS25 92 A7
HEM/SK/SE WF9 225 J7
HEM/SK/SE WF9 247 M2
HUDS HD4 215 H8
OSS WF5 174 F8
STKB/PEN S36 269 M5
Field Pl WKFDW/WTN WF2 12 A4
Field Rd HOLM/MEL HD9 254 D2
MILN OL16 206 F7
The Fields EARD/LOFT WF3 154 F5
Fields End STKB/PEN S36 271 K6
Fieldshead Bungalows
MAR/SLWT HD7 212 E7
Fieldside CUL/QBY BD13 79 M8
Field Side HFAX HX1 10 A3
Fieldside Rd HEM/SK/SE WF9 223 K4
Fields Ri HUDE HD5 193 K5
Fields Rd KBTN HD8 215 M3
LM/WK BD12 149 G1
Field St BFD BD1 5 G6
DEWS * WF13 173 G8
ROCH OL11 228 C2
Fields Wy HUDE HD5 193 K5
Field Ter MSTN/BAR LS15 111 J6
Field Top Rd BRIG HD6 170 B6
Field Vw CAS WF10 157 J8
HIPP HX3 146 B4
Field Wy KBTN HD8 238 A6
Fieldway CLAY BD14 125 K2
ILK LS29 39 G2
MILN OL16 228 D3
Fieldway Av BRAM LS13 107 J2
Fieldway Cha RTHW LS26 155 M1
Fieldway Cl BRAM LS13 107 J2
Fieldway Ri BRAM LS13 107 H2
Fife St BSLY S70 260 F6
Fifth Av BFDE BD3 105 L5
RTHW LS26 133 J8
Fifth Av West LVSG WF15 171 K2
Filbert St HUDN HD2 14 E2
Filey Av BSLYN/ROY S71 243 M2
Filey St BFD BD1 5 H7
MILN OL16 206 E4
Filley Royd CLECK BD19 149 M8
Fillingfir Dr BHP/TINH LS16 86 B6
Fillingfir Rd BHP/TINH LS16 86 B6
Fillingfir Wk BHP/TINH LS16 86 B6
Finance St LIT OL15 207 G1
Finch Av WKFDW/WTN WF2 220 F1
Finching Gv MIRF WF14 172 C6
Finchley St WBOW BD5 126 F3
Finchley Wy MOR LS27 152 C3
Finch St WBOW BD5 126 F2
Findon Ter IDLE BD10 106 A2
Fine Garth Cl BSPA/BRAM LS23 69 M3
Fingall Rd AWLS/ASK DN6 249 H4
Fink Hl HORS LS18 85 J6
Finkil St BRIG HD6 170 A1
Finkin Av EARD/LOFT WF3 177 G4
Finkin Cft EARD/LOFT WF3 177 G4
Finkin La EARD/LOFT WF3 177 G4
Finkle Hl GFTH/SHER LS25 116 A5
Finkle La MOR LS27 129 L8
Finkle St HOR/CROF WF4 220 B7
LUD/ILL HX2 166 F2
PONT WF8 180 F5
Finsbury Dr ECHL BD2 83 H8
Finsbury Rd LDS LS1 6 E6
Finthorpe La HUDE HD5 215 J3
Fir Av MIRF WF14 194 F1
Firbank Gn ECHL * BD2 105 M4
Firbank Gv MSTN/BAR LS15 111 G8
Fir Bank Rd ROY/SHW OL2 228 F8
Firbarn Cl MILN OL16 206 F7
Firbeck BGLY BD16 80 D6
Firbeck Rd BSPA/BRAM LS23 69 M3
Fire Station Yd ROCH OL11 206 B8
Firethorn Cl GIR * BD8 104 C6
Firgrove Av MILN OL16 206 F6
Firgrove Gdns MILN OL16 206 F6
Firham Cl BSLYN/ROY S71 243 J2
Fir La ROY/SHW OL2 228 F8
Fir Pde DEWS WF13 194 F1
Fir Rd HUDW HD3 191 M8
The Firs BSLY S70 261 L8
BSLYN/ROY S71 243 J2
SCFT LS14 67 L7
Firs La STKB/PEN S36 257 M7
First Av AL/HA/HU LS17 68 A1
BFDE BD3 105 L5
GFTH/SHER LS25 116 D7
HEM/SK/SE WF9 223 J2
HEM/SK/SE WF9 225 J7
HEM/SK/SE WF9 246 B5
HIPP HX3 168 D2
HOR/CROF WF4 197 H5
HUDE HD5 193 H7
KGHY BD21 2 E7
LVSG WF15 171 L1
PDSY/CALV LS28 107 G5
RTHW LS26 133 H7
WBY LS22 48 B1
WKFDE WF1 176 D4
WOR/ARM LS12 108 F7
YEA LS19 84 E1
Fir St HWTH BD22 78 E8
KGHY BD21 79 K2
TOD OL14 163 J6
First St LM/WK BD12 127 G8
Firth Av BEE/HOL LS11 131 J4
BRIG HD6 170 C3
CUD/GR S72 262 C1
Firthcliffe Dr LVSG WF15 172 D1
Firthcliffe Gv LVSG WF15 172 D1
Firthcliffe La LVSG WF15 172 D1
Firthcliffe Mt LVSG WF15 150 D8
Firthcliffe Pde LVSG WF15 172 D1
Firthcliffe Pl LVSG WF15 172 E1
Firthcliffe Rd LVSG WF15 172 D1
Firthcliffe Ter LVSG WF15 172 D1
Firthcliffe Vw LVSG WF15 172 D1
Firthcliffe Wk LVSG WF15 172 D1
Firth Cl EARD/LOFT WF3 177 G1
Firthfield La HEM/SK/SE WF9 225 G2
Firthfields GFTH/SHER LS25 113 J7
Firth Gv BEE/HOL LS11 131 J4
Firth House La BRIG HD6 170 D7
GTL/HWG HX4 189 L6
Firth La WIL/AL BD15 102 E1
Firth Mt BEE/HOL LS11 131 J4
Firth Rd BEE/HOL LS11 131 J4
HTON BD9 104 C3
Firth St BRIG HD6 170 C5
BSLYN/ROY * S71 261 H4
CHAL LS7 7 K6
CUL/QBY BD13 102 F8
KBTN HD8 238 A6
SKP/WHF BD23 16 C4
Firths Yd DEWS * WF13 173 L4
Firth Ter OSM LS9 7 L6
Firth Vw BEE/HOL LS11 131 J4
Fir Tree Ap AL/HA/HU LS17 87 K3
Firtree Av GFTH/SHER LS25 113 K8
Fir Tree Cl AL/HA/HU LS17 87 L2
Firtree Crs TAD LS24 71 K4
Fir Tree Dr AWLS/ASK DN6 227 L3
Fir Tree Gdns AL/HA/HU LS17 87 K2
IDLE BD10 83 M8
Fir Tree Gn AL/HA/HU LS17 87 L2
Fir Tree Gv AL/HA/HU LS17 87 L3
Fir Tree La AL/HA/HU LS17 87 L3
Fir Tree Ri AL/HA/HU LS17 87 L3
Fir Tree V AL/HA/HU LS17 87 L3
Fir Tree Vw RTHW LS26 157 G3
Firville Av NORM WF6 178 C5
Firville Crs NORM WF6 178 D5
Fir Wk DEWS WF13 194 F1
Firwood Cl TOD OL14 163 J5
Fishbeck La AIRE BD20 36 C2
Fish Dam La BSLYN/ROY S71 243 M6
Fishergate KNOT WF11 181 M1
Fisher Gn HOLM/MEL HD9 236 A2
Fisher Gv OSS WF5 197 H2
Fisher St KNOT WF11 182 A2
Fisher Wy HECK WF16 173 G3
Fishpond La HOR/CROF WF4 220 B1
Fishponds Dr HOR/CROF WF4 220 B1
Fish St LDS LS1 7 H9
Fishwick St MILN OL16 206 C8
Fitton St MILN OL16 206 C6
ROY/SHW OL2 229 H7
Fitts La AL/HA/HU LS17 45 J6
Fitzgerald St WBOW BD5 4 D9
Fitzroy Dr RHAY LS8 88 C8
Fitzroy Rd BFDE BD3 5 M6
Fitzwilliam Rd WMB/DAR S73 263 L8
Fitzwilliam St BOW BD4 5 G9
BSLY S70 260 F5
HEM/SK/SE WF9 223 K5
HUD HD1 14 D6
Five Acres DOD/DAR S75 259 H1
Five Lane Ends BHP/TINH LS16 64 F6
HOLM/MEL * HD9 254 A1
Five Oaks BAIL BD17 82 D3
Fixby Av LUD/ILL HX2 168 A1
Fixby La EARL WF12 194 F8
Fixby Park Dr HUDN HD2 192 A4
Fixby Rd HUDN HD2 192 C1
Flagship Sq EARL WF12 174 C4
Flannel St WHIT * OL12 206 C6
Flanshaw Av
WKFDW/WTN WF2 176 A8
Flanshaw Crs
WKFDW/WTN WF2 176 A8
Flanshaw Gv
WKFDW/WTN WF2 176 A8
Flanshaw La
WKFDW/WTN WF2 175 M8
Flanshaw Rd
WKFDW/WTN WF2 176 A8
Flanshaw St
WKFDW/WTN WF2 176 A8
Flanshaw Vw
WKFDW/WTN WF2 176 A8
Flanshaw Wy
WKFDW/WTN WF2 175 L7
Flasby St KGHY BD21 3 G2
Flash La MIRF WF14 172 D8
Flass La CAS WF10 179 J3
Flat Nook BGLY * BD16 81 K3
The Flats YEA * LS19 62 E8
Flats La MSTN/BAR LS15 90 F8
Flavell Cl HEM/SK/SE WF9 246 D5
Flawith Dr ECHL BD2 105 M4
Flaxen Ct WBSY BD6 126 F5
Flax Meadow HUDW HD3 191 J4
Flax Pl OSM LS9 9 L2
Flaxton Cl BEE/HOL LS11 8 E9
Flaxton Gdns BEE/HOL LS11 8 E9
Flaxton Gn ECHL BD2 105 M4
Flaxton Pl GTHN BD7 125 M2
Flaxton St BEE/HOL LS11 8 E9
Flaxton Vw BEE/HOL LS11 8 F9
Fledborough Rd WBY LS22 47 L1
Fleece St KGHY BD21 3 H5
MILN OL16 206 B7
WBSY BD6 126 B7
Fleet Hill Crs BSLYN/ROY S71 261 J1
Fleet La CUL/QBY BD13 124 F6
RTHW LS26 155 M1
Fleet St KBTN HD8 239 M5
Fleet Thro Rd HORS LS18 85 K8
Fleetwood Av BSLYN/ROY S71 261 J1
Fleminghouse La HUDE HD5 215 J1
Fleming Pl BSLY S70 261 G6
Fleming St BTLY WF17 173 L1
Fletcher Av AIRE BD20 36 A4
Fletcher Crs BRIG HD6 170 A8
Fletcher La SHPY BD18 104 F1
Fletcher Rd WBSY BD6 126 D5
Fletcher St ROCH OL11 228 C1
Fletton Ter ECHL BD2 105 K4
Flexbury Av MOR LS27 152 C3
Flight Hl HOLM/MEL HD9 267 L1
Flight House Rd
RPDN/SBR HX6 188 B2
Flint La HOLM/MEL HD9 268 C1
Flintmill La BSPA/BRAM LS23 48 F3
Flinton Gv ECHL BD2 105 M3
Flint St HUDN HD2 15 G1
Flockton Av BOW BD4 127 J2
Flockton Cl BOW BD4 127 J2
Flockton Crs BOW BD4 127 J2
Flockton Dr BOW BD4 127 J2
Flockton Gv BOW BD4 127 J2
Flockton Rd BOW BD4 127 J2
KBTN HD8 238 D3
Floral Av CHAL LS7 87 L8
Floreat Cl BTLY WF17 151 J6
Florence Av OSM LS9 110 C4
WIL/AL BD15 80 D8
Florence Gv OSM LS9 110 C4
Florence Mt OSM * LS9 110 C4
Florence Pl OSM LS9 110 C4
Florence St BFDE BD3 105 L8
CAS WF10 157 M6
HFAX HX1 10 D6
MILN OL16 206 D8
OSM LS9 110 C4
Florence Ter MOR LS27 152 D2
Florida Rd WIL/AL BD15 103 J2
Florist St KGHY BD21 3 M1
Flossmore Wy MOR LS27 129 L7
Flounders Hl FEA/AMT WF7 202 B8
Flower Acre ELL HX5 169 H8
Flower Bank ECHL BD2 105 H2
RPDN/SBR HX6 167 H3
Flower Cl YEA LS19 62 C7
Flower Ct ECHL * BD2 105 L3
Flower Cft HWTH BD22 2 B9
Flower Garth IDLE BD10 83 M8
Flower Hvn HTON BD9 103 M2
Flower Hl HTON BD9 104 B2
Flowerlands HIPP HX3 148 A5
Flower Scar Rd TOD OL14 140 A8
Floyd St WBOW BD5 126 D3
Flush LVSG WF15 172 D2
Flush House La
HOLM/MEL HD9 253 J3
Fold Grassmoor
HOLM/MEL HD9 236 C3
The Foldings KBTN HD8 239 J4
Foldings Av CLECK BD19 149 H6
Foldings Cl CLECK BD19 149 G6
Foldings Ct CLECK BD19 149 G6
Foldings Gv CLECK BD19 149 G6
Foldings Pde CLECK BD19 149 G6
Foldings Rd CLECK BD19 149 G6
The Fold MSTN/BAR LS15 112 A2
Fold La HBR HX7 120 C8
HWTH BD22 54 E3
Foljambe St WKFDW/WTN WF2 12 F6
Folkestone St BFDE BD3 5 M5
Folkton Holme ECHL BD2 105 M4
Follett Av HUDS HD4 213 L4
Follifoot La PBR HG3 27 H5
PBR HG3 28 D2
Follifoot Rd PBR HG3 27 G2
Follingworth La
MAR/SLWT HD7 211 L5
Follingworth Rd BTLY WF17 174 A1
The Folly Hall Gdns WBSY BD6 126 D6
Folly Hall HUD HD1 214 C2
Folly Hall Av WBSY BD6 126 D6
Folly Hall La HBR HX7 165 M4
Folly Hall Rd EARD/LOFT WF3 153 G6
Folly Hall Wk WBSY BD6 126 D6
Folly La BEE/HOL LS11 8 E8
BSPA/BRAM LS23 69 M4
STKB/PEN S36 257 H8
Folly Rd HUDN HD2 192 C3
Folly Vw BSPA/BRAM LS23 69 M4
Folly View Rd HWTH * BD22 78 F8
Folly Wk WHIT OL12 206 B5
Fontmell Cl BOW BD4 128 A4
Football YEA LS19 62 E8
Forber Gv BOW BD4 128 A1
Forber Pl MSTN/BAR LS15 111 G7
Ford CUL/QBY BD13 124 E6
Ford Dr MIRF WF14 194 A1
Ford Hl CUL/QBY BD13 124 E6
Ford Houses BAIL * BD17 83 H3
Ford St HEM/SK/SE WF9 223 K5
KGHY BD21 3 L1
Fore La RPDN/SBR HX6 167 J3
Fore Lane Av RPDN/SBR HX6 167 H3
Foreside Bottom La
CUL/QBY BD13 123 M2
Foreside La CUL/QBY BD13 123 K1
Forest Av LUD/ILL HX2 146 A3
Forest Bank MOR LS27 129 L7
Forest Cl WKFDE WF1 177 G5
Forest Crs LUD/ILL HX2 146 A2
Forest Ga OT LS21 41 J7
Forest Gn LUD/ILL HX2 146 A3
Forest Hill Gdns HUDW * HD3 190 C6
Forest Hill Rd GTL/HWG HX4 189 M5
Forest Rdg EARD/LOFT WF3 153 L5
Forest Rd BSLYN/ROY S71 243 H6
HUDE HD5 215 G1
Forest Wy HOLM/MEL HD9 236 A2
Forge Gn PBR HG3 28 A1
Forge Hill La KNOT WF11 182 A1
Forge La AL/HA/HU LS17 66 F5
EARL WF12 195 K2
HOR/CROF WF4 197 L6
LVSG WF15 172 D4
WOR/ARM LS12 108 F6
Forge Rw WOR/ARM LS12 129 M3
Forge Vw AIRE BD20 56 E1
Forman's Dr EARD/LOFT WF3 154 C3
Formby Av HUDN HD2 192 B3
Formby Ct BSLYN/ROY S71 243 M8
Forrest Av HUDW HD3 191 M7
Forrester Cl HEM/SK/SE WF9 223 J3
Forrester Dr ROY/SHW OL2 229 M6
Forrester's Cl AWLS/ASK DN6 227 L3
Forster Ct BFD BD1 4 F5
Forster Dr HECK WF16 173 G3
Forster Pl WOR/ARM LS12 130 C2
Forster Sq BFD BD1 5 G6
Forster St MID LS10 9 L6
Forsythia Av EARD/LOFT WF3 153 L7
Fort Ann Rd BTLY WF17 174 B2
Fortis Wy HUDW HD3 191 G6
Fortshot La AL/HA/HU LS17 66 D5
Forum Vw PONT WF8 225 J1
Foss Av WBY LS22 29 M7
Fosse Wy GFTH/SHER LS25 113 K8
Foster Av AIRE BD20 35 M4
CUL/QBY BD13 103 H8
HUDS HD4 213 L4
NORM WF6 178 C5
Foster Cl ILK LS29 40 B6
MOR LS27 152 C1
Foster Crs MOR LS27 152 C1
Foster Gdns HWTH BD22 2 B5
Foster La HBR HX7 143 J2
Foster Park Gv CUL/QBY BD13 102 A5
Foster Park Rd CUL/QBY BD13 102 A5
Foster Park Vw CUL/QBY BD13 102 A5
Foster Place La
HOLM/MEL HD9 255 H4
Foster Rd KGHY BD21 2 E9
Foster Sq MID LS10 131 M6
Foster St BSLY S70 261 M6
CUL/QBY BD13 124 F5
MOR * LS27 152 C2
Foster Wk GFTH/SHER LS25 116 A7
Foston Cl ECHL BD2 106 A4
Foston La ECHL BD2 105 M4
Fothergill Av FEA/AMT WF7 202 A8
Foulcauseway La OT LS21 41 M7
Foul Clough Rd TOD OL14 162 E7
Foulds Rd COL BB8 74 D3
Foulds' Ter BGLY BD16 81 J2
Foundry Ap OSM LS9 110 D4
Foundry Av RHAY LS8 110 D3
Foundry Dr RHAY LS8 110 D3
Foundry Hl BGLY BD16 81 H3
Foundry La BOW BD4 127 K1
KNOT WF11 182 C2
OSM LS9 111 G3
PDSY/CALV LS28 107 G4
Foundry Mill Crs SCFT LS14 111 G3
Foundry Mill Dr SCFT LS14 111 G3
Foundry Mill Gdns SCFT LS14 111 G1
Foundry Mill Mt SCFT LS14 111 H3
Foundry Mill St SCFT LS14 111 H3
Foundry Mill Ter SCFT LS14 111 H3
Foundry Mill Vw SCFT LS14 111 H3
Foundry Mill Wk SCFT LS14 111 H3
Foundry Pl OSM LS9 110 D3
Foundry St BEE/HOL LS11 8 E3
BRIG HD6 170 E5
BSLY S70 261 G6
CLECK BD19 149 M6
DEWS WF13 173 M6
DEWS WF13 195 G1
HFAX HX1 11 H4
OSM LS9 9 L1
RPDN/SBR HX6 167 K3
Foundry St North LUD/ILL HX2 146 B2
Foundry Wk RHAY LS8 110 D3
Fountain Cl DOD/DAR S75 242 A5
LVSG WF15 172 B5
Fountain Ct BSLYN/ROY S71 243 G5
LUD/ILL * HX2 146 A6
Fountain Dr LVSG WF15 172 B5
Fountain Gv HUDS HD4 213 L2
Fountains Av BSPA/BRAM LS23 48 E7
BTLY WF17 173 H2
Fountain St CUL/QBY BD13 102 F8
CUL/QBY BD13 125 G5
HECK WF16 172 E1
HFAX HX1 11 G6
LDS LS1 6 D8
LM/WK BD12 126 E8
LVSG WF15 172 B5
MOR LS27 152 B4
RPDN/SBR * HX6 188 F2
TOD OL14 142 A8
Fountains Wy BSLYN/ROY S71 261 M3
WKFDE WF1 177 H5
Fountain Ter LM/WK BD12 148 F4
Fountain Wy SHPY BD18 82 E7
Four Acres MIRF WF14 194 C3
Fourlands Ct IDLE BD10 83 L6
Fourlands Crs IDLE * BD10 83 L6
Fourlands Dr IDLE BD10 83 L6
Fourlands Gdns IDLE BD10 83 L6
Fourlands Gv IDLE BD10 83 L6
Fourlands Rd IDLE BD10 83 L6
Four Lane Ends EARL WF12 196 A4
Four Lanes Cl DOD/DAR S75 260 A1
Fourteenth Av WOR/ARM LS12 109 G8
Fourth Av BFDE BD3 105 L5
KGHY BD21 2 D7
LVSG WF15 171 K1
RTHW LS26 133 J7
WBY LS22 48 B2
WKFDE WF1 176 D4
Fourth Ct BEE/HOL LS11 8 C4
Fourth St HOR/CROF WF4 200 D7
LM/WK BD12 127 G8
Fowlers Garth HWTH BD22 78 F5
Fowler's Pl PDSY/CALV LS28 107 G4
Fowler St BOW * BD4 127 K1
Foxbridge Wy NORM WF6 179 G3
Foxcliff KNOT WF11 159 M5
Fox Cl KBTN HD8 217 M8
Fox Ct GTL/HWG HX4 168 F7
Fox Covert Rd or Whin Covert La
PONT WF8 227 G4
Foxcroft Cl CUL/QBY BD13 124 E7
HDGY LS6 108 D1
Foxcroft Dr BRIG HD6 170 A6
Foxcroft Gn HDGY LS6 108 D1
Foxcroft Mt HDGY LS6 108 D1
Foxcroft Rd HDGY LS6 108 D1
Foxcroft St LIT OL15 207 H1
Foxcroft Wk HDGY LS6 108 D1
Foxcroft Wy HDGY LS6 108 D1
Foxen La RPDN/SBR HX6 166 E8
Foxfields STKB/PEN S36 271 J5
Foxfield Wk BSLY S70 261 M8

Foxglove Av *RHAY* LS8 ....88 E8
Foxglove Folly
  WKFDW/WTN WF2 ....176 A6
Foxglove Rd *BTLY* WF17 ....151 G4
  HUDE HD5 ....215 G2
Fox Heads La *PBR* HG3 ....28 C6
Fox HI *ROY/SHW* OL2 ....229 G6
Foxhill *WBY* LS22 ....30 E4
Foxhill Av *BHP/TINH* LS16 ....86 F5
Foxhill CI *CUL/QBY* BD13 ....124 F5
Foxhill Ct *BHP/TINH* LS16 ....86 F5
Foxhill Crs *BHP/TINH* LS16 ....86 F5
  CUL/QBY BD13 ....124 F5
Foxhill Gn *BHP/TINH* LS16 ....86 F5
  CUL/QBY BD13 ....124 F5
The Foxhills *BHP/TINH* LS16 ....85 M2
Foxhole La *PDSY/CALV* LS28 ......84 D8
Foxholes CI *WHIT* OL12 ....206 C5
Foxholes Crs *PDSY/CALV* LS28 ....84 D8
Fox Holes Gv *STKB/PEN* S36 .....268 F1
Foxholes La *NORM* WF6 ....178 B1
Foxholes Rd *WHIT* OL12 ....206 C5
Fox La *GFTH/SHER* LS25 ....139 K6
  HOR/CROF WF4 ....198 B7
  WKFDW/WTN WF2 ....176 A6
Foxlow Av *HUDE* HD5 ....193 G6
Fox Royd Av *MIRF* WF14 ....172 B8
Foxroyd CI *BSLYN/ROY* S71 ......262 B6
Fox Royd Dr *MIRF* WF14 ....172 B8
Foxroyd La *EARL* WF12 ....195 J3
Fox Royd La *MIRF* WF14 ....172 B8
Foxstone Ri *BAIL* BD17 ....83 G3
Foxstones La *RPDN/SBR* HX6 ....188 F4
Fox St *BGLY* BD16 ....81 H3
  BTLY WF17 ....173 M2
  CLECK BD19 ....149 K7
  HUD HD1 ....14 F7
  MILN OL16 ....206 D6
  MILN OL16 ....207 G8
  WBOW BD5 ....126 E3
Fox Ter *PONT* WF8 ....181 C4
Fox Vw *DEWS* WF13 ....173 J4
Fox Wy *MID* LS10 ....9 M6
Fox Wood Av *RHAY* LS8 ....111 K4
Fox Wood CI *RHAY* LS8 ....111 G1
Fox Wood Farm Wy *RHAY* LS8 ...111 G1
Fox Wood Gv *RHAY* LS8 ....111 G1
Fox Wood Ri *RHAY* LS8 ....111 K4
Fox Wood Wk *RHAY* LS8 ....111 G1
Foxwood Wk *WBY* LS22 ....30 B7
Frain CI *PONT* WF8 ....181 C7
Fraisthorpe Md *ECHL* BD2 ....105 M4
France Fold *HOLM/MEL* HD9 .....236 B1
Frances Av *HUDS* HD4 ....213 K3
Frances Rd *EARL* WF12 ....174 B7
Frances St *BRIG* HD6 ....170 C3
  KGHY BD21 ....2 D3
  MILN OL16 ....206 F3
  PDSY/CALV LS28 ....106 C4
France St *BTLY* WF17 ....174 A2
Francis Av *HUDS* HD4 ....213 J3
Francis CI *HFAX* HX1 ....10 D6
Francis Gv *BEE/HOL* LS11 ....131 K3
Francis Gv *HOR/CROF* WF4 ....200 D3
Francis St *BOW* BD4 ....5 J9
  CAS WF10 ....158 A6
  CHAL LS7 ....7 L2
  FEA/AMT WF7 ....223 M1
  HECK WF16 ....173 G3
  HFAX HX1 ....10 D7
  HUDS HD4 ....213 J2
  MIRF WF14 ....194 B1
Francis Vw *MIRF* WF14 ....194 B1
Francus Rd *BSLYN/ROY* S71 .....243 L5
Frank CI *EARL* WF12 ....196 A4
Frankland Gv *CHAL* LS7 ....7 L2
Frankland PI *CHAL* LS7 ....7 M3
Frank La *EARL* WF12 ....196 A4
  KBTN HD8 ....239 L1
  LUD/ILL HX2 ....144 D4
Franklin St *HFAX* HX1 ....10 B6
  MILN OL16 ....228 E1
Frank Peel CI *HECK* WF16 ....172 F2
Frank PI *GTHN* BD7 ....126 D2
Frank St *GTHN* BD7 ....126 D2
  HFAX HX1 ....10 C7
Fraser Av *HORS* LS18 ....85 J6
Fraser Rd *PDSY/CALV* LS28 ....84 B8
Fraser St *GIR* BD8 ....4 B3
  MILN OL16 ....228 D2
  OSM LS9 ....110 B5
  ROY/SHW OL2 ....229 J4
Freakfield La *LVSG* WF15 ....171 K4
Frederick Av *BSLY* S70 ....260 F6
  OSM LS9 ....110 C8
  WKFDE WF1 ....13 L9
Frederick CI *IDLE* BD10 ....83 H5
Frederick St *BFDE* BD3 ....5 H7
  HUDS HD4 ....213 J1
  KGHY BD21 ....3 J4
  LIT OL15 ....185 J4
  LVSG WF15 ....172 D3
  PDSY/CALV LS28 ....106 C3
  WKFDE WF1 ....12 F2
Frederic St *BOW* BD4 ....127 L3
Fred's PI *BOW* BD4 ....127 L3
Fred St *KGHY* BD21 ....2 E6
Freeholds Rd *WHIT* OL12 ....162 A8
Freehold St *ROCH* OL11 ....228 A1
Freely La *BSPA/BRAM* LS23 ....69 M4
Freeman Rd *HIPP* HX3 ....169 J1
Freemans Wy *WBY* LS22 ....30 B8
Freemans Yd *BSLY* S70 ....261 H6
Freemont St *BRAM* LS13 ....107 J4
Freemans Wy *NORM* WF6 ....178 A2
Free School La *HFAX* HX1 ....168 A4
Freeston Ct *NORM* WF6 ....178 D3
Freeston Dr *NORM* WF6 ....178 D3
Freestone Ms *WOR/ARM* LS12 ...107 L7
Freestone Wy *NORM* WF6 ....178 A2
Freetrade St *ROCH* OL11 ....228 A1
Fremantle Gv *BOW* BD4 ....127 L8
Fremantle PI *MSTN/BAR* LS15 ...111 G4
French St *AWLS/ASK* DN6 ....249 J5

Frensham Av *MOR* LS27 ....152 B3
Frensham Dr *CAS* WF10 ....158 F8
  GTHN BD7 ....125 M3
Frensham La *GTHN* BD7 ....125 M4
Frensham Wy *GTHN* BD7 ....125 M3
Freshfield Gdns *WIL/AL* BD15 ...103 K5
Freston Av *WKFDE* WF1 ....177 M8
Freston Dr *WKFDE* WF1 ....177 L8
Friar Ct *IDLE* BD10 ....83 L8
Friar PI *HUDN* HD2 ....193 H1
Friar's CI *FEA/AMT* WF7 ....201 M2
Friars Crs *ROCH* OL11 ....228 B4
Friars Nook *PONT* WF8 ....181 H7
Friar's Rd *BSLYN/ROY* S71 ....262 A3
Friarwood La *PONT* WF8 ....180 F6
Frickley Bridge La *CUD/GR* S72 ...245 G2
Frickley La *BTLY* DN5 ....247 H8
Frieldhurst La *TOD* OL14 ....140 E5
Friendly Av *RPDN/SBR* HX6 ......167 J1
Friendly Fold Rd *HIPP* HX3 ....146 A4
Friendly St *CUL/QBY* BD13 ....102 F8
  HIPP HX3 ....146 A4
  HUD HD1 ....15 G5
Frieston *WHIT* OL12 ....206 B6
Frimley Dr *WBOW* BD5 ....126 E4
Frith St *HWTH* BD22 ....79 C6
Frizingham Rd *HTON* BD9 ....104 E3
Frizley Gdns *HTON* BD9 ....104 E3
Frobisher Gv
  WKFDW/WTN WF2 ....198 A1
Frobisher Rd *LIT* OL15 ....185 L5
Frodingham Vls *ECHL* BD2 ....105 M4
Frogmoor La *LM/WK* BD12 ....149 H1
Frontline Ct *RHAY* LS8 ....88 C8
Front Rw *BEE/HOL* LS11 ....8 C8
Front St *BEE/HOL* LS11 ....8 E8
  BSPA/BRAM LS23 ....69 L3
  CAS WF10 ....158 B8
  PONT WF8 ....180 E6
Frost HI *LVSG* WF15 ....172 D2
Fruit St *KGHY* BD21 ....3 L3
Fryergate *WKFDW/WTN* WF2 ...176 B7
Fryston Common La
  GFTH/SHER LS25 ....138 D6
Fryston La *KNOT* WF11 ....159 J7
Fryston Rd *CAS* WF10 ....158 D8
Fuchsia Cft *RTHW* LS26 ....134 A8
Fulford Av *HUDN* HD2 ....192 C4
Fulford CI *NORM* WF6 ....178 F5
Fulford St *CAS* WF10 ....157 L7
Fulford Wk *ECHL* BD2 ....105 M4
Fulham La *AWLS/ASK* DN6 ....205 L3
Fulham PI *BEE/HOL* LS11 ....8 E9
Fulham St *BEE/HOL* LS11 ....8 E9
Fullerton Ct *AWLS/ASK* DN6 .....249 H4
Fullerton St *BFDE* BD3 ....5 J7
Fullshaw La *HEM* S36 ....269 K7
Fullwood Dr *MAR/SLWT* HD7 ...212 C3
Fulmar Ct *MID* LS10 ....153 M1
Fulmar Ms *GIR* * BD8 ....103 L3
Fulmar Rd *CAS* WF10 ....157 L8
Fulmer CI *BSLYN/ROY* S71 ....243 K8
Fulneck *PDSY/CALV* LS28 ....129 G1
Fulneck CI *HUDN* HD2 ....192 B3
Fulstone Hall La
  HOLM/MEL HD9 ....237 J7
Fulstone Rd *KBTN* HD8 ....237 K6
Fulton St *BFD* BD1 ....4 D6
Fulwood Gv *WKFDW/WTN* WF2 ...220 D1
Furnace Gv *LM/WK* BD12 ....149 H1
Furnace Inn St *BOW* BD4 ....127 M1
Furnace La *BIRK/DRI* BD11 ....128 C8
Furnace La *LM/WK* BD12 ....149 H1
Furnbrook Gdns *HUDE* HD5 ......193 L7
Furness Av *LIT* OL15 ....185 J8
  LUD/ILL HX2 ....145 M2
  WKFDW/WTN WF2 ....176 A4
Furness CI *MILN* OL16 ....207 G8
Furness Crs *LUD/ILL* HX2 ....145 M1
Furness Dene *BSLYN/ROY* S71 ...261 M1
Furness Dr *LUD/ILL* HX2 ....145 M2
  WKFDW/WTN WF2 ....176 A4
Furness Gdns *LUD/ILL* HX2 ....146 A2
Furness Gv *LUD/ILL* HX2 ....145 M2
Furness PI *LUD/ILL* HX2 ....145 M2
Further Heights Rd *WHIT* OL12 ...206 A4
Furzegate *MILN* OL16 ....228 E3
Fusden La *CLECK* BD19 ....150 C5
Fyfe Crs *BAIL* BD17 ....82 F4
Fyfe Gv *BAIL* BD17 ....83 G4
Fyfe La *BAIL* BD17 ....83 G4
Fylde CI *BSLYN/ROY* S71 ....243 M8

G

The Gables *BAIL* BD17 ....83 G3
  HWTH BD22 ....2 D5
Gables CI *GLE* DN14 ....161 K7
The Gabriels *ROY/SHW* OL2 ......229 H7
Gadding Moor Rd
  STKB/PEN S36 ....258 B6
Gagewell Dr *HOR/CROF* WF4 ...197 K4
Gagewell La *HOR/CROF* WF4 ....197 K4
Gagewell Vw *HOR/CROF* WF4 ...197 K4
Gainest *LUD/ILL* HX2 ....168 B1
Gainford Dr *GFTH/SHER* LS25 ...113 H8
Gain La *BFDE* BD3 ....106 A5
Gainsborough CI *BFDE* BD3 ....105 J4
Gainsborough Ct
  SKP/WHF BD23 ....16 A2
Gainsborough Dr *ROCH* OL11 ....228 A3
Gainsborough Wy
  BSLYN/ROY S71 ....261 K3
  EARD/LOFT WF3 ....177 G3
Gainsbro Dr *BHP/TINH* LS16 ....86 D1
Gaisby La *ECHL* BD2 ....104 E2
Gaisby Mt *SHPY* BD18 ....104 F1
Gaisby PI *SHPY* BD18 ....82 F8
Gaisby Ri *SHPY* BD18 ....82 F8
Gaitskell Ct *BEE/HOL* LS11 ....8 D6
Gaitskell Gra *BEE/HOL* LS11 ....8 D6
Gaitskell Wk *BEE/HOL* LS11 ....8 D5
Galefield Gn *WBSY* BD6 ....126 B8
Gale La *OT* LS21 ....24 E7
Gales Ter *ROCH* OL11 ....228 A1

Gale St *KGHY* BD21 ....3 G3
  WHIT OL12 ....206 B3
Gall La *TOD* OL14 ....140 E3
Gallogate La *AL/HA/HU* LS17 ....44 B4
Gallon Cft *HEM/SK/SE* WF9 ......247 G5
Galloway Ct *PDSY/CALV* LS28 ...106 C6
Galloway La *PDSY/CALV* LS28 ...106 C5
Galloway Rd *IDLE* BD10 ....83 M7
Galloway St *HUD* HD1 ....15 H3
Gallows La *HOR/CROF* WF4 ......220 B5
Gallows La *CAS* WF10 ....158 E7
  OT LS21 ....41 L6
Galpharm Wy *DOD/DAR* S75 ....260 A6
Galsworthy Av *HTON* BD9 ....103 M3
Gamble HI *BRAM* LS13 ....107 M6
Gamble Hill CI *BRAM* LS13 ....107 M6
Gamble Hill Dr *BRAM* LS13 ....107 M6
Gamble Hill Gn *BRAM* LS13 ....107 M6
Gamble Hill Lawn *BRAM* LS13 ...107 M6
Gamble Hill PI *BRAM* LS13 ....107 M6
Gamble Hill Ri *BRAM* LS13 ....107 M6
Gamble Hill Vw *BRAM* LS13 ......107 M6
Gamble La *WOR/ARM* LS12 ......107 G6
Gamel Vw *AIRE* BD20 ....35 K8
Game Scar La or Goose Eye Brow
  HWTH BD22 ....56 D8
The Gang *WOR/ARM* LS12 ....108 E6
Ganners CI *BRAM* LS13 ....107 L2
Ganners Gn *BRAM* LS13 ....107 L2
Ganners Gv *BRAM* LS13 * 107 M2
Ganners HI *BRAM* LS13 ....107 M6
Ganners La *BRAM* LS13 ....107 L2
Ganners Mt *BRAM* LS13 ....107 L2
Ganners Ri *BRAM* LS13 ....107 M2
Ganners Rd *BRAM* LS13 ....107 M2
Ganners Wk *BRAM* LS13 ....107 L2
Ganners Wy *BRAM* LS13 ....107 L2
Gannerthorpe CI *LM/WK* BD12 ...148 E3
Gannet CI *CAS* WF10 ....157 L8
Ganny Rd *BRIG* HD6 ....170 D4
Ganton CI *HDGY* LS6 ....6 E1
Ganton PI *BSLYN/ROY* S71 ....243 C7
Ganton Wy *HUDN* HD2 ....192 B3
Gaol La *HFAX* HX1 ....11 H5
Garden CI *AIRE* BD20 ....34 D8
  CLECK BD19 ....172 C1
  GFTH/SHER LS25 ....115 M7
  LIT OL15 ....207 H4
  LM/WK BD12 ....148 E2
  OSS WF5 ....197 G3
Garden Ct *BSLY* S70 ....260 D5
Garden Dr *DEWS* WF13 ....173 G8
Gardeners St *MID* LS10 ....9 K8
Gardener's Sq *HIPP* HX3 ....147 L6
Garden Fld *LM/WK* BD12 ....148 E3
Garden Fold *HIPP* HX3 ....147 L6
Garden House CI
  BSLYN/ROY S71 ....261 L1
  RTHW LS26 ....156 F3
Garden House La
  EARD/LOFT WF3 ....153 J6
Garden La *GFTH/SHER* LS25 .....115 M7
  HTON BD9 ....104 B3
  KNOT WF11 ....182 C1
  MILN OL16 ....206 C6
  RPDN/SBR HX6 ....167 K7
Garden Pde *CLECK* BD19 ....150 C8
Garden PI *DEWS* WF13 ....173 H5
Garden Rd *BRIG* HD6 ....170 B2
The Gardens *BGLY* BD16 ....81 M3
  HFAX HX1 ....168 E1
  MID LS10 ....153 L2
  MOR LS27 ....152 M4
  PDSY/CALV LS28 ....106 C3
Gardens Rd *DEWS* WF13 ....173 G8
Gardens St *HTON* BD9 ....104 C3
Garden St *BSLY* S70 ....261 H6
  CAS WF10 ....157 M8
  CAS WF10 ....158 C3
  DEWS WF13 ....173 G8
  FEA/AMT WF7 ....223 M1
  HECK WF16 ....172 F3
  HUD HD1 ....214 B2
  HWTH BD22 ....79 H6
  MILN OL16 ....229 K2
  NORM WF6 ....178 A3
  NORM * WF6 ....178 C4
  TOD OL14 ....141 K8
  WKFDE WF1 ....12 C4
Garden St North *HIPP* HX3 ....11 J4
Garden Ter *HBR* * HX7 ....143 J3
  HOR/CROF WF4 ....219 M2
  HTON BD9 ....104 C3
  ROY/SHW OL2 ....228 E7
Garden Vw *BGLY* BD16 ....81 L3
  CLECK BD19 ....150 C8
Garden Village
  GFTH/SHER LS25 ....114 C7
Garden Wk *CLECK* BD19 ....150 C8
Garden Wy *LIT* OL15 ....207 H4
Gardiner Rw *BOW* BD4 ....127 K4
Gare Forth Av *AIRE* BD20 ....35 L8
Garfield Av *GIR* BD8 ....104 D4
Garfield PI *MAR/SLWT* HD7 ......233 H2
Garfield St *HIPP* * HX3 ....10 D1
  TOD OL14 ....140 E5
  WIL/AL BD15 ....103 J5
Garforth CI *NORM* WF6 ....178 A3
Garforth Dr *MIRF* WF14 ....172 C7
Garforth Dr *NORM* WF6 ....178 A3
Garforth Rd *KGHY* BD21 ....3 M2
Garforth St *HUDS* HD4 ....213 L7
Gargrave Ap *OSM* LS9 ....110 B6
Gargrave Ct *BRIG* HD6 ....169M7
Gargrave Ct *OSM* LS9 ....110 B5
Gargrave Crs *HEM/SK/SE* WF9 ...223 L8
Gargrave PI *HEM/SK/SE* WF9 ...223 L8
  OSM LS9 ....110 B5
Garibaldi St *BFDE* BD3 ....106 A7
Garland Dr *MSTN/BAR* LS15 .....111M7
Garlick St *BRIG* HD6 ....170 A8
Garmil Head La
  HEM/SK/SE WF9 ....223 H1
Garmont Ms *CHAL* * LS7 ....87 M8

Garmont Rd *CHAL* LS7 ....87 M8
Garner La *HOLM/MEL* HD9 ....235 M2
  KBTN HD8 ....215 M7
Garnet Av *BEE/HOL* * LS11 ....131 L3
Garnet Crs *BEE/HOL* * LS11 ....131 L3
Garnet Gv *BEE/HOL* LS11 ....131 L3
Garnet La *TAD* LS24 ....71 H6
Garnet Pde *BEE/HOL* LS11 ....131 L4
Garnet PI *BEE/HOL* LS11 ....131 L4
Garnet Rd *BEE/HOL* LS11 ....131 L4
Garnet Ter *BEE/HOL* LS11 ....131 L4
Garnett St *BFDE* BD3 ....5 J6
  DEWS WF13 ....173 H3
  HBR HX7 ....143 J3
  OT LS21 ....41 J6
Garnet Vw *BEE/HOL* LS11 ....131 L3
Garret Gv *ROY/SHW* OL2 ....229 L7
Garrett CI *KBTN* HD8 ....239 H4
Garsdale Av *IDLE* BD10 ....83 L7
Garsdale Crs *BAIL* BD17 ....83 G2
Garsdale Fold *WBY* LS22 ....47 J5
Garsdale Rd *HUDS* HD4 ....214 D4
Garsdale Wk *KNOT* WF11 ....182 C1
The Garth *GFTH/SHER* LS25 ......113 J7
  OSM LS9 ....9 L1
  WBY LS22 ....47 K6
Garth Av *AL/HA/HU* LS17 ....87 K5
  NORM WF6 ....178 C6
  WBY LS22 ....47 K6
Garth Barn CI *HTON* BD9 ....104 C3
Garth CI *SEL* YO8 ....139 M4
Garth Dr *AL/HA/HU* LS17 ....87 K5
  SEL YO8 ....139 M4
Garth End *WBY* LS22 ....47 K6
Garth Land Wy *BOW* BD4 ....127 L3
Garth La *SEL* YO8 ....139 M4
Garth MI *GLE* DN14 ....161 J7
Garth Rectory
  HEM/SK/SE WF9 ....223 M7
Garth Rd *AL/HA/HU* LS17 ....87 K5
  SEL YO8 ....139 M4
Garth St *CAS* WF10 ....157 L7
  KGHY BD21 ....2 D1
Garth Vw *SEL* YO8 ....139 M4
Garthwaite Mt *WIL/AL* BD15 .....103 K4
Garth Wk *AL/HA/HU* LS17 ....87 K5
Garth Willow *BULY* LS4 ....89 K6
Garth Willow Av *SCFT* LS14 ....89 K6
Garth Willow CI *SCFT* LS14 ....89 K6
Garton Av *OSM* LS9 ....110 C7
Garton Dr *IDLE* BD10 ....105 M1
Garton Gv *OSM* LS9 ....110 C7
Garton Rd *OSM* LS9 ....110 C7
Garton Ter *OSM* LS9 ....110 C7
Garton Vw *OSM* LS9 ....110 C7
Garvey Vw *WBOW* BD5 ....127 G2
Garwick Ter *GTL/HWG* HX4 ....168 C7
Gascoigne Av *MSTN/BAR* LS15 ....90 F8
Gascoigne Ct *MSTN/BAR* LS15 ....90 F8
Gascoigne Rd *EARD/LOFT* WF3 ..154 A5
  MSTN/BAR LS15 ....90 F8
Gascoigne St *LDS* LS1 ....9 G1
Gascoigne Vw *MSTN/BAR* LS15 ...90 F8
Gashouse La *WBY* LS22 ....48 A1
Gaskell CI *LIT* * OL15 ....185 J8
Gaskell Dr *HOR/CROF* WF4 ......197 J4
Gaskell St *HUDS* HD4 ....213 J2
Gasson St *HUDS* HD4 ....213 J1
Gas St *HWTH* * BD22 ....78 F7
  ROCH OL11 ....206 B4
  SKP/WHF BD23 ....16 B3
Gas Works La *BSPA/BRAM* LS23 ...49 H7
  ELL HX5 ....169 H7
Gas Works Rd *KGHY* BD21 ....58 B7
  RPDN/SBR HX6 ....167 M2
Gasworks St *HUD* HD1 ....15 H5
  LVSG WF15 ....172 D2
Gate CI *DOD/DAR* S75 ....260 B6
Gatefield Mt *LM/WK* BD12 ....126 D8
Gate Foot La *KBTN* HD8 ....237 L8
Gate Head *MAR/SLWT* HD7 ......233 J1
Gatehead Bank
  MAR/SLWT HD7 ....233 K1
Gate Head La *GTL/HWG* HX4 ....168 B8
  HOLM/MEL HD9 ....255 D6
Gatehouse *LIT* * OL15 ....185 M8
Gate House CI *RTHW* LS26 ....133M7
Gateland Dr *AL/HA/HU* LS17 ......89 C2
Gateland La *AL/HA/HU* LS17 ......89 C2
Gateon House La
  AL/HA/HU LS17 ....67 J2
Gate St *ROCH* OL11 ....228 B1
Gatesgarth Crs *HUDW* HD3 ....191 H6
Gateway *BGLY* BD16 ....80 C5
Gate Way Dr *YEA* LS19 ....62 C8
Gateways *WKFDE* WF1 ....176 E1
Gathorne St *BRIG* HD6 ....170 D3
  GTHN BD7 ....126 D2
  RHAY LS8 ....7 M3
Gathorne Ter *RHAY* LS8 ....7 M3
Gaukroger La *HFAX* HX1 ....11 J9
Gauk St *KNOT* WF11 ....159 J2
  KNOT WF11 ....159 L6
Gavin CI *BFDE* BD3 ....106 A4
Gawber Rd *DOD/DAR* S75 ....260 E3
Gawsworth CI *ROY/SHW* OL2 ....229 H7
Gawthorpe Dr *BGLY* BD16 ....81 H1
Gawthorpe Green La
  HUDE HD5 ....194 M8
Gawthorpe La *KBTN* HD8 ....215 M1
  OSS WF5 ....174 F5
Gay La *OT* LS21 ....41 J7
  TAD LS24 ....95 H8
Gayle CI *LM/WK* BD12 ....148 E4
Gayle Ct *BSLY* S70 ....260 F4
Gaynor St *BFD* BD1 ....4 C5
Gaythorne Rd *ECHL* BD2 ....105 L4
  WBOW BD5 ....127 G4
Gaythorne Ter *CLAY* BD14 ....125 L2
Gaythorn Ter *HIPP* HX3 ....147 L5
Geary CI *WKFDW/WTN* WF2 .....175 M6
Geary Dr *WKFDW/WTN* WF2 ....175 M6
Geecroft La *WBY* LS22 ....46 E1
Geelong CI *ECHL* BD2 ....105 H3
Gelder Ct *WKFDW/WTN* WF2 ...175 M6
Gelder Cft *WKFDW/WTN* * WF2 ...175 M6

Gelderd CI *WOR/ARM* LS12 ......130 F2
Gelderd La *WOR/ARM* LS12 ......130 F2
Gelderd PI *BEE/HOL* LS11 ....8 A3
Gelderd Rd *BTLY* WF17 ....151 H4
  MOR LS27 ....130 A7
Gelder Rd *WOR/ARM* LS12 ....108 D7
Geneva Gv *WKFDE* WF1 ....176 E7
Genista Dr *MID* LS10 ....131M6
Genn La *BSLY* S70 ....260 F8
Genoa CI *WMB/DAR* S73 ....263 G7
Gentian Ct *WKFDW/WTN* WF2 ...176 A6
George-a-Green Rd
  WKFDW/WTN WF2 ....198 A2
George & Crown Yd
  WKFDE WF1 ....12 E4
George Av *HUDN* HD2 ....14 B2
George Buckley Ct
  HEM/SK/SE WF9 ....246 C4
George La *HOR/CROF* WF4 ....221 C8
  RPDN/SBR HX6 ....188 C4
George Sq *BSLY* * S70 ....261 G5
  HFAX HX1 ....11 G6
George's Sq *CUL/QBY* BD13 ....79 M8
  KGHY BD21 ....2 F6
George's St *LUD/ILL* HX2 ....146 B3
George St *AWLS/ASK* DN6 ....249 K4
  BAIL * BD17 ....82 E5
  BFD BD1 ....5 H7
  BRIG HD6 ....170 C4
  BSLY S70 ....261 G5
  BTLY WF17 ....173 L2
  CLECK BD19 ....149M6
  CUD/GR S72 ....222 F8
  CUD/GR S72 ....244 E6
  CUD/GR S72 ....263M7
  CUL/QBY * BD13 ....102 F8
  CUL/QBY BD13 ....102 F8
  DEWS WF13 ....173 H6
  DEWS WF13 ....173 L6
  DEWS WF13 ....195 G1
  DOD/DAR S75 ....242 D5
  ELL HX5 ....191 H1
  FEA/AMT WF7 ....200 F1
  FEA/AMT WF7 ....201 L1
  GTL/HWG HX4 ....168 F7
  HBR HX7 ....144 A6
  HECK WF16 ....172 F2
  HEM/SK/SE WF9 ....224 A8
  HFAX HX1 ....11 G6
  HOR/CROF WF4 ....197 K5
  HOR/CROF WF4 ....222 D5
  HUDS HD4 ....214 A2
  HUDW HD3 ....191 K5
  HUDW HD3 ....213 K1
  ILK LS29 ....19 H6
  LDS LS1 ....7 H9
  LIT * OL15 ....207 K1
  LVSG WF15 ....172 C2
  MILN OL16 ....206 D6
  NORM WF6 ....178 B3
  OSS WF5 ....174 E7
  ROY/SHW OL2 ....229 L6
  RPDN/SBR HX6 ....167 K3
  SHPY BD18 ....82 B6
  SKP/WHF BD23 ....16 B3
  TOD OL14 ....163 K1
  WKFDE WF1 ....12 D4
  WKFDE WF1 ....176 D1
  YEA LS19 ....84 D2
George Yd *BSLY* S70 ....261 G5
Georgia Ms *OSS* WF5 ....197 H2
Gerald CI *BSLY* S70 ....261 L7
Gerald Crs *BSLY* S70 ....261M6
Gerald PI *BSLY* S70 ....261 L7
Gerald Rd *BSLY* S70 ....261 L7
Geraldton Av *ECHL* BD2 ....105 G3
Gerald Wk *BSLY* S70 ....261 L7
Gerard Av *MOR* LS27 ....152 B2
Gernhill Av *HUDN* HD2 ....192 B1
Gerrard St *HFAX* HX1 ....10 E6
  ROCH OL11 ....228 C5
Gervase Rd *HOR/CROF* WF4 .....197 J5
Ghyllbank *AIRE* * BD20 ....36 A4
The Ghyll *BGLY* BD16 ....81 J6
  HUDN HD2 ....192 C2
Ghyll Beck Dr *OT* LS21 ....40 F3
  YEA LS19 ....85 J3
Ghyll CI *AIRE* BD20 ....56 E1
Ghyll Dr *HWTH* BD22 ....78 E8
Ghyll Mt *YEA* LS19 ....62 B8
Ghyll Rd *HDGY* LS6 ....86 C8
Ghyll Royd *GSLY* LS20 ....62 A7
Ghyllroyd Av *BIRK/DRI* BD11 ....150 D1
Ghyllroyd Dr *BIRK/DRI* BD11 ....150 D1
Ghyll Wy *AIRE* BD20 ....16 C6
Ghyll Wd *ILK* LS29 ....38 A3
Ghyll Wood Dr *BGLY* BD16 ....81 J6
Gibbet St *HFAX* HX1 ....10 A6
Gibb La *LUD/ILL* HX2 ....145 K3
Gibb St *HWTH* BD22 ....54 E8
Gib La *KBTN* HD8 ....239 J4
Gibraltar Av *HFAX* HX1 ....146 A8
Gibraltar Island Rd *MID* LS10 ....132 B2
Gibraltar Rd *HFAX* HX1 ....146 A7
  PDSY/CALV LS28 ....106 C2
Gibriding La *HOLM/MEL* HD9 ....253 H3
Gibside La *AIRE* BD20 ....34 B4
Gibson Av *WKFDW/WTN* WF2 ...176 C4
Gibson Dr *MSTN/BAR* LS15 ......111 L2
Gibson La *GFTH/SHER* LS25 .....135 K5
Gibson St *BFDE* BD3 ....5 J8
  HUDW HD3 ....191 L4
  TOD OL14 ....163 L1
Gilbert Cha *KSTL* LS5 ....108 D3
Gilbert CI *KSTL* LS5 ....108 D3
Gilbert Gv *BSLY* S70 ....261M6
  HUDS HD4 ....213 M3
Gilbert HI *STKB/PEN* S36 ....269 L4
Gilbert St *BULY* LS4 ....108 D3
Gilbert St *PDSY/CALV* * LS28 ....106 F4
Gilbrook Wy *MILN* OL16 ....228 D4
Gilcar St *NORM* WF6 ....178 F2
Gilcar Wy *NORM* WF6 ....178 F2

Gilderdale Cl *ROY/SHW* OL2 ....229 K6
Gildersome Cross *MOR* * LS27 ......129 L8
Gildersome La *MOR* LS27 ....129 K6
Gildersome Sp *MOR* LS27 ....151 M8
Gilead Rd *HUDW* HD3 ....191 G7
Giles Hill La *HIPP* HX3 ....125 J7
Giles St *HOLM/MEL* HD9 ....236 B6
  WBSY BD6 ....126 C5
Gillann St *KNOT* WF11 ....182 C2
Gill Bank Rd *ILK* LS29 ....20 C8
Gill Beck Cl *BAIL* BD17 ....83 G2
Gill Cl *ILK* LS29 ....18 F6
Gillemere Gv *ROY/SHW* OL2 ....229 L7
Gillett Dr *RTHW* LS26 ....155 H1
Gillett La *RTHW* LS26 ....155 H1
Gilling Av *GFTH/SHER* LS25 ....113 K6
Gillingham Gn *BOW* BD4 ....128 A3
Gillion Crs *HOR/CROF* WF4 ....220 A1
Gill La *HOLM/MEL* HD9 ....254 A4
  HWTH BD22 ....54 D3
  HWTH BD22 ....78 C2
  ILK LS29 ....19 L7
  WBY LS22 ....46 B3
  YEA LS19 ....84 C1
Gillroyd La *MAR/SLWT* HD7 ....212 F7
Gillroyd Pl *MOR* LS27 ....152 D3
Gillroyd Ri *GTHN* BD7 ....104 D7
Gill Sike Av *WKFDW/WTN* WF2 .....198 B2
Gill Sike Bungalows
  WKFDW/WTN WF2 ....198 B2
Gill Sike Gv *WKFDW/WTN* WF2 .....198 B2
Gill Sike Rd *WKFDW/WTN* WF2 .....198 B2
The Gills *OT* LS21 ....41 J4
Gillstone Dr *HWTH* BD22 ....78 F8
Gill St *WKFDE* WF1 ....12 C1
Gill's Yd *WKFDE* WF1 ....12 E1
Gillygate *PONT* WF8 ....180 F6
Gilmour St *HIPP* HX3 ....10 C2
Gilpin Pl *WOR/ARM* LS12 ....108 F8
Gilpin St *BFDE* BD3 ....5 M5
  WOR/ARM LS12 ....108 F8
Gilpin Ter *WOR/ARM* LS12 ....108 F8
Gilpin Vw *WOR/ARM* LS12 ....108 F8
Gilstead Ct *BGLY* BD16 ....81 L3
Gilstead Dr *BGLY* BD16 ....81 L3
Gilstead La *BGLY* BD16 ....81 L3
Gilstead Wy *ILK* LS29 ....38 D1
Gilthwaites Crs *KBTN* HD8 ....239 J7
Gilthwaites Gv *KBTN* HD8 ....239 J8
Gilthwaites La *KBTN* HD8 ....239 J7
Gilthwaites Top *KBTN* HD8 ....239 J7
Gilynda Cl *GIR* BD8 ....104 A7
Gindhill La *OT* LS21 ....25 J7
Gin La *FEA/AMT* WF7 ....200 E2
The Ginnel *AL/HA/HU* LS17 ....67 L4
Gipsy La *BEE/HOL* LS11 ....131 J6
  DOD/DAR S75 ....242 B1
  RTHW LS26 ....133 K8
  WKFDW/WTN WF2 ....199 G7
Gipsy Md *RTHW* LS26 ....133 K8
Gipsy St *BFDE* BD3 ....106 A6
Gipton Ap *OSM* LS9 ....110 F5
Gipton Av *RHAY* LS8 ....7 M3
Gipton Ga East *OSM* LS9 ....110 E3
Gipton Ga West *RHAY* LS8 ....110 D3
Gipton Sq *OSM* LS9 ....110 F5
Gipton St *RHAY* LS8 ....7 M2
Gipton Wood Av *RHAY* LS8 ....110 C1
Gipton Wood Crs *RHAY* LS8 ....110 C1
Gipton Wood Gv *RHAY* LS8 ....110 C1
Gipton Wood Pl *RHAY* LS8 ....110 D1
Gipton Wood Rd *RHAY* LS8 ....110 D1
Girlington Rd *GIR* BD8 ....104 B5
Girnhill La *FEA/AMT* WF7 ....201 L2
Gisbourne Rd *HUDN* HD2 ....193 G1
Gisburn Rd *ROCH* OL11 ....228 C3
Gisburn St *KGHY* BD21 ....2 E3
Gissing Rd *WKFDW/WTN* WF2 ......197 M2
The Glade *PDSY/CALV* LS28 ....106 C4
  SCFT LS14 ....67 K7
Gladstonbury Av *WKFDE* WF1 ....177 H5
  YEA LS19 ....84 D1
Gladstone Crs *ROCH* OL11 ....228 C3
Gladstone Rd *HFAX* * HX1 ....10 D5
Gladstone St *BFDE* BD3 ....105 L7
  BGLY * BD16 ....81 H4
  CLECK BD19 ....149 M7
  CUL/QBY BD13 ....125 H5
  FEA/AMT WF7 ....179 M7
  GTL/HWG HX4 ....190 C2
  KGHY BD21 ....2 E6
  NORM WF6 ....178 E3
  PDSY/CALV LS28 ....106 E3
  SKP/WHF BD23 ....16 B1
  TOD OL14 ....140 D7
  WIL/AL BD15 ....103 K5
Gladstone Ter *CAS* WF10 ....158 A6
  MOR * LS27 ....152 C2
Gladstone Vw *HIPP* HX3 ....169 G3
Gladwin St *BTLY* WF17 ....173 K2
Glaisdale Cl *AIRE* BD20 ....36 A4
Glaisdale Ct *WIL/AL* BD15 ....103 J3
Glaisdale Gv *HIPP* HX3 ....147 M7
Glamis Cl *GFTH/SHER* LS25 ....113 K6
Glanville Ter *RTHW* LS26 ....155 G1
Glasshouse St *MID* LS10 ....9 K6
Glasshouse Vw *MID* LS10 ....153 K2
Glastonbury *WHIT* * OL12 ....206 A6
Glastonbury Dr *HUDN* HD3 ....213 H1
Glazier Rd *CUL/QBY* BD13 ....124 E4
Gleanings Av *LUD/ILL* HX2 ....145 L7
Gleanings Dr *LUD/ILL* HX2 ....145 K7
Glebe Av *KSTL* LS5 ....108 D2
Glebe Cl *COP/BISH* YO23 ....73 J7
  KBTN HD8 ....217 M7
Glebe Field Cha *WBY* LS22 ....29 L8
Glebe Field Cl *WBY* LS22 ....29 M8
Glebe Field Cft *WBY* LS22 ....29 M8
Glebe Field Dr *WBY* LS22 ....29 L8
Glebe Field Garth *WBY* LS22 ....29 L8
Glebe Field Holt *WBY* LS22 ....29 M8
Glebe Ga *EARL* WF12 ....196 A5
Glebelands Cl *GFTH/SHER* LS25 .....113 H6
Glebelands Dr *HDGY* LS6 ....86 F8
Glebe La *KNOT* WF11 ....182 B2
Glebe Mt *PDSY/CALV* LS28 ....107 G8
Glebe Pl *KSTL* LS5 ....108 C2
Glebe Rd *AWLS/ASK* DN6 ....227 M5

Glebe St *CAS* WF10 ....157 M7
  HUDW HD3 ....14 A4
  NORM WF6 ....178 E6
  PDSY/CALV LS28 ....107 G8
  ROY/SHW OL2 ....229 K7
Glebe Ter *HDGY* LS6 ....86 F7
Gledcliffe *HFAX* HX1 ....11 H4
Gleddings Cl *HFAX* HX3 ....168 C3
Gledhill Av *STKB/PEN* S36 ....270 E5
Gledhill Cl *ROY/SHW* OL2 ....229 J5
Gledhill Rd *BFDE* BD3 ....5 M7
Gledhill St *TOD* OL14 ....141 K8
Gledhill Ter *DEWS* WF13 ....173 H6
Gledholt Bank *HUD* HD1 ....14 B7
Gledholt Rd *HUD* HD1 ....14 A5
Gledhow Av *RHAY* LS8 ....88 B6
Gledhow Ct *CHAL* LS7 ....88 A7
Gledhow Dr *HWTH* BD22 ....100 C2
Gledhow Grange Vw *RHAY* LS8 ....88 B7
Gledhow Grange Wk *RHAY* LS8 ....88 B7
Gledhow La *CHAL* LS7 ....87 M7
Gledhow Mt *RHAY* LS8 ....7 M4
Gledhow Park Av *CHAL* LS7 ....88 A8
Gledhow Park Crs *CHAL* * LS7 ....88 A8
Gledhow Park Dr *CHAL* LS7 ....87 M8
Gledhow Park Rd *CHAL* LS7 ....88 A8
Gledhow Park Vw *CHAL* LS7 ....88 A8
Gledhow Pl *RHAY* LS8 ....7 M4
Gledhow Ri *RHAY* LS8 ....88 D8
Gledhow Ter *RHAY* LS8 ....7 M4
Gledhow Towers *RHAY* LS8 ....88 A7
Gledhow Valley Rd *CHAL* LS7 ....87 M6
Gledhow Wood Av *RHAY* LS8 ....88 B7
Gledhow Wood Cl *RHAY* LS8 ....88 B7
Gledhow Wood Ct *RHAY* LS8 ....110 C1
Gledhow Wood Gv *RHAY* LS8 ....88 B7
Gledhow Wood Rd *RHAY* LS8 ....88 B8
Gledmow Lane End *CHAL* LS7 ....87 M7
Glenaire *SHPY* BD18 ....83 G5
Glenaire Dr *BAIL* BD17 ....82 C5
Glen Av *BTLY* WF17 ....151 M8
  TOD OL14 ....141 H7
Glenavon Dr *ROY/SHW* OL2 ....229 H6
Glenbrook Dr *GTHN* BD7 ....104 A7
Glencoe Cl *GFTH/SHER* LS25 ....135 H6
Glencoe Cft *GFTH/SHER* LS25 ....135 H6
Glencoe Gdns *GFTH/SHER* LS25 .....135 H6
Glencoe Ter *GFTH/SHER* LS25 ....135 H6
  LVSG WF15 ....172 D3
Glencoe Vw *OSM* LS9 ....110 B8
Glencote Cl *CAS* WF10 ....157 J8
Glen Dl *BGLY* BD16 ....81 H7
Glendale *HOR/CROF* WF4 ....197 H5
  GFTH/SHER LS25 ....113 H4
Glendale Cl *DOD/DAR* S75 ....260 D5
  WBSY BD6 ....126 C7
Glendale Dr *WBSY* BD6 ....126 C7
Glendare Av *GTHN* BD7 ....104 B8
Glendare Rd *GTHN* BD7 ....104 B8
Glendare Ter *GTHN* BD7 ....104 B8
Glen Dene *BGLY* BD16 ....81 H7
  EARL * WF12 ....174 B6
  ILK LS29 ....61 K2
Glendower Pk *BHP/TINH* LS16 ....86 F4
Gleneagles Cl *BOW* BD4 ....127 K6
Gleneagles Rd *AL/HA/HU* LS17 ....87 K2
  FEA/AMT WF7 ....179 M5
Gleneagles Wy *HUDN* HD2 ....192 B3
Glenfield *SHPY* BD18 ....83 G5
Glen Field Av *HUDN* HD2 ....193 H3
Glen Field Av *WBSY* * BD6 ....126 F6
  WBY LS22 ....48 B3
Glenfields Cl *BRAM* LS13 ....107 J3
Glenfields Gdns *BRAM* LS13 ....107 J3
Glen Lee La *KGHY* BD21 ....79 M2
Glenlee Rd *GTHN* BD7 ....104 B8
Glenlow Rd *BTLY* WF17 ....174 B3
Glenlyon Av *KGHY* BD21 ....57 J5
Glenlyon Dr *KGHY* BD21 ....57 J5
Glenmere Mt *YEA* LS19 ....62 F7
Glenmoor Av *BSLY* S70 ....260 D6
Glenmore Cl *ECHL* BD2 ....105 J5
Glenmore Ct *BHP/TINH* LS16 ....64 A3
Glen Mt *BGLY* BD16 ....81 H7
  HIPP HX3 ....146 A4
  ILK LS29 ....61 K3
  MOR LS27 ....152 D3
Glen Mount Cl *HIPP* HX3 ....146 A4
Glenn Wy *HOR/CROF* WF4 ....200 C7
Glen Ri *BGLY* BD17 ....82 A1
Glen Rd *BGLY* BD16 ....81 L1
  BHP/TINH LS16 ....86 A6
  MOR LS27 ....152 D3
Glenrose Dr *GTHN* BD7 ....104 A8
Glenroyal Buildings *BAIL* * BD17 ......82 D6
Glenroyd *SHPY* BD18 ....83 G5
Glenroyd Av *WBSY* BD6 ....126 F7
Glenroyd Cl *PDSY/CALV* LS28 ....106 E4
Glensdale Gv *OSM* LS9 ....110 B7
Glensdale Mt *OSM* LS9 ....110 B7
Glensdale Rd *OSM* LS9 ....110 B7
Glensdale St *OSM* LS9 ....110 B7
Glensdale Ter *OSM* LS9 ....110 B7
Glenside Av *SHPY* BD18 ....83 G5
Glenside Cl *HUDW* HD3 ....191 M6
Glen Side Rd *MAR/SLWT* HD7 ....212 C7
Glenstone Gv *GIR* BD8 ....104 B7
Glen Ter *HFAX* HX1 ....168 D1
The Glen *TOD* OL14 ....141 H7

Glenthorpe Av *OSM* LS9 ....110 C6
Glenthorpe Crs *OSM* LS9 ....110 C6
Glenthorpe Ter *OSM* LS9 ....110 C6
Glenton Sq *HTON* BD9 ....104 C4
Glen Vw *BGLY* BD16 ....80 D5
  HFAX HX1 ....10 F9
Glenview Av *HTON* BD9 ....104 A3
Glenview Cl *SHPY* BD18 ....81 L7
Glenview Dr *BGLY* BD16 ....81 L8
Glenview Gv *SHPY* BD18 ....81 M7
Glen View Rd *BGLY* BD16 ....81 L1
  HBR HX7 ....143 G3
  KBTN HD8 ....238 C4
Glenview Rd *SHPY* BD18 ....81 M7
Glen View St *TOD* OL14 ....140 E5
Glenview Ter *SHPY* BD18 ....82 B6
Glen Wy *BGLY* BD16 ....59 L8
Glenwood Av *BAIL* BD17 ....82 A2
Global Av *BEE/HOL* LS11 ....131 G5
Globe Ct *LVSG* WF15 ....172 D2
Globe Fold *GIR* BD8 ....4 A3
Globe Rd *WOR/ARM* LS12 ....8 C2
Glossop Cl *LDS* LS6 ....6 E1
Glossop Mt *HDGY* LS6 ....6 E1
Glossop St *HDGY* LS6 ....6 E1
Glossop Vw *HDGY* LS6 ....6 E1
Gloucester Av *BEE/HOL* LS11 ....131 G5
  BFDE BD3 ....105 M5
  WHIT OL12 ....206 F2
Gloucester Ct
  WKFDW/WTN WF2 ....109 G6
  WOR/ARM * LS12 ....109 G6
Gloucester Gv
  WKFDW/WTN WF2 ....197 M1
Gloucester Pl
  WKFDW/WTN WF2 ....197 M1
Gloucester Rd *BGLY* BD16 ....81 K4
  WKFDW/WTN WF2 ....197 L1
Gloucester Ter *WOR/ARM* LS12 ....109 G7
Glover Cl *WBSY* BD6 ....127 G2
Glovershaw La *BAIL* BD17 ....60 A8
Clover Wy *BEE/HOL* LS11 ....131 L4
Clydegate *WBOW* BD5 ....4 E7
Clyndon Ct *BTLY* WF17 ....170 D6
Glynn Ter *GIR* BD8 ....104 D6
Glynwed St *SKP/WHF* BD23 ....16 A3
Gobind Marg *BFDE* BD3 ....5 J6
Godfrey Rd *HIPP* HX3 ....168 E4
Godfrey St *GIR* BD8 ....103 M7
Godley Branch Rd *HIPP* HX3 ....11 L4
Godley Gdns *HIPP* HX3 ....147 H5
Godley La *HIPP* HX3 ....11 M3
Godley Rd *HIPP* HX3 ....11 H3
Godley St *BSLYN/ROY* S71 ....243 M2
Godly Cl *RPDN/SBR* HX6 ....188 E5
Godly La *RPDN/SBR* HX6 ....188 E5
Godwin St *BFD* BD1 ....4 E6
Goff Well La *KGHY* BD21 ....79 L4
Goit Stock La *BGLY* BD16 ....80 D6
Goit Stock Ter *BGLY* BD16 ....80 D6
Golcar Brow Rd
  HOLM/MEL HD9 ....234 E4
Goldbourne Dr *ROY/SHW* OL2 ....229 K6
Goldcrest Av *GIR* BD8 ....103 K7
Goldcrest Ct *HUDS* HD4 ....214 A7
Gold Cft *BSLY* S70 ....261 J6
Golden Butts Rd *ILK* LS29 ....38 E2
Golden Sq *HOR/CROF* WF4 ....197 K5
Golden St *ROY/SHW* OL2 ....230 A6
Golden Ter *WOR/ARM* LS12 ....130 C2
Golden View Dr *KGHY* BD21 ....58 B9
Goldfields Av *GTL/HWG* HX4 ....168 C6
Goldfields Cl *GTL/HWG* HX4 ....168 C6
Goldfields Vw *GTL/HWG* HX4 ....168 D6
Goldfields Wy *GTL/HWG* HX4 ....168 C6
Goldington Av *HUDW* HD3 ....191 H6
Goldington Dr *HUDW* HD3 ....191 G8
Gold St *BSLY* S70 ....261 J6
Goldthorpe Vis
  AWLS/ASK * DN6 ....227 M3
Golf Av *LUD/ILL* HX2 ....145 L1
Golf Crs *LUD/ILL* HX2 ....145 L1
Golf La *MOR* LS27 ....152 A6
Golf Links Av *TAD* LS24 ....71 K4
Golf Links Ct *TAD* LS24 ....71 L4
Golf Links Crs *TAD* LS24 ....71 L4
Gomersal La *CLECK* BD19 ....150 C7
Gomersal Rd *CLECK* BD19 ....150 E8
Gondal Ct *WBOW* BD5 ....126 E3
Goodbard Houses *LDS* * LS1 ....6 F7
Gooder Av *BSLYN/ROY* S71 ....243 L3
Gooder La *BRIG* HD6 ....170 C5
Gooder St *BRIG* HD6 ....170 C4
Good Hope Cl *NORM* WF6 ....178 E4
Goodman St *MID* LS10 ....9 M6
Goodrich *ROCH* OL11 ....206 A8
Goodrick La *AL/HA/HU* LS17 ....65 K7
Good Shepherd Cl *MILN* OL16 ....206 C6
Goods La *EARL* WF12 ....173 M7
Goodwin Pl *HUDN* HD2 ....193 H1
Goodwin Rd *WOR/ARM* LS12 ....108 E8
Goodwood *EARL/LOFT* WF3 ....153 M3
Goodwood Av
  GFTH/SHER LS25 ....135 H4
Goody Cross La *RTHW* LS26 ....134 D3
Goose Cote La *HWTH* BD22 ....79 G4
Goose Cote Wy *HWTH* BD22 ....79 G3
Goosedale Ct *BOW* BD4 ....128 C5
Goose Eye *HWTH* BD22 ....56 D8
Goosefield Ri *GFTH/SHER* LS25 ....134 F1
Goosegate *LUD/ILL* * HX2 ....124 B8
Goose Gn *HOLM/MEL* HD9 ....254 C1
Goose Green La *COL* BB8 ....74 D4
Goose Hi *HECK* WF16 ....172 F2
Goosehill La *NORM* WF6 ....178 A1
Goosehole La *HEM/SK/SE* WF9 ....247 K5
Goose La *GSLY* LS20 ....60 D7
  WHIT OL12 ....206 B6
Goose West La *RPDN/SBR* HX6 ....167 G4
Gordale Cl *BTLY* WF17 ....173 K1
Gordon Av *OSS* * WF5 ....174 F4
Gordon Ct *ILK* OL15 ....185 K8
  MIRF WF14 ....172 C4
Gordon Dr *HDGY* LS6 ....86 C8
Gordon Pl *HEM/SK/SE* WF9 ....247 M7
Gordon St *AIRE* BD20 ....55 M1
  BSLY S70 ....262 A6

CLAY * BD14 ....125 K2
COL BB8 ....74 A1
EARD/LOFT WF3 ....154 A6
ELL HX5 ....169 H8
FEA/AMT WF7 ....179 M7
HIPP HX3 ....146 D4
HWTH * BD22 ....79 G6
ILK LS29 ....38 E2
KGHY BD21 ....2 E4
MAR/SLWT HD7 ....212 C6
MILN OL16 ....229 K3
ROCH OL11 ....228 C1
ROY/SHW OL2 ....229 K7
RPDN/SBR HX6 ....167 J3
WBOW BD5 ....5 G9
WKFDE WF1 ....199 G4
Gordon Ter *AIRE* BD20 ....34 B3
  IDLE BD10 ....83 K5
  MAR/SLWT HD7 ....212 F4
Goring Park Av *OSS* WF5 ....197 J2
Gorrel St *ROCH* * OL11 ....228 C1
Gorse Av *BAIL* BD17 ....82 A4
Gorse La *GFTH/SHER* LS25 ....137 K1
Gorse Lea *MID* LS10 ....131 M6
Gorse Rd *HUDW* HD3 ....191 L8
  MILN OL16 ....207 H8
Gorsley Bank *LIT* OL15 ....185 L7
Gorton St *SKP/WHF* * BD23 ....16 C3
Goschen St *SKP/WHF* * BD23 ....16 C3
Gosling La *GTL/HWG* HX4 ....189 H4
Gosport Cl *HUDW* HD3 ....190 C6
Gosport La *GTL/HWG* HX4 ....190 B1
Gosside Gv *WOR/ARM* LS6 ....178 F5
Gothic Mt *FEA/AMT* WF7 ....179 J6
Gothic St *CUL/QBY* BD13 ....125 G5
Gotts Park Av *WOR/ARM* LS12 ....108 B5
Gotts Park Crs *WOR/ARM* LS12 ....108 B5
Gotts Park Vw *WOR/ARM* LS12 ....108 B4
Gotts Rd *WOR/ARM* LS12 ....8 B1
Gott's Ter *AIRE* BD20 ....57 J4
Gott St *HWTH* BD22 ....79 H6
Gough La *RPDN/SBR* HX6 ....166 D8
Goulbourne St *KGHY* BD21 ....2 E7
Governor's Yd *WKFDE* WF1 ....176 F7
Gowers St *MILN* OL16 ....206 D7
Gower St *LDSU* LS2 ....7 J8
  WBOW BD5 ....127 G2
Gracechurch St *GIR* BD8 ....4 C4
Grace Leather La *BTLY* WF17 ....174 A1
Grace St *BSLYN/ROY* S71 ....244 B8
  KGHY BD21 ....3 K5
  LDS LS1 ....6 D9
  WHIT * OL12 ....206 C4
Gracey La *WBSY* BD6 ....126 B5
Grafton Cl *BAIL* BD17 ....82 F2
  KNOT WF11 ....182 B1
Grafton Ct *MILN* * OL16 ....206 D8
Grafton Pl *HIPP* HX3 ....146 C3
Grafton Rd *KGHY* BD21 ....2 C5
Grafton St *BSLY* S70 ....260 F5
  BTLY WF17 ....173 M3
  CAS WF10 ....158 A8
  CHAL LS7 ....7 H7
  KGHY BD21 ....2 E7
  MILN OL16 ....206 D8
  WBOW BD5 ....4 D9
Gragwood Cl *HORS* LS18 ....85 L6
Graham Dr *CAS* WF10 ....158 D7
Graham Gv *BULY* LS4 ....108 F3
Graham St *BULY* LS4 ....108 F3
  HTON BD9 ....104 C4
Graham Ter *BULY* LS4 ....108 F3
Graham Vw *BULY* LS4 ....108 F3
Graham Wk *MOR* LS27 ....129 M7
Graingers Wy *WOR/ARM* LS12 ....8 B7
Grains Rd *ROY/SHW* OL2 ....229 L7
Grain St *WBOW* BD5 ....126 D3
Gramfield Rd *HUDS* HD4 ....213 K3
Grammar School St *BFD* BD1 ....4 E4
Grampian Av
  WKFDW/WTN WF2 ....198 A3
Grampian Cl *DOD/DAR* S75 ....260 D4
  KBTN HD8 ....238 B3
Grampian Wy *ROY/SHW* OL2 ....229 J6
Granary Ct *ECHL* BD2 ....105 L1
Granary Whf *LDS* * LS1 ....8 C7
Granby Av *HDGY* LS6 ....108 F1
Granby Ct *HEM/SK/SE* WF9 ....247 J1
Granby Dr *AIRE* BD20 ....58 B5
Granby La *HDGY* LS6 ....108 F1
Granby Flats *HUD* HD1 ....14 A8
Granby Gv *HDGY* LS6 ....108 F1
Granby Pl *HDGY* LS6 ....108 F1
Granby Rd *HDGY* LS6 ....108 F2
Granby St *BOW* BD4 ....5 H9
  CUL/QBY BD13 ....125 G5
Granby Ter *HDGY* LS6 ....108 F1
Granby Vw *HDGY* LS6 ....108 F1
Grandage Ter *GIR* BD8 ....104 D6
Grand Ar *LDS* LS1 ....7 J8
Grand Cross Rd *HUDE* HD5 ....193 G8
Grandidge St *ROCH* OL11 ....228 A1
Grandsmere Pl *HIPP* HX3 ....168 D2
Grand Stand Rd
  EARD/LOFT WF3 ....176 B1
  GFTH/SHER LS25 ....113 K7
Grange Av *BFDE* BD3 ....106 B6
  BOW BD4 ....128 C6
  BSPA/BRAM LS23 ....49 J3
  BTLY WF17 ....173 K3
  CHAL LS7 ....7 L1
  GFTH/SHER LS25 ....113 H8
  HEM/SK/SE WF9 ....247 J3
  HUDN HD2 ....192 B5
  ILK LS29 ....38 D7
  LUD/ILL HX2 ....146 B1
  MAR/SLWT HD7 ....233 J2
  MILN OL16 ....229 H2
  PBR HG3 ....28 E3
  SHPY BD18 ....82 A4

TAD LS24 ....72 A2
WIL/AL BD15 ....103 L6
YEA LS19 ....62 E8
Grange Bank *HIPP* HX3 ....125 L8
Grange Bank Cl *HUDE* HD5 ....15 L4
Grange Br *AIRE* BD20 ....35 J6
Grange Castle *YEA* LS19 ....62 F8
Grange Cl *AL/HA/HU* LS17 ....67 M2
  CUD/GR S72 ....245 H3
  HEM/SK/SE WF9 ....247 J3
  HORS LS18 ....85 H6
  HUDW HD3 ....190 C6
  ILK LS29 ....38 F2
  KNOT WF11 ....181 M2
  MID LS10 ....9 K7
Grange Ct *AL/HA/HU* LS17 ....87 L1
  BGLY BD16 ....81 J7
  HIPP HX3 ....169 J3
  MSTN/BAR LS15 ....90 B8
Grange Crs *AIRE* BD20 ....58 A5
  BSLYN/ROY S71 ....262 A4
  CHAL LS7 ....7 L1
  TAD LS24 ....71 M2
  YEA LS19 ....62 E8
Grange Cft *AL/HA/HU* LS17 ....87 L1
Grange Dr *GIR* BD8 ....103 L6
  KBTN HD8 ....217 M6
  OSS WF5 ....197 H3
Grange Est *ILK* LS29 ....38 F2
Grangefield Av *BTLY* WF17 ....173 K3
  ILK LS29 ....40 B5
Grangefield Rd
  PDSY/CALV LS28 ....107 G5
Grange Fields Mt *RTHW* LS26 ....132 B8
Grange Fields Rd *MID* LS10 ....132 B8
Grange Fields Wy *RTHW* LS26 ....132 B8
Grange Gv *AIRE* BD20 ....58 A5
  BFDE BD3 ....106 B6
Grange Hts *HIPP* HX3 ....169 J3
Grange Holt *AL/HA/HU* LS17 ....87 L1
Grange La *AWLS/ASK* DN6 ....249 J2
  BRIG HD6 ....171 G4
  BSLYN/ROY S71 ....262 A5
  GFTH/SHER LS25 ....135 K4
  HOR/CROF WF4 ....217 M2
  HWTH BD22 ....78 B3
  KBTN HD8 ....237 M3
  UPML OL3 ....231 H8
Grange Mt *YEA* LS19 ....62 E8
Grange Pk *BAIL* BD17 ....83 G3
  HIPP HX3 ....168 D3
Grange Park Av *RHAY* LS8 ....110 F1
Grange Park Cl *CAS* WF10 ....157 J1
  MOR * LS27 ....111 G1
  RHAY LS8 ....111 G1
Grange Park Crs *RHAY* LS8 ....110 F1
Grange Park Dr *BGLY* BD16 ....81 J6
  MOR LS27 ....130 D7
Grange Park Gv *RHAY* LS8 ....110 F1
Grange Park Ms *MOR* LS27 ....130 D7
Grange Park Pl *RHAY* LS8 ....111 G1
Grange Park Ri *RHAY* LS8 ....110 F1
Grange Park Rd *BGLY* BD16 ....81 J6
  RHAY LS8 ....110 F1
Grange Park Ter *RHAY* LS8 ....111 G1
Grange Park Wk *RHAY* LS8 ....110 F1
Grange Park Wy *MOR* * LS27 ....130 D7
The Grange Rd *BHP/TINH* LS16 ....86 D5
Grange Rd *AIRE* BD20 ....34 F5
  AIRE BD20 ....56 C1
  AIRE BD20 ....58 A5
  AWLS/ASK DN6 ....227 M5
  BGLY BD16 ....81 K2
  BSLYN/ROY S71 ....243 J3
  BTLY WF17 ....173 J3
  BTLY WF17 ....174 A2
  CAS WF10 ....158 F5
  CLECK BD19 ....149 L6
  CUD/GR S72 ....245 H4
  EARL WF12 ....174 C3
  HUDW HD3 ....191 G8
  ILK LS29 ....40 A5
  MID LS10 ....9 K7
  TAD LS24 ....72 A2
  WIL/AL BD15 ....103 L6
  YEA LS19 ....62 E8
Grange St *HIPP* HX3 ....10 C1
  KGHY BD21 ....3 H3
  WKFDW/WTN WF2 ....12 A4
Grange Ter *CHAL* LS7 ....7 K1
  MAR/SLWT HD7 ....233 J2
  MOR LS27 ....130 D7
  PDSY/CALV LS28 ....107 G6
  SHPY BD18 ....82 D8
  WIL/AL BD15 ....103 L6
Grange Valley Rd *BTLY* WF17 ....174 B2
Grange Vw *BFDE* * BD3 ....106 B6
  CHAL LS7 ....7 K1
  EARL WF12 ....195 M6
  HEM/SK/SE WF9 ....223 M8
  MSTN/BAR LS15 ....111 M8
  OT LS21 ....41 H5
  PDSY/CALV LS28 ....107 G6
  TAD LS24 ....93 M2
Grange View Gdns
  AL/HA/HU LS17 ....89 H5
Grangeway *GIR* BD8 ....103 L6
  HEM/SK/SE WF9 ....223 M7
Grangewood Ct *WKFDE* WF1 ....176 F1
Grangewood Gdns
  BHP/TINH LS16 ....86 D5
Granhamthorpe *BRAM* LS13 ....107 H2
Granny Av *MOR* LS27 ....130 E6
Granny Hall Gv *BRIG* HD6 ....170 B2
Granny Hall La *BRIG* HD6 ....170 B2
Granny Hall Pk *BRIG* HD6 ....170 B2
Granny Hill Ter *HFAX* HX1 ....168 A1
Granny La *MIRF* WF14 ....194 D3
  WOR/ARM LS12 ....130 C1
Grant Av *RHAY* LS8 ....7 L4
Grantham Pl *GTHN* BD7 ....4 B9
  HIPP HX3 ....146 D4
Grantham Rd *GTHN* BD7 ....4 A9
  HIPP HX3 ....146 D4
Grantham Ter *GTHN* BD7 ....4 B9
Grantley Pl *HUDN* HD2 ....192 F1
Grantley St *WKFDE* WF1 ....13 G1
Grantley Wy *WKFDE* WF1 ....13 H1

Granton Rd *CHAL* LS7 ....109 M1
Granton St *BFDE* BD3 ....105 L7
Grant St *BFDE* BD3 ....5 K5
  HWTH BD22 ....2 C5
  HWTH BD22 ....100 E4
Granville Av *PONT* * WF8 ....180 M1
Granville Ct *MILN* OL16 ....229 K3
  OT * LS21 ....41 H7
Granville Mt *OT* LS21 ....41 H7
Granville Pl *WIL/AL* BD15 ....103 K5
Granville Rd *HTON* BD9 ....104 D1
  OSM LS9 ....7 M6
Granville St *CAS* WF10 ....179 L1
  CLAY BD14 ....125 L1
  COL BB8 ....74 A1
  DEWS WF13 ....173 K6
  DOD/DAR S75 ....260 F3
  ELL * HX5 ....169 H8
  FEA/AMT WF7 ....201 L2
  KGHY BD21 ....2 E4
  LVSG WF15 ....172 D3
  NORM WF6 ....178 D4
  PDSY/CALV LS28 ....106 E6
  PDSY/CALV LS28 ....107 H4
  SKP/WHF BD23 ....16 A2
  TOD * OL14 ....163 J5
Granville Ter *BGLY* BD16 ....81 J3
  HUD HD1 ....14 A9
  SHPY BD18 ....104 D1
  YEA LS19 ....62 E7
Grape St *HFAX* HX1 ....10 E6
  KGHY BD21 ....3 J3
  MID LS10 ....9 J6
  WIL/AL BD15 ....103 L5
Grasleigh Av *WIL/AL* BD15 ....103 J3
Grasleigh Wy *WIL/AL* BD15 ....103 J3
Grasmere Av *WBY* LS22 ....47 L1
Grasmere Cl *CAS* WF10 ....159 G5
  STKB/PEN S36 ....270 F2
  WOR/ARM LS12 ....108 F8
Grasmere Crs *DOD/DAR* S75 ....242 C3
Grasmere Dr *ELL* HX5 ....169 K7
  WBY LS22 ....47 L1
Grasmere Rd *AWLS/ASK* DN6 ....249 L5
  BSLYN/ROY S71 ....261 J5
  EARL WF12 ....174 A4
  ECHL BD2 ....105 J3
  HOLM/MEL HD9 ....235 G5
  HUD HD1 ....14 A5
  LM/WK BD12 ....149 G5
  ROY/SHW OL2 ....228 F8
  WKFDW/WTN WF2 ....176 A7
  WOR/ARM LS12 ....108 F8
Grasmere St *WHIT* OL12 ....206 B5
Grasscroft *HUDE* HD5 ....215 H4
Grasscroft Av *HOLM/MEL* HD9 ....236 A2
Grasscroft Rd *HOLM/MEL* HD9 ....236 A2
  HUD HD1 ....191 M7
Grassington Rd *SKP/WHF* BD23 ....16 B1
Gratrix La *OT* LS21 ....25 H6
Grattan Rd *BFD* BD1 ....4 D6
Graveleythorpe Ri
  MSTN/BAR LS15 ....111 K5
Graveleythorpe Rd
  MSTN/BAR LS15 ....111 K5
Gravelly Hill La *AL/HA/HU* LS17 ....43 J3
Gray Av *SHPY* BD18 ....104 F1
Gray Ct *MSTN/BAR* * LS15 ....111 M6
Gray Hall Cl *GTL/HWG* * HX4 ....190 B3
Grayrigg Cl *MSTN/BAR* LS15 ....111 G7
Grayrigg Ct *MSTN/BAR* LS15 ....110 F7
Grayshon Dr *WBSY* BD6 ....126 E5
Grayshon St *BIRK/DRI* BD11 ....151 G1
Grayson Crest *BULY* LS4 ....108 D3
Grayson Hts *BULY* LS4 ....108 D3
Gray's Rd *BSLYN/ROY* S71 ....243 L5
Gray St *LVSG* WF15 ....172 A2
Grayswood Crs *BOW* BD4 ....127 M3
Grayswood Dr *BOW* BD4 ....127 M2
Great Albion St *HFAX* HX1 ....11 G5
Great Ben La *MAR/SLWT* HD7 ....212 A2
Great Bent Cl *WHIT* OL12 ....206 F2
Great Cliffe Rd *DOD/DAR* S75 ....260 A6
Great Cross St *BFD* BD1 ....5 G7
Great Edge Rd *LUD/ILL* HX2 ....145 H8
Greatfield Cl *OSS* WF5 ....197 G1
Greatfield Dr *OSS* WF5 ....175 G8
Greatfield Gdns *OSS* WF5 ....175 G8
Greatfield Rd *OSS* WF5 ....197 G1
Great Gates Cl *ROCH* OL11 ....228 C2
Great Gates Rd *ROCH* OL11 ....228 C4
Great George St *LDS* LS1 ....6 B7
  MILN OL16 ....229 K3
Great Horton Rd *GTHN* BD7 ....4 A9
Great House La
  RPDN/SBR HX6 ....188 C3
Great House Rd *TOD* OL14 ....142 A6
Great Howarth *WHIT* OL12 ....206 D2
Great Meadow *ROY/SHW* OL2 ....229 H5
Great Northern Rd *KGHY* BD21 ....3 H6
Great Northern St *MOR* LS27 ....152 C3
Great North Rd *AWLS/ASK* DN6 ....249 H8
  GFTH/SHER LS25 ....114 A4
Great Pasture *ILK* LS29 ....40 B4
Great Pond St *DEWS* * WF13 ....195 H1
Great Russell Ct *GTHN* BD7 ....4 A6
Great Russell St *GTHN* BD7 ....104 D7
Great Wilson St *BEE/HOL* LS11 ....8 F5
Greatwood Av *SKP/WHF* BD23 ....16 C3
Great Wood St *BTLY* WF17 ....173 L2
Greave *CUD* HUDN HD2 ....192 D2
Greavefield La *PONT* WF8 ....181 K6
Greave House Dr *LUD/ILL* HX2 ....144 F7
Greave House Flds
  LUD/ILL HX2 ....145 G6
Greave House La *KBTN* HD8 ....215 M3
Greave House Pk *LUD/ILL* HX2 ....144 F7
Greave House Ter *KBTN* HD8 ....215 M3
Greave Rd *HOLM/MEL* HD9 ....254 C6
  RPDN/SBR HX6 ....166 A8
Greaves Av *WKFDW/WTN* WF2 ....197 L1
Greaves Cft *KBTN* HD8 ....215 M3
Greaves Fold *DOD/DAR* S75 ....260 D4
  GTL/HWG HX4 ....190 E2
Greaves Rd *DEWS* WF13 ....173 L5
Greaves Smithy *ILK* LS29 ....19 L7
Greaves St *CAS* WF10 ....157 M6

  ROY/SHW OL2 ....229 L7
  WBOW BD5 ....126 F3
Greave St *TOD* OL14 ....163 M1
Greek St *CAS* WF10 ....158 A6
  LDS LS1 ....6 F9
The Green *AL/HA/HU* LS17 ....87 M4
  BGLY BD16 ....59 G7
  BGLY BD16 ....59 J8
  BGLY BD16 ....59 L8
  BGLY * BD16 ....81 M3
  BOW BD4 ....128 B7
  BTLY WF17 ....151 H4
  CAS WF10 ....158 F6
  COL BB8 ....52 B8
  FEA/AMT WF7 ....202 A2
  GFTH/SHER LS25 ....113 J8
  GFTH/SHER LS25 ....135 J5
  GSLY LS20 ....62 A6
  HOR/CROF WF4 ....200 E4
  HOR/CROF WF4 ....220 C7
  HORS LS18 ....85 K6
  HUDN HD2 ....192 F1
  MAR/SLWT * HD7 ....233 H2
  MIRF WF14 ....172 A5
  OSS WF5 ....196 F2
  OT LS21 ....41 H5
  PDSY/CALV LS28 ....106 F2
  STKB/PEN S36 ....270 F2
  WKFDW/WTN WF2 ....176 A3
The Green Vw *CUD/GR* S72 ....244 D2
Green Abbey *HOLM/MEL* HD9 ....254 D7
Greenacre Av *LM/WK* BD12 ....148 F4
Green Acre Cl *BAIL* BD17 ....82 F5
Greenacre Cl *LM/WK* BD12 ....148 F4
Greenacre Ct *GFTH/SHER* LS25 ....113 J7
  LM/WK BD12 ....148 F4
Greenacre Dr *KBTN* HD8 ....257 G3
Greenacre Pk *YEA* LS19 ....84 D1
Greenacre Park Av *YEA* LS19 ....84 D1
Greenacre Park Ms *YEA* LS19 ....84 E1
Greenacre Park Ri *YEA* LS19 ....84 D1
Greenacre Rd *WOR/ARM* * WF9 ....225 L6
Green Acres *FEA/AMT* WF7 ....202 A3
  HOR/CROF WF4 ....198 C7
  STKB/PEN S36 ....271 G3
Greenacres *HIPP* HX3 ....125 M8
  OSS WF5 ....174 F5
  SKP/WHF BD23 ....16 D1
Greenacres Av *HIPP* HX3 ....125 M8
Green Acres Cl *KBTN* * HD8 ....217 L8
Greenacres Cl *OSS* WF5 ....174 F5
Greenacres Ct *LM/WK* BD12 ....158 C6
Greenacres Dr *BTLY* WF17 ....151 J4
  HIPP HX3 ....125 M8
  KGHY BD21 ....57 H5
Greenacres Gv *HIPP* HX3 ....125 M8
Greenacre Wk *HOR/CROF* WF4 ....222 E4
Greenacre Wy *LM/WK* BD12 ....148 F4
Green Av *AIRE* BD20 ....35 M4
  GFTH/SHER LS25 ....135 H3
  HECK WF16 ....173 G2
Green Balk La *KBTN* HD8 ....216 B3
Greenbank *BSLYN/ROY* S71 ....243 H5
Green Bank *CLECK* BD19 ....150 B8
  EARD/LOFT WF3 ....154 F5
Greenbank Cl *CAS* WF10 ....179 J1
Greenbank Dr *LIT* OL15 ....207 H3
Greenbank Gv *NORM* WF6 ....178 A3
Greenbank Rd *NORM* WF6 ....178 A3
  WHIT OL12 ....206 C4
  WIL/AL BD15 ....103 L6
Greenbanks Av *HORS* LS18 ....85 K4
Greenbanks Cl *HORS* LS18 ....85 L4
Greenbanks Dr *HORS* LS18 ....85 K4
Greenbank Wk *CUD/GR* S72 ....245 H7
Green Bridge Cl *ROCH* OL11 ....228 B2
Green Cha *HDGY* * LS6 ....87 G7
Green Cliff *HOLM/MEL* HD9 ....236 B1
Greencliffe Av *BAIL* BD17 ....82 D5
Green Cl *AIRE* BD20 ....16 E8
  AIRE BD20 ....35 H8
  BTLY WF17 ....174 A2
  DEWS WF13 ....173 A2
  GIR BD8 ....104 A6
  HDGY * LS6 ....87 H7
Green Ct *CLECK* BD19 ....149 H6
  GTHN BD7 ....126 B1
  MSTN/BAR LS15 ....90 A7
Green Crs *HDGY* LS6 ....87 G7
  MAR/SLWT HD7 ....213 G1
Green Cft *HEM/SK/SE* WF9 ....223 K4
Greencroft Av *WORS* LS14 ....147 K3
Greencroft Cl *IDLE* BD10 ....83 J7
Greendale Ct *HOLM/MEL* HD9 ....236 B1
Greendown Cl *ILK* LS29 ....38 F2
Green End *BRIG* HD6 ....170 C5
  CLAY BD14 ....125 K2
Green End La
  WKFDW/WTN WF2 ....12 D9
Green End Rd *AIRE* BD20 ....59 G5
  WBSY BD6 ....126 D6
Greenfell Cl *HWTH* BD22 ....2 C7
Greenfield Av *GFTH/SHER* LS25 ....135 J4
  CSLY LS20 ....61 K7
  HIPP HX3 ....148 C7
  HUDW HD3 ....191 J7
  MOR LS27 ....129 K7
  OSS WF5 ....197 J2
  SHPY BD18 ....82 E8
Greenfield Ct *GFTH/SHER* LS25 ....135 J4
  HWTH BD22 ....2 D5
Greenfield Crs *CUL/QBY* BD13 ....80 B3
Greenfield Dr *CLECK* BD19 ....149 H6
  MOR LS27 ....129 K7
Greenfield Garth
  GFTH/SHER LS25 ....135 J4
Greenfield La *BOW* BD4 ....127 K8
  CSLY LS20 ....61 J7
  GTHN BD7 ....126 B2
  IDLE BD10 ....83 K5
  MILN OL16 ....206 F3

  ROCH OL11 ....228 C2
  ROY/SHW OL2 ....229 K8
Greenfield Mt
  WKFDW/WTN WF2 ....176 B4
Greenfield Pl *GIR* * BD8 ....4 B1
  HIPP HX3 ....148 C7
Greenfield Ri *GFTH/SHER* LS25 ....135 J4
Greenfinch Gv *HUDS* HD4 ....214 A7
Greenfold La *WBY* LS22 ....48 B1
Greenfoot La *DOD/DAR* S75 ....260 F3
Green Gdns *MAR/SLWT* HD7 ....213 G1
Greengate *AIRE* BD20 ....35 M4
Greengate Cl *WHIT* OL12 ....206 F2
Green Gate La *MAR/SLWT* HD7 ....234 C7
Green Gate Rd
  HOLM/MEL HD9 ....253 J2
Greengate Rd *KGHY* BD21 ....3 G7
Greengates Av *LM/WK* BD12 ....148 E5
Green Grove Bank *MILN* OL16 ....206 E3
Green Haggs La *PBR* HG3 ....28 A4
Green Hall Pk *HIPP* HX3 ....147 M1
Green Head Av *HUDE* HD5 ....215 H1
Green Head Dr *AIRE* BD20 ....57 J4
Green Head La *AIRE* BD20 ....57 J4
  LA BRIG HD6 ....170 A8
  HUDE HD5 ....215 H1
Green Head Mt *AIRE* BD20 ....57 J4
Greenhead Rd *BHP/TINH* LS16 ....86 D6
  HUD HD1 ....14 C7
  LUD/ILL HX2 ....145 K8
Greenhill Av *BSLYN/ROY* S71 ....261 G3
  PONT WF8 ....181 G8
  ROY/SHW OL2 ....229 G5
Greenhill Bank Rd
  HOLM/MEL HD9 ....254 F1
Green Hill Cha *WOR/ARM* LS12 ....108 D8
Green Hill Cl *WOR/ARM* LS12 ....108 B5
Greenhill Crs *WOR/ARM* LS12 ....108 D8
Green Hill Cft *WOR/ARM* LS12 ....108 D8
Green Hill Dr *BGLY* BD16 ....59 G7
Green Hill Dr *BRAM* LS13 ....108 A5
Green Hill Gdns
  WOR/ARM LS12 ....108 D8
Green Hill Gv *STKB/PEN* S36 ....258 C8
Green Hill Holt
  WOR/ARM * LS12 ....108 D8
Greenhill La *BFDE* BD3 ....105 L7
  BGLY BD16 ....59 H8
  OSS * WF5 ....196 F2
Green Hill La *HWTH* BD22 ....54 D5
Green Hill Mt *BRAM* LS13 ....108 A5
Greenhill Mt *WOR/ARM* LS12 ....108 D8
Greenhill Pl *BRAM* LS13 ....108 A5
Green Hill Pl *BRAM* LS13 ....108 A5
Greenhill Rd *HUDW* HD3 ....191 G7
  WKFDE WF1 ....13 H1
Greenhills *YEA* LS19 ....84 B4
Greenhill St *BFDE* BD3 ....105 L8
Green Hill Wy *BRAM* LS13 ....108 A5
Greenholme Cl *ILK* LS29 ....40 B4
Greenholme Ct *BOW* BD4 ....128 B4
Green House Hl *KBTN* HD8 ....238 E2
Green House La *KBTN* HD8 ....238 E2
Greenhouse Rd *HUDN* HD2 ....192 C4
Greenhow Cl *BULY* LS4 ....108 F4
Greenhow Gdns *BULY* LS4 ....108 F4
Greenhow Pk *ILK* LS29 ....39 M5
Greenhow Rd *BULY* LS4 ....108 F4
Greenhow Wk *BULY* LS4 ....108 F4
Greenland Av *CUL/QBY* * BD13 ....125 J4
Greenland Av *CUL/QBY* BD13 ....125 G6
Greenland Rd *HBR* HX7 ....119 L8
Greenland Vls *CUL/QBY* BD13 ....125 G6
Green La *AIRE* BD20 ....17 J8
  AIRE BD20 ....34 D8
  AIRE BD20 ....35 J8
  AL/HA/HU LS17 ....44 C7
  AWLS/ASK DN6 ....249 J3
  BAIL BD17 ....82 C3
  BAIL BD17 ....82 D5
  BEE/HOL LS11 ....131 K5
  BHP/TINH LS16 ....85 M2
  BRIG HD6 ....170 A1
  BRIG HD6 ....171 H4
  BSPA/BRAM LS23 ....49 G7
  CAS WF10 ....135 M8
  CAS WF10 ....158 B4
  CAS WF10 ....179 L1
  CLECK BD19 ....149 M4
  CUD/GR S72 ....244 D2
  DOD/DAR S75 ....242 E5
  HECK WF16 ....172 E2
  HOR/CROF WF4 ....222 D6
  KBTN HD8 ....239 G7
  KBTN HD8 ....239 J8
  LM/WK BD12 ....149 J2
  PDSY/CALV LS28 ....106 F8
  STKB/PEN S36 ....258 C8
  WKFDW/WTN WF2 ....199 J7
Greenside Av *DOD/DAR* S75 ....242 E5
  HUDE HD5 ....215 J1
  WOR/ARM LS12 ....130 D1
Greenside Ct *HOR/CROF* WF4 ....200 D7
  MOR * LS27 ....129 M7
Greenside Crs *HUDE* HD5 ....215 J1
Greenside Dr *HUDE* HD5 ....215 J1
  WOR/ARM LS12 ....130 E1

  HEM/SK/SE WF9 ....246 D4
  HIPP HX3 ....11 M7
  HIPP HX3 ....147 G1
  HIPP HX3 ....148 A1
  HOLM/MEL HD9 ....235 G5
  HOLM/MEL HD9 ....254 C4
  HOR/CROF WF4 ....196 B4
  HOR/CROF WF4 ....197 H8
  HOR/CROF WF4 ....197 M6
  HOR/CROF WF4 ....218 F1
  HOR/CROF WF4 ....221 J8
  HORS LS18 ....85 K7
  HWTH BD22 ....78 B2
  HWTH BD22 ....78 H4
  IDLE BD10 ....83 J6
  IDLE BD10 ....83 L6
  ILK LS29 ....19 G5
  ILK LS29 ....39 L8
  ILK LS29 ....40 A3
  KBTN HD8 ....256 D4
  LM/WK BD12 ....148 E4
  LM/WK BD12 ....149 H2
  LUD/ILL HX2 ....144 F5
  LUD/ILL HX2 ....168 A1
  LVSG WF15 ....171 M3
  MAR/SLWT HD7 ....233 H2
  MSTN/BAR LS15 ....111 K5
  OT LS21 ....41 H5
  PDSY/CALV LS28 ....106 F8
  PONT WF8 ....180 F7
  PONT WF8 ....203 G1
  RPDN/SBR HX6 ....188 D3
  RTHW LS26 ....157 H5
  SCFT LS14 ....89 J6
  STKB/PEN S36 ....258 E7
  TAD LS24 ....71 K7
  WBY LS22 ....47 H6
  WHIT OL12 ....206 A6
  WKFDW/WTN WF2 ....176 A6
  WOR/ARM LS12 ....129 L1
  YEA LS19 ....84 B1
Green Lane Cl *HOR/CROF* WF4 ....196 B7
Green Lane Ter
  MAR/SLWT HD7 ....190 E8
Greenlawns Cl *HOLM/MEL* HD9 ....253 M1
Greenlay Dr *WKFDW/WTN* WF2 ....175 K4
Green Lea *RTHW* LS26 ....133 L8
Greenlea Av *YEA* LS19 ....62 B8
Green Lea La *BSPA/BRAM* LS23 ....49 G7
Greenlea Cl *YEA* LS19 ....84 B1
Greenlea Mt *YEA* LS19 ....62 B8
Greenlea Rd *YEA* LS19 ....62 B8
  YEA LS19 ....84 B1
Greenlees Cl *WHIT* OL12 ....206 B6
Greenlea St *MSTN* LS9 ....110 E4
Green Meadow *COL* BB8 ....74 D4
  WHIT OL12 ....206 F2
  WIL/AL BD15 ....102 F2
Greenmires La *OT* LS21 ....25 H6
Greenmoor Av
  EARD/LOFT WF3 ....154 E5
  WOR/ARM LS12 ....107 M7
Greenmoor Cl *EARD/LOFT* WF3 ....154 E5
Greenmoor Crs
  EARD/LOFT WF3 ....154 F6
Green Mt *BOW* * BD4 ....127 M3
  HUDE HD5 ....15 M7
  OSS * WF5 ....196 F2
Greenmount Ct
  BEE/HOL * LS11 ....131 K3
Greenmount La *BEE/HOL* LS11 ....8 E9
Greenmount Pl *BEE/HOL* LS11 ....8 E9
Green Mount Rd
  CUL/QBY BD13 ....103 G8
Greenmount St *BEE/HOL* LS11 ....8 E9
Greenmount Ter *BEE/HOL* LS11 ....8 E9
Green Pk *AL/HA/HU* LS17 ....88 A4
  WKFDE WF1 ....13 J2
Green Park Av *HIPP* HX3 ....168 E4
  OSS WF5 ....197 G2
Green Park Dr *HIPP* HX3 ....168 E4
Green Park Rd *HIPP* HX3 ....168 E4
Green Park St *HIPP* HX3 ....168 E3
Green Pasture Cl *OSM* LS9 ....110 E6
Green Pl *ECHL* * BD2 ....105 K4
Green Rd *BAIL* BD17 ....82 D4
  HDGY LS6 ....87 G6
  LVSG WF15 ....172 C1
  STKB/PEN S36 ....270 F4
Green Rw *RTHW* LS26 ....156 F5
Green Royd *GTL/HWG* HX4 ....168 B3
Greenroyd Av *CLECK* BD19 ....149 M4
  HIPP HX3 ....168 D3
Greenroyd Cl *HIPP* HX3 ....168 D4
Greenroyd Ct *PONT* WF8 ....203 L1
Greenroyd Crs *HFAX* * HX1 ....10 A2
Greenroyd Cft *HUDN* HD2 ....14 A1
Greenroyd Dr *AIRE* BD20 ....55 M2
Greenroyde *ROCH* * OL11 ....228 A1
Greenroyd La *LUD/ILL* HX2 ....146 A5
Greens End Rd
  HOLM/MEL HD9 ....234 F4
Greenset Vw *BSLYN/ROY* S71 ....243 G5
Greenside *CLECK* BD19 ....150 A7
  CUD/GR S72 ....244 D2
  DOD/DAR S75 ....242 E5
  HECK WF16 ....172 E2
  HOR/CROF WF4 ....222 D6
  KBTN HD8 ....239 G7
  KBTN HD8 ....239 J8
  LM/WK BD12 ....149 J2
  PDSY/CALV LS28 ....106 F8
  STKB/PEN S36 ....258 C8
  WKFDW/WTN WF2 ....199 J7
Greenside Av *DOD/DAR* S75 ....242 E5
  HUDE HD5 ....215 J1
  WOR/ARM LS12 ....130 D1
Greenside Ct *HOR/CROF* WF4 ....200 D7
  MOR * LS27 ....129 M7
Greenside Crs *HUDE* HD5 ....215 J1
Greenside Dr *HUDE* HD5 ....215 J1
  WOR/ARM LS12 ....130 E1

Greenside Gv *PDSY/CALV* LS28 ....106 F3
Greenside La *CUL/QBY* BD13 ....79 M3
  GIR BD8 ....104 B7
Greenside Mt *MIRF* WF14 ....172 D7
Greenside Pk *HOR/CROF* WF4 ....200 D5
Greenside Pl *DOD/DAR* S75 ....242 D5
Green Side Rd *HUDS* HD4 ....237 H3
Greenside Rd *MIRF* WF14 ....172 D7
  WOR/ARM LS12 ....130 D1
Greenside Ter *WOR/ARM* LS12 ....130 D1
Greenside Wk *WOR/ARM* LS12 ....130 D1
Green's Sq *LUD/ILL* HX2 ....146 A6
Green St *BFD* BD1 ....5 K4
  CAS WF10 ....157 M5
  GTL/HWG HX4 ....190 D2
  HUD HD1 ....14 C5
  HWTH BD22 ....54 E3
  HWTH BD22 ....78 E8
  HWTH BD22 ....100 E4
Greensway *GFTH/SHER* LS25 ....113 J8
Green Sykes Rd *AIRE* BD20 ....56 B6
Green Ter *BEE/HOL* LS11 ....9 G7
  ECHL BD2 ....105 K4
Green Terrace Sq *HFAX* HX1 ....168 C4
Greenthorpe Hl *BRAM* LS13 ....108 A7
Greenthorpe Mt *BRAM* LS13 ....108 A6
Greenthorpe Rd
  WOR/ARM LS12 ....108 A7
Greenthorpe St *BRAM* LS13 ....108 A7
Greenthorpe Wk *BRAM* LS13 ....108 A6
Greenthwaite Cl *KGHY* BD21 ....2 D1
Greenton Av *CLECK* BD19 ....149 G5
Greenton Crs *CUL/QBY* BD13 ....124 F6
Greentop *HOR/CROF* WF4 ....200 D7
  PDSY/CALV LS28 ....106 F3
Green Top *WOR/ARM* LS12 ....130 D1
Green Top Gdns
  WOR/ARM LS12 ....130 D1
Green Top St *GIR* BD8 ....104 A7
Greenups Ter *RPDN/SBR* HX6 ....167 K2
Green Vw *HDGY* LS6 ....87 G7
  SCFT LS14 ....67 L6
Greenview Cl *OSM* LS9 ....110 E4
Greenview Ct *OSM* LS9 ....110 E4
Green View Ct *RHAY* LS8 ....88 C6
Greenville Av *WOR/ARM* LS12 ....130 D1
Greenville Dr *LM/WK* BD12 ....127 G3
Greenville Gdns
  WOR/ARM LS12 ....130 D1
The Greenway *BFDE* BD3 ....5 L3
Green Wy *AIRE* BD20 ....34 C3
  LUD/ILL HX2 ....124 A6
  SCFT LS14 ....67 L6
Greenway *GSLY* LS20 ....61 L7
  HOLM/MEL HD9 ....236 D5
  MAR/SLWT HD7 ....213 H1
  MSTN/BAR LS15 ....111 L5
  ROY/SHW OL2 ....229 H5
Greenway Cl *MSTN/BAR* LS15 ....111 L5
Greenway Dr *WIL/AL* BD15 ....103 K7
Greenway Rd *WBOW* BD5 ....127 G4
Greenwell Ct *OSM* LS9 ....110 E6
Greenwell Rw *CLAY* BD14 ....125 K2
Greenwood Av *EARL* WF12 ....174 A7
  ECHL BD2 ....105 J1
  HEM/SK/SE WF9 ....225 L1
Greenwood Cl *NORM* WF6 ....178 D7
Greenwood Dr *ECHL* BD2 ....105 J2
  HDGY LS6 ....87 G6
Greenwood Mt *ECHL* BD2 ....105 J2
  HDGY LS6 ....87 G6
Green Wood Pk *HDGY* LS6 ....87 G6
Greenwood Rd *BAIL* BD17 ....82 D5
  EARD/LOFT WF3 ....153 H1
  WKFDE WF1 ....13 H1
Greenwood Rw
  PDSY/CALV LS28 ....107 H7
Greenwood St *DEWS* WF13 ....173 K6
  HBR HX7 ....143 J3
  HUDS HD4 ....214 C2
  LIT OL15 ....207 K1
  MILN OL16 ....206 B7
Greenwood Ter *BSLY* LS70 ....261 G4
Greetland Rd *GTL/HWG* HX4 ....189 J1
Greggs Ct *BSLY* LS70 ....261 M4
Gregory Ct *CLAY* BD14 ....125 L2
Gregory Crs *GTHN* BD7 ....126 A4
Gregory Dr *KBTN* HD8 ....216 B8
Gregory La *HUDE* HD5 ....194 C7
Gregory Rd *CAS* WF10 ....180 A1
Gregory Springs La
  MIRF WF14 ....194 C4
Gregory Springs Mt
  MIRF WF14 ....194 D4
Gregory Springs Rd
  MIRF WF14 ....194 D3
Gregory St *BTLY* * WF17 ....174 A1
Grenfell Dr *BFDE* BD3 ....105 M4
Grenfell Rd *BFDE* BD3 ....105 M6
Grenfell Ter *BFDE* BD3 ....105 M6
Grenley St *KNOT* WF11 ....182 C2
Grenville Pl *DOD/DAR* S75 ....260 E3
Grenville Wk *HOR/CROF* WF4 ....220 B3
Gresham Av *ECHL* BD2 ....105 H2
Gresley Rd *KGHY* BD21 ....3 H5
Grey Cl *WKFDE* WF1 ....176 D3
Grey Ct *WKFDE* WF1 ....176 D3
Greycourt Cl *ECHL* BD2 ....83 J8
  HFAX HX1 ....10 C8
Greyfriars Av *HUDN* HD2 ....193 G2
Greyfriar Wk *GTHN* BD7 ....126 A3
Grey Gables *HOR/CROF* WF4 ....197 G8
Grey Scar Rd *HWTH* BD22 ....78 C4
Greyshiels Av *HDGY* LS6 ....108 C2
Greystone Av *ELL* HX5 ....191 G1
Greystone Cl *BSPA/BRAM* LS23 ....49 G7
  ILK LS29 ....40 A4
Greystone Ct *BRIG* HD6 ....170 C7
Greystone Crs *IDLE* BD10 ....83 L8
Grey Stone La *TOD* OL14 ....142 B6
Greystone Mt *MSTN/BAR* LS15 ....111 G7
Greystone Pk *GFTH/SHER* LS25 ....92 A5
Greystones Cl *GFTH/SHER* LS25 ....92 A5
Greystones Ct *RHAY* LS8 ....88 C7
Greystones Dr *HWTH* BD22 ....79 H3
  OSS WF5 ....197 G2
Grey Stones La *HBR* HX7 ....121 K1

Greystones La HWTH BD22 55 M8
Greystones Mt HWTH BD22 79 H4
Greystones Ri HWTH BD22 79 H3
Greystones Rd LUD/ILL HX2 145 G7
Grey St WKFDE WF1 176 D3
Griffe Dr LM/WK BD12 148 E5
Griffe Gdns HWTH BD22 78 D4
Griffe Head Crs LM/WK * BD12 148 E4
Griffe Head Rd LM/WK BD12 148 E4
Griffe Rd HWTH BD22 77 M6
LM/WK BD12 148 E4
Griff House La EARD/LOFT WF3 153 K6
Grime La HOLM/MEL HD9 255 L5
HOR/CROF WF4 200 D3
Grimescar Mdw HUDN HD2 191 M4
Grimescar Rd HUDW HD3 191 L3
Grimethorpe St
HEM/SK/SE WF9 247 H4
Grimpit Hl HOR/CROF * WF4 221 J8
Grimscar Av HUDN HD2 192 B5
Grimthorpe Av HDGY * LS6 108 E1
Grimthorpe Pl HDGY LS6 108 F1
Grimthorpe St HDGY LS6 108 F1
Grimthorpe Ter HDGY LS6 108 F1
Grisedale Av HUDN HD2 192 B5
ROY/SHW OL2 228 E6
Grizedale Cl WBY LS22 29 K8
Grosmont Rd BRAM LS13 107 L4
Grosmont Ter BRAM LS13 107 L3
Grosvenor Av HEM/SK/SE WF9 225 J7
KBTN HD8 216 A3
PONT WF8 180 C5
SHPY BD18 82 B6
Grosvenor Dr BSLY S70 260 E5
Grosvenor Gdns AL/HA/HU LS17 43 L3
Grosvenor Hl CHAL LS7 7 G4
Grosvenor Mt HDGY LS6 109 H2
Grosvenor Pk CHAL LS7 87 L7
Grosvenor Park Gdns HDGY LS6 6 B1
Grosvenor Rd BTLY WF17 151 M8
GIR BD8 4 C2
HDGY LS6 6 B1
HUDE HD5 193 G8
SHPY BD18 82 B7
Grosvenor St COL BB8 74 B1
EARL WF12 173 L7
ELL HX5 169 H8
HECK WF16 172 F1
WKFDE WF1 13 L9
Grosvenor Ter GIR BD8 4 C2
HDGY LS6 109 H2
HECK * WF16 172 F2
HFAX * HX1 10 D6
WBY LS22 30 A8
Grosvenor Wy KBTN HD8 216 A3
Grouse Moor La
CUL/QBY BD13 124 E4
Grouse St KGHY BD21 3 H3
WHIT OL12 206 B5
The Grove AL/HA/HU LS17 46 D8
AL/HA/HU LS17 87 H1
BAIL BD17 82 E2
BGLY BD16 59 G8
BTLY WF17 151 J7
CUD/GR S72 244 D5
EARD/LOFT WF3 153 K6
GFTH/SHER LS25 135 J5
HECK WF16 150 E8
HEM/SK/SE WF9 247 H2
HIPP HX3 147 L6
HOLM/MEL HD9 235 H5
HOR/CROF WF4 222 C5
HORS LS18 85 K6
HUDN HD2 192 D4
IDLE BD10 83 K7
IDLE BD10 83 M7
ILK LS29 38 C2
NORM * WF6 178 D4
PDSY/CALV LS28 106 F7
ROY/SHW OL2 229 J8
RTHW LS26 134 D4
SHPY BD18 82 A7
SKP/WHF BD23 16 E3
WKFDW/WTN WF2 199 K7
YEA LS19 62 D8
YEA LS19 84 C2
Grove Av HDGY LS6 87 G8
HEM/SK/SE WF9 224 A8
HEM/SK/SE WF9 246 E4
HIPP HX3 146 B4
ILK LS29 38 B3
PDSY/CALV LS28 106 F7
PONT * WF8 181 G6
SHPY BD18 104 D1
Grove Cl CLECK BD19 150 D5
ECHL BD2 105 J2
STKB/PEN S36 270 F5
Grove Ct HDGY LS6 87 G8
HIPP HX3 146 C4
PDSY/CALV LS28 106 F7
Grove Crs BSPA/BRAM LS23 49 G7
GFTH/SHER LS25 138 A3
LUD/ILL HX2 144 F7
WKFDW/WTN WF2 199 K7
Grove Crs South
BSPA/BRAM LS23 49 G8
Grove Cft HIPP HX3 146 B4
Grove Dr HEM/SK/SE WF9 246 D4
HIPP HX3 146 B3
Grove Edge HIPP HX3 146 B4
Grove Farm Cl BHP/TINH LS16 86 B2
Grove Farm Crs BHP/TINH LS16 86 A3
Grove Farm Cft BHP/TINH LS16 86 A2
Grove Farm Dr BHP/TINH LS16 86 A2
Grove Gdns BSPA/BRAM LS23 49 H7
EARL WF12 174 C8
HDGY LS6 87 G8
HIPP HX3 146 C4
Grovehall Av BEE/HOL LS11 131 H5
Grovehall Dr BEE/HOL LS11 131 H4
Grovehall La PONT WF8 181 K6
Grovehall Pde BEE/HOL LS11 131 H5
Grovehall Rd BEE/HOL LS11 131 H5
Grove Head HEM/SK/SE WF9 246 D4
Grove House Crs ECHL BD2 105 J2
Grove House Dr ECHL BD2 105 J3
Grove House Rd ECHL BD2 105 J2
Grovelands ECHL BD2 105 J3
Grove La CLECK BD19 150 D5
HDGY LS6 109 G1
HEM/SK/SE WF9 224 A8
HEM/SK/SE WF9 225 G3
HEM/SK/SE WF9 246 D4
KNOT WF11 182 A2
Grove Lea Cl HEM/SK/SE WF9 224 A8
Grove Lea Crs PONT WF8 181 G7
Grove Lea Wk PONT WF8 181 G7
Grove Marsh Lea
HEM/SK/SE * WF9 224 B7
Grove Mt HEM/SK/SE WF9 246 D4
PONT * WF8 181 G6
Grove Nook HUDW HD3 191 H8
Grove Pk HIPP HX3 146 B3
HOR/CROF WF4 197 M8
Grove Pl BSPA/BRAM LS23 49 G7
HEM/SK/SE WF9 224 A8
Grove Ri AL/HA/HU LS17 87 H1
PONT * WF8 181 G6
Grove Rd BSPA/BRAM LS23 49 G7
DOD/DAR * S75 242 C5
ELL HX5 169 J7
HBR HX7 143 J2
HDGY LS6 87 G8
HECK WF16 173 G2
HOR/CROF WF4 197 J5
HORS LS18 85 K6
HUD HD1 15 H4
ILK LS29 38 A2
ILK LS29 61 J2
MID LS10 9 L9
MSTN/BAR LS15 111 J7
PDSY/CALV LS28 106 F7
PONT WF8 180 F6
SHPY BD18 104 D1
WKFDE WF1 12 F4
Grove Royd HIPP HX3 146 C4
Groves Hall Rd DEWS WF13 173 H6
Grove Sq CLECK * BD19 150 D5
HIPP HX3 146 B4
Grove St BRIG HD6 170 D4
BSLYN/ROY S71 261 J5
DEWS WF13 173 L6
HECK WF16 173 G2
HEM/SK/SE WF9 246 D4
HUDW HD3 191 G8
LDS LS1 6 C9
LVSG WF15 172 D4
MAR/SLWT HD7 212 B5
MIRF WF14 172 D8
OSS WF5 196 F2
PDSY/CALV * LS28 107 G4
ROCH OL11 228 A1
RPDN/SBR HX6 167 M2
WKFDE WF1 13 G4
Grove St South HFAX * HX1 10 B6
Grove Ter GTHN * BD7 4 D7
HBR HX7 144 A6
HEM/SK/SE WF9 224 A8
PDSY/CALV LS28 106 F7
Groveville HIPP HX3 147 L5
Groveway ECHL BD2 105 J2
Grove Wy HEM/SK/SE WF9 246 D4
Grovewood HDGY LS6 86 F8
Grudgby La STKB/PEN S36 271 J8
Grunberg Rd HDGY LS6 108 F1
Grunberg St HDGY * LS6 108 F1
Guard House Av HWTH BD22 2 C5
Guard House Dr HWTH BD22 2 C4
Guard House Gv HWTH BD22 2 B5
Guard House Rd HWTH BD22 2 C5
Guernsey Rd EARL WF12 174 B4
Guest La DOD/DAR S75 259 J6
Guest Rd DOD/DAR S75 260 F3
Guildford Rd BSLYN/ROY S71 243 K2
Guildford St HBR HX7 143 J4
MILN OL16 206 C7
OSS WF5 196 F2
Guild Wy LUD/ILL HX2 145 K8
Guillemot Ap MOR LS27 152 F3
Guiseley Dr ILK LS29 61 K4
The Gully KBTN HD8 255 L1
Gulley Rd OSM LS9 132 F3
Gully Ter HOLM/MEL HD9 254 D2
Gunson Crs OSS WF5 174 F8
Gunter Rd WBY LS22 30 C8
Gunthwaite La KBTN HD8 257 H3
Gunthwaite Top KBTN * HD8 257 H3
Gurbax Ct BFDE BD3 106 A7
Gurney Cl WBOW BD5 126 F3
Guygroft OT LS21 41 H6
Guys Cft WKFDW/WTN WF2 197 L2
Guy St BOW BD4 5 G8
Gwyn Holme DEWS * WF13 173 H4
Gwynne Av BFDE BD3 106 A5
Gynn La HOLM/MEL HD9 236 C2
Gypsy Ct CAS WF10 158 E8
Gypsy La CAS WF10 158 E8
Gypsy Wood Cl
MSTN/BAR LS15 111 M7
Gypsy Wood Crest
MSTN/BAR LS15 111 M7

H

Hacking La HEM/SK/SE WF9 247 K3
Hackings Av STKB/PEN S36 270 E5
Hadassah St HIPP HX3 168 F2
Haddingley La KBTN HD8 255 M3
Haddlesey Rd KNOT WF11 161 J4
Haddon Av BULY LS4 108 E4
HIPP HX3 168 E3
Haddon Cl CLECK BD19 150 D6
DOD/DAR S75 260 A7
HEM/SK/SE WF9 247 J1
Haddon Pl BULY LS4 108 E4
Haddon Rd BSLYN/ROY S71 243 K8
BULY LS4 108 F4
Haddon St ROCH OL11 228 A1
Haddon Wy ROY/SHW OL2 229 L6
Hadfield Rd HECK WF16 172 F1
Hadleigh Ct AL/HA/HU LS17 87 M4
Hadleigh Ri PONT WF8 180 D8
Hadrian Cl CAS WF10 158 E5
Hadrian's Cl HUDW HD3 191 G6
PONT WF8 225 J1
Hag Farm Rd ILK LS29 40 A7
Hagg La GFTH/SHER LS25 139 H2
MIRF WF14 194 D3
Haggroyd La HOLM/MEL HD9 236 D4
Haggs Hill Rd OSS WF5 197 J1
Haggs La WKFDW/WTN WF2 197 L1
Haggs Rd PBR HG3 27 K1
Hagg Wood Rd
HOLM/MEL HD9 236 D4
Hag Hill La KBTN HD8 217 M8
Hag La HIPP HX3 146 E3
Hague Crs HEM/SK/SE WF9 246 A1
Hague Park Cl
HEM/SK/SE * WF9 246 D3
Hague Park La
HEM/SK/SE WF9 246 D3
Hague Park Wk
HEM/SK/SE WF9 246 D3
Hague Ter HEM/SK/SE WF9 224 A8
Haigh Av RTHW LS26 132 F7
Haigh Beck Vw IDLE BD10 83 L7
Haigh Cl STKB/PEN S36 258 B8
Haigh Cnr IDLE BD10 83 M7
Haigh Cft BSLYN/ROY S71 243 K2
Haigh Cross HUDW * HD3 191 H4
Haigh Fold ECHL BD2 105 L3
Haigh Gdns RTHW LS26 132 E7
Haigh Hall IDLE BD10 83 M7
Haigh La DOD/DAR S75 241 K2
HIPP HX3 168 F2
HOLM/MEL HD9 236 B6
HOR/CROF WF4 217 J4
STKB/PEN S36 258 C7
Haigh Ms DOD/DAR * S75 241 L1
Haigh Moor Av
EARD/LOFT WF3 153 G8
Haigh Moor Crs
EARD/LOFT WF3 153 G8
Haigh Moor Rd
EARD/LOFT WF3 175 G1
Haigh Moor St WKFDE WF1 176 F6
Haigh Moor Vw
EARD/LOFT WF3 153 G8
Haigh Moor Wy
BSLYN/ROY S71 243 K2
Haigh Park Rd MID LS10 132 D4
Haigh Rd RTHW LS26 133 H8
Haighside RTHW LS26 132 E8
Haighside Cl RTHW LS26 132 E8
Haighside Dr RTHW LS26 132 E8
Haighside Wy RTHW LS26 132 E8
Haighs Sq HUDE HD5 15 M5
Haigh St BOW BD4 127 K3
BRIG HD6 170 C3
GTL/HWG HX4 168 C7
HFAX HX1 10 B4
HUDS HD4 214 A3
ROCH OL11 206 C8
Haigh Ter RTHW LS26 132 E7
Haigh Vw RTHW LS26 132 E7
Haigh Wood Crs BHP/TINH LS16 85 M3
Haigh Wood Gn
BHP/TINH * LS16 85 M4
Haigh Wood Rd BHP/TINH LS16 85 L3
Hailhead Dr PONT WF8 181 H5
Haincliffe Rd KGHY BD21 79 K2
Haines Pk RHAY * LS8 7 L4
Hainsworth Moor Crs
CUL/QBY BD13 124 F6
Hainsworth Moor Dr
CUL/QBY BD13 124 F6
Hainsworth Moor Garth
CUL/QBY BD13 124 F6
Hainsworth Moor Gv
CUL/QBY BD13 124 F6
Hainsworth Moor Vw
CUL/QBY BD13 124 F6
Hainsworth Rd AIRE BD20 36 B6
Hainsworth Sq
PDSY/CALV LS28 106 F3
Hainsworth St RTHW LS26 155 G2
WOR/ARM * LS12 109 G8
Hainworth Crag Rd KGHY BD21 79 J4
Hainworth La KGHY BD21 79 K3
Hainworth Rd KGHY BD21 79 K3
Hainworth Wood Rd
KGHY BD21 79 K2
Hainworth Wood Rd North
KGHY BD21 3 G9
Haise Mt DOD/DAR S75 242 C5
Halcyon Hl CHAL LS7 87 L6
Halcyon Wy WBOW BD5 126 E3
Haldane Cl CUD/GR S72 245 H3
Haldane Crs WKFDE WF1 177 G6
Hales Rd WOR/ARM LS12 130 D1
Halesworth Crs BOW BD4 128 A3
Haley Ct HIPP HX3 11 G3
Haley Hl HFAX HX1 11 G3
Half Acre Rd CUL/QBY BD13 102 D7
Half House La BRIG HD6 169 M1
Half Mile BRAM LS13 107 G4
Half Mile Cl PDSY/CALV LS28 107 H4
Half Mile Ct PDSY/CALV LS28 107 H4
Half Mile Gdns BRAM LS13 107 H4
Half Mile Gn PDSY/CALV LS28 107 H4
Half Mile La BRAM LS13 107 H3
Half Moon La WKFDE WF1 177 K7
Half Moon St HUD HD1 14 F7
Halfpenny La FEA/AMT WF7 180 B8
Half St KGHY BD21 2 F3
Halifax La HBR HX7 142 A2
LUD/ILL HX2 145 G6
Halifax Old Rd HIPP HX3 147 K6
HUDN HD2 192 B4
Halifax Rd BRFD/BLYE BB10 96 D5
BRIG HD6 170 C4
CLECK BD19 149 G7
CUL/QBY BD13 79 M8
CUL/QBY BD13 124 E8
CUL/QBY BD13 124 A2
DEWS WF13 173 H3
ELL HX5 169 G7
HIPP HX3 147 K2
HUDW HD3 191 L5
HWTH BD22 79 H7
LIT OL15 186 B7
LUD/ILL HX2 123 M2
LVSG WF15 171 L1
MAR/SLWT HD7 212 D1
MILN OL16 206 D5
RPDN/SBR HX6 188 F2
STKB/PEN S36 257 L8
TOD OL14 140 B8
TOD OL14 163 L1
WBSY BD6 126 B7
Halifax St BSLYN/ROY S71 261 G2
Haliwell St LIT OL15 207 L1
Hallam La OT LS21 40 C1
Hallamshire Ms
WKFDW/WTN WF2 197 L2
Hallam's Yd SKP/WHF BD23 16 B2
Hallas Gv HUDE HD5 215 G1
Hallas La CUL/QBY BD13 80 B8
KBTN HD8 216 C8
Hallas Rd KBTN HD8 216 B8
Hall Av AIRE BD20 55 M2
HUD HD1 14 C9
IDLE BD10 105 M1
Hall Balk La DOD/DAR S75 260 F3
Hallbank Cl WBOW BD5 126 F5
Hall Bank Dr BGLY BD16 81 H2
Hallbank Dr WBOW BD5 126 F5
Hall Bank La HBR HX7 144 A6
Hall Bower La HUDS HD4 214 D6
Hallcliffe BAIL BD17 82 F2
Hall Cliffe Ct HOR/CROF WF4 197 J4
Hall Cliffe Crs HOR/CROF WF4 197 J4
Hall Cliffe Gv HOR/CROF WF4 197 K4
Hall Cliffe Ri HOR/CROF WF4 197 K4
Hall Cliffe Rd HOR/CROF WF4 197 K4
Hall Cl AIRE BD20 55 L2
BHP/TINH LS16 64 A2
BSPA/BRAM LS23 49 G7
HIPP HX3 147 J3
HOLM/MEL HD9 235 H4
ILK LS29 39 M5
LVSG WF15 172 C3
Hall Ct KNOT WF11 159 L6
Hall Cft HOR/CROF WF4 197 G8
SKP/WHF BD23 16 A2
Hallcroft Cl HOR/CROF WF4 197 K5
Hallcroft Dr HOR/CROF WF4 197 K6
ILK LS29 19 K7
Hallcroft Gdns MILN OL16 207 G8
Hallcroft Ri BSLYN/ROY S71 243 K3
Hall Cross Gv HUDS HD4 214 E3
Hall Cross Rd HUDE HD5 214 E3
Hall Dr AIRE BD20 55 M2
BHP/TINH LS16 64 A2
ILK LS29 39 M5
LVSG WF15 172 D4
Hall Farm Gv STKB/PEN S36 258 C8
Hall Farm Pk GFTH/SHER LS25 114 B6
Hallfield Av GFTH/SHER LS25 114 B7
Hallfield Crs WBY LS22 48 B1
Hallfield Dr BAIL BD17 82 E3
Hall Field La HOR/CROF WF4 222 C7
Hallfield La WBY LS22 30 B8
Hallfield Pl BFD BD1 4 E3
Hallfield Rd GIR BD8 4 D4
Hallfield St BFD BD1 4 E4
Hallfield Ter GFTH/SHER LS25 114 B7
Hall Gdns AIRE BD20 35 G5
Hall Garth Cl TAD LS24 95 G1
Hall Garth Rd PONT WF8 225 J1
Hall Ga STKB/PEN S36 270 F3
Hall Green La AL/HA/HU LS17 26 A7
GTL/HWG HX4 188 F6
Hall Gv DOD/DAR S75 242 E5
HDGY LS6 6 A4
Halliday Av WOR/ARM LS12 108 C6
Halliday Dr WOR/ARM LS12 108 C6
Halliday Gv WOR/ARM LS12 108 C6
Halliday Mt WOR/ARM * LS12 108 C6
Halliday Pl WOR/ARM LS12 108 C6
Halliday Rd GFTH/SHER LS25 113 G7
WOR/ARM LS12 108 C6
Halliday St PDSY/CALV LS28 107 G6
Hallilley St DEWS WF13 173 K6
Hall Ing La HOLM/MEL HD9 236 D1
Halling Pl TOD OL14 163 J2
Hall Ing Rd HOLM/MEL HD9 236 F2
Hall Ings BFD BD1 5 G6
HIPP HX3 169 J3
Halliwell St MILN OL16 207 G7
WHIT OL12 206 A6
Hall La BHP/TINH LS16 64 A8
BOW BD4 5 H9
CAS WF10 136 B8
CHAL LS7 109 M1
EARL WF12 196 A4
GFTH/SHER LS25 137 H1
HEM/SK/SE WF9 225 K8
HIPP HX3 147 H2
HOR/CROF WF4 220 B2
HORS LS18 85 J5
KBTN HD8 216 A7
MAR/SLWT HD7 190 C8
OT LS21 22 B8
OT LS21 42 C4
SHPY BD18 82 E6
TAD LS24 117 G1
WOR/ARM LS12 107 L8
WOR/ARM LS12 108 F7
Hall Lee Rd HUDW HD3 191 L5
Hall Mdw COL BB8 74 D3
Hall Ms BSPA/BRAM LS23 49 G7
Hall Orchards Av WBY LS22 30 B8
The Hallows KGHY BD21 2 C2
Hallowes Gv CUL/QBY BD13 101 M1
Hallowes Park Rd
CUL/QBY BD13 101 M1
Hallows Ct HUDE * HD5 215 H3
Hallows Rd KGHY BD21 3 M1
Hall Park Av HOR/CROF WF4 200 B4
HORS LS18 85 K5
LVSG WF15 172 C4
Hall Park Cl HORS LS18 85 J5
Hall Park Ct GFTH/SHER LS25 135 K5
Hall Park Cft GFTH/SHER LS25 135 K6
Hall Park Garth HORS LS18 85 J5
Hall Park Mdw
GFTH/SHER LS25 135 K6
Hall Park Mt HORS * LS18 85 J5
Hall Park Orch
GFTH/SHER LS25 135 J6
Hall Park Ri GFTH/SHER * LS25 135 K5
HORS LS18 85 J5
Hall Park Rd BSPA/BRAM LS23 49 K2
Hall Pl BSLYN/ROY S71 261 L2
OSM LS9 110 B7
Hall Ri BHP/TINH LS16 64 A3
ILK LS29 39 M5
Hall Rise Cl BHP/TINH LS16 64 A3
Hall Rise Cft BHP/TINH LS16 64 A3
Hall Rd COL BB8 74 D3
IDLE BD10 105 M1
RTHW LS26 134 D5
WKFDW/WTN WF2 197 M2
WOR/ARM LS12 108 E7
Hall Royd SHPY BD18 82 D7
Hallroyd Crs TOD OL14 163 L1
Hall Royd La DOD/DAR S75 259 J8
Hallroyd Pl TOD * OL14 163 L1
Hallroyd Rd TOD OL14 141 L8
Hall Royd Wk DOD/DAR S75 259 J8
Halls La CUL/QBY BD13 102 A1
Hall Stone Ct HIPP * HX3 147 L1
Hall St AIRE BD20 34 F7
BRIG HD6 170 D4
FEA/AMT WF7 202 A2
HFAX HX1 10 F5
HUDW HD3 191 H7
HWTH BD22 78 E8
HWTH BD22 78 F3
WBSY BD6 126 E5
Hall St North HIPP HX3 146 D4
Hall Ter AIRE * BD20 58 B5
Hall Wy AIRE BD20 55 L2
Hallwood Gn IDLE BD10 106 A1
Halstead Dr ILK LS29 40 C8
Halstead Gv DOD/DAR S75 242 C4
Halstead La HUDS HD4 237 H6
Halstead Pl GTHN BD7 126 C3
Halsteads Wy AIRE BD20 35 K8
Halton Cl HUDE HD5 215 H2
Halton Moor Av OSM LS9 110 F7
Halton Moor Rd OSM LS9 110 F8
Halton Pl GTHN BD7 126 D3
Halton St FEA/AMT WF7 179 M7
The Hame GTL/HWG * HX4 190 B3
Hamber Cote La AIRE BD20 36 B4
Hamble Ct DOD/DAR * S75 242 E6
Hambledon Av BOW BD4 127 K5
HOLM/MEL HD9 235 H5
Hambleton Bank LUD/ILL HX2 145 K1
Hambleton Cl DOD/DAR S75 260 D4
Hambleton Crs LUD/ILL HX2 145 K1
Hambleton Dr LUD/ILL HX2 145 J1
Hambleton St WKFDE WF1 176 F7
Hamel Ri HEM/SK/SE WF9 223 M8
Hamer Hall Crs WHIT OL12 206 D4
Hamer La MILN OL16 206 D5
Hamilton Av CHAL LS7 7 L1
Hamilton Ct NORM WF6 178 D3
Hamilton Gdns CHAL LS7 7 K2
Hamilton Pl CHAL LS7 7 L2
Hamilton Ter CHAL LS7 7 M2
Hamilton Vw CHAL LS7 7 L1
Hammer La HOR/CROF WF4 200 D2
Hammerstone Leach La
ELL HX5 190 F1
Hammerstones Rd ELL HX5 168 F8
Hammerton Dr
GFTH/SHER LS25 135 J1
Hammerton Farm Av
HOR/CROF WF4 222 D5
Hammerton Gv
PDSY/CALV LS28 107 H7
Hammerton Rd HUDN HD2 192 C4
Hammerton St BFDE BD3 5 J7
PDSY/CALV LS28 107 G7
Hammond Crs BIRK/DRI BD11 128 F7
Hammond Pl HTON BD9 104 C3
Hammond Rd KNOT WF11 181 M3
Hammond St HFAX HX1 10 B7
HUDN HD2 192 D5
OSM * LS9 9 M4
Hammonds Yd HUD * HD1 14 F7
Hamm Strasse BFD BD1 4 F4
Hampden Cl KNOT WF11 181 K1
Hampden Pl HFAX HX1 10 E6
WBOW BD5 126 F2
Hampden Rd ROY/SHW OL2 229 M8
Hampden St WBOW BD5 126 F2
Hamper La STKB/PEN S36 258 B8
Hampole Balk AWLS/ASK DN6 249 H5
Hampole Field La
AWLS/ASK DN6 248 B5
Hampshire Cl ILK LS29 38 F2
PONT WF8 181 G3
Hampshire St HUDE HD5 15 L7
Hampson St BTLY WF17 151 J7
Hampton Pl IDLE BD10 83 K6
OSM LS9 110 B7
Hampton St HFAX HX1 10 A9
Hampton Ter OSM LS9 110 B7
Hamworth Dr HWTH BD22 78 F4
Hamza St BTLY WF17 173 K2
Hanbury Cl BSLYN/ROY S71 261 M2
Hanbury Gdns
GFTH/SHER LS25 113 H6
Hanby Av NORM WF6 178 B3
Hand Bank La MIRF WF14 194 C4
Hand Carr La LUD/ILL HX2 144 D7
Handel St GTHN BD7 4 B5
MAR/SLWT HD7 212 F2
Handel Ter HUDE * HD5 15 L8
Handsworth Rd
WKFDW/WTN WF2 220 C2
Hanging Chadder La
ROY/SHW OL2 228 E7
Hanging Gate La HWTH BD22 100 C1
Hangingroyd Cl HBR HX7 143 J3
Hangingroyd La HBR HX7 143 J3
Hangingroyd Rd HBR HX7 143 J3
Hanging Stone Rd HUDS HD4 214 B7
Hangingstone Rd ILK LS29 38 F4
Hanging Stones La
RPDN/SBR HX6 189 G1
Hanging Wood Wy
CLECK BD19 149 L4

Hangthwaite Rd
AWLS/ASK DN6 ....249 M7
Hanley Rd MOR LS27 ....152 C3
Hannah Ct LM/WK BD12 ......148 E3
Hannas Royd DOD/DAR S75 ...260 C7
Hannerton Rd ROY/SHW OL2 ...229 M6
Hanover Av BVRD LS3 ....6 C7
Hanover Cl GIR BD8 ....104 C5
Hanover Crs PONT WF8 ....202 E1
Hanover Gdns DEWS WF13 ......173 K6
WBOW * BD5 ....126 F1
Hanover La BVRD LS3 ....6 D8
Hanover Mt BVRD LS3 ....6 B7
Hanover Pl BTLY WF17 ....173 M1
KNOT WF11 ....159 L5
Hanover Sq BFD BD1 ....4 D3
BVRD LS3 ....6 C7
Hanover St AIRE BD20 ....34 F5
BTLY WF17 ....173 L1
DEWS WF13 ....173 K6
HFAX HX1 ....10 F7
KGHY BD21 ....3 G5
LIT OL15 ....207 J1
RPDN/SBR HX6 ....167 M1
WKFDW/WTN WF2 ....12 A4
Hanover Wk LDS * LS1 ....6 D8
ILK LS29 ....40 C7
Hansby Av SCFT LS14 ....111 K1
Hansby Bank SCFT LS14 ....111 K1
Hansby Cl SCFT LS14 ....111 K1
Hansby Dr SCFT LS14 ....111 K1
Hansby Gdns SCFT LS14 ....111 K1
Hansby Ga SCFT LS14 ....111 K1
Hansby Pl SCFT LS14 ....111 K2
Hanson Av NORM WF6 ....178 D5
Hanson Ct LM/WK BD12 ....148 E4
Hanson Fold LM/WK BD12 ......148 E3
Hanson La HFAX HX1 ....10 C5
HUDS HD4 ....214 A4
Hanson Mt LM/WK BD12 ....148 E4
Hanson Rd BRIG HD6 ....170 A6
HOLM/MEL HD9 ....234 E5
Hanson St BSLY S70 ....261 H5
Hanworth Rd LM/WK BD12 ......126 E8
Harbeck Dr BTLY WF17 ....80 D6
Harborough Hill Rd
BSLYN/ROY S71 ....261 H4
Harbour Crs WBSY BD6 ....126 C6
Harbour La MILN OL16 ....229 H1
Harbour La North MILN OL16 ...207 H8
Harbour Pk WBSY BD6 ....126 B7
Harbour Rd WBSY BD6 ....126 C7
Harclo Rd KGHY BD21 ....3 L2
Harcourt Av CUL/QBY BD13 ......102 F7
Harcourt Dr ILK LS29 ....19 H5
MOR LS27 ....152 B1
Harcourt Pl LDS LS1 ....6 C9
Harcourt St BOW BD4 ....127 K3
WKFDW/WTN WF2 ....198 B1
Hardaker La BAIL * BD17 ....82 C4
Hardakers Ap FEA/AMT WF7 ....224 E1
Hardaker's La FEA/AMT WF7 .....202 A8
Hardaker St GIR * BD8 ....4 C4
Hardcastle Av PONT WF8 ....180 E5
Hardcastle La HOR/CROF WF4 ...217 M3
Harden Brow La BGLY BD16 ......80 C5
Harden Cl DOD/DAR S75 ....260 C4
STKB/PEN S36 ....270 F4
Harden Gv IDLE BD10 ....106 A3
KGHY BD21 ....3 M9
Harden Hill Rd HOLM/MEL HD9 ..235 G6
Harden Hills ROY/SHW OL2 .....229 M6
Harden La BGLY BD16 ....80 D6
Harden Moss Rd
HOLM/MEL HD9 ....234 F7
Harden Rd BGLY BD16 ....80 C5
KGHY BD21 ....3 M9
Hardgate La HWTH BD22 ....79 H8
Hardie Rd HOR/CROF WF4 ......222 E5
Hardings La AIRE BD20 ....35 G7
ILK LS29 ....20 C5
Hard Ings Rd KGHY BD21 ....3 H1
Hardistry Dr PONT WF8 ....180 D4
Hardknot Cl CTHN BD7 ....126 A3
Hard La WHIT OL12 ....184 C6
Hard Nese La HWTH BD22 ....100 B5
Hard Platts La GTL/HWG HX4 ...190 B3
Hardrow Gn WOR/ARM LS12 ...130 F1
Hardrow Gv WOR/ARM LS12 ...130 E1
Hardrow Rd WOR/ARM LS12 ...130 E1
Hardrow Ter WOR/ARM * LS12 ..130 F1
Hardwick Cl HOR/CROF WF4 ....222 C6
Hardwick Cft PONT WF8 ....180 E7
Hardwick Crs BSLYN/ROY S71 ...243 J7
PONT WF8 ....202 F1
Hardwick Cft CHAL * LS7 ....87 M8
Hardwick St ROCH OL11 ....228 A2
Hardwick Gv DOD/DAR S75 .....260 B8
Hardwick La HOR/CROF WF4 ....201 K5
Hardwick Rd FEA/AMT WF7 .....201 L2
PONT WF8 ....180 E8
PONT WF8 ....203 H3
Hardwick St KGHY BD21 ....3 G2
Hardy Av MOR LS27 ....130 E6
WBSY BD6 ....126 E6
Hardy Cl ROCH OL11 ....228 B3
Hardy Ct MOR LS27 ....152 D2
Hardy Cft WKFDE WF1 ....13 G3
Hardy Gv BEE/HOL LS11 ....131 J3
Hardy Pl BRIG HD6 ....170 A1
Hardy St BEE/HOL LS11 ....131 J3
BOW BD4 ....5 G8
BRIG HD6 ....170 D3
MOR LS27 ....152 D2
Hardy Ter BEE/HOL LS11 ....131 J3
Hardy Vw BEE/HOL LS11 ....131 J3
Hareball Av WKFDW/WTN WF2 ..176 A1
Harecroft Rd OT LS21 ....41 J5
Hare Farm Av WOR/ARM LS12 ..107 M7
Hare Farm Cl WOR/ARM LS12 ...107 M7
Harefield Av ROCH OL11 ....228 B1
Harefield East
MSTN/BAR LS15 ....111 G7
Harefield Dr BTLY WF17 ....151 J3
Harefield Rd PONT WF8 ....181 H6
Harefield West
MSTN/BAR LS15 ....111 G7

Harefield Pk HUDN HD2 ....191 L4
Harehill Av TOD OL14 ....141 J8
Harehill Cl IDLE BD10 ....83 K5
Harehill Rd IDLE BD10 ....83 K5
Hare Hill Rd LIT OL15 ....185 J8
Harehills Av RHAY LS8 ....110 B2
Harehills La HWTH BD22 ....77 L5
OSM LS9 ....110 D4
Harehills Park Av OSM * LS9 ....110 D4
Harehills Park Ter OSM LS9 ......110 D4
Harehills Park Vw OSM LS9 ......110 D4
Harehills Pl RHAY LS8 ....110 B3
Harehills Rd RHAY LS8 ....110 B2
Harehill St TOD OL14 ....141 J8
Hare La PDSY/CALV LS28 ....129 G1
Hare Park Av LVSG WF15 ....171 L2
Hare Park Cl LVSG WF15 ....171 L1
Hare Park La HOR/CROF WF4 ....200 B7
LVSG WF15 ....171 L2
Hare Park Mt WOR/ARM LS12 ..107 L7
Hares Av RHAY LS8 ....110 B2
Hares Mt RHAY LS8 ....7 M1
Hares Rd RHAY LS8 ....7 M1
Hares Ter RHAY LS8 ....110 B2
Hare St HFAX HX1 ....10 B6
ROCH OL11 ....228 B1
Hares Vw RHAY LS8 ....110 B2
Harewood Av AIRE BD20 ....56 C1
AL/HA/HU LS17 ....45 K8
BSLY S70 ....260 D5
HECK WF16 ....173 C3
LUD/ILL HX2 ....145 M6
NORM WF6 ....178 E3
PONT WF8 ....181 C6
Harewood Cl KNOT WF11 ....181 L2
Harewood Crs HWTH BD22 ....79 C3
Harewood Dr
WKFDW/WTN WF2 ....175 M5
Harewood Ga AL/HA/HU LS17 ....45 J7
Harewood Gv AL/HA/HU LS17 ....45 K8
Harewood La HEM/SK/SE WF9 ..225 L6
PONT WF8 ....226 B4
Harewood Ms AL/HA/HU LS17 ....45 J7
PONT WF8 ....181 C6
Harewood Mt HEM/SK/SE WF9 ..235 H4
PONT WF8 ....181 C6
Harewood Pl LUD/ILL HX2 ....146 A8
Harewood Ri HWTH BD22 ....79 H3
Harewood Rd AL/HA/HU LS17 .....46 D7
HWTH BD22 ....79 G4
ROY/SHW OL2 ....229 L6
SKP/WHF BD23 ....16 A2
WKFDE WF1 ....177 H6
Harewood St BFDE BD3 ....5 L5
LDSU LS2 ....7 H9
Harewood Wy BRAM LS13 ....107 K6
Hargrave Crs ILK LS29 ....61 H2
Hargreaves Av
EARD/LOFT WF3 ....177 G1
Hargreaves Cl MOR LS27 ....130 B7
Harker Rd WBSY BD6 ....126 E7
Harker St KNOT WF11 ....182 D2
Harker Ter PDSY/CALV LS28 .....106 F5
Harland Cl ECHL BD2 ....105 C4
Harland Sq LDSU LS2 ....6 D3
Harlech Av BEE/HOL LS11 ....131 J4
Harlech Crs BEE/HOL LS11 ....131 K4
Harlech Gv BEE/HOL LS11 ....131 J4
Harlech Mt BEE/HOL LS11 ....131 J4
Harlech Park Ct BEE/HOL LS11 ..131 K1
Harlech Rd BEE/HOL LS11 ....131 K4
Harlech St BEE/HOL LS11 ....131 K4
Harlech Ter BEE/HOL LS11 ....131 K4
Harlech Wy GFTH/SHER LS25 ....113 K7
Harley Av BRAM LS13 ....107 J6
Harley Cl BRAM LS13 ....107 J6
Harley Ct BRAM LS13 ....107 J6
Harley Dr BRAM LS13 ....107 J6
Harley Gdns PDSY/CALV LS28 ...107 J6
Harley Gn BRAM LS13 ....107 J6
Harley Ri BRAM LS13 ....107 J6
Harley Rd BRAM LS13 ....107 J6
Harley St BRIG HD6 ....170 C5
TOD OL14 ....141 K8
Harley Ter BRAM LS13 ....107 K6
Harley Vw BRAM LS13 ....107 J6
Harley Wk BRAM LS13 ....107 J6
Harley Wd TOD OL14 ....141 G6
Harlington Ct MOR LS27 ....152 C4
Harlington Rd MOR LS27 ....152 C4
Harlow Ct RHAY LS8 ....88 E7
Harlow Rd GTHN BD7 ....126 C1
Harmby Cl AWLS/ASK DN6 ....249 H4
Harmon Cl BOW BD4 ....127 L6
Harold Av BSLYN/ROY S71 ....262 A2
MOR LS27 ....109 G4
Harold Gdns MOR LS27 ....152 E1
Harold Gv HDGY LS6 ....109 G4
Harold Mt HDGY LS6 ....109 G4
Harold Pl HDGY LS6 ....109 G4
Harold Rd HDGY LS6 ....109 G4
Harold Sq HDGY LS6 ....109 G4
Harold St BGLY BD16 ....81 G2
HDGY LS6 ....109 G4
MILN OL16 ....206 E4
Harold Ter HDGY LS6 ....109 G4
Harold Vw HDGY LS6 ....109 G4
Harold Wk HDGY LS6 ....109 G4
Harpe Inge HUDE HD5 ....193 G7
Harper Av IDLE BD10 ....83 K5
Harper Crs IDLE BD10 ....83 L5
Harper Ga BOW BD4 ....128 B2
Harper Gv AIRE BD20 ....55 M2
IDLE BD10 ....83 K5
Harper La YEA LS19 ....62 D8
Harper Royd La
RPDN/SBR HX6 ....167 K4
Harpers Sq ROY/SHW OL2 ....229 L7
Harpers Sq AIRE BD20 ....55 M2
Harp St LDSU LS2 ....9 J1
ROCH OL11 ....228 A1
Harp Rd HUDW HD3 ....213 K1
Harrap St WKFDW/WTN WF2 ...175 M8
Harrier Cl GIR BD8 ....103 K7
Harrier Wy MOR LS27 ....152 F2
Harriet Cl BSLY * S70 ....261 J7

Harriet St BRIG HD6 ....170 C2
CHAL LS7 ....7 K2
GIR BD8 ....104 D6
Harriett St MILN OL16 ....206 C7
Harrington Cl BSLYN/ROY S71 ...262 A2
Harrington Dr BTLY WF17 ....173 L3
KGHY BD21 ....3 G5
Harrington Ter GTHN BD7 ....126 C1
Harris Ct GTHN BD7 ....126 C3
Harrison Crs OSM LS9 ....110 F5
Harrison La HOLM/MEL HD9 .....235 G2
Harrison Rd HFAX HX1 ....11 G7
HOR/CROF WF4 ....200 B5
Harrisons Av PDSY/CALV LS28 ...107 H4
Harrison St BGLY BD16 ....81 J4
LDS LS1 ....7 H8
TOD * OL14 ....140 D5
Harris St BFD BD1 ....5 J6
BGLY BD16 ....81 J4
Harrogate Av ECHL BD2 ....105 J4
Harrogate Pl BFDE BD3 ....105 J4
Harrogate Ringway PBR HG3 .....26 C4
Harrogate Rd AL/HA/HU LS17 .....43 M1
AL/HA/HU LS17 ....44 F2
AL/HA/HU LS17 ....87 M4
CHAL * LS7 ....87 L8
ECHL BD2 ....105 L3
IDLE BD10 ....83 M8
KNA HG5 ....28 E1
PBR HG3 ....26 E5
WBY LS22 ....29 H6
YEA LS19 ....84 D2
Harrogate St BFDE BD3 ....105 J4
Harrogate Ter BFDE BD3 ....105 J4
Harrogate Vw AL/HA/HU LS17 ....88 E1
Harrop Av MOR LS27 ....152 D4
Harrop Gv MOR LS27 ....152 D4
Harrop La WIL/AL BD15 ....102 D3
Harrop Ter MOR LS27 ....152 D4
Harrop Well La PONT WF8 ....180 F6
Harrowby Crs BHP/TINH LS16 .....86 D7
Harrowby Rd BHP/TINH LS16 .....86 D7
Harrow Ms ROY/SHW OL2 ....229 K6
Harrow St HEM/SK/SE WF9 ......247 G3
HFAX HX1 ....10 B6
ROCH * OL11 ....228 D4
Harry La CLAY BD14 ....125 K2
HWTH BD22 ....100 D3
Harry Rd DOD/DAR S75 ....260 D3
Harry St BOW BD4 ....127 L3
Hartcliff La STKB/PEN S36 ....270 E3
Hartcliffe La STKB/PEN S36 ......270 A5
Hartcliff Hill Rd STKB/PEN S36 ..270 B6
Hartcliff Nick STKB/PEN S36 .....270 A6
Hartcliff Rd STKB/PEN S36 ....269 L6
STKB/PEN S36 ....270 C6
Harthill MOR LS27 ....129 M7
Harthill Av MOR LS27 ....129 M7
Harthill Cl MOR LS27 ....129 M7
Harthill La MOR LS27 ....129 M7
Harthill Paddock MOR LS27 .....129 M7
Harthill Ri MOR LS27 ....129 M7
Hartington Dr BSLYN/ROY S71 ...261 H2
Hartington St BTLY WF17 ....173 L3
KGHY BD21 ....3 G3
Hartington Ter GTHN BD7 ....126 C1
Hartland Rd BOW BD4 ....128 A2
Hartlebury ROCH * OL11 ....206 A8
Hartley Av HDGY LS6 ....6 E1
Hartley Ct LVSG WF15 ....172 C3
Hartley Crs HDGY LS6 ....6 E1
Hartley Gdns HDGY LS6 ....6 E1
Hartley Gv HDGY LS6 ....6 D1
Hartley Hl LDSU LS2 ....7 H7
Hartley La ROCH OL11 ....228 A3
Hartley Park Av PONT WF8 ....180 D6
Hartley Park Vw PONT WF8 ......180 D6
Hartley Pl HWTH BD22 ....54 F3
MOR * LS27 ....152 D2
Hartley's Buildings MOR LS27 ..152 D3
Hartley's Sq AIRE BD20 ....58 F5
Hartleys Ter COL BB8 ....74 A2
Hartley St BOW BD4 ....127 J1
CAS WF10 ....157 L7
DEWS WF13 ....173 L5
HFAX HX1 ....10 C4
LIT OL15 ....207 J1
MILN * OL16 ....206 F7
MOR LS27 ....130 D7
MOR LS27 ....152 D2
WHIT OL12 ....184 E8
Hartley Ter FEA/AMT WF7 ....201 L2
Hartlington Ct BAIL * BD17 ....83 G3
Hartman Pl HTON * BD9 ....104 B4
Harton Cl ROY/SHW OL2 ....229 J8
Hartshead Hall La LVSG WF15 ...171 L6
Hartshead La LVSG WF15 ....171 K4
Hart St GTHN BD7 ....126 C1
HUDS HD4 ....214 C4
Hartwell Rd HDGY LS6 ....109 G4
Harvard St ROCH OL11 ....228 C2
Harvelin Pk TOD OL14 ....164 C1
Harvest Ct PONT WF8 ....181 G3
Harvey Royd HUDE HD5 ....215 J2
Harvey St BSLY S70 ....260 F6
WHIT OL12 ....206 D5
WKFDE WF1 ....13 K8
Harwill Ap MOR LS27 ....130 E7
Harwill Av MOR LS27 ....130 E7
Harwill Cft MOR LS27 ....130 E7
Harwill Gv MOR LS27 ....130 E7
Harwill Ri MOR LS27 ....130 E7
Harwill Rd MOR LS27 ....130 E7
Harwood Cl HUDE HD5 ....215 H1
WKFDW/WTN WF2 ....199 G5
Harwood St LIT OL15 ....207 H1
Harworth Rd BSLYN/ROY S71 ....262 A4
Haselden Crs
WKFDW/WTN WF2 ....197 M1
Haselden Rd
WKFDW/WTN WF2 ....197 M1
Haslam Cl BFDE BD3 ....5 K4
Haslam Gv SHPY BD18 ....83 G8
Haslemere Cl BOW BD4 ....127 M3
Haslewood Cl OSM LS9 ....7 M9
Haslewood Ct OSM LS9 ....110 B6
Haslewood Dene OSM LS9 ....110 B6
Haslewood Dr OSM LS9 ....110 B6
Haslewood Gdns OSM LS9 ....110 B6
Haslewood Gn OSM LS9 ....110 B6

Haslewood Ms OSM LS9 ....110 B6
Haslewood Pl OSM LS9 ....110 B6
Haslewood Sq OSM LS9 ....110 B6
Haslewood Vw OSM LS9 ....110 B6
Hasley Rd ILK LS29 ....40 D5
Haslingden Dr HTON BD9 ....104 B4
Hassocks La HOLM/MEL HD9 .....235 L2
Hassocks Rd HOLM/MEL HD9 ....234 E3
Haste St CAS WF10 ....157 K6
Hastings Av WBOW BD5 ....126 F4
WKFDW/WTN WF2 ....198 E4
NORM WF6 ....178 A2
Hastings Crs CAS WF10 ....158 D7
Hastings Gv WKFDW/WTN WF2 ..198 E4
Hastings Pl WBOW BD5 ....126 F4
Hastings St CUD/GR S72 ....245 J7
ROCH OL11 ....228 B1
WBOW BD5 ....126 F4
Hastings Ter WBOW BD5 ....126 F4
Hastings Wk CAS WF10 ....158 D7
Hatchet La LM/WK BD12 ....149 J2
Hatfield Cl BSLYN/ROY S71 ......243 G1
Hatfield Pl HOR/CROF WF4 ....222 B6
Hatfield Rd ECHL BD2 ....105 K4
Hatfield St WKFDE WF1 ....176 E4
Hatfield Vw WKFDE WF1 ....176 E4
Hathaway Av HTON BD9 ....103 M3
Hathaway Dr SCFT LS14 ....89 K6
Hathaway La SCFT LS14 ....89 K6
Hathaway Ms SCFT LS14 ....89 K5
Hathershelf La LUD/ILL HX2 ......144 C1
Hatton Cl WBSY BD6 ....126 F6
Haugh End La RPDN/SBR HX6 ...167 J4
Haugh Head Rd STKB/PEN S36 ..258 D3
Haugh La MILN OL16 ....229 L2
Haugh Rd TOD OL14 ....142 A3
Haugh Shaw Cft HFAX HX1 ....10 D7
Haugh Shaw Rd HFAX HX1 ....10 C7
Haugh Shaw Rd West
HFAX HX1 ....168 B1
Haughs La HUDD HD3 ....191 H7
Haughs Rd HUDW HD3 ....191 J7
Hauxley Ct ILK LS29 ....38 F1
Hauxwell Cl AWLS/ASK DN6 ......249 H4
Hauxwell Dr YEA LS19 ....62 D8
Havelock Sq CUL/QBY BD13 ......103 G3
Havelock St BSLY S70 ....260 F6
CUL/QBY BD13 ....103 G8
DEWS WF13 ....195 G1
GTHN BD7 ....126 B2
Havelocks BHP/TINH LS16 ....86 A3
Haven Cha BHP/TINH LS16 ....86 A3
Haven Ct BHP/TINH LS16 ....86 A3
PONT WF8 ....202 D1
Haven Cft BHP/TINH LS16 ....86 B3
Haven Gdns BHP/TINH LS16 ....86 A3
Haven Garth BHP/TINH LS16 ....86 A3
Haven Gn BHP/TINH LS16 ....86 A3
Haven La HBR HX7 ....143 K6
Haven Mt BHP/TINH LS16 ....86 A3
Haven Ri BHP/TINH LS16 ....86 A3
Haven St TOD * OL14 ....163 L1
Haven Vw BHP/TINH LS16 ....86 A3
Havercroft OSS WF5 ....197 H3
WOR/ARM LS12 ....130 A1
Havercroft La PONT WF8 ....204 A1
Havercroft Rd CUD/GR S72 ....223 G8
Havercroft Wy BTLY WF17 ....173 H1
The Haverlands
HEM/SK/SE WF9 ....224 A8
Haverdale Ri DOD/DAR S75 ......260 F3
Haverdale Rd HOR/CROF WF4 ...222 E5
Haveroid La HOR/CROF WF4 .....220 B2
Haveroid Wy HOR/CROF WF4 ....220 A1
Haverthwaites Dr
GFTH/SHER LS25 ....92 A5
Havertop La NORM WF6 ....179 H4
Haw Av YEA LS19 ....62 E6
Hawber Cote Dr AIRE * BD20 ......36 B4
Hawber La AIRE BD20 ....36 B5
Haw Cliff La HUDS HD4 ....237 H5
Haw Ct DOD/DAR S75 ....259 H6
Hawes Av HUDW HD3 ....191 K8
WBOW BD5 ....126 E4
Hawes Cl CAS WF10 ....158 D6
Hawes Crs WBOW BD5 ....126 E4
Hawes Dr COL BB8 ....52 B8
WBOW BD5 ....126 E4
Hawes Gv WBOW BD5 ....126 E4
Hawes Mt WBOW BD5 ....126 E4
Hawes Rd WBOW BD5 ....126 E4
Hawes Ter WBOW BD5 ....126 E4
Haweswater Cl WBY LS22 ....47 L1
Haw Hill Vw NORM WF6 ....178 D3
Hawkcliffe Vw AIRE BD20 ....35 L5
Hawke Av HECK WF16 ....173 C1
Hawke Wy LM/WK BD12 ....127 G8
Hawkhill Av GSLY LS20 ....61 M6
MSTN/BAR LS15 ....111 K3
Hawkhill Dr MSTN/BAR LS15 .....111 K3
Hawkhill Gdns MSTN/BAR LS15 ..111 K3
Hawkhills CHAL LS7 ....88 A7
Hawkhurst Rd WOR/ARM LS12 ..108 E8
Hawkingcroft Rd
HOR/CROF WF4 ....197 H5
Hawkins Dr CHAL LS7 ....7 G4
Hawkins Wy LIT OL15 ....185 L5
Hawkroyd Bank Rd HUDS HD4 ...214 A7
Hawksbridge La HWTH BD22 ....100 B3
Hawkshead Cl WBOW BD5 ....127 G1
Hawkshead Crs SCFT LS14 ....111 H3
Hawkshead Dr ROY/SHW OL2 ...127 G1
WBOW BD5 ....127 G1
Hawkshead Rd ROY/SHW OL2 ...229 J6
Hawkshead Wk WBOW * BD5 ....127 G1
Hawkshead Wy WBOW * BD5 ....127 G1
Hawksley Ct MOR LS27 ....130 B7
Hawksmoor Dr ROY/SHW OL2 ...229 K6
Hawk's Nest Gdns East
AL/HA/HU LS17 ....87 M2
Hawk's Nest Gdns South
AL/HA/HU LS17 ....87 M2

Hawk's Nest Gdns West
AL/HA/HU LS17 ....87 M2
Hawk's Nest Ri AL/HA/HU LS17 ..87 M2
Hawkstone Av GSLY LS20 ....61 L7
Hawkstone Vw GSLY LS20 ....61 L7
Hawk St KGHY BD21 ....3 J3
Hawkswood Av HTON BD9 ....104 B3
KSTL LS5 ....86 A7
Hawkswood Crs KSTL LS5 ....86 A7
Hawkswood Gv KSTL LS5 ....86 A7
Hawkswood Mt KSTL LS5 ....86 A7
Hawkswood Pl KSTL LS5 ....86 B8
Hawkswood St KSTL LS5 ....86 B8
Hawkswood Ter KSTL LS5 ....86 B8
Hawksworth Av GSLY LS20 ....61 M7
Hawksworth Cl ILK LS29 ....61 J3
Hawksworth Dr ILK LS29 ....61 J3
Hawksworth La GSLY LS20 ....61 H5
Hawksworth Rd BAIL BD17 ....82 C1
HORS LS18 ....85 M7
Hawkwell Bank
BSLYN/ROY S71 ....262 C1
Haw La YEA LS19 ....62 E6
Hawley Cl MOR LS27 ....152 B4
Hawley St COL BB8 ....74 E1
Hawley Ter IDLE BD10 ....106 A2
Hawley Wy MOR LS27 ....152 B4
Haworth Cl BSLYN/ROY S71 ......261 K3
MIRF WF14 ....172 B8
Haworth Gv HTON BD9 ....104 A3
Haworth La YEA LS19 ....84 A3
Haworth Rd BTLY WF17 ....151 K4
CUL/QBY BD13 ....79 J8
HWTH BD22 ....79 C6
WIL/AL BD15 ....102 C2
Haworth to Hebden Bridge Wk
HBR HX7 ....99 G3
HBR HX7 ....99 L7
HBR HX7 ....120 E4
Haw Park La
WKFDW/WTN WF2 ....221 K4
Hawshaw Rd HWTH BD22 ....53 M1
Hawswater Pl KNOT WF11 ....182 K5
The Hawthorns AIRE BD20 ....34 E8
OSS WF5 ....197 G3
WKFDE WF1 ....176 F1
Hawthorn Av BFDE BD3 ....106 A6
BTLY WF17 ....173 J3
HOR/CROF WF4 ....200 A5
KNOT WF11 ....181 M7
TAD LS24 ....71 K5
YEA LS19 ....62 D7
Hawthorn Cl BRIG HD6 ....170 E3
ILK LS29 ....18 F6
TAD LS24 ....71 L5
WKFDW/WTN WF2 ....175 K3
Hawthorn Ct EARD/LOFT WF3 ...154 E5
Hawthorn Crs CHAL * LS7 ....87 M7
ROY/SHW * OL2 ....229 K8
YEA LS19 ....62 D7
Hawthorn Cft TAD LS24 ....71 K5
Hawthorn Dr BRAM LS13 ....106 F1
IDLE BD10 ....83 L7
YEA LS19 ....62 D7
Hawthorne Av CAS WF10 ....158 D8
FEA/AMT WF7 ....201 L2
HEM/SK/SE WF9 ....223 M8
SHPY BD18 ....104 F1
WBY LS22 ....29 M7
Hawthorne Cl HOR/CROF WF4 ...217 M3
KBTN HD8 ....215 M3
MOR LS27 ....129 M7
Hawthorne Ct DOD/DAR S75 .....241 K6
Hawthorne Crs AWLS/ASK DN6 ..249 J3
DOD/DAR S75 ....260 A6
HEM/SK/SE WF9 ....223 L8
Hawthorne Dr MOR LS27 ....129 M7
Hawthorne Gdns
BHP/TINH LS16 ....86 D1
Hawthorne La MILN OL16 ....229 J3
Hawthorne Mt NORM WF6 ....178 D7
Hawthorne Ri SCFT LS14 ....89 L6
Hawthorne St AIRE BD20 ....35 M5
BSLY S70 ....261 G6
CUD/GR S72 ....244 E3
Hawthorne Vw MOR LS27 ....130 A7
Hawthorne Wy CUD/GR S72 ......244 E3
KBTN HD8 ....238 B2
Hawthorn Gv DOD/DAR S75 .....259 J6
FEA/AMT WF7 ....224 B1
ILK LS29 ....40 B7
RTHW LS26 ....155 H2
Hawthorn La CHAL * LS7 ....87 M7
Hawthorn Mt CHAL * LS7 ....87 M7
Hawthorn Pl TOD * OL14 ....141 K8
Hawthorn Rd CHAL * LS7 ....87 M7
MAR/SLWT HD7 ....212 A5
YEA LS19 ....62 D7
Hawthorn St BFDE BD3 ....106 A6
HFAX * HX1 ....10 C9
HIPP * HX3 ....147 M6
Hawthorn Ter HFAX * HX1 ....10 C9
HUDS HD4 ....213 L2
OSS WF5 ....197 G3
Hawthorn V CHAL * LS7 ....87 M7
Hawthorn Vw BAIL BD17 ....82 F3
CHAL * LS7 ....87 M7
Hawthorn Wk LIT OL15 ....207 H1
Hawtop La DOD/DAR S75 ....220 B8
Hayburn Gdns BTLY WF17 ....173 K1
Hayburn Rd BTLY WF17 ....173 J1
Haycliffe Av GTHN BD7 ....126 C4
Haycliffe Dr GTHN BD7 ....126 B4
Haycliffe Gv GTHN BD7 ....126 C4
Haycliffe Hill Rd WBOW BD5 .....126 D4
Haycliffe La WBSY BD6 ....126 D4
Haycliffe Rd WBOW BD5 ....126 C4
Haycliffe Ter GTHN BD7 ....126 D3
Hayden St BFDE BD3 ....5 L8
Haydn Av EARD/LOFT WF3 ....155 G4
Haydn's Ter PDSY/CALV LS28 ....107 G4
Hayes Cft BSLY S70 ....261 H5
The Hayfields HWTH BD22 ....78 E6
Hayfield Av BSPA/BRAM LS23 .....48 C5
HUDW HD3 ....191 J7
Hayfield Cl DOD/DAR S75 ....260 A7
HOLM/MEL HD9 ....254 F2
Hayfield Ter WOR/ARM LS12 .....108 E8

Haygill Nook *SKP/WHF* BD23 ....17 M4
Hayhills La *AIRE* BD20 ....35 M2
Hayhills Rd *AIRE* BD20 ....36 A4
Hayleigh Av *BRAM* LS13 ....107 L3
Hayleigh Mt *BRAM* LS13 ....107 L4
Haylock Cl *DOD/DAR* S75 ....260 A3
Hayne La *HOR/CROF* WF4 ....218 A1
Haynes St *KGHY* BD21 ....3 J5
WHIT OL12 ....206 B6
Hays La *LUD/ILL* HX2 ....123 K7
Hayson Cl *EARL* WF12 ....174 B5
Haythorns Av *AIRE* BD20 ....35 M5
Haythorns Mt *AIRE* BD20 ....35 M5
Hayton Dr *WBY* LS22 ....48 B2
Hayton Wood Vw
GFTH/SHER LS25 ....92 A6
The Haywain *ILK* LS29 ....38 F3
Haywood Av *HUD* HD3 ....191 L8
Hazel Av *EARL* WF12 ....174 D7
MILN OL16 ....229 J3
SCFT LS14 ....89 L6
Hazel Bank *WKFDW/WTN* WF2 ....176 A6
Hazel Beck *BGLY* BD16 ....81 H6
Hazel Cl *BIRK/DRI* BD11 ....128 C8
EARL WF12 ....174 D7
PBR HG3 ....26 D2
Hazel Ct *RTHW* LS26 ....155 H2
WKFDW/WTN WF2 ....176 C6
Hazel Crs *EARL* WF12 ....174 D7
Hazelcroft *IDLE* BD10 ....105 M2
Hazel Cft *SHPY* BD18 ....82 F7
Hazeldene *CUL/QBY* BD13 ....124 F6
Hazel Dr *EARL* WF12 ....174 D7
PBR HG3 ....26 D2
Hazel Gdns *CAS* WF10 ....180 F1
Hazel Gv *AIRE* BD20 ....55 L1
BTLY WF17 ....173 J2
HIPP HX3 ....148 C7
HOR/CROF WF4 ....217 M3
HUDN HD2 ....192 D1
PONT WF8 ....181 G4
Hazel Grove Rd *AIRE* BD20 ....55 L1
Hazelheads *BAIL* BD17 ....82 E1
Hazelhurst Av *BGLY* BD16 ....81 H6
Hazelhurst Brow *HTON* BD9 ....103 M4
Hazelhurst Rd *BFDE* BD3 ....105 L1
PDSY/CALV LS28 ....107 H7
Hazel Hurst Gv *CUL/QBY* BD13 ....124 F5
Hazel Hurst Rd *CUL/QBY* BD13 ....124 F7
Hazelhurst St *HTON* BD9 ....103 M4
Hazelhurst Ter *HTON* BD9 ....103 M4
Hazel La *AWLS/ASK* DN6 ....248 C5
Hazelmere Av *BGLY* BD16 ....81 J6
Hazel Mt *SHPY* BD18 ....82 E7
Hazel Ri *RTHW* LS26 ....156 F5
Hazel Rd *KNOT* WF11 ....182 A3
Hazelshaw *DOD/DAR* S75 ....260 C6
Hazel Wk *HTON* BD9 ....103 M4
Hazelwood Av *AIRE* BD20 ....58 B5
GFTH/SHER LS25 ....135 J1
Hazelwood Ct *WKFDE* WF1 ....176 F1
Hazelwood Rd
HEM/SK/SE WF9 ....223 K5
HTON BD9 ....103 L3
WKFDE WF1 ....176 F1
Hazelwood St *TOD* OL14 ....163 K4
Hazledene Crs *CUD/GR* S72 ....244 E5
Hazledene Rd *CUD/GR* S72 ....244 D5
Headfield Rd *EARL* WF12 ....173 L8
HUDS HD4 ....214 C3
Headfield Vw *EARL* WF12 ....195 M2
Headingley Av *HDGY* LS6 ....108 E1
Headingley Cl *HDGY* LS6 ....108 F2
Headingley La *HDGY* LS6 ....109 G2
Headingley Mt *HDGY* LS6 ....108 E1
Headingley Rd *AWLS/ASK* DN6 ....227 M3
Headingley Vw *HDGY* LS6 ....108 F2
Headland Gv *WBSY* BD6 ....126 B5
Headland La *EARL* WF12 ....174 D8
Headlands Av *OSS* WF5 ....196 E1
Headlands Cl *LVSG* WF15 ....172 D3
Headlands Gv *OSS* WF5 ....196 E1
Headlands La *KNOT* WF11 ....182 A2
PONT WF8 ....180 E5
Headlands Pk *OSS* WF5 ....196 E1
Headlands Rd *HUD* HD1 ....14 E4
LVSG WF15 ....172 C2
OSS WF5 ....196 E1
Headlands St *LVSG* WF15 ....172 D3
WHIT OL12 ....206 A5
Headlands Wk *OSS* WF5 ....196 F1
Headley La *BSPA/BRAM* LS23 ....70 A5
CUL/QBY BD13 ....124 F7
The Headrow *LDS* LS1 ....6 F8
Headwell La *TAD* LS24 ....115 L1
Heald Cl *LIT* OL15 ....207 J3
Healdfield Rd *CAS* WF10 ....158 B6
Healds Av *LVSG* WF15 ....172 D2
Healds Rd *DEWS* WF13 ....173 J4
Heald St *CAS* WF10 ....158 B6
Healdwood Cl *CAS* WF10 ....158 C6
Healdwood Rd *CAS* WF10 ....158 C6
Healey Av *BGLY* BD16 ....81 J4
Healey Cl *BTLY* WF17 ....173 H1
Healey Crs *OSS* WF5 ....196 F3
Healey Croft La
EARD/LOFT WF3 ....153 K7
Healey Dr *OSS* WF5 ....196 F3
Healey Farm *KBTN* HD8 ....238 A3
Healey Green La *HUDE* HD5 ....194 B7
Healey La *BGLY* BD16 ....81 J4
BTLY WF17 ....173 H2
EARL WF12 ....195 M4
WHIT OL12 ....206 A4
Healey Rd *OSS* WF5 ....196 E3
Healey St *BTLY* WF17 ....173 H1
MILN OL16 ....206 A8
Healey Wood Crs *BRIC* HD6 ....170 C6
Healey Wood Gdns *BRIC* HD6 ....170 C6
Healey Wood Gv *BRIC* HD6 ....170 C6
Healey Wood Rd *BRIC* HD6 ....170 C6
Healing St *ROCH* OL11 ....228 C1
Heap La *BFDE* BD3 ....5 J4
Heap St *BFDE* BD3 ....5 J5
HIPP HX3 ....146 E4
Heath Av *HIPP* HX3 ....168 D2

Heathcliff *HWTH* BD22 ....78 D7
Heathcliffe Cl *BTLY* WF17 ....151 H3
Heath Cl *EARL* WF12 ....174 D6
MAR/SLWT HD7 ....213 G7
Heath Crs *BFDE* BD3 ....16 E8
BEE/HOL LS11 ....131 G3
Heathcroft Crs *BEE/HOL* LS11 ....131 G4
Heathcroft Dr *BEE/HOL* LS11 ....131 G4
Heathcroft Lawn
BEE/HOL LS11 ....131 G4
Heathcroft Ri *BEE/HOL* LS11 ....131 G4
Heathcroft V *BEE/HOL* LS11 ....131 G4
Heathdale Ms *HUDN* HD2 ....192 B5
Heath Dr *AIRE* BD20 ....16 E8
BSPA/BRAM LS23 ....48 D7
Heather Av *ROY/SHW* OL2 ....229 M6
Heather Bank *LIT* OL15 ....185 M8
Heatherbank Av *HWTH* BD22 ....79 H2
Heather Bank Cl
CUL/QBY BD13 ....101 L1
Heather Cl *EARD/LOFT* WF3 ....176 F1
HEM/SK/SE WF9 ....246 F3
OSS WF5 ....197 H3
Heather Ct *BTLY* WF17 ....151 G4
EARD/LOFT WF3 ....176 F1
HUDW HD3 ....191 H6
Heathercroft *CHAL* LS7 ....88 A8
Heather Cft *HOR/CROF* WF4 ....200 E3
Heatherdale Ct
EARD/LOFT WF3 ....153 G6
Heatherdale Dr
EARD/LOFT WF3 ....153 G6
Heatherdale Rd
EARD/LOFT WF3 ....152 F6
Heatherdene *TAD* LS24 ....71 M2
Heather Dr *LUD/ILL* HX2 ....145 J3
Heatherfield Crs *HUD* HD1 ....191 M8
Heatherfield Rd *HUD* HD1 ....191 M8
Heather Fold *KBTN* HD8 ....239 H4
Heather Gdns *BRAM* LS13 ....108 A6
SCFT LS14 ....67 L7
Heather Gv *BRAM* LS13 ....107 M6
HTON BD9 ....103 K3
KGHY BD21 ....2 B3
Heathergrove Fold *HUDE* HD5 ....2 B3
Heather Knowle *DOD/DAR* S75 ....260 C7
Heatherlands Av
CUL/QBY BD13 ....101 M4
Heather Ri *ILK* LS29 ....40 A6
Heather Rd *BAIL* BD17 ....82 F2
HOLM/MEL HD9 ....234 F5
The Heathers *HOR/CROF* WF4 ....200 E3
Heather Side *BAIL* BD17 ....82 D2
Heatherstones *HIPP* HX3 ....168 D2
Heather V *SCFT* LS14 ....67 K7
Heather Vw *BGLY* BD16 ....81 M1
HOR/CROF WF4 ....200 E3
OSS WF5 ....196 F1
SKP/WHF BD23 ....16 D3
Heathfield *BHP/TINH* LS16 ....86 C2
MIRF WF14 ....172 B8
Heathfield Av *ELL* HX5 ....169 K7
Heathfield Cl *BGLY* BD16 ....81 J2
EARD/LOFT WF3 ....153 H7
Heathfield Gv *GTHN* BD7 ....126 A2
HIPP * HX3 ....168 E2
Heathfield La *BSPA/BRAM* LS23 ....48 D6
Heathfield Ms *MAR/SLWT* HD7 ....213 G2
Heathfield Pl *HIPP* HX3 ....168 E2
Heathfield Ri *RPDN/SBR* HX6 ....188 E5
Heathfield Rd *MAR/SLWT* HD7 ....213 G2
OSS WF5 ....174 E6
Heathfield St *ELL* HX5 ....169 J8
Heathfield Ter *HDGY* LS6 ....86 F8
Heath Gdns *HIPP* HX3 ....168 E2
Heath Gv *AIRE* BD20 ....16 E8
BEE/HOL LS11 ....131 G3
BTLY WF17 ....174 B2
HUDS HD4 ....214 A4
PDSY/CALV LS28 ....106 E7
Heath Hall *HFAX* HX1 ....168 E1
Heath Hall Av *BOW* BD4 ....127 K5
Heath Hill Rd *LUD/ILL* HX2 ....145 J4
Heath House La
MAR/SLWT HD7 ....212 D2
Heath House Mi
MAR/SLWT * HD7 ....212 D2
Heath La *HIPP* HX3 ....168 E2
Heath Lea *HFAX* HX1 ....11 G8
Heathmoor Cl *IDLE* BD10 ....83 J7
LUD/ILL HX2 ....123 M8
Heathmoor Mt *LUD/ILL* HX2 ....123 M8
Heathmoor Park Rd
LUD/ILL HX2 ....123 M8
Heathmoor Wy *LUD/ILL* HX2 ....123 M8
Heath Mt *BEE/HOL* LS11 ....131 G3
HFAX HX1 ....168 D2
Heath Mount Rd *BRIC* HD6 ....170 C6
Heathness Rd *ILK* LS29 ....38 B3
Heath Pk *HUDW* HD3 ....191 G6
Heath Park Av *HFAX* HX1 ....168 E1
Heath Pl *BEE/HOL* LS11 ....131 G3
Heath Ri *BEE/HOL* LS11 ....131 G3
Heath Ter *BFDE* BD3 ....5 M6
Heath Vw *HFAX* HX1 ....11 H8
Heath View St *HFAX* HX1 ....11 H8
Heath Vw *EARL* WF12 ....174 D6
Heathwood Dr *MAR/SLWT* HD7 ....212 E1
Heathy Av *LUD/ILL* HX2 ....146 C1
Heathy La *LUD/ILL* HX2 ....124 B8
Heatley Rd *MILN* OL16 ....206 D7
Heaton Av *AIRE* BD20 ....58 E7
CLECK BD19 ....149 L7
EARL WF12 ....174 A6
HUDE HD5 ....193 L7

Heaton Cl *BGLY* BD16 ....81 K2
Heaton Crs *BGLY* * BD16 ....81 K2
BGLY BD16 ....81 K2
HUDE HD5 ....193 L4
Heaton Fold La *HUD* HD1 ....191 M8
Heaton Gdns *HUD* HD1 ....191 M8
Heaton Gra *BTLY* WF17 ....174 A3
Heaton Gv *CLECK* BD19 ....149 L7
HTON BD9 ....104 B3
SHPY BD18 ....82 E7
Heaton Hl *WBSY* BD6 ....126 A7
Heaton Moor Rd *HUDE* HD5 ....193 L5
Heaton Park Dr *HTON* BD9 ....104 B3
Heaton Park Rd *HTON* BD9 ....104 A3
Heaton Rd *BTLY* WF17 ....151 L7
HTON BD9 ....104 C3
HUD HD1 ....191 M8
Heaton Royds *SHPY* * BD18 ....104 B1
Heaton Royds La *SHPY* BD18 ....104 B1
Heaton St *BEE/HOL* LS11 ....8 E3
BOW BD4 ....5 J9
BRIG HD6 ....170 C4
CLECK BD19 ....149 M6
FEA/AMT WF7 ....224 A1
MILN OL16 ....229 J1
Heator La *KBTN* HD8 ....238 C7
Hebble Brook Cl *LUD/ILL* HX2 ....145 L2
Hebble Butt Cl *MILN* * OL16 ....207 G8
Hebble Dr *HOLM/MEL* HD9 ....236 C7
Hebble End *HBR* HX7 ....143 H3
Hebble Gdns *LUD/ILL* HX2 ....146 A5
Hebble La *HFAX* HX1 ....10 A1
HOLM/MEL HD9 ....234 F6
Hebble Ms *LUD/ILL* HX2 ....10 A1
Hebble St *DEWS* WF13 ....195 H1
HUD HD1 ....15 G3
Hebble Vale Dr *LUD/ILL* HX2 ....146 A4
Hebble Vw *WBSY* BD6 ....126 A4
Hebden Ap *SCFT* LS14 ....89 K8
Hebden Bridge Rd *HWTH* BD22 ....100 A7
Hebden Cl *SCFT* LS14 ....89 K8
Hebden Gn *SCFT* LS14 ....89 K8
Hebden Pth *SCFT* LS14 ....89 K8
Hebden Pl *SCFT* LS14 ....89 K8
Hebden Rd *HWTH* BD22 ....78 F7
Heber Cl *AIRE* BD20 ....36 B6
Heber Pl *LIT* OL15 ....207 K1
Heber's Ghyll Dr *ILK* LS29 ....38 A3
Heber's Gv *ILK* LS29 ....38 A3
Heber St *KGHY* BD21 ....2 E5
Heckmondwike Rd
DEWS WF13 ....173 H5
Hector Av *MILN* OL16 ....206 C6
Hector Cl *WBSY* BD6 ....126 E5
Heddon Cl *WBOW* BD5 ....127 G1
Heddon Gv *WBOW* BD5 ....4 F9
Heddon St *HDGY* LS6 ....87 G8
Heddon Wk *WBOW* BD5 ....127 G1
Hedge Cl *GIR* BD8 ....103 M5
Hedge Hill Rd *STKB/PEN* * S36 ....270 C3
Hedge La *DOD/DAR* S75 ....241 M7
Hedge Side *GIR* BD8 ....104 A6
Hedge Top La *HIPP* HX3 ....147 J3
Hedge Wy *GIR* BD8 ....104 A5
Hedley Cha *WOR/ARM* LS12 ....109 G7
Hedley Crs *WKFDE* WF1 ....176 D3
Hedley Gdns *WOR/ARM* LS12 ....109 G7
Hedley Gn *WOR/ARM* LS12 ....109 G7
Heeley Rd *WKFDW/WTN* WF2 ....220 C2
Heelis St *BSLY* S70 ....261 H6
Heidelberg Rd *HTON* BD9 ....104 C4
Height Gn *RPDN/SBR* HX6 ....167 K2
Height La *HWTH* BD22 ....100 F4
SKP/WHF BD23 ....17 M3
Height Rd *HBR* HX7 ....143 M2
The Heights *HOLM/MEL* HD9 ....254 E3
Heights Av *WHIT* OL12 ....206 A5
Heights Bank *WOR/ARM* LS12 ....108 B7
Heights Cl *WHIT* OL12 ....206 A4
WOR/ARM LS12 ....108 A6
Heights Dr *MAR/SLWT* HD7 ....212 D1
WOR/ARM LS12 ....108 B7
Heights Garth *WOR/ARM* LS12 ....108 A7
Heights La *AIRE* BD20 ....35 K2
BGLY BD16 ....59 J7
HECK WF16 ....173 G3
HTON BD9 ....103 M3
UPML OL3 ....230 F7
WHIT OL12 ....206 A5
WOR/ARM LS12 ....108 A7
Heights Pde *WOR/ARM* LS12 ....108 A7
Heights Vw *MAR/SLWT* * HD7 ....212 D1
Heights Wy *WOR/ARM* LS12 ....108 B7
Helena Cl *BSLY* S70 ....260 F6
Helena Ct *GFTH/SHER* LS25 ....135 H6
Helena Pl *GFTH/SHER* LS25 ....135 H6
Helena Wy *BOW* BD4 ....127 L6
Helen Rose Ct *SHPY* BD18 ....83 G5
Helensburgh Cl *DOD/DAR* S75 ....260 E4
Helen St *HUDS* HD4 ....214 A3
SHPY BD18 ....82 B6
Hellewell St *WBSY* BD6 ....126 B7
Hell La *WKFDE* WF1 ....199 M2
Hellwood La *SCFT* LS14 ....67 L7
Helme La *HOLM/MEL* HD9 ....235 G3
Helme Pk *HOLM/MEL* HD9 ....234 F5
Helmet La *HOLM/MEL* HD9 ....234 F5
Helme St *HOLM/MEL* HD9 ....193 L1
RPDN/SBR HX6 ....166 E6
Helmsley Wy *ROY/SHW* OL2 ....229 K6
Helmsley Ct *MID* LS10 ....153 J1
Helmsley Dr *BHP/TINH* LS16 ....86 D7
Helmsley Rd *BHP/TINH* LS16 ....86 D7
BSPA/BRAM LS23 ....48 E7
WKFDW/WTN WF2 ....199 C5
Helston Cl *BSLYN/ROY* S71 ....261 K3
Helston Crs *BSLYN/ROY* S71 ....261 K3
Helston Garth *MID* LS10 ....153 J1
Helston Gv *HOLM/MEL* HD9 ....236 A2
Helston Pl *MID* LS10 ....153 J1
Helston Rd *MID* LS10 ....131 J8
NORM WF6 ....178 D3

Helston St *MID* LS10 ....131 H8
Helston Wk *MID* LS10 ....153 H1
Helston Wy *MID* LS10 ....131 J8
Helted Wy *HUDE* HD5 ....215 G3
Hemingway Cl *MID* LS10 ....9 M7
Hemingway Garth *MID* LS10 ....9 M9
Hemingway Gn *MID* LS10 ....9 J9
Hemingway Rd *IDLE* BD10 ....83 H6
Hemishor Dr *RTHW* LS26 ....135 G6
Hemsby Gv *KGHY* * BD21 ....79 J2
Hemsby Rd *CAS* WF10 ....157 L7
Hemsby St *KGHY* BD21 ....79 J2
Hemsworth La
HEM/SK/SE WF9 ....223 J2
Hemsworth Rd
HEM/SK/SE WF9 ....246 A1
Henacrewood Ct
CUL/QBY BD13 ....125 G7
Henbury St *CHAL* LS7 ....7 K6
Henconner Av *CHAL* LS7 ....87 L8
Henconner Crs *CHAL* LS7 ....87 L8
Henconner Dr *CHAL* LS7 ....87 L8
Henconner Gdns *CHAL* LS7 ....87 L8
Henconner Gv *CHAL* LS7 ....87 L8
Henconner La *BRAM* LS13 ....107 M5
CHAL LS7 ....87 L8
Henconner Rd *CHAL* LS7 ....87 L8
Hendal La *WKFDW/WTN* WF2 ....220 C1
Henderson Av *NORM* WF6 ....178 D6
Henderson Gln *BSLYN/ROY* S71 ....243 J3
Henderson Pl *WBSY* BD6 ....126 E5
Henderson St *LIT* OL15 ....207 J1
WHIT OL12 ....206 D4
Henderville St *LIT* OL15 ....185 J8
Hendford Dr *BFDE* BD3 ....5 K5
Hendriff Pl *WHIT* * OL12 ....206 D4
Hen Holme La *AIRE* BD20 ....36 A7
Henley Av *BRAM* LS13 ....107 L4
EARL WF12 ....196 A4
WBOW BD5 ....127 C4
YEA LS19 ....84 F3
Henley Cl *YEA* LS19 ....84 F3
Henley Ct *WBOW* BD5 ....127 H4
Henley Crs *BRAM* LS13 ....107 L4
YEA LS19 ....84 F3
Henley Cft *HUDE* HD5 ....193 G8
Henley Dr *FEA/AMT* WF7 ....201 M3
YEA LS19 ....84 E3
Henley Gv *BRAM* LS13 ....107 L4
WBOW BD5 ....127 C4
Henley Hl *YEA* LS19 ....84 F3
Henley Mt *YEA* LS19 ....84 F3
Henley Pl *BRAM* LS13 ....107 L4
Henley Rd *BRAM* LS13 ....107 L4
EARL WF12 ....196 A4
WBOW BD5 ....127 C4
WHIT OL12 ....206 A5
ROCH OL11 ....228 A1
Henley Ter *BRAM* LS13 ....107 L4
Henley Vw *BRAM* LS13 ....107 L4
Henrietta St *BTLY* WF17 ....173 L1
Henry Av *HOR/CROF* WF4 ....222 E6
Henry Cl *CUD/GR* S72 ....244 D3
Henry Frederick Av *HUDS* HD4 ....213 L7
Henry Moore Ct *CAS* WF10 ....158 D7
Henry Ralph Av *HUDS* HD4 ....213 L5
Henry St *BRIC* HD6 ....170 C2
BTLY WF17 ....173 L4
CLAY BD14 ....125 L2
CUL/QBY BD13 ....102 F3
HFAX HX1 ....10 C7
HUD HD1 ....14 E7
KGHY BD21 ....3 G4
LIT OL15 ....207 H3
ROCH OL11 ....206 B8
SKP/WHF BD23 ....16 B4
WKFDW/WTN WF2 ....12 A3
Henry Ter *YEA* LS19 ....62 B7
Henshall St *BSLY* S70 ....261 J6
Henshaw Av *YEA* LS19 ....62 D8
Henshaw Crs *YEA* LS19 ....62 D8
Henshaw La *YEA* LS19 ....62 D8
Henshaw Ov *YEA* LS19 ....62 D8
Henshaw Rd *TOD* OL14 ....163 J5
Henson Gv *CAS* WF10 ....158 D8
Henthorn St *ROY/SHW* OL2 ....229 K8
Hepton Ct *OSM* LS9 ....110 D5
Hepton Dr *HBR* HX7 ....143 H2
Heptonstall Rd *HBR* HX7 ....143 H5
Hepworth Av *MOR* LS27 ....130 D6
Hepworth Cl *HOLM/MEL* HD9 ....255 G3
Hepworth Crs *HOLM/MEL* HD9 ....255 G3
MOR LS27 ....130 D6
Hepworth Dr *MIRF* WF14 ....172 B8
Hepworth La *MIRF* WF14 ....172 B8
Hepworth Rd *HOLM/MEL* HD9 ....255 G3
Hepworth St *CAS* WF10 ....158 D7
Herbalist St *WOR/ARM* LS12 ....109 G8
Herbert Pl *BFDE* BD3 ....106 A6
Herbert St *BGLY* BD16 ....81 J3
CAS WF10 ....157 M7
CLAY BD14 ....125 J2
HFAX HX1 ....10 A7
SHPY BD18 ....82 B6
WBOW BD5 ....126 F2
Hereford Cl *HEM/SK/SE* WF9 ....223 K3
ROY/SHW OL2 ....229 H7
Hereford Rd *ROCH* OL11 ....228 C1
Hereford Wy *BOW* * BD4 ....127 J2
Heritage Ms *HFAX* * HX1 ....11 J7
Heritage Pk *BGLY* BD16 ....59 J8
Heritage Rd *BTLY* WF17 ....173 C2
Heritage Wy *HWTH* BD22 ....78 D7
Hermitage Pk *KBTN* HD8 ....216 A4
Hermit La *DOD/DAR* S75 ....260 D6
Hermit St *HWTH* BD22 ....79 J4
Hermon Av *HFAX* HX1 ....10 C4
Hermon Gv *HFAX* HX1 ....10 C4
Hermon Rd *MSTN/BAR* LS15 ....111 K5
Hermon St *MSTN/BAR* LS15 ....111 K5
Heron Cl *AIRE* BD20 ....35 K3
AL/HA/HU LS17 ....88 B2
CUL/QBY BD13 ....124 C7
Heron Ct *MOR* LS27 ....152 F2
Heron Gv *AL/HA/HU* LS17 ....88 C2
Herriot Ms *CAS* WF10 ....180 F1

Herschel Rd *GIR* BD8 ....103 L7
Hertford Cha *MSTN/BAR* LS15 ....111 L8
Hertford Cl *MSTN/BAR* LS15 ....111 M8
Hertford Cft *MSTN/BAR* LS15 ....111 M8
Hertford Fold *MSTN/BAR* LS15 ....111 L8
Hertford Lawn
MSTN/BAR LS15 ....111 L8
Hertfordshire Park Cl
ROY/SHW OL2 ....229 K6
Heseltine La *HBR* HX7 ....165 J2
Heshbon St *BOW* BD4 ....127 L3
Hesketh Av *EARD/LOFT* WF3 ....152 F6
KSTL LS5 ....108 C2
Hesketh La *EARD/LOFT* WF3 ....152 F6
Hesketh Mt *KSTL* LS5 ....108 C1
Hesketh Pl *KSTL* LS5 ....108 C1
Hesketh Rd *KSTL* LS5 ....108 C1
Hesketh Ter *KSTL* LS5 ....108 C1
Heslington Rd *HUDW* HD3 ....206 E7
Hessle Av *HDGY* LS6 ....109 G3
Hessle Common La
HOR/CROF WF4 ....201 M7
Hessle La *HOR/CROF* WF4 ....201 M6
Hessle Mt *HDGY* LS6 ....109 G3
Hessle Pl *HDGY* LS6 ....109 G3
Hessle Rd *HDGY* LS6 ....109 G3
Hessle Ter *HDGY* * LS6 ....109 G3
Hessle Vw *HDGY* LS6 ....109 G3
Hessle Wk *HDGY* LS6 ....109 G3
Hetchell Vw *AL/HA/HU* LS17 ....67 M4
Hetton Dr *BFDE* BD3 ....105 M8
Hetton Rd *RHAY* LS8 ....110 D2
Heuthwaite Av *WBY* LS22 ....48 B2
Hever Gv *HUDE* * HD5 ....193 J7
Heversham Av *ROY/SHW* OL2 ....229 M7
Hew Clews *GTHN* BD7 ....126 A3
The Hey *ROY/SHW* * OL2 ....230 A5
Hey Beck La *EARL* WF12 ....174 E1
Heybeck Wk *BOW* BD4 ....128 B4
Hey Bottom La *WHIT* OL12 ....184 C8
Heybrook St *MILN* OL16 ....206 D6
Heycliffe Rd *HOLM/MEL* HD9 ....254 D1
Hey Crs *HOLM/MEL* HD9 ....234 F4
Heyden Br *GLSP* SK13 ....265 M8
Heyford Ct *ECHL* BD2 ....104 F3
Heygate Cl *BAIL* BD17 ....82 F2
Heygate La *BAIL* BD17 ....82 F2
BSPA/BRAM LS23 ....70 B2
Hey Head La *LIT* OL15 ....185 K5
TOD OL14 ....141 M7
Hey La *HUDE* HD5 ....214 F3
HUDS HD4 ....214 D7
HUDW HD3 ....189 L7
Heys Av *CUL/QBY* BD13 ....103 H8
Heys Cl *KNOT* WF11 ....182 C2
Heys Crs *CUL/QBY* BD13 ....103 J8
Heys Gdns *HOLM/MEL* HD9 ....236 E6
Heysham Dr *BOW* BD4 ....128 B3
Heysham Gn *BSLYN/ROY* S71 ....261 M1
Hey Slack La *KBTN* HD8 ....255 L4
Heys La *LUD/ILL* HX2 ....122 E8
MAR/SLWT HD7 ....211 M4
RPDN/SBR HX6 ....188 F5
Heys Rd *HOLM/MEL* HD9 ....236 E6
Hey St *BRIG* HD6 ....170 D2
GTHN BD7 ....4 C8
MILN OL16 ....206 D6
Heywood Cl *WHIT* OL12 ....184 E8
Heywood Pl *HFAX* HX1 ....10 D5
Heywood St *HFAX* HX1 ....10 C4
Hibbert Ter *BSLY* * S70 ....261 H7
Hibson Cl *WHIT* OL12 ....184 E8
Hick La *BTLY* WF17 ....173 M1
Hicks La *RTHW* LS26 ....156 F3
Hickson Dr *BSLYN/ROY* S71 ....262 A2
Hick St *BFD* * BD1 ....5 H6
Higgin Farm *LUD/ILL* * HX2 ....166 E1
Higgin La *LUD/ILL* HX2 ....169 G1
Higham And Dob La
RPDN/SBR HX6 ....166 E2
Higham Common Rd
DOD/DAR S75 ....260 A2
Higham La *DOD/DAR* S75 ....260 A3
Higham Vw *DOD/DAR* S75 ....241 M7
Higham Wy *GFTH/SHER* LS25 ....113 H6
High Ash *AL/HA/HU* LS17 ....88 A1
SHPY BD18 ....83 G7
High Ash Av *AL/HA/HU* LS17 ....88 B1
KBTN HD8 ....240 B4
High Ash Cl *HOR/CROF* WF4 ....221 H8
High Ash Dr *AL/HA/HU* LS17 ....88 A1
High Ash Mt *AL/HA/HU* LS17 ....88 A1
High Ash Pk *WIL/AL* BD15 ....103 H5
High Bank *AIRE* BD20 ....16 B1
High Bank Ap *MSTN/BAR* LS15 ....111 M7
High Bank Cl *ILK* LS29 ....19 H6
MSTN/BAR LS15 ....111 M7
High Bank Gdns
MSTN/BAR LS15 ....112 A7
High Bank Ga
MSTN/BAR * LS15 ....111 M7
High Bank La *SHPY* BD18 ....81 M8
STKB/PEN S36 ....269 M1
High Bank Pl *MSTN/BAR* LS15 ....111 M7
Highbank Rd *MILN* OL16 ....229 L3
High Banks Cl *AIRE* BD20 ....58 B4
High Bank Vw *MSTN/BAR* LS15 ....111 M7
High Binns La *HWTH* BD22 ....100 F3
High Bradley La *AIRE* BD20 ....16 B1
Highbridge La *KBTN* HD8 ....239 L1
Highbridge Ter *WBOW* BD5 ....127 H5
High Brook Fall
EARD/LOFT WF3 ....154 E8
High Brooms *HUDN* HD2 ....192 M3
High Bury Cl *CUL/QBY* BD13 ....124 E6
Highbury Cl *HDGY* LS6 ....87 G8
Highbury La *HDGY* LS6 ....87 G8
Highbury Pl *BRAM* LS13 ....107 J6
HDGY LS6 ....87 G8
Highbury Rd *HDGY* LS6 ....87 G8
Highbury St *HDGY* LS6 ....87 G8
Highbury Ter *HDGY* LS6 ....87 G8
Highbury Wy *ROY/SHW* OL2 ....228 F8
High Busy La *SHPY* BD18 ....83 J5

High Cliffe *BULY* LS4 ......108 E3
Highcliffe Av *HUDN* HD2 ......192 B4
Highcliffe Dr *MAR/SLWT* HD7 ......145 M7
Highcliffe Rd *BTLY* WF17 ......173 L3
  MOR LS27 ......152 B2
High Cliffe Ter *WBY* LS22 ......48 A1
High Cl *DOD/DAR* S75 ......241 M5
  GSLY LS20 ......61 K6
  HUDE HD5 ......215 G3
  MAR/SLWT HD7 ......213 G6
  OSS WF5 ......174 F5
  YEA LS19 ......84 D3
High Ct *HBR* HX7 ......120 F8
  LDSU LS2 ......9 J1
High Court La *LDSU* LS2 ......9 J2
High Crest *MAR/SLWT* HD7 ......213 G4
High Cft *CUL/QBY* BD13 ......125 C5
  HIPP HX3 ......146 B4
Highcroft *HOLM/MEL* HD9 ......254 A1
  WBY LS22 ......47 J6
Highcroft Cl *PDSY/CALV* LS28 ......106 A4
High Croft Crs *HUDE* HD5 ......215 H3
High Croft Dr *BSLYN/ROY* S71 ......243 H6
Highcroft Gdns *KGHY* BD21 ......58 B8
High Croft Rd *TOD* OL14 ......141 L8
Highcroft Wy *WHIT* OL12 ......206 B2
High Cross La *HIPP* HX3 ......125 J7
Highdale *EARL* WF12 ......174 A4
Highdale Cft *IDLE* BD10 ......83 K6
Higher Ashenhurst *TOD* OL14 ......141 J7
Higher Back La *HBR* HX7 ......142 A2
Higher Bank Rd *OL15* OL15 ......207 J3
Higher Brockwell
  RPDN/SBR HX6 ......167 H3
Higher Calderbrook Rd
  LIT OL15 ......185 L5
Higher Cleggswood Av
  LIT OL15 ......207 J3
Higher Coach Rd *BGLY* BD16 ......81 M4
Higher Downs *GIR* BD8 ......103 M6
Higher Grange Rd
  PDSY/CALV LS28 ......107 G6
Higher Intake Rd *ECHL* BD2 ......105 L5
Higher Lodge St *AIRE* BD20 ......34 D8
Higher Park Royd Dr
  RPDN/SBR HX6 ......167 G7
Higher Ri *ROY/SHW* OL2 ......229 J5
Higher School St *SHPY* BD18 ......82 B6
Higher Shore Rd *WHIT* OL12 ......185 G7
Higher Wheat La *MILN* OL16 ......206 E6
Higherwood Cl *KGHY* BD21 ......3 M5
Highfell Ri *HWTH* BD22 ......79 G1
High Fernley Ct *LM/WK* BD12 ......148 E2
High Fernley Rd *LM/WK* BD12 ......148 C3
Highfield *BOW* BD4 ......127 M5
  EARL/LOFT WF3 ......152 F5
  HIPP HX3 ......147 K1
Highfield Av *BRIG* HD6 ......148 D6
  BSLY S70 ......261 H8
  BSLYN/ROY S71 ......243 J8
  COL BB8 ......52 A5
  GTL/HWG HX4 ......168 D6
  HIPP HX3 ......125 M7
  HOLM/MEL HD9 ......234 F3
  IDLE BD10 ......83 J7
  KBTN HD8 ......256 C2
  PONT WF8 ......180 E7
  WOR/ARM LS12 ......130 F1
Highfield Cl *AIRE* BD20 ......58 E5
  FEA/AMT WF7 ......179 M6
  MOR LS27 ......130 A7
  WOR/ARM LS12 ......130 F1
Highfield Ct *HWTH* BD22 ......78 E4
  KBTN HD8 ......238 A8
  LVSG * WF15 ......172 B4
Highfield Crs *BAIL* BD17 ......82 E2
  HBR HX7 ......143 J2
  HOLM/MEL HD9 ......234 F3
  HOR/CROF WF4 ......196 E6
  HTON BD9 ......103 M2
  PDSY/CALV LS28 ......106 F6
  RTHW LS26 ......133 L7
  WOR/ARM LS12 ......108 F8
Highfield Dr *BTLY* WF17 ......151 G4
  CAS WF10 ......157 H1
  GFTH/SHER LS25 ......135 M3
  HTON BD9 ......103 M2
  LVSG WF15 ......172 A2
  MOR LS27 ......129 M7
  WKFDW/WTN WF2 ......176 A6
  YEA LS19 ......84 E3
Highfield Gdns *EARL* WF12 ......195 M3
  HTON BD9 ......103 M3
  MOR LS27 ......129 M7
  WOR/ARM LS12 ......108 E8
Highfield Garth
  WOR/ARM LS12 ......130 F1
Highfield Gra *HOR/CROF* WF4 ......197 J5
Highfield Gn *CAS* WF10 ......135 M4
  GFTH/SHER LS25 ......116 A4
  PDSY/CALV LS28 ......106 F6
Highfield Gv *CAS* WF10 ......135 M8
  ELL HX5 ......169 G6
  IDLE BD10 ......83 J8
High Field La *HWTH* BD22 ......78 E3
  RPDN/SBR HX6 ......166 F8
Highfield La *AIRE* BD20 ......36 A4
  AWLS/ASK DN6 ......205 K4
  DEWS WF13 ......173 K4
  GFTH/SHER LS25 ......136 F2
  HOLM/MEL HD9 ......234 E4
  HUDE HD5 ......215 L1
  KGHY BD21 ......2 D3
  MSTN/BAR LS15 ......112 F1
  RTHW LS26 ......133 L7
Highfield Ms *AIRE* BD20 ......58 E5
  BAIL BD17 ......82 E2
Highfield Mt *EARL* WF12 ......196 A5
  RTHW LS26 ......133 L8
Highfield Pl *CAS*, WF10 ......135 J8
  GIR BD8 ......4 B1
  HEM/SK/SE WF9 ......223 L8
  HFAX HX1 ......10 B8
  MOR LS27 ......152 D3
Highfield Range
  WMB/DAR S73 ......263 J7

Highfield Ri *WKFDW/WTN* WF2 ......176 A6
Highfield Rd *BRAM* LS13 ......107 M4
  BRIG HD6 ......170 A6
  CLECK BD19 ......149 L7
  ELL HX5 ......169 H8
  GFTH/SHER LS25 ......92 A6
  HOLM/MEL * HD9 ......234 F3
  HOR/CROF WF4 ......197 J5
  HOR/CROF WF4 ......218 F1
  HTON BD9 ......104 E1
  IDLE BD10 ......83 J8
  KBTN HD8 ......216 A7
  KGHY BD21 ......2 C3
  LUD/ILL HX2 ......145 G6
  MAR/SLWT HD7 ......212 B3
  MILN OL16 ......207 J8
  PDSY/CALV LS28 ......106 E6
  PONT WF8 ......180 E8
  WMB/DAR S73 ......263 J8
High Fields *LUD/ILL* HX2 ......168 A2
Highfields *HOR/CROF* WF4 ......218 F1
  HOR/CROF WF4 ......222 F4
  STKB/PEN S36 ......258 B8
Highfields Rd *DOD/DAR* S75 ......241 K6
  HUD HD1 ......14 D5
  KGHY BD21 ......2 F4
  PDSY/CALV LS28 ......106 E6
Highfield St *BRAM* * LS13 ......107 M4
  HUD HD1 ......14 D5
  KGHY BD21 ......2 F4
  PDSY/CALV LS28 ......106 E6
Highfield Ter *EARL* WF12 ......195 M3
  HFAX * HX1 ......10 B8
  PDSY/CALV LS28 ......106 E6
  SHPY BD18 ......82 A6
Highfield Vw *MOR* LS27 ......130 A7
Highfield Vls *GFTH/SHER* LS25 ......116 A8
High Fold *HWTH* BD22 ......2 B9
  YEA LS19 ......84 C1
High Fold La *AIRE* BD20 ......57 J4
Highgate *AIRE* BD20 ......34 E7
  HTON BD9 ......104 B2
Highgate Av *KBTN* HD8 ......216 B3
Highgate Cl *CUL/QBY* BD13 ......125 L4
Highgate Crs *KBTN* HD8 ......216 A3
Highgate Dr *KBTN* HD8 ......216 B3
  ROY/SHW OL2 ......228 D7
Highgate Gdns *LUD/ILL* HX2 ......146 A6
Highgate Gv *CLAY* BD14 ......125 L4
  HUDE * HD5 ......193 M4
  KBTN HD8 ......215 M3
Highgate La *CUL/QBY* BD13 ......125 K4
  EARL WF12 ......173 M6
Highgate St *BTLY* WF17 ......174 B3
Highgate Wk *KBTN* * HD8 ......216 B3
High Gn *KBTN* HD8 ......216 B4
High Green Dr *AIRE* BD20 ......35 M4
High Green Rd *NORM* WF6 ......178 A2
Highgrove Ct *NORM* WF6 ......178 B1
High Grove La *HIPP* HX3 ......11 L9
High Holly Garth *KGHY* BD21 ......3 K7
High House Av *ECHL* BD2 ......105 J2
High House Edge
  MAR/SLWT HD7 ......212 E7
High House La *LUD/ILL* HX2 ......144 C2
  MAR/SLWT HD7 ......212 D7
High House Rd *ECHL* BD2 ......105 J2
High Hoyland La *DOD/DAR* S75 ......240 D7
High Keep Fold
  HOR/CROF WF4 ......220 B3
Highlands Cl *PONT* WF8 ......181 H3
The Highlands *LVSG* WF15 ......171 M1
Highlands *LIT* OL15 ......207 J3
Highlands Cl *GTHN* BD7 ......126 A3
  RTHW LS26 ......132 B3
Highlands Dr *RTHW* LS26 ......132 B6
Highlands La *LUD/ILL* HX2 ......124 B3
Highlands Rd *ROY/SHW* OL2 ......229 H6
Highlands Wk *RTHW* LS26 ......132 B6
Highland Ville *HIPP* HX3 ......147 M6
High La *HBR* HX7 ......165 L3
  HOLM/MEL HD9 ......254 E3
  HUDS HD4 ......214 D4
  HWTH BD22 ......54 D5
  LUD/ILL HX2 ......145 K6
  PBR HG3 ......28 B6
  STKB/PEN S36 ......256 F7
High Lea *MAR/SLWT* HD7 ......233 H2
Highlea Cl *YEA* LS19 ......84 B1
Highlee La *RPDN/SBR* HX6 ......167 H7
High Lee La *STKB/PEN* S36 ......271 H1
High Lees Rd *LUD/ILL* HX2 ......145 K1
High Level Rd *ROCH* OL11 ......206 C8
High Level Wy *HFAX* HX1 ......10 B3
Highley Hall Cft *BRIG* HD6 ......170 F4
Highley Pk *BRIG* HD6 ......171 G4
High Meadow *KGHY* BD21 ......57 J5
High Mdw *EARL* WF12 ......195 L5
  GTL/HWG HX4 ......168 D7
  WIL/AL BD15 ......102 D1
  WKFDW/WTN WF2 ......199 K8
High Mill *ILK* * LS29 ......19 J5
High Mill La *ILK* LS29 ......19 J5
Highmoor *BAIL* BD17 ......82 C3
High Moor Av *AL/HA/HU* LS17 ......88 A4
High Moor Cl *AL/HA/HU* LS17 ......88 A4
High Moor Crs *AL/HA/HU* LS17 ......88 A4
Highmoor Crs *BRIG* HD6 ......170 F3
High Moor Dr *AL/HA/HU* LS17 ......88 A3
High Moor La *AL/HA/HU* LS17 ......88 A3
Highmoor La *BRIG* HD6 ......170 F3
  CLECK BD19 ......171 J1
High Moor Rd *PBR* HG3 ......25 L4
Highmoor Wk *BAIL* BD17 ......82 C4
Highoak Garth *HWTH* BD22 ......78 E4
High Oxford St *CAS* WF10 ......157 L7
High Park Crs *HTON* BD9 ......104 A3
High Park Dr *HTON* BD9 ......103 M3
High Park Gv *HTON* BD9 ......104 A3
High Poplars *ECHL* BD2 ......105 H4
High Rdg *HOR/CROF* WF4 ......197 G8
High Ridge Av *RTHW* LS26 ......132 G7
High Ridge Gv *RTHW* LS26 ......133 G8
High Ridge Pk *RTHW* LS26 ......133 G7
High Ridge Wy *BHP/TINH* LS16 ......64 D4
High Rd *EARL* WF12 ......174 A7
Highroad Well La *LUD/ILL* HX2 ......145 L7
Highroyd *KBTN* HD8 ......216 B3

High Royd Av *CUD/GR* S72 ......244 D8
Highroyd Crs *HUDE* HD5 ......15 L7
Highroyd La *HUDE* HD5 ......15 L7
High Royd La *STKB/PEN* S36 ......271 J1
High Royds Dr *ILK* LS29 ......61 J3
High Spring Gardens La
  KGHY BD21 ......2 D1
High Spring Rd *KGHY* BD21 ......58 B8
Highstone Av *BSLY* S70 ......261 G7
Highstone Crs *BSLY* S70 ......261 G7
Highstone La *BSLY* S70 ......261 H8
High Stones Rd *HBR* HX7 ......166 A3
Highstone V *BSLY* S70 ......261 G7
High St *AIRE* BD20 ......55 M1
  AIRE BD20 ......56 E1
  AWLS/ASK DN6 ......227 L6
  AWLS/ASK DN6 ......227 M3
  AWLS/ASK DN6 ......249 L6
  BRIG HD6 ......170 D3
  BSLY S70 ......261 G4
  BSLYN/ROY S71 ......243 K3
  BSLYN/ROY S71 ......261 L2
  BSPA/BRAM LS23 ......48 D6
  BSPA/BRAM LS23 ......69 M4
  BSPA/BRAM LS23 ......70 A1
  BTLY WF17 ......151 G4
  BTLY WF17 ......174 B3
  CAS WF10 ......157 L7
  CLECK BD19 ......149 M6
  COL BB8 ......74 A1
  CUD/GR S72 ......244 E4
  CUD/GR S72 ......245 H8
  CUD/GR S72 ......245 G1
  CUD/GR S72 ......263 M4
  CUL/QBY BD13 ......102 E8
  CUL/QBY BD13 ......125 G5
  DEWS WF13 ......173 K7
  DOD/DAR S75 ......242 C4
  DOD/DAR S75 ......259 H7
  DOD/DAR S75 ......260 B8
  EARL WF12 ......174 B7
  EARL WF12 ......195 L5
  GFTH/SHER LS25 ......135 K5
  GFTH/SHER LS25 ......138 A2
  GTL/HWG * HX4 ......168 F7
  GTL/HWG HX4 ......190 A3
  HECK WF16 ......172 F3
  HEM/SK/SE WF9 ......225 J7
  HEM/SK/SE WF9 ......247 K3
  HFAX HX1 ......10 F7
  HOLM/MEL * HD9 ......236 B2
  HOR/CROF WF4 ......197 J5
  HOR/CROF WF4 ......200 A2
  HOR/CROF WF4 ......200 B6
  HOR/CROF WF4 ......220 A1
  HOR/CROF WF4 ......220 B7
  HUD HD1 ......14 A8
  HUD HD1 ......14 F8
  IDLE BD10 ......83 K6
  KBTN HD8 ......240 B4
  KGHY BD21 ......2 F5
  KNOT WF11 ......159 L5
  KNOT * WF11 ......181 L1
  LIT OL15 ......207 H1
  LUD/ILL HX2 ......145 G5
  MAR/SLWT HD7 ......212 D1
  MOR LS27 ......152 C4
  NORM WF6 ......178 B3
  NORM WF6 ......178 D4
  OSS WF5 ......174 E5
  PBR HG3 ......28 A4
  PDSY/CALV LS28 ......106 F3
  ROY/SHW OL2 ......229 K8
  SKP/WHF BD23 ......16 C2
  STKB/PEN S36 ......270 F4
  TAD LS24 ......71 L3
  WBSY BD6 ......126 E5
  WBY LS22 ......48 A1
  WHIT OL12 ......206 B6
  YEA LS19 ......62 D7
High Street Ct *LUD/ILL* HX2 ......145 G5
High Sunderland La *HIPP* HX3 ......11 J1
Highthorne Ct *AL/HA/HU* LS17 ......88 B1
Highthorne Gn *ROY/SHW* OL2 ......228 E6
Highthorne La *AL/HA/HU* LS17 ......88 B2
  WOR/ARM * LS12 ......108 C6
Highthorne Mt *AL/HA/HU* LS17 ......88 B2
Highthorne St
  WOR/ARM * LS12 ......108 C6
Highthorne Vw
  WOR/ARM * LS12 ......108 D6
High Thorns *DOD/DAR* S75 ......259 H6
Hightown La *HOLM/MEL* HD9 ......254 C1
Hightown Rd *CLECK* BD19 ......149 M7
Hightown Vw *LVSG* WF15 ......171 M1
High Trees Ct *GFTH/SHER* LS25 ......116 A7
High Trees La *GTL/HWG* HX4 ......167 M8
High Vw *BSLYN/ROY* S71 ......243 K3
  HOR/CROF WF4 ......220 A3
High View Cl *WMB/DAR* S73 ......263 J8
Highway *GSLY* LS20 ......61 K5
Highway *GSLY* LS20 ......61 K5
High Ways *SCFT* LS14 ......111 G5
High Weardley La *OT* LS21 ......44 C8
High Well Hill La *CUD/GR* S72 ......222 E8
High Wheatley *ILK* LS29 ......39 G3
High Wicken Cl *CUL/QBY* BD13 ......102 E8
High Wd *ILK* LS29 ......39 H3
Highwood Av *AL/HA/HU* LS17 ......87 L3
Highwood Cl *DOD/DAR* S75 ......241 L6
Highwood Crs *AL/HA/HU* LS17 ......87 L3
High Woodlands
  EARD/LOFT WF3 ......153 L7
High Wood La *KBTN* HD8 ......238 D1
High Wood Rd *BTLY* WF17 ......151 J2
Higson Ct *HUDE* HD5 ......193 J7
Hilberoyd Rd *BTLY* WF17 ......173 M2
Hilda St *HTON* BD9 ......104 D2
  OSS WF5 ......197 G2
Hild Av *CUD/GR* S72 ......262 F2
Hillam Common La
  GFTH/SHER LS25 ......138 F8
Hillam Hall La *GFTH/SHER* LS25 ......138 E8
Hillam Hall Vw
  GFTH/SHER LS25 ......138 D8
Hillam La *GFTH/SHER* LS25 ......160 A1

Hillam Rd *ECHL* BD2 ......104 F3
  SEL YO8 ......139 L7
Hillam St *WBOW* BD5 ......126 D3
Hillary Pl *LDSU* LS2 ......6 E1
Hillary Rd *SHPY* BD18 ......83 G7
Hillary St *DEWS* WF13 ......173 H3
Hillbro Ct *KGHY* BD21 ......2 D1
Hillbrook Ri *ILK* LS29 ......38 B3
Hill Brow Cl *WIL/AL* BD15 ......103 J5
Hill Cl *BAIL* BD17 ......82 D4
  HUDW HD3 ......191 H5
  PONT WF8 ......180 F7
Hill Clough Gv *HWTH* BD22 ......56 E7
Hillcote Dr *WBOW* BD5 ......127 G2
Hillcourt Av *BRAM* LS13 ......107 L3
Hillcourt Cft *BRAM* LS13 ......107 L3
Hill Court Dr *BRAM* LS13 ......107 L3
Hillcourt Gv *BRAM* LS13 ......107 L2
Hill Crs *BTLY* WF17 ......151 J5
  ILK LS29 ......40 B7
  YEA LS19 ......84 E1
Hill Crest *HOR/CROF* WF4 ......222 F5
  WBY LS22 ......47 G6
Hillcrest *BHP/TINH* * LS16 ......63 J7
  GFTH/SHER LS25 ......138 D7
  HEM/SK/SE * WF9 ......223 M8
  NORM WF6 ......178 A2
  TAD LS24 ......71 K4
Hill Crest Av *CUL/QBY* BD13 ......101 M5
  BTLY WF17 ......173 J1
  CAS WF10 ......158 F3
  CHAL LS7 ......7 M2
  CUL/QBY BD13 ......125 H6
Hillcrest Cl *CAS* WF10 ......158 F8
  TAD LS24 ......71 K4
Hill Crest Dr *CUL/QBY* BD13 ......101 M5
Hillcrest Dr *CAS* WF10 ......158 F8
  CUL/QBY BD13 ......125 H6
Hillcrest Mt *BHP/TINH* LS16 ......86 A2
  CAS WF10 ......158 F8
  CLECK BD19 ......149 H7
Hill Crest Mt *CUL/QBY* BD13 ......101 M5
Hillcrest Pl *CHAL* LS7 ......7 M1
Hillcrest Ri *BHP/TINH* LS16 ......86 A2
Hill Crest Rd *CUL/QBY* BD13 ......101 M5
  CUL/QBY BD13 ......102 F7
  EARL WF12 ......195 L1
Hillcrest Rd *CAS* WF10 ......159 G8
  CUL/QBY BD13 ......125 H6
Hillcrest Vw *CHAL* LS7 ......7 M1
Hill Cft *CUL/QBY* BD13 ......103 G7
Hill Croft Cl *PONT* WF8 ......203 H1
Hill Dr *FEA/AMT* WF7 ......202 C6
Hill End *EARL* WF12 ......174 A6
Hill End Cl *HIPP* HX3 ......148 C4
Hill End Crs *WOR/ARM* LS12 ......108 B6
Hill End Gv *GTHN* BD7 ......126 A3
Hill End La *CUL/QBY* BD13 ......80 A6
  CUL/QBY BD13 ......124 F6
  HWTH BD22 ......54 A4
Hill End Rd *DOD/DAR* S75 ......242 E7
  WOR/ARM LS12 ......108 B6
Hillesley Rd *EARL* WF12 ......174 C3
Hillfold *HEM/SK/SE* WF9 ......247 K3
Hill Foot *SHPY* BD18 ......81 M7
Hillfoot Av *PDSY/CALV* LS28 ......106 D6
Hillfoot Crs *PDSY/CALV* LS28 ......106 D6
Hill Foot La *PBR* HG3 ......26 C2
Hillfoot Dr *PDSY/CALV* LS28 ......106 D6
Hillfoot Ri *PDSY/CALV* LS28 ......106 D6
Hillgarth *EARL* WF12 ......195 M3
  KNOT WF11 ......182 A3
Hill Green Ct *BOW* BD4 ......129 G4
Hill Gv *HUDW* HD3 ......191 H5
Hill Grove Lea *HUDW* HD3 ......191 H5
Hill Gv South *MID* LS10 ......132 B7
Hillhead Dr *BTLY* WF17 ......151 H5
Hill House Edge La
  HWTH BD22 ......100 D6
Hill House La *HOLM/MEL* HD9 ......253 M4
Hillhouse La *HUD* HD1 ......14 F7
Hill House Rd *HOLM/MEL* HD9 ......254 A4
Hilliam Hall Cl *GFTH/SHER* LS25 ......138 D7
Hillidge Rd *MID* LS10 ......9 J8
Hillidge Sq *MID* LS10 ......9 J7
Hillingdon Wy *AL/HA/HU* LS17 ......87 J1
Hillings La *ILK* LS29 ......60 F2
Hill Lands *LM/WK* BD12 ......148 D2
Hilla La *COL* BB8 ......52 D8
  HOLM/MEL HD9 ......254 A1
Hill Mount Pleasant *MID* LS10 ......153 L1
Hill Park Av *HIPP* HX3 ......10 A1
Hill Park Cv *DOD/DAR* S75 ......260 B6
Hill Ri *BTLY* WF17 ......174 B2
  SKP/WHF BD23 ......16 B1
Hill Rise Av *BRAM* LS13 ......107 L2
Hill Rise Gv *BRAM* LS13 ......107 L2
Hill Rd *CAS* WF10 ......158 B7
  WOR/ARM WF2 ......220 E2
Hillside *BSLYN/ROY* S71 ......262 C6
  GFTH/SHER LS25 ......113 J8
  KBTN HD8 ......239 H8
  KNOT WF11 ......159 M7
  PBR HG3 ......28 A1
Hill Side Av *HOLM/MEL* HD9 ......255 M8
Hillside Av *GSLY* LS20 ......61 M3
  HUDN HD2 ......192 D4
  HWTH BD22 ......78 D4
  LUD/ILL HX2 ......144 F7
  ROY/SHW OL2 ......229 M7
  RPDN/SBR HX6 ......167 H3
Hill Side Buildings
  BEE/HOL LS11 ......8 D7
Hillside Cl *GFTH/SHER* LS25 ......138 D7
  ILK LS29 ......19 G6
  STKB/PEN S36 ......258 B8
  WKFDW/WTN WF2 ......197 M3
Hillside Ct *CHAL* LS7 ......88 A7
  HEM/SK/SE WF9 ......247 J2

Hillside Crs *CUD/GR* S72 ......245 A1
  HUDS HD4 ......214 C4
  SKP/WHF BD23 ......16 E3
Hillside Gv *CUD/GR* S72 ......245 G1
  HWTH BD22 ......78 D4
  PDSY/CALV LS28 ......107 J3
Hill Side Mt *PDSY/CALV* LS28 ......107 G4
Hillside Mt *CUD/GR* S72 ......245 A4
  PDSY/CALV LS28 ......107 J3
  PONT WF8 ......181 G6
Hill Side Ri *GSLY* LS20 ......61 M4
Hill Side Rd *BFDE* BD3 ......5 J5
  BGLY BD16 ......81 K3
Hillside Rd *CHAL* LS7 ......87 M7
  FEA/AMT WF7 ......202 C8
  PBR HG3 ......26 F2
  PONT WF8 ......181 G6
  SHPY BD18 ......82 B8
Hillside Ter *BAIL* * BD17 ......82 E2
Hillside Vw *MAR/SLWT* HD7 ......212 F5
  PDSY/CALV LS28 ......107 H7
  RPDN/SBR HX6 ......167 J2
Hill St *BEE/HOL* LS11 ......8 A9
  BOW BD4 ......5 L9
  BSLYN/ROY S71 ......262 A6
  CLECK BD19 ......149 L7
  HFAX HX1 ......10 F8
  HOLM/MEL HD9 ......255 G5
  HWTH BD22 ......78 E8
  MILN OL16 ......206 C7
  OSM LS9 ......15 H6
  ROY/SHW OL2 ......229 L8
  WBSY BD6 ......126 C5
Hillthorpe Ct *MID* LS10 ......153 L3
Hillthorpe Dr *PONT* WF8 ......225 J1
Hillthorpe Ri *PDSY/CALV* LS28 ......129 G3
Hillthorpe Rd *PDSY/CALV* LS28 ......129 G3
Hillthorpe Sq *PDSY/CALV* LS28 ......129 G3
Hillthorpe St *PDSY/CALV* * LS28 ......129 G3
Hillthorpe Ter
  PDSY/CALV * LS28 ......129 G3
Hilltop *CUD/GR* S72 ......245 H3
Hill Top *CAS* WF10 ......157 H7
  DOD/DAR S75 ......259 G2
  HEM/SK/SE * WF9 ......223 J8
  HFAX HX1 ......168 A1
  ILK LS29 ......38 C4
  ILK LS29 ......40 A5
  KNOT WF11 ......182 B2
Hill Top Av *BSLYN/ROY* S71 ......243 D5
  RHAY LS8 ......110 B2
Hilltop Cl *CAS* WF10 ......158 C5
Hill Top Ct *EARD/LOFT* WF3 ......153 G8
  HEM/SK/SE * WF9 ......223 K3
  HOR/CROF WF4 ......221 K8
  TAD LS24 ......71 K7
  WOR/ARM LS12 ......108 B6
Hill Top Cottages *HTON* BD9 ......104 A4
Hill Top Ct *EARD/LOFT* WF3 ......153 G8
  WKFDW/WTN * WF2 ......220 E2
Hill Top Crs *MIRF* WF14 ......194 A5
Hill Top Cft *HUDS* HD4 ......213 L8
Hill Top Dr *HUDW* HD3 ......191 J6
  ROCH OL11 ......228 C4
Hill Top Farm *KBTN* HD8 ......238 D1
Hill Top Gdns
  EARD/LOFT * WF3 ......153 G8
Hill Top Gn *EARD/LOFT* WF3 ......152 F8
Hill Top Gv *EARD/LOFT* WF3 ......153 G8
  WIL/AL BD15 ......103 J5
Hill Top La *BGLY* BD16 ......59 H5
  DOD/DAR S75 ......260 D3
  EARD/LOFT WF3 ......152 F8
  HBR HX7 ......165 K3
  HOR/CROF WF4 ......201 L5
  PBR HG3 ......26 B2
  WIL/AL BD15 ......103 J5
Hill Top Ms *KNOT* WF11 ......182 B2
Hill Top Mt *RHAY* LS8 ......110 B2
Hill Top Pl *HDGY* LS6 ......6 A4
  RHAY LS8 ......110 B2
Hill Top Rd *CUL/QBY* BD13 ......102 D7
  HOLM/MEL HD9 ......254 D4
  HOR/CROF WF4 ......217 M3
  HUD HD1 ......14 A9
  HUDE HD5 ......15 L6
  HUDW HD3 ......191 H5
  HWTH BD22 ......78 D4
  KGHY BD21 ......79 J5
  MAR/SLWT HD7 ......212 B5
  WKFDW/WTN WF2 ......220 F2
  WOR/ARM LS12 ......108 B6
Hill Top Vw *EARD/LOFT* WF3 ......152 F8
  HOLM/MEL HD9 ......254 D6
Hill Top Wk *HWTH* BD22 ......2 A4
Hill Top Wy *HWTH* BD22 ......2 A4
Hill Vw *LUD/ILL* HX2 ......124 B7
Hillview Gdns *HIPP* HX3 ......147 J5
Hill View Pl *CHAL* * LS7 ......87 M7
Hill View Ter *CHAL* * LS7 ......87 M7
Hillway *GSLY* LS20 ......61 L1
Hillworth Village *KGHY* * BD21 ......2 D1
Hilmian Wy *HEM/SK/SE* WF9 ......246 B1
Hilton Av *SHPY* BD18 ......104 D1
Hilton Ct *BHP/TINH* LS16 ......63 J2
Hilton Crs *BAIL* BD17 ......82 E4
Hilton Dr *SHPY* BD18 ......104 D1
Hilton Gra *BHP/TINH* LS16 ......63 J2
Hilton Gv *GTHN* BD7 ......104 C8
  RHAY LS8 ......110 B1
  SHPY BD18 ......104 D1
Hilton Ms *BHP/TINH* LS16 ......63 J3
Hilton Pl *RHAY* LS8 ......110 B2
Hilton Rd *GTHN* BD7 ......104 C8
  RHAY LS8 ......110 B2
  SHPY BD18 ......104 D1
Hilton St *DOD/DAR* S75 ......260 F4
  HBR HX7 ......143 J3
  RHAY * LS8 ......110 B2
Hilton Ter *RHAY* * LS8 ......110 B2
Hinchcliffe Av *OSS* WF5 ......197 H1
Hinchliffe St *BFDE* BD3 ......5 L3
Hinchliffe Av *BAIL* BD17 ......82 F4
Hind Ct *HOLM/MEL* HD9 ......234 E3
Hindle Pl *MOR* * LS27 ......130 D7

Hin - Hou 303

Hindle St BSLY S70 260 F5
Hindley Rd LVSG WF15 172 C3
Hindley Wk GTHN BD7 125 M4
Hinds Crs HEM/SK/SE WF9 247 H3
Hind St LM/WK BD12 148 E4
Hinsley Ct HDGY LS6 109 G1
Hinton WHIT * OL12 206 A6
Hinton Cl PONT WF8 181 G3
Hinton La KNOT WF11 159 J8
Hions Cl BRIG HD6 170 C6
Hipswell St BFDE BD3 105 L6
Hird Av WBSY BD6 126 E6
Hird Rd LM/WK BD12 126 F8
Hird St BAIL BD17 82 D6
BEE/HOL LS11 8 D9
KGHY BD21 2 E8
Hirds Yd SKP/WHF BD23 16 B3
Hirst Av HECK WF16 172 F1
Hirst Ct HBR HX7 143 K3
Hirstlands Av OSS WF5 174 E7
Hirstlands Dr OSS WF5 174 E6
Hirst La HOLM/MEL HD9 255 K2
SHPY BD18 82 A6
Hirst Lodge Ct ECHL BD2 105 H2
Hirst Mill Crs SHPY BD18 82 A5
Hirst Rd DEWS WF13 173 L5
WKFDW/WTN WF2 197 M1
Hirst St CAS WF10 135 G7
TOD * OL14 140 D5
Hirst Wood Crs SHPY BD18 82 A6
Hirst Wood Rd SHPY BD18 81 M6
Hive St HWTH BD22 2 D7
Hobart Rd CAS WF10 158 F6
EARL WF12 174 B5
Hobberley La AL/HA/HU LS17 89 H3
Hobb Nook La OT LS21 22 C7
Hob Cote La HWTH BD22 78 B5
Hobcroft Ter AWLS/ASK DN6 249 K5
Hob La HUDS HD4 213 K4
HWTH BD22 77 L7
RPDN/SBR HX6 167 K5
RPDN/SBR HX6 188 E1
Hockney Rd GIR BD8 104 D6
Hodder Av LIT OL15 185 H8
Hodge La PONT WF8 205 G8
Hodgewood La PONT WF8 181 M8
Hodgkinson Av STKB/PEN S36 270 F3
Hodgson Av AL/HA/HU LS17 88 C3
BFDE BD3 105 M6
Hodgson Crs AL/HA/HU LS17 88 C3
Hodgson Fold ILK LS29 18 F5
Hodgson La BIRK/DRI BD11 128 D7
Hodgson's La GFTH/SHER LS25 116 C5
Hodgson St MOR LS27 152 E5
WKFDE WF1 176 D7
Hodroyd Cl CUD/GR S72 244 F5
Hodroyd Cottages
CUD/GR S72 245 H4
Hodster La CUD/GR S72 263 M2
Hoffman St HUDS HD4 213 J2
Hogarth Rd ROCH OL11 228 B4
Hog Close La HOLM/MEL HD9 255 L6
Hogley La HOLM/MEL HD9 253 L2
Holays HUDE HD5 193 G7
Holbeck La BEE/HOL LS11 8 B4
Holbeck Moor Rd BEE/HOL LS11 8 C6
Holbeck Towers BEE/HOL LS11 8 C6
Holborn Ap HDGY LS6 6 D2
Holborn Ct HDGY LS6 6 E3
WBSY BD6 126 E8
Holborn Gdns HDGY LS6 6 D2
Holborn Gn HDGY LS6 6 D2
Holborn Gv HDGY LS6 6 D3
Holborn St HDGY LS6 6 E2
Holborn Ter HDGY LS6 6 E3
Holborn Vw HDGY LS6 6 D2
Holborn Wk HDGY LS6 6 D3
Holby Sq WKFDW/WTN * WF2 197 L2
Holden Ct BSLY S70 261 G5
Holden Ing Wy BTLY WF17 151 J2
Holden La AIRE BD20 36 D7
BAIL BD17 82 F2
Holden St WHIT * OL12 206 C4
Holderness Rd KNOT WF11 182 A1
Holderness St TOD OL14 163 L1
Holdforth Cl WOR/ARM LS12 109 G7
Holdforth Gdns
WOR/ARM LS12 109 G7
Holdforth Gn WOR/ARM LS12 109 G8
Holdforth Pl WOR/ARM LS12 109 G7
Holdsworth Av HECK WF16 151 G7
Holdsworth Ct CLECK BD19 149 M7
Holdsworth Rd LUD/ILL HX2 124 C7
Holdsworth St BFD BD1 5 G4
CLECK BD19 149 M6
SHPY BD18 82 E8
Holdsworth Ter HFAX HX1 168 F1
Hole Bottom Rd TOD OL14 141 K8
Hole La AIRE BD20 35 K2
Holes La KNOT WF11 182 A2
Holford Wk MILN OL16 206 F7
Holgate Crs HEM/SK/SE WF9 223 L7
Holgate Gdns HEM/SK/SE WF9 223 L7
Holgate Mt BSLY S70 261 H8
Holgate Rd PONT WF8 202 E1
Holgate Vw CUD/GR S72 245 J3
Holker St GIR BD8 104 D6
KGHY BD21 3 G3
Holland Ri WHIT * OL12 206 A6
Holland Rd GFTH/SHER LS25 135 L4
Holland St BTLY WF17 173 M1
MILN OL16 206 F2
WHIT OL12 206 A6
Hollas La RPDN/SBR HX6 168 A4
Hollerton La EARD/LOFT WF3 153 H6
The Hollies WOR/ARM * LS12 108 E7
Hollin Av HUDW HD3 191 M7
Hollinbank La HECK WF16 173 G1
Hollin Brigg La
HOLM/MEL HD9 253 L4
Hollin Close La ECHL BD2 105 G3
Hollin Ct BHP/TINH * LS16 86 F7
Hollin Crs BHP/TINH LS16 86 F7
Hollin Cft DOD/DAR S75 260 C6
Hollin Dr BHP/TINH LS16 86 F7
HOR/CROF WF4 220 A1
Hollin Edge KBTN HD8 239 J8
Hollin Gdns BHP/TINH LS16 86 E7
Hollin Ga OT LS21 40 F4
The Hollings RTHW LS26 156 D3
Hollingbourne Rd
MSTN/BAR LS15 112 B4
Hollin Greaves La HIPP HX3 11 H1
Hollings HWTH * BD22 78 C7
Hollings Rd GIR BD8 104 D6
Hollings Sq GIR BD8 104 D6
Hollings St BGLY BD16 81 K7
GIR BD8 104 D6
Hollings Ter GIR BD8 104 D6
Hollingthorpe Av
HOR/CROF WF4 220 A3
Hollingthorpe Ct
HOR/CROF WF4 220 A4
Hollingthorpe Gv
HOR/CROF WF4 220 A3
Hollingthorpe La
HOR/CROF WF4 220 A3
Hollingthorpe Rd
HOR/CROF WF4 220 A3
Hollington St COL BB8 74 D1
Hollingwood Av GTHN BD7 126 B2
Hollingwood Dr GTHN BD7 126 A2
Hollingwood Ga ILK LS29 38 A3
Hollingwood La GTHN BD7 126 A3
Hollingwood Mt GTHN BD7 126 A2
Hollingwood Ri ILK LS29 38 A3
Hollingworth Fold LIT * OL15 207 L4
Hollingworth La KNOT WF11 182 C2
TOD OL14 163 K6
Hollingworth Rd LIT * OL15 207 K2
Hollin Hall Dr ILK LS29 38 A3
Hollin Hall La HUDE HD5 193 M4
MAR/SLWT HD7 212 F1
Hollin Hall Rd SHPY BD18 82 A8
Hollin Head BAIL BD17 83 H2
Hollin Hill Av RHAY LS8 110 E1
Hollinhirst La HOR/CROF WF4 219 H1
Hollin House La
HOLM/MEL HD9 255 H1
KBTN HD8 240 B7
Hollin La BHP/TINH LS16 86 F7
HBR HX7 144 C1
HOR/CROF WF4 197 M8
RPDN/SBR HX6 167 K5
RPDN/SBR HX6 188 C3
SHPY BD18 82 F8
STKB/PEN S36 269 J2
Hollin Mt BHP/TINH LS16 86 E7
Hollin Park Av RHAY LS8 110 F1
Hollin Park Ct PDSY/CALV LS28 84 C8
Hollin Park Crs RHAY LS8 110 F1
Hollin Park Dr PDSY/CALV LS28 84 C8
Hollin Park Mt RHAY LS8 110 F1
Hollin Park Pl RHAY LS8 110 E1
Hollin Park Rd PDSY/CALV LS28 84 C8
RHAY LS8 110 E1
Hollin Park Ter RHAY LS8 110 E1
Hollin Ri SHPY * BD18 82 E8
Hollin Rd BHP/TINH LS16 86 F7
SHPY BD18 82 E8
Hollinroyd Rd EARL WF12 174 A6
The Hollins TOD OL14 141 K8
Hollins Av DEWS WF13 173 H4
Hollins Bank RPDN/SBR HX6 167 K2
Hollins Bank La AIRE BD20 56 F2
Hollins Beck Cl
GFTH/SHER LS25 135 J6
Hollins Bungalows
RPDN/SBR * HX6 167 K1
Hollins Cl AIRE BD20 57 H4
Hollins Gln MAR/SLWT HD7 212 C6
Hollins Gv CAS WF10 135 H8
Hollins Hey Rd GTL/HWG HX4 190 F2
Hollins Hl BAIL BD17 61 K8
Hollins La AIRE BD20 57 H3
LUD/ILL HX2 145 L1
LUD/ILL HX2 166 D1
MAR/SLWT HD7 211 M8
RPDN/SBR HX6 167 K1
Hollins Meadow TOD OL14 163 J5
Hollins Mill La RPDN/SBR HX6 167 J2
Hollins Mt HEM/SK/SE WF9 223 L7
Hollins Pk GFTH/SHER LS25 135 J5
Hollins Pl HBR HX7 143 J3
TOD OL14 163 J5
Hollins Rd DEWS WF13 173 H4
TOD OL14 163 J4
Hollins Rw MAR/SLWT HD7 212 C6
Hollins St TOD OL14 163 K6
Hollin St RPDN/SBR HX6 167 G5
Hollin Ter HUDW HD3 191 L7
SHPY * BD18 82 E8
Hollin Vw BHP/TINH LS16 86 F7
Hollin Wood Cl SHPY BD18 82 A7
Hollinwood Vw AIRE BD20 58 F7
Hollis Pl BVRD LS3 6 A7
The Hollow HOLM/MEL HD9 234 E4
Hollowdene DOD/DAR S75 260 D3
Hollowfield Cft LM/WK BD12 149 K1
Hollowgate HOLM/MEL HD9 254 C1
Hollowspell WHIT OL12 206 E3
Holly Ap OSS WF5 174 F6
Holly Av BHP/TINH LS16 85 M3
Holly Bank FEA/AMT WF7 202 B8
GFTH/SHER LS25 113 K8
HDGY LS6 86 F8
HEM/SK/SE * WF9 223 M7
Hollybank Av BTLY WF17 151 K7
KBTN HD8 238 E8
Holly Bank Ct HUDW * HD3 191 J7
Holly Bank Dr HIPP HX3 147 M6
Hollybank Gdns GTHN BD7 126 A3
Hollybank Gv GTHN BD7 126 A3
Holly Bank Pk BRIG HD6 170 B6
BRIG HD6 170 A6
Holly Bank Rd HUDW HD3 191 K5
Hollybank Rd GTHN BD7 126 A3
Holly Bush Ct BSPA/BRAM LS23 49 G7
Hollybush Gn WBY LS22 47 L6
Holly Cl HEM/SK/SE WF9 247 H4
HOR/CROF WF4 200 A5
MID LS10 153 K2
Holly Ct EARD/LOFT WF3 153 G8
WKFDE WF1 176 E1
Holly Crs HOR/CROF WF4 200 A5
RPDN/SBR HX6 188 E3
Hollycroft Ct BHP/TINH LS16 86 C3
Holly Dene OSS WF5 174 F6
Holly Dr BHP/TINH LS16 85 M3
Hollyfield Av HUDW HD3 191 J7
Hollygarth La GLE DN14 161 J7
Holly Gv BTLY WF17 173 K2
CUD/GR S72 245 J3
HFAX HX1 10 C7
HUDW HD3 191 L5
Holly Hall La LM/WK BD12 148 E2
Holly Mede OSS WF5 174 F6
Hollynsmill GTL/HWG HX4 168 F7
Hollyoake Av MAR/SLWT HD7 212 E6
Holly Pk AL/HA/HU LS17 43 L1
HORS LS18 85 H6
Holly Park Dr GTHN BD7 126 A2
Holly Park Gv GTHN * BD7 126 A2
Holly Park Mills
PDSY/CALV * LS28 84 C8
PDSY/CALV * LS28 107 G2
Holly Rd BSPA/BRAM LS23 48 E6
HUD HD1 214 A2
Hollyshaw Crs MSTN/BAR LS15 111 L6
Hollyshaw Gv MSTN/BAR LS15 111 L6
Hollyshaw La MSTN/BAR LS15 111 L6
Hollyshaw St MSTN/BAR LS15 111 L6
Hollyshaw Ter MSTN/BAR LS15 111 L6
Hollyshaw Wk MSTN/BAR LS15 111 L5
Holly St HEM/SK/SE WF9 223 M7
WBSY BD6 125 M4
WHIT OL12 184 E8
WKFDW/WTN WF2 176 B7
Holly Ter HUD HD1 15 G3
Holly Tree La MSTN/BAR LS15 112 A8
Hollywell Gv WOR/ARM LS12 108 D6
Hollywell La WOR/ARM LS12 108 D6
Holman Av GFTH/SHER LS25 135 H1
Holmcliffe Av HUDS HD4 214 B5
Holmclose HOLM/MEL HD9 253 K4
Holmdale Crs HOLM/MEL HD9 236 B6
Holmdene Dr MIRF WF14 172 C8
Holme Av HUDE HD5 215 G1
Holmebank Ms
HOLM/MEL HD9 236 D3
Holme Cl AIRE BD20 34 F8
HOR/CROF WF4 217 G1
Holme Ct HOLM/MEL HD9 237 G7
Holme Crs COL BB8 74 D3
Holme Cft HOR/CROF WF4 198 B7
Holme Dr LUD/ILL HX2 145 K8
Holme Farm WBSY BD6 125 M5
Holme Farm Ct
WOR/ARM LS12 129 M3
Holme Farm La
BSPA/BRAM LS23 68 B3
Holme Fld OSS WF5 174 E7
Holmefield Rd AIRE BD20 55 M1
HUDW HD3 191 G8
Holmefield Vw BOW BD4 128 A2
Holme Gv ILK LS29 40 B7
Holme House La HWTH BD22 78 E1
LUD/ILL HX2 145 G2
Holme House Rd TOD OL14 140 E5
Holme House St LIT OL15 185 M5
Holme Ings ILK LS29 19 L7
Holme La AIRE BD20 55 M1
BOW BD4 128 A5
HOLM/MEL HD9 237 G7
MAR/SLWT HD7 211 L6
WKFDW/WTN WF2 198 D4
Holme Leas Dr OSS WF5 174 E7
Holme Mill La HWTH BD22 2 A6
Holme Pk ILK LS29 40 B7
Holme Park Ct HUDS * HD4 214 B6
Holme Pl HBR HX7 143 J2
Holme Rd LUD/ILL HX2 145 K8
Holmeside Cl HUDS HD4 214 A6
Holme South LVSG WF15 172 D2
Holmes Rd RPDN/SBR HX6 167 L2
Holmes St BEE/HOL LS11 9 G4
GIR BD8 4 C4
WHIT OL12 206 E3
Holmes Ter LUD/ILL HX2 145 M6
Holme St BRIG HD6 148 C7
COL BB8 74 D1
HBR HX7 143 J3
HWTH BD22 100 E4
LVSG WF15 172 D2
TOD OL14 141 G7
WBOW BD5 126 F2
Holme Styes La
HOLM/MEL HD9 254 A5
Holme Ter LIT OL15 185 M5
Holme Top La WBOW BD5 126 F2
Holme Top St WBOW BD5 126 F2
Holme Valley Circular Wk
HOLM/MEL HD9 236 A7
HOLM/MEL HD9 237 H6
HOLM/MEL HD9 237 K7
HOLM/MEL HD9 255 K2
HUDS HD4 214 A7
HUDS HD4 237 G2
Holme View Dr
HOLM/MEL HD9 253 M1
Holme View Pk
HOLM/MEL HD9 254 A1
Holme View Rd DOD/DAR S75 241 K6
Holme Wy OSS WF5 174 E7
Holme Well Rd MID LS10 154 A1
Holme Wood Rd BOW BD4 127 M3
HWTH BD22 2 B7
Holme Woods La
HOLM/MEL HD9 266 B1
Holmfield KBTN * HD8 240 B4
Holmfield Av WKFDW/WTN WF2 12 D9
Holmfield Cha EARD/LOFT WF3 155 K8
Holmfield Cl KBTN HD8 240 B4
PONT WF8 181 H3
Holmfield Dr MAR/SLWT HD7 213 H2
RHAY LS8 88 B5
Holmfield Gv WKFDW/WTN WF2 12 D9
Holmfield La PONT WF8 181 H2
WKFDW/WTN WF2 12 D8
Holmfield Rd KBTN HD8 240 B4
Holmfirth Rd HOLM/MEL HD9 235 G5
HOLM/MEL HD9 236 F7
KBTN HD8 237 M8
Holmsley Av HEM/SK/SE WF9 246 C4
Holmsley Crest RTHW LS26 133 J7
Holmsley Field Ct RTHW LS26 133 L8
Holmsley Field La RTHW LS26 133 K8
Holmsley Garth RTHW LS26 133 K7
Holmsley Gv HEM/SK/SE WF9 246 C4
Holmsley La CUD/GR S72 246 A4
RTHW LS26 133 K8
Holmsley Mt HEM/SK/SE WF9 246 C4
Holmwood Av HDGY LS6 87 G6
Holmwood Cl HDGY LS6 87 H6
Holmwood Crs HDGY LS6 87 G7
Holmwood Dr HDGY LS6 87 G6
Holmwood Gv HDGY LS6 87 H6
Holmwood Mt HDGY LS6 87 H6
Holroyd Hl WBSY BD6 126 E5
Holroyd St CHAL LS7 7 K5
MILN OL16 206 C7
Holsworthy Rd BOW BD4 128 A3
The Holt SHPY BD18 82 E7
Holt Av BHP/TINH LS16 86 E1
HUDN HD2 192 E3
Holtby Gv BRIG HD6 148 C7
Holt Cl BHP/TINH LS16 86 E2
Holt Crs BHP/TINH LS16 86 B1
Holtdale Ap BHP/TINH LS16 86 A1
Holtdale Av BHP/TINH LS16 86 B1
Holtdale Cl BHP/TINH LS16 86 B1
Holtdale Cft BHP/TINH LS16 86 B1
Holtdale Dr BHP/TINH LS16 86 B1
Holtdale Fold BHP/TINH LS16 86 B1
Holtdale Gdns BHP/TINH LS16 86 B1
Holtdale Garth BHP/TINH LS16 86 B1
Holtdale Gn BHP/TINH LS16 86 B1
Holtdale Gv BHP/TINH LS16 86 A1
Holtdale Lawn BHP/TINH LS16 86 B1
Holtdale Pl BHP/TINH LS16 86 B1
Holtdale Rd BHP/TINH LS16 86 B1
Holtdale Vw BHP/TINH LS16 86 B1
Holtdale Wy BHP/TINH LS16 86 B1
Holt Dr BHP/TINH LS16 86 C1
Holt Farm Cl BHP/TINH LS16 86 B1
Holt Farm Ri BHP/TINH LS16 86 B1
Holt Gdns BHP/TINH LS16 86 E1
IDLE BD10 83 H6
Holt Garth BHP/TINH LS16 86 C1
Holt Ga BHP/TINH LS16 86 C1
Holt Head Rd MAR/SLWT HD7 212 D8
Holt La BHP/TINH LS16 86 C1
HOLM/MEL HD9 236 B8
Holt Park Ap BHP/TINH LS16 86 C1
Holt Park Av BHP/TINH LS16 86 C1
Holt Park Cl BHP/TINH LS16 86 C1
Holt Park Crs BHP/TINH LS16 86 C1
Holt Park Dr BHP/TINH LS16 86 C1
Holt Park Gdns BHP/TINH LS16 86 C1
Holt Park Ga BHP/TINH LS16 86 C1
Holt Park Gra BHP/TINH LS16 86 C1
Holt Park Gn BHP/TINH LS16 86 C1
Holt Park Gv BHP/TINH LS16 86 B1
Holt Park La BHP/TINH LS16 86 C1
Holt Park Ri BHP/TINH LS16 86 C1
Holt Park Rd BHP/TINH LS16 86 C1
Holt Park V BHP/TINH LS16 86 C1
Holt Park Wy BHP/TINH LS16 86 C1
Holt Ri BHP/TINH LS16 86 C1
Holt Rd BHP/TINH LS16 86 C1
Holts La CLAY BD14 125 K1
Holts Ter HIPP HX3 168 F2
WHIT OL12 206 A4
Holt St LIT OL15 185 M4
MILN * OL16 229 J1
Holt Vw BHP/TINH LS16 86 C1
Holt Wy BHP/TINH LS16 86 C1
Holwick Cl DOD/DAR * S75 259 H6
Holwick Ct BSLY * S70 261 G5
Holybrook Av IDLE BD10 83 M8
Holycroft St KGHY BD21 2 E7
Holyoake Av BGLY BD16 81 H5
BTLY WF17 173 J1
Holyoake St TOD OL14 140 C5
Holyoake Ter HOR/CROF WF4 197 G5
MAR/SLWT HD7 212 E5
Holyrood Crs NORM WF6 178 B2
Holy Rood La GFTH/SHER LS25 137 G6
Holy St ROCH OL11 228 D4
Holywell Ash La GIR BD8 4 D2
Holywell Gdns CAS WF10 158 B8
Holywell La AL/HA/HU LS17 88 F1
CAS WF10 158 C8
Holywell Mt CAS WF10 158 D8
Homefield Av MOR LS27 152 C4
Home Lea RTHW LS26 132 F7
Home Lea Dr RTHW LS26 132 F7
The Homestead HECK WF16 173 G2
Homestead Dr
WKFDW/WTN WF2 176 B8
Homestead Gdns WHIT OL12 206 F1
Home View Ter GIR BD8 104 D5
Honey Head La
HOLM/MEL HD9 236 B3
Honey Hole Cl TOD OL14 163 K2
Honey Hole Rd TOD OL14 163 K2
Honey Pot La BAIL * BD17 82 D3
Honeysuckle Cl
WKFDW/WTN WF2 176 A7
Honeysuckle Dr EARL WF12 195 M3
Honeywell Cl BSLYN/ROY S71 261 H3
Honeywell Gv BSLYN/ROY S71 261 H2
Honeywell La DOD/DAR S75 261 G3
Honeywell Pl BSLYN/ROY S71 261 H3
Honeywell St BSLYN/ROY S71 261 H3
Honley Rd HUDS HD4 214 E8
Honley Sq HOR/CROF WF4 197 J5
Honoria St HUD HD1 14 F1
The Hoods BRIG HD6 170 B7
Hood St HEM/SK/SE WF9 247 G6
HUDS HD4 214 B6
Hooton Crs HOR/CROF WF4 222 C5
Hoowood La HOLM/MEL HD9 253 G3
Hopbine Av WBOW BD5 127 G4
Hopbine Rd WBOW BD5 127 G4
Hope Av SHPY BD18 82 F6
WBOW BD5 126 E4
Hopefield Cha EARD/LOFT WF3 154 D2
Hopefield Cl RTHW LS26 154 D2
Hopefield Ct EARD/LOFT WF3 153 L7
EARD/LOFT WF3 154 D2
HOLM/MEL HD9 254 C7
Hopefield Crs RTHW LS26 154 D2
Hopefield Dr EARD/LOFT WF3 154 D2
Hopefield Gdns
EARD/LOFT WF3 154 D2
Hopefield Gn RTHW LS26 154 D2
Hopefield Gv
EARD/LOFT * WF3 154 D2
Hopefield Ms EARD/LOFT WF3 154 D2
Hopefield Pl RTHW LS26 154 D2
Hopefield Vw RTHW LS26 154 D2
Hopefield Wk RTHW LS26 154 D2
Hopefield Wy BOW BD4 127 K5
EARD/LOFT WF3 154 D2
Hope Hall St HFAX HX1 11 H8
Hope Hall Ter HFAX HX1 11 H8
Hope Hill Vw BGLY BD16 81 J7
Hope La BAIL BD17 82 D3
Hope Pl KGHY BD21 2 F8
Hope Rd LDSU LS2 7 K8
Hopes Farm Mt RTHW * LS26 132 B7
Hopes Farm Rd RTHW LS26 132 B7
Hopes Farm Vw RTHW LS26 132 B7
Hope St BSLYN/ROY S71 244 B8
CAS WF10 158 E3
DEWS WF13 173 L5
DOD/DAR S75 242 E6
DOD/DAR S75 260 F4
HBR HX7 143 J3
HFAX HX1 10 E5
HUDW * HD3 213 K1
MOR LS27 152 C2
NORM WF6 178 C6
OSS WF5 197 H2
ROY/SHW OL2 229 K7
RPDN/SBR HX6 167 L3
WHIT OL12 206 B6
Hope St East CAS * WF10 157 M6
Hope St West CAS * WF10 157 L7
Hope Vw SHPY BD18 82 E7
Hopewell Pl HDGY * LS6 109 G4
Hopewell St BSLY S70 261 M6
Hopewell Ter GFTH/SHER LS25 135 K5
Hopewell Vw MID LS10 153 M1
Hopewell Wy HOR/CROF WF4 220 A1
Hopkinson Dr BOW BD4 127 L6
Hopkinson Rd HUDN HD2 192 D2
Hopkinson St COL * BB8 74 D3
LUD/ILL HX2 146 B2
Hopkin St BOW BD4 128 A5
Hopps's Rd AIRE BD20 34 E7
Hops La HIPP HX3 145 M4
Hopton Av BOW BD4 127 K5
MIRF WF14 194 A4
Hopton Dr MIRF WF14 194 A4
Hopton Hall La HUDE HD5 194 B6
Hopton La MIRF WF14 194 A4
Hopton Ms WOR/ARM LS12 108 D7
Hopton New Rd MIRF WF14 194 C3
Hopwood Bank HORS LS18 85 L4
Hopwood Cl HORS LS18 85 L4
Hopwood Gv CAS WF10 158 D7
Hopwood La HFAX HX1 10 A7
Hopwood Rd HORS LS18 85 L4
Hopwood St BSLY S70 261 G4
Horace Waller VC Pde
EARL WF12 174 C4
Horbury Ms HOR/CROF WF4 197 H4
Horbury Rd CUD/GR S72 244 D6
OSS WF5 197 G3
WKFDW/WTN WF2 12 A4
Horest La UPML OL3 230 D6
Horley Green Rd HIPP HX3 11 L2
Hornbeam Av
WKFDW/WTN WF2 176 C6
Hornbeam Cl WIL/AL BD15 103 H2
Hornbeam Wy SCFT LS14 89 L6
Hornby St BSLY S70 261 H7
HFAX HX1 10 B9
Hornby Ter HFAX * HX1 10 B8
Horncastle St CLECK BD19 150 A7
Horncastle Vw HOR/CROF WF4 222 F5
Horn Cote La HOLM/MEL HD9 237 J8
Horn Cft DOD/DAR S75 259 G1
Horner Av BTLY WF17 151 H8
Horner Crs BTLY WF17 151 H8
Hornes La DOD/DAR S75 242 E5
Horne St HFAX HX1 10 E5
WKFDW/WTN WF2 12 D6
Hornington Br COP/BISH YO23 73 G6
Horn La AIRE BD20 35 L1
HOLM/MEL HD9 237 J8
STKB/PEN S36 256 C5
Hornsea Dr WIL/AL BD15 102 E2
Hornthwaite Hill Rd
STKB/PEN S36 270 B4
Horse Bank Dr HUDS * HD4 214 A4
Horse Carr Vw BSLYN/ROY S71 262 C6
Horse Croft La KBTN HD8 238 D3
Horse Fair PONT WF8 180 F6
Horsefair WBY LS22 48 A1
Horsehold La HBR HX7 143 G4
Horsehold Rd HBR HX7 143 G4
Horse Pond La HUDW HD3 190 C7
Horsewood Cl BSLY S70 260 D6
Horsfall St HFAX HX1 168 C1
MOR LS27 130 B8
TOD OL14 142 A8
Horsfall Vls TOD * OL14 142 A8
Horsfield Cl COL BB8 74 B1
Horsforth New Rd BRAM LS13 85 G8
Horsham Ct HWTH BD22 79 G1
Horsham Rd BOW * BD4 128 A4
Horsley St WBSY BD6 126 E5
Horsman St BOW BD4 128 A5
Horton Cl BRAM LS13 107 H2
Horton Garth BRAM * LS13 107 H2
Horton Grange Rd GTHN BD7 104 D8
Horton Hall Cl WBOW BD5 126 F1
Horton Park Av GTHN BD7 126 D1
Horton Ri BRAM LS13 107 H2
Horton St HECK WF16 172 F3
HFAX HX1 11 H7
OSS WF5 174 E8
Hospital La BHP/TINH LS16 86 B4
Hospital Rd AIRE BD20 58 C5
Hostingley La EARL WF12 196 B5
Hothfield St AIRE BD20 35 M5
Hough HIPP HX3 147 J4

Hough End Av *BRAM* LS13 ....**107** M5
Hough End Cl *BRAM* * LS13 ....**107** M5
Hough End Cres *BRAM* LS13 ....**107** M5
Hough End Crs *BRAM* LS13 ....**107** L5
Hough End Gdns *BRAM* LS13 ....**107** M5
Hough End La *BRAM* LS13 ....**107** L5
Hough Gv *BRAM* LS13 ....**107** L4
Hough La *BRAM* LS13 ....**107** L4
Houghley Av *WOR/ARM* LS12 ......**108** A4
Houghley Cl *BRAM* LS13 ....**108** A4
Houghley Crs *WOR/ARM* LS12 .....**108** A4
Houghley La *WOR/ARM* LS13 ......**108** A4
Houghley Pl *WOR/ARM* LS12 ......**108** A4
Houghley Rd *WOR/ARM* LS12 ......**108** A4
Houghley Sq *WOR/ARM* LS12 ......**108** A4
Hough Side Cl *PDSY/CALV* LS28 ...**107** K7
Hough Side La
    PDSY/CALV LS28 ....**107** J7
Hough Side Rd
    PDSY/CALV LS28 ....**107** J7
Hough Ter *BRAM* LS13 ....**107** L4
Houghton Av *KNOT* WF11 ....**181** K2
Houghton Cl *MILN* OL16 ....**206** E8
Houghton Pl *BFD* BD1 ....**4** D4
Hough Top *BRAM* LS13 ....**107** J6
Hough Tree Rd *BRAM* LS13 ....**107** L6
Hoults La *GTL/HWG* HX4 ....**168** D6
Houndhill La *FEA/AMT* WF7 ....**202** B2
House Ct *KBTN* HD8 ....**257** K1
House Grove Dr *KBTN* HD8 ....**240** A4
Hovingham Av *RHAY* LS8 ....**110** C2
Hovingham Gv *RHAY* LS8 ....**110** C2
Hovingham Mt *RHAY* LS8 ....**110** C2
Hovingham St *MILN* OL16 ....**206** D6
Hovingham Ter *RHAY* LS8 ....**110** C2
Howard Av *HUDW* HD3 ....**191** L6
    MSTN/BAR LS15 ....**111** H7
Howard Ct *MSTN/BAR* LS15 ....**111** H7
Howard Crs *HOR/CROF* WF4 ......**198** A4
Howard Dr *FEA/AMT* WF7 ....**224** B2
Howard Pl *BTLY* WF17 ....**173** L3
    MILN OL16 ....**206** B6
Howard Rd *HUDW* HD3 ....**191** L6
Howards Dean *HWTH* BD22 ....**78** F5
Howard St *BSLY* S70 ....**261** M4
    BTLY WF17 ....**173** L3
    HFAX HX1 ....**10** C4
    OSS WF5 ....**174** F7
    ROY/SHW OL2 ....**229** J7
    WBOW BD5 ....**4** D8
    WHIT OL12 ....**206** B6
    WKFDE WF1 ....**176** E7
Howard Wy *HOLM/MEL* HD9 .....**235** G8
    LIT OL15 ....**185** L5
Howarth Av *ECHL* BD2 ....**105** J1
Howarth Crs *ECHL* * BD2 ....**105** J1
Howarth Cross St *MILN* OL16 .....**206** D4
Howarth Farm Wy *WHIT* OL12 ...**206** A4
Howarth La *HUDS* HD4 ....**214** A3
Howarth Pl *CHAL* LS7 ....**7** H6
Howarth Sq *MILN* OL16 ....**206** C6
Howarth St *LIT* OL15 ....**185** K4
Howbeck Av *AIRE* BD20 ....**58** C5
Howbeck Dr *AIRE* BD20 ....**58** C5
Howcans La *HIPP* HX3 ....**146** C2
Howcroft Gdns
    WKFDW/WTN WF2 ....**199** G7
    AWLS/ASK DN6 ....**249** G5
Howden Av *AIRE* BD20 ....**57** J4
Howdenbrook *HIPP* HX3 ....**125** M7
Howden Cl *BOW* BD4 ....**128** B4
    DOD/DAR S75 ....**242** B3
    HUDS HD4 ....**213** H4
Howden Clough Rd *MOR* LS27 ....**151** L3
Howden Gdns *HDGY* LS6 ....**109** G4
Howden Pl *HDGY* LS6 ....**109** G4
Howden Rd *AIRE* BD20 ....**36** D5
Howden Wy *WKFDE* WF1 ....**13** J3
Howell Av *CUD/GR* S72 ....**246** A4
Howes La *HIPP* HX3 ....**147** H3
Howgate *IDLE* BD10 ....**83** L6
Howgate Hl *HIPP* HX3 ....**169** H1
Howgate Rd *MAR/SLWT* HD7 .....**212** B6
Howgill Gn *WBSY* BD6 ....**126** C8
Howhill Quarry Rd *PBR* HG3 ......**25** M7
Howley Mill La *BTLY* WF17 ....**151** M7
Howley Park Cl *MOR* LS27 ....**152** B4
Howley Park Rd *MOR* LS27 ....**152** B4
Howley Park Rd East
    MOR LS27 ....**152** C5
Howley St *BTLY* WF17 ....**151** M8
Howroyd La *EARL* WF12 ....**195** G7
    GTL/HWG HX4 ....**189** K2
Howroyd's Yd *OSS* WF5 ....**174** E5
Howson Cl *GSLY* LS20 ....**62** B6
Hoxton Mt *BEE/HOL* LS11 ....**8** A9
Hoxton St *GIR* BD8 ....**104** C6
Hoylake Av *HUDN* HD2 ....**192** B3
Hoyland Cl *STKB/PEN* S36 ....**269** M3
Hoyland Rd *WKFDW/WTN* WF2 ...**220** D1
Hoyle Court Av *BAIL* BD17 ....**83** G3
Hoyle Court Dr *BAIL* BD17 ....**83** G3
Hoyle Court Rd *BAIL* BD17 ....**83** G3
Hoyle Fold *HWTH* BD22 ....**2** A8
Hoyle House Fold
    MAR/SLWT HD7 ....**212** B6
Hoyle Ing Rd *CUL/QBY* BD13 .....**103** H4
Hoyle Mill Rd *BSLY* S70 ....**261** M6
    HEM/SK/SE WF9 ....**223** L4
Hoyle's Ter *MILN* OL16 ....**207** G8
Hubberton Green Rd
    RPDN/SBR HX6 ....**166** C3
Hubert St *BFDE* BD3 ....**5** M8
    HUDW HD3 ....**191** G5
    LUD/ILL * HX2 ....**145** M7
Huddersfield Rd *BRIG* HD6.....**170** D4
    BTLY WF17 ....**151** G7
    DEWS WF13 ....**173** H3
    DEWS WF13 ....**194** F1
    DOD/DAR S75 ....**241** K1
    DOD/DAR S75 ....**241** L5
    DOD/DAR S75 ....**260** E2
    ELL HX5 ....**168** F5
    ELL HX5 ....**169** H7

HIPP HX3 ....**168** E2
HOLM/MEL HD9 ....**235** G4
HOLM/MEL HD9 ....**236** C8
HOLM/MEL HD9 ....**236** F7
HOLM/MEL HD9 ....**236** C1
HOR/CROF WF4 ....**219** H6
HUDW HD3 ....**191** J2
KBTN HD8 ....**238** F3
LM/WK BD12 ....**148** A4
MILN OL16 ....**229** L2
MIRF WF14 ....**171** M8
MIRF WF14 ....**172** B5
STKB/PEN S36 ....**257** H6
UPML OL3 ....**231** L7
UPML OL3 ....**231** M8
UPML OL3 ....**231** L1
Huddleston Ct *EARL* WF12 ....**174** B6
Hud Hl *HIPP* HX3 ....**147** K2
Hudroyd *HUDE* HD5 ....**215** H3
The Hudson *LM/WK* BD12 ....**148** E3
Hudson Av *GTHN* BD7 ....**126** D2
    HOR/CROF WF4 ....**221** K8
Hudson Cl *GTHN* BD7 ....**126** D3
    TAD LS24 ....**71** M1
    WBY LS22 ....**48** A1
Hudson Crs *GTHN* BD7 ....**126** D3
Hudson Gdns *GTHN* BD7 ....**126** D2
Hudson Gv *OSM* LS9 ....**110** C5
Hudson Ms *BSPA/BRAM* LS23 .....**49** G7
Hudson Pl *OSM* * LS9 ....**110** C5
Hudson Rd *OSM* LS9 ....**110** C5
Hudson St *BFDE* BD3 ....**105** M7
    OSM LS9 ....**110** C5
    PDSY/CALV * LS28 ....**106** F5
    TOD OL14 ....**140** E5
Hudson Vw *TAD* LS24 ....**71** M2
Hudson Wy *TAD* LS24 ....**71** M1
Hudswell Rd *MID* LS10 ....**9** J7
Hudswell St *WKFDE* WF1 ....**13** K9
Hughenden Vw *MOR* * LS27 ......**130** C8
Hughendon Dr *CUL/QBY* BD13 ...**103** J1
Hughendon Wk
    CUL/QBY BD13 ....**103** J8
    MILN OL16 ....**206** C6
Hughtrede St *MILN* * OL16 .....**228** D3
Hugill St *CUL/QBY* BD13 ....**102** F8
Hulbert Cft *HUDE* HD5 ....**215** H2
Hulbert St *BGLY* BD16 ....**81** J4
Hullenedge Gdns *ELL* HX5 ....**168** F8
Hullenedge La *GTL/HWG* HX4 ....**168** F8
Hullenedge Rd *ELL* HX5 ....**169** G8
Hullen Rd *ELL* HX5 ....**168** F8
Hullett Cl *HBR* HX7 ....**144** B5
Hullett Dr *HBR* HX7 ....**144** B5
Hull St *MOR* LS27 ....**152** D2
Hulme Sq *CAS* WF10 ....**158** F5
Humber Cl *AWLS/ASK* DN6 ......**249** J5
    MAR/SLWT HD7 ....**212** F5
Humber Ct *AWLS/ASK* DN6 ......**249** J5
Humber Rd *MILN* OL16 ....**207** J8
Humberside Wy
    BSLYN/ROY S71 ....**243** M8
Humboldt St *BFD* BD1 ....**5** J6
Hume Crest *BTLY* WF17 ....**173** L1
Hume St *MILN* OL16 ....**228** C1
Humley Rd *WKFDW/WTN* WF2 ...**220** D1
Hundhill La *PONT* WF8 ....**202** F4
Hungate Cl *TAD* LS24 ....**93** J8
Hungate La *RTHW* LS26 ....**156** B5
Hungate Rd *GFTH/SHER* LS25 ...**116** A6
Hungerford Rd *HUDW* HD3 ......**191** M6
Hunger Hl *HFAX* HX1 ....**11** H8
    ILK LS29 ....**20** E7
    MOR LS27 ....**152** C3
Hunger Hills Av *HORS* LS18 .....**85** J5
Hunger Hills Dr *HORS* LS18 ......**85** J5
Hunningley La *BSLY* S70 ....**261** M6
Hunslet Green Wy *MID* LS10 .....**9** J7
Hunslet Hall Rd *BEE/HOL* LS11 ...**8** E7
Hunslet La *MID* LS10 ....**9** J5
Hunslet Rd *MID* LS10 ....**9** J3
Hunston Av *HUDW* HD3 ....**191** M6
Hunsworth La *BIRK/DRI* BD11 ....**128** A8
    CLECK BD19 ....**149** M5
Hunt Cl *BSLYN/ROY* * S71 ....**261** L2
Hunters Cottages
    DOD/DAR * S75 ....**260** C5
Hunters Ct *HTON* BD9 ....**103** L2
Hunters Gn *CUL/QBY* BD13 .....**79** M7
Hunters Hill La *UPML* OL3 ....**231** L8
Hunter's La *MILN* OL16 ....**206** B6
    TOD OL14 ....**141** J8
Hunters Meadow *AIRE* BD20 .....**36** A4
Hunters Park Av *CLAY* BD14 .....**125** M1
Hunters Ri *DOD/DAR* S75 ....**260** C5
Hunter's Wy *WBY* LS22 ....**30** A7
Huntingdon Av *HUDN* HD2 ......**193** H1
Huntingdon Rd *BRIG* HD6 ....**170** E5
Huntock Pl *BRIG* HD6 ....**170** B1
Huntsman Fold
    WKFDW/WTN WF2 ....**175** M8
Huntsmans Cl *BGLY* BD16 ......**81** L1
    HUDS HD4 ....**213** M6
    KGHY HD21 ....**2** D3
Huntsmans Wy
    HEM/SK/SE WF9 ....**225** G4
Hunt St *CAS* WF10 ....**157** K6
    CAS WF10 ....**157** M6
Huntwick Av *FEA/AMT* WF7 .....**201** L2
Huntwick Crs *FEA/AMT* WF7 .....**201** L3
Huntwick Dr *FEA/AMT* WF7 .....**201** K3
Huntwick La *FEA/AMT* WF7 .....**201** H3
Huntwick Rd *FEA/AMT* WF7 .....**201** L3
Hurricane Cl *GFTH/SHER* LS25 ...**138** C6
Hurrs Rd *SKP/WHF* BD23 ....**16** D2
Hurstead Gn *WHIT* OL12 ....**206** F2
Hurstead La *MILN* OL16 ....**207** H8
Hurst Knowle *HUDE* HD5 ....**215** J2
Hurst La *MIRF* WF14 ....**194** D3
Hurst Meadow *MILN* OL16 ......**228** D4
Hurst Rd *HBR* HX7 ....**143** K2
Hurst St *ROCH* OL11 ....**228** B7
Hurstville Av *BIRK/DRI* BD11 .....**128** B8

Hurstwood *HUDN* HD2 ....**193** G2
Huskar Cl *DOD/DAR* S75 ....**259** H6
Husler Gv *CHAL* LS7 ....**7** J3
Husler Pl *CHAL* LS7 ....**7** J3
The Hustings *LVSG* * WF15 ......**172** C2
Hustlergate *BFD* BD1 ....**4** F6
Hustlers Rw *HDGY* LS6 ....**86** F6
Hustler St *BFDE* BD3 ....**5** L7
Hutchinson's Pl *KSTL* LS5 ....**108** C3
Hutson St *WBOW* BD5 ....**126** F2
Hutton Dr *HECK* WF16 ....**173** G2
    HEM/SK/SE WF9 ....**247** J2
Hutton Rd *WBOW* BD5 ....**126** E4
Hutton St *RYKW* YO26 ....**33** K4
Hutton Ter *IDLE* BD10 ....**105** M1
Huttons Ct *CUL/QBY* BD13 ......**107** C7
Hydale Cl *KGHY* BD21 ....**3** L8
Hydale Cl *LM/WK* BD12 ....**126** E8
Hyde Gv *KGHY* BD21 ....**3** J2
Hyde Pk *HFAX* HX1 ....**10** D8
    WKFDE WF1 ....**13** K5
Hyde Park Cl *HDGY* LS6 ....**6** A4
Hyde Park Cnr *HDGY* LS6 ....**6** B2
Hyde Park Pl *HDGY* LS6 ....**6** B2
Hyde Park Rd *HDGY* LS6 ....**6** A4
    HFAX HX1 ....**10** C9
Hyde Park Ter *HDGY* LS6 ....**6** A4
Hyde Pl *LDSU* LS2 ....**6** C6
Hyde St *IDLE* BD10 ....**83** K5
    LDSU LS2 ....**6** C7
Hyde Ter *LDSU* LS2 ....**6** C6
Hydro Cl *ILK* LS29 ....**39** H3
Hyne Av *BOW* BD4 ....**127** L5
Hyrst Garth *BTLY* WF17 ....**173** K4
Hyrstlands Rd *BTLY* WF17 ......**173** K3
Hyrst Wk *BTLY* WF17 ....**173** L3

I

Ian Frazer Ct *ROCH* OL11 ......**228** B2
Ibberson Av *DOD/DAR* S75 ......**242** C6
Ibbetson Cl *MOR* LS27 ....**130** C7
Ibbetson Ct *MOR* LS27 ....**130** C7
Ibbetson Cft *MOR* LS27 ....**130** C7
Ibbetson Dr *MOR* LS27 ....**130** C7
Ibbetson Ov *MOR* LS27 ....**130** C7
Ibbetson Ri *MOR* LS27 ....**130** C7
Ibbetson Rd *MOR* LS27 ....**130** C7
Ibbotroyd Av *TOD* OL14 ....**141** J7
Ibbotson Flats *HUD* HD1 ....**15** G6
Ibbottson St *WKFDE* WF1 ......**13** L9
Ibsley *WHIT* * OL12 ....**206** A6
Ida St *MID* LS10 ....**132** C4
    WBOW BD5 ....**126** E3
Iddesleigh St *BOW* BD4 ....**105** L8
Idlecroft Rd *IDLE* BD10 ....**83** K6
Idle Rd *ECHL* BD2 ....**105** J3
Idlethorp Wy *IDLE* BD10 ....**83** L7
Ilbert Av *BOW* BD4 ....**127** L5
Ilford St *MOR* LS27 ....**152** D2
Ilkley Hall Ms *ILK* LS29 ....**38** D3
Ilkley Hall Pk *ILK* LS29 ....**38** D3
Ilkley Rd *AIRE* BD20 ....**58** B4
    ILK LS29 ....**19** K7
    ILK LS29 ....**39** M3
    ILK LS29 ....**41** G7
Illingworth Av *BTLY* * WF17 ....**150** F5
Illingworth Crs *LUD/ILL* HX2 ....**124** A7
    NORM WF6 ....**178** A2
Illingworth Ct *LUD/ILL* HX2 ....**124** A7
    YEA LS19 ....**84** E1
Illingworth Gdns *LUD/ILL* HX2 ..**124** A8
Illingworth Gv *LUD/ILL* HX2 ....**124** A7
Illingworth Rd *LM/WK* BD12 ....**149** H2
    LUD/ILL HX2 ....**124** A7
Illingworth St *OSS* WF5 ....**196** F1
Illingworth Wy *LUD/ILL* HX2 ....**124** A7
Ilisley Rd *WMB/DAR* S73 ....**263** J8
Ilminster *ROCH* * OL11 ....**206** A8
Imperial Ar *HUD* HD1 ....**14** F7
Imperial Av *WKFDW/WTN* WF2 ..**176** B4
The Incline *HIPP* HX3 ....**11** K4
Inchfield Rd *TOD* OL14 ....**163** J6
Independent St *WBOW* BD5 .....**126** E3
Indoor Market *MILN* * OL16 ....**206** A7
Indus Cl *HECK* WF16 ....**173** G2
Industrial Av *BTLY* * WF17 .....**150** F5
Industrial Pk *RPDN/SBR* HX6 ....**167** K2
Industrial St *BGLY* BD16 ....**81** H3
    BRIG HD6 ....**170** D3
    CLECK BD19 ....**149** H6
    HOR/CROF WF4 ....**197** L6
    HUDS HD4 ....**214** C3
    LVSG WF15 ....**172** A2
    OSM LS9 ....**110** B5
    TOD OL14 ....**163** K1
    WKFDE * WF1 ....**12** C4
Industrial Ter *HFAX* HX1 ....**168** D1
Industry Rd *BSLYN/ROY* S71 ....**243** L7
    WHIT OL12 ....**206** B5
Industry St *LIT* OL15 ....**207** K1
    TOD OL14 ....**163** J5
Infirmary Rd *DEWS* WF13 ......**173** K5
Infirmary St *BFD* BD1 ....**4** E5
    LDS LS1 ....**6** F9
Ingbirchworth La
    STKB/PEN S36 ....**257** J7
Ingbirchworth Rd
    STKB/PEN S36 ....**270** C2
Ingdale Dr *HOLM/MEL* HD9 .....**236** D8
Ing Fld *LM/WK* BD12 ....**149** J2
Ingfield Av *HUDE* HD5 ....**15** M7
    OSS WF5 ....**175** G8
Ingham Cl *LUD/ILL* HX2 ....**124** B6
Ingham Cft *MIRF* WF14 ....**194** E2
Ingham Garth *MIRF* WF14 ......**194** E1
Ingham La *LUD/ILL* HX2 ....**124** B6
Ingham Rd *EARL* WF12 ....**195** M3
Ingham's Av *PDSY/CALV* LS28 ...**106** D6
Ingham's Ct *HIPP* * HX3 ....**10** D1
Inghams La *LIT* OL15 ....**207** K1
Inghams Ter *PDSY/CALV* LS28 ...**106** D6

Ingham St *MID* LS10 ....**9** K5
Ingham's Vw
    PDSY/CALV LS28 ....**106** D6
Ing Head *MAR/SLWT* HD7 ......**212** A5
Inghead Gdns *HIPP* HX3 ....**147** K2
Ing Head La *HUDS* HD4 ....**237** H3
Ing La *HUDS* HD4 ....**214** C4
Ingle Av *MOR* LS27 ....**130** B8
Ingleborough Cl *BOW* BD4 ......**128** A3
Ingleborough Dr *MOR* LS27 .....**152** A4
Ingleby Cl *ROY/SHW* OL2 ....**229** J6
Ingleby Dr *TAD* LS24 ....**71** M2
Ingleby Pl *GTHN* BD7 ....**104** C8
Ingleby Rd *GIR* BD8 ....**104** C7
Ingleby St *GIR* BD8 ....**104** C7
Ingleby Wy *MID* LS10 ....**132** A7
    ROY/SHW OL2 ....**229** J6
Ingle Ct *KBTN* HD8 ....**215** M2
    MOR LS27 ....**130** B8
Ingle Crs *MOR* LS27 ....**152** C1
Ingledew Ct *AL/HA/HU* LS17 ....**87** M2
Ingledew Crs *RHAY* LS8 ....**88** D4
Ingledew Dr *RHAY* LS8 ....**88** D5
Ingle Gv *MOR* LS27 ....**152** B1
Ingle Rw *CHAL* LS7 ....**87** L8
Ingleton Cl *BEE/HOL* LS11 .....**131** K3
Ingleton Dr *MSTN/BAR* LS15 ....**111** C7
Ingleton Gv *BEE/HOL* LS11 .....**131** K3
Ingleton Pl *BEE/HOL* LS11 .....**131** K3
Ingleton Rd *HUDS* HD4 ....**214** D4
Ingleton St *BEE/HOL* LS11 .....**131** K3
Ingleton Wk *BSLY* * S70 ....**260** F4
Inglewood *DOD/DAR* S75 ....**242** B5
Inglewood Dr *AL/HUDW* HD3 ...**191** L5
Inglewood Dr *OT* LS21 ....**41** H7
    SCFT LS14 ....**111** K3
Inglewood Pl *SCFT* LS14 ....**111** K3
Inglewood Ter *HDGY* * LS6 .....**6** C1
Inglis St *LIT* OL15 ....**185** K8
Ingram Cl *BEE/HOL* LS11 ....**8** B5
Ingram Ct *BEE/HOL* LS11 ....**8** B5
Ingram Crs *BEE/HOL* * LS11 ....**8** A7
    KNOT WF11 ....**181** M3
Ingram Gdns *BEE/HOL* LS11 ....**8** B5
Ingram Pde *RTHW* LS26 ....**155** G1
Ingram Rd *BEE/HOL* LS11 ......**8** B7
Ingram Rw *BEE/HOL* LS11 ......**8** F4
Ingram Sq *HFAX* * HX1 ....**168** C1
Ingram St *BEE/HOL* LS11 ......**8** C1
    HFAX HX1 ....**168** C1
    KGHY BD21 ....**79** K3
Ingram Vw *BEE/HOL* LS11 ......**8** B6
Ingrow Br *KGHY* * BD21 ....**79** K2
Ingrow La *HWTH* BD22 ....**79** H2
The Ings *BRIC* HD6 ....**148** C8
    KBTN HD8 ....**240** B4
Ings Av *GSLY* LS20 ....**61** M4
Ings Cl *HEM/SK/SE* WF9 ....**246** F5
    HOR/CROF WF4 ....**222** E5
Ings Ct *GSLY* LS20 ....**61** L3
Ings Crs *EARL* WF12 ....**195** L4
    GSLY LS20 ....**61** L3
    LVSG WF15 ....**172** C2
    OSM LS9 ....**110** D7
Ings Dr *AIRE* BD20 ....**16** E8
    RTHW LS26 ....**157** C3
Ings Holt *HEM/SK/SE* WF9 .....**246** F3
    OSM LS9 ....**34** C2
    AWLS/ASK DN6 ....**249** J5
    BSPA/BRAM LS23 ....**49** J5
    CAS WF10 ....**157** M3
    CAS WF10 ....**158** B5
    CUD/GR S72 ....**263** L6
    EARL WF12 ....**195** L4
    GLE DN14 ....**161** J7
    GSLY LS20 ....**61** L4
    MAR/SLWT HD7 ....**233** J2
    TAD LS24 ....**50** C6
Ings Mere Ct *KNOT* WF11 .....**159** J2
Ings Mill Av *KBTN* HD8 ....**240** B3
Ings Mill Dr *KBTN* HD8 ....**240** B4
Ings Rd *AIRE* BD20 ....**35** K7
    BTLY WF17 ....**151** K8
    EARL WF12 ....**174** A5
    HECK WF16 ....**172** F2
    HEM/SK/SE WF9 ....**223** K5
    HUDE HD5 ....**215** J2
    LVSG WF15 ....**172** D1
    OSM LS9 ....**110** D7
    TAD LS24 ....**95** C1
    WKFDE WF1 ....**12** D4
Ings St *BFDE* BD3 ....**105** M8
Ings Vw *CAS* WF10 ....**158** D6
    RTHW LS26 ....**157** C3
Ings Wll *LVSG* WF15 ....**172** E4
Ings Wy *AIRE* BD20 ....**36** B6
    GIR BD8 ....**104** A6
    KBTN HD8 ....**216** B3
    STKB/PEN S36 ....**256** F5
Ingswell Av *HOR/CROF* WF4 .....**221** H7
Ingswell Dr *HOR/CROF* WF4 .....**221** H7
Ingthorns La *GFTH/SHER* LS25 ..**138** C6
Ingthorpe La *GFTH/SHER* LS25 ..**138** C6
Ingthorpe Wy
    GFTH/SHER LS25 ....**138** C5
Ingwell Ct *WKFDE* WF1 ....**13** G3
Ingwell St *WKFDE* WF1 ....**13** G3
Ingwell Ter *CLECK* BD19 ....**150** A7
Inholmes La *TAD* LS24 ....**49** L2
    TAD LS24 ....**71** K3
Inkerman Ct *KBTN* HD8 ....**257** J1
Inkerman St *BOW* BD4 ....**127** M2
    ECHL BD2 ....**105** M2
    WHIT * OL12 ....**206** B5
Inkerman Wy *KBTN* HD8 ....**257** H1
Inkersley Ri *BFD* BD1 ....**4** E2
Ink St *MILN* OL16 ....**206** D7
Inner Hey *MAR/SLWT* HD7 .....**233** J2
The Innings *IDLE* BD10 ....**83** J7
Innovation Wy *DOD/DAR* S75 ...**260** C2
Institute Rd *ECHL* BD2 ....**105** L1
Institute St *AIRE* BD20 ....**34** E8
The Intake *GFTH/SHER* LS25 ....**135** K5
Intake *MAR/SLWT* HD7 ....**213** G1
Intake Cl *EARD/LOFT* WF3 .....**177** H1
Intake Crs *COL* BB8 ....**52** B8

Intake Gdns *DOD/DAR* S75 .....**260** B8
Intake Gv *ECHL* BD2 ....**105** L4
Intake La *AIRE* BD20 ....**56** C2
    BRAM LS13 ....**107** H3
    BTLY WF17 ....**151** H6
    CUD/GR S72 ....**244** B6
    DOD/DAR S75 ....**260** D4
    EARD/LOFT WF3 ....**177** H1
    HOLM/MEL HD9 ....**234** B2
    HOR/CROF WF4 ....**219** M7
    HUDS HD4 ....**213** H7
    KNOT WF11 ....**161** J5
    MID LS10 ....**153** L3
    OSS WF5 ....**197** G1
    SCFT LS14 ....**89** M3
    YEA LS19 ....**84** F3
Intake Mt *MID* LS10 ....**153** L3
Intake Rd *ECHL* BD2 ....**105** L4
    MAR/SLWT HD7 ....**211** L4
    PDSY/CALV LS28 ....**107** L3
Intake Sq *MID* LS10 ....**153** L3
Intake Vw *MID* LS10 ....**153** L3
Intercity Wy *PDSY/CALV* LS28 ...**107** J5
Intermezzo Dr *MID* LS10 ......**132** C6
Invargarry Cl *GFTH/SHER* LS25 ..**113** K6
Inverness Rd *GFTH/SHER* LS25 ..**113** K7
Invertrees Av *YEA* LS19 ....**84** E2
Iona Pl *HIPP* HX3 ....**146** D4
Iona St *HIPP* HX3 ....**10** F1
Ipswich St *ROCH* OL11 ....**228** B5
Iqbal Ct *BFDE* * BD3 ....**105** M8
Ireland Crs *BHP/TINH* LS16 .....**86** B3
Ireland St *BGLY* BD16 ....**81** C3
Ireland Ter *BGLY* BD16 ....**81** C3
Ireton St *GTHN* BD7 ....**104** D8
Iron Rw *ILK* LS29 ....**40** B5
Iron St *CLECK* BD19 ....**149** L7
Ironwood Ap *SCFT* LS14 ....**111** K3
Ironwood Crs *SCFT* LS14 ....**111** K3
Ironwood Vw *SCFT* LS14 ....**111** J2
Irving St *HFAX* HX1 ....**10** A9
Irving Ter *CLAY* BD14 ....**125** L3
Irwell St *BOW* BD4 ....**127** J1
Irwin Ap *MSTN/BAR* LS15 ......**111** H7
Irwin Av *WKFDE* WF1 ....**177** G7
Irwin Crs *WKFDE* WF1 ....**177** G7
Irwin Pl *PDSY/CALV* LS28 .....**106** F4
Isaac St *GIR* BD8 ....**104** D6
Isabella St *WHIT* OL12 ....**206** C4
Isherwood St *ROCH* OL11 ......**228** C1
The Island *HOR/CROF* * WF4 ...**197** G6
Island Dr *HOLM/MEL* HD9 ......**236** E4
Islay Cl *RTHW* LS26 ....**155** J1
Isles St *GIR* BD8 ....**104** B6
Issott St *BSLYN/ROY* S71 ......**261** H3
Ivanhoe Rd *GTHN* BD7 ....**126** D1
Iveagh St *MILN* OL16 ....**206** D8
Ive House La *LUD/ILL* HX2 .....**145** G6
Iver Wy *SHPY* BD18 ....**82** C7
Iveson Ap *BHP/TINH* LS16 .....**86** C4
Iveson Cl *BHP/TINH* LS16 ......**86** B4
Iveson Crs *BHP/TINH* LS16 .....**86** C4
Iveson Dr *BHP/TINH* LS16 ......**86** B4
Iveson Gdns *BHP/TINH* LS16 ...**86** B4
Iveson Garth *BHP/TINH* LS16 ...**86** C4
Iveson Gn *BHP/TINH* LS16 .....**86** B4
Iveson Gv *BHP/TINH* LS16 .....**86** C4
Iveson Lawn *BHP/TINH* LS16 ...**86** C4
Iveson Ri *BHP/TINH* LS16 ......**86** C4
Ives St *BAIL* BD17 ....**82** D6
Ivory St *BEE/HOL* LS11 ....**9** J5
Ivy Av *OSM* LS9 ....**110** D6
Ivy Bank La *HWTH* BD22 ......**78** E8
Ivy Cha *BRAM* LS13 ....**107** K7
Ivy Cl *HEM/SK/SE* WF9 ....**247** H5
    PBR HG3 ....**28** A1
    ROY/SHW OL2 ....**229** K7
    WKFDE WF1 ....**177** G6
Ivy Ct *CUD/GR* S72 ....**244** D8
Ivy Crs *HIPP* HX3 ....**148** A3
    OSM LS9 ....**110** C6
Ivy Farm Cl *BSLYN/ROY* S71 ....**243** M5
Ivy Gdns *BRAM* LS13 ....**107** M2
    CAS WF10 ....**180** F1
Ivy Garth *CHAL* LS7 ....**87** M8
Ivy Gv *OSM* LS9 ....**110** D6
    SHPY BD18 ....**82** A7
    WKFDE WF1 ....**177** G6
Ivy House Rd *WBOW* BD5 ......**127** G5
Ivy La *BSPA/BRAM* LS23 ......**48** E6
    LUD/ILL HX2 ....**123** M8
    WIL/AL BD15 ....**103** J5
    WKFDE WF1 ....**177** G6
Ivy Mt *MAR/SLWT* HD7 ....**212** B5
    OSM LS9 ....**110** C6
Ivy Pl *AIRE* BD20 ....**34** E7
    BRAM LS13 ....**107** M2
Ivy Rd *KGHY* BD21 ....**3** M6
    OSM LS9 ....**110** C7
    SHPY BD18 ....**82** A7
Ivy St *BRIG* HD6 ....**170** B3
    FEA/AMT WF7 ....**179** M8
    HFAX HX1 ....**11** J3
    HUD HD1 ....**15** J8
    HUDS HD4 ....**213** L2
    KGHY BD21 ....**2** F3
    OSM LS9 ....**110** C6
Ivy Ter *BRIG* HD6 ....**170** B3
    BSLY * S70 ....**261** J6
    HEM/SK/SE WF9 ....**247** H5
    HIPP HX3 ....**148** A7
    OSM LS9 ....**110** C6
Ivy Vw *OSM* LS9 ....**110** C6

J

Jacana Wy *CUL/QBY* BD13 .....**125** L3
Jacinth Ct *HUDN* HD2 ....**192** E4
Jack Br *HBR* HX7 ....**142** C1
Jack Close Orch
    BSLYN/ROY S71 ....**243** J7

Jackdaw La *BSPA/BRAM* LS23 .....48 E6
Jack Field La *AIRE* BD20 .....55 J2
Jack Hl *HUDN* HD2 .....14 E1
Jack Hill La *OT* LS21 .....23 H1
Jackie Smart Ct *CHAL* LS7 .....7 L2
Jackie Smart Rd *WBOW* BD5 .....127 G2
Jack La *BEE/HOL* LS11 .....8 E5
DEWS WF13 .....173 M4
MID LS10 .....9 K7
Jackman Dr *HORS* LS18 .....85 M7
Jackroyd La *HUDS* HD4 .....214 D2
MIRF WF14 .....194 A4
Jackson Av *RHAY* LS8 .....88 B7
Jackson Hill La *CUL/QBY* BD13 .....125 H7
Jackson La *GTL/HWG* HX4 .....189 J1
Jackson Mdw *GTL/HWG* HX4 .....189 J1
Jackson Rd *CHAL* LS7 .....7 G3
Jackson's La *AIRE* BD20 .....35 C1
EARL WF12 .....195 J4
PONT WF8 .....204 A7
Jackson St *AIRE* BD20 .....55 M1
BFDE BD3 .....5 K8
CUD/GR S72 .....244 C2
MILN OL16 .....206 D8
WHIT OL12 .....184 B8
Jacksons Yd *BSLY* * S70 .....260 F5
Jack Taylor Ct *WHIT* * OL12 .....206 D5
Jacky La *HWTH* BD22 .....78 E8
Jacobs Hall Ct *DOD/DAR* * S75.....241 L6
WBOW BD5 .....127 C1
Jacob's Rw *HUD4* HD4 .....214 B3
Jacob St *LDSU* LS2 .....7 J7
WBOW BD5 .....126 F2
Jacob's Well La *WKFDE* WF1 .....12 E1
Jacques Gv *AIRE* BD20 .....36 B5
Jacques Pl *BSLYN/ROY* S71 .....261 J4
Jaggar La *HUDE* HD5 .....236 D2
Jagger Green La *HUDW* HD3 .....190 D4
Jagger La *HUDE* HD5 .....193 J6
KBTN HD8 .....217 C7
Jail Rd *BTLY* WF17 .....173 H1
Jakeman Ct *EARD/LOFT* WF3 .....153 C6
Jakeman Ct *EARD/LOFT* WF3 .....153 C6
Jakeman Dr *EARD/LOFT* WF3 .....153 C6
James Av *AIRE* BD20 .....56 C1
RHAY LS8 .....88 B6
James Butterworth Ct
MILN OL16 .....206 D8
James Butterworth St
MILN OL16 .....206 D7
James Cl *GFTH/SHER* LS25 .....113 J4
James Ct *WBY* LS22 .....47 K6
James Duggan Av
FEA/AMT WF7 .....179 L8
James Ga *BFD* BD1 .....4 E6
James Gibbs Ct *FEA/AMT* * WF7.....179 M8
James Hill St *LIT* * OL15 .....207 K1
James La *HUDS* HD4 .....213 J8
James Mason Ct *WHIT* OL12 .....191 M7
James Rd *AWLS/ASK* DN6 .....249 M7
ROY/SHW OL2 .....229 K6
James St *AIRE* * BD20 .....34 F7
BFD BD1 .....4 E5
BIRK/DRI * BD11 .....128 C8
BRIG HD6 .....170 C2
BSLYN/ROY S71 .....261 H4
BTLY WF17 .....173 K2
CAS WF10 .....157 M5
COL * BB8 .....74 A1
CUD/GR S72 .....245 K8
CUL/QBY BD13 .....102 F7
DEWS WF13 .....173 K5
GTL/HWG HX4 .....190 D2
HWTH BD22 .....78 D4
LIT OL15 .....207 H1
LVSG WF15 .....172 D3
MAR/SLWT HD7 .....212 C5
MAR/SLWT HD7 .....212 F2
MIRF WF14 .....172 C7
WHIT OL12 .....206 A6
WIL/AL BD15 .....103 L5
YEA LS19 .....84 D2
Jamie Ct *IDLE* BD10 .....83 M8
Jane La *CUL/QBY* BD13 .....101 M5
SHPY BD18 .....82 B6
WHIT OL12 .....162 A8
WHIT OL12 .....206 A6
Janesway *GFTH/SHER* LS25 .....135 H4
Janet St *HWTH* BD22 .....79 G6
Jaques Ct *HDGY* LS6 .....108 D2
Jardine Av *FEA/AMT* WF7 .....179 M8
Jardine Rd *BGLY* BD16 .....81 J3
Jarratt St *GIR* BD8 .....104 D5
Jarratt St East *GIR* BD8 .....104 D5
Jarrom Cl *BOW* BD4 .....127 M2
Jarvis Sq *EARD/LOFT* WF3 .....154 C3
Jarvis St *WHIT* OL12 .....206 B5
Jarvis Wk *EARD/LOFT* WF3 .....154 C3
Jason Ter *BTLY* * WF17 .....151 J4
Jasper La *PBR* HG3 .....27 K8
Jasper St *HFAX* HX1 .....10 B1
IDLE BD10 .....83 K6
Javelin Cl *IDLE* BD10 .....83 K8
Jay House La *BRIG* HD6 .....170 F1
Jay St *HWTH* BD22 .....78 F8
Jean Av *MSTN/BAR* LS15 .....111 J3
Jebb La *DOD/DAR* S75 .....241 H2
Jefferson Wy *WHIT* OL12 .....206 B3
Jenkin Dr *HOR/CROF* WF4 .....197 H5
Jenkin La *HOR/CROF* WF4 .....197 J5
Jenkin Rd *HOR/CROF* WF4 .....197 H5
Jenkinson Cl *BEE/HOL* LS11 .....8 D6
Jenkinson Lawn *BEE/HOL* LS11.....8 D6
Jenkinsons Pl *MID* LS10 .....131 M6
Jenkinson St *BTLY* WF17 .....173 L4
Jenkyn La *KBTN* HD8 .....237 M6
Jennetts Crs *OT* LS21 .....41 H7
Jennings Cl *AIRE* BD20 .....36 A6
Jennings Pl *GTHN* BD7 .....126 C2
Jennings St *GTHN* BD7 .....126 C2
Jenny Gill Crs *SKP/WHF* BD23 .....16 D3
Jenny La *BAIL* BD17 .....82 F2
MIRF WF14 .....172 D7
Jensen Av *DEWS* WF13 .....173 H3
Jepheys Pl *WHIT* OL12 .....206 B5
Jepheys St *WHIT* OL12 .....206 B5
Jepson La *ELL* HX5 .....169 H8

Jeremy La *HECK* WF16 .....172 F2
Jer Gv *WBSY* BD6 .....126 A4
Jer La *WBSY* BD6 .....126 A4
Jermyn St *BFDE* BD3 .....5 G5
WHIT OL12 .....206 C6
Jerrold St *LIT* OL15 .....207 K1
Jerry Clay Dr
WKFDW/WTN WF2 .....176 A4
Jerry Clay La
WKFDW/WTN WF2 .....175 M3
Jerry Cft *SKP/WHF* BD23 .....16 C2
Jerry Fields Rd *LUD/ILL* HX2 .....144 F8
Jerry La *AIRE* BD20 .....37 H5
RPDN/SBR HX6 .....167 J3
Jersey Ct *EARL* WF12 .....174 B4
Jerusalem La *LUD/ILL* HX2 .....144 F2
Jerusalem Rd *MAR/SLWT* HD7.....212 D7
Jervaulx Crs *GIR* BD8 .....4 B3
Jervaulx Ct *GIR* BD8 .....4 B3
Jerwood Hill Cl *HIPP* HX3 .....11 K2
HTON BD9 .....104 B4
Jesmond Av *BSLYN/ROY* S71 .....243 K3
Jesmond Gv *DEWS* WF13 .....173 K5
HTON BD9 .....104 B4
Jessamine Av *BEE/HOL* LS11 .....131 H5
Jessamine St *DEWS* WF13 .....194 F1
Jesse St *GIR* BD8 .....103 M7
WBOW BD5 .....127 C1
Jessop Av *HUDE* HD5 .....215 J3
Jessop Fold *HOLM/MEL* HD9 .....236 B3
Jessop St *CAS* WF10 .....157 M6
WKFDW/WTN WF2 .....12 E7
Jewitt La *WBY* LS22 .....47 L7
Jew La *HWTH* BD22 .....100 E4
Jew Leys La *COP/BISH* YO23 .....73 M8
Jilley Royd La *HUDN* HD2 .....192 C2
Jill La *MIRF* WF14 .....172 E7
Jim Allen La *LUD/ILL* HX2 .....144 E5
Jim La *HUD* HD1 .....191 M8
Jinnah Ct *GIR* BD8 .....4 C3
Jinny Moor La *RTHW* LS26 .....134 A6
Jin-whin Hl *CAS* WF10 .....157 H6
Joan Royd *HECK* WF16 .....150 F8
Joan Royd La *STKB/PEN* S36 .....270 D5
Joba Av *BFDE* BD3 .....5 M6
Jockey Rd *STKB/PEN* S36 .....271 L4
Joffre Av *CAS* WF10 .....158 A4
John Ashworth St *WHIT* OL12 .....206 D5
John Booth Cl *LVSG* WF15 .....172 B4
John Carr Av *HOR/CROF* WF4 .....197 J4
John Charles Wy
WOR/ARM LS12 .....130 F2
John Eastwood Homes
TOD OL14 .....163 J5
John Escritt Rd *BGLY* BD16 .....81 J4
John Haigh Rd *MAR/SLWT* HD7.....212 C6
John Nelson Cl *BTLY* * WF17 .....151 H5
Johnny La *OT* LS21 .....41 J8
John O'gaunts Wk *RTHW* LS26 .....133 H8
John Ormsby VC Wy
EARL WF12 .....174 C3
John Roberts Ct *ROCH* * OL11 .....228 A1
Johns Av *EARD/LOFT* WF3 .....154 E8
John's Crs *WKFDW/WTN* WF2 .....176 A4
Johns La *ELL* HX5 .....191 H2
Johnson St *BFDE* BD3 .....105 M7
BGLY BD16 .....81 H3
DOD/DAR S75 .....260 F4
MIRF WF14 .....194 B3
Johnson Ter *MOR* LS27 .....152 D2
Johnston *WHIT* * OL12 .....206 A6
Johnston Av *LIT* * OL15 .....207 H3
Johnston St *HDGY* LS6 .....8 E1
WKFDE WF1 .....13 H3
John St *AWLS/ASK* DN6 .....249 L8
BFD BD1 .....4 E5
BOW BD4 .....128 A5
BRIG HD6 .....170 C3
BSLY S70 .....261 H5
BTLY WF17 .....151 G5
CAS WF10 .....157 L8
CLAY BD14 .....125 L2
CUD/GR S72 .....263 M7
CUL/QBY BD13 .....101 M6
CUL/QBY BD13 .....102 F7
DEWS WF13 .....173 L4
DEWS WF13 .....195 G1
ELL HX5 .....169 H8
GTL/HWG HX4 .....168 G6
HDGY LS6 .....109 G3
HECK * WF16 .....172 F3
HEM/SK/SE WF9 .....247 H4
HFAX HX1 .....11 G6
HUDS HD4 .....213 K2
HWTH BD22 .....78 F4
LIT OL15 .....207 J1
MILN OL16 .....206 E3
SHPY BD18 .....82 C6
WKFDE WF1 .....13 H3
YEA LS19 .....84 D2
John St West *RPDN/SBR* HX6 .....167 K2
John William St *CLECK* BD19 .....149 M6
ELL HX5 .....169 H8
HUD HD1 .....14 F5
LVSG WF15 .....172 E2
Jonathan Garth *ILK* * LS29 .....19 G6
Jones St *MILN* OL16 .....206 D8
Jons Av *HEM/SK/SE* WF9 .....246 C4
Jordan Av *ROY/SHW* OL2 .....229 M6
Joseph Av *HIPP* HX3 .....147 J4
Josephine Rd *HUDS* HD4 .....213 J3
Joseph St *BFD* BD1 .....5 J6
BOW BD4 .....128 A5
BSLY S70 .....261 G6
CUD/GR S72 .....245 J8
LIT OL15 .....185 K8
MID LS10 .....9 L7
Josephs Well *LDS* * LS1 .....6 C4
Joshua St *TOD* OL14 .....141 M8
Jos La *KBTN* HD8 .....238 A6
Jos Wy *KBTN* HD8 .....238 A5
Jowett House La
DOD/DAR S75 .....258 D2
Jowett Park Crs *IDLE* BD10 .....83 J4
Jowett's La *AIRE* BD20 .....17 M6

Jowett St *BFD* BD1 .....4 B5
Joy St *WHIT* OL12 .....206 B4
Jubilee Av *KBTN* HD8 .....238 C4
NORM WF6 .....178 C6
WKFDE WF1 .....176 E2
Jubilee Ct *SHPY* * BD18 .....82 E6
Jubilee Crs *HOR/CROF* WF4 .....200 D3
WKFDE WF1 .....176 E2
Jubilee Cft *BIRK/DRI* BD11 .....129 H7
Jubilee Dr *KGHY* BD21 .....2 C9
Jubilee La *HUDS* HD4 .....213 H3
Jubilee Pl *MOR* LS27 .....152 D2
Jubilee Rd *HIPP* HX3 .....168 F4
HBR HX7 .....144 A5
HIPP HX3 .....11 K8
HOR/CROF WF4 .....220 B3
MOR LS27 .....152 D2
ROY/SHW OL2 .....229 L7
Jubilee St North *HIPP* HX3 .....146 C2
Jubilee Ter *HIPP* * HX3 .....11 K8
MOR LS27 .....152 D2
RPDN/SBR HX6 .....167 G8
Jubilee Trees *ILK* LS29 .....39 L7
Jubilee Wy *PONT* WF8 .....180 E6
SHPY BD18 .....82 F6
Judd Field La *STKB/PEN* S36 .....270 D8
Judy Haigh La *EARL* WF12 .....195 M6
Judy La *HUDN* HD2 .....192 D3
Judy Rw *BSLYN/ROY* S71 .....261 L2
Julian Dr *CUL/QBY* BD13 .....125 L4
Julian St *HUDE* * HD5 .....215 G1
Julia St *WHIT* OL12 .....206 A6
Julie Av *HOR/CROF* WF4 .....220 A1
Jumb Beck Cl *ILK* LS29 .....40 B6
Jumble Dyke *BRIG* HD6 .....170 B6
Jumble Hole Rd *TOD* OL14 .....142 D4
Jumbles St *EARD/LOFT* WF3 .....154 E5
Jumbles La *EARD/LOFT* WF3 .....154 E5
Jumble Wd *KBTN* HD8 .....215 M3
Jumples *LUD/ILL* HX2 .....145 M2
Jumples Cl *LUD/ILL* HX2 .....145 M2
Jumps La *HBR* HX7 .....143 H5
TOD OL14 .....141 G5
Junction Aly *MILN* OL16 .....206 B7
Junction La *OSS* WF5 .....197 J2
Junction Rd *BAIL* BD17 .....82 E6
DEWS WF13 .....195 K7
Junction St *BSLY* S70 .....261 K6
MID LS10 .....9 H4
June St *KGHY* BD21 .....3 H2
Juniper Av *RTHW* LS26 .....133 M7
Juniper Dr *MILN* OL16 .....206 F8
Juniper Gv *HUDS* HD4 .....213 M8
Juniper Pl *HOR/CROF* WF4 .....110 D5
Justin St *HUDS* HD4 .....213 J5

K

Kaffir Rd *HUDW* HD3 .....191 M6
Karnac Rd *RHAY* LS8 .....110 B2
Karon Dr *HOR/CROF* WF4 .....197 K5
Kathan Cl *MILN* OL16 .....206 D7
Katherine St *SHPY* BD18 .....82 B6
Katrina Gv *FEA/AMT* WF7 .....201 M3
Kaycell St *BOW* BD4 .....127 K4
Kay Cl *MOR* LS27 .....130 B7
Kaye La *HUDE* HD5 .....214 F4
Kaye St *BSLYN/ROY* S71 .....261 H4
EARL WF12 .....173 M8
HECK WF16 .....172 F3
Kay's Ter *BSLY* S70 .....262 A7
Kay St *HTON* BD9 .....104 E1
ROCH OL11 .....228 A1
WKFDE WF1 .....13 H3
Kearby Cliff *WBY* LS22 .....45 M4
Keats Av *TOD* OL14 .....141 M8
Keats Cl *PONT* WF8 .....180 F4
Keats Dr *HECK* WF16 .....173 G4
Keats Gv *EARD/LOFT* WF3 .....155 G4
STKB/PEN S36 .....270 F2
Keat St *HUDS* HD4 .....214 A2
Kebble St *CLECK* BD19 .....150 D7
Keble Garth *GFTH/SHER* LS25 .....135 L5
Kebroyd La *RPDN/SBR* HX6 .....167 G7
Kebroyd Mt *RPDN/SBR* HX6 .....167 G7
Kebs Rd *HBR* HX7 .....141 K3
Kedleston Rd *RHAY* LS8 .....88 B3
Kedleston Rd *RHAY* LS8 .....88 B3
Keel Moorings *BRAM* LS13 .....107 H1
Keelham Dr *YEA* LS19 .....84 E2
Keel La *AIRE* BD20 .....57 J4
Keel Moorings *BRAM* LS13 .....141 M4
Keenan St *HEM/SK/SE* WF9 .....247 G5
Keeper La *BOW* BD4 .....128 F3
HOR/CROF WF4 .....220 F8
Keeton St *OSM* LS9 .....110 B6
Keighley Cl *LUD/ILL* HX2 .....123 M8
Keighley Dr *LUD/ILL* HX2 .....146 A2
Keighley Rd *AIRE* BD20 .....16 C8
AIRE BD20 .....34 E3
AIRE BD20 .....34 F7
AIRE BD20 .....55 G8
BGLY BD16 .....59 G8
BGLY BD16 .....80 C3
BGLY BD16 .....81 G1
COL BB8 .....53 K7
COL BB8 .....74 C3
COL BB8 .....74 D1
CUL/QBY BD13 .....79 M6
CUL/QBY BD13 .....101 M3
HBR HX7 .....121 J5
HTON BD9 .....104 E3
HWTH BD22 .....54 E3
HWTH BD22 .....79 G3
HWTH BD22 .....100 A4
ILK LS29 .....38 A6
LUD/ILL HX2 .....123 M6
SKP/WHF BD23 .....16 B4
Kell Beck *OT* LS21 .....41 H4

Keir Ter *BSLY* * S70 .....260 F4
Kelburn Gv *HWTH* BD22 .....78 D3
Kelby St *DOD/DAR* S75 .....260 E5
Kelcbar Cl *TAD* LS24 .....71 K2
Kelcbar Hl *TAD* LS24 .....71 J2
Kelcbar Wy *TAD* LS24 .....71 K2
Kelcliffe Av *GSLY* LS20 .....62 A5
Kelcliffe La *GSLY* LS20 .....61 M7
Keldholme Cl *BRAM* LS13 .....107 G1
Keldholme Rd *BRAM* LS13 .....107 H1
Keldregate *HUDN* HD2 .....193 G2
Kell Beck *OT* LS21 .....41 H4
Kelloe St *CLECK* BD19 .....149 L5
Kell St *BGLY* BD16 .....81 J3
Kelmore Gv *WBSY* BD6 .....126 A4
Kelmscott Av *MSTN/BAR* LS15.....111 M3
Kelmscott Crs *MSTN/BAR* LS15.....111 M3
Kelmscott Gdns
MSTN/BAR LS15 .....112 A3
Kelmscott Garth
MSTN/BAR LS15 .....112 A3
Kelmscott Gn *MSTN/BAR* LS15.....111 M3
Kelmscott La *MSTN/BAR* LS15.....111 M3
Kelsall Av *HDGY* LS6 .....109 G4
Kelsall Gv *HDGY* LS6 .....109 G5
Kelsall Pl *HDGY* LS6 .....109 G4
Kelsall Rd *HDGY* LS6 .....109 G4
Kelsall St *MOR* * OL16 .....206 B6
Kelsall Ter *HDGY* LS6 .....109 G4
Kelsey St *HFAX* HX1 .....10 B4
Kelsey Ter *BSLY* * S70 .....261 H7
Kelso Gdns *LDSU* LS2 .....6 B6
Kelso Gv *HUDE* HD5 .....193 J8
Kelso Pl *LDSU* LS2 .....6 C6
Kelso Rd *LDSU* LS2 .....6 B6
Kelso St *LDSU* LS2 .....6 B6
Kelvin Av *HUDE* HD5 .....193 G8
LUD/ILL HX2 .....145 M7
Kelvin Crs *LUD/ILL* HX2 .....145 L7
Kelvin Rd *ELL* HX5 .....169 G8
Kelvin Wy *ECHL* BD2 .....105 J2
Kemp's Br *WKFDW/WTN* WF2 .....12 A4
Kemps Wy *HOLM/MEL* HD9 .....255 G4
Kempton Rd *GFTH/SHER* LS25 .....135 J4
Kemsing Wk *MSTN/BAR* LS15 .....112 B3
Ken Churchill Dr
HOR/CROF WF4 .....197 J4
Kendal Bank *BVRD* LS3 .....6 B7
Kendal Cl *BVRD* LS3 .....6 B7
CAS WF10 .....159 G7
Kendal Cft *CAS* WF10 .....159 G7
Kendal Dr *CAS* WF10 .....158 F6
HOR/CROF WF4 .....199 L4
MSTN/BAR LS15 .....111 C8
ROY/SHW OL2 .....229 M7
Kendal Gdns *CAS* WF10 .....158 F7
RYKW YO26 .....32 C1
Kendal Garth *CAS* WF10 .....159 G7
Kendal Gv *BSLYN/ROY* S71 .....262 C6
BVRD LS3 .....6 C7
Kendal La *BVRD* LS3 .....6 B7
Kendall Av *SHPY* BD18 .....82 A6
Kendal Mellor Ct *KGHY* BD21 .....2 F4
Kendal Ri *BVRD* LS3 .....6 B7
HOR/CROF WF4 .....199 J8
WKFDW/WTN WF2 .....199 J8
Kendal Rd *BVRD* LS3 .....6 C7
Kendal St *KGHY* BD21 .....3 J6
Kendal Wk *BVRD* * LS3 .....6 B7
Kendell St *MID* LS10 .....9 H2
Kendray St *BSLY* S70 .....261 H5
Kenilworth *ROCH* * OL11 .....206 A8
Kenilworth Av *MOR* LS27 .....129 M8
Kenilworth Cl *MIRF* WF14 .....172 B8
Kenilworth Dr *BRIG* HD6 .....148 C8
Kenilworth Gdns *MOR* LS27 .....129 M7
Kenilworth Rd *MILN* OL16 .....228 G6
WOR/ARM LS12 .....130 C1
Kenilworth St *BOW* BD4 .....127 J2
Kenion St *MILN* OL16 .....206 B7
Kenley Av *WBSY* BD6 .....126 C5
Kenley Mt *WBSY* BD6 .....126 C5
Kenley Pde *GTHN* BD7 .....126 B4
Kenmore Av *CLECK* BD19 .....149 L6
Kenmore Cl *CLECK* BD19 .....149 L6
Kenmore Crs *CLECK* BD19 .....149 L6
WBSY BD6 .....126 C4
Kenmore Dr *CLECK* BD19 .....149 L6
WBSY BD6 .....126 C4
Kenmore Gv *CLECK* BD19 .....149 L6
WBSY BD6 .....126 C4
Kenmore Rd *CLECK* BD19 .....149 L6
EARD/LOFT WF3 .....176 B1
WBSY BD6 .....126 C4
Kenmore Vw *CLECK* BD19 .....149 L6
Kenmore Wy *CLECK* BD19 .....149 L6
Kennedy Av *HUDN* HD2 .....192 C1
Kennedy Cl *BTLY* WF17 .....174 B3
STKB/PEN S36 .....269 M3
Kennel La *HWTH* BD22 .....100 A4
RPDN/SBR HX6 .....166 C5
Kennels La *SCFT* LS14 .....68 B6
Kennerleigh Av
MSTN/BAR LS15 .....111 M5
Kennerleigh Crs
MSTN/BAR LS15 .....111 M5
Kennerleigh Dr
MSTN/BAR LS15 .....111 L5
Kennerleigh Garth
MSTN/BAR LS15 .....111 M5
Kennerleigh Gln
MSTN/BAR LS15 .....111 L5

Kennerleigh Gv
MSTN/BAR LS15 .....111 M5
Kennerleigh Ri
MSTN/BAR LS15 .....111 L5
Kennerleigh Wk
MSTN/BAR LS15 .....111 L5
Kenneth St *BEE/HOL* LS11 .....8 A6
Kennet La *GFTH/SHER* LS25 .....113 J8
Kennion St *WBOW* BD5 .....126 F1
Kensington Av *ROY/SHW* OL2 .....228 E8
SCFT LS14 .....68 C8
STKB/PEN S36 .....270 C2
Kensington Cl *BTLY* WF17 .....173 K2
HIPP HX3 .....168 C2
MILN OL16 .....207 J8
Kensington Gdns *MID* LS10 .....132 B7
Kensington Rd *DOD/DAR* S75 .....260 F3
HIPP HX3 .....168 C2
WKFDE WF1 .....176 D6
Kensington St *GIR* BD8 .....104 C5
KGHY BD21 .....2 E7
ROCH OL11 .....228 A2
Kensington Ter *HDGY* LS6 .....6 A2
Kenstone Crs *IDLE* BD10 .....83 J7
Kent Av *AIRE* BD20 .....35 M5
Kent Cl *BSLYN/ROY* S71 .....243 L2
PDSY/CALV LS28 .....107 J7
Kent Crs *PDSY/CALV* LS28 .....107 J7
Kent Dr *PDSY/CALV* LS28 .....107 J7
Kentmere Ap *SCFT* LS14 .....111 J1
Kentmere Av *GFTH/SHER* LS25 .....113 K8
LM/WK BD12 .....149 G5
SCFT LS14 .....89 H7
WHIT OL12 .....206 D3
Kentmere Cl *SCFT* LS14 .....111 H1
Kentmere Crs *SCFT* LS14 .....89 H8
Kentmere Gdns *SCFT* LS14 .....89 H8
Kentmere Ga *SCFT* LS14 .....89 H8
Kentmere Gn *SCFT* LS14 .....89 H8
Kentmere Ri *SCFT* LS14 .....111 J1
Kent Ms *BGLY* BD16 .....81 K4
Kenton Dr *HOR/CROF* WF4 .....198 C7
Kenton Rd *ROY/SHW* OL2 .....229 J7
Kenton Wy *BOW* * BD4 .....128 A3
Kent Rd *BGLY* BD16 .....81 K3
PDSY/CALV LS28 .....107 J7
Kent St *HFAX* HX1 .....10 F7
ROCH OL11 .....206 B8
Kenwood Cl *BSLY* S70 .....261 M6
Kenworthy Cl *BHP/TINH* LS16 .....86 C1
Kenworthy Gdns
BHP/TINH LS16 .....86 C1
Kenworthy Garth
BHP/TINH LS16 .....86 C1
Kenworthy Ga *BHP/TINH* LS16 .....86 C1
Kenworthy La *RPDN/SBR* HX6 .....167 G8
Kenworthy Ri *BHP/TINH* LS16 .....86 C1
Kenworthy Rd *BSLY* S70 .....261 G7
Kenworthy St *MILN* OL16 .....206 E7
Kenworthy Ter *MILN* OL16 .....206 E7
Kenworthy V *BHP/TINH* LS16 .....86 C1
Kenya Mt *HWTH* BD22 .....2 A3
Kenyon Bank *KBTN* HD8 .....257 H7
Kenyon La *LUD/ILL* HX2 .....145 M7
Kenyon St *HEM/SK/SE* WF9 .....247 J5
Kepler Gv *RHAY* LS8 .....7 M4
Kepler Mt *RHAY* LS8 .....7 M4
Kepler Ter *RHAY* LS8 .....7 M4
Kepstorn Cl *KSTL* LS5 .....108 C1
Kepstorn Ri *KSTL* LS5 .....108 C1
Kepstorn Rd *BHP/TINH* LS16 .....86 D7
Keren Gv *WKFDW/WTN* WF2 .....176 A4
Keresforth Cl *BSLY* S70 .....260 E6
Keresforth Ct *BSLY* S70 .....260 E6
Keresforth Hall Rd *BSLY* S70 .....260 F7
Keresforth Hill Rd *BSLY* S70 .....260 E7
Keresforth Rd *DOD/DAR* S75 .....260 B8
Kerry Garth *HORS* LS18 .....85 K5
Kerry Hl *HORS* LS18 .....85 K6
Kerry St *HORS* LS18 .....85 K5
Kershaw Av *CAS* WF10 .....158 D7
Kershaw Ct *LUD/ILL* * HX2 .....144 F6
Kershaw Crs *LUD/ILL* HX2 .....144 F7
Kershaw Dr *LUD/ILL* HX2 .....144 F6
Kershaw La *KNOT* WF11 .....181 M3
Kershaw Rd *TOD* OL14 .....163 J5
Kershaw St *BFDE* BD3 .....105 M7
ROY/SHW OL2 .....229 K7
WHIT * OL12 .....206 B6
Kershaw St East
ROY/SHW OL2 .....229 K7
Kertland St *EARL* WF12 .....173 L7
Kester Rd *BTLY* WF17 .....173 H1
Kesteven Cl *BOW* BD4 .....128 B4
Kesteven Ct *BOW* BD4 .....128 B4
Kesteven Rd *BOW* BD4 .....128 A4
Kestrel Bank *HUDS* HD4 .....214 A4
Kestrel Cl *AL/HA/HU* LS17 .....88 B2
Kestrel Dr *AWLS/ASK* DN6 .....249 H6
ECHL BD2 .....105 J2
WKFDW/WTN WF2 .....220 F1
Kestrel Gra *AL/HA/HU* LS17 .....67 L1
Kestrel Mt *ECHL* BD2 .....105 J2
Kestrel Vw *CLECK* BD19 .....149 M5
Keswick Av *HUDW* HD3 .....191 J5
Keswick Cl *HIPP* HX3 .....169 G3
TOD OL14 .....141 H7
Keswick Dr *CAS* WF10 .....159 G4
WKFDW/WTN WF2 .....176 A7
Keswick Gra *AL/HA/HU* LS17 .....67 L1
Keswick Rd *DOD/DAR* S75 .....242 C4
Keswick St *BOW* BD4 .....127 M1
Keswick Vw *AL/HA/HU* LS17 .....68 A1
Keswick Wk *BSLYN/ROY* S71 .....262 C4
Kettle La *MAR/SLWT* HD7 .....211 K8
Kettleman Br *TAD* LS24 .....72 A5
Kettlethorpe Hall Dr
WKFDW/WTN WF2 .....198 D2
Kettlethorpe Rd
WKFDW/WTN WF2 .....220 D1
Ketton Wk *DOD/DAR* S75 .....260 E3
Kew Hl *HUDW* HD3 .....191 H3
Kew Rd *ROCH* OL11 .....228 C3
Kexbrough Dr *DOD/DAR* S75 .....241 L6

Key Hill La CUD/GR S72 ....245 H3
Keystone Av CAS WF10 ....180 A1
Key Syke La TOD OL14 ....163 L1
Khalaq Ct BFDE BD3 ....5 M4
Khus Wk KGHY BD21 ....79 L2
Kibroyd Dr DOD/DAR S75 ....241 L7
Kidacre St BEE/HOL LS11 ....9 H5
Kiddal La MSTN/BAR LS15 ....91 G3
Kidroyd La HUDE HD5 ....214 F2
Kilburn Fold HUD5 ....15 K9
Kilburn Rd WOR/ARM LS12 ....108 E7
Kilby St WKFDE WF1 ....176 D7
Kildare Crs ROCH OL11 ....228 C4
  WIL/AL BD15 ....103 J5
Kildare Ter WOR/ARM LS12 ....109 G8
Killingbeck Br SCFT LS14 ....111 G5
Killingbeck Dr SCFT LS14 ....111 G5
Killinghall Av ECHL BD2 ....5 M1
Killinghall Dr ECHL BD2 ....5 M1
Killinghall Gv ECHL BD2 ....5 L1
Killinghall Rd BFDE BD3 ....105 L5
Kiln Bent Rd HOLM/MEL HD9 ....253 D8
Kiln Ct HUDW HD3 ....191 G5
Kilner Bank HUDE HD5 ....15 K4
Kilnerdeyne Ter MILN * OL16 ....206 A8
Kilner Rd WBSY * BD6 ....126 C5
Kiln Fold BRIG HD6 ....170 F3
Kiln HI MAR/SLWT HD7 ....212 C6
Kiln hill La AIRE BD20 ....17 J8
Kilnhouse Bank La
  HOLM/MEL HD9 ....253 K5
Kilnhurst La TOD OL14 ....163 M2
Kilnhurst Mt TOD OL14 ....163 L1
Kilnhurst Rd TOD OL14 ....163 L1
Kiln La HBR HX7 ....120 E3
  KBTN HD8 ....240 B1
  MILN OL16 ....207 H8
Kilnsea Mt BOW BD4 ....128 A3
Kilnsey Fold AIRE BD20 ....35 M4
Kilnsey Gv WKFDE WF1 ....177 G7
Kilnsey HI BTLY WF17 ....173 M4
Kilnsey Ms BAIL BD17 ....82 D3
Kilnsey Rd BFDE BD3 ....5 M7
  WKFDE WF1 ....177 G6
Kilnshaw La HBR HX7 ....143 H6
Kiln Wk WBSY BD6 ....206 A4
Kilroyd Dr CLECK BD19 ....149 M4
Kilroyd La CLECK BD19 ....150 A4
Kimberley PI HIPP HX3 ....146 C2
  OSM LS9 ....110 D4
Kimberley Rd OSM LS9 ....110 D4
Kimberley St BFDE BD3 ....105 L8
  BRIG HD6 ....170 D3
  FEA/AMT WF7 ....179 L8
  HIPP HX3 ....146 C2
  WKFDE WF1 ....13 H8
Kimberley Vw OSM LS9 ....110 D5
Kimberly CI PONT WF8 ....225 K1
Kinara CI KGHY BD21 ....3 M1
Kinder Av HUDS HD4 ....213 H4
Kinders Fold LIT OL15 ....185 H7
Kineholme Dr OT LS21 ....40 F8
Kine Moor La STKB/PEN S36 ....258 F8
King Alfred St ROY/SHW OL2 ....229 K7
King Alfred's Dr HDGY LS6 ....87 J5
King Alfred's Wy HDGY LS6 ....87 J5
King Charles St LDS * LS1 ....7 G9
King Cliffe Rd HUDN HD2 ....14 E1
King CI AL/HA/HU LS17 ....87 H2
King Cross Rd HFAX HX1 ....10 B9
King Cross St HFAX HX1 ....10 C9
King Dr AL/HA/HU LS17 ....87 H2
  HORS LS18 ....85 K6
King Edward Crs HORS LS18 ....85 L5
King Edward Rd
  CUL/QBY BD13 ....102 F8
King Edwards Gdns BSLY S70 ....260 F6
King Edward St AIRE BD20 ....55 M1
  BSLYN/ROY S71 ....243 M8
  EARL WF12 ....195 K3
  HEM/SK/SE WF9 ....224 A8
  HFAX * HX1 ....11 H6
  LDS LS1 ....7 H9
  NORM WF6 ....178 C4
King Edwin's Ct RHAY LS8 ....110 C1
Kingfield GSLY LS20 ....62 B3
Kingfisher CI AL/HA/HU LS17 ....88 D2
  HOR/CROF WF4 ....198 B7
Kingfisher Ct KGHY BD21 ....3 H5
Kingfisher Gv GIR BD8 ....103 L7
  HUDS HD4 ....214 A4
  WKFDE/WTN WF2 ....220 F1
Kingfisher Ms MOR LS27 ....152 E3
Kingfisher Reach WBY LS22 ....47 J5
Kingfisher Wy AL/HA/HU LS17 ....88 D2
King George Av CHAL LS7 ....87 M7
  HORS LS18 ....85 L5
  MOR LS27 ....130 D8
King George Cft MOR LS27 ....152 D1
King George Gdns CHAL * LS7 ....87 M7
King George Rd HORS LS18 ....85 L5
King George St WKFDE WF1 ....176 C3
King George Ter BSLY * S70 ....261 K6
King La AL/HA/HU LS17 ....65 G7
  AL/HA/HU LS17 ....87 J2
  AL/HA/HU LS17 ....87 K4
King Royd La HOR/CROF WF4 ....201 L8
Kings Ap BRAM LS13 ....108 A4
Kings Av CAS WF10 ....158 C4
  HDGY LS6 ....109 G5
  ILK LS29 ....38 C2
  NORM WF6 ....178 B1
King's Bridge Rd HUD HD1 ....214 D2
Kingsbury PI HFAX HX1 ....10 B6
Kings Cha RTHW LS26 ....133 H8
Kings CI FEA/AMT WF7 ....223 M1
  ILK LS29 ....38 A2
  OSS WF5 ....174 E7
  OT LS21 ....41 G7
  PONT WF8 ....180 E7
Kings Crs PONT WF8 ....181 G7

Kings Cft HEM/SK/SE WF9 ....246 D4
  OSS WF5 ....174 E6
King's Croft Gdns
  AL/HA/HU LS17 ....87 M5
Kingsdale Av BIRK/DRI BD11 ....129 G8
  ECHL BD2 ....105 J3
Kingsdale Ct SCFT LS14 ....89 H8
Kingsdale Crs ECHL BD2 ....105 J3
Kingsdale Dr ECHL BD2 ....105 J3
Kingsdale Gdns BIRK/DRI BD11 ....129 G8
  ECHL BD2 ....105 G8
King's Dr BTLY WF17 ....151 G4
  ECHL BD2 ....83 H8
  NORM WF6 ....178 D1
Kingsfield RTHW LS26 ....154 D1
King's Ga BGLY BD16 ....4 F1
Kings Gv BGLY BD16 ....81 J3
  WHIT OL12 ....206 F2
Kings Head Buildings
  HUD * HD1 ....14 F7
Kings Head Dr MIRF * WF14 ....172 B8
Kings Head Rd MIRF WF14 ....172 B8
Kings Lea HIPP HX3 ....168 D4
  LVSG WF15 ....172 E4
  OSS WF5 ....174 E6
Kingsley Av BHP/TINH LS16 ....86 D1
  BIRK/DRI BD11 ....150 D2
  ECHL BD2 ....105 G3
  FEA/AMT WF7 ....179 M6
  HOR/CROF WF4 ....200 A3
  HUDS HD4 ....214 A2
  KNOT WF11 ....181 L1
  RPDN/SBR HX6 ....167 H3
  WKFDE WF1 ....176 D1
  WKFDW/WTN WF2 ....198 E8
Kingsley CI BIRK/DRI BD11 ....150 D2
  BSLYN/ROY S71 ....243 J8
  HOR/CROF WF4 ....200 A4
  WKFDE WF1 ....176 D1
  WKFDW/WTN WF2 ....198 E8
Kingsley Crs BAIL BD17 ....82 E4
  BIRK/DRI BD11 ....150 D2
Kingsley Dr BHP/TINH LS16 ....86 D1
  BIRK/DRI BD11 ....150 D2
  CAS WF10 ....180 F1
Kingsley Garth WKFDE WF1 ....176 D1
Kingsley PI HFAX HX1 ....10 B8
Kingsley Rd BHP/TINH LS16 ....86 D1
  COL BB8 ....52 F8
Kings Md RTHW LS26 ....133 J8
Kingsmead SCFT LS14 ....89 J6
Kingsmead Dr SCFT LS14 ....89 H5
Kings Meadow OSS WF5 ....174 E7
Kings Meadow CI WBY LS22 ....29 M7
Kings Meadow Dr WBY LS22 ....29 M7
Kings Meadow Gv WBY LS22 ....29 M7
Kings Meadow Ms WBY LS22 ....29 M7
Kingsmill CI MOR LS27 ....152 B3
King's Mill La HUDS HD4 ....214 D2
King's Mt CHAL LS7 ....87 L6
  KNOT WF11 ....181 K1
Kings Paddock OSS WF5 ....174 E7
King's PI HDGY LS6 ....109 G4
King's Rd BGLY BD16 ....81 G1
  BHP/TINH LS16 ....64 C5
  CUD/GR S72 ....244 E5
  ECHL BD2 ....83 H8
  HDGY LS6 ....109 G4
  ILK LS29 ....38 B2
  MILN OL16 ....228 D1
  NORM WF6 ....156 A8
  ROY/SHW OL2 ....229 J8
King's St CUD/GR S72 ....245 J8
  SKP/WHF BD23 ....16 D2
Kingston Av HUDE HD5 ....193 G8
Kingston CI HFAX HX1 ....10 B7
  ROY/SHW OL2 ....229 K7
  WIL/AL BD15 ....102 E2
Kingston Crs SEL YO8 ....139 M4
Kingston Dr HFAX HX1 ....10 A7
  NORM WF6 ....178 C5
  ROY/SHW OL2 ....228 E8
  SEL YO8 ....139 M4
Kingstone PI BSLY S70 ....260 F7
Kingston Gdns
  MSTN/BAR LS15 ....111 K3
Kingston Gv IDLE BD10 ....83 K5
Kingston Rd IDLE BD10 ....83 K5
Kingston St HFAX HX1 ....10 B7
Kingston Ter LDSU LS2 ....6 E4
King St AIRE * BD20 ....36 A5
  BIRK/DRI BD11 ....129 H8
  BRIG HD6 ....170 D4
  BSLY S70 ....261 H6
  CAS WF10 ....158 A8
  CLECK BD19 ....150 A6
  COL BB8 ....74 A1
  HBR HX7 ....143 G3
  HBR HX7 ....144 A6
  HECK WF16 ....172 F2
  HEM/SK/SE WF9 ....223 K5
  HFAX HX1 ....11 J5
  HOR/CROF WF4 ....196 F5
  HUD HD1 ....15 G7
  HUDW HD3 ....191 K6
  IDLE BD10 ....105 L1
  KBTN HD8 ....239 J4
  KGHY BD21 ....2 E1
  LDS LS1 ....8 E1
  MILN OL16 ....206 B7
  MIRF WF14 ....194 C3
  MOR LS27 ....152 C3
  NORM WF6 ....178 C5
  OSS WF5 ....197 G2
  OSS WF5 ....106 E6
  PONT WF8 ....180 E6
  RPDN/SBR * HX6 ....167 G3
  TOD OL14 ....141 M8
  WKFDE WF1 ....12 E2
  YEA LS19 ....59 J4
  YEA LS19 ....62 C7
  YEA LS19 ....84 C2
King St East ROCH OL11 ....228 A1
King St South ROCH OL11 ....228 A1

Kings Vw HIPP HX3 ....169 J2
Kingsway AIRE BD20 ....58 C5
  AL/HA/HU LS17 ....43 M2
  BGLY BD16 ....81 J4
  BIRK/DRI BD11 ....129 H8
  BTLY WF17 ....151 G4
  DOD/DAR S75 ....242 C5
  EARD/LOFT WF3 ....177 H4
  ECHL BD2 ....83 H8
  GFTH/SHER LS25 ....112 F8
  HOLM/MEL HD9 ....255 H5
  HUDN HD2 ....192 B3
  HUDN HD2 ....192 E2
  MSTN/BAR LS15 ....111 L6
  NORM WF6 ....178 C6
  OSS WF5 ....174 E7
  PONT WF8 ....180 F3
  SKP/WHF BD23 ....16 D2
Kingsway CI OSS WF5 ....174 D7
Kingsway Ct OSS WF5 ....174 E7
Kingsway Dr ILK LS29 ....38 C2
Kingsway Garth
  GFTH/SHER LS25 ....112 E8
Kingswear CI MSTN/BAR LS15 ....111 M5
Kingswear Crs MSTN/BAR LS15 ....111 M5
Kingswear Garth
  MSTN/BAR LS15 ....111 M5
Kingswear Gln MSTN/BAR LS15 ....111 M5
Kingswear Gv MSTN/BAR LS15 ....111 M5
Kingswear Pde
  MSTN/BAR LS15 ....111 M5
Kingswear Ri MSTN/BAR LS15 ....111 M5
Kingswear Vw MSTN/BAR LS15 ....111 M5
Kingswell Av WKFDE WF1 ....176 E2
Kingswood Av HIPP HX3 ....88 C3
Kingswood Crs RHAY LS8 ....88 B3
Kingswood Dr RHAY LS8 ....88 B3
Kingswood Gdns RHAY LS8 ....88 B3
Kingswood Gn HIPP HX3 ....147 H5
Kingswood Gv RHAY LS8 ....88 C3
Kingswood PI GTHN BD7 ....126 C2
Kingswood St GTHN BD7 ....126 C2
Kingswood Ter GTHN * BD7 ....126 C2
Kingwell Sts ROY/SHW OL2 ....261 H8
Kinnaird CI BTLY WF17 ....174 A1
Kinsley House Crs
  HEM/SK/SE WF9 ....223 J4
Kinsley St HEM/SK/SE WF9 ....223 K5
Kipling CI HUDS HD4 ....213 M3
Kipling Gv IDLE BD10 ....83 M7
Kipling PI PONT WF8 ....180 F4
Kippax Mt OSM LS9 ....110 B7
Kippax PI OSM LS9 ....110 B7
Kipping La CUL/QBY BD13 ....102 F8
Kipping PI CUL/QBY BD13 ....102 F8
Kirby Cote La HBR HX7 ....165 M3
Kirby St KGHY BD21 ....3 J2
Kirk Beston CI BEE/HOL LS11 ....131 G4
Kirkbourne Gv BAIL BD17 ....83 G4
Kirk Bridge La HOLM/MEL HD9 ....236 F7
Kirkbridge Wy
  HEM/SK/SE WF9 ....247 H3
Kirkburn PI GTHN BD7 ....104 D8
Kirkby Av BSLYN/ROY S71 ....243 J6
  GFTH/SHER LS25 ....135 J1
Kirkby CI HEM/SK/SE WF9 ....246 E3
Kirkbygate HEM/SK/SE WF9 ....246 A1
Kirkby La HOR/CROF WF4 ....217 L6
  PBR HG3 ....45 M2
Kirkby Leas HFAX HX1 ....11 G8
Kirkby Rd HEM/SK/SE WF9 ....224 A8
Kirk CI EARL WF12 ....174 D6
Kirk Cross Crs BSLYN/ROY S71 ....243 L4
Kirkdale CAS WF10 ....158 E7
Kirkdale Av WOR/ARM LS12 ....130 D3
Kirkdale Crs WOR/ARM LS12 ....130 D3
Kirkdale Dr HOR/CROF WF4 ....197 M8
  WOR/ARM LS12 ....130 D2
Kirkdale Gdns WOR/ARM LS12 ....130 C2
Kirkdale Mt WOR/ARM LS12 ....130 D3
Kirkdale Ter WOR/ARM LS12 ....130 D3
Kirkdale Vw WOR/ARM LS12 ....130 D3
Kirk Dr BAIL BD17 ....82 F2
Kirkfield Av SCFT LS14 ....68 C8
Kirkfield CI DOD/DAR S75 ....259 H2
Kirkfield Crs SCFT LS14 ....68 C8
Kirkfield Dr MSTN/BAR LS15 ....111 L7
Kirkfield Gdns MSTN/BAR LS15 ....111 M7
Kirkfield La SCFT LS14 ....68 C8
Kirkfields BAIL BD17 ....83 G2
Kirkfield Vw MSTN/BAR LS15 ....111 M7
Kirkfield Wy BSLYN/ROY S71 ....243 L4
Kirkgate AIRE BD20 ....35 G6
  AIRE BD20 ....36 A5
  BFD BD1 ....6 A4
  BTLY WF17 ....150 F5
  BTLY WF17 ....174 B3
  GFTH/SHER LS25 ....116 A6
  HUD HD1 ....15 G7
  LDSU LS2 ....6 E2
  OT LS21 ....41 J6
  SHPY BD18 ....82 C7
  TAD LS24 ....71 M3
  WKFDE WF1 ....12 F2
Kirkgate La CUD/GR S72 ....222 E8
Kirkham Av WKFDW/WTN WF2 ....175 K3
Kirkham CI BSLYN/ROY S71 ....261 L3
Kirkham PI BSLYN/ROY S71 ....243 M7
Kirkham Rd GTHN * BD7 ....104 D8
Kirkham St BRAM LS13 ....107 H1
Kirkhaw La KNOT WF11 ....159 K8
Kirkhill Bank STKB/PEN S36 ....270 E6
Kirklands Av BAIL BD17 ....83 G3
Kirklands CI BAIL BD17 ....83 G4
  YEA LS19 ....62 C7
Kirklands Gdns BAIL BD17 ....83 G3
Kirklands La BAIL BD17 ....83 G3
Kirklands Vls BAIL * BD17 ....83 G3
Kirk La HIPP HX3 ....147 L6
  RYKW YO26 ....32 B1
  YEA LS19 ....62 C7
  YEA LS19 ....84 C7
Kirklea KBTN HD8 ....238 E8
Kirk Lea Crs HUDW HD3 ....191 L6
Kirklees PDSY/CALV LS28 ....107 G2

Kirklees Cft PDSY/CALV LS28 ....106 F2
Kirklees Dr PDSY/CALV LS28 ....106 F2
Kirklees Garth PDSY/CALV LS28 ....106 F2
Kirklees Ri PDSY/CALV LS28 ....106 F2
Kirklees Wy BIRK/DRI BD11 ....150 B1
  BTLY WF17 ....151 L5
  CLECK BD19 ....149 J3
  EARL WF12 ....174 A7
  HOLM/MEL HD9 ....255 H5
  HUDN HD2 ....192 B3
  HUDN HD2 ....192 E2
  KBTN HD8 ....237 L7
  KBTN HD8 ....238 D6
  KBTN HD8 ....239 K7
  MAR/SLWT HD7 ....210 F5
  MAR/SLWT HD7 ....212 C1
  MAR/SLWT HD7 ....233 K8
  OSS WF5 ....196 D2
Kirkley Av LM/WK BD12 ....148 E5
Kirkstall WHIT * OL12 ....206 A6
Kirkstall Av KSTL LS5 ....108 B3
  LIT OL15 ....185 J8
Kirkstall Gv GIR BD8 ....103 M7
Kirkstall Hl BULY LS4 ....108 B3
Kirkstall La KSTL LS5 ....108 D2
Kirkstall Mt KSTL LS5 ....108 B3
Kirkstall Rd BSLYN/ROY S71 ....243 G7
Kirkstone Av HUDE HD5 ....15 K6
Kirkstone Dr CLECK BD19 ....150 D6
  LUD/ILL HX2 ....145 K6
  ROY/SHW OL2 ....228 E8
Kirkthorpe La WKFDE WF1 ....177 K3
Kirkwall Av OSM LS9 ....110 D7
Kirkwall Dr BOW BD4 ....128 A3
Kirkwood Av BHP/TINH LS16 ....85 M7
Kirkwood CI BHP/TINH LS16 ....85 M1
Kirkwood Crs BHP/TINH LS16 ....85 M1
Kirkwood Dr BHP/TINH LS16 ....85 M1
  HUDW HD3 ....191 G5
Kirkwood Gdns BHP/TINH LS16 ....86 A1
Kirkwood Gn HUDW HD3 ....191 G5
Kirkwood Gv BHP/TINH LS16 ....85 M2
  EARD/LOFT WF3 ....153 M5
Kirkwood La BHP/TINH LS16 ....85 M1
Kirkwood Ri BHP/TINH LS16 ....86 A1
Kirkwood Vw BHP/TINH LS16 ....86 A1
Kirkwood Wy BHP/TINH LS16 ....86 A1
Kismet Gdns BFDE BD3 ....105 L6
Kistyaen Gdns HOLM/MEL HD9 ....234 D2
Kitchener Av OSM LS9 ....110 D5
Kitchener Gv OSM LS9 ....110 D5
Kitchener Mt OSM LS9 ....110 D5
Kitchener PI OSM LS9 ....110 D5
  OSM LS9 ....110 D5
  RTHW LS26 ....133 L4
Kitchen Fold MAR/SLWT HD7 ....212 C6
Kitchen St MILN OL16 ....206 D3
Kite Ms GIR BD8 ....103 L7
Kit La AIRE BD20 ....17 L8
Kitson CI WOR/ARM LS12 ....108 E8
Kitson Dr BSLYN/ROY S71 ....261 L8
Kitson Gdns WOR/ARM LS12 ....108 E8
Kitson Hill Crs MIRF WF14 ....172 A8
Kitson Hill Rd MIRF WF14 ....172 A8
Kitson La RPDN/SBR HX6 ....167 M5
Kitson Rd MID LS10 ....9 J6
Kitson St EARD/LOFT WF3 ....152 F5
  OSM LS9 ....110 B7
  SHPY BD18 ....82 E7
Kitson Wood Rd TOD OL14 ....141 G6
Kitter St WHIT OL12 ....206 D3
Kliffen PI HIPP HX3 ....168 F2
Knaresborough Dr HUDN HD2 ....192 C4
Knaresborough Rd WBY LS22 ....29 L1
Knavesmire RTHW LS26 ....154 D1
Knightsbridge Wk BOW BD4 ....127 K6
Knightsclose MSTN/BAR LS15 ....111 L6
Knights Cft WBY LS22 ....30 E1
Knightscroft Av RTHW LS26 ....133 G8
Knightscroft Dr RTHW LS26 ....133 G8
Knightscroft Pde
  HEM/SK/SE WF9 ....247 J4
Knight's Fold GTHN BD7 ....126 C2
Knightshill MSTN/BAR LS15 ....111 M6
Knight St HFAX HX1 ....10 B9
  HUD HD1 ....15 G5
Knightsway EARD/LOFT WF3 ....154 D5
  GFTH/SHER LS25 ....134 F1
  MSTN/BAR LS15 ....111 L6
  WKFDW/WTN WF2 ....198 E8
The Knoll BSPA/BRAM LS23 ....69 L3
  PDSY/CALV LS28 ....106 C3
  ROY/SHW * OL2 ....229 L8
Knoll CI OSS WF5 ....174 F7
Knoll La HOLM/MEL HD9 ....235 M6
Knoll Pk EARD/LOFT WF3 ....153 M7
Knoll Park Dr BAIL BD17 ....82 D5
Knoll Wood Pk HORS LS18 ....85 M6
Knott Hill St WHIT OL12 ....162 A8
Knottingley Rd PONT WF8 ....181 J4
Knotta CI AIRE BD20 ....56 B1
  YEA LS19 ....85 G5
Knotts Rd TOD OL14 ....140 F6
Knotty La KBTN HD8 ....216 C3
Knowle Av BULY LS4 ....108 F3
  HUDE HD5 ....215 G1
Knowle CI BULY LS4 ....108 F3
Knowle La HOLM/MEL HD9 ....235 K4
  LM/WK BD12 ....148 F4
Knowle Mt BULY LS4 ....108 F3
Knowle Park Av KBTN HD8 ....238 D6
Knowle PI BULY LS4 ....108 F3
Knowler CI LVSG WF15 ....172 C2
Knowler HI LVSG WF15 ....172 C2
Knowle Rd BSLY S70 ....261 G6
  BULY * LS4 ....108 F3
  MAR/SLWT HD7 ....212 C6
Knowler Wy LVSG WF15 ....172 C2
Knowles Av BOW BD4 ....127 M4
Knowles Hl DEWS WF13 ....173 H5
Knowles Hill Rd DEWS WF13 ....173 H5
Knowles La BOW BD4 ....127 M4
  BTLY * WF17 ....173 K2

CLECK BD19 ....150 A3
Knowle Spring Rd KGHY * BD21 ....2 D6
Knowles Rd BRIG HD6 ....170 C6
  BTLY WF17 ....173 K2
Knowle St BOW BD4 ....127 L5
  CUL/QBY BD13 ....101 M4
  STKB/PEN S36 ....271 H4
Knowles Vw BOW BD4 ....127 M4
The Knowle KBTN HD8 ....238 C6
Knowle Ter BULY LS4 ....108 E4
Knowle Top Dr HIPP HX3 ....148 A6
Knowle Top Rd HIPP HX3 ....148 A6
Knowl Gv MIRF WF14 ....194 C1
Knowl Rd HOLM/MEL HD9 ....252 F2
  MAR/SLWT HD7 ....213 G2
  MILN OL16 ....206 F8
  MIRF WF14 ....194 C1
  ROY/SHW OL2 ....229 L8
Knowl Syke St WHIT OL12 ....184 F7
Knowl Vw LIT OL15 ....207 H4
Knowlwood Rd TOD OL14 ....163 J3
Knowsley Av TOD * OL14 ....163 J5
Knowsley Crs WHIT OL12 ....162 A6
Knowsley St BFDE BD3 ....5 K7
  BSLY S70 ....260 F5
  WHIT OL12 ....206 A6
Knowsthorpe Crs OSM LS9 ....110 B8
Knowsthorpe Ga OSM LS9 ....132 B3
Knowsthorpe La OSM LS9 ....132 B1
  OSM LS9 ....132 F4
Knowsthorpe Rd OSM LS9 ....132 D3
Knowsthorpe Wy OSM LS9 ....132 D2
Knox St BRAM LS13 ....106 F1
Knutsford Gv BOW BD4 ....128 A4
Knutsford Ms BOW * BD4 ....128 A4
Komla CI BFD BD1 ....5 H5
Krive La MAR/SLWT HD7 ....234 A1
Kyffin Av MSTN/BAR LS15 ....111 G7
Kyffin PI BOW BD4 ....128 A3

L

Laburnum Av ROY/SHW OL2 ....229 K8
Laburnum CI EARD/LOFT WF3 ....153 L7
Laburnum Ct HOR/CROF WF4 ....197 H5
Laburnum Dr BAIL BD17 ....82 F2
Laburnum Gv BRIG HD6 ....148 C8
  CLECK BD19 ....150 C5
  HOR/CROF WF4 ....197 H5
  HWTH BD22 ....79 G6
  KBTN HD8 ....239 J5
  MAR/SLWT HD7 ....213 H4
Laburnum La MILN OL16 ....229 J3
Laburnum PI GIR BD8 ....4 B2
  IDLE BD10 ....84 A6
Laburnum Rd DEWS WF13 ....173 G4
  SHPY BD18 ....104 F1
  WKFDE WF1 ....12 D1
Laburnum St BFDE BD3 ....4 B2
  PDSY/CALV LS28 ....106 C3
Laburnum Ter HUD * HD1 ....15 G3
  ROCH OL11 ....228 A2
Laburnum Wy LIT OL15 ....207 H1
Laceby CI IDLE BD10 ....83 L9
Laceby Ct BSLY S70 ....260 E7
Lacey St DEWS WF13 ....173 K6
Lachman Rd COL BB8 ....74 D3
Lacy Av TOD OL14 ....163 J5
Lacy Gv WBY LS22 ....48 B3
Lacy St HEM/SK/SE WF9 ....223 L7
Lacy Wy ELL HX5 ....169 J6
Ladbroke Gv BOW * BD4 ....128 A5
Ladderbanks La BAIL BD17 ....82 F2
Ladock CI BSLYN/ROY S71 ....261 K3
Lady Ann Rd BTLY WF17 ....173 M1
Lady Balk La PONT WF8 ....180 F4
Lady Beck CI LDSU LS2 ....7 J3
Ladybower Av HUDS HD4 ....213 G4
Lady CI OSS WF5 ....174 E6
Lady Gap La AWLS/ASK DN6 ....249 L1
Lady Heton Av MIRF WF14 ....172 B8
Lady Heton CI MIRF * WF14 ....172 A8
Lady Heton Dr MIRF WF14 ....172 A8
Lady Heton Gv MIRF WF14 ....172 A8
Ladyhouse CI MILN OL16 ....229 J2
Lady House La MILN OL16 ....229 H1
Lady La BGLY BD16 ....59 J3
  LDSU LS2 ....7 H5
  WKFDE WF1 ....12 D4
Lady Pk AL/HA/HU LS17 ....88 B2
Lady Park Av BGLY BD16 ....59 J3
Lady Park Ct AL/HA/HU * LS17 ....88 B2
Lady Pit La BEE/HOL LS11 ....8 E7
Ladyroyd Cft CUD/GR S72 ....244 D8
Ladyroyd Dr BIRK/DRI BD11 ....128 A3
Ladysmith Rd CUL/QBY BD13 ....124 E6
Ladywell CI WBOW BD5 ....127 G3
Ladywell La LVSG WF15 ....171 K3
Ladywood Gra RHAY * LS8 ....88 F3
Ladywood Md RHAY LS8 ....88 F3
Ladywood Rd CUD/GR S72 ....245 K8
  RHAY LS8 ....88 D7
Ladywood Ter HFAX HX1 ....10 C3
Lady Wood Rd RHAY LS8 ....88 D7
Ladywood Wy DEWS WF13 ....194 F2
Lafflands La HOR/CROF WF4 ....222 C5
Lairds Wy STKB/PEN S36 ....271 G3
Lairum Ri BSPA/BRAM LS23 ....69 M1
Laisterdyke BFDE BD3 ....105 M8
Laisteridge La GTHN BD7 ....4 B8
  WBOW BD5 ....126 E1
Laith CI BHP/TINH LS16 ....86 B3
Laithe Av HOLM/MEL HD9 ....253 L4
Laithe Bank Dr
  HOLM/MEL HD9 ....253 L3
Laithe CI AIRE BD20 ....35 M4
Laithe Cft DOD/DAR S75 ....260 B7
Laithe Croft Rd BTLY WF17 ....174 A1
Laithe Gv WBSY BD6 ....126 C5
Laithe Rd WBSY BD6 ....126 C5
Laithes Cha WKFDW/WTN WF2 ....175 M4
Laithes CI BSLYN/ROY S71 ....243 K7
  WKFDW/WTN WF2 ....175 M7
Laithes Crs BSLYN/ROY S71 ....243 K7
  WKFDW/WTN WF2 ....175 M7

Laithes Cft EARL WF12 ......174 A7
Laithes Dr WKFDW/WTN WF2 ......175 M7
Laithes Fold
WKFDW/WTN WF2 ......175 M7
Laithes La BSLYN/ROY S71 ......243 H7
Laith Garth BHP/TINH LS16 ......86 B3
Laith Gn BHP/TINH LS16 ......86 B3
Laith Rd BHP/TINH LS16 ......86 B3
Laith Staid La GFTH/SHER LS25 ......115 K6
Lake Bank LIT OL15 ......207 J5
Lakeland Cl CUD/GR S72 ......262 D1
Lakeland Crs AL/HA/HU LS17 ......65 J8
Lakeland Dr AL/HA/HU LS17 ......65 K8
ROY/SHW * OL2 ......228 E6
Lakeland Wy
WKFDW/WTN WF2 ......199 J8
Lake Lock Dr EARD/LOFT WF3 ......177 H1
Lake Lock Gv EARD/LOFT WF3 ......177 H1
Lake Lock Rd EARD/LOFT WF3 ......177 H1
Lake Rw BOW BD4 ......5 M9
Lakeside AIRE BD20 ......59 C4
Lake Side LIT OL15 ......207 J4
Lakeside Cl ILK LS29 ......38 C1
Lakeside Ct HUDW HD3 ......191 K6
Lakeside Gdns YEA LS19 ......84 E2
Lakeside Mdw PONT WF8 ......180 F3
Lakeside Rd WOR/ARM LS12 ......108 A8
Lakeside Ter YEA LS19 ......84 E2
Lakeside Vw YEA LS19 ......84 E2
Lake St BOW BD4 ......5 M9
KGHY BD21 ......3 L1
Lake Ter MID LS10 ......131 M4
Lake Vw HFAX HX1 ......10 F3
PONT WF8 ......180 E3
WKFDW/WTN WF2 ......220 E2
Lake View Ct RHAY LS8 ......88 C6
Lake Yd EARD/LOFT WF3 ......177 J1
Lamb Cote Rd HUDN HD2 ......170 D4
Lambecroft BSLYN/ROY S71 ......243 L5
Lambe Flatt DOD/DAR * S75 ......241 L6
Lambert Av RHAY LS8 ......88 B3
Lambert Cl GTL/HWG HX4 ......168 F7
Lambert Dr RHAY LS8 ......88 B8
Lambert Fold DOD/DAR S75 ......260 C7
Lambert Pl ECHL BD2 ......105 K4
Lambert Rd BSLY S70 ......261 L7
Lambert St COL BB8 ......74 E4
GTL/HWG HX4 ......168 F7
SKP/WHF BD23 ......16 C3
Lambert Wk BSLY S70 ......261 L6
Lambeth St COL BB8 ......74 D1
Lamb Hall Rd HUDW HD3 ......191 G6
Lamb Hey MAR/SLWT * HD7 ......212 D5
Lamb Inn Rd KNOT WF11 ......182 C2
Lamb La BSLYN/ROY S71 ......261 L1
Lambourne Av IDLE BD10 ......105 M1
Lambourne Gv MID OL16 ......229 H1
Lambra Rd BSLY S70 ......261 H5
Lambton Gv RHAY LS8 ......110 B2
Lambton Pl RHAY LS8 ......110 B2
Lambton St RHAY * LS8 ......110 B2
Lambton Ter RHAY LS8 ......110 B2
Lambton Vw RHAY * LS8 ......110 B2
Lamma Well Rd
HOLM/MEL HD9 ......254 C4
Lampards Cl WIL/AL BD15 ......103 J4
Lamplands BTLY WF17 ......151 M7

Lane Head Ri DOD/DAR S75 ......242 C4
Lane Head Rd DOD/DAR S75 ......258 F3
DOD/DAR S75 ......259 L1
KBTN HD8 ......238 A7
RPDN/SBR HX6 ......188 L1
Lane House La COL BB8 ......74 E4
Lane House Rd HWTH BD22 ......54 B2
The Lanes PDSY/CALV LS28 ......107 H6
WIL/AL BD15 ......102 D2
Laneside KBTN HD8 ......216 C7
MOR LS27 ......130 D7
Laneside Av ROY/SHW OL2 ......229 M7
Lane Side Cl LM/WK BD12 ......148 E2
Laneside Cl LIT OL15 ......185 J8
MOR LS27 ......130 D7
Laneside Fold MOR LS27 ......130 D8
Lane Side La HUDE HD5 ......193 L7
Laneside St TOD OL14 ......163 J2
The Lane AL/HA/HU LS17 ......87 L1
OSM LS9 ......9 L2
Lane Top BRIG * HD6 ......148 F7
Lang Av BSLYN/ROY S71 ......262 A4
Langbar Ap SCFT LS14 ......111 M1
Langbar Av HTON BD9 ......103 M3
Langbar Cl SCFT LS14 ......89 M8
Langbar Garth SCFT LS14 ......89 M8
Langbar Gn SCFT LS14 ......89 M8
Langbar Gv SCFT LS14 ......111 M1
Langbar Rd ILK LS29 ......20 C8
SCFT LS14 ......111 M1
Langcliffe Cl DOD/DAR S75 ......242 C4
Lang Crs BSLYN/ROY S71 ......262 A4
GIR BD8 ......104 A6
HDGY LS6 ......108 L1
LM/WK BD12 ......149 G5
MILN OL16 ......228 E6
NORM WF6 ......178 C2
Langdale Cl CAS WF10 ......159 G4
WBY LS22 ......29 M8
Langdale Ct BGLY BD16 ......81 J2
Langdale Crs LUD/ILL HX2 ......146 A5
FEA/AMT WF7 ......202 E7
HUDE HD5 ......15 K5
NORM WF6 ......178 C1
WKFDW/WTN WF2 ......176 A8
Langdale Gdns HDGY LS6 ......108 L2
Langdale Ms NORM * WF6 ......178 C2
Langdale Mt
WKFDW/WTN WF2 ......199 J8
Langdale Ri COL BB8 ......52 B8
Langdale Sq
WKFDW/WTN WF2 ......176 B8
Langdale St ELL HX5 ......169 H8
Langdale Ter HDGY LS6 ......108 L2
Langden Cl ROY/SHW OL2 ......229 J6
Langdon Wk BSLY S70 ......260 F4
Langford Cl DOD/DAR S75 ......260 C7
Langford La ILK LS29 ......40 B5
Langford Ride ILK LS29 ......40 B5
Langford Rd ILK LS29 ......40 A5
Lang Kirk Cl AIRE BD20 ......35 G6
Langlands Rd BGLY BD16 ......81 J2
Lang La ECHL * BD2 ......104 F2
MAR/SLWT * HD7 ......211 K4
Langley Av BGLY BD16 ......81 J2
BOW BD4 ......127 L5
BRAM LS13 ......107 J2
Langley Cl BRAM LS13 ......107 J2
BRAM LS13 ......107 K3
Langley Crs BAIL BD17 ......83 C3
BRAM LS13 ......107 K3
Langley Garth BRAM LS13 ......107 J2
Langley Gv BGLY BD16 ......81 J2
Langley La BAIL BD17 ......83 G2
KBTN HD8 ......240 A2
Langley Mt BRAM LS13 ......107 J2
Langley Pl BRAM LS13 ......107 J2
BRAM LS13 ......107 J2
Langley Rd BGLY BD16 ......81 J2
BRAM LS13 ......107 J2
Langport Cl CUL/QBY BD13 ......125 H5
Langroyd Rd COL BB8 ......52 B8
COL BB8 ......74 A1
Langsett Cft HUDN HD2 ......193 G1
Langsett Rd BSLYN/ROY S71 ......243 G7
WKFDW/WTN WF2 ......220 D1
Langthorne Ct MOR LS27 ......152 E4
Langthwaite La
HEM/SK/SE WF9 ......247 G4
Langthwaite Rd
HEM/SK/SE WF9 ......246 F5
Langton Av BOW BD4 ......127 K5
Langton Cl CLECK BD19 ......150 C4
Langton Gn WOR/ARM LS12 ......108 B8
Langton St RPDN/SBR HX6 ......167 K1
Langtons Whf LDSU LS2 ......9 J2
Langton Ter ROCH OL11 ......228 A2
Langwith Av WBY LS22 ......47 J6
Langwith Dr WBY LS22 ......47 G6
Langwith Valley Rd WBY LS22 ......47 G6
Lansdale Ct BOW BD4 ......128 B4
Lansdowne Av CAS WF10 ......158 B7
Lansdowne Cl BAIL BD17 ......83 H3
BTLY WF17 ......151 M8
Lansdowne Crs DOD/DAR S75 ......241 M7
Lansdowne Pl WBOW BD5 ......6 E4
Lansdowne St WOR/ARM LS12 ......8 D1
Lanshaw Bank SKP/WHF BD23 ......19 K1
Lanshaw Cl MID LS10 ......132 A8
Lanshaw Crs MID LS10 ......154 A1
Lanshaw Pl MID LS10 ......132 A8
Lanshaw Rd MID LS10 ......132 A8
Lanshaw Ter MID LS10 ......154 A1
Lanshaw Vw MID LS10 ......132 A8
Lanshaw Wk MID LS10 ......132 A8
Lanyon Wy BSLYN/ROY S71 ......261 K3
Lapage St BFDE BD3 ......105 L7
Lapage Ter BFDE * BD3 ......105 L7
Lapwing Cl GIR BD8 ......103 K6
Larch Av HOLM/MEL HD9 ......236 C6
Larch Cl BTLY WF17 ......151 J4

HUDE * HD5 ......193 K5
HWTH BD22 ......78 F4
LVSG WF15 ......172 C3
NORM WF6 ......178 D6
Larch Dl HUDN HD2 ......192 C2
Larch Dr WBSY BD6 ......126 E7
Larchfield Pl BSLYN/ROY S71 ......261 M1
Larchfield Rd MID LS10 ......9 L7
Larchfield Wy HOR/CROF WF4 ......222 D5
Larch Gv BGLY BD16 ......81 H1
Larch Hl WBSY BD6 ......126 F7
Larch Hill Crs WBSY BD6 ......126 F6
Larch La GFTH/SHER LS25 ......113 K8
Larchmont CLAY BD14 ......125 L2
Larch Pl BSLY S70 ......261 L8
Larch Rd KGHY BD21 ......79 K2
Larchway MILN OL16 ......206 F7
Larch Wd SCFT LS14 ......67 L7
Larkfield Av YEA LS19 ......84 E2
Larkfield Crs YEA LS19 ......84 E2
Larkfield Dr YEA LS19 ......84 E2
Larkfield Mt YEA LS19 ......84 E2
Larkfield Rd PDSY/CALV LS28 ......107 G6
YEA LS19 ......84 E2
Lark Hl BTLY WF17 ......151 J5
Larkhill Cl RHAY LS8 ......88 B4
Lark Hill Dr CLECK BD19 ......149 K7
Larkhill Gn AL/HA/HU LS17 ......88 A5
Larkhill Pl WHIT OL12 ......206 A5
Larkhill Rd AL/HA/HU LS17 ......88 A6
Larkhill Vw RHAY LS8 ......88 A5
Larkhill Wk RHAY LS8 ......88 A5
Larkhill Wy AL/HA/HU LS17 ......88 A5
Larks Hl PONT WF8 ......180 D8
Larkspur Wy
WKFDW/WTN WF2 ......176 A7
Lark St BGLY LS29 ......81 H3
COL BB8 ......52 A8
HWTH BD22 ......78 F4
HWTH BD22 ......78 F4
KGHY BD21 ......2 E3
Larwood Av IDLE BD10 ......106 A2
Lascelles Hall Rd HUDE HD5 ......193 K7
Lascelles Mt RHAY * LS8 ......110 B3
Lascelles Pl RHAY LS8 ......110 B3
Lascelles Rd HECK WF16 ......173 G3
Lascelles Rd East RHAY * LS8 ......110 B3
Lascelles Rd West RHAY * LS8 ......110 B3
Lascelles St RHAY LS8 ......110 B3
Lascelles Ter RHAY LS8 ......110 B3
Lascelles Vw RHAY LS8 ......110 B3
Lastingham Gn WBSY * BD6 ......126 A5
Latchmere Av BHP/TINH LS16 ......86 B6
Latchmere Cl BHP/TINH LS16 ......86 C6
Latchmere Crest
BHP/TINH LS16 ......86 B6
Latchmere Cross
BHP/TINH LS16 ......86 B6
Latchmere Dr BHP/TINH LS16 ......86 B6
Latchmere Rd BHP/TINH LS16 ......86 B6
Latchmere Vw BHP/TINH LS16 ......86 B6
Latchmere Wk BHP/TINH LS16 ......86 B6
Latchmore Rd WOR/ARM LS12 ......130 F2
Latham Ct BSLY * S70 ......150 D4
Latham Ct CLECK BD19 ......150 C3
Latham Lea CLECK BD19 ......150 C3
Latimer St BFDE BD3 ......105 M8
Latin St MILN OL16 ......206 A8
Launceston Dr BOW BD4 ......128 A4
Laund Rd HUDW HD3 ......191 G5
Launton Wy WBOW BD5 ......126 F2
Laura St BRIG HD6 ......170 C5
HIPP HX3 ......11 G2
WOR/ARM LS12 ......8 B3
Laurel Av BSLY S70 ......261 M7
Laurel Bank BGLY * BD16 ......81 M2
Laurel Bank Cl LUD/ILL HX2 ......124 C8
Laurel Bank Ct BULY LS4 ......108 E2
Laurel Cl AL/HA/HU LS17 ......67 L1
ELL HX5 ......169 G8
HIPP HX3 ......125 L7
Laurel Ct MILN * OL16 ......206 D8
OSS WF5 ......174 E8
Laurel Crs KGHY BD21 ......2 E3
BTLY WF17 ......151 J7
Laurel Fold WOR/ARM * LS12 ......108 E7
Laurel Gv AIRE BD20 ......35 M5
BGLY BD16 ......81 G1
BTLY WF17 ......151 J7
KGHY BD21 ......2 E3
WOR/ARM LS12 ......108 E7
Laurel Hill Av MSTN/BAR LS15 ......111 M7
Laurel Hill Cft
MSTN/BAR * LS15 ......111 M7
Laurel Hill Gdns
MSTN/BAR LS15 ......111 M7
Laurel Hill Gv MSTN/BAR LS15 ......111 M7
Laurel Hill Vw MSTN/BAR LS15 ......111 M7
Laurel Hill Wy MSTN/BAR LS15 ......111 M8
Laurel Mt CHAL * LS7 ......109 M1
HFAX * HX1 ......10 D9
PDSY/CALV LS28 ......107 G6
Laurel Pk WIL/AL BD15 ......102 E3
Laurel Pl MID LS10 ......153 K3
WOR/ARM LS12 ......108 E7
The Laurels BGLY * BD16 ......81 K3
EARL WF12 ......174 C4
Laurels Dr LIT OL15 ......207 H4
Laurel St BFDE BD3 ......105 L8
HFAX HX1 ......10 D9
WOR/ARM LS12 ......108 E7
Laurel Ter AWLS/ASK DN6 ......249 J4
PDSY/CALV LS28 ......107 G6
Laurence Ct RTHW LS26 ......133 M7
Laurie Pl WHIT * OL12 ......206 B5
Lavender Cl HUDN HD4 ......213 M8
Lavender Cft HECK WF16 ......173 G2
Lavender Hl AWLS/ASK DN6 ......249 J4
Lavender Wk OSM LS9 ......110 B7
Lavenham Pl AWLS/ASK DN6 ......249 J4
Laverhills LVSG WF15 ......171 M1
Laverock Crs BRIG HD6 ......170 B1
Laverock La BRIG HD6 ......170 B1

Laverton Rd BOW BD4 ......127 K2
Lavinia Ter CLAY BD14 ......125 M2
Lawcliffe Crs HWTH BD22 ......78 F6
Law Cl WBY LS22 ......30 E7
Law Common Rd
HOLM/MEL HD9 ......268 A1
Lawefield Av RTHW LS26 ......132 C8
Lawefield La WKFDW/WTN WF2 ......12 B5
Lawefield Wy WKFDW/WTN WF2 ......12 B5
Lawflat WHIT OL12 ......206 A5
Lawkholme La KGHY BD21 ......3 F2
Law La HIPP HX3 ......169 J1
ILK LS29 ......40 B5
Lawn Av AWLS/ASK DN6 ......249 K8
Lawndale Fold DOD/DAR * S75 ......242 B5
Lawn Rd ILK LS29 ......40 B5
The Lawns HOR/CROF WF4 ......196 C8
Lawns Av AL/HA/HU LS17 ......87 H1
WOR/ARM LS12 ......129 M3
Lawns Cl NORM WF6 ......178 A2
WOR/ARM LS12 ......129 M3
Lawns Ct WKFDW/WTN WF2 ......176 A1
Lawns Crs WOR/ARM LS12 ......129 M3
Lawns Cft WOR/ARM LS12 ......129 M3
Lawns Dene WOR/ARM LS12 ......129 M3
Lawns Dr WOR/ARM LS12 ......129 M3
Lawns Gn WOR/ARM LS12 ......129 M3
Lawns Hall Cl BHP/TINH LS16 ......86 D3
Lawns La MID LS10 ......9 J3
WKFDW/WTN WF2 ......176 A1
WOR/ARM LS12 ......129 M1
Lawns Mt WOR/ARM LS12 ......129 M3
Lawns Sq WOR/ARM LS12 ......129 M3
Lawns Ter EARD/LOFT WF3 ......153 M7
WOR/ARM LS12 ......129 M3
Lawnswood Gdns
BHP/TINH LS16 ......86 D4
Lawnswood Rd KGHY BD21 ......2 B5
RHAY LS8 ......110 E2
Lawrence Av PONT WF8 ......180 D6
RHAY LS8 ......110 E2
Lawrence Crs HECK WF16 ......150 F8
RHAY LS8 ......110 E2
Lawrence Dr GTHN BD7 ......126 A4
Lawrence Gdns RHAY LS8 ......110 E1
HUD HD1 ......14 A5
RHAY LS8 ......110 E2
Lawrence St HIPP * HX3 ......10 D1
Lawrence Wk RHAY LS8 ......110 E2
Law Slack Rd HOLM/MEL HD9 ......267 M1
Lawson St BRIG HD6 ......170 D4
Lawson St BFDE BD3 ......5 J3
WOR/ARM * LS12 ......108 D7
Law St BOW BD4 ......127 L4
BTLY WF17 ......151 H6
CLECK BD19 ......149 M5
TOD OL14 ......140 D5
Lawton St HUDS HD4 ......214 C3
WHIT OL12 ......206 C5
Laxton Rd BSLYN/ROY S71 ......243 H6
Laycock La HWTH BD22 ......56 E8
Laycock Pl CHAL LS7 ......7 J1
Laycock St MILN OL16 ......206 F3
Lay Garth Cl RTHW * LS26 ......155 G1
Laygarth Dr HUDE HD5 ......193 L8
Lay Garth Gdns RTHW LS26 ......154 F2
Lay Garth Gn RTHW LS26 ......155 G2
Lay Garth Md RTHW LS26 ......155 G2
Lay Garth Pl RTHW LS26 ......155 G2
Lay Garth Sq RTHW LS26 ......155 G2
Laythe Barn Cl MILN OL16 ......207 G8
Layton Av YEA LS19 ......85 G3
Layton Cl YEA LS19 ......85 G3
Layton Crs YEA LS19 ......84 F3
Layton Dr YEA LS19 ......85 G4
Layton La YEA LS19 ......85 G4
Layton Mt YEA LS19 ......84 F3
Layton Park Av YEA LS19 ......85 G4
Layton Park Cl YEA LS19 ......84 F3
Layton Park Cft YEA LS19 ......85 G4
Layton Park Dr YEA LS19 ......85 G4
Layton Ri HORS LS18 ......85 H3
Layton Rd YEA LS19 ......85 G3
Lazenby Dr WBY LS22 ......29 M8
Lazenby Fold WBY LS22 ......29 M8
Lea Av HIPP HX3 ......168 E3
Leabank Av GFTH/SHER LS25 ......135 J1
Leach Cl MILN OL16 ......206 E4
Leach Crs AIRE BD20 ......58 A4
Leach Ri AIRE BD20 ......58 A4
Leach Rd AIRE BD20 ......57 M4
Leach St MILN OL16 ......229 H1
ROY/SHW OL2 ......229 L8
Leach Wy AIRE BD20 ......58 A4
Lea Cl BRIG HD6 ......170 C2
Lea Ct GTHN BD7 ......126 A4
Lea Cft BSPA/BRAM LS23 ......69 M1
OT LS21 ......41 J7
Leadenhall St HFAX HX1 ......10 B9
Lea Dr KBTN HD8 ......238 B6
Leadwell La EARD/LOFT WF3 ......154 D3
Lea Farm Dr KSTL LS5 ......86 B8
Lea Farm Gv KSTL LS5 ......86 B8
Lea Farm Mt KSTL LS5 ......86 B8
Lea Farm Pl KSTL LS5 ......86 A7
Lea Farm Rd KSTL LS5 ......86 A7
Lea Farm Rw KSTL LS5 ......86 B7
Lea Farm Wk KSTL LS5 ......86 B7
Leafield Av ECHL BD2 ......105 J1
Leafield Bank HUDW HD3 ......191 G8
Leafield Cl AL/HA/HU LS17 ......87 K4
HUDN HD2 ......192 F2
Leafield Crs ECHL BD2 ......105 K3
Leafield Dr ECHL BD2 ......105 K3
PDSY/CALV LS28 ......107 H8
Leafield Gra AL/HA/HU LS17 ......87 K4
Leafield Ter ECHL BD2 ......105 J3
Leafield Wy ECHL BD2 ......105 L3
Leafland St HFAX HX1 ......10 C6
Leaf St CAS WF10 ......157 L7

HWTH * BD22 ......79 G6
Leafsway WBSY * BD6 ......126 B8
Lea Head KBTN HD8 ......238 A6
Leah Pl WOR/ARM LS12 ......8 A4
Leah St LIT * OL15 ......207 K1
Leake St CAS WF10 ......158 A7
Leak Hall Crs KBTN HD8 ......239 H8
Leak Hall La KBTN HD8 ......239 H8
Lea La FEA/AMT WF7 ......202 A2
HUDS HD4 ......213 L8
Lea Mill Park Cl YEA LS19 ......62 C7
Lea Mill Park Dr YEA LS19 ......62 C7
Leamington Dr IDLE BD10 ......83 L6
Leamington St HTON BD9 ......104 D4
WHIT OL12 ......206 A6
Leamside Wk BOW BD4 ......128 A4
Lea Park Cft RTHW LS26 ......132 B7
Lea Park Cl RTHW LS26 ......132 B7
Lea Park Dr RTHW LS26 ......132 B7
Lea Park Gdns RTHW LS26 ......132 B7
Lea Park Garth RTHW * LS26 ......132 B7
Lea Park Gv RTHW LS26 ......132 B7
Lea Park V RTHW LS26 ......132 B7
Leapings La STKB/PEN S36 ......270 B3
Learise HOLM/MEL HD9 ......236 B3
Lea Rd BSLYN/ROY S71 ......243 K7
BTLY WF17 ......151 H7
Learoyd St HUD HD1 ......15 H4
Leas Gdns HOLM/MEL HD9 ......255 G2
Leaside Dr CUL/QBY BD13 ......102 F7
Lea Side Gdns HUDW HD3 ......191 G8
Leasowe Av MID LS10 ......132 A4
Leasowe Cl MID LS10 ......132 A4
Leasowe Gdns MID LS10 ......132 A4
Leasowe Garth MID LS10 ......132 A4
Leasowe Rd MID LS10 ......132 A4
Lea St HUD HD1 ......14 F2
HUDN HD3 ......191 L5
Leatham Av FEA/AMT WF7 ......202 A2
Leatham Crs FEA/AMT WF7 ......202 A2
Leatham Dr FEA/AMT WF7 ......202 A2
Leatham Park Rd
FEA/AMT WF7 ......202 A2
Leatham Royd
MAR/SLWT * HD7 ......233 H2
The Lea GFTH/SHER LS25 ......135 H1
Leather Bank ILK LS29 ......40 A3
Leathley Av ILK LS29 ......61 K3
Leathley Br OT LS21 ......42 C5
Leathley Crs ILK LS29 ......61 K3
Leathley La ILK LS29 ......61 K3
OT LS21 ......42 C3
Leathley Rd ILK LS29 ......61 K2
MID LS10 ......9 J5
Leathley St MID LS10 ......9 J5
The Leavens IDLE BD10 ......83 M6
Leaventhorpe Av GIR BD8 ......103 L7
Leaventhorpe Cl GIR BD8 ......103 M7
Leaventhorpe Gv
CUL/QBY BD13 ......103 L8
Leaventhorpe La
CUL/QBY BD13 ......103 L8
GIR BD8 ......103 M7
Lea Vw BTLY WF17 ......151 H7
Leavington Cl LM/WK BD12 ......126 D8
Leaway WHIT OL12 ......184 C4
Ledbury Av MID LS10 ......154 A2
Ledbury Cl MID LS10 ......154 B2
Ledbury Dr EARD/LOFT WF3 ......154 B2
Ledbury Gn MID LS10 ......154 A2
Ledbury Gv MID * LS10 ......154 A2
Ledbury Pl BOW BD4 ......127 L5
Ledbury Rd BSLYN/ROY S71 ......243 H8
Ledgard Dr HOR/CROF WF4 ......198 B7
Ledgard Wy WOR/ARM LS12 ......108 E6
Ledgate La GFTH/SHER LS25 ......159 M2
Ledger La EARD/LOFT WF3 ......154 E2
WKFDE WF1 ......176 D1
Ledger Pl WKFDE WF1 ......176 D2
Ledston Av GFTH/SHER LS25 ......135 J1
Ledston Mill La CAS WF10 ......136 A4
Lee Bank HIPP HX3 ......10 E2
Lee Beck Gv EARD/LOFT WF3 ......155 G2
Lee Bottom Rd TOD OL14 ......164 C1
Lee Br HFAX HX7 ......10 E1
Lee Brig NORM WF6 ......178 B3
Leech La BGLY BD16 ......80 B6
Lee Cl WIL/AL BD15 ......80 E8
Lee Clough Dr HBR HX7 ......144 B5
Lee Ct KGHY BD21 ......58 B7
OSS WF5 ......197 H2
Leeds & Bradford Rd
PDSY/CALV LS28 ......107 H4
Leeds Barnsdale Rd CAS WF10 ......157 J8
Leeds Country Wy
AL/HA/HU LS17 ......65 M2
BHP/TINH LS16 ......64 E6
HORS LS18 ......85 J1
MOR LS27 ......129 J7
MOR LS27 ......152 B7
OSS WF5 ......175 L7
PDSY/CALV LS28 ......106 B3
RTHW LS26 ......134 C6
SCFT LS14 ......68 A7
SCFT LS14 ......90 D3
WKFDE WF1 ......176 F4
Leeds La RTHW LS26 ......134 C6
Leeds Old Rd BFDE BD3 ......105 M6
HECK WF16 ......172 E1
Leeds Rd AL/HA/HU LS17 ......67 M3
BFD BD1 ......5 J6
BFDE BD3 ......105 M7
BHP/TINH LS16 ......63 M3
BTLY WF17 ......151 J4
CAS WF10 ......135 H8
CAS WF10 ......179 M1
EARD/LOFT WF3 ......154 D4
EARL WF12 ......154 E8
ECHL BD2 ......105 K3
GFTH/SHER LS25 ......135 H2
GSLY LS20 ......62 A6
HIPP HX3 ......147 J5
HIPP HX3 ......147 M6
HUD HD1 ......15 K2
HUDN HD2 ......193 G4
ILK LS29 ......38 E1
LVSG WF15 ......172 C4

Entry	Ref	Page
MIRF WF14		172 A6
MSTN/BAR LS15		112 A2
OSS WF5		174 E5
OT LS21		41 K7
PBR HD3		27 G2
RTHW LS26		132 E6
RTHW LS26		156 D3
SHPY BD18		82 F6
TAD LS24		71 H4
WBY LS22		47 H1
WKFDE WF1		176 D6
YEA LS19		84 E3
Leeds St KGHY BD21		2 E5
Leefield Rd HECK WF16		151 G8
Leef St HUDE HD5		15 L7
Lee Gn MIRF WF14		172 C8
Lee Head HUDN HD2		14 C2
Leeke Av HOR/CROF WF4		197 J4
Lee La BGLY BD16		80 E7
DOD/DAR S75		243 G4
FEA/AMT WF7		202 D6
HIPP HX3		146 F3
HORS LS18		85 K4
HWTH BD22		100 B3
KBTN LS27		216 A8
STKB/PEN S36		269 H2
TOD OL14		164 A3
WIL/AL BD15		80 D8
Lee La East HORS LS18		85 K4
Lee La West HORS LS18		85 H4
Lee Mill Rd HBR HX7		143 J1
Leeming St BFD		5 G4
Lee Moor La EARD/LOFT WF3		155 G6
Lee Moor Rd EARD/LOFT WF3		155 H8
Lee Mount Gdns HIPP HX3		10 C1
Lee Mount Rd HIPP HX3		10 C1
Lee Orchards BSPA/BRAM LS23		48 F6
Lee Rd DEWS WF13		194 F1
Lees Av EARL WF12		195 L2
STKB/PEN S36		270 F3
Lees Bank Av HWTH BD22		79 G6
Lees Bank Dr HWTH * BD22		79 G6
Lees Bank HI HWTH BD22		79 G6
Lees Bank Rd HWTH BD22		79 G6
Lees CI CUL/QBY BD13		79 L8
HUDE HD5		193 H7
Lees Crs HOR/CROF WF4		198 B7
Lees Dr EARL * WF12		195 L2
Lees Hall Rd EARL WF12		195 L2
Lees Holm EARL WF12		195 L2
Lees House Rd EARL WF12		195 L1
Leeside Av HUDN HD2		192 D0
Leeside Rd HECK WF16		151 G8
Lees La HWTH BD22		78 F6
PDSY/CALV LS28		106 B2
Lees Mill La MAR/SLWT HD7		212 D5
Lees Moor Rd CUL/QBY BD13		79 L8
Lees Rd ROY/SHW OL2		229 K7
Lees St ROY/SHW OL2		229 K7
Lee St BFD BD1		4 E7
BRIG HD6		170 C2
CUL/QBY BD13		124 F6
DEWS WF13		173 G8
LIT OL15		185 K8
LVSG WF15		172 C1
WKFDE WF1		12 E2
Leesworth Ct HWTH * BD22		79 G6
Lee Wy KBTN HD8		216 A7
Lee Wood Rd HBR HX7		121 H8
Legion Av GFTH/SHER LS25		138 A3
Legrams Av GTHN BD7		126 B1
Legrams La GTHN BD7		104 C8
Legrams Mill La GTHN BD7		104 C8
Legrams St GTHN BD7		104 D7
Legrams Ter GTHN BD7		4 A6
Leicester CI LDSU LS2		6 F4
Leicester Gv LDSU LS2		6 F4
Leicester PI LDSU LS2		6 F4
Leicester St BOW BD4		127 L4
ROCH OL11		228 C1
Leicester Ter HIPP HX3		168 D2
Leigh Av EARD/LOFT WF3		153 J6
Leigh CI BSLYN/ROY S71		261 H3
Leighton La LDS * LS1		6 D8
Leighton PI LDS * LS1		6 D8
Leigh Vw EARD/LOFT WF3		153 H6
Leisure La KBTN HD8		218 A6
Leith CI EARL WF12		196 A5
Leith St KGHY BD21		2 E3
Lemans Dr DEWS WF13		173 H3
Lemington Av HFAX HX1		10 D8
WBOW BD5		126 E4
Lemon St HFAX HX1		10 A4
Lemon Tree CI PONT WF8		180 D8
Lenacre La KBTN HD8		216 F5
Lenham CI MOR LS27		152 C3
Lenhurst Av WOR/ARM LS12		108 C3
Lennerton La GFTH/SHER LS25		117 G8
Lennie St KGHY BD21		2 E7
Lennon Dr GIR BD8		104 D5
Lennox Dr WKFDW/WTN WF2		197 M4
Lennox Gdns MSTN/BAR LS15		111 J7
Lennox Rd BULY LS4		108 C5
TOD OL14		140 C5
Lenny Balk AWLS/ASK DN6		248 A7
Lens Dr BAIL BD17		82 E2
Lentilfield St HIPP HX3		146 A4
Lentilfield Ter HIPP HX3		146 A4
Lenton Dr BEE/HOL LS11		131 L4
Lenton Vls IDLE BD10		83 K5
Leodis Ct BEE/HOL LS11		8 D7
Leodis Wy RTHW LS26		132 D6
Leonardin La ROY/SHW OL2		229 H6
Leonard's PI BGLY BD16		81 J4
Leonard St BGLY BD16		81 J4
HUDN HD2		192 D3
LM/WK BD12		148 F3
Leopold Gdns CHAL LS7		7 L3
Leopold Gv CHAL LS7		7 L3
CHAL LS7		7 K3
OSS WF5		197 J2
Lepton Gdns BSLY S70		261 M8
Lepton La KBTN HD8		216 C5
Lepton PI MOR LS27		129 M7
Lesley Wy HUDS HD4		213 J5
Leslie Av YEA LS19		62 D6
Leslie Rd BSLY S70		261 M7
Leslie St HUDN HD2		14 D1
Leslie Ter HDGY LS6		6 D1
Lesmere Gv BD7		126 B4
Lessarna Ct BOW * BD4		127 L1
Letchworth Av ROCH OL11		228 C1
Levens Bank MSTN/BAR LS15		110 F8
Levens CI MSTN/BAR LS15		111 G8
Levens Garth MSTN/BAR LS15		111 G8
Levens PI MSTN/BAR LS15		111 G8
Leventhorpe Ct RTHW LS26		155 L1
Leventhorpe Wy RTHW LS26		155 L1
Leveret Wy BTLY WF17		151 K5
Lever St WBSY BD6		126 C5
Levita Gv BOW BD4		127 M2
Levita PI BOW BD4		127 M2
MSTN/BAR LS15		111 G6
Lewin Gv CAS WF10		158 F6
Lewis CI CUL/QBY BD13		124 F5
Lewisham CI ROY/SHW * OL2		228 E8
Lewisham Ct ROY/SHW * OL2		228 E8
Lewisham Rd MAR/SLWT HD7		212 B5
Lewisham St MOR LS27		152 A3
Lewis Rd BSLYN/ROY S71		262 A2
Lewis St HFAX HX1		10 F4
Lexington CI BOW BD4		127 K6
Leyburn Av HECK WF16		173 C1
MIRF WF14		147 M6
Leyburn Gv BGLY BD16		81 J2
SHPY BD18		82 C7
Leyburn Rd AWLS/ASK DN6		249 H4
Leyfield BAIL BD17		82 C3
Leyfield Bank HOLM/MEL HD9		236 E7
Leyfield Rd MILN OL16		206 F8
Ley Fleaks Rd IDLE BD10		83 K7
Leygards La HOLM/MEL HD9		234 D5
Leyland CI COL BB8		74 D3
Leyland Cft HUDN HD2		171 G8
Leyland Rd BTLY WF17		150 F5
CAS WF10		158 A6
The Leylands DOD/DAR S75		260 C2
Leylands Av HTON BD9		104 C8
Leylands Gv HTON BD9		104 B8
Leylands La HTON BD9		104 B8
KGHY BD21		3 J6
Leylands Rd LDSU LS2		7 K7
Leylands Ter HTON BD9		104 B3
Ley La WOR/ARM LS12		108 F6
Leymoor Rd MAR/SLWT HD7		212 F1
Leys CI IDLE BD10		83 J5
Leysholme Dr WOR/ARM LS12		108 D8
Leysholme Dr WOR/ARM LS12		108 D8
Leysholme Ter WOR/ARM LS12		108 C8
Leysholme Vw WOR/ARM LS12		108 C8
Leyside Dr WIL/AL BD15		103 K4
Leys La AWLS/ASK DN6		248 F5
BSPA/BRAM LS23		48 D6
KBTN HD8		217 K8
KNOT WF11		182 B4
PONT WF8		204 E7
Leys Rd PONT WF8		182 B8
Leyton Crs IDLE * BD10		83 K7
Leyton Dr IDLE BD10		83 K7
Leyton Gv IDLE BD10		83 K7
Leyton St WHIT OL12		206 C4
Leyton Ter IDLE BD10		83 K7
Ley Top La WIL/AL BD15		103 L6
Leywell Ter WOR/ARM LS12		108 C6
Libbey St GIR BD8		104 D5
Lichen CI GTHN BD7		126 C3
Lichfield Mt ECHL BD2		105 G2
Lichfield Rd EARL WF12		174 B6
Lichfield Ter MILN OL16		228 E2
Lickless Av HORS LS18		85 M5
Lickless Dr HORS LS18		85 M5
Lickless Gdns HORS LS18		85 M5
Lickless Ter HORS LS18		85 M5
Lidgate CI DEWS WF13		173 L4
Lidgate Crs HEM/SK/SE WF9		246 F4
Lidgate La CUD/GR S72		244 D3
DEWS WF13		173 L4
Lidget Av GTHN * BD7		126 B1
Lidget HI PDSY/CALV LS28		107 G6
Lidget La HOR/CROF WF4		200 F4
Lidget PI GTHN BD7		126 B1
Lidget Rd AIRE BD20		34 E1
Lidget St HUDW HD3		191 K5
Lidgett Av RHAY LS8		88 B7
Lidgett Crs RHAY LS8		88 B6
Lidget Ter CLAY BD14		125 M2
Lidgett Gv RHAY LS8		88 B6
Lidgett HI RHAY LS8		88 B7
Lidgett La GFTH/SHER LS25		113 G8
KBTN HD8		239 H5
Lidgett Mt RHAY LS8		88 B5
Lidgett Park Av RHAY LS8		88 B5
Lidgett Park Gdns RHAY LS8		88 B5
Lidgett Park Gv RHAY LS8		88 B6
Lidgett Park Ms RHAY LS8		88 B5
Lidgett Park Rd RHAY LS8		88 B5
Lidgett Park Vw RHAY LS8		88 B5
Lidgett PI RHAY LS8		88 B6
Lidgett Ri KBTN HD8		239 H5
Lidgett Wk RHAY LS8		88 B6
Lidget Wy BSLYN/ROY S71		243 L2
Lifton PI LDSU LS2		6 C5
Light Bank La AIRE BD20		36 E2
Lightburn Av LIT OL15		207 L4
Lightcliffe Rd BRIG HD6		170 C2
Lightcliffe Royd La GTL/HWG HX4		167 L8
Lightenfield La HUDS HD4		213 L8
Lightfoot Av CAS WF10		157 M8
Lightfoot CI CAS WF10		157 M8
Lighthazles Chapel Rd RPDN/SBR HX6		166 D6
Lighthazles Rd RPDN/SBR HX6		166 D7
Light La WKFDW/WTN WF2		176 A7
Lightowler CI HFAX HX1		10 D5
Lightowler Rd HFAX HX1		10 D5
Lightowlers La LIT OL15		185 M7
Lightowler St WBSY BD6		126 E5
Lightridge CI HUDN HD2		192 B2
Lightridge Rd HUDN HD2		192 B1
Lilac Av MILN OL16		229 J3
WKFDW/WTN WF2		12 B1
Lilac CI BRIG HD6		170 E3
ILK LS29		19 J6
Lilac Gv BOW BD4		105 M8
CLECK BD19		150 C5
SHPY BD18		104 F1
Lilac Ov GFTH/SHER LS25		138 D8
Lilac Rd ROCH OL11		228 B4
The Lilacs GSLY LS20		62 A5
Lilac St COL BB8		52 B8
HUDS HD4		10 D2
Lilac View CI ROY/SHW OL2		229 M8
Liley La HUDE HD5		194 B6
Lilian St BOW BD4		127 L3
Lillands Av BRIG HD6		170 B4
Lillands La BRIG HD6		170 B4
Lillands Ter BRIG HD6		170 B4
Lilley St HEM/SK/SE WF9		223 M8
Lilley Ter HEM/SK/SE WF9		246 D4
Lilly La HIPP HX3		11 J7
Lilly St BOW BD4		127 L3
Lilycroft Rd GIR BD8		104 C5
Lilycroft Wk HTON BD9		104 C4
Lilydene Av CUD/GR S72		245 H7
Lily St GIR BD8		18 F6
MILN OL16		207 H8
TOD OL14		141 G6
Lilythorne Av IDLE BD10		83 L6
Lime Av HBR HX7		143 H3
HOLM/MEL HD9		236 E6
TOD OL14		141 J8
Lime CI ILK LS29		18 F6
KGHY BD21		2 C1
Lime Crs HEM/SK/SE WF9		247 G5
WKFDW/WTN WF2		199 H5
Lime Fld MILN OL16		207 G7
Lime Gv BSLYN/ROY S71		243 L5
HEM/SK/SE WF9		247 G5
LIT OL15		207 H1
MAR/SLWT HD7		213 G1
ROY/SHW OL2		228 F8
YEA LS19		84 C2
Lime Kiln La WBY LS22		29 L5
Lime Pit La EARD/LOFT WF3		177 H2
Limers Ga TOD OL14		162 B3
WHIT OL12		206 B1
Limes Av DOD/DAR S75		242 E4
DOD/DAR S75		260 D3
HIPP HX3		168 E2
Limes CI DOD/DAR S75		242 E4
Lime St BGLY BD16		81 H3
COL BB8		52 A8
GTHN BD7		126 C2
HUDS HD4		214 A3
HWTH BD22		78 B8
KGHY BD21		2 E5
OSS WF5		197 G2
TOD OL14		141 J8
Limesway DOD/DAR S75		260 D3
Lime Tree Av AL/HA/HU LS17		88 A4
BSPA/BRAM LS23		48 F6
BTLY WF17		173 J2
PONT WF8		180 D6
Lime Tree Court Ct HEM/SK/SE * WF9		223 L8
Lime-tree Crs GFTH/SHER LS25		135 L8
Lime Tree Gdns BSPA/BRAM LS23		49 G7
Lime Tree Gv BIRK/DRI * BD11		128 C7
Lime Tree Sq SHPY BD18		81 M6
Limetrees PONT WF8		181 J2
Limewood Ap SCFT LS14		89 J7
Limewood Rd SCFT LS14		89 J8
Linburn CI BSLYN/ROY S71		243 J2
Linby Rd BSLYN/ROY S71		243 H6
Lincoln Av HECK WF16		172 B4
LVSG WF15		172 B4
Lincoln CI ROCH OL11		206 C8
Lincoln Ct HUDE * HD5		193 J7
Lincoln Crs HEM/SK/SE WF9		247 J2
Lincoln Dr LIT OL15		207 J3
LVSG WF15		172 C4
Lincoln Green Ct OSM LS9		7 L7
Lincoln Green Rd OSM LS9		7 L7
Lincoln Gv HUDE HD5		215 J2
Lincoln Leach Ct ROCH * OL11		228 B1
Lincoln Rd EARL WF12		174 B5
OSM LS9		7 L6
Lincoln St CAS WF10		158 A6
HUD HD1		15 J7
ROCH OL11		206 C8
TOD OL14		140 D5
WKFDW/WTN WF2		176 D7
Lincoln Wk GFTH/SHER LS25		135 L4
Lincoln Wy HIPP HX3		10 F7
Lincombe Bank RHAY LS8		88 A6
Lincombe Dr RHAY LS8		88 A7
Lincombe Mt RHAY LS8		88 A6
Lincombe Ri RHAY LS8		88 A6
Lincroft Av HUDE HD5		215 G1
Lincs Wold LVSG WF15		171 K2
Lindale CI FEA/AMT WF7		202 E7
ROY/SHW OL2		228 E7
Lindale CI MID LS10		131 M7
Lindale Garth WKFDW/WTN WF2		175 M5
Lindale Gv WKFDW/WTN WF2		175 L4
Lindale Mt WKFDW/WTN WF2		175 L5
Lindale La WKFDW/WTN WF2		175 L5
Linden Av BEE/HOL LS11		8 F9
BFDE BD3		106 A6
TOD OL14		141 J8
Linden CI BHP/TINH LS16		86 F7
BRIG HD6		170 E3
CAS WF10		158 F8
EARL WF12		174 D7
KNOT WF11		181 L2
Linden Gdns BEE/HOL LS11		131 L3
Linden Gv BEE/HOL LS11		9 G9
Linden Mt BEE/HOL LS11		8 F9
Linden PI BEE/HOL LS11		131 L3
HBR * HX7		143 J2
Linden Ri KGHY BD21		3 L8
Linden Rd BEE/HOL * LS11		8 F9
ELL HX5		169 G8
HBR HX7		143 J2
HBR HX7		143 M5
HIPP HX3		168 E2
HUDN HD2		192 B5
Linden Ter HBR * HX7		180 E6
Linden Wy WBY LS22		29 M7
Lindholme Rd BSLYN/ROY S71		243 H6
Lindhurst Rd BSLYN/ROY S71		243 H6
Lindisfarne WHIT OL12		206 A6
Lindisfarne Rd SHPY BD18		82 B7
Lindley Av HUDW HD3		191 J3
Lindley Br OT LS21		42 A1
Lindley Dr GTHN BD7		126 B4
Lindley Moor Rd HUDW HD3		190 F6
Lindley Rd ELL HX5		191 H2
WBOW BD5		126 F3
Lindley St HUDW HD3		213 J1
SKP/WHF BD23		16 B4
Lindrick Ct CR S72		244 E5
Lindrick Gv LUD/ILL HX2		124 B7
Lindrick Wk LUD/ILL HX2		124 B7
Lindrick Wy LUD/ILL HX2		124 B7
Lindsay Acre EARD/LOFT WF3		153 J6
Lindsay Av WKFDW/WTN WF2		197 L1
Lindsay Rd GFTH/SHER LS25		113 M3
Lindsey Ct OSM LS9		7 M7
Lindsey Gdns OSM LS9		7 L7
Lindsey Mt OSM LS9		7 M6
Lindsey Rd OSM LS9		7 M7
Lindwell Av GTL/HWG HX4		168 E2
Lindwell Gv GTL/HWG HX4		168 E2
Linefield Rd BTLY WF17		173 H1
Lineham Ct LVSG WF15		172 C4
Lineholme Av TOD OL14		141 G7
Lineside Cottages EARL * WF12		195 J3
Linfit Fold MAR/SLWT HD7		212 C6
Linfit La KBTN HD8		216 D6
MAR/SLWT HD7		212 C6
Lingard St DOD/DAR S75		260 F4
Lingards Rd MAR/SLWT HD7		212 A4
Lingards Ter MAR/SLWT * HD7		211 L8
Lingard St BFD BD1		5 K4
DOD/DAR S75		260 F3
Ling Bob LUD/ILL HX2		145 M6
Ling Bob Cft LUD/ILL HX2		145 M5
Lingcrag Gdns HWTH BD22		54 F3
Ling Cft BSPA/BRAM LS23		48 D6
Lingcroft La WBY LS22		31 J3
Lingdale Rd LM/WK BD12		126 C8
Lingfield Ap AL/HA/HU LS17		87 K3
Lingfield Bank AL/HA/HU LS17		87 K3
Lingfield CI AL/HA/HU LS17		87 L3
WBSY BD6		125 L4
Lingfield Crs AL/HA/HU LS17		87 K3
HWTH BD22		79 J5
Lingfield Dr AL/HA/HU LS17		87 L3
Lingfield Ga AL/HA/HU LS17		87 K3
Lingfield Gn AL/HA/HU LS17		87 K3
Lingfield Gv AL/HA/HU LS17		87 L3
WIL/AL BD15		102 F3
Lingfield Mt AL/HA/HU LS17		87 L3
Lingfield Rd AL/HA/HU LS17		87 K3
WIL/AL BD15		102 F3
Lingfield Ter WBSY BD6		125 L4
Lingfield Vw AL/HA/HU LS17		87 K3
Lingfield Wk AL/HA/HU LS17		87 K3
Ling La AL/HA/HU LS17		67 H7
Ling Park Ap WIL/AL BD15		102 E2
Ling Park Av WIL/AL BD15		102 F3
Ling Royd Av LUD/ILL HX2		145 M6
Lings La PONT WF8		226 C6
Lingthwaite DOD/DAR S75		260 C7
Lingwell Ap MID LS10		153 L2
Lingwell Av MID LS10		153 L2
Lingwell Cha EARD/LOFT WF3		154 E8
Lingwell Ct EARD/LOFT WF3		176 C1
MID LS10		153 L2
Lingwell Crs MID LS10		153 L2
Lingwell Gdns MID LS10		153 L2
Lingwell Gate Crs WKFDE WF1		176 D1
Lingwell Gate Dr WKFDE WF1		176 C1
Lingwell Gate La EARD/LOFT WF3		154 C6
Lingwell Gn MID LS10		153 L2
Lingwell Gv MID LS10		153 L2
Lingwell Ms MID * LS10		153 L2
Lingwell Nook La EARD/LOFT WF3		154 C6
Lingwell Rd MID LS10		153 L1
Lingwell Vw MID * LS10		153 L2
Lingwood Av GIR BD8		104 B5
Lingwood Rd GIR BD8		104 B5
Lingwood Ter GIR BD8		104 B5
The Link DOD/DAR S75		260 C8
PONT WF8		180 E8
ROY/SHW OL2		229 H5
RTHW LS26		134 D3
The Links BEE/HOL LS11		131 J7
FEA/AMT WF7		179 M6
TAD LS24		71 L4
Links Av CLECK BD19		149 M5
Links Vw DOD/DAR S75		242 D4
Linkway AWLS/ASK * DN6		227 M3
BGLY BD16		81 J7
Linnet CI GIR * BD8		103 L6
MIRF WF14		194 B1
Linnet Ct MOR LS27		152 F3
Linnet Gv WKFDW/WTN WF2		220 F1
Linnet St KGHY BD21		3 L1
Linney La ROY/SHW OL2		229 L7
Linnhe Av WBSY BD6		126 B8
Linshaws Rd HOLM/MEL HD9		267 H1
Linton Av AIRE BD20		36 A4
AL/HA/HU LS17		88 B2
BTLY WF17		173 J1
WBY LS22		29 M8
Linton CI AL/HA/HU LS17		88 A2
BSLY S70		260 E5
WBY LS22		172 B1
Linton Common WBY LS22		47 J5
Linton Ct SKP/WHF BD23		16 B3
Linton Crs AL/HA/HU LS17		88 A2
Linton Gv AL/HA/HU LS17		88 A2
BRIG HD6		170 A6
Linton Hills Rd WBY LS22		47 L1
Linton La WBY LS22		29 L7
Linton Mdw WBY LS22		47 L1
Linton Ri AL/HA/HU LS17		88 A2
NORM WF6		178 F5
Linton Rd WBY LS22		47 L1
WKFDE WF1		13 M2
Linton St WBOW BD4		127 H2
HWTH BD22		2 A9
Linton Vw AL/HA/HU LS17		88 A1
Lion Chambers HUD * HD1		14 F6
Lionel St OSS WF5		197 G2
Liphill Bank Rd HOLM/MEL HD9		253 L1
Lippersley La AIRE BD20		18 C3
Lipscomb St HUDW HD3		213 K1
Liquorice Wy PONT WF8		180 E6
Lisbon Sq LDS LS1		6 C9
Lisbon St LDS LS1		6 C9
Lisheen Av CAS WF10		158 A8
Lisheen Gv CAS WF10		158 A7
Liskeard Ct MILN OL16		206 F4
Lisker Av OT LS21		41 K7
Lisker Ct OT LS21		41 K7
Lisker Dr OT LS21		41 K7
Lisle St WHIT OL12		206 C6
Lismore CI RTHW LS26		155 H1
Lismore Rd KGHY BD21		2 E5
Lister Av BOW BD4		127 K3
Lister CI FEA/AMT WF7		201 L1
Lister CI HFAX HX1		11 G6
Listerdale LVSG WF15		172 C1
Lister Gdns GIR BD8		104 E4
Lister HI AIRE BD20		55 M2
HORS LS18		85 L4
Listerhills Rd GTHN BD7		4 A1
Lister La ECHL BD2		105 H4
HFAX HX1		10 D6
Lister Rd FEA/AMT WF7		201 K1
Lister's Rd HIPP HX3		11 L4
Lister St BOW BD4		127 L4
BRIG HD6		170 C3
CAS WF10		157 L6
HFAX HX1		10 D6
HUDE HD5		193 G8
ILK LS29		38 C2
KGHY BD21		2 E5
Lister Vw GIR BD8		104 E4
Lister Wk MOR LS27		130 B8
Listing Av LVSG WF15		172 D1
Listing Ct LVSG WF15		172 D1
Listing Dr LVSG WF15		172 D1
Listing La LVSG WF15		172 D1
Litell Royd FEA/AMT WF7		200 F1
Little Baines St HFAX HX1		10 C5
Littlebeck Dr BGLY BD16		81 L3
Little Bradley GTL/HWG HX4		168 B8
Little Brunswick St HUD HD1		14 E6
Little Cake HOLM/MEL HD9		254 E4
Little Catterton La TAD LS24		72 C1
Little Church La RTHW LS26		156 E4
Little Clegg Rd LIT OL15		207 H4
Little Cote IDLE BD10		83 J5
Little Cross St WBOW BD5		127 G4
Little Fold HUDS * HD4		214 A6
Little Fountain St MOR LS27		152 C2
Little Green La HECK WF16		172 E1
Little Hemsworth HEM/SK/SE WF9		224 A8
Little Hew Royd IDLE BD10		83 H6
Littleholme St TOD OL14		163 J3
Little Horton Gn WBOW BD5		126 E1
Little Horton La WBOW BD5		4 F8
Little Howarth Wy WHIT * OL12		206 E2
Little Ings CI TAD LS24		95 C6
Little King St LDS LS1		8 F1
Littlelands BGLY BD16		81 J7
Littlelands Ct BGLY * BD16		81 J7
Little La AIRE BD20		59 G6
AWLS/ASK DN6		205 J7
EARD/LOFT WF3		155 G3
FEA/AMT WF7		202 A2
HBR HX7		99 K8
HEM/SK/SE WF9		225 K7
HEM/SK/SE WF9		247 H3
HEM/SK/SE WF9		247 K3
HOLM/MEL * HD9		236 E8
HTON BD9		104 B4
ILK LS29		38 C2
MOR LS27		152 F3
Little Lane Ct MOR LS27		130 E6
Littlemoor Ct PDSY/CALV LS28		107 H8
Littlemoor Crs PDSY/CALV LS28		129 G1
Littlemoor Crs South PDSY/CALV LS28		129 G1
Littlemoor Gdns LUD/ILL HX2		124 A8
PDSY/CALV LS28		129 G1
Littlemoor Gv MIRF WF14		194 B3
Little Moor PI WOR/ARM LS12		108 D7
Littlemoor Rd LUD/ILL HX2		124 A8
MIRF WF14		194 B3
PDSY/CALV LS28		107 G8

Littlemoor Vw
  PDSY/CALV LS28 ....107 H8
Little Neville St LDS LS1 ....8 F2
Little New Cl DOD/DAR S75 ....260 D5
Little Pk IDLE BD10 ....84 A5
Little Queen St LDS LS1 ....6 D9
Littlethorpe Hl LVSG WF15 ....171 M4
Littlethorpe La LVSG WF15 ....171 M4
Little Westfields
  BSLYN/ROY * S71 ....243 L3
Littlewood Cl WBSY BD6 ....126 E5
Littlewood Cft HUDS HD4 ....214 C4
Little Wood Dr CLECK BD19 ....149 M4
Little Woodhouse BRIG HD6 ....170 C4
Little Woodhouse St LDSU LS2 ....6 D7
Littleworth La BSLYN/ROY S71 ....261 M3
Litton Cft WKFDE WF1 ....13 L1
Littondale La BAIL BD17 ....83 G2
Litton Rd HWTH BD22 ....2 C7
Litton Wk BSLY S70 ....260 F4
Litton Wy SCFT LS14 ....89 K6
Liversedge Hall La LVSG WF15 ....172 C3
Livingstone Crs
  BSLYN/ROY S71 ....261 K1
Livingstone Rd SHPY BD18 ....104 F2
Livingstone St HIPP HX3 ....10 D1
Livingstone St North
  LUD/ILL HX2 ....146 C1
Livingstone Ter BSLY * S70 ....261 G6
Livinia Gv CHAL LS7 ....6 F4
Livsey St MILN OL16 ....206 C7
Lloyds Dr LM/WK BD12 ....127 G8
Lloyd St TOD OL14 ....141 K8
Lobley Cl WHIT OL12 ....206 D4
Lobley St HECK WF16 ....173 G2
Locherbie Gn WIL/AL * BD15 ....103 J5
Lochy Rd WBSY BD6 ....126 B8
Lockbridge Wy HUDS HD4 ....213 K2
Lockeaflash Crs BSLY S70 ....261 M8
Locke Av BSLY S70 ....261 G7
Locke Rd DOD/DAR S75 ....260 C6
Locke St BSLY S70 ....260 F7
Lockhart St MILN OL16 ....228 D1
Lock La CAS WF10 ....157 M5
  NORM WF6 ....156 B8
Locksley Rd BRIG HD6 ....170 F5
The Locks BGLY BD16 ....81 H2
Lock St EARL WF12 ....195 M2
  HIPP * HX3 ....11 M3
  TOD OL14 ....163 J3
Lockton Ct TAD LS24 ....94 F8
Lock Vw ELL HX5 ....169 J6
Lock Wy DEWS WF13 ....195 G2
Lockwood Av MIRF WF14 ....172 C7
Lockwood Cl BEE/HOL LS11 ....131 K5
  HUDW HD3 ....191 L1
Lockwood Ct BEE/HOL LS11 ....131 L5
Lockwood La BSLY S70 ....261 M6
Lockwood Pk BEE/HOL LS11 ....131 L5
Lockwood Rd HUD HD1 ....214 B3
Lockwood Scar HUDS HD4 ....214 B3
Lockwood St LM/WK BD12 ....149 G1
  SHPY * BD18 ....82 B6
  WBSY BD6 ....126 E5
Lockwood's Yd HUD HD1 ....14 F7
Lockwood Wy BEE/HOL LS11 ....131 L5
Locomotion Br HUD HD1 ....15 H6
Lode Pit La BGLY BD16 ....81 M2
The Lodge MAR/SLWT HD7 ....213 G4
Lodge Av CAS WF10 ....158 E7
  ELL HX5 ....169 L7
Lodge Bank LIT OL15 ....207 H3
Lodge Cl HUDS HD4 ....214 A5
Lodge Dr ELL HX5 ....169 L7
  MIRF WF14 ....194 E2
Lodge Farm Cl EARL WF12 ....195 M2
Lodge Farm Gdns NORM WF6 ....178 A4
Lodge Gate Cl CUL/QBY BD13 ....102 A5
Lodge Hl BAIL BD17 ....82 B3
Lodge Hill Cl WOR/ARM LS12 ....129 M3
Lodge Hill Rd OSS WF5 ....174 F6
Lodge La BEE/HOL LS11 ....8 D9
  HOR/CROF WF4 ....200 A4
  LUD/ILL * HX2 ....145 G1
  LVSG WF15 ....172 F4
  WKFDW/WTN WF2 ....220 F2
Lodge Pl ELL * HX5 ....169 L7
Lodge Rd AWLS/ASK DN6 ....249 K4
  PDSY/CALV LS28 ....106 F6
Lodges Cl HOR/CROF WF4 ....222 D4
Lodge St CUL/QBY BD13 ....79 M8
  HEM/SK/SE WF9 ....223 M6
  KBTN HD8 ....239 J4
  LDS LS1 ....6 E5
  LIT OL15 ....185 K8
  WHIT OL12 ....184 E8
Lodge Ter BEE/HOL * LS11 ....131 K4
Lodore Pl ECHL BD2 ....105 K3
Lodore Rd ECHL BD2 ....105 J3
Lofthouse Pl LDSU LS2 ....6 F5
Lofthouse Ter CHAL LS7 ....7 G5
Loft St GIR BD8 ....104 B6
Logwood St HUD HD1 ....214 C2
Loiner Ct OSM LS9 ....132 E1
Lomax St WHIT OL12 ....206 B6
Lombard Ct DOD/DAR S75 ....261 G3
Lombardi Ct OSS WF5 ....197 H2
Lombard St HFAX HX1 ....10 B9
  MSTN/BAR LS15 ....111 H7
  YEA LS19 ....84 C2
Lomond Av HORS LS18 ....85 K2
Lomond Ter MILN OL16 ....228 E2
Londesboro Gv OSM LS9 ....110 C7
Londesboro Ter OSM LS9 ....110 C7
London La YEA LS19 ....84 C2
London Rd MAR/SLWT HD7 ....212 C5
  RPDN/SBR HX6 ....167 J4
  TAD LS24 ....115 M2
  TOD OL14 ....164 D1
London Spring Rd
  RPDN/SBR HX6 ....188 C2
London St YEA LS19 ....84 C2
Long Acre BSLYN/ROY S71 ....243 K5
Longacre CAS WF10 ....157 M8
Longacre La HWTH BD22 ....78 F6
Longacres HWTH BD22 ....79 G6

Long Acre Wk PBR HG3 ....26 F3
Longbottom Av AIRE BD20 ....36 B5
  RPDN/SBR HX6 ....167 G3
Longbottom Ter HIPP * HX3 ....168 F2
Longbow Cl HUDN HD2 ....192 F1
Longcar La BSLY S70 ....260 F6
Longcauseway EARL WF12 ....173 M6
The Long Cswy
  BRFD/BLYE BB10 ....140 C1
  LUD/ILL HX2 ....144 C8
Long Cswy BHP/TINH LS16 ....86 C1
  BSLYN/ROY S71 ....261 L3
  EARD/LOFT WF3 ....177 H1
  EARL WF12 ....195 M3
  HBR HX7 ....142 A2
  HBR HX7 ....101 J5
  OSM LS9 ....132 B1
  RPDN/SBR HX6 ....188 B6
  TOD OL14 ....164 B3
  WKFDE WF1 ....176 F6
Long Cl LM/WK BD12 ....148 D2
  LUD/ILL HX2 ....144 C1
Long Close La HEM/SK/SE WF9 ....225 K8
  HOLM/MEL HD9 ....237 K8
  OSM LS9 ....110 B7
Long Crest PONT WF8 ....181 G8
Long Cft DOD/DAR S75 ....242 D5
Longcroft HUDE HD5 ....215 H3
  KGHY BD21 ....3 H6
Longcroft Pl BFD BD1 ....4 D6
  ILK LS29 ....39 G3
Long Croft St MAR/SLWT HD7 ....213 G2
Longdale Dr HEM/SK/SE WF9 ....247 G2
Long Dam La HOR/CROF WF4 ....222 C2
Longden Av HUDS HD4 ....213 L4
Longdike Ct GFTH/SHER LS25 ....135 K5
Longdike La GFTH/SHER LS25 ....135 L6
Longdon Av KBTN HD8 ....216 A3
Long Edge Low Rd
  RPDN/SBR HX6 ....166 D4
Long Edge Rd RPDN/SBR HX6 ....166 D4
Long Fallas Crs BRIG HD6 ....170 D7
Longfellow Gv
  EARD/LOFT WF3 ....155 G8
Longfield Av HIPP HX3 ....147 J5
  HUDE HD5 ....15 M5
  MAR/SLWT HD7 ....213 G1
  PDSY/CALV LS28 ....107 H7
  TOD OL14 ....163 K2
Longfield Cl HUDE HD5 ....15 M5
  TOD OL14 ....163 K2
Longfield Ct HECK WF16 ....172 F2
  PDSY/CALV LS28 ....107 H7
Longfield Dr BOW BD4 ....127 L3
  BRAM LS13 ....107 H2
  DOD/DAR S75 ....242 D5
  FEA/AMT WF7 ....202 E7
  MSTN/BAR LS15 ....111 J6
Longfield Garth BRAM LS13 ....107 H1
Longfield Gv PDSY/CALV LS28 ....107 H7
  TOD OL14 ....163 K2
Longfield Mt PDSY/CALV LS28 ....107 H7
Longfield Rd HECK WF16 ....172 F2
  PDSY/CALV LS28 ....107 H7
  ROY/SHW OL2 ....229 J8
  TOD OL14 ....163 K1
  WKFDW/WTN WF2 ....176 B7
Longfield Ter PDSY/CALV LS28 ....107 G7
  WKFDW/WTN WF2 ....176 B7
Longford Ter GTHN BD7 ....126 B1
Long Ga HBR HX7 ....55 L7
  RPDN/SBR HX6 ....188 L7
Long Grove Av HUDE HD5 ....193 G8
Long Heads La
  GFTH/SHER LS25 ....138 B5
Long Hey La TOD OL14 ....163 L3
Long Heys GTL/HWG HX4 ....168 B8
Long Hill End HWTH BD22 ....54 C5
Long Hill Rd HUDN HD2 ....192 D2
Longhouse Dr CUL/QBY BD13 ....101 M6
Longhouse La CUL/QBY BD13 ....101 M6
Long Ing HOLM/MEL HD9 ....253 M3
Long Ing Rd HOLM/MEL HD9 ....254 C7
Longlands Av CUL/QBY BD13 ....101 M5
  MAR/SLWT HD7 ....212 A5
Longlands Bank
  HOLM/MEL HD9 ....236 D7
Longlands Cl OSS WF5 ....175 G8
Longlands Dr DOD/DAR S75 ....242 D6
  HWTH BD22 ....78 F6
Longlands La WBY LS22 ....46 L1
Longlands Rd DEWS WF13 ....173 J4
  MAR/SLWT HD7 ....212 A5
  OSS WF5 ....175 G8
Longlands St BFD BD1 ....4 D5
Long La BGLY BD16 ....80 C5
  COL BB8 ....52 F6
  CUL/QBY BD13 ....124 F7
  EARL WF12 ....174 B8
  FEA/AMT WF7 ....202 D5
  HBR HX7 ....143 G5
  HBR HX7 ....164 F3
  HIPP HX3 ....146 A4
  HIPP HX3 ....147 H8
  HOLM/MEL HD9 ....236 B3
  HOR/CROF WF4 ....216 F5
  HTON BD9 ....103 M1
  HUDE HD5 ....193 G6
  HWTH BD22 ....54 D1
  KBTN HD8 ....238 A3
  KBTN HD8 ....240 B3
  MSTN/BAR LS15 ....90 A7
  PONT WF8 ....181 M8
  PONT WF8 ....226 E5
  RPDN/SBR HX6 ....167 J4
  STKB/PEN S36 ....271 H5
  WIL/AL BD15 ....102 F5
Long Lee La KGHY BD21 ....3 K8
Long Lee Ter KGHY BD21 ....3 M8
Longley Cl DOD/DAR S75 ....260 A2
Longley Edge La
  HOLM/MEL HD9 ....254 D5
Longley Edge Rd
  HOLM/MEL HD9 ....254 C5
Longley La HOLM/MEL HD9 ....254 C5
  HUDE HD5 ....214 E4

  RPDN/SBR HX6 ....167 H6
Longley Rd HUDE HD5 ....214 F2
Longley St DOD/DAR S75 ....260 A2
Longman Rd BSLY S70 ....261 G3
Long Meadow COL * BB8 ....74 C1
  SKP/WHF BD23 ....16 D1
Long Meadow Ct
  GFTH/SHER LS25 ....135 J1
Long Meadow Ga
  GFTH/SHER LS25 ....135 H1
Long Mdw BHP/TINH LS16 ....64 A4
  ECHL BD2 ....105 G2
  GFTH/SHER LS25 ....135 H1
  ILK LS29 ....40 A4
Long Moor La KBTN HD8 ....238 E5
Long Preston Cha IDLE * BD10 ....84 A7
Long Reach LUD/ILL HX2 ....145 J3
Long Riddings ILK LS29 ....19 G5
Long Rdg BRIG HD6 ....170 C7
Longridge Rd BSLYN/ROY S71 ....243 M8
Long Rw HOR/CROF WF4 ....200 C1
  HORS LS18 ....85 L5
  LM/WK BD12 ....148 F1
Longroyd Av BEE/HOL LS11 ....131 L3
Longroyd Crs BEE/HOL LS11 ....131 L3
  MAR/SLWT HD7 ....212 A5
Longroyd Crs North
  BEE/HOL LS11 ....9 G9
Longroyd Dr BAIL BD17 ....83 G2
Longroyde Cl BRIG HD6 ....170 B6
Longroyde Gv BRIG HD6 ....170 B6
Longroyde Rd BRIG HD6 ....170 B5
Longroyd Farm
  HOR/CROF WF4 ....196 D7
Longroyd Gv BEE/HOL LS11 ....131 L3
Longroyd La HUD HD1 ....14 B9
Longroyd Pl BEE/HOL LS11 ....131 L3
  HUD HD1 ....14 B9
Long Royd Rd RPDN/SBR HX6 ....166 E4
Longroyd St BEE/HOL LS11 ....131 L3
Longroyd St North
  BEE/HOL LS11 ....9 H9
Longroyd Ter MID LS10 ....131 L3
Longroyd Vw BEE/HOL LS11 ....131 L3
Long Rushes ROY/SHW OL2 ....229 H6
Long Shaw La TOD OL14 ....164 B2
Longside La GTHN BD7 ....4 B7
Longsight Rd DOD/DAR S75 ....242 C5
Long St BOW BD4 ....5 L9
Long Thorpe La
  EARD/LOFT WF3 ....154 C5
Long Tongue Scrog La
  HUDE HD5 ....193 M7
Long Wall HUDS HD4 ....169 G8
Longwood Av BGLY BD16 ....81 G1
Longwood Cl AL/HA/HU LS17 ....88 D1
  EARD/LOFT * WF3 ....152 F6
Longwood Ct AL/HA/HU LS17 ....88 D1
Longwood Crs AL/HA/HU LS17 ....88 D1
Longwood Edge Rd
  HUDW HD3 ....191 G6
Longwood Fold
  EARD/LOFT WF3 ....153 G6
Longwood Garth
  EARD/LOFT WF3 ....153 G6
Longwood Ga HUDW HD3 ....191 H8
Longwood House Rd
  HUDN * HD2 ....192 C3
  HUDW HD3 ....213 K1
Longwoods Wk KNOT WF11 ....182 C1
Longwood V EARD/LOFT WF3 ....153 G6
Longwood Vw AL/HA/HU LS17 ....88 D1
Longwood Vw AL/HA/HU LS17 ....88 D1
Lonsbrough Av HECK WF16 ....172 F1
Lonsbrough Flats HUD HD1 ....15 G6
Lonsdale Av BSLYN/ROY S71 ....262 D6
  BTLY WF17 ....151 H7
  MILN OL16 ....228 D1
Lonsdale Cl MID LS10 ....131 M5
Lonsdale Mdw
  BSPA/BRAM LS23 ....48 F7
Lonsdale Ri EARD/LOFT WF3 ....153 G6
Lonsdale St BFDE BD3 ....5 L4
Lonsdale Ter LVSG * WF15 ....172 C2
Lord La HWTH BD22 ....78 D6
Lordsfield Pl BOW BD4 ....127 M5
Lord's La BRIG HD6 ....170 D5
Lord Sq WIL * OL16 ....206 B7
Lord St BSLYN/ROY S71 ....261 L4
  DEWS * WF13 ....173 H2
  EARL * WF12 ....174 D7
  HFAX HX1 ....10 F6
  HUD HD1 ....15 G6
  KGHY BD21 ....3 G4
  MAR/SLWT HD7 ....212 B5
  RPDN/SBR HX6 ....167 L1
  TOD OL14 ....163 J3
  WKFDE WF1 ....13 L9
  WOR/ARM LS12 ....8 A3
Lord Ter WOR/ARM LS12 ....8 A3
Loris St BOW BD4 ....127 M5
Lorne St BOW BD4 ....127 K3
  HWTH BD22 ....79 H6
  KGHY BD21 ....3 L3
  WHIT OL12 ....206 D3
Lorry Bank CHAL LS7 ....7 G1
Loscoe Cl NORM WF6 ....179 G5
Loscoe La NORM WF6 ....179 G4
Loshpot La WBY LS22 ....30 C4
Lothersdale Rd AIRE BD20 ....34 C7
Lotherton La GFTH/SHER LS25 ....92 B8
Lotherton Wy
  GFTH/SHER LS25 ....113 H6
Loughrigg Av ROY/SHW OL2 ....228 E6
Loughrigg St WBOW BD5 ....127 J3
Loughrigg Wk FEA/AMT WF7 ....224 A1
Louisa St WOR/ARM LS12 ....157 L6
  IDLE * BD10 ....83 K6
Louis Av WBOW BD5 ....126 E5
Louis Ct CHAL LS7 ....7 K2
Louise Cl WHIT OL12 ....206 E3
Louise Gdns WHIT OL12 ....206 D3

Louise St WHIT OL12 ....206 D3
Louis Gv CHAL LS7 ....7 L3
Louis Le Prince Ct RHAY LS8 ....110 B3
Louis St CHAL LS7 ....7 K2
Lovaine Gv WKFDW/WTN WF2 ....198 F5
Love La CAS WF10 ....157 L8
  HFAX HX1 ....10 F8
  OSS WF5 ....174 E8
  PONT WF8 ....180 D7
  RTHW LS26 ....155 G1
Love Lane Ter PONT WF8 ....180 D6
Lovell Park Cl CHAL LS7 ....7 J6
Lovell Park Ct CHAL LS7 ....7 H6
Lovell Park Ga CHAL LS7 ....7 H6
Lovell Park Gra CHAL LS7 ....7 J6
Lovell Park Hts CHAL LS7 ....7 J6
Lovell Park Hl CHAL LS7 ....7 H6
Lovell Park Ms CHAL LS7 ....7 H6
Lovell Park Rd CHAL LS7 ....7 H6
Lovell Vw HOR/CROF WF4 ....200 C6
Low Ash Av SHPY BD18 ....82 F7
Low Ash Crs SHPY BD18 ....83 G7
Low Ash Dr SHPY BD18 ....82 F7
Low Ash Gv SHPY BD18 ....82 F7
Low Ash Rd SHPY BD18 ....83 G7
Low Bank Dr HWTH BD22 ....78 D3
Low Bank La HWTH BD22 ....78 D3
Low Banks AIRE * BD20 ....58 B4
Low Bank St PDSY/CALV LS28 ....106 E3
Low Cliff Wk HECK WF16 ....173 G4
Low Cl BGLY BD16 ....81 K4
  ILK LS29 ....20 D8
Low Close St LDSU LS2 ....6 D7
Low Cft BSLYN/ROY S71 ....243 M3
Lowcroft WBY LS22 ....47 J6
Low Crompton Rd
  ROY/SHW OL2 ....228 D7
Lowdale EARL WF12 ....174 A4
Lowell Av GTHN BD7 ....126 B1
Lowell Gv BRAM LS13 ....107 J6
Lowell Pl BRAM LS13 ....107 J6
Lower Ashgrove WBOW BD5 ....4 D8
Lower Back La HBR * HX7 ....142 B2
Lower Bankhouse
  PDSY/CALV LS28 ....128 F2
Lower Bank Houses
  GTL/HWG * HX4 ....189 M4
Lower Basinghall St LDS LS1 ....6 F9
Lower Bower La DEWS WF13 ....173 H1
Lower Brock Well La
  RPDN/SBR HX6 ....167 H5
Lower Brunswick St LDSU LS2 ....7 J7
Lower Cambridge St
  CAS WF10 ....157 M6
Lower Castlereagh St
  BSLY * S70 ....261 G5
Lower Clifton St
  RPDN/SBR * HX6 ....167 L2
Lower Clyde St RPDN/SBR HX6 ....167 L3
Lower Common La KBTN HD8 ....240 G5
Lower Constable Rd ILK LS29 ....38 F3
Lower Cow Cl LM/WK * BD12 ....149 H4
Lower Cross St HFAX HX1 ....11 J4
Lower Crow Nest Dr BRIG HD6 ....148 F5
Lower Denby La KBTN HD8 ....257 J3
Lower Edge Rd ELL HX5 ....169 K7
Lower Ellistones
  GTL/HWG * HX4 ....168 C7
Lower Ferney Lee TOD OL14 ....141 J8
Lowerfields Ri ROY/SHW OL2 ....229 K6
Lower Finkil St BRIG HD6 ....170 A1
Lower Fitzwilliam St HUD HD1 ....15 G5
Lower Fold BRIG HD6 ....170 B8
  HOLM/MEL HD9 ....236 B1
Lower Ga HUDW HD3 ....213 K1
Lower George St TOD OL14 ....163 K1
  WBSY * BD6 ....126 D5
Lower Globe St GIR BD8 ....4 A4
Lower Gra HUDN HD2 ....171 G8
Lower Grattan Rd BFD BD1 ....4 C6
Lower Greave Rd
  HOLM/MEL HD9 ....235 K6
Lower Green Av CLECK BD19 ....149 H6
Lower Hall Cl LVSG WF15 ....172 B2
Lower Hall Crs HUDE HD5 ....193 L8
Lower Hall Dr LVSG WF15 ....172 B2
Lower Hall La LVSG WF15 ....172 B2
Lower Hall Mt LVSG WF15 ....172 B2
Lower Hall Rd HUDE HD5 ....193 L8
Lower Heights Rd
  CUL/QBY BD13 ....102 E6
Lower Hey HOLM/MEL HD9 ....234 F4
Lower High Royds
  DOD/DAR S75 ....242 C6
Lower Holme BAIL BD17 ....82 E5
Lower House Cl SHPY BD18 ....83 H5
Lower House La KBTN HD8 ....216 C4
  WHIT OL12 ....184 D7
Lowerhouses La HUDE HD5 ....214 F2
Lowerhouses Rd HUDW * HD3 ....191 K8
Lower Kipping La
  CUL/QBY BD13 ....102 F8
Lower Kirkgate HFAX HX1 ....11 L6
Lower Laith Av TOD OL14 ....163 L1
Lower La BIRK/DRI BD11 ....149 M1
  BOW BD4 ....127 L2
  CLECK BD19 ....150 D7
  HBR HX7 ....142 A3
  HOLM/MEL HD9 ....235 M2
  MILN OL16 ....228 F2
Lower Langwith WBY LS22 ....47 J2
Lower Lark HI CLECK BD19 ....149 K7
Lower Maythorn La
  HOLM/MEL HD9 ....253 M1
Lower Mdw HOLM/MEL HD9 ....235 M1
Lower Mickletown RTHW LS26 ....157 G3
Lower Mill Bank Rd
  RPDN/SBR HX6 ....166 F7
Lower Newlands BRIG HD6 ....170 D5
Lower Northcroft
  HEM/SK/SE WF9 ....247 J5
Lower Northfield La
  HEM/SK/SE WF9 ....246 E3
Lower North St BTLY WF17 ....173 K2
Lower Oxford St CAS WF10 ....157 M7

Lower Park Gn AIRE BD20 ....35 L5
Lower Park Royd Dr
  RPDN/SBR HX6 ....167 G7
Lower Peel St DEWS WF13 ....173 L5
Lower Quarry Rd HUDN HD2 ....171 J7
Lower Range HIPP * HX3 ....11 H2
Lower Rd HUDW HD3 ....189 H8
Lower Rushton Rd BFDE BD3 ....106 A7
Lower School St LM/WK BD12 ....126 B8
  SHPY * BD18 ....82 B6
Lower Sheriff St WHIT OL12 ....206 A6
Lower Station Rd NORM WF6 ....178 C4
Lower St MILN OL16 ....228 C2
Lower Thomas St BSLY S70 ....261 G6
Lower Tofts Rd
  PDSY/CALV LS28 ....107 G7
Lowertown HWTH BD22 ....100 E4
Lower Town St BRAM LS13 ....107 M4
Lower Tweedale St ROCH OL11 ....206 D7
Lower Union St SKP/WHF BD23 ....16 B3
Lower Unwin St STKB/PEN S36 ....270 C4
Lower Viaduct St HUD HD1 ....15 G2
Lower Warrengate WKFDE WF1 ....13 G2
Lower Wellhouse Rd
  MAR/SLWT HD7 ....212 F3
Lower Wellington Rd ILK LS29 ....38 C5
Lower Westfield Rd GIR * BD8 ....104 C5
Lower Wheat End MILN OL16 ....206 D6
Lower Wortley Rd
  WOR/ARM LS12 ....130 D1
Lower Wyke Gn LM/WK BD12 ....148 D6
Lower Wyke La LM/WK BD12 ....148 E6
Lowestwood La
  MAR/SLWT HD7 ....212 F4
Loweswater Av WBSY BD6 ....126 B8
Low Farm RTHW LS26 ....135 G6
Low Farm Cl COP/BISH YO23 ....73 J7
Low Farm La FEA/AMT WF7 ....202 C8
Lowfield Cl LM/WK BD12 ....149 G1
Lowfield Crs AIRE BD20 ....36 B5
  HEM/SK/SE WF9 ....224 A7
Lowfield La SKP/WHF BD23 ....19 H1
Lowfield Rd DEWS WF13 ....173 H6
  GFTH/SHER LS25 ....139 G6
  HEM/SK/SE WF9 ....224 A7
Low Fields Av BEE/HOL LS11 ....131 G2
Lowfields Cl ELL HX5 ....169 J6
Low Fields Rd WOR/ARM LS12 ....130 F2
Lowfields Wy ELL HX5 ....169 J6
Low Fold AIRE BD20 ....35 L8
  CLECK BD19 ....149 H6
  ECHL BD2 ....105 H4
Low Garth Link
  GFTH/SHER LS25 ....116 A7
Low Garth Rd GFTH/SHER LS25 ....116 A7
Low Ga HEM/SK/SE WF9 ....247 J3
  HOLM/MEL HD9 ....254 C2
Low Gate La UPML OL3 ....231 H5
Low Gipton Crs OSM LS9 ....110 F3
Low Grange Crs MID LS10 ....132 A5
Low Grange Vw MID LS10 ....132 A6
Low Gn FEA/AMT WF7 ....202 D7
  GTHN BD7 ....126 C3
  KNOT WF11 ....182 D2
  YEA LS19 ....84 E3
Low Green Ter GTHN BD7 ....126 D3
Low Hall Pl BEE/HOL LS11 ....8 A4
Low Hall Rd ILK LS29 ....61 K2
  YEA LS19 ....84 F6
Low HI WHIT OL12 ....206 A3
Low Hills La HUDW HD3 ....191 J5
Lowhouse Cl MILN OL16 ....207 J5
Low House Dr AIRE BD20 ....36 A6
Low House Fold LVSG WF15 ....172 B2
Lowlands Cl BSLYN/ROY S71 ....261 M1
Lowlands Rd MIRF WF14 ....194 D3
Low La AIRE BD20 ....34 A3
  AIRE BD20 ....35 L1
  AIRE BD20 ....36 B3
  BRIG HD6 ....148 E8
  BTLY WF17 ....151 G5
  CLAY BD14 ....125 J1
  CUL/QBY BD13 ....124 C3
  HBR HX7 ....122 C7
  HOR/CROF WF4 ....196 D5
  HORS LS18 ....85 M4
  OT LS21 ....25 H8
  PBR BD23 ....28 B6
Low Mdw ROY/SHW OL2 ....228 F8
Low MI ILK * LS29 ....19 L7
Low Mill La DEWS WF13 ....194 F2
  ILK LS29 ....19 K6
  KGHY BD21 ....3 J4
Low Mill Rd OSS WF5 ....196 E3
Low Mills GSLY * LS20 ....62 A6
Low Mills Rd WOR/ARM LS12 ....130 B3
Low Moor Crs HOR/CROF WF4 ....220 B3
Low Moor La HOR/CROF WF4 ....219 M5
Low Moor Side
  WOR/ARM LS12 ....129 K4
Low Moorside Cl
  WOR/ARM * LS12 ....130 A3
Low Moor Side La
  WOR/ARM LS12 ....129 L4
Low Moor St LM/WK BD12 ....126 F8
Low Moor Ter LUD/ILL HX2 ....145 M8
Lowood La BTLY WF17 ....151 G3
Low Park Rd ILK LS29 ....39 K1
Low Pasture Cl DOD/DAR S75 ....260 C4
Low Rd DEWS WF13 ....173 H6
  EARL WF12 ....174 A4
  EARL WF12 ....195 L5
  GLE DN14 ....161 M8
  HUDS HD4 ....214 B6
  MID LS10 ....9 M8
  STKB/PEN S36 ....271 M5
Lowry Rd EARD/LOFT WF3 ....153 G5
Lowry Vw KGHY BD21 ....3 H7
Low Shops La RTHW LS26 ....132 E3
Low's PI WHIT OL12 ....206 C4
Low St DEWS * WF13 ....173 L5
  DOD/DAR S75 ....260 D8
  EARD/LOFT WF3 ....153 G5
  GFTH/SHER LS25 ....116 A7
  GFTH/SHER LS25 ....138 B3
  KGHY BD21 ....3 G5

KNOT WF11 ....159 L7
Lowswater Rd KNOT WF11 ....182 A4
Lowther Av GFTH/SHER LS25 ....113 G8
ROY/SHW OL2 ....228 E6
Lowther Crs RTHW LS26 ....134 B4
Lowther Dr GFTH/SHER LS25 ....113 G8
RTHW LS26 ....134 B4
Lowther Rd ROCH OL11 ....228 A2
Lowther St RHAY LS8 ....110 B2
Low Town KBTN HD8 ....238 D1
Low Vw DOD/DAR S75 ....260 A7
Low Wy BSPA/BRAM LS23 ....48 F8
BSPA/BRAM LS23 ....69 M4
Low Well Rd WBOW * BD5 ....126 F3
Low Whitehouse Rw MID * LS10 ....9 K6
Low Wd WIL/AL BD15 ....102 F2
Low Wood Ct AIRE * BD20 ....57 K3
Low Wood Ri ILK LS29 ....39 H3
Loxley Gv WBY LS22 ....29 M6
Loxley Mt AWLS/ASK DN6 ....227 L6
Loxley Rd BSLYN/ROY S71 ....262 B3
Loxley St BTLY WF17 ....151 J7
Lucas Ct CHAL LS7 ....7 G2
Lucas Gv North RYKW YO26 ....32 A1
Lucas Gv South RYKW YO26 ....32 A1
Lucas Pl HDGY LS6 ....6 D1
Lucas Rd RYKW YO26 ....32 A1
Lucas St HDGY LS6 ....6 D1
Luck La HUDW HD3 ....191 L8
Lucknow St ROCH OL11 ....228 B1
Lucy Av MSTN/BAR LS15 ....111 C6
Lucy Hall Dr BAIL BD17 ....82 A4
Lucy St HIPP HX3 ....11 K3
Luddenden La HUDW * HX2 ....144 F7
Ludgate Rd ROCH OL11 ....228 C4
Ludhill La HOLM/MEL HD9 ....236 F1
Ludlam St WBOW BD5 ....127 G1
Ludlow Av GFTH/SHER LS25 ....113 K7
Ludolf Dr AL/HA/HU LS17 ....89 G2
Ludwell Cl EARL WF12 ....196 B5
Ludwood Cl HOLM/MEL HD9 ....236 E6
Lugano Gv WMB/DAR S73 ....263 G8
Luke La HOLM/MEL HD9 ....236 E6
Luke Rd WBOW BD5 ....126 F2
Lulworth Av MSTN/BAR LS15 ....111 M6
Lulworth Cl BSLY S70 ....261 K6
MSTN/BAR LS15 ....111 M5
Lulworth Crs MSTN/BAR LS15 ....111 M5
Lulworth Garth
MSTN/BAR LS15 ....111 M6
Lulworth Gv BOW BD4 ....127 M4
Lulworth Vw MSTN/BAR LS15 ....111 M6
Lulworth Wk MSTN/BAR LS15 ....111 M6
Lumb Bottom BIRK/DRI BD11 ....129 H7
Lumbfoot Rd HWTH BD22 ....78 A7
Lumb Gill La ILK LS29 ....19 K8
Lumb La GIR BD8 ....4 B1
HIPP HX3 ....146 D4
HUDS HD4 ....214 F6
HWTH BD22 ....54 C5
LUD/ILL HX2 ....123 H7
LVSG WF15 ....172 B4
RPDN/SBR HX6 ....166 E7
Lumb Rd HBR HX7 ....142 F1
Lumbutts La TOD OL14 ....164 B2
Lumbutts Rd TOD OL14 ....163 M3
Lumby Cl PDSY/CALV LS28 ....129 H1
Lumby La AL/HA/HU LS17 ....46 C3
GFTH/SHER LS25 ....138 B4
PDSY/CALV LS28 ....129 H1
Lumby St IDLE * BD10 ....83 K6
Lumley Av BULY LS4 ....108 F3
CAS WF10 ....157 J7
Lumley Gv BULY LS4 ....108 F3
Lumley Hl CAS WF10 ....157 J7
Lumley Mt BULY LS4 ....108 F3
Lumley Pl BULY LS4 ....108 F3
Lumley Rd BULY LS4 ....108 F3
EARL WF12 ....174 A4
Lumley St BULY LS4 ....108 F3
CAS WF10 ....157 K7
Lumley Ter BULY LS4 ....108 F3
Lumley Vw BULY LS4 ....108 F3
Lumley Wk BULY LS4 ....108 F3
Lunan Pl RHAY LS8 ....110 B2
Lund Av BSLYN/ROY S71 ....262 B3
Lund Cl BSLYN/ROY S71 ....262 B3
Lund Crs BSLYN/ROY S71 ....262 B3
Lund Dr HECK WF16 ....173 G3
Lund Head La PBR HG3 ....45 L1
Lund Hill La BSLYN/ROY S71 ....244 B2
Lund La BSLYN/ROY S71 ....262 B3
HWTH BD22 ....56 D8
Lund Sike La GFTH/SHER LS25 ....138 C3
Lund St BGLY BD16 ....81 J3
GIR BD8 ....104 A1
KGHY BD21 ....3 G3
Lune St COL BB8 ....74 A2
Lunnfields La KNOT WF11 ....159 K2
Lunn La GLE DN14 ....161 L3
Lunn Rd CUD/GR S72 ....244 D8
Lupset Crs WKFDW/WTN WF2 ....198 D5
Lupton Av OSM LS9 ....110 C6
Lupton St GIR BD8 ....4 D2
MID LS10 ....9 L9
Lustre St KGHY BD21 ....2 D5
Luther Pl HUDW HD3 ....14 A3
Luther Wy ECHL BD2 ....105 H3
Luton St HFAX HX1 ....10 B5
HUDS HD4 ....213 H3
KGHY BD21 ....2 F5
Lutterworth Dr AWLS/ASK DN6 ....249 J8
Luttrell Cl BHP/TINH LS16 ....86 C4
Luttrell Crs BHP/TINH LS16 ....86 C4
Luttrell Gdns BHP/TINH LS16 ....86 C4
Luttrell Pl BHP/TINH LS16 ....86 C4
Luttrell Rd BHP/TINH LS16 ....86 C4
The Lutyens ILK LS29 ....38 B2
Luxor Av RHAY LS8 ....110 B2
Luxor Rd RHAY LS8 ....110 B2
Luxor St RHAY LS8 ....110 C2
Luxor Vw RHAY LS8 ....110 B2
Lyceum Pas MILN * OL16 ....206 B7
Lydbrook Pk HIPP HX3 ....168 C4

Lyddon Ter LDSU LS2 ....6 C5
Lydford ROCH * OL11 ....206 A8
Lydgate HIPP HX3 ....147 J5
KBTN HD8 ....216 C3
OSM LS9 ....110 B5
Lydgate Cl HOLM/MEL HD9 ....234 F7
Lydgate Dr HOLM/MEL HD9 ....236 F7
KBTN HD8 ....216 C3
Lydgate Pk HIPP HX3 ....148 A7
Lydgate Pl PDSY/CALV LS28 ....84 C7
Lydgate Ri HEM/SK/SE * WF9 ....246 F3
Lydgate Rd BTLY WF17 ....174 B1
KBTN HD8 ....238 A6
Lydgate St PDSY/CALV LS28 ....84 C7
Lydget Ct AIRE BD20 ....57 J5
Lydgetts HOLM/MEL HD9 ....253 M1
Lydia St LDSU LS2 ....7 J8
Lyefield Wk MILN OL16 ....206 D8
Lyme Cha SCFT LS14 ....111 H4
Lymington Dr BOW BD4 ....128 A2
Lynch Av OSM WF5 ....197 J2
Lynda Gv OSM WF5 ....197 J2
Lyndale GFTH/SHER LS25 ....135 J6
Lyndale Cls HECK WF16 ....173 G2
Lyndale Dr LIT OL15 ....185 J8
SHPY BD18 ....83 H7
WKFDW/WTN WF2 ....176 A4
Lyndale Gv NORM WF6 ....178 E5
Lyndale Ms DEWS WF13 ....173 H5
Lyndale Rd BGLY BD16 ....81 L1
Lyndale Ct WBSY BD6 ....126 C7
Lyndean Gdns IDLE BD10 ....83 J7
Lynden Av SHPY BD18 ....83 G6
Lynden Ct WBSY BD6 ....126 C7
Lyndhurst Av HUDW HD6 ....170 C7
Lyndhurst Cl MSTN/BAR LS15 ....90 B7
Lyndhurst Crs MSTN/BAR LS15 ....90 B7
Lyndhurst Dr AWLS/ASK DN6 ....227 M3
Lyndhurst Gv WIL/AL BD15 ....103 L5
Lyndhurst Grove Rd BRIG HD6 ....170 C7
Lyndhurst Rd BRIG HD6 ....170 C6
HUDW HD3 ....191 K6
MSTN/BAR LS15 ....90 B8
Lyndhurst Vw MSTN/BAR LS15 ....90 B8
Lyndon Av BSPA/BRAM LS23 ....69 L3
GFTH/SHER LS25 ....113 G7
Lyndon Cl BSPA/BRAM LS23 ....69 L3
Lyndon Crs BSPA/BRAM LS23 ....69 L3
Lyndon Rd BSPA/BRAM LS23 ....69 L3
Lyndon Sq BSPA/BRAM LS23 ....69 L3
Lyndon Ter BGLY BD16 ....81 J3
Lyndon Wy BSPA/BRAM LS23 ....69 L3
Lyndum Gv GFTH/SHER LS25 ....135 J4
Lyndum Vls AWLS/ASK * DN6 ....227 L3
Lynfield Dr HTON BD9 ....103 M3
LVSG WF15 ....171 K1
Lynfield Mt SHPY BD18 ....83 G6
Lynmoor Ct IDLE BD10 ....83 H7
Lynndale Av AIRE BD20 ....34 F7
HUDN HD2 ....192 B5
Lynnfield Gdns MSTN/BAR LS15 ....90 B8
Lynnwood Gdns
PDSY/CALV LS28 ....106 E8
Lynsey Gdns BOW BD4 ....127 K7
Lynthorne Rd HTON BD9 ....104 D2
Lynton Av BSPA/BRAM LS23 ....48 F6
EARD/LOFT WF3 ....154 A4
HTON BD9 ....104 B3
HUD HD1 ....14 C7
Lynton Dr AIRE BD20 ....58 B5
HTON BD9 ....104 A4
SHPY BD18 ....82 C7
Lynton Gv CUL/QBY LS28 ....124 B5
Lynton Pl DOD/DAR S75 ....241 M6
Lynton Ter CLECK * BD19 ....149 M6
Lynton Vls HTON BD9 ....104 B4
Lynwood Av RTHW LS26 ....133 M8
SHPY BD18 ....83 G6
WOR/ARM LS12 ....130 E2
Lynwood Cl BIRK/DRI BD11 ....150 D1
FEA/AMT WF7 ....201 G2
Lynwood Ct HWTH BD22 ....79 G1
Lynwood Crs HEM/SK/SE WF9 ....223 H3
HFAX HX1 ....10 A9
PONT WF8 ....180 F8
RTHW LS26 ....133 M8
WOR/ARM LS12 ....130 E2
Lynwood Dr BSLYN/ROY S71 ....243 L5
WKFDW/WTN WF2 ....198 D3
Lynwood Garth
WOR/ARM LS12 ....130 E1
Lynwood Gv WOR/ARM LS12 ....130 E2
Lynwood Ms BOW BD4 ....128 B4
Lynwood Mt WOR/ARM LS12 ....130 E1
Lynwood Ri WOR/ARM LS12 ....130 E1
Lynwood Vw WOR/ARM LS12 ....130 E1
Lyon Rd AIRE BD20 ....35 H8
PONT WF8 ....180 F8
Lyon St CUL/QBY BD13 ....102 F7
CUL/QBY BD13 ....125 H5
ROY/SHW OL2 ....229 K7
Lytham Av BSLYN/ROY S71 ....261 M1
Lytham Cl NORM WF6 ....178 F5
SKP/WHF BD23 ....16 E3
Lytham Dr CUL/QBY BD13 ....125 K4
Lytham Gdns SKP/WHF BD23 ....16 E3
Lytham Gv WOR/ARM LS12 ....130 C2
Lytham Pl WOR/ARM LS12 ....130 C2
Lytham St WHIT OL12 ....206 A3
Lyttleton Crs STKB/PEN S36 ....270 E5
Lytton Rd GIR BD8 ....104 B6
Lytton St HIPP HX3 ....11 H2
MID LS10 ....9 K9

M

Mabel Royd GTHN BD7 ....126 B1
Mabel St COL BB8 ....74 B1
HBR HX7 ....144 A5
Mabgate OSM LS9 ....7 K7
Mabgate Gn OSM LS9 ....7 K8
Macaulay Rd HUDN HD2 ....14 C1
Macaulay St OSM LS9 ....7 L8
Macham St HUD HD1 ....214 B2

Mackie Hill Cl HOR/CROF WF4 ....219 M2
Mackingstone Dr HWTH BD22 ....78 D3
Mackingstone La HWTH BD22 ....78 D3
Mackinnon Av NORM WF6 ....178 E3
Mackintosh Homes
LUD/ILL HX2 ....168 C2
Maclure Rd ROCH OL11 ....206 B8
Macturk Gr GIR * BD8 ....104 C5
Maddocks St SHPY BD18 ....82 C6
Madeley Rd HOR/CROF WF4 ....222 E6
Madeley Sq CAS WF10 ....158 E5
Maden's Sq LIT OL15 ....207 K1
Madgin La HUDS HD4 ....213 J8
Madison Av BOW BD4 ....128 A5
Madni Cl HFAX HX1 ....10 E6
Mafeking Av BEE/HOL LS11 ....131 J5
Mafeking Gv BEE/HOL LS11 ....131 J5
Mafeking Mt BEE/HOL LS11 ....131 J5
Magdalene Cl BHP/TINH LS16 ....86 F7
Magdalene Flds NORM WF6 ....178 F5
Magdalene Rd
WKFDW/WTN WF2 ....197 L1
Magdalen Rd HOLM/MEL HD9 ....234 F7
Maggot La STKB/PEN S36 ....271 M4
Magna Gv WKFDW/WTN WF2 ....198 F5
Magnolia Cl CUD/GR S72 ....244 F4
Magnolias BTLY WF17 ....151 G7
Magpie Cl WBSY BD6 ....125 L5
Magpie La MOR LS27 ....152 D3
Maidstone St BFDE BD3 ....105 L7
Maidwell Wy WBSY BD6 ....126 C8
Mail Cl MSTN/BAR LS15 ....112 A3
Main Av HUDS HD4 ....213 H3
Main Ga HOLM/MEL HD9 ....255 G4
Main Rd AIRE BD20 ....35 G6
AIRE BD20 ....56 C1
AIRE BD20 ....58 F6
CUL/QBY BD13 ....101 M6
Mainspring Rd WIL/AL BD15 ....102 E1
Main St AIRE BD20 ....34 B4
AIRE BD20 ....34 E8
AIRE BD20 ....34 E1
AIRE BD20 ....34 E4
AIRE BD20 ....55 M1
AL/HA/HU LS17 ....44 B4
AL/HA/HU LS17 ....67 L1
AL/HA/HU LS17 ....88 F1
AWLS/ASK DN6 ....205 H3
AWLS/ASK DN6 ....248 D5
BAIL BD17 ....83 L1
BGLY BD16 ....81 H3
BGLY BD16 ....81 K8
BSPA/BRAM LS23 ....49 J2
CAS WF10 ....157 K2
CAS WF10 ....158 A1
COP/BISH YO23 ....73 M5
CUD/GR S72 ....222 F8
EARD/LOFT WF3 ....153 M7
EARD/LOFT WF3 ....154 F3
GFTH/SHER LS25 ....92 A7
GFTH/SHER LS25 ....113 G7
GFTH/SHER LS25 ....138 C6
GFTH/SHER LS25 ....160 A3
GLE DN14 ....161 J7
GSLY LS20 ....61 G6
HEM/SK/SE WF9 ....225 G4
HEM/SK/SE WF9 ....225 M6
HWTH BD22 ....77 M8
HWTH BD22 ....78 E7
ILK LS29 ....19 G6
ILK LS29 ....40 A4
ILK LS29 ....61 H2
LM/WK BD12 ....127 G8
LM/WK BD12 ....148 E2
MSTN/BAR LS15 ....90 B8
MSTN/BAR LS15 ....90 F7
OT LS21 ....42 E7
PBR HG3 ....26 E2
PONT WF8 ....204 F8
RTHW LS26 ....156 F3
SCFT LS14 ....90 B2
TAD LS24 ....50 A7
TAD LS24 ....93 K8
TAD LS24 ....94 F7
TAD LS24 ....94 F1
TAD LS24 ....115 M1
WBY LS22 ....29 M5
WBY LS22 ....31 K4
WBY LS22 ....46 D1
WBY LS22 ....47 K4
WIL/AL BD15 ....102 E1
Maister Pl HWTH BD22 ....78 D3
Maitland Cl WHIT OL12 ....206 E3
WIL/AL BD15 ....103 K7
Maitland Pl BEE/HOL LS11 ....8 D7
Maitland St TOD OL14 ....163 J6
Maizebrook DEWS WF13 ....173 G6
Maize St HWTH BD22 ....79 J2
Major St MILN OL16 ....207 H8
WKFDW/WTN WF2 ....12 D8
Malais La AIRE BD20 ....55 J1
Malcolm Cl BSLY S70 ....261 M6
Maldon St ROCH OL11 ....228 B1
Malham Av BRIG HD6 ....170 A6
HTON BD9 ....103 L3
Malham Cl CUD/GR S72 ....244 E3
SCFT LS14 ....111 J2
Malham Ct BSLY * S70 ....260 F4
Malham Dr BTLY WF17 ....173 J1
LVSG WF15 ....172 B5
Malham Rd BRIG HD6 ....170 A7
WKFDE WF1 ....13 L1
Malham Sq WKFDE WF1 ....13 M1
Maliff Rd BRFD/BLYE BB10 ....96 D4
Malincroft DOD/DAR S75 ....242 D6
Malin Rd EARL WF12 ....174 B3
Mallard Av WKFDW/WTN WF2 ....220 L1
Mallard Cl IDLE BD10 ....105 L1
RTHW LS26 ....132 B7
Mallard Ct GIR BD8 ....103 L1
Mallard Rd CAS WF10 ....157 L8
The Mallards AIRE BD20 ....36 A5
Mallard Vw HWTH BD22 ....100 D4
Mallard Wy MAR/SLWT HD7 ....212 B6
MOR LS27 ....152 D2
Mallinson St DEWS WF13 ....173 J5
Mallory Cl GTHN BD7 ....104 D3
Mallory Wy CUD/GR S72 ....244 E7

Mallow Cft MILN OL16 ....228 E2
Malmesbury Cl BOW BD4 ....128 A4
WOR/ARM LS12 ....108 E8
Malmesbury Gv
WOR/ARM LS12 ....108 E8
Malmesbury Pl
WOR/ARM LS12 ....108 E8
Malmesbury St
WOR/ARM LS12 ....108 E8
Malmesbury Ter
WOR/ARM LS12 ....108 E8
Malsis Rd KGHY BD21 ....2 D7
Maltby Ct MSTN/BAR * LS15 ....111 M7
Malthouse Cl SCFT LS14 ....67 L6
Malthouse La PBR HG3 ....26 E3
Malthouse Rd BSLYN/ROY S71 ....261 H5
The Maltings EARD/LOFT WF3 ....154 D3
HDGY * LS6 ....109 G4
MIRF WF14 ....194 B1
PONT WF8 ....180 F5
Maltings Ct BEE/HOL LS11 ....9 G8
Maltings Rd BEE/HOL LS11 ....9 H8
LUD/ILL HX2 ....145 M4
Malt Kiln Cft
WKFDW/WTN WF2 ....199 G5
Maltkiln Dr HOR/CROF WF4 ....219 M6
Maltkiln La CAS WF10 ....158 A6
Malt Kiln La CUL/QBY BD13 ....124 D1
GFTH/SHER LS25 ....135 K5
Malt Kiln Ter TAD LS24 ....71 K7
Malton Pl BSLYN/ROY S71 ....243 G7
Malton Rd HEM/SK/SE WF9 ....225 M6
Malton St HIPP HX3 ....146 E4
RPDN/SBR HX6 ....167 K1
Malt St HWTH BD22 ....79 J2
Malvern Brow HTON BD9 ....103 M4
Malvern Cl CAS WF10 ....179 H1
DOD/DAR S75 ....260 D4
MILN OL16 ....207 J7
ROY/SHW OL2 ....229 H6
Malvern Crs AIRE BD20 ....57 M3
Malvern Gv BEE/HOL LS11 ....8 C8
HTON BD9 ....103 M5
Malvern Ri BEE/HOL LS11 ....8 C8
HUDS HD4 ....214 C3
Malvern Rd BEE/HOL LS11 ....8 C8
EARL WF12 ....174 A5
HTON BD9 ....103 M5
HUDS HD4 ....214 D2
KNOT WF11 ....182 A2
Malvern St BEE/HOL LS11 ....8 C8
Malvern Vw BEE/HOL LS11 ....8 C8
Manchester Rd HUD HD1 ....14 C9
HUDS HD4 ....213 M2
MAR/SLWT HD7 ....232 C6
ROCH OL11 ....206 A8
STKB/PEN S36 ....269 L5
WBSY BD6 ....126 F6
Manchester Rd Linthwaite
MAR/SLWT HD7 ....212 C6
Manchester Rd Marsden
MAR/SLWT HD7 ....233 J2
Manchester Rod Slaithwaite
MAR/SLWT HD7 ....211 M7
Mandale Gv WBSY BD6 ....125 M6
Mandale Rd WBSY BD6 ....125 M6
Mandarin Wy RTHW LS26 ....132 B7
Mandeville Crs WBSY BD6 ....126 B6
Mangrill La BSPA/BRAM LS23 ....68 F8
Manitoba Pl CHAL LS7 ....88 A8
Mankinholes Bank TOD OL14 ....164 B2
Manley Ct GFTH/SHER LS25 ....135 H1
Manley Dr WBY LS22 ....29 K8
Manley Gv ILK LS29 ....38 F2
Manley Ri ILK LS29 ....38 F3
Manley Rd ILK LS29 ....38 F3
Manley St BRIG HD6 ....170 C3
Mannerley Gv CLECK BD19 ....150 D8
Mannheim Rd HTON BD9 ....104 C4
Manningham La GIR BD8 ....4 C1
Mannville Gv HWTH BD22 ....2 C7
Mannville Pl HWTH BD22 ....2 C7
Mannville Rd KGHY BD21 ....2 C7
Mannville St HWTH BD22 ....2 C7
Mannville Ter BD7 ....4 D8
Mannville Wk HWTH * BD22 ....2 C7
Mannville Wy HWTH BD22 ....2 C7
Manor Av HDGY LS6 ....109 G2
OSS WF5 ....197 H3
Manor Cha RYKW YO26 ....33 H2
Manor Cl AWLS/ASK DN6 ....227 L3
BHP/TINH LS16 ....63 M3
BIRK/DRI BD11 ....129 C7
GIR BD8 ....103 M6
HEM/SK/SE WF9 ....225 G4
HIPP HX3 ....168 D2
HOR/CROF WF4 ....221 H7
OSS WF5 ....197 H3
PONT WF8 ....226 F1
RTHW LS26 ....133 G8
YEA LS19 ....62 D7
Manor Cottage Ms SCFT LS14 ....67 L8
Manor Ct AL/HA/HU LS17 ....89 G7
BGLY * BD16 ....81 J7
KNOT WF11 ....159 L7
OSS WF5 ....197 H3
Manor Crs CUD/GR S72 ....245 H6
OT LS21 ....42 E7
RTHW LS26 ....154 F1
WKFDW/WTN WF2 ....198 A2
WKFDW/WTN WF2 ....199 J6
Manor Cft CUD/GR S72 ....244 F1
HBR HX7 ....143 K3
MSTN/BAR LS15 ....111 J7
Manorcroft NORM WF6 ....178 D4
Manor Dr BGLY BD16 ....81 J7
CUD/GR S72 ....222 E8
FEA/AMT WF7 ....179 L5
HBR HX7 ....143 K3
HDGY LS6 ....109 G3
HIPP HX3 ....168 D2
HOR/CROF WF4 ....200 C7
HOR/CROF WF4 ....217 M3
KBTN HD8 ....239 J5
MIRF WF14 ....171 M7
OSS WF5 ....197 H3

Manor Farm
HEM/SK/SE * WF9 ....225 G4
Manor Farm Cl AWLS/ASK DN6 ....249 K8
BGLY BD16 ....81 K8
BSLYN/ROY S71 ....243 M6
MID LS10 ....131 M8
Manor Farm Crs MOR LS27 ....130 E6
Manor Farm Dr BTLY WF17 ....152 B8
MID LS10 ....131 L8
MOR LS27 ....130 E6
Manor Farm Gdns MID LS10 ....131 L8
Manor Farm Gn MID LS10 ....131 L8
Manor Farm Gv MID LS10 ....131 L8
Manor Farm Ri MID LS10 ....131 M8
Manor Farm Rd
HOR/CROF WF4 ....220 A2
MID LS10 ....131 L8
Manor Farm Wy MID LS10 ....153 L7
Manorfield Dr HOR/CROF WF4 ....197 J4
Manorfields Av
HOR/CROF WF4 ....200 C6
Manorfields Ct HOR/CROF WF4 ....200 C6
Manor Fold BGLY BD16 ....81 K8
Manor Gdns BSLYN/ROY S71 ....262 C6
CUL/QBY BD13 ....101 M1
EARL * WF12 ....174 C4
OT LS21 ....42 E7
SCFT LS14 ....68 C3
Manor Garth GFTH/SHER LS25 ....136 F6
MSTN/BAR LS15 ....111 L7
PBR HG3 ....28 E3
WKFDW/WTN WF2 ....199 J6
Manor Garth Rd EARL WF12 ....174 B7
GFTH/SHER LS25 ....135 K4
Manor Gra KBTN HD8 ....237 M6
Manor Gv AIRE BD20 ....58 C6
BSLYN/ROY S71 ....243 K3
CAS WF10 ....158 A8
CHAL LS7 ....87 M8
CUD/GR S72 ....245 H6
HEM/SK/SE WF9 ....246 C5
OSS WF5 ....197 H3
Manor Haigh Rd
WKFDW/WTN WF2 ....198 A3
Manor Heath Rd HIPP HX3 ....168 D3
Manor House Cft
BHP/TINH LS16 ....86 F3
Manor House La AL/HA/HU LS17 ....88 E3
Manor House Rd WIL/AL BD15 ....80 E8
Manor La OSS WF5 ....197 H3
SHPY BD18 ....82 D7
STKB/PEN S36 ....271 L5
TAD LS24 ....50 F4
UPML OL3 ....232 A6
Manorley La HIPP HX3 ....126 A8
Manor Mill La BEE/HOL LS11 ....131 G5
Manor Occupation Rd
BSLYN/ROY S71 ....243 K2
Manor Pk CAS WF10 ....136 A8
DOD/DAR S75 ....259 H7
EARL WF12 ....174 D3
GIR BD8 ....103 M6
HWTH BD22 ....54 E3
HWTH BD22 ....78 E4
MIRF WF14 ....171 L7
PONT WF8 ....203 M1
SCFT LS14 ....67 L7
Manor Park Av CAS WF10 ....157 K1
PONT WF8 ....181 H3
Manor Park Gdns CLECK BD19 ....150 C3
Manor Park Wy KBTN HD8 ....215 M4
Manor Ri HUD HD1 ....214 D2
ILK LS29 ....38 F2
KBTN HD8 ....239 J5
WKFDW/WTN WF2 ....199 J6
Manor Rd AIRE BD20 ....57 J4
BEE/HOL LS11 ....8 E4
BGLY BD16 ....81 K7
BTLY WF17 ....174 B1
COL BB8 ....52 A7
CUD/GR S72 ....244 C8
DEWS WF13 ....173 K7
GLE DN14 ....161 H7
HOR/CROF WF4 ....197 J5
HORS LS18 ....85 J6
HUDS HD4 ....215 H8
KBTN HD8 ....240 C2
MAR/SLWT HD7 ....212 F2
MOR LS27 ....130 E6
OSS WF5 ....197 J2
ROY/SHW OL2 ....229 J7
RTHW LS26 ....132 F8
TAD LS24 ....71 L6
TAD LS24 ....71 M2
WKFDW/WTN WF2 ....198 B3
WKFDW/WTN WF2 ....199 J7
Manor Rw BFD BD1 ....4 E4
WBSY BD6 ....126 E7
Manor Sq YEA LS19 ....62 D7
Manorstead KBTN HD8 ....239 J5
Manor St BSLYN/ROY S71 ....243 M6
CHAL LS7 ....7 K5
CLECK BD19 ....149 M7
EARL WF12 ....173 M6
ECHL BD2 ....105 K3
HUDS HD4 ....214 D2
OT LS21 ....41 J6
Manor Ter ECHL BD2 ....105 K3
HDGY LS6 ....109 G2
Manor Vw CAS WF10 ....180 A1
CUD/GR S72 ....244 E4
HDGY LS6 ....109 G2
PDSY/CALV LS28 ....107 G7
Manor Wy AIRE BD20 ....55 L2
BTLY WF17 ....174 B1
Manscombe Rd WIL/AL BD15 ....103 L5
Manse Crs ILK LS29 ....40 A4
Manse Dr HUDS HD4 ....213 J3
Mansel Ms BOW BD4 ....128 A5
Manse Rd ILK LS29 ....40 A5
Manse St BFDE BD3 ....105 L7
Manse Wy AIRE BD20 ....34 E8
Mansfield Av BGLY BD16 ....81 L1
Mansfield Crs AWLS/ASK DN6 ....249 K6
Mansfield Rd BSLYN/ROY S71 ....243 M6
GIR BD8 ....104 C4
ILK LS29 ....40 A5
Mansion Gdns HUDS HD4 ....213 J3

Mansion Ga CHAL LS7 ...... 87 M8
Mansion Gate Dr CHAL LS7 ...... 88 A8
Mansion La HIPP HX3 ...... 168 E2
  RHAY LS8 ...... 88 D5
Manston Ap MSTN/BAR LS15 ...... 111 J3
Manston Av MSTN/BAR LS15 ...... 111 J3
Manston Crs MSTN/BAR LS15 ...... 111 J3
Manston Dr MSTN/BAR LS15 ...... 111 J3
Manston Gdns MSTN/BAR LS15 ...... 111 M3
Manston Gv MSTN/BAR LS15 ...... 111 J3
Manston La MSTN/BAR LS15 ...... 112 A4
Manston Ri MSTN/BAR LS15 ...... 111 J3
Manston Wy MSTN/BAR LS15 ...... 111 J3
Mantley La ROY/SHW OL2 ...... 230 C7
Manygates Av WKFDE WF1 ...... 13 H9
Manygates Ct WKFDE WF1 ...... 13 H8
Manygates Crs WKFDE WF1 ...... 13 H9
Manygates La
  WKFDW/WTN WF2 ...... 198 F4
Manygates Pk WKFDE WF1 ...... 13 H8
Manywells Brow
  CUL/QBY BD13 ...... 101 L3
Manywells Crs CUL/QBY BD13 ...... 101 M1
Manywells La CUL/QBY BD13 ...... 101 K1
Maple Av BFDE BD3 ...... 106 A6
  HWTH BD22 ...... 78 F4
  MAR/SLWT HD7 ...... 213 H1
  PONT WF8 ...... 202 C1
Maple Cl BSLY S70 ...... 261 K7
  CAS WF10 ...... 179 K1
  GFTH/SHER LS25 ...... 138 A3
  HUDE HD5 ...... 193 L6
  ROY/SHW * OL2 ...... 229 H6
Maple Ct OSS WF5 ...... 197 C5
Maple Cft AL/HA/HU LS17 ...... 88 A3
  WOR/ARM LS12 ...... 129 M1
Maple Dr PONT WF8 ...... 180 E8
  WBY LS22 ...... 30 A7
  WOR/ARM LS12 ...... 129 M1
Maple Fold WOR/ARM LS12 ...... 129 M1
Maple Gdns AL/HA/HU LS17 ...... 68 A1
Maple Gv CLECK BD19 ...... 150 C5
  HUDN HD2 ...... 192 C2
  KGHY BD21 ...... 2 C1
  PONT WF8 ...... 202 C1
  WOR/ARM LS12 ...... 129 M1
Maple Ri RTHW * LS26 ...... 155 C2
Maple Rd DOD/DAR S75 ...... 242 C5
  EARL WF12 ...... 174 D7
Maple St HFAX HX1 ...... 10 B9
  HUD HD1 ...... 15 J9
  TOD OL14 ...... 163 J7
  WKFDW/WTN WF2 ...... 176 B6
Maple Wk EARL WF12 ...... 174 D7
Maple Wy SCFT LS14 ...... 89 L6
Maplin Av HUDW HD3 ...... 191 M5
Maplin Dr HUDW HD3 ...... 191 H5
Mapplewell Crs OSS WF5 ...... 197 C5
Mapplewell Dr DOD/DAR S75 ...... 242 E6
  OSS WF5 ...... 197 C5
Marbridge Ct WBSY BD6 ...... 126 C4
Marchant St CAS WF10 ...... 157 L6
Marchbank Rd BFDE BD3 ...... 105 L6
March Cote La BGLY BD16 ...... 81 J8
March St MILN OL16 ...... 206 C7
  NORM WF6 ...... 178 C5
Marchwood Gv CLAY BD14 ...... 125 M1
Marcroft Pl ROCH OL11 ...... 228 C2
Marcus Wy HUDW HD3 ...... 190 F5
Mardale Av ROY/SHW OL2 ...... 228 C6
Mardale Crs SCFT LS14 ...... 111 J3
Mardale Rd EARL WF12 ...... 174 A4
Mardyke WHIT * OL12 ...... 206 M4
Margaret Av AL/HA/HU LS17 ...... 67 M2
  MILN OL16 ...... 206 E7
Margaret Cl MOR LS27 ...... 130 E8
Margaret St HFAX HX1 ...... 10 E1
  KGHY BD21 ...... 2 D3
  ROY/SHW * OL2 ...... 229 K8
  WKFDE WF1 ...... 176 C2
  WKFDE WF1 ...... 176 D7
Margate RTHW * LS26 ...... 133 L8
Margate Rd BOW BD4 ...... 127 J2
Margate St CUD/GR S72 ...... 245 C7
  RPDN/SBR HX6 ...... 167 J3
Margerison Crs ILK LS29 ...... 39 C3
Margerison Rd ILK LS29 ...... 39 C3
Margetson Rd BIRK/DRI BD11 ...... 151 H1
Margroy Cl WHIT OL12 ...... 206 C4
Marian Gv BEE/HOL * LS11 ...... 131 K3
Marian Rd HDGY LS6 ...... 6 E2
Marian Ter HDGY LS6 ...... 6 E2
Maria St ILK LS29 ...... 40 A4
Marie Cl HUDE HD5 ...... 193 L8
Marigold St ROCH OL11 ...... 228 B1
Marina Crs MOR LS27 ...... 152 B3
Marina Ter MAR/SLWT HD7 ...... 213 C1
Marine Villa Rd KNOT WF11 ...... 182 B2
Marion Av WKFDW/WTN WF2 ...... 175 M6
Marion Cl HEM/SK/SE WF9 ...... 246 C4
Marion Dr SHPY BD18 ...... 82 E7
Marion St WKFDW/WTN WF2 ...... 175 M6
  BRIG HD6 ...... 170 C2
  GTHN BD7 ...... 4 A5
Marizon Gv WKFDE * WF1 ...... 176 E7
Mark Bottoms La
  HOLM/MEL HD9 ...... 236 B8
Mark Cl IDLE BD10 ...... 83 L6
Markenfield Rd ROY/SHW OL2 ...... 229 H7
Market Ar CLECK * BD19 ...... 150 C1
Market Av HUD HD1 ...... 14 F7
Market Balcony HFAX * HX1 ...... 11 H6
Market Cl BSLYN/ROY S71 ...... 261 J5
Market Ct CUL/QBY BD13 ...... 103 C8
Market Hl BSLY S70 ...... 261 C5
Market Pde BSLY * S70 ...... 261 H5
Market Pl CLECK BD19 ...... 150 A7
  COL BB8 ...... 74 A1
  CUD/GR S72 ...... 244 D7
  HECK WF16 ...... 172 F5
  HUD HD1 ...... 14 F7
  KGHY BD21 ...... 3 C5
  MAR/SLWT HD7 ...... 212 B6
  MAR/SLWT HD7 ...... 233 H2
  NORM WF6 ...... 178 C4
  OT LS21 ...... 41 J6
  PDSY/CALV LS28 ...... 107 G7

PONT WF8 ...... 180 F6
  WBY LS22 ...... 48 A1
Market Sq SHPY BD18 ...... 82 D6
Market St AIRE BD20 ...... 56 E1
  BFD BD1 ...... 4 F6
  BGLY BD16 ...... 81 H3
  BRIG HD6 ...... 170 D4
  BSLY S70 ...... 261 C5
  BTLY WF17 ...... 151 L5
  CLECK BD19 ...... 150 A7
  COL BB8 ...... 74 A1
  CUD/GR S72 ...... 244 D7
  CUL/QBY BD13 ...... 102 F8
  DEWS WF13 ...... 173 M6
  FEA/AMT WF7 ...... 179 L8
  HBR HX7 ...... 143 H3
  HECK WF16 ...... 172 F3
  HEM/SK/SE WF9 ...... 223 M7
  HFAX HX1 ...... 11 H6
  HOLM/MEL HD9 ...... 254 C1
  HUD HD1 ...... 14 A9
  HUD HD1 ...... 14 F7
  HUD HD3 ...... 213 K1
  KGHY BD21 ...... 3 C6
  NORM WF6 ...... 178 C4
  OT LS21 ...... 41 J7
  ROY/SHW OL2 ...... 229 K8
  SHPY BD18 ...... 82 D7
  STKB/PEN S36 ...... 270 F3
  WBSY * BD6 ...... 126 E5
  WKFDE WF1 ...... 12 E3
Market Street Ar LDS LS1 ...... 9 H1
Market Wk HUD * HD1 ...... 14 F7
  MAR/SLWT * HD7 ...... 233 H2
Market Wy WKFDE WF1 ...... 12 F2
Markfield Av LM/WK BD12 ...... 148 E1
Markfield Cl LM/WK BD12 ...... 148 E1
Markfield Dr LM/WK BD12 ...... 148 E1
Markham Av AWLS/ASK DN6 ...... 249 L5
  RHAY LS8 ...... 110 B2
  YEA LS19 ...... 84 E1
Markham Crs YEA LS19 ...... 84 E1
Markham Cft YEA LS19 ...... 84 E1
Markham St WKFDW/WTN WF2 ...... 12 B3
Markington Pl MID LS10 ...... 153 L3
Mark La ROY/SHW OL2 ...... 229 M8
  TOD OL14 ...... 141 H7
  WBY LS22 ...... 30 A5
Mark St BSLY S70 ...... 261 C5
  HUD HD1 ...... 14 A8
  LVSG WF15 ...... 172 D2
  WBOW BD5 ...... 127 C3
  WHIT * OL12 ...... 206 D5
  WKFDE WF1 ...... 12 F6
Marland Rd KGHY BD21 ...... 3 M3
Marlbeck Cl HOLM/MEL HD9 ...... 236 B3
Marlborough Av HIPP HX3 ...... 168 C2
Marlborough Cft
  HEM/SK/SE WF9 ...... 247 H2
Marlborough Dr TAD LS24 ...... 71 K4
Marlborough Gdns
  DEWS WF13 ...... 173 K4
  LDSU LS2 ...... 6 E5
Marlborough Gra LDS LS1 ...... 6 C8
Marlborough Rd GIR BD8 ...... 4 B1
  HBR HX7 ...... 143 J3
  HUDN * HD2 ...... 192 D1
  SHPY BD18 ...... 82 C7
Marlborough Sq ILK LS29 ...... 38 F3
Marlborough St KGHY BD21 ...... 3 J5
  LDS LS1 ...... 6 C8
  OSS WF5 ...... 196 E1
  WKFDW/WTN WF2 ...... 12 B3
Marlborough Ter BSLY S70 ...... 261 G6
  DEWS * WF13 ...... 173 K4
  HBR HX7 ...... 143 J3
Marldon Rd HIPP HX3 ...... 147 J5
Marley Cl GIR BD8 ...... 104 A6
Marley Ct AIRE BD20 ...... 58 F7
Marley Gv BEE/HOL LS11 ...... 131 K3
Marley La CUL/QBY BD13 ...... 125 C3
Marley Pl BEE/HOL LS11 ...... 131 K3
Marley Rd KGHY BD21 ...... 58 B6
Marley St BEE/HOL LS11 ...... 131 K3
  BFDE BD3 ...... 5 J6
  KGHY BD21 ...... 2 F7
Marley Ter BEE/HOL LS11 ...... 131 K3
Marley Vw AIRE BD20 ...... 58 F7
  BEE/HOL LS11 ...... 131 K3
Marlfield Rd ROY/SHW OL2 ...... 229 H6
Marling Rd HUDW HD3 ...... 191 K3
Marlo Rd EARL WF12 ...... 174 C4
Marlott Rd SHPY BD18 ...... 82 F6
Marlow Cl HUDE HD5 ...... 193 H8
Marlowe Cl PDSY/CALV LS28 ...... 129 H1
Marlowe Ct GFTH/SHER LS25 ...... 113 H7
Marlow St KGHY BD21 ...... 3 M3
Marl Pit Hl PONT WF8 ...... 180 C8
Marlpit La PONT WF8 ...... 181 K8
Marmion Av GIR BD8 ...... 103 L7
Marne Av CLAY BD14 ...... 125 L3
Marne Crs IDLE BD10 ...... 83 K7
Marquis Av LM/WK BD12 ...... 149 K1
Marriner Rd KGHY BD21 ...... 3 G7
Marriner's Dr HTON BD9 ...... 104 D2
Marriott Gv WKFDW/WTN WF2 ...... 199 H6
Marsala Wk WMB/DAR S73 ...... 263 H8
Marsden Av BEE/HOL LS11 ...... 131 J4
Marsden Cl MILN OL16 ...... 228 J4
Marsden Ga GTL/HWG HX4 ...... 190 A6
Marsden La BEE/HOL LS11 ...... 131 J4
Marsden Mt BEE/HOL LS11 ...... 131 J4
Marsden St KBTN HD8 ...... 239 J6
Marsden Vw BEE/HOL LS11 ...... 131 J4
Marsett Wy SCFT LS14 ...... 89 K6
Marsh HOLM/MEL HD9 ...... 236 B2
  PDSY/CALV LS28 ...... 106 F7
Marshall Av HOR/CROF WF4 ...... 220 B3
  MSTN/BAR LS15 ...... 111 M4
Marshall Crs MOR LS27 ...... 152 D4
Marshall Dr HEM/SK/SE WF9 ...... 247 G3

Marshall Mill Ct KBTN HD8 ...... 239 M5
Marshall St BEE/HOL LS11 ...... 8 E4
  EARD/LOFT WF3 ...... 177 H1
  KGHY BD21 ...... 57 K5
  MILN OL16 ...... 206 E7
  MIRF WF14 ...... 194 C3
  MOR LS27 ...... 152 C2
  MSTN/BAR LS15 ...... 111 L4
  YEA LS19 ...... 62 D7
Marshall Ter MSTN/BAR LS15 ...... 111 L4
Marsham Gv HUDW * HD3 ...... 191 L7
Marsh Ct CUL/QBY BD13 ...... 106 E7
Marsh Cft KNOT WF11 ...... 159 L7
Marsh Delves La MAR/SLWT HD7 ...... 147 H8
Marsh Hall La HUDS HD4 ...... 237 H3
Marsh La BIRK/DRI BD11 ...... 150 C2
  COP/BISH YO23 ...... 73 J8
  GLE DN14 ...... 161 J7
  HBR HX7 ...... 142 C3
  HIPP HX3 ...... 147 H8
  HWTH BD22 ...... 100 E2
  KBTN HD8 ...... 237 L8
  KNOT WF11 ...... 160 B8
  OSM LS9 ...... 7 L9
  OSM LS9 ...... 9 K1
Marsh Platt La
  HOLM/MEL HD9 ...... 236 C2
Marsh Rd CAS WF10 ...... 179 J1
  HOLM/MEL HD9 ...... 254 F3
Marsh St CLECK BD19 ...... 150 A8
  HDGY LS6 ...... 6 D2
  RTHW LS26 ...... 155 C2
  WBOW BD5 ...... 126 F4
Marsh Ter PDSY/CALV LS28 ...... 106 E7
Marsh V HDGY LS6 ...... 6 D2
Marshway HFAX HX1 ...... 10 D4
Marsh Wy WKFDE WF1 ...... 12 F1
Marsland Av WKFDE WF1 ...... 13 H3
Marsland Ct CLECK BD19 ...... 149 M4
Marsland Pl BFDE BD3 ...... 105 M7
  WKFDE WF1 ...... 13 H2
Marsland St WKFDE WF1 ...... 13 H2
Marsland Ter WKFDE WF1 ...... 13 H2
Marston Av MOR LS27 ...... 152 C3
Marston Cl CUL/QBY BD13 ...... 125 H5
Marston Ct CAS WF10 ...... 157 J8
Marston Crs BSLYN/ROY S71 ...... 243 H8
Marston Mt OSM LS9 ...... 7 L6
Marston Rd RYKW YO26 ...... 32 F1
Marston Wk NORM WF6 ...... 178 A2
Marston Wy WBY LS22 ...... 29 L8
Marten Dr HUDS HD4 ...... 213 M7
Marten Gv WBOW BD5 ...... 126 E3
Marten Rd WBOW BD5 ...... 126 E3
Martha's Ter MILN OL16 ...... 206 E3
Martin Bank Wd HUDE HD5 ...... 15 L9
Martin Cl MOR LS27 ...... 152 E2
Martin Ct MSTN/BAR LS15 ...... 111 M6
Martindale Dr BRAM LS13 ...... 108 A5
Martindale Wk AWLS/ASK DN6 ...... 249 L6
Martin Frobisher Dr
  NORM WF6 ...... 178 B3
Martingale Dr EARD/LOFT WF3 ...... 153 L3
Martin Green La GTL/HWG HX4 ...... 168 C7
Martin Gv WKFDW/WTN WF2 ...... 199 G8
Martin's Rd BSLYN/ROY S71 ...... 262 A3
Martin St BRIG * HD6 ...... 170 D3
  BTLY WF17 ...... 151 C5
Martin Ter BULY LS4 ...... 108 E4
Martlett Dr WBOW BD5 ...... 127 H4
Marton Av HEM/SK/SE WF9 ...... 223 L8
Marton Ct BFDE BD3 ...... 105 M7
Marwood Rd WOR/ARM LS12 ...... 107 M7
Mary Ann Cl BSLYN/ROY S71 ...... 261 M4
Maryfield Av MSTN/BAR LS15 ...... 111 J4
Maryfield Cl MSTN/BAR LS15 ...... 111 J4
Maryfield Gdns
  MSTN/BAR LS15 ...... 111 J4
Maryfield Gn MSTN/BAR LS15 ...... 111 J4
Maryfield Ms MSTN/BAR LS15 ...... 111 J4
Maryfield V MSTN/BAR LS15 ...... 111 J4
Marygate WKFDE WF1 ...... 12 E2
Mary's Pl DOD/DAR S75 ...... 260 D4
Mary St AIRE BD20 ...... 35 C5
  BOW BD4 ...... 127 L1
  BRIG HD6 ...... 170 C2
  CUL/QBY BD13 ...... 102 A5
  CUL/QBY BD13 ...... 102 F8
  DOD/DAR S75 ...... 259 M2
  EARD/LOFT WF3 ...... 154 A6
  HBR HX7 ...... 100 E4
  LM/WK BD12 ...... 148 E2
  MILN OL16 ...... 206 F2
  PDSY/CALV LS28 ...... 107 G2
  SHPY BD18 ...... 82 B6
Maryville Av BRIG HD6 ...... 170 B1
Masefield Av HTON BD9 ...... 103 L3
Masefield St GSLY LS20 ...... 62 B6
Masham Gv WOR/ARM LS12 ...... 108 F7
Masham Pl HTON BD9 ...... 104 B4
Masham St WOR/ARM LS12 ...... 108 F7
Masonic St HFAX HX1 ...... 146 A8
Mason St HBR HX7 ...... 143 H3
  MILN * OL16 ...... 206 B7
Masons Wy BSLY S70 ...... 261 L8
Maspin Moor Rd
  GFTH/SHER LS25 ...... 139 J8
Massey Flds HWTH BD22 ...... 78 F6
Master La LUD/ILL HX2 ...... 168 E2
Matherville HNDN WF9 ...... 239 J5
Matlock Rd BSLYN/ROY S71 ...... 243 K8
Matrix Wy HEM/SK/SE WF9 ...... 10 C1
  HUDS HD4 ...... 213 M2
Matterdale Cl EARL WF12 ...... 174 A4
Matterdale Rd EARL WF12 ...... 174 A4
Matthew Cl AIRE BD20 ...... 58 A5
  COL BB8 ...... 74 A2
Matthew Gv HOLM/MEL HD9 ...... 234 E4
Matthew La AIRE BD20 ...... 34 E1

HOLM/MEL HD9 ...... 234 B8
  TOD OL14 ...... 142 A7
Matty Marsden La OSS WF5 ...... 197 G4
Maud Av BEE/HOL LS11 ...... 131 J4
Maude Av BAIL BD17 ...... 82 E4
Maude Crs RPDN/SBR HX6 ...... 167 G3
Maude St GTL/HWG HX4 ...... 168 F7
  HIPP HX3 ...... 146 C2
  LDSU LS2 ...... 9 J2
Maud La OT LS21 ...... 23 J2
Maud Pl BEE/HOL LS11 ...... 131 K3
Maudsley St BFDE BD3 ...... 5 K6
Maud St BFDE BD3 ...... 5 L7
  WHIT OL12 ...... 206 C4
Maufe Wy ILK LS29 ...... 38 D3
Maureen St OL14 ...... 206 C4
Maurice Av BRIG HD6 ...... 170 B2
Mavis Av BHP/TINH LS16 ...... 64 A8
  DEWS WF13 ...... 173 J8
Mavis Gv BHP/TINH LS16 ...... 86 A1
  MILN OL16 ...... 207 J8
Mavis La BHP/TINH LS16 ...... 64 A8
Mavis Rd DEWS WF13 ...... 173 H3
Mavis St BFDE BD3 ...... 5 J8
  DEWS WF13 ...... 173 J8
Mawcroft Cl YEA LS19 ...... 84 C1
Mawcroft Grange Dr YEA LS19 ...... 84 C1
Mawfield Rd DOD/DAR S75 ...... 260 B2
Mawson St SHPY BD18 ...... 82 B6
Maw St BOW BD4 ...... 127 H1
Maxwell Av DEWS WF13 ...... 173 L4
Maxwell Rd ILK LS29 ...... 38 F1
  WBSY BD6 ...... 126 B6
Maxwell St FEA/AMT WF7 ...... 201 L1
May Av CUL/QBY BD13 ...... 103 G8
Mayberry Dr DOD/DAR S75 ...... 259 H5
Maybury Pl HOR/CROF WF4 ...... 198 C6
May Bush Rd WKFDE WF1 ...... 13 K9
May Day Gn BSLY S70 ...... 261 C5
May Day Green Ar BSLY * S70 ...... 261 H5
Mayfair WBOW BD5 ...... 126 F2
Mayfair Av GTL/HWG HX4 ...... 190 B4
Mayfair Pl HEM/SK/SE WF9 ...... 223 M7
Mayfair Wy BOW BD4 ...... 127 M4
Mayfield BSLYN/ROY S71 ...... 261 K2
  STKB/PEN S36 ...... 271 K5
Mayfield Av BRIG HD6 ...... 148 D6
  HFAX HX1 ...... 10 C8
  HUDE HD5 ...... 193 H8
Mayfield Cl AIRE BD20 ...... 34 E8
  ILK LS29 ...... 38 F2
Mayfield Ct OSS WF5 ...... 197 G3
Mayfield Crs BSLY S70 ...... 261 G8
Mayfield Dr AIRE BD20 ...... 58 E6
  HFAX HX1 ...... 10 C8
Mayfield Gdns HFAX HX1 ...... 10 C8
  OSS WF5 ...... 174 E6
Mayfield Gv BAIL BD17 ...... 82 F3
  BRIG HD6 ...... 148 D6
  HFAX HX1 ...... 10 C8
  HUDE HD5 ...... 193 H8
  WIL/AL BD15 ...... 80 C8
Mayfield Mt HFAX * HX1 ...... 10 C8
Mayfield Pl LM/WK BD12 ...... 148 E3
  LM/WK BD12 ...... 148 E3
Mayfield Ri HOR/CROF WF4 ...... 222 C5
  LM/WK BD12 ...... 148 E3
Mayfield Rd HBR HX7 ...... 143 J2
  ILK LS29 ...... 38 F2
  KGHY BD21 ...... 2 E3
  MSTN/BAR LS15 ...... 111 K6
  MILN OL16 ...... 206 D5
Mayfield Ter South HFAX * HX1 ...... 10 C8
Mayfield Vw LM/WK BD12 ...... 148 E3
Mayfields Wy HEM/SK/SE WF9 ...... 246 D5
Mayfield Ter CLAY BD14 ...... 125 L2
  HFAX HX1 ...... 10 B5
  LM/WK BD12 ...... 148 F3
  MILN OL16 ...... 206 D5
Mayflower St MID LS10 ...... 132 C4
Maylea Dr OT LS21 ...... 40 F8
Mayman Cl BTLY WF17 ...... 173 K1
Mayman La BTLY WF17 ...... 173 K1
Maynes Cl EARL WF12 ...... 195 M4
Mayo Av WBOW BD5 ...... 126 F4
Mayo Cl RHAY LS8 ...... 88 B8
Mayo Crs WBOW BD5 ...... 127 G5
Mayo Dr WBOW BD5 ...... 127 G5
Mayo Gv WBOW BD5 ...... 127 G5
Mayo Rd WBOW BD5 ...... 127 G5
Mayors Wk CAS WF10 ...... 159 G7
  PONT WF8 ...... 180 F7
Mayor's Walk Av PONT WF8 ...... 180 F7
Mayors Walk Cl PONT WF8 ...... 180 F7
Maypole Rd HUDN HD2 ...... 192 E3
Mayster Gv BRIG HD6 ...... 170 A7
Mayster Rd BRIG HD6 ...... 170 A7
May St CLECK BD19 ...... 149 M6
  HUDS HD4 ...... 213 M2
  HWTH BD22 ...... 78 F8
  KGHY BD21 ...... 3 H2
May Ter BSLY S70 ...... 261 C8
  OSM LS9 ...... 110 B8
Maythorne Av BTLY WF17 ...... 173 J3
Maythorne Cl DOD/DAR S75 ...... 242 E6
Maythorne Crs CLAY BD14 ...... 125 M2
Maythorne Dr CLAY BD14 ...... 126 A2
May Tree Cl CLAY BD14 ...... 125 M1
Mayville Av AIRE BD20 ...... 58 E6
  HDGY LS6 ...... 109 G3
Mayville Pl HDGY LS6 ...... 109 G3
Mayville Rd HDGY LS6 ...... 109 G3
Mayville St HDGY LS6 ...... 108 F3
Mayville Ter HDGY LS6 ...... 109 G3
Mazebrook Av CLECK BD19 ...... 150 A4
Mazebrook Crs CLECK BD19 ...... 150 A4
McBride Wy WBY LS22 ...... 48 B1
McLaren Av HEM/SK/SE WF9 ...... 225 M6
McLaren Flds BRAM LS13 ...... 107 M4
McLintock Wy BSLY S70 ...... 260 F5
McMahon Dr CUL/QBY BD13 ...... 125 L4
McMillan Gdns WBSY BD6 ...... 126 F7
McNaught St MILN OL16 ...... 206 D8
The Meade GFTH/SHER LS25 ...... 113 H7
Mead Cl MSTN/BAR * LS15 ...... 112 A8
Mead Gv MSTN/BAR LS15 ...... 112 A8

Meadow Av CUD/GR S72 ...... 262 F2
Meadow Bank DEWS WF13 ...... 173 H6
  WKFDE WF1 ...... 202 C5
  HOLM/MEL HD9 ...... 236 B8
  HOR/CROF WF4 ...... 222 C5
Meadowbank Av WIL/AL BD15 ...... 103 K5
Meadow Bank Crs MIRF WF14 ...... 194 A3
Meadow Bottom Rd TOD OL14 ...... 141 K8
Meadow Brook Cl NORM WF6 ...... 178 E5
Meadow Cl AIRE BD20 ...... 34 C4
  AL/HA/HU LS17 ...... 67 M1
  BGLY BD16 ...... 80 D5
  BSPA/BRAM LS23 ...... 48 E6
  BTLY WF17 ...... 151 J5
  HIPP HX3 ...... 125 M8
  LVSG WF15 ...... 172 B5
  WKFDE WF1 ...... 176 F1
Meadow Ct BRIG HD6 ...... 171 C4
  CAS WF10 ...... 158 F8
  HEM/SK/SE WF9 ...... 247 K3
  OSS WF5 ...... 174 E7
  WIL/AL BD15 ...... 103 J2
Meadow Crs BSLYN/ROY S71 ...... 243 M3
  CUD/GR S72 ...... 245 H7
  HIPP HX3 ...... 146 A4
Meadow Cft AIRE BD20 ...... 34 B3
  AL/HA/HU LS17 ...... 67 L1
  BEE/HOL LS11 ...... 8 E5
  CUD/GR S72 ...... 244 E3
  GTL/HWG HX4 ...... 189 K2
  HEM/SK/SE WF9 ...... 245 M1
  HUDN HD2 ...... 193 H1
  HWTH BD22 ...... 57 C8
  WKFDE WF1 ...... 176 E1
Meadowcroft HOLM/MEL HD9 ...... 236 A2
  ILK LS29 ...... 61 H3
Meadow Croft Cl IDLE BD10 ...... 83 H6
Meadowcroft Cl WKFDE WF1 ...... 176 F1
Meadowcroft Crs CAS WF10 ...... 158 C6
Meadowcroft La
  RPDN/SBR HX6 ...... 189 G1
Meadowcroft Ms CAS WF10 ...... 158 C6
  OSM * LS9 ...... 9 M2
Meadowcroft Ri BOW BD4 ...... 127 L6
Meadowcroft Rd WKFDE WF1 ...... 176 F1
Meadow Dr BSLYN/ROY S71 ...... 261 M2
  HIPP HX3 ...... 146 A4
  LVSG WF15 ...... 172 B5
Meadow End BHP/TINH LS16 ...... 64 A4
Meadowfield MILN OL16 ...... 228 D3
Meadowfield Cl
  HEM/SK/SE * WF9 ...... 223 J8
Meadowfield Ri
  EARD/LOFT WF3 ...... 155 K8
Meadowfields Cl
  HOR/CROF WF4 ...... 200 C6
Meadowfields Dr
  HOR/CROF WF4 ...... 200 C6
Meadow Garth BHP/TINH LS16 ...... 64 B4
  TAD LS24 ...... 72 A1
  WKFDE WF1 ...... 176 E1
Meadowgate OSS WF5 ...... 174 E7
Meadowgate Cft
  EARD/LOFT WF3 ...... 154 D4
Meadowgate Dr
  EARD/LOFT WF3 ...... 154 D5
Meadowgate V
  EARD/LOFT WF3 ...... 154 D5
Meadow Gn MAR/SLWT HD7 ...... 212 F6
Meadowhurst Gdns
  PDSY/CALV LS28 ...... 106 F7
Meadowland Ri CUD/GR S72 ...... 262 E1
Meadowlands CLECK BD19 ...... 149 C5
Meadow La AIRE BD20 ...... 34 B3
  BEE/HOL LS11 ...... 9 C4
  DEWS WF13 ...... 173 L5
  DOD/DAR S75 ...... 242 A4
  HIPP HX3 ...... 146 A4
  LVSG WF15 ...... 172 B5
  MAR/SLWT HD7 ...... 212 B5
  ROY/SHW OL2 ...... 229 J8
  WKFDW/WTN WF2 ...... 176 B4
Meadow Lea PDSY/CALV LS28 ...... 34 E8
Meadow Pk HUDE HD5 ...... 193 K4
Meadow Park Crs
  PDSY/CALV LS28 ...... 106 D4
Meadow Park Dr
  PDSY/CALV LS28 ...... 106 D4
Meadow Ri HEM/SK/SE WF9 ...... 223 L8
  ROY/SHW OL2 ...... 229 J5
  SKP/WHF BD23 ...... 16 D1
Meadow Rd BEE/HOL LS11 ...... 8 F5
  BSLYN/ROY S71 ...... 243 M3
  CAS WF10 ...... 179 K1
  GFTH/SHER LS25 ...... 113 J7
  IDLE BD10 ...... 84 A6
The Meadows BHP/TINH LS16 ...... 86 A1
  GFTH/SHER LS25 ...... 138 C6
  GFTH/SHER LS25 ...... 138 A3
  KBTN HD8 ...... 257 H1
  WBSY BD6 ...... 126 E5
Meadowside MILN OL16 ...... 229 L2
Meadows Morvern
  HEM/SK/SE WF9 ...... 224 B7
Meadow St BSLYN/ROY S71 ...... 261 H4
  HUD HD1 ...... 191 M7
Meadow V HOR/CROF WF4 ...... 218 F5
  WKFDE WF1 ...... 176 E1
Meadow Va AL/HA/HU LS17 ...... 87 J1
Meadow Vw GFTH/SHER LS25 ...... 116 B6
  HDGY LS6 ...... 109 G3
  HWTH BD22 ...... 78 F4
  KBTN HD8 ...... 239 K5
  LM/WK BD12 ...... 148 E5
  MSTN/BAR LS15 ...... 91 G6
  OSS WF5 ...... 174 E7
  STKB/PEN S36 ...... 258 B8
Meadow Wk CHAL LS7 ...... 88 A8
  HEM/SK/SE WF9 ...... 224 F3
  HIPP HX3 ...... 146 A4
  LIT * WF15 ...... 207 H1
Meadow Wy AL/HA/HU LS17 ...... 87 J1
  CAS WF10 ...... 158 C6
  EARD/LOFT WF3 ...... 152 F7
  FEA/AMT WF7 ...... 202 C5
  TAD LS24 ...... 72 A2

Mead Rd MSTN/BAR LS15 ....112 A8
Meadstead Dr BSLYN/ROY S71 .243 K5
Mead St HUDN HD2 ....14 F1
Mead Vw BOW * BD4 ....128 A3
Mead Wy KBTN HD8 ....216 A7
  MSTN/BAR LS15 ....112 A8
Meadway FEA/AMT WF7 ....178 E2
  WBSY BD6 ....126 B8
Meagill Ri OT LS21 ....40 F4
Meal Hill La HOLM/MEL HD9 .255 H4
  MAR/SLWT HD7 ....212 A3
Meal Hill Rd HOLM/MEL HD9 .253 H5
Mean La HOLM/MEL HD9 ....235 G8
  HWTH BD22 ....77 M6
Meanwood Cl CHAL LS7 ....6 F1
Meanwood Gv HDGY LS6 ....87 G5
Meanwood Gv CHAL LS7 ....7 J5
  CHAL LS7 ....109 J1
Meanwood Mt CHAL LS7 ....7 H5
Meanwood Valley Dr CHAL LS7 .87 H8
Meanwood Valley Gn CHAL LS7 .87 H8
Meanwood Valley Gv CHAL LS7 .87 H8
Meanwood Valley Mt CHAL LS7 .87 H8
Mearclough Rd
  RPDN/SBR HX6 ....167 M2
Mears Cl STKB/PEN S36 ....271 G3
Medeway PDSY/CALV LS28 ....106 E4
Medhurst Av GFTH/SHER LS25..135 K4
Medina Wy DOD/DAR S75 ....260 A1
Medley La HIPP HX3 ....147 H2
Medley St CAS WF10 ....158 A7
  WHIT OL12 ....206 B5
Medlock Rd HOR/CROF WF4 .197 J5
Medway CUL/QBY BD13 ....125 H6
  HUDE * HD5 ....193 K4
Medway Av GFTH/SHER LS25....135 J1
Medway Cl DOD/DAR S75 ....260 B1
Medway Rd ROY/SHW OL2 ....229 J6
Meeting House La
  MAR/SLWT HD7 ....212 C2
Meggison Gv WBOW BD5 ....126 E2
Meg La HUDW HD3 ....213 K1
Megnaway WBOW BD5 ....127 G2
Melba Rd GTHN BD7 ....126 D3
Melbourne Av
  WKFDW/WTN WF2 ....176 B3
Melbourne Cl ROCH OL11 ....228 C4
Melbourne Gv BFDE BD3 ....106 A4
  BRAM LS13 ....107 L4
Melbourne Ms
  WKFDW/WTN WF2 ....176 A2
Melbourne Pl WBOW BD5 ....4 D9
Melbourne Rd ROCH OL11 ....228 C4
  TOD OL14 ....163 J5
Melbourne St HBR HX7 ....143 H3
  HIPP HX3 ....10 D1
  LDSU LS2 ....7 J7
  LVSG WF15 ....172 D3
  MOR LS27 ....152 D2
  PDSY/CALV LS28 ....106 F4
  SHPY BD18 ....82 C6
Melbourne Ter WBOW BD5 ....4 E9
Melcombe Wk BOW BD4 ....128 A2
Melford Cl DOD/DAR S75 ....242 D5
Melford St BOW BD4 ....127 L4
Mellor Brook MAR/SLWT HD7 .212 B2
Mellor La HOLM/MEL HD9 ....253 K2
Mellor Mill La GTL/HWG HX4 .190 D2
Mellor St BRIG HD6 ....170 D4
  HFAX HX1 ....168 C1
Mellwood La HEM/SK/SE WF9 .247 G3
Melrose Whit * OL12 ....206 A6
Melrose Av LIT OL15 ....185 J7
Melrose Cl HUDE HD5 ....193 H8
Melrose Dr ILK LS29 ....40 A4
Melrose Gv HORS LS18 ....86 A6
Melrose Pl HORS LS18 ....85 M6
  PDSY/CALV LS28 ....106 F4
Melrose St GTHN BD7 ....126 C2
  HIPP HX3 ....10 D1
Melrose Ter ELL * HX5 ....169 H8
Melrose Wk HORS LS18 ....85 M6
Melrose Wy BSLYN/ROY S71 .261 M4
Meltham House La
  HOLM/MEL HD9 ....255 H2
Meltham Mills Rd
  HOLM/MEL HD9 ....235 H4
Meltham Rd HOLM/MEL HD9 .235 L3
  HUDS HD4 ....213 M8
  MAR/SLWT HD7 ....233 K2
Melton Av EARD/LOFT WF3 ....154 B2
Melton Cl EARD/LOFT WF3 ....154 B1
  HEM/SK/SE WF9 ....247 J1
Melton Garth EARD/LOFT WF3 .154 B2
Melton Rd HOR/CROF WF4 ....220 C2
Melton St BTLY WF17 ....151 K8
Melton Ter IDLE BD10 ....106 A1
Melton Wy LVSG WF15 ....172 B5
Melville Cl HDGY LS6 ....6 E2
Melville Gdns HDGY LS6 ....6 F1
Melville La ILK LS29 ....39 G2
Melville Pl HDGY LS6 ....6 F1
Melville Rd HDGY LS6 ....6 E1
Melville St GTHN BD7 ....4 A6
Melvinia Crs DOD/DAR S75 ....260 F2
Memorial Cottages
  WOR/ARM * LS12 ....129 M3
Memorial Dr HDGY LS6 ....87 H7
Mendip Av HUDW HD3 ....191 J5
Mendip Cl DOD/DAR S75 ....260 D4
  GFTH/SHER LS25 ....135 H1
Mendip Dr MILN OL16 ....207 J8
Mendip Rd EARL WF12 ....174 B5
Mendips Cl ROY/SHW OL2 ....229 H6
Mendip Wy LM/WK BD12 ....126 D8
Menin Dr BAIL BD17 ....82 D1
Menston Old La ILK LS29 ....40 B8
Menston Dr MILN OL16 ....206 F7
Mentmore Rd MILN OL16 ....206 F7
Mercer Cl HUDS HD4 ....213 L7
Merchants Ct BOW BD4 ....127 J1
Merchants Quay OSM * LS9 ....9 K2
Mercia Wy MSTN/BAR LS15 ....112 A3
Mercury Rw OT LS21 ....41 J7
Merefield Av ROCH OL11 ....228 A1
Merefield St ROCH OL11 ....228 A1
Merefield Ter ROCH * OL11 ......228 A1

Merefield Wy CAS WF10 ....180 A1
Mere La ROCH OL11 ....228 B1
Mere St ROCH OL11 ....206 B8
Merewood Rd CAS WF10 ....157 H7
Meriden Av GFTH/SHER LS25..135 H1
Merinall Cl MILN OL16 ....206 E7
Merlin Cl AWLS/ASK DN6 ....249 K8
  LIT OL15 ....207 J4
  MOR LS27 ....152 E3
Merlin Ct BTLY WF17 ....151 H6
  HUDS HD4 ....214 A7
  KGHY * BD21 ....2 F8
Merlin Gv GIR BD8 ....103 L7
Merlin Rd MILN OL16 ....207 H8
Merlinwood Dr BAIL BD17 ....82 F2
Merlyn-rees Av MOR LS27 ....152 C2
Merrion Pl LDS LS1 ....7 H8
Merrion St LDSU LS2 ....7 G8
Merrivale Rd WIL/AL BD15 ....103 J6
Merrybank La AL/HA/HU LS17 ....43 K1
Merrybents St TOD OL14 ....163 M1
Merrydale Rd BOW BD4 ....127 J8
Merryman Hall MILN * OL16....206 D4
Mersey St GIR BD8 ....104 D5
Merton Av PDSY/CALV LS28 ....106 F4
Merton Cl GFTH/SHER LS25 ....135 L4
Merton Dr GFTH/SHER LS25 ....106 E4
Merton Fold WBOW BD5 ....127 G2
Merton Gdns PDSY/CALV LS28..106 E4
Merton Rd GTHN BD7 ....4 C9
Merton St HUD HD1 ....14 D8
Merville Av BAIL BD17 ....82 E1
Metcalfe St BOW BD4 ....127 K2
Methley Br RTHW LS26 ....157 H6
Methley Dr CHAL LS7 ....87 M8
Methley Gv CHAL LS7 ....87 L8
Methley La CHAL LS7 ....87 M8
  RTHW LS26 ....156 A2
Methley Mt CHAL LS7 ....87 M8
Methley Pl CHAL LS7 ....87 L8
Methley Rd CAS WF10 ....157 J6
Methley St CUD/GR S72 ....244 D6
Methley Ter CHAL LS7 ....87 L8
Methley Vw CHAL LS7 ....87 L8
Methuen Ov LM/WK BD12 ....148 E5
The Mews NORM WF6 ....178 D3
Mews Ct FEA/AMT WF7 ....201 M1
Mexborough Av CHAL LS7 ....7 J1
Mexborough Dr CHAL LS7 ....7 J1
Mexborough Gv CHAL LS7 ....7 J1
Mexborough Pl CHAL LS7 ....7 J2
Mexborough Rd CHAL LS7 ....7 J1
  SHPY BD18 ....104 F1
Mexborough St CHAL LS7 ....7 J1
Meynell Ap BEE/HOL LS11 ....8 C6
Meynell Av RTHW LS26 ....155 G1
Meynell Ct MSTN/BAR LS15 ....111 M7
Meynell Hts BEE/HOL LS11 ....8 C5
Meynell Mt RTHW LS26 ....155 H1
Meynell Rd MSTN/BAR LS15 ....111 M8
Meynell Sq BEE/HOL LS11 ....8 C5
Meynell Wk BEE/HOL LS11 ....8 C6
Meyrick Av WBY LS22 ....30 C8
Meyrick Dr DOD/DAR S75 ....241 M7
Miall St HFAX HX1 ....10 C4
  ROCH OL11 ....206 C8
Michael Av EARD/LOFT WF3....177 G1
Michael Rd BSLYN/ROY S71 ....262 A4
Michael's Est CUD/GR S72 ....245 J7
Mickelden Wy DOD/DAR S75 ..260 C5
Mickle Ct CAS WF10 ....157 L7
Mickledore Cl GTHN * BD7 ....126 A3
Mickledore Rdg GTHN BD7 ....126 A3
Micklefield Ct YEA LS19 ....84 C1
Micklefield La YEA LS19 ....84 C2
Micklefield Ms YEA * LS19 ....84 C2
Micklefield Rd YEA LS19 ....84 D2
Micklegate PONT WF8 ....180 F5
Micklemoss Dr CUL/QBY BD13 ..124 E4
Micklethwaite Dr
  CUL/QBY BD13 ....125 G6
Micklethwaite La BGLY BD16....59 G8
Micklethwaite Rd
  WHIT * OL12 ....220 B3
Micklethwaite Vw WBY LS22......48 A3
Micklethwaite Rd RTHW LS26..156 B3
Mickley St WOR/ARM LS12 ....108 E7
Middlebrook Crs GIR BD8 ....103 M8
Middlebrook Dr GIR BD8 ....103 M7
Middlebrook Hl GIR BD8 ....103 M7
Middlebrook Ri GIR BD8 ....103 M7
Middlebrook Vw GIR BD8 ....104 A7
Middlebrook Wk GIR BD8 ....104 A7
Middlebrook Wy GIR BD8 ....103 M8
Middleburn Cl BSLY S70 ....261 J7
Middlecliffe Dr STKB/PEN S36..268 F1
Middlecliff La CUD/GR S72 ....263 L6
Middlecroft Cl RTHW LS26 ....132 B6
Middlecroft Rd RTHW LS26 ....132 B6
Middle Cross St
  WOR/ARM LS12 ....108 C7
Middle Dean St GTL/HWG HX4..168 E7
Middle Field La
  HOR/CROF WF4 ....220 A8
Middlefield La PONT WF8 ....226 E1
Middle Field Rd DOD/DAR S75 ..259 M6
Middlegate BTLY WF17 ....151 G5
Middlegate Ct BOW BD4 ....127 K6
Middle Hall Cl LVSG WF15 ....172 B2
Middleham Ct BOW * BD4 ....128 A3
Middle La CLAY BD14 ....125 L1
  HOR/CROF WF4 ....200 D7
  KNOT WF11 ....182 C3
  WBY LS22 ....47 L4
Middlemoor SCFT LS14 ....89 K6
Middle Oxford St CAS WF10....157 L7
Middle Rd DEWS WF13 ....173 J4
  EARL WF12 ....174 A7
  OSM LS9 ....132 F3
Middlesex St BSLY S70 ....261 H7
Middle St RPDN/SBR HX6 ....167 G4
Middlethorne Cl AL/HA/HU LS17..88 D2
Middlethorne Ct
  AL/HA/HU LS17 ....88 C1

Middlethorne Ms
  AL/HA/HU LS17 ....88 D1
Middlethorne Ri AL/HA/HU LS17..88 C2
Middleton Av ILK LS29 ....38 D1
  OSM LS9 ....110 B5
Middleton Cl MOR LS27 ....152 D2
Middleton Gv BEE/HOL LS11 ..131 K4
  MOR * LS27 ....152 D2
Middleton La EARD/LOFT WF3..153 M4
Middleton Park Av MID LS10 ..153 L2
Middleton Park Crs MID LS10 ..153 L2
Middleton Park Gn MID LS10 ..153 L2
Middleton Park Gv MID LS10 ..153 K1
Middleton Park Mt MID LS10 ..153 L2
Middleton Park Pl MID * LS10 ..153 L2
Middleton Park Rd MID LS10 ..153 L1
Middleton Park Ter MID LS10 ..153 K2
Middleton Rd ILK LS29 ....38 C2
  MID LS10 ....132 A5
  MOR LS27 ....152 D2
Middleton St GIR BD8 ....104 D5
Middleton Ter MOR LS27 ....152 E2
Middleton Wy KNOT WF11 ....182 B2
Middleway AIRE BD20 ....36 B5
Middle Wood La WHIT OL12 ..185 G8
Midge Hall Cl ILK LS29 ....40 A5
Midgeham Gv HBR HX7 ....121 J8
Midgehole Rd HBR HX7 ....121 J6
Midgeley Rd BAIL BD17 ....82 C5
Midgley Gdns HDGY LS6 ....6 D2
Midgley Pl HDGY LS6 ....6 E2
Midgley Ri PONT WF8 ....180 F3
Midgley Rd HBR HX7 ....144 C5
  ILK LS29 ....40 A5
Midgley St COL BD8 ....74 A2
Midgley Ter HDGY LS6 ....6 E2
Midhope Wy DOD/DAR S75 ....260 C5
Midhurst Gv DOD/DAR S75 ....260 A1
Midhurst St ROCH OL11 ....228 B1
Midland Cl MID LS10 ....132 B3
Midland Garth MID LS10 ....9 M9
Midland Hl BGLY BD16 ....81 H3
Midland Pas HDGY LS6 ....6 B2
Midland Rd BAIL BD17 ....82 F4
  BSLYN/ROY S71 ....243 M2
  GIR BD8 ....104 F4
  HDGY LS6 ....6 B2
  HTON BD9 ....104 E1
  MID LS10 ....132 A3
  PONT WF8 ....181 G5
Midland Ter ECHL BD2 ....105 G4
  HTON BD9 ....104 E1
  KGHY * BD21 ....3 G2
Mid Point BFDE BD3 ....106 B6
Midway HUDS HD4 ....213 J8
Midway Av BGLY BD16 ....81 J7
Milan Rd RHAY LS8 ....110 B3
Milan St RHAY LS8 ....110 C3
Milbury Dr LIT OL15 ....207 J4
Milden Pl BSLY S70 ....261 J7
Mildred Sylvester Wy
  NORM WF6 ....179 G4
Mile Cross Gdns HFAX HX1 ....146 A8
Mile Cross Pl HFAX HX1 ....146 A8
Mile Cross Rd HFAX HX1 ....146 A8
Mile Cross Ter HFAX HX1 ....146 A8
Mile End HOLM/MEL HD9 ....234 F5
Milefield La CUD/GR S72 ....245 G7
Milefield Vw CUD/GR S72 ....245 H7
Miles Garth AL/HA/HU LS17 ......47 H8
Miles Hill Av CHAL LS7 ....87 K8
Miles Hill Crs BOW BD4 ....127 L5
  CHAL LS7 ....87 K8
Miles Hill Dr BOW BD4 ....127 L5
  CHAL LS7 ....87 K8
Miles Hill Mt CHAL LS7 ....87 J8
Miles Hill Pl CHAL LS7 ....87 K8
Miles Hill Rd CHAL LS7 ....87 K8
Miles Hill St CHAL LS7 ....87 K8
Miles Hill Ter CHAL LS7 ....87 K8
Miles Hill Vw CHAL LS7 ....87 K8
Mileswood Cl CUD/GR S72 ....263 M3
Mile Thorn St HFAX HX1 ....10 B6
Milford Crs LIT OL15 ....185 K8
Milford Gv CLECK BD19 ....150 C3
Milford Pl BULY LS4 ....108 F5
  HTON BD9 ....104 C3
Milford Rd GFTH/SHER LS25 ..138 B1
Milford St HUD HD1 ....14 F9
  WHIT OL12 ....206 B5
Milgate St BSLYN/ROY S71 ....243 M2
Milkstone Pl ROCH * OL11 ....206 B8
Milkstone Rd ROCH OL11 ....206 B8
Milk St ROCH OL11 ....206 B8
Millars Wk HEM/SK/SE WF9 ..246 C5
Mill Av HUDE HD5 ....193 J7
Millbank PDSY/CALV LS28 ....107 H8
Mill Bank Cl RPDN/SBR HX6 ..166 F7
Millbank Ct PDSY/CALV LS28 ..129 H1
Mill Bank Rd HOLM/MEL HD9 ..235 G5
  RPDN/SBR HX6 ....166 E7
Mill Banks AIRE BD20 ....36 A6
Millbeck Ap MOR LS27 ....152 E2
Millbeck Cl GIR BD8 ....103 L8
Millbeck Dr BGLY BD16 ....80 C5
Millbeck Gn WBY LS22 ....47 K6
Millbrae Gdns ROY/SHW OL2 ..229 H7
Mill Br SKP/WHF BD23 ....16 B2
Millbrook Cl ROY/SHW OL2....229 M8
Millbrook Gdns DEWS WF13 ..173 J4
Mill Carr Hill Rd BOW BD4 ....127 K8
Mill Cl FEA/AMT WF7 ....202 C6
  GFTH/SHER LS25 ....138 D7
  HEM/SK/SE WF9 ....246 C4
  HOLM/MEL HD9 ....234 F4
  PBR HC3 ....28 E3
Mill Ct HWTH BD22 ....100 E4
Mill Cft HWTH BD22 ....54 E3
  MOR LS27 ....129 M7

  ROY/SHW OL2 ....229 L8
Millcroft EARD/LOFT WF3 ....155 G8
  OT LS21 ....42 F7
Millcroft Cl EARD/LOFT WF3....154 F8
Millcroft La UPML OL3 ....231 H8
Millcroft Ri EARD/LOFT WF3 ..155 G8
Mill Dam BSPA/BRAM LS23 ....70 A1
Mill Dam La PONT WF8 ....181 G4
Millennium Ct PDSY/CALV * LS28..107 H6
Millennium Rd AIRE BD20 ....16 C6
Millennium Sq LDS LS1 ....6 F7
Millennium Wy BEE/HOL LS11 ..131 K5
Miller Av WKFDW/WTN WF2 ..198 F4
Miller Ct WKFDW/WTN WF2 ..220 D3
Miller Garth FEA/AMT WF7 ....224 C1
Millergate BFD BD1 ....4 E6
Miller Hl KBTN HD8 ....257 J1
Miller Hill Bank HD8 ....257 J1
Miller Meadow Cl
  ROY/SHW OL2 ....229 L6
Millers Ct LVSG WF15 ....172 D4
Millers Cft BTLY WF17 ....151 K5
Millers Dr MOR LS27 ....130 B8
Millersdale Cl BOW BD4 ....127 J7
Millgarth Ct WBY LS22 ....47 K6
Millgarth St LDSU LS2 ....7 J9
Millgate ELL HX5 ....169 H7
  FEA/AMT WF7 ....224 C1
  HUD HD1 ....14 A9
  HUDS HD4 ....215 K4
Mill Ga MILN OL16 ....206 D4
Mill Grath PONT WF8 ....180 E7
Mill Gn BEE/HOL LS11 ....8 A4
Mill Green Cl SCFT LS14 ....111 L1
Mill Green Gdns SCFT LS14 ....111 L1
Mill Green Garth SCFT * LS14 ..111 L1
Mill Green Pl SCFT LS14 ....111 L2
Mill Green Rd SCFT LS14 ....111 L1
Mill Green Vw SCFT LS14 ....111 K1
Mill Gv BRIG HD6 ....170 D4
Millhaven Ms GIR BD8 ....104 E4
Mill Hey HWTH BD22 ....78 F7
Mill Hl FEA/AMT WF7 ....202 C6
  HWTH BD22 ....78 D7
  LDS LS1 ....9 G1
  NORM WF6 ....178 C5
  PDSY/CALV LS28 ....129 G1
  RTHW LS26 ....155 G1
Mill Hill Av PONT WF8 ....180 D2
Mill Hill Cl PONT WF8 ....203 M1
Mill Hill Gn RTHW * LS26 ....155 G1
Mill Hill La BRIG HD6 ....170 B2
  BRIG HD6 ....171 H5
  PONT WF8 ....180 D7
Mill Hill Rd PONT WF8 ....180 D4
Mill Hill Sq RTHW LS26 ....155 G1
Mill Hill Top BGLY BD16 ....80 D6
Mill House Cl WHIT OL12 ....206 E5
Mill House La RPDN/SBR HX6 ..167 H4
Millhouse St STKB/PEN S36 ....269 M3
Mill House Ri BOW * BD4 ....127 K5
Milligan Av ECHL * BD2 ....105 H1
Milligan Ct BGLY BD16 ....80 C5
Milligans Pl AIRE * BD20 ....34 C7
Mill La AIRE BD20 ....16 E8
  AIRE BD20 ....56 E1
  AL/HA/HU LS17 ....67 M3
  AWLS/ASK DN6 ....249 K8
  AWLS/ASK DN6 ....249 H4
  BIRK/DRI BD11 ....128 C8
  BOW BD4 ....129 J3
  BRAM LS13 ....107 J3
  BRIG HD6 ....170 D4
  BSPA/BRAM LS23 ....49 G6
  BTLY WF17 ....151 K4
  BTLY WF17 ....173 M2
  CAS WF10 ....157 M5
  CAS WF10 ....178 F2
  CLECK BD19 ....149 M3
  COP/BISH YO23 ....33 M1
  CUL/QBY BD13 ....124 C4
  DOD/DAR S75 ....242 A5
  EARD/LOFT WF3 ....153 M6
  EARL WF12 ....174 C7
  FEA/AMT WF7 ....178 E8
  FEA/AMT WF7 ....224 C1
  GFTH/SHER LS25 ....138 D7
  GSLY LS20 ....60 F6
  GTL/HWG HX4 ....190 E2
  HEM/SK/SE WF9 ....246 D5
  HEM/SK/SE WF9 ....247 K2
  HIPP HX3 ....126 A8
  HIPP HX3 ....146 D4
  HOR/CROF WF4 ....217 M3
  HOR/CROF WF4 ....221 G7
  HOR/CROF WF4 ....222 D5
  HUDE HD5 ....193 K1
  HWTH BD22 ....78 D4
  HWTH BD22 ....100 E3
  LUD/ILL HX2 ....123 L7
  MOR LS27 ....129 M7
  OT LS21 ....41 J6
  OT LS21 ....42 F7
  PBR HC3 ....26 F2
  PBR HC3 ....28 E3
  PONT WF8 ....181 H5
  RTHW LS26 ....156 F3
  SKP/WHF BD23 ....16 B3
  STKB/PEN S36 ....256 F6
  STKB/PEN S36 ....270 B3
  TAD LS24 ....71 L6
  TAD LS24 ....71 M2
  TAD LS24 ....95 M4
  WBOW BD5 ....127 G1
  WBY LS22 ....46 A3
Millmoor Cl HTON BD9 ....103 M4
Mill Moor Rd HOLM/MEL HD9 ..234 D6

Millom Cl MILN OL16 ....206 F7
Mill Pk MIRF WF14 ....194 B4
Mill Pit La RTHW LS26 ....132 F7
Mill Pond Cl HDGY LS6 ....87 G8
Mill Pond Gv HDGY LS6 ....87 G8
Mill Pond La HDGY LS6 ....87 G8
Mill Pond Sq HDGY LS6 ....87 G7
Mill Race Fold HOLM/MEL HD9..236 E6
Mill Rd DEWS WF13 ....173 L4
Mill Rw AIRE BD20 ....35 H8
Mill Royd St BRIG HD6 ....170 D4
Millshaw BEE/HOL LS11 ....130 F5
Millshaw La HOLM/MEL HD9 ..255 J4
Millshaw Mt BEE/HOL LS11 ....131 G6
Millshaw Park Av MOR LS27 ..130 F6
Millshaw Park Cl
  BEE/HOL LS11 ....130 F5
Millshaw Park La
  BEE/HOL LS11 ....130 F5
Millshaw Park Wy
  BEE/HOL LS11 ....130 F5
Millshaw Rd BEE/HOL LS11 ....131 G2
Millside CUD/GR S72 ....244 E3
Millside Wk CUD/GR S72 ....244 E3
  MOR LS27 ....152 E2
Millstone Cl FEA/AMT WF7 ....224 C1
Millstone Ri LVSG WF15 ....172 D4
Millstones STKB/PEN S36 ....271 L3
Mill St AIRE BD20 ....56 A1
  BFD 5 G4
  BTLY WF17 ....151 G6
  CAS WF10 ....157 K7
  CUL/QBY BD13 ....79 M8
  HEM/SK/SE WF9 ....246 C4
  HIPP HX3 ....168 C5
  HUDS HD4 ....214 A2
  MOR LS27 ....152 C3
  OSM LS9 ....9 L1
  WBSY BD6 ....126 C5
Mill St East EARL WF12 ....173 M8
Mill St West EARL WF12 ....173 L7
Mill Vw HEM/SK/SE WF9 ....223 L8
  ILK LS29 ....40 A4
  KNOT WF11 ....181 K2
Millward St HOR/CROF WF4 ..222 C5
Millwater Av EARL WF12 ....195 K1
Millwood La TOD OL14 ....163 L1
Millwright St LDSU LS2 ....7 K7
Milne Ct MSTN/BAR LS15 ....111 M8
Milner Av STKB/PEN S36 ....270 D3
Milner Bank OT LS21 ....40 F8
Milner Cl GTL/HWG HX4 ....168 E7
Milner Gdns OSM * LS9 ....110 B8
Milner Ing LM/WK BD12 ....148 E2
Milner La EARD/LOFT WF3 ....154 C3
  GTL/HWG HX4 ....168 E7
  SCFT LS14 ....68 B6
  TAD LS24 ....93 J7
Milner Rd BAIL BD17 ....82 D5
Milner's La PONT WF8 ....203 M2
Milner's Rd YEA LS19 ....62 B7
Milner St HFAX HX1 ....10 E1
  HUDS HD4 ....214 A3
  OSS * WF5 ....174 E5
Milner Wy OSS WF5 ....175 G8
Milne's Av WKFDW/WTN WF2 ..198 B3
Milnes Gv CAS WF10 ....158 D7
Milnes St BSLY * S70 ....261 J6
  WOR/ARM LS12 ....109 G8
Milne St DOD/DAR S75 ....260 A2
  ROY/SHW OL2 ....229 K8
Milngate Cl MILN OL16 ....228 E3
Miln Rd HUD HD1 ....14 E2
Milnrow Rd LIT OL15 ....207 H4
  MILN OL16 ....206 D7
  ROY/SHW OL2 ....229 K7
Milnthorpe Cl
  BSPA/BRAM LS23 ....69 L3
Milnthorpe Crs
  WKFDW/WTN WF2 ....198 F2
Milnthorpe Dr
  WKFDW/WTN WF2 ....198 F2
Milnthorpe Gdns
  BSPA/BRAM LS23 ....69 L3
Milnthorpe Garth
  BSPA/BRAM LS23 ....69 L3
Milnthorpe Gn
  WKFDW/WTN WF2 ....198 F2
Milnthorpe La BSPA/BRAM LS23..69 L3
Milnthorpe Wy
  BSPA/BRAM LS23 ....69 L3
Milroyd Crs BTLY WF17 ....151 J4
Milton Av LVSG WF15 ....172 E3
  RPDN/SBR HX6 ....167 L1
Milton Cl HOR/CROF WF4 ....197 M8
  LVSG WF15 ....172 E4
Milton Crs WKFDW/WTN WF2 ..197 L2
Milton Dr HEM/SK/SE WF9 ....223 K4
  LVSG WF15 ....172 E4
  MSTN/BAR LS15 ....90 B7
Milton Gdns LVSG WF15 ....172 E3
Milton Gv DEWS WF13 ....173 L4
Milton Pl HFAX HX1 ....10 E6
  OSS WF5 ....174 F7
Milton Rd AWLS/ASK DN6 ....249 L5
  LVSG WF15 ....172 E3
  PBR HC3 ....26 F2
  WKFDW/WTN WF2 ....197 L2
Milton Sq HECK WF16 ....172 E5
Milton St CAS WF10 ....157 L6
  CUD/GR S72 ....263 K4
  CUL/QBY BD13 ....101 M6
  GTHN BD7 ....4 B6
  HECK WF16 ....172 E5
  MILN OL16 ....206 B6
  RPDN/SBR HX6 ....167 K1
  SKP/WHF BD23 ....16 C3
Milton Ter CLECK BD19 ....149 L8
  HFAX * HX1 ....10 E6
  KSTL LS5 ....108 C2
Minden Cl PONT WF8 ....180 C7
Minden Wy PONT WF8 ....180 C6
Minerva St HUDS HD4 ....213 H5
Minnie St HWTH BD22 ....78 E8

KGHY BD21 2 E7
Minorca Mt CUL/QBY BD13 101 M5
Minster Wy BSLYN/ROY S71 261 M3
Minsthorpe La
HEM/SK/SE WF9 225 J8
HEM/SK/SE WF9 247 G3
Mint St ECHL BD2 105 K4
HUDW HD3 191 M7
Miramar HUDN HD2 192 F1
Mire Rdg COL BB8 74 C3
Mires La TAD LS24 94 F4
Mirey Butt La KNOT WF11 181 M3
Mirey La RPDN/SBR HX6 166 D3
Mirfield Av ECHL BD2 105 J1
Miry La HBR HX7 144 B8
HOLM/MEL HD9 236 A5
LVSG WF15 171 L2
MSTN/BAR LS15 91 H4
YEA LS19 62 D7
Mission St BRIG HD6 170 E5
Mistral Cl LM/WK BD12 148 E4
Mistral Gv LVSG WF15 171 K1
Mistress La WOR/ARM LS12 108 E6
Mitcham Dr HTON BD9 104 C4
Mitchell Av HUDE HD5 215 J1
Mitchell Cl IDLE BD10 83 L5
Mitchell Hey WHIT OL12 206 A7
Mitchell La AIRE BD20 36 A5
IDLE BD10 83 L5
Mitchell Sq WBOW BD5 127 G2
Mitchell St BRIG HD6 170 C3
HBR HX7 143 J4
KGHY BD21 3 J3
MILN OL16 206 E3
RPDN/SBR HX6 167 L2
TOD OL14 141 G7
Mitchell Ter BGLY BD16 81 H5
Mitchelson Av DOD/DAR S75 260 A7
Mitchel Sq AIRE BD20 36 A5
Mitford Pl WOR/ARM LS12 108 F7
Mitford Rd WOR/ARM LS12 108 F7
Mitford Ter WOR/ARM LS12 108 F7
Mitford Vw WOR/ARM LS12 108 F7
Mitre Ct BOW BD4 127 M3
Mitre St DEWS WF13 173 J6
HUDW HD3 14 A4
Mitton St WBOW BD5 126 E3
Mixenden Cl LUD/ILL HX2 145 L1
Mixenden La LUD/ILL HX2 123 M8
Mixenden Rd LUD/ILL HX2 145 L1
Mizzy Rd WHIT OL12 206 A5
Moat Hl BTLY WF17 151 H4
Moat Hill Farm Dr BTLY WF17 151 J4
Modder Av WOR/ARM LS12 108 D7
Modder Pl WOR/ARM LS12 108 D7
Modd La HOLM/MEL HD9 254 B2
Model Av WOR/ARM LS12 108 F7
Model Rd WOR/ARM LS12 108 F7
Model Ter WOR/ARM LS12 108 F7
Modena Ct WMB/DAR S73 263 G8
Moderna Wy HBR HX7 144 B6
Moffat Cl WBSY BD6 126 B7
Moles Head MAR/SLWT HD7 190 E8
Molesworth St MILN OL16 206 C7
Molly Hurst La HOR/CROF WF4 220 B7
Mona St DOD/DAR S75 260 F4
MAR/SLWT HD7 212 B5
WKFDW/WTN WF2 176 A8
Monckton Dr CAS WF10 158 E8
Monckton Rd
WKFDW/WTN WF2 198 C4
Mond Av BFDE BD3 105 M5
Monk Barn Cl BGLY * BD16 81 J2
Monk Bridge Av HDGY LS6 87 G8
Monk Bridge Dr HDGY LS6 87 H8
Monk Bridge Pl HDGY LS6 87 G8
Monk Bridge Rd HDGY LS6 87 G8
Monk Bridge Ter HDGY LS6 87 G8
Monkfield MIRF WF14 172 A8
Monkhill Av PONT WF8 180 F4
Monkhill Dr PONT WF8 180 F4
Monkhill La PONT WF8 180 F3
Monkhill Mt PONT WF8 180 F4
Monk Ings BTLY WF17 150 F5
Monk Ings Av BTLY WF17 150 E5
Monkmans Wharfe AIRE BD20 35 M5
Monks Cl MILN OL16 207 G8
Monk St GTHN BD7 4 B6
WKFDE WF1 13 G4
Monks Wy BSLYN/ROY S71 261 M3
Monkswood KSTL LS5 86 B8
Monkswood Av SCFT LS14 89 H6
Monkswood Bank SCFT LS14 89 H6
Monkswood Cl SCFT LS14 89 H6
Monkswood Dr SCFT LS14 89 H6
Monkswood Ga SCFT * LS14 89 J6
Monkswood Gn SCFT LS14 89 H6
Monkswood Hl SCFT LS14 89 H6
Monkswood Ri SCFT LS14 89 H6
Monkswood Wk SCFT LS14 89 J6
Monk Ter BSLYN/ROY S71 262 A1
Monkton Wy BSLYN/ROY S71 243 L1
Monkwood Rd WKFDE WF1 176 D1
Monmouth St COL BB8 74 C1
ROCH OL11 206 B8
Monsal Crs BSLYN/ROY S71 243 J7
Monson Av PDSY/CALV LS28 84 D8
Mons Rd TOD OL14 141 H7
Montagu Av RHAY LS8 110 E1
Montagu Ct RHAY LS8 88 D8
Montagu Crs RHAY LS8 110 E1
Montagu Dr RHAY LS8 110 D1
Montague Crs
GFTH/SHER LS25 113 J6
Montague Pl GFTH/SHER LS25 113 J7
Montague St COL BB8 52 A8
CUD/GR S72 244 E6
RPDN/SBR HX6 167 J3
WBOW BD5 126 E3
Montagu Gdns RHAY LS8 110 D1
Montagu Gv RHAY LS8 110 E1
Montagu Pl RHAY LS8 110 D1
Montagu Ri RHAY LS8 110 E2
Montagu Rd WBY LS22 30 C8
Montagu Vw RHAY LS8 110 D1
Montcalm Crs EARD/LOFT WF3 177 H3
MID LS10 132 A4
Montfort Cl HORS LS18 85 K3
Montgomery ROCH * OL11 206 A8
Montgomery St SKP/WHF BD23 16 C3
Montpelier Ter HDGY LS6 109 H2
Montreal Av CHAL LS7 87 M8
Montreal St TOD * OL14 163 J5
Montreal Ter BRAM LS13 107 J6
Montrose Av DOD/DAR S75 242 B5
Montrose St ECHL BD2 104 F2
Montserrat Rd BOW BD4 128 B5
Monument La PONT WF8 181 G7
Monument Ms PONT WF8 181 G7
Moody St BOW BD4 5 G9
Moor Allerton Av
AL/HA/HU LS17 88 A4
Moor Allerton Crs
AL/HA/HU LS17 88 A4
Moor Allerton Dr
AL/HA/HU LS17 88 B4
Moor Allerton Gdns
AL/HA/HU LS17 87 M4
Moor Av BSPA/BRAM LS23 48 F8
EARD/LOFT WF3 155 G8
MSTN/BAR LS15 111 H7
Moorbank Cl DOD/DAR S75 260 E2
Moor Bank La MILN OL16 228 F2
Moorbottom CLECK BD19 149 K8
Moor Bottom HOLM/MEL HD9 236 B2
Moor Bottom La BGLY BD16 81 J3
GTL/HWG HX4 168 C5
HBR HX7 166 C1
KGHY BD21 79 K4
RPDN/SBR HX6 167 J6
Moor Bottom Rd
GTL/HWG HX4 189 H1
Moorbottom Rd HUD HD1 214 A2
Moor Bottom Rd LUD/ILL HX2 124 B8
Moorbridge Cft
GFTH/SHER LS25 116 B7
Moorbrow HOLM/MEL HD9 254 E4
Moor Cl HUDS HD4 213 L5
MID LS10 131 M4
Moor Close Av CUL/QBY BD13 124 E6
Moor Close Farm Ms
CUL/QBY BD13 124 E6
Moor Close La CUL/QBY BD13 124 E6
Moor Close Pde
CUL/QBY BD13 124 E5
Moor Close Rd CUL/QBY BD13 124 E6
Moorcock Rd HBR HX7 141 L1
Moor Cottage Cl HUDS HD4 213 M7
Moor Crs BEE/HOL LS11 9 G8
SKP/WHF BD23 16 D2
Moor Crescent Cha
BEE/HOL LS11 9 G7
Moorcrest Ri DOD/DAR S75 242 D4
Moor Crest Rd HUDS HD4 213 L3
Moor Cft BGLY BD16 81 K1
BHP/TINH LS16 86 F2
Moorcroft DEWS WF13 173 J5
ROCH OL11 228 B3
Moorcroft Av BFDE BD3 105 M5
HWTH BD22 78 F3
Moorcroft Avenues
MAR/SLWT HD7 212 F1
Moorcroft Dr BOW BD4 128 B5
DEWS WF13 173 H5
Moorcroft Park Dr
HOLM/MEL HD9 236 F7
Moorcroft Rd BOW BD4 128 B5
DEWS WF13 173 H5
Moorcroft Ter BOW BD4 128 B6
Moor Dr HDGY LS6 87 G8
HWTH BD22 78 E3
OT LS21 41 M6
PDSY/CALV LS28 129 H1
Moore Av GTHN BD7 126 B4
Moor Edge High Side
BGLY BD16 80 C4
Moorehouse Gv OSM LS9 7 L6
Moor End Av LUD/ILL HX2 145 L5
Moor End Gdns LUD/ILL HX2 145 M5
Moor End La DEWS WF13 173 H4
RPDN/SBR HX6 167 M4
Moor End Rd HUDS HD4 214 A3
LUD/ILL HX2 145 K4
Moor End Vw LUD/ILL HX2 146 A5
Moore St MILN OL16 206 B7
Moore Vw GTHN BD7 126 B4
Moor Farm Gdns CHAL * LS7 87 L7
Moorfield MOR LS27 129 L7
Moorfield Av BFDE BD3 105 M5
CLECK BD19 149 G7
ILK LS29 61 H2
LIT OL15 185 J7
WOR/ARM LS12 108 C6
Moorfield Cl YEA LS19 62 F8
Moorfield Ct HOR/CROF WF4 217 G2
YEA LS19 62 F8
Moorfield Crs HEM/SK/SE WF9 223 L8
PDSY/CALV LS28 106 F8
WOR/ARM LS12 108 C6
YEA LS19 62 E8
Moorfield Cft YEA LS19 62 F8
Moorfield Dr BAIL BD17 82 E1
HWTH BD22 78 F3
YEA LS19 62 F8
Moorfield Gdns
PDSY/CALV LS28 106 E8
Moorfield Gv PDSY/CALV LS28 106 E8
WOR/ARM LS12 108 C6
Moorfield Hamlet
ROY/SHW OL2 229 H7
Moorfield Ms ROY/SHW * OL2 229 K7
Moorfield Pl HEM/SK/SE WF9 223 L8
IDLE BD10 83 K6
WHIT * OL12 206 A5
Moorfield Rd BGLY BD16 81 J7
Moor Field Rd GTL/HWG HX4 189 J6
Moorfield Rd HUDN HD2 192 D5
ILK LS29 39 G2
WOR/ARM LS12 108 C6
YEA LS19 62 F8
Moorfields AL/HA/HU * LS17 87 M4
BRAM LS13 107 L3
Moorfield St HFAX HX1 10 D9
LDSU LS2 6 D3
WOR/ARM LS12 108 C6
Moorfield Vw LVSG WF15 172 A5
Moorfield Wy CLECK BD19 149 G7
Moor Flatts Av MID LS10 153 L1
Moor Flatts Rd MID LS10 153 L1
Moorfoot La AIRE BD20 34 C3
Moorgarth Av BFDE BD3 105 M5
Moorgate BAIL BD17 82 E2
Moor Ga TOD OL14 163 L3
Moorgate Av BFDE BD3 105 L5
GFTH/SHER LS25 135 J3
Moorgate Cl GFTH/SHER LS25 135 J4
Moorgate Dr GFTH/SHER LS25 135 K4
Moor Gate La WHIT OL12 185 G7
Moorgate Ri GFTH/SHER LS25 135 J4
Moorgate Rd GFTH/SHER LS25 135 J3
Moorgate St HFAX * HX1 10 B9
Moor Grange Ri BHP/TINH LS16 86 C6
Moor Grange Vw
BHP/TINH LS16 86 C6
Moor Green Cl DOD/DAR S75 260 C4
Moor Gv EARD/LOFT WF3 155 G8
HIPP HX3 125 L7
PDSY/CALV LS28 129 H1
Moorhead Cl HOLM/MEL HD9 234 F4
Moorhead Crs SHPY BD18 82 A7
Moorhead La SHPY BD18 82 A7
Moorhead Ter SHPY BD18 82 A7
Moor Hey La ELL HX5 191 L1
GTL/HWG HX4 190 A5
Moor Hill Ct HUDW * HD3 191 G6
Moor Hill Rd HUDW HD3 191 H6
Moorhouse Av BEE/HOL LS11 131 H5
EARD/LOFT WF3 155 K7
ECHL BD2 105 J1
WKFDW/WTN WF2 176 B8
Moorhouse Cl EARD/LOFT WF3 155 K7
HWTH BD22 100 E3
NORM WF6 178 E3
Moorhouse Ct
HEM/SK/SE WF9 247 J5
HWTH BD22 100 E3
Moorhouse Crs
WKFDW/WTN WF2 12 A2
Moorhouse Farm MILN OL16 207 G8
Moor House Fold MILN OL16 207 G8
Moorhouse Gap
AWLS/ASK DN6 248 B5
Moorhouse Gv
EARD/LOFT WF3 155 K7
Moorhouse La AWLS/ASK DN6 247 L6
DOD/DAR S75 241 L1
HOR/CROF WF4 222 E2
HWTH BD22 100 D2
Moorhouse Ter
EARD/LOFT WF3 155 K8
Moorhouse Vw
EARD/LOFT WF3 155 K8
HEM/SK/SE WF9 247 K4
The Moorings AL/HA/HU LS17 88 A1
IDLE BD10 83 M6
MID LS10 132 D3
Moor Knoll Cl EARD/LOFT WF3 153 M6
Moor Knoll Dr EARD/LOFT WF3 153 L6
Moor Knoll La EARD/LOFT WF3 153 L5
Moorland Av BAIL BD17 82 F2
BGLY BD16 59 L8
BSLY S70 260 D6
DOD/DAR S75 242 D4
GSLY LS20 62 A5
HDGY LS6 6 A4
MILN OL16 229 H1
MOR LS27 129 K6
Moorland Cl LUD/ILL HX2 146 A3
MAR/SLWT HD7 213 G7
MOR LS27 129 L6
Moorland Crs AL/HA/HU LS17 87 L5
BAIL BD17 82 F2
DOD/DAR S75 242 D4
GSLY LS20 62 A4
ILK LS29 61 J1
ILK LS29 61 K4
MOR LS27 129 K6
Moorland Dr AL/HA/HU LS17 87 L5
BIRK/DRI BD11 128 D7
GSLY LS20 62 A4
HOR/CROF WF4 220 B4
PDSY/CALV LS28 106 C6
Moorland Gdns AL/HA/HU LS17 87 M4
Moorland Garth AL/HA/HU LS17 87 L5
Moorland Gv AL/HA/HU LS17 87 L4
PDSY/CALV LS28 106 C6
Moorland Ings AL/HA/HU LS17 87 L5
Moorland Pl LM/WK BD12 149 G1
Moorland Ri AL/HA/HU LS17 87 L5
HOLM/MEL HD9 234 E5
Moorland Rd BHP/TINH LS16 63 L4
BIRK/DRI BD11 129 G8
HDGY LS6 6 B4
PDSY/CALV LS28 106 C5
The Moorlands AL/HA/HU LS17 88 A2
WBY LS22 48 B1
Moorlands HOLM/MEL HD9 254 E3
ILK LS29 38 C4
Moorlands Av BFDE BD3 105 M5
BIRK/DRI BD11 128 C7
DEWS WF13 173 K5
HWTH BD22 79 H2
LUD/ILL HX2 146 A3
MIRF * WF14 172 B8
OSS WF5 174 E6
YEA LS19 62 F8
Moorlands Ct GTL/HWG * HX4 168 D6
WBY LS22 48 B1
Moorlands Crs HUDW HD3 190 F5
Moorlands Dr LUD/ILL HX2 146 A4
YEA LS19 62 F8
Moorlands Pl HFAX HX1 168 D1
Moorlands Rd BIRK/DRI BD11 128 C7
DEWS WF13 173 K6
GTL/HWG HX4 168 D6
HUDW HD3 190 F5
Moorlands St ROY/SHW OL2 229 L7
Moorland St WHIT OL12 206 A5
Moorlands Vw HFAX HX1 168 D1
WBY LS22 48 B1
Moorland Ter CUD/GR S72 262 E1
GFTH/SHER LS25 113 G8
KGHY BD21 58 B8
Moorland Vw AL/HA/HU LS17 87 L4
BRAM LS13 107 K2
KBTN HD8 217 J7
KBTN HD8 240 C4
LM/WK BD12 149 G1
RPDN/SBR HX6 167 H3
Moorland Wk AL/HA/HU LS17 87 L4
Moor La AIRE BD20 56 B1
AL/HA/HU LS17 67 J1
BSPA/BRAM LS23 48 F1
BTLY WF17 151 H6
CLECK BD19 150 D4
GFTH/SHER LS25 116 C6
GSLY LS20 62 A4
HOLM/MEL HD9 236 A7
HUDS HD4 213 M7
HUDS HD4 237 G1
ILK LS29 18 F6
ILK LS29 18 C4
ILK LS29 39 M6
ILK LS29 61 G2
KBTN HD8 216 C7
LUD/ILL HX2 146 A2
OT LS21 22 D6
OT LS21 40 D3
PBR HG3 45 L3
PONT WF8 203 G2
PONT WF8 203 H1
RYKW YO26 32 D4
TAD LS24 51 L5
TAD LS24 71 H6
TAD LS24 95 M4
TOD OL14 163 K3
WBY LS22 48 B6
Moorlea Dr BAIL BD17 82 F3
Moorleigh Cl GFTH/SHER LS25 135 K4
Moorleigh Dr GFTH/SHER LS25 135 K4
Moor Park Av HDGY LS6 86 F8
HUDS HD4 213 L5
Moor Park Cl ILK LS29 18 F6
Moor Park Ct EARL * WF12 174 A5
Moor Park Crs ILK LS29 18 F6
Moor Park Dr BFDE BD3 105 M6
HDGY LS6 86 F8
ILK LS29 18 F6
Moor Park Gdns EARL WF12 174 A6
Moor Park Gv ILK LS29 19 G6
Moor Park La EARL WF12 174 A6
Moor Park Mt HDGY LS6 86 F7
Moor Park Rd BFDE * BD3 105 L6
Moor Park Vls HDGY LS6 87 G8
Moor Park Wy ILK LS29 19 G6
Moor Rd BEE/HOL LS11 9 G8
BHP/TINH LS16 63 M4
EARD/LOFT WF3 155 G8
FEA/AMT WF7 201 M1
GFTH/SHER LS25 116 B6
HDGY LS6 86 F8
ILK LS29 39 H5
LIT OL15 185 L5
MID LS10 131 M4
Moor Royd HIPP HX3 168 C2
HOLM/MEL HD9 236 A3
Moorroyd St OSS WF5 174 E6
Moorshutt Rd
HEM/SK/SE WF9 223 L8
Moor Side BSPA/BRAM LS23 48 D6
Moorside BAIL BD17 82 F1
CLECK BD19 149 J8
HTON BD9 104 A4
ROCH OL11 228 B3
Moorside Ap BIRK/DRI BD11 151 H1
Moorside Av AIRE BD20 56 C1
BIRK/DRI BD11 128 C7
BIRK/DRI BD11 151 H1
DEWS WF13 173 H4
ECHL BD2 105 M4
HUDS HD4 213 M2
STKB/PEN S36 270 E4
Moorside Cl BIRK/DRI BD11 151 H1
DOD/DAR S75 242 D6
ECHL BD2 105 L3
Moorside Crs BIRK/DRI BD11 151 H1
DEWS WF13 173 H4
HOR/CROF WF4 220 B4
Moorside Cft ECHL BD2 105 L4
Moorside Dr BIRK/DRI BD11 151 H1
BRAM LS13 107 L2
Moorside End DEWS WF13 173 H4
Moorside Gdns BIRK/DRI BD11 151 H1
ECHL BD2 105 L3
LUD/ILL HX2 146 B2
Moorside Gn BIRK/DRI BD11 129 H8
Moor Side La HWTH BD22 100 B1
MAR/SLWT HD7 211 M3
Moorside La BFDE BD3 105 M7
ILK LS29 37 G2
OT LS21 22 B7
Moorside Maltings
BEE/HOL LS11 9 G8
Moorside Mt BIRK/DRI BD11 151 G1
Moorside Pde BIRK/DRI BD11 151 H1
Moorside Pl BFDE BD3 105 M7
DEWS WF13 173 H4
Moorside Ri CLECK BD19 149 K7
Moorside Rd BFDE BD3 105 M7
BIRK/DRI BD11 151 G1
DEWS WF13 173 H4
ECHL BD2 105 L3
HOLM/MEL HD9 236 A3
HUDE HD5 193 L4
WIL/AL BD15 102 E2
Moorside St BRAM LS13 107 L2
LM/WK BD12 126 D8
Moorside Ter BIRK/DRI BD11 151 G1
BRAM LS13 107 L2
ECHL BD2 105 M4
Moorside V BIRK/DRI BD11 129 H8
Moorside Vw BIRK/DRI BD11 151 H1
Moorside Wk BIRK/DRI BD11 151 H1
Moor Stone Pl HIPP * HX3 147 L1
Moor St CUL/QBY * BD13 125 G5
HWTH BD22 78 F3
ROY/SHW OL2 229 J8
Moor Ter ECHL BD2 105 L5
Moorthorpe Av BFDE BD3 105 M5
Moortop BIRK/DRI BD11 128 F8
Moor Top BIRK/DRI BD11 150 F1
MIRF WF14 172 A8
OT LS21 61 M1
WOR/ARM LS12 129 L4
Moor Top Av FEA/AMT WF7 224 A1
HUDS HD4 237 H4
Moor Top Dr HEM/SK/SE WF9 245 M1
Moor Top Gdns LUD/ILL HX2 124 A7
Moor Top La HOR/CROF WF4 216 F5
Moor Top Rd HUDE HD5 193 L4
LM/WK BD12 126 D8
LUD/ILL HX2 145 K6
Moor Vw BEE/HOL LS11 8 D6
BOW * BD4 128 C6
HECK WF16 173 G4
HOLM/MEL HD9 234 E3
HOR/CROF WF4 220 B1
MIRF WF14 172 C5
Moor View Av SHPY BD18 82 C6
Moor View Cl CAS WF10 158 B7
Moor View Ct AIRE BD20 58 E7
IDLE * BD10 83 J5
Moorview Cft ILK LS29 61 H1
Moorview Dr BGLY BD16 81 G8
SHPY BD18 83 H7
Moorview Gv KGHY BD21 3 K8
Moorview Rd SKP/WHF BD23 16 D3
Moorview Wy SKP/WHF BD23 16 D3
Moorville Av BFDE BD3 105 M5
Moorville Cl BEE/HOL LS11 8 E8
Moorville Ct BEE/HOL LS11 8 D7
Moorville Dr BIRK/DRI BD11 128 C7
Moorville Gv BEE/HOL LS11 8 D7
Moorville Rd BEE/HOL LS11 8 E7
Moorway GSLY LS20 61 K5
Moor Wy HWTH BD22 78 E3
Moorwell Pl ECHL BD2 105 K2
Moravian Pl WBOW * BD5 126 F2
Morefield Bank
HOLM/MEL HD9 236 E6
Moresby Rd WBSY BD6 126 A8
Moresdale La SCFT LS14 111 H3
Morgan St LIT OL15 207 K1
Morlands Cl DEWS WF13 173 H3
Morley Av BFDE BD3 105 M5
KNOT WF11 182 C2
Morley Carr Rd LM/WK BD12 148 F1
Morley Fold KBTN HD8 257 H1
Morley Hall La LUD/ILL HX2 144 E8
Morley La HUDS HD4 213 J2
Morley St GTHN BD7 4 D8
MILN OL16 206 D5
Morningside GIR BD8 104 D5
Morningside Cl MILN * OL16 206 D8
Morning St KGHY BD21 79 K2
Mornington Rd BGLY BD16 81 J3
ILK LS29 38 E2
ROCH OL11 228 B4
Mornington St KGHY BD21 2 F3
Mornington Vls GIR BD8 4 C1
Morpeth Pl OSM LS9 9 L3
Morpeth St CUL/QBY BD13 125 G5
GTHN BD7 4 B6
Morphet Ter CHAL * LS7 7 H6
Morrell Crs WKFDW/WTN WF2 176 B3
Morris Av KSTL LS5 108 C1
Morris Cl HEM/SK/SE WF9 223 K4
Morris Gv KSTL LS5 108 C2
Morris La KSTL LS5 108 C1
Morris Mt KSTL LS5 108 C2
Morrison Pl WMB/DAR S73 263 J8
Morrison Rd WMB/DAR S73 263 H8
Morrison St CAS WF10 158 A7
Morris Pl MOR LS27 152 B1
Morris Vw KSTL LS5 108 C2
Morritt Av MSTN/BAR LS15 111 K5
Morritt Gv MSTN/BAR LS15 111 H6
Mortech Pk MSTN/BAR * LS15 90 F7
Mortimer Av BFDE BD3 105 M5
BTLY WF17 173 H1
Mortimer Dr STKB/PEN S36 270 E5
Mortimer Ri OSS WF5 175 G8
Mortimer Rw BFDE BD3 105 M8
HOR/CROF WF4 197 H5
Mortimer St BTLY WF17 173 H1
CLECK * BD19 149 M7
GIR BD8 104 B6
Mortimer Ter BTLY WF17 173 H1
Morton Cl BSLYN/ROY S71 261 M1
Morton Crs CAS WF10 158 B7
Morton Gn HUDE HD5 215 J2
Morton Gv AIRE BD20 58 F6
EARL WF12 195 K3
Morton La AIRE BD20 58 F7
Morton Pde WKFDW/WTN WF2 12 B3
Morton Rd BOW BD4 127 M1
The Mortons HUDW * HD3 191 H6
Mortons Cl HIPP HX3 169 G3
Morton Wy HUDW HD3 191 G5
Morton Wood Gv
HOLM/MEL HD9 254 F3
Morwick Gv MSTN/BAR LS15 90 A8
Moselden La RPDN/SBR HX6 188 E8
Moseley Pl HDGY LS6 6 F2
Moseley Wood Ap
BHP/TINH LS16 85 M2
Moseley Wood Av
BHP/TINH LS16 63 M8
Moseley Wood Bank
BHP/TINH LS16 85 M1
Moseley Wood Cl
BHP/TINH LS16 85 M2
Moseley Wood Crs B
HP/TINH LS16 85 M1
Moseley Wood Cft HORS LS18 85 L2
Moseley Wood Dr
BHP/TINH LS16 85 M1
Moseley Wood Gdns
BHP/TINH LS16 85 M2
Moseley Wood Gn
BHP/TINH LS16 85 M1
Moseley Wood Gv
BHP/TINH LS16 85 M1
Moseley Wood La
BHP/TINH LS16 64 A8
Moseley Wood Ri
BHP/TINH LS16 85 L1
Moseley Wood Vw
BHP/TINH LS16 64 A8

Moseley Wood Wk
BHP/TINH LS16 85 M1
Moseley Wood Wy
BHP/TINH LS16 63 M8
Moser Av ECHL BD2 105 J1
Moser Crs ECHL BD2 105 J1
Moss Av MILN OL16 206 E8
Moss Bridge Rd BRAM LS13 107 H1
MILN OL16 206 D8
Moss Carr Av KGHY BD21 80 B1
Moss Carr Gv KGHY * BD21 80 B1
Moss Carr Rd KGHY BD21 80 B1
Mossdale Av HTON BD9 103 L3
Moss Dr LUD/ILL HX2 124 A8
Moss Edge Rd HOLM/MEL HD9 253 L6
Moss End La HWTH BD22 54 A4
Moss Gdns AL/HA/HU LS17 87 J1
Moss Gate Rd ROY/SHW OL2 229 K5
Moss Gv ROY/SHW OL2 229 G5
Moss Hall La HBR HX7 142 A2
Moss Hey St ROY/SHW OL2 229 K8
Moss La HBR HX7 143 J2
LUD/ILL HX2 124 A8
MILN OL16 206 C8
Mossley Rd STKB/PEN S36 270 E8
Moss Mill St MILN OL16 228 D1
Moss Ri AL/HA/HU LS17 87 J1
HOLM/MEL HD9 254 A1
Moss Rw WIL/AL BD15 80 E8
Moss Side HTON BD9 104 A4
Moss Side La MILN OL16 228 E1
Moss Side St WHIT OL12 184 A1
Moss St CAS WF10 157 K6
CUL/QBY BD13 102 E7
HUDS HD4 214 D2
HWTH BD22 79 G6
MILN OL16 206 D8
Moss Syke SCFT LS14 67 L5
Moss Ter MILN OL16 206 C8
Mosstree Cl CUL/QBY BD13 124 E4
Moss Va AL/HA/HU LS17 87 J1
Mossy Bank Cl CUL/QBY BD13 125 G4
Mostyn Gv WBSY BD6 126 C6
Mostyn Mt HIPP HX3 146 C3
Mostyn Wk HOR/CROF WF4 220 B3
Motley La GSLY LS20 62 A4
Mottram St BSLYN/ROY S71 261 H4
Moule Ri GFTH/SHER LS25 113 K5
Moulson Ct WBOW BD5 127 G3
Mountain Crs EARL WF12 195 M4
Mountain Rd EARL WF12 195 M4
Mountain Vw LUD/ILL HX2 124 C8
SHPY BD18 82 F8
Mountain Wy HUDE HD5 193 L7
The Mount AL/HA/HU LS17 65 K8
BTLY WF17 151 G4
CAS WF10 158 E7
GFTH/SHER LS25 135 J5
MSTN/BAR LS15 90 F8
MSTN/BAR LS15 111 K5
PONT WF8 180 E6
TOD OL14 141 L8
WKFDW/WTN WF2 175 M5
WKFDW/WTN WF2 198 B3
YEA * LS19 84 F3
Mount Av CUD/GR S72 245 J6
ECHL BD2 105 K1
HECK WF16 151 G8
HEM/SK/SE WF9 223 M6
HUDW HD3 190 E5
LIT OL15 185 J7
LUD/ILL HX2 145 L7
WHIT OL12 207 G2
WKFDW/WTN WF2 176 B2
Mountbatten Av WKFDE WF1 176 E1
WKFDW/WTN WF2 199 G7
Mountbatten Crs WKFDE WF1 176 E1
Mountbatten Gdns HUDW HD3 191 K7
Mountbatten Gv WKFDE WF1 176 E2
Mountcliffe Vw MOR LS27 130 D7
Mount Cl BSLY S70 261 H7
Mount Ct PDSY/CALV LS28 107 G6
Mount Crs CLECK BD19 149 M6
LUD/ILL HX2 145 L7
WKFDW/WTN WF2 198 B3
Mount Dr AL/HA/HU LS17 65 K8
Mountfield Av HUDE HD5 215 K2
Mountfield Rd HUDE HD5 215 K1
Mountfields HIPP HX3 148 A6
Mountfields Wk
HEM/SK/SE WF9 246 D5
Mount Gdns AL/HA/HU LS17 65 K8
CLECK BD19 149 M6
Mount Gv ECHL BD2 105 K1
Mountjoy Rd HUD HD1 14 C5
Mount La BRIG HD6 170 A7
TOD OL14 140 E3
Mountleigh Cl BOW BD4 127 J8
Mount Pellon LUD/ILL HX2 10 A3
Mount Pellon Rd LUD/ILL HX2 146 A6
Mount Pl SHPY BD18 82 D6
Mount Pleasant AIRE BD20 58 E7
BRAM LS13 107 K2
CAS WF10 158 B8
CUD/GR S72 245 J6
CUL/QBY BD13 101 M6
EARL * WF12 174 A7
GFTH/AMT WF7 202 B8
GFTH/SHER LS25 135 K6
GIR * BD8 104 E4
GSLY LS20 62 A4
HUD HD1 214 B3
ILK LS29 19 H6
KBTN HD8 217 M7
LIT * OL15 185 L6
WBSY BD6 126 A7
Mount Pleasant Av HFAX HX1 10 E4
RHAY LS8 110 B1
Mount Pleasant Dr HBR HX7 144 A5
Mount Pleasant Gdns
RHAY * LS8 110 B1
Mount Pleasant La HUDE HD5 215 L2
Mount Pleasant Rd
PDSY/CALV LS28 107 G6
Mount Pleasant St
FEA/AMT WF7 179 M8
HUDE HD5 15 L6
TOD OL14 140 C5
Mount Pleasant Vw TOD OL14 163 J1
Mount Preston LDSU LS2 6 C6
Mount Preston St LDSU LS2 6 C6
Mount Ri AL/HA/HU LS17 65 K8
Mount Rd CUD/GR S72 245 J6
EARD/LOFT WF3 155 H8
ECHL BD2 105 K1
HUD HD1 191 M8
MAR/SLWT HD7 232 D5
WBSY BD6 126 C5
Mount Royd AWLS/ASK * DN6 227 K3
GIR BD8 104 E4
Mount Scar Vw
HOLM/MEL HD9 254 F2
Mountside Cl WHIT OL12 206 B4
Mount St BFDE BD3 5 K7
BSLY S70 261 G6
BSLYN/ROY S71 262 B6
BTLY WF17 173 M3
CLECK BD19 149 M6
ECHL BD2 105 K1
HFAX HX1 10 F6
HUD HD1 214 B3
HUDS * HD4 213 J2
HWTH BD22 2 D5
RPDN/SBR HX6 167 K2
WHIT * OL12 206 A6
Mount St West LUD/ILL * HX2 146 A6
Mount Tabor Rd LUD/ILL HX2 145 H2
Mount Tabor St
PDSY/CALV * LS28 106 E7
Mount Ter BTLY WF17 173 L3
ECHL BD2 105 K1
LUD/ILL HX2 146 A6
Mount Vernon Av BSLY S70 261 H7
Mount Vernon Crs BSLY S70 261 J8
Mount Vernon Rd BSLY S70 261 H8
YEA LS19 84 E2
Mount Vw HWTH BD22 78 D4
LUD/ILL HX2 145 J3
Mount View Ct CLECK BD19 149 L6
Mount View Rd
HOLM/MEL HD9 255 G4
ROY/SHW OL2 229 L8
Mount Wk CAS WF10 157 M8
Mount Zion Rd HUDE HD5 15 K7
Mousehole La MIRF WF14 194 F5
Moverley Flatts PONT WF8 181 G7
Mowat Ct LVSG WF15 171 K1
Mowbray Cha RTHW LS26 133 J7
Mowbray Cl CUL/QBY BD13 101 L1
Mowbray Ct SCFT LS14 111 J3
Mowbray Crs SCFT LS14 111 J3
Moxon Cl PONT WF8 180 F8
Moxon Gv WKFDE WF1 176 D3
Moxon Pl WKFDW/WTN WF2 197 L1
Moxon Sq WKFDE WF1 176 F7
Moxon St WKFDE WF1 176 E2
Moxon Wy WKFDE WF1 176 E2
Moynihan Cl RHAY LS8 110 D2
Mozley Dr LUD/ILL HX2 124 B8
Mucky La BSLYN/ROY S71 262 C5
GTL/HWG HX4 190 F2
Muddy La WBY LS22 47 K3
Muffit La CLECK BD19 150 F6
Muff St BOW BD4 5 L9
Mug Mill La EARL WF12 196 A6
Mugup La HOLM/MEL HD9 255 G5
Muir Ct HDGY LS6 108 F2
Muirfield Av FEA/AMT WF7 179 L5
Muirfield Dr WKFDW/WTN WF2 198 C4
Muirhead Ct BOW BD4 128 A4
Muirhead Dr BOW BD4 128 A4
Muirhead Fold BOW BD4 128 A4
The Muirlands HUDN HD2 193 G1
Mulberry Av BHP/TINH LS16 86 F2
Mulberry Cl ROCH OL11 228 A1
Mulberry Ct MAR/SLWT HD7 213 G1
Mulberry Garth BHP/TINH LS16 86 F3
BSPA/BRAM LS23 49 G6
Mulberry Pl HOR/CROF WF4 222 E5
Mulberry Ri BHP/TINH LS16 86 F2
Mulberry St HUD HD1 15 K8
KGHY BD21 3 J3
MID LS10 9 J5
PDSY/CALV LS28 107 G7
Mulberry Ter HUD * HD1 14 F3
Mulberry Vw BHP/TINH LS16 86 F3
Mulcture Hall Rd HFAX HX1 11 J5
Mulehouse La HUDW HD3 190 D5
Mulgrave St BFDE BD3 5 L8
Mullberry Gdns RTHW LS26 156 D4
Mullins Ct OSM LS9 110 B8
Mullion Av HOLM/MEL HD9 236 A2
Mumford St WBOW BD5 127 G3
Munby St GIR BD8 104 A7
Muncaster Rd
GFTH/SHER LS25 113 K6
Munster St BOW BD4 127 K3
Munton Cl WBSY * BD6 126 A8
Murdoch Pl BSLYN/ROY S71 243 G7
Murdoch St KGHY BD21 58 B6
Murgatroyd St SHPY BD18 82 D6
WBOW BD5 127 G3
Muriel St MILN OL16 228 D1
Murray Rd HUDN HD2 14 C3
Murray St WBOW * BD5 126 E3
Murton Cl SCFT LS14 111 J2
Musabbir Sq WHIT * OL12 206 C6
Museum Ct ECHL BD2 105 L4
Museum St OSM LS9 110 B5
Musgrave Bank BRAM LS13 108 A4
Musgrave Buildings
PDSY/CALV LS28 107 H6
Musgrave Dr ECHL BD2 105 L4
Musgrave Gv ECHL BD2 105 L4
Musgrave Mt BRAM LS13 108 A4
ECHL BD2 105 L4
Musgrave Ri BRAM LS13 108 A4
Musgrave Rd ECHL BD2 105 L4
Musgrave St BTLY * WF17 151 G5
Musgrave Vw BRAM LS13 108 A4
Mushroom St CHAL LS7 7 K6
Musselburgh St GTHN BD7 4 A5
Mutton La WIL/AL BD15 102 F4
Myers Av ECHL BD2 105 J2
Myers Cft HUDE HD5 193 H8
OT LS21 41 J7
Myers La ECHL BD2 105 J2
Mylor Ct BSLYN/ROY S71 261 L3
Myrtle Av BGLY * BD16 81 H4
DEWS WF13 195 G1
LUD/ILL HX2 146 A2
Myrtle Ct BGLY BD16 81 H4
Myrtle Dr HWTH BD22 79 H5
LUD/ILL HX2 146 A2
Myrtle Gdns LUD/ILL HX2 146 A2
Myrtle Gv BGLY BD16 81 H4
HUDW HD3 191 K8
LUD/ILL HX2 146 A2
Myrtle Pl BGLY BD16 81 H3
LUD/ILL HX2 146 A2
Myrtle Rd DEWS * WF13 195 G1
ELL HX5 191 H1
Myrtle St BFDE BD3 105 L8
BGLY BD16 81 J3
DOD/DAR S75 260 E4
HUD HD1 15 G4
Myson Av PONT WF8 181 H2
Mytholm Bank HBR * HX7 143 G3
Mytholm Cl HBR HX7 143 H3
Mytholmes La HWTH BD22 78 E7

N

Nabbs La MAR/SLWT HD7 212 B6
Nabb Vw HOLM/MEL * HD9 254 D2
The Nab MIRF WF14 172 A8
Nab Crs HOLM/MEL HD9 234 E4
Nabcroft La HUDS HD4 213 M3
Nabcroft Ri HUDS * HD4 213 M2
Nab End La GTL/HWG HX4 168 F7
Nab La BTLY WF17 151 J4
MIRF WF14 172 B8
SHPY BD18 81 M7
Naburn Ap SCFT LS14 89 K5
Naburn Cl SCFT LS14 89 K7
Naburn Dr SCFT LS14 89 K7
Naburn Gn SCFT LS14 89 K7
Naburn Pl SCFT LS14 89 K6
Naburn Rd SCFT LS14 89 K7
Naburn Vw SCFT LS14 89 L7
Nab Vw AIRE BD20 36 B3
Nab Water La HWTH BD22 100 E8
Nab Wood Bank SHPY BD18 81 M7
Nab Wood Cl SHPY * BD18 82 A7
Nab Wood Crs SHPY BD18 81 M7
Nab Wood Dr BGLY BD16 81 M8
Nab Wood Gdns SHPY BD18 82 A7
Nab Wood Gv SHPY BD18 81 M7
Nab Wood Mt SHPY BD18 81 M7
Nab Wood Pl SHPY BD18 81 M7
Nab Wood Ri SHPY BD18 81 M7
Nab Wood Rd SHPY BD18 81 M8
Nab Wood Ter SHPY BD18 81 M7
Nairn Cl HUDS HD4 213 L4
Nall St MILN OL16 207 G8
Nancroft Crs WOR/ARM LS12 108 E7
Nancroft Ter WOR/ARM LS12 108 E7
Nancy Crs CUD/GR S72 245 K8
Nancy Rd CUD/GR S72 245 K8
Nanny Goat La
GFTH/SHER LS25 113 G6
Nanny La TAD LS24 95 G8
Nanny Marr Rd WMB/DAR S73 263 K8
Nansen Av BRAM LS13 107 K4
Nansen Gv BRAM LS13 107 K4
Nansen Mt BRAM LS13 107 K4
Nansen Pl BRAM LS13 107 K4
Nansen St BRAM LS13 107 J4
Nansen Ter BRAM LS13 107 K4
Nansen Vw BRAM LS13 107 K4
Nantwich Av WHIT OL12 206 B3
Naomi Rd HUDS HD4 214 C4
Napier Mt BSLY S70 261 H8
Napier Rd BFDE BD3 105 M7
ELL HX5 169 G8
Napier St BFDE BD3 105 M7
CUL/QBY BD13 125 H5
KGHY BD21 3 J6
ROY/SHW OL2 229 K6
Napier Ter BFDE BD3 105 M7
Naples St GIR BD8 104 D5
Nares St HWTH BD22 79 G6
KGHY BD21 2 E4
Narrow La BGLY BD16 80 D5
The Narrows BGLY BD16 80 D5
Naseby Gdns OSM * LS9 7 L7
Naseby Garth OSM LS9 7 L7
Naseby Gra OSM LS9 7 L8
Naseby Pl OSM LS9 7 L8
Naseby Ri CUL/QBY BD13 125 H5
Naseby Ter OSM LS9 7 M8
Naseby Vw OSM * LS9 7 L8
Naseby Wk OSM LS9 7 M8
Nashville Rd HWTH BD22 2 D7
Nashville St HWTH BD22 2 D7
Nashville Ter HWTH BD22 2 D7
Nassau Pl CHAL LS7 7 L1
Nathan La RPDN/SBR HX6 166 E7
National Rd MID LS10 9 M7
Nat La AL/HA/HU LS17 43 J1
Natty Fields Cl LUD/ILL HX2 124 A7
Natty La LUD/ILL HX2 124 A7
Nature Wy WBSY BD6 126 A7
Navigation Cl ELL HX5 169 J6
Navigation Ri HUDS HD4 213 K2
Navigation Rd CAS WF10 157 M5
EARL WF12 195 K2
HIPP HX3 11 K7
Navigation Wk MID LS10 9 H2
Navvy La BSLYN/ROY S71 221 M7
Naylor Ct DEWS WF13 173 M5
Naylor Gv DOD/DAR S75 260 B7
Naylor La LUD/ILL HX2 144 E6
Naylors Garth HDGY LS6 109 H1
Naylor St DEWS WF13 173 K4
HFAX HX1 10 A5
OSS WF5 174 E6
Naze Rd TOD OL14 163 H3
Neale Rd HUD HD1 214 B3
Neale St HBR HX7 143 J4
Neal St WBOW BD5 4 E8
Near Bank KBTN HD8 238 D4
Nearcliffe Rd HTON BD9 104 C4
Near Crook SHPY BD18 83 H5
Near La HOLM/MEL HD9 235 G4
Neath Gdns OSM LS9 110 F3
Necropolis Rd GTHN BD7 126 B1
Ned Hill Rd LUD/ILL HX2 124 A4
Ned La BOW BD4 128 B2
MAR/SLWT HD7 212 B6
Needles Inn La RTHW LS26 133 L7
Needlewood DOD/DAR S75 260 B8
Nell Gap Av HOR/CROF WF4 196 C7
Nell Gap Crs HOR/CROF WF4 196 C7
Nell Gap La HOR/CROF WF4 196 D7
Nelson Av BSLYN/ROY S71 261 J2
Nelson Ct MOR LS27 152 B4
Nelson Cft GFTH/SHER LS25 112 F8
Nelson Pl CUL/QBY BD13 125 G5
MOR LS27 152 C1
Nelson Rd ILK LS29 38 D2
Nelson St BFD BD1 4 F7
BSLY S70 261 G5
BTLY WF17 151 H5
BTLY * WF17 173 J1
CUD/GR S72 245 G1
CUL/QBY BD13 125 G5
DEWS * WF13 173 L6
HUD HD1 214 B2
HWTH BD22 79 G6
LIT OL15 207 K1
LVSG WF15 172 D3
MILN OL16 206 B7
NORM WF6 178 E3
OT LS21 41 J7
RPDN/SBR HX6 167 M2
SKP/WHF BD23 16 C3
WIL/AL BD15 103 L5
Nene St WBOW BD5 126 E2
Nepshaw La MOR LS27 152 B1
Nepshaw La North MOR LS27 152 A1
Nepshaw La South MOR LS27 151 M2
Neptune St OSM LS9 9 K2
Nesfield Cl MID LS10 132 B8
Nesfield Crs MID LS10 132 B8
Nesfield Gdns MID LS10 132 A8
Nesfield Garth MID LS10 132 A8
Nesfield Rd ILK LS29 38 B1
MID LS10 132 A8
Nesfield St BFD BD1 4 D3
Nesfield Vw ILK LS29 38 A2
MID LS10 132 A8
Nesfield Wk MID LS10 132 A8
Nessfield Dr HWTH BD22 2 B8
Nessfield Gv HWTH BD22 2 B8
Nessfield Rd HWTH BD22 2 B8
Nestfield Cl PONT WF8 180 F3
Nest La HBR HX7 143 M6
Neston Cl ROY/SHW OL2 229 M7
Neston Rd MILN OL16 228 E2
Neston Wy OSS * WF5 174 F5
Netherby St BFDE BD3 5 M6
Nethercliffe Rd GSLY LS20 61 M4
Nether Cl HUDE HD5 193 G6
Nether Crs HUDE HD5 193 G6
Nethercroft DOD/DAR S75 260 A1
Netherdale Ct WBY LS22 30 C8
Netherend Rd MAR/SLWT HD7 212 B5
Netherfield Av HOR/CROF WF4 218 F1
Netherfield Cl CAS WF10 179 H1
KBTN HD8 216 B8
YEA LS19 62 D7
Netherfield Crs
HOR/CROF WF4 218 F1
Netherfield Dr GSLY LS20 61 M4
HOLM/MEL HD9 236 C7
Netherfield Pl CLECK BD19 150 A7
HOR/CROF WF4 196 F8
Netherfield Rd DEWS WF13 195 G1
ILK LS29 61 L3
Nethergill La AIRE BD20 34 A4
Nether Hall Av HUDE HD5 193 G6
Netherhall Rd BAIL BD17 82 F3
Nether House La
STKB/PEN S36 269 M7
Netherhouse Rd
ROY/SHW OL2 229 J7
Netherhouses HOLM/MEL HD9 253 M1
Netherlands Av WBSY BD6 126 E7
Netherlands Sq WBSY BD6 126 F7
Nether La HOLM/MEL HD9 252 D3
Netherlea Dr HOLM/MEL HD9 236 B7
Netherley Dr MAR/SLWT HD7 233 G4
Netherly Brow OSS WF5 197 G3
Nether Moor Rd HUDS HD4 213 K6
Nether Moor Vw BGLY BD16 81 J3
Netheroyd FEA/AMT WF7 200 E1
Netheroyd Hill Rd HUDN HD2 192 B3
Netheroyd Pl HOR/CROF WF4 200 D3
Nether Rd DOD/DAR S75 259 J5
Nether St PDSY/CALV LS28 106 F2
Netherthong Rd
HOLM/MEL HD9 235 H6
Netherton Fold HUDS HD4 213 L8
Netherton Hall Dr
HOR/CROF WF4 196 F8
Netherton Hall Gdns
HOR/CROF WF4 197 G8
Netherton La HOR/CROF WF4 196 F8
Netherton Moor Rd HUDS HD4 213 M7
Netherwood Cl HUDN HD2 192 C3
Netley Av WHIT OL12 206 B3
Nettle Gv HIPP HX3 147 H5
Nettleton Av MIRF WF14 194 B1
Nettleton Cha OSS WF5 174 E5
Nettleton Cl BOW BD4 128 F4
Nettleton Ct MSTN/BAR LS15 111 M6
Nettleton Hill Rd
MAR/SLWT HD7 190 D8
Nettleton Rd HUDE HD5 193 J6
MIRF WF14 194 B1
Nettleton St EARD/LOFT WF3 155 K8
OSS WF5 174 E8
Neville Ap OSM LS9 110 E8
Neville Av BOW BD4 127 K5
BSLY S70 261 M7
OSM LS9 110 E8
Neville Cl BSLY S70 261 M7
HEM/SK/SE WF9 246 E3
OSM LS9 110 E8
Neville Crs BSLY S70 261 M7
OSM LS9 110 F6
Neville Garth OSM LS9 110 E8
Neville Gv HUDE HD5 215 H2
OSM LS9 110 E8
RTHW LS26 134 C4
Neville Mt OSM LS9 110 E8
Neville Pde OSM LS9 110 E8
Neville Pl OSM LS9 110 F7
Neville Rd BOW BD4 127 K2
OSM LS9 110 F6
OT LS21 41 K7
WKFDW/WTN WF2 197 L1
Neville Rw OSM LS9 110 E8
Neville Sq OSM LS9 110 F7
Neville St BEE/HOL LS11 8 F2
CLECK BD19 150 A8
KGHY * BD21 3 J3
NORM WF6 178 D5
SKP/WHF BD23 16 C2
WKFDE WF1 13 L7
Neville Ter OSM LS9 110 E8
Neville Vw OSM LS9 110 E8
Neville Wk OSM LS9 110 E8
Nevill Gv HTON BD9 103 M3
Nevins Rd DEWS WF13 172 F8
Nevison Av PONT WF8 181 G3
Nevis St ROCH OL11 228 C4
New Adel Av BHP/TINH LS16 86 C3
New Adel Gdns BHP/TINH LS16 86 C3
New Adel La BHP/TINH LS16 86 C3
Newall Av OT LS21 41 H5
Newall Carr Rd OT LS21 23 G8
Newall Cl ILK LS29 61 K1
OT LS21 41 H5
Newall Crs HEM/SK/SE WF9 223 H3
Newall Hall Pk OT LS21 41 J5
Newall St LIT OL15 185 K8
TOD OL14 163 J6
WBOW BD5 126 F2
New Ar HEM/SK/SE * WF9 246 D4
Newark Cl DOD/DAR S75 242 D4
Newark Park Wy
ROY/SHW OL2 228 E8
Newark Rd BGLY BD16 81 G1
WHIT OL12 206 B3
Newark Sq WHIT OL12 206 B3
Newark St BOW BD4 5 K9
Newark V EARD/LOFT WF3 154 C3
New Augustus St BFD BD1 5 H7
New Av HUDE HD5 193 K5
New Bank HIPP HX3 11 J3
New Bank Ri BOW BD4 127 M3
New Bank St MOR LS27 152 D1
Newbarn Cl ROY/SHW OL2 229 J7
New Barn St MILN OL16 228 C1
ROY/SHW OL2 229 J7
New Bath St COL BB8 74 A1
New Bbrighton BGLY BD16 81 J8
Newbold Moss MILN OL16 206 D7
Newbold St MILN OL16 206 E6
New Bond St HFAX HX1 10 F6
Newbridge Gv BSLYN/ROY S71 261 K3
New Bridge Rd
HOLM/MEL HD9 234 D4
New Briggate LDSU LS2 7 H8
New Broad La MILN OL16 228 E3
New Brook St ILK LS29 38 D1
New Brunswick St HFAX HX1 10 F5
WKFDE WF1 12 F6
New Buildings Pl MILN * OL16 206 B6
Newburn Rd GTHN BD7 126 D1
Newbury Dr HEM/SK/SE WF9 247 J1
Newbury Rd BRIG HD6 170 B7
Newbury Wk HUDE HD5 193 L5
Newby Garth AL/HA/HU LS17 88 D1
Newby Rd AIRE BD20 34 F6
Newby St AIRE * BD20 34 F7
Newcastle Cl BIRK/DRI BD11 150 F1
Newcastle Farm Ct
KNOT WF11 159 J2
New Chapel Av STKB/PEN S36 270 E5
New Cl DOD/DAR S75 259 H6
SHPY BD18 81 M7
New Close Av AIRE * BD20 36 A5
New Close La AWLS/ASK DN6 227 G7
MAR/SLWT HD7 211 K5
New Close Rd SHPY BD18 81 M7
New Clough Rd
RPDN/SBR HX6 167 M4
Newcombe St ELL HX5 191 J1
New Cottages OSS * WF5 196 F1
New Craven Ga BEE/HOL LS11 9 H7
New Crs HORS LS18 85 K6
New Cft HORS LS18 85 K6
New Cross St LM/WK BD12 149 K1
WBOW BD5 127 G4
Newdale Av CUD/GR S72 262 C1
New Dales La AIRE BD20 16 D8
New Farmers Hl RTHW LS26 133 M7
Newfield Av BSLYN/ROY S71 261 M2
CAS WF10 158 A7
NORM WF6 178 E5
New Field Cl MILN OL16 206 D6
Newfield Cl NORM WF6 178 E5
Newfield Ct NORM WF6 178 E4
Newfield Crs GFTH/SHER LS25 135 K2
NORM WF6 178 E5
Newfield Dr GFTH/SHER LS25 135 K1
ILK LS29 61 J2
Newfield Head La MILN OL16 229 K1
Newfield La GFTH/SHER LS25 136 F6
Newfield Vw MILN OL16 207 J8
New Fold HOLM/MEL HD9 254 C2
WBSY BD6 126 A7
Newforth Gv WBOW * BD5 126 E4
New Ga HOLM/MEL HD9 254 E5
Newgate MILN OL16 206 B7
MIRF WF14 194 C2
PONT WF8 180 E6
Newgate La HOLM/MEL HD9 235 G4
Newgate St BTLY WF17 174 B3
New Grove Dr HUDE HD5 193 G7
New Hall Ap HOR/CROF WF4 218 A2
Newhall Bank MID LS10 153 M1
Newhall Cha MID LS10 131 M8
New Hall Cl HOR/CROF WF4 220 A2
Newhall Cl MID LS10 131 M8

New - Nor 315

Newhall Crs MID LS10 131 M8
Newhall Cft MID LS10 131 M8
Newhall Dr WBSY BD6 127 H6
Newhall Gdns MID LS10 153 M1
Newhall Garth MID LS10 153 M1
Newhall Ga MID LS10 131 M7
Newhall Gn MID LS10 131 M8
New Hall La HOR/CROF WF4 218 B3
Newhall La MIRF WF14 194 D4
Newhall Mt MID LS10 153 M1
WBSY BD6 127 H6
Newhall Rd BOW * BD4 127 K5
MID LS10 131 M8
New Hall Rd PONT WF8 181 G3
New Hall Wy HOR/CROF WF4 218 B3
New Hey Rd BOW BD4 127 J2
HUDW HD3 191 K2
HUDW HD3 211 L2
Newhey Rd MILN OL16 229 J2
Newhill HEM/SK/SE WF9 246 D5
Newhill Rd BSLYN/ROY S71 261 J1
Newhold GFTH/SHER LS25 113 J6
New Holme Rd HWTH BD22 78 F8
Newhouse Cl WHIT OL12 184 E8
New House La CUL/QBY BD13 125 K6
Newhouse Pl HUD HD1 14 D5
New House Rd HUDN HD2 192 F2
New Houses CUL/QBY * BD13 125 H5
Newill Cl WBOW BD5 127 H4
Newington Av CUD/GR S72 244 D6
New Inn St WOR/ARM LS12 108 C7
New John St BFD * BD1 4 E6
New Kirkgate SHPY * BD18 82 D6
New Laithe Cl HUDE HD5 214 E4
SKP/WHF BD23 16 D1
New Laithe Hl HUDS HD4 214 E4
New Laithe La HOLM/MEL HD9 254 D1
New Laithe Rd HUDE HD5 214 E4
HWTH BD22 77 G6
WBSY * BD6 126 C5
Newlaithes Crs NORM WF6 178 E4
Newlaithes Gdns HORS LS18 85 K7
Newlaithes Garth HORS LS18 85 J8
Newlaithes Rd HORS LS18 85 K8
Newland Av CUD/GR S72 244 C8
Newland Ct HUDN HD2 14 C1
WKFDE WF1 199 G4
Newland La NORM WF6 178 A5
Newland Rd BSLYN/ROY S71 243 G7
HUDE HD5 193 J7
The Newlands RPDN/SBR HX6 167 G4
Newlands PDSY/CALV LS28 106 F4
YEA LS19 62 C6
Newlands Av AWLS/ASK DN6 249 G4
BFDE BD3 105 M5
HIPP HX3 147 J2
KBTN HD8 240 B4
RPDN/SBR HX6 167 G3
WHIT OL12 206 B3
YEA LS19 62 C7
Newlands Cl BRIG HD6 170 D5
WHIT OL12 206 B3
Newlands Crs MOR LS27 152 F2
Newlands Dr AIRE BD20 34 F7
BGLY BD16 81 G1
EARD/LOFT WF3 177 G1
HIPP HX3 147 J3
MOR LS27 152 F2
Newlands Gv HIPP HX3 147 J3
Newlands Pl BFDE BD3 5 K3
Newlands Ri YEA LS19 62 C7
Newlands Rd LUD/ILL HX2 145 K7
Newland St KNOT WF11 181 K1
WKFDE WF1 199 G4
Newlands Wk EARD/LOFT WF3 177 G1
Newland Vw NORM WF6 178 B4
New La AIRE BD20 35 H4
BEE/HOL LS11 8 F3
BOW BD4 105 M8
BOW BD4 128 D4
CLECK BD19 149 J8
COP/BISH YO23 51 M1
EARD/LOFT WF3 153 L6
GFTH/SHER LS25 115 M8
GLE DN14 161 K8
HBR HX7 142 F3
HBR HX7 165 M2
HEM/SK/SE WF9 225 J8
HIPP HX3 168 D4
HIPP HX3 168 F2
HOR/CROF WF4 198 A6
HUDW HD3 210 F2
KBTN HD8 239 K5
KNOT WF11 159 M3
LUD/ILL HX2 166 D1
MAR/SLWT HD7 190 D8
MAR/SLWT HD7 212 C3
MID LS10 153 K1
MOR LS27 129 J6
OT LS21 24 F6
New Lane Crs HEM/SK/SE WF9 225 J7
Newlay Cl IDLE BD10 84 A7
Newlay Gv HORS LS18 85 K8
Newlay La BRAM LS13 107 L2
HORS LS18 85 K7
Newlay Lane Pl BRAM LS13 107 L2
Newlay Wood Av HORS LS18 85 L7
Newlay Wood Cl HORS LS18 85 L7
Newlay Wood Crs HORS LS18 85 L7
Newlay Wood Dr HORS LS18 85 L7
Newlay Wood Gdns
HORS * LS18 85 L7
Newlay Wood Ri HORS LS18 85 K7
Newlay Wood Rd HORS LS18 85 K7
New Lennerton La
GFTH/SHER LS25 117 H7
Newley Av BTLY WF17 151 H6
Newley Mt HORS LS18 85 K8
New Line IDLE BD10 84 A7
New Lodge Crs
BSLYN/ROY S71 243 G7
New Longley La
RPDN/SBR HX6 167 J5
Newlyn Dr BSLYN/ROY S71 261 K3
WKFDW/WTN WF2 198 F4
Newlyn Rd AIRE BD20 58 C5
Newman Av BSLYN/ROY S71 243 L5
Newman St BOW BD4 127 K4
MILN OL16 206 E3
New Market OT LS21 41 J7
Newmarket Ap OSM LS9 132 D1
Newmarket Gn OSM LS9 110 C8
Newmarket La
EARD/LOFT WF3 155 L6
OSM LS9 132 D1
New Market St LDS LS1 9 H1
Newmarket St SKP/WHF BD23 16 C2
New Mill La BSPA/BRAM LS23 70 A1
New Mill Rd HOLM/MEL HD9 236 D8
HOLM/MEL HD9 236 C2
New Mill St LIT OL15 207 J1
New North Pde HUD HD1 14 E6
New North Rd HECK WF16 172 E1
HUD HD1 14 C4
MAR/SLWT HD7 212 C4
New Occupation La
PDSY/CALV LS28 106 E8
New Otley Rd BFDE BD3 5 J4
New Oxford St COL BB8 74 A1
New Park Av PDSY/CALV LS28 107 G3
New Park Cl PDSY/CALV LS28 107 G3
New Park Cft PDSY/CALV LS28 107 G3
New Park La OSS WF5 175 K6
New Park Pl PDSY/CALV LS28 107 G3
New Park Rd CUL/QBY BD13 124 F5
New Park St MOR LS27 152 B3
New Park V PDSY/CALV LS28 107 G3
New Park Vw PDSY/CALV LS28 106 F4
New Park Wk
PDSY/CALV * LS28 106 F3
New Park Wy PDSY/CALV LS28 107 G3
New Popplewell La
CLECK BD19 149 H6
Newport Av BRAM LS13 107 J4
Newport Crs BULY LS4 108 F3
Newport Gdns HDGY LS6 108 F3
Newport Mt HDGY LS6 108 F3
Newport Pl GIR BD8 4 A3
Newport Rd GIR BD8 4 A2
Newport St PONT WF8 180 E5
Newport Vw HDGY * LS6 108 F3
New Princess St BEE/HOL LS11 8 E5
New Pudsey Sq
PDSY/CALV LS28 106 E5
New Rd AIRE BD20 36 A5
AWLS/ASK DN6 227 J6
BSPA/BRAM LS23 69 M3
COP/BISH YO23 73 L4
CUL/QBY BD13 101 M6
DOD/DAR S75 240 D8
DOD/DAR S75 242 C4
DOD/DAR S75 242 E5
EARD/LOFT WF3 154 F3
FEA/AMT WF7 178 F6
GFTH/SHER LS25 136 F4
GTL/HWG HX4 168 C7
GTL/HWG HX4 190 C5
HBR HX7 120 A8
HBR HX7 143 H4
HBR HX7 144 A6
HBR HX7 165 M5
HEM/SK/SE WF9 224 F4
HFAX HX1 11 H7
HOLM/MEL HD9 236 C7
HOR/CROF WF4 196 B8
HOR/CROF WF4 196 C7
HOR/CROF WF4 197 K5
HOR/CROF WF4 201 K5
HOR/CROF WF4 220 D8
HUDE HD5 193 K4
HUDW HD3 190 E4
KNOT WF11 181 J1
LIT OL15 207 G2
LUD/ILL HX2 144 F5
PONT WF8 204 E4
STKB/PEN S36 258 A5
TAD LS24 94 D1
TOD OL14 140 E1
TOD OL14 142 B6
TOD OL14 164 C2
YEA LS19 62 B7
New Rd East CLECK BD19 149 G6
New Rd Side HORS LS18 85 J7
YEA LS19 84 D2
New Road Sq BRIG * HD6 170 A8
New Rw COL BB8 74 E2
HOLM/MEL HD9 254 C1
HTON BD9 104 A4
WKFDW/WTN WF2 175 K4
New Row La STKB/PEN S36 257 G6
New Royd STKB/PEN S36 269 M3
Newroyd Rd WBOW BD5 127 G4
Newsam Ct MSTN/BAR * LS15 111 J7
Newsam Dr MSTN/BAR LS15 111 G7
Newsam Green Rd
MSTN/BAR LS15 133 M4
New Shaw La HBR HX7 142 B1
Newsholme La HOR/CROF WF4 198 B7
Newsholme New Rd
HWTH BD22 78 C2
New Smithy Av STKB/PEN S36 270 C2
New Smithy Dr STKB/PEN S36 270 C2
Newsome Av HUDS HD4 214 C5
Newsome Rd HUDS HD4 214 D2
Newsome Rd South
HUDS HD4 214 C6
Newsome St DEWS WF13 173 K5
New Station St LDS LS1 8 F1
Newstead WHIT * OL12 206 A6
Newstead Av HEM/SK/SE WF9 223 J3
HFAX HX1 146 A7
WKFDE WF1 176 C2
Newstead Crs HEM/SK/SE WF9 223 J2
Newstead Dr HEM/SK/SE WF9 223 J3
Newstead Gdns HFAX HX1 146 A7
Newstead Gv HEM/SK/SE WF9 223 J3
HFAX HX1 146 A7
Newstead Heath HFAX HX1 146 A7
Newstead La HOR/CROF WF4 223 G3
Newstead Pl HFAX HX1 146 A7
Newstead Rd BSLYN/ROY S71 243 G6
WKFDE WF1 12 D1
Newstead Ter HEM/SK/SE WF9 223 J3
HFAX HX1 146 A7
Newstead Vw
HEM/SK/SE WF9 223 H3
Newstead Wk WBOW * BD5 126 F2
New St AWLS/ASK DN6 249 M5
BOW BD4 127 K6
BRIG HD6 148 D7
BRIG HD6 170 F4
BSLY S70 261 G6
BSLYN/ROY S71 243 L3
BSLYN/ROY S71 262 A6
BTLY WF17 174 A3
CAS WF10 158 A6
CLECK BD19 150 B8
CUD/GR S72 222 F8
CUD/GR S72 245 J8
CUL/QBY BD13 101 M6
DOD/DAR S75 242 D5
DOD/DAR S75 260 B8
EARL WF12 174 B7
FEA/AMT WF7 224 B1
GFTH/SHER LS25 135 K5
GTL/HWG HX4 190 B3
HEM/SK/SE WF9 223 L4
HEM/SK/SE * WF9 247 G3
HIPP HX3 169 J2
HOLM/MEL HD9 234 F4
HOLM/MEL HD9 236 B2
HOR/CROF WF4 197 K5
HORS LS18 85 K6
HUD HD1 14 A8
HUD HD1 14 F8
HUDE HD5 193 L6
HUDS HD4 213 J2
HUDS HD4 213 L7
HWTH BD22 78 E8
IDLE BD10 83 K6
KBTN HD8 239 J5
KBTN HD8 239 M5
LIT OL15 207 H2
LM/WK BD12 149 K1
LUD/ILL * HX2 146 A6
MAR/SLWT HD7 212 C5
MAR/SLWT HD7 213 G2
MILN OL16 229 J1
OSS WF5 197 G1
PDSY/CALV LS28 106 F5
PDSY/CALV LS28 107 G8
TAD LS24 71 M3
WHIT OL12 206 A4
New Street Cl PDSY/CALV LS28 107 G8
New Street Gdns
PDSY/CALV LS28 107 G8
New Street Gv
PDSY/CALV LS28 107 G8
New Sturton La
GFTH/SHER LS25 113 K7
New Tanhouse MIRF WF14 194 B1
New Temple Ga
MSTN/BAR LS15 111 J8
Newthorpe Rd AWLS/ASK DN6 227 L2
Newton Av WKFDE WF1 176 D4
Newton Cl AIRE BD20 35 M5
RTHW LS26 154 D2
WKFDE WF1 176 D5
Newton Ct RHAY LS8 88 E8
WKFDE WF1 176 D2
Newton Dr CAS WF10 158 D7
WKFDE WF1 176 D3
Newton Garth CHAL LS7 110 A1
Newton Gn WKFDE WF1 176 D5
Newton Gv CHAL LS7 109 M2
TOD OL14 141 H7
Newton Hill Rd CHAL LS7 109 M1
Newton La CAS WF10 157 M2
WKFDE WF1 176 D3
Newton Lodge Cl CHAL LS7 109 L1
Newton Lodge Dr CHAL LS7 109 L1
Newton Pde CHAL * LS7 109 M1
Newton Pk BRIG HD6 148 B8
Newton Park Ct CHAL * LS7 110 A1
Newton Park Dr CHAL LS7 110 A1
Newton Park Vw CHAL LS7 110 A2
Newton Pl WBOW BD5 126 F2
Newton Rd CHAL LS7 110 A2
Newton St BSLY S70 260 F5
MILN OL16 228 D1
RPDN/SBR * HX6 167 K2
WBOW BD5 127 G3
Newton Vw CHAL LS7 109 M1
Newton Vls CHAL * LS7 87 L8
Newton Wk CHAL LS7 110 A2
Newton Wy BAIL * BD17 82 E2
Newtown Av BSLYN/ROY S71 243 K2
CUD/GR S72 262 D1
New Town Ct HWTH BD22 2 D5
Newtown Gn CUD/GR S72 262 D1
Newtown St COL BB8 74 A2
ROY/SHW OL2 229 K8
New Wk RHAY LS8 88 D5
New Wy BTLY WF17 173 L1
GSLY LS20 61 L5
New Wellgate CAS WF10 158 B8
New Wls WKFDE WF1 12 F4
New Wells Ter WKFDE * WF1 12 F4
New Windsor Dr RTHW LS26 133 H8
New Works Rd LM/WK BD12 148 E1
New York La YEA LS19 84 F4
New York Rd LDSU LS2 7 J8
New York St LDSU LS2 9 H1
Nibshaw La CLECK BD19 150 C6
Nibshaw Rd CLECK BD19 150 C6
Nice Av RHAY LS8 110 B2
Nice St RHAY LS8 110 C2
Nice Vw RHAY LS8 110 B2
Nicholas Cl GTHN BD7 104 B7
Nicholas St BSLY S70 260 F5
Nichols Cl WBY LS22 47 L1
Nicholson Av DOD/DAR S75 260 A2
Nicholson Ct RHAY * LS8 88 C8
Nicholson St CAS WF10 157 L7
ROCH OL11 228 B1
Nichols Wy WBY LS22 47 K1
Nickleby Rd OSM LS9 110 C6
Nicolsons Pl AIRE BD20 36 A5
Nidd Ap WBY LS22 29 M6
Nidd Ct AIRE BD20 36 A6
Nidderdale Cl
GFTH/SHER LS25 135 K1
Nidderdale Wk BAIL BD17 83 G2
Nidd St BFDE BD3 5 M7
Nields Rd MAR/SLWT HD7 212 B6
Nigher Moss Av MILN OL16 206 E8
Nighthorne Av BFDE BD3 105 L5
Nightingale Crest
WKFDW/WTN WF2 197 L2
Nightingale St KGHY * BD21 3 H2
Nightingale Wk BGLY BD16 81 L2
Nijinsky Wy MID LS10 132 D5
Nile Crs HWTH BD22 2 A7
Nile St HUD HD1 14 D9
HWTH * BD22 2 A7
HWTH BD22 79 G6
LDSU LS2 7 J8
MILN OL16 206 C6
Nina Rd GTHN BD7 126 B3
Ninelands La GFTH/SHER LS25 135 J1
Ninelands Sp GFTH/SHER LS25 113 H8
Ninelands Vw GFTH/SHER LS25 113 J7
Ninevah La CAS WF10 157 H1
HEM/SK/SE WF9 224 F3
Nineveh Gdns BEE/HOL LS11 8 D5
Nineveh Pde BEE/HOL LS11 8 D6
Nineveh Rd BEE/HOL LS11 8 C5
Ninth Av LVSG WF15 171 K1
Nippet La OSM LS9 7 M8
Nixon Av OSM LS9 110 D7
Nixon Cl EARL WF12 196 B5
Noble Ct HUDS HD4 213 M8
Noble Meadow WHIT * OL12 206 F2
Noble St GTHN BD7 126 D1
Nog La HTON BD9 104 C2
Nook Farm Av WHIT OL12 206 B3
Nook Gdns MSTN/BAR LS15 90 B6
Nook Gn EARD/LOFT WF3 153 H7
EARL WF12 195 M4
The Nooking
WKFDW/WTN WF2 175 K3
Nook La HBR HX7 143 M2
RPDN/SBR HX6 166 B6
STKB/PEN S36 271 G5
Nook Rd MSTN/BAR LS15 90 B6
The Nooks MOR LS27 129 M7
The Nook AL/HA/HU LS17 87 M1
CLECK BD19 150 A6
EARD/LOFT WF3 153 G8
GFTH/SHER LS25 138 A2
RPDN/SBR HX6 167 K3
STKB/PEN S36 258 C8
Nook Wk DEWS WF13 173 H6
Noon Cl EARD/LOFT WF3 177 G1
Noon Sun St WHIT OL12 206 B5
Nopper Rd HUDS HD4 213 H7
Nora Pl BRAM LS13 107 J3
Nora Rd BRAM LS13 107 J3
Nora Ter BRAM LS13 107 J3
Norbeck Dr HWTH BD22 79 G6
Norbury Rd IDLE BD10 106 A1
Norbury St MILN * OL16 228 D2
Norcliffe La HIPP HX3 147 J8
Norcroft BSLY S70 261 H8
Norcroft Brow GTHN BD7 4 C7
Norcroft La DOD/DAR S75 259 G3
Norcroft St BFD BD1 4 B6
Norcross Av HUDW HD3 191 J7
Norfield HUDN HD2 192 C2
Norfolk Av BTLY WF17 173 K3
Norfolk Cl BSLYN/ROY S71 261 K2
CHAL LS7 87 M7
KNOT WF11 159 K6
LIT OL15 185 L6
ROY/SHW OL2 229 H7
RTHW LS26 155 M1
Norfolk Dr RTHW LS26 155 M1
Norfolk Gdns BFD BD1 4 F7
CHAL LS7 87 M7
RYKW YO26 32 B1
Norfolk Gn CHAL LS7 87 M7
Norfolk Mt CHAL LS7 87 M7
Norfolk Pl CHAL LS7 87 M7
HFAX HX1 10 D8
Norfolk St BGLY BD16 81 J3
BTLY WF17 173 K2
COL BB8 74 A1
HBR HX7 143 J4
ROCH OL11 206 A8
Norfolk Ter CHAL * LS7 87 M7
Norfolk Vw CHAL LS7 87 M7
Norfolk Wk CHAL LS7 87 M7
Norgarth Cl BTLY WF17 174 B1
Norham Gv LM/WK BD12 148 F4
Norland Rd RPDN/SBR HX6 167 K3
RPDN/SBR HX6 167 M5
Norland St GTHN BD7 126 B3
Norland Town Rd
RPDN/SBR HX6 167 M4
Norland Vw RPDN/SBR HX6 167 M2
Norman Av ECHL BD2 105 K1
ELL HX5 169 J8
Norman Cl BSLYN/ROY S71 261 L2
Norman Crs ECHL BD2 105 K1
Norman Dr MIRF WF14 172 B8
Norman Gv ECHL BD2 105 K1
ELL * HX5 169 J8
KSTL LS5 108 C2
Norman La ECHL BD2 105 K1
Norman Mt ECHL BD2 105 K1
KSTL LS5 108 C2
Normanon Pl BEE/HOL LS11 8 D7
Norman Pl RHAY LS8 88 C4
Norman Rd KBTN HD8 257 H1
MIRF WF14 172 B8
Norman Rw KSTL LS5 108 C2
Norman St BGLY * BD16 81 J3
ELL HX5 169 J8
HFAX HX1 10 A9
KSTL LS5 108 C2
SHPY BD18 82 F7
Normans Wy
WKFDW/WTN WF2 199 H5
Norman Ter ECHL BD2 105 K1
ELL HX5 169 J8
RHAY LS8 88 C4
Normanton Gv BEE/HOL LS11 8 C7
Normanton St HOR/CROF WF4 197 L6
Normanton Vw NORM WF6 178 D6
Norman Vw KSTL LS5 108 C2
Norreys St MILN OL16 206 C6
Norridge Bottom
HOLM/MEL HD9 254 C1
Norris Cl HUDE HD5 215 J2
Northorpe La LVSG WF15 172 C4
Nortech Cl CHAL LS7 7 K5
Northallerton Rd BFDE BD3 5 H2
North Ap TAD LS24 92 C2
North Av AIRE BD20 55 L2
CAS WF10 157 H7
HEM/SK/SE WF9 247 H4
HOR/CROF WF4 197 L5
HTON BD9 104 F3
OT LS21 41 J6
PONT WF8 180 C6
WKFDE WF1 176 E6
North Baileygate PONT WF8 180 F5
North Bank Rd BGLY BD16 103 J1
BTLY WF17 173 J1
HUDN HD2 14 C1
North Bolton LUD/ILL HX2 123 M7
North Br HFAX HX1 11 H4
North Bridge St HFAX HX1 11 H4
North Broadgate La HORS LS18 85 L5
Northbrook Cft CHAL * LS7 87 M7
Northbrook Pl CHAL LS7 87 M7
North Brook St BFD BD1 5 G4
Northbrook St CHAL LS7 87 M7
North Byland LUD/ILL HX2 124 A7
North Carr HUDE HD5 193 G7
North Cliffe Av CUL/QBY BD13 103 H8
North Cliffe Cl CUL/QBY * BD13 103 G8
North Cliffe Dr CUL/QBY BD13 103 G8
North Cliffe Gv CUL/QBY BD13 103 G7
North Cliffe La CUL/QBY BD13 103 H7
Northcliffe Rd SHPY BD18 82 C8
North Cl BSLYN/ROY S71 243 L3
FEA/AMT WF7 179 L5
RHAY LS8 88 F8
Northcote OSS WF5 174 E5
Northcote Crs BEE/HOL LS11 8 F7
Northcote Dr BEE/HOL LS11 8 E7
Northcote Fold WBY LS22 47 K4
Northcote Gn BEE/HOL LS11 8 F7
Northcote Rd ECHL BD2 105 K4
Northcote Ter DOD/DAR S75 260 E4
North Ct LDSU LS2 7 H8
North Court Gv WBY LS22 30 A8
North Crs GFTH/SHER LS25 116 A5
HEM/SK/SE WF9 247 K2
Northcroft HEM/SK/SE WF9 247 J3
Northcroft Av
HEM/SK/SE WF9 247 J3
North Croft Grove Rd ILK LS29 38 C2
Northcroft Ri HTON BD9 104 A5
North Cross Rd HUDN HD2 192 B4
North Cut BRIG HD6 170 A4
Northdale Av WBOW BD5 126 E4
Northdale Crs WBOW BD5 126 E4
Northdale Mt WBOW BD5 126 E4
Northdale Rd HTON BD9 104 D1
North Dean Av HWTH BD22 57 G7
North Dean Rd GTL/HWG HX4 168 B5
North Dene Rd AIRE BD20 36 A4
Northdowns Rd ROY/SHW OL2 229 H6
North Dr BHP/TINH LS16 64 B4
GFTH/SHER LS25 116 A5
MAR/SLWT HD7 213 G1
Northedge La HIPP HX3 147 M5
Northedge Meadow IDLE BD10 83 K8
Northedge Pk HIPP HX3 147 M6
Northern Cl GTHN BD7 126 B4
Northern St LDS LS1 8 D1
North Farm Rd RHAY LS8 110 D3
North Fld DOD/DAR S75 259 H6
Northfield Av HEM/SK/SE WF9 246 D2
KNOT WF11 182 B2
OSS WF5 174 F8
RTHW LS26 154 E2
Northfield Cl AWLS/ASK DN6 205 H3
ELL * HX5 169 H8
Northfield Ct TAD LS24 94 F7
Northfield Crs BGLY BD16 81 J7
Northfield Dr PONT WF8 181 H5
Northfield Gdns WBSY BD6 126 E5
Northfield Gv HEM/SK/SE WF9 246 D3
HUD HD1 214 A2
WBSY BD6 126 E5
North Field La KBTN HD8 239 J4
Northfield La AWLS/ASK DN6 205 G2
GFTH/SHER LS25 137 M1
HEM/SK/SE WF9 246 D3
HOR/CROF WF4 197 L5
KBTN HD8 216 A6
Northfield La KNOT WF11 182 F8
Northfield Pl DEWS WF13 173 K5
GIR BD8 4 B1
RTHW LS26 154 D2
WBY LS22 30 A8
North Field Rd AWLS/ASK DN6 248 A6
Northfield Rd DEWS WF13 173 K5
HOR/CROF WF4 200 D3
KNOT WF11 182 B2
OSS WF5 174 F8
WBSY BD6 126 D5
Northfields BSPA/BRAM LS23 49 J3
Northfields La TAD LS24 94 F6
Northfield St DEWS WF13 173 L5
HEM/SK/SE WF9 246 D3
Northfield Ter CUL/QBY BD13 125 J5
HOR/CROF * WF4 197 L4
North Fold IDLE BD10 83 K6
North Ga MIRF WF14 193 M4
Northgate BAIL BD17 82 E2
BFD BD1 4 E5
CLECK BD19 150 A7
CUD/GR S72 223 G8
DEWS WF13 173 M6
DOD/DAR S75 260 E3
ELL HX5 169 H7
GTL/HWG HX4 190 D2
HBR HX7 143 H1
HECK WF16 172 E2
HFAX HX1 11 H5
HOLM/MEL HD9 214 D8
HOLM/MEL HD9 236 C1
HOR/CROF WF4 197 J4
HUD HD1 15 G4
HUDE HD5 215 H3

PONT WF8 180 F5
RTHW LS26 133 L8
WKFDE WF1 12 F2
Northgate Cl PONT WF8 180 F5
Northgate La WBY LS22 47 J2
WBY LS22 47 K3
Northgate Ldg PONT WF8 180 F5
Northgate Ri WBY LS22 47 K4
Northgates WBY LS22 48 A1
North Grange Ms HDGY LS6 6 A1
North Grange Mt HDGY LS6 109 G1
North Grange Rd HDGY LS6 109 G2
North Gv WBY LS22 30 A8
North Grove Av WBY LS22 30 A7
North Grove Cl RHAY LS8 88 F8
North Grove Crs WBY LS22 30 A7
North Grove Dr RHAY LS8 88 F8
WBY LS22 30 A7
North Grove Mt WBY LS22 30 A8
North Grove Ri RHAY LS8 88 F8
North Grove Rd WBY LS22 30 A7
North Grove Wy WBY LS22 30 A7
North Hall Av IDLE BD10 83 J4
North Hl SCFT LS14 67 M5
North Hill Cl RHAY LS8 88 E8
North Hill Dr HUDE HD5 193 L6
North Hill Rd HDGY LS6 6 A1
North Holme St BFD BD1 4 F4
North King St BTLY WF17 173 M2
Northlands BSLYN/ROY S71 243 L2
North La MAR/SLWT HD7 211 M5
RHAY LS8 88 F8
RTHW LS26 133 L8
STKB/PEN S36 258 B4
WHIT OL12 206 B6
Northlea Av IDLE BD10 83 J5
North Lingwell Rd MID LS10 153 L1
North Lodge Fold DEWS WF13 173 H3
North Lodge La PONT WF8 204 B2
North Md BHP/TINH LS16 64 B4
North Moor La HUDE HD5 193 L4
Northolme Av BHP/TINH LS16 86 D7
Northolme Crs BHP/TINH LS16 86 D7
Northorpe Ct MIRF WF14 172 E7
Northorpe La MIRF WF14 172 E7
Northowram Gn HIPP HX3 147 J2
North Pde BFD BD1 4 E5
BHP/TINH LS16 86 C6
HFAX HX1 11 G5
ILK LS29 38 E2
ILK LS29 40 A4
MILN OL16 229 L2
OT LS21 41 J6
SKP/WHF BD23 16 C4
WIL/AL BD15 103 J4
North Park Av RHAY LS8 88 B6
North Park Gv RHAY LS8 88 C6
North Park La AWLS/ASK DN6 249 L4
North Park Rd HTON BD9 104 D3
RHAY LS8 88 C6
North Park St DEWS WF13 173 J5
North Park Ter HTON BD9 104 E4
North Pkwy SCFT LS14 111 G1
North Pl DOD/DAR S75 260 D3
North Pollard St HFAX HX1 11 H4
North Queen St KGHY BD21 3 G4
North Ri HUDN HD2 192 E4
North Rd AIRE BD20 55 L1
BSLYN/ROY S71 243 M2
DEWS WF13 172 F8
HORS LS18 85 K3
KBTN HD8 216 A7
KNOT WF11 159 J2
MSTN/BAR LS15 111 L4
OSM LS9 132 E3
WBSY BD6 126 D6
North Road Ter WKFDE WF1 176 D7
Northrop Cl GIR BD8 104 C5
North Rw KBTN HD8 237 M6
North Royds Wd
BSLYN/ROY S71 243 H5
Northside Av GTHN BD7 104 C8
Northside Rd GTHN BD7 104 C8
Northside Ter GTHN BD7 104 B8
North's Pl MIRF WF14 172 C7
Northstead DEWS WF13 172 F8
North St AIRE BD20 34 F7
AIRE BD20 36 A4
AIRE BD20 55 M1
BFD BD1 5 H5
CAS WF10 157 L6
CAS WF10 158 E4
CHAL LS7 7 J5
DEWS WF13 173 L5
GTL/HWG HX4 168 F7
GTL/HWG HX4 190 D2
HECK WF16 172 F3
HEM/SK/SE WF9 246 D3
HUD HD1 214 A2
HWTH BD22 78 D7
IDLE BD10 83 K4
ILK LS29 19 J6
KGHY BD21 3 G5
LM/WK BD12 149 J2
MILN OL16 206 C6
MIRF WF14 194 B3
NORM WF6 178 C6
OT LS21 41 J6
PDSY/CALV LS28 107 G6
WBY LS22 48 A1
WMB/DAR S73 263 J8
YEA LS19 84 D2
North Ter BTLY WF17 151 H5
MSTN/BAR * LS15 111 L4
YEA LS19 62 D7
Northumberland St HUD HD1 14 F6
Northumberland Wy
BSLYN/ROY S71 262 B6
North Vw AIRE BD20 35 H8
EARL WF12 173 M8
ILK LS29 61 J2
KNOT WF11 182 A1
WIL/AL BD15 102 E1
WIL/AL BD15 103 J5
North View Rd BFDE BD3 105 H4
BOW BD4 128 C7
North View St KGHY BD21 57 L5
PDSY/CALV LS28 107 G4
North View Ter DEWS * WF13 173 K4
HWTH BD22 78 E6
PDSY/CALV LS28 107 G4
North Wk BGLY BD16 80 C5
HEM/SK/SE WF9 223 M6
North Wy HUDN HD2 193 G2
RHAY LS8 88 F8
Northway MIRF WF14 172 B7
Northway Crs MIRF WF14 172 B7
Northway Gdns MIRF WF14 172 B6
Northwell Ga OT LS21 41 G5
North West Rd HDGY LS6 6 F3
North Wing BFDE BD3 5 H4
Northwood Cl PDSY/CALV LS28 129 H1
RTHW LS26 133 L7
Northwood Crs IDLE BD10 83 L7
Northwood Falls RTHW LS26 133 L7
Northwood Gdns
MSTN/BAR LS15 112 A7
Northwood Mt
PDSY/CALV LS28 129 H1
Northwood Pk KBTN HD8 216 A7
RTHW LS26 133 L7
Northwood Vw
PDSY/CALV LS28 129 H1
Norton & Kirk Smeaton Rd
PONT WF8 226 F1
Norton Cl ELL HX5 191 H1
LUD/ILL HX2 145 K7
Norton Dr LUD/ILL HX2 145 K7
Norton Fold ECHL * BD2 105 K1
Norton Mill La AWLS/ASK DN6 227 L2
Norton Rd RHAY LS8 88 C3
WHIT OL12 206 B3
WKFDE WF1 176 F7
Norton St AIRE BD20 35 M5
ELL HX5 191 H1
WKFDE WF1 13 K7
Norton Wy MOR LS27 130 B8
Norville Crs WMB/DAR S73 263 K8
Norwich Av MID LS10 131 M4
Norwich St ROCH OL11 228 C1
Norwood PONT WF8 203 J1
Norwood Av BIRK/DRI BD11 150 D2
ILK LS29 40 B5
SHPY BD18 82 D8
Norwood Bottom Rd OT LS21 23 H3
Norwood Cl ILK LS29 40 B5
ROY/SHW OL2 229 J6
Norwood Crs CLECK BD19 150 D2
PDSY/CALV LS28 107 H4
Norwood Dr BIRK/DRI BD11 150 D2
BTLY WF17 151 H6
CUD/GR S72 245 J3
DOD/DAR S75 260 A1
Norwood Green Hl HIPP HX3 148 B4
Norwood Gv BIRK/DRI BD11 150 D2
HDGY LS6 109 G3
Norwood La PBR HG3 24 D1
STKB/PEN S36 270 B1
Norwood Mt HDGY LS6 109 G3
Norwood Pk HUDW HD3 191 M5
Norwood Pl HDGY LS6 109 G3
SHPY BD18 82 D8
Nor Wood Rd HEM/SK/SE WF9 245 M1
Norwood Rd HDGY LS6 109 G3
HUDN HD2 192 A4
SHPY BD18 82 D8
Norwood St NORM WF6 178 F3
SHPY BD18 82 D8
WBOW BD5 126 F4
Norwood Ter HDGY LS6 109 G3
ILK LS29 40 B5
SHPY BD18 82 D8
Norwood Vw HDGY * LS6 109 G3
Nostell Cl GIR BD8 4 C3
Nostell Fold DOD/DAR S75 260 B8
Nostell La HOR/CROF WF4 222 D4
Noster Gv BEE/HOL LS11 8 B9
Noster Hl BEE/HOL LS11 131 H3
Noster Pl BEE/HOL LS11 8 B9
Noster Rd BEE/HOL LS11 131 H3
Noster St BEE/HOL LS11 8 B9
Noster Ter BEE/HOL LS11 8 B9
Noster Vw BEE/HOL LS11 8 B9
Nottingham Cl BSLYN/ROY S71 262 C7
EARD/LOFT * WF3 154 C3
Nottingham St BFDE BD3 106 A7
Notton La HOR/CROF WF4 221 L7
Nova La BTLY WF17 150 F4
Nowell Ap OSM LS9 110 D5
Nowell Av OSM LS9 110 D5
Nowell Cl OSM LS9 110 D5
Nowell Ct OSM LS9 110 D5
Nowell Crs OSM LS9 110 D5
Nowell End Rw OSM LS9 110 D5
Nowell Gdns OSM LS9 110 D5
Nowell Gv OSM LS9 110 D5
Nowell La OSM LS9 110 D5
Nowell Mt OSM LS9 110 D5
Nowell Pde OSM LS9 110 D5
Nowell Pl HUDE HD5 215 H2
OSM LS9 110 D5
Nowell St DEWS WF13 173 K5
OSM LS9 110 D5
Nowell's Yd DEWS WF13 173 K6
Nowell Ter OSM LS9 110 D5
Nowell Vw OSM * LS9 110 D5
Nowell Wk OSM LS9 110 D5
Noyna Av COL BB8 52 A5
Noyna Vw COL BB8 52 A7
Nunburnholme Wk IDLE BD10 83 L8
Nunington Av WOR/ARM LS12 108 E6
Nunington St WOR/ARM LS12 108 E6
Nunington Ter WOR/ARM LS12 108 E6
Nunington Vw WOR/ARM LS12 108 E5
Nunlea Royd BRIG HD6 148 C8
Nunnery La BRIG HD6 169 M7
Nunns Av FEA/AMT WF7 201 L3
Nunn's Cl FEA/AMT WF7 201 L2
Nunns Ct FEA/AMT WF7 201 L3
Nunn's Cft FEA/AMT WF7 201 M2
Nunn's Gn FEA/AMT WF7 201 M2
Nunn's La FEA/AMT WF7 201 M2
Nunroyd HECK WF16 172 F1
Nunroyd Av GSLY LS20 62 B6
Nunroyd Gv AL/HA/HU LS17 87 M5
Nunroyd Lawn
AL/HA/HU * LS17 87 M5
Nunroyd Rd AL/HA/HU LS17 87 M5
Nunroyd Ter AL/HA/HU LS17 87 M5
Nunthorpe Rd BRAM LS13 107 H1
Nurser La WBOW BD5 126 E2
Nurser Pl WBOW BD5 126 E2
Nursery Av LUD/ILL HX2 146 B3
Nursery Cl AIRE BD20 57 J3
AL/HA/HU LS17 87 L2
BAIL * BD17 82 A4
Nursery Gdns BSLY S70 262 A7
MILN * OL16 206 E6
Nursery Garth WBY LS22 30 B8
Nursery Gv AL/HA/HU LS17 87 J2
LUD/ILL HX2 146 B3
Nursery La AL/HA/HU LS17 87 L2
HIPP HX3 146 B3
ILK LS29 19 J6
RPDN/SBR HX6 188 D3
Nursery Mt MID LS10 132 A5
Nursery Mount Rd MID LS10 132 A5
Nursery Rd GSLY LS20 61 M3
GTHN BD7 126 B4
Nursery St BSLY S70 261 G6
EARL WF12 195 L2
Nursery Wy BSPA/BRAM LS23 48 D6
BSPA/BRAM LS23 69 M1
Nursery Wood Rd BTLY WF17 173 M4
Nussey Av BTLY WF17 151 G4
Nutclough Rd HBR HX7 143 K2
Nutfield St TOD OL14 141 K8
Nuttall Rd BFDE BD3 5 J5
Nutter La CLECK BD19 150 E4
Nutter St CLECK BD19 149 L7
Nutting Grove Ter
WOR/ARM LS12 130 A1
Nutwood Wk WBSY BD6 126 A8

O

Oak Av BGLY BD16 81 H5
COP/BISH YO23 73 L8
EARD/LOFT WF3 177 H2
GFTH/SHER LS25 113 H7
GIR BD8 104 E4
HOLM/MEL HD9 234 E3
HUDE HD5 215 G1
HUDW HD3 213 G1
ILK LS29 40 B6
MOR LS27 152 D3
NORM WF6 178 C6
ROY/SHW OL2 228 F8
RPDN/SBR HX6 167 K1
TOD OL14 141 J8
Oak Bank BGLY BD16 81 H5
SHPY BD18 104 F1
Oakbank Av HWTH BD22 2 A9
Oakbank Broadway
HWTH BD22 79 H2
Oakbank Ct HWTH BD22 79 H2
Oakbank Crs HWTH BD22 79 H2
Oakbank Dr HWTH BD22 2 A9
Oakbank Gv HWTH BD22 2 B9
Oakbank La HWTH BD22 79 H2
Oakbank Mt HWTH BD22 79 H2
Oakburn Rd ILK LS29 38 C3
Oakcliffe Rd WHIT OL12 206 E2
Oak Crs GFTH/SHER LS25 113 H7
MSTN/BAR LS15 111 H7
Oakdale BGLY BD16 81 J1
Oakdale Av SHPY BD18 82 F8
WBSY BD6 126 D5
Oakdale Cl EARD/LOFT WF3 154 D8
HIPP HX3 146 C4
IDLE BD10 106 A3
Oakdale Crs HUDW HD3 191 J6
WBSY BD6 126 D5
Oakdale Dr IDLE BD10 106 A3
SHPY BD18 83 G8
Oakdale Garth SCFT LS14 89 K5
Oakdale Gv SHPY BD18 83 G8
Oakdale Meadow SCFT LS14 89 K5
Oakdale Pk OT LS21 42 F8
Oakdale Rd SHPY BD18 83 G8
Oakdale Ter WBSY BD6 126 D5
Oakdean HUDN HD2 192 C2
Oakdene Cl PDSY/CALV LS28 129 H1
Oakdene Ct AL/HA/HU LS17 88 C2
Oakdene Dr AL/HA/HU LS17 88 C2
HOR/CROF WF4 200 D6
Oakdene Gdns AL/HA/HU LS17 88 C2
Oakdene V AL/HA/HU LS17 88 C2
Oakdene Wy AL/HA/HU LS17 88 C2
Oak Dr GFTH/SHER LS25 113 H7
MAR/SLWT HD7 212 F3
Oakenshaw Ct LM/WK BD12 148 E4
Oakenshaw La CLECK BD19 149 J3
WKFDW/WTN WF2 199 J6
Oakenshaw St WKFDE WF1 13 L9
Oakes Av HOLM/MEL HD9 236 E5
Oakes Fold KBTN HD8 216 C3
Oakes La HOLM/MEL HD9 236 E4
Oakes Rd South HUDW HD3 191 K7
Oakes St WKFDW/WTN WF2 175 M8
Oakfield HDGY LS6 109 G1
Oakfield Av BGLY BD16 81 L4
RTHW * LS26 133 G8
Oakfield Cl ELL HX5 169 G8
GFTH/SHER LS25 113 H8
ILK LS29 40 C8
Oakfield Ct DOD/DAR * S75 242 C5
Oakfield Crs KNOT WF11 182 B3
Oakfield Dr BAIL BD17 82 F4
MIRF WF14 194 B3
Oakfield Gv HTON BD9 104 E4
KBTN HD8 239 J5
Oakfield Pk PONT WF8 225 K2
Oakfield Rd HUDN HD2 192 A5
HWTH BD22 79 J2
Oakfield Ter SHPY BD18 82 F7
Oakfield Wk DOD/DAR S75 260 D4
Oak Gv GFTH/SHER LS25 113 J7
HWTH BD22 79 J3
MOR LS27 152 D3
Oakhall Pk CUL/QBY BD13 102 F7
Oak Hall Pk HOR/CROF WF4 219 L2
Oakhall Park Av
CUL/QBY BD13 102 F7
Oakham Pl DOD/DAR S75 260 E3
Oakhampton Ct RHAY LS8 88 E7
Oakham Wk BOW * BD4 127 J2
Oak Hl LIT OL15 207 H1
RPDN/SBR HX6 167 G6
Oak Hill Rd BRIG HD6 170 D3
Oakhill Rd BTLY WF17 151 J7
Oakhurst Av BEE/HOL LS11 131 H5
Oakhurst Gv BEE/HOL LS11 131 H5
Oakhurst Mt BEE/HOL LS11 131 H5
Oakhurst Rd BEE/HOL LS11 131 J5
Oakhurst St BEE/HOL LS11 131 H5
Oakland Ct KBTN HD8 216 B7
Oakland Dr HOR/CROF WF4 218 E1
Oakland Rd HOR/CROF WF4 218 F1
WKFDE WF1 13 J9
Oaklands BRIG HD6 170 B5
EARD/LOFT WF3 154 C3
IDLE BD10 83 J6
ILK LS29 38 B4
SHPY BD18 81 M7
Oaklands Av BHP/TINH LS16 86 F3
BRAM LS13 107 G1
BSLYN/ROY S71 261 M2
HIPP HX3 147 J3
Oaklands Cl BHP/TINH LS16 86 F3
HOLM/MEL HD9 236 C7
Oaklands Cft
WKFDW/WTN WF2 199 K8
Oaklands Dr BHP/TINH LS16 86 F3
BTLY WF17 174 B1
HUDE HD5 215 H1
Oaklands Fold BHP/TINH LS16 86 F3
Oaklands Gv BHP/TINH LS16 86 F3
Oaklands Rd BRAM LS13 107 G1
Oakland St AIRE BD20 35 M5
Oak La GIR BD8 104 E4
HFAX HX1 10 C5
RPDN/SBR HX6 167 G6
Oaklea Cl DOD/DAR S75 242 D4
Oaklea Gdns BHP/TINH LS16 86 F4
Oaklea Hall Cl BHP/TINH LS16 86 F4
Oaklea Rd MSTN/BAR LS15 90 B8
Oak Leigh DOD/DAR S75 259 G2
Oakleigh Av CLAY BD14 125 K3
HIPP HX3 168 E3
WKFDW/WTN WF2 198 A1
Oakleigh Cl CLAY BD14 125 K2
HOR/CROF WF4 200 E2
Oakleigh Gdns CLAY * BD14 125 K3
Oakleigh Gv CLAY BD14 125 K3
Oakleigh Rd CLAY BD14 125 K3
Oakleigh Ter CLAY BD14 125 K2
Oakleigh Vw BAIL BD17 82 D3
Oakley Gv BEE/HOL LS11 131 L3
Oakley St EARD/LOFT WF3 154 A5
Oakley Ter BEE/HOL LS11 131 L4
Oakley Vw BEE/HOL LS11 131 L4
Oak Mt GIR BD8 104 F4
HIPP * HX3 148 A7
TOD OL14 141 K8
Oak Park Ri BSLY * S70 261 J7
Oak Pl GFTH/SHER LS25 113 G7
HFAX HX1 10 C6
RPDN/SBR HX6 167 K1
Oak Rdg WBY LS22 47 L1
Oakridge Av ILK LS29 61 K2
Oakridge Ct BGLY BD16 81 J2
Oak Ri CLECK BD19 149 M4
Oak Rd CHAL LS7 109 M1
CUD/GR S72 244 F4
GFTH/SHER LS25 113 G7
HUDN HD2 193 J1
MOR LS27 152 B4
MSTN/BAR LS15 111 H7
WBY LS22 30 F1
WOR/ARM LS12 109 G7
Oak Royd GFTH/SHER LS25 113 H7
Oakroyd RTHW LS26 155 H2
Oakroyd Av WBSY BD6 126 E6
Oakroyd Cl BIRK/DRI BD11 150 C1
BRIG HD6 170 D1
Oakroyd Dr BIRK/DRI BD11 150 C2
BRIG HD6 170 D1
Oakroyd Fold MOR * LS27 130 E6
Oakroyd Mt PDSY/CALV LS28 107 G6
Oakroyd Rd WBSY BD6 126 E6
Oakroyd Ter BAIL BD17 82 F4
GIR BD8 104 F4
MOR * LS27 130 E6
PDSY/CALV LS28 107 G6
Oakroyd Vls GIR BD8 104 F4
The Oaks HOR/CROF WF4 200 D2
MOR LS27 130 D7
Oak Scar La HOLM/MEL HD9 254 F4
Oaks Crs BSLY S70 261 L6
Oaks Dr GIR BD8 103 L6
Oaks Farm Dr DOD/DAR S75 242 B6
Oaksfield RTHW LS26 156 F4
Oaks Fold KBTN * HD8 216 C3
WBOW BD5 127 G3
Oaks Green Mt BRIG HD6 170 B7
Oaks La BSLY S70 261 L6
BSPA/BRAM LS23 48 F6
GIR BD8 103 L5
Oaks Rd BTLY WF17 174 A2
Oak St BSLY S70 260 F5
CLAY BD14 125 K2
COL BB8 52 B8
CUD/GR S72 263 K1
ELL HX5 169 H8
HBR HX7 143 J3
HECK WF16 172 E2
HEM/SK/SE WF9 247 G5
HOR/CROF WF4 200 C7
HWTH BD22 78 F7
HWTH BD22 100 E3
LIT OL15 207 L1
MILN OL16 206 B7
MILN OL16 229 J3
MOR LS27 130 D7
PDSY/CALV LS28 106 E6
ROY/SHW OL2 229 L8
RPDN/SBR HX6 167 K1
TOD OL14 163 J2
WKFDE WF1 176 E2
Oaks Wood Dr DOD/DAR S75 242 B6
Oak Ter COL * BB8 53 G8
HFAX * HX1 10 C5
HUDN * HD2 192 D5
LIT OL15 185 M4
Oak Tree Av CUD/GR S72 244 D7
KBTN HD8 215 M3
Oak Tree Cl DOD/DAR S75 241 M6
OSM LS9 110 E3
Oak Tree Ct AIRE BD20 35 M4
Oak Tree Crs OSM LS9 110 E3
Oak Tree Dr RHAY LS8 110 E3
Oak Tree Gv HEM/SK/SE WF9 224 B8
OSM LS9 110 E3
Oaktree La HEM/SK/SE WF9 224 E1
Oak Tree Meadow
WKFDW/WTN WF2 199 J8
Oak Tree Mt OSM LS9 110 E3
Oak Tree Pl OSM LS9 110 E3
Oak Tree Rd KBTN HD8 215 M3
Oak Tree Ter KBTN HD8 215 M3
Oak Tree Wk OSM LS9 110 E3
Oak Vw AIRE BD20 36 A4
Oak Vls GIR BD8 104 F4
Oakville Rd HBR HX7 142 F4
Oakway BIRK/DRI BD11 150 D2
Oakwell Av BTLY WF17 151 H8
PONT WF8 180 E8
RHAY LS8 88 C8
WOR/ARM LS12 108 F7
Oakwell Cl BIRK/DRI BD11 151 J1
GTHN BD7 126 D3
HEM/SK/SE WF9 223 J4
Oakwell Ct BRAM LS13 107 K3
Oakwell Crs RHAY LS8 88 C8
Oakwell Dr RHAY LS8 88 C8
Oakwell Gdns RHAY LS8 88 C8
Oakwell Gv BRAM LS13 107 K3
Oak Well La BSLY S70 261 J6
Oakwell Mt RHAY LS8 88 C8
Oakwell Ov RHAY LS8 88 C8
Oakwell Rd BIRK/DRI BD11 151 J1
Oakwell Ter BSLYN/ROY S71 261 J6
PDSY/CALV * LS28 106 F3
Oakwell Vw BSLYN/ROY S71 261 J6
Oakwell Wy BTLY WF17 151 J3
Oakwood WKFDW/WTN * WF2 197 M3
Oakwood Av BIRK/DRI BD11 150 C1
BSLYN/ROY S71 243 K2
ECHL BD2 104 F2
RHAY LS8 88 D8
WKFDW/WTN WF2 197 M1
Oakwood Boundary Rd
RHAY LS8 88 D8
Oakwood Cl NORM WF6 178 B2
TAD LS24 94 E8
Oakwood Cottages
BGLY * BD16 59 J8
Oakwood Ct GIR BD8 4 A4
RHAY LS8 88 E8
Oakwood Crs BSLYN/ROY S71 243 K3
Oakwood Dr BGLY BD16 81 H1
HEM/SK/SE WF9 246 B1
NORM WF6 178 B2
RHAY LS8 88 D8
RTHW LS26 132 F7
Oakwood Gdns RHAY LS8 88 D8
Oakwood Garth RHAY LS8 88 E8
Oakwood Gra RHAY LS8 88 E8
Oakwood Grange La RHAY LS8 88 E8
Oakwood Gn RHAY LS8 88 E8
Oakwood Gv GIR BD8 104 C5
HOR/CROF WF4 197 L5
RHAY LS8 88 D8
Oakwood La OSM LS9 110 F3
RHAY LS8 88 D8
Oakwood Mt RHAY LS8 88 D8
Oakwood Nook RHAY LS8 88 D8
Oakwood Pk RHAY LS8 110 E1
Oakwood Pl RHAY LS8 88 D8
Oakwood Ri RHAY LS8 88 E8
Oakwood Rd BSLYN/ROY S71 243 K2
BTLY WF17 174 A1
Oak Wood Rd WBY LS22 29 M7
Oakwood Sq DOD/DAR S75 241 K6
Oakwood Ter PDSY/CALV LS28 107 G8
Oakwood Vw RHAY * LS8 88 E8
Oakwood Wk RHAY LS8 88 D8
Oakworth Cl DOD/DAR S75 260 D3
Oakworth Hall HWTH BD22 78 E4
Oakworth Rd HWTH BD22 79 H2
KGHY BD21 2 B9
Oasby Cft BOW BD4 128 A5
Oast House Cft
EARD/LOFT WF3 154 D3
Oastler Av HUD HD1 14 C7
Oastler Pl LM/WK BD12 126 F8
Oastler Rd PDSY/CALV LS28 84 D8
SHPY BD18 82 B6
Oastler St DEWS WF13 173 K6
Oates St DEWS WF13 173 M6
Oatland Cl CHAL LS7 7 H4
Oatland Ct CHAL LS7 7 H5
Oatland Dr CHAL LS7 7 H5
Oatland Gdns CHAL LS7 7 J5
Oatland Gn CHAL LS7 7 H4
Oatland Hts CHAL LS7 7 H5
Oatland La CHAL LS7 7 G4
Oatland Pl CHAL LS7 7 G3
Oatland Rd CHAL LS7 7 G4
Oatlands Dr OT LS21 41 H5
Oat St HWTH * BD22 79 J2
Oban Cl EARD/LOFT WF3 152 F5
Oban Pl WOR/ARM LS12 108 D6
Oban St WOR/ARM LS12 108 D6
Oban Ter WOR/ARM LS12 108 D6
Oberon Crs WMB/DAR S73 263 H8
Occupation La BHP/TINH LS16 63 K3
DEWS WF13 173 H3
HOLM/MEL HD9 236 F5
HWTH BD22 78 F2
LUD/ILL HX2 124 A8
PDSY/CALV LS28 106 E8
TAD LS24 91 M2
Occupation Rd HUDN * HD2 192 E3
HUDW HD3 191 K6
Ochrewell Av HUDN HD2 193 G3

Octagon Ter LUD/ILL HX2 168 A2
Odda La GSLY LS20 61 G5
Oddfellows' Ct BFD BD1 4 E6
Oddfellows St BRIG HD6 170 D3
CLECK BD19 149 H6
MIRF WF14 194 C1
Oddfellow St MOR LS27 152 C2
Oddy Pl WBSY BD6 126 D5
Oddy's Fold HDGY LS6 87 G6
Oddy St BOW BD4 128 A5
Odsal Pl WBSY BD6 126 F6
Odsal Rd WBSY BD6 126 E5
Offley La HEM/SK/SE WF9 201 K8
Ogden Crs CUL/QBY BD13 101 M4
Ogden La BRIG HD6 170 B6
CUL/QBY BD13 101 M4
LUD/ILL HX2 123 M4
MILN OL16 229 M1
Ogden St RPDN/SBR HX6 167 J3
Ogden View Cl LUD/ILL HX2 123 M7
Ogilby Ct RTHW LS26 133 K7
Ogilby Ms RTHW LS26 133 K7
O'Grady Sq OSM LS9 110 B7
Old Allen Rd CUL/QBY BD13 102 C3
Old Anna La or Long La
STKB/PEN S36 270 C2
Old Bank HIPP HX3 11 K5
MAR/SLWT HD7 212 B6
Old Bank Fold HUDE * HD5 15 L8
Old Bank Rd EARL WF12 174 A6
MIRF WF14 172 C7
Old Bar La HOLM/MEL HD9 255 K6
Old Barn Cl AL/HA/HU LS17 87 J1
Old Bell Ct HFAX * HX1 11 G8
Old Bent La WHIT OL12 184 C7
Old Brandon La AL/HA/HU LS17 89 G2
Old Brewery Gdns TAD LS24 72 A2
Old Bridge Ri ILK LS29 38 C2
Old Brook Cl ROY/SHW OL2 229 M6
Old Brow La MILN OL16 206 E3
Old Canal Rd BFD BD1 4 F2
Old Cawsey RPDN/SBR HX6 167 L2
Old Church St OSS WF5 196 F1
Old Clay Dr WHIT OL12 206 F2
Old Cl BEE/HOL LS11 130 F6
Old Cock Yd HFAX * HX1 11 H6
Old Corn Mill La GTHN * BD7 126 C2
Old Crown Rd
WKFDW/WTN WF2 197 M3
Old Dalton La KGHY BD21 3 J4
Old Earth ELL HX5 169 K7
Oldfarm Ap BHP/TINH LS16 86 B6
Oldfarm Cl BHP/TINH LS16 86 C6
Old Farm Crs BOW * BD4 127 K3
Oldfarm Cross BHP/TINH LS16 86 C6
Oldfarm Dr BHP/TINH LS16 86 C6
Oldfarm Garth BHP/TINH LS16 86 C6
Oldfarm Pde BHP/TINH LS16 86 C6
Oldfarm Wk BHP/TINH LS16 86 B6
Oldfield Av WOR/ARM LS12 108 E8
Oldfield Ct CHAL LS7 88 A8
Old Fieldhouse La HUDN HD2 192 F4
Oldfield La HECK WF16 172 F3
HWTH BD22 77 M6
HWTH BD22 78 C7
KBTN HD8 240 B4
WBY LS22 48 A5
WOR/ARM LS12 108 F8
Oldfield Rd HOLM/MEL HD9 236 A5
Oldfield St HIPP HX3 146 C2
HUDS HD4 214 A2
WOR/ARM LS12 108 E8
Old Forge Ms BHP/TINH LS16 63 M3
Old Garth Cft KNOT WF11 159 J2
Old Ga HBR HX7 143 J3
HOLM/MEL HD9 253 G7
Oldgate HUD HD1 15 G7
Oldgate La GFTH/SHER LS25 115 L2
Old Great North Rd
KNOT WF11 159 K5
KNOT WF11 159 L8
Old Gnd MAR/SLWT HD7 211 J6
Old Guy Rd CUL/QBY BD13 124 D4
Old Hall Cl AIRE BD20 34 D8
HWTH * BD22 78 E8
Old Hall La KBTN HD8 240 A1
Old Hall Ms BTLY * WF17 151 L7
Old Hall Rd AIRE BD20 34 D8
AWLS/ASK * DN6 249 J5
BTLY WF17 151 L7
EARD/LOFT WF3 153 H6
Old Hall Wy AIRE BD20 34 C8
Oldham Rd MILN OL16 206 B7
ROCH OL11 228 C1
RPDN/SBR HX6 210 A1
UPML OL3 230 C8
Oldham Wy MILN OL16 229 H5
ROY/SHW OL2 230 C4
UPML OL3 231 L3
Old Haworth La YEA LS19 62 D7
Old Hollings Hl BAIL BD17 61 L8
Old Laithe La HBR HX7 143 L1
Old La BEE/HOL LS11 131 H4
BHP/TINH LS16 63 J3
BIRK/DRI BD11 129 J7
BIRK/DRI BD11 150 C1
BRIG HD6 170 D3
BWCK/EAR BB18 52 B2
GSLY LS20 61 G6
HBR HX7 121 K6
HIPP HX3 10 E1
HOLM/MEL HD9 252 E2
HUDN HD2 192 F2
HWTH BD22 54 E4
HWTH BD22 77 H7
ILK LS29 19 L8
ILK LS29 38 F3
LUD/ILL HX2 144 F5
MAR/SLWT HD7 211 M7
MAR/SLWT HD7 212 D1
RYKW YO26 33 J3
SEL YO8 139 L5
WHIT OL12 162 A8
Old Langley La BAIL BD17 82 F2
Old Lee Bank HIPP HX3 10 E2
Old Leeds Rd HUD HD1 15 H6
Old Lees Rd HBR HX7 143 J2
Old Lindley Rd HUDW HD3 190 E4
Old London Rd TAD LS24 71 J8
Old Main St BGLY BD16 81 H3
Old Manchester Rd
STKB/PEN S36 269 G6
Old Manor Dr STKB/PEN S36 271 K5
Old Manse Cft HWTH * BD22 100 E3
Old Market HFAX HX1 11 H6
Old Marsh PDSY/CALV LS28 106 E7
Old Mill Cl HEM/SK/SE WF9 223 L7
ILK LS29 40 B4
Old Mill Dr COL BB8 74 B2
Old Mill La BSLY S70 261 G4
BSPA/BRAM LS23 70 A1
CHPT/GREN S35 271 M8
Old Mill Rd BAIL * BD17 82 C6
Oldmill St WHIT OL12 206 B6
Old Mill Vw EARL WF12 195 K1
Old Mill Yd OSS * WF5 196 E3
Old Moll Rd HOLM/MEL HD9 235 M1
Old Mount Farm
HOR/CROF WF4 220 C7
Old Mount Rd MAR/SLWT HD7 233 G3
Old Oak Cl BHP/TINH LS16 86 C7
Old Oak Dr BHP/TINH LS16 86 B7
Old Oak Garth BHP/TINH LS16 86 B7
Old Oak Lawn BHP/TINH LS16 86 C7
The Old Orch OT LS21 42 E7
Old Oxenhope La HWTH BD22 100 D1
Old Pack Horse Rd UPML OL3 231 K8
Old Park Rd IDLE BD10 83 L7
RHAY LS8 88 C7
Old Pool Bank BHP/TINH LS16 63 K2
Old Popplewell La CLECK BD19 149 G6
Old Power Wy ELL HX5 169 J6
Old Quarry La GFTH/SHER LS25 137 M5
Old Riding La LUD/ILL HX2 145 H3
Old Rd AL/HA/HU LS17 44 F4
BSLYN/ROY S71 261 J1
COP/BISH YO23 73 K5
CUL/QBY BD13 101 M6
CUL/QBY BD13 103 H8
GTHN BD7 126 A4
HBR HX7 121 J4
HOLM/MEL HD9 253 M3
HOR/CROF WF4 196 B8
MILN OL16 207 G2
MOR LS27 130 E6
Oldroyd Av CUD/GR S72 245 J8
Oldroyd Crs BEE/HOL LS11 131 G4
Oldroyd Rd TOD OL14 163 M1
Oldroyd Wy DEWS WF13 173 K6
Old Run Rd MID LS10 131 M4
Old Run Vw MID LS10 131 M6
The Old Sawmills
RPDN/SBR HX6 188 E4
Old School Ct CAS WF10 179 L1
Old School La HUDE HD5 215 H3
Old School Ms MOR LS27 130 E6
Old Schools Gdns HIPP HX3 11 H2
Old Shaw La HBR HX7 142 B2
Old Side Ct AIRE BD20 59 G5
Old Souls Wy BGLY BD16 59 G8
Old South St HUD HD1 14 E7
Old Station Rd LUD/ILL HX2 144 F7
Old Station Wy ILK LS29 19 H6
Old Stone Brow
BWCK/EAR BB18 52 C2
Old Stone Trough La
BWCK/EAR BB18 52 C1
Old St AWLS/ASK DN6 248 B5
Old Town Mill La HBR HX7 143 K1
Old Vicarage La
GFTH/SHER LS25 138 D6
Old Village St AWLS/ASK DN6 249 J2
Old Wakefield Rd HUDE HD5 15 L8
Old Well Head HFAX HX1 11 G8
Old Westgate EARL WF12 173 L6
Old Whack House La YEA LS19 62 B8
Old Wood La BGLY BD16 60 C4
The Old Woodyard
HOR/CROF WF4 218 E4
Old Yew La HOLM/MEL HD9 254 A4
Olicana Pk ILK LS29 38 C1
Olive Gv GIR BD8 104 A6
Oliver Cl LIT OL15 207 H1
Oliver Gdns MIRF WF14 172 B7
Oliver Hl HORS LS18 85 L7
Oliver Mdw ELL HX5 169 J6
Oliver Rd HECK WF16 173 G1
Olivers Mt PONT WF8 181 G6
Oliver St BOW BD4 5 J9
Olive St HUD HD1 15 G1
Olive Ter MAR/SLWT * HD7 211 L8
Ollerdale Av WIL/AL BD15 103 J3
Ollerdale Cl WIL/AL BD15 103 J4
Ollerton WHIT * OL12 206 A6
Ollerton Rd BSLYN/ROY S71 243 H6
Olney ROCH * OL11 206 A8
Olney St MAR/SLWT HD7 212 B5
Olympic Pk LM/WK BD12 149 G1
Omar St HECK WF16 172 E2
One Acre Garth SEL YO8 139 M4
One Ash Cl WHIT OL12 206 B4
Onslow Crs BOW BD4 127 K4
Ontario Pl CHAL LS7 87 M8
Opal St HWTH BD22 79 J2
Orange St BFDE BD3 105 L8
HFAX HX1 11 G5
Orange Ter HUD * HD1 14 F3
Orange Tree Gv
EARD/LOFT WF3 153 L7
Orchan Rd TOD OL14 141 H7
The Orchard AWLS/ASK DN6 227 L6
FEA/AMT WF7 179 M5
HOR/CROF WF4 200 B5
KGHY BD21 58 B7
MIRF WF14 172 D7
NORM WF6 178 C6
OSS WF5 196 F1
PONT WF8 203 H1
WKFDW/WTN WF2 176 B3
Orchard Av EARD/LOFT WF3 177 H1
Orchard Cl AWLS/ASK DN6 227 M3
BSLYN/ROY S71 261 L1
DOD/DAR S75 242 D5
EARD/LOFT WF3 153 M8
GFTH/SHER LS25 138 D6
GFTH/SHER LS25 138 A3
HOLM/MEL HD9 235 H5
HOR/CROF WF4 197 J4
LUD/ILL HX2 145 M8
TAD LS24 115 M1
WKFDW/WTN WF2 176 A3
Orchard Ct BSPA/BRAM LS23 69 M4
HUDW HD3 191 H8
Orchard Cft DOD/DAR S75 260 C8
WKFDW/WTN WF2 176 A4
WKFDW/WTN WF2 199 J7
Orchard Dr AWLS/ASK DN6 227 M3
CUD/GR S72 222 F8
FEA/AMT WF7 224 C1
HOR/CROF WF4 198 B7
KNOT WF11 159 K1
SEL YO8 139 M4
WBY LS22 47 K3
Orchard Gdns HOR/CROF WF4 198 B7
Orchard Gv IDLE BD10 83 M7
ILK LS29 61 J2
ROY/SHW OL2 229 J7
Orchard Head Crs PONT WF8 181 G2
Orchard Head Dr PONT WF8 181 G3
Orchard Head La PONT WF8 181 G2
Orchard La ILK LS29 19 J6
PONT WF8 203 L2
TAD LS24 116 A2
Orchard Lees HUDE HD5 193 L6
Orchard Mt MSTN/BAR LS15 111 L4
Orchard Pl CUD/GR S72 262 E1
Orchard Ri RPDN/SBR HX6 167 H4
Orchard Rd HUDE HD5 193 L6
MSTN/BAR LS15 111 K4
WKFDW/WTN WF2 199 G5
The Orchards BGLY BD16 81 J1
CLECK BD19 150 E6
MSTN/BAR LS15 111 K4
RTHW LS26 156 E4
Orchard Sq MSTN/BAR LS15 111 K4
Orchard St EARL WF12 173 L8
HUDS HD4 214 C2
OT LS21 41 K7
Orchard St West HUDW HD3 213 J1
Orchard Ter DOD/DAR S75 259 H2
HUDS HD4 214 D2
Orchard Vw HEM/SK/SE * WF9 246 E4
Orchard Wk BSLYN/ROY * S71 261 H3
HBR HX7 144 B5
Orchard Wy BRIG HD6 170 C2
RTHW LS26 133 G8
Orchid Cl SHPY BD18 104 F1
Orchid Ct EARD/LOFT WF3 154 D4
Orchid Crest HEM/SK/SE WF9 225 J7
Oriel St ROCH OL11 228 B1
Oriel Wy BSLYN/ROY S71 261 M3
Oriental St WOR/ARM LS12 108 E7
Orion Crs MID LS10 132 A7
Orion Dr MID LS10 132 A7
Orion Gdns MID LS10 132 B7
Orion Vw MID LS10 132 B7
Orion Wk MID LS10 132 B6
Orlando Cl MIRF WF14 172 B7
Orleans St WBSY BD6 126 B7
Ormonde Dr WIL/AL BD15 103 J6
Ormond Rd WBSY BD6 126 D6
Ormondroyd Av WBSY BD6 126 E6
Ormond St GTHN BD7 126 C2
Orron St LIT OL15 207 J1
Orville Gdns HDGY LS6 109 G2
Orwell Cl CAS WF10 180 E1
Osborne Av HOR/CROF WF4 197 L3
Osborne Ms BSLY * S70 261 J6
Osborne Pl TOD OL14 163 L1
Osborne Rd HUD HD1 14 D3
Osborne St BSLY S70 261 J6
HBR * HX7 143 J3
HFAX HX1 10 B4
HUDE HD5 15 M8
ROCH OL11 228 A1
ROY/SHW OL2 229 K8
WBOW BD5 126 F1
Osbourne Ct BRAM LS13 107 M5
Osbourne Dr CUL/QBY BD13 125 G5
Osmondthorpe La OSM LS9 110 E7
Osmondthorpe Ter OSM LS9 110 D6
Osprey Cl AL/HA/HU LS17 88 B2
AWLS/ASK DN6 249 K8
WBY LS22 47 K5
Osprey Ct GIR * BD8 103 L7
Osprey Dr HUDS HD4 214 A7
Osprey Gv AL/HA/HU LS17 88 B2
Osprey Meadow MOR LS27 152 F2
Ossett La EARL WF12 174 B7
Osterley Gv IDLE BD10 106 A1
Oswald St MILN OL16 206 C6
ROY/SHW OL2 229 L6
SHPY BD18 82 F7
Oswaldthorpe Av BFDE BD3 105 M5
Otley La YEA LS19 62 D7
Otley Mt AIRE * BD20 58 F6
Otley Old Rd BHP/TINH LS16 86 A1
HORS LS18 63 J5
Otley Rd BAIL BD17 83 H3
BFDE BD3 5 H5
BGLY BD16 59 J5
BGLY BD16 60 B5
BHP/TINH LS16 64 D7
GSLY LS20 61 L5
ILK LS29 40 C6
OT LS21 44 C7
PBR HG3 25 H3
SHPY BD18 82 D8
SKP/WHF BD23 16 D2
Otley St HFAX HX1 10 A5
KGHY BD21 2 F7
SKP/WHF BD23 16 C2
Ottawa Pl CHAL LS7 87 M8
Otterburn Cl WBOW BD5 126 F1
Otterburn Gdns BHP/TINH LS16 86 D3
Otterburn St KGHY * BD21 3 G1
Otter Lee La RPDN/SBR HX6 166 E6
Otters Holt HOR/CROF WF4 198 B7
Otterwood Bank WBY LS22 30 B7
Ouchthorpe La WKFDE WF1 176 E3
Ouldfield Cl MILN * OL16 206 D8
Oulton Dr CUD/GR S72 244 E7
RTHW LS26 155 L3
Oulton La RTHW LS26 133 L7
RTHW LS26 155 J1
Oulton Ter GTHN BD7 4 A9
Ounsworth St BOW BD4 127 K2
Ouse Dr WBY LS22 29 M6
Ouslethwaite Ct BSLY S70 261 G8
Ouson Gdns BSLYN/ROY S71 243 L5
Ouston Cl TAD LS24 72 A3
Ouston La TAD LS24 72 A3
Outcote Bank HUD HD1 14 E9
Outdoor Market MILN * OL16 206 B6
Out Gang BRAM LS13 107 M3
Outgang La BRAM LS13 108 A3
Outlands Ri IDLE BD10 83 M6
Out La HOLM/MEL HD9 236 B6
KBTN HD8 217 L7
Outside La HWTH BD22 100 B4
Outwood Av HORS LS18 85 M7
Outwood Cha HORS LS18 85 M6
Outwood La HORS LS18 85 L7
TAD LS24 95 G3
Outwood Park Ct WKFDE WF1 176 D2
Outwood Wk HORS LS18 85 L7
Ouzelwell Crs EARL WF12 195 J3
Ouzelwell La EARL WF12 195 J3
Ouzelwell Rd EARL WF12 195 K2
Ouzlewell Gn EARD/LOFT WF3 154 F4
The Oval AWLS/ASK DN6 249 H8
BGLY BD16 81 K4
GIR BD8 104 A6
GLE DN14 183 H1
GSLY LS20 61 L6
HOLM/MEL HD9 236 B7
HOR/CROF WF4 221 K8
LVSG WF15 171 L1
MID LS10 9 K8
OT LS21 41 H5
RTHW LS26 155 H2
SCFT LS14 111 H4
SKP/WHF BD23 16 D3
Ovenden Av HIPP HX3 10 C1
Ovenden Cl HIPP * HX3 10 D1
Ovenden Crs HIPP HX3 146 C4
Ovenden Gn HIPP HX3 146 C4
Ovenden Pk LUD/ILL * HX2 146 B2
Ovenden Rd HIPP HX3 146 C3
Ovenden Road Ter HIPP HX3 146 C4
Ovenden Ter HIPP HX3 146 C4
Ovenden Wy HIPP HX3 146 B4
Ovenden Wood Rd
LUD/ILL HX2 145 L4
Overburn Rd AIRE BD20 55 M2
Overdale RPDN/SBR HX6 167 G7
Overdale Av AL/HA/HU LS17 88 C1
BSLY S70 261 K8
Overdale Cl WBY LS22 29 M8
Overdale Ct SKP/WHF BD23 16 C1
Overdale Dr SHPY BD18 83 H5
Overdale Mt LUD/ILL HX2 167 M1
Overdale Ter HWTH * BD22 78 E7
MSTN/BAR LS15 111 J6
Overfield Wy WHIT OL12 206 B4
Over Hall Cl MIRF WF14 172 D8
Over Hall Pk MIRF WF14 172 D8
Over Hall Rd MIRF WF14 172 D8
Overland Crs IDLE BD10 83 M6
Over La YEA LS19 84 E3
Overthorpe Av EARL WF12 195 M5
Overthorpe Rd EARL WF12 195 M4
Overton Dr WBSY BD6 125 M4
Overt St ROCH OL11 228 B1
Ovington Dr BOW BD4 128 A4
Owen Ct BGLY BD16 59 J8
Owlcotes Dr PDSY/CALV LS28 106 E6
Owlcotes Gdns
PDSY/CALV LS28 106 E6
Owlcotes Garth
PDSY/CALV LS28 106 D6
Owlcotes La PDSY/CALV LS28 106 D5
Owlcotes Rd PDSY/CALV LS28 106 D6
Owlcotes Ter PDSY/CALV LS28 106 E6
Owler Bars Rd HOLM/MEL HD9 234 E4
Owler Ings Rd BRIG HD6 170 C4
Owler La BTLY WF17 151 G3
Owler Mdw HECK WF16 172 E1
Owler Park Rd ILK LS29 20 B8
Owlers Cl HUDN HD2 193 H1
Owler's La HEM/SK/SE WF9 225 H2
Owlet Hurst La LVSG WF15 172 D4
Owlet Rd SHPY BD18 82 E7
Owlett Md EARD/LOFT WF3 154 A5
Owlett Mead Cl
EARD/LOFT WF3 154 A5
Owl La EARL WF12 174 C4
Owl Ms HUDE HD5 193 L8
Owl Rdg MOR LS27 152 E3
Owl St KGHY BD21 3 J3
Owston La AWLS/ASK DN6 249 M4
Owston Rd AWLS/ASK DN6 249 L6
Ox Close La WBY LS22 29 L8
Oxfield Ct HUDE HD5 193 J8
Oxford Av GSLY LS20 61 M5
Oxford Cl CLECK BD19 150 D6
CUL/QBY BD13 124 E7
Oxford Court Gdns CAS * WF10 157 L7
Oxford Crs CLAY BD14 125 K2
HIPP HX3 168 F2
Oxford Dr CLECK BD19 150 D6
GFTH/SHER LS25 135 J5
Oxford La HIPP HX3 168 F2
Oxford Pl BAIL BD17 82 F4
BFDE BD3 5 H3
BSLYN/ROY S71 262 A6
HUD HD1 214 A3
LDS LS1 6 E8
MILN OL16 228 C1
PDSY/CALV LS28 107 G5
Oxford Rd CHAL LS7 7 G3
CLECK BD19 150 D4
CUL/QBY * BD13 124 E6
DEWS WF13 173 J5
ECHL BD2 105 J4
GSLY LS20 61 M5
HFAX HX1 11 G8
WKFDE WF1 176 D6
Oxford Rw LDS LS1 6 E8
Oxford St BSLY S70 261 J7
BSLYN/ROY S71 262 A6
BTLY WF17 173 K2
CLAY BD14 125 K2
COL BB8 74 A1
EARD/LOFT WF3 154 A6
FEA/AMT WF7 201 M1
GSLY LS20 62 A5
HBR HX7 143 H3
HEM/SK/SE WF9 247 H4
HUD HD1 14 F4
HWTH BD22 2 D6
NORM WF6 178 E3
ROY/SHW OL2 229 K7
RPDN/SBR HX6 167 M1
TOD OL14 163 K1
WKFDE WF1 13 J8
Oxford Ter BTLY WF17 173 M2
Oxford Wk CLECK BD19 150 D6
Oxford Wy WHIT OL12 206 A4
Ox Hey La UPML OL3 231 G5
Ox Heys Mdw CUL/QBY BD13 103 J8
Ox Lee La HOLM/MEL HD9 255 G6
Oxley Gdns WBSY BD6 126 E7
Oxley Rd HUDN HD2 192 E2
Oxley St GIR BD8 4 B4
OSM LS9 110 B7
Oxmoor La GFTH/SHER LS25 117 L3
TAD LS24 95 J8
Oxspring La STKB/PEN S36 271 K3
Oxspring Rd STKB/PEN S36 270 F6
Oxton Dr TAD LS24 72 A3
Oxton La TAD LS24 72 A3
Oxton Mt OSM LS9 110 B6
Oxton Rd BSLYN/ROY S71 243 J6
Oxton Wy OSM LS9 110 B6
Oyster Cl MOR LS27 152 E3
Ozar St BEE/HOL LS11 8 C5

P

Pacaholme Rd
WKFDW/WTN WF2 175 M6
Packer St MILN OL16 206 B7
Pack Horse Cl KBTN HD8 240 C2
Pack Horse Gn DOD/DAR S75 259 H6
Pack Horse Wk HUD * HD1 15 G7
Padan St HIPP HX3 168 F2
Pad Cote La HWTH BD22 54 C6
The Paddock AIRE BD20 36 A5
AL/HA/HU LS17 46 E8
AWLS/ASK DN6 249 L8
BAIL BD17 83 H2
CAS WF10 158 E8
CLECK * BD19 149 H6
CUL/QBY BD13 79 M8
EARL WF12 174 B8
GFTH/SHER LS25 160 A2
HDGY LS6 87 H7
HOR/CROF WF4 220 C7
HUDE HD5 193 L6
ILK * LS29 19 J5
KNOT WF11 182 B3
NORM WF6 178 D5
RTHW LS26 155 G1
SCFT LS14 90 B1
WKFDE * WF1 176 C4
WMB/DAR S73 263 J8
Paddock HTON BD9 104 E2
Paddock Br WBY LS22 47 K5
Paddock Cl DOD/DAR S75 242 E5
GFTH/SHER LS25 113 J8
LM/WK BD12 148 E5
Paddock Dr BIRK/DRI BD11 151 G1
Paddock Foot HUD HD1 14 B9
Paddock Gn AL/HA/HU LS17 67 L1
Paddock Gv CUD/GR S72 244 E7
Paddock House La WBY LS22 46 C2
Paddock La BGLY BD16 59 M8
LUD/ILL HX2 145 L6
Paddock Rd DOD/DAR S75 242 E5
HIPP HX3 147 G1
KBTN HD8 216 C7
The Paddocks PBR HG3 28 A1
Paddocks Church BRIG HD6 171 G4
Paddock Vw CAS WF10 158 D8
Paddy Bridge Rd HBR * HX7 143 M5
Padgum BAIL BD17 82 E2
Padley Cl DOD/DAR S75 260 A7
Padma Cl GTHN BD7 104 D7
Padstow Gdns MID LS10 153 J1
Pagan St WHIT OL12 206 B6
Page Hl LUD/ILL HX2 146 A4
Page St HUD HD1 15 G8
Paget Crs HUDN HD2 191 M5
Paget St KGHY BD21 2 D5
Pagewood Ct IDLE BD10 83 J5
Painter La SEL YO8 139 M3
Painthorpe La HOR/CROF WF4 220 B3
Paisley Gv WOR/ARM * LS12 108 D6
Paisley Pl WOR/ARM * LS12 108 D6
Paisley Rd WOR/ARM * LS12 108 D6
Paisley St WOR/ARM LS12 108 D6
Paisley Ter WOR/ARM * LS12 108 D6
Pakington St WBOW BD5 126 F2
Palace House Rd HBR HX7 143 J4
Palatine St MILN OL16 206 E7
Pale La SKP/WHF BD23 16 A6
Palermo Fold WMB/DAR S73 263 H8
Paleside La OSS WF5 174 F7
Palesides Av OSS WF5 174 F6
Palestine Rd HBR HX7 143 J2
Paley Rd BOW BD4 127 J2
Paley Ter BOW BD4 127 J2
Palin Av BFDE BD3 105 M5
Pall Ml BSLY S70 261 H5
Palma St TOD OL14 140 D5
Palm Cl WBSY BD6 126 D6
Palmer Cl STKB/PEN S36 270 E5
Palmer Rd BFDE BD3 5 M4
Palmer's Av HEM/SK/SE WF9 247 J4
Palmerston St ECHL * BD2 105 K4
Palm St DOD/DAR S75 260 E3
HIPP HX3 146 D4
HUDS HD4 214 D2
Panelagh Av IDLE BD10 106 A1
Pannal Av PBR HG3 26 F3
WKFDE WF1 177 G6
Pannal Bank PBR HG3 26 F3

Pannal Gn PBR HG3 ....26 F2
Pannal Rd PBR HG3 ....27 J2
Pannal St GTHN BD7 ....126 C3
Panorama Dr ILK LS29 ....38 A4
The Parade BGLY BD16 ....81 J7
  BRAM * LS13 ....107 L4
  BTLY * WF17 ....151 H3
  BTLY * WF17 ....173 J2
  HDGY LS6 ....108 F1
  OSM LS6 ....9 L2
  YEA * LS19 ....62 B8
Paradise La LUD/ILL HX2 ....145 K8
  TAD LS24 ....92 D1
Paradise Rd HTON * BD9 ....104 B2
Paradise St BFD BD1 ....4 C5
  HFAX HX1 ....10 F7
  PDSY/CALV LS28 ....106 F3
Parish Ghyll Dr ILK LS29 ....38 B3
Parish Ghyll La ILK LS29 ....38 B3
Parish Ghyll Rd ILK LS29 ....38 C3
Parish Ghyll Wk ILK LS29 ....38 C3
Parish Wy BSLYN/ROY S71 ....261 M3
Paris Rd HOLM/MEL HD9 ....254 F3
The Park DOD/DAR S75 ....259 G2
Park Av AIRE BD20 ....55 M1
  AWLS/ASK DN6 ....249 L6
  BGLY BD16 ....81 H4
  BIRK/DRI BD11 ....129 C8
  BSLY S70 ....261 G5
  BSLYN/ROY S71 ....243 H7
  BSLYN/ROY S71 ....243 M3
  CAS WF10 ....157 L2
  CAS WF10 ....158 B7
  CUD/GR S72 ....244 D7
  CUD/GR S72 ....245 J6
  CUD/GR S72 ....245 K3
  DEWS WF13 ....173 K6
  EARD/LOFT WF3 ....154 E7
  ELL HX5 ....169 G8
  GFTH/SHER LS25 ....115 M7
  GFTH/SHER LS25 ....135 L5
  HEM/SK/SE WF9 ....246 D4
  HUD HD1 ....14 D6
  HWTH BD22 ....78 F4
  IDLE BD10 ....83 K4
  KBTN HD8 ....238 C3
  KBTN HD8 ....240 B3
  KGHY BD21 ....2 E7
  LVSG WF15 ....172 C4
  MIRF WF14 ....194 D2
  MOR LS27 ....152 B3
  MSTN/BAR LS15 ....111 M4
  NORM WF6 ....178 D4
  PONT WF8 ....180 D6
  PONT WF8 ....203 L1
  RHAY LS8 ....88 D7
  RTHW LS26 ....134 C6
  SHPY BD18 ....82 C6
  SKP/WHF * BD23 ....16 B2
  STKB/PEN S36 ....270 E4
  WKFDE WF1 ....176 C2
  WKFDE WF1 ....177 M7
  WKFDW/WTN WF2 ....12 C6
  WOR/ARM LS12 ....108 D6
  YEA LS19 ....62 C7
Park Cliffe Rd ECHL BD2 ....105 J4
Park Cl BGLY BD16 ....81 J2
  BIRK/DRI BD11 ....129 C8
  BRAM LS13 ....107 L3
  BTLY WF17 ....173 K3
  CUL/QBY BD13 ....124 F5
  DOD/DAR S75 ....242 E6
  HIPP HX3 ....148 A7
  HOR/CROF WF4 ....222 D5
  IDLE BD10 ....105 L1
  KBTN HD8 ....238 B3
  KGHY BD21 ....3 G8
  LUD/ILL HX2 ....145 K5
  PONT WF8 ....203 L1
Park Copse HORS LS18 ....85 J5
Park Cottages ROY/SHW OL2 ....229 H6
Park Ct OSS WF5 ....197 H2
  OT LS21 ....42 F8
Park Crs BFDE BD3 ....105 J4
  BSLYN/ROY S71 ....243 M3
  CAS WF10 ....158 E7
  GSLY LS20 ....61 L6
  HIPP HX3 ....10 C1
  ILK LS29 ....19 J6
  MOR LS27 ....129 M8
  RHAY LS8 ....88 D5
  RTHW LS26 ....133 J8
  WOR/ARM LS12 ....108 D6
Park Crest HEM/SK/SE WF9 ....223 M8
Park Cft BTLY WF17 ....173 J2
  DEWS WF13 ....173 K6
Parkcroft PDSY/CALV LS28 ....106 F4
Park Cross St LDS LS1 ....6 E9
Park Dl CAS WF10 ....158 E5
  ILK LS29 ....61 J2
Parkdale Dr RPDN/SBR HX6 ....167 C7
Park Dene HFAX * HX1 ....10 C7
Park Dr AIRE BD20 ....55 M1
  AWLS/ASK DN6 ....227 M5
  BGLY BD16 ....81 K1
  BTLY WF17 ....173 K3
  EARD/LOFT WF3 ....154 E7
  HORS LS18 ....85 H6
  HTON BD9 ....104 D2
  HUD HD1 ....14 B5
  KBTN HD8 ....238 B3
  MIRF WF14 ....194 D2
Park Drive Rd KGHY BD21 ....3 C8
Park Dr South HUD HD1 ....14 B6
Park Edge Cl RHAY LS8 ....88 E7
Park Cross St LDS LS1 ....6 E9
Parker Av NORM WF6 ....178 A2
Parker La MIRF WF14 ....194 E2
Parker Rd EARL WF12 ....195 L3
  HOR/CROF WF4 ....197 L5
Parker's La AIRE BD20 ....57 J3
Parker St AIRE BD20 ....34 F7
  BSLY S70 ....260 F5
  EARD/LOFT WF3 ....153 L7
  LVSG WF15 ....172 C4
Park Fld ILK LS29 ....61 J2
Parkfield Av BEE/HOL LS11 ....131 J3
  ELL HX5 ....169 H8
  MIRF WF14 ....194 E2

Parkfield Cl GFTH/SHER LS25 ....135 K4
  PDSY/CALV LS28 ....106 F7
Parkfield Ct SCFT * LS14 ....111 C3
Parkfield Crs MIRF WF14 ....194 E2
Parkfield Cft MIRF WF14 ....194 E2
Parkfield Dr BSPA/BRAM LS23 ....48 E6
  CUL/QBY BD13 ....124 F5
  RPDN/SBR HX6 ....167 J4
Parkfield Gv BEE/HOL LS11 ....131 J3
Parkfield La FEA/AMT WF7 ....179 L4
  RPDN/SBR HX6 ....167 M3
Parkfield Mt BEE/HOL LS11 ....131 H3
  PDSY/CALV LS28 ....107 G7
Parkfield Pl BEE/HOL LS11 ....131 J3
Parkfield Rd BEE/HOL LS11 ....131 J3
  GIR BD8 ....104 F4
  SHPY BD18 ....82 A6
Parkfield Rw BEE/HOL LS11 ....131 J3
  ROCH OL11 ....228 D4
  OSS WF5 ....197 J1
Parkfield Ter PDSY/CALV LS28 ....107 G5
  SCFT LS14 ....111 C3
Park Gdns LUD/ILL HX2 ....167 M1
  OSS WF5 ....197 H2
Park Ga BFDE BD3 ....5 H5
Parkgate HEM/SK/SE WF9 ....246 D5
  HUDS HD4 ....214 B6
Parkgate Av WKFDE WF1 ....13 K2
Park Gate Cl HORS LS18 ....85 K6
Park Gate Rd MAR/SLWT HD7 ....211 K8
Park Ga West HIPP * HX3 ....169 C4
Park Gn AIRE BD20 ....35 L4
  NORM WF6 ....178 B5
Park Gv BSLY S70 ....261 G6
  CUL/QBY BD13 ....124 F5
  HDGY LS6 ....86 F8
  HIPP HX3 ....147 H5
  HOR/CROF WF4 ....197 H4
  HORS LS18 ....85 H5
  HTON BD9 ....104 E2
  HUD HD1 ....14 D7
  MIRF WF14 ....194 E2
  MOR LS27 ....129 M8
  RTHW LS26 ....134 D6
  SHPY BD18 ....82 B6
  YEA LS19 ....62 C7
Park Grove Rd
  WKFDW/WTN WF2 ....12 A5
Parkhead Cl BSLYN/ROY S71 ....243 J2
Park Head La HOLM/MEL HD9 ....254 A2
  KBTN HD8 ....256 B1
Park Hl DOD/DAR S75 ....241 K8
  HUDN HD2 ....171 H8
Park Hill Cl GIR BD8 ....103 M5
Parkhill Crs WKFDE WF1 ....13 K2
Park Hill Dr GIR BD8 ....103 M5
Park Hill Gv WKFDE WF1 ....13 L3
Park Hill La WKFDE WF1 ....13 L3
Park Holme CHAL LS7 ....110 A2
Parkhome Est RTHW * LS26 ....134 D5
Park House Cl LM/WK BD12 ....127 C7
Park House Ct STKB/PEN S36 ....257 G6
Park House Crs LM/WK BD12 ....127 G7
Park House Dr EARL WF12 ....195 M2
Park House Gn PBR HG3 ....28 F4
Park House Gv LM/WK * BD12 ....127 G7
Park House La LM/WK BD12 ....126 F8
Park House Wk LM/WK BD12 ....127 G7
Parkin Hall La RPDN/SBR HX6 ....166 D4
Parkin House La
  STKB/PEN S36 ....269 M8
Parkin La IDLE BD10 ....84 B6
  TOD OL14 ....140 F8
Parkinson Ap GFTH/SHER LS25 ....113 H6
Parkinson Cl WKFDE WF1 ....13 K1
Parkinson Rd CUL/QBY BD13 ....102 A5
Parkinson St WBOW BD5 ....126 F2
Parkin St LVSG WF15 ....171 L1
Parkland Av MOR LS27 ....152 A3
Parkland Dr HDGY LS6 ....87 J5
  IDLE BD10 ....83 D7
  TAD LS24 ....72 A2
Parkland Gdns HDGY LS6 ....87 J6
Parklands BHP/TINH LS16 ....63 M3
  CAS WF10 ....158 A7
  ILK LS29 ....38 F2
  OSS WF5 ....197 H2
Park Lands PBR HG3 ....28 E4
Parklands ROY/SHW OL2 ....228 E8
  ROY/SHW OL2 ....229 M6
Parklands Av HOR/CROF WF4 ....197 G5
Parklands Cl HOR/CROF WF4 ....197 G5
Parklands Crs BHP/TINH LS16 ....64 A3
  HOR/CROF WF4 ....197 G5
Parklands Ga BHP/TINH LS16 ....64 A3
  RPDN/SBR HX6 ....167 G5
Parklands Ter HDGY LS6 ....87 H6
Parkland Vw YEA LS19 ....62 C6
Park La AIRE BD20 ....55 M1
  AWLS/ASK DN6 ....205 J3
  BAIL BD17 ....83 H2
  BVRD LS3 ....6 B8
  CAS WF10 ....157 K1
  CLAY BD14 ....125 K2
  CUD/GR S72 ....263 K3
  CUL/QBY BD13 ....125 H5
  GFTH/SHER LS25 ....135 L6
  GFTH/SHER LS25 ....136 C6
  GSLY LS20 ....61 G6
  GTL/HWG HX4 ....190 B5
  HBR * HX7 ....143 L6
  HIPP HX3 ....169 G4
  HOLM/MEL * HD9 ....235 G4
  HOR/CROF WF4 ....219 G7
  HUDS HD4 ....214 C7
  HWTH BD22 ....54 B4
  KBTN HD8 ....239 J1
  KBTN HD8 ....256 C1
  KGHY BD21 ....3 H8
  MAR/SLWT HD7 ....212 F2
  MILN * OL16 ....206 B6

PBR HG3 ....28 E4
  PONT WF8 ....180 A5
  RHAY LS8 ....88 D4
  RTHW LS26 ....155 H1
  RTHW LS26 ....156 C5
  STKB/PEN S36 ....270 F3
  STKB/PEN S36 ....271 J7
  WBOW BD5 ....126 F2
  WBY LS22 ....46 D1
Park Lane Ms AL/HA/HU LS17 ....88 B2
Park Lea HUDN HD2 ....171 H8
  MID * LS10 ....153 L1
Park Lodge Ct WKFDE WF1 ....13 J2
Park Lodge Crs WKFDE WF1 ....13 J2
Park Lodge Gv WKFDE WF1 ....13 H2
Park Lodge La WKFDE WF1 ....13 H2
Park Lodge Vw KBTN HD8 ....239 J5
Park Md IDLE BD10 ....83 K4
Parkmere Cl BOW BD4 ....127 K7
Park Ms OT LS21 ....42 F8
Park Mill La OSS WF5 ....175 J7
Park Mill Wy KBTN HD8 ....240 B3
Park Mt KSTL LS5 ....108 D2
  OT LS21 ....63 K1
  PBR HG3 ....28 E4
  WOR/ARM LS12 ....108 C6
Park Mount Av BAIL BD17 ....83 G3
Park Pde DEWS WF13 ....173 K7
  MOR * LS27 ....152 B3
  OSM LS9 ....110 C8
  ROY/SHW OL2 ....229 L5
Park Pl HFAX * HX1 ....10 C8
  IDLE BD10 ....83 K4
  LDS LS1 ....6 D9
  PONT WF8 ....180 D6
Park Pl East HIPP HX3 ....148 A7
Park Pl West HIPP HX3 ....148 A7
Park Ri BRAM LS13 ....107 L2
  CAS WF10 ....158 B7
Park Rd AIRE BD20 ....34 E7
  BGLY BD16 ....81 H3
  BRAM LS13 ....107 L3
  BSLY S70 ....261 G5
  BSPA/BRAM LS23 ....48 E6
  BTLY WF17 ....173 M1
  CAS WF10 ....180 C1
  CUD/GR S72 ....245 J7
  CUD/GR S72 ....245 K3
  DEWS WF13 ....173 H8
  EARL WF12 ....173 J5
  EARL WF12 ....174 B7
  ELL HX5 ....169 H6
  GSLY LS20 ....61 M7
  HECK WF16 ....172 F2
  HFAX HX1 ....10 E7
  HUDS HD4 ....214 A2
  HWTH BD22 ....54 E3
  IDLE BD10 ....83 K4
  IDLE BD10 ....105 M1
  ILK LS29 ....61 J2
  KBTN HD8 ....240 B3
  MSTN/BAR LS15 ....133 M1
  PONT WF8 ....180 C3
  RPDN/SBR HX6 ....167 L2
  SHPY BD18 ....82 E7
  TOD OL14 ....141 K8
  WBOW BD5 ....127 G1
  WBSD BD6 ....126 E7
  WHIT OL12 ....206 D5
  WOR/ARM LS12 ....108 C6
  YEA LS19 ....62 C7
  YEA LS19 ....84 D2
Park Rd West HUD4 ....213 L2
Park Rw BRIG * HD6 ....170 D4
  LDS LS1 ....6 F9
  PDSY/CALV LS28 ....107 G5
Park Side CLECK BD19 ....150 C7
  HOLM/MEL HD9 ....255 C7
  HOR/CROF WF4 ....217 L3
  HORS LS18 ....85 J6
  HUDE HD5 ....193 L5
Parkside BGLY BD16 ....81 J2
  CLECK BD19 ....149 M7
  DOD/DAR * S75 ....260 F2
  HOR/CROF WF4 ....196 D8
Parkside Av CUL/QBY BD13 ....124 F5
  HDGY LS6 ....87 H7
Park Side Av ROY/SHW OL2 ....229 L6
Parkside Cl HDGY LS6 ....87 H6
Parkside Ct HWTH BD22 ....79 C6
Parkside Crs HDGY LS6 ....87 H6
Parkside Gdns HDGY LS6 ....87 H7
Parkside Gn HDGY LS6 ....87 H7
Parkside Gv HTON BD9 ....104 C3
Parkside La BEE/HOL LS11 ....131 L5
  EARD/LOFT WF3 ....177 G4
Parkside Lawns HDGY LS6 ....87 H7
Parkside Mt BEE/HOL LS11 ....131 J5
Parkside Pde BEE/HOL LS11 ....131 J5
Parkside Pl HDGY LS6 ....87 H6
  PDSY/CALV LS28 ....106 F4
Parkside Rd HDGY LS6 ....87 G5
  TOD OL14 ....140 D5
  WBOW BD5 ....127 G4
Parkside Rw BEE/HOL LS11 ....131 J5
Parkside Ter CUL/QBY BD13 ....79 M8
Parkside Vw HDGY LS6 ....87 H6
Parkside Wk PDSY/CALV LS28 ....107 G4
Park Spring Gdns BRAM LS13 ....107 K5
Park Spring Ri BRAM LS13 ....107 K5
Park Spring Rd CUD/GR S72 ....245 H8
Park Sq EARD/LOFT WF3 ....154 E7
  OSS WF5 ....197 H2
  OT LS21 ....42 F8
  WBSD BD6 ....126 B6
Park Sq East LDS LS1 ....6 E9
Park Sq North LDS LS1 ....6 E9
Park Sq South LDS LS1 ....6 E9
Park Sq West LDS LS1 ....6 E9
Parkstone AIRE BD20 ....171 H8
Parkstone Av BHP/TINH LS16 ....86 C5
Parkstone Dr IDLE BD10 ....105 L1
Parkstone Gn BHP/TINH LS16 ....86 C5
Parkstone Gv BHP/TINH LS16 ....86 C5
Parkstone Mt BHP/TINH LS16 ....86 C5
Parkstone Pl BHP/TINH * LS16 ....86 C5
Park Stone Ri HIPP HX3 ....125 K8

Park St AIRE BD20 ....34 F7
  BRIG HD6 ....170 D4
  BSLY S70 ....261 G6
  BTLY WF17 ....151 G6
  CLECK BD19 ....149 K8
  CLECK BD19 ....150 E6
  DEWS WF13 ....173 M5
  HECK WF16 ....172 F2
  HOR/CROF WF4 ....197 J5
  HWTH BD22 ....78 F7
  LDS LS1 ....6 E8
  MAR/SLWT HD7 ....190 E8
  MILN OL16 ....206 B8
  MOR LS27 ....130 E6
  OSS WF5 ....197 H2
  ROY/SHW OL2 ....229 K8
  RPDN/SBR HX6 ....167 L2
  SHPY BD18 ....82 C6
  SKP/WHF BD23 ....16 B2
  WKFDE WF1 ....13 G4
  WOR/ARM LS12 ....108 C6
  YEA LS19 ....62 C7
Park Ter HDGY LS6 ....86 F8
  HFAX * HX1 ....10 C6
  HIPP HX3 ....147 H5
  KGHY BD21 ....3 K4
  OT LS21 ....63 J1
Park Top PDSY/CALV LS28 ....107 G5
The Park Towngate HIPP HX3 ....169 J3
Park Vw BEE/HOL LS11 ....131 J3
  BRAM LS13 ....107 L3
  BSLYN/ROY S71 ....243 M2
  CAS WF10 ....158 E8
  CLECK BD19 ....149 L6
  CUD/GR S72 ....244 E6
  CUD/GR S72 ....245 K3
  DOD/DAR S75 ....260 B7
  EARD/LOFT WF3 ....154 E8
  HEM/SK/SE * WF9 ....246 F3
  HFAX HX1 ....10 C7
  HIPP HX3 ....147 J5
  HOLM/MEL HD9 ....254 F3
  LIT OL15 ....188 K8
  MAR/SLWT * HD7 ....233 J2
  PDSY/CALV LS28 ....107 G7
  RTHW LS26 ....134 C5
  WKFDW/WTN * WF2 ....176 A8
Park View Av HDGY LS6 ....108 F3
  HIPP HX3 ....147 J5
  HWTH BD22 ....79 C6
Parkview Ct RHAY LS8 ....88 D4
  SHPY * BD18 ....82 C7
Park View Crs RHAY LS8 ....88 D5
Park View Gv BULY LS4 ....108 B4
Park View Rd BULY LS4 ....108 F4
  DOD/DAR S75 ....260 A5
  HTON BD9 ....104 D4
Park View Ter HTON BD9 ....104 D3
  YEA LS19 ....84 D2
Park Vls RHAY LS8 ....88 C4
Park Villas Dr PONT WF8 ....180 D5
Parkville Pl BRAM LS13 ....107 L3
Park Wy AWLS/ASK DN6 ....249 K8
  BAIL BD17 ....82 B5
  ILK LS29 ....61 J2
  OT LS21 ....42 F8
Parkway AIRE BD20 ....56 D1
  CUL/QBY BD13 ....124 F5
  HOR/CROF WF4 ....200 B4
  KGHY BD21 ....3 C9
  MOR LS27 ....127 H5
  WBOW BD5 ....127 H5
Parkway Cl SCFT LS14 ....111 G2
Parkways RTHW LS26 ....133 K8
Parkways Av RTHW LS26 ....155 K1
Parkways Cl RTHW LS26 ....133 K8
Parkways Ct RTHW LS26 ....133 K8
Parkways Dr RTHW LS26 ....133 K8
Parkways Garth RTHW * LS26 ....155 K1
Parkways Gv RTHW LS26 ....133 K8
Park West RTHW LS26 ....155 H1
Park Willow RTHW LS26 ....125 M8
Park Wood Av BEE/HOL LS11 ....131 H7
Parkwood Av RHAY LS8 ....88 C7
Parkwood Cl KBTN HD8 ....238 B3
Park Wood Cl SKP/WHF BD23 ....16 A1
Park Wood Crs RHAY LS8 ....88 C6
Park Wood Crs BEE/HOL LS11 ....131 H7
Park Wood Dr BEE/HOL LS11 ....131 H6
Parkwood Gdns
  PDSY/CALV LS28 ....84 C8
  RHAY LS8 ....88 C7
Parkwood Ri KGHY BD21 ....3 H7
Park Wood Rd BEE/HOL LS11 ....131 H7
Parkwood Rd MAR/SLWT HD7 ....191 G8
  PDSY/CALV LS28 ....84 C8
  SHPY BD18 ....82 B7
Parkwood St KGHY BD21 ....3 J6
Parkwood Vw RHAY LS8 ....88 C6
Parkwood Wy RHAY LS8 ....88 C7
Parliament Pl WOR/ARM LS12 ....108 F6
Parliament Rd WOR/ARM LS12 ....108 F7
Parliament St
  WKFDW/WTN WF2 ....12 C3
Parlington Ct MSTN/BAR LS15 ....91 C7
Parlington Dr GFTH/SHER LS25 ....92 A7
Parlington La GFTH/SHER LS25 ....92 A8
  GFTH/SHER LS25 ....113 J2
Parlington Meadow
  MSTN/BAR LS15 ....91 G8
Parlington Vls GFTH/SHER LS25 ....92 A7
Parma St WBOW BD5 ....127 G1
Parnaby Av MID LS10 ....132 B5
Parnaby Rd MID LS10 ....132 B5
Parnaby St MID LS10 ....132 B5
Parnaby Ter MID LS10 ....132 B5
Parratt Rw BFDE BD3 ....105 M7
Parrock La HBR HX7 ....143 L5
Parrott St BOW BD4 ....127 M5
Parry La BOW BD4 ....127 L1
Parsonage La BRIG HD6 ....170 C4
Parsonage Rd BOW BD4 ....127 M1
  RTHW LS26 ....156 F3
  WBOW BD5 ....127 G3

Parsonage St HIPP HX3 ....11 J7
Parsonage Wk MILN * OL16 ....207 N3
Parson La HOR/CROF WF4 ....220 C7
Parsons Gn WBY LS22 ....48 B1
Parson's La ILK LS29 ....18 E4
Parsons Rd HTON BD9 ....104 C2
Parson St KGHY BD21 ....3 J3
Partons Pl EARD/LOFT WF3 ....154 E8
Partridge Cl MOR LS27 ....152 F2
Partridge Crs EARL WF12 ....196 B5
The Pass MILN OL16 ....206 C6
Pasture Av CHAL LS7 ....87 M7
  GFTH/SHER LS25 ....116 C6
  HWTH BD22 ....78 E5
Pasture Cl CLAY BD14 ....125 M2
  SKP/WHF BD23 ....16 D1
Pasture Ct GFTH/SHER LS25 ....116 C6
Pasture Crs CHAL LS7 ....87 M7
Pasture Dr CAS WF10 ....157 M8
Pasture Cv CHAL LS7 ....87 M7
Pasture La CHAL LS7 ....87 M7
  CLAY BD14 ....125 M2
  WBY LS22 ....46 A5
Pasture Mt WOR/ARM LS12 ....108 D6
Pasture Pde CHAL LS7 ....87 M7
Pasture Pl CHAL LS7 ....87 M7
Pasture Ri CLAY BD14 ....125 M2
Pasture Rd BAIL BD17 ....82 F4
  RHAY LS8 ....110 A2
Pasture Side Ter East
  CLAY BD14 ....125 M2
Pasture Side Ter West
  CLAY BD14 ....125 L2
Pasture St CHAL * LS7 ....87 M7
Pastures Wy MAR/SLWT HD7 ....212 F1
Pasture Ter CHAL LS7 ....87 M7
Pasture Vw GFTH/SHER LS25 ....116 B6
  WOR/ARM LS12 ....108 D6
Pasture View Rd RTHW LS26 ....154 F1
Pasture Wk CLAY BD14 ....125 L2
Pasture Wy CAS WF10 ....157 J8
  GFTH/SHER LS25 ....116 C6
Pateley Crs HUDN HD2 ....192 B4
Patent St HTON BD9 ....104 C4
Paternoster La GTHN BD7 ....4 A5
Paterson Av WKFDW/WTN WF2 ....12 B3
Patience La NORM WF6 ....178 A3
Patricia Gdns RPDN/SBR * HX6 ....168 B2
Patterdale Ap WBY LS22 ....47 K1
Patterdale Dr HUDE HD5 ....15 L6
Patterdale Rd EARL WF12 ....174 A4
Patte Roale Cl AWLS/ASK DN6 ....249 L5
Patterson Ct
  WKFDW/WTN WF2 ....176 B3
Pattie St KGHY BD21 ....57 K5
Pauline Ter CAS WF10 ....157 L7
Paul La HOR/CROF WF4 ....216 B3
  HUDE HD5 ....193 L1
Pavement La LUD/ILL HX2 ....124 F7
Pavilion Cl CUD/GR S72 ....245 J3
  WHIT OL12 ....206 B4
Pavilion Ms BULY LS4 ....108 E3
Pavilion Wy HOLM/MEL HD9 ....235 G2
Paw Hill La STKB/PEN S36 ....269 L6
Paw La CUL/QBY BD13 ....125 H7
Pawson St BOW BD4 ....105 M8
  EARD/LOFT WF3 ....154 A6
  EARD/LOFT WF3 ....154 D4
  MOR LS27 ....152 A3
Paxton Av AWLS/ASK DN6 ....249 L5
Peabody St HIPP HX3 ....10 C1
Peace Hall Dr HUDE HD5 ....215 L1
Peace St BOW BD4 ....127 L1
Peach Tree Cl PONT * WF8 ....180 B4
Peacock Av WKFDW/WTN WF2 ....176 B7
Peacock Ct YEA LS19 ....62 E8
Peacock Gn MOR LS27 ....152 E3
Peacock Gv WKFDW/WTN WF2 ....176 B7
Peak Rd BSLYN/ROY * S71 ....243 J7
Peak Vw DEWS WF13 ....173 H4
Pearl St BTLY WF17 ....151 J8
  HWTH BD22 ....79 J2
Pear Pl TOD OL14 ....140 C7
Pearson Av HDGY LS6 ....109 G3
Pearson Cl MILN OL16 ....207 N3
Pearson Gv HDGY LS6 ....109 G3
Pearson La HTON BD9 ....103 M5
Pearson Rd WBSD BD6 ....126 F6
Pearson Rw LM/WK BD12 ....148 F1
Pearson's La EARL WF12 ....195 H7
Pearson St BFDE BD3 ....105 L8
  CLECK BD19 ....149 K8
  MID LS10 ....9 J6
  MILN OL16 ....206 E6
  NORM WF6 ....178 C1
  PDSY/CALV LS28 ....84 D7
Pearson Ter HDGY LS6 ....109 G3
Pear St HFAX HX1 ....10 A7
  HUDS HD4 ....214 A2
  HWTH BD22 ....79 J3
  HWTH * BD22 ....100 E4
Pear Tree Acre
  BSPA/BRAM LS23 ....49 G5
Pear Tree Cl CUD/GR S72 ....263 M4
  PONT WF8 ....180 B6
Pear Tree Ct AIRE BD20 ....36 A3
Peartree Field La PONT WF8 ....225 L2
Pear Tree Gdns MSTN/BAR LS15 ....91 G8
Pear Tree La HEM/SK/SE WF9 ....223 M7
  HOLM/MEL HD9 ....235 G2
Peasborough Vw ILK LS29 ....40 B7
Pease Cl PONT WF8 ....180 F8
Peasefold GFTH/SHER LS25 ....135 K5
Peasehill Cl BSLY S70 ....261 G6
  YEA LS19 ....84 E2
Peaseland Av CLECK BD19 ....149 M7
Peaseland Cl CLECK BD19 ....149 M7
Peaseland Rd CLECK BD19 ....149 M7
Peat Ponds HUDW HD3 ....191 G5
Peckett Cl HUDW HD3 ....191 L7
Peckover Dr PDSY/CALV LS28 ....106 B3
Peckover St BFD BD1 ....5 H6
Pedler Brow La WHIT OL12 ....185 G8
Peebles Cl HUDN HD3 ....191 J5
Peel Av BTLY WF17 ....173 L1
Peel Cl BOW BD4 ....128 A1
  HOR/CROF WF4 ....197 K5

Peel Cottage Rd TOD OL14 ...163 J5
Peel Cott St TOD OL14 ...163 J6
Peel Pde BSLY S70 ...261 G5
Peel Park Dr ECHL BD2 ...105 K4
Peel Park Ter ECHL BD2 ...105 K4
Peel Park Vw BFDE BD3 ...5 J1
Peel Pl BSLYN/ROY S71 ...261 J3
  ILK LS29 ...40 A5
Peel Rw IDLE BD10 ...126 C3
Peel Sq BFD BD1 ...4 D4
  BSLY S70 ...261 G5
Peel St BGLY BD16 ...81 K3
  BSLY S70 ...261 G5
  CUL/QBY BD13 ...102 F8
  CUL/QBY BD13 ...125 H5
  HECK WF16 ...172 E2
  HOR/CROF WF4 ...197 K5
  HUD HD1 ...14 F8
  LIT OL15 ...207 K1
  MAR/SLWT HD7 ...233 H2
  MOR LS27 ...152 D2
  RPDN/SBR * HX6 ...167 K2
  WHIT OL12 ...206 A6
  WIL AL BD15 ...102 E2
Peep Green Rd LVSG WF15 ...171 L3
Pegholme Dr OT LS21 ...40 F8
Pelham Ct EARD/LOFT * WF3 ...153 M3
  ECHL BD2 ...105 K3
Pelham Pl CHAL LS7 ...87 L7
Pelham Rd ECHL BD2 ...105 K3
Pell Ct HOLM/MEL HD9 ...236 E7
Pell La HOLM/MEL HD9 ...236 E8
Pellentine Rd PBR HG3 ...28 A1
Pellon La HFAX HX1 ...10 A3
Pellon New Rd LUD/ILL HX2 ...146 A6
Pellon St TOD OL14 ...163 K6
Pellon Ter IDLE BD10 ...83 K5
Pellon Wk IDLE BD10 ...83 K5
Pemberton Dr GTHN BD7 ...4 C8
Pemberton Rd CAS WF10 ...158 D6
Pemberton Wy ROY/SHW OL2 ...229 K6
Pembroke Ct MOR LS27 ...152 B1
  WHIT * OL12 ...206 B5
Pembroke Ri GFTH/SHER LS25 ...135 L4
Pembroke Rd PDSY/CALV LS28 ...107 G6
Pembroke Rd LIT OL15 ...185 K8
  SKP/WHF BD23 ...16 B3
  WBOW BD5 ...127 G2
Pembury Mt MSTN/BAR LS15 ...112 B3
Penarth Av HEM/SK/SE WF9 ...225 J7
Penarth Rd MSTN/BAR LS15 ...111 K4
Penarth Ter HEM/SK/SE WF9 ...225 H7
Penda's Dr MSTN/BAR LS15 ...111 M4
Penda's Gv MSTN/BAR LS15 ...111 M3
Penda's Wk MSTN/BAR LS15 ...111 M4
Penda's Wy MSTN/BAR LS15 ...112 A4
Pendennis ROCH * OL11 ...206 A8
Pendennis Av HEM/SK/SE WF9 ...247 G2
Pendil Cl MSTN/BAR LS15 ...111 L6
Pendle Ct CUL/QBY BD13 ...125 G7
Pendle Rd BGLY BD16 ...81 K3
Pendle Wy COL BB8 ...75 L5
  COL BB8 ...75 C1
Pendragon ECHL * BD2 ...105 J3
Pendragon La ECHL BD2 ...105 K3
Penfield Gv CLAY BD14 ...125 L2
Penfield Rd BIRK/DRI BD11 ...129 H8
Pengarth BGLY BD16 ...81 K1
Pengeston Rd STKB/PEN S36 ...270 D4
Penistone Boundary Wk
  STKB/PEN S36 ...257 H8
  STKB/PEN S36 ...258 E6
  STKB/PEN S36 ...269 K1
  STKB/PEN S36 ...271 J1
Penistone Ct STKB/PEN * S36 ...271 G8
Penistone Ms HWTH * BD22 ...78 E7
Penistone Rd HOLM/MEL HD9 ...237 H8
  HOLM/MEL HD9 ...255 G7
  HUDE HD5 ...215 K1
Penlands Crs MSTN/BAR LS15 ...111 M7
Penlands Lawn
  MSTN/BAR LS15 ...111 M7
Penlands Wk MSTN/BAR LS15 ...111 M7
Penlington Ct HEM/SK/SE WF9 ...245 M1
Penmore Cl ROY/SHW OL2 ...229 L7
Penn Cl ECHL BD2 ...105 K3
Penn Dr CLECK BD19 ...149 M8
Penn Gv CLECK BD19 ...149 M8
Pennine Cl CUL/QBY BD13 ...124 F7
  HOLM/MEL HD9 ...253 M1
  WKFDW/WTN WF2 ...198 A4
Pennine Crs HUDW HD3 ...191 G6
Pennine Dr KBTN HD8 ...239 M4
  MILN OL16 ...207 J8
  WHIT OL12 ...184 E8
Pennine Gdns MAR/SLWT HD7 ...212 F5
Pennine Gv TOD OL14 ...141 L8
Pennine Ri KBTN HD8 ...239 M4
Pennine Rd EARL WF12 ...174 A6
Pennine V ROY/SHW OL2 ...229 L6
Pennine Vw BTLY WF17 ...151 J4
  DOD/DAR S75 ...242 C4
  HBR HX7 ...142 B2
  HEM/SK/SE WF9 ...225 J6
  HUDE HD5 ...193 L4
  LIT OL15 ...185 M4
  MAR/SLWT HD7 ...212 F5
Pennine Wy DOD/DAR S75 ...260 D4
  GLSP SK13 ...264 C6
  HBR HX7 ...119 M3
  HBR HX7 ...120 D8
  HEM/SK/SE WF9 ...224 B7
  HUDW HD3 ...209 L8
  HWTH BD22 ...76 E3
  KBTN HD8 ...239 M4
  LIT OL15 ...186 D7
  UPML OL3 ...231 M3
Pennington Gv HDGY LS6 ...6 D1
Pennington La RTHW LS26 ...155 K4
Pennington Pl HDGY LS6 ...6 D1
Pennington St HDGY LS6 ...6 D1
Pennington Ter HDGY LS6 ...6 D2
  WBOW * BD5 ...126 C3
Pennithorne Av BAIL BD17 ...82 C3
Penn St HFAX HX1 ...10 C4

MILN OL16 ...206 B6
Pennwell Fold SCFT LS14 ...112 A1
Pennwell Garth SCFT LS14 ...111 M1
Pennwell Gn SCFT LS14 ...111 M1
Pennwell Lawn SCFT LS14 ...111 M1
Pennygate BGLY BD16 ...59 M8
Penny Hill Dr CLAY BD14 ...125 M2
Penny La HUDE HD5 ...215 K1
Penny Lane Wy MID LS10 ...9 J8
Penny Spring HUDE HD5 ...215 G3
Penraevon Av CHAL LS7 ...7 G2
Penraevon St CHAL LS7 ...7 G2
Penrhyn Wk BSLYN/ROY S71 ...262 C6
Penrith Crs CAS WF10 ...159 G4
Penrith Gv BSLYN/ROY S71 ...262 B6
  WOR/ARM LS12 ...108 E8
Penrith St ROCH OL11 ...228 B1
Penrose Beck Dr
  FEA/AMT WF7 ...224 A1
Penrose Dr GTHN BD7 ...126 B3
Penrose Pl WKFDW/WTN WF2 ...220 B1
Penryn Av HUDE HD5 ...193 L6
Pentland Av CLAY BD14 ...125 M2
Pentland Cl HWTH * BD22 ...2 D6
Pentland Dr GFTH/SHER LS25 ...135 H1
Pentland Gv
  WKFDW/WTN WF2 ...198 A3
Pentland Rd EARL WF12 ...173 M8
Pentland Wy MOR LS27 ...152 C3
Penzance Ct GIR BD8 ...104 D6
Pepper Gdns BRAM LS13 ...108 A2
Pepper La BRAM LS13 ...107 M2
  MID LS10 ...132 B3
Peppermint Cl MILN OL16 ...229 L2
Pepper Rd MID LS10 ...132 B4
Pepper Royd St DEWS WF13 ...173 M5
Percival Ct HUDW HD3 ...191 H8
Percival St BFDE BD3 ...5 K6
  HUDW HD3 ...191 H8
  LDSU LS2 ...6 F7
Percy St BGLY BD16 ...81 J3
  COL BB8 ...52 A8
  HUDN HD2 ...192 C5
  KGHY BD21 ...79 K2
  MILN OL16 ...228 D1
  WOR/ARM LS12 ...108 F8
Peregrine Av MOR LS27 ...152 F2
Peregrine Dr HUDS HD4 ...214 A7
Peregrine Wy WBSY BD6 ...125 L5
Peridot Fold HUDN HD2 ...192 E4
Per La LUD/ILL HX2 ...123 M7
Permain Ct HUDS HD4 ...214 D3
Perseverance La GTHN BD7 ...126 C3
Perseverance Rd
  CUL/QBY BD13 ...124 C3
Perseverance St BAIL * BD17 ...82 C7
  BSLY S70 ...260 F5
  CAS WF10 ...157 L6
  HUDS HD4 ...214 C3
  LM/WK BD12 ...148 E2
  PDSY/CALV LS28 ...106 E7
  RPDN/SBR HX6 ...167 K2
Perseverance Ter HFAX HX1 ...168 C1
  RTHW LS26 ...155 G2
Perseverance St HUDS HD4 ...213 H3
Pershore WHIT OL12 ...206 A6
Perth Av ECHL BD2 ...105 G3
Perth Dr EARD/LOFT WF3 ...153 H6
Perth Mt HORS LS18 ...85 K2
Perth Rd ROCH OL11 ...228 D4
Peterborough Pl ECHL BD2 ...105 K3
Peterborough Rd ECHL BD2 ...105 K4
Peterborough Ter ECHL BD2 ...105 K4
Peterfoot Wy BSLYN/ROY S71 ...243 K5
Petergate BFD BD1 ...5 G5
Peter Hl BTLY WF17 ...173 M4
Peterhouse Dr OT LS21 ...41 L7
Peter La LUD/ILL HX2 ...145 K7
  MOR LS27 ...152 F1
Petersfield Av MID LS10 ...132 A7
Peterson Rd WKFDE WF1 ...13 G3
Peter St COL * BB8 ...74 A2
Pether Hl GTL/HWG HX4 ...190 B3
Petrel Cl WBSY BD6 ...125 L5
Petrel Wy MOR LS27 ...152 E3
Petrie Crs BRAM LS13 ...106 F1
Petrie Gv BFDE BD3 ...106 A7
Petrie Rd BFDE BD3 ...106 A7
Petrie St BRAM LS13 ...106 F1
  WHIT * OL12 ...206 B5
Petts Crs LIT OL15 ...185 J8
Petworth Cft BSLYN/ROY S71 ...243 K2
Petyt Gv SKP/WHF BD23 ...16 C2
Peverell Cl BOW BD4 ...128 A3
Peverils Crs BSLYN/ROY S71 ...243 J7
Peveril Mt ECHL BD2 ...105 L4
Pexwood Rd TOD OL14 ...163 H3
Pheasant Dr BTLY WF17 ...151 J3
Pheasant St KGHY BD21 ...3 J5
Philip Garth WKFDE WF1 ...176 D1
Philip La SEL YO8 ...139 L2
Philippa Wy WOR/ARM LS12 ...130 E3
Philip Rd BSLY S70 ...261 M7
Philip's Gv EARD/LOFT WF3 ...154 E8
Philip's La PONT WF8 ...203 L1
Philip St ROCH OL11 ...228 B1
Phillips St CAS WF10 ...157 K6
Phil May Ct WOR/ARM LS12 ...109 G7
Phoebe La HIPP HX3 ...168 F2
Phoenix Av KBTN HD8 ...217 M8
Phoenix Ct BTLY WF17 ...174 B1
  TOD OL14 ...163 M1
  WKFDW/WTN WF2 ...12 B3
Phoenix St BRIG HD6 ...170 D4
  LIT OL15 ...185 K8
  TOD OL14 ...141 M8
Phoenix Wy BOW BD4 ...106 A8
Piccadilly BFD BD1 ...4 F5
Pickard Bank HDGY LS6 ...109 H1
Pickard Ct MSTN/BAR LS15 ...111 L6
Pickard La AIRE BD20 ...36 A4
Pickard Wy DEWS WF13 ...173 K5
Pickering Av GFTH/SHER LS25 ...113 C7

Pickering Dr OSS WF5 ...174 E5
Pickering La OSS WF5 ...174 D5
The Pickerings CUL/QBY BD13 ...125 C6
Pickering St WOR/ARM LS12 ...108 F6
Pickering St WOR/ARM LS12 ...108 F6
Pickersgill St OSS WF5 ...174 E6
Pickford St HUDS HD4 ...213 J2
Pick Haven Garth GLE DN14 ...161 M8
Pick Hill Rd HOLM/MEL HD9 ...234 F3
Picklesfield DEWS WF13 ...173 K4
Pickles La GTHN BD7 ...126 B3
  KBTN HD8 ...239 K5
Pickles St BSLY S70 ...261 K6
  KGHY BD21 ...2 F8
Pickrowfield La
  GFTH/SHER LS25 ...117 G3
Pickthall Ter TOD OL14 ...163 M1
Pickup St MILN OL16 ...206 C7
Pickwood La RPDN/SBR HX6 ...168 A4
Picton St GIR BD8 ...4 C2
Picton Wy HUDE HD5 ...193 J7
Pictureville BFD BD1 ...4 E7
Piece Wood Rd BHP/TINH LS16 ...85 M3
Piethorne Cl MILN OL16 ...229 L2
Pigeon Cote Cl SCFT LS14 ...89 J8
Pigeon Cote Rd SCFT LS14 ...89 H8
Piggott St BRIG HD6 ...170 C3
Pighill Nook Rd
  GFTH/SHER LS25 ...139 H7
Pighill Top La MAR/SLWT HD7 ...212 A4
Pike End Rd RPDN/SBR HX6 ...188 D6
Pike Law La MAR/SLWT HD7 ...212 D1
Pike Law Rd MAR/SLWT HD7 ...212 D1
Pike Lowe Gv DOD/DAR S75 ...242 F6
Pikes Gv ROCH OL11 ...228 B1
Pilden La EARD/LOFT WF3 ...153 L7
Pilgrim Av DEWS WF13 ...173 H7
Pilgrim Crs DEWS WF13 ...173 H7
Pilgrim Dr DEWS WF13 ...173 H7
Pilkington St WKFDW/WTN WF2 ...12 B8
Pilley Hl DOD/DAR S75 ...260 B8
Pilling La KBTN HD8 ...239 K4
Pilling Top La KBTN HD8 ...238 D2
Pill White La OT LS21 ...24 B8
Pilmer Ct WKFDW/WTN WF2 ...197 M2
Pilot St OSM LS9 ...7 L6
Pincheon St WKFDE * WF1 ...13 G2
Pindar Oaks Cottages
  BSLY S70 ...261 K6
Pindar Oaks St BSLY S70 ...261 K6
Pindar St BSLY S70 ...261 K6
Pinder Av WOR/ARM LS12 ...130 B3
Pinderfields Rd WKFDE WF1 ...176 E7
Pinder Gv WOR/ARM LS12 ...130 B3
Pinders Crs KNOT WF11 ...181 L1
Pinders Garth KNOT WF11 ...181 L1
Pinders Green RTHW LS26 ...156 E5
Pinders Green Dr RTHW LS26 ...156 E5
Pinders Green Fold
  RTHW LS26 ...156 E5
Pinder's Gv WKFDE WF1 ...177 G6
Pinder St WOR/ARM LS12 ...130 B2
Pine Cl BSLY S70 ...261 L8
  CAS WF10 ...158 A8
  SKP/WHF BD23 ...16 A2
  WBY LS22 ...30 A7
Pine Ct HUDS HD4 ...213 M8
  LDSU LS2 ...9 J1
Pine Cft KGHY BD21 ...2 C1
Pinedale BGLY BD16 ...81 H1
Pine Gv BTLY WF17 ...173 K2
  ROY/SHW OL2 ...228 F8
Pinehall Dr BSLYN/ROY S71 ...261 M2
Pine Rd TOD OL14 ...141 M7
The Pines AL/HA/HU LS17 ...43 L3
Pines Gdns ILK LS29 ...38 B3
Pine St BFD BD1 ...5 H5
  HEM/SK/SE WF9 ...247 G5
  HFAX HX1 ...11 C7
  HUD HD1 ...15 H6
  HWTH BD22 ...78 E8
  LIT OL15 ...185 K8
  MILN OL16 ...206 D7
  MILN OL16 ...206 D7
Pine Tree Av BSPA/BRAM LS23 ...49 G6
  PONT WF8 ...180 D8
Pine Tree La GFTH/SHER LS25 ...138 D8
Pinewood Av
  WKFDW/WTN WF2 ...175 M8
Pinewood Cl CUD/GR S72 ...263 M3
  ILK LS29 ...38 C3
Pinewood Gdns GTL/HWG HX4 ...190 D2
Pinewood Pl KNOT WF11 ...182 A3
The Pinfold SKP/WHF BD23 ...16 B1
Pinfold Av GFTH/SHER LS25 ...116 B6
Pinfold Ct BSLYN/ROY S71 ...262 A6
  EARL WF12 ...196 A4
  GFTH/SHER LS25 ...116 B6
  GTL/HWG HX4 ...189 J1
  HOR/CROF WF4 ...217 L4
  KNOT WF11 ...181 L1
  MIRF WF14 ...194 D1
  WBY LS22 ...31 L5
Pinfold Cft GFTH/SHER LS25 ...116 B6
  MSTN/BAR * LS15 ...111 K6
Pinfold Cft CLAY BD14 ...125 J2
Pinfold Garth GFTH/SHER LS25 ...116 C6
Pinfold Gv MSTN/BAR LS15 ...111 J1
  WKFDW/WTN WF2 ...198 F5
Pinfold Hl BSLY S70 ...261 J8
  DEWS WF13 ...173 K7
  MSTN/BAR LS15 ...111 K7
Pinfold La AWLS/ASK DN6 ...227 M3
  BHP/TINH LS16 ...64 A8
  BSLYN/ROY S71 ...243 L4
  ELL HX5 ...169 M8
  GFTH/SHER LS25 ...113 H7
  HOR/CROF WF4 ...217 L4
  HUDW HD3 ...211 L1
  KBTN HD8 ...216 C3
  MAR/SLWT HD7 ...212 C2
  MIRF WF14 ...194 D1
  MSTN/BAR LS15 ...111 J6

PONT WF8 ...226 F1
RPDN/SBR HX6 ...166 F2
RTHW LS26 ...157 G4
WKFDW/WTN WF2 ...199 G5
WOR/ARM LS12 ...108 D6
Pinfold Mt MSTN/BAR LS15 ...111 K7
Pinfold Ri GFTH/SHER LS25 ...92 B6
Pinfold Sq MSTN/BAR LS15 ...111 K7
Pinfold Wy GFTH/SHER LS25 ...116 C6
Pingle Ri KBTN HD8 ...239 J7
Pinhaw Rd SKP/WHF BD23 ...16 C4
Pin Hill La LUD/ILL HX2 ...144 F5
Pink St HWTH BD22 ...78 E8
Pinnacle La HBR HX7 ...143 G5
Pinnacle Vw HWTH BD22 ...54 E3
Pinnar St HIPP HX3 ...169 H1
Pioneer St EARL WF12 ...195 L3
  LIT OL15 ...207 K1
  ROCH OL11 ...206 C8
  TOD * OL14 ...163 J7
Pioneer Vls MILN * OL16 ...230 A1
Pioneer Wy CAS WF10 ...179 G1
Pipe & Nook La
  WOR/ARM LS12 ...108 B7
Pipercroft WBSY BD6 ...126 A8
Piper Hl KNOT WF11 ...159 J1
Piper La HWTH BD22 ...54 F5
  OT LS21 ...41 H7
Piper Well La KBTN HD8 ...238 D2
Pipit Meadow MOR LS27 ...152 E3
Pippin's Ap NORM WF6 ...178 D3
Pippins Green Av
  WKFDW/WTN WF2 ...175 K4
Pirie Cl ECHL BD2 ...105 H3
Pitchstone Ct WOR/ARM LS12 ...107 M2
Pitcliffe Wy WBOW BD5 ...127 G2
Pitfall St LDS LS1 ...9 L4
Pit Field Rd EARD/LOFT WF3 ...154 F4
Pit Hl HIPP HX3 ...11 M8
Pit La CLECK BD19 ...150 D4
  CUL/QBY BD13 ...101 L5
  CUL/QBY BD13 ...124 F2
  DEWS WF13 ...173 H4
  GFTH/SHER LS25 ...114 C3
  GFTH/SHER LS25 ...136 A2
  ROY/SHW OL2 ...228 F6
  RTHW LS26 ...156 F3
Pits La CLECK BD19 ...149 G8
Pitt Hill La GTL/HWG HX4 ...189 L4
Pitt Rw LDS LS1 ...9 G2
Pitts St BOW BD4 ...127 M2
Pitt St BSLY S70 ...261 G5
  KGHY BD21 ...3 J5
  LVSG WF15 ...172 C4
  TOD OL14 ...163 M1
  WHIT OL12 ...206 B6
Pitt St West BSLY S70 ...260 F5
Place's Rd OSM LS9 ...9 M2
Plaid Rw OSM LS9 ...7 M9
Plain La RPDN/SBR HX6 ...166 E4
Plains La ELL HX5 ...169 K7
  MAR/SLWT HD7 ...233 J1
Plane St HUDS HD4 ...214 D3
  TOD OL14 ...141 G7
Plane Tree Av AL/HA/HU LS17 ...88 D2
Plane Tree Cl AL/HA/HU LS17 ...88 D2
Plane Tree Cft AL/HA/HU LS17 ...88 C2
Plane Tree Gv YEA LS19 ...62 F8
Plane Tree Nest La
  LUD/ILL HX2 ...146 A8
Plane Tree Ri AL/HA/HU * LS17 ...88 D2
Plane Tree Rd RPDN/SBR HX6 ...167 K1
Plane Trees LUD/ILL HX2 ...145 M6
Plane Trees Cl CLECK BD19 ...149 M3
Planetrees St WIL/AL BD15 ...103 J5
Planetrees Wl WIL/AL BD15 ...103 J5
Planetrees Rd BFDE BD3 ...105 M8
Planet Rd AWLS/ASK DN6 ...249 L7
Plantation Av AL/HA/HU LS17 ...88 C2
  BSLYN/ROY S71 ...243 M3
  MSTN/BAR LS15 ...111 M3
Plantation Dr HUDS HD4 ...214 C5
Plantation Gdns AL/HA/HU LS17 ...88 D1
Plantation Pl BOW BD4 ...127 L2
Plantation Wy BAIL BD17 ...82 F3
Platt Cl MILN OL16 ...229 L2
Platting La ROCH OL11 ...228 C2
Platt La MAR/SLWT HD7 ...212 C5
Playfair Rd MID LS10 ...131 M4
Playhouse Sq OSM LS9 ...7 K9
The Pleasance RTHW LS26 ...134 C5
Pleasant Ct HDGY LS6 ...6 C2
Pleasant Mt BEE/HOL LS11 ...8 C5
Pleasant Pl BEE/HOL LS11 ...8 C5
Pleasant St BEE/HOL LS11 ...8 B5
  GTHN BD7 ...126 C2
Pleasant Ter BEE/HOL LS11 ...8 C5
Pleasant Vw CUD/GR S72 ...262 E2
Pledwick Crs
  WKFDW/WTN WF2 ...198 F8
Pledwick Dr WKFDW/WTN WF2 ...220 F1
Pledwick Gv
  WKFDW/WTN WF2 ...220 E1
Pledwick La WKFDW/WTN WF2 ...220 F1
Pledwick Ri WKFDW/WTN WF2 ...198 F8
Plevna La MID LS10 ...132 C4
Plevna Ter BGLY BD16 ...81 H7
Plimsoll St BOW BD4 ...127 J2
  HEM/SK/SE WF9 ...223 M7
Ploughcroft La HIPP HX3 ...146 D4
The Plough Garth GLE DN14 ...161 M8
Ploughmans Cft ECHL BD2 ...105 G2
Plover Dr BTLY WF17 ...173 K2
Plover Rd HUDW HD3 ...191 K6
Plover St KGHY BD21 ...3 G6
  WBOW BD5 ...126 E3
Plover Wy MOR LS27 ...152 E3
Plumber St BSLY S70 ...260 F5
Plumpton Av ECHL BD2 ...83 H8
Plumpton Cl ECHL BD2 ...105 J4
Plumpton Dr ECHL BD2 ...83 H8
Plumpton End ECHL BD2 ...83 H8
Plumpton Gdns ECHL BD2 ...83 H8
Plumpton Lea ECHL BD2 ...83 H8
Plumpton Md ECHL BD2 ...83 H8
Plumpton Pl WKFDW/WTN WF2 ...12 B3

Plumpton Rd ROCH OL11 ...228 D6
  WKFDW/WTN WF2 ...12 B3
Plumpton St GIR BD8 ...104 C6
  WKFDW/WTN WF2 ...12 B4
Plumpton Ter
  WKFDW/WTN WF2 ...12 B4
Plumpton Vw ECHL BD2 ...83 H8
Plum St HFAX HX1 ...10 B8
  HWTH BD22 ...79 J3
Plum Tree Cl PONT WF8 ...180 D8
Plymouth Gv HFAX * HX1 ...10 C3
Poet's Pl HORS LS18 ...85 L4
Pogmoor La DOD/DAR S75 ...260 D5
Pogmoor Rd DOD/DAR S75 ...260 D5
Pog Well La DOD/DAR S75 ...259 M4
Pohlman St HFAX * HX1 ...10 B9
Pole Ga HUDW HD3 ...211 M3
Pole Gate Branch HUDW HD3 ...211 M2
Pole Rd HWTH BD22 ...56 B2
Pollard Av BGLY BD16 ...81 K1
  CLECK BD19 ...150 D5
Pollard Cl CLECK BD19 ...150 D5
Pollard Gv LIT OL15 ...185 L6
Pollard La BFDE BD3 ...5 M1
  BRAM LS13 ...85 L8
Pollard's Flds KNOT WF11 ...181 K1
Pollard St South HUDW HD3 ...213 K1
Pollard Wy CLECK BD19 ...150 D5
Pollit Av RPDN/SBR HX6 ...167 K3
Pollitt St DOD/DAR S75 ...260 E5
Pollyfox Wy DOD/DAR S75 ...260 A7
Polperro Cl NORM WF6 ...178 D3
Pomfret Pl GFTH/SHER LS25 ...113 K6
Pomona St ROCH OL11 ...228 B1
Pond Cl HUDS HD4 ...214 B4
Pond Common La
  STKB/PEN S36 ...271 K8
Ponden La HWTH BD22 ...77 J8
Ponderosa Gv RHAY LS8 ...110 B3
Pondfields Cl GFTH/SHER LS25 ...135 K5
Pondfields Crest
  GFTH/SHER LS25 ...135 K5
Pondfields Dr GFTH/SHER LS25 ...135 K4
Pondfields Ri GFTH/SHER LS25 ...135 K5
Pond La KBTN HD8 ...216 C4
Pond St BSLY S70 ...261 G6
  KGHY BD21 ...3 H4
Ponker La CLECK BD19 ...239 C6
Ponker Nook La KBTN HD8 ...239 K1
Pontefract Av OSM LS9 ...110 B7
Pontefract La MSTN/BAR LS15 ...133 L4
  OSM LS9 ...110 B7
Pontefract Lane Cl OSM LS9 ...110 B7
Pontefract Rd BSLYN/ROY S71 ...261 K5
  CAS WF10 ...158 A7
  CUD/GR S72 ...244 E5
  FEA/AMT WF7 ...201 L2
  FEA/AMT WF7 ...202 C6
  HEM/SK/SE WF9 ...224 B5
  HOR/CROF WF4 ...200 A4
  MID LS10 ...132 C4
  NORM WF6 ...178 F3
  PONT WF8 ...181 J2
Pontefract St OSM LS9 ...110 B7
Pontefract Ter
  HEM/SK/SE WF9 ...224 A8
Pontey Dr HUDE HD5 ...215 K1
Pontey Mt HUDE HD5 ...215 K1
Ponyfield Cl HUDN HD2 ...14 B1
Pool Bank Cl OT LS21 ...42 F7
Pool Bank Ct OT LS21 ...42 F8
Pool Bank New Rd
  BHP/TINH LS16 ...63 K2
Pool Br OT LS21 ...42 E6
Pool Ct BFDE BD3 ...5 K4
Poole Crs MSTN/BAR LS15 ...111 K4
Poole La GFTH/SHER LS25 ...160 A3
Poole Mt MSTN/BAR LS15 ...111 K5
Poole Rd MSTN/BAR LS15 ...111 K5
Poole Sq MSTN/BAR LS15 ...111 K5
Pool Hill La KBTN HD8 ...257 L1
Pool Rd OT LS21 ...41 L6
  OT LS21 ...42 B6
Pools La BSLYN/ROY S71 ...244 A3
Pool St KGHY BD21 ...3 L1
Popeley Rd HECK WF16 ...150 E8
Pope St KGHY BD21 ...3 K3
  NORM WF6 ...178 D1
Poplar Av CAS WF10 ...158 E7
  CUD/GR S72 ...244 E4
  GFTH/SHER LS25 ...113 G7
  GTHN BD7 ...126 B4
  HOLM/MEL HD9 ...236 E5
  MSTN/BAR LS15 ...111 M4
  RPDN/SBR HX6 ...167 K1
  SHPY BD18 ...104 C1
  TOD OL14 ...141 J7
  WBY LS22 ...30 A7
  WKFDW/WTN WF2 ...197 M1
Poplar Cl BRAM LS13 ...108 B6
  ILK LS29 ...40 B6
Poplar Ct ELL * HX5 ...169 H8
Poplar Crs EARD/LOFT WF3 ...152 E2
  LUD/ILL HX2 ...124 B7
  SHPY BD18 ...104 C1
Poplar Cft BRAM LS13 ...108 A6
Poplar Dr AIRE BD20 ...58 E7
  HORS LS18 ...85 H5
  NORM WF6 ...178 C1
  SHPY BD18 ...104 C1
Poplar Gdns BRAM LS13 ...108 A6
Poplar Garth BRAM LS13 ...108 A6
Poplar Gate WOR/ARM LS12 ...108 A6
Poplar Gv BGLY BD16 ...80 C8
  BSLYN/ROY S71 ...262 A2
  CLECK BD19 ...149 G8
  GTHN BD7 ...126 B4
  KNOT WF11 ...182 A4
  PONT WF8 ...180 D6
  SHPY BD18 ...104 C1
Poplar Ri BRAM LS13 ...108 A5
  KBTN HD8 ...239 K5
Poplar Rd AWLS/ASK DN6 ...249 K5
  GTHN BD7 ...126 C4

SHPY BD18....................104 E1
The Poplars *AIRE* BD20.......55 L2
BHP/TINH LS16...............64 B4
GSLY LS20....................62 A4
HDGY LS6....................109 G2
HIPP * HX3..................148 C4
KNOT WF11...................182 D4
Poplars Park Rd *ECHL* BD2....104 F2
Poplar Sq *PDSY/CALV* LS28....106 F4
Poplars Rd *BSLY* S70.........261 K7
Poplar St *CUD/GR* S72........263 K1
EARD/LOFT WF3...............154 E8
HIPP HX3.....................11 G3
HUDE HD5.....................15 K9
HUDN HD2....................192 C5
Poplar Ter *AIRE* BD20.........58 F7
BSLYN/ROY S71...............243 M2
HEM/SK/SE WF9...............247 J4
HUDE HD4.....................15 M8
Poplar Vw *AL/HA/HU* * LS17....89 H3
BRAM LS13...................108 A6
BRIG HD6....................148 C8
GTHN BD7....................126 A4
Poplarwood Gdns *IDLE* BD10...106 A1
Popley Dr *HOLM/MEL* HD9......234 F5
Popples Dr *LUD/ILL* HX2......124 B7
Poppleton Ct *EARD/LOFT* WF3..153 C5
Poppleton Dr *EARD/LOFT* WF3..153 G5
Poppleton Ri *EARD/LOFT* WF3..153 G6
Poppleton Rd *EARD/LOFT* WF3..153 G5
Poppleton Wy
EARD/LOFT WF3...............153 G6
Popple Wells La *LUD/ILL* HX2.145 H1
Poppy Ct *WBSY* * BD6.........126 E3
Porritt St *CLECK* BD19.......149 M5
Portage Av *MSTN/BAR* LS15....111 H7
Portage Crs *MSTN/BAR* LS15...111 H7
Portal Crs *MIRF* WF14........172 C6
Portal Dr *MIRF* WF14.........172 C6
Porter Av *DOD/DAR* S75.......260 E4
Porter Ter *DOD/DAR* S75......260 D4
Portland Av *PONT* WF8........180 D5
Portland Cl *HUDW* * HD3......191 L7
Portland Crs *LDSU* LS2.........6 E7
Portland Ga *LDSU* LS2..........6 F7
Portland Pl *BGLY* BD16........81 J4
HEM/SK/SE WF9...............225 J7
HFAX HX1.....................11 H8
Portland Rd *HIPP* HX3.........11 H3
WOR/ARM LS12................108 E8
Portland Wy *LDSU* LS2..........6 F7
Portman St *PDSY/CALV* LS28....84 C1
Portobello Gv
WKFDW/WTN WF2...............13 G9
Portobello Rd *WKFDE* WF1......13 G9
Portsmouth Av *BFDE* BD3........5 H2
Portwood St *HTON* BD9........103 M4
Post Hill Ct *WOR/ARM* LS12...107 M7
IDLE BD10...................105 L1
Post Office Rd *FEA/AMT* WF7..201 M1
Post Office St *CLECK* BD19...150 B8
Pothouse Rd *WBSY* BD6........126 D6
Pot La *AIRE* BD20.............35 K8
Potovens La
WKFDW/WTN WF2..............176 B3
Potter Av *WKFDW/WTN* WF2.....198 A2
Potter Brow Rd *BAIL* BD17.....60 E7
Potternewton Av *CHAL* LS7.....87 K8
Potternewton Crs *CHAL* LS7....87 J8
Potternewton Gdns *CHAL* * LS7.87 J8
Potternewton Hts *CHAL* LS7....87 K8
Potternewton La *CHAL* LS7.....87 J8
Potternewton Mt *CHAL* LS7.....87 K8
Potternewton Vw *CHAL* * LS7...87 K8
Potters Cft *EARD/LOFT* WF3...154 E8
Potters Ga *HOLM/MEL* HD9.....255 M6
Potters Wk *MAR/SLWT* HD7.....213 C2
Potterton Br *MSTN/BAR* LS15...91 C5
Potterton Cl *MSTN/BAR* LS15...91 C7
Potterton La *MSTN/BAR* LS15...91 C7
Pottery La *KNOT* WF11........181 M1
RTHW LS26...................133 M7
Pottery Rd *MID* LS10...........9 J7
Pottery St *CAS* WF10.........157 K6
HUDW HD3....................191 G6
Potts' Ter *NORM* WF6.........178 C6
Poulton Pl *BEE/HOL* LS11.......9 H9
Poulton St *BSLYN/ROY* S71....243 M8
Poverty La *RPDN/SBR* HX6.....166 C5
Powell Av *WBOW* BD5.........126 E2
Powell Rd *BGLY* BD16..........81 J3
SHPY BD18...................104 F1
Powell St *CAS* WF10..........157 M6
HECK WF16...................172 F5
HEM/SK/SE WF9...............246 F3
HFAX HX1.....................11 G6
Poxton Gv *HEM/SK/SE* WF9.....247 G5
Prail Cl *PONT* WF8...........181 H7
Pratt La *MIRF* WF14..........172 C8
SHPY BD18....................82 E8
Premiere Pk *ILK* LS29.........38 A3
Prescott St *HFAX* HX1.........11 H8
MILN OL16...................206 E4
Prescott Ter *WIL/AL* BD15....103 K5
Preston La *LUD/ILL* HX2......145 L4
RTHW LS26...................135 G2
Preston Pde *BEE/HOL* LS11....131 J4
Preston St *HFAX* HX1..........10 D6
Preston St *BTLY* WF17........173 L1
EARL WF12...................174 A7
GTHN BD7.....................4 A5
Preston Vw *RTHW* LS26........134 D5
Prestwich Dr *HUDN* HD2.......192 B4
Prestwick Cl *OT* LS21.........40 F1
Prestwick Fold *OSS* WF5......174 F7
Pretoria St *CAS* WF10........158 A7

FEA/AMT WF7.................179 L8
MAR/SLWT HD7................212 B5
WKFDE WF1....................13 H9
Priest Bank Rd *AIRE* BD20.....35 G6
Priest Croft La *BSLYN/ROY* S71.245 F1
Priest Hill Gdns *WBY* LS22....29 M7
PDSY/CALV LS28..............106 D4
Priesthorpe Av
PDSY/CALV LS28..............106 C4
Priesthorpe Ct
PDSY/CALV LS28..............106 F2
Priesthorpe La
PDSY/CALV LS28..............106 D3
Priesthorpe Rd
PDSY/CALV LS28..............106 C2
HECK WF16...................150 F8
WBSY BD6....................126 D6
Priestley Cl *PDSY/CALV* LS28.107 H6
Priestley Ct *PDSY/CALV* LS28.107 H6
Priestley Dr *PDSY/CALV* LS28.107 H6
Priestley Gdns *HECK* WF16....172 E1
PDSY/CALV LS28..............107 H6
Priestley Gv *HUDS* HD4.......214 B5
Priestley Pl *RPDN/SBR* HX6...167 J3
Priestley Sq *BTLY* WF17......151 G4
Priestley St *CUL/QBY* BD13...102 F8
Priestley Ter *WBSY* BD6......126 E5
Priestley Vw *PDSY/CALV* LS28.107 H6
Priestley Wy *PDSY/CALV* LS28.107 H6
Priestley Wy *ROY/SHW* OL2....229 M7
Priestman Cl *GIR* BD8..........4 A1
Priestman St *GIR* BD8..........4 A2
Priestthorpe Cl *BGLY* BD16....81 J2
Priestthorpe La *BGLY* BD16....81 J2
Priestthorpe Rd *BGLY* BD16....81 J3
Primitive St *EARD/LOFT* WF3..154 F3
HUD HD1.....................15 G6
Primley Gdns *AL/HA/HU* LS17...87 L2
Primley Park Av *AL/HA/HU* LS17.87 L2
Primley Park Cl *AL/HA/HU* LS17.87 M2
Primley Park Crs
AL/HA/HU LS17...............87 L2
Primley Park Dr *AL/HA/HU* LS17.87 M1
Primley Park Garth
AL/HA/HU LS17...............87 M1
Primley Park Gn *AL/HA/HU* LS17.87 M1
Primley Park La *AL/HA/HU* LS17.87 M2
Primley Park Mt *AL/HA/HU* LS17.87 M2
Primley Park Ri *AL/HA/HU* LS17.87 M2
Primley Park Rd *AL/HA/HU* LS17.87 L2
Primley Park Vw
AL/HA/HU LS17...............87 L1
Primley Park Wk
AL/HA/HU LS17...............87 M2
Primley Park Wy
AL/HA/HU LS17...............87 L1
Primrose Av *MSTN/BAR* LS15...111 J5
RTHW LS26...................134 D5
Primrose Bank *BGLY* BD16......81 K4
Primrose Cl *MSTN/BAR* LS15...111 J6
PONT WF8....................180 F7
Primrose Ct *AL/HA/HU* * LS17..87 M1
Primrose Crs *MSTN/BAR* LS15..111 J5
Primrose Dene *KNOT* WF11.....159 M7
Primrose Dr *BGLY* BD16........81 L4
CAS WF10....................158 D8
MSTN/BAR LS15...............111 J6
Primrose Gdns *BTLY* WF17.....152 A8
MSTN/BAR LS15...............111 J5
Primrose Garth
MSTN/BAR LS15...............111 J6
Primrose Gv *HUDS* HD4........214 C3
KGHY BD21....................3 M4
Primrose Hl *BTLY* WF17.......151 M8
KNOT WF11...................182 C1
PDSY/CALV LS28..............107 G5
SKP/WHF BD23.................16 B2
Primrose Hill Cl *RTHW* LS26..134 D5
Primrose Hill Dr *RTHW* LS26..134 D5
Primrose Hill Gn *RTHW* LS26..134 D6
Primrose Hill Rd *HUDS* HD4...214 C2
Primrose La *BEE/HOL* LS11......9 H9
BGLY BD16....................81 K5
BSPA/BRAM LS23...............48 E7
ECHL BD2....................104 F2
HOR/CROF WF4................197 M8
KBTN HD8....................215 M4
LVSG WF15...................172 B2
MIRF WF14...................172 E1
MSTN/BAR LS15...............111 H7
Primrose Rd *MSTN/BAR* LS15...111 J6
Primrose St *GIR* BD8..........4 B3
HUDS HD4....................214 C2
KGHY BD21....................3 M4
Primrose V *KNOT* WF11........182 C1
Primrose Wk *MOR* LS27........130 E6
Primrose Wy *HIPP* HX3........125 M7
Prince Arthur St *DOD/DAR* S75.260 F4
Prince Edward Gv
WOR/ARM LS12................130 C2
Prince Edward Rd
WOR/ARM LS12................130 C2
Prince Henry Rd *OT* LS21......41 J5
Princeroyd Wy *GTHN* BD7.....104 C7
Prince's Av *RHAY* LS8.........88 D7
Princes Ct *AL/HA/HU* * LS17...87 L1
Prince's Crs *ECHL* BD2.......105 C3
SKP/WHF BD23................16 C2
Princes Dr *SKP/WHF* BD23......16 C2
Prince's Ga *HIPP* HX3........168 D2
Princess Alexandra Wk
HUD HD1.....................15 G7
Princess Av *EARL* WF12.......174 D4
HEM/SK/SE WF9...............247 H4
WHIT OL12...................206 E2
Princess Cl *EARL* WF12.......174 C4
Princess Ct *AL/HA/HU* LS17....87 M3
NORM WF6....................178 C5
Princess Crs *EARL* WF12......174 C7
Princess Flds *MSTN/BAR* LS15.111 M8
Princess Rd *EARL* WF12.......174 C6
ILK LS29....................38 C3

MILN OL16...................206 F7
ROY/SHW OL2.................229 J8
Princess Royal Wy *PBR* HG3....26 F4
Princess St *BRIG* HD6........170 D4
BSLY S70....................261 G5
BTLY WF17...................151 L8
CAS WF10....................158 A5
CUD/GR S72..................245 J8
DOD/DAR S75.................242 C5
EARL WF12...................174 C6
GTL/HWG HX4.................168 F7
HFAX HX1....................11 H5
HUD HD1.....................14 F8
NORM WF6....................178 D4
RPDN/SBR HX6................167 L2
WHIT OL12...................206 B5
WKFDE WF1...................198 F4
YEA LS19....................84 C2
Princes St *HECK* WF16........173 G2
WBSY BD6....................126 A7
WBSY BD6....................126 D6
Princeville Rd *GTHN* BD7.....104 C7
Princeville St *GTHN* BD7.....104 D7
Prince Wood La *HUDN* HD2.....191 L4
Priordale Rd *FEA/AMT* WF7....201 K2
Priors Ter *GTL/HWG* * HX4....190 B2
Prior St *KGHY* BD21...........3 K2
Priory Cl *BGLY* BD16..........81 J2
MIRF WF14...................172 A8
NORM WF6....................178 B2
WBY LS22....................30 B8
Priory Ct *GIR* * BD8..........4 C3
Priory Crs *BSLYN/ROY* S71....262 A3
Priory Gv *BGLY* BD16..........81 J2
Priory Ms *EARD/LOFT* WF3.....155 H8
Priory Park Gv
GFTH/SHER LS25..............138 C6
Priory Pl *BSLYN/ROY* S71.....262 A4
HUDN HD2....................193 H1
Priory Rdg *HOR/CROF* WF4.....200 C6
Priory Rd *BRIG* HD6..........170 E5
BSLYN/ROY S71...............262 A3
FEA/AMT WF7.................201 L2
Priory Sq *WKFDW/WTN* WF2.....199 J7
Priory Wk *MIRF* WF14.........172 A8
Priory Wy *MIRF* WF14.........172 A8
Privilege St *WOR/ARM* LS12...108 D8
Proctor St *BOW* BD4..........127 M5
Prod Ga *BAIL* BD17............82 B4
Prod La *BAIL* BD17............82 A4
Progress Av *BGLY* BD16........80 C5
Prospect Av *BRAM* LS13.......107 L3
GFTH/SHER LS25..............116 B7
LUD/ILL HX2.................168 A3
NORM WF6....................178 D3
PDSY/CALV LS28..............106 F6
SHPY BD18....................82 E7
Prospect Bank
BSPA/BRAM LS23...............69 M3
Prospect Cl *LUD/ILL* HX2.....168 A3
SHPY BD18....................82 E7
Prospect Ct *LUD/ILL* HX2.....145 K6
TAD LS24....................71 M2
Prospect Crs *HWTH* BD22.......79 G1
MID LS10...................131 M4
Prospect Dr *HWTH* BD22........79 G1
TAD LS24....................71 M2
Prospect Gdns
MSTN/BAR LS15...............111 J6
Prospect Gv *PDSY/CALV* LS28..106 F6
SHPY BD18....................82 E7
Prospect La *BIRK/DRI* BD11...150 D1
Prospect Mt *HWTH* BD22........79 G1
SHPY BD18....................82 E7
Prospect Pl *BRIG* HD6........170 C4
EARD/LOFT WF3...............154 D4
ECHL BD2....................105 L4
HORS LS18...................85 K6
HTON BD9....................104 B5
LUD/ILL HX2.................146 B3
RPDN/SBR * HX6..............166 F3
RTHW LS26...................155 H2
SKP/WHF BD23................16 B2
Prospect Rd *BFDE* BD3.........81 L1
CLECK BD19..................149 M6
HECK WF16...................150 E8
HUDH HD3....................191 H8
ILK LS29....................40 B6
LVSG WF15...................171 M4
OSS WF5.....................174 F8
OSS WF5.....................196 F1
Prospect Sq *PDSY/CALV* LS28..106 F4
Prospect St *AIRE* * BD20......34 F7
BOW BD4.....................5 H9
BSLY S70....................260 F5
BTLY * WF17.................151 L8
CLECK BD19..................149 M7
CUD/GR S72..................244 D7
CUL/QBY * BD13..............103 G8
HIPP HX3....................11 J3
HOR/CROF WF4................197 L6
HUD HD1.....................14 D8
HWTH BD22....................78 A7
IDLE BD10...................105 L1
LIT * OL15..................185 K8
PDSY/CALV LS28..............106 E6
ROCH OL11...................228 A2
SHPY BD18....................82 E7
WBSY BD6....................126 B7
YEA LS19....................84 E3
Prospect Ter *BRAM* LS13......107 L3
CLECK BD19..................149 M6

GFTH/SHER LS25..............114 C8
HBR * HX7...................143 G3
LVSG WF15...................172 C2
RTHW LS26...................155 H2
WIL/AL BD15.................103 L5
Prospect Vw *AWLS/ASK* * DN6..227 L3
BRAM LS13...................107 L3
LVSG WF15...................171 M4
Prospect Wk *SHPY* BD18........82 E7
Prosper St *MID* LS10..........9 L7
Providence Av *BAIL* BD17......82 E2
HDGY LS6....................6 D1
Providence Ct *BSLY* S70......261 G6
MOR * LS27..................152 C1
Providence Crs *HWTH* BD22.....78 E4
Providence Gn *PONT* WF8......181 G3
Providence La *HWTH* BD22......78 E4
Providence Pl *BRIC* * HD6....170 E5
GFTH/SHER LS25..............113 C7
PDSY/CALV * LS28............107 G5
RTHW LS26...................157 K3
Providence Rd *HDGY* LS6.......6 D1
Providence Rw *BAIL* BD17......82 E2
LUD/ILL HX2.................146 B3
Providence St *BFD* BD1.........4 D6
CLECK * BD19................149 G6
CLECK * BD19................150 A6
EARL WF12...................174 B7
ELL HX5.....................169 H7
OSM LS9.....................9 M1
PDSY/CALV LS28..............106 F4
TOD OL14....................163 J7
WKFDE WF1...................12 E1
Providence Ter *CUL/QBY* BD13.102 F8
LDSU LS2....................6 E5
Providential St
HOR/CROF WF4................217 K3
Provident St *ROY/SHW* * OL2..229 K7
Prune Park La *WIL/AL* BD15...103 G3
Psalters Dr *STKB/PEN* S36....271 J5
Pudding La *TOD* OL14.........140 E4
Pudsey Rd *BRAM* LS13.........107 K3
TOD OL14....................140 D5
Pugneys Rd *WKFDW/WTN* WF2....198 D6
Pule Green La *HIPP* HX3......146 D3
Pullan Av *ECHL* BD2..........105 L2
Pullan Dr *ECHL* BD2..........105 L2
Pullan Gv *ECHL* BD2..........105 L2
Pullan La *BAIL* BD17..........83 L1
Pullan St *WBOW* BD5..........126 E1
Pullman St *ROCH* OL11........228 B1
Pumphouse La *MIRF* WF14......172 D8
Pump La *DEWS* WF13...........173 M8
EARD/LOFT WF3...............175 G1
KBTN HD8....................216 E7
Purbeck Ct *BOW* * BD4........128 A4
Purbeck Gv *GFTH/SHER* LS25...113 H4
Purcell Dr *AIRE* BD20.........35 M4
Purley Wk *WBSY* BD6..........126 D6
Purlwell Av *BTLY* WF17.......173 K5
Purlwell Crs *BTLY* WF17......173 L5
Purlwell Hall Rd *BTLY* WF17..173 L3
Purlwell La *BTLY* WF17.......173 K5
Purprise La *HBR* HX7.........121 J5
Purston La *FEA/AMT* WF7......202 B5
Purston Park Ct *FEA/AMT* WF7.201 M2
Pye La *DOD/DAR* S75..........242 C6
Pye Nest Av *LUD/ILL* HX2.....167 M1
Pye Nest Dr *LUD/ILL* HX2.....168 A2
Pye Nest Gdns *LUD/ILL* HX2...168 A1
Pye Nest Gv *LUD/ILL* HX2.....167 M1
Pye Nest Ri *LUD/ILL* HX2.....168 A2
Pye Nest Rd *RPDN/SBR* HX6....167 M2
Pyenot Av *CLECK* BD19........150 A8
Pyenot Dr *CLECK* BD19........150 A8
Pyenot Gdns *CLECK* BD19......150 A8
Pyenot Hall La *CLECK* BD19...150 A7
Pymont Ct *EARD/LOFT* WF3.....154 E5
Pymont Dr *RTHW* LS26.........133 K7
Pymont Gv *RTHW* LS26.........133 K7
Pymroyd La *HUDS* HD4.........213 J3
Pynate St *MID* LS10...........9 L6
Pynate Rd *BTLY* WF17.........151 J8
Pyrah Rd *DEWS* WF13..........173 L5
Pyrah St *DEWS* WF13..........173 L5
LM/WK BD12..................148 B7

Q

Quail St *KGHY* * BD21.........3 J3
Quaker La *BSLYN/ROY* S71.....262 C6
CLECK BD19..................149 M8
HUD HD1.....................14 A9
LVSG WF15...................171 M4
WBOW BD5....................126 D3
Quakers La *RPDN/SBR* HX6.....188 F4
YEA LS19....................84 D1
Quarmby Cft *HUDW* HD3........191 J7
Quarmby Rd *HUDW* HD3.........191 K8
Quarrie Dene Ct *CHAL* * LS7...87 L8
The Quarry *AL/HA/HU* LS17.....65 J8
Quarry Av *KNOT* WF11.........182 C3
Quarry Bank Cl *CUD/GR* S72...244 D8
Quarry Bank Ct *KSTL* LS5......86 B3
Quarry Cl *DOD/DAR* S75.......241 M6
HOLM/MEL HD9................236 E4
Quarry Ct *CAS* WF10..........157 M8
HUDW HD3....................191 H7
Quarry Dene *BHP/TINH* LS16....86 A6
Quarrydene Dr *CAS* WF10......158 D8
Quarry Dene Pk *BHP/TINH* LS16.86 A6
Quarry Dr *HUDE* HD5..........193 K8
Quarry Farm Rd *OT* LS21......63 J1
Quarryfields *MIRF* WF14......172 D7
Quarry Gdns *AL/HA/HU* LS17....87 K4
Quarry Hl *HOR/CROF* WF4......197 H5
HUDE HD5....................215 K2
OSM LS9.....................7 K9
RPDN/SBR HX6................167 K3
RTHW LS26...................133 L8
Quarry Hill La *WBY* LS22......29 M8
Quarry La *BTLY* WF17.........151 H5
HEM/SK/SE WF9...............225 J6
HUDE HD5....................193 K8

HUDS HD4....................213 L7
MOR LS27....................152 C7
MOR LS27....................152 D4
Quarry Mt *HDGY* LS6..........109 J2
Quarry Mount St *HDGY* LS6......6 D1
Quarry Mount Ter *HDGY* LS6.....6 D1
HDGY LS6....................6 D2
MIRF WF14...................171 M8
Quarry Pl *ECHL* BD2..........105 K4
HDGY LS6....................6 D2
Quarry Rd *CLECK* BD19........149 L7
CLECK BD19..................150 D7
DEWS WF13...................173 K7
HIPP HX3....................146 A4
HUD HD1.....................14 A6
HUDS HD4....................213 K3
LVSG WF15...................172 C2
OT LS21.....................63 J1
RTHW LS26...................133 M8
Quarryside Rd *MIRF* WF14.....172 A8
Quarry St *BSLY* S70..........261 H6
BSLYN/ROY S71...............261 J1
CUD/GR S72..................244 D7
FEA/AMT WF7.................224 B1
HDGY LS6....................6 D2
HTON BD9....................104 C2
KGHY BD21....................3 K5
WHIT OL12...................184 A1
WHIT OL12...................206 A5
Quarry Vw *DEWS* WF13.........173 K5
Quayside *BAIL* BD17...........82 D6
Quay St *HUD* HD1..............15 H6
Quebec St *ELL* HX5...........169 J8
KGHY BD21....................2 F5
LDS LS1.....................6 E9
TOD OL14....................163 J5
WKFDW/WTN WF2...............12 C3
Queen Elizabeth Dr
NORM WF6....................178 C6
Queen Elizabeth Gdns
HUD HD1.....................14 D6
Queen Elizabeth Gv
WKFDE WF1...................177 G7
Queen Elizabeth Rd
WKFDE WF1...................177 G7
Queen Elizabeth St
WKFDE WF1...................176 C2
Queen Margarets Av
KNOT WF11...................159 M6
Queen Margarets Cl
KNOT * WF11.................159 M6
Queen Margaret's Dr
KNOT WF11...................159 M6
Queens Ar *LDS* LS1............7 G3
Queen's Av *CUD/GR* S72.......263 M7
DOD/DAR S75.................260 F4
ECHL BD2....................105 L3
PONT WF8....................180 C7
WHIT OL12...................206 E2
Queensbury Av *WKFDE* WF1.....176 C1
Queensbury Ct *NORM* WF6......178 E5
Queensbury Rd *HIPP* HX3......146 C1
Queensbury Sq
CUL/QBY BD13................125 G5
Queens Cl *BGLY* BD16..........81 K4
CHAL LS7....................87 L5
Queenscourt *MOR* * LS27......152 C2
Queen's Crs *HOR/CROF* WF4....200 E2
OSS WF5.....................196 F1
Queen's Dr *CUD/GR* S72.......244 D3
CUD/GR S72..................244 D4
DOD/DAR S75.................260 B7
DOD/DAR S75.................260 E3
EARD/LOFT WF3...............154 F3
HIPP HX3....................169 J2
ILK LS29....................38 B3
OSS WF5.....................197 G2
PDSY/CALV LS28..............106 F6
ROCH OL11...................228 A3
WKFDW/WTN WF2...............176 A5
Queens Drive Cl *OSS* WF5.....197 G2
Queen's Drive La *ILK* LS29....38 B3
Queens Gdns *DOD/DAR* S75.....260 E3
ILK LS29....................38 C2
OSS WF5.....................196 F1
TAD LS24....................71 L4
Queen's Ga *HIPP* HX3.........168 D2
Queensgate *BFD* BD1...........4 E6
Queensgate *HUD* HD1..........14 F9
Queensgate Dr *ROY/SHW* OL2...228 M4
Queensgate Market Ar
HUD * HD1...................15 G8
Queens Gv *KGHY* BD21..........2 E9
MOR LS27....................152 B3
Queenshill Av *AL/HA/HU* LS17..87 L4
Queenshill Cl *AL/HA/HU* * LS17.87 L4
Queenshill Ct *AL/HA/HU* * LS17.87 L3
Queenshill Crs *AL/HA/HU* LS17.87 L3
Queenshill Dr *AL/HA/HU* LS17..87 L4
Queenshill Gdns *AL/HA/HU* LS17.87 K4
Queenshill Garth
AL/HA/HU LS17...............87 L4
Queenshill Rd *AL/HA/HU* LS17..87 L4
Queenshill Vw *AL/HA/HU* LS17..87 L4
Queenshill Wk *AL/HA/HU* LS17..87 L4
Queenshill Wy *AL/HA/HU* LS17..87 L4
Queens Md *HIPP* * HX3........147 J3
Queens Mill Rd *HUD* HD1......214 C2
Queens Park Av *CAS* WF10.....158 B8
Queen's Park Dr *CAS* WF10....158 C7
Queen's Pl *MOR* LS27.........152 C2
OT LS21.....................41 J7
SHPY BD18....................82 E6
Queen's Prom *MOR* LS27.......152 C2
Queen Sq *LDSU* LS2...........7 G3
Queen's Ri *ECHL* BD2.........105 H3
Queen's Rd *AWLS/ASK* DN6.....249 L6
BGLY BD16....................59 G8
BSLYN/ROY S71...............261 H5
BSPA/BRAM LS23...............48 E7
CAS WF10....................158 A8
CUD/GR S72..................244 A5
ECHL BD2....................105 C4
HDGY LS6....................109 G4
HFAX HX1....................10 B4
HIPP HX3....................148 B4
HUDW HD3....................14 C1

ILK LS29 38 C3
KGHY BD21 2 E9
LIT OL15 207 K1
MOR LS27 152 B3
PONT WF8 180 C7
SHPY BD18 82 B6
Queen's Ct LDS LS1 9 H1
Queens Sq HUD HD1 15 M1
PONT WF8 180 C7
Queen's St SKP/WHF BD23 16 D2
Queen's Ter OSS WF5 196 F1
Queensthorpe Av BRAM LS13 107 M6
Queensthorpe Cl BRAM LS13 108 A6
Queensthorpe Ri BRAM LS13 107 M6
Queen St AIRE BD20 36 A5
AIRE BD20 56 E1
BAIL BD17 82 E5
BGLY BD16 81 H3
BSLY S70 261 H5
CAS WF10 158 A5
CLECK BD19 150 A8
CLECK BD19 150 D4
DEWS WF13 173 G8
EARD/LOFT WF3 153 M6
EARD/LOFT WF3 154 F3
EARL WF12 174 C6
GTL/HWG HX4 168 E8
HBR * HX7 144 A6
HECK WF16 172 E3
HEM/SK/SE WF9 247 H4
HOR/CROF WF4 197 J5
HUD HD1 15 G7
HWTH BD22 54 E3
IDLE BD10 83 M7
KBTN HD8 239 J4
LDS LS1 8 D1
LIT OL15 207 K1
MID LS10 132 C4
MIRF WF14 194 C2
MOR LS27 152 C2
NORM WF6 178 C4
OSS WF5 196 F1
PONT WF8 180 D6
ROY/SHW OL2 229 K8
RPDN/SBR HX6 167 G3
RTHW LS26 135 G8
STKB/PEN S36 271 G3
TOD OL14 163 K1
WBSY BD6 126 A7
WHIT OL12 206 B6
WIL/AL BD15 102 E2
WKFDE WF1 12 E3
WKFDE WF1 176 D2
WMB/DAR S73 263 K6
YEA LS19 84 D2
Queen St South HUD HD1 15 G9
Queens Vw LIT OL15 207 J3
SCFT * LS14 111 K1
Queen's Wk OSS WF5 197 H1
Queens Wy KBTN HD8 238 C1
Queensway BGLY BD16 81 K4
BSLYN/ROY S71 243 L2
DOD/DAR S75 263 E3
GFTH/SHER LS25 112 F7
GSLY LS20 62 B5
HFAX HX1 10 A4
MOR LS27 152 C2
MSTN/BAR LS15 111 L6
PONT WF8 181 H3
ROCH OL11 228 C2
RTHW LS26 133 G8
Queenswood Cl HDGY LS6 86 C7
Queenswood Ct HDGY LS6 108 D2
Queenswood Dr HDGY LS6 86 C8
Queenswood Gdns HDGY LS6 108 E2
Queenswood Gn HDGY LS6 86 C7
Queenswood Hts HDGY LS6 108 D1
Queenswood Mt HDGY LS6 108 D1
Queenswood Ri HDGY LS6 108 D2
Queenswood Rd HDGY LS6 108 D1
Queen Victoria Crs HIPP HX3 147 K3
Queen Victoria St LDS LS1 7 H9
ROCH OL11 228 C3
Quernmore Dr BWCK/EAR BB18 52 C1
Quern Wy WMB/DAR S73 263 J8
Quincy Cl ECHL BD2 105 L2
Quinton WHIT * OL12 206 A6

R

Raby Av CHAL LS7 7 J2
Raby Pk WBY LS22 47 M1
Raby St CHAL LS7 7 J2
Raby Ter CHAL LS7 7 J2
Racca Av KNOT WF11 182 D2
Racca Gn KNOT WF11 182 C2
Race Common Av
STKB/PEN S36 270 E6
Racecommon La BSLY S70 260 F7
Racecommon Rd BSLY S70 260 F6
Race Moor La HWTH BD22 78 D3
Race St BSLY S70 261 G5
Rachael St HOR/CROF WF4 197 H5
Racton St MAR/SLWT HD7 212 B5
Radcliffe Av ECHL BD2 105 J1
Radcliffe Gdns
PDSY/CALV LS28 107 G7
Radcliffe La LUD/ILL HX2 144 E4
PDSY/CALV LS28 107 G7
Radcliffe Pl WKFDE WF1 12 E2
Radcliffe Rd BSLYN/ROY S71 243 H6
HUDS HD4 213 K2
MAR/SLWT HD7 212 C5
WKFDW/WTN WF2 197 M2
Radcliffe St KBTN HD8 239 H4
Radfield Dr WBSY BD6 127 G6
Radford Park Av
HEM/SK/SE WF9 246 D5
Radnor St BFDE BD3 105 L7
WOR/ARM LS12 109 G8
Radwell Dr WBOW BD5 4 E9
Raeburn Dr WBSY BD6 126 C7
Rae Ct EARD/LOFT WF3 177 G1
Rae Rd SHPY BD18 82 C8
Rafborn Av HUDW HD3 191 G5
Raglan Av HWTH BD22 2 B6
Raglan Cl CAS WF10 157 J6
Raglan Ct HFAX HX1 10 D5
Raglan Rd HDGY LS6 6 D2
Raglan St BFDE BD3 105 M7
CUL/QBY BD13 125 G5
HFAX HX1 10 D5
HWTH BD22 2 B6
TOD OL14 163 K1
Raglan Ter BFDE BD3 106 A7
Raikes Av SKP/WHF BD23 16 B1
Raikes La BOW BD4 128 A7
BOW BD4 128 C4
BTLY WF17 151 G4
Raikes Rd SKP/WHF BD23 16 B1
Raikeswood Crs SKP/WHF BD23 16 A1
Raikes Wood Dr BOW BD4 128 A7
Raikeswood Dr SKP/WHF BD23 16 A1
Raikeswood Rd SKP/WHF BD23 16 A1
Railes Cl LUD/ILL HX2 144 F5
Railsfield Mt BRAM LS13 107 L4
Railsfield Ri BRAM LS13 107 L5
Railsfield Wy BRAM LS13 107 L4
Railway Av PONT WF8 180 E5
Railway Rd IDLE BD10 83 K6
MSTN/BAR LS15 111 M4
Railway St BOW BD4 127 L5
BRIG HD6 170 D5
CLECK BD19 149 M7
DEWS WF13 173 H8
EARL WF12 173 M6
HECK WF16 172 F3
HUD HD1 14 F6
KGHY * BD21 57 L5
LIT OL15 207 K1
MILN OL16 206 C8
MILN OL16 229 L2
OSM LS9 9 L1
TOD OL14 141 K8
Railway Ter EARD/LOFT WF3 153 L5
HEM/SK/SE WF9 223 J3
HIPP HX3 168 C4
NORM WF6 178 C4
Railway Vw CAS WF10 157 K7
ROY/SHW OL2 229 L5
Rainbow Ms WBSY * BD6 126 B8
Raincliffe Gv OSM LS9 110 C6
Raincliffe Mt OSM * LS9 110 C7
Raincliffe Rd OSM LS9 110 C6
Raincliffe St OSM LS9 110 C6
Raincliffe Ter OSM * LS9 110 C7
Raines Crest MILN OL16 207 J8
Raines Dr AIRE BD20 34 E1
Rainford Dr BSLYN/ROY S71 243 M8
Rainsborough Av KNOT WF11 181 L3
Rainton Gv DOD/DAR S75 260 D3
Raistrick Wy SHPY BD18 82 F6
Rake HBR HX7 143 H6
Rake Head Barn La TOD OL14 163 J6
Rake Head Rd HOLM/MEL HD9 253 G7
Rakehill Rd MSTN/BAR LS15 90 B7
Rake Ter LIT OL15 185 L8
Rakewood Rd LIT OL15 207 K3
Raleigh Gdns LIT OL15 185 L5
Raleigh St HFAX * HX1 10 B9
Raley St BSLY S70 260 F7
Ralph Garth RYKW YO26 32 C1
Ralph St WHIT OL12 206 C5
The Rampart COP/BISH YO23 73 J8
Rampart Rd HDGY LS6 6 C2
Ramsay Pl MILN OL16 206 C6
Ramsay St MILN OL16 206 C6
Ramsay Ter MILN OL16 206 C6
Ramsden Av GTHN BD7 126 A1
Ramsden Cl KNOT WF11 159 L6
Ramsden Ct GTHN BD7 126 C2
Ramsden La TOD OL14 163 G7
Ramsden Mill Bottom
MAR/SLWT * HD7 213 H3
Ramsden Mill La MAR/SLWT HD7 213 G5
Ramsden Pl CLAY BD14 125 K1
Ramsden Rd HOLM/MEL HD9 253 K7
WHIT OL12 184 E7
Ramsden St CAS WF10 179 L1
GFTH/SHER LS25 135 H6
HIPP HX3 146 A4
HUD HD1 14 F8
MAR/SLWT HD7 213 G2
TOD OL14 163 J7
Ramsden Wood Rd TOD OL14 163 H7
Ramsey Crs HOR/CROF WF4 196 D7
Ramsey Rd HOR/CROF WF4 196 C7
Ramsey St WBOW BD5 126 F3
Ramsey Vw HOR/CROF WF4 196 C7
Ramsgate EARD/LOFT WF3 154 D5
Ramsgate Crs EARD/LOFT WF3 154 D5
Ramsgate St HFAX HX1 10 A5
Ramshaw Dr SKP/WHF BD23 16 C5
Ramshead Ap SCFT LS14 89 J8
Ramshead Cl SCFT LS14 89 J7
Ramshead Crs SCFT LS14 89 H7
Ramshead Dr SCFT LS14 89 H7
Ramshead Gdns SCFT LS14 89 H7
Ramshead Gv SCFT LS14 89 J8
Ramshead Hl SCFT LS14 89 J8
Ramshead Pl SCFT LS14 89 J8
Ramshead Vw SCFT LS14 89 J8
Randall Pl HTON BD9 104 C3
Randall Well St BFD BD1 4 D7
Randolph St BFDE BD3 106 A6
BRAM LS13 107 J4
HIPP HX3 11 G3
Random Cl HWTH BD22 2 A9
Rand Pl GTHN BD7 4 A9
Rand St GTHN BD7 4 A9
Ranelagh Av IDLE BD10 106 A1
Raneley Gv ROCH OL11 228 C4
Range Bank HIPP HX3 11 H2
Range Bank Top HIPP HX3 11 H1
Range Ct HIPP HX3 11 G2
Range Gdns HIPP HX3 11 H2
Range La HIPP HX3 11 H3
UPML OL3 230 F5
Range St HIPP HX3 11 G1
Rankin's Well Rd SKP/WHF BD23 16 D2
Ransdale Dr WBOW BD5 126 F3
Ransdale Gv WBOW BD5 126 F3
Ransdale Rd WBOW BD5 126 F3
Ranter's Fold HOR/CROF WF4 197 J5
Raper Vw GFTH/SHER LS25 92 A6
Rapes Hwy UPML OL3 231 J1
Rashcliffe Hill Rd HUD HD1 214 B2
Rastrick Common BRIG HD6 170 C6
Rathbone St MILN OL16 206 E7
Rathlin Rd EARL WF12 174 B4
Rathmell Rd MSTN/BAR LS15 111 H8
Rathmell St WBOW BD5 126 F5
Ratten Rw DOD/DAR S75 260 A8
Ratten Row Rd RPDN/SBR HX6 166 E5
Raven Cl FEA/AMT WF7 179 K5
Ravenfield Dr BSLYN/ROY S71 243 J8
Raven La CUD/GR S72 222 C8
Raven Rd HDGY LS6 109 G2
Raven Royd BSLYN/ROY S71 243 H5
Ravens Av DEWS WF13 173 J8
HUDE HD5 215 G1
Ravenscar Av RHAY LS8 88 C8
Ravenscar Mt RHAY LS8 88 C8
Ravenscar Ter RHAY LS8 88 C8
Ravenscar Vw RHAY * LS8 88 C8
Ravenscar Wk RHAY * LS8 88 C8
Ravenscliffe Av IDLE BD10 106 A1
Ravenscliffe Rd PDSY/CALV LS28 84 A8
Ravens Cl DOD/DAR S75 242 D6
Ravens Crs DEWS WF13 173 J8
Ravensdeane HUDW * HD3 191 M6
Ravensfield Rd DEWS WF13 173 J8
Ravens Gv DEWS WF13 173 J8
Ravenshaw Cl DOD/DAR S75 260 D3
Ravenshouse Rd DEWS WF13 173 H7
Ravensknowle Rd HUDE HD5 215 G1
Ravens Lodge Ter DEWS * WF13 173 J8
Ravensmead FEA/AMT WF7 202 B1
Ravens Mt PDSY/CALV LS28 107 H7
Ravens St DEWS WF13 195 H1
Ravensthorpe Rd EARL WF12 195 H2
Ravenstone Dr GTL/HWG HX4 168 E8
Raven St BGLY BD16 81 J3
HFAX HX1 10 B5
HUD HD1 213 M1
KGHY BD21 2 F4
Ravens Vw AIRE * BD20 55 M2
Ravensville AIRE BD20 35 G8
Ravens Wk DEWS WF13 173 J8
Ravens Wy HOLM/MEL HD9 255 G2
Ravenswharf Rd DEWS WF13 173 J8
Ravenswood GTL/HWG * HX4 168 B7
Ravensworth Cl MSTN/BAR LS15 112 B3
Ravensworth Wy MSTN/BAR LS15 112 B3
Raven Ter GIR BD8 103 L7
Rawden Hl OT LS21 44 A8
Rawdon Dr YEA LS19 84 D3
Rawdon Hall Dr YEA LS19 84 D3
Rawdon Rd HORS LS18 85 G5
HWTH BD22 78 E7
Rawdon St HWTH BD22 2 C7
Raw End Rd LUD/ILL HX2 145 J6
Rawfield La GFTH/SHER LS25 137 L8
Rawfolds Av BTLY WF17 151 H4
Rawfolds Wy CLECK BD19 150 A8
Rawgate Av CAS WF10 157 H6
Raw Hl BRIG * HD6 170 B6
Raw La HBR HX7 143 M3
LUD/ILL HX2 145 M1
TAD LS24 94 A1
Rawling St KGHY BD21 2 E9
Rawling Wy HDGY LS6 109 H1
Raw Nook LM/WK BD12 149 H1
Raw Nook Rd HUDW HD3 191 G6
Rawroyds GTL/HWG HX4 190 E2
Rawson Av BFDE BD3 105 M6
HIPP HX3 168 D3
Rawson Pl BFD BD1 4 E5
RPDN/SBR HX6 167 J3
Rawson Rd BFD BD1 4 D5
Rawson Sq BFD BD1 4 E5
IDLE BD10 83 K5
Rawson St HFAX HX1 11 G6
LM/WK BD12 148 F2
Rawson St North HIPP HX3 10 E1
Rawson Ter BEE/HOL * LS11 131 L3
Rawtenstall Bank HBR HX7 143 G2
Rawthorpe Crs HUDE HD5 193 G6
Rawthorpe La HUDE HD5 15 M5
Rawthorpe Ter HUDE HD5 193 G6
Rayfield WKFDW/WTN WF2 198 B1
Ray Ga HBR HX7 122 B7
HOLM/MEL HD9 236 F6
HUDW HD3 190 F6
Raygill Cl AL/HA/HU LS17 88 D1
Raylands Cl MID LS10 132 B8
Raylands Ct MID LS10 132 B8
Raylands Fold MID LS10 132 B8
Raylands Garth MID LS10 132 B8
Raylands La MID LS10 132 B8
Raylands Pl MID LS10 132 B8
Raylands Rd MID LS10 132 B8
Raylands Wy MID LS10 154 B1
Rayleigh St BOW BD4 127 J2
Raymond Av CUD/GR S72 245 J8
Raymond Dr WBOW BD5 127 G4
Raymond Rd BSLY S70 261 M7
Raymond St WBOW BD5 127 G4
Raynbron Crs WBOW BD5 127 H4
Raynel Ap BHP/TINH LS16 86 B3
Raynel Cl BHP/TINH LS16 86 C2
Raynel Dr BHP/TINH LS16 86 C3
Raynel Gdns BHP/TINH LS16 86 C2
Raynel Garth BHP/TINH LS16 86 C3
Raynel Gn BHP/TINH LS16 86 C3
Raynel Mt BHP/TINH LS16 86 B2
Raynel Wy BHP/TINH LS16 86 B2
Rayner Av GIR BD8 104 B5
HECK WF16 150 F8
Rayner Dr BRIG HD6 170 C2
Rayner Mt WIL/AL BD15 103 K6
Rayner Rd BRIG HD6 170 C2
Rayners Av LVSG WF15 171 L2
Rayner St HOR/CROF WF4 197 J5
Raynham Crs HWTH BD22 57 G6
Raynor Cl HUDW HD3 191 L7
Raynville Ap BRAM LS13 108 A4
Raynville Av BRAM LS13 108 A3
Raynville Crs WOR/ARM LS12 108 B4
Raynville Dr BRAM LS13 108 A4
Raynville Gv BRAM LS13 108 A3
Raynville Mt BRAM LS13 108 A3
Raynville Pl WOR/ARM LS12 108 A3
Raynville Ri BRAM LS13 108 A4
Raynville Rd WOR/ARM LS12 108 B3
Raynville St BRAM LS13 108 A3
Raynville Ter BRAM LS13 108 A3
Raynville Wk BRAM LS13 108 A4
Ray St HUD HD1 15 G4
Raywood Cl YEA LS19 62 C6
Reap Hirst Rd HUDN HD2 191 M4
Reasbeck Ter BSLYN/ROY S71 261 H1
Rebecca Ms BSLY * S70 261 H6
Rebecca Rw BSLY S70 261 H6
Rebecca St GIR BD8 4 C4
Recreation Av BEE/HOL * LS11 8 C7
Recreation Crs BEE/HOL LS11 8 B7
Recreation Gv BEE/HOL LS11 8 B7
Recreation La ELL HX5 169 G8
Recreation Mt BEE/HOL LS11 8 B7
Recreation Pl BEE/HOL LS11 8 B7
Recreation Rd RPDN/SBR HX6 167 K2
Recreation Rw BEE/HOL LS11 8 B7
Recreation St BEE/HOL LS11 8 B7
Recreation Ter BEE/HOL LS11 8 B7
Recreation Vw BEE/HOL LS11 8 B7
Rectory Cl BSLYN/ROY S71 243 M5
COP/BISH YO23 73 J7
GFTH/SHER LS25 113 H7
MAR/SLWT HD7 233 H2
Rectory Dr BTLY WF17 151 J5
HUDE HD5 193 K7
Rectory Gdn KBTN HD8 217 M7
Rectory La KBTN HD8 217 M7
SKP/WHF BD23 16 C2
Rectory Rw KGHY BD21 2 F5
Rectory St CAS WF10 157 M6
OSM LS9 7 M6
Rectory Vw EARL WF12 196 A3
Rectory Wy BSLYN/ROY S71 261 M3
Red Beck Rd HIPP HX3 147 H5
Red Beck V SHPY BD18 104 C1
Red Brink La RPDN/SBR HX6 166 D4
Redbrook Ct DOD/DAR S75 260 E2
Redbrook Rd DOD/DAR S75 260 C2
Redbrook Vw DOD/DAR S75 260 E2
Redbrook Wk DOD/DAR S75 260 E2
Redburn Av SHPY BD18 104 C1
Redburn Dr SHPY BD18 104 C1
Redburn Rd SHPY BD18 104 C1
Redcar La AIRE BD20 56 D4
Redcar Rd IDLE BD10 84 A8
Redcar St HFAX HX1 10 A5
WHIT OL12 206 A6
Redcliffe Av KGHY BD21 2 D4
Redcliffe Cl DOD/DAR S75 260 D2
Redcliffe Gv KGHY BD21 2 C4
Redcliffe St KGHY BD21 2 C4
Redcross St WHIT OL12 206 B6
Redcross St North
WHIT * OL12 206 A5
Red Deer Park La
HOR/CROF WF4 217 G1
Reddisher Rd MAR/SLWT HD7 233 G2
Red Doles La HUD HD1 192 E5
Red Doles Rd HUDN HD2 192 E4
Reddyshore TOD * OL14 185 L2
Reddyshore Brow LIT OL15 185 L6
Reddyshore Scout Ga
TOD OL14 185 K1
Redesdale Gdns BHP/TINH LS16 86 D3
Redfearn Av HECK WF16 172 F1
Redfearn St BSLYN/ROY S71 261 H4
Red Hall Ap SCFT LS14 89 J5
Red Hall Av AL/HA/HU LS17 89 H5
Redhall Cl BEE/HOL LS11 131 G5
Red Hall Ct SCFT LS14 89 J5
Redhall Cres BEE/HOL LS11 131 G5
Red Hall Cft SCFT LS14 89 J6
Red Hall Dr SCFT LS14 89 K5
Red Hall Gdns AL/HA/HU LS17 89 H5
Red Hall Garth SCFT LS14 89 J5
Redhall Ga BEE/HOL LS11 131 G5
Red Hall Gn SCFT LS14 89 J5
Red Hall La AL/HA/HU LS17 89 H5
WKFDE WF1 176 C5
Red Hall Vw SCFT * LS14 89 J5
Red Hall Wk SCFT LS14 89 J5
Red Hall Wy SCFT LS14 89 J5
Redhill Av BSLY S70 261 L7
CAS WF10 158 B8
EARD/LOFT WF3 175 G1
Redhill Cl EARD/LOFT WF3 175 G1
Redhill Crs EARD/LOFT WF3 175 G1
Redhill Dr CAS WF10 158 C7
EARD/LOFT WF3 175 G1
Redhill Gdns CAS WF10 158 C8
Red Hill La GFTH/SHER LS25 137 L5
Redhill Mt CAS WF10 158 C7
Redhill Rd CAS WF10 158 C7
Redhill Vw CAS WF10 158 C8
Red House La AWLS/ASK DN6 248 F8
AWLS/ASK DN6 249 J7
Redhouse La CHAL * LS7 88 A7
Red Laithes La DEWS WF13 173 G8
Redland Cl LIT OL15 185 K8
Redland Crs HEM/SK/SE WF9 223 K4
Redland Dr KBTN HD8 216 A7
Redland Gv DOD/DAR S75 242 D4
Red La FEA/AMT WF7 201 G1
HOLM/MEL HD9 234 D4
PDSY/CALV LS28 106 E3
WHIT OL12 206 D4
WKFDE WF1 200 A1
Red Lodge Cl RHAY LS8 110 F2
Redman Garth HWTH BD22 78 D7
Redmayne Gv KNOT WF11 181 M2
Redmire Ct SCFT LS14 111 J2
Redmire Dr SCFT LS14 111 J2
Redmire St BFDE BD3 106 A7
Redmire Vw SCFT LS14 111 J2
Redruth Dr NORM WF6 178 D3
Redshaw Rd WOR/ARM LS12 108 F8
Redthorne Wy CUD/GR S72 244 D3
Redthorpe Crest
DOD/DAR S75 260 C2
Red V CLECK BD19 150 D4
Redvers Cl BHP/TINH LS16 86 C5
Redwood Av BSLYN/ROY S71 243 L3
EARD/LOFT WF3 153 J6
Redwood Cl KGHY BD21 3 L8
RTHW LS26 134 A8
Redwood Dr HUDN HD2 192 F1
Redwood Gv HOR/CROF WF4 200 E2
HUDE HD5 15 L7
Redwood Park Gv MILN * OL16 206 F7
Redwood Wy YEA LS19 62 B7
Reed Hl MILN * OL16 206 B6
Reedling Dr MOR LS27 152 E3
Reed Rd WOR/ARM LS12 108 E8
Reedsdale Av MOR LS27 129 L7
Reedsdale Dr MOR LS27 129 L7
Reedsdale Gdns MOR LS27 129 L7
Reedshaw La HWTH BD22 54 B5
Reed St HUD HD1 191 M7
Rees Wy BFDE BD3 5 H3
Reeth Rd BRIG HD6 170 A6
Reevy Av WBSY BD6 126 B6
Reevy Crs WBSY BD6 126 A7
Reevy Dr WBSY BD6 126 C6
Reevylands Dr WBSY BD6 126 C6
Reevy Rd WBSY BD6 126 B6
Reevy Rd West WBSY BD6 126 A6
Reevy St WBSY BD6 126 C5
Reform St CLECK BD19 150 D5
WHIT OL12 206 B5
Refuge St ROY/SHW OL2 229 K8
Regal Ar HUDE * HD5 15 M7
Regal Cl RPDN/SBR HX6 188 E5
Regal Dr RPDN/SBR HX6 188 E5
Regency Ct GIR BD8 104 C6
HDGY LS6 109 G2
ILK LS29 38 C3
Regency Gdns
EARD/LOFT WF3 153 J6
Regency Park Gv
PDSY/CALV LS28 129 G1
Regency Park Rd
PDSY/CALV LS28 129 G1
Regency Rd MIRF WF14 194 C2
Regency Vw BFDE BD3 105 J4
Regent Av COL BB8 52 A8
HORS LS18 85 L7
SKP/WHF BD23 16 D1
Regent Cl BRIG HD6 170 A8
Regent Ct LDS * LS1 9 H1
Regent Crs BSLYN/ROY S71 243 H7
CUD/GR S72 245 G1
HORS LS18 85 K7
SKP/WHF BD23 16 D1
Regent Dr SKP/WHF BD23 16 D2
Regent Gdns BSLY S70 261 G4
Regent Ms BTLY WF17 174 B2
Regent Pde RPDN/SBR * HX6 167 L2
Regent Park Av HDGY LS6 6 B1
Regent Park Cross Av HDGY LS6 6 B1
Regent Park Ter HDGY LS6 6 B1
Regent Pl HBR HX7 143 J3
IDLE BD10 83 J5
RPDN/SBR HX6 167 K1
Regent Rd HORS LS18 85 K7
HUDE HD5 193 L4
HUDW HD3 14 A4
ILK LS29 38 C2
SKP/WHF BD23 16 D1
Regents Pk WKFDE WF1 13 J3
Regent St BSLY S70 261 G4
CAS WF10 157 L7
CHAL LS7 87 L7
CUD/GR S72 245 G1
CUL/QBY BD13 125 H5
FEA/AMT WF7 201 M1
HBR HX7 143 J3
HECK WF16 172 E3
HEM/SK/SE WF9 223 L7
HEM/SK/SE WF9 247 G3
HFAX HX1 10 F7
HOR/CROF WF4 197 H5
IDLE BD10 83 J5
IDLE * BD10 83 M7
LIT OL15 207 K1
MIRF WF14 194 C3
NORM WF6 178 E3
OSM LS9 7 K8
TOD * OL14 163 J5
WHIT OL12 206 B5
WKFDE WF1 13 K7
Regent St South BSLY * S70 261 H4
Regent Ter HDGY LS6 6 A5
Regina Crs CUD/GR S72 245 G3
HOR/CROF WF4 222 E5
Regina Dr CHAL LS7 87 M8
Reginald Mt CHAL LS7 109 M2
Reginald Pl CHAL LS7 109 M2
Reginald Rd BSLY S70 261 M7
Reginald Rw CHAL LS7 109 M2
Reginald St CHAL LS7 109 M2
WBOW BD5 126 F3
Reginald Ter CHAL LS7 109 M2
Reginald Vw CHAL LS7 109 M2
Reid Park Av HOR/CROF WF4 197 G5
Reighton Cft IDLE BD10 84 A8
The Rein SCFT LS14 89 H8
Rein Closet GFTH/SHER LS25 92 A6
Rein Gdns EARD/LOFT WF3 152 E6
Rein Ms EARD/LOFT WF3 152 E6
Rein Rd BRAM LS13 85 L8
EARD/LOFT WF3 152 E6
Reins Av BAIL BD17 82 D5
Reins Rd BRIG HD6 170 A6
Rein St MOR LS27 152 E5
Reinwood Av HUDW HD3 191 K8
RHAY LS8 110 F1
Reinwood Rd HUDW HD3 191 K8
Rembrandt Av
EARD/LOFT WF3 153 H6
Renald La STKB/PEN S36 258 A7
Renee Cl BOW BD4 127 L6
Renfield Gv NORM WF6 178 F3
Renshaw St IDLE BD10 83 K5
Renton Av GSLY LS20 61 M5
Renton Dr GSLY LS20 61 M6
Repton Rd AWLS/ASK DN6 249 K6
Reservoir Farm Ct
HOR/CROF WF4 222 F4
Reservoir Pl CUL/QBY BD13 124 E4
Reservoir Rd HWTH BD22 78 A7
LUD/ILL HX2 146 A6

Reservoir Side Rd
  MAR/SLWT HD7 .....213 G7
Reservoir St DEWS WF13 .....173 J5
  MILN OL16 .....206 E6
Reservoir Vw CUL/QBY BD13...102 E8
  KBTN HD8 .....239 G4
Restmore Av GSLY LS20 .....61 M3
Retford Av MILN OL16 .....228 D2
Retford Pl GTHN BD7 .....4 B3
Reuben St LVSG WF15 .....172 C1
Reva Cl BGLY BD16 .....81 K2
Reva Syke Rd CLAY BD14 ...125 K3
Revel Garth KBTN HD8 .....257 J1
Revie Rd BEE/HOL LS11 .....8 A9
Reydon Wk WBSY BD6 .....126 B5
Reyhill Gv WBOW BD5 .....126 E6
Reyner House Ms WBOW BD5 ...4 F4
Reynolds Av GTHN BD7.....126 A1
Rhine St BOW BD4 .....127 J1
Rhodes Av HECK WF16 .....150 F8
Rhodes Crs PONT WF8 .....180 F8
  ROCH OL11 .....228 B3
Rhodes Gdns EARD/LOFT WF3...154 E8
Rhode's Hill La
  BSPA/BRAM LS23 .....70 A3
Rhodesia Av HIPP HX3 .....168 E3
  WIL/AL BD15 .....103 L6
Rhodesia St AIRE BD20 .....34 F8
Rhodes La BSPA/BRAM LS23 ...48 D8
Rhodes Pl SHPY BD18 .....82 D6
Rhodes St CAS WF10 .....157 K7
  HFAX HX1 .....10 E6
  LVSG WF15 .....172 E2
  SHPY BD18 .....82 C6
  WHIT OL12 .....206 D3
Rhodes Ter BSLY * S70 .....261 J6
  WOR/ARM LS12 .....109 G8
Rhodes Wy GIR BD8 .....103 M5
Rhodesway GIR BD8 .....103 M7
Rhondda Pl WBSY BD6 .....126 B8
Rhum Cl WBSY BD6 .....126 B8
Rhyddings Av FEA/AMT WF7...224 B1
Rhyddings Dr FEA/AMT WF7 ...224 B2
Rhylstone Mt GTHN BD7.....104 B7
Rhyl St FEA/AMT WF7 .....179 M8
Ribble Av LIT OL15 .....185 H8
Ribblesdale Av
  GFTH/SHER LS25 .....113 K8
Ribble St KGHY BD21 .....3 M3
Ribbleton Gv BFDE BD3 .....5 J4
Riber Av BSLYN/ROY S71 ...243 J7
Ribstone St HBR HX7 .....144 A5
Ribston Rd PBR HG3 .....29 C1
Riccall Nook IDLE BD10.....83 M8
Rice St HUD HD1 .....15 G8
Richard Av BSLYN/ROY S71 ...243 J8
Richard Rd BSLYN/ROY S71 ...243 J8
  DOD/DAR S75 .....241 M6
Richardshaw La
  PDSY/CALV LS28 .....107 G5
Richardshaw Rd
  PDSY/CALV LS28 .....107 H5
Richardson Av WBSY BD6 ...126 E6
Richardson Crs OSM LS9 .....110 D7
Richardson Rd OSM LS9 .....110 D7
Richardson Sq HUD * HD1 .....14 E7
Richardson St LM/WK BD12...149 J2
Richard St BFDE BD3 .....5 J6
  BRIG HD6 .....170 C2
  BSLY S70 .....260 F5
  ROCH S70 .....206 C8
  WKFDE * WF1 .....176 E7
Richard Thorpe Av MIRF WF14...194 D1
Rich Ga HOLM/MEL HD9 .....254 C4
Richmond Av DOD/DAR S75...241 M7
  HDGY LS6 .....109 G3
  HUDN HD2 .....192 C4
  KNOT WF11 .....181 K1
  RPDN/SBR HX6 .....167 H3
Richmond Cl BRAM LS13 ...107 J4
  HFAX HX1 .....10 F4
  MILN OL16 .....228 E3
  MOR LS27 .....152 C3
  RTHW * LS26 .....133 H7
Richmond Ct HOR/CROF WF4...200 C6
  HUDS HD4 .....213 H3
  RTHW * LS26 .....133 H8
Richmond Cft OSM LS9 .....110 B7
Richmondfield Av
  MSTN/BAR LS15 .....91 G8
Richmondfield Cl
  MSTN/BAR LS15 .....91 G8
Richmondfield Crs
  MSTN/BAR LS15 .....91 G8
Richmondfield Cross
  MSTN/BAR LS15 .....91 G8
Richmondfield Dr
  MSTN/BAR LS15 .....91 G8
Richmondfield Garth
  MSTN/BAR LS15 .....91 G8
Richmondfield Gv
  MSTN/BAR LS15 .....91 G8
Richmondfield La
  MSTN/BAR LS15 .....91 G8
Richmondfield Mt
  MSTN/BAR LS15 .....91 G8
Richmondfield Wy
  MSTN/BAR LS15 .....91 G8
Richmond Flats HUD HD1 .....15 G8
Richmond Gdns
  PDSY/CALV LS28 .....107 J2
  RPDN/SBR HX6 .....167 H3
Richmond Garth OSS WF5 ...197 H2
Richmond Green St OSM LS9...9 M2
Richmond Gv CLECK BD19 ...150 D4
Richmond Hill Ap OSM LS9 ...9 M2
Richmond Hill Cl OSM LS9 ...9 M2
Richmond Lea MIRF WF14 ...172 C8
Richmond Ms SHPY BD18.....82 B6
Richmond Mt HDGY LS6.....109 G3
Richmond Park Av WF15...172 C3
Richmond Pl SHPY BD18.....82 B6
Richmond Rd GTHN BD7 .....4 B6
  HDGY LS6 .....109 G3
  HECK WF16 .....151 G6
  HEM/SK/SE WF9 .....225 K7
  HFAX HX1 .....10 F4
  PDSY/CALV LS28 .....106 C6

SHPY * BD18 .....82 B6
  WKFDE WF1 .....176 D6
Richmond St BSLY * S70 .....260 F5
  CLECK BD19 .....149 M7
  HFAX HX1 .....10 F4
  KGHY BD21 .....2 E3
  OSM LS9 .....9 L2
  TOD * OL14 .....163 L1
Richmond Ter OT LS21 .....41 H7
  PDSY/CALV LS28 .....107 J7
Richmond Wy
  GFTH/SHER LS25 .....135 H1
Rickard St WOR/ARM LS12 .....8 A3
Ridding Ga OT LS21 .....41 G5
Riddings Cl HEM/SK/SE WF9...245 M1
  HUDN HD2 .....192 F3
Riddings Ri HUDN HD2 .....192 F3
Riddings Rd HUDN HD2 .....193 G3
Riddlesden St AIRE * BD20...58 B5
Ridehalgh La BRFD/BLYE BD10...96 B3
Rider St OSM LS9 .....6 E1
Rider St OSM LS9 .....7 L8
The Ridge WBY LS22 .....47 K3
Ridge Av HOR/CROF WF4 ...196 C3
Ridge Bank TOD OL14 .....163 K1
Ridge Cl GSLY LS20 .....61 L6
  HUDS HD4 .....214 C3
  KBTN HD8 .....239 J5
Ridgedale Mt PONT WF8 ...180 E2
Ridgefield St CAS WF10 .....157 M7
Ridge Gv CHAL LS7 .....109 J2
Ridge Hl BRIG HD6 .....170 A5
Ridge La AIRE BD20 .....17 L7
Ridge Lea BRIG HD6 .....170 B5
Ridge Mt HDGY LS6 .....6 C1
Ridgemount Rd AIRE BD20...58 A4
Ridge Rd GFTH/SHER LS25...135 M4
  HDGY LS6 .....6 F1
  HOR/CROF WF4 .....196 C3
  TOD OL14 .....163 K1
Ridgestone Av
  HEM/SK/SE WF9 .....224 A7
Ridge St HUDS HD4 .....214 C3
Ridge Ter HDGY LS6 .....109 C3
Ridge Vw HRAV LS17 .....107 L6
Ridge View Dr HUDN HD2 ...191 M4
Ridge View Gdns IDLE BD10...83 L7
Ridge View Rd BRIG * HD6...170 C5
Ridgewalk Wy BSLY S70 .....261 H8
Ridge Wy RHAY LS8 .....88 B8
The Ridgeway KNOT WF11...182 B3
Ridgeway CUL/QBY BD13.....125 H6
  GSLY LS20 .....61 L6
  HUDE HD5 .....193 G7
  SHPY BD18 .....83 G8
  SKP/WHF BD23 .....88 B8
Ridgeway Cl HUDE HD5 .....193 G7
  RHAY LS8 .....88 B8
Ridgeway Crs BSLYN/ROY S71...243 L5
Ridgeway Dr BTLY WF17 .....151 J5
Ridgeway Gdns BRIG HD6 ...170 A1
Ridgeway Mt HWTH BD22 .....2 A9
The Ridgeways
  MAR/SLWT HD7 .....212 F6
Ridgeway Cl KNOT WF11 ...182 B3
Ridgeway Ter HDGY * LS6.....6 D1
Ridgewood Cl BAIL BD17.....83 G3
Ridgill Av AWLS/ASK DN6 ...249 J5
Ridgway Cl WMB/DAR S73 ...263 J8
Riding Head La LUD/ILL HX2...145 C5
Riding Hl HIPP HX3 .....126 A8
Riding La LUD/ILL HX2 .....145 L3
The Ridings AIRE BD20 .....57 K3
  BSLYN/ROY S71 .....261 L1
Ridings Av BSLYN/ROY S71...261 K1
Ridings Cl EARD/LOFT WF3...154 D8
Ridings Ct EARD/LOFT WF3...154 D8
Ridings Flds HOLM/MEL HD9...236 E3
  HOLM/MEL HD9 .....236 E7
  MAR/SLWT HD7 .....212 E2
Ridings Ms EARD/LOFT WF3...154 D8
Ridings Rd EARL WF12 .....173 M6
Riding St BTLY WF17 .....151 J4
Ridings Wy EARD/LOFT WF3...154 D8
  WBSY BD6 .....126 A6
Ridingwood Ri KBTN HD8 ...240 A4
Ridleys Fold ILK LS29 .....19 H6
Rievaulx Av GIR BD8 .....4 B3
Rievaulx Cl BSPA/BRAM LS23...48 E7
Riffa La OT LS21 .....42 E3
Rifle Flds HUD HD1 .....14 D7
Rifle St HUD HD1 .....15 G8
Rigg La FEA/AMT WF7 .....202 E6
Rightox Rd HOLM/MEL HD9...236 E3
Rigton Ap OSM LS9 .....7 M8
Rigton Bank AL/HA/HU LS17...67 M2
Rigton Cl OSM LS9 .....110 B6
Rigton Gn AL/HA/HU LS17...68 A2
  OSM LS9 .....7 M8
Rigton Hl AL/HA/HU LS17...25 M7
Rigton Lawn OSM LS9 .....7 M8
Rigton Ms OSM LS9 .....7 M8
Rigton St WBOW BD5 .....126 F3
Riley La KBTN HD8 .....238 A1
  LUD/ILL HX2 .....124 B6
Riley Pk KBTN HD8 .....216 B8
Riley St HUDS HD4 .....214 D2
Rillbank La BVRD LS3 .....109 G5
Rillbank St BVRD LS3 .....6 A6
Rillington Md IDLE BD10.....83 M8
Rillside AIRE BD20 .....238 B5
Rills Md OT LS21 .....41 J7
Rimbswell Holt IDLE BD10...84 A8
Ringby La HIPP HX3 .....146 D2
Ringby Ter HIPP * HX3 .....146 D4
Ring Lows La WHIT OL12 ...206 C2
Ring Rd Adel BHP/TINH LS16...86 A7
Ring Rd Beeston
  WOR/ARM LS12 .....130 E3
Ring Rd Beeston Pk
  BEE/HOL LS11 .....131 H4
Ring Rd Bramley BRAM LS13...107 M6
Ring Rd Cross Gates
  MSTN/BAR LS15 .....111 L3

Ring Rd Farnley
  WOR/ARM LS12 .....107 M7
Ring Rd Farsley
  PDSY/CALV LS28 .....106 E3
Ring Rd Halton
  MSTN/BAR LS15 .....111 L5
Ring Rd Horsforth HORS LS18...86 A6
Ring Rd Meanwood
  BHP/TINH LS16 .....87 G4
Ring Rd Middleton MID LS10...153 M1
Ring Rd Moortown
  AL/HA/HU LS17 .....87 J4
Ring Rd Seacroft SCFT LS14...89 J3
Ring Rd Shadwell
  AL/HA/HU LS17 .....88 E4
Ring Rd Weetwood
  BHP/TINH LS16 .....86 E5
Ring Rd West Pk
  BHP/TINH LS16 .....86 C5
Ringstone Gv CUD/GR S72 ...245 J3
Ringway GFTH/SHER LS25 ...112 F8
Ringwood Av SCFT LS14 .....89 H6
Ringwood Ct WKFDE * WF1...176 F1
Ringwood Crs SCFT LS14 .....89 J5
Ringwood Dr SCFT LS14 .....89 J5
Ringwood Edge GTL/HWG HX4...168 E8
Ringwood Gdns SCFT LS14 ...89 J6
Ringwood Mt SCFT LS14 .....89 J6
Ringwood Rd WBOW BD5 ...126 D3
Ringwood Wy
  HEM/SK/SE WF9 .....224 B7
Rink St BTLY WF17 .....173 M3
Ripley Cl NORM WF6 .....178 F4
Ripley Ct NORM WF6 .....178 D6
Ripley Dr NORM WF6 .....178 F3
Ripley Gv DOD/DAR S75 ...260 D2
Ripley La GSLY LS20 .....62 A4
  LVSG WF15 .....172 B2
Ripley Rd AIRE BD20 .....58 B5
  ECHL BD2 .....105 L2
  PONT WF8 .....180 F3
Ripley St AIRE BD20 .....35 K8
  ECHL BD2 .....105 L2
  PDSY/CALV LS28 .....107 G7
Ripon Av HUDN HD2 .....192 C4
Ripon Rd EARL WF12 .....174 B6
Ripon St HFAX HX1 .....146 A8
Ripon Ter HIPP HX3 .....10 F1
Rippenden New Bank
  RPDN/SBR HX6 .....189 G2
Rippenden Old Bank
  RPDN/SBR HX6 .....189 G2
Rippenden Old La
  RPDN/SBR HX6 .....188 C3
Rippenden Rd LIT OL15 .....208 F8
  UPML OL3 .....230 F4
Risedale Av BTLY WF17 .....151 K4
Risedale Cl BTLY WF17 .....151 K4
The Rise HIPP HX3 .....147 J4
  KNOT WF11 .....159 L6
  KSTL LS5 .....108 C1
Rise La TOD OL14 .....163 K1
Rishworth Av KBTN HD8 ...217 M8
Rishworth Cl
  WKFDW/WTN WF2 .....176 A4
Rishworth Hall Cl
  RPDN/SBR HX6 .....188 D5
Rishworthian Ct HIPP * HX3...10 D5
Rishworth Mill La
  RPDN/SBR HX6 .....188 F6
Rishworth New Rd
  RPDN/SBR HX6 .....188 D5
Rishworth Ri ROY/SHW OL2...229 H5
Rishworth Rd EARL WF12 ...173 M6
  GTL/HWG HX4 .....189 J3
  HWTH BD22 .....2 B7
Rivadale Vw ILK LS29 .....38 D2
Rivelin Rd CAS WF10 .....157 L8
Riverdale GLE DN14 .....161 J7
  WBY LS22 .....48 B2
Riverdale Av EARD/LOFT WF3...177 H4
Riverdale Cl EARD/LOFT WF3...177 H4
Riverdale Crs EARD/LOFT WF3...177 H4
Riverdale Dr EARD/LOFT WF3...177 H4
Riverdale Gdns OT LS21 .....41 J6
  EARD/LOFT WF3 .....177 H4
Riverdale Rd EARD/LOFT WF3...177 H4
  OT LS21 .....41 J6
River Holme Vw
  HOLM/MEL HD9 .....236 E4
Rivermead MILN OL16 .....229 K3
  WKFDW/WTN WF2 .....13 G9
River Mt AIRE BD20 .....58 B5
River Pk HOLM/MEL HD9 ...236 B1
River Pl MILN * OL16 .....207 H8
Riverside KBTN HD8 .....240 A4
  KGHY BD21 .....3 L4
Riverside Av OT LS21 .....41 K4
Riverside Cl OT LS21 .....41 K5
  WMB/DAR S73 .....263 L8
Riverside Crs OT LS21 .....41 K5
Riverside Ct CLECK BD19 ...149 M5
  MILN OL16 .....206 D4
  OT LS21 .....41 K4
Riverside Est BAIL BD17.....82 C6
Riverside Pk OT LS21 .....41 K5
Riverside Vls WKFDW/WTN WF2...12 F9
Riverside Wk ILK LS29 .....38 B1
Riverstone Br LIT OL15 .....207 J1
River St BRIG HD6 .....170 C5
  COL BB8 .....74 E3
  HWTH * BD22 .....78 F7
  KGHY BD21 .....3 L1
  MILN OL16 .....206 B7
  TOD OL14 .....163 L4
River Vw BSPA/BRAM LS23...49 H7
  MIRF WF14 .....171 M8
River Wk BGLY BD16 .....81 H3
Riverwood Dr HIPP HX3 .....168 D4
Riviera Gdns CHAL LS7 .....87 L3
Rivington Dr WHIT * OL12...206 B5
Rivington St WHIT * OL12...206 B5
Rivock Av AIRE BD20 .....35 M8
  AIRE BD20 .....57 H3
Rivock Gv AIRE BD20 .....57 H4
Riverside Dr MILN OL16 .....206 E4

Roach Grange Av
  GFTH/SHER LS25 .....135 J3
Roach Pl MILN OL16 .....206 C6
Roach V MILN OL16 .....206 B4
Roads Ford Av MILN OL16...207 H7
Roaine Dr HOLM/MEL HD9...254 D3
Roans Brae IDLE BD10 .....84 A8
Robb Av BEE/HOL LS11 .....131 J5
Robbins Ter FEA/AMT WF7...179 M8
Robb St BEE/HOL LS11 .....131 J5
Roberson Ter CLECK BD19 ...150 C6
Robert Av BSLYN/ROY S71 ...261 M4
Roberts Av OSM LS9 .....110 D4
Roberts Ct OSM LS9 .....110 D4
Robertsgate EARD/LOFT WF3...154 D5
Robertshaw Rd HBR HX7 ...143 H3
Robertson Av HUD HD6 .....170 C6
Roberts Pl BFD BD1 .....4 D5
  OSM LS9 .....110 D5
Robert's St CLECK BD19 .....149 H7
  CUD/GR * S72 .....244 D7
  HWTH BD22 .....56 E8
  PDSY/CALV LS28 .....106 F5
  RTHW * LS26 .....133 L8
Robert St North HIPP HX3 ...146 E4
Roberttown La LVSG WF15...172 A5
Robin Cha PDSY/CALV LS28...107 H7
Robin Cl ECHL BD2 .....105 L2
  PONT WF8 .....180 F3
Robin Dr AIRE BD20 .....35 K8
  ECHL BD2 .....105 L2
Robin Hl BTLY WF17 .....151 J5
Robin Hood Av
  BSLYN/ROY S71 .....243 M2
Robin Hood Crs
  WKFDW/WTN WF2 .....197 M4
Robin Hood Gv HUDN HD2...192 E2
Robin Hood Hl HUDS HD4 ...214 B7
Robin Hood Rd HUDN HD2...192 E2
Robin Hood St CAS * WF10...158 A7
Robin Hood Wy BRIG HD6 ...171 G4
Robin La BSLYN/ROY S71 ...243 M2
  DEWS WF13 .....173 H3
  HEM/SK/SE WF9 .....245 J1
  PDSY/CALV LS28 .....107 G7
Robin Rocks HOLM/MEL HD9...236 E4
Robin Royd Av MIRF WF14...172 C6
Robin Royd Cft MIRF WF14...172 C6
Robin Royd Dr MIRF WF14...172 C6
Robin Royd Garth
  MIRF * WF14 .....172 C6
Robin Royd Gv MIRF * WF14...172 C6
Robin Royd La MIRF WF14 ...172 C7
The Robins ILK LS29 .....40 A6
Robin's Gv RTHW LS26 .....155 H1
Robinson Ct GTHN BD7 .....104 B8
Robinson La GFTH/SHER LS25...135 K4
Robinson St CAS WF10 .....157 K3
  HUD HD1 .....15 H9
  MILN OL16 .....206 C7
  PONT WF8 .....180 F5
Robin St HUD HD1 .....213 M1
  WBOW * BD5 .....126 E2
Rob Royd DOD/DAR S75 .....260 B8
Rob Royd La BSLY S70 .....260 F8
Robson Cl PONT WF8 .....180 F8
Robsons Dr HUDE HD5 .....15 M6
Robsons Rd WKFDE * WF1 .....12 D5
Rochdale Rd GTL/HWG HX4...168 A7
  HUDW HD3 .....212 A1
  LUD/ILL HX2 .....167 M1
  MILN OL16 .....206 F7
  MILN OL16 .....229 G5
  ROY/SHW OL2 .....228 B8
  RPDN/SBR HX6 .....167 H4
  RPDN/SBR HX6 .....187 H5
  TOD OL14 .....163 J4
  UPML OL3 .....230 D3
Roche Cl BSLYN/ROY S71 ...261 K3
Rocheford Cl MID LS10 .....132 B5
Rocheford Gdns MID LS10...132 B5
Rocheford Gv MID LS10 .....132 B5
Rocheford Wk MID LS10 .....132 B5
Rochester Dr HOR/CROF WF4...197 J3
Rochester Dr HOR/CROF WF4...197 L3
Rochester Gdns BRAM LS13...107 H2
Rochester Pl ELL * HX5 .....169 H8
Rochester Rd BSLYN/ROY S71...261 K2
  BTLY WF17 .....151 G3
Rochester St BFDE BD3 .....105 L7
  SHPY BD18 .....82 E8
Rochester Ter HDGY LS6 ...108 F2
Rochester Wynd
  AL/HA/HU LS17 .....88 C2
Roch St MILN OL16 .....206 D5
The Rock MAR/SLWT * HD7...213 G6
Rockcliffe Av BAIL BD17.....82 E5
Rock Edge LVSG WF15 .....172 C1
Rockery Rd HORS LS18 .....85 L4
Rockery Rd HORS LS18 .....85 L4
Rockfield Ter YEA LS19 .....62 F1
Rock Fold MAR/SLWT HD7...212 F2
Rock Hl CAS WF10 .....158 C8
Rockhill Cl BTLY WF17 .....151 H5
Rockhill La BOW BD4 .....127 J7
Rock House Dr DEWS WF13...173 L4
Rockingham Cl
  MSTN/BAR LS15 .....112 B3
  ROY/SHW OL2 .....229 G2
Rockingham Ct TAD LS24 .....93 M2
Rockingham La
  HEM/SK/SE WF9 .....225 C1
Rockingham Rd
  MSTN/BAR LS15 .....112 B3
Rockingham St
  BSLYN/ROY S71 .....261 G2
  CUD/GR * S72 .....245 J7
  HEM/SK/SE WF9 .....223 J5
Rockingham Wy
  MSTN/BAR LS15 .....112 B3

Rockland Crs GTHN BD7 .....126 A1
Rocklands Av BAIL BD17.....82 E7
Rocklands Pl BAIL BD17.....82 E7
Rock La BRAM LS13 .....107 K3
  CUL/QBY BD13 .....102 C8
  MAR/SLWT HD7 .....212 C4
Rockley Cl HUDE HD5 .....215 G3
Rockley Dr WKFDW/WTN WF2...198 D8
Rockley Grange Gdns
  GFTH/SHER LS25 .....134 F7
Rockley Mdw BSLY S70 .....260 F1
Rockley St EARL WF12 .....173 M6
Rockmill Rd HOLM/MEL HD9...236 E4
Rock Side Rd STKB/PEN S36...270 C3
Rocks Rd HIPP HX3 .....168 C3
Rock St BRIG HD6 .....170 C3
  BSLY * S70 .....260 F4
  HUDW * HD3 .....191 G7
Rocks Vw CUL/QBY BD13 ...168 C2
Rockley St EARL WF12 .....152 D8
  EARL * WF12 .....152 D8
  GIR BD8 .....4 D1
  HUDW HD3 .....191 J4
  MOR LS27 .....152 D1
  MSTN/BAR LS15 .....111 M1
Rock Vw GTL/HWG HX4 .....190 E2
  MAR/SLWT HD7 .....233 H3
Rockville Ter HFAX HX1 .....168 C1
Rockwell Cl DOD/DAR * S75...242 B8
  HUDN HD2 .....171 G8
  SKP/WHF BD23 .....16 A2
Rockwood Cl HOR/CROF WF4...197 M6
  PDSY/CALV LS28 .....106 B8
Rockwood Crs HOR/CROF WF4...197 M6
  PDSY/CALV LS28 .....106 C8
Rockwood Dr SKP/WHF BD23...16 A1
Rockwood Gv PDSY/CALV LS28...106 C8
Rockwood Hill Ct
  PDSY/CALV LS28 .....106 C4
Rockwood Ri KBTN HD8 .....239 J7
Rockwood Rd PDSY/CALV LS28...106 C4
Roderick St WOR/ARM LS12...108 D7
Rodger La WKFDW/WTN WF2...176 B4
Rodin Av GIR BD8 .....103 M7
Rodley La KBTN HD8 .....217 M7
  PDSY/CALV LS28 .....106 F5
Rodney Yd WKFDE WF1 .....12 F5
Rods Mills La MOR LS27 .....152 D3
Roebuck St BTLY WF17 .....151 H5
Roeburn Cl DOD/DAR S75 ...242 C4
Roehampton Ri
  BSLYN/ROY S71 .....262 B6
Roe La KNOT WF11 .....161 H2
Roger Ct ECHL BD2 .....5 M1
Roger Dr WKFDW/WTN WF2...198 D5
Roger Fold GFTH/SHER LS25...135 K5
Roger Ga HBR HX7 .....143 L5
Roger Rd BSLYN/ROY S71 ...262 A4
Rogers Ct EARD/LOFT WF3...155 H8
Rogerson Sq BRIG 170 C3
Rogers Pl PDSY/CALV LS28 ...107 H6
Roils Head Rd LUD/ILL HX2...145 K7
Rokeby Gdns HDGY LS6 .....108 E1
  IDLE BD10 .....84 A8
Roker La PDSY/CALV LS28 ...129 H1
Rolleston Rd AWLS/ASK DN6...249 K6
Rolling Br TAD LS24 .....72 D1
Roman Av HUDW HD3 .....190 F5
  RHAY LS8 .....88 C3
Romanby Shaw IDLE BD10 ...83 M8
Roman Cl HUDW HD3 .....190 F5
  TAD LS24 .....71 M2
Roman Crs RHAY LS8 .....88 D4
Roman Dr HUDW HD3 .....190 F5
  RHAY LS8 .....88 D4
Roman Gdns RHAY LS8 .....88 C4
Roman Gv RHAY LS8 .....88 C4
Roman Pl RHAY LS8 .....88 C4
Roman Rdg AWLS/ASK DN6...249 G7
Roman Ri PONT WF8 .....202 F4
Roman Ri BTLY WF17 .....151 H6
  DOD/DAR S75 .....241 M7
Roman Ter RHAY LS8 .....88 C4
Roman Vw RHAY LS8 .....88 C4
Rombalds Av WOR/ARM LS12...108 D8
Rombalds Crs AIRE BD20 .....36 B6
  WOR/ARM LS12 .....108 C5
Rombalds Dr BGLY BD16 .....81 K3
  SKP/WHF BD23 .....16 C4
Rombalds Gv WOR/ARM LS12...108 C5
Rombalds La ILK LS29 .....39 G3
Rombalds Pl WOR/ARM LS12...108 C5
Rombalds St WOR/ARM LS12...108 C5
Rombalds Ter WOR/ARM LS12...108 C5
Rombald's Vw ILK LS29 .....38 F1
  OT LS21 .....40 F4
  WOR/ARM LS12 .....108 C5
Romford Av MOR LS27 .....152 C3
Romille St SKP/WHF BD23 .....16 B3
Romney Av ROCH OL11 .....228 A4
Romney Mt PDSY/CALV LS28...129 J1
Romsey WHIT * OL12 .....206 A6
Romsey Cl HUDW HD3 .....191 H5
Romsey Gdns BOW BD4 .....127 M3
Romsey Ms BOW BD4 .....127 M3
Rona Cft RTHW LS26 .....155 J1
Ronald Dr GTHN BD7 .....104 C7
Roods La HOLM/MEL HD9 ...253 J3
Rookdale Cl DOD/DAR S75 ...260 D2
Rookery Cottages OSS * WF5...196 F3
Rookery La HIPP HX3 .....168 F3
Rookes Av WBSY BD6 .....126 E6
Rookes La HIPP HX3 .....148 C5
Rookhill Dr PONT WF8 .....181 G7
Rookhill Mt PONT WF8 .....181 H8
Rookhill Rd PONT WF8 .....181 H8
Rook La BOW BD4 .....127 K4
Rooks Av CLECK BD19 .....149 L6
Rooks Cl LM/WK BD12 .....148 F5
Rook's Nest Rd WKFDE WF1...176 E2
Rook St BGLY BD16 .....81 H3
  HUD HD1 .....14 E5
Rockwith Pde IDLE BD10.....83 M8
Rookwood
  GFTH/SHER LS25 .....135 J6
  OSM LS9 .....110 D9

Rookwood Crs OSM LS9 ....110 E6
Rookwood Gdns OSM LS9 ....110 E7
Rookwood Hl OSM LS9 ....110 E6
Rookwood Mt OSM LS9 ....110 E6
Rookwood Pde OSM LS9 ....110 F6
Rookwood Pl OSM LS9 ....110 E6
Rookwood Rd OSM LS9 ....110 E7
Rookwood Sq OSM LS9 ....110 F6
Rookwood St OSM LS9 ....110 E7
Rookwood Ter OSM LS9 ....110 E6
Rookwood V OSM LS9 ....110 E7
Rookwood Vw OSM LS9 ....110 E6
Rooley Av WBSY BD6 ....126 F6
Rooley Banks RPDN/SBR HX6 ....167 G3
Rooley Cl WBOW BD5 ....127 G5
Rooley Crs WBSY BD6 ....127 G6
Rooley Hts RPDN/SBR HX6 ....166 F3
Rooley La RPDN/SBR HX6 ....166 F4
WBOW BD5 ....126 F5
Roomfield St TOD OL14 ....163 K1
Rooms Fold MOR LS27 ....130 C8
Rooms La MOR LS27 ....130 B6
Ropefield Wy WHIT OL12 ....206 A3
Roper Av RHAY LS8 ....88 B6
Ropergate PONT WF8 ....180 E6
Ropergate Service Rd
PONT WF8 ....180 E6
Roper Gn LUD/ILL HX2 ....145 M2
Roper Gv RHAY LS8 ....88 B6
Roper La LUD/ILL HX2 ....124 B6
Rope St WHIT OL12 ....206 B6
Rope Wk KNOT WF11 ....182 C2
LUD/ILL HX2 ....123 H7
SKP/WHF BD23 ....16 C2
Roscoe St CHAL LS7 ....7 K4
Roseate Gn MOR LS27 ....152 E3
Rose Av GFTH/SHER LS25 ....116 A8
HEM/SK/SE WF9 ....225 H7
HORS LS18 ....85 J6
HUDS HD4 ....213 H3
HUDW HD3 ....191 L8
LIT OL15 ....207 L1
WMB/DAR S73 ....263 H7
Rose Bank GIR BD8 ....4 B1
ILK LS29 ....40 A6
Rosebank Crs HDGY LS6 ....6 A5
Rosebank Gdns BVRD LS3 ....6 A6
Rose Bank Pl GIR BD8 ....104 A7
Rosebank Rd BVRD LS3 ....6 A6
Rose Bank Rd TOD OL14 ....163 J2
Rosebank Rw BVRD LS3 ....6 A6
Rosebank St BTLY WF17 ....151 K8
Roseberry St HWTH BD22 ....78 F4
TOD OL14 ....140 D5
Rosebery Av HIPP HX3 ....168 F2
SHPY BD18 ....82 E7
Rosebery Mt SHPY BD18 ....82 E7
Rosebery Rd GIR BD8 ....104 E4
Rosebery St ELL HX5 ....169 H8
HUDN HD2 ....14 D1
PDSY/CALV LS28 ....106 E6
Rosebery Ter BSLY S70 ....261 H6
HFAX HX1 ....10 C3
PDSY/CALV LS28 ....107 H4
Rosebud Wk RHAY LS8 ....7 L4
Rosechapel Cl WBSY * BD6 ....126 B8
Rosecliffe Mt BRAM LS13 ....107 K3
Rosecliffe Ter BRAM LS13 ....107 K4
Rose Cl HEM/SK/SE WF9 ....225 J7
Rose Cottages GTL/HWG * HX4 ....190 A4
Rose Ct GFTH/SHER LS25 ....113 J7
Rose Crs GFTH/SHER LS25 ....116 A8
Rose Cft AL/HA/HU LS17 ....46 E8
Rosedale PBR HG3 ....26 E2
RTHW LS26 ....133 H8
Rosedale Av HUDE HD5 ....15 M8
LVSG WF15 ....171 M4
WIL/AL BD15 ....103 H4
WKFDW/WTN WF2 ....199 G6
Rosedale Bank MID LS10 ....131 M5
Rosedale Cl BAIL BD17 ....82 C4
HEM/SK/SE WF9 ....225 K7
NORM WF6 ....178 F5
PBR HG3 ....26 E2
Rosedale Gdns BSLY S70 ....260 E5
MID LS10 ....131 M5
Rosedale Gn MID LS10 ....131 M5
Rosedale Ri BSPA/BRAM LS23 ....48 E7
Rosedale Wk MID LS10 ....131 M5
Rose Farm Ap NORM WF6 ....178 B2
Rose Farm Cl NORM WF6 ....178 B1
Rose Farm Fold NORM WF6 ....178 B1
Rose Farm Ri NORM WF6 ....178 B1
Rosefield Crs MILN OL16 ....206 E7
Rose Garth HOR/CROF WF4 ....200 B5
ILK LS29 ....39 L7
Rosegarth Av HOLM/MEL HD9 ....236 E7
Rose Gv HBR HX7 ....144 A6
HEM/SK/SE WF9 ....225 J7
RPDN/SBR HX6 ....167 H1
RTHW LS26 ....132 F8
Rose Heath LUD/ILL HX2 ....123 M7
Rose Hl MAR/SLWT * HD7 ....233 J2
Rosehill Av HEM/SK/SE WF9 ....223 L8
Rose Hill Cl STKB/PEN S36 ....270 F4
Rosehill Cottages
DOD/DAR * S75 ....260 C8
Rosehill Ct BSLY S70 ....261 G4
Rosehill Crs LM/WK BD12 ....148 E2
Rose Hill Dr DOD/DAR S75 ....260 B7
HUDW HD3 ....191 M5
Rose La FEA/AMT WF7 ....223 M2
TAD LS24 ....94 D8
Rose Lea Cl GFTH/SHER LS25 ....138 D8
Roselee Cl HIPP HX3 ....169 G3
Rosemary Av WOR/ARM LS12 ....108 F7
Rosemary Ct TAD LS24 ....71 M2
Rosemary Dr LIT OL15 ....185 H8
Rosemary La BRIG HD6 ....170 C6
HIPP HX3 ....169 G3
Rosemary Rw TAD LS24 ....71 M2
Rose Mdw HWTH BD22 ....79 G1
Rosemont Av BRAM * LS13 ....107 L4
PDSY/CALV LS28 ....107 H6
Rosemont Dr PDSY/CALV LS28 ....107 H6
Rosemont Gv BRAM LS13 ....107 K4
Rosemont La BAIL BD17 ....82 F4
Rosemont Pl BRAM LS13 ....107 K4
Rosemont Rd BRAM LS13 ....107 L4
Rosemont St BRAM LS13 ....107 L4
PDSY/CALV LS28 ....107 H6
Rosemont Ter BRAM LS13 ....107 L4
PDSY/CALV LS28 ....107 H6
Rosemont Vw BRAM LS13 ....107 K4
Rosemont Wk BRAM LS13 ....107 L4
Rose Mt BOW * BD4 ....128 C6
ECHL BD2 ....105 J3
HUDN HD2 ....191 M5
LUD/ILL * HX2 ....168 C2
Rosemount Av ELL HX5 ....169 J8
Rosemount Cl KGHY * BD21 ....2 F4
Rose Mount Pl WOR/ARM LS12 ....108 F8
Rosemount Wk KGHY * BD21 ....2 F4
Roseneath Pl WOR/ARM LS12 ....108 F8
Roseneath St WOR/ARM LS12 ....108 F8
Roseneath Ter WOR/ARM LS12 ....108 F8
Rose Pl LUD/ILL HX2 ....167 G1
Rose St GIR BD8 ....104 D5
HFAX HX1 ....10 B4
HORS LS18 ....85 J6
KGHY BD21 ....58 B7
TOD OL14 ....163 K1
Rose Ter BTLY * WF17 ....151 J4
HFAX HX1 ....10 C5
HUD * HD1 ....15 G3
LUD/ILL * HX2 ....168 C2
Rose Tree Av CUD/GR S72 ....244 D7
Rose Tree Ct CUD/GR S72 ....244 D7
Roseville Rd RHAY LS8 ....7 L5
Roseville St RHAY LS8 ....7 M4
Roseville Wy RHAY LS8 ....7 L5
Rosewood Av GFTH/SHER LS25 ....135 H3
KGHY BD21 ....58 B5
Rosewood Ct RTHW LS26 ....133 H7
Rosewood Gv BOW BD4 ....127 M1
Rosgill Dr SCFT LS14 ....111 H1
Rosgill Wk SCFT LS14 ....111 H1
Rosley Mt WBSY BD6 ....126 B8
Rosley St COL BB8 ....74 D1
Roslyn Av HUDS HD4 ....213 L7
Roslyn Pl GTHN BD7 ....104 D8
Rossall Gv RHAY * LS8 ....110 B2
Rossall Rd RHAY LS8 ....110 B2
WHIT OL12 ....206 C4
Rossefield Ap BRAM LS13 ....107 M5
Rossefield Av BRAM LS13 ....107 M4
HUDN HD2 ....14 A1
Rossefield Cha BRAM LS13 ....107 M4
Rossefield Cl BRAM * LS13 ....107 M4
Rossefield Dr BRAM LS13 ....107 M4
Rossefield Gv BRAM LS13 ....107 M4
Rossefield Lawn BRAM LS13 ....107 M4
Rossefield Pk HTON BD9 ....104 D2
Rossefield Pl BRAM LS13 ....107 M4
Rossefield Rd HTON BD9 ....104 C2
Rossefield Ter BRAM LS13 ....107 M4
Rossendale Cl ROY/SHW OL2 ....229 M7
Rossendale Pl SHPY BD18 ....82 C7
Rossendale Wy BCUP OL13 ....162 C7
WHIT OL12 ....184 C3
Rosse St GIR BD8 ....104 C8
SHPY BD18 ....82 D6
Rossett Green La HARS HG2 ....26 D1
Ross Gv BRAM LS13 ....107 K2
Rossington Gv RHAY LS8 ....7 M1
Rossington Pl RHAY LS8 ....7 M1
Rossington Rd RHAY LS8 ....110 C1
Rossington St LDSU LS2 ....6 F8
Rossiter Dr KNOT WF11 ....181 M3
Rosslyn Av FEA/AMT WF7 ....224 B1
Rosslyn Cl FEA/AMT WF7 ....224 B1
Rosslyn Ct EARL WF12 ....174 B7
FEA/AMT WF7 ....224 B1
Rosslyn Gv FEA/AMT WF7 ....224 B1
HWTH BD22 ....78 E8
Rossmore Dr WIL/AL BD15 ....103 L5
Rossyde AWLS/ASK * DN6 ....227 M3
Rosy St HWTH BD22 ....79 H6
Rotcher La MAR/SLWT HD7 ....212 A6
Rotcher Rd HOLM/MEL HD9 ....254 C2
Rothbury Gdns BHP/TINH LS16 ....86 D3
Rotherham Rd BSLYN/ROY S71 ....243 J8
BSLYN/ROY S71 ....261 L3
Rothery Ct HFAX * HX1 ....10 D4
Rothesay Ter GTHN BD7 ....4 A9
MILN OL16 ....228 E2
Roth St HWTH BD22 ....79 G6
Rothwell La RTHW LS26 ....155 J1
Rothwell Mt HFAX HX1 ....10 E9
Rothwell Rd HFAX HX1 ....10 E9
Rothwell St HUDE HD5 ....193 G8
WHIT OL12 ....206 C5
Roughaw Cl SKP/WHF BD23 ....16 B4
Roughaw Rd SKP/WHF BD23 ....16 C4
Roughbirchworth La
STKB/PEN S36 ....271 J6
Rough Hall La LUD/ILL HX2 ....145 G1
Rough Hey Wk MILN OL16 ....206 D8
Rough Side La TOD OL14 ....163 L2
Round Close Rd
HOLM/MEL HD9 ....254 D8
Roundell Av BOW BD4 ....127 K6
Roundhay Av RHAY LS8 ....110 B1
Roundhay Crs RHAY LS8 ....110 B1
Roundhay Gdns RHAY * LS8 ....110 B1
Roundhay Gv RHAY LS8 ....110 B1
Roundhay Mt RHAY LS8 ....110 B1
Roundhay Park La
AL/HA/HU LS17 ....88 D1
Roundhay Pl RHAY LS8 ....110 A2
Roundhay Rd CHAL LS7 ....7 K4
Roundhay Vw RHAY * LS8 ....110 B1
Roundhead Fold IDLE BD10 ....84 A6
Round Hl DOD/DAR S75 ....242 C5
LUD/ILL HX2 ....124 B8
Roundhill Av BGLY BD16 ....81 K7
Round Hill Cl CUL/QBY BD13 ....125 K4
Roundhill Mt BGLY BD16 ....81 K7
Roundhill Pl BFD BD1 ....4 D5
Roundhill Rd CAS WF10 ....157 M7
Roundhill St WBOW BD5 ....126 F2
Round Ings Rd HUDW HD3 ....190 B7
Round St WBOW BD5 ....127 G3
WKFDE WF1 ....13 K7
Round Thorn Pl GIR * BD8 ....104 C6
Roundway HOLM/MEL HD9 ....236 B3
The Roundway MOR LS27 ....152 A2
Roundwell Rd LVSG WF15 ....171 L1
Roundwood SHPY BD18 ....82 A7
Round Wood Av HUDE HD5 ....193 J8
Roundwood Av BAIL BD17 ....83 H3
IDLE BD10 ....106 A1
Roundwood Crs
WKFDW/WTN WF2 ....197 L1
Roundwood Gln IDLE BD10 ....84 A8
Roundwood Ri
WKFDW/WTN WF2 ....197 M2
Roundwood Rd BAIL BD17 ....83 G3
OSS WF5 ....197 J2
Roundwood Vw IDLE BD10 ....84 A8
Rouse Fold BOW BD4 ....5 H9
Rouse Mill La BTLY WF17 ....173 M2
Rouse St LVSG WF15 ....172 C2
The Rowans BAIL BD17 ....82 B3
BHP/TINH LS16 ....64 B4
BRAM LS13 ....107 H3
Rowan Av BFDE BD3 ....106 A7
HUDS HD4 ....213 M8
NORM WF6 ....178 C6
Rowan Avenue Ms HUDS HD4 ....213 M8
Rowanberry Cl ECHL BD2 ....105 K2
Rowan Cl BSLY S70 ....261 H7
BTLY WF17 ....151 J4
Rowan Ct ECHL * BD2 ....105 L5
RTHW LS26 ....134 A8
WKFDW/WTN WF2 ....176 B6
YEA LS19 ....84 D1
Rowan Dr BRIG HD6 ....170 E3
DOD/DAR S75 ....260 D3
Rowan Garth AIRE BD20 ....34 F8
Rowan Pl GFTH/SHER LS25 ....113 K8
Rowan St AIRE BD20 ....57 J4
Rowantree Av BAIL BD17 ....82 D2
Rowantree Dr IDLE BD10 ....83 L8
Rowanwood Gdns IDLE * BD10 ....106 A1
Row Ga KBTN HD8 ....237 M7
Rowgate KBTN HD8 ....238 C8
Rowland Ct MILN * OL16 ....206 D8
Rowland La HBR HX7 ....143 L3
Rowland Pl BEE/HOL LS11 ....131 K3
Rowland Rd BEE/HOL LS11 ....131 K3
DOD/DAR S75 ....260 E3
Rowlands Av HEM/SK/SE WF9 ....225 J7
HUDE HD5 ....193 H8
Rowland St BSLYN/ROY S71 ....243 M2
MILN OL16 ....206 D8
SKP/WHF BD23 ....16 C3
Rowland Ter BEE/HOL LS11 ....131 L3
Row La MAR/SLWT HD7 ....211 L6
RPDN/SBR HX6 ....166 F3
Rowlestone Ri IDLE BD10 ....84 A8
Rowley Dr ILK LS29 ....39 H3
KBTN HD8 ....215 M3
Rowley La HEM/SK/SE WF9 ....247 J5
KBTN HD8 ....215 M4
Rowsley St KGHY BD21 ....3 J4
Row St HUDS HD4 ....214 A2
Rowton Thorpe IDLE BD10 ....84 A8
Roxburghe Dl NORM WF6 ....178 F5
Roxburgh Gv WIL/AL BD15 ....103 K6
Roxby Cl OSM LS9 ....7 M9
Roxby St WBOW BD5 ....126 F3
Roxholme Av CHAL LS7 ....110 A1
Roxholme Gv CHAL LS7 ....110 A1
Roxholme Pl CHAL LS7 ....110 A1
Roxholme Ter CHAL LS7 ....110 A1
Royal Cl GTHN BD7 ....126 B3
MID LS10 ....131 M4
Royal Ct DOD/DAR S75 ....242 A8
MID LS10 ....131 M4
PONT WF8 ....202 D1
Royal Dr MID LS10 ....131 M4
Royal Gdns MID LS10 ....131 M4
Royal Park Av HDGY LS6 ....6 A4
Royal Park Gv HDGY LS6 ....6 A3
Royal Park Mt HDGY LS6 ....6 A3
Royal Park Rd HDGY LS6 ....109 G4
Royal Park Ter HDGY LS6 ....6 A3
Royal Park Vw HDGY LS6 ....6 A3
Royal Pl MID LS10 ....131 M4
Royal St BSLY S70 ....261 G5
MILN OL16 ....206 E4
Royal Ter BSPA/BRAM LS23 ....49 G6
HUDW HD3 ....213 J1
Royd Av BGLY BD16 ....81 K3
CUD/GR S72 ....244 D8
DOD/DAR S75 ....242 D5
HECK WF16 ....150 F8
HUDW HD3 ....191 J3
HUDW HD3 ....213 J1
STKB/PEN S36 ....269 M3
Royd Cl AIRE BD20 ....34 F8
Royd Crs HBR HX7 ....144 B5
HFAX * HX1 ....10 A4
Royd Cft HUDW HD3 ....191 K8
Royden Gv HTON BD9 ....104 C4
Royd Field La STKB/PEN S36 ....270 F6
Roydfield St HUDN HD2 ....192 D4
Royd Head Farm OSS WF5 ....196 E1
Royd House Gv KGHY BD21 ....3 L8
Royd House La
MAR/SLWT HD7 ....212 F5
Royd House Rd KGHY BD21 ....3 M8
Royd House Wk KGHY BD21 ....3 M8
Royd House Wy KGHY BD21 ....3 L8
Royd Ings Av KGHY BD21 ....3 J1
Roydlands St HIPP HX3 ....147 M6
Royd La DOD/DAR S75 ....259 M3
HIPP HX3 ....146 C3
HOLM/MEL HD9 ....254 A4
KGHY BD21 ....57 K5
LUD/ILL HX2 ....124 A7
RPDN/SBR HX6 ....188 E1
STKB/PEN S36 ....269 M2
TOD OL14 ....141 K7
Royd Moor La
HEM/SK/SE WF9 ....224 C5
Royd Moor Rd BOW BD4 ....128 B5
STKB/PEN S36 ....269 M1
Royd Mt HIPP HX3 ....146 E4
HOLM/MEL HD9 ....254 C2
Roydon Gv HTON BD9 ....104 C4
Royd Pl HIPP HX3 ....146 E4
Royd Rd HOLM/MEL HD9 ....235 G6
TOD OL14 ....141 J8
The Royds HOLM/MEL HD9 ....254 C1
KBTN HD8 ....240 C3
Royds Av BIRK/DRI BD11 ....150 D1
BRIG HD6 ....148 D6
CAS WF10 ....158 E6
HOLM/MEL HD9 ....236 F8
HUDW HD3 ....191 K8
MAR/SLWT HD7 ....212 F4
OSS WF5 ....174 E6
Roydscliffe Dr HTON BD9 ....104 B2
Roydscliffe Rd HTON BD9 ....104 A3
Royds Cl HOLM/MEL HD9 ....236 F8
WOR/ARM LS12 ....130 E2
Royds Crs BRIG HD6 ....148 D7
Roydsdale Wy BOW BD4 ....127 J8
Royds Dr HOLM/MEL HD9 ....236 F8
Royds Farm Rd BEE/HOL LS11 ....130 E4
Royds Gv WKFDE WF1 ....176 E1
Royds Hall Av WBSY BD6 ....126 E6
Royds Hall La LM/WK BD12 ....148 C1
WBSY BD6 ....126 C8
Royds Hall Rd WOR/ARM LS12 ....130 E2
Royds La RTHW LS26 ....155 J2
WOR/ARM LS12 ....130 E3
Royds Pk KBTN HD8 ....239 J8
Royds Park Crs LM/WK BD12 ....148 F2
Royds Pl MILN OL16 ....228 C1
Royds St LIT OL15 ....207 L1
MAR/SLWT HD7 ....233 H3
MILN OL16 ....228 D1
MILN OL16 ....229 J1
Royds St West MILN OL16 ....228 C1
Roydstone Rd BFDE BD3 ....105 M6
Roydstone Ter BFDE BD3 ....105 M6
Royd St BTLY WF17 ....174 A3
CUL/QBY BD13 ....102 E8
HUDW HD3 ....213 J1
HWTH BD22 ....54 E3
KGHY BD21 ....57 K4
MAR/SLWT HD7 ....212 B5
TOD OL14 ....141 J8
WIL/AL BD15 ....102 E1
Royds Vw MAR/SLWT HD7 ....212 F5
Royd Ter HBR HX7 ....143 J3
Royd Vw HBR HX7 ....144 A5
Royd Vls HBR * HX7 ....143 J3
Royd Wy KGHY BD21 ....3 H1
Royd Wd CLECK BD19 ....149 M8
Roydwood Ter CUL/QBY BD13 ....79 M8
Roydwood Ter Back
CUL/QBY BD13 ....79 M8
Royle Fold HECK WF16 ....172 F2
Royles Cl HEM/SK/SE WF9 ....246 E4
Royles Head La HUDW HD3 ....191 G8
Roy Rd WBSY BD6 ....125 M5
Royston Cl EARD/LOFT WF3 ....153 M8
Royston Hl EARD/LOFT WF3 ....153 M8
Royston La BSLYN/ROY S71 ....243 L4
Royston Rd CUD/GR S72 ....244 C5
Ruby St BTLY WF17 ....151 J8
CHAL LS7 ....7 L6
HWTH BD22 ....79 J2
Rud Broom La STKB/PEN S36 ....270 D3
Rudding Av WIL/AL BD15 ....103 J5
Rudding Crs WIL/AL BD15 ....103 J4
Rudding Dr BTLY WF17 ....151 H8
Rudding La PBR HG3 ....26 A4
Rudding St HUDS HD4 ....213 M2
Rudd St GTHN BD7 ....126 C3
Rudgate RYKW YO26 ....31 L3
TAD LS24 ....49 L2
TAD LS24 ....70 F1
Rudgate Pk BSPA/BRAM LS23 ....49 J3
Rud La HBR HX7 ....165 H3
Rudman St WHIT OL12 ....206 A4
Rudstone Gv GFTH/SHER LS25 ....116 A6
Rudyard Gv ROCH OL11 ....228 B4
Ruffield Side LM/WK BD12 ....148 E1
Rufford Av BSLYN/ROY S71 ....243 J6
YEA LS19 ....62 D8
Rufford Bank YEA LS19 ....62 E8
Rufford Cl HOR/CROF WF4 ....222 C6
ROY/SHW OL2 ....229 H7
YEA LS19 ....62 E8
Rufford Crs YEA LS19 ....62 E8
Rufford Dr YEA LS19 ....62 E8
Rufford Pl HFAX * HX1 ....168 D2
Rufford Rdg YEA LS19 ....62 E8
Rufford Ri YEA LS19 ....62 D8
Rufford Rd ELL HX5 ....169 G8
HIPP HX3 ....168 D2
HUDW HD3 ....213 H1
Rufford St BFDE BD3 ....105 L7
WKFDW/WTN WF2 ....176 B8
Rufford Vls HIPP HX3 ....168 D2
Rufus St KGHY BD21 ....3 H2
WBOW BD5 ....126 D3
Rugby Av HIPP HX3 ....146 B3
Rugby Dr HIPP HX3 ....146 B3
Rugby Gdns HIPP HX3 ....146 B3
Rugby Mt HIPP HX3 ....146 B3
Rugby Pl GTHN BD7 ....104 D8
Rugby Rd WHIT OL12 ....206 C5
Rugby Ter HIPP HX3 ....146 B3
Rumble Rd EARL WF12 ....174 B5
Rumbold Rd HUDW HD3 ....191 M7
Rumple Cft OT LS21 ....41 G4
Runswick Av BEE/HOL LS11 ....8 B6
Runswick Gv WBOW BD5 ....126 F5
Runswick Pl BEE/HOL LS11 ....8 B6
Runswick St BEE/HOL LS11 ....8 B6
WBOW BD5 ....126 F5
Runswick Ter BEE/HOL LS11 ....8 C6
WBOW BD5 ....126 F5
The Runtlings OSS WF5 ....196 D1
Runtlings La OSS WF5 ....196 E2
Rupert Rd ILK LS29 ....38 C1
Rupert St HWTH BD22 ....79 H6
KGHY * BD21 ....3 H2
Ruscombe Pl BSLYN/ROY S71 ....243 L5
Rush Bank ROY/SHW OL2 ....229 H6
Rush Cft IDLE BD10 ....83 H5
Rushcroft Rd ROY/SHW OL2 ....229 H6
Rushdene Ct LM/WK BD12 ....148 E5
Rushfield V KBTN HD8 ....215 L2
Rushmoor Rd BOW BD4 ....127 M4
Rush Mt ROY/SHW OL2 ....229 H5
Rusholme Dr PDSY/CALV LS28 ....106 E3
Rushton Av BFDE BD3 ....106 A6
Rushton Hill Cl LUD/ILL HX2 ....145 L5
Rushton Rd BFDE BD3 ....105 M6
Rushton St HFAX HX1 ....10 B4
PDSY/CALV LS28 ....84 D8
Rushton Ter BFDE BD3 ....106 A7
Rushworth Cl DOD/DAR S75 ....241 L6
EARD/LOFT WF3 ....177 G1
Rushworth St HIPP * HX3 ....10 D1
Ruskin Av HTON BD9 ....103 M3
WKFDE WF1 ....176 C4
Ruskin Cl CAS WF10 ....158 D6
Ruskin Ct WKFDE WF1 ....176 B4
Ruskin Crs GSLY LS20 ....62 B6
Ruskin Dr CAS WF10 ....158 D6
Ruskin Gv HUDN HD2 ....192 F3
Ruskin Pl CAS WF10 ....158 D6
Ruskin Rd ROCH OL11 ....228 A4
Ruskin St PDSY/CALV LS28 ....106 E5
Ruskin Ter HIPP HX3 ....10 D1
Russell Av CUL/QBY BD13 ....125 G6
HOR/CROF WF4 ....220 B4
Russell Cl BSLYN/ROY S71 ....261 K1
BTLY WF17 ....173 L1
HECK WF16 ....173 G3
Russell Hall La CUL/QBY BD13 ....125 G5
Russell Rd CUL/QBY BD13 ....124 F6
Russell St CUL/QBY BD13 ....125 G5
DEWS WF13 ....173 J5
HFAX HX1 ....11 H6
KGHY BD21 ....2 F5
LDS LS1 ....6 F9
SHPY BD18 ....104 E1
SKP/WHF BD23 ....16 C3
TOD OL14 ....163 L1
WBOW BD5 ....4 D9
WKFDE WF1 ....12 F6
Russell Wy BRIG HD6 ....170 D2
The Russets WKFDW/WTN WF2 ....199 G8
Russett Gv HUDS HD4 ....214 D3
Rustic Av HIPP HX3 ....169 J2
Ruswarp Crs IDLE BD10 ....83 M8
Ruth St HUDS HD4 ....214 C4
Ruthven Vw RHAY LS8 ....110 C3
Rutland ROCH * OL11 ....206 A8
Rutland Av PONT WF8 ....202 F1
WKFDW/WTN WF2 ....198 E4
Rutland Cl GFTH/SHER LS25 ....135 K4
RTHW LS26 ....133 M8
Rutland Dr GFTH/SHER LS25 ....135 K4
HOR/CROF WF4 ....199 L3
Rutland Mt BVRD LS3 ....6 B8
Rutland Rd BTLY WF17 ....151 M8
HOR/CROF WF4 ....217 L3
HUDW HD3 ....213 H1
Rutland St BOW BD4 ....127 J2
COL BB8 ....74 B1
KGHY BD21 ....2 F8
LDS LS1 ....6 C8
Rutland Ter BVRD LS3 ....6 B8
Rutland Wy DOD/DAR S75 ....260 E3
ROY/SHW OL2 ....229 L6
Ryan Gv HWTH BD22 ....56 F6
Ryan Pl RHAY LS8 ....110 C2
Ryan St WBOW BD5 ....126 F3
Ryburn Ct HFAX HX1 ....10 B5
Ryburn La RPDN/SBR HX6 ....189 G1
Ryburn Pl WKFDW/WTN WF2 ....12 D6
Ryburn Rd HUDW HD3 ....191 K7
Ryburn St RPDN/SBR HX6 ....167 K3
Ryburn Ter HFAX HX1 ....10 B5
Ryburn Vw LUD/ILL HX2 ....168 A1
RPDN/SBR HX6 ....188 E3
Rycroft Av BGLY BD16 ....81 J8
BRAM LS13 ....107 J5
Rycroft Cl BRAM LS13 ....107 K5
Rycroft Dr BRAM LS13 ....107 K5
Rycroft Gdns BRAM LS13 ....107 K5
Rycroft St SHPY BD18 ....82 F8
Rycroft Towers BRAM LS13 ....107 J5
Rydal Av GFTH/SHER LS25 ....113 G8
HTON BD9 ....104 E2
ROY/SHW OL2 ....228 E6
Rydal Cl STKB/PEN S36 ....270 F2
Rydal Crs MOR LS27 ....152 F1
WKFDW/WTN WF2 ....176 A7
Rydal Dr HUDE HD5 ....15 L6
MOR LS27 ....152 F1
WKFDW/WTN WF2 ....176 A7
Rydale Ct OSS WF5 ....196 F2
Rydale Ms OSS WF5 ....196 F2
Rydal Gv LVSG WF15 ....172 C5
Rydall Pl BEE/HOL LS11 ....8 B6
Rydall St BEE/HOL LS11 ....8 B6
Rydall Ter BEE/HOL LS11 ....8 B6
Rydal Pl COL BB8 ....74 C1
Rydal Rd AWLS/ASK DN6 ....249 L5
Rydal St CAS WF10 ....158 F6
HWTH BD22 ....2 D6
Rydal Ter BSLYN/ROY S71 ....261 J5
Ryder Cl PONT WF8 ....180 D6
Ryder Gdns RHAY LS8 ....88 C7
Rydings Av BRIG HD6 ....170 C3
Rydings Cl BRIG HD6 ....170 C3
Rydings Dr BRIG HD6 ....170 B3
Rydings La WHIT OL12 ....184 C8
Rydings Rd WHIT OL12 ....206 D2
Ryebank HOLM/MEL HD9 ....254 D2
Ryebread CAS WF10 ....158 A5
Rye Close La HOLM/MEL HD9 ....252 F2
Rye Cft BGLY BD16 ....80 B5
Rye Cft BSLYN/ROY S71 ....243 J8
LUD/ILL HX2 ....124 B8
Ryecroft Av AWLS/ASK DN6 ....227 L3
HOR/CROF WF4 ....222 E4
Ryecroft Cl WKFDE WF1 ....176 D1
Ryecroft Crs LUD/ILL HX2 ....145 M5
Ryecroft Dr HUDW HD3 ....191 J5
Ryecroft La HOLM/MEL HD9 ....254 E3
LUD/ILL HX2 ....145 M6
Ryecroft Rd AIRE BD20 ....34 D7
AWLS/ASK DN6 ....227 L3
BGLY BD16 ....79 M4
Ryecroft St OSS WF5 ....174 E8
Ryecroft Ter LUD/ILL HX2 ....145 M5
Ryecroft Wy AIRE BD20 ....34 E8
Ryedale HUDE HD5 ....193 K4

Ryedale Av KNOT WF11 182 A4
WOR/ARM LS12 130 D2
Ryedale Cl NORM * WF6 178 C1
TAD LS24 94 F2
Ryedale Ct SCFT LS14 111 H1
Ryedale Holt WOR/ARM LS12 130 D1
Ryedale Pk ILK LS29 38 F3
Ryedale Pl NORM WF6 178 C1
Ryedale Wy EARD/LOFT WF3 153 G7
WIL/AL BD15 103 J4
Ryefield Av CLAY BD14 125 K1
Rye Field La HUDW HD3 189 H8
Rye Field La West HUDW HD3 189 H8
Ryefields HOLM/MEL HD9 254 F2
Ryefields Av HUDW HD3 191 J7
Ryefields Rd MAR/SLWT HD7 213 G2
Rye Garth WBY LS22 29 M6
Ryeland Cl MILN OL16 228 D2
Ryelands Gv HTON BD9 103 M2
Ryeland St AIRE BD20 34 F8
Rye La LUD/ILL HX2 145 L5
Rye Pl SCFT LS14 111 H5
Rye St HWTH BD22 79 K2
Ryhill Pits La HOR/CROF WF4 221 M5
Rylands Av BGLY BD16 81 K3
Rylands Meadow HWTH BD22 79 G6
Rylstone Gdns BFDE BD3 5 K1
Rylstone Gv WKFDE WF1 177 G6
Rylstone Rd BAIL BD17 82 B4
Rylstone St KGHY BD21 3 K2
Rylstone Wk BSLY S70 261 M8
Ryndleside HUDW HD3 191 H5
Ryshworth Av AIRE BD20 58 F7
Ryton Dl IDLE BD10 84 A8

S

Sable Crest ECHL BD2 105 H2
Sackup La DOD/DAR S75 242 B5
Sackville Ap CHAL LS7 7 H3
Sackville Cl ROY/SHW OL2 229 J5
Sackville Rd AIRE BD20 36 A4
Sackville St BFD BD1 4 E6
BSLY S70 260 F4
CHAL LS7 7 H3
DEWS WF13 173 G8
HBR HX7 143 J3
SKP/WHF BD23 16 C3
TOD OL14 163 L1
Saddlers Cft CAS WF10 158 D8
Saddlers La KNOT WF11 159 L5
Saddler St LM/WK BD12 148 E2
Saddlers Wy RYKW YO26 33 J3
Saddleworth Rd GTL/HWG HX4 169 G7
GTL/HWG HX4 189 K1
HUDW HD3 210 D4
Sadler Cl BHP/TINH LS16 86 E2
Sadler Copse BHP/TINH LS16 86 E2
Sadler Ga BSLY S70 261 G4
Sadler Wy BHP/TINH LS16 86 E2
Saffron Dr WIL/AL BD15 103 J5
Sagar La TOD OL14 140 F4
Sagar Pl HDGY LS6 108 F2
Sagar St CAS WF10 157 M6
Sage St WBOW BD5 126 E2
Sahara Ct GIR BD8 104 F4
St Abbs Cl WBSY BD6 126 E7
St Abbs Dr WBSY BD6 126 E7
St Abbs Fold WBSY BD6 126 E7
St Abbs Ga WBSY BD6 126 E7
St Abbs Wk WBSY BD6 126 E7
St Abbs Wy WBSY BD6 126 E7
St Aidan's Rd BAIL BD17 82 F4
RTHW LS26 135 G6
St Aiden's Wk OSS WF5 197 J2
St Alban Cl OSM LS9 110 E5
St Alban Crs OSM LS9 110 E5
St Alban Gv OSM * LS9 110 E5
St Alban Mt OSM LS9 110 E5
St Alban Rd OSM LS9 110 E5
St Alban's Av HIPP HX3 168 E3
HUDW HD3 191 J3
St Albans Cft HIPP HX3 168 F2
St Albans Pl LDSU LS2 7 H7
St Alban's Rd HIPP HX3 168 E3
St Alban's St MILN OL16 206 A8
St Albans Ter ROCH * OL11 206 A8
St Alban Vw OSM LS9 110 E5
St Andrew's Av MOR LS27 152 A3
St Andrew's Cl BRAM LS13 107 G1
MOR LS27 152 A3
WHIT OL12 207 G2
YEA LS19 62 E7
St Andrews Ct BVRD LS3 6 B8
St Andrew's Crs LM/WK BD12 149 J2
St Andrews Cft AL/HA/HU LS17 87 K2
St Andrews Dr AL/HA/HU LS17 87 L2
BRIG HD6 170 C2
DOD/DAR S75 242 C5
FEA/AMT WF7 179 L5
HUDE HD5 193 K6
KNOT WF11 181 L1
St Andrew's Gv MOR LS27 152 B3
St Andrew's Pl BVRD LS3 6 B8
GTHN BD7 4 A7
St Andrew's Rd CAS WF10 158 E5
HUD HD1 15 J7
YEA LS19 62 E7
St Andrew's St BVRD LS3 6 B8
St Andrew's Vls GTHN BD7 4 A6
St Andrews Wk AL/HA/HU LS17 87 L2
St Andrews Wy
BSLYN/ROY S71 262 C7
St Anne's Cl EARL WF12 195 M2
St Anne's Dr BSLYN/ROY S71 243 M7
BULY LS4 108 E2
St Anne's Gn BULY LS4 108 E2
St Anne's Rd HDGY LS6 108 E1
HIPP HX3 168 E4
St Anne's St HOR/CROF WF4 222 D5
LDS LS1 6 F8
St Ann's Av BULY LS4 108 F4
St Ann's Cl BULY LS4 108 E2
St Ann's Gdns BULY LS4 108 E3
St Ann's La KSTL LS5 108 E2
St Ann's Mt BULY LS4 108 F3
St Ann's Ri BULY LS4 108 D3
St Ann's Rd MILN OL16 206 E6
St Ann's Sq BULY LS4 108 E3
OSM * LS9 7 L9
RPDN/SBR HX6 167 L2
St Ann's Wy BULY LS4 108 E3
St Anthony's Dr BEE/HOL LS11 131 H4
St Anthony's Rd BEE/HOL LS11 131 G4
St Anuil GIR * BD8 104 D5
St Augustine's Ter BFDE BD3 5 J2
HFAX * HX1 10 C5
St Austell Dr DOD/DAR S75 260 A2
St Barnabas Rd BEE/HOL LS11 8 F4
LVSG WF15 171 L1
St Barnabas's Dr LIT OL15 185 J8
St Bartholomew's Cl
WOR/ARM LS12 108 E7
St Bartholomews Ct
WKFDW/WTN WF2 197 L2
St Barts Ter BSLY * S70 261 H6
St Benedicts Cha BRAM LS13 107 M1
St Benedicts Dr BRAM LS13 107 M1
St Bernard's Av PONT WF8 180 D6
St Bevan's Rd HIPP HX3 168 E3
St Blaise Ct WBOW BD5 4 F8
St Blaise Wy BFD BD1 4 F5
St Boltophs Cl KNOT * WF11 182 C2
St Catherine's Crs BRAM LS13 107 M2
St Catherine's Dr BRAM LS13 107 M2
St Catherine's Gn BRAM LS13 107 M2
St Catherine's Hl BRAM LS13 107 M2
St Catherine St WKFDE WF1 13 K8
St Catherines Vls WKFDE WF1 13 M8
St Catherine's Wk RHAY LS8 88 C8
St Catherines Wy
DOD/DAR S75 260 D4
St Chad's Av BRIG * HD6 170 A1
HDGY LS6 86 E8
St Chad's Cl MILN * OL16 206 B7
St Chads Ct MILN * OL16 206 B7
St Chad's Dr HDGY LS6 86 E8
St Chad's Ri HDGY LS6 86 E8
St Chad's Rd GIR BD8 104 D5
HDGY LS6 86 F8
St Chad's Vw HDGY LS6 108 E1
St Christopher's Av RTHW LS26 155 H1
St Christophers Cl
BSLYN/ROY S71 262 C7
St Christophers Dr ILK LS29 19 H7
St Clair Gn WKFDW/WTN WF2 175 M6
St Clair Rd OT LS21 41 K7
St Clair St OT LS21 41 K6
WKFDE WF1 13 G3
St Clare's Av ECHL BD2 105 M4
St Clements Av RTHW LS26 155 G1
St Clements Cl BSLYN/ROY S71 262 C7
RTHW LS26 154 F2
St Clements Ri RTHW LS26 154 F1
St Cuthbert's Ct
FEA/AMT * WF7 202 C5
St Cyprians Gdns OSM * LS9 110 D4
St David's Dr BSLYN/ROY S71 262 B6
St Davids Rd OT LS21 41 G4
St Edmunds Cl CAS WF10 158 E6
St Edwards Av BSLY S70 260 F6
St Edwards Cl KNOT WF11 160 A7
St Elmo Gv OSM LS9 110 C6
St Eloi Av BAIL BD17 82 E2
St Enoch's Rd WBSY BD6 126 D5
St Francis Bvd BSLYN/ROY S71 243 M7
St Francis Gdns HUDN HD2 192 C1
St Francis Pl BEE/HOL LS11 8 E3
St George's Av HUDW HD3 191 J3
RTHW LS26 132 E7
St Georges Ct HOR/CROF WF4 222 F4
St George's Crs HFAX HX1 10 D3
RTHW LS26 132 E7
St Georges Ms
WKFDW/WTN WF2 220 C1
St George's Pl WBOW BD5 4 E9
St George's Rd BSLY S70 261 G5
HIPP HX3 10 D2
HOLM/MEL HD9 254 F2
LDS LS1 6 E7
WKFDW/WTN WF2 197 M3
St George's Sq HBR * HX7 143 J3
HUD HD1 14 F6
St George's St HBR HX7 143 J3
HUD HD1 14 F7
St Georges Wk
WKFDW/WTN WF2 198 D8
St Giles Av PONT WF8 180 D6
St Giles Cl BRIG HD6 170 A1
St Giles Garth BHP/TINH LS16 63 M3
St Giles Rd HIPP HX3 148 A8
St Helena Rd WBSY BD6 126 D5
St Helens Av BHP/TINH LS16 86 F3
BSLYN/ROY S71 261 K1
HEM/SK/SE WF9 223 L7
St Helen's Bvd BSLYN/ROY S71 243 K8
St Helens Cl BHP/TINH LS16 86 F3
St Helens Cft BHP/TINH LS16 86 E3
St Helen's Dr GFTH/SHER LS25 114 B6
St Helen's Fld HUDS HD4 215 J4
St Helens Gdns BHP/TINH LS16 86 E3
St Helen's Ga HUDE HD5 215 J4
St Helens Gv BHP/TINH LS16 86 E3
WKFDW/WTN WF2 199 H6
St Helen's La BHP/TINH LS16 86 D3
St Helen's Pl CAS WF10 158 A7
St Helens St MID LS10 9 K6
St Helens Wy BHP/TINH LS16 86 F3
BSLYN/ROY S71 261 M1
ILK LS29 38 F2
St Helier Dr DOD/DAR S75 260 D4
St Helier Gv BAIL BD17 82 F2
St Hilda Av BSLY S70 260 E5
St Hilda's Av OSM LS9 110 B8
St Hilda's Crs OSM * LS9 110 B8
St Hilda's Gv OSM LS9 110 B8
St Hilda's Mt OSM LS9 110 B8
St Hilda's Pl OSM LS9 110 B8
St Hilda's Rd OSM LS9 110 B8
St Hilda's Ter BFDE BD3 106 A6
St Ians Cft ILK LS29 19 H7
St Ives Cl PONT WF8 180 F3
St Ives Crs CAS WF10 180 E1
St Ive's Gdns HIPP * HX3 168 E3
St Ives Gv BGLY BD16 80 E4
WOR/ARM LS12 108 C6
St Ives Mt WOR/ARM LS12 108 C6
St Ives Pl BGLY BD16 80 E4
St Ives Rd BGLY BD16 80 E4
HIPP HX3 168 D3
St James Ap SCFT LS14 111 J2
St James Av HORS LS18 85 L5
St Jame's Cl MILN OL16 228 E6
WOR/ARM LS12 108 A6
St James Ct HFAX HX1 11 G5
HOR/CROF WF4 222 E5
St James Crs PDSY/CALV LS28 106 D7
St James Dr HORS LS18 85 M5
St James Ms WOR/ARM LS12 108 B6
St James Ri WKFDW/WTN WF2 197 L2
St James Rd HFAX HX1 11 G5
ILK LS29 38 C3
St James's Ct OSM LS9 7 M4
WKFDW/WTN WF2 12 D6
St James's Market BFDE * BD3 5 J8
St James's Ms WOR/ARM LS12 108 B6
St James's Pk WKFDE WF1 13 J3
St James's Rd HUD HD1 191 M7
St James's Sq WBOW * BD5 127 G1
St James's St WBY LS22 48 A1
St James St BTLY WF17 173 L1
HECK WF16 172 F3
HFAX HX1 11 G5
MILN OL16 207 H8
ROY/SHW OL2 229 K7
St James Ter HORS LS18 85 M5
St James Wk HORS LS18 85 M5
St James Wy HOR/CROF WF4 220 A1
HUDE HD5 15 L4
St John Pde DEWS WF13 173 K6
St Johns STKB/PEN S36 258 B8
St John's Av DOD/DAR S75 260 A2
HDGY LS6 6 B5
HUDE HD5 193 K5
HUDS HD4 214 C4
ILK LS29 19 H6
OSS WF5 197 J1
PDSY/CALV LS28 106 F4
SCFT LS14 90 B1
WKFDE WF1 176 D6
St John's Cha WKFDE WF1 176 D7
St Johns Cl CLECK * BD19 150 A7
DEWS * WF13 173 K6
DOD/DAR S75 260 A8
GFTH/SHER LS25 92 A5
HBR * HX7 143 J3
HDGY LS6 6 A5
OSS WF5 197 J1
RPDN/SBR HX6 188 E5
STKB/PEN S36 270 E4
St John's Ct BAIL BD17 83 G4
KBTN * HD8 216 B3
MILN * OL16 206 D8
SCFT * LS14 90 B1
TAD LS24 94 F1
WKFDE WF1 176 D7
YEA LS19 62 C8
St John's Crs GIR BD8 104 A6
HUD HD1 14 E3
NORM WF6 178 C7
OSS WF5 197 J1
St John's Cft WKFDE WF1 176 C7
St John's Dr AL/HA/HU LS17 25 M7
HUD HD1 14 E3
MILN OL16 206 D8
YEA LS19 62 C8
St John's Garth
GFTH/SHER LS25 92 A6
St John's Gv HDGY LS6 6 A4
WKFDE WF1 176 E6
St John's La HFAX HX1 11 G8
St Johns Ms WKFDE * WF1 176 D6
St John's Mt WKFDE WF1 176 C6
St John's North WKFDE WF1 176 D7
St John's Pk ILK LS29 61 H1
St John's Pl BIRK/DRI * BD11 128 C8
HFAX * HX1 11 G8
St John's Rd AIRE BD20 57 J4
BSLY S70 261 G6
BSPA/BRAM LS23 48 F8
BVRD LS3 6 B6
CUD/GR S72 244 D8
HUD HD1 14 E2
HUDE HD5 193 L5
ILK LS29 39 G2
YEA LS19 62 C8
St John's Sq WKFDE WF1 176 D7
St John's St AIRE BD20 34 C4
AIRE BD20 36 A5
HOR/CROF WF4 197 G5
RTHW LS26 155 L1
St Johns Ter HDGY LS6 6 B5
St John St BRIG HD6 170 C5
DEWS WF13 173 K6
St John's Vw BSPA/BRAM LS23 48 E7
St Johns Vls CUD/GR * S72 244 D8
St John's Wk BSLYN/ROY S71 243 M3
St Johns Wy HWTH BD22 2 B7
YEA LS19 62 C8
St John Wk DEWS WF13 173 K6
St Joseph's Dr MILN OL16 228 D2
St Joseph's Mt PONT WF8 180 D7
St Joseph's St TAD LS24 71 L3
St Jude's Pl GIR BD8 4 D3
St Jude's St BFD BD1 4 C3
HFAX HX1 168 D1
St Julien's Mt DOD/DAR S75 259 G2
St Julien's Wy DOD/DAR S75 259 G2
St Laurence's Cl SHPY BD18 104 F1
St Lawrence Cl
PDSY/CALV LS28 106 F7
St Lawrence Md
PDSY/CALV LS28 106 F8
St Lawrence St CHAL * LS7 87 M8
St Lawrence Ter
PDSY/CALV LS28 107 G8
St Leonards Cl ILK LS29 19 H7
St Leonards Ct HTON BD9 104 B5
St Leonard's Gv GIR BD8 104 B5
St Leonard's Rd GIR BD8 104 B5
St Leonards Wy
BSLYN/ROY S71 262 C7
St Lucius's Cl HUDS HD4 215 G8
St Luke's Cl BSPA/BRAM LS23 69 M1
BTLY * WF17 174 A2
CLECK BD19 149 K7
WBOW BD5 126 F1
St Luke's Crs BEE/HOL LS11 8 D7
St Luke's Gn BEE/HOL LS11 8 D8
St Luke's Rd BEE/HOL LS11 8 D8
St Luke's St BEE/HOL LS11 8 D8
St Luke St ROCH * OL11 228 B1
St Luke's Vw BEE/HOL LS11 8 D8
St Lukes Wy BSLYN/ROY * S71 261 L3
St Margaret's Av BOW BD4 127 M4
HORS LS18 85 K5
RHAY LS8 88 C8
RTHW LS26 156 F3
St Margaret's Cl HORS LS18 85 K4
St Margarets Ct
HEM/SK/SE WF9 225 K8
St Margaret's Dr HORS LS18 85 K4
RHAY LS8 88 C8
St Margaret's Gv RHAY LS8 88 C8
St Margaret's Pl GTHN BD7 126 D1
St Margaret's Rd GTHN BD7 104 D8
HORS LS18 85 K4
RTHW LS26 156 F3
St Margaret's Ter GTHN BD7 126 D1
ILK LS29 38 D3
St Margaret's Vw RHAY LS8 88 C8
St Mark's Av LDSU LS2 6 D4
LM/WK BD12 148 E1
St Mark's Rd HUDW HD3 191 J8
LDSU LS2 6 D3
St Mark's St LDSU LS2 6 D4
WKFDE WF1 176 F6
St Mark's Ter LM/WK BD12 148 E1
St Marks Vw HUDW HD3 191 J8
St Martin's Av CHAL LS7 109 L1
GTHN BD7 4 A6
OT LS21 41 H4
St Martins Cl DOD/DAR S75 260 D4
FEA/AMT WF7 201 L2
St Martin's Crs CHAL LS7 109 M1
St Martin's Dr CHAL * LS7 87 M8
St Martin's Gdns CHAL LS7 109 L1
St Martin's Gv CAS WF10 157 K8
CHAL LS7 109 M1
St Martin's Rd CHAL LS7 109 M1
St Martins Ter CHAL * LS7 109 M1
St Martin's Vw BRIG HD6 170 C3
CHAL LS7 109 M1
St Mary Magdalenes Cl
GIR * BD8 4 B3
St Mary's Av BTLY WF17 173 J3
HOLM/MEL HD9 236 B6
LM/WK BD12 148 E4
MIRF WF14 172 E8
NORM WF6 178 B2
RTHW LS26 134 C5
St Mary's Cl CHAL LS7 109 M1
EARD/LOFT WF3 152 E7
GFTH/SHER LS25 113 H8
HEM/SK/SE WF9 247 J4
ILK LS29 38 E2
LM/WK BD12 148 D4
MILN OL16 228 D1
WOR/ARM LS12 108 F8
St Mary's Ct CAS WF10 157 K2
CHAL LS7 109 M1
St Mary's Crs HOLM/MEL HD9 236 B6
LM/WK BD12 148 D5
St Mary's Dr LM/WK BD12 148 E4
St Mary's Gdns LM/WK BD12 148 E4
St Mary's Garth AL/HA/HU LS17 67 K1
St Mary's Ga BSLY S70 261 G4
ELL HX5 169 H7
ROY/SHW * OL2 229 K7
WHIT OL12 206 A7
St Mary's La HUDE HD5 193 L7
OSM LS9 7 L8
St Mary's Mt LM/WK BD12 148 D5
St Mary's Park Ap
WOR/ARM LS12 108 B6
St Mary's Park Ct
WOR/ARM * LS12 108 B6
St Mary's Park Crs
WOR/ARM LS12 108 B6
St Mary's Park Gn
WOR/ARM * LS12 108 B6
St Mary's Pl BSLY S70 261 G4
EARL WF12 173 L8
St Mary's Ri HOLM/MEL HD9 236 B6
St Mary's Rd AIRE BD20 58 B4
BOW BD4 127 M1
CHAL LS7 109 M1
HOLM/MEL HD9 236 B6
HOLM/MEL HD9 236 B1
HTON BD9 104 E4
NORM WF6 178 B3
St Mary's Sq HOLM/MEL HD9 236 B1
LM/WK BD12 148 D4
MOR * LS27 152 C2
St Mary's St BSPA/BRAM LS23 48 F6
OSM LS9 7 K8
STKB/PEN S36 270 F3
St Mary St HFAX HX1 10 E7
St Mary's Wk GFTH/SHER LS25 114 B7
MIRF WF14 172 E8
St Mary's Wy HOLM/MEL HD9 236 B6
St Matthew Rd DEWS WF13 173 K6
St Matthews Cl WIL/AL BD15 102 D2
St Matthew's Dr HIPP HX3 147 J3
St Matthews Gv WIL/AL BD15 102 D2
St Matthew's Rd WBSY BD6 126 F5
St Matthew's St BEE/HOL LS11 8 C5
St Matthew's Wk CHAL LS7 87 L6
St Matthews Wy
BSLYN/ROY S71 261 L3
St Matthias Ct BULY LS4 108 F4
St Matthias' St BULY LS4 108 F4
St Matthias Ter BULY LS4 108 F4
St Merrion Crs HIPP HX3 11 M9
St Michael's Av
BSLYN/ROY S71 243 M8
PONT WF8 180 D6
St Michael's Cl CAS WF10 157 M7
EARL WF12 196 A4
KBTN * HD8 217 M7
WKFDW/WTN WF2 12 A
St Michael's Crs HDGY LS6 108 F
St Michael's Gdns KBTN HD8 217 L
St Michaels Gn NORM WF6 178 C
St Michael's Gv HDGY LS6 108 F
St Michael's La HDGY LS6 108 F
St Michael's Mt EARL WF12 196 A
St Michael's Rd GIR BD8 4 B
HDGY LS6 108 F
St Michael's Ter HDGY LS6 108 F
St Michaels Vls HDGY LS6 108 F
St Michaels Wy ILK LS29 19 H
ILK LS29 40 B
St Nicholas Rd ILK LS29 38 C
St Nicholas St CAS WF10 157 M
St Oswald Av PONT WF8 180 D
St Oswald Rd
WKFDW/WTN WF2 197 L
St Oswalds Garth GSLY LS20 62 A
St Oswalds Pl OSS WF5 175 G
St Oswald St CAS * WF10 157 M
St Owens Dr DOD/DAR S75 260 D
St Paulinus Cl DEWS WF13 173 K
St Paul's Av BIRK/DRI BD11 150 D
WBSY BD6 126 D
St Pauls Cl GIR * BD8 4 A
HEM/SK/SE * WF9 225 M
St Pauls Ct PONT WF8 181 G
St Paul's Dr WKFDW/WTN WF2 175 M
St Paul's Gv ILK LS29 38 F
WBSY BD6 126 D
St Paul's Pde BSLYN/ROY S71 262 B
St Paul's Pl LDS * LS1 6 E
St Pauls Ri ILK LS29 19 H
St Paul's Rd BIRK/DRI BD11 150 C
DOD/DAR S75 260 E
GIR BD8 104 E
HFAX HX1 10 A
HUDE HD5 193 K
KGHY BD21 3 J
MIRF WF14 194 C
SHPY BD18 82 C
WBSY BD6 126 D
St Paul's St HUD HD1 15 G
LDS LS1 6 D
MOR * LS27 152 C
St Paul's Ter MIRF WF14 194 C
St Paul's Wk
WKFDW/WTN WF2 175 M
St Peg Cl CLECK BD19 150 A
St Peg La CLECK BD19 150 A
St Peter's Av RPDN/SBR HX6 167 H
RTHW LS26 155 H
St Peter's Cl BTLY WF17 150 F
MIRF * WF14 194 B
St Peters Ct BEE/HOL LS11 9 G
BRAM LS13 107 M
HOR/CROF WF4 197 J
ILK LS29 19 H
St Peter's Crs EARD/LOFT WF3 155 K
HUDE HD5 193 K
MOR LS27 130 C
St Peter's Gdns BRAM LS13 107 L
St Peter's Garth SCFT LS14 68 C
St Peters Ga OSS WF5 174 F
St Peter's Gv HOR/CROF * WF4 197 K
St Peter's Mt BRAM LS13 107 L
St Peter's Sq OSM LS9 7 K
St Peter's St HUD HD1 15 G
LDSU LS2 7 J
MILN OL16 206 D
St Peter's Ter BSLY * S70 261 J
St Peter's Wy ILK LS29 61 H
St Philip's Av MID LS10 153 K
St Philip's Cl DEWS * WF13 173 M
ILK LS29 40 B
MID LS10 153 L
St Philips Ct HUDW HD3 191 K
St Philip's Dr ILK LS29 40 B
St Philip's Wy ILK LS29 40 B
St Phillips Ct GIR BD8 104 B
St Richards Rd OT LS21 41 H
St Stephen's Cl SKP/WHF BD23 16 B
St Stephen's Ct AIRE BD20 35 L
HIPP * HX3 168 C
OSM * LS9 110 B
St Stephen's Rd AIRE BD20 56 E
HUD * HD1 214 B
OSM LS9 110 B
PDSY/CALV LS28 84 C
WBOW BD5 126 F
St Stephen's St HIPP HX3 168 C
St Stephen's Ter WBOW * BD5 127 G
St Stephen's Wy COL BB8 74 B
Saint St GTHN BD7 126 C
St Swithins Dr EARD/LOFT WF3 177 H
St Swithins Gv
EARD/LOFT * WF3 177 H
St Thomas Gdns HUDN HD2 171 H
St Thomas Rd FEA/AMT WF7 201 M
St Thomas Rw LDSU LS2 7 J
St Thomas's Rd DOD/DAR S75 260 C
St Vincent Av AWLS/ASK DN6 249 H
St Vincent Rd PDSY/CALV LS28 107 G
St Wilfred's St PDSY/CALV LS28 84 D
St Wilfrid's Av RHAY LS8 110 C
St Wilfrid's Circ RHAY LS8 110 D
St Wilfrid's Cl GTHN BD7 126 B
St Wilfrid's Crs GTHN BD7 126 B
RHAY LS8 110 D
St Wilfrid's Dr RHAY LS8 110 C
St Wilfrid's Garth RHAY LS8 110 D
St Wilfrid's Gv RHAY LS8 110 D
St Wilfrid's Rd GTHN BD7 126 B
St Winifred's Cl LUD/ILL * HX2 145 M
Salcombe Cl DOD/DAR S75 242 E
Salcombe Pl BOW BD4 128 A
Salem Pl GFTH/SHER LS25 113 G
MID LS10 9 H
Salem St BFD BD1 4 E
CUL/QBY * BD13 124 F
HBR HX7 143 J
Salerno Wy WMB/DAR S73 263 G
Sale St LIT OL15 185 K
Salford Wy TOD OL14 163 J
Salik Gdns ROCH OL11 228 B
Salisbury Av BAIL BD17 82 E
WOR/ARM LS12 108 E

alisbury Cl EARL WF12 ......174 B6
NORM WF6 ......178 D3
alisbury Gv WOR/ARM LS12 ......108 E6
alisbury Ms HORS LS18 ......85 M4
alisbury Pl HIPP HX3 ......10 F1
PDSY/CALV LS28 ......84 C8
alisbury Rd CLECK BD19 ......149 H6
HTON BD9 ......104 E1
HWTH BD22 ......2 D7
LM/WK BD12 ......126 E8
WOR/ARM LS12 ......108 E6
alisbury St DOD/DAR S75 ......260 F3
PDSY/CALV LS28 ......84 C8
ROY/SHW OL2 ......229 H6
RPDN/SBR HX6 ......167 J3
SKP/WHF BD23 ......16 A2
YEA LS19 ......84 D2
alisbury Ter HIPP HX3 ......10 F1
WOR/ARM LS12 ......108 E6
alisbury Vw WOR/ARM LS12 ......108 E6
alkeld St ROCH OL11 ......228 B1
almon Crs HORS LS18 ......85 L5
al Nook Cl LM/WK BD12 ......126 F7
al Royd Rd LM/WK BD12 ......149 G1
altaire Rd BGLY BD16 ......59 M8
SHPY BD18 ......82 C6
altburn Pl HFAX HX1 ......10 A5
altburn Rd HTON BD9 ......104 B4
alt Drake RPDN/SBR HX6 ......166 D6
alt Royd Rd ......
alterhebble Hl HIPP HX3 ......168 F4
alterlee HIPP HX3 ......10 C4
alter Hill La STKB/PEN S36 ......271 G8
alter Oak Cft BSLYN/ROY S71 ......243 L5
alter Rake Ga TOD OL14 ......163 K6
alter Rw PONT WF8 ......180 F6
altersbrook Rd
WMB/DAR S73 ......263 H7
altersgate Av KNOT WF11 ......182 A1
alter St DEWS WF13 ......173 K4
alter's Wy STKB/PEN S36 ......270 F4
alt Horn Cl LM/WK BD12 ......149 H1
altonstall La LUD/ILL HX2 ......144 F1
alt Pie Aly WKFDW/WTN WF2 ......12 C4
alts Dr LIT OL15 ......185 J8
alts Mill Rd BAIL BD17 ......82 D6
alts St ROY/SHW OL2 ......229 K7
alt St GIR BD8 ......4 A2
HFAX HX1 ......10 C4
amlesbury Cl ROY/SHW OL2 ......229 J7
amson St LVSG WF15 ......172 D2
amuel Dr EARD/LOFT WF3 ......177 G1
amuel Rd DOD/DAR S75 ......260 D3
amuel Sq DOD/DAR S75 ......260 D3
amuel St KGHY * BD21 ......3 G4
andal Av WKFDW/WTN WF2 ......199 G5
andal Cliff WKFDW/WTN WF2 ......199 G6
andale Wk BD6 ......126 B7
andal Hall Cl
WKFDW/WTN WF2 ......199 H6
andal Hall Ms
WKFDW/WTN WF2 ......199 G5
andall Cl GFTH/SHER LS25 ......135 K4
andall Magna WBSY BD6 ......126 A3
andal Ri PONT WF8 ......225 J1
andal Rd BAIL BD17 ......82 E4
andal Wy BTLY WF17 ......151 H5
andbeck Cl BSLYN/ROY S71 ......261 H3
andbeck La WBY LS22 ......30 B7
andbeck Pk WBY LS22 ......30 B7
andbeck Wy WBY LS22 ......30 B7
andbed Ct MSTN/BAR LS15 ......111 M3
andbed Ter MSTN/BAR LS15 ......111 M3
and Beds CUL/QBY BD13 ......125 G5
andbeds HOLM/MEL HD9 ......214 B8
andbeds Crs LUD/ILL HX2 ......146 A5
andbeds Rd LUD/ILL HX2 ......146 A6
andbeds Ter LUD/ILL HX2 ......146 A6
andbrook Pk ROCH * OL11 ......228 A2
andbrook Rd ROCH OL11 ......228 A2
andene Av HUDS HD4 ......213 L4
andene Rd HUDS HD4 ......213 L4
anderling Ct GIR * BD8 ......103 L7
anderling Garth MID LS10 ......153 M1
anderling Wy MID LS10 ......153 M1
anderson Av NORM WF6 ......178 C5
WBSY BD6 ......126 E5
anderson La RTHW LS26 ......155 J4
anderson St WKFDE WF1 ......13 H3
andfield Av HDGY LS6 ......87 G8
andfield Garth HDGY LS6 ......87 G8
andfield Rd IDLE BD10 ......83 K8
MILN OL16 ......228 D1
andfield Ter TAD LS24 ......72 A2
andfield Vw HDGY LS6 ......87 G8
andford Ct BSLY S70 ......260 F6
andford Pl KSTL LS5 ......108 C2
andford Rd BFDE BD3 ......105 L7
HEM/SK/SE WF9 ......247 J1
KSTL LS5 ......108 D3
andforth Av HIPP HX3 ......146 E4
andgate Dr GFTH/SHER LS25 ......135 K4
andgate La HEM/SK/SE WF9 ......223 L1
andgate Ri GFTH/SHER LS25 ......135 L5
andgate Ter GFTH/SHER LS25 ......135 L5
andhall Av LUD/ILL HX2 ......145 M7
andhall Dr LUD/ILL HX2 ......145 M6
andhall La LUD/ILL HX2 ......145 M6
andhall La LUD/ILL HX2 ......145 M7
andhill Cl AL/HA/HU LS17 ......88 A2
andhill Dr AL/HA/HU LS17 ......88 A2
CUD/GR S72 ......245 H5
and Hill La AL/HA/HU LS17 ......87 M3
and Hill Lawn PONT WF8 ......180 E7
and Hill Lawns AL/HA/HU LS17 ......87 M3
andhill Mt AL/HA/HU LS17 ......87 M1
IDLE BD10 ......83 K8
andhill Ov AL/HA/HU LS17 ......88 A1
andhill Ri PONT WF8 ......180 F2
Sand Hole La ROCH OL11 ......228 B5
Sandholme Crs HIPP HX3 ......147 M7
Sandholme Dr IDLE BD10 ......83 L8
ILK LS29 ......40 B7
OSS WF5 ......196 F1

Sandhurst Av RHAY LS8 ......110 C3
Sandhurst Gv RHAY LS8 ......110 C3
Sandhurst Pl RHAY LS8 ......110 C3
Sandhurst Rd RHAY LS8 ......110 C3
Sandhurst Ter RHAY LS8 ......110 C3
Sandiford Cl MSTN/BAR LS15 ......111 M3
Sandiford Ter MSTN/BAR LS15 ......111 M3
Sandiway Bank EARL WF12 ......195 M3
San La GFTH/SHER LS25 ......138 A3
Sandleas Wy MSTN/BAR LS15 ......112 B4
Sandlewood Cl BEE/HOL LS11 ......8 C6
Sandlewood Gn BEE/HOL LS11 ......8 D8
Sandmead Cl BOW BD4 ......128 A3
MOR LS27 ......130 C8
Sandmead Cft MOR LS27 ......130 C8
Sandmead Wy MOR LS27 ......130 C8
Sandmoor Av AL/HA/HU LS17 ......65 M8
Sandmoor Cl AL/HA/HU LS17 ......87 M1
CUL/QBY BD13 ......103 C8
Sandmoor Dr AL/HA/HU LS17 ......65 M8
HUDN HD3 ......191 J5
Sandmoor Gdns HIPP HX3 ......147 K2
Sandmoor Garth IDLE BD10 ......83 K5
Sandmoor Gn AL/HA/HU LS17 ......65 L8
Sandmoor La AL/HA/HU LS17 ......65 M8
Sandmoor Ms AL/HA/HU LS17 ......87 M1
Sandon Gv MID * LS10 ......132 A4
Sandon Mt MID LS10 ......132 A4
Sandown Av HOR/CROF WF4 ......200 B5
LUD/ILL HX2 ......146 A2
Sandown Rd LUD/ILL HX2 ......146 A2
Sandpiper Ap MOR LS27 ......152 E3
Sandpiper Ms GIR BD8 ......103 L7
Sandringham Ap
AL/HA/HU LS17 ......88 A3
Sandringham Cl CLAY * BD14 ......125 M1
MOR LS27 ......152 E1
PONT WF8 ......202 E1
STKB/PEN S36 ......270 C2
Sandringham Ct CLAY BD14 ......125 M1
Sandringham Crs
AL/HA/HU LS17 ......87 M3
PDSY/CALV LS28 ......107 G8
Sandringham Dr
AL/HA/HU LS17 ......87 M3
MILN OL16 ......207 J8
Sandringham Gdns
AL/HA/HU LS17 ......87 M3
Sandringham Gn
AL/HA/HU * LS17 ......88 A3
Sandringham Mt
AL/HA/HU LS17 ......87 M3
Sandringham Rd CLAY BD14 ......125 M1
KNOT WF11 ......159 M7
WBY LS22 ......30 A1
Sandringham Wy
AL/HA/HU LS17 ......87 M3
ROY/SHW OL2 ......228 E8
Sandrock Rd PONT WF8 ......181 G4
Sandsend Cl HTON BD9 ......103 M3
Sands House La HUDS HD4 ......213 K5
Sandside Cl WBOW BD5 ......127 H4
Sands La EARL WF12 ......173 M7
HUDE HD5 ......194 B8
MIRF WF14 ......194 F3
Sands Rd EARL WF12 ......174 A8
Sands Ter HUDN * HD2 ......193 G4
Sandstone Cl HOLM/MEL HD9 ......236 B3
Sandstone Dr WOR/ARM LS12 ......107 L7
Sandstone La HUDS HD4 ......213 K3
Sandstone Rd MILN OL16 ......207 H7
Sand St HUD HD1 ......15 H8
HWTH BD22 ......78 E8
KGHY BD21 ......3 G3
Sandwath La TAD LS24 ......94 D7
Sandway MSTN/BAR LS15 ......111 K4
Sandway Gdns
MSTN/BAR LS15 ......111 K4
Sandway Gv MSTN/BAR LS15 ......111 K4
Sandwell St MAR/SLWT HD7 ......212 B5
Sandwich Crs HUDN HD2 ......192 B3
Sandyacres RTHW LS26 ......133 H8
Sandyacres Crs RTHW LS26 ......133 H8
Sandyacres Dr RTHW LS26 ......133 H8
Sandy Bank ROY/SHW OL2 ......229 H6
Sandy Bank Av RTHW LS26 ......133 H8
Sandy Banks BGLY BD16 ......80 C6
Sandy Beck WIL/AL BD15 ......103 J3
Sandybridge La CUD/GR S72 ......244 D5
Sandy Dyke La RPDN/SBR HX6 ......167 G6
Sandyfields Vw
AWLS/ASK DN6 ......249 K5
Sandyfoot GTL/HWG HX4 ......189 K2
Sandyforth La HWTH BD22 ......53 M4
Sandy Ga AL/HA/HU LS17 ......44 F7
HBR HX7 ......143 K3
HOLM/MEL HD9 ......254 C2
KGHY BD21 ......2 C2
Sandy Gate La FEA/AMT WF7 ......202 E3
Sandygate La HEM/SK/SE WF9 ......223 L1
Sandygate Ter BOW WF12 ......127 M1
Sandy Gv RTHW LS26 ......133 H8
Sandylands HUD HD4 ......213 M8
Sandy La HOR/CROF WF4 ......196 D5
HUDS HD4 ......213 J2
Sandy Lobby OT LS21 ......42 E8
Sandymoor WIL/AL BD15 ......103 J2
Sandy Wk BHP/TINH S16 ......64 B4
WKFDE WF1 ......12 C1
Sandy Wy YEA LS19 ......62 D7
Sandywood St KGHY BD21 ......3 J5
Sangster Wy WBOW BD5 ......127 J5
Santa Monica Crs IDLE BD10 ......83 J7
Santa Monica Gv IDLE BD10 ......83 J7
Santa Monica Rd IDLE BD10 ......83 J7
Santingley La HOR/CROF WF4 ......200 C8
Sanworth St TOD OL14 ......163 J1
Sapgate La CUL/QBY BD13 ......103 G8
Saplin St GIR BD8 ......104 D5
Sapphire St BTLY WF17 ......151 J8
Sarah Butterworth Ct
MILN * OL16 ......206 D7
Sarah Butterworth St
MILN OL16 ......206 D8
Sarah St EARD/LOFT WF3 ......153 M6

ROCH OL11 ......206 C8
Sardinia St MID LS10 ......9 J6
Saunders Cl HUDW HD3 ......191 L7
Saunderson Rd STKB/PEN S36 ......270 D2
Saunters Wy NORM WF6 ......178 C2
Savile Av CHAL LS7 ......7 J2
IDLE BD10 ......83 L8
KBTN HD8 ......217 M7
Savile Cl BRIG HD6 ......170 F3
Savile Ct MIRF * WF14 ......172 C8
Savile Crs HFAX HX1 ......10 F3
Savile Dr CHAL LS7 ......7 J2
HFAX HX1 ......10 E8
HOR/CROF WF4 ......197 J4
Savile Gln HFAX HX1 ......10 F3
Savile Gn EARL WF12 ......11 G8
Savile Gv EARL WF12 ......173 L7
Savile La BRIG HD6 ......170 F3
Savile Lea HFAX HX1 ......10 F8
Savile Ms EARL WF12 ......195 L1
Savile Mt CHAL LS7 ......7 J2
Savile Pde HFAX HX1 ......168 D1
Savile Pk HFAX HX1 ......168 C1
Savile Park Gdns HFAX HX1 ......168 D1
Savile Park Rd CLECK BD19 ......149 M3
HFAX HX1 ......10 E8
Savile Park St HFAX HX1 ......168 C1
Savile Park Ter HFAX * HX1 ......168 C1
Savile Pit La EARL WF12 ......174 C5
Savile Pl CHAL LS7 ......7 J2
MIRF WF14 ......172 C8
Savile Rd CAS WF10 ......157 L6
CHAL LS7 ......7 J2
EARL WF12 ......195 L1
ELL HX5 ......169 H4
HBR HX7 ......143 G3
HFAX HX1 ......10 F8
HUDW HD3 ......191 L6
RTHW LS26 ......156 F3
Savile Royd HFAX HX1 ......10 E9
Savile St BTLY WF17 ......173 M3
CLECK BD19 ......149 M5
DEWS WF13 ......173 L4
HUDW HD3 ......213 J1
KBTN HD8 ......217 M7
Savile Ter HFAX HX1 ......10 D9
Savile Wk CUD/GR S72 ......245 K3
Savile Wy ELL HX5 ......169 J6
Savile Ct EARD/LOFT WF3 ......154 E5
Savile Ct OT LS21 ......41 H7
Savile Crs CUD/GR S72 ......244 D7
KBTN * HD8 ......239 M5
OSS WF5 ......197 H2
WKFDW WF1 ......176 E7
Saville Ter BSLY * S70 ......261 G6
Savins Mill Wy KSTL LS5 ......108 C2
Sawley Av LIT OL15 ......185 J7
Sawley St KGHY BD21 ......2 E7
Saw Mill St BEE/HOL LS11 ......8 E3
Sawood La HUWTH BD22 ......101 H6
Sawrey Pl WBOW BD5 ......4 D8
Saw Wells La TAD LS24 ......116 A2
Sawyer St WHIT OL12 ......206 B5
Sawyers Garth ILK LS29 ......19 J6
Sawyer St WHIT OL12 ......206 B5
Saxon Av HEM/SK/SE WF9 ......246 B4
Saxon Cl HEM/SK/SE WF9 ......226 A7
KBTN HD8 ......217 L8
Saxon Ga AL/HA/HU LS17 ......87 K4
Saxon Gn AL/HA/HU LS17 ......87 J4
Saxon Gv AL/HA/HU LS17 ......87 J4
HEM/SK/SE WF9 ......246 B4
Saxon Mt AL/HA/HU LS17 ......87 K3
HEM/SK/SE WF9 ......246 B4
Saxon Rd AL/HA/HU LS17 ......87 J4
Saxon St CUD/GR S72 ......244 D7
GIR BD8 ......4 A4
HFAX HX1 ......10 A5
TOD OL14 ......163 J5
Saxon Wy CAS WF10 ......158 C6
Saxton Av WBSY BD6 ......126 B5
Saxton Ct GFTH/SHER LS25 ......113 H6
TAD LS24 ......93 K7
Saxton Gdns OSM * LS9 ......9 L1
Saxton La OSM LS9 ......9 L1
TAD LS24 ......93 K8
Saxton Pl HUDE HD5 ......215 J2
Saxton St LVSG WF15 ......172 E1
Sayers Cl KSTL LS5 ......108 C2
Sayle Av BOW BD4 ......127 K6
Sayner La MID LS10 ......9 J4
Sayner Rd MID LS10 ......9 J4
Scalebor Park Cl ILK LS29 ......40 A6
Scale Hl HUDN HD2 ......192 C4
OT LS21 ......42 D3
Scaley St BFDE BD3 ......105 M7
Scaly Ga HOLM/MEL HD9 ......255 J1
HOLM/MEL HD9 ......255 J1
Scammonden Rd
GTL/HWG HX4 ......189 H7
RPDN/SBR HX6 ......167 J8
Scape Vw MAR/SLWT HD7 ......213 G2
Scarborough Mdw MIRF * WF14 ......194 C1
Scarborough La
EARD/LOFT WF3 ......152 F6
Scarborough Rd SHPY BD18 ......82 C7
Scarborough St
EARD/LOFT WF3 ......152 F5
EARL WF12 ......173 M8
Scarborough Ter EARL WF12 ......173 M8
Scar Bottom La GTL/HWG HX4 ......168 B7
Scarbro' Jct BRAM LS13 ......107 M5
Scarcroft La SCFT LS14 ......67 M6
Scarfield Cl BSLYN/ROY S71 ......262 B6
Scarfold HOLM/MEL HD9 ......254 C1
Scargill Ct OSM LS9 ......110 B5
Scargill Gra OSM LS9 ......110 B5
Scar Gv HUDS HD4 ......214 B4
Scar Head Rd RPDN/SBR HX6 ......167 K4
Scar Hole La HOLM/MEL HD9 ......255 J2
Scarhouse La MAR/SLWT HD7 ......213 G2

Scar La BSLYN/ROY S71 ......262 B6
MAR/SLWT HD7 ......213 H2
Scarlet Hts CUL/QBY BD13 ......125 H5
Scarr Bottom Rd LUD/ILL HX2 ......168 B2
Scarr Dr WHIT OL12 ......206 B4
Scarr End La DEWS WF13 ......173 H4
EARL WF12 ......196 B1
Scarr End Vw DEWS WF13 ......173 H4
Scarr La ROY/SHW OL2 ......229 L7
Scarsdale La AL/HA/HU LS17 ......47 G8
Scarsdale Rdg AL/HA/HU LS17 ......47 G8
Scarth Av OSM LS9 ......110 C4
Scarthingwell Crs TAD LS24 ......93 K7
Scarthingwell La TAD LS24 ......93 K7
Scarth Ter EARD/LOFT WF3 ......155 K8
Scar Top GTL/HWG * HX4 ......168 B7
Scar Top La HUDS HD4 ......213 M8
Scar Top Rd HWTH BD22 ......77 H7
Scarwood Cl BGLY BD16 ......81 J2
Scatcherd Gv MOR LS27 ......152 B2
Scatcherd La MOR LS27 ......152 C1
Scatcherd Park Av MOR LS27 ......152 C1
Scawthorpe Ct PONT WF8 ......181 H5
Sceptone Gv CUD/GR S72 ......244 E3
Schofield Ct MOR * LS27 ......152 C2
Schofield Dr WMB/DAR S73 ......263 J8
Schofield Hall Rd LIT OL15 ......207 M5
Schofield La HUDE HD5 ......15 L8
Schofield Pl WMB/DAR S73 ......263 J8
Schofield Rd WMB/DAR S73 ......263 H8
Schofield St LIT OL15 ......185 L8
LIT OL15 ......185 M4
MILN OL16 ......229 J1
ROCH OL11 ......228 C2
Scholars Wk ECHL BD2 ......105 K3
Schole Av STKB/PEN S36 ......270 E3
Scholebrook La BOW BD4 ......128 E3
Schole Hill La STKB/PEN S36 ......270 F4
Scholemoor Av GTHN BD7 ......126 A1
Scholemoor La GTHN BD7 ......126 A1
Scholemoor Rd GTHN BD7 ......126 B1
Scholes La CLECK BD19 ......149 H6
GTL/HWG HX4 ......168 C5
HWTH BD22 ......78 B5
MSTN/BAR LS15 ......90 A6
Scholes Moor Rd
HOLM/MEL HD9 ......254 E5
Scholes Rd CAS WF10 ......158 F5
HOLM/MEL HD9 ......255 G2
HUDN HD2 ......192 C4
Scholes St WBOW BD5 ......126 F4
Scholey Av BRIG HD6 ......170 C6
Scholey Rd BRIG HD6 ......170 C6
Scholfield St TOD OL14 ......141 K8
School Av DEWS WF13 ......173 H5
HOR/CROF WF4 ......200 C4
LUD/ILL HX2 ......124 D7
RPDN/SBR HX6 ......189 G2
WOR/ARM LS12 ......107 M3
School Cote Brow LUD/ILL HX2 ......124 D8
School Crs DEWS WF13 ......173 H5
LUD/ILL HX2 ......124 D7
WKFDW/WTN WF2 ......197 M2
School Cft KNOT WF11 ......159 L6
RTHW LS26 ......133 G8
School Dr KNOT WF11 ......181 L1
Schoolgate MSTN/BAR LS15 ......91 G1
School Gn BHP/TINH S16 ......64 A4
BRIG HD6 ......170 C4
CUL/QBY BD13 ......103 J8
School Green Av
CUL/QBY BD13 ......103 H8
School Gv DEWS WF13 ......173 H5
School Hl CUD/GR S72 ......244 D7
HUDS HD4 ......213 J7
KBTN HD8 ......216 B8
WKFDW/WTN WF2 ......220 D2
School Houses HUDW * HD3 ......191 H6
School Land La HBR HX7 ......120 D3
School La AL/HA/HU LS17 ......66 D6
AL/HA/HU LS17 ......67 L1
BSPA/BRAM LS23 ......49 G7
CAS WF10 ......158 B8
CHAL LS7 ......87 L7
COL BB8 ......53 G8
DEWS WF13 ......173 H5
GFTH/SHER LS25 ......92 A7
GFTH/SHER LS25 ......138 A3
HDGY LS6 ......86 A6
HIPP HX3 ......169 J3
HOR/CROF WF4 ......197 J5
HOR/CROF WF4 ......222 D5
HUD HD1 ......14 A9
HUDE HD5 ......193 K7
HUDS HD4 ......214 B6
ILK LS29 ......19 G6
KBTN HD8 ......217 M7
KBTN HD8 ......239 J8
LUD/ILL HX2 ......124 B6
LVSG WF15 ......171 M4
MAR/SLWT HD7 ......190 D8
MAR/SLWT HD7 ......211 L8
MILN OL16 ......206 B7
MSTN/BAR LS15 ......111 J6
MSTN/BAR LS15 ......112 A7
PBR HG3 ......28 E3
TOD OL14 ......163 K1
WBY LS22 ......47 K6
WKFDW/WTN WF2 ......197 M3
School Ms MILN * OL16 ......229 K2
School Pl LM/WK * BD12 ......148 E2
School Rd HWTH BD22 ......2 A5
MAR/SLWT HD7 ......190 D8
PONT WF8 ......181 D7
WBY LS22 ......30 B8
WKFDW/WTN WF2 ......197 M3
School Sq BFDE BD3 ......105 M7
School St West HUDW HD3 ......191 K6

CLAY BD14 ......125 K2
CLECK BD19 ......149 H5
CUD/GR S72 ......244 D6
CUD/GR S72 ......263 M4
CUL/QBY BD13 ......79 M8
CUL/QBY * BD13 ......102 A6
DEWS WF13 ......194 F5
DOD/DAR S75 ......242 A5
DOD/DAR S75 ......242 E5
DOD/DAR S75 ......242 F3
EARD/LOFT WF5 ......174 F1
EARL WF12 ......173 L6
EARL WF12 ......174 D6
GTL/HWG HX4 ......168 D6
HBR HX7 ......143 J3
HEM/SK/SE WF9 ......225 M6
HFAX HX1 ......11 J7
HOLM/MEL HD9 ......236 B1
HOLM/MEL HD9 ......236 B1
HOLM/MEL HD9 ......254 C1
HUDE HD5 ......15 M8
LIT OL15 ......207 G2
LM/WK BD12 ......126 E8
LM/WK BD12 ......149 G2
LVSG WF15 ......172 A4
LVSG WF15 ......172 A4
MOR LS27 ......130 E6
MOR LS27 ......152 D2
OSS WF5 ......174 E5
PDSY/CALV LS28 ......106 F3
PDSY/CALV LS28 ......106 F8
WHIT * OL12 ......206 B5
WIL/AL BD15 ......102 L1
WMB/DAR S73 ......263 K8
School St West HUDW HD3 ......191 K6
School Vw HDGY LS6 ......109 G3
School Wk HWTH BD22 ......2 B5
School Yd SKP/WHF * BD23 ......16 C2
School Yard Vw HIPP * HX3 ......11 H2
Sconce La BAIL BD17 ......60 C6
Scopsley Gn EARL WF12 ......195 G6
Scopsley La EARL WF12 ......194 F5
Scorcher Hills La
AWLS/ASK DN6 ......249 H2
Score Cft KBTN HD8 ......239 J4
Score Hl HIPP HX3 ......147 J2
Scoresby St BFD BD1 ......5 H6
Scotchman Cl MOR LS27 ......152 B4
Scotchman La MOR LS27 ......152 A6
Scotchman Rd HTON BD9 ......104 B4
Scotgate Rd HOLM/MEL HD9 ......235 M2
Scotland Cl HORS LS18 ......85 K3
Scotland La HORS LS18 ......63 J7
Scotland Mill La BHP/TINH S16 ......87 H4
Scotland St CLECK BD19 ......150 C5
Scotland Wy HORS LS18 ......85 J2
Scotland Wood Rd
AL/HA/HU LS17 ......87 H4
Scott Av HECK WF16 ......150 F8
Scott Cl AIRE BD20 ......55 M1
HECK * WF16 ......173 G2
RTHW LS26 ......134 C5
Scott Dr HOR/CROF WF4 ......200 C4
Scott Gn MOR LS27 ......129 K6
Scott Green Crs MOR LS27 ......129 K6
Scott Green Dr MOR LS27 ......129 K6
Scott Green Gv MOR * LS27 ......129 K6
Scott Green Mt MOR LS27 ......129 K6
Scott Green Vw MOR LS27 ......129 K6
Scott Hall Av CHAL LS7 ......109 L2
Scott Hall Dr CHAL LS7 ......7 H2
Scott Hall Gn CHAL LS7 ......109 L1
Scott Hall Gv CHAL LS7 ......109 L1
Scott Hall Pl CHAL LS7 ......109 L1
Scott Hall Rd CHAL LS7 ......87 K8
Scott Hall Rw CHAL LS7 ......7 H1
Scott Hall Sq CHAL LS7 ......109 L1
Scott Hall St CHAL LS7 ......7 G1
Scott Hall Ter CHAL LS7 ......109 L1
Scott Hall Wk CHAL LS7 ......87 L8
Scott Hl KBTN HD8 ......240 B3
Scott La AIRE BD20 ......58 A4
CLECK BD19 ......149 M6
CLECK BD19 ......152 A3
WBY LS22 ......48 A1
Scott La West AIRE BD20 ......57 M4
Scott Ms WBY LS22 ......48 A1
Scotts Hill Cl SCFT LS14 ......90 B1
Scott St KGHY BD21 ......2 F4
PDSY/CALV LS28 ......107 L4
TOD OL14 ......163 J6
Scott V HUDN HD2 ......192 F3
Scott Wood La CHAL LS7 ......109 K1
Scotty Bank BRIG * HD6 ......170 C4
Scotty Croft La BRIG HD6 ......170 C4
Scout Bottom La HBR HX7 ......144 B6
Scout Cl HBR HX7 ......144 B6
Scout Hill Rd DEWS WF13 ......173 J8
Scout La MAR/SLWT HD7 ......211 K5
Scout Rd HBR HX7 ......144 A6
Scowcroft La ROY/SHW OL2 ......229 J4
Scrapers La TOD OL14 ......141 K6
Scriftain La WBY LS22 ......30 A5
Seacroft Av SCFT LS14 ......111 K1
Seacroft Cl SCFT LS14 ......111 K1
Seacroft Crs SCFT LS14 ......111 K1
Seacroft Ga SCFT * LS14 ......111 K1
Seaforth Av OSM LS9 ......110 C3
Seaforth Gn OSM LS9 ......110 C3
Seaforth Mt OSM LS9 ......110 C3
Seaforth Pl OSM LS9 ......110 C3
Seaforth Rd OSM LS9 ......110 C3
Seaforth Ter OSM LS9 ......110 C3
Seagrave Rd HUDS HD4 ......213 L3
Seaton St BFDE BD3 ......6 A4
Seckar La HOR/CROF WF4 ......220 C4
Secker St WKFDW/WTN WF2 ......12 D8
Second Av AL/HA/HU LS17 ......68 A1
BFDE BD3 ......105 L5
HEM/SK/SE WF9 ......223 J2
HEM/SK/SE WF9 ......225 M6
HEM/SK/SE WF9 ......246 B5
HIPP HX3 ......168 D2
HOR/CROF WF4 ......197 H5
HUDE HD5 ......193 H7
KGHY BD21 ......2 E7

LVSG WF15 ....171 K2
RTHW LS26 ....133 H7
WBY LS22 ....48 B1
WKFDE WF1 ....176 D4
WOR/ARM LS12 ....109 G7
YEA LS19 ....84 E1
Second St LM/WK BD12 ..127 G8
Sedan St HFAX * HX1 ......11 C7
Sedbergh Cl MSTN/BAR LS15 ..110 F7
Sedbergh Dr ILK LS29 .....38 E3
Sedbergh Pk ILK LS29 .....38 E3
Sedburgh Rd HIPP HX3 ....11 J9
Sedge Gv HWTH BD22 .....78 E6
Sedge Ri TAD LS24 ....71 J4
Sedgewick St BTLY WF17 ..151 G5
Sedgley Av MILN OL16 .....228 D2
Sedgwick Cl GIR BD8 ....4 C4
Seed Hill Ter LM/ILL HX2 ..123 L8
Seed St LM/WK BD12 ......126 F8
Sefton Av BEE/HOL LS11 ...131 J3
   BRIG HD6 ....170 B1
Sefton Ct HDGY LS6 ....86 F8
Sefton Crs BRIG HD6 ....170 B1
   ILK LS29 ....38 D3
Sefton Dr BRIG HD6 ....170 B1
Sefton Gv ECHL BD2 ....105 K3
Sefton La HOLM/MEL HD9 ..234 F4
Sefton Pl KGHY BD21 ....3 G3
Sefton Ri EARL WF12 ....195 M2
Sefton St BEE/HOL LS11 ....131 J3
   COL BB8 ....74 B1
   HFAX HX1 ....10 D4
   KGHY BD21 ....3 G2
   ROCH OL11 ....228 A1
Sefton Ter BEE/HOL LS11 ..131 J3
   HFAX HX1 ....10 D4
Selborne Gv HTON BD9 ....104 D3
   KGHY BD21 ....2 D8
Selborne Mt HTON BD9 ....104 E4
Selborne Ter HTON BD9 ....104 D4
   SHPY BD18 ....82 D8
Selborne Vls CLAY BD14 ...125 L3
   HTON BD9 ....104 D4
Selbourne Av EARL WF12 ..173 L8
Selbourne Cl DOD/DAR S75 ..260 A1
Selbourne Dr EARL WF12 ..195 L1
Selbourne Rd EARL WF12 ..195 L1
Selby Av OSM LS9 ....111 G6
Selby Cl MILN OL16 ....207 G8
Selby Rd BSLYN/ROY * S71 ..243 H7
   GFTH/SHER LS25 ....134 F1
   MSTN/BAR LS15 ....112 C8
   SCFT LS14 ....110 F5
Selby St MILN OL16 ....206 D6
   WKFDE WF1 ....176 E7
Seldon St WBOW BD5 .....126 D3
Selene Cl CLECK BD19 .....150 E4
Sellars Fold GTHN * BD7 ..126 C2
Sellerdale Av LM/WK BD12 ..148 F4
Sellerdale Dr LM/WK BD12 ..148 F4
Sellerdale Ri LM/WK BD12 ..148 F4
Sellerdale Wy LM/WK BD12 ..148 F5
Selso Rd EARL WF12 ....174 B5
Seminary St LDSU LS2 ....6 D6
Semon Av ECHL BD2 ....105 H1
Senior St DEWS WF13 ......173 K7
Senior Wy WBOW BD5 ....4 E8
   HUDE HD5 ....15 M8
Sennen Cft BSLYN/ROY S71 ..261 K3
Sentry HOLM/MEL HD9 ....236 B1
Sergeantson St HUD HD1 ...14 F7
Serpentine Rd CLECK BD19 ..149 M6
Servia Dr CHAL LS7 ....6 F3
Servia Gdns CHAL LS7 ....7 G3
Servia Hl CHAL LS7 ....6 F3
Servia Rd HDCY LS6 ....6 F3
Service Rd OSM LS9 ....14 E4
Sessions House Yd PONT WF8 ..180 E5
Seth Ter BSLY S70 ....261 J6
Sevenoaks Md WIL/AL BD15 ..103 K5
Seventh Av LVSG WF15 .....171 K1
   RTHW LS26 ....133 J8
Severn Dr GFTH/SHER LS25 ..135 K1
   MILN OL16 ....207 J8
Severn Rd ECHL BD2 ....105 J4
   MID LS10 ....132 B3
Severn Wy MID LS10 ....132 B2
Sewage Works Rd OSM LS9 ..132 G3
Sewell Rd BFDE BD3 ....5 M7
Sewerbridge La FEA/AMT WF7 ..179 H5
Seymour Gv MILN OL16 ....228 D3
Seymour St BFDE BD3 ....5 K7
   WKFDW/WTN WF2 ....12 C1
Seymour Wk HOLM/MEL HD9 ..235 G4
Shackleton St TOD OL14 ...140 F4
Shackleton Vw STKB/PEN S36 ..270 F4
Shade St TOD OL14 ....163 J3
Shadwell La AL/HA/HU LS17 ..87 M4
Shadwell Park Av
   AL/HA/HU LS17 ....88 E1
Shadwell Park Cl
   AL/HA/HU LS17 ....88 E1
Shadwell Park Ct
   AL/HA/HU LS17 ....88 E2
Shadwell Park Dr
   AL/HA/HU LS17 ....88 E2
Shadwell Park Gdns
   AL/HA/HU LS17 ....88 E1
Shadwell Park Gv
   AL/HA/HU LS17 ....88 E2
Shadwell Wk AL/HA/HU LS17 ..88 A3
Shady La AIRE BD20 ....34 B3
Shaftesbury Av BRIG HD6 ..170 D7
   GLE DN14 ....183 H1
   HTON BD9 ....103 M4
   LIT OL15 ....207 H4
   RHAY LS8 ....88 C5
   SHPY BD18 ....82 E7
Shaftesbury Dr WHIT OL12 ..184 F8
Shaftesbury Pde OSM * LS9 ..110 E5
Shaftesbury Rd RHAY LS8 ..88 C4
Shaftesbury St BSLY S70 ..261 M6
Shafton Hall Dr CUD/GR S72 ..244 D3
Shafton La BEE/HOL LS11 ....8 B6
Shafton Pl BEE/HOL LS11 .....8 B6
Shafton St BEE/HOL LS11 ....8 C6
Shafton Vw BEE/HOL LS11...8 B6

Shakespeare Ap OSM LS9 ..110 B5
Shakespeare Av
   AWLS/ASK DN6 ....227 L4
   NORM WF6 ....178 C7
   OSM LS9 ....110 B5
   TOD OL14 ....141 M8
Shakespeare Cl LIT OL15 ..185 L5
   OSM LS9 ....110 B5
Shakespeare Ct OSM LS9 ..110 B5
Shakespeare Crs CAS WF10 ..180 F1
Shakespeare Gdns OSM LS9 ..110 B5
Shakespeare Gra OSM LS9 ..110 B5
Shakespeare Lawn OSM LS9 ..110 B5
Shakespeare Rd GSLY LS20 ..62 A6
Shakespeare St HFAX HX1 ..11 H7
   OSM LS9 ....110 B4
Shakespeare Towers OSM LS9 ..110 B4
Shalimar St HFAX HX1 ......10 A5
The Shambles WBY LS22 ....48 A1
Shambles St BSLY S70 .....261 C5
Shann Av KGHY BD21 ....2 B3
Shann Crs KGHY BD21 ....2 B3
Shann La KGHY BD21 ....2 B3
Shannon Cl BRIG HD6 ......170 A7
Shannon Dr HUDW HD3 ....190 F5
Shannon Rd BRIG HD6 .....170 A7
   OSM * LS9 ....7 M9
Shannon St OSM LS9 ....7 L9
Shann St SHPY BD18 ....104 F2
Shapla Cl HUDN HD2 ....2 C6
Share Hl MAR/SLWT HD7 ..212 E9
Sharp Av WBSY BD6 ....126 E6
Sharpe St BFD BD1 ....4 E8
   HECK WF16 ....172 F3
Sharphaw Av SKP/WHF BD23 ..16 C4
Sharp House Rd MID LS10 ..154 A2
Sharp La HUDS HD4 ....215 H5
   MID LS10 ....154 A1
Sharp Ms HDGY LS6 ....109 H1
Sharp Rw PDSY/CALV LS28 ..107 H8
Sharp Royd HUDE HD5 .....215 J3
Sharp St DEWS WF13 ......173 M6
   WBSY BD6 ....126 E5
Shaw Av NORM WF6 ....178 E4
Shaw Barn Cft WBY LS22 ....47 L1
Shaw Barn La WBY LS22 ....47 L1
Shaw Booth La LUD/ILL HX2 ..145 H2
Shaw Cl GFTH/SHER LS25 ..135 J1
   GTL/HWG HX4 ....190 D2
   NORM WF6 ....178 E4
Shawfield Av HOLM/MEL HD9 ..253 M2
Shawfield Rd BSLYN/ROY S71 ..243 L8
Shaw Fields La MAR/SLWT HD7 ..211 L6
Shaw Fold WKFDW/WTN WF2 ..199 C5
Shaw Ga MAR/SLWT HD7 ..212 A8
Shaw Hl HFAX HX1 ....11 J9
Shaw Hill La HIPP HX3 ......11 J9
Shaw La BSLY S70 ....260 E5
   BSLYN/ROY S71 ....244 A5
   DOD/DAR S75 ....244 A5
   ELL HX5 ....169 L7
   GSLY LS20 ....62 B5
   GTL/HWG HX4 ....190 D2
   HDGY LS6 ....86 F8
   HIPP HX3 ....125 H8
   HIPP HX3 ....168 F2
   HOLM/MEL HD9 ....253 M2
   HUDS HD4 ....213 K2
   HUDW HD3 ....190 E6
   KGHY BD21 ....79 M3
   MAR/SLWT HD7 ....190 D7
   MAR/SLWT HD7 ....211 J3
   MILN OL16 ....207 H5
   PBR HG3 ....25 K3
   PBR HG3 ....28 D2
   RPDN/SBR HX6 ....167 L5
   RPDN/SBR HX6 ....188 E4
   TOD OL14 ....140 D3
Shaw Lane Gdns GSLY LS20 ..62 B5
Shaw Leys YEA LS19 ....62 C6
Shaw Ri NORM * WF6 ......178 E4
Shaw Rd MILN OL16 ....229 K3
   MILN OL16 ....207 J8
Shaw Royd YEA LS19 ....62 C6
Shaws La MSTN/BAR LS15 ...90 E8
   RPDN/SBR HX6 ....166 C5
Shaw St BSLY S70 ....260 F6
   CLECK * BD19 ....149 K7
   GTL/HWG HX4 ....190 D2
   LM/WK BD12 ....148 F4
   MIRF WF14 ....194 C1
   WHIT OL12 ....206 D4
Shaw Wood Rd TOD OL14 ..142 B8
Shay Cl HTON BD9 ....104 A2
Shay Ct HOR/CROF WF4 ...200 A5
   LDSU LS2 ....6 E3
Shay Crs HTON BD9 ....104 A2
Shay Dr HTON BD9 ....104 A2
Shayfield La EARD/LOFT WF3 ..154 F3
Shay Fold HTON BD9 ....104 A2
Shay Gap Rd HWTH * BD22 ..56 E7
Shay Ga WIL/AL * BD15 ....103 C2
Shay Gra HTON BD9 ....104 A1
Shay Gv HTON BD9 ....104 A2
Shay La HOLM/MEL HD9 ...253 G3
   HOR/CROF WF4 ....199 M5
   HTON BD9 ....104 A1
   LUD/ILL HX2 ....146 C2
   WIL/AL BD15 ....103 C2
Shay St HDGY LS6 ....6 E3
Shay Syke HFAX HX1 ....11 H8
Sheaf Cl BSLY S70 ....261 M7
Sheaf St MID LS10 ....9 J3
Shearbridge Gn GTHN BD7 ....4 A7
Shearbridge Pl GTHN BD7 ....4 A7
Shearbridge St GTHN BD7 ....4 B9
Sheardale HOLM/MEL HD9 ..236 A4
Shearing Cross Gdns HUD HD1 ..15 G2
Shed St KGHY BD21 ....3 G4
Sheep Hill La CUL/QBY BD13 ..125 K4
Sheepridge Gv HUDN HD2 ..192 G5
Sheepridge Rd HUDN HD2 ..192 G5
Sheepscar Gv CHAL LS7 ......7 J6
Sheepscar St North CHAL LS7 ..7 H2
Sheepscar St South CHAL LS7 ..7 K5
Sheepscar Wy CHAL LS7 .....7 J3
Sheep St SKP/WHF BD23 ....16 B2

Sheepwalk La CAS WF10 ...158 F8
   HEM/SK/SE WF9 ....226 A6
Sheerien Cl BSLYN/ROY S71 ..243 G6
Sheffield Rd BSLY S70 .....261 H6
   HOLM/MEL HD9 ....255 C1
   STKB/PEN S36 ....271 H4
Sheldon Rdg BOW BD4 .....127 K7
Sheldrake Av GIR BD8 ......103 L7
Sheldrake Rd CAS WF10 ...157 M8
Shelf Hall La HIPP HX3 .....147 K1
Shelf Moor HIPP HX3 ....125 L7
Shelf Moor Rd HIPP HX3 ..125 L7
Shelf Rd HBR HX7 ....143 H3
Shelldrake Dr MID LS10 ...153 M1
Shelley Av HECK * WF16 ...173 G4
   STKB/PEN S36 ....270 F2
Shelley Cl RTHW LS26 .....155 L3
   STKB/PEN S36 ....270 F2
Shelley Ct BGLY BD16 ....81 J3
   HOR/CROF WF4 ....197 L4
Shelley Crs RTHW LS26 ....155 L3
   KNOT WF11 ....181 K2
Shelley Dr BSLYN/ROY S71 ..261 K3
Shelley Gv GIR BD8 ....104 A6
Shelley La KBTN HD8 ....238 C1
Shelley Woodhouse La
   KBTN HD8 ....238 F4
Shell La PDSY/CALV LS28 ..106 D2
Shepcote Cl BHP/TINH LS16 ..86 B3
Shepcote Crs BHP/TINH LS16 ..86 B3
Shepherd La STKB/PEN * S36 ..261 M6
Shepherds Gv HUDN HD2 ..193 G3
   RHAY LS8 ....7 M1
Shepherd's La CHAL LS7 ..110 A2
   RHAY LS8 ....7 M1
Shepherds Pl RHAY * LS8 ..110 B2
Shepherds Thorn La
   HUDN HD2 ....170 E8
Shepherd St WHIT * OL12 ..206 B2
Shepherds Wy MILN OL16 ..229 G1
Shepley Mt MIRF WF14 .....172 D7
Shepley Rd HUDS HD4 .....237 L4
Shepley St WKFDE WF1 .....13 L1
Shepstye Rd HOR/CROF WF4 ..197 J6
Sherborne Cl HWTH BD22 ..79 G1
Sherborne Rd GTHN BD7 ....4 B8
   IDLE BD10 ....83 K5
Sherbrooke Av
   MSTN/BAR LS15 ....111 H7
Sherburn Ap SCFT LS14 .....89 L8
Sherburn Cl AWLS/ASK DN6 ..249 G4
   BIRK/DRI BD11 ....128 D8
Sherburn Gv BIRK/DRI BD11 ..128 D8
Sherburn Pl SCFT LS14 .....89 L8
Sherburn Rd BRIG HD6 .....169 M8
   BSLYN/ROY S71 ....243 G7
   SCFT LS14 ....89 L8
Sherburn Rd North SCFT LS14 ..89 K6
Sheridan Cl PDSY/CALV LS28 ..107 H8
Sheridan Ct BSLYN/ROY S71 ..261 K3
   PDSY/CALV * LS28 ....107 H8
Sheridan St BOW BD4 ......127 J2
   WKFDE WF1 ....176 F1
Sheridan Wy PDSY/CALV LS28 ..107 G8
Sheriff La BGLY BD16 ....81 L2
Sheriff St MILN OL16 ....229 J1
   WHIT OL12 ....206 B1
Sherwell Av WIL/AL BD15 ..103 L5
Sherwell Ri WIL/AL BD15 ..103 L5
Sherwood Av CLECK BD19 ..150 D6
   HUDN HD2 ....193 H1
Sherwood Cl AWLS/ASK DN6 ..227 L5
   BGLY BD16 ....81 L1
   CLECK * BD19 ....150 D6
   DEWS WF13 ....173 H3
Sherwood Dr AWLS/ASK DN6 ..249 G4
   HUDS HD4 ....213 L8
   WKFDW/WTN WF2 ....220 B1
Sherwood Gdns
   EARD/LOFT * WF3 ....154 D4
Sherwood Gn EARD/LOFT WF3 ..154 D4
   WKFDW/WTN WF2 ....197 M2
Sherwood Pl ECHL BD2 .....105 K4
Sherwood Rd BRIG HD6 ....170 E4
Sherwood St BSLYN/ROY S71 ..261 H5
Sherwood Wy CUD/GR S72 ..244 C5
   ROY/SHW OL2 ....229 G6
Shetcliffe La BOW BD4 .....127 L6
Shetcliffe Rd BOW BD4 ....127 K6
Shetland Cl ECHL BD2 ......105 H2
Shibden Dr BTLY WF17 .....151 L8
Shibden Garth HIPP HX3 ...147 H6
Shibden Grange Dr HIPP HX3 ..147 H5
Shibden Hall Cft HIPP HX3 ..147 H6
Shibden Hall Rd HIPP HX3 ..147 H6
Shibden Head La
   CUL/QBY BD13 ....124 E7
Shibden Vw CUL/QBY BD13 ..124 F7
Shield Cl MSTN/BAR LS15 ..112 A3
Shield Hall La RPDN/SBR HX6 ..166 C2
Shill Bank Av MIRF WF14 ..172 E8
Shill Bank La MIRF WF14 ..172 E8
Shillbank Vw MIRF WF14 ..172 E8
Shilling St WKFDE WF1 .....176 F1
Shipley Airedale Rd BFDE BD3 ..5 G3
Shipley Fields Rd SHPY BD18 ..104 D1
Ship St BRIG HD6 ....170 C4
Shipton Ms MOR LS27 ......152 D3
Ship Yd WKFDE WF1 ....13 G4
Shirburn ROCH * OL11 .....206 A8
Shire Cl WBSY BD6 ....126 B7
Shire Oak Rd HDGY LS6 ....109 G1
Shire Oak St HDGY LS6 ....108 F1
Shires Gv EARD/LOFT WF3 ..177 H1
Shires Hl HUD HD1 ....14 B9
Shirland Av BSLYN/ROY S71 ..243 J3
Shirley Av CLECK BD19 .....150 D6
   LM/WK BD12 ....148 D5
Shirley Cl OT LS21 ....41 K6
Shirley Crs LM/WK BD12 ..148 D5
Shirley Dr BRAM LS13 ......107 L2
Shirley Gv CLECK BD19 ....150 D6
   HIPP HX3 ....148 D5
Shirley Mt CLECK BD19 ....150 D6
Shirley Pde CLECK BD19 ..150 C6

Shirley Pl CLECK BD19 .....150 C6
   LM/WK BD12 ....148 E5
Shirley Rd BOW BD4 ....127 M5
   CLECK BD19 ....150 D6
   HIPP HX3 ....104 D8
Shirley St HWTH BD22 ......78 D7
   SHPY BD18 ....82 B6
Shirley Ter CLECK BD19 ...150 D6
Shirley Wk CLECK BD19 ...150 D6
Shoebridge Av AIRE BD20 ..35 H8
Shoebroad La TOD OL14 ...163 K2
Shoe Market PONT WF8 ...180 E6
Sholebroke Av CHAL LS7 ..109 M2
Sholebroke Mt CHAL LS7 ..109 L2
Sholebroke Pl CHAL LS7 ..109 M2
Sholebroke St CHAL LS7 ..109 L2
Sholebroke Ter CHAL LS7 ..109 M1
Sholebroke Vw CHAL LS7 ..109 M2
Shoolaboards La PONT WF8 ..181 H6
Shop La EARD/LOFT WF3 ..154 D6
   HUDE HD5 ....193 L5
   HWTH BD22 ....54 D1
Shore End La HBR HX7 .....122 C7
Shorefield Cl MILN OL16 ..207 H7
Shore Fold LIT OL15 ....185 H8
Shore Gn TOD OL14 ....140 E4
Shore Hall La STKB/PEN S36 ..270 A4
Shoreham Rd WOR/ARM LS12 ..108 E8
Shore Hl LIT OL15 ....185 L8
Shore Lea LIT OL15 ....185 H8
Shore Mt LIT OL15 ....185 H8
Shore New Rd TOD OL14 ..140 D4
Shore Rd LIT OL15 ....185 H7
Shore St HUDE HD5 ....207 H8
Shortbank Cl SKP/WHF BD23 ..16 D3
Shortbank Rd SKP/WHF BD23 ..16 C2
Short Cl LM/WK BD12 ......148 D1
Shortfield Ct BSLYN/ROY S71 ..243 G6
Short La CHAL * LS7 ....87 L7
Short Rw EARL WF12 ....174 C7
   FEA/AMT WF7 ....201 L1
Shortway CUL/QBY BD13 ..103 J8
   PDSY/CALV LS28 ....106 C5
Showfield Cl GFTH/SHER LS25 ..116 A4
Shrewsbury Cl STKB/PEN S36 ..270 F3
Shrewsbury Rd STKB/PEN S36 ..270 F3
Shroggs Head Cl
   WMB/DAR S73 ....263 K8
Shroggs Rd HFAX HX1 ....10 D3
Shroggs St HFAX HX1 ....10 D4
Shroggs Vue Ter HFAX HX1 ..10 D4
The Shutt HOR/CROF WF4 ..197 K6
Shuttle Eye Wy
   HOR/CROF WF4 ....217 G2
Shuttleworth La GIR BD8 ..103 M6
Shuttocks Cl GFTH/SHER LS25 ..135 J3
Shuttocks Fold
   GFTH/SHER LS25 ....135 K3
Shutts La HIPP HX3 ....148 A3
Sickleholme Ct HUDN HD2 ..193 G3
Sickle St CLECK BD19 ......150 D6
Sicklinghall Rd WBY LS22 ...47 H1
Sidcop Rd CUD/GR S72 .....244 D5
Siddal Gv HIPP HX3 ....168 F2
Siddal La HIPP HX3 ....169 G3
Siddal St BEE/HOL LS11 .....8 E4
Siddal New Rd HIPP HX3 ..168 F1
Siddal Top La HIPP HX3 ...169 G3
Siddal Vw HIPP HX3 ....169 G2
Side Copse OT LS21 ....41 K6
Side La HUDW HD3 ....191 H8
Sides Rd PONT WF8 ....180 F8
Sidgwick Ct SKP/WHF BD23 ..16 D3
The Sidings GSLY LS20 ......61 M5
   SHPY * BD18 ....82 E6
Sidney St LDS LS1 ....7 H9
Siegen Cl MOR LS27 ....152 C2
Siena Cl WMB/DAR S73 ....263 G2
Siggett La TOD OL14 ....141 H8
Sigott St HUDW HD3 ....191 H8
Sike Cl DOD/DAR S75 ......241 G5
Sike La HOLM/MEL HD9 ....254 F1
   STKB/PEN S36 ....270 C5
   WKFDW/WTN WF2 ....221 K1
Sikes Cl HUDE HD5 ....215 H3
Silcoates Av WKFDW/WTN WF2 ..176 A6
Silcoates Cl WKFDW/WTN WF2 ..176 A5
Silcoates Dr WKFDW/WTN WF2 ..176 A5
Silcoates La WKFDW/WTN WF2 ..175 M5
Silcoates St WKFDW/WTN WF2 ..176 B6
Silk Mill Ap BHP/TINH LS16 ..86 A4
Silk Mill Av BHP/TINH LS16 ..85 M3
Silk Mill Bank BHP/TINH LS16 ..85 M3
Silk Mill Cl BHP/TINH LS16 ..86 A4
Silk Mill Dr BHP/TINH LS16 ..85 M3
Silk Mill Gdns BHP/TINH LS16 ..85 M4
Silk Mill Gn BHP/TINH LS16 ..86 A4
Silk Mill Ms BHP/TINH LS16 ..86 A4
Silk Mill Rd BHP/TINH LS16 ..85 M4
Silk Mill Wy BHP/TINH LS16 ..86 A4
Silkstone Cl GFTH/SHER LS25 ..113 K5
Silkstone Crs NORM * WF6 ..178 B2
   WKFDW/WTN WF2 ....198 E8
Silkstone La DOD/DAR S75 ..259 H4
Silkstone Wy MSTN/BAR LS15 ..111 L5
Silk St HTON BD9 ....104 C4
Silsden Br AIRE BD20 ....35 M7
Silsden Rd AIRE BD20 ....34 F1
   AIRE BD20 ....58 B2
   ILK LS29 ....18 D7
Silson La BAIL BD17 ....83 G2
Silver Birch Av LM/WK BD12 ..148 A5
Silver Birch Cl LM/WK BD12 ..148 F4
Silver Birch Dr LM/WK BD12 ..148 F4
Silver Birch Gv LM/WK BD12 ..148 F4
Silverdale Av AIRE BD20 ....58 A5
   AL/HA/HU LS17 ....88 D1
   GSLY LS20 ....62 A6
Silverdale Cl GSLY LS20 .....62 A7
Silverdale Dr BSLYN/ROY S71 ..261 M1
   GSLY LS20 ....62 A6
Silverdale Gra GSLY LS20 ..62 A7
Silverdale Gv GSLY LS20 ....61 M7
Silverdale Mt GSLY LS20 ....62 A7

Silverdale Rd GSLY LS20 ....61 M7
   WBOW BD5 ....127 C6
Silver Hl MILN OL16 ....207 H1
Silverhill Dr BFDE BD3 ....105 M4
Silverhill Rd BFDE BD3 ....105 L3
Silver La YEA LS19 ....62 D7
Silver Royd Av WOR/ARM LS12 ..108 B8
Silver Royd Cl WOR/ARM LS12 ..108 B8
Silver Royd Garth
   WOR/ARM LS12 ....108 B8
Silver Royd Gv WOR/ARM LS12 ..108 B8
Silver Royd Hl WOR/ARM LS12 ..108 B8
Silver Royd Pl WOR/ARM LS12 ..108 B8
Silver Royd Rd WOR/ARM LS12 ..108 B8
Silver Royd St WOR/ARM LS12 ..108 B8
Silver Royd Ter
   WOR/ARM LS12 ....108 B8
Silverstone Av CUD/GR S72 ..244 E5
Silver St BEE/HOL LS11 ....8 D
   BSLY S70 ....261 G
   DOD/DAR S75 ....260 B
   GIR BD8 ....104 D
   HFAX HX1 ....11 G
   HUD HD1 ....15 K
   KNOT WF11 ....159 J
   TOD OL14 ....163 J
   WKFDE WF1 ....12 E
   WHIT OL12 ....176 D
Silver St East HUD HD1 .....15 K
Silver St West HUD HD1 ....15 K
Silverwood Av LUD/ILL HX2 ..145 L
Silwood Dr ECHL BD2 ......105 L
Simbach Cl SKP/WHF BD23 ..16 D
Simeon St TOD OL14 ....163 J
Simes St BFD BD1 ....4 D
Simm Carr La HIPP HX3 ...146 F
Simmonds La HFAX HX1 .....11 J
Simmons Ct OSM LS9 ......110 B
Simmons Wy RHAY LS8 ....110 D
Simms Dene WIL/AL BD15 ..103 J
Simon Cl BOW BD4 ....128 B
Simon Green Rd
   MAR/SLWT HD7 ....212 D
Simon St MILN OL16 ....207 H
Simpson Gv IDLE BD10 ......83 L
   WOR/ARM LS12 ....108 F
Simpson Rd HBR HX7 ......247 M
   HEM/SK/SE WF9 ....247 K
Simpsons La KNOT WF11 ..181 M
Simpson St EARD/LOFT WF3 ..154 A
   HIPP HX3 ....146 D
   KGHY BD21 ....3 K
Sim Royd La STKB/PEN S36 ..257 M
Sinclair Garth
   WKFDW/WTN WF2 ....199 G
Sinclair Rd ECHL BD2 ......105 H
Sinden Ms IDLE BD10 ....83 K
Singleton St BFD BD1 ....4 F
Sion Hl HIPP HX3 ....169 G
Sir George Martin Dr
   BHP/TINH LS16 ....86 F
Sir Isaac Holden Pl GTHN BD7 ..104 D
Sir John's La GFTH/SHER LS25 ..115 M
Sir Karl Cohen Sq
   WOR/ARM LS12 ....108 D
Sir Wilfred Pl IDLE * BD10 ..83 K
Siskin Ct MOR LS27 ....152 C
Sisley La TOD OL14 ....164 C
Sissons Av MID LS10 ....153 K
Sissons Crs MID LS10 ......153 K
Sissons Dr MID LS10 ....153 K
Sissons Gn MID LS10 ......153 K
Sissons Gv MID LS10 ......153 K
Sissons La MID LS10 ....153 K
Sissons Mt MID LS10 ......153 K
Sissons Pl MID LS10 ....153 K
Sissons Rd MID LS10 ......153 K
Sissons Rw MID LS10 ......153 K
Sissons St MID LS10 ....153 K
Sissons Ter MID LS10 .....153 K
Sissons Vw MID LS10 ......153 K
Sitka Cl BSLYN/ROY S71 ..243 K
Siward St HEM/SK/SE WF9 ..223 J
Sixroad La AWLS/ASK DN6 ..249 J
Sixth Av BFDE BD3 ....105 L
   LVSG WF15 ....171 K
   RTHW LS26 ....133 J
Sizers Ct YEA LS19 ....84 C
Skelbrooke Dr PONT WF8 ..202 F
Skelda Ri ILK LS29 ....24 A
Skelf St TAD LS24 ....95 G
Skellow Hall Gdns
   AWLS/ASK DN6 ....249 H
Skellow Rd AWLS/ASK DN6 ..249 J
Skelton Av DOD/DAR S75 ..242 D
   OSM LS9 ....110 D
Skelton Crs HUDS HD4 .....213 K
   OSM LS9 ....110 D
Skelton Grange Rd MID LS10 ..132 D
Skelton Mt OSM LS9 ....110 D
Skelton Pl OSM LS9 ....110 D
Skelton Rd OSM LS9 ....110 D
Skeltons La SCFT LS14 ......89 K
Skelton St COL BB8 ....74 A
   OSM LS9 ....110 D
Skelton Ter OSM LS9 ....110 D
Skelton Wk IDLE BD10 ......83 M
Skelwith Ap SCFT LS14 .....111 J
Skibeden Ct SKP/WHF * BD23 ..16 D
Skinner La GIR BD8 ....104 C
   LDSU LS2 ....7 K
   PONT WF8 ....180 F
Skinner St LDS LS1 ....6 F
Skinpit La STKB/PEN S36 ..258 D
Skipton Av HUDN HD2 .....192 D
Skipton New Rd COL BB8 ...52 A
   COL BB8 ....52 A
Skipton Old Rd COL BB8 ....52 A
   COL BB8 ....52 A
Skipton Ri GFTH/SHER LS25 ..113 K
Skipton Rd AIRE BD20 ....16 E
   AIRE BD20 ....16 E
   AIRE BD20 ....34 E
   AIRE BD20 ....34 G
   AIRE BD20 ....35 H
   COL BB8 ....52 A
   COL BB8 ....52 A

ILK LS29 ... 18 F5
ILK LS29 ... 37 M1
KCHY BD21 ... 3 G1
SKP/WHF BD23 ... 16 D1
Skipton St BTLY WF17 ... 173 L4
Skircoat Gn HIPP HX3 ... 168 E4
Skircoat Green Rd HIPP HX3 ... 168 E4
Skircoat Moor Cl LUD/ILL * HX2 ... 168 C2
Skircoat Moor Rd LUD/ILL HX2 ... 168 C2
Skircoat Rd HFAX HX1 ... 11 H9
Skirrow St BGLY BD16 ... 81 K8
Skye Rd HTON BD9 ... 104 C3
Skye Vw RTHW LS26 ... 155 H1
Slack Bottom Rd WBSY BD6 ... 126 C6
Slackcote La UPML OL3 ... 230 E7
Slack Ga WHIT OL12 ... 184 A6
Slack Gate La UPML OL3 ... 230 F6
Slack House La HBR HX7 ... 121 K8
Slack La CUD/GR S72 ... 244 D1
GTL/HWG HX4 ... 189 J3
HBR HX7 ... 144 D2
HOLM/MEL HD9 ... 254 D2
HOR/CROF WF4 ... 200 B6
HUDW HD3 ... 190 C6
HWTH BD22 ... 78 D3
RPDN/SBR HX6 ... 166 B5
RPDN/SBR HX6 ... 188 B1
UPML OL3 ... 230 F8
WKFDW/WTN WF2 ... 220 D2
Slacks La MAR/SLWT HD7 ... 211 J6
MAR/SLWT HD7 ... 234 A1
Slack St MILN OL16 ... 206 C7
Slack Top La HOLM/MEL HD9 ... 255 L5
Slade Cl BSPA/BRAM LS23 ... 48 F7
Slade La AIRE BD20 ... 58 A4
BRIG HD6 ... 170 B8
Sladen St KGHY BD21 ... 2 D5
WHIT OL12 ... 206 B9
Slades La HOLM/MEL HD9 ... 235 G2
Slades Rd MAR/SLWT HD7 ... 212 D2
Slade Wk BTLY WF17 ... 151 H5
Slaidburn Cl MILN OL16 ... 229 H1
Slaithwaite Av EARL WF12 ... 195 L2
Slaithwaite Cl EARL WF12 ... 195 L2
Slaithwaite Ga MAR/SLWT HD7 ... 212 D2
Slaithwaite Rd EARL WF12 ... 195 M2
HOLM/MEL HD9 ... 234 D2
Slant La KBTN HD8 ... 216 A7
MAR/SLWT HD7 ... 213 G4
STKB/PEN S36 ... 269 M2
Slater Av HBR HX7 ... 143 J2
Slater Ing La HBR HX7 ... 142 E1
Slaters Rd PDSY/CALV LS28 ... 107 G5
Slates La ILK LS29 ... 20 D7
Slaymaker La HWTH BD22 ... 78 E3
Slead Av BRIG HD6 ... 170 B2
Slead Ct BRIG HD6 ... 170 B2
Slead Crs BRIG HD6 ... 170 B2
Slead Gv BRIG HD6 ... 170 B2
Slead Royd BRIG HD6 ... 170 B2
Sledbrook Crs STKB/PEN S36 ... 255 L8
Sledgate La MAR/SLWT HD7 ... 234 A1
Sledmere Cl SCFT LS14 ... 89 L8
Sledmere Garth SCFT LS14 ... 89 L8
Sledmere La SCFT LS14 ... 89 L8
Sledmere Pl SCFT LS14 ... 89 L8
Sleep Hill La HEM/SK/SE WF9 ... 226 A7
The Sleights AL/HA/HU LS17 ... 43 K2
Sleights La AL/HA/HU LS17 ... 45 K8
Sleningford Gv SHPY BD18 ... 82 A6
Sleningford Ri BGLY BD16 ... 81 G1
Sleningford Rd BGLY BD16 ... 81 H1
SHPY BD18 ... 82 A6
Slice La TAD LS24 ... 72 D3
Slingsby Cl IDLE BD10 ... 83 H6
Slipper La MIRF WF14 ... 172 A6
Slippery Ford La HWTH BD22 ... 55 L7
Slippy La LUD/ILL HX2 ... 145 L1
Sloan Sq GIR BD8 ... 104 D6
Slutwell La PONT WF8 ... 180 F6
Smalewell Cl PDSY/CALV LS28 ... 106 E8
Smalewell Dr PDSY/CALV LS28 ... 106 E8
Smalewell Gdns PDSY/CALV LS28 ... 106 E8
Smalewell Gn PDSY/CALV LS28 ... 106 E8
Smalewell Rd PDSY/CALV LS28 ... 106 E8
Smallbrook Rd ROY/SHW OL2 ... 229 K4
Small La MAR/SLWT HD7 ... 212 F2
STKB/PEN S36 ... 258 D6
Small Lees Rd RPDN/SBR HX6 ... 188 F3
Small Page Fold CUL/QBY * BD13 ... 125 G5
Smallpage Yd WKFDE WF1 ... 12 F2
Small Shaw La HBR HX7 ... 121 K8
Smallwood Gdns EARL WF12 ... 174 C4
Smallwood Rd EARL WF12 ... 174 C4
Smawell La HOR/CROF WF4 ... 221 K7
Smawthorne Av WF10 ... 157 M7
Smawthorne Gv CAS WF10 ... 157 M7
Smawthorne La CAS WF10 ... 157 M7
Smeatley's La PONT WF8 ... 205 G7
Smeaton Ap MSTN/BAR LS15 ... 112 A3
Smeaton Gv RTHW LS26 ... 126 B5
Smeaton Rd HEM/SK/SE WF9 ... 225 M6
Smiddles La WBOW BD5 ... 126 C4
Smiddy HI BSPA/BRAM LS23 ... 49 J2
Smirthwaite St WKFDE WF1 ... 176 E6
Smirthwaite Vw NORM WF6 ... 178 C5
Smith Av WBSY BD6 ... 126 C5
Smith Crs BRIG HD6 ... 170 A6
Smitherds St KGHY BD21 ... 2 F7
Smithfield Av HIPP HX3 ... 147 L6
Smith HI MILN OL16 ... 207 H8
Smith House Crs BRIG HD6 ... 170 D1
Smith House Gv BRIG HD6 ... 170 C1
Smith House La BRIG HD6 ... 170 C1
Smithies La BSLYN/ROY S71 ... 261 G2
BTLY WF17 ... 151 G6
LVSG WF15 ... 172 E4
Smithies Moor Crs BTLY WF17 ... 151 G7
Smithies Moor La BTLY WF17 ... 151 G7
Smithies Moor Ri BTLY WF17 ... 151 H6
Smithies Moor St BSLYN/ROY S71 ... 261 G2
Smith La HTON BD9 ... 104 A4
Smith Rd DEWS WF13 ... 173 H5

GTHN BD7 ... 126 D3
Smiths Av HUDW HD3 ... 191 M7
Smithson Av CAS WF10 ... 158 D8
Smithson St RTHW LS26 ... 155 H2
Smith's Ter HIPP HX3 ... 146 C3
Smith St BGLY BD16 ... 81 K8
BOW BD4 ... 127 K6
CAS WF10 ... 158 B5
CAS WF10 ... 158 B5
GTHN BD7 ... 4 C6
KGHY BD21 ... 2 D1
LIT OL15 ... 207 K1
LVSG WF15 ... 172 D3
MILN OL16 ... 206 B7
Smithville AIRE BD20 ... 58 B5
Smith Wy OSS WF5 ... 175 G8
Smithwell La HBR HX7 ... 143 L5
Smithy Bridge Rd LIT OL15 ... 207 G2
Smithy Brook La EARL WF12 ... 196 B5
Smithy Carr La BRIG HD6 ... 170 C2
Smithy Cl HOR/CROF WF4 ... 200 B6
KBTN HD8 ... 239 J5
Smithy Clough La RPDN/SBR HX6 ... 188 C3
Smithy HI CUL/QBY BD13 ... 102 A8
KBTN HD8 ... 257 H3
WBSY BD6 ... 126 E5
Smithy La AL/HA/HU LS17 ... 67 L4
BHP/TINH LS16 ... 64 A8
EARD/LOFT WF3 ... 153 H6
GTL/HWG HX4 ... 188 F7
HBR HX7 ... 142 C1
HOLM/MEL HD9 ... 253 L4
HOR/CROF WF4 ... 218 B2
HUDE HD5 ... 15 K8
ILK LS29 ... 21 K7
ILK LS29 ... 40 A6
KBTN HD8 ... 239 J5
TAD LS24 ... 95 G1
WIL/AL BD15 ... 80 E8
Smithy Mills La BHP/TINH LS16 ... 86 F4
Smithy Place La HOLM/MEL HD9 ... 236 D4
Smithy St HFAX HX1 ... 11 L6
Smithy Wk EARL WF12 ... 196 B5
Smithy Wood La DOD/DAR S75 ... 260 B8
Smyth St WKFDE WF1 ... 12 D3
Snail La HBR HX7 ... 143 K6
Snailsden Wy DOD/DAR S75 ... 242 F6
Snaith Wood Dr YEA LS19 ... 84 E5
Snaith Wood Ms YEA LS19 ... 84 E5
Snape Dr GTHN BD7 ... 125 M4
Snapes Fold HUDE HD5 ... 215 H2
Snape St KGHY BD21 ... 79 L2
Snapethorpe Crs WKFDW/WTN WF2 ... 197 M2
Snapethorpe Ga WKFDW/WTN WF2 ... 197 L2
Snapethorpe Rd WKFDW/WTN WF2 ... 197 M2
Snell Gv COL BB8 ... 52 B8
Snelsins La CLECK BD19 ... 149 L5
Snelsins Rd CLECK BD19 ... 149 L5
Snetterton Cl CUD/GR S72 ... 244 E7
Snittle Rd HOLM/MEL HD9 ... 254 D7
Snowden Ap BRAM LS13 ... 108 A3
Snowden Carr Rd OT LS21 ... 22 C5
Snowden Cl BRAM LS13 ... 107 M4
Snowden Crs BRAM LS13 ... 107 M4
Snowden Fold BRAM LS13 ... 107 M4
Snowden Gv BRAM LS13 ... 107 M4
Snowden Lawn BRAM LS13 ... 107 M4
Snowden Rd SHPY BD18 ... 82 F8
Snowden Royd BRAM LS13 ... 107 M4
Snowden St BFD BD1 ... 4 E4
Snowdens Wk CLAY BD14 ... 125 M2
Snowden V BRAM LS13 ... 107 M4
Snowdon Av KNOT WF11 ... 181 L2
Snowdon St BTLY WF17 ... 173 K2
ROCH OL11 ... 228 C4
Snowdrop Ms WIL/AL BD15 ... 103 K6
Snow Hill Cl WKFDE * WF1 ... 176 C5
Snow Hill Ri WKFDE WF1 ... 176 C5
Snow Hill Vw WKFDE WF1 ... 176 D6
Snug La HOLM/MEL HD9 ... 255 J5
Snydale Av NORM WF6 ... 178 A5
Snydale Cl NORM WF6 ... 178 C5
Snydale Ct NORM WF6 ... 178 C5
Snydale Gv NORM WF6 ... 178 C5
Snydale Rd CUD/GR S72 ... 244 D7
NORM WF6 ... 178 D5
Soaper House La HIPP HX3 ... 147 L4
Soaper La HIPP HX3 ... 125 M4
Sod House Gn HIPP HX3 ... 146 C3
Soho Dr WKFDW/WTN WF2 ... 12 A3
Soho St BFD BD1 ... 4 D6
HFAX HX1 ... 10 B6
Solid HUDS HD4 ... 214 B4
Solomon Hl LUD/ILL HX2 ... 144 F5
Solway Rd BTLY WF17 ... 174 B1
Somerdale Cl BRAM LS13 ... 107 M5
Somerdale Gdns BRAM LS13 ... 107 M5
Somerdale Gv BRAM LS13 ... 107 M5
Somerdale Wk BRAM LS13 ... 107 M5
Somerset Av BAIL BD17 ... 82 D2
BRIG HD6 ... 170 D7
ROY/SHW OL2 ... 229 H7
Somerset Crs HUD HD1 ... 15 J8
Somerset Rd HUD HD1 ... 15 J8
PDSY/CALV LS28 ... 107 G6
Somerset St CUD/GR S72 ... 244 D8
Somers Pl LDS * LS1 ... 6 D9
Somers St LDS LS1 ... 6 D9
Somerton Dr BOW BD4 ... 127 M4
Somerville Av SCFT LS14 ... 111 H4
WBSY BD6 ... 126 D5
Somerville Dr SCFT LS14 ... 111 H4
Somerville Gn SCFT LS14 ... 111 H4
Somerville Gv SCFT LS14 ... 111 H4
Somerville Mt SCFT LS14 ... 111 H4
Somerville Pk WBSY BD6 ... 126 D7
Somerville Vw SCFT LS14 ... 111 H4
Sonning Rd WIL/AL BD15 ... 103 K6
Soothill La BTLY WF17 ... 174 B1
Sorbus Wy BRIG HD6 ... 216 A3
Sorrel Cl PONT WF8 ... 180 F7
Sorrel Dr LIT OL15 ... 185 H8

Sorrento Wy WMB/DAR S73 ... 263 H8
Sorrin Cl IDLE BD10 ... 83 J7
Sotheron Cft PONT WF8 ... 203 L1
Soureby Cross Wy BOW BD4 ... 128 B7
Sourhall Ct TOD OL14 ... 140 F8
Sourhall Rd TOD OL14 ... 162 F1
South Accommodation Rd MID LS10 ... 9 K5
Southampton St BFDE BD3 ... 5 H2
South Ap BSPA/BRAM LS23 ... 69 H6
South Av GFTH/SHER LS25 ... 92 A4
HOR/CROF WF4 ... 197 L5
South Baileygate PONT WF8 ... 181 G5
South Bank AL/HA/HU LS17 ... 46 E8
CUL/QBY BD13 ... 125 H5
South Bank Rd BTLY WF17 ... 151 J8
South Bolton LUD/ILL HX2 ... 123 M7
South Brook Ter GTHN * BD7 ... 4 D7
South Cliffe CUL/QBY BD13 ... 102 F8
Southcliffe Dr BAIL BD17 ... 82 D5
Southcliffe Wy BAIL BD17 ... 82 E5
South Cl BSLYN/ROY S71 ... 243 L4
GSLY LS20 ... 61 K6
South Clough Head LUD/ILL HX2 ... 145 J7
Southcote Pl IDLE BD10 ... 83 K6
South Crs DOD/DAR S75 ... 260 B7
South Cft CUD/GR S72 ... 244 E3
KBTN HD8 ... 239 J5
South Croft Av BIRK/DRI BD11 ... 128 C8
South Croft Dr BIRK/DRI BD11 ... 128 C8
South Croft Ga BIRK/DRI BD11 ... 128 C8
South Cross Rd HUDN HD2 ... 192 B4
Southdale Gdns OSS WF5 ... 196 F1
Southdale Rd OSS WF5 ... 196 F2
Southdown Cl HTON BD9 ... 104 A4
Southdown Rd BAIL BD17 ... 82 D5
Southdowns Cl ROY/SHW OL2 ... 229 H6
South Dr BSLYN/ROY S71 ... 243 L4
GSLY LS20 ... 61 K6
PDSY/CALV LS28 ... 106 F3
WKFDW/WTN WF2 ... 198 F5
South Drive Farm AWLS/ASK DN6 ... 249 J5
South Edge KGHY BD21 ... 2 C3
SHPY BD18 ... 82 A7
Southedge Cl HIPP HX3 ... 147 L7
South End Av BRAM LS13 ... 107 M5
South End Gv BRAM LS13 ... 107 M5
South End Mt BRAM LS13 ... 107 M5
South End Ter BRAM LS13 ... 107 M5
Southern Rd HUDS HD4 ... 213 J3
Southey Cl LIT OL15 ... 207 H4
Southey St SKP/WHF BD23 ... 16 C3
South Farm Crs OSM LS9 ... 110 E4
South Farm Rd OSM LS9 ... 110 E4
Southfield BHP/TINH LS16 ... 64 B4
HBR HX7 ... 143 H2
Southfield Av AIRE BD20 ... 58 B4
AL/HA/HU LS17 ... 88 A4
FEA/AMT WF7 ... 201 K2
WBSY BD6 ... 126 E6
Southfield Cl HOR/CROF WF4 ... 197 K5
WKFDW/WTN WF2 ... 176 A5
Southfield Ct KBTN HD8 ... 216 B7
Southfield Dr AIRE BD20 ... 58 C4
AL/HA/HU LS17 ... 88 A4
Southfield Fold HOR/CROF WF4 ... 197 K6
Southfield La GLE DN14 ... 183 M3
GTHN BD7 ... 126 C3
HOR/CROF WF4 ... 197 K6
ILK LS29 ... 19 H6
South Field La RYKW YO26 ... 32 A3
Southfield Mt AIRE BD20 ... 58 C4
WOR/ARM LS12 ... 108 E7
Southfield Rd BGLY BD16 ... 81 J5
CUD/GR S72 ... 262 E2
HOR/CROF WF4 ... 200 D2
HUDE HD5 ... 215 H3
ILK LS29 ... 19 H6
ILK LS29 ... 40 A5
KNOT WF11 ... 182 B3
WBOW BD5 ... 126 E3
Southfield Sq GIR BD8 ... 4 B2
Southfields Vw HOR/CROF WF4 ... 218 F1
Southgate BFD BD1 ... 4 E7
CUD/GR S72 ... 223 G8
DOD/DAR S75 ... 260 B3
EARL WF12 ... 173 L6
ELL HX5 ... 169 H7
GSLY LS20 ... 61 K7
HFAX HX1 ... 11 H6
HOLM/MEL HD9 ... 236 B2
HUD HD1 ... 15 G6
PONT WF8 ... 180 F6
RTHW LS26 ... 133 L8
STKB/PEN S36 ... 271 G4
WKFDE WF1 ... 12 F3
South Gv BRIG HD6 ... 169 M1
SHPY BD18 ... 81 M7
South Hill Cl MID LS10 ... 132 B7
South Hill Cft MID * LS10 ... 132 B7
South Hill Dr BGLY BD16 ... 81 K3
South Hill Gdns RTHW LS26 ... 132 B7
South Hill Ri MID LS10 ... 132 B7
South Hill Wy MID LS10 ... 132 B7
Southlands BAIL BD17 ... 82 D5
HUDE HD5 ... 193 K5
LUD/ILL HX2 ... 124 D7
Southlands Av AIRE * BD20 ... 58 C5
AL/HA/HU LS17 ... 87 L6
BGLY BD16 ... 81 J5
CUL/QBY BD13 ... 103 K8
YEA LS19 ... 84 A4
Southlands Cl GFTH/SHER LS25 ... 138 D7

HEM/SK/SE WF9 ... 225 G4
Southlands Crs AL/HA/HU LS17 ... 87 L6
Southlands Dr AIRE * BD20 ... 58 C5
AL/HA/HU LS17 ... 87 L6
HUDN HD2 ... 192 D3
Southlands Gv AIRE BD20 ... 58 C5
BGLY BD16 ... 81 H5
CUL/QBY BD13 ... 103 K8
Southlands Gv West AIRE BD20 ... 58 C4
Southlands Mt AIRE BD20 ... 58 C5
Southlands Rd AIRE BD20 ... 58 C4
South La DOD/DAR S75 ... 258 D5
ELL HX5 ... 191 H2
HIPP HX3 ... 125 K7
HOR/CROF WF4 ... 218 F2
South Lane Gdns ELL HX5 ... 191 H1
South Lea EARD/LOFT * WF3 ... 153 H5
Southlea Av HWTH BD22 ... 79 G4
Southlea Cl LM/WK BD12 ... 149 J1
South Lee HORS LS18 ... 85 K5
Southleigh Av BEE/HOL LS11 ... 131 J6
Southleigh Crs BEE/HOL LS11 ... 131 J6
Southleigh Cft BEE/HOL LS11 ... 131 K6
Southleigh Dr BEE/HOL LS11 ... 131 J6
Southleigh Gdns BEE/HOL LS11 ... 131 J6
Southleigh Gra BEE/HOL LS11 ... 131 K6
Southleigh Gv BEE/HOL LS11 ... 131 J6
Southleigh Rd BEE/HOL LS11 ... 131 J6
Southleigh Vw BEE/HOL LS11 ... 131 J6
South Md BHP/TINH LS16 ... 64 B4
Southmere Av GTHN BD7 ... 126 C3
Southmere Crs GTHN BD7 ... 126 C3
Southmere Dr GTHN BD7 ... 126 C3
Southmere Gv GTHN BD7 ... 126 C3
Southmere Ov GTHN BD7 ... 126 C4
Southmere Rd GTHN BD7 ... 126 C3
Southmere Ter GTHN BD7 ... 126 C3
Southmoor La KNOT WF11 ... 182 E4
Southmoor Rd CUD/GR S72 ... 245 M4
South Mt AL/HA/HU LS17 ... 46 D8
South Nelson St MOR LS27 ... 152 D1
Southolme Cl KSTL LS5 ... 108 B1
Southowram Bank HIPP HX3 ... 11 L6
South Pde CLECK BD19 ... 149 L6
ELL HX5 ... 191 H1
GIR BD8 ... 4 D2
GTL/HWG HX4 ... 190 B3
HDGY LS6 ... 108 F1
HFAX HX1 ... 11 J8
ILK LS29 ... 38 C2
LDS LS1 ... 6 F9
MILN OL16 ... 206 B9
MOR LS27 ... 152 D2
OSS WF5 ... 197 J2
PDSY/CALV LS28 ... 107 G8
WKFDE WF1 ... 12 E3
South Parade Cl PDSY/CALV LS28 ... 106 F3
South Pkwy OSM LS9 ... 110 E3
South Park Wy WKFDW/WTN WF2 ... 176 B2
South Parkway Ap OSM LS9 ... 111 G3
South Pl DOD/DAR S75 ... 260 D3
South Point MID * LS10 ... 9 L5
South Queen St MOR LS27 ... 152 D3
South Rdg GFTH/SHER LS25 ... 135 J5
South Rd CUL/QBY BD13 ... 101 M1
DOD/DAR S75 ... 260 B6
HTON BD9 ... 104 B3
OSM LS9 ... 132 E3
South Royd HUDE HD5 ... 215 J2
South Royde Av HIPP HX3 ... 168 E3
Southroyd Ri PDSY/CALV LS28 ... 129 G1
South Sq CUL/QBY BD13 ... 102 F8
South St BRIG HD6 ... 170 C3
BSLY S70 ... 260 E5
CUL/QBY BD13 ... 101 M6
CUL/QBY BD13 ... 102 E7
DOD/DAR S75 ... 260 B8
EARL WF12 ... 173 L6
EARL WF12 ... 173 M8
HEM/SK/SE WF9 ... 224 A8
HFAX HX1 ... 10 F7
HOLM/MEL HD9 ... 236 C6
HOR/CROF WF4 ... 222 F5
HUD HD1 ... 213 M1
HUDS HD4 ... 213 M1
KGHY BD21 ... 79 K2
LM/WK BD12 ... 149 J2
LVSG WF15 ... 172 D2
MILN OL16 ... 206 C6
MIRF WF14 ... 194 B3
MOR LS27 ... 152 D2
NORM WF6 ... 178 A4
OSS WF5 ... 196 F2
WBOW BD5 ... 126 E3
WKFDE WF1 ... 13 H4
South Ter OSS WF5 ... 197 G3
South Terrace Ct MILN OL16 ... 228 C1
South Vw AIRE BD20 ... 34 F5
AIRE BD20 ... 58 D5
BAIL BD17 ... 82 A3
CAS WF10 ... 158 A4
CAS WF10 ... 180 A1
FEA/AMT WF7 ... 179 M8
HIPP HX3 ... 169 J2
HOLM/MEL HD9 ... 255 H3
HUD HD1 ... 213 M1
HUD HD22 ... 78 E7
IDLE BD10 ... 83 M7
ILK LS29 ... 61 J3
PDSY/CALV LS28 ... 106 E5
PDSY/CALV LS28 ... 107 H7
RTHW LS26 ... 132 F2
TAD LS24 ... 51 J3
WBY LS22 ... 30 A6
YEA LS19 ... 62 A7
South View Cl BOW BD4 ... 128 A7
YEA LS19 ... 62 A7
South View Cottages AL/HA/HU * AIRE * BD20 ... 58 C5
South View Ct HIPP HX3 ... 147 M8
South View Dr BOW BD4 ... 128 B7
South View Gdns PONT WF8 ... 180 F5
South View Gv CLECK * BD19 ... 150 D7
South View Rd BOW BD4 ... 128 B7

MID LS10 ... 132 A5
MILN OL16 ... 207 H5
YEA LS19 ... 62 D7
South View St TOD OL14 ... 140 E5
South View Ter AIRE BD20 ... 35 M5
BAIL * BD17 ... 82 E3
HFAX HX1 ... 10 B1
HOR/CROF WF4 ... 217 G2
MILN OL16 ... 207 G2
YEA LS19 ... 62 E8
Southwaite La SCFT LS14 ... 111 H2
Southwaite Pl SCFT LS14 ... 111 H2
South Wk BGLY BD16 ... 80 C5
South Wy BOW BD4 ... 128 A7
SHPY BD18 ... 81 M7
Southway BGLY BD16 ... 81 L1
GSLY LS20 ... 61 K6
HORS LS18 ... 85 J3
HUDW HD3 ... 191 L5
ILK LS29 ... 38 F3
MIRF WF14 ... 172 B7
Southwell Av HUDW HD3 ... 191 M5
Southwell La HOR/CROF WF4 ... 197 A6
Southwell St DOD/DAR S75 ... 260 F4
Southwood Av HOLM/MEL HD9 ... 236 D1
Southwood Cl SCFT LS14 ... 111 L2
Southwood Crs SCFT LS14 ... 111 L2
Southwood Ga MSTN/BAR LS15 ... 111 L2
Sovereign Cl BTLY WF17 ... 151 H5
Sovereign St AL/HA/HU LS17 ... 66 A3
Sovereign Gdns NORM WF6 ... 178 C4
Sovereign Quay LDS * LS1 ... 9 H2
Sovereign St HFAX * HX1 ... 10 F8
LDS LS1 ... 8 F2
Sovereign's Wy EARL WF12 ... 195 K3
Sowden Buildings BEE/HOL * LS11 ... 105 K4
Sowden Gra CUL/QBY BD13 ... 102 F8
Sowden Rd HTON BD9 ... 103 M3
Sowden St GTHN * BD7 ... 126 D3
Sowden's Yd HDGY * LS6 ... 86 F8
Sowerby Croft La RPDN/SBR HX6 ... 167 K3
Sowerby La LUD/ILL HX2 ... 144 D8
Sowerby New Rd RPDN/SBR HX6 ... 167 K3
Sowerby St RPDN/SBR HX6 ... 167 K3
Sowgate La PONT WF8 ... 181 J3
Sowood Av OSS WF5 ... 197 G3
Sowood Ct OSS WF5 ... 197 G3
Sowood Gdns OSS WF5 ... 197 G3
Sowood Gra OSS WF5 ... 197 G3
Sowood La EARL WF12 ... 195 K3
OSS WF5 ... 197 H3
Sowood St BULY LS4 ... 108 E4
Sow Vw OSS WF5 ... 197 H2
Soyland Town Rd RPDN/SBR HX6 ... 166 F8
Spa Bottom HUDE HD5 ... 215 L1
Spa Croft Rd OSS WF5 ... 197 J2
Spa Flds MAR/SLWT HD7 ... 212 D5
Spa Gv WKFDW/WTN WF2 ... 198 A3
Spaines Rd HUDN HD2 ... 192 C5
Spa La BGLY BD16 ... 81 J1
BSPA/BRAM LS23 ... 49 G7
MAR/SLWT HD7 ... 212 D5
OSS WF5 ... 197 J3
Spa Ms BSPA/BRAM LS23 ... 49 G7
Sparable La WKFDE WF1 ... 13 H9
Sparkfields DOD/DAR S75 ... 242 D6
Spark House La RPDN/SBR HX6 ... 167 L3
Spark La DOD/DAR S75 ... 242 D7
Sparks Rd HUDW HD3 ... 191 K7
Spark St HUDW HD3 ... 191 C8
Sparrow HI MILN OL16 ... 206 A7
Spartal La GFTH/SHER LS25 ... 136 A6
Spartan Rd LM/WK BD12 ... 148 F1
Sparth La HOLM/MEL HD9 ... 253 K2
Spa St BTLY WF17 ... 173 L1
OSS WF5 ... 197 K2
Spawd Bone La KNOT WF11 ... 182 A3
Spa Well Gv CUD/GR S72 ... 245 J3
Speak Cl WKFDE WF1 ... 177 H6
Speakers Ct DEWS WF13 ... 173 K6
Spear Fir AL/HA/HU LS17 ... 67 J4
Spearhead Wy KGHY BD21 ... 3 H3
Speedwell Mt HDGY LS6 ... 6 F7
Speedwell Rd CAS WF10 ... 157 G8
Speedwell St HDGY LS6 ... 6 F7
HUD * HD1 ... 213 M1
Speeton Av WBSY BD6 ... 126 A4
Speeton Gv GTHN BD7 ... 125 M4
Spen Ap BHP/TINH LS16 ... 86 B7
Spen Bank BHP/TINH LS16 ... 86 B7
CLECK BD19 ... 150 B7
Spence La WOR/ARM LS12 ... 8 A3
Spenceley St LDSU LS2 ... 6 D4
Spencer Av AIRE BD20 ... 36 A4
GTHN BD7 ... 125 L2
MOR LS27 ... 152 C1
Spencer Cl AIRE BD20 ... 35 G7
Spencer La HBR HX7 ... 143 C5
Spencer Mt RHAY LS8 ... 7 M2
Spencer Pl RHAY LS8 ... 7 M3
Spencer Rd GSLY LS20 ... 62 B6
GTHN BD7 ... 126 D1
Spencer St AIRE BD20 ... 55 M1
BSLY S70 ... 261 G6
KBTN HD8 ... 239 J4
KGHY BD21 ... 2 E4
MIRF WF14 ... 194 C3
Spencer Wk SKP/WHF BD23 ... 16 E3
Spen Cl BOW BD4 ... 127 K7
Spen Common La TAD LS24 ... 70 A8
Spen Crs BHP/TINH LS16 ... 86 B7
Spen Dr BHP/TINH LS16 ... 86 B7
Spenfield Ct LVSG WF15 ... 172 C4
Spen Fold LIT OL15 ... 207 J2
Spen Gdns BHP/TINH LS16 ... 86 B6
Spen La RYKW YO26 ... 33 L7
Spen Gn BHP/TINH LS16 ... 86 B7
Spen La CLECK BD19 ... 150 B6
HDGY LS6 ... 86 C6
Spen Ms BHP/TINH LS16 ... 86 C7

Spennithorne Av
  BHP/TINH LS16 ....86 C5
Spennithorne Dr
  BHP/TINH LS16 ....86 C5
Spennithorne Rd
  AWLS/ASK DN6 ....249 G4
Spen Rd *BHP/TINH* LS16 ....86 D6
Spenser Ri *GSLY* LS20 ......62 B6
Spenser Rd *GSLY* LS20 ......62 B6
Spenslea Gv *MOR* LS27 ....152 C4
Spen Vale St *HECK* WF16 ..172 F3
Spen Valley Heritage Trail
  BTLY WF17 ....150 F3
  CLECK BD19 ....150 A4
Spen Valley Rd *DEWS* WF13 ..173 G8
Spen Vw *DEWS* WF13 ......173 G6
Spen View La *BOW* BD4 ....127 K7
Spen Wk *BHP/TINH* LS16 ....86 B7
Spenwood Rd *LIT* OL15 ....207 H1
Spey Cl *DOD/DAR* S75 ......242 E7
Spibey Crs *RTHW* LS26 ......132 F7
Spibey La *RTHW* LS26 ......132 F7
Spicer House La *STKB/PEN* S36 ..256 D7
Spicer St *WBOW* * BD5 ......126 E3
Spiers Garth *WBSY* BD6 ....126 F5
The Spindles *MID* LS10 ....131 M6
Spindle St *LUD/ILL* HX2 ....146 C1
Spinkfield Rd *HUDN* HD2 ....14 C3
Spink La *PONT* WF8 ....180 F5
Spink Pl *GIR* BD8 ....4 B4
Spinks Gdns *SCFT* LS14 ....111 K2
Spink Well La *EARD/LOFT* WF3 ..153 H5
Spinkwell Rd *DEWS* WF13 ..173 L5
The Spinners *HWTH* BD22 ....78 E8
Spinners Cha *PDSY/CALV* LS28..107 G7
Spinners Gdns *WHIT* OL12 ..206 E2
Spinners Gn *WHIT* OL12 ....206 B4
Spinners Wy *CLECK* BD19 ..149 H6
  MIRF WF14 ....194 C3
The Spinney *AIRE* BD20 ....58 F6
  AL/HA/HU LS17 ....88 A4
  BRIG HD6 ....170 C1
  HBR * HX7 ....143 K4
  IDLE BD10 ....84 C4
  OSM * LS9 ....9 M2
  SKP/WHF BD23 ....17 M1
  WBY LS22 ....29 M8
  WKFDW/WTN WF2 ....199 G8
Spinneyfield *HUDN* HD2 ....192 C3
Spinneyfield Ct *OSM* LS9 ....9 M2
Spinning Mill Ct *SHPY* BD18 ..82 A6
Spion Kop *SCFT* LS14 ......90 B1
Spire Ct *HUDW* HD3 ....14 A4
Spitalgap La *PONT* WF8 ....181 K7
Spitfire Wy *GFTH/SHER* LS25 ..126 B4
Spittal Hardwick La *CAS* WF10 ..180 E1
Spittlerush La *PONT* WF8 ..227 J2
Spofforth Hl *WBY* LS22 ......29 L8
Spofforth La *PBR* HG3 ......28 B1
  WBY LS22 ....29 J2
Spofforth Wk *GFTH/SHER* LS25 ..113 K7
Spokeshave Wy *MILN* OL16 ..206 E4
Spout Fold *WKFDW/WTN* WF2...175 M8
Spout Hl *BRIC* HD6 ....170 A8
Spout House La *BRIC* HD6 ..148 A8
Spring Av *KGHY* BD21 ......3 M7
  MOR LS27 ....129 L6
Springbank *GFTH/SHER* LS25..134 E1
Spring Bank Av *MOR* LS27 ..129 L7
  PDSY/CALV LS28 ....107 G3
Springbank Cl *BSLYN/ROY* S71 ..243 L6
  PDSY/CALV LS28 ....107 G3
Spring Bank Crs *HDGY* LS6 ..109 G2
Springbank Crs
  GFTH/SHER LS25 ....112 E8
  HUD HD1 ....15 L1
  MOR LS27 ....129 L6
Spring Bank Cft
  HOLM/MEL HD9 ....253 M2
Spring Bank Dr *LVSG* WF15 ..172 D4
Springbank Dr
  PDSY/CALV LS28 ....107 G3
Springbank Gv
  PDSY/CALV LS28 ....107 G3
Springbank Ms
  HOLM/MEL * HD9 ....236 D3
Spring Bank Pl *GIR* BD8 ......4 C1
Springbank Ri *KGHY* BD21 ..79 L2
Springbank Ri *PDSY/CALV* LS28...107 G3
Springbank Rd *HUD* HD1 ....15 L1
  MOR LS27 ....129 L6
  PDSY/CALV LS28 ....106 F3
Springcliffe *GIR* BD8 ......104 D5
Springcliffe St *GIR* BD8 ....104 D5
Spring Cl *BGLY* BD16 ....81 K4
  GFTH/SHER LS25 ....113 J6
  GFTH/SHER LS25 ....113 K8
  KGHY BD21 ....3 M7
  MOR LS27 ....130 C7
Spring Close Av *OSM* LS9 ..9 M3
Spring Close Gdns *OSM* LS9 ..110 B8
Spring Close St *OSM* LS9 ....9 M3
Spring Close Wk *OSM* LS9 ..110 B8
Spring Ct *WIL/AL* * BD15 ....103 J3
Spring Dl *HOLM/MEL* HD9 ..236 B1
Springdale Crs *IDLE* BD10 ..83 L6
Springdale St *HUD* HD1 ....214 B2
Spring Dr *KGHY* BD21 ......3 M7
Springfield *BSPA/BRAM* LS23...48 E6
  BSPA/BRAM LS23 ....69 M1
  HUDW HD3 ....190 D6
  RPDN/SBR HX6 ....167 J3
Springfield Av *BTLY* WF17 ..173 K1
  GTHN BD7 ....126 B1
  HEM/SK/SE WF9 ....224 A8
  HOLM/MEL HD9 ....236 B3
  ILK LS29 ....38 E2
  KBTN HD8 ....240 A4
  LIT OL15 ....185 J7
  MAR/SLWT HD7 ....212 A7

MOR LS27 ....130 C8
  PONT WF8 ....181 G5
Springfield Bungalows
  CLECK * BD19 ....150 A7
Springfield Cl *HORS* LS18 ..86 A5
  KBTN HD8 ....240 A4
  MID LS10 ....132 C4
Springfield Ct *GFTH/SHER* LS25..116 B5
  KGHY BD21 ....2 C2
Springfield Crs *MOR* LS27 ..130 C8
  PONT WF8 ....227 G1
Springfield Dr *KBTN* HD8 ..256 C2
  LVSG WF15 ....171 L1
Springfield Gdns *HORS* LS18 ..85 M5
  KGHY BD21 ....2 D2
Springfield Gra
  WKFDW/WTN WF2 ....175 M8
Springfield Gn *MID* * LS10 ..132 A4
Springfield Gv *BGLY* BD16 ..81 H2
  BRIC HD6 ....170 C2
Springfield La *BOW* BD4 ....129 C4
  KBTN HD8 ....216 A7
  LVSG WF15 ....172 A1
  MILN OL16 ....206 F3
  MOR LS27 ....130 C8
  ROY/SHW OL2 ....228 E7
Springfield Mt
  HEM/SK/SE WF9 ....247 G5
  HORS LS18 ....85 L5
  ILK LS29 ....19 H5
  LDSU LS2 ....6 C6
  WOR/ARM * LS12 ....108 C7
Springfield Pk *MIRF* WF14 ..194 D1
Springfield Pl *BSLY* S70 ..260 F5
  GIR BD8 ....8 D3
  MID LS10 ....132 A4
Springfield Ri *HORS* LS18 ..85 M5
  RTHW LS26 ....155 H2
Springfield Rd *BAIL* BD17 ..82 D2
  CUD/GR S72 ....245 H7
  ELL HX5 ....169 K7
  GFTH/SHER LS25 ....116 B5
  GSLY LS20 ....62 A6
  KGHY BD21 ....3 H2
  MOR LS27 ....130 C8
Springfields *DOD/DAR* S75 ..260 C2
  KNOT WF11 ....182 D3
  SKP/WHF BD23 ....16 D2
Springfields Av *KNOT* WF11 ..182 D2
Springfield St *BSLY* S70 ....260 E5
  GIR BD8 ....8 D3
  RTHW LS26 ....103 C8
Springfield Ter *CLECK* BD19 ..149 H5
  DEWS * WF13 ....173 L5
  GIR * BD8 ....4 B3
  GSLY LS20 ....62 A6
  PDSY/CALV LS28 ....106 F5
Spring Gdns *AL/HA/HU* LS17 ..45 J7
  BFD BD1 ....4 D3
  BIRK/DRI BD11 ....129 H8
  BRIG * HD6 ....170 C2
  BSLYN/ROY S71 ....261 L2
  BTLY * WF17 ....173 K1
  HOLM/MEL HD9 ....254 A1
  MOR LS27 ....130 E7
Spring Gardens La *KGHY* BD21 ..2 E1
Spring Gardens Mt *KGHY* BD21..2 E1
Spring Gardens Rd *HTON* BD9 ..104 C3
Spring Garden St
  CUL/QBY BD13 ....125 G5
Spring Gv *COL* BB8 ....52 E8
  HBR HX7 ....143 J2
  HFAX HX1 ....146 A7
Spring Grove St *HUD* HD1 ..14 E8
Spring Grove Vw *HDGY* LS6 ..109 G4
Spring Grove Wk *HDGY* * LS6..109 G4
Spring Hall Ct *HFAX* HX1 ..147 K1
Spring Hall Ct *HFAX* HX1 ..146 A6
Spring Hall Dr *HFAX* HX1 ..146 A8
Spring Hall Gdns *HFAX* HX1 ..146 A7
Spring Hall Gv *LUD/ILL* HX2 ..146 A7
Spring Hall La *HFAX* HX1 ..146 A7
Spring Hall Pl *HFAX* HX1 ..146 A7
Spring Head La
  MAR/SLWT HD7 ....233 H1
Spring Head Rd *CUL/QBY* BD13...103 G8
  HWTH BD22 ....78 E6
Springhead Rd *RTHW* LS26 ..133 J8
Spring Hl *BAIL* BD17 ....82 B3
  BHP/TINH LS16 ....87 G2
  CHAL LS7 ....7 G1
  SHPY BD18 ....83 C7
Springhill Av *HOR/CROF* WF4 ..200 C5
Springhill Cl *WKFDE* WF1 ..176 C1
Springhill Ct *TAD* LS24 ....71 M2
Springhill Dr *HOR/CROF* WF4..200 C5
Springhill Gv *HOR/CROF* WF4 ..200 C5
Springhill Mt *HOR/CROF* WF4 ..200 C6
Springhills *WKFDE* WF1 ....176 C1
Spring Hill Ter *HDGY* LS6 ....87 G8
Spring Holes La *CUL/QBY* BD13...102 E7
Springhurst Rd *SHPY* BD18 ..82 C7
Spring La *BGLY* BD16 ....59 M8
  BSLYN/ROY S71 ....243 L6
  BTLY WF17 ....151 K7
  DOD/DAR S75 ....242 E2
  GTL/HWG HX4 ....168 C2
  HOLM/MEL HD9 ....253 M4
  HOLM/MEL HD9 ....254 A2
  HOLM/MEL HD9 ....255 C1
  HOR/CROF WF4 ....200 D7
  PBR HG3 ....26 E2
  PBR HG3 ....45 H2
  RYKW YO26 ....33 K4
  WBY LS22 ....48 E1
Springlodge Pl *GIR* BD8 ......4 D2
Springmead Dr
  GFTH/SHER LS25 ....115 H8
Spring Mill La *OSS* WF5 ....175 H8
Spring Mill St *WBOW* BD5 ..127 G1
Spring Mill Wk *MILN* OL16 ..206 E4
Spring Mt *KGHY* BD21 ......3 M8
Spring Park Rd *WIL/AL* BD15 ..102 C1
Spring Pl *GTHN* BD7 ....4 B9
  KGHY BD21 ....3 M8
Spring Ri *KGHY* BD21 ......3 M7
  ROY/SHW OL2 ....229 J5

SKP/WHF BD23 ....17 M1
Spring Rd *HDGY* LS6 ....108 F2
Spring Rw *BGLY* BD16 ......80 D5
  COL * BB8 ....52 E8
  KGHY BD21 ....2 F7
Springroyd Ter *GIR* BD8 ..104 B6
Spring Side Ri *MAR/SLWT* HD7 ..212 F1
Springs La *BSPA/BRAM* LS23 ..31 H8
  ILK LS29 ....38 D2
Springs Pavement *ILK* * LS29 ..38 D2
Springs Rd *BAIL* BD17 ......84 A1
  HOLM/MEL HD9 ....252 D3
Springstone Av
  HEM/SK/SE WF9 ....224 A7
  OSS WF5 ....174 F7
Spring St *BRIG* HD6 ....170 C4
  BSLY S70 ....261 G6
  DEWS WF13 ....173 L5
  HUD HD1 ....14 D7
  IDLE BD10 ....83 K8
  KGHY BD21 ....3 H2
  LVSG WF15 ....172 D2
  MAR/SLWT HD7 ....212 B6
  MAR/SLWT HD7 ....233 H3
  RPDN/SBR HX6 ....188 F2
  TOD OL14 ....140 E5
Springswood Av *SHPY* BD18 ..82 C7
Springswood Pl *SHPY* BD18 ..82 C7
Springswood Rd *SHPY* BD18 ..82 C7
Spring Ter *HIPP* HX3 ....11 J4
  KGHY BD21 ....3 M6
  MILN * OL16 ....229 K3
  RPDN/SBR HX6 ....167 L4
Springvale *GIR* HOR/CROF* WF4 ..200 D3
Springvale Gv *STKB/PEN* S36..271 G3
Springvale Ri *HEM/SK/SE* WF9...223 M6
Spring Vale Rd
  HEM/SK/SE WF9 ....246 E2
Spring Vale Ter *LIT* OL15 ..207 K1
Spring Valley Av *BRAM* LS13 ..107 L5
Spring Valley Cl *BRAM* LS13 ..107 L5
Spring Valley Crs *BRAM* LS13 ..107 K5
Spring Valley Cft *BRAM* LS13 ..107 L5
Spring Valley Dr *BRAM* LS13 ..107 L5
Spring Valley St *LVSG* WF15 ..172 C1
Spring Valley Vw *BRAM* LS13 ..107 L5
Spring Valley Wk *BRAM* LS13 ..107 L5
Spring Vw *MOR* LS27 ....129 M6
  OSS WF5 ....175 H8
Spring Vls *TOD* OL14 ......140 D5
Springville Gdns
  HEM/SK/SE WF9 ....225 K7
Spring Wy *KGHY* BD21 ......3 M7
Springwell Av *RTHW* LS26 ..134 C5
Springwell Cl *HWTH* BD22 ..54 F3
  YEA LS19 ....62 E8
Springwell Ct *BEE/HOL* LS11 ..8 B5
  EARD/LOFT WF3 ....155 C5
Springwell Dr *WBOW* BD5 ..127 G2
Springwell Rd *RTHW* LS26 ..134 C5
  WOR/ARM LS12 ....8 B3
Springwell St *BEE/HOL* LS11 ..8 B5
Springwell Vw *BEE/HOL* LS11 ..8 C4
Spring Wood Av *HIPP* HX3 ..168 D4
Springwood Av *HUD* HD1 ..14 C8
  WBOW BD5 ....127 H3
Spring Wood Dr *HIPP* HX3 ..168 D4
Spring Wood Gdns *HIPP* * HX3 ..168 D5
  WBOW BD5 ....127 H4
Springwood Gdns *RHAY* LS8 ..88 C8
Springwood Gv *RHAY* LS8 ..88 C8
Springwood Hall Gdns
  HUD HD1 ....14 C8
Springwood Rd
  HOLM/MEL HD9 ....236 E6
  RHAY LS8 ....88 D8
  YEA LS19 ....84 C3
Springwood Sq *HUD* * HD1 ..14 E7
Springwood St *HUD* HD1 ..14 E8
Springwood Ter *ECHL* BD2 ..105 G4
Springwood Vw
  STKB/PEN S36 ....271 H4
Sprinkwell Cl *BFDE* BD3 ....5 G2
Spruce Av *BSLYN/ROY* S71 ..243 K3
Spruce Dr *HUDW* HD3 ......213 M8
Spruce Drive Ms *HUDS* HD4 ..213 M8
Spruce Hts *BRIG* HD6 ......148 C8
Spruce St *KGHY* BD21 ......3 J3
Sprutts La *HBR* HX7 ....121 K7
Spur Dr *MSTN/BAR* LS15 ..112 A3
Spurr Gv *WKFDW/WTN* WF2 ..199 K8
Spurrier's Av *KNOT* WF11 ..181 L3
Spurr St *BTLY* WF17 ....173 M2
The Square *BSLY* S70 ......260 E6
  BSPA/BRAM LS23 ....49 G7
  CAS WF10 ....158 E7
  CUD/GR S72 ....245 K8
  GFTH/SHER LS25 ....135 J5
  GIR BD8 ....103 J7
  KBTN * HD8 ....238 A6
  KNOT WF11 ....159 L8
  TAD LS24 ....72 A2
Square Rd *HFAX* HX1 ....11 J6
  TOD OL14 ....163 J6
Square St *BOW* BD4 ....127 J1
Squire Gn *GIR* BD8 ....104 B5
Squirrel Cl *DEWS* WF13 ....173 H3
Squirrel Ct *HUDN* HD2 ....191 L4
Squirrel Ditch *HUDS* HD4 ..214 E3
Squirrel Hall Dr *DEWS* WF13 ..173 H3
Squirrel La *CUL/QBY* BD13 ..124 D1
Squirrels Drey *HOR/CROF* WF4 ..198 B7
Squirrel Wk *DEWS* WF13 ..173 H3
The Stables *WKFDW/WTN* WF2 ..199 J7
Stable Fold *LM/WK* BD12 ..148 E4
Stableford Gdns *HUDN* HD2 ..191 M4
Stableford Mnr
  MAR/SLWT HD7 ....213 G1
Stable La *HIPP* HX3 ....10 E1
Stablers Wk *NORM* WF6 ..178 C2
Stables La *BSPA/BRAM* LS23 ..49 G7
Stacey Crs *CUD/GR* S72 ....245 H7
Stackgarth *BRIG* HD6 ......170 C4
Stackhills Rd *TOD* OL14 ....163 L1
Stacks La *HBR* HX7 ....166 B1

Stadium Rd *WBSY* BD6 ......126 F6
Stadium Wy *BEE/HOL* LS11 ..131 G3
  HDE/SK/SE WF9 ....247 K1
  HUDE HD5 ....15 J4
Stafford Av *HIPP* HX3 ......168 E2
Stafford Hill La *HUDE* HD5 ..193 L6
Stafford Pde *HIPP* HX3 ....168 E3
Stafford Rd *HIPP* HX3 ......168 E3
Stafford Sq *HIPP* HX3 ......168 F3
Stafford St *BOW* BD4 ......127 K2
  CAS WF10 ....157 L5
Stafford Ter *WKFDW/WTN* WF2...176 B8
Stainbeck Av *CHAL* LS7 ....87 H8
Stainbeck Cnr *CHAL* LS7 ....87 L7
Stainbeck Gdns *CHAL* LS7 ....87 K8
  WBSY BD6 ....125 M6
Stainbeck La *CHAL* LS7 ....87 J7
Stainbeck Rd *CHAL* LS7 ....87 J8
Stainbeck Wk *CHAL* LS7 ....87 K8
Stainborough Cl *DOD/DAR* S75..260 B8
Stainborough Rd
  DOD/DAR S75 ....260 B8
Stainburn Av *AL/HA/HU* LS17..88 A5
  CAS WF10 ....180 C1
Stainburn Cl *OT* LS21 ......42 C4
Stainburn Crs *AL/HA/HU* LS17 ..87 M5
Stainburn Dr *AL/HA/HU* LS17 ..87 M5
Stainburn Gdns *AL/HA/HU* LS17 ..88 A5
Stainburn La *OT* LS21 ......42 C4
Stainburn Mt *AL/HA/HU* LS17 ..88 A6
Stainburn Rd *AL/HA/HU* LS17 ..87 M6
Stainburn Ter *AL/HA/HU* LS17 ..87 M6
Stainburn Vw *AL/HA/HU* LS17 ..88 A5
Staincliffe Cl *DEWS* WF13 ..173 H6
Staincliffe Crs *DEWS* WF13 ..173 H4
Staincliffe Hall Rd *BTLY* WF17..173 H3
Staincliffe Mill Yd
  DEWS * WF13 ....173 J3
Staincliffe Rd *DEWS* WF13 ..173 H4
Staincross Common
  DOD/DAR S75 ....242 D4
Staincross Av *HUDS* HD4 ..213 L4
Staines Cft *HUDE* HD5 ......195 G8
Stainland Dean *GTL/HWG* HX4..189 M5
Stainland Rd *GTL/HWG* HX4 ..189 J2
  GTL/HWG HX4 ....190 B3
  HUDW HD3 ....190 C6
Stainley Cl *DOD/DAR* S75 ..260 C6
Stainmore Cl *DOD/DAR* S75 ..259 H6
  SCFT LS14 ....111 J3
Stainmore Pl *SCFT* LS14 ....111 J3
Stainton Cl *BSLYN/ROY* S71 ..243 G8
  WBSY BD6 ....126 A6
Stainton La *EARD/LOFT* WF3 ..154 F2
Staircase La *OT* LS21 ....63 M1
Stairfoot Cl *BHP/TINH* LS16 ..86 F1
Stair Foot La *BHP/TINH* LS16 ..86 F1
Stairfoot Vw *BHP/TINH* LS16 ..86 F1
Staithe Av *MID* LS10 ......153 M1
Staithe Cl *MID* LS10 ......153 M1
Staithe Gdns *MID* LS10 ..153 M1
Staithgate La *WBSY* BD6 ..127 H6
Stake La *HBR* HX7 ....144 A7
Stake Lane Bank
  HOLM/MEL HD9 ....254 D1
Stallabrass St *GIR* BD8 ......4 B4
Stalley Royd La
  HOLM/MEL HD9 ....255 H3
Stamford Av *CAS* WF10 ....157 J8
Stamford St *BOW* BD4 ......5 L9
  MILN OL16 ....206 D8
Stamford Wy *DOD/DAR* S75 ..242 D4
Stammergate La *WBY* LS22 ..47 K4
Stamp Hill Cl *ILK* LS29 ....18 F6
Stanacre Pl *BFDE* BD3 ......5 H2
Stanage La *HIPP* HX3 ......125 J7
Stanbury Cl *DOD/DAR* S75 ..260 D3
Stancliffe Wy *HUDE* HD5 ..193 K5
Standale Av *PDSY/CALV* LS28 ..106 F6
Standale Crs *PDSY/CALV* LS28..106 F6
Standale Ri *PDSY/CALV* LS28 ..106 F6
Standard Dr *HUDS* HD4 ....213 K4
Standbridge Cl
  WKFDW/WTN WF2 ....220 C1
Stand Bridge Garth
  HOR/CROF WF4 ....198 B8
Standbridge La
  WKFDW/WTN WF2 ....198 E7
  WKFDW/WTN WF2 ....220 B1
Standedge Foot Rd *UPML* OL3..231 M7
Standedge Trail
  MAR/SLWT HD7 ....232 D2
  UPML OL3 ....231 M7
  UPML OL3 ....232 B6
Standhill Crs *BSLYN/ROY* S71 ..243 G2
Standiforth La *HUDE* HD5 ..193 G7
Standiforth Rd *HUDE* HD5 ..15 M7
Standish Crs *HEM/SK/SE* WF9..246 E2
Standroyd Dr *COL* BB8 ......74 C1
Standroyd Rd *COL* BB8 ......74 C1
Stanhall Av *PDSY/CALV* LS28 ..106 F5
Stanhope Av *DOD/DAR* S75 ..259 H1
  HORS LS18 ....85 L4
Stanhope Cl *HORS* LS18 ....85 L4
Stanhope Dr *HORS* LS18 ....85 K6
Stanhope Gdns *DOD/DAR* S75...260 H1
  EARD/LOFT WF3 ....154 A5
Stanhope Gv *EARD/LOFT* WF3 ..154 A5
Stanhope St *BSLY* S70 ....260 F5
  KBTN HD8 ....239 M7
  ROCH OL11 ....228 B1

Stanley Av *OSM* LS9 ....110 A3
Stanley Cottages *NORM* WF6 ..178 C1
Stanley Dr *RHAY* LS8 ....88 D2
Stanley Garth *HECK* * WF16 ..173 G6
Stanley La *GTL/HWG* HX4 ..190 B3
  LVSG WF15 ....172 C2
  WKFDE WF1 ....176 F4
Stanley Pl *BTLY* WF17 ......130 C4
  OSM LS9 ....110 C3
  WHIT OL12 ....207 H1
Stanley Rd *BSLY* S70 ......262 A3
  CHAL LS7 ....7 H1
  ECHL BD2 ....104 F1
  HFAX HX1 ....10 A1
  HUDW HD3 ....191 J1
  HUDW HD3 ....191 L3
  HWTH BD22 ....79 J1
  LVSG WF15 ....172 C2
  OSM LS9 ....110 B3
  WKFDE WF1 ....176 F4
Stanley St *BGLY* BD16 ......81 .
  BRIG HD6 ....170 D.
  BSLY S70 ....260 F.
  CAS WF10 ....158 A.
  CLECK BD19 ....149 M.
  CUD/GR S72 ....262 E.
  FEA/AMT WF7 ....179 M.
  HUDS HD4 ....214 A.
  HWTH BD22 ....79 G.
  IDLE BD10 ....83 K.
  KGHY * BD21 ....3 G.
  RPDN/SBR HX6 ....167 L.
  SHPY BD18 ....104 E.
  WHIT OL12 ....206 A.
  WKFDE WF1 ....176 F.
Stanley Ter *OSM* LS9 ......110 C.
Stanley Vw *WOR/ARM* LS12 ..108 E.
Stanmoor Dr *EARD/LOFT* WF3...155 C.
Stanmore Av *BULY* LS4 ....108 E.
Stanmore Crs *BULY* LS4 ....108 E.
Stanmore Gv *BULY* LS4 ....108 E.
Stanmore Hl *BULY* LS4 ....108 E.
Stanmore Mt *BULY* LS4 ....108 E.
Stanmore Pl *BULY* LS4 ......108 E.
  GTHN BD7 ....126 C.
Stanmore Rd *BULY* LS4 ....108 E.
Stanmore St *BULY* LS4 ......108 E.
Stanmore Ter *BULY* LS4 ....108 E.
Stanmore Vw *BULY* LS4 ....108 E.
Stannard Well Dr
  HOR/CROF WF4 ....197 K.
Stannard Well La
  HOR/CROF WF4 ....197 K.
Stannary Pl *HFAX* HX1 ......10 .
Stannery End La *HBR* HX7 ..144 B.
Stanneybrook Cl *MILN* OL16 ..206 D.
Stanney Cl *MILN* OL16 ......229 G.
Stanney Rd *MILN* OL16 ....206 D.
Stanningley Av *LUD/ILL* HX2 ..145 K.
Stanningley By-Pass
  PDSY/CALV LS28 ....106 E.
Stanningley Dr *LUD/ILL* HX2 ..145 K.
Stanningley Gv *HECK* WF16 ..172 E.
Stanningley Rd *LUD/ILL* HX2 ..145 K.
  PDSY/CALV LS28 ....107 H.
Stansfeld Cl *CAS* WF10 ....158 D.
  HFAX HX1 ....10 D.
Stansfield Cl *RPDN/SBR* HX6 ..167 K.
Stansfield Dr *CAS* WF10 ....158 E.
Stansfield Hall *LIT* OL15 ..185 L.
Stansfield Hall Rd *TOD* OL14 ..141 K.
Stansfield Mill La
  RPDN/SBR HX6 ....167 H.
Stansfield Rd *CAS* WF10 ....158 D.
  TOD OL14 ....163 K.
Stansfield St *TOD* OL14 ....141 K.
Stan Va *PONT* WF8 ....205 G.
Stanwell Av *HUDW* HD3 ..191 M.
Stapper Gn *WIL/AL* BD15 ..80 D.
Starbeck Rd *WKFDE* WF1 ..177 G.
Starfield Av *LIT* OL15 ......207 H.
Starkey La *AIRE* BD20 ......35 G.
Starkie St *KGHY* BD21 ......2 F.
Star La *BSLY* S70 ....261 G.
Starmire *HWTH* BD22 ......54 D.
Starring La *LIT* OL15 ......207 G.
Starring Rd *WHIT* OL12 ....207 G.
Starring Wy *LIT* OL15 ......207 H.
Star St *WBOW* BD5 .... F.
Starwort Cl *PONT* WF8 ....180 F.
Station Ap *HOLM/MEL* HD9 ..236 D.
  ILK LS29 ....40 A.
  TOD OL14 ....163 K.
Station Av *BRAM* LS13 ....107 K.
Station Ct *GSLY* * LS20 ....61 M.
Station Crs *WOR/ARM* LS12 ..108 D.
Stationers Entry *MILN* OL16 ..206 B.
Station Est *TAD* * LS24 ....71 L.
Station Flds *GFTH/SHER* LS25..113 H.
Station Forecourt *BFD* * BD1 ..4 F.
Station La *BIRK/DRI* BD11 ..128 D.
  EARD/LOFT WF3 ....153 M.
  EARD/LOFT WF3 ....153 M.
  FEA/AMT WF7 ....201 L.
  HUDS HD4 ....214 B.
  KBTN HD8 ....238 B.
  LVSG WF15 ....172 E.
  MAR/SLWT HD7 ....212 F.
  PONT WF8 ....180 F.
  RTHW LS26 ....133 M.
  SCFT LS14 ....68 B.
  WBY LS22 ....47 K.
Station Mt *BRAM* LS13 ....107 K.
Station Pde *KSTL* LS5 ......86 D.
  TOD OL14 ....140 C.
Station Pl *BRAM* LS13 ....107 K.
Station Rd *AIRE* BD20 ......34 .
  AIRE BD20 ....54 .
  AWLS/ASK DN6 ....249 .
  AWLS/ASK DN6 ....205 .
  BAIL BD17 ....61 K.
  BAIL BD17 ....82 .
  BFD BD1 ....
  BIRK/DRI BD11 ....129 G.
  BRIG HD6 ....170 .
  BSLY S70 ....260 .
  BSLYN/ROY S71 ....243 .
  BSLYN/ROY S71 ....261 .

BTLY WF17 ....173 M2
CAS WF10 ....157 L2
CAS WF10 ....157 M6
CLAY BD14 ....125 L2
CUL/QBY BD13 ....79 L8
CUL/QBY BD13 ....102 A6
CUL/QBY BD13 ....125 C5
DOD/DAR S75 ....242 A5
EARL WF12 ....174 B8
EARL WF12 ....195 L1
FEA/AMT WF7 ....202 C7
GFTH/SHER LS25 ....135 H6
GSLY LS20 ....61 M5
GTL/HWG HX4 ....190 D2
HBR WF17 ....143 J4
HECK WF16 ....172 E3
HEM/SK/SE WF9 ....224 A7
HEM/SK/SE WF9 ....247 J3
HIPP HX5 ....147 L7
HIPP HX5 ....148 C4
HOLM/MEL HD9 ....235 G6
HOLM/MEL HD9 ....236 C1
HOLM/MEL HD9 ....254 C1
HOR/CROF WF4 ....222 C5
HORS LS18 ....85 L4
HUDN HD2 ....193 J1
HUDS HD4 ....237 L8
HWTH BD22 ....78 E7
HWTH BD22 ....78 H4
HWTH BD22 ....100 E4
ILK LS29 ....38 D2
ILK LS29 ....40 A6
ILK LS29 ....61 J2
KBTN HD8 ....215 L3
KBTN HD8 ....238 A6
KBTN HD8 ....239 J2
KNOT * WF11 ....181 L1
LIT OL15 ....207 K1
LM/WK BD12 ....149 G1
LUD/ILL HX2 ....144 F7
MAR/SLWT HD7 ....212 B5
MAR/SLWT HD7 ....212 F2
MAR/SLWT HD7 ....233 H2
MILN OL16 ....229 H1
MIRF WF14 ....194 C2
MOR LS27 ....152 C1
MSTN/BAR LS15 ....90 B7
MSTN/BAR LS15 ....111 L4
NORM WF6 ....178 B3
OSS WF5 ....196 F1
OT LS21 ....27 L3
OT LS21 ....64 B1
PBR HG3 ....26 F2
ROCH OL11 ....206 B8
RPDN/SBR HX6 ....167 L3
RTHW LS26 ....156 D3
SHPY BD18 ....82 D6
TAD LS24 ....71 L3
TAD LS24 ....94 E8
TOD OL14 ....140 E5
WIL/AL BD15 ....102 B3
WOR/ARM LS12 ....108 D7
Station St *HOLM/MEL* HD9 ....234 M4
HUD HD1 ....14 F6
PDSY/CALV LS28 ....106 F8
WKFDE WF1 ....199 G4
Station Ter *BRAM* LS13 ....107 L4
CAS WF10 ....157 L2
Station to Station Wk *LIT* OL15.............207 M7
MAR/SLWT HD7 ....231 L1
Station Vw *AIRE* BD20 ....56 F1
HWTH BD22 ....100 E3
MSTN/BAR LS15 ....111 L5
Station Wy *WOR/ARM* LS12 ....108 D7
Staups La *HBR* HX7 ....142 B4
HIPP HX5 ....147 H5
Staveley La *ROY/SHW* OL2 ....229 M8
Staveley Dr *SHPY* BD18 ....81 M7
Staveley Gv * *WBTH* BD22 ....79 J3
Staveley Ms *BGLY* * BD16 ....81 J2
Staveley Rd *BGLY* BD16 ....81 J1
GTHN BD7 ....104 D8
HWTH BD22 ....79 J3
SHPY BD18 ....81 M6
Staveley Wy *HWTH* BD22 ....79 J2
Stavely Ms *BGLY* * BD17 ....13 H5
Staverton Gv *CUL/QBY* BD13 ....103 G7
Staverton St *LUD/ILL* HX2 ....146 A7
Stavordale *WHIT* OL12 ....206 A6
Staybrite Av *BGLY* BD16 ....81 J7
Staygate Gn *WBSY* BD6 ....127 G5
Staynton Crs *HUDN* HD2 ....193 H1
Stead Ga *KBTN* HD8 ....238 F4
Stead Hill Wy *IDLE* BD10 ....83 H5
Stead La *HUDE* HD5 ....193 K6
ILK LS29 ....39 K6
RPDN/SBR HX6 ....188 E4
SCFT LS14 ....90 C1
Steadman St *BFDE* BD3 ....5 M7
Steadman Ter *BFDE* BD3 ....5 M7
Stead Rd *BOW* BD4 ....128 A6
Stead St *BAIL* BD17 ....82 D6
HFAX * HX1 ....10 F6
Stead's Yd *HORS* LS18 ....85 L4
Steanard La *MIRF* WF14 ....194 E3
Steander *OSM* LS9 ....9 K2
Steele La *GTL/HWG* HX4 ....189 L5
Steeplands *HUDN* HD7 ....171 H8
Steep La *HBR* HX7 ....166 C2
STKB/PEN S36 ....271 H2
Steeple Av *HOR/CROF* WF4 ....217 G2
Steep Riding *HOLM/MEL* HD9 ....236 A6
Steeton Gv *AIRE* BD20 ....35 L8
Steeton Hall Gdns *AIRE* BD20 ....35 L8
Steeton Wy *GFTH/SHER* LS25 ....137 L3
Steincroft Rd *GFTH/SHER* LS25.............138 B3
Stella Gdns *PONT* WF8 ....181 H4
Stell Hl *HWTH* BD22 ....78 F1
Stennard Island *WKFDE* WF1.............13 H5
Stephen Cl *HIPP* HX3 ....147 J3
Stephen Crs *ECHL* BD2 ....105 J3
Stephen Rd *WBOW* BD6 ....126 B4
Stephenson Cl *EARL* WF12 ....174 A5
Stephenson Dr
WOR/ARM LS12 ....129 M3
Stephenson Rd *WIL/AL* BD15...102 F4
Stephenson St *GTHN* BD7 ....126 D3

Stephenson Wy
WKFDW/WTN WF2 ....176 B1
WOR/ARM LS12 ....129 M3
Stepping Stones *AIRE* BD20 ....59 G6
Steps La *RPDN/SBR* HX6 ....167 L1
Steps Meadow *WHIT* OL12 ....206 D2
Sterling Ct *EARD/LOFT* WF3 ....153 G4
Sterling Wy *EARD/LOFT* WF3 ....152 F4
Sterne Hl *LUD/ILL* HX2 ....168 B2
Stevenson Av *CAS* WF10 ....180 E1
Stevenson Dr *DOD/DAR* S75 ....260 A7
Stewart Cl *ECHL* BD2 ....105 L1
MSTN/BAR LS15 ....111 L7
Stewart Pl *BEE/HOL* * LS11 ....8 D9
Stewart Royd *HECK* * WF16 ....173 G2
Stewart St *HWTH* BD22 ....79 G6
MILN OL16 ....229 K3
Sticker La *BOW* BD4 ....127 L3
Stile Common Rd *HUDS* HD4 ....214 D3
Stile Hill Wy *MSTN/BAR* LS15 ....112 A7
Stilemoor Ri *TOD* OL14 ....141 J7
Stile Rd *TOD* OL14 ....141 J7
Stillwell Dr *WKFDW/WTN* WF2 ....199 G5
Stillwell Garth
WKFDW/WTN WF2 ....199 G6
Stillwell Gv *WKFDW/WTN* WF2...199 G6
Stirling Crs *BOW* BD4 ....128 A3
HORS LS18 ....85 J2
Stirling Rd *ILK* LS29 ....39 M5
Stirling St *AIRE* BD20 ....36 A4
HFAX HX1 ....10 E7
Stirling Wy *GFTH/SHER* LS25 ....113 K7
Stirrup Gv *ECHL* BD2 ....105 H2
Stirton St *WBOW* BD5 ....126 F3
Stithy St *OSS* WF5 ....174 E6
Stiups La *MILN* OL16 ....228 E2
Stock Cl *WHIT* OL12 ....206 A4
Stockeld La *WBY* LS22 ....28 B3
Stockeld Rd *ILK* LS29 ....38 C2
Stockeld Wy *ILK* LS29 ....38 C1
Stockerhead La
MAR/SLWT HD7 ....212 C6
Stock Gv *MILN* OL16 ....207 H7
Stockheld La *MSTN/BAR* LS15 ....90 B5
Stock Hey La *TOD* OL14 ....142 D8
Stockhill Fold *IDLE* BD10 ....83 M6
Stockhill Rd *IDLE* BD10 ....83 M7
Stockhill St *DEWS* WF13 ....173 J6
Stockingate *HEM/SK/SE* WF9 ....246 D5
Stockinger La *ILK* LS29 ....19 H7
Stocking La *GFTH/SHER* LS25...92 B8
GFTH/SHER LS25 ....138 E8
KNOT WF11 ....182 E2
SEL YO8 ....139 L5
Stock La *LUD/ILL* HX2 ....145 K8
Stocks Ap *SCFT* LS14 ....111 K2
Stocks Av *HBR* HX7 ....143 M6
Stocks Bank Rd *MIRF* WF14 ....171 M7
Stocks Crs *HBR* HX7 ....143 M6
Stocks Dr *KBTN* HD8 ....237 M6
Stocks Gdns *HBR* HX7 ....143 M6
Stocks Hl *BEE/HOL* LS11 ....8 C5
ILK LS29 ....61 H2
WOR/ARM LS12 ....108 E6
Stocks Hill Cl *AIRE* * BD20 ....58 F5
Stocks La *BTLY* WF17 ....173 L1
CUL/QBY BD13 ....125 K5
DOD/DAR S75 ....260 F4
HBR HX7 ....143 M6
HUDS HD4 ....237 K5
LUD/ILL HX2 ....145 G5
RPDN/SBR HX6 ....167 G3
Stocksmoor Rd
HOR/CROF WF4 ....218 A7
Stocks Moor Rd *HUDS* HD4 ....237 K4
Stocks Ri *SCFT* LS14 ....111 K2
Stocks Rd *SCFT* LS14 ....111 K2
Stocks St *CHAL* LS7 ....7 G2
Stocks Wk *HUDE* HD5 ....215 H3
Stockton St *LIT* OL15 ....207 J1
Stockwell Dr *BTLY* WF17 ....151 M8
Stockwell Hl *HUDS* HD4 ....214 B6
Stod Fold *LUD/ILL* HX2 ....123 L6
Stoke St *MILN* OL16 ....206 D8
Stone Acre Hts
HOLM/MEL * HD9 ....235 H5
Stone Arches *WBOW* BD5 ....127 G2
Stonebridge Ap
WOR/ARM * LS12 ....108 A8
Stonebridge Av
WOR/ARM LS12 ....108 B8
Stonebridge Gv
WOR/ARM LS12 ....108 A8
Stonebridge La
WOR/ARM LS12 ....108 A8
Stonebridge Wk *KBTN* HD8 ....238 B5
Stone Brig Gn *RTHW* LS26 ....154 F2
Stone Brig La *RTHW* LS26 ....155 G2
Stonechat Ri *MOR* LS27 ....152 E2
Stonecliffe Cl *CUL/QBY* BD13 ....168 C2
Stonecliffe Crs *WOR/ARM* LS12 ....108 A8
Stonecliffe Dr *HOR/CROF* WF4 ....196 D7
WOR/ARM LS12 ....108 A8
Stonecliffe Garth
WOR/ARM LS12 ....108 A8
Stonecliffe Gv *WOR/ARM* LS12 ....108 A8
Stonecliffe Mt *WOR/ARM* LS12 ....108 A8
Stonecliffe Ter *WOR/ARM* LS12...107 M8
WOR/ARM LS12 ....129 M1
Stone Ct *AIRE* BD20 ....58 F6
CUD S72 ....245 G3
Stonecroft *EARD/LOFT* WF3 ....177 G1
ECHL BD2 ....105 L2
Stonecroft Gdns *KBTN* HD8 ....238 A6
Stonecroft Mt *LUD/ILL* HX2 ....167 L1
Stonedale Cl *OT* LS21 ....43 C8
Stonedene Pk *WBY* LS22 ....30 A8
Stonefield *SCFT* LS14 ....67 M2
Stonefield Av *HUDS* HD4 ....213 K3
Stonefield Cl *IDLE* BD10 ....105 K1
Stonefield Pl *BTLY* WF17 ....151 H5
Stonefield Rd *HUDS* HD4 ....213 K3
Stonefield St *CLECK* BD19 ....149 J8
DEWS WF13 ....173 J5
MILN OL16 ....229 H1

Stonefleece Ct
HOLM/MEL HD9 ....236 B3
Stonegarth Cl *CUD/GR* S72 ....244 D8
Stonegate *BGLY* BD16 ....81 J1
CHAL LS7 ....7 H2
OSS WF5 ....197 G3
Stonegate Ap *CHAL* * LS7 ....87 H8
Stonegate Cha *CHAL* LS7 ....87 J7
Stonegate Cl *AL/HA/HU* LS17...87 M3
Stonegate Crs *CHAL* LS7 ....87 J7
Stonegate Dr *PONT* WF8 ....180 B8
Stonegate Farm Cl *CHAL* LS7 ....87 H7
Stonegate Gdns *CHAL* LS7 ....87 H7
Stonegate Gn *CHAL* LS7 ....87 H7
FEA/AMT WF7 ....224 A1
Stonegate Ms *CHAL* LS7 ....87 H8
Stonegate Pl *CHAL* * LS7 ....87 H8
Stonegate Rd *AL/HA/HU* LS17...87 J6
IDLE BD10 ....83 L8
Stonegate Wk *CHAL* LS7 ....87 J8
Stone Gv *AIRE* BD20 ....56 E1
Stone Hall Rd *ECHL* BD2 ....105 K2
Stone Head La *HWTH* BD22 ....53 M2
Stone Hl *BGLY* BD16 ....81 K2
Stonehill Ri *CUD/GR* S72 ....244 D8
STKB/PEN S36 ....270 E5
Stonehouse Dr *CUL/QBY* BD13...124 E6
Stonehurst *EARD/LOFT* WF3 ....111 M2
Stonehurst Rd *MIRF* WF14 ....172 C8
Stonehyrst Av *DEWS* WF13 ....173 M5
Stone La *HWTH* BD22 ....100 D4
Stonelea *GTL/HWG* HX4 ....189 J1
Stonelea Cl *DOD/DAR* S75 ....259 H6
Stonelea Ct *CHAL* LS7 ....87 J7
HDGY LS6 ....108 F1
Stone Lea Gv
HEM/SK/SE * WF9 ....247 J4
Stoneleigh *CUL/QBY* BD13 ....125 H5
Stoneleigh Ct *KBTN* HD8 ....238 C3
Stoneleigh Cft *BSLY* * S70 ....261 H7
Stonely Dr *TOD* OL14 ....163 J7
Stone Mill Ap *HDGY* LS6 ....87 J7
Stone Mill Ct *HDGY* LS6 ....87 G7
Stone Mill Wy *HDGY* LS6 ....87 G7
Stone Pits La *MOR* LS27 ....151 M1
Stones Dr *RPDN/SBR* HX6 ....188 D4
Stones Hey Ga *HBR* * HX7 ....120 E8
Stones La *MAR/SLWT* HD7 ....212 E6
MAR/SLWT HD7 ....212 F3
TOD OL14 ....163 G2
Stones Rd *TOD* OL14 ....163 H2
Stones Ter *TOD* * OL14 ....163 J4
Stone St *BAIL* BD17 ....83 C4
BFD BD1 ....4 F5
BSLYN/ROY S71 ....261 G2
WIL/AL BD15 ....103 J3
Stone Vls *FEA/AMT* * WF7 ....224 A1
HDGY LS6 ....86 F8
Stone Wood La *KBTN* HD8 ....237 L5
Stoney Back La *HUDS* HD4 ....214 A4
Stoney Bank La
HOLM/MEL HD9 ....236 F6
Stoney Bank St *DEWS* WF13 ....173 J8
Stoney Battery *HFAX* HX1 ....11 H3
Stoney Battery Rd *HUDN* HD3 ....213 M2
Stoneybrook Cl
HOR/CROF WF4 ....219 H6
Stoney Cft *CLECK* BD19 ....150 D7
Stoney Cross La *AIRE* BD20 ....57 K4
Stoney Cross St *HUDS* HD4 ....214 A4
Stoney Ford La *HUDE* HD5 ....193 K5
Stoneyhurst Sq *BOW* BD4 ....128 A3
Stoney La *AL/HA/HU* LS17 ....89 J1
BTLY WF17 ....151 M8
COL BB8 ....52 A5
HIPP HX3 ....146 C3
HIPP HX3 ....148 C7
HOR/CROF WF4 ....220 B3
HORS LS18 ....85 K6
HUDW HD3 ....191 H8
ILK LS29 ....39 L8
UPML OL3 ....230 F7
WKFDW/WTN WF2 ....175 M1
Stoney Ridge Av *WIL/AL* BD15...103 K1
Stoney Ridge Rd *BGLY* BD16 ....103 L1
Stoney Ri *WBTH* * LS18 ....85 K6
Stoney Rock Ct *OSM* LS9 ....110 B5
Stoney Rock Gv *OSM* LS9 ....110 B5
Stoney Rock La *OSM* LS9 ....110 B5
Stoney Royd *BSLYN/ROY* S71 ....243 H5
Stoney Royd La *TOD* OL14 ....141 H6
Stoney Royd Ter *HIPP* HX5 ....168 F2
Stoneys Fold *WIL/AL* BD15 ....80 B7
Stoneythorpe *HORS* LS18 ....85 K6
Stonie Heyes Av *WHIT* OL12 ....206 D4
Stony Croft La *AWLS/ASK* DN6 ....249 J2
GTL/HWG HX4 ....189 K2
Stony Ga *HOLM/MEL* HD9 ....254 A4
Stony La *ECHL* BD2 ....105 L1
GTL/HWG HX4 ....168 C6
HBR HX7 ....142 F4
HIPP HX3 ....169 L2
HOLM/MEL HD9 ....236 B1
RPDN/SBR HX6 ....188 F1
TOD OL14 ....141 C5
WIL/AL BD15 ....103 H4
Stony Royd *PDSY/CALV* LS28 ....106 E3
Stony Royd La *HBR* * HX7 ....165 J2
Stoodley Cl *TOD* OL14 ....164 C1
Stoodley Gra *TOD* * OL14 ....164 C1
Stoodley La *TOD* OL14 ....142 C7
Stoodley Ter *LUD/ILL* HX2 ....146 A8
Stopford La *LIT* OL15 ....207 G2
Stopford Garth
WKFDW/WTN WF2 ....199 G6
Store St *ROY/SHW* OL2 ....229 L6
Storey Pl *SCFT* LS14 ....111 C5
Storie Crs *WKFDW/WTN* WF2 ....199 G6
Stormer Hill La *RPDN/SBR* HX6 ....167 M4
Storr Hl *LM/WK* BD12 ....148 E2
Storrs Hill Rd *OSS* WF5 ....197 G4
Storrs La *STKB/PEN* S36 ....271 L4
Storrs Mill La *BSLYN/ROY* S71 ....263 G4

Storrs Wood Vw *CUD/GR* S72 ....262 F2
Storth Av *HUDS* HD4 ....213 H3
Storthes Hall La *WBTH* HD8 ....237 K1
Storth Pl *HUDN* HD2 ....14 C1
Storths Rd *HUDN* HD2 ....192 B5
Stottercliffe Rd *STKB/PEN* S36 ....270 E3
Stott Hl *BFD* BD1 ....5 G5
Stott Rd *HDGY* * LS6 ....109 G3
Stott St *MILN* OL16 ....206 F3
MILN OL16 ....229 H2
WHIT OL12 ....206 B5
WOR/ARM LS12 ....108 F7
Stott Ter *ECHL* BD2 ....105 M2
Stourton Rd *ILK* LS29 ....38 B1
Stowe Gv *OSM* LS9 ....110 E6
Stowell Mill St *WBOW* BD5 ....126 F2
Stradmore Rd *CUL/QBY* BD13 ....102 A6
Strafford Av *BSLY* S70 ....261 H8
Strafford Wk *DOD/DAR* S75 ....260 B8
Strafford Wy *IDLE* BD10 ....84 A6
Straightacres La *IDLE* BD10 ....105 M1
Straight La *AWLS/ASK* DN6 ....248 D2
ILK LS29 ....36 F1
LUD/ILL HX2 ....145 M1
Strait La *AL/HA/HU* LS17 ....43 J1
Straits *BAIL* BD17 ....82 C2
Stralau St *BTLY* WF17 ....151 L8
Strands Ct *HOR/CROF* WF4 ....197 G8
Strangford Ct *IDLE* BD10 ....83 M6
Stranglands La *KNOT* WF11 ....159 H8
Stratford Av *BEE/HOL* LS11 ....131 K3
ROCH OL11 ....228 A1
Stratford Cl *MAR/SLWT* HD7 ....213 G1
Stratford Gn *GTHN* BD7 ....126 D3
Stratford St *BEE/HOL* LS11 ....131 K3
Stratford Ter *BEE/HOL* LS11 ....131 K3
Strathallan Dr *BAIL* BD17 ....82 F3
Stratheden Rd
WKFDW/WTN WF2 ....12 B1
Strathmore Av *OSM* LS9 ....110 C4
Strathmore Dr *BAIL* BD17 ....82 D2
OSM LS9 ....110 C3
Strathmore Gdns
HEM/SK/SE * WF9 ....247 K2
Strathmore Rd *ILK* LS29 ....39 G3
Strathmore St *OSM* LS9 ....110 C4
Strathmore Vw *OSM* LS9 ....110 C4
Stratton Cl *BRIG* HD6 ....170 D5
Stratton Pk *BRIG* HD6 ....170 D5
Stratton Rd *BRIG* HD6 ....170 D5
Stratton Vw *BOW* * BD4 ....128 A2
Stratus Cl *FEA/AMT* WF7 ....224 B2
Strawberry Av
GFTH/SHER LS25 ....113 G8
LVSG WF15 ....172 C2
Strawberry Bank *LVSG* WF15...172 C2
Strawberry Flds *KGHY* BD21 ....3 G3
Strawberry Gdns
BSLYN/ROY S71 ....261 G2
Strawberry La *WOR/ARM* LS12 ....108 E7
Strawberry Rd *WOR/ARM* LS12...108 E7
Strawberry St *AIRE* BD20 ....35 M5
KGHY BD21 ....3 G3
Stream Head Rd
CUL/QBY BD13 ....102 D4
Streamside *HDGY* LS6 ....87 G8
Streamside Fold *HBR* * HX7 ....144 A6
The Street *ILK* LS29 ....18 F6
Street 1 *BSPA/BRAM* LS23 ....49 J6
Street 2 *BSPA/BRAM* LS23 ....49 J5
Street 3 *BSPA/BRAM* LS23 ....49 K5
Street 5 *BSPA/BRAM* LS23 ....49 K4
Street 6 *BSPA/BRAM* LS23 ....49 K3
Street 7 *BSPA/BRAM* LS23 ....49 K3
Street 8 *BSPA/BRAM* LS23 ....49 L4
Street Furlong La *PONT* WF8 ....181 K7
Street Head La *HWTH* BD22 ....78 A5
Street La *AIRE* BD20 ....58 D3
AL/HA/HU LS17 ....87 M4
MOR * LS27 ....129 L7
Strelley Rd *BSLYN/ROY* S71 ....243 G6
Strensall Gn *WBSY* BD6 ....126 A6
Stretchgate La *LUD/ILL* HX2 ....146 A6
Stretton Cl *FEA/AMT* WF7 ....179 J5
Stretton Rd *BSLYN/ROY* S71 ....261 J2
Strickland Av *AL/HA/HU* LS17...89 H2
Strickland Cl *AL/HA/HU* LS17...89 H2
Strickland Crs *AL/HA/HU* LS17...89 H2
Strickland Rd *HEM/SK/SE* WF9 ....225 M6
Strikes La *AIRE* BD20 ....56 A3
Strines Moor Rd
HOLM/MEL HD9 ....254 E7
Strines St *TOD* OL14 ....163 J7
Stringer House La *KBTN* HD8 ....217 J7
Stringer La *HOR/CROF* WF4 ....197 K5
Strong Close Gv *KGHY* BD21 ....3 L4
Strong Close Rd *KGHY* BD21 ....3 L4
Strong Close Wy *KGHY* BD21 ....3 L4
Stuart Gv *MAR/SLWT* HD7 ....212 C6
NORM WF6 ....178 C2
Stuart Pl *HUDN* HD2 ....193 H1
Stuart Rd *PONT* WF8 ....180 B1
Stuart St *CAS* WF10 ....158 A6
MILN OL16 ....206 D8
PONT WF8 ....180 B1
Stubbin Fold *HOLM/MEL* HD9 ....253 L3
Stubbing Brink *HBR* HX7 ....143 G3
Stubbing Dr *HBR* HX7 ....143 G3
Stubbing Holme Rd *HBR* HX7 ....143 H3
Stubbing La *GTL/HWG* HX4 ....190 A1
RPDN/SBR HX6 ....167 G6
Stubbings Cl *HBR* HX7 ....144 A6
Stubbings Rd *BAIL* BD17 ....82 B4
Stubbings St *HBR* HX7 ....144 A6
Stubbing Wy *SHPY* BD18 ....82 E8
Stubbs La *HOLM/MEL* HD9 ....253 J3
KBTN HD8 ....239 K8
Stubbs Br *AWLS/ASK* DN6 ....248 C3
KNOT WF11 ....183 J3
Stubbs La *AWLS/ASK* DN6 ....227 M1
EARD/LOFT WF3 ....154 A7
KNOT WF11 ....182 C7
Stubbs Rd *PONT* WF8 ....227 J1
Stubham Ri *ILK* LS29 ....38 C1

Stubley Farm Rd *HECK* WF16 ....150 E8
Stubley Gdns *LIT* OL15 ....207 J1
Stubley Holme *TOD* OL14 ....140 C5
Stubley La *LIT* OL15 ....207 J1
TOD OL14 ....140 C5
Stubley Mill Rd *LIT* OL15 ....207 G2
Stubley St *HECK* WF16 ....150 E8
Stubley St *WKFDE* * WF1 ....12 D3
Stubs Beck La *CLECK* BD19 ....149 L4
Studfold Vw *SCFT* LS14 ....111 J3
Studio Rd *BVRD* 109 G5
Studley Av *WBSY* BD6 ....126 D7
Studley Cl *AIRE* BD20 ....58 F5
Studley Crs *BGLY* BD16 ....81 K3
Studley Rd *ECHL* BD2 ....105 H4
Stump Cross *HIPP* HX3 ....147 H5
Stumpcross Ct *PONT* WF8 ....181 J3
Stumpcross La *PONT* WF8 ....181 J3
Stumpcross Wy *PONT* WF8 ....181 J3
Stunstead Rd *COL* BB8 ....74 E3
Stunsteds Rd *CLECK* BD19 ....149 M6
Sturges Gv *ECHL* BD2 ....105 K4
Sturton Av *GFTH/SHER* LS25 ....113 J6
Sturton Grange La
GFTH/SHER LS25 ....113 K7
Sturton Gv *LUD/ILL* HX2 ....124 J7
Sturton La *GFTH/SHER* LS25 ....113 J6
LUD/ILL HX2 ....124 A8
Stutely Gv *HUDN* HD2 ....193 G3
Stutton Rd *TAD* LS24 ....71 K6
Styebank La *RTHW* LS26 ....133 H8
Styes La *RPDN/SBR* HX6 ....166 F2
Stygate La *AWLS/ASK* DN6 ....227 L4
Sty La *BGLY* BD16 ....59 H8
Styveton Wy *AIRE* BD20 ....35 K8
Sude Hl *HOLM/MEL* HD9 ....237 H8
Sude Hill Ter *HOLM/MEL* HD9 ....237 H8
Sudforth La *GLE* DN14 ....183 J1
Sudlow St *MILN* OL16 ....206 D4
Suffield Crs *MOR* LS27 ....129 K6
Suffield Dr *MOR* LS27 ....129 K6
Suffield Rd *MOR* LS27 ....129 K6
Suffolk Av *BTLY* WF17 ....173 J3
Suffolk Ct *YEA* LS19 ....62 D7
Suffolk Pl *ECHL* BD2 ....105 H2
Suffolk St *BTLY* WF17 ....173 K2
ROCH OL11 ....206 B8
Sufton St *HUDN* HD2 ....14 D1
Sugar Hl *ILK* LS29 ....19 H6
Sugar Hill Cl *RTHW* LS26 ....155 L3
Sugar La *EARL* WF12 ....174 A6
WKFDE WF1 ....13 J7
Sugar Well Ap *CHAL* * LS7 ....109 K1
Sugar Well Ct *CHAL* * LS7 ....109 K2
Sugar Well Mt *CHAL* LS7 ....109 J1
Sugar Well Rd *CHAL* LS7 ....109 J1
Sugden Cl *BRIG* HD6 ....170 C6
Sugden St *BFD* BD1 ....4 E5
LM/WK BD12 ....149 H2
Sulby Gv *BSLY* S70 ....261 M8
IDLE BD10 ....84 A8
Sullivan Cl *HUDS* HD4 ....213 M3
Sullivan Gv *HEM/SK/SE* WF9 ....246 D5
Summerbank Cl
BIRK/DRI BD11 ....129 H7
Summerbridge Cl *BTLY* WF17 ....151 J8
Summerbridge Crs
CLECK BD19 ....150 D4
IDLE BD10 ....105 M1
Summerbridge Dr *IDLE* BD10 ....105 M1
Summer Castle *MILN* * OL16 ....206 B7
Summerdale *CLECK* BD19 ....150 D4
Summerdale Rd *CUD/GR* S72 ....262 C1
Summerfield Av *BRAM* LS13 ....107 J3
BRIG HD6 ....148 D8
Summerfield Cl *BAIL* BD17 ....82 C3
KNOT WF11 ....160 A6
Summerfield Dr *BAIL* BD17 ....82 D3
BRAM LS13 ....107 J3
KNOT WF11 ....159 M6
Summerfield Gdns *BRAM* LS13 ....107 J3
Summerfield Gn *BAIL* BD17 ....82 D3
BRAM LS13 ....107 J3
Summerfield Gv *BAIL* BD17 ....82 C3
KBTN HD8 ....215 M4
Summerfield Pk *BAIL* BD17 ....82 D3
Summerfield Pl *BRAM* LS13 ....107 J3
Summerfield Rd *BRAM* LS13 ....107 H3
IDLE BD10 ....83 L8
TOD OL14 ....163 J3
Summergate Pl *HFAX* HX1 ....10 A8
Summergate St *HFAX* HX1 ....10 B8
Summer Hall Ing *LM/WK* BD12 ....148 D2
Summerhill Av *AIRE* BD20 ....35 M8
Summerhill Dr *AIRE* BD20 ....35 M8
Summerhill Gdns *RHAY* LS8 ....88 D3
Summerhill Gv
GFTH/SHER LS25 ....112 F8
Summerhill La *AIRE* BD20 ....35 M8
Summerhill Pl *RHAY* LS8 ....88 D3
Summerhill Rd
GFTH/SHER LS25 ....112 F7
Summer Hill Rd *RTHW* LS26 ....156 F3
Summer Hill St *GTHN* BD7 ....126 C1
Summerlands Gv *WBOW* BD5 ....127 J4
Summer La *BSLY* S70 ....260 F4
BSLYN/ROY S71 ....243 K2
KBTN HD8 ....217 M8
Summer Lea *IDLE* BD10 ....83 J9
Summer Meadow *PONT* * WF8 ....180 E7
Summer Rd *BSLYN/ROY* S71 ....243 K2
Summerscale St *HFAX* * HX1 ....10 C4
Summerseat Pl *GTHN* BD7 ....126 D1
Summer St *BSLY* S70 ....260 F4
HFAX HX1 ....10 B3
HUD * HD1 ....214 B2
HUDS HD4 ....213 M8
MILN OL16 ....206 C7
Summervale *HOLM/MEL* HD9 ....236 C8
Summerville Rd *GTHN* BD7 ....4 A7
PDSY/CALV LS28 ....106 E4
Summit St *KGHY* * BD21 ....2 F3
Sunbeam Av *BEE/HOL* LS11 ....131 K3
Sunbeam Gv *BEE/HOL* LS11 ....131 K3
Sunbeam Pl *BEE/HOL* LS11 ....131 K3
Sunbeam Ter *BEE/HOL* LS11 ....131 K3
EARD/LOFT * WF3 ....153 G5
Sunbridge Rd *BFD* BD1 ....4 B4

Sunbury Gv *HUDE* HD5 ....193 G8
Sun Ct *FEA/AMT* WF7 ....179 L5
Sunderland Ct *BRIG* HD6 ....170 C3
Sunderland Rd *AIRE* BD20 ....34 F1
  HTON BD9 ....104 D4
Sunderland St *HFAX* HX1 ....10 F6
  HWTH BD22 ....79 H6
  KGHY BD21 ....2 F7
Sunderland Ter *BSLY* S70 ....261 J6
Sundown Av *GTHN* BD7 ....126 A2
Sun Fld *PDSY/CALV* LS28 ....106 F5
Sunfield Cl *PDSY/CALV* LS28 ....106 F4
Sunfield Dr *PDSY/CALV* LS28 ....106 F4
Sunfield Gdns
  PDSY/CALV * LS28 ....106 F4
Sunfield Pl *PDSY/CALV* LS28 ....106 F4
Sun Fold *HFAX* HX1 ....11 J8
Sunhill Cl *MILN* OL16 ....228 D4
Sun Hill Dr *BAIL* BD17 ....82 A3
Sunhurst Cl *HWTH* BD22 ....78 E4
Sunhurst Dr *HWTH* BD22 ....78 E4
Sun La *HWTH* BD22 ....78 A7
  ILK LS29 ....39 M4
  WKFDE WF1 ....13 G3
Sunmoor Dr *SKP/WHF* BD23 ....16 D2
Sunningdale *GFTH/SHER* LS25 ....114 B7
  GIR BD8 ....103 M6
Sunningdale Av *AL/HA/HU* LS17 ....87 J2
  DOD/DAR S75 ....242 C5
Sunningdale Crs
  CUL/QBY BD13 ....102 A1
Sunningdale Cft *HUDN* HD2 ....192 B3
Sunningdale Dr *AL/HA/HU* LS17 ....87 J2
  CUD/GR S72 ....244 E5
Sunningdale Gn *AL/HA/HU* LS17 ....87 J2
Sunningdale Rd *HUDS* HD4 ....213 M3
Sunningdales *NORM* WF6 ....178 F5
Sunny Av *HEM/SK/SE* WF9 ....225 J7
  HEM/SK/SE WF9 ....247 K4
Sunny Bank *CHAL* LS7 ....110 B1
  HEM/SK/SE WF9 ....223 J1
  HOR/CROF WF4 ....222 C5
  KNOT WF11 ....182 C2
  NORM WF6 ....178 C6
  SHPY BD18 ....82 D7
  HBR HX7 ....144 A5
Sunnybank *KBTN* HD8 ....257 H1
Sunnybank Av *BFDE* BD3 ....106 B5
  HORS LS18 ....85 K7
Sunny Bank Av *MIRF* WF14 ....172 C4
  WBOW BD5 ....126 F5
Sunnybank Cl *CLECK* BD19 ....149 H8
Sunnybank Ct *YEA* LS19 ....62 F7
Sunnybank Crs *GTL/HWG* HX4 ....168 C7
  YEA LS19 ....62 F7
Sunny Bank Dr *CUD/GR* S72 ....262 D2
  MIRF WF14 ....172 B6
  RPDN/SBR HX6 ....167 L2
Sunnybank Dr *GTL/HWG* HX4 ....168 D7
Sunnybank Gv *BFDE* BD3 ....106 B5
Sunny Bank Gv *CHAL* LS7 ....110 A1
  MIRF WF14 ....172 C1
Sunny Bank La *BTLY* WF17 ....151 M7
  HBR HX7 ....165 L2
  HIPP HX3 ....147 K8
Sunnybank La *BFDE* BD3 ....106 B5
  GTL/HWG HX4 ....168 D7
Sunny Bank Pde *MIRF* WF14 ....172 B6
Sunny Bank Rd *AIRE* BD20 ....34 E8
  BRIG HD6 ....170 B3
  BTLY WF17 ....151 M8
  DOD/DAR S75 ....259 H6
  HOLM/MEL HD9 ....234 E4
  LUD/ILL HX2 ....145 K1
  MAR/SLWT HD7 ....212 D3
  MIRF WF14 ....172 C6
  WBOW BD5 ....126 F5
Sunnybank Rd
  GFTH/SHER LS25 ....114 D8
  GTL/HWG HX4 ....168 C7
  HORS LS18 ....85 K7
  HUDW HD3 ....191 M6
Sunnybank St *OSS* WF5 ....196 E1
Sunny Bank St *RPDN/SBR* HX6 ....167 L2
Sunny Bank Ter *HIPP* * HX3 ....11 G2
  TOD OL14 ....140 D5
Sunny Bank Vw *RHAY* LS8 ....110 B1
Sunny Bank Wk *MIRF* WF14 ....172 C6
Sunnybank Woods *BTLY* WF17 ....151 M8
Sunnybrae Crs *BGLY* BD16 ....81 K4
Sunny Brow *HUDS* HD4 ....214 B6
Sunny Brow La *HTON* BD9 ....103 M4
Sunnycliffe *AIRE* BD20 ....58 F6
Sunnydale Av *BRIG* HD6 ....170 C6
Sunnydale Crs *OT* LS21 ....40 F8
Sunnydale Gv *KGHY* BD21 ....58 B8
Sunnydale Pk *AIRE* BD20 ....59 G5
  OSS WF5 ....197 G1
Sunnydale Rdg *OT* LS21 ....40 F8
Sunnydale Rd *OSS* WF5 ....197 G1
Sunnydale Ter *OSS* WF5 ....197 G1
Sunnydene *SCFT* LS14 ....111 H5
Sunnyfield *EARD/LOFT* WF3 ....153 L8
Sunnyfield Dr *HEM/SK/SE* WF9 ....223 J3
Sunny Gv *MOR* LS27 ....130 E6
Sunny Heys Rd
  HOLM/MEL HD9 ....234 D4
Sunny Heys West
  HOLM/MEL HD9 ....234 F3
Sunny Hl *WKFDW/WTN* WF2 ....175 M5
Sunnyhill Av *HUDE* HD5 ....193 K4
Sunny Hill Av *HWTH* BD22 ....2 B8
Sunny Hill Cl
  WKFDW/WTN WF2 ....176 A4
Sunnyhill Crs
  WKFDW/WTN WF2 ....175 M4
Sunnyhill Cft
  WKFDW/WTN WF2 ....175 M4
Sunny Hill Gv *HWTH* BD22 ....2 B8
Sunny Lea *MAR/SLWT* HD7 ....233 J2
Sunny Lea Ter *WBSY* * BD6 ....126 F4
Sunnylee Est *OT* * LS21 ....41 J6
Sunny Md *HUDE* HD5 ....193 J8
Sunnymead *KBTN* HD8 ....239 M4
Sunny Mt *AIRE* BD20 ....58 E7
  BGLY BD16 ....80 D5
  KGHY BD21 ....2 E3

Sunnymount *HWTH* BD22 ....56 F6
Sunnyridge Av
  PDSY/CALV LS28 ....106 D7
Sunnyside *BRIG* HD6 ....170 D7
  GTL/HWG HX4 ....190 B5
  HECK WF16 ....172 F3
  HUDW HD3 ....14 A3
  TOD OL14 ....163 J1
Sunnyside Av *EARD/LOFT* WF3 ....152 F6
  LVSG WF15 ....172 B4
Sunnyside Rd *BRAM* LS13 ....107 K5
Sunny Side La *HIPP* * HX3 ....11 H2
Sunnyvale Mt *HEM/SK/SE* WF9 ....247 G3
Sunnyview *EARD/LOFT* WF3 ....153 L7
Sunnyview Av *BEE/HOL* LS11 ....131 H5
Sunny View Crs *HUDN* HD2 ....192 F3
Sunnyview Gdns
  BEE/HOL LS11 ....131 H3
Sunnyview Ter *BEE/HOL* LS11 ....131 H3
Sunny View Ter *CUL/QBY* BD13 ....124 E6
Sunnywood House
  HOLM/MEL HD9 ....235 M2
Sunroyd Av *HOR/CROF* WF4 ....197 K4
Sunroyd Hl *HOR/CROF* WF4 ....197 K4
Sunset Av *HDGY* LS6 ....87 G6
Sunset Dr *HDGY* LS6 ....87 G7
  ILK LS29 ....38 F1
Sunset Hilltop *HDGY* LS6 ....87 G6
Sunset Mt *HDGY* LS6 ....87 G6
Sunset Ri *HDGY* LS6 ....87 G6
Sunset Rd *HDGY* LS6 ....87 G6
Sunset Vw *HDGY* LS6 ....87 G7
Sunshine Ct *WBSY* BD6 ....126 B7
Sun St *AIRE* BD20 ....34 B4
  AIRE BD20 ....56 B1
  BFDE BD3 ....5 H4
  COL BB8 ....74 A1
  HWTH BD22 ....54 E3
  KGHY BD21 ....3 G6
  PDSY/CALV LS28 ....106 F5
  YEA LS19 ....62 E7
Sun Ter *TOD* * OL14 ....140 D5
Sun Vale Av *TOD* OL14 ....140 D5
Sun Wy *HIPP* HX3 ....169 H1
Sunways *MIRF* WF14 ....172 A7
Sun Wood Av *HIPP* HX3 ....147 K2
Surat Rd *MAR/SLWT* HD7 ....212 B4
Suresnes Rd *KGHY* BD21 ....2 F5
Surgery St *HWTH* BD22 ....78 E8
Surma Cl *MILN* OL16 ....228 D1
Surrey Av *ROY/SHW* OL2 ....229 H7
Surrey Cl *BSLY* S70 ....261 H7
Surrey Gv *PDSY/CALV* LS28 ....107 G6
  WBOW BD5 ....127 G2
Surrey Park Cl *ROY/SHW* * OL2 ....229 K6
Surrey Rd *PDSY/CALV* LS28 ....107 G6
Surrey St *BTLY* WF17 ....173 M1
  HFAX HX1 ....146 A8
  KGHY BD21 ....3 L2
  TOD * OL14 ....141 K8
Sussex Av *HORS* LS18 ....85 L3
  MID LS10 ....132 B3
Sussex Cl *HEM/SK/SE* WF9 ....223 M6
Sussex Crs *CAS* WF10 ....159 G7
Sussex Gdns *MID* LS10 ....132 B3
Sussex Gn *MID* LS10 ....132 B3
Sussex Pl *MID* LS10 ....132 B3
Sussex St *BTLY* WF17 ....173 M1
  KGHY BD21 ....3 L2
  OSM LS9 ....9 M2
  ROCH * OL11 ....206 B8
Sutcliffe Cl *LIT* OL15 ....185 K8
  LUD/ILL HX2 ....146 A6
Sutcliffe Wood La *HIPP* HX3 ....147 L8
Sutherland Av *RHAY* LS8 ....88 C5
Sutherland Crs *RHAY* LS8 ....88 C4
Sutherland Dr *HUDS* HD4 ....213 L5
Sutherland Mt *OSM* LS9 ....110 C4
Sutherland Rd *HIPP* HX3 ....148 A6
  OSM LS9 ....110 C4
Sutherland St
  WOR/ARM * LS12 ....109 G8
Sutherland Ter *OSM* LS9 ....110 C4
Sutton Ap *SCFT* LS14 ....111 C5
Sutton Av *BSLYN/ROY* S71 ....243 H6
  ECHL BD2 ....105 H1
  HUDE HD5 ....193 J6
Sutton Crs *BOW* BD4 ....128 A2
  SCFT LS14 ....111 C5
Sutton Dr *CUL/QBY* BD13 ....101 M1
  HUDE HD5 ....193 J6
Sutton Gv *BOW* BD4 ....128 A1
  MOR LS27 ....152 C3
Sutton La *AIRE* BD20 ....56 A1
  KNOT WF11 ....159 M7
Sutton Rd *AWLS/ASK* DN6 ....227 L6
  BOW BD4 ....128 A1
Sutton St *WOR/ARM* LS12 ....8 B3
Suzanne Crs *HEM/SK/SE* WF9 ....247 G3
Swadford St *SKP/WHF* BD23 ....16 B2
Swaindrod La *LIT* OL15 ....186 A7
Swaine Hill Crs *YEA* LS19 ....62 C7
Swaine Hill St *YEA* LS19 ....62 C7
Swaine Hill Ter *YEA* LS19 ....62 C7
Swain House Crs *ECHL* BD2 ....105 J1
Swain House Rd *ECHL* BD2 ....105 J1
Swain Mt *ECHL* BD2 ....105 J1
Swain St *WHIT* * OL12 ....206 A5
Swale Crs *GFTH/SHER* LS25 ....113 K8
Swales Moor Rd *HIPP* HX3 ....146 E1
Swales' Yd *PONT* WF8 ....180 E6
Swallow Av *WOR/ARM* LS12 ....108 C9
Swallow Cl *AL/HA/HU* LS17 ....88 B2
  DOD/DAR S75 ....241 M6
  OT LS21 ....42 F8
Swallow Crs *WOR/ARM* LS12 ....108 C9
Swallow Dr *AL/HA/HU* LS17 ....88 B2
  OT LS21 ....42 F8
Swallow Fold *GIR* BD8 ....103 L7
Swallow Garth
  WKFDW/WTN WF2 ....220 F1
Swallow Gv *HUDS* HD4 ....214 A8
Swallow Hl *BTLY* WF17 ....151 J5
Swallow Hill Rd *DOD/DAR* S75 ....242 C7
Swallow La *MAR/SLWT* HD7 ....212 L1
Swallow Mt *WOR/ARM* LS12 ....108 C7
Swallow St *HECK* WF16 ....172 E3

KGHY BD21 ....3 J3
Swallow V *MOR* LS27 ....152 F2
Swan Av *BGLY* BD16 ....81 L3
Swan Bank Ct *HOLM/MEL* HD9 ....254 C2
Swan Bank La *HOLM/MEL* HD9 ....11 K9
  HOLM/MEL HD9 ....254 C2
Swan St *ROY/SHW* * OL2 ....229 K8
Swanee Rd *BSLY* S70 ....261 K8
Swanhill La *PONT* WF8 ....180 F7
Swan La *HUDS* HD4 ....214 A3
  HUDW * HD3 ....190 D5
Swan St *WBOW* BD5 ....4 E9
Swarcliffe Ap *SCFT* LS14 ....111 L2
Swarcliffe Av *SCFT* LS14 ....111 L2
Swarcliffe Bank *SCFT* LS14 ....111 L1
Swarcliffe Dr *SCFT* LS14 ....111 L2
Swarcliffe Dr East
  MSTN/BAR LS15 ....111 M2
Swarcliffe Gn *SCFT* LS14 ....111 M2
Swarcliffe Rd *SCFT* LS14 ....111 L1
Swardale Gn *SCFT* LS14 ....111 L2
Swardale Rd *SCFT* LS14 ....111 L2
Swarland Gv *WBOW* BD5 ....127 G1
Sweeming La *GTL/HWG* HX4 ....168 B8
Sweep La *HOLM/MEL* HD9 ....254 D5
Sweetbriar Cl *ROY/SHW* OL2 ....229 K7
Sweet Briar Cl *WHIT* OL12 ....206 A4
Sweet Briar La *WHIT* * OL12 ....206 A4
Sweet St *BEE/HOL* LS11 ....8 F4
Sweet St West *BEE/HOL* LS11 ....8 F4
Swift's Fold *HOLM/MEL* HD9 ....236 B1
Swift St *DOD/DAR* S75 ....260 F4
Swift Wy *WKFDW/WTN* WF2 ....220 F1
Swillington La *RTHW* LS26 ....134 B5
Swincar Av *YEA* LS19 ....62 D7
Swincliffe Cl *CLECK* BD19 ....150 C2
Swincliffe Crs *CLECK* BD19 ....150 C3
Swincroft *OSS* WF5 ....197 G1
Swindon La *PBR* HD3 ....26 E6
  PBR HD3 ....45 H1
Swindon Rd *DEWS* WF13 ....173 L6
Swinegate *LDS* LS1 ....9 G3
Swine La *AIRE* BD20 ....58 D6
  HOR/CROF WF4 ....201 G8
  HOR/CROF WF4 ....222 E3
Swine Lane Br *AIRE* BD20 ....58 E6
Swine Market La *HBR* HX7 ....165 J2
Swineshead La *TOD* OL14 ....163 K3
Swineshead Rd *TOD* OL14 ....163 J3
Swinnow Av *BRAM* LS13 ....107 J5
Swinnow Cl *BRAM* LS13 ....107 J5
Swinnow Crs *PDSY/CALV* LS28 ....107 J5
Swinnow Dr *BRAM* LS13 ....107 J5
Swinnow Gdns *BRAM* LS13 ....107 J5
Swinnow Garth
  PDSY/CALV LS28 ....107 J6
Swinnow Gn *PDSY/CALV* LS28 ....107 H6
Swinnow Gv *BRAM* LS13 ....107 J5
Swinnow La *BRAM* LS13 ....107 J4
Swinnow Pl *PDSY/CALV* LS28 ....107 J5
Swinnow Rd *PDSY/CALV* LS28 ....107 J5
Swinnow Vw *BRAM* LS13 ....107 J5
Swinnow Wk *BRAM* LS13 ....107 J5
Swinton Pl *GTHN* BD7 ....126 D1
Swinton Ter *HFAX* HX1 ....10 A1
Swires La *AIRE* BD20 ....34 B1
Swires Rd *ECHL* BD2 ....5 M1
  HFAX HX1 ....10 B8
Swires Ter *HFAX* HX1 ....10 F8
Swiss St *CAS* WF10 ....158 A5
Swithenbank Av *OSS* WF5 ....174 E6
Swithenbank St *OSS* WF5 ....174 E5
Swithen Hl *DOD/DAR* S75 ....241 K2
Swithens Av *RTHW* LS26 ....155 H3
Swithens Dr *RTHW* LS26 ....155 G2
Swithens Gv *RTHW* LS26 ....155 G2
Swithen's La *RTHW* LS26 ....155 H4
Swithen's St *RTHW* LS26 ....155 H3
Swordfish Wy
  GFTH/SHER LS25 ....116 D7
Sybil St *LIT* OL15 ....185 J8
The Sycamores *BHP/TINH* LS16 ....64 B5
  DEWS WF13 ....173 K4
  GSLY LS20 ....62 A4
  HOR/CROF WF4 ....197 L5
  WIL/AL * BD15 ....102 C2
Sycamore Av *BGLY* BD16 ....81 H4
  CUD/GR S72 ....244 D7
  CUD/GR S72 ....263 K6
  GFTH/SHER LS25 ....135 H4
  GTHN BD7 ....104 B7
  HOLM/MEL HD9 ....234 F5
  HUDW HD3 ....213 H1
  KNOT WF11 ....181 M3
  MILN OL16 ....229 J3
  MSTN/BAR LS15 ....111 J6
  RHAY LS8 ....110 B1
  TOD OL14 ....141 J7
  WKFDW/WTN WF2 ....176 B4
  WKFDW/WTN WF2 ....176 B7
Sycamore Cha
  PDSY/CALV LS28 ....107 H7
Sycamore Cl *BFDE* BD3 ....5 J3
  BHP/TINH LS16 ....64 B5
  CHAL LS7 ....87 H7
  HDGY LS6 ....6 C1
  KBTN * HD8 ....216 B3
  KNOT WF11 ....181 M4
  LIT OL15 ....207 H1
Sycamore Copse
  WKFDW/WTN WF2 ....198 B1
Sycamore Ct *KBTN* HD8 ....216 B7
  PONT WF8 ....181 G4
  RHAY LS8 ....88 E8
Sycamore Cft *BEE/HOL* LS11 ....8 A5
Sycamore Dr *BRIG* HD6 ....148 C8
  BSLYN/ROY S71 ....243 J1
  CLECK BD19 ....149 K7
  ELL HX5 ....168 F4
  ILK LS29 ....24 E5
Sycamore Fold *BEE/HOL* LS11 ....8 A5
Sycamore Gn *KBTN* HD8 ....239 G7
  NORM WF6 ....178 C6
  WKFDW/WTN WF2 ....176 B7
Sycamore La *HOR/CROF* WF4 ....219 H6
Sycamore Ri *HOLM/MEL* HD9 ....236 F7

Sycamore Rd *HEM/SK/SE* WF9 ....223 L8
Sycamore Rw *BRAM* LS13 ....107 J2
Sycamore St *DOD/DAR* S75 ....260 E4
  WKFDE WF1 ....13 K7
Sycamore Vw *HWTH* BD22 ....2 B7
Sycamore Wk *PDSY/CALV* LS28 ....106 F4
  STKB/PEN S36 ....270 F3
Sycamore Wy *BTLY* WF17 ....151 H5
  FEA/AMT WF7 ....179 M8
Sydenham Pl *BFDE* BD3 ....105 J4
Sydenham Rd *BEE/HOL* LS11 ....8 A4
Sydenham St *BEE/HOL* LS11 ....8 A4
Sydney Gdns *LIT* OL15 ....185 L5
Sydney St *BGLY* BD16 ....81 J3
  LVSG WF15 ....172 D3
  PDSY/CALV LS28 ....106 F4
  RTHW LS26 ....133 M8
Syke Av *EARD/LOFT* WF3 ....152 F7
  EARL WF12 ....174 B6
Syke Cl *EARD/LOFT* WF3 ....152 E7
Syke Cft *BSLYN/ROY* S71 ....243 L1
Syke Gdns *EARD/LOFT* WF3 ....152 F7
Syke Gn *SCFT* LS14 ....67 L6
Syke Gv *EARL* WF12 ....174 B6
Syke House La *GTL/HWG* HX4 ....168 B8
Syke Ing Cl *EARL* WF12 ....174 C7
Syke La *CUL/QBY* BD13 ....125 G7
  EARL WF12 ....174 B7
  HIPP HX3 ....148 A5
  LUD/ILL HX2 ....123 M4
  RPDN/SBR HX6 ....167 J3
  SCFT LS14 ....67 J6
  WHIT OL12 ....206 B2
Syke Pde *EARD/LOFT* * WF3 ....152 E6
Syke Rd *EARD/LOFT* WF3 ....152 F7
  EARL WF12 ....174 B6
  LIT OL15 ....207 L4
  WBY LS22 ....48 C1
  WHIT OL12 ....206 B7
Sykes Av *DOD/DAR* S75 ....260 F4
  MIRF WF14 ....172 B8
Sykes Cl *BTLY* WF17 ....152 A8
Sykes Ct *MILN* OL16 ....206 D8
Sykes Ga *HBR* HX7 ....165 K7
Syke Side *AIRE* BD20 ....57 K4
Sykes La *AIRE* BD20 ....35 M6
  EARL WF12 ....174 C2
  HWTH BD22 ....78 F3
  LM/WK BD12 ....149 J2
Sykes Rd *BTLY* WF17 ....152 A8
Sykes St *BSLY* S70 ....260 F7
  CAS WF10 ....157 M6
  CLECK BD19 ....149 M7
  MILN OL16 ....206 D7
  MILN OL16 ....229 J2
Syke St *EARL* WF12 ....174 B7
Syke Ter *EARD/LOFT* * WF3 ....152 E7
Syke Vw *EARL* WF12 ....174 B6
Sylhet Cl *BFD* BD1 ....4 D4
Sylvan Av *CUL/QBY* BD13 ....124 F6
Sylvester Av *NORM* WF6 ....178 C6
Symons St *WKFDW/WTN* WF2 ....12 D6
Syringa Av *WIL/AL* BD15 ....103 J2
Syringa St *HUDW* HD3 ....191 M7

T

Tabbs Ct *CLECK* BD19 ....149 H5
Tabbs La *CLECK* BD19 ....149 G5
Tadman St *WKFDE* WF1 ....12 F6
Tagore Ct *BOW* BD4 ....105 M8
Talbot & Falcon Yd *WKFDE* WF1 ....12 E2
Talbot Av *AL/HA/HU* LS17 ....88 A4
  BULY LS4 ....108 E3
  HUDW HD3 ....191 L6
Talbot Ct *RHAY* LS8 ....88 B5
Talbot Crs *RHAY* LS8 ....88 B4
Talbot Fold *RHAY* LS8 ....88 B5
Talbot Gdns *RHAY* LS8 ....88 B4
Talbot Gv *RHAY* LS8 ....88 B4
Talbot Mt *BULY* LS4 ....108 E3
Talbot Ri *RHAY* LS8 ....88 B4
Talbot Rd *RHAY* LS8 ....88 B4
  STKB/PEN S36 ....270 E3
Talbot Rw *BTLY* WF17 ....173 M1
Talbot St *BTLY* WF17 ....173 L2
  GTHN BD7 ....104 D7
  KGHY BD21 ....2 C5
  NORM WF6 ....178 C4
  ROCH OL11 ....206 B8
Talbot St *BULY* LS4 ....108 E3
  RTHW LS26 ....155 G2
Talbot Vw *BULY* LS4 ....108 E3
Tallow Ms *KBTN* HD8 ....239 J5
Tall Trees *AL/HA/HU* LS17 ....87 L3
Tall Trees Dr *FEA/AMT* WF7 ....179 M6
Tamar Cl *DOD/DAR* S75 ....260 A3
Tamar St *WBOW* BD5 ....126 E2
Tame Barn Cl *MILN* * OL16 ....207 J8
Tame La *UPML* OL3 ....230 E7
Tammy Hall St *WKFDE* * WF1 ....12 E2
Tamworth St *BOW* BD4 ....106 A8
Tandem Wy *HUDE* HD5 ....193 K8
Tandle Hill Rd *ROY/SHW* OL2 ....228 D8
Tandlewood Pk *ROY/SHW* OL2 ....228 D7
Tanfield Cl *BSLYN/ROY* S71 ....243 J2
Tanfield Dr *ILK* LS29 ....40 A4
Tanfield Rd *HUD* HD1 ....14 D2
Tanglewood Ct *WBSY* BD6 ....126 B5
Tanhouse Hl *HIPP* HX3 ....147 L7
Tanhouse La *MIRF* WF14 ....194 D7
Tanhouse Pk *HIPP* HX3 ....147 L7
Tanhouse St *DEWS* WF13 ....173 H8
Tanhouse Vw *HIPP* * HX3 ....147 L7
Tank Rw *BSLY* S70 ....261 M5
Tan La *BOW* BD4 ....127 K8
Tannerbrook Cl *CLAY* BD14 ....125 M2
Tanner Hill Rd *GTHN* BD7 ....126 D4
Tanners *MAR/SLWT* HD7 ....212 B7
Tanner St *LVSG* WF15 ....171 K1
Tannery Ct *IDLE* BD10 ....83 M6
  PDSY/CALV * LS28 ....107 H7

Tannery Sq *HDGY* LS6 ....87 G2
Tanpit La *AWLS/ASK* DN6 ....227 M4
Tanpits *HBR* * HX7 143
Tanshelf Dr *PONT* WF8 ....180 E5
Tanton Crs *CLAY* BD14 ....125 M5
Tanton Wk *CLAY* BD14 ....125 M5
Tanyard Av *HUDW* HD3 191
Tanyard Cft *CUD/GR* S72 245
Tanyard Fold *HOR/CROF* WF4 ....220 C2
Tanyard Rd *HUDS* HD4 ....213 K4
  HUDW HD3 191
Tarn *BAIL* * BD17 83
Tarn Cl *CAS* WF10 ....159 C2
Tarn Ct *HWTH* BD22 2
  WKFDE WF1 ....176 D2
Tarnhill Ms *WBOW* BD5 ....127 G1
Tarn Hows Wk *FEA/AMT* WF7 ....202 A4
Tarn La *AL/HA/HU* LS17 ....66 F7
  HWTH BD22 ....56 E2
Tarn Rd *FEA/AMT* WF7 ....202 A4
Tarnside Cl *MILN* OL16 ....206 E8
Tarnside Dr *SCFT* LS14 111
Tarn View Rd *YEA* LS19 ....62 E8
Tarn Vis *ILK* * LS29 ....38 E1
Tatefield Cl *GFTH/SHER* LS25 135
Tatefield Pl *GFTH/SHER* LS25 135
Tateley Cl *OSS* WF5 ....174 F4
Tateley La *OSS* WF5 ....174 E6
Tate Naylor St *DEWS* * WF13 ....173 K4
Tatham St *MILN* OL16 ....206 C7
Tatham Wy *RHAY* LS8 ....88 E2
Tatton St *SHPY* BD18 ....82 C7
Taunton St *WKFDE* WF1 ....13 L1
Tavern St *WKFDE* WF1 ....13 H1
Tavistock Rd *ROCH* OL11 ....228 B8
Tavistock Wy
  WKFDW/WTN WF2 ....220 B1
Tavora St *WKFDE* WF1 ....176 E2
Tavy Cl *DOD/DAR* S75 ....260 A4
Tawny Beck *WOR/ARM* LS12 ....107 L2
Tawny Cl *BOW* BD4 ....128 A2
Tay Cl *DOD/DAR* S75 ....242 E1
Taylor Av *AIRE* BD20 ....35 M4
Taylor Cl *OSS* WF5 ....197 H4
Taylor Crs *CUD/GR* S72 ....263 K6
  OSS WF5 ....197 H5
Taylor Dr *OSS* WF5 ....197 H4
Taylor Gv *RTHW* LS26 ....157 G2
Taylor Hall La *MIRF* WF14 ....172 A4
  MIRF WF14 ....172 A4
Taylor Hill Rd *HUDS* HD4 ....214 A4
Taylor La *LUD/ILL* HX2 ....124 C2
  MAR/SLWT HD7 ....212 D2
  MSTN/BAR LS15 ....90 C7
Taylor Rd *WBSY* BD6 ....126 F7
Taylor Rw *BSLY* S70 ....261 H4
Taylors Cl *SCFT* LS14 ....111 K4
Taylors Pl *WHIT* * OL12 ....206 B4
Taylor St *BTLY* WF17 ....173 L1
  CLECK BD19 ....149 L4
  MAR/SLWT HD7 ....213 G4
  WHIT OL12 ....206 B2
Tealbeck Ap *OT* LS21 ....41 K4
Tealby Cl *BHP/TINH* LS16 ....86 A4
Teal Cl *CAS* WF10 ....157 M4
Teal Ct *AIRE* BD20 ....35 K1
Teal Dr *MOR* LS27 ....152 F7
Teall Ct *OSS* WF5 ....197 K3
Teall St *OSS* WF5 ....197 H4
  WKFDE WF1 ....12 F6
Teal Ms *MID* LS10 ....153 M1
Teal St *WKFDE* WF1 ....12 F6
Teasdale St *BOW* BD4 ....127 K4
Teasel Cl *LM/WK* BD12 149
Tebbet Pl *HECK* * WF16 173
Technology Dr *BTLY* WF17 ....174 A4
Teddington Av *HUDE* HD5 ....193 K4
Tees St *MILN* * OL16 ....206 C7
  WBOW BD5 ....126 E4
Telephone Pl *CHAL* LS7 ....7 M1
Telford Cl *AIRE* BD20 ....36 E2
  CAS WF10 ....157 M4
  MID LS10 ....132 A4
Telford Pl *MID* LS10 ....132 A4
Telford Ter *MID* LS10 ....132 A4
Telford Wy *ROCH* OL11 ....228 C2
  WKFDW/WTN WF2 ....176 A4
Telscombe Dr *BOW* BD4 ....127 M1
Temperance Flds *CLECK* BD19 ....149 H4
Tempest Av *WMB/DAR* S73 263
Tempest Pl *BEE/HOL* LS11 ....8 E1
Tempest Rd *HEM/SK/SE* WF9 ....246 B1
Templar Gdns *WBY* LS22 ....30 E3
Templar La *LDSU* LS2 ....7 L3
  MSTN/BAR LS15 ....111 M4
Templar Pl *LDSU* LS2 ....7 L3
Templars Cl *GTL/HWG* HX4 ....168 C2
  WKFDE WF1 ....13 M1
Templars Wy *GFTH/SHER* LS25 ....113 H7
  GIR BD8 ....104 A1
Temple Av *MSTN/BAR* LS15 ....111 J6
  RTHW LS26 ....133 L4
Temple Bank Flats *HTON* * BD9 ....104 A4
Temple Cl *HUD* HD1 ....14 F7
  MSTN/BAR LS15 ....111 J6
Temple Ct *MSTN/BAR* LS15 ....111 H6
  RTHW LS26 ....133 L4
Temple Crs *BEE/HOL* LS11 ....8 C8
Temple Gdns *NORM* WF6 ....178 E6
Temple Ga *MSTN/BAR* LS15 ....111 J6
Templegate Av
  MSTN/BAR LS15 ....111 J7
Templegate Cl
  MSTN/BAR LS15 ....111 J6
Templegate Crs
  MSTN/BAR LS15 ....111 J7
Temple Gate Dr
  MSTN/BAR LS15 ....111 H7
Templegate Gn
  MSTN/BAR LS15 ....111 J6
Templegate Ri *MSTN/BAR* LS15 ....111 J7
Templegate Rd
  MSTN/BAR LS15 ....111 J7
Templegate Vw
  MSTN/BAR LS15 ....111 J7

Templegate Wk
  MSTN/BAR LS15 ....111 K7
Templegate Wy
  MSTN/BAR LS15 ....111 K8
Temple Gn *RTHW* LS26 ....133 J7
Temple La *LIT* OL15 ....185 L6
  MSTN/BAR LS15 ....111 K7
Temple Lea *MSTN/BAR* LS15 ....111 J7
Temple Moor
  MSTN/BAR * LS15 ....111 K6
Templenewsam Rd
  MSTN/BAR LS15 ....111 H7
Templenewsam Vw
  MSTN/BAR LS15 ....111 H8
Temple Park Cl
  MSTN/BAR LS15 ....111 J7
Temple Park Gdns
  MSTN/BAR LS15 ....111 J7
Temple Park Gn
  MSTN/BAR LS15 ....111 J7
Temple Rhydding Dr *BAIL* BD17 ....82 E4
Temple Ri *MSTN/BAR* LS15 ....111 J8
Temple Rd *DEWS* WF13 ....173 J7
Temple Row Cl
  MSTN/BAR LS15 ....112 A8
Templestowe Crs
  MSTN/BAR LS15 ....111 L5
Templestowe Dr
  MSTN/BAR LS15 ....111 L6
Templestowe Gdns
  MSTN/BAR LS15 ....111 K6
Templestowe HI
  MSTN/BAR LS15 ....111 K5
Temple St *CAS* WF10 ....157 L7
  COL BB8 ....52 L8
  HTON BD9 ....104 D4
  HUDW HD3 ....191 K5
  KGHY BD21 ....2 F5
Temple Vw *EARD/LOFT* WF3 ....154 E5
Temple View Gv *OSM* LS9 ....110 C7
Temple View Pl *OSM* LS9 ....110 B7
Temple View Rd *OSM* LS9 ....110 B7
Temple View Ter *OSM* LS9 ....110 B7
Temple Vue *HDGY* LS6 ....86 F8
Temple Wk *MSTN/BAR* LS15 ....111 K6
Temple Wy *BSLYN/ROY* S71 ....261 M3
Ten Lands La *HOR/CROF* WF4 ....222 E7
Tennis Av *BOW* BD4 ....128 A5
Tennis Wy *BAIL* BD17 ....82 C5
Tennyson Av *AWLS/ASK* DN6 ....227 L5
  EARD/LOFT WF3 ....155 G8
  RPDN/SBR HX6 ....167 H3
  TOD OL14 ....141 M8
Tennyson Cl *PDSY/CALV* LS28 ....107 H8
  STKB/PEN S36 ....270 F2
Tennyson Pl *BFDE* BD3 ....5 L3
  CLECK BD19 ....149 M6
  WBSY BD6 ....126 D6
Tennyson St *GSLY* LS20 ....62 B6
  HIPP HX3 ....10 D1
  KGHY BD21 ....2 E6
  MOR LS27 ....152 D2
  PDSY/CALV LS28 ....107 H8
  ROCH OL11 ....228 C1
Tennyson Ter *MOR* * LS27 ....152 D2
Tennyson Wy *PONT* WF8 ....180 F3
Tenter Cl *BTLY* WF17 ....151 L8
  KBTN HD8 ....239 J4
Tentercroft *WHIT* * OL12 ....206 A7
Tentercroft Ct *DEWS* WF13 ....173 M5
Tenterden Wy *MSTN/BAR* LS15 ....112 B3
Tenterfield Ri *HIPP* HX3 ....147 J5
Tenterfield Rd *OSS* WF5 ....197 G1
Tenterfields *IDLE* BD10 ....84 A6
  LUD/ILL HX2 ....167 G1
Tenter HI *BSPA/BRAM* LS23 ....69 K4
  CLAY BD14 ....125 K2
  HOLM/MEL HD9 ....255 H2
Tenter Hill La *HUDN* HD2 ....192 F2
Tenters Gv *HUDN* HD2 ....192 B3
Tenter La *STKB/PEN* S36 ....271 J8
Tenters Cl *KNOT* WF11 ....181 L1
Tenth Av *LVSG* WF15 ....171 K1
Ten Yards La *CUL/QBY* BD13 ....102 B5
Ternhill Gv *WBOW* BD5 ....4 E9
Tern Pk *WBY* LS22 ....47 J5
Tern St *WBOW* BD5 ....126 E3
The Terrace *PDSY/CALV* LS28 ....129 G2
Terrace Gdns *HIPP* HX3 ....10 E2
Terrington Crest *CLAY* BD14 ....125 M2
Terry Rd *LM/WK* BD12 ....149 G1
Tetley Dr *BIRK/DRI* BD11 ....150 D2
Tetley La *HIPP* HX3 ....147 J4
Tetley Pl *ECHL* BD2 ....105 H3
Tetley St *BFD* BD1 ....4 D6
Teville Ct *BOW* BD4 ....127 J2
Tewit Cl *LUD/ILL* HX2 ....124 B7
Tewit Gn *LUD/ILL* HX2 ....124 B7
Tewit Hall Gdns *LUD/ILL* HX2 ....124 B8
Tewit Hall Rd *BFDE* BD3 ....105 L6
Tewit La *LUD/ILL* HX2 ....124 B7
Tewitt Cl *AIRE* BD20 ....35 K8
Tewitt La *BGLY* BD16 ....59 K8
  CUL/QBY BD13 ....102 C4
Tew St *WKFDW/WTN* WF2 ....12 E6
Texas St *MOR* LS27 ....152 D4
Thackeray *MOR* LS27 ....213 M3
Thackeray Rd *IDLE* BD10 ....105 M2
Thacker Gate Rd *HBR* HX7 ....166 D2
Thackley Av *IDLE* BD10 ....83 J4
Thackley Ct *BAIL* BD17 ....82 E6
Thackley Old Rd *SHPY* BD18 ....82 F6
Thackley Rd *IDLE* BD10 ....83 J4
Thackley Vw *IDLE* BD10 ....83 J4
Thackray Av *HECK* WF16 ....173 G1
Thackray Rd *PONT* WF8 ....180 F5
Thackray St *LUD/ILL* HX2 ....145 M7
  MOR LS27 ....152 C3
Thames Dr *GFTH/SHER* LS25 ....113 J8
Thames Rd *MILN* OL16 ....207 J8
Thames Steet *MILN* OL16 ....206 D8

Thanes Cl *HUDN* HD2 ....192 A4
Thanet Garth *AIRE* BD20 ....36 B6
Thane Wy *MSTN/BAR* LS15 ....112 A3
Thatchers Wy *CLECK* BD19 ....150 C5
Theakston Md *CLAY* BD14 ....125 L1
Thealby Cl *OSM* LS9 ....7 L8
Thealby Lawn *OSM* LS9 ....7 L7
Thealby Pl *OSM* LS9 ....7 L7
Thearne Gn *CLAY* BD14 ....125 M2
Theodore St *BEE/HOL* LS11 ....131 J5
Thetford *WHIT* * OL12 ....206 A6
Thewlis La *HUDS* HD4 ....213 K4
Thickett La *STKB/PEN* S36 ....271 C6
Thick Hollins Dr
  HOLM/MEL HD9 ....235 H5
Thick Hollins Rd
  HOLM/MEL HD9 ....235 H6
The Thimbles *WHIT* OL12 ....206 F2
Thimble Cl *WHIT* OL12 ....206 F2
Third Av *BFDE* BD3 ....105 L5
  HEM/SK/SE WF9 ....225 J6
  HIPP HX3 ....168 D2
  KGHY BD21 ....2 E7
  LVSG WF15 ....171 K1
  RTHW LS26 ....133 H7
  WBY LS22 ....48 B1
  WOR/ARM LS12 ....108 F8
Third St *LM/WK* BD12 ....127 G8
Thirkleby Royd *CLAY* BD14 ....125 L2
Thirlmere Av *COL* BB8 ....52 B8
Thirlmere Cl *BEE/HOL* LS11 ....131 G6
Thirlmere Dr *CAS* WF10 ....158 F7
  EARD/LOFT WF3 ....153 M3
  WBY LS22 ....47 K1
Thirlmere Gdns *BEE/HOL* LS11 ....131 G6
  ECHL BD2 ....105 K4
Thirlmere Gv *ROY/SHW* OL2 ....228 F3
Thirlmere Rd *BSLYN/ROY* S71 ....261 J5
  EARL WF12 ....174 B4
  WKFDW/WTN WF2 ....176 A3
Thirsk Av *GFTH/SHER* LS25 ....135 J4
Thirsk Gra *CLAY* BD14 ....125 L2
Thirsk Gv *EARD/LOFT* WF3 ....153 M3
Thirsk Rw *LDS* LS1 ....8 E1
Thirstin Rd *HOLM/MEL* HD9 ....236 A1
Thirteenth Av *LVSG* WF15 ....171 K1
Thistle Cl *HUDN* HD2 ....192 A4
Thistle Dr *HEM/SK/SE* WF9 ....225 H7
Thistle Hill Av *HUDE* HD5 ....215 L1
Thistle St *HUD* HD1 ....15 H3
Thistle Wy *MOR* LS27 ....151 M1
Thistlewood Rd
  EARD/LOFT WF3 ....176 F1
Thistlefields *MILN* * OL16 ....207 G7
Thomas Cl *WBSY* BD6 ....126 E5
Thomas St *BRIG* HD6 ....170 C5
  BSLY S70 ....261 G6
  BTLY WF17 ....151 K8
  CAS WF10 ....158 A5
  ELL HX5 ....169 J8
  HDGY LS6 ....6 D2
  HECK WF16 ....172 F3
  HEM/SK/SE WF9 ....224 A8
  HFAX HX1 ....11 H6
  HUD HD1 ....214 A2
  HUDW HD3 ....191 J5
  HWTH BD22 ....78 F8
  LVSG WF15 ....171 K1
  MILN OL16 ....206 C6
  ROY/SHW OL2 ....229 L8
  TOD OL14 ....140 E5
Thomas St South *HFAX* HX1 ....10 B7
Thomas St West *HFAX* HX1 ....168 C1
Thompson Av *CAS* WF10 ....159 G8
  ECHL BD2 ....105 H1
Thompson Dr
  WKFDW/WTN WF2 ....176 B3
Thompson Gn *BAIL* BD17 ....82 C4
Thompson La *BAIL* BD17 ....82 C5
Thompson St *HFAX* HX1 ....10 F5
  SHPY BD18 ....82 C6
Thompson's Yd *WKFDE* WF1 ....12 D2
Thong La *HOLM/MEL* HD9 ....236 C6
Thoresby Av *BSLYN/ROY* S71 ....261 K2
Thoresby Dr *CLECK* BD19 ....150 D6
Thoresby Gv *GTHN* BD7 ....126 A3
Thoresby Pl *LDS* LS1 ....6 B8
Thornaby Dr *CLAY* BD14 ....125 L2
Thornacre Crs *SHPY* BD18 ....83 G8
Thornacre Rd *SHPY* BD18 ....83 G7
Thorn Av *EARL* WF12 ....195 L5
  HTON BD9 ....103 L2
Thorn Bank Av *HWTH* BD22 ....79 G2
Thornberry Dr *LVSG* WF15 ....171 K1
Thornbridge Ms *ECHL* BD2 ....105 K2
Thornbury *ROCH* * OL11 ....206 A9
Thornbury Av *BFDE* BD3 ....105 M6
Thornbury Crs *BFDE* BD3 ....105 M6
Thornbury Dr *BFDE* BD3 ....105 M6
Thornbury Gv *BFDE* BD3 ....105 M6
Thornbury Pk
  WKFDW/WTN WF2 ....198 B2
Thornbury Rd *BFDE* BD3 ....105 M7
  WKFDW/WTN WF2 ....198 B2
Thornbury St *BFDE* BD3 ....105 M7
Thornbush Wy *HECK* WF16 ....206 E6
Thorncliffe Av *ROY/SHW* OL2 ....228 E8
Thorncliffe Est *BTLY* WF17 ....173 J3
Thorncliffe La *KBTN* HD8 ....217 M7
Thorncliffe Pk *ROY/SHW* OL2 ....228 E8
Thorncliffe Rd *BTLY* WF17 ....173 J3
  GIR BD8 ....4 D1
  HWTH BD22 ....2 A6
Thorncliffes *HEM/SK/SE* * WF9 ....246 B1
Thorncliffe St *HUDW* HD3 ....191 K5
Thorncliff Green Rd *KBTN* HD8 ....216 D7
Thorncliff La *KBTN* HD8 ....217 L8
Thorn Cl *RHAY* LS8 ....110 D3
  SHPY BD18 ....83 G8
Thorn Crs *RHAY* LS8 ....110 D3
Thorncroft Rd *WBSY* BD6 ....126 C5
Thorndale Ri *ECHL* BD2 ....105 G2
Thorndene Wy *BOW* BD4 ....128 C7
Thorn Dr *CUL/QBY* BD13 ....124 E7

HTON BD9 ....103 M2
RHAY LS8 ....110 D3
Thorne Cl *BSLYN/ROY* S71 ....243 G7
  NORM WF6 ....178 E5
  PDSY/CALV LS28 ....106 D6
Thorne End Rd *DOD/DAR* S75 ....242 D4
Thornefield Crs
  EARD/LOFT WF3 ....152 F6
Thorne Gv *RTHW* LS26 ....133 H8
Thornely Av *DOD/DAR* S75 ....260 B6
Thorner Gv *AIRE* BD20 ....36 A4
Thorner La *BSPA/BRAM* LS23 ....68 F4
  SCFT LS14 ....67 M6
  SCFT LS14 ....90 A4
Thorne Rd *HUD* HD1 ....214 A2
Thorner Rd *BSPA/BRAM* LS23 ....68 F6
Thornes Farm Ap *OSM* LS9 ....132 F1
Thornes Farm Wy *OSM* LS9 ....132 F1
Thornes La *WKFDW/WTN* WF2 ....12 C6
Thornes Lane Whf *WKFDE* WF1 ....13 C6
Thornes Moor Av
  WKFDW/WTN WF2 ....12 A9
Thornes Moor Cl
  WKFDW/WTN WF2 ....12 A8
Thornes Moor Dr
  WKFDW/WTN WF2 ....12 A9
Thornes Moor Rd
  WKFDW/WTN WF2 ....12 A9
Thornes Pk *BRIG* HD6 ....170 C5
  SHPY BD18 ....104 F1
Thornes Park Ct
  WKFDW/WTN WF2 ....12 C8
Thornton Ter *GTL/HWG* HX4 ....190 C2
Thorney La *LUD/ILL* HX2 ....144 F4
Thornfield *BGLY* BD16 ....81 G2
Thornfield Av *HUD* HD4 ....214 A3
  PDSY/CALV LS28 ....106 C3
  WBSY BD6 ....126 E6
Thornfield Ct *MSTN/BAR* LS15 ....111 K4
Thornfield Drive Dr
  MSTN/BAR LS15 ....111 K4
Thornfield Ms *BGLY* BD16 ....59 G7
  MSTN/BAR LS15 ....111 K4
Thornfield Mt *BTLY* WF17 ....151 J5
Thornfield Pl *ECHL* BD2 ....105 L3
Thornfield Ri *GTL/HWG* HX4 ....168 D7
Thornfield Rd *BHP/TINH* LS16 ....86 D6
Thornfield St *GTL/HWG* HX4 ....168 D7
Thornfield Wy *MSTN/BAR* LS15 ....111 K4
Thorn Garth *CLECK* BD19 ....149 L8
  KGHY BD21 ....57 J7
Thorn Gv *COL* BB8 ....52 B8
  HTON BD9 ....103 M2
  RHAY LS8 ....110 D3
Thornham Ct *MILN* OL16 ....228 E6
Thornham La *ROY/SHW* OL2 ....228 B6
Thornham New Rd *ROCH* OL11 ....228 C5
Thornham Old Rd
  ROY/SHW OL2 ....228 C7
Thornham Rd *ROY/SHW* OL2 ....228 F7
Thorn HI *GTL/HWG* HX4 ....190 B4
Thornhill Av *HUDW* HD3 ....191 L7
  HWTH BD22 ....79 G3
  SHPY BD18 ....104 F1
Thornhill Back Rd *HUDW* HD3 ....191 J8
Thornhill Bridge La *BRIG* HD6 ....170 C3
Thornhill Cl *HOR/CROF* WF4 ....196 D7
  PDSY/CALV LS28 ....84 D7
  WKFDW/WTN WF2 ....199 J7
Thornhill Cft
  WKFDW/WTN WF2 ....199 J7
  WOR/ARM LS12 ....108 D8
Thornhill Dr *PDSY/CALV* LS28 ....84 C6
  SHPY BD18 ....104 F1
  WKFDW/WTN WF2 ....199 J7
Thornhill Gv *AIRE* BD20 ....35 K8
  PDSY/CALV LS28 ....84 D7
  SHPY BD18 ....104 F1
Thornhill Hey *GTL/HWG* HX4 ....190 B4
Thornhill Park Av *EARL* WF12 ....195 K8
Thornhill Pl *BFDE* BD3 ....106 A6
  WOR/ARM LS12 ....108 D8
Thornhill Rd *AIRE* BD20 ....35 K8
  BRIG HD6 ....170 B6
  CAS WF10 ....158 A8
  EARL WF12 ....173 K8
  EARL WF12 ....196 C6
  HUDW HD3 ....191 J8
  HUDW HD3 ....191 M6
  WOR/ARM LS12 ....108 D8
Thornhill St Bungalows
  WKFDE WF1 ....12 F4
Thornhill Ter *BFDE* BD3 ....105 M6
Thornie Bank *EARL* * WF12 ....173 M8
Thorn La *HTON* BD9 ....103 M2
  RHAY LS8 ....88 B8
Thornlea Cl *YEA* LS19 ....84 B1
Thornleigh *EARL* WF12 ....173 M8
Thornleigh Av
  WKFDW/WTN WF2 ....12 E8
Thornleigh Crs
  WKFDW/WTN WF2 ....12 E7
Thornleigh Cft
  WKFDW/WTN WF2 ....12 E7
Thornleigh Dr *LVSG* WF15 ....172 D1
  WKFDW/WTN WF2 ....12 E8
Thornleigh Gdns *OSM* * LS9 ....110 B8
Thornleigh Garth
  WKFDW/WTN WF2 ....12 E8
Thornleigh Gv *OSM* LS9 ....110 B8
Thornleigh Mt *OSM* LS9 ....110 B8
Thornleigh Rd *HUDS* HD4 ....213 K3
  WKFDW/WTN WF2 ....12 E7
Thornleigh St *OSM* LS9 ....110 B8
Thornleigh Vw *OSM* LS9 ....110 B8
Thornmead Rd *BAIL* BD17 ....82 F4
Thorn Mt *RHAY* LS8 ....110 D2
Thorn Rd *EARL* WF12 ....195 L5
Thorn Royd Dr *BOW* BD4 ....128 B4

Thornsgill Av *BOW* BD4 ....127 L3
Thorn St *BTLY* * WF17 ....151 G5
  GIR BD8 ....104 B5
  HWTH BD22 ....79 G6
Thorn Ter *RHAY* LS8 ....110 D3
Thornton Av *WOR/ARM* LS12 ....108 C7
Thornton Cl *BTLY* WF17 ....151 H3
Thornton Ct *GIR* BD8 ....104 B6
Thornton Gdns
  WOR/ARM LS12 ....108 C7
Thornton La *WBOW* BD5 ....126 E3
Thornton Lodge Rd *HUD* HD1 ....214 A2
Thornton Moor Rd
  HWTH BD22 ....101 J7
Thornton Old Rd *GIR* BD8 ....103 M7
Thornton Rd *BRIG* HD6 ....170 A6
  BSLY S70 ....261 L7
  CUL/QBY BD13 ....103 H8
  CLAY BD13 ....124 B1
  EARL WF12 ....195 K2
  GIR BD8 ....104 D6
Thornton St *HFAX* HX1 ....10 A9
  ILK LS29 ....40 A4
  ROCH * OL11 ....228 B1
Thornton Ter *BSLY* S70 ....261 L7
  HFAX HX1 ....10 B9
Thornton View Rd *CLAY* BD14 ....125 L2
Thorntonville *CLECK* BD19 ....150 B8
Thorntree Av *HOR/CROF* WF4 ....200 A5
Thorntree Cl *PONT* WF8 ....203 M2
Thorntree Ct *HOR/CROF* WF4 ....200 A5
Thorn Tree St *HFAX* HX1 ....10 B9
Thorn Vw *HBR* HX7 ....144 A6
  HIPP HX3 ....146 E4
  RHAY LS8 ....110 D3
Thornville *MOR* LS27 ....130 D7
Thornville Av *HDGY* * LS6 ....109 G4
Thornville Crs *HDGY* LS6 ....109 G3
Thornville Gv *HDGY* LS6 ....109 G3
Thornville Mt *DEWS* WF13 ....173 J8
  HDGY LS6 ....109 G3
Thornville Pl *DEWS* * WF13 ....173 J8
  HDGY LS6 ....109 G4
Thornville Rd *HDGY* * LS6 ....109 G4
Thornville Rw *HDGY* * LS6 ....109 G4
Thornville St *DEWS* * WF13 ....173 J8
  HDGY LS6 ....109 G4
Thornville Ter *DEWS* * WF13 ....173 J8
  HDGY LS6 ....109 G4
Thornville Wk *DEWS* WF13 ....173 J8
Thorn Wk *RHAY* LS8 ....110 E3
Thornwell Gv *CUD/GR* S72 ....244 C8
Thorp Arch Pk *BSPA/BRAM* LS23 ....49 G6
Thorp Av *HOLM/MEL* HD9 ....254 D2
Thorpe Av *CUL/QBY* BD13 ....103 J8
Thorpe Cl *GSLY* LS20 ....61 K6
Thorpe Ct *MID* LS10 ....153 L3
Thorpe Crs *MID* LS10 ....153 L3
Thorpe Dr *GSLY* LS20 ....61 K5
Thorpe Gdns *MID* LS10 ....153 L2
Thorpe Garth *MID* LS10 ....153 L3
Thorpe Green Dr *HUDW* HD3 ....191 G8
Thorpe Gv *CUL/QBY* BD13 ....103 K8
  MID LS10 ....153 L2
Thorpe La *EARD/LOFT* WF3 ....153 G5
  GSLY LS20 ....61 J6
  HEM/SK/SE WF9 ....225 H3
  HUDE HD5 ....215 H3
Thorpe Lower La
  EARD/LOFT WF3 ....154 B4
Thorpe Mill Ct
  RPDN/SBR * HX6 ....167 G7
Thorpe Mt *MID* LS10 ....153 K3
Thorpe Pl *MID* LS10 ....153 L2
Thorpe Rd *CUL/QBY* BD13 ....103 J8
  EARD/LOFT WF3 ....153 M7
  MID LS10 ....153 L2
  PDSY/CALV LS28 ....106 F6
Thorpes Av *KBTN* HD8 ....239 J7
Thorpes Crs *KBTN* HD8 ....239 J5
Thorpe Sq *MID* LS10 ....153 M3
Thorpe St *HIPP* HX3 ....146 D4
  KGHY BD21 ....3 G2
  MID LS10 ....153 L2
  MSTN/BAR LS15 ....111 J6
Thorpe Ter *MID* LS10 ....153 L2
Thorpe Vw *EARD/LOFT* WF3 ....154 A4
  MID LS10 ....153 L3
  OSS WF5 ....174 F6
  WKFDW/WTN WF2 ....176 B8
Thorp Garth *IDLE* BD10 ....83 K7
Thraves Av *NORM* WF6 ....178 D3
Three Nooks La *CUD/GR* S72 ....244 D5
Three Sisters Sq *HUD* HD1 ....14 F7
Threshfield Crs *BIRK/DRI* BD11 ....128 F7
Thrice Fold *IDLE* BD10 ....83 H5
Thrift Wy *BGLY* BD16 ....81 H4
Throstle Av *MID* LS10 ....153 K3
Throstle Bank *LUD/ILL* HX2 ....168 B1
Throstle Crest *FEA/AMT* WF7 ....179 J6
Throstle Dr *MID* LS10 ....153 J3
Throstle HI *MID* LS10 ....153 L3
Throstle La *LUD/ILL* HX2 ....167 H1
  MID LS10 ....153 K3
Throstle Nest *MID* LS10 ....173 J2
Throstle Nest Cl *OT* LS21 ....40 F4
Throstle Nest Rd *AIRE* * BD20 ....36 A4
Throstle Nest Vw *HORS* LS18 ....85 L1
Throstle Pde *MID* LS10 ....153 K3
Throstle Pl *MID* LS10 ....153 K3
Throstle Rw *MID* LS10 ....153 K3
Throstle Sq *MID* LS10 ....153 M2
Throstle St *MID* LS10 ....153 K3

Throstle Ter *MID* LS10 ....153 L3
Throstle Vw *MID* LS10 ....153 M3
Throstle Wk *MID* LS10 ....153 K3
Throxenby Wy *CLAY* BD14 ....125 L2
Thrum Hall Dr *HFAX* HX1 ....146 A7
Thrum Hall La *HFAX* HX1 ....10 A5
  WHIT OL12 ....206 A3
Thrumpton Rd *BSLYN/ROY* S71 ....243 H5
Thrush Hill Rd *HBR* HX7 ....143 M6
Thrush St *KGHY* BD21 ....3 J2
Thruxton Cl *CUD/GR* S72 ....244 E6
Thryberg St *BFDE* BD3 ....5 K7
Thunder Bridge La *KBTN* HD8 ....237 M3
Thunderton La *RPDN/SBR* HX6 ....166 D4
Thurgoland Bank
  STKB/PEN S36 ....271 M6
Thurgory Ga *KBTN* HD8 ....215 M3
Thurgory La *KBTN* HD8 ....216 B2
Thurley Dr *BOW* BD4 ....127 K4
Thurley Rd *BOW* BD4 ....127 K4
Thurlstone Rd *STKB/PEN* S36 ....270 D2
Thurnscoe Rd *BFD* BD1 ....4 D3
Thurrish La *HBR* HX7 ....121 K1
Thursby St *BFDE* BD3 ....5 L6
Thurston Gdns *WIL/AL* BD15 ....103 K6
Thurstonland Bank Rd
  HOLM/MEL HD9 ....236 F5
Thurstonland Rd *HUDS* HD4 ....237 G1
Thwaite Ga *MID* LS10 ....132 B3
Thwaite La *MID* LS10 ....132 D3
Thwaites Av *ILK* LS29 ....38 E2
Thwaites Brow Rd *KGHY* BD21 ....3 M4
Thwaites La *KGHY* BD21 ....3 M4
Tib Garth *WBY* LS22 ....47 K3
Tichborne Rd *WBOW* * BD5 ....127 G3
Tichborne Rd West
  WBOW BD5 ....127 G3
Tichborne St *LVSG* WF15 ....172 A2
Tichbourne St *BTLY* WF17 ....173 H2
Tickhill St *BFDE* BD3 ....5 L7
Tiding Field La *MAR/SLWT* HD7 ....211 M4
Tidswell St *HECK* WF16 ....173 G2
Tiflis St *WHIT* OL12 ....206 A6
Tilbury Av *BEE/HOL* LS11 ....8 B8
Tilbury Gv *BEE/HOL* LS11 ....8 B8
Tilbury Mt *BEE/HOL* LS11 ....8 B8
Tilbury Pde *BEE/HOL* LS11 ....8 B8
Tilbury Rd *BEE/HOL* LS11 ....8 B8
Tilbury Rw *BEE/HOL* LS11 ....8 A8
Tilbury Ter *BEE/HOL* LS11 ....8 B8
Tilbury Vw *BEE/HOL* * LS11 ....8 B8
Tile Cl *SKP/WHF* BD23 ....16 D3
Tile La *BHP/TINH* LS16 ....86 F3
Tile St *GIR* BD8 ....104 D5
Tiley Sq *WBOW* BD5 ....126 E3
Till Carr La *HIPP* HX3 ....148 C7
Tiliotson Av *RPDN/SBR* HX6 ....167 J3
Tillotson Ct *AIRE* * BD20 ....34 C4
Tillotson St *AIRE* * BD20 ....34 C4
Timber St *ELL* HX5 ....169 H8
  KGHY BD21 ....3 L3
Timberwood *KBTN* HD8 ....237 M2
Timble Dr *BGLY* BD16 ....81 K2
Timmey La *RPDN/SBR* HX6 ....167 J1
Timothy La *BTLY* WF17 ....151 M7
Tinderley Gv *HUDE* HD5 ....215 G2
Tingley Av *EARD/LOFT* WF3 ....153 K8
Tingley Common *MOR* LS27 ....152 D4
Tingley Crs *EARD/LOFT* WF3 ....152 E5
Tinker La *HOLM/MEL* HD9 ....234 C5
  HUDE HD5 ....216 C4
Tinkingfield La *WBY* LS22 ....31 L6
Tinkler's La *KNOT* WF11 ....161 J3
Tinkler Stile *SHPY* BD18 ....83 H6
Tinsel Rd *EARL* WF12 ....174 B5
Tinshill Av *BHP/TINH* LS16 ....86 A3
Tinshill Cl *BHP/TINH* LS16 ....86 A3
Tinshill Crs *BHP/TINH* LS16 ....86 A2
Tinshill Dr *BHP/TINH* LS16 ....86 A2
Tinshill Garth *BHP/TINH* LS16 ....86 A2
Tinshill Gv *BHP/TINH* LS16 ....86 A2
Tinshill La *BHP/TINH* LS16 ....85 M3
Tinshill Mt *BHP/TINH* LS16 ....86 A2
Tinshill Rd *BHP/TINH* LS16 ....85 M3
Tinshill Vw *BHP/TINH* LS16 ....86 A3
Tinsworth Rd
  WKFDW/WTN WF2 ....220 C2
Tintagel Cl *NORM* WF6 ....178 D3
Tintern Av *GIR* BD8 ....103 M7
  HUDW HD3 ....213 H1
  LIT OL15 ....185 J7
  WOR/ARM LS12 ....206 A4
Tippaty La *KNOT* WF11 ....160 C7
Tipping La *KBTN* HD8 ....239 G3
Tippit La *CUD/GR* S72 ....262 E1
Tisma Dr *BOW* BD4 ....127 L6
Tithe Barn Cl *WHIT* * OL12 ....206 F2
Tithe Barn La *AL/HA/HU* LS17 ....67 K4
Tithe Barn Rd *KNOT* WF11 ....182 C2
Tithe Barn St *EARL* WF12 ....173 M6
  HOR/CROF WF4 ....200 C7
Tithe Barn La *BRIG* HD6 ....170 E6
Tithe House Wy *HUDN* HD2 ....177 A3
Titus La *KBTN* HD8 ....216 F8
Titus St *SHPY* BD18 ....104 E3
Tivoli Pl *ILK* LS29 ....38 E3
  WBOW BD5 ....126 E3
Tivy Dl *DOD/DAR* S75 ....259 G2
Tivy Dale Cl *DOD/DAR* S75 ....259 G2
Tivvydale Dr *DOD/DAR* S75 ....242 A7
Tivy Dale Dr *DOD/DAR* S75 ....259 G2
Toad Carr *TOD* * OL14 ....141 J8
Toad La *WHIT* OL12 ....206 A6
Toby Wood La *KBTN* HD8 ....256 F7
Tockwith Rd *RYKW* YO26 ....32 E1
  RYKW YO26 ....32 E1
  RYKW YO26 ....33 J3
Todd St *MILN* OL16 ....206 C7
Todley Hall Rd *HWTH* BD22 ....56 B8
Todmorden Rd *LIT* OL15 ....185 L8
  TOD OL14 ....162 B2
Todwell La *WBOW* BD5 ....126 E3
Toft La *HUDS* HD4 ....215 H8

Tofts Av LM/WK BD12 ...148 E4
Tofts Gv BRIG HD6 ...170 B7
Tofts Grove Gdns BRIG HD6 ...170 B7
Toftshaw Fold BOW BD4 ...127 M6
Toftshaw La BOW BD4 ...128 A6
Toftshaw New Rd BOW BD4 ...127 M6
Tofts House Cl PDSY/CALV LS28 ...107 G7
Tofts La HUDS * HD4 ...215 H8
  PBR HG3 ...28 A1
Tofts Rd CLECK BD19 ...149 M7
  PDSY/CALV LS28 ...106 F7
Toft St WOR/ARM LS12 ...108 F8
Toll Bar Cl SEL YO8 ...139 M4
Tollbar Cl STKB/PEN S36 ...271 K6
Toll Bar La WKFDW/WTN WF2 ...175 M5
Toll Bar Rd CAS WF10 ...157 H7
Toll Bar Wy TAD LS24 ...72 B1
Toller Dr HTON BD9 ...104 A3
Toller Gv HTON BD9 ...104 B3
Toller La HTON BD9 ...104 B3
Toller Pk HTON BD9 ...104 B3
Tollgate Wy MILN OL16 ...206 E6
Tolson Crs HUDE HD5 ...193 H7
Tolson St DEWS * WF13 ...173 L5
  OSS WF5 ...174 D6
Tolsons Yd HUDE HD5 ...15 L8
Tolworth Fold WIL/AL BD15 ...103 J6
Tomahawk Trail CAS WF10 ...180 B1
Tombridge Crs
  HEM/SK/SE WF9 ...223 J5
Tom Cat La WBSY LS22 ...31 L5
Tom Dando Cl NORM WF6 ...179 G4
Tom La HUDS HD4 ...213 K3
  HWTH BD22 ...53 L1
Tomling Cote La AIRE BD20 ...36 C6
Tomlinson Wy
  GFTH/SHER LS25 ...115 M7
Tomlinson Yd HUD HD1 ...15 G6
Tommy La MAR/SLWT HD7 ...213 G5
Tom Wood Ash La
  HEM/SK/SE WF9 ...225 M7
Tonbridge Cl WBSY BD6 ...126 B6
Tonbridge St LDS LS1 ...6 D6
Tong Av WOR/ARM LS12 ...107 M8
Tong Dr WOR/ARM LS12 ...107 M8
Tonge St ROCH * OL11 ...206 C8
Tong Ga WOR/ARM LS12 ...107 M8
Tong Gn WOR/ARM LS12 ...107 M8
Tong La BOW BD4 ...128 E6
Tong Rd WOR/ARM LS12 ...129 K2
Tong St BOW BD4 ...127 M5
Tongue La HDGY LS6 ...87 H5
Tong Wy WOR/ARM LS12 ...107 M7
Tootal St WKFDE WF1 ...13 G6
Toothill La BRIG HD6 ...170 C7
Toothill Bank BRIG HD6 ...170 C7
Toothill La BRIG HD6 ...170 C8
Toot Hill La RPDN/SBR HX6 ...166 D4
Toothill La South HUDN HD2 ...192 B1
Topaz Cl HUDN HD1 ...192 E4
Topcliffe Av MOR LS27 ...152 F2
Topcliffe Gv MOR LS27 ...152 E4
Topcliffe La MOR LS27 ...152 E4
Topcliffe Md MOR LS27 ...152 F2
Topcliffe Rd BSLYN/ROY S71 ...261 J1
Topfield Fold MOR LS27 ...152 E4
Top Fold BSLYN/ROY * S71 ...262 C6
  KNOT WF11 ...159 J2
Top House Farm Ms
  KNOT WF11 ...159 J2
Top La COL BB8 ...74 E2
  HOR/CROF WF4 ...218 F5
  OT LS21 ...23 J7
Top Meadow WHIT OL12 ...194 B4
Top Moor Side BEE/HOL LS11 ...8 C6
Top of the Hi HUDS HD4 ...237 G4
Top Orch HOR/CROF WF4 ...222 D5
Top O' Th' Bank HUDS HD4 ...237 G5
Top O' Th' Close Rd TOD OL14 ...163 K8
Top O' Th' Hill Rd TOD OL14 ...163 J5
Top Rd KBTN HD8 ...239 G7
Top Rw BSLYN/ROY * S71 ...262 C6
Top Stone Cl GFTH/SHER LS25 ...160 A3
Top St HEM/SK/SE WF9 ...223 L7
Tor Av LM/WK BD12 ...148 E5
Tor Cl BSLYN/ROY S71 ...261 J1
Torcote Crs HUDN HD2 ...192 E1
Tordoff Av GTHN BD7 ...126 A1
Tordoff Gn WBSY BD6 ...126 D6
Tordoff Rd LM/WK BD12 ...127 G8
Tordoff Ter KSTL * LS5 ...108 C2
Toronto Pl CHAL LS7 ...87 M8
Torre Cl OSM LS9 ...110 C6
Torre Crs OSM LS9 ...110 D5
  WBSY BD6 ...125 M5
Torre Dr OSM LS9 ...110 C5
Torre Gv OSM LS9 ...110 C5
  WBSY BD6 ...125 M5
Torre Hl OSM LS9 ...110 D6
Torre La OSM LS9 ...110 C5
Torre Mt OSM LS9 ...110 C5
Torre Pl OSM LS9 ...110 C5
Torre Rd OSM LS9 ...110 B6
  WBSY BD6 ...125 M5
Torre Sq OSM LS9 ...110 D5
Torre Vw OSM LS9 ...110 C5
Torre Wk OSM LS9 ...110 D5
Torridon Crs WBSY BD6 ...126 A8
Torridon Rd EARL WF12 ...174 A4
Tor Vw HOLM/MEL HD9 ...236 E4
Totley Cl BSLYN/ROY S71 ...243 K7
Totties La HOLM/MEL HD9 ...254 F1
Toulston La TAD LS24 ...70 B4
The Tower Dr OT LS21 ...43 G8
Tower Av HEM/SK/SE WF9 ...225 J6
Tower Cswy TOD OL14 ...140 D6
Tower Crs TAD LS24 ...71 K2
Tower Gdns LUD/ILL HX2 ...168 B2
Tower Gv WOR/ARM LS12 ...108 C6
Tower Hl RPDN/SBR HX6 ...167 K2
Tower House St LDSU LS2 ...7 G7
Tower La WOR/ARM LS12 ...108 B6
Tower Rd WOR/ARM LS12 ...108 B6
Tower Rd OSM LS9 ...132 F2
  SHPY BD18 ...82 A6
Towers Cl HOR/CROF WF4 ...200 B6
Towers La HOR/CROF WF4 ...200 D5
Towers Paddock CAS WF10 ...158 C7

The Towers WOR/ARM LS12 ...108 C6
Towers Sq HDGY LS6 ...87 J6
Tower St BSLY S70 ...261 G2
  ECHL BD2 ...105 K4
  TOD OL14 ...140 C5
Towers Wy HDGY LS6 ...87 J6
Tower Vw HFAX HX1 ...168 A1
Towlerton La
  WKFDW/WTN WF2 ...176 A4
The Town EARL WF12 ...195 M4
Town Av HUD HD1 ...15 J3
Town Cl HORS LS18 ...85 K5
Townclose Vw
  GFTH/SHER LS25 ...135 H6
Town Crs HUD HD1 ...15 J2
Town End GFTH/SHER LS25 ...113 G6
  GTHN BD7 ...126 C2
  HUDE HD5 ...215 G2
  MAR/SLWT HD7 ...212 F2
  MOR LS27 ...129 M7
  OSS WF5 ...196 F1
Town End Av FEA/AMT WF7 ...202 E7
  HOLM/MEL HD9 ...236 E8
Town End Cl AIRE * BD20 ...34 E8
Town End Crs HOLM/MEL HD9 ...236 E8
Town End La KBTN HD8 ...216 C2
Townend Pl AIRE BD20 ...34 E8
  PDSY/CALV LS28 ...107 H6
Town End Rd CLAY BD14 ...125 K1
  HOLM/MEL HD9 ...236 D8
Townend Rd WOR/ARM LS12 ...130 D1
Town End Vw HOLM/MEL HD9 ...236 D8
Townfield WIL/AL BD15 ...102 E1
Townfield La HBR HX7 ...143 H1
Town Fields Rd ELL HX5 ...169 G8
Townfold OSS WF5 ...175 G8
Town Ga CLECK BD19 ...149 H6
  GSLY LS20 ...62 A5
  HBR HX7 ...143 H1
  HIPP HX3 ...147 J3
  HOLM/MEL HD9 ...236 B6
  HOLM/MEL HD9 ...253 M1
  HOLM/MEL HD9 ...254 C1
  HOLM/MEL HD9 ...255 G4
  KBTN HD8 ...216 A6
  KBTN HD8 ...216 C2
  LUD/ILL HX2 ...144 D5
  MAR/SLWT HD7 ...233 H2
  PDSY/CALV LS28 ...84 D7
  RPDN/SBR HX6 ...166 F3
Towngate BRIG HD6 ...170 F3
  DOD/DAR S75 ...242 D5
  DOD/DAR S75 ...259 H6
  HIPP HX3 ...147 L6
  HIPP HX3 ...169 J2
  HUDS HD4 ...214 C4
  LM/WK BD12 ...147 M8
  MIRF WF14 ...172 D8
  OSS WF5 ...197 G1
  SHPY BD18 ...82 F7
  STKB/PEN S36 ...270 C2
Towngate Gv BRIG HD6 ...170 F3
Town Gate Cl GSLY LS20 ...62 A5
Towngate Rd BTLY WF17 ...173 J1
Town Hall Sq YEA LS19 ...62 D7
Town Hall St ELL HX5 ...169 H8
  HOLM/MEL HD9 ...254 C1
  KGHY BD21 ...3 G5
  MIRF * WF14 ...194 C2
  RPDN/SBR HX6 ...167 K3
Town Hall St East HFAX * HX1 ...11 H5
Town Hall Wy EARL * WF12 ...173 M6
Townhead Fold ILK LS29 ...19 G6
Town Hl BSPA/BRAM LS23 ...69 M4
Town Hill St BGLY * BD16 ...81 K8
Town House Rd LIT OL15 ...185 K8
Town La IDLE BD10 ...83 K6
Townley Av HIPP HX3 ...169 J2
Townley Rd HOLM/MEL OL16 ...207 H8
  WKFDW/WTN WF2 ...197 M1
Townley St COL BB8 ...74 A1
Town Mill Brow WHIT * OL12 ...206 B7
Town Moor HUDS HD4 ...237 H4
Town Pl HUD HD1 ...15 J3
Town Rd HUDE HD5 ...193 L5
Town St BEE/HOL LS11 ...131 H4
  BIRK/DRI BD11 ...128 C8
  BRAM LS13 ...107 H1
  CHAL LS7 ...87 M7
  DEWS WF13 ...173 L4
  EARD/LOFT WF3 ...154 F3
  EARL WF12 ...174 B7
  GSLY LS20 ...62 A5
  HEM/SK/SE WF9 ...223 L7
  HORS LS18 ...85 K6
  MID LS10 ...153 L1
  MOR LS27 ...129 M7
  PDSY/CALV LS28 ...106 F4
  PDSY/CALV LS28 ...107 G4
  WOR/ARM LS12 ...108 C6
  YEA LS19 ...62 D7
  YEA LS19 ...84 F5
Town Street Ms CHAL LS7 ...87 M7
Town Street Wk CHAL LS7 ...87 M7
Town Ter HUD HD1 ...15 J3
Town Wells Dr PDSY/CALV LS28 ...84 D8
Towton Dr CAS WF10 ...157 J8
Track Mt BTLY WF17 ...173 K4
Track Rd BTLY WF17 ...173 K4
Trafalgar Cl HUDN HD2 ...192 D2
Trafalgar Gdns MOR LS27 ...152 C3
Trafalgar Rd DEWS WF13 ...173 K5
  ILK LS29 ...38 D2
Trafalgar Sq HFAX HX1 ...10 C1
Trafalgar St AWLS/ASK DN6 ...249 L5
  BFD BD1 ...4 E4
  BTLY WF17 ...173 J1
  HFAX HX1 ...10 C1
  LDSU LS2 ...7 J8
  MILN OL16 ...206 C6
Trafford Av OSM LS9 ...110 D4
Trafford Gv OSM LS9 ...110 C5
Trafford Rd AWLS/ASK DN6 ...287 M3
Trafford St ROCH OL11 ...228 A1
Trafford Ter OSM LS9 ...110 D4
Traith Ct BTLY * WF17 ...151 G8
Tramways LM/WK BD12 ...149 H1

Tranbeck Rd GSLY LS20 ...61 K5
Tranfield Av GSLY LS20 ...61 L5
Tranfield Cl GSLY LS20 ...61 L5
Tranfield Gdns GSLY LS20 ...61 L5
Tranmere Ct GSLY LS20 ...61 K5
Tranmere Dr GSLY LS20 ...61 K5
Tranquility MSTN/BAR LS15 ...111 L4
Tranquility Ct MSTN/BAR LS15 ...111 L4
Trans Pennine Trail
  BSLYN/ROY S71 ...244 A7
  EARD/LOFT WF3 ...177 J3
  MID LS10 ...9 K2
  RTHW LS26 ...134 A7
  RTHW LS26 ...156 B7
  WKFDE WF1 ...199 J2
Transperience Wy
  LM/WK BD12 ...127 H8
Transvaal Ter BTLY WF17 ...151 K7
Trans Wk TAD LS24 ...95 G5
Tranter Gv BOW BD4 ...128 A1
Tranter Pl MSTN/BAR LS15 ...111 K5
Travis St MILN OL16 ...229 K2
  ROY/SHW OL2 ...229 K7
Trawden Rd COL BB8 ...74 D1
Tredgold Av BHP/TINH LS16 ...64 A4
Tredgold Cl BHP/TINH LS16 ...64 A4
Tredgold Crs BHP/TINH LS16 ...64 A4
Tredgold Garth BHP/TINH LS16 ...64 A4
Tredis Cl BSLYN/ROY S71 ...261 K3
Treecrest Ri DOD/DAR S75 ...261 G2
Treelands DOD/DAR S75 ...260 D3
Tree La LUD/ILL HX2 ...145 H1
Trees St GIR BD8 ...4 A1
Tree Tops Ct RHAY LS8 ...88 C4
Tree Top Vw CUL/QBY BD13 ...124 E4
Trefoil Wy LIT OL15 ...185 H8
Trelawn Av HDGY LS6 ...108 F1
Trelawn Pl HDGY LS6 ...108 F1
Trelawn St HDGY LS6 ...108 F1
Trelawn Ter HDGY LS6 ...108 F1
Tremont Gdns MID LS10 ...132 A4
Trenam Park Dr IDLE BD10 ...83 J4
Trenance Dr SHPY BD18 ...82 B7
Trenance Gdns GTL/HWG HX4 ...168 B7
Trenholme Av LM/WK BD12 ...126 D8
Trenic Crs HDGY LS6 ...108 F3
Trenic Dr HDGY LS6 ...108 F3
Trent Av GFTH/SHER LS25 ...135 J1
  MILN OL16 ...207 J8
  NORM WF6 ...178 C2
Trentham Av BEE/HOL LS11 ...131 K4
Trentham Gv BEE/HOL LS11 ...131 K4
Trentham Pl BEE/HOL LS11 ...131 K4
Trentham Rw BEE/HOL LS11 ...131 K4
Trentham St BEE/HOL LS11 ...131 K4
Trenton Dr GIR BD8 ...4 B2
Trenton Rd EARL WF12 ...174 B4
Trent Rd OSM LS9 ...110 B6
  ROY/SHW OL2 ...229 J6
Trent St BEE/HOL LS11 ...8 E5
  MILN OL16 ...206 D8
Trescoe Av WOR/ARM LS12 ...108 A5
Tresham Ct EARL WF12 ...174 B4
Trevelyan Sq LDS * LS1 ...9 G1
Trevelyan St BRIG HD6 ...170 C1
  HUDE HD5 ...15 M8
Trewan Ct BSLYN/ROY S71 ...261 K3
The Triangle HUD HD1 ...14 B9
Triath Ct BTLY WF17 ...151 G8
Trilby St WKFDE WF1 ...13 G1
Trimmingham La LUD/ILL HX2 ...145 M8
Trimmingham Rd LUD/ILL HX2 ...145 M8
Trimmingham Vls
  LUD/ILL * HX2 ...146 A8
Trinity Church Ga WKFDE WF1 ...12 F3
Trinity Cl LUD/ILL HX2 ...124 C8
Trinity Ct HEM/SK/SE WF9 ...247 J2
  HOLM/MEL HD9 ...236 B2
Trinity Dr KBTN HD8 ...257 H1
Trinity Fold HFAX * HX1 ...11 G7
Trinity Gv BRIG * HD6 ...170 C2
Trinity Mt DEWS * WF13 ...173 L4
Trinity Pl BGLY BD16 ...81 J4
  HFAX HX1 ...11 G7
Trinity Ri OT LS21 ...41 K7
Trinity Rd HFAX HX1 ...11 G7
  WBOW BD5 ...4 C9
Trinity St BTLY WF17 ...173 L4
  HBR HX7 ...143 H5
  HFAX HX1 ...11 G7
  HUD HD1 ...15 G6
  HUD HD1 ...14 E7
  KGHY BD21 ...3 H2
  MIRF WF14 ...194 C2
  PONT WF8 ...180 F5
  WKFDE WF1 ...13 L8
Trinity Street Ar LDS LS1 ...7 G9
Trinity Ter BTLY WF17 ...150 F5
Trinity Vw HIPP HX3 ...11 K8
  LM/WK BD12 ...127 G7
  OSS WF5 ...174 F7
Trinity Wk LM/WK BD12 ...127 G7
Trip Garth WBY LS22 ...47 K4
Trip La WBY LS22 ...47 H4
Tristram Av WBOW BD5 ...127 J4
Triumph Cl BEE/HOL LS11 ...8 C4
Troon Dr HUDN HD2 ...192 B3
Troon Wy WKFDW/WTN WF2 ...198 C4
Trooper La HIPP HX3 ...11 K8
Trooper Ter HIPP HX3 ...11 K8
Trough La HEM/SK/SE WF9 ...247 J5
  HWTH BD22 ...101 J5
Trough Well La
  WKFDW/WTN WF2 ...176 A3
Trowell Wy BSLYN/ROY S71 ...243 H6
Troydale Gdns PDSY/CALV LS28 ...129 K1
Troydale Gv PDSY/CALV LS28 ...129 K1
Troydale La PDSY/CALV LS28 ...107 J8
Troy HI MOR LS27 ...152 C1
Troy Ri MOR LS27 ...152 D1
Troy Rd HORS LS18 ...85 L4
  MOR LS27 ...152 C1
Trueman Av HECK WF16 ...173 G2
Trueman Ct LM/WK BD12 ...127 G4
Trueman Ter BSLYN/ROY S71 ...262 A4
Truncliffe WBSY BD5 ...126 F5
Trundles La KNOT WF11 ...182 D2
Truro Av BSLYN/ROY S71 ...261 K3

Truro Dr NORM WF6 ...178 D3
Truro St WOR/ARM LS12 ...108 C6
Truro Wk NORM WF6 ...178 D3
Trust Fold GFTH/SHER LS25 ...159 M3
Tubby La HUDN HD2 ...192 D5
Tubs La HUDN * HD2 ...82 F7
Tudor Cl PDSY/CALV LS28 ...106 E4
Tudor Cft HUDN HD2 ...202 E1
Tudor Ct HEM/SK/SE WF9 ...247 H3
  WHIT OL12 ...206 D5
Tudor Cft HUDN HD2 ...193 H1
Tudor Gdns BEE/HOL LS11 ...131 G4
Tudor Lawns RHAY LS8 ...88 D7
  WKFDW/WTN WF2 ...176 A1
Tudor St MAR/SLWT HD7 ...212 C6
  ROY/SHW OL2 ...229 K7
  WBOW BD5 ...126 F2
Tuel La WHIT * OL12 ...195 K3
Tuel Lane RPDN/SBR HX6 ...167 L2
Tufton St AIRE BD20 ...35 M4
Tulip Gv WHIT OL12 ...206 A3
Tulip St HWTH BD22 ...100 E1
  MID LS10 ...131 M3
Tumbling Cl OSS WF5 ...175 G8
Tumbling HI PONT WF8 ...203 J1
Tumbling Hill St GTHN BD7 ...4 C7
Tumbling La BSLYN/ROY S71 ...244 B8
Tune St BSLY S70 ...261 J6
Tun La CUL/QBY BD13 ...222 F7
Tunnacliffe Rd HUDS HD4 ...214 D3
Tunnel St CUL/QBY BD13 ...101 M6
  HUDS HD4 ...213 J7
Tunnicliffe Pl AIRE BD20 ...35 M5
Tunshill La MILN OL16 ...207 L8
Tunstall Gn BOW BD4 ...128 A3
Tunstall Rd BEE/HOL LS11 ...131 L3
Tunwell La ECHL BD2 ...105 L2
Tunwell St ECHL BD2 ...105 L2
Tup La HOR/CROF WF4 ...222 E6
Turbary Av PDSY/CALV LS28 ...107 G4
Turbary Wk MILN OL16 ...206 F8
Turbid La HUDS HD4 ...213 J8
Turbury La GTL/HWG HX4 ...168 A6
Turf Ct CUL/QBY BD13 ...101 L1
Turf Hill Rd MILN OL16 ...228 D2
Turf House Cl LIT * OL15 ...185 H7
Turf La CUL/QBY BD13 ...79 L8
Turgate La RPDN/SBR HX6 ...166 B5
Turley Cote La HUDW HD3 ...190 E5
Turlow Ct OSM LS9 ...9 K2
Turnberry Av AL/HA/HU LS17 ...87 K2
Turnberry Cl AL/HA/HU LS17 ...87 K2
  AIRE BD20 ...57 J3
  NORM WF6 ...178 F5
Turnberry Dr AL/HA/HU LS17 ...87 K2
  EARD/LOFT WF3 ...152 F6
Turnberry Gdns
  EARD/LOFT WF3 ...152 F6
  AL/HA/HU LS17 ...87 K2
  CUD/GR * S72 ...244 E5
Turnberry Pl AL/HA/HU LS17 ...87 K2
Turnberry Ri AL/HA/HU LS17 ...87 K2
Turnberry Vw AL/HA/HU LS17 ...87 K2
Turnbridge Rd HUDE HD5 ...15 J6
Turner Av BTLY * WF17 ...173 L1
  GTHN BD7 ...126 B1
Turner Av North LUD/ILL HX2 ...145 M1
Turner Av South LUD/ILL HX2 ...146 A2
Turner Cl EARD/LOFT WF3 ...153 G6
Turner Crs OT LS21 ...41 J5
Turner Dr EARD/LOFT WF3 ...153 G6
Turner La HIPP HX3 ...11 K2
  ILK LS29 ...18 E6
Turner Pl GTHN BD7 ...126 D1
Turner's Ct HIPP HX3 ...146 D4
Turner's Pl WHIT OL12 ...206 A3
Turner St PDSY/CALV LS28 ...106 F3
  WHIT OL12 ...206 A5
Turners Yd PDSY/CALV LS28 ...106 F3
Turner Vw LUD/ILL * HX2 ...146 A2
Turney St HIPP HX3 ...146 C4
Turnfield Cl MILN OL16 ...206 F3
Turnhill Rd MILN OL16 ...228 D3
Turnip La EARL WF12 ...195 M5
Turn O' The Nook OSS WF5 ...174 E8
Turnough Rd MILN OL16 ...207 H8
Turnpike La WBY LS22 ...31 L5
Turnpike Rd TAD LS24 ...72 B1
Turnpike St ELL HX5 ...169 J7
Turnshaw Rd HWTH BD22 ...78 B4
Turnshaws Av KBTN HD8 ...216 C8
Turnshaws Cl KBTN HD8 ...216 C7
Turnsteads Av CLECK BD19 ...149 K6
Turnsteads Cl CLECK BD19 ...149 L6
Turnsteads Crs CLECK BD19 ...149 L6
Turnsteads Dr CLECK BD19 ...149 L6
Turnsteads Mt CLECK BD19 ...149 L6
Turnstone Ct MID LS10 ...153 M1
The Turnways HDGY LS6 ...108 E2
Turpin La GFTH/SHER LS25 ...138 D3
Turret Hall Rd HBR HX7 ...142 E4
Turret Royd Rd HBR HX7 ...142 E4
Turton Gn MOR LS27 ...129 M7
Turton St WKFDE WF1 ...13 L5
Turton V MOR LS27 ...129 M8
Turver's La KNOT WF11 ...183 G2
Turvin Rd RPDN/SBR HX6 ...186 F4
Tuscany Wy NORM WF6 ...156 D8
Tuxford Crs BSLYN/ROY S71 ...261 M4
Twain Crs CAS WF10 ...180 C5
Tweedale Gdns DEWS WF13 ...173 K6
Tweedale St DEWS * WF13 ...173 K6
  ROCH OL11 ...228 A1
Tweed Cl BTLY WF17 ...151 J5
Tweedy St WIL/AL BD15 ...102 E1
Twelfth Av LVSG WF15 ...171 K1
Twibell St BSLYN/ROY S71 ...261 J3
Twickenham Ct GIR BD8 ...104 F4
Twinegate WHIT OL12 ...206 A3
Twitch HI HOR/CROF WF4 ...197 K5
Twivey St CAS WF10 ...157 L7
Two Acre Dr ROY/SHW OL2 ...229 H6
Two Bridges Rd MILN OL16 ...229 K3
Two Laws Rd HWTH BD22 ...76 E5
Tyas Gv OSM LS9 ...110 D7

Tyas La MAR/SLWT HD7 ...211 K4
Tyburn La KBTN HD8 ...217 K4
Tydeman Wk MILN OL16 ...229
Tyersal Av BOW BD4 ...106 C5
Tyersal Cl BOW BD4 ...106 C5
Tyersal Crs BOW BD4 ...106 C5
Tyersal Dr BOW BD4 ...106 C5
Tyersal Garth BOW BD4 ...106 C5
Tyersal Gv BOW BD4 ...106 C5
Tyersal La BOW BD4 ...128 C1
  PDSY/CALV LS28 ...106 C5
Tyersal Pk BOW BD4 ...106 C5
Tyersal Rd BOW BD4 ...106 C5
Tyersal Ter BOW BD4 ...106 C5
Tyersal Vw BOW BD4 ...106 C5
Tyersal Wk BOW BD4 ...106 C5
Tyers Hill Cottages
  BSLYN/ROY * S71 ...262 F3
Tyler Cl NORM WF6 ...179 C
Tyndale Av HOR/CROF WF4 ...197 H
Tyndale St HWTH BD22 ...173 G
Tyndale Wk BTLY WF17 ...173 G
Tynedale Ct CHAL LS7 ...87
Tyne St BFDE BD3 ...5 L
  BFD BD1 ...3
Tynwald Cl AL/HA/HU * LS17 ...87 H
Tynwald Dr AL/HA/HU LS17 ...87 H
Tynwald Gn AL/HA/HU LS17 ...87 H
Tynwald Hl AL/HA/HU LS17 ...87 H
Tynwald Mt AL/HA/HU LS17 ...87 H
Tynwald Rd AL/HA/HU LS17 ...87 H
Tynwald Wk AL/HA/HU LS17 ...87 H
Tyrrel Ct WKFDW/WTN WF2 ...175 M
Tyrrell St BFD BD1 ...4 F
Tyson St HFAX HX1 ...146 A

U

Ulla Gn TAD LS24 ...95 C
Ullesthorpe WHIT * OL12 ...206 A
Ullswater Av EARL WF12 ...174 A
  ROY/SHW OL2 ...228 F
Ullswater Cl EARL WF12 ...174 A
Ullswater Crs MSTN/BAR LS15 ...111 C
  RTHW LS26 ...133
Ullswater Dr WBSY BD6 ...126 E
  WBY LS22 ...29 L
Ullswater Ri WBY LS22 ...29 L
Ullswater Rd BSLYN/ROY S71 ...262 D
  EARL WF12 ...174 A
Ulster Av ROCH OL11 ...228 A
Una Pl HUDN HD2 ...14 F
Uncouth Rd MILN OL16 ...207 C
Underbank Av TOD OL14 ...142 C
Underbank Old Rd
  HOLM/MEL HD9 ...254 C
Undercliffe La BFDE BD3 ...5 L
Undercliffe Old Rd ECHL BD2 ...5 L
Undercliffe Ri ILK LS29 ...39 C
Undercliffe Rd ECHL BD2 ...105 L
Undercliffe St BFDE BD3 ...5 L
Underwood WHIT * OL12 ...206 A
Underwood Av BSLY S70 ...261 K
Underwood Dr YEA LS19 ...84 C
Underwood Wy ROY/SHW OL2 ...229 M
Union Bank Yd HUD * HD1 ...14 F
Union Ct BSLY S70 ...261 L
Union Gv LVSG WF15 ...172 C
Union House La CLAY BD14 ...125 L
Union La LUD/ILL HX2 ...123 M
Union Pl BEE/HOL LS11 ...8 E
Union Rd GTHN BD7 ...126 C
  LVSG WF15 ...172 C
  WBSY BD6 ...126 E
  WHIT OL12 ...207 C
Union Sq WKFDE WF1 ...12 F
Union St BAIL BD17 ...82 F
  BGLY BD16 ...
  BSLY S70 ...261 H
  BTLY WF17 ...151 C
  COL BB8 ...74 A
  CUL/QBY * BD13 ...125 L
  DEWS WF13 ...173 L
  GTL/HWG HX4 ...168 F
  HEM/SK/SE WF9 ...224 A
  HFAX HX1 ...11 H
  HUD HD1 ...15 C
  HUDW HD3 ...191 C
  LDSU LS2 ...7 J
  LVSG WF15 ...172 C
  MAR/SLWT HD7 ...212 C
  MOR LS27 ...130 B
  OSS WF5 ...174 F
  OT LS21 ...41 H
  RPDN/SBR HX6 ...167 L
  RPDN/SBR HX6 ...167 L
  WHIT OL12 ...206 D
  WKFDE WF1 ...12 F
Union St South HFAX * HX1 ...11 H
  TOD OL14 ...163 H
Union Ter CHAL LS7 ...87 M
  SKP/WHF BD23 ...16 F
Union Yd IDLE BD10 ...83 L
Unity Cl HDGY LS6 ...86 D
Unity Ct DEWS WF13 ...173 L
Unity St AIRE BD20 ...58 A
  EARD/LOFT WF3 ...154 F
  HBR HX7 ...143 H
  TOD OL14 ...163 H
Unity St North BGLY BD16 ...81 J
Unity St South BGLY BD16 ...81 J
Unity Ter HFAX HX1 ...146 F
University Rd LDSU LS2 ...9 M
University St CAS WF10 ...157 M
Unwin Crs STKB/PEN S36 ...270 F
Unwin Pl HTON BD9 ...104 B
Unwin St STKB/PEN S36 ...270 F
The Uplands PONT WF8 ...180 F
Upland Crs RHAY LS8 ...110 C
Upland Gdns RHAY LS8 ...110 C
Upland Gv RHAY LS8 ...110 C
Upland Rd RHAY LS8 ...110 C
Uplands HUDN HD2 ...192 E
  KGHY BD21 ...3 H
  SKP/WHF BD23 ...16 F
Uplands Av CUL/QBY BD13 ...125 L

DOD/DAR S75 ...241 L6
Uplands Cl CUL/QBY BD13 ...125 K4
Uplands Crs CUL/QBY BD13 ...125 K4
Uplands Dr MIRF WF14 ...172 C8
Uplands Gv CUL/QBY BD13 ...125 K4
Upper Accommodation Rd
OSM LS9 ...9 M1
Upper Ada St SHPY BD18 ...82 B6
Upper Addison St BOW BD4 ...5 H9
Upper Allerton La
WIL/AL BD15 ...103 G6
Upper Ash Gv HEM/SK/SE WF9 ...247 J3
Upper Ashley La SHPY * BD18 ...82 D6
Upper Bank End Rd
HOLM/MEL HD9 ...254 D3
Upper Bank Houses
GTL/HWG * HX4 ...189 M2
Upper Barker St LVSG WF15 ...172 C2
Upper Basinghall St LDS LS1 ...6 F9
Upper Batley La BTLY WF17 ...151 K6
Upper Batley Low La
BTLY WF17 ...173 M5
Upper Battye St HECK WF16 ...172 F1
Upper Bell Hall HFAX HX1 ...168 C1
Upper Bolton Brow
RPDN/SBR HX6 ...167 M1
Upper Bonegate BRIG HD6 ...170 D3
Upper Brig Royd
RPDN/SBR HX6 ...188 F2
Upper Brow Rd HUDW HD3 ...213 M1
Upper Butts CLECK BD19 ...149 M7
Upper Calton St KGHY BD21 ...2 E8
Upper Camroyd St
DEWS WF13 ...173 M5
Upper Carr La CUL/QBY LS28 ...84 C8
Upper Carr St LVSG WF15 ...172 C1
Upper Castle St WBOW BD5 ...127 G1
Upper Chelsea St KGHY BD21 ...2 E8
Upper Cliffe Rd DOD/DAR S75 ...260 A6
Upper Clough Rd
MAR/SLWT HD7 ...212 E6
Upper Commercial St
BTLY WF17 ...173 L1
Upper Common La KBTN HD8 ...240 E6
Upper Croft BTLY WF17 ...173 K2
Upper Cross St * DEWS WF13 ...173 L5
Upper Ellistones Ct
GTL/HWG HX4 ...168 C8
Upper Ferndown Gn
WIL/AL * BD15 ...103 J5
Upperfield Dr MAR/SLWT HD7 ...212 E6
Upper Field House La
RPDN/SBR HX6 ...166 F4
Upper Field La DOD/DAR S75 ...240 F1
Upper Folderings
DOD/DAR S75 ...260 B7
Upper Forest Rd
BSLYN/ROY S71 ...243 H6
Upper Forge HFAX HX1 ...11 G6
Upper Fountaine St LDS LS1 ...6 F8
Upper Fountain St
RPDN/SBR HX6 ...167 K2
Upper Fyfe La BAIL BD17 ...83 G3
Upper Ga HOLM/MEL HD9 ...255 G4
Upper George St HECK WF16 ...172 F2
HUD HD1 ...14 D7
WBSY * BD6 ...126 D5
WHIT * OL12 ...206 B5
Upper Grange Av WIL/AL BD15 ...103 H6
Upper Green Av CLECK * BD19 ...149 H6
EARD/LOFT * WF3 ...152 F7
Upper Green La BRIG HD6 ...170 A1
Upper Green Wy
EARD/LOFT WF3 ...152 F7
Upper Hagg Rd
HOLM/MEL HD9 ...236 D5
Upper Hall Fold GTL/HWG HX4 ...189 K2
Upper Hall Vw HIPP HX3 ...147 J3
Upper Hatfield Pl
HOR/CROF WF4 ...222 F4
Upper Haugh Shaw HFAX HX1 ...10 D9
Upper Hayes Cl MILN OL16 ...206 E6
Upper Headley
CUL/QBY * BD13 ...124 F1
Upperhead Rw HUD HD1 ...14 E7
Upper Heaton La HUDE HD5 ...193 K3
Upper Heights Rd
CUL/QBY BD13 ...102 E6
Upper High Royds
DOD/DAR S75 ...242 C6
Upper House Cl LVSG WF15 ...171 L2
Upper House Rd
HOLM/MEL HD9 ...254 E6
Upper House St BOW BD4 ...127 K1
Upper Kirkgate HFAX HX1 ...11 J4
HIPP HX3 ...147 H2
KBTN HD8 ...217 M8
TOD OL14 ...141 M5
Upper Langwith WBY LS22 ...47 G6
Upper Lombard St YEA LS19 ...84 C2
Upper Lumb La HBR HX7 ...165 L2
Upper Lunns Cl
BSLYN/ROY S71 ...244 A3
Upper Marsh HIPP HX3 ...169 H1
Upper Marsh La HWTH BD22 ...100 B1
Upper Martin Gn
GTL/HWG HX4 ...168 C7
Upper Mary St SHPY BD18 ...82 B6
Upper May Day Green Ar
BSLY * S70 ...261 H6
Upper Maythorn La
HOLM/MEL HD9 ...255 M6
Upper Mdw CUL/QBY BD13 ...125 G6
HOLM/MEL HD9 ...253 M1
Uppermoor PDSY/CALV LS28 ...106 E7
Uppermoor Cl PDSY/CALV LS28 ...106 E7
Upper Mosscar St BFDE BD3 ...5 K6
Upper Mount St BTLY WF17 ...173 L3
HUD HD1 ...214 B2
Upper New St BSLY * S70 ...261 H6
Upper Nidd St BFD3 ...5 M7
Upper North St BTLY WF17 ...173 L2
LDSU LS2 ...6 F3
Upper Parish Ghyll La ILK LS29 ...38 B3
Upper Peel St DEWS * WF13 ...173 M5
Upper Piccadilly BFD * BD1 ...4 E5

Upper Quarry Rd HUDN HD2 ...171 J8
Upper Raglan St TOD * OL14 ...141 K8
Upper Range DEWS WF13 ...11 H1
Upper Rd DEWS WF13 ...173 K4
Upper Royd HIPP HX3 ...147 L6
Upper Rushton Rd BFDE BD3 ...105 M5
Upper Sackville St
SKP/WHF BD23 ...16 C3
Upper School St AIRE BD20 ...56 E1
Upper Seymour St BFDE BD3 ...5 L7
Upper Sheffield Rd BSLY S70 ...261 J8
Upper South St DEWS WF13 ...173 L5
Upper Station Rd BTLY WF17 ...173 M1
Upper Stone Dr MILN OL16 ...206 F8
Upper Sutherland Rd
HIPP HX3 ...148 A6
Upperthong La
HOLM/MEL HD9 ...254 B1
Upper Town St BRAM LS13 ...107 L3
Upper Union St SKP/WHF BD23 ...16 B3
Upper Warrengate WKFDE WF1 ...13 G2
Upper Washer La LUD/ILL HX2 ...168 B1
Upper Wellhouse Rd
MAR/SLWT HD7 ...212 E6
Upper Westlock Av OSM LS9 ...110 C5
Upper West St BTLY * WF17 ...174 A1
Upper Willow Hall LUD/ILL HX2 ...145 M8
Upperwood Hall
WMB/DAR * S73 ...263 H8
Upper Woodlands Rd GIR BD8 ...104 C5
Upperwood Rd WMB/DAR S73 ...263 G8
Upper Woodview Pl
BEE/HOL * LS11 ...131 K4
Upper Wortley Dr
WOR/ARM * LS12 ...108 D7
Upper Wortley Rd
WOR/ARM LS12 ...108 D7
Upper York St WKFDE WF1 ...12 E1
Upton ROCH OL11 ...206 A6
Upton St BTLY WF17 ...151 K8
Upwood La AIRE BD20 ...58 F4
Ure Crs GIR BD8 ...4 B3
Ure Gv WBY LS22 ...29 M6
Usher St BOW BD4 ...127 J1
Uttley St HIPP * HX3 ...146 D4

V

Vaal St BSLY S70 ...261 K6
The Vale HDGY LS6 ...109 H1
WBY LS22 ...47 J6
Vale Av KNOT WF11 ...181 M2
RHAY LS8 ...88 C3
Vale Cl HUDE HD5 ...215 H3
Vale Cottages LIT OL15 ...207 J1
Vale Crs KNOT WF11 ...181 M2
Vale Crest KNOT WF11 ...181 M2
Vale Gv AIRE BD20 ...35 M5
CUL/QBY BD13 ...125 H6
Vale Head Gv KNOT WF11 ...181 M2
Vale Head Mt KNOT WF11 ...181 M2
Vale Mill La HWTH BD22 ...78 F5
Valentine Ct CUL/QBY BD13 ...103 G7
ROY/SHW OL2 ...229 M8
Valestone Av HEM/SK/SE WF9 ...224 A7
Vale St BRIG HD6 ...170 C3
KGHY BD21 ...3 L1
Vale Vw FEA/AMT WF7 ...202 D7
The Valley AL/HA/HU LS17 ...65 J7
Valley Av HEM/SK/SE WF9 ...247 K3
HIPP HX3 ...148 B6
Valley Cl AL/HA/HU LS17 ...87 J1
Valley Ct AL/HA/HU LS17 ...87 M6
BFD BD1 ...4 F1
CAS WF10 ...179 J1
Valley Crs WKFDW/WTN WF2 ...176 B4
Valley Dr EARL WF12 ...196 A5
ILK LS29 ...38 F1
MSTN/BAR LS15 ...111 K5
RTHW LS26 ...135 G6
WKFDW/WTN WF2 ...176 B5
Valley Farm Rd RTHW LS26 ...132 C5
Valley Farm Wy RTHW LS26 ...132 C5
Valley Fold CUL/QBY BD13 ...125 G6
Valley Gdns CHAL LS7 ...87 L6
PONT WF8 ...204 A2
Valley Gn PDSY/CALV LS28 ...107 H8
Valley Gv LUD/ILL HX2 ...124 B7
PDSY/CALV LS28 ...107 H8
Valley Head HUDW HD3 ...191 L4
Valley Mt BRAM LS13 ...107 J6
GFTH/SHER LS25 ...135 J4
Valley Pde GIR BD8 ...4 D2
Valley Pl BFD BD1 ...4 E1
Valley Rdg GFTH/SHER LS25 ...135 H4
Valley Ri BRAM LS13 ...107 L1
ROY/SHW OL2 ...229 J5
Valley Rd BFD BD1 ...4 F3
BRAM LS13 ...107 L1
CLECK BD19 ...150 A6
DOD/DAR S75 ...242 C5
EARL WF12 ...196 B5
GFTH/SHER LS25 ...135 H3
HBR HX7 ...143 J3
ILK LS29 ...38 F1
LVSG WF15 ...172 C1
MOR LS27 ...152 D1
OSS WF5 ...182 F5
PDSY/CALV LS28 ...107 H8
PONT WF8 ...204 A2
ROCH OL11 ...228 A2
SHPY BD18 ...82 D8
Valley Sq PDSY/CALV LS28 ...107 H8
Valley St HEM/SK/SE WF9 ...247 H4
Valley Ter AL/HA/HU LS17 ...88 B3
Valley Vw AIRE BD20 ...34 E7
BAIL BD17 ...82 D5
BGLY BD16 ...80 D5
HEM/SK/SE WF9 ...247 K3
LUD/ILL HX2 ...124 B7
Valley View Ct HWTH BD22 ...79 G3
Valley View Gdns HWTH * BD22 ...79 G6
Valley View Gv ECHL BD2 ...105 J4
Valley View Rd HBR HX7 ...143 H2

OSS WF5 ...196 F2
Valley Wy LUD/ILL HX2 ...124 B7
Vancouver Pl CHAL LS7 ...88 A8
Varley Rd MAR/SLWT HD7 ...212 B8
Varley St CUL BB8 ...52 A8
PDSY/CALV LS28 ...106 F5
Vaughan Av AWLS/ASK DN6 ...227 M5
DOD/DAR S75 ...260 D3
Vaughan St BFD BD1 ...4 C5
HFAX HX1 ...10 A9
Vavasour Ct MILN * OL16 ...206 D8
Vavasour St MILN OL16 ...206 D8
Vaynor WHIT * OL12 ...206 A6
Velvet Wood Cl DOD/DAR S75 ...260 C3
Venables Av COL BB8 ...52 B8
Ventnor Cl CLECK BD19 ...150 D4
OSS WF5 ...196 F1
Ventnor Dr OSS WF5 ...196 F1
Ventnor St BFDE BD3 ...5 K6
ROCH OL11 ...228 B1
Ventnor Ter HIPP HX3 ...168 D2
Ventnor Wy OSS WF5 ...196 F1
Vento Cl WBSY BD6 ...126 D6
Verdant Wy MILN OL16 ...228 E3
Verdun Rd WBSY BD6 ...126 C6
Vere Sq WBOW BD5 ...127 G2
Verity Sp SCFT LS14 ...111 G6
Verity St BOW BD4 ...128 B7
Verity Vw SCFT LS14 ...111 G5
Vermont St BRAM LS13 ...107 H3
Verner St FEA/AMT WF7 ...201 L2
Vernon Av HUD HD1 ...14 C5
Vernon Cl BSLY S70 ...261 H7
HUD HD1 ...14 C5
Vernon Ct KGHY BD21 ...2 F7
Vernon Pl ECHL BD2 ...105 K4
PDSY/CALV LS28 ...107 G4
WKFDW/WTN WF2 ...12 B5
Vernon Rd COL BB8 ...52 F8
LDS LS1 ...6 E6
LVSG WF15 ...172 D2
Vernon St BSLYN/ROY S71 ...261 H4
HWTH BD22 ...79 H6
LDSU LS2 ...6 F7
TOD OL14 ...163 J3
Vernon St North
BSLYN/ROY S71 ...261 H4
Vernon Wy DOD/DAR S75 ...260 D3
Vesper Cl KSTL LS5 ...86 A8
Vesper Ct KSTL LS5 ...86 A8
Vesper Gdns KSTL LS5 ...108 B1
Vesper Gate Crs KSTL LS5 ...108 B1
Vesper Gate Dr KSTL LS5 ...86 B8
Vesper Gate Mt KSTL LS5 ...86 B8
Vesper Gv KSTL LS5 ...108 C2
Vesper La KSTL LS5 ...108 B1
Vesper Mt KSTL LS5 ...108 C2
Vesper Pl KSTL LS5 ...108 C2
Vesper Ri KSTL LS5 ...86 A8
Vesper Rd KSTL LS5 ...86 A8
Vesper Wk KSTL LS5 ...86 A8
Vesper Wy KSTL LS5 ...85 M8
Vestry St BOW BD4 ...127 K3
Viaduct Rd WOR/ARM LS12 ...108 F5
Viaduct St HUD HD1 ...14 F5
MAR/SLWT HD7 ...212 C5
MOR LS27 ...129 L8
Vicarage Av KSTL LS5 ...108 D2
Vicarage Cl HEM/SK/SE WF9 ...246 E5
LM/WK BD12 ...148 E4
WKFDE WF1 ...176 D1
Vicarage Ct CLECK BD19 ...149 M6
BRIG HD6 ...170 B6
FEA/AMT WF7 ...179 M6
OT LS21 ...41 J7
Vicarage Dr MILN OL16 ...206 B3
PDSY/CALV LS28 ...106 F7
Vicarage Gdns BIRK/DRI BD11 ...150 C1
BRIG HD6 ...170 B6
FEA/AMT WF7 ...179 M6
Vicarage La BSLYN/ROY S71 ...243 L3
BSPA/BRAM LS23 ...69 M4
FEA/AMT WF7 ...179 M6
Vicarage Meadow MIRF WF14 ...194 E1
Vicarage Rd EARL WF12 ...173 M6
EARL WF12 ...195 L1
HDGY LS6 ...6 A4
HUDW HD3 ...191 J8
SHPY BD18 ...83 G6
Vicarage St KSTL LS5 ...108 D2
ROY/SHW OL2 ...229 K7
Vicarage St North WKFDE WF1 ...13 L1
Vicarage St South WKFDE WF1 ...13 L1
Vicarage Ter KSTL LS5 ...108 D2
Vicarage Vw KSTL LS5 ...108 D2
Vicarage Wk ROY/SHW OL2 ...229 J8
Vicar La BFD BD1 ...5 G7
LDS LS1 ...7 H9
OSS WF5 ...197 G2
Vicar Park Dr LUD/ILL HX2 ...145 K6
Vicar's Dr MILN OL16 ...206 B7
Vicar's Ga MILN OL16 ...206 A7
Vicars Rd RHAY LS8 ...110 B2
Vicars Ter CAS WF10 ...157 K2
RHAY * LS8 ...110 B2
Vickerman Crs HUDS HD4 ...214 B5
Vickerman St HFAX HX1 ...10 B8
Vickers Av HEM/SK/SE WF9 ...247 G5
KSTL LS5 ...108 B3
Vickersdale PDSY/CALV LS28 ...107 G4
Vickers St CAS WF10 ...157 M7
MOR LS27 ...152 B4

SHPY BD18 ...82 B6
WKFDW/WTN WF2 ...12 A2
YEA LS19 ...62 F7
Victoria Cl CAS WF10 ...157 K2
HORS LS18 ...38 B2
ILK LS29 ...38 B2
YEA LS19 ...62 F7
Victoria Ct HEM/SK/SE WF9 ...225 J7
KGHY BD21 ...2 E4
Victoria Court Ms HDGY * LS6 ...109 G3
Victoria Crs BSLY S70 ...260 F4
DEWS WF13 ...173 J4
ELL HX5 ...169 H8
HORS LS18 ...85 J7
PDSY/CALV LS28 ...106 E7
Victoria Crs West
DOD/DAR S75 ...260 F4
Victoria Dr EARL WF12 ...195 L2
ECHL BD2 ...105 M2
HIPP HX3 ...147 K3
HORS LS18 ...85 J7
ILK LS29 ...38 B2
MOR LS27 ...130 D8
Victoria Gdns HORS LS18 ...85 J7
ILK LS29 ...38 B2
OSM LS9 ...110 C6
WKFDW/WTN WF2 ...197 M3
Victoria Grange Dr MOR LS27 ...152 C1
Victoria Gv HORS LS18 ...85 J8
ILK LS29 ...38 B2
OSM LS9 ...110 C6
Victoria Houses KSTL * LS5 ...108 B1
MAR/SLWT HD7 ...212 E2
Victoria La HUD HD1 ...15 G8
MAR/SLWT HD7 ...212 E2
Victoria Ms ELL * HX5 ...169 H8
HORS LS18 ...85 J7
KGHY BD21 ...2 D4
MOR LS27 ...152 C1
Victoria Park Av BRAM LS13 ...108 A3
Victoria Park Gv BRAM LS13 ...108 A3
Victoria Park St KGHY * BD21 ...3 J3
Victoria Park Vw KGHY BD21 ...3 J3
Victoria Pl BEE/HOL LS11 ...8 F3
BRIG HD6 ...170 D5
CAS WF10 ...157 M6
HUDE HD5 ...15 M8
HUDS HD4 ...213 J8
MIRF WF14 ...194 B1
YEA LS19 ...62 C7
Victoria Ri PDSY/CALV LS28 ...106 E7
Victoria Rd AIRE BD20 ...34 E8
AWLS/ASK DN6 ...249 M8
BEE/HOL LS11 ...8 F3
BRIG HD6 ...148 D7
BSLY S70 ...260 F4
BSLYN/ROY S71 ...243 M2
CLECK BD19 ...150 E6
DEWS WF13 ...173 L5
EARL WF12 ...195 L2
ECHL BD2 ...105 L2
ELL HX5 ...169 G8
GSLY LS20 ...61 M6
HBR HX7 ...143 J2
HDGY LS6 ...109 G3
HFAX HX1 ...10 C5
HIPP HX3 ...147 M7
HOLM/MEL HD9 ...234 D1
HUD HD1 ...214 B2
HWTH BD22 ...54 F3
HWTH BD22 ...78 F7
HWTH BD22 ...78 F4
ILK LS29 ...38 B2
KGHY BD21 ...2 E7
KSTL LS5 ...108 C2
LVSG WF15 ...172 C3
PDSY/CALV LS28 ...106 F4
PDSY/CALV * LS28 ...106 F4
RPDN/SBR HX6 ...167 K3
RTHW LS26 ...132 F8
SHPY BD18 ...82 B6
TOD OL14 ...141 K8
WBSY BD6 ...126 C6
Victoria Springs
HOLM/MEL HD9 ...254 A2
Victoria Sq LDS LS1 ...7 H9
Victoria St AIRE BD20 ...55 M1
BAIL BD17 ...82 D6
BFD BD1 ...4 D3
BRIG HD6 ...170 D5
BSLY S70 ...261 G4
BSLY S70 ...261 M6
BTLY WF17 ...151 H5
BTLY WF17 ...151 K8
BVRD LS3 ...6 B7
CAS WF10 ...157 K2
CAS WF10 ...157 K6
CHAL LS7 ...87 L7
CLAY BD14 ...125 K2
CLECK BD19 ...149 M6
CUD/GR S72 ...244 D7
CUL/QBY BD13 ...80 A8
CUL/QBY BD13 ...125 H5
DEWS WF13 ...173 G8
ECHL BD2 ...105 L4
FEA/AMT WF7 ...201 M1
FEA/AMT WF7 ...223 M1
GTL/HWG HX4 ...168 F7
HECK WF16 ...172 F2
HEM/SK/SE WF9 ...224 A8
HFAX HX1 ...11 G5
HOLM/MEL HD9 ...254 C1
HOR/CROF WF4 ...197 H5
HUD HD1 ...214 D2
HUDE HD5 ...15 M8
HUDN HD2 ...193 G3
HUDW HD3 ...191 L6
IDLE BD10 ...83 K4
KBTN HD8 ...240 A4
LIT OL15 ...207 K1
MAR/SLWT HD7 ...233 H2
MID LS10 ...9 K4
MOR LS27 ...130 E7
MOR LS27 ...152 B1

PDSY/CALV LS28 ...84 C8
PONT WF8 ...180 E3
ROY/SHW OL2 ...229 K7
RPDN/SBR HX6 ...167 K3
SKP/WHF BD23 ...16 B2
STKB/PEN S36 ...270 F4
TOD OL14 ...140 E5
WBY LS22 ...48 A1
WHIT OL12 ...206 B5
WIL/AL BD15 ...102 E2
WIL/AL BD15 ...103 J3
WKFDE WF1 ...176 D2
WKFDW/WTN WF2 ...12 A1
WMB/DAR S73 ...263 K8
Victoria Ter BSLY S70 ...261 J6
BVRD LS3 ...6 B7
HDGY LS6 ...86 B8
HFAX * HX1 ...10 C7
KGHY BD21 ...3 J4
KSTL LS5 ...108 C2
LUD/ILL HX2 ...167 G1
MAR/SLWT * HD7 ...233 J3
PDSY/CALV LS28 ...107 H4
SKP/WHF BD23 ...16 B2
Victoria Wk HORS LS18 ...85 J7
Victoria Wy WKFDE WF1 ...176 D3
Victor Rd HEM/SK/SE WF9 ...246 K4
HTON BD9 ...104 D4
Victor St AWLS/ASK DN6 ...249 K6
BFDE BD3 ...106 A7
BTLY WF17 ...173 M1
CAS WF10 ...179 L1
HEM/SK/SE WF9 ...247 H4
HTON BD9 ...104 D4
Victor Ter BSLY S70 ...261 J6
HFAX HX1 ...10 C3
HTON BD9 ...104 D4
Victory Av HUDW HD3 ...213 K1
Victory La EARD/LOFT WF3 ...177 J4
The View AL/HA/HU LS17 ...65 H8
RHAY LS8 ...88 B6
View Croft Rd BAIL BD17 ...82 D6
Viewland Ct CUD/GR S72 ...262 E1
Viewlands HUDN HD2 ...192 C2
Viewlands Cl STKB/PEN S36 ...270 F1
Viewlands Mt ILK LS29 ...61 M1
View Rd KGHY BD21 ...2 D1
STKB/PEN S36 ...270 C2
Vignola Ter CLAY BD14 ...125 L1
Viking Av KBTN HD8 ...217 M8
Viking Rd PONT WF8 ...181 G6
Villa Cl FEA/AMT WF7 ...202 D6
The Village BSPA/BRAM LS23 ...49 G5
HUDS HD4 ...215 H8
HUDS HD4 ...237 G5
The Village St BULY LS4 ...108 F4
Village Av BULY LS4 ...108 F4
Village Farm Ct GLE DN14 ...161 K7
Village Ms WIL/AL * BD15 ...102 E1
Village Pl BULY LS4 ...108 F4
Village Rd BHP/TINH LS16 ...65 H4
Village St AWLS/ASK DN6 ...249 M8
HIPP HX3 ...148 B4
Village Ter BULY LS4 ...108 F3
Villa Gv BGLY BD16 ...81 J2
Villa Mt LM/WK BD12 ...148 E5
Villa Rd BGLY BD16 ...81 J2
Villa St RPDN/SBR HX6 ...167 L2
Villier Ct WIL/AL BD15 ...103 K5
Vincent Av AIRE BD20 ...56 C1
Vincent Rd BSLYN/ROY S71 ...262 D4
Vincent St BFD * BD1 ...4 D6
COL BB8 ...74 B1
HFAX HX1 ...10 B7
MILN * OL16 ...228 C1
Vine Av CLECK BD19 ...149 L6
Vine Cl BRIG HD6 ...170 F4
BSLYN/ROY S71 ...261 G2
ROY/SHW OL2 ...229 K7
Vine Ct BRIG HD6 ...170 F4
MILN OL16 ...206 D7
Vine Crs CLECK BD19 ...149 L6
Vine Garth BRIG HD6 ...170 F4
Vine Gv BRIG HD6 ...170 F4
Vine Pl ROCH OL11 ...228 B1
Vinery Av OSM LS9 ...110 C6
Vinery Cl KBTN HD8 ...240 B4
Vinery Gv OSM LS9 ...110 C6
Vinery Mt OSM LS9 ...110 C7
Vinery Pl OSM LS9 ...110 C7
Vinery Rd BULY LS4 ...108 D4
Vinery St OSM LS9 ...110 C6
Vinery Ter OSM LS9 ...110 C7
Vinery Vw OSM LS9 ...110 C7
Vine St CLECK BD19 ...149 M6
GTHN BD7 ...126 D1
HUD HD1 ...15 H2
Vine Ter CUL/QBY BD13 ...102 F8
HFAX HX1 ...10 F8
Vine Ter East GIR BD8 ...104 A6
Vine Ter West GIR BD8 ...104 A6
Vineyard Cl WHIT OL12 ...184 E7
Violet St HFAX HX1 ...10 C5
HWTH BD22 ...100 E1
Violet St North HFAX HX1 ...10 C4
Virginia Ct EARD/LOFT WF3 ...154 C8
Virginia Dr EARD/LOFT WF3 ...154 C8
Virginia Gdns EARD/LOFT WF3 ...154 C8
Virginia Rd HUDW HD3 ...191 L7
Virginia St CLAY BD14 ...125 L3
ROCH * OL11 ...228 C2
Vissett Cl HEM/SK/SE WF9 ...223 K8
Vissitt La HEM/SK/SE WF9 ...223 J8
Vivian Pl GTHN BD7 ...126 C3
Vivian St ROCH OL11 ...228 A1
Vivien Rd GIR BD8 ...103 L6
Vulcan Cl DEWS WF13 ...173 L6
Vulcan Gdns DEWS * WF13 ...173 L6
Vulcan Rd DEWS WF13 ...173 K6
Vulcan St BOW BD4 ...127 M5
BRIG HD6 ...170 E5
TOD OL14 ...163 J5

W

Waarburton KBTN HD8 ....217 L8
Waddington Fold MILN OL16 ...228 E4
Waddington Rd DOD/DAR S75 ...260 D4
Waddington St KGHY * BD21 ....3 G7
Wade House Av HIPP HX3 ....125 L8
Wade House Rd HIPP HX3 ....147 L1
Wade La LDSU LS2 ....7 G7
Wade St BFD BD1 ....4 E7
  DOD/DAR S75 ....260 D4
  HFAX HX1 ....11 H5
  PDSY/CALV LS28 ....106 F3
Wadhouse La HOR/CROF WF4 ...198 B6
Wadlands Cl PDSY/CALV LS28 ....106 E2
Wadlands Dr PDSY/CALV LS28 ....106 E3
Wadlands Gv PDSY/CALV LS28 ...106 E2
Wadlands Ri PDSY/CALV LS28 ....106 E3
Wadman Rd HOLM/MEL HD9 ...254 C1
Wadsworth La HWTH BD22 ....143 L5
Wadsworth St HFAX HX1 ....10 B4
Waggon La HEM/SK/SE WF9 ....225 K7
Wagon La BGLY BD16 ....81 J5
Wain Brow HUDS HD4 ....214 B6
Waincliffe Dr BEE/HOL LS11 ...131 H5
Waincliffe Garth
  BEE/HOL LS11 ....131 H5
Waincliffe Mt BEE/HOL LS11 ...131 H6
Waincliffe Pl BEE/HOL LS11 ...131 H6
Waincliffe Ter BEE/HOL LS11 ...131 H6
Wain Cl GFTH/SHER LS25 ....137 K4
Waindale Cl LUD/ILL HX2 ....145 J3
Waindale Crs LUD/ILL HX2 ....145 J3
Waindyke Wy NORM WF6 ....178 F4
Waingap Ri WHIT OL12 ....206 B2
Waingate MAR/SLWT HD7 ....212 F6
Waingate Pk MAR/SLWT HD7 ...212 F5
Wainhouse Rd HFAX HX1 ....10 A9
Wainman's Cl HWTH BD22 ....54 F2
Wainman St BAIL BD17 ....82 D6
  BAIL BD17 ....82 F2
  HFAX HX1 ....10 B5
Wain Pk HUDS HD4 ....214 B6
Wainscott Cl HBR HX7 ....121 K8
Wainsgate HBR HX7 ....121 K8
Wainsgate La HBR HX7 ....121 K8
Wainstalls La LUD/ILL HX2 ....145 G1
Wainstalls Lodge La
  LUD/ILL HX2 ....145 G1
Wainstalls Rd LUD/ILL HX2 ...123 H8
Waites Cft WKFDW/WTN * WF2 ...175 K4
Waite St WKFDW/WTN WF2 ....176 A8
Waithlands Rd MILN OL16 ....206 D8
Wakefield Av SCFT LS14 ....111 H5
Wakefield Crs EARL WF12 ....174 E4
Wakefield Ga LUD/ILL HX2 ....168 B2
Wakefield Old Rd EARL * WF12 ...173 M6
Wakefield Rd BFD BD1 ....5 H8
  BIRK/DRI BD11 ....151 L1
  BOW BD4 ....127 K2
  BRIG HD6 ....170 F5
  DOD/DAR S75 ....242 F5
  EARL WF12 ....173 M6
  FEA/AMT WF7 ....201 H1
  FEA/AMT WF7 ....223 M1
  GFTH/SHER LS25 ....112 E8
  HEM/SK/SE WF9 ....223 J3
  HIPP HX3 ....148 B7
  HIPP HX3 ....168 C4
  HOR/CROF WF4 ....197 L4
  HUDE HD5 ....15 L8
  KBTN HD8 ....240 B3
  LVSG WF15 ....172 D2
  MID LS10 ....132 B4
  MOR LS27 ....151 L1
  NORM WF6 ....178 C5
  OSS WF5 ....175 K8
  PONT WF8 ....180 D7
  RPDN/SBR HX6 ....168 A2
  RTHW LS26 ....134 B6
  RTHW LS26 ....154 D1
Walden Dr HTON BD9 ....103 L3
Walden St CAS WF10 ....157 M7
Walden Stubbs Rd
  AWLS/ASK DN6 ....227 M2
Waldorf Wy WKFDW/WTN WF2 ...12 E5
Walesby Ct BHP/TINH LS16 ....86 A6
Walford Av OSM LS9 ....110 C6
Walford Gv OSM LS9 ....110 C6
Walford Mt OSM LS9 ....110 C6
Walford Rd OSM LS9 ....110 C6
Walford Ter OSM LS9 ....110 C6
Walkden St WHIT * OL12 ....206 B5
Walker Av BSTH BD7 ....126 A1
  WKFDW/WTN WF2 ....176 B7
Walker Cl AIRE BD20 ....34 D8
Walker Dr GIR BD8 ....104 C6
Walkergate OT LS21 ....41 J7
  PONT WF8 ....181 G5
Walker Gn EARL WF12 ....196 A5
Walker La HBR HX7 ....143 L1
  HOR/CROF WF4 ....197 L4
  RPDN/SBR HX6 ....167 M2
Walker Pl MOR * LS27 ....130 C7
  SHPY BD18 ....82 F6
Walker Rd HORS LS18 ....85 K5
  LM/WK BD12 ....149 H2
Walkers Gn WOR/ARM LS12 ....130 C2
Walker's La AIRE BD20 ....17 M7
  WOR/ARM LS12 ....130 C2
Walkers Mt BTLY WF17 ....173 L3
  HDGY LS6 ....109 H1
Walker's Pl AIRE BD20 ....36 A6
Walkers Rw YEA LS19 ....62 C8
Walker's Ter WKFDE * WF1 ...12 D2
Walker St BOW WF4 ....127 K6
  CLECK BD19 ....149 H5
  CLECK BD19 ....149 M6
  DEWS WF13 ....194 F2
  EARL WF12 ....195 M2
  MILN OL16 ....206 D7
Walker Ter BOW BD4 ....127 J2
  CUL/QBY BD13 ....101 L1
Walker Wd BAIL BD17 ....82 B4
Walkley Av HECK WF16 ....172 F4

Walkley Gv HECK WF16 ....172 F3
Walkley La HECK WF16 ....173 G4
Walkley Ter HECK WF16 ....173 G4
The Walk KGHY BD21 ....3 H6
  MILN OL16 ....206 B7
  PDSY/CALV LS28 ....106 C4
Walk Royd Hl DOD/DAR S75 ...241 K4
Wallace Gdns EARD/LOFT WF3 ...154 D8
Wallhead Rd MILN OL16 ....206 F7
Wallingford Mt WIL/AL BD15 ...103 K7
Wallis St GIR BD8 ....104 C7
Wall Nook La KBTN HD8 ....237 M8
Wallroyds KBTN HD8 ....257 C1
Wall St BSLY S70 ....261 G6
  HWTH BD22 ....2 B7
Walmer Gv PDSY/CALV LS28 ...129 H1
Walmer Vls GIR BD8 ....4 C1
Walmsley Av LIT OL15 ....207 H3
Walmsley Dr HEM/SK/SE WF9 ...225 K7
Walmsley Rd HDGY LS6 ....109 G3
Walney Fold BSLYN/ROY S71 ...243 M8
Walnut Av EARL WF12 ....174 C7
  WKFDW/WTN WF2 ....176 B7
Walnut Cl BSLY * S70 ....261 H7
  EARL WF12 ....174 C8
  SCFT LS14 ....89 L6
  TAD LS24 ....93 K8
Walnut Crs EARL WF12 ....174 C7
  WKFDW/WTN WF2 ....176 B7
Walnut Dr EARL WF12 ....174 D7
  NORM WF6 ....178 C7
  PONT WF8 ....180 D8
Walnut Gv EARL WF12 ....174 C7
Walnut La EARL WF12 ....174 C8
Walnut Pl EARL WF12 ....174 C7
Walnut Rd EARL WF12 ....174 C8
Walnut St BFDE BD3 ....105 L8
  HEM/SK/SE WF9 ....247 H5
  HFAX HX1 ....10 C6
  KGHY BD21 ....79 K2
Walpole Rd HUDS HD4 ....213 M3
Walpole St MILN OL16 ....206 C7
Walsham La HBR HX7 ....120 E3
Walshaw St GTHN BD7 ....126 C2
Walsh La BGLY BD16 ....59 H8
  HIPP HX3 ....10 E1
  WOR/ARM LS12 ....129 L4
Walsh Sq HFAX * HX1 ....168 C1
Walsh St HFAX HX1 ....10 B5
Walter Clough La HIPP HX3 ...169 K1
Walter Crs OSM LS9 ....110 B7
Walter St BULY LS4 ....108 F5
  ECHL BD2 ....104 F2
  OSM LS9 ....83 K6
Waltham Dr AWLS/ASK DN6 ...249 G4
Waltham St BSLY S70 ....261 H6
Waltin Rd HOLM/MEL HD9 ....254 B5
Walton Av PBR HG3 ....27 C3
Walton Cha BSPA/BRAM LS23 ...49 H3
Walton Cft HUDE HD5 ....193 G8
Walton Dr BIRK/DRI BD11 ....129 H8
Walton Garth BIRK/DRI BD11 ...151 L1
Walton Head La PBR HG3 ....26 E5
Walton La BRIG HD6 ....171 C1
  WKFDW/WTN WF2 ....199 H6
Walton Pk PBR HG3 ....27 C3
Walton Pl PBR HG3 ....26 F3
Walton Rd BSPA/BRAM LS23 ....49 H4
  HEM/SK/SE WF9 ....225 M6
  WBY LS22 ....48 B1
Walton Station La
  WKFDW/WTN WF2 ....199 G7
Walton St BEE/HOL LS11 ....8 L4
  BOW BD4 ....5 H9
  DOD/DAR S75 ....260 E3
  HWTH BD22 ....54 E3
  MID LS10 ....9 L8
  RPDN/SBR HX6 ....167 M2
  SKP/WHF BD23 ....16 B5
Walton St North DOD/DAR S75 ...260 D3
Walton Vw HOR/CROF WF4 ....200 B6
Waltroyd La BSLYN/ROY S19 ...149 L7
Wansford Ct BOW BD4 ....128 A4
Wanstead Crs WIL/AL BD15 ...103 K6
Wapping Nick La HUDW HD3 ...191 G3
Wapping Rd BFDE BD3 ....5 G3
Ward Bank Rd HOLM/MEL HD9 ...254 C2
Ward Fall HOR/CROF WF4 ....220 B3
Ward La EARD/LOFT WF3 ....177 J4
  MID LS10 ....131 M5
Wardle Crs HWTH BD22 ....2 B7
Wardle Edge WHIT OL12 ....206 D3
Wardle Fold WHIT OL12 ....184 E7
Wardle Gdns WHIT OL12 ....206 E3
Wardle Rd WHIT OL12 ....206 E1
Wardle St LIT * OL15 ....185 J8
Wardman St KGHY BD21 ....3 L1
Ward Place La
  HOLM/MEL HD9 ....254 B3
Ward's End HFAX HX1 ....11 H7
Wards Hl BTLY WF17 ....173 L3
Wards Hill Ct BTLY * WF17 ....173 L1
Ward Sq HUD * HD1 ....14 E7
Ward St DEWS WF13 ....173 M5
  GTHN BD7 ....126 C3
  KGHY BD21 ....2 E4
  MID LS10 ....9 J5
  SKP/WHF BD23 ....16 C1
  STKB/PEN S36 ....270 E4
Wareham Cnr BOW BD4 ....128 A4
Wareham Gv DOD/DAR S75 ....260 C6
Warehouse Hill Rd
  MAR/SLWT HD7 ....233 H2
Warehouse St BTLY WF17 ....173 M2
Wareings Yd BATT OL11 ....228 C2
War Field La WBY LS22 ....31 G2
Warhurst Rd ELL HX5 ....175 M7
Waring Wy EARL WF12 ....174 A5
Warlbeck ILK LS29 ....38 E2
Warley Av BFDE BD3 ....105 M4

Warley Dene LUD/ILL HX2 ....145 K8
Warley Dr BFDE BD3 ....105 M7
Warley Edge La LUD/ILL HX2 ...145 J7
Warley Gv BFDE BD3 ....105 M6
  LUD/ILL HX2 ....145 M7
Warley Rd LUD/ILL HX2 ....145 M8
Warley St HFAX HX1 ....10 C7
  LIT OL15 ....185 K3
Warley Town La LUD/ILL HX2 ...145 J7
Warley Vw LUD/ILL HX2 ....145 M7
Warley Wise La COL BB8 ....53 J3
Warley Wood Av LUD/ILL HX2 ...167 H1
Warley Wood La LUD/ILL HX2 ...145 G8
Warmfield La WKFDE WF1 ....178 A7
Warmfield Vw WKFDE WF1 ...177 H7
Warm La YEA LS19 ....84 C1
Warmleigh Pk CUL/QBY BD13 ...124 D5
Warneford Av OSS WF5 ....174 F7
Warneford Rd HUDS HD4 ....213 J2
Warneford Rd HUDS HD4 ....213 J2
Warner Av DOD/DAR S75 ....260 E4
Warner Pl DOD/DAR S75 ....260 E4
Warner Rd DOD/DAR S75 ....260 D4
Warrel's Av BRAM LS13 ....107 L4
Warrel's Ct BRAM LS13 ....107 L4
Warrel's Gv BRAM LS13 ....107 L4
Warrel's Mt BRAM LS13 ....107 L4
Warrel's Pl BRAM LS13 ....107 L4
Warrel's Rd BRAM LS13 ....107 L3
Warrel's Rw BRAM * LS13 ....107 L4
Warrel's Ter BRAM LS13 ....107 L4
Warren Av BGLY BD16 ....81 K1
  KNOT WF11 ....181 M3
  WKFDW/WTN WF2 ....198 F4
Warren Cl BSLYN/ROY S71 ....243 M1
  LVSG WF15 ....172 D4
Warren Ct WKFDE WF1 ....13 H2
Warren Crs BSLY S70 ....261 H7
Warren Dr BGLY BD16 ....81 K2
  FEA/AMT WF7 ....179 J6
Warrenfield Ct HUDN HD2 ....192 F3
Warren House La HUDW HD3 ...191 J3
  YEA LS19 ....62 F5
Warren La BGLY BD16 ....81 K2
  DOD/DAR S75 ....242 E2
  OT LS21 ....43 J7
  TAD LS24 ....70 D5
Warren Pk BRIG HD6 ....148 A8
Warren Park Cl BRIG HD6 ....170 A1
Warren Pl BSLY S70 ....261 H7
Warren Quarry La BSLY S70 ...261 H6
Warren Rd FEA/AMT WF7 ....201 K1
Warrenside HUDN HD2 ....193 G2
Warrens La BTLY WF17 ....150 F1
Warren St EARL WF12 ....173 M8
Warrenton Pl GTHN * BD7 ....126 C1
Warren Vw BSLY S70 ....261 H6
Warrington Ter
  MAR/SLWT * HD7 ....233 G2
Warsop Rd BSLYN/ROY S71 ...243 J3
Warton Av BOW BD4 ....127 K5
Warwick Av MAR/SLWT HD7 ...213 G2
Warwick Cl BOW BD4 ....127 K2
  HFAX * HX1 ....168 D1
Warwick Dr BOW BD4 ....127 K2
Warwick Rd BOW BD4 ....127 K2
  BSLYN/ROY S71 ....261 K3
  BTLY WF17 ....173 L3
Warwick St WHIT OL12 ....206 D4
  WKFDE WF1 ....13 L9
Wasdale Crs WKFDW/WTN WF2 ...176 A7
Wasdale Rd WKFDW/WTN WF2 ...176 A7
Washburn Ct WBY LS22 ....29 M6
Washburn Dr AIRE BD20 ....34 E8
Washer La LUD/ILL HX2 ....168 B2
Washfold Rd HBR HX7 ....165 J7
Washington Pl BRAM LS13 ....107 J6
Washington St BRAM LS13 ....107 J6
  BVRD LS3 ....109 G6
  GIR BD8 ....104 B5
  HIPP HX3 ....10 D1
Washington Ter BRAM LS13 ....107 J6
Washpit New Rd
  HOLM/MEL HD9 ....254 C4
Wasp Av ROCH OL11 ....228 C3
Wasp Nest Rd HUDN HD2 ....14 F1
Waste La HBR HX7 ....121 J1
  HUDE HD5 ....215 G3
  MIRF WF14 ....194 C3
Wastwater Dr WBSY BD6 ....126 B8
Watchit Hole La PONT WF8 ...225 L2
Watercock St BOW BD4 ....127 J1
Watercroft HUDE HD5 ....215 H3
Waterfall Fold PONT WF8 ....181 G2
Waterfield Pl BSLYN/ROY S71 ...262 A6
Waterfront Ms IDLE BD10 ....84 A6
Watergate HIPP HX3 ....147 L7
  HUD HD1 ....15 H6
  PONT WF8 ....180 E6
  RTHW LS26 ....156 D5
Watergate Rd DEWS WF13 ....173 K7
Water Green La
  RPDN/SBR HX6 ....166 C8
Water Hall La STKB/PEN S36 ...270 F2
Waterhall Vw STKB/PEN S36 ...270 F2
Water Hill La RPDN/SBR HX6 ...166 F7
Waterhouse Cl WHIT OL12 ....206 E1
Waterhouse Gv
  WKFDW/WTN WF2 ....12 B3
Waterhouse St HFAX HX1 ....11 G6
  KGHY BD21 ....2 E4
  WHIT OL12 ....206 B6
Watering Place Rd
  STKB/PEN S36 ....270 C3
Waterloo Av MID LS10 ....132 B4

MILN OL16 ....229 J1
  PDSY/CALV LS28 * 106 F3
  PONT WF8 ....181 H3
  PONT WF8 ....202 F4
  PONT WF8 ....205 G8
  WOR/ARM LS12 ....107 M7
Water Lane Cl HOR/CROF WF4 ...196 F6
Waterloo Cl CAS WF10 ....179 H1
  HOLM/MEL HD9 ....254 A6
Waterloo Crs BRAM LS13 ....107 M3
  IDLE BD10 ....84 B6
Waterloo Fold LM/WK BD12 ....148 E2
Waterloo Gv PDSY/CALV LS28 ...106 D7
Waterloo La BRAM LS13 ....107 M3
Waterloo Mt PDSY/CALV LS28 ...106 D6
Waterloo Rd BGLY BD16 ....81 H3
  BRIG HD6 ....170 C3
  BSLY S70 ....260 F5
  HUDE HD5 ....193 G7
  PDSY/CALV LS28 ....106 D6
Waterloo St MID LS10 ....9 H2
  WKFDE WF1 ....13 G6
Waterloo Ter LUD/ILL HX2 ....145 L8
Waterloo Wy BRAM LS13 ....107 M3
Waterman Cl WOR/ARM LS12 ...206 E6
Watermill Cl MILN OL16 ....206 F8
Water Rw HOLM/MEL HD9 ....237 G8
Water Royd Av MIRF WF14 ...172 C8
Water Royd Crs MIRF * WF14 ...172 C8
Water Royd Dr DOD/DAR S75 ...260 B7
  MIRF WF14 ....172 C8
Water Royd La MIRF WF14 ....172 C8
Waterside AIRE BD20 ....36 B6
  BGLY BD16 ....80 F1
  HIPP HX3 ....11 J8
  HUD HD1 ....14 B4
  HUDS HD4 ....214 B4
  HWTH BD22 ....100 E4
Waterside Fold HBR HX7 ....143 J2
Waterside La MILN OL16 ....206 D6
Waterside Rd MID LS10 ....132 C4
Waterside Wk HUDS HD5 ....193 M1
Watersole La WBY LS22 ....48 C3
Waters Rd MAR/SLWT HD7 ....232 E1
Water Stalls Rd
  RPDN/SBR HX6 ....166 A6
Water St BRIG HD6 ....170 C3
  HOLM/MEL HD9 ....253 M3
  HUD HD1 ....14 D8
  KBTN HD8 ....239 M5
  MILN OL16 ....206 B7
  RPDN/SBR HX6 ....167 K3
  SKP/WHF BD23 ....16 B2
Waterton Cl HEM/SK/SE WF9 ...246 F3
  WKFDW/WTN WF2 ....199 H7
Waterton Gv
  WKFDW/WTN WF2 ....198 B1
Waterton Rd
  WKFDW/WTN WF2 ....197 M2
Water Vw CAS WF10 ....157 M6
Waterview Ct MILN OL16 ....229 K3
Waterwheel Ri HUDS HD4 ....213 M4
Waterwood Cl
  EARD/LOFT WF3 ....153 H7
Waterworks Rd BTLY WF17 ...173 H2
Watery La HOLM/MEL HD9 ....253 H6
Watford Av HIPP HX3 ....148 B3
Wath La TAD LS24 ....94 F2
Watkin Av CUL/QBY BD13 ....103 H8
Watkinson Av LUD/ILL HX2 ...146 B3
Watkinson Dr LUD/ILL HX2 ...146 B2
Watkinson Rd LUD/ILL HX2 ...146 B2
Watkin St MILN OL16 ....228 D2
Watling Rd CAS WF10 ....158 F5
Watmough St GTHN BD7 ....126 C3
Watnall Rd BSLYN/ROY S71 ...243 H6
Watroyd La MAR/SLWT HD7 ...212 D3
Watson Av EARL WF12 ....174 D6
Watson Crs WKFDE WF1 ....177 G2
Watson Mill La RPDN/SBR HX6 ...167 K3
Watson Rd SCFT LS14 ....111 K3
Watson's Houses
  SKP/WHF BD23 ....16 B2
Watson's La TAD LS24 ....70 F1
Watson St MOR LS27 ....152 B3
  NORM WF6 ....178 C4
Wattle Syke WBY LS22 ....47 M5
Watts St CLAY BD14 ....125 K2
  WHIT OL12 ....206 C6
Watt St BOW BD4 ....127 M1
Watty Hall Av WBSY BD6 ....126 C4
Watty Hall La WBSY BD6 ....126 C4
Watty Hall Rd WBSY BD6 ....126 C4
Watty La TOD OL14 ....163 H3
Wauchope St
  WKFDW/WTN WF2 ....12 D6
Wauds Gates BAIL BD17 ....82 E5
Waulkmill Cl HEM/SK/SE WF9 ...225 J7
Wavell Garth
  WKFDW/WTN WF2 ....199 H7
Wavell Gv WKFDW/WTN WF2 ...199 G7
Waveney Dr DOD/DAR S75 ....260 A3
Waveney Rd ROY/SHW OL2 ....229 J6
  WOR/ARM LS12 ....108 E8
Waverley WHIT * OL12 ....206 A6
Waverley Av AIRE BD20 ....58 D6
  GTHN BD7 ....126 A3
Waverley Crs HIPP HX3 ....147 L7
Waverley Garth BEE/HOL LS11 ...8 L5
Waverley Pl GTHN BD7 ....126 D1
Waverley Rd ELL HX5 ....191 H1
  GTHN BD7 ....126 D1
  HUD HD1 ....14 D5
Waverley St EARL WF12 ....173 L7
  MAR/SLWT HD7 ....212 D5
Waverley Ter GTHN BD7 ....126 D1
  HUD HD1 ....191 M7

Wayside Ter AL/HA/HU LS17 ...43 M3
Weardale Cl BOW BD4 ....127 L5
Weardley La AL/HA/HU LS17 ...44 D8
Weatherall Pl AWLS/ASK DN6 ...249 H4
Weatherhill Crs HUDW HD3 ...191 J4
Weather Hill La HBR HX7 ....166 A1
  HOLM/MEL HD9 ....254 A6
Weather Hill Rd HUDW HD3 ...191 J3
Weatherhouse Ter
  LUD/ILL HX2 ....145 M5
Weaver Cl DOD/DAR S75 ....260 A3
Weaver Cottages
  HWTH * BD22 ....100 E4
Weaver Gdns MOR LS27 ....152 F3
Weavers Ct HOLM/MEL HD9 ...235 H4
  WOR/ARM LS12 ....108 D7
Weavers Cft IDLE BD10 ....83 J4
  PDSY/CALV LS28 ....107 H8
Weavers Gra GSLY LS20 ....62 A5
Weavers Hl HWTH BD22 ....78 B8
Weavers Rd PONT WF8 ....181 G5
Weavers Rw PDSY/CALV LS28 ...107 H9
Weaver St BULY LS4 ....108 F5
Weavers Wk AIRE BD20 ....36 A4
  KBTN HD8 ....239 H7
Weaverthorpe Rd BOW BD4 ....128 A6
Webb Dr ECHL BD2 ....105 J4
Webb's Ter HIPP HX3 ....105 K3
Weber Ct BFDE * BD3 ....105 L7
Webster Hl EARL WF12 ....173 L6
Webster Pl NORM WF6 ....178 C4
Webster Rw WOR/ARM LS12 ...108 D8
Webster St BFDE BD3 ....5 L4
  DEWS * WF13 ....173 L6
Wedgemoor Cl LM/WK BD12 ...148 E2
Wedgewood Dr RHAY LS8 ....88 C6
Wedgewood Gv RHAY LS8 ....88 C6
Weedling Ga TAD LS24 ....71 K6
Weedon St MILN OL16 ....206 D6
Weeland Av HOR/CROF WF4 ...200 D3
Weeland Ct KNOT WF11 ....182 C2
Weeland Crs HOR/CROF WF4 ...200 E2
Weeland Dr HOR/CROF WF4 ...200 C4
Weeland Rd HOR/CROF WF4 ...183 G2
  KNOT WF11 ....183 G2
Weetlands Cl GFTH/SHER LS25 ...135 K4
Weeton La AL/HA/HU LS17 ....43 M3
Weet Shaw La CUD/GR S72 ....244 C5
Weetwood Av BHP/TINH LS16 ...86 E6
Weetwood Crs BHP/TINH LS16 ...86 F6
Weetwood Grange Gv
  BHP/TINH LS16 ....86 D6
Weetwood House Ct
  BHP/TINH LS16 ....86 D6
Weetwood La BHP/TINH LS16 ...86 E5
  GIR BD8 ....104 C6
Weetwood Mill La
  BHP/TINH LS16 ....86 D6
Weetwood Park Dr
  BHP/TINH LS16 ....86 D6
Weetwood Rd BHP/TINH LS16 ...86 D6
  GIR BD8 ....104 C6
Weetwood Wk BHP/TINH LS16 ...86 F7
Weetworth Av CAS WF10 ....158 A8
Weetworth Pk CAS WF10 ....158 A8
Weir Rd MILN OL16 ....207 G7
Weir Side MAR/SLWT * HD7 ...233 H2
Weir St TOD OL14 ....163 J3
Weir Vw CAS WF10 ....157 M6
Welbeck Av LIT OL15 ....185 J8
Welbeck Cl MILN OL16 ....207 G8
Welbeck Dr GTHN BD7 ....126 A2
Welbeck Ri GTHN BD7 ....125 M2
Welbeck Rd BTLY WF17 ....151 H4
  MILN OL16 ....228 D2
  OSM LS9 ....110 C7
Welbeck St CAS * WF10 ....157 M6
  DOD/DAR S75 ....260 F4
  WKFDE WF1 ....13 H8
  WKFDE WF1 ....13 K7
  WKFDE WF1 ....13 L7
Welburn Av BHP/TINH LS16 ....86 D7
  HIPP HX3 ....147 M7
Welburn Cl WKFDW/WTN WF2 ...199 H5
Welburn Dr BHP/TINH LS16 ....86 D7
Welburn Gv BHP/TINH LS16 ....86 D7
Welburn Mt WBSY BD6 ....126 A6
Welbury Dr GIR BD8 ....104 E4
Weldon Ct BOW BD4 ....128 A2
Weldon Dr HUDW HD3 ....190 C6
Welfare Av MSTN/BAR LS15 ....91 G7
Welham St BFDE BD3 ....5 J3
Welland Ct DOD/DAR S75 ....260 A3
Welland Dr GFTH/SHER LS25 ...113 J8
Welland Rd ROY/SHW OL2 ....229 J6
Wellands La CLECK BD19 ....149 K7
Wellands La CLECK BD19 ....149 K7
Wellands Ter BFDE BD3 ....105 L7
Well Cl RTHW LS26 ....135 G6
  YEA LS19 ....84 E3
Well Close Ri LDSU LS2 ....7 G5
Well Close St BRIG HD6 ....170 C3
Wellcroft OT LS21 ....41 J7
Well Cft SHPY BD18 ....82 D7
Wellcroft Gv EARD/LOFT WF3 ...153 H7
Wellesley Gn
  WKFDW/WTN WF2 ....176 A2
Wellesley Pk LUD/ILL * HX2 ...146 A7
Wellfield Av HOR/CROF WF4 ...217 G3
Wellfield Cl HOR/CROF WF4 ...217 G3
  MAR/SLWT HD7 ....213 G4
Wellfield Gv STKB/PEN S36 ....270 F1
Wellfield La ILK LS29 ....40 A4
Wellfield Pl ROCH OL11 ....228 C4
Wellfield Rd DOD/DAR S75 ....260 F3
  HUDW HD3 ....191 L8
Wellfield Ter ROCH OL11 ....228 C4
Wellfold Bank HUDS HD4 ....213 L4
Well Garth HFAX HX1 ....10 F9
Well Garth MSTN/BAR LS15 ...111 L4
Well Garth Bank BRAM LS13 ...107 K2
Well Garth Mt MSTN/BAR LS15 ...111 L4
Well Garth Vw BRAM LS13 ....107 L2
Wellgate CAS WF10 ....158 B8

DOD/DAR S75 ....242 D5
GTL/HWG HX4 ....168 E6
MAR/SLWT HD7 ....212 D3
Well Green Gdns
HOLM/MEL HD9 ....236 B7
Well Green La BRIG HD6 ....170 B1
Well Gv BRIG HD6 ....170 B1
HUDN HD2 ....192 E3
Wellhead Cl BHP/TINH LS16 ....64 A2
Well Head Dr HFAX HX1 ....11 G8
Well Head La HFAX HX1 ....11 G8
RPDN/SBR HX6 ....166 E4
Well Heads CUL/QBY BD13 ....102 C8
Well Hi HOLM/MEL HD9 ....236 B2
OT LS21 ....41 H7
YEA LS19 ....62 D7
Well Hill Gv BSLYN/ROY S71 ..243 F3
Well Hill Rd HOLM/MEL HD9 ..254 D2
Wellholme BRIG HD6 ....170 D3
Well Holme Md
WOR/ARM LS12 ....130 A3
Wellhouse Av MIRF WF14 .....172 C7
Wellhouse Av WOR/ARM LS12 ..8 A1
Wellhouse Cl MIRF WF14 ......172 C7
Wellhouse Crs RHAY LS8 ....110 C1
Wellhouse Dr RHAY LS8 ....110 C1
Wellhouse Gdns RHAY LS8 ....110 C1
Wellhouse La HUDE HD5 ......193 J5
MIRF WF14 ....172 C7
Well House La STKB/PEN S36 ...257 K8
STKB/PEN S36 ....270 F2
Well House Rd RHAY LS8 ......110 C1
Wellhouse Wy STKB/PEN S36 ..270 F1
Well Road Cl LUD/ILL HX2 .....145 M7
Wellington Ar BRIG * HD6 .....170 C4
Wellington Br WOR/ARM LS12 ..8 A1
Wellington Bridge St BVRD LS3 ..6 B9
LDS LS1 ....8 B1
Wellington Cl BSLYN/ROY S71 ..261 K2
Wellington Ct BIRK/DRI BD11 ..128 C8
BTLY * WF17 ....173 K1
LUD/ILL HX2 ....146 A5
Wellington Crs SHPY BD18 ......82 C7
Wellington Gdns BRAM LS13 ..107 M3
Wellington Garth BRAM LS13 ..107 M2
Wellington Gv BRAM LS13 ......107 M2
ECHL BD2 ....105 K4
PDSY/CALV LS28 ....106 E7
Wellington Hl SCFT LS14 ....89 J4
Wellingtonia Dr
AWLS/ASK DN6 ....227 L5
Wellington Mt BRAM LS13 .....107 M2
Wellington Pl BSLY * S70 ....260 F5
KNOT WF11 ....181 M7
MILN OL16 ....206 C6
Wellington Rd EARL WF12 .....173 L6
ECHL BD2 ....105 K4
KGHY BD21 ....3 H6
TOD OL14 ....163 K1
WIL/AL BD15 ....102 E2
WOR/ARM LS12 ....8 A2
Wellington Rd East
DEWS * WF13 ....173 L6
Wellington St BFD * BD1 ....5 G5
BGLY BD16 ....81 H3
BOW BD4 ....105 M4
BSLY S70 ....261 G5
BTLY WF17 ....173 K1
BTLY WF17 ....173 L1
BVRD LS3 ....6 B9
CAS WF10 ....157 K6
CUL/QBY BD13 ....125 H5
DEWS WF13 ....173 L6
ECHL BD2 ....105 K3
HUDW HD3 ....191 K6
IDLE BD10 ....83 K7
LIT OL15 ....207 K1
LVSG WF15 ....172 D3
MILN OL16 ....207 J8
MOR LS27 ....152 C2
SKP/WHF BD23 ....16 C3
WHIT OL12 ....206 B5
WIL/AL BD15 ....103 L5
WKFDW/WTN WF2 ....176 A7
Wellington St South HFAX HX1 ..11 J7
Wellington St West HFAX HX1 ..10 E8
Wellington Ter BRAM LS13 ....107 M2
MAR/SLWT * HD7 ....233 J2
Well l' Th' La ROCH OL11 ......228 C1
Well La BRIG HD6 ....171 G4
BSLYN/ROY S71 ....261 L1
BTLY WF17 ....173 K1
CHAL LS7 ....87 M7
DEWS WF13 ....173 H6
GFTH/SHER LS25 ....135 J5
GFTH/SHER LS25 ....138 A2
GSLY LS20 ....62 A5
HFAX HX1 ....11 J5
YEA LS19 ....84 E3
Well Road Cl LUD/ILL HX2 .....145 M7
Well Royd Av LUD/ILL HX2 ....145 L7
The Wells LUD/ILL HX2 ....145 L7
LUD/ILL * HX2 ....168 A1
Wells Ct OSS WF5 ....196 E1
Wells Cft HDGY LS6 ....87 G7
Wellsley Ct MAR/SLWT * HD7 ..213 J1
Wells Mt KBTN HD8 ....238 C3
Wells Prom ILK LS29 ....38 D3
Wells Rd EARL WF12 ....195 M4
GSLY LS20 ....62 A5
ILK LS29 ....38 C4
Wells St CUD/GR S72 ....244 D8
DOD/DAR S75 ....242 A6
Wellstone Av BRAM LS13 .....107 K5
Wellstone Dr BRAM LS13 ......107 K6
Wellstone Gdns BRAM LS13 ..107 K5
Wellstone Garth BRAM LS13 ..107 K5
Wellstone Gn BRAM LS13 ......107 K5
Wellstone Ri BRAM LS13 ....107 K6
Wellstone Rd BRAM LS13 ......107 K6
Wellstone Wy BRAM LS13 .....107 K6
Well St BFD BD1 ....5 G6
BSLY * S70 ....260 F5
CUL/QBY BD13 ....101 M6
EARL WF12 ....174 A6
GTL/HWG HX4 ....190 D2
HUD HD1 ....14 C9
KGHY BD21 ....2 F4

LVSG WF15 ....172 C1
ROCH OL11 ....228 C1
TOD OL14 ....163 K2
WIL/AL BD15 ....102 E1
Wells Wk ILK LS29 ....38 D3
Wellsyke Rd AWLS/ASK DN6 ..249 M7
Wellthorne Av STKB/PEN S36 ..257 G5
Wellthorne La STKB/PEN S36 ..256 F7
Well Vw GSLY LS20 ....62 A5
Welton Gv HDGY LS6 ....109 G3
Welton Mt HDGY LS6 ....109 G3
Welton Pl HDGY LS6 ....109 G3
Welton Rd HDGY LS6 ....109 G3
Welwyn Av BTLY WF17 ....151 H8
SHPY BD18 ....83 H7
Welwyn Dr BAIL BD17 ....82 E4
SHPY BD18 ....83 H7
Welwyn Rd EARL WF12 ....174 B3
Wembly Av CUL/QBY BD13 ...103 H8
Wenborough La BOW BD4 ......128 B3
Wendel Av MSTN/BAR LS15 ....90 A7
Wendron Cl LVSG WF15 ....172 B5
Wendron Wy IDLE BD10 ....83 K7
Wenlock St BFDE BD3 ....5 J7
Wenning St KGHY BD21 ....3 M3
Wensley Av CHAL LS7 ....87 L7
SHPY BD18 ....82 C7
Wensley Bank CUL/QBY BD13 ..102 E8
Wensley Bank Ter
CUL/QBY BD13 ....102 E8
Wensley Bank West
CUL/QBY BD13 ....102 E8
Wensley Crs CHAL LS7 ....87 L7
WOR/ARM LS12 ....108 B4
Wensleydale Av SKP/WHF BD23 ..16 C2
WOR/ARM LS12 ....108 B4
Wensleydale Crs
WOR/ARM LS12 ....108 B4
Wensleydale Dr
WOR/ARM LS12 ....108 B4
Wensleydale Ms
WOR/ARM LS12 ....108 B4
Wensleydale Ri BAIL BD17 ......83 G2
Wensleydale Rd BFDE BD3 .....106 A7
Wensley Dr CHAL LS7 ....87 K6
PONT WF8 ....181 G8
Wensley Gn CHAL LS7 ....87 K7
Wensley Gv BRIG HD6 ....170 A6
Wensley Lawn MID LS10 ....153 L2
Wensley Rd BSLYN/ROY S71 ..243 G7
CHAL LS7 ....87 K6
Wensley St East
HOR/CROF WF4 ....197 J5
Wensley Vw CHAL LS7 ....87 L7
Went Ap FEA/AMT WF7 ....201 L3
Wentbridge La PONT WF8 .....203 L8
Wentbridge Rd FEA/AMT WF7 ..202 A2
Wentcliffe Rd KNOT WF11 .....181 K2
Went Cft PONT WF8 ....202 F1
Wentdale Rd PONT WF8 ....205 G8
Went Fold PONT WF8 ....202 F1
Went Garth PONT WF8 ....202 E1
Went Gv FEA/AMT WF7 ....201 L2
Went Hill La FEA/AMT WF7 ...202 C6
Went La HOR/CROF WF4 ......201 J8
Went Vw PONT WF8 ....225 J1
Went View Ct PONT WF8 ......203 H7
Wentwell Rd FEA/AMT WF7 ...200 F1
Wentworth Av AL/HA/HU LS17 ..87 K2
KBTN HD8 ....217 L8
Wentworth Cl HOR/CROF WF4 ..220 B7
ILK LS29 ....61 J2
Wentworth Ct BRIG HD6 ....170 B7
Wentworth Crs AL/HA/HU LS17 ..87 L2
DOD/DAR S75 ....242 E6
STKB/PEN S36 ....270 F3
Wentworth Dr DOD/DAR S75 ..242 E6
HEM/SK/SE WF9 ....246 D3
HOR/CROF WF4 ....200 C6
KBTN HD8 ....217 L8
LUD/ILL HX2 ....124 B7
Wentworth Ga WBY LS22 ....29 K8
Wentworth Gv LUD/ILL HX2 ...124 B7
Wentworth Mdw
STKB/PEN S36 ....270 E2
Wentworth Ms STKB/PEN S36 ..270 F3
Wentworth Park Ri PONT WF8 ..203 M1
Wentworth Rd DOD/DAR S75 ..241 L6
DOD/DAR S75 ....242 E6
FEA/AMT WF7 ....201 K2
STKB/PEN S36 ....270 E2
Wentworth St BSLYN/ROY S71 ..261 G3
HUD HD1 ....14 D5
WKFDE WF1 ....176 D6
Wentworth Ter
HEM/SK/SE WF9 ....223 K3
WKFDE * WF1 ....176 D7
Wentworth Wy AL/HA/HU LS17 ..87 L2
DOD/DAR S75 ....260 B8
WKFDW/WTN WF2 ....199 G5
Wepener Rd OSM LS9 ....110 D5
Wepener Pl OSM LS9 ....110 D5
Wescoe Hill La AL/HA/HU LS17 ..43 M4
Wesleyan Ter BOW * BD4 ......127 L3
Wesley Ap BEE/HOL LS11 ......131 H4
Wesley Av LM/WK BD12 ....126 F7
WOR/ARM LS12 ....108 E7
Wesley Av South LM/WK BD12 ..127 G8
Wesley Cl BTLY WF17 ....151 G5
WHIT OL12 ....206 D4
Wesley Ct BEE/HOL LS11 ....131 H4
HDGY LS6 ....6 D2
HFAX * HX1 ....11 H5
OSS WF5 ....174 E8
Wesley Cft BEE/HOL LS11 ....8 A9
Wesley Dr LM/WK BD12 ....127 G7
Wesley Garth BEE/HOL LS11 ..131 H4
Wesley Gn BEE/HOL LS11 ......131 H4
Wesley Gv IDLE BD10 ....83 L3
Wesley Hall Ct
EARD/LOFT * WF3 ....177 H4
Wesley Pl AIRE BD20 ....36 A5
DEWS * WF13 ....173 L6
FEA/AMT WF7 ....201 M4
KGHY BD21 ....79 K3
OSM LS9 ....9 M1

WOR/ARM LS12 ....108 E7
Wesley Rd PDSY/CALV LS28 ..106 E5
Wesley Rw PDSY/CALV * LS28 ..107 G6
Wesley Sq PDSY/CALV LS28 ...107 G6
Wesley St BEE/HOL LS11 ....131 G3
BRAM LS13 ....107 G1
BSLY S70 ....261 H5
CAS WF10 ....157 M6
CAS WF10 ....179 L1
CLECK BD19 ....149 M6
HEM/SK/SE WF9 ....247 G4
MILN OL16 ....207 G8
MOR LS27 ....152 C2
OSS WF5 ....174 E8
OT LS21 ....41 J6
PDSY/CALV LS28 ....106 F3
WHIT OL12 ....206 D3
WKFDE WF1 ....13 K8
Wesley Ter BRAM LS13 ....107 H1
BRAM LS13 ....107 M3
KBTN HD8 ....239 H8
PDSY/CALV LS28 ....107 G5
Wesley Vw BRAM * LS13 ....107 H1
Wessenden Cl DOD/DAR S75 ..260 C5
Wessenden Head Rd
HOLM/MEL HD9 ....234 D6
Wessenden Rd MAR/SLWT HD7 ..233 H5
Wessex Park Cl ROY/SHW OL2 ..229 K6
West Acres KNOT WF11 ....159 M6
West Av BAIL BD17 ....82 E2
BSPA/BRAM LS23 ....48 E6
HEM/SK/SE WF9 ....225 J7
HEM/SK/SE WF9 ....247 K2
HIPP HX3 ....148 C7
HIPP HX3 ....168 D2
HOLM/MEL HD9 ....236 A2
HOR/CROF WF4 ....197 L5
HUDW HD3 ....191 L5
PONT WF8 ....180 C6
RHAY LS8 ....88 E6
West Bank HWTH BD22 ....2 B3
LUD/ILL HX2 ....145 M2
West Bank Cl HWTH BD22 ....2 A3
West Bank Gv AIRE BD20 ....58 A4
West Bank Ri HWTH BD22 ....2 A3
West Bank Rd AIRE BD20 ....57 M4
SKP/WHF BD23 ....16 A2
West Bolton LUD/ILL HX2 ......123 M7
Westborough Dr LUD/ILL HX2 ..145 M7
Westbourne Av BEE/HOL LS11 ..131 K3
GFTH/SHER LS25 ....112 F8
Westbourne Cl OT LS21 ....41 G8
WKFDW/WTN WF2 ....198 E8
Westbourne Crs
GFTH/SHER LS25 ....112 F8
PONT WF8 ....180 D7
Westbourne Dr
GFTH/SHER LS25 ....112 F8
GSLY LS20 ....61 L5
ILK LS29 ....61 J1
Westbourne Gdns
GFTH/SHER LS25 ....112 F8
Westbourne Gv DOD/DAR S75 ..260 F3
GFTH/SHER LS25 ....112 F8
HIPP HX3 ....168 F3
OT LS21 ....41 G7
Westbourne Mt BEE/HOL LS11 ..131 K3
PONT WF8 ....180 D7
Westbourne Pl BEE/HOL LS11 ..131 K3
PDSY/CALV LS28 ....106 F5
Westbourne Rd GIR * BD8 ......104 D4
HUDW HD3 ....191 M7
PONT WF8 ....180 E7
Westbourne St BEE/HOL LS11 ..131 K3
Westbourne Ter DOD/DAR S75 ..260 F3
GFTH/SHER LS25 ....112 E8
HIPP HX3 ....168 F3
Westbrook Cl HORS LS18 ....85 K4
West Brook La HFAX HX1 ....10 F4
Westbrook Dr HUDE HD5 ......193 K4
Westbrook La HORS LS18 ....85 K4
Westburn Av HWTH BD22 ....2 A8
Westburn Crs HWTH BD22 ....2 A8
Westburn Gv HWTH BD22 ....2 B8
Westburn Pl HWTH BD22 ....2 A8
Westbury Cl BOW BD4 ....127 M1
DOD/DAR S75 ....260 D2
Westbury Gv MID LS10 ....132 B4
Westbury Mt RTHW LS26 ....132 B5
Westbury Pl HFAX HX1 ....146 A8
Westbury Pl North MID LS10 ..132 B4
Westbury Pl South RTHW LS26 ..132 B5
Westbury Rd WBSY BD6 ....125 M5
Westbury St BOW BD4 ....127 M1
ELL HX5 ....169 J7
MID LS10 ....132 B5
Westbury Ter HFAX HX1 ....146 A8
RTHW LS26 ....132 B5
West Busk La OT LS21 ....40 F8
West Byland LUD/ILL HX2 ......123 M7
West Carr La HUDW HD3 ....211 G4
West Chevin Rd OT LS21 ....61 M1
Westcliffe Dr LUD/ILL HX2 .....145 M7
Westcliffe Av BAIL BD17 ....82 D2
Westcliffe Ri CLECK BD19 ......149 L7
Westcliffe Rd CLECK BD19 .....149 L6
SHPY BD18 ....82 D7
West Cl HUDN HD2 ....192 D4
NORM WF6 ....178 C4
PONT WF8 ....203 G1
Westcombe Av RHAY LS8 ....88 C4
Westcombe Ct LM/WK BD12 ..148 C7
West Cote Dr IDLE BD10 ....83 H5
West Ct RHAY LS8 ....88 C7
West Crs STKB/PEN S36 ....271 J4
West Cft AIRE BD20 ....55 C7
ILK LS29 ....19 H6
LM/WK BD12 ....148 E3
Westcroft HOLM/MEL HD9 ....236 A2
Westcroft Av HIPP HX3 ....147 K2
Westcroft Dr OSS WF5 ....174 E4
Westcroft Rd GTHN BD7 ....126 C2
HEM/SK/SE WF9 ....223 M7
West Di BSPA/BRAM LS23 ....48 E5

Westdale Dr PDSY/CALV LS28 ..106 F6
Westdale Gdns
PDSY/CALV LS28 ....106 F6
Westdale Gv PDSY/CALV LS28 ..106 F6
Westdale Ri PDSY/CALV LS28 ..106 F6
Westdale Rd PDSY/CALV LS28 ..106 F6
West Dene AIRE BD20 ....36 A4
AL/HA/HU LS17 ....88 B1
West Dr HWTH BD22 ....100 E3
PONT WF8 ....181 G7
West Edge Rd PONT WF8 ....203 M8
West End BSPA/BRAM LS23 ....48 E6
CUL/QBY BD13 ....124 F6
HFAX * HX1 ....146 A8
MOR LS27 ....129 L7
WOR/ARM LS12 ....129 M3
West End Ap MOR LS27 ....152 A3
TAD LS24 ....94 F1
West End Av BSLYN/ROY S71 ..243 J3
FEA/AMT WF7 ....179 K5
HOLM/MEL HD9 ....236 E8
STKB/PEN S36 ....269 M3
West End Crs BSLYN/ROY S71 ..243 J3
West End Dr CLECK BD19 ......149 K8
HORS LS18 ....85 H5
West End Gv HORS LS18 ....85 H5
West End La HORS LS18 ....85 H4
West End Pl BEE/HOL LS11 ......8 C4
West End Ri HORS LS18 ....85 H5
West End Ter AWLS/ASK DN6 ..227 L3
HFAX * HX1 ....146 A8
MAR/SLWT HD7 ....212 C2
PDSY/CALV LS28 ....84 D8
Westend St BFD BD1 ....4 D5
West End Ter ECHL BD2 ....105 K1
GSLY LS20 ....61 L5
HBR HX7 ....144 A5
SHPY BD18 ....82 C6
Westercroft La HIPP HX3 ....147 K3
Westercroft Vw HIPP HX3 ......147 K3
Westerley Cl KBTN HD8 ....238 C3
Westerley Crs AIRE BD20 ....35 L5
Westerley La KBTN HD8 ....238 C3
Westerly Cft WOR/ARM LS12 ..108 E6
Westerly Ri WOR/ARM LS12 ..108 E6
Westerly Wy KBTN HD8 ....238 C3
Westerman Cl FEA/AMT * WF7 ..179 M8
Westerman St WKFDE WF1 ......13 K9
Western Av AIRE BD20 ....57 M3
BTLY WF17 ....151 J5
PONT WF8 ....181 H5
Western Ct PONT WF8 ....181 H5
Western Gales Wy NORM WF6 ..178 F5
Western Gv WOR/ARM LS12 ..130 D1
Western Mt WOR/ARM LS12 ..130 D1
Western Pl CUL/QBY BD13 .....125 K5
Western Rd HUDS HD4 ....213 J2
SKP/WHF BD23 ....16 D3
WOR/ARM LS12 ....130 D1
Western St BSLY S70 ....261 G4
WOR/ARM LS12 ....130 D1
Western Wy WBSY BD6 ....126 C7
Westerton Cl EARD/LOFT WF3 ..153 K7
Westerton Ct LM/WK BD12 ....149 K1
Westerton Rd EARD/LOFT WF3 ..152 F7
Westerton Wk
EARD/LOFT WF3 ....153 K6
West Farm Av MID LS10 ....153 K4
Westfell Cl HWTH BD22 ....2 B7
Westfell Rd HWTH BD22 ....2 B7
Westfell Wy HWTH BD22 ....2 B7
Westfield CUL/QBY BD13 ....103 J8
HBR HX7 ....143 L1
PDSY/CALV LS28 ....106 F5
Westfield Av CAS WF10 ....179 L2
EARL WF12 ....174 C6
HOLM/MEL HD9 ....234 E3
HUDW HD3 ....191 M7
KBTN HD8 ....239 H5
KNOT WF11 ....182 B3
PONT WF8 ....180 E8
STKB/PEN S36 ....270 C2
WOR/ARM LS12 ....108 B6
YEA LS19 ....62 B8
Westfield Cl GFTH/SHER LS25 ..137 M3
HECK * WF16 ....172 E1
RTHW LS26 ....154 E2
YEA LS19 ....62 B8
Westfield Ct GFTH/SHER LS25 ..138 B2
HOR/CROF WF4 ....197 H4
HUDE HD5 ....15 M6
MIRF WF14 ....194 C1
RTHW LS26 ....154 E2
Westfield Crs AIRE BD20 ....58 B4
ECHL BD2 ....5 L1
HDGY LS6 ....6 A5
HOR/CROF WF4 ....222 C5
OSS WF5 ....196 E1
SHPY BD18 ....83 G8
TAD LS24 ....71 L3
WKFDW/WTN WF2 ....175 K4
Westfield Dr AIRE BD20 ....58 B5
HIPP HX3 ....147 M7
KBTN HD8 ....239 H5
OSS WF5 ....196 E1
YEA LS19 ....62 A8
West Field La HOLM/MEL HD9 ..236 A6
Westfield La GFTH/SHER LS25 ..135 H4
GFTH/SHER LS25 ....137 J4
HEM/SK/SE WF9 ....247 H5
IDLE BD10 ....83 H7
KBTN HD8 ....217 G6

LM/WK BD12 ....148 F5
PONT WF8 ....203 L3
PONT WF8 ....227 G3
STKB/PEN S36 ....270 C2
Westfield Ms YEA LS19 ....62 B5
Westfield Ov YEA LS19 ....62 B8
Westfield Pk WKFDE WF1 .....176 E6
Westfield Pl CLECK BD19 ....149 K5
HFAX * HX1 ....10 C8
WKFDW/WTN WF2 ....175 K4
Westfield Rd AIRE BD20 ....58 B5
BVRD LS3 ....6 A6
CLAY BD14 ....125 K2
HECK WF16 ....172 E1
HEM/SK/SE WF9 ....223 H6
HOR/CROF WF4 ....197 H4
HTON BD9 ....104 C4
KNOT WF11 ....182 B3
MOR * LS27 ....152 C2
RTHW LS26 ....154 E2
RYKW YO26 ....32 A1
WKFDE WF1 ....176 D6
Westfields BSLYN/ROY S71 .....243 J2
CAS WF10 ....179 L1
Westfields Av MIRF WF14 ......194 C1
Westfield Sq TAD LS24 ....71 L2
Westfields Rd MIRF WF14 ......194 C1
Westfield St BSLY * S70 ....260 F5
HECK WF16 ....172 E1
HFAX HX1 ....10 C3
OSS WF5 ....196 E1
Westfield Ter BAIL BD17 ....82 E2
CAS WF10 ....157 J1
CHAL LS7 ....87 L6
CLAY BD14 ....125 K2
ECHL BD2 ....5 L1
HFAX HX1 ....10 C3
TAD LS24 ....71 L3
WKFDE WF1 ....176 E6
Westfield Vw WKFDE WF1 .....176 E6
West Garth TAD LS24 ....94 F1
Westgarth WBY LS22 ....47 K3
West Ga HOLM/MEL HD9 ......254 B6
WBY LS22 ....48 A1
Westgate BAIL BD17 ....82 E2
BRIG HD6 ....171 G4
BSLY S70 ....261 G5
BSLYN/ROY S71 ....261 K2
CLECK BD19 ....149 L7
EARL WF12 ....173 M6
ECHL BD2 ....105 L2
ELL HX5 ....169 H7
GIR BD8 ....4 C4
GSLY LS20 ....61 K6
HEM/SK/SE WF9 ....223 L8
HFAX HX1 ....11 H6
HOLM/MEL HD9 ....234 F4
HOLM/MEL HD9 ....236 B2
HUD HD1 ....14 F7
HUDE HD5 ....215 H4
LDS LS1 ....6 C9
LVSG WF15 ....172 C2
OT LS21 ....41 H7
SHPY BD18 ....82 B5
SKP/WHF BD23 ....16 B2
STKB/PEN S36 ....270 F4
TAD LS24 ....71 L3
WKFDW/WTN WF2 ....12 D3
Westgate Ct EARD/LOFT WF3 ..154 D6
Westgate End
WKFDW/WTN WF2 ....12 B4
Westgate Gdns KGHY BD21 .....2 F6
Westgate Gv EARD/LOFT WF3 ..154 D6
Westgate Hill St BOW BD4 .....128 C6
Westgate La EARD/LOFT WF3 ..154 D6
Westgate Market HFAX HX1 ....11 H6
Westgate Ter BOW BD4 ....128 C6
West Grange Cl MID LS10 ......131 M5
West Grange Dr MID LS10 .....131 M5
West Grange Fold MID LS10 ...131 M5
West Grange Gdns MID LS10 ..131 M5
West Grange Garth MID LS10 ..131 M5
West Grange Wk MID LS10 ....131 M5
West Gv BAIL BD17 ....82 E2
BSLYN/ROY S71 ....243 J3
West Grove Av HUDE HD5 ......15 M6
Westgrove Ct CLECK BD19 .....149 L6
West Grove St
PDSY/CALV * LS28 ....106 F5
West Grove Ter HFAX HX1 ....10 E8
West Hall La ILK LS29 ....19 J4
Westhaven CUD/GR * S72 ......262 E4
West Hi ROCH * OL11 ....206 A8
West Hill Av CHAL LS7 ....87 L7
Westhill Av CUL/QBY BD13 ....102 A1
West Hill St HFAX HX1 ....10 E6
Westholme Rd HFAX HX1 ....10 A6
Westholme St BFD BD1 ....4 D7
West Ings Ct KNOT WF11 ......182 C1
West Ings Crs KNOT WF11 .....182 D1
West Ings La KNOT WF11 ......182 C1
West Ings Ms KNOT WF11 .....182 D1
West Ings Wy KNOT WF11 .....182 D1
Westland Ct AIRE BD20 ....35 G8
Westland Rd BEE/HOL LS11 ...131 J5
Westlands RYKW YO26 ....32 D5
Westlands Dr WIL/AL BD15 ....103 K5
Westlands Gv WIL/AL BD15 ....103 L5
Westland Sq BEE/HOL LS11 ...131 K6
West La AIRE BD20 ....34 B3
AIRE BD20 ....34 C1
AIRE BD20 ....55 L3
BAIL BD17 ....82 C2
BSPA/BRAM LS23 ....48 D5
CLECK BD19 ....150 D5
CUL/QBY BD13 ....102 F8
HIPP HX3 ....169 A3
HOR/CROF WF4 ....200 D5
HWTH BD22 ....2 D2
HWTH BD22 ....78 D7
OT LS21 ....40 A1
Westlea Av KGHY BD21 ....58 B5
West Lea Cl AL/HA/HU LS17 ....87 K5
West Lea Crs EARD/LOFT WF3 ..152 F7
YEA LS19 ....62 B8
West Lea Dr AL/HA/HU LS17 ...87 K5

West Lea Gdns *AL/HA/HU* LS17 ......87 K5
West Lea Garth *AL/HA/HU* LS17 ...87 K5
West Lea Gv *YEA* LS19 ....62 B8
West Leeds St *HWTH* BD22 ....2 D5
Westleigh *BGLY* BD16 ....81 J2
Westleigh Cl *BAIL* BD17 ....82 C4
Westleigh Dr *BAIL* BD17 ....82 C4
Westleigh Rd *BAIL* BD17 ....82 C3
Westleigh Wy *BAIL* BD17 ....82 B4
Westley Av *HOLM/MEL* HD9 ....236 B6
Westlock Av *OSM* LS9 ....110 C5
West Ldg *ILK* LS29 ....40 A6
West Lodge Gv *HUDW* HD3 ....191 K2
West Lodge Gdns *CHAL* LS7 ....87 L8
West Md *CAS* WF10 ....158 C7
Westminster Cl *ROY/SHW* OL2 ....229 K6
Westminster Av *CLAY* BD14 ....125 J2
  ROY/SHW OL2 ....228 E8
Westminster Cl *BRAM* LS13 ....107 H2
Westminster Crs *CLAY* BD14 ....125 J2
  MSTN/BAR LS15 ....111 G8
  PBR HG3 ....26 E3
Westminster Cft *BRAM* * LS13 ....107 H2
Westminster Dr *BRAM* LS13 ....107 H2
  CLAY BD14 ....125 J2
  PBR HG3 ....26 D3
Westminster Gdns *CLAY* BD14 ....125 J2
Westminster Ga *PBR* HG3 ....26 E2
Westminster Gv *PBR* HG3 ....26 E2
Westminster Pl *BFDE* BD3 ....5 H2
Westminster Ri *PBR* HG3 ....26 E1
Westminster Rd *BFDE* BD3 ....5 H2
  PBR HG3 ....26 D2
Westminster Ter *BFDE* BD3 ....5 H3
Westmoor Av *BAIL* BD17 ....82 D2
Westmoor Cl *BAIL* * BD17 ....82 D2
West Moor Crs *DOD/DAR* S75 ....260 C5
West Moorlands Av
  DEWS * WF13 ....173 K5
Westmoor Pl *BRAM* LS13 ....107 K5
Westmoor Rd *BRAM* LS13 ....107 K5
West Moor Rd
  HEM/SK/SE WF9 ....223 J4
Westmoor St *BRAM* LS13 ....107 K5
Westmoreland Mt
  BRAM * LS13 ....107 M2
Westmoreland St
  SKP/WHF BD23 ....16 E1
Westmorland Dr *WHIT* OL12 ....184 F8
Westmorland St *WKFDE* WF1 ....12 F2
West Mt *TAD* LS24 ....71 K4
West Mount Pl *HFAX* HX1 ....10 C4
West Mount St *BEE/HOL* * LS11 ....8 D9
Westmount St *PONT* WF8 ....180 E6
Westoff La *CUD/GR* S72 ....222 E7
Weston Av *CUL/QBY* BD13 ....124 F6
  MILN OL16 ....228 D2
Weston Crs *OT* LS21 ....41 G5
Weston Dr *OT* LS21 ....40 F4
Weston La *OT* LS21 ....41 G5
Weston Moor Rd *OT* LS21 ....22 F6
Weston Park Vw *OT* LS21 ....40 F4
Weston Rdg *OT* LS21 ....41 G4
Weston St *HWTH* BD22 ....2 A9
  MILN OL16 ....207 H8
Weston Vale Rd
  CUL/QBY BD13 ....124 E6
Westover Gdns
  PDSY/CALV LS28 ....106 E8
Westover Gn *BRAM* * LS13 ....107 L3
Westover Gv *BRAM* * LS13 ....107 L3
Westover Mt *BRAM* * LS13 ....107 L3
Westover Rd *BRAM* LS13 ....107 L3
Westover Ter *BRAM* * LS13 ....107 L3
Westover Vw *BRAM* LS13 ....107 L3
West Pde *BHP/TINH* LS16 ....86 C6
  HFAX HX1 ....10 E7
  ILK LS29 ....38 E2
  RPDN/SBR HX6 ....167 M2
  RTHW LS26 ....155 H1
  WKFDE WF1 ....12 F3
West Parade Ct *WKFDE* WF1 ....12 E4
West Parade Flats *HFAX* HX1 ....10 F7
West Parade St *WKFDE* WF1 ....12 F4
West Pk *BHP/TINH* LS16 ....86 C6
  GSLY LS20 ....61 L4
West Park Av *RHAY* LS8 ....88 C3
West Park Cl *RHAY* LS8 ....88 C3
West Park Crs *RHAY* LS8 ....88 C3
West Park Dr *BHP/TINH* LS16 ....86 C6
  PONT WF8 ....203 M4
West Park Dr East *RHAY* LS8 ....88 C3
West Park Dr West *RHAY* LS8 ....88 B3
West Park Gv *BTLY* WF17 ....173 J1
  RHAY LS8 ....88 C3
West Park Pl *RHAY* LS8 ....88 C4
West Park Rd *BTLY* WF17 ....173 H2
  GIR BD8 ....104 B6
West Parks *PDSY/CALV* LS28 ....106 F7
West Park St *BRIG* HD6 ....170 D4
  DEWS WF13 ....173 K5
West Park Ter *BTLY* WF17 ....173 J1
  GIR * BD8 ....104 B6
West Pasture La *HORS* LS18 ....85 H5
West Pinfold *BSLYN/ROY* S71 ....243 L3
West Pl *HUDE* HD5 ....15 M6
Westridge Dr *HUDS* HD4 ....213 J3
West Rd *DOD/DAR* S75 ....260 D4
  OSM LS9 ....132 E3
West Rd North *OSM* LS9 ....132 E3
Westroyd *PDSY/CALV* LS28 ....106 E8
Westroyd Av *PDSY/CALV* LS28 ......106 E8
West Royd *WIL/AL* BD15 ....102 E1
West Royd Av *ECHL* * BD2 ....105 K2
  HFAX HX1 ....10 B9
  MIRF WF14 ....194 C1
  SHPY BD18 ....82 F6
Westroyd Av *CLECK* BD19 ....149 M3
Westroyd Cl *PDSY/CALV* LS28 ......106 E8
West Royd Crs *SHPY* BD18 ....83 G6
West Royd Dr *MIRF* WF14 ....172 C8
  SHPY BD18 ....83 G6
Westroyd Gdns
  PDSY/CALV LS28 ....106 E8

West Royd Gv *MIRF* WF14 ....172 C8
  SHPY BD18 ....83 G6
West Royd Pk *SHPY* BD18 ....83 G6
West Royd Pk *MIRF* WF14 ....172 C8
West Royd Rd *SHPY* BD18 ....83 G6
West Royd Ter *SHPY* BD18 ....83 G6
West Royd Vls *HFAX* HX1 ....10 C9
West Scausby Pk *LUD/ILL* HX2 ......124 A7
West Shaw La *HWTH* BD22 ....100 C3
West Side Ct *GIR* BD8 ....104 B5
West Slaithwaite Rd
  MAR/SLWT HD7 ....211 L7
West St *BAIL* BD17 ....82 E2
  BFD BD1 ....5 G7
  BIRK/DRI BD11 ....151 G1
  BRIG HD6 ....148 D7
  BRIG HD6 ....170 C3
  BSLYN/ROY S71 ....243 M2
  BTLY WF17 ....173 M1
  BVRD LS3 ....6 A8
  CAS WF10 ....157 L6
  CLECK BD19 ....149 M7
  CLECK BD19 ....150 C5
  COL BB8 ....74 A2
  CUD/GR S72 ....245 G1
  EARL WF12 ....173 L7
  ECHL BD2 ....105 K3
  GTL/HWG HX4 ....190 D2
  HECK WF16 ....172 E2
  HEM/SK/SE WF9 ....223 L7
  HEM/SK/SE WF9 ....246 B4
  HEM/SK/SE WF9 ....247 K2
  HFAX HX1 ....10 C5
  HIPP HX3 ....147 K2
  HOR/CROF WF4 ....222 E5
  HUDW HD3 ....191 J5
  LIT OL15 ....207 K1
  MILN OL16 ....206 C6
  MILN OL16 ....206 F7
  MOR LS27 ....152 D3
  NORM WF6 ....178 C4
  PDSY/CALV LS28 ....107 G6
  RPDN/SBR HX6 ....167 K3
  WKFDW/WTN WF2 ....198 B1
West Vw *WOR/ARM* LS12 ....131 C1
  BEE/HOL LS11 ....8 D9
  BOW BD4 ....127 J2
  BSLY S70 ....261 G1
  CUD/GR S72 ....262 E1
  DEWS WF13 ....173 K4
  FEA/AMT WF7 ....223 M1
  GFTH/SHER LS25 ....114 D8
  GFTH/SHER LS25 ....116 A8
  GFTH/SHER LS25 ....135 K4
  GTL/HWG HX4 ....190 C2
  HIPP HX3 ....146 D4
  HUD HD1 ....213 M1
  LIT OL15 ....207 L1
  NORM WF6 ....178 B3
  OT LS21 ....41 K6
  OT LS21 ....43 H8
  RTHW LS26 ....155 L1
  SKP/WHF BD23 ....17 M1
  WBY LS22 ....29 K2
  WKFDW/WTN WF2 ....175 K4
  YEA LS19 ....62 B7
West View Av *CAS* WF10 ....158 C7
  HFAX HX1 ....146 A7
  ILK LS29 ....40 A5
  SHPY BD18 ....83 G7
West View Cl *SHPY* BD18 ....83 G7
West View Ct *YEA* * LS19 ....62 B7
West View Crs *HFAX* HX1 ....146 A8
West View Dr *LUD/ILL* HX2 ....145 M7
Westview Gv *KGHY* BD21 ....2 D7
West View Ri *HUD* HD1 ....213 M1
West View Rd *HIPP* * HX3 ....146 D4
  ILK LS29 ....40 A5
West View Ter *GIR* * BD8 ....104 A7
  LUD/ILL * HX2 ....146 A6
Westview Wy *KGHY* BD21 ....2 B7
West Villa Rd *GSLY* LS20 ....62 A5
Westville Av *ILK* LS29 ....38 C2
Westville Cl *ILK* LS29 ....38 C2
Westville Rd *DOD/DAR* S75 ....260 F3
  ILK LS29 ....38 C2
Westville Wy *CUL/QBY* BD13 ....102 F8
Westward Ho *HIPP* HX3 ....146 C2
  MILN OL16 ....207 H8
West Wy *BSLY* S70 ....261 H8
  SHPY BD18 ....81 M7
Westway *BTLY* WF17 ....174 B3
  GFTH/SHER LS25 ....112 F8
  GSLY LS20 ....61 K6
  HTON BD9 ....103 L4
  KGHY BD21 ....2 B1
  MIRF WF14 ....172 B7
  PDSY/CALV LS28 ....106 E3
  ROY/SHW * OL2 ....229 K8
Westways *WKFDW/WTN* WF2 ....176 B3
Westways Cl
  WKFDW/WTN WF2 ....176 B4
Westways Gv *RHAY* LS8 ....88 E7
Westways Ri
  WKFDW/WTN WF2 ....176 B4
West Wells Crs *OSS* WF5 ....196 E1
West Wells Rd *OSS* WF5 ....196 E1
West Winds *ILK* LS29 ....61 G1
Westwinn Garth *SCFT* LS14 ....89 L6
Westwinn Vw *SCFT* LS14 ....89 L6
Westwood Av *ECHL* BD2 ....105 K1
  HOLM/MEL HD9 ....236 E2
Westwood Ct *BSLY* S70 ....261 G4
West Wood Dr *MID* S10 ....153 J1
Westwood Dr *ILK* LS29 ....38 B4
Westwood Edge Rd
  MAR/SLWT HD7 ....212 C3

Westwood Fold
  MAR/SLWT HD7 ....212 D4
Westwood Gv *ECHL* BD2 ....105 K1
Westwood Ri *ILK* LS29 ....38 B4
  MOR LS27 ....130 C8
West Wood Rd *MOR* LS27 ....153 H2
Westwood Rd *CAS* WF10 ....179 K1
  OSS WF5 ....197 H1
Westwood Side *MOR* LS27 ....130 C7
Westwoodside *MOR* LS27 ....130 D7
Westwood St *HUDN* * HD2 ....171 J8
Westwood Wy
  BSPA/BRAM LS23 ....48 F7
Wetherby Grange Pk
  WBY * LS22 ....48 C3
Wetherby Gv *BULY* LS4 ....108 E4
Wetherby La *WBY* LS22 ....30 E1
Wetherby Pl *BULY* LS4 ....108 F4
Wetherby Rd *AL/HA/HU* LS17 ....67 M2
  BSPA/BRAM LS23 ....49 G2
  BSPA/BRAM LS23 ....69 L3
  RHAY LS8 ....88 D7
  RYKW YO26 ....32 B5
  RYKW YO26 ....33 J3
  SCFT LS14 ....89 J3
  TAD LS24 ....71 K2
  WBY LS22 ....30 A6
  WBY LS22 ....46 F1
  WBY LS22 ....47 M5
  WBY LS22 ....48 A3
Wetherby Ter *BULY* LS4 ....108 E4
Wetherhill St *BTLY* WF17 ....173 K1
Wetlands St *HOLM/MEL* HD9 ....235 G5
Wetton Ct *BFDE* BD3 ....105 M7
Weydale Av *HUDW* HD3 ....191 J6
Weyhill Dr *WIL/AL* BD15 ....103 K6
Weymouth Av *HUDW* HD3 ....191 K7
  WIL/AL BD15 ....103 J6
Whack House Cl *YEA* LS19 ....62 C8
Whales La *GLE* DN14 ....183 M1
Whaley Rd *DOD/DAR* S75 ....260 B1
Whalley Av *LIT* OL15 ....185 J8
Whalley Cl *MILN* * OL16 ....207 G8
Whalley La *CUL/QBY* BD13 ....101 M4
Wham La *UPML* OL3 ....230 T5
Whams Rd *STKB/PEN* S36 ....269 G4
Wharfe Bank *WBY* LS22 ....47 G6
Wharfe Cl *BHP/TINH* LS16 ....86 F2
Wharfe Crs *OT* LS21 ....42 F7
Wharfedale Av *CHAL* LS7 ....109 K2
Wharfedale Cl *SKP/WHF* BD23 ....16 D2
Wharfedale Ct *OT* LS21 ....41 K6
  SCFT LS14 ....111 H1
Wharfedale Crs
  GFTH/SHER LS25 ....135 H1
  KBTN HD8 ....239 K5
Wharfedale Dr *ILK* LS29 ....38 E3
  NORM WF6 ....178 C2
Wharfedale Gdns *BAIL* BD17 ....83 G2
Wharfedale Gv *HDGY* LS6 ....6 E1
Wharfedale Lawns *WBY* LS22 ....48 A1
Wharfedale Ms *HIPP* HX3 ....125 K8
Wharfedale Mt *HIPP* HX3 ....125 K8
Wharfedale Pl *HDGY* LS6 ....6 E1
Wharfedale Ri
  EARD/LOFT WF3 ....152 F7
  HTON BD9 ....103 L4
Wharfedale Rd *BOW* BD4 ....127 J7
  DOD/DAR S75 ....260 C3
Wharfedale St *HDGY* LS6 ....6 E1
Wharfedale Vw *HDGY* LS6 ....109 K2
  ILK LS29 ....19 G6
  ILK LS29 ....61 J2
Wharfe Gra *WBY* LS22 ....47 M1
Wharfe Gv *WBY* LS22 ....47 M1
Wharfe La *WBY* LS22 ....45 L4
Wharfe Ms *ILK* * LS29 ....61 K2
  WBY * LS22 ....48 A1
Wharfe Pk *ILK* LS29 ....19 J6
Wharfe Rein *WBY* LS22 ....47 G6
Wharfeside La *ILK* LS29 ....38 E1
Wharfe St *OT* LS21 ....41 K6
Wharfe Vw *PBR* HG3 ....27 K7
  WBY LS22 ....47 M1
Wharfe View Rd *ILK* LS29 ....38 D2
Wharf St *BAIL* BD17 ....82 D6
  BFDE BD3 ....5 G4
  BRIG HD6 ....170 D4
  BSLYN/ROY S71 ....261 J3
  EARL WF12 ....173 M7
  LDSU LS2 ....9 J1
  RPDN/SBR HX6 ....167 L2
  TOD OL14 ....163 J5
Wharncliffe *DOD/DAR* S75 ....260 C8
Wharncliffe Crs *ECHL* BD2 ....105 M2
Wharncliffe Dr *ECHL* BD2 ....105 M2
Wharncliffe Gv *ECHL* BD2 ....105 M2
  SHPY BD18 ....82 D8
Wharncliffe Rd *SHPY* BD18 ....104 D1
  WKFDW/WTN WF2 ....220 C1
Wharncliffe St *BSLY* S70 ....260 F5
  BSLYN/ROY S71 ....243 M6
The Whartons *OT* LS21 ....41 J4
Wharton St *LVSG* WF15 ....172 D2
Wheat Cl *DEWS* WF13 ....173 H6
  HOLM/MEL HD9 ....253 M4
Wheatcroft *CAS* WF10 ....158 D8
Wheatcroft Av *BTLY* WF17 ....173 L2
Wheatdale Rd *TAD* LS24 ....94 F2
Wheater Rd *GTHN* * BD7 ....126 C1
Wheat Field Av *HUDW* HD3 ....191 J7
Wheatfield Ct *PDSY/CALV* LS28 .....106 F8
Wheathead Crs *HWTH* BD22 ....79 G1
Wheat Head Dr *HWTH* BD22 ....79 G1
Wheathead La *HWTH* BD22 ....79 G1
Wheathill St *ROCH* OL11 ....228 C2
Wheathouse Rd *HUDN* HD2 ....14 D1
Wheathouse Ter *HUDN* HD2 ....14 D1
The Wheatings *OSS* WF5 ....197 H1
Wheatlands *ILK* LS29 ....38 E1
  PDSY/CALV LS28 ....106 C3
Wheatlands Av *AIRE* BD20 ....34 E7
  HTON BD9 ....104 A4
Wheatlands Crs *HTON* BD9 ....104 A4
Wheatlands Dr *HTON* BD9 ....104 A4
  LVSG * WF15 ....172 B4
Wheatlands Gv *HTON* BD9 ....104 A4

Wheatlands La *AIRE* BD20 ....34 E7
Wheatlands Sq *HTON* BD9 ....104 A4
Wheatley Av *ILK* LS29 ....39 G3
  NORM WF6 ....178 D5
Wheatley Cl *BSLYN/ROY* S71 ....261 H2
  HIPP HX3 ....10 C1
Wheatley Dr *MIRF* WF14 ....194 C3
Wheatley Gdns *ILK* LS29 ....39 G3
Wheatley Gv *ILK* LS29 ....39 G3
Wheatley Hill La *HUDN* HD8 ....240 A6
Wheatley La *HIPP* HX3 ....10 C1
  ILK LS29 ....39 G3
Wheatley Ri *DOD/DAR* S75 ....242 D4
Wheatley Rd *BSLY* S70 ....262 A7
  HIPP HX3 ....146 B4
  ILK LS29 ....38 E3
Wheaton Av *MSTN/BAR* LS15 ....111 J6
Wheatroyd Crs *OSS* WF5 ....196 F5
Wheatroyd La *HUDE* HD5 ....215 G4
Wheat St *HWTH* BD22 ....79 J2
Wheelwright Av
  WOR/ARM LS12 ....130 C1
Wheelwright Cl
  WOR/ARM LS12 ....130 C1
Wheelwright Dr *DEWS* WF13 ....173 K4
  MILN OL16 ....206 E3
Wheelwright St *EARL* * WF12 ....173 L6
Wheldale La *CAS* WF10 ....159 G4
Wheldon Rd *CAS* WF10 ....158 A6
  CAS WF10 ....158 F3
Whernside Mt *GTHN* BD7 ....126 A4
Whernside Wy *LUD/ILL* HX2 ....145 J3
Wherwell Rd *BRIG* HD6 ....170 D5
Whetley Cl *GIR* BD8 ....4 B3
Whetley Gv *GIR* BD8 ....104 C5
Whetley Hill *GIR* BD8 ....104 D5
Whetley La *GIR* BD8 ....104 C5
Whetley Ter *GIR* BD8 ....4 B3
Whewell St *BTLY* WF17 ....151 G5
Whiddon Cft *ILK* LS29 ....61 H1
Whimbrel Cl *BFDE* BD3 ....103 L7
Whimbrel Ms *MOR* LS27 ....152 E3
Whinbeck Av *NORM* WF6 ....178 F5
Whinberry Pl *BTLY* WF17 ....151 H3
Whinbrook Crs *AL/HA/HU* LS17 ....87 L5
Whinbrook Gdns
  AL/HA/HU LS17 ....87 L5
Whinbrook Gv *AL/HA/HU* LS17 ....87 L5
Whinby Cft *DOD/DAR* S75 ....260 B7
Whinby Rd *DOD/DAR* S75 ....259 M6
Whin Cl *HEM/SK/SE* WF9 ....245 M1
Whincop Av *CAS* WF10 ....157 H7
Whincover Cl *WOR/ARM* LS12 ....130 B1
Whincover Cross
  WOR/ARM LS12 ....130 B1
Whincover Dr *WOR/ARM* LS12 ......130 A1
Whincover Gdns
  WOR/ARM LS12 ....130 B1
Whincover Gv *WOR/ARM* LS12 ......130 B1
Whincover Hl *WOR/ARM* LS12 ....130 B1
Whincover Mt *WOR/ARM* LS12 ......130 B1
Whincover Rd *WOR/ARM* LS12 ......130 A1
Whincover Vw *WOR/ARM* LS12 .....130 B1
Whinfell Cl *AWLS/ASK* DN6 ....249 K8
Whinfield *BHP/TINH* LS16 ....86 D2
Whinfield Av *HWTH* BD22 ....57 G6
Whinfield Cl *HWTH* BD22 ....2 A3
Whinfield Dr *HWTH* BD22 ....57 G6
Whingate *WOR/ARM* LS12 ....108 C7
Whingate Av *WOR/ARM* LS12 ....108 C7
Whingate Gn *WOR/ARM* LS12 ....108 C7
Whingate Gv *WOR/ARM* LS12 ....108 C7
Whingate Rd *WOR/ARM* LS12 ....108 C7
Whingrove Av *HEM/SK/SE* WF9 .....234 E5
Whin Knoll Av *KGHY* BD21 ....2 B3
Whin La *GFTH/SHER* LS25 ....137 J3
Whinmoor Cl *DOD/DAR* S75 ....259 H5
Whinmoor Ct *SCFT* LS14 ....89 J5
Whinmoor Crs *SCFT* LS14 ....89 J5
Whinmoor Dr *DOD/DAR* S75 ....259 H5
Whinmoor Gdns *SCFT* LS14 ....89 J5
Whinmoor La *AL/HA/HU* LS17 ....89 G3
Whin Moor La *DOD/DAR* S75 ....258 E6
Whinmoor Vw *DOD/DAR* S75 ....259 H5
Whinmoor Wy *DOD/DAR* S75 ....259 H6
Whinmore Gdns *CLECK* BD19 ....150 E7
Whin Mt *NORM* WF6 ....178 E6
Whinney Brow *IDLE* BD10 ....83 H6
Whinney Cl *FEA/AMT* WF7 ....200 F1
Whinney Hill Pk *BRIG* HD6 ....170 C1
Whinney La *FEA/AMT* WF7 ....200 F1
Whinney Moor Av
  WKFDW/WTN WF2 ....197 M3
Whinney Royd La *HIPP* HX3 ....147 J1
Whinny Gill Rd *SKP/WHF* BD23 ....16 D3
Whins La *BSPA/BRAM* LS23 ....49 H5
  PBR HG3 ....26 C6
Whin St *HWTH* BD22 ....2 C4
Whirlaw Av *TOD* OL14 ....141 K7
Whirlaw La *TOD* OL14 ....141 K6
Whiskers La *HIPP* HX3 ....147 G3
Whisperwood Cl *WKFDE* * WF1 ......176 F1
Whisperwood Rd *WKFDE* WF1 ....176 F1
Whitacre Cl *HUDN* HD2 ....193 G3
Whitacre St *HUDN* HD2 ....193 G3
Whitaker Av *ECHL* BD2 ....105 L3
Whitaker St *BTLY* WF17 ....173 M2
  PDSY/CALV LS28 ....106 F4
Whitaker Wk *HWTH* * BD22 ....100 K8
Whitbourne Av *BSLYN/ROY* S71 ....261 H1
Whitby Av *HUDN* HD2 ....192 C4
Whitby Crs *EARL* WF12 ....174 D6
Whitby Rd *GIR* BD8 ....104 C5
Whitby St *ROCH* OL11 ....228 C2
Whitby Ter *GIR* BD8 ....104 C5
Whitcliffe Rd *CLECK* BD19 ....149 L6
Whitcliffe Sq *CLECK* BD19 ....149 M6
White Abbey Rd *GIR* BD8 ....4 B3
White Apron St
  HEM/SK/SE WF9 ....246 D4
Whitebeam La *MILN* OL16 ....229 J3
Whitebeam Ms *MID* LS10 ....131 M6
Whitebeam Pk *HUDN* HD2 ....191 M4
White Birch Ter *HIPP* HX3 ....146 B4
Whitebridge Crs *OSM* LS9 ....111 G5

Whitebridge Sp *SCFT* LS14 ....111 K5
Whitebridge Vw *OSM* LS9 ....111 G5
White Castle Ct *CUL/QBY* BD13 ....124 E4
Whitechapel Cl *RHAY* LS8 ....88 D7
Whitechapel Gv *CLECK* BD19 ....149 J5
Whitechapel Rd *CLECK* BD19 ....149 K6
Whitechapel Wy *RHAY* LS8 ....88 D8
Whitecliffe Crs *RTHW* LS26 ....134 C4
Whitecliffe Dr *RTHW* LS26 ....134 C4
Whitecliffe Ri *RTHW* LS26 ....134 C4
Whitecote Gdns *BRAM* LS13 ....107 K2
Whitecote Hl *BRAM* LS13 ....107 K2
Whitecote La *BRAM* LS13 ....107 K1
  GFTH/SHER LS25 ....137 J5
Whitecote Ri *BRAM* LS13 ....107 K2
Whitecroft Av *ROY/SHW* OL2 ....200 C6
Whitecroft Rd *HOR/CROF* WF4 ....200 D2
  ROY/SHW OL2 ....229 M7
White Cross *HUDN* HD2 ....193 G1
White Cross Av *CUD/GR* S72 ....262 D4
White Cross Ct *CUD/GR* S72 ....262 E1
White Cross Gdns *CUD/GR* S72 .....222 E8
White Cross Mt *CUD/GR* S72 ....262 E1
White Cross Rd *CUD/GR* S72 ....262 D5
  EARL WF12 ....174 A5
Whitefield La *GLE* DN14 ....183 M5
Whitefield Pl *GIR* BD8 ....104 C6
White Ga *HOLM/MEL* HD9 ....236 B1
  LUD/ILL HX2 ....123 M7
Whitegate Dr *HIPP* HX3 ....168 F2
Whitegate Hl *PONT* WF8 ....203 M5
Whitegate La *PONT* WF8 ....203 G7
Whitegate Rd *HIPP* HX3 ....168 F1
White Gate Rd
  HOLM/MEL HD9 ....253 M5
Whitegate Rd *HUDS* HD4 ....214 D2
Whitegates Cl
  WKFDW/WTN WF2 ....176 B5
Whitegates Gv *KBTN* HD8 ....215 M4
Whitegates Ter *HIPP* HX3 ....168 F2
Whitegate Top *HIPP* HX3 ....169 G2
Whitehall Av *LM/WK* BD12 ....148 E5
  MIRF WF14 ....172 C7
  WKFDE WF1 ....176 C5
Whitehall Crs *WKFDE* WF1 ....176 C5
Whitehall Cft *RTHW* LS26 ....155 H1
Whitehall Est *WOR/ARM* * LS12 .....130 B2
Whitehall Fold *HBR* * HX7 ....143 H1
Whitehall Gv *BIRK/DRI* BD11 ....150 D7
Whitehall Quay *LDS* LS1 ....8 E7
Whitehall Rd *LM/WK* BD12 ....149 G5
  MAR/SLWT HD7 ....212 D6
  WOR/ARM LS12 ....8 A3
  WOR/ARM LS12 ....109 G8
Whitehall Rd East
  BIRK/DRI BD11 ....150 D7
Whitehall Rd West
  CLECK BD19 ....149 M4
Whitehall St *HIPP* HX3 ....147 M6
  WHIT OL12 ....206 B6
  WKFDW/WTN WF2 ....176 B8
Whitehall Wy *DEWS* WF13 ....173 M6
White Hart Dr *HUDS* HD4 ....214 C3
White Hart Fold
  HEM/SK/SE WF9 ....225 M4
  RPDN/SBR HX6 ....188 E3
Whitehaven Cl *WBSY* BD6 ....126 B7
Whitehead Gv *ECHL* BD2 ....105 L3
Whitehead La *HOLM/MEL* HD9 ......213 H8
  HUDS HD4 ....214 B8
Whitehead Pl *ECHL* BD2 ....105 L3
Whitehead's Ter *HFAX* * HX1 ....10 B5
  MILN * OL16 ....207 G8
  MILN OL16 ....229 M2
  ROY/SHW OL2 ....229 H6
White Hi *MAR/SLWT* HD7 ....211 J2
White Hill Av *BSLY* S70 ....260 C5
Whitehill Cottages
  LUD/ILL HX2 ....146 A1
Whitehill Crs *LUD/ILL* HX2 ....146 A1
Whitehill Dr *LUD/ILL* HX2 ....124 A8
Whitehill Gn *LUD/ILL* HX2 ....124 B8
Whitehill Gv *BSLY* * S70 ....260 D5
Whitehill Rd *HWTH* BD22 ....77 L1
  LUD/ILL HX2 ....146 A1
White Hill Ter *BSLY* * S70 ....260 C5
White Holme Dr *OT* LS21 ....43 G6
White Horse Cl *BTLY* WF17 ....151 K4
White Horse Fold *CAS* WF10 ....158 A4
White Horse Mdw *MILN* * OL16 .....228 B4
White Horse Ms *PBR* HG3 ....28 E6
White Horse Yd *WKFDE* WF1 ....12 E1
Whitehouse Av *RTHW* LS26 ....134 C1
Whitehouse Bungalows
  WKFDW/WTN * WF2 ....12 C1
Whitehouse Crs *RTHW* LS26 ....135 G1
Whitehouse Dr *RTHW* LS26 ....134 F1
Whitehouse La *RTHW* LS26 ....135 G1
  YEA LS19 ....63 H1
Whitehouse St *MID* LS10 ....9 K1
White Laith Av *SCFT* LS14 ....89 K1
White Laithe Ap *SCFT* LS14 ....89 K1
White Laithe Cl *SCFT* LS14 ....89 K1
White Laithe Cft *SCFT* LS14 ....89 K1
White Laithe Gdns *SCFT* * LS14 ....89 K1
White Laithe Garth *SCFT* LS14 ....89 K1
White Laithe Gn *SCFT* LS14 ....89 L1
White Laithe Rd *SCFT* LS14 ....89 K1
White Laithe Wk *SCFT* LS14 ....89 K1
White Lands *YEA* LS19 ....84 C2
White Lee Av *COL* BB8 ....74 B4
White Lee Cl *BTLY* WF17 ....151 G4
White Lee Gdns *HBR* HX7 ....144 B4
White Lee Rd *MID* LS10 ....131 M4
White Lee Side *HECK* WF16 ....151 G4
Whitelees Rd *LIT* OL15 ....207 J4
Whiteley Av *RPDN/SBR* HX6 ....167 J5

White Ley Bank
  HOLM/MEL HD9 ....237 J7
Whiteley Cft OT LS21 ....41 J7
Whiteley Croft Ri OT LS21 ....41 J7
Whiteley Croft Rd OT LS21 ....41 J7
White Ley Rd AWLS/ASK DN6 ....227 C5
Whiteley St FEA/AMT WF7 ....201 L1
  HFAX HX1 ....10 F7
  HUDS HD4 ....213 K2
Whitelock St CHAL LS7 ....7 J6
White Moss Cl FEA/AMT WF7 ....202 B8
Whiteplatts St TOD OL14 ....141 K8
White Rose Av
  GFTH/SHER LS25 ....113 H7
  HUDE HD5 ....193 H7
Whiterose Md
  GFTH/SHER * LS25 ....113 J7
White Rose Wy
  GFTH/SHER LS25 ....113 J7
White Slack Ga TOD OL14 ....163 H8
White's Rd WKFDE WF1 ....13 G2
White's Ter GIR BD8 ....104 D5
Whitestone Crs YEA LS19 ....62 D7
Whitestone La HUD HD1 ....15 G2
White's Vw GIR BD8 ....104 D6
White St RTHW LS26 ....133 M8
White Walls La
  HOLM/MEL HD9 ....253 H3
Whiteways ECHL BD2 ....105 J4
Whitewell Cl MILN OL16 ....206 E6
Whitewell Green La ELL HX5 ....169 K7
White Wells Gdns
  HOLM/MEL HD9 ....254 F3
White Wells Rd
  HOLM/MEL HD9 ....254 F3
Whitewood Cl BSLYN/ROY S71 ....243 K4
Whitfield Av MID LS10 ....9 L8
Whitfield Crs MILN OL16 ....229 K3
Whitfield Dr MILN OL16 ....229 C1
Whitfield Gdns MID * LS10 ....9 L8
Whitfield Pl MILN OL16 ....229 K3
Whitfield Ri ROY/SHW OL2 ....229 J5
Whitfield Sq MILN OL16 ....229 K3
Whitfield St CLECK BD19 ....149 M6
  RHAY LS8 ....110 B3
Whitfield Wy MID LS10 ....9 L7
Witham Cl BSPA/BRAM LS23 ....48 F6
Whitkirk Cl MSTN/BAR LS15 ....112 A4
Whitkirk La MSTN/BAR LS15 ....111 M6
Whitlam St SHPY BD18 ....82 B6
Whitley Dr LUD/ILL HX2 ....124 B8
Whitley Gdns RHAY LS8 ....7 M3
Whitley La HIPP HX3 ....169 J1
Whitley Pl CAS WF10 ....157 K2
  KGHY BD21 ....2 B8
  STKB/PEN S36 ....256 B8
Whitley Spring Crs OSS WF5 ....175 H8
Whitley Spring Rd OSS WF5 ....175 H8
Whitley St BFDE BD3 ....5 J8
  BGLY BD16 ....81 H3
Whitley Wy HOR/CROF WF4 ....217 G1
Whittaker Dr LIT OL15 ....207 H4
Whittaker Fold LIT * OL15 ....208 A1
Whittaker La LIT OL15 ....207 M2
Whitteron Cl HUDW * HD3 ....191 K5
Whittle Crs CLAY BD14 ....125 K1
Whittle Dr ROY/SHW OL2 ....229 M6
Whittle St LIT OL15 ....207 H1
Whitty La LUD/ILL HX2 ....145 K8
Whitwell Av ELL HX5 ....169 K7
Whitwell Dr ELL HX5 ....169 K7
Whitwell St BOW BD4 ....127 L1
Whitwood Common La
  CAS WF10 ....179 H1
Whitwood La CAS WF10 ....157 G8
  CLECK BD19 ....148 E2
Whitworth Rd DEWS * WF13 ....173 K7
  WHIT OL12 ....204 B4
Whitworth St MILN * OL16 ....206 A4
  MILN OL16 ....208 H7
Wholestone Ga
  MAR/SLWT HD7 ....212 D1
Whytecote End LM/WK BD12 ....148 E2
Wibsey Bank WBSY BD6 ....126 F5
Wibsey Park Av WBSY BD6 ....126 B6
Wicken Cl IDLE BD10 ....83 L8
Wicken La CUL/QBY BD13 ....102 E7
Wickleden Ga HOLM/MEL HD9 ....254 F3
Wickliffe Pl ROCH OL11 ....206 B8
Widdop Rd HBR HX7 ....120 E7
Wide La HWTH BD22 ....78 C3
  MOR LS27 ....152 F2
Wigan St BFD BD1 ....4 D5
Wigeon Ap MOR LS27 ....152 E2
Wiggan La HUDN HD2 ....192 F3
Wighill Garth TAD LS24 ....71 M2
Wighill La BSPA/BRAM LS23 ....49 L4
  TAD LS24 ....50 D7
  TAD LS24 ....51 G2
Wighill St AIRE BD20 ....55 M1
Wightman St BFDE BD3 ....105 J4
Wignall St KGHY BD21 ....57 K5
Wigton Cha AL/HA/HU LS17 ....88 C1
Wigton Ga AL/HA/HU LS17 ....66 A8
Wigton Gn AL/HA/HU LS17 ....66 B8
Wigton Gv AL/HA/HU LS17 ....66 A8
Wigton La AL/HA/HU LS17 ....66 A8
Wigton Park La AL/HA/HU LS17 ....66 B8
Wike La AL/HA/HU LS17 ....66 D3
Wike Ridge Av AL/HA/HU LS17 ....88 C1
Wike Ridge Cl AL/HA/HU LS17 ....66 C8
Wike Ridge Ct AL/HA/HU LS17 ....66 D8
Wike Ridge Fold AL/HA/HU LS17 ....66 C8

Wike Ridge Gv AL/HA/HU LS17 ....88 D1
Wike Ridge La AL/HA/HU LS17 ....88 D1
Wike Ridge Ms AL/HA/HU LS17 ....88 D1
Wike Ridge Mt AL/HA/HU LS17 ....88 D1
Wike Rd BSLYN/ROY S71 ....262 A4
Wilbrook Ri DOD/DAR S75 ....260 C2
Wilby La BSLY S70 ....261 J6
Wilcock La AIRE BD20 ....35 H2
Wild Gv OT LS21 ....106 C7
Wildhouse La LIT OL15 ....207 H5
Wildspur Cottages
  HOLM/MEL * HD9 ....255 G1
Wildspur Gv HOLM/MEL HD9 ....255 G2
Wild St ROY/SHW OL2 ....229 L8
Wild's Yd WKFDE WF1 ....12 F4
Wilford Rd BSLYN/ROY S71 ....243 G5
Wilfred Av MSTN/BAR LS15 ....111 K6
Wilfred St CLAY BD14 ....125 M2
  MSTN/BAR LS15 ....111 K6
Wilfrid Ter WOR/ARM LS12 ....130 C2
Wilkinson Fold LM/WK * BD12 ....148 E4
Wilkinson St BSLY S70 ....261 H6
Wilkinson Ter GTHN BD7 ....104 B8
Wilkinson Wy OT LS21 ....41 G5
Wilkin St KGHY BD21 ....2 F4
Willans Av RTHW LS26 ....133 G7
Willan's Rd DEWS WF13 ....173 L6
Willerton Cl EARL WF12 ....174 D3
Willgutter La HWTH BD22 ....78 B5
William Av MSTN/BAR LS15 ....111 G6
William Henry St BRIG * HD6 ....170 D3
  ROCH OL11 ....228 C2
  SHPY * BD18 ....82 B6
William Hey St OSM * LS9 ....110 D4
William Horsfall St HUDS HD4 ....213 H3
William Prince Gv WKFDE WF1 ....13 K7
William Ri MSTN/BAR LS15 ....111 G6
Williams Dr AIRE BD20 ....56 D1
Williamson St HFAX HX1 ....10 C4
Williams Rd AIRE BD20 ....56 D1
William St BOW BD4 ....127 M1
  BOW BD4 ....127 M5
  BRIG BD6 ....170 C5
  CAS WF10 ....157 M5
  CAS WF10 ....158 A5
  CAS WF10 ....158 A4
  COL BB8 ....74 A2
  CUL/QBY BD13 ....101 M3
  DEWS WF13 ....173 H3
  DEWS WF13 ....195 G1
  EARL * WF12 ....174 A5
  HDGY LS6 ....109 G3
  HUD HD1 ....15 G1
  HUDS HD4 ....213 L2
  LIT OL15 ....207 J1
  LVSG WF15 ....172 C2
  MILN OL16 ....206 F2
  MOR LS27 ....130 C6
  PDSY/CALV LS28 ....106 C7
  ROCH OL11 ....206 B8
  WBOW * BD5 ....4 E8
  WBSY BD6 ....126 B7
  WKFDE WF1 ....13 G4
William Vw MSTN/BAR LS15 ....111 G6
Willington Rd AWLS/ASK DN6 ....249 J5
Willis St OSM LS9 ....9 M2
Willman Rd BSLYN/ROY S71 ....262 B3
Willoughby Ter BEE/HOL LS11 ....8 B6
Willow Ap BULY LS4 ....109 G5
Willow Av BSPA/BRAM LS23 ....48 F8
  BULY LS4 ....109 G5
  ECHL BD2 ....83 J8
Willow Bank BSLYN/ROY S71 ....260 F2
  HFAX HX1 ....10 C9
  HUDW * HD3 ....191 M6
  TOD OL14 ....141 K8
Willow Bank Dr PONT WF8 ....181 G4
Willowbank Gv HUDE HD5 ....193 K5
Willow Beck HOR/CROF WF4 ....221 J7
Willowbridge La CAS WF10 ....157 H8
Willowbridge Wy CAS WF10 ....157 H8
Willowbrook AWLS/ASK DN6 ....249 H4
Willow Brook Rd
  DOD/DAR S75 ....242 C6
Willow Cl BULY LS4 ....109 G5
  CLECK BD19 ....150 D7
  CUD/GR S72 ....244 D7
  ILK LS29 ....40 A5
  LUD/ILL HX2 ....145 M8
  WBSY BD6 ....126 F7
Willow Cft BTLY WF17 ....151 J9
  FEA/AMT WF7 ....179 L5
  OT LS21 ....42 F8
  WKFDW/WTN WF2 ....175 M7
Willow Crs BSPA/BRAM LS23 ....48 F8
  ECHL BD2 ....83 J8
  MSTN/BAR LS15 ....111 H7
  NORM WF6 ....178 C6
  RPDN/SBR HX6 ....167 L1
Willow Cft CLECK BD19 ....149 L7
Willow Dene Av LUD/ILL HX2 ....167 M1
Willowdene La PONT WF8 ....180 F3
Willow Dene La CUD/GR S72 ....245 J1
Willow Dr HEM/SK/SE WF9 ....245 L1
  LUD/ILL HX2 ....145 M8
  WBSY BD6 ....126 F7
  WKFDE WF1 ....13 J9
Willowfield Av LUD/ILL HX2 ....167 M1
Willowfield Cl LUD/ILL HX2 ....145 M8
Willowfield Crs IDLE BD10 ....83 J8
  LUD/ILL HX2 ....145 M8
Willowfield Dr LUD/ILL HX2 ....167 M1
Willowfield St LUD/ILL HX2 ....167 M1
Willow Flds KBTN HD8 ....216 C3
Willowfield St CLAY BD14 ....104 D8
Willowfield Ter LUD/ILL HX2 ....168 A1
  LUD/ILL HX2 ....145 M8
Willow Gdns CAS WF10 ....158 F8
  ECHL BD2 ....83 J8
  GSLY LS20 ....62 A5
  WKFDW/WTN WF2 ....175 M7
Willow Garth HEM/SK/SE WF9 ....247 K6
Willow Garth Av AIRE BD20 ....34 F6

Willowgarth Cl
  HOR/CROF WF4 ....222 C6
Willow Gld BSPA/BRAM LS23 ....69 M1
Willow Gn WKFDE WF1 ....176 D3
Willow Gv BSPA/BRAM LS23 ....48 F8
  ECHL BD2 ....83 J8
  GFTH/SHER LS25 ....135 H3
  MAR/SLWT HD7 ....213 G1
  OSS WF5 ....197 G2
Willow Hall Dr RPDN/SBR HX6 ....167 L1
Willow Hall La RPDN/SBR HX6 ....167 L1
Willow La BSPA/BRAM LS23 ....48 F8
  FEA/AMT WF7 ....179 L5
  HUD HD1 ....14 E2
  NORM WF6 ....177 M7
  WKFDW/WTN WF2 ....175 M7
Willow La East FEA/AMT WF7 ....179 L5
Willow Ms WKFDW/WTN WF2 ....175 M7
Willow Mt WKFDW/WTN WF2 ....175 M7
Willow Pk PONT WF8 ....181 H6
Willow Ri LUD/ILL HX2 ....145 L7
  LIT OL15 ....207 H3
  LUD/ILL HX2 ....145 M8
  TAD LS24 ....71 K4
Willow Rd AWLS/ASK DN6 ....227 G5
  BTLY WF17 ....174 A2
  BULY LS4 ....109 G5
  CAS WF10 ....157 M8
  KNOT WF11 ....182 C1
  PDSY/CALV LS28 ....106 E4
  WKFDW/WTN WF2 ....175 M7
The Willows AL/HA/HU LS17 ....87 L4
  BGLY BD16 ....80 D5
  HOR/CROF WF4 ....197 J5
  HUD HD1 ....124 A7
  SEL YO8 ....139 M4
Willows La MILN OL16 ....206 F8
Willow St BSLY S70 ....260 F6
  CLECK BD19 ....149 M5
  GIR BD8 ....104 C6
  HFAX HX1 ....10 C6
  RPDN/SBR HX6 ....167 L2
Willow Terrace Rd LDSU LS2 ....6 D6
Willow Tree Cl KGHY BD21 ....3 K8
Willow Tree Gdns BGLY BD16 ....81 L1
  ILK LS29 ....40 B5
Willow V WBY LS22 ....29 M7
Willow Vls IDLE BD10 ....83 J8
Willow Wk LVSG WF15 ....172 C3
Willow Well Rd
  MSTN/BAR LS15 ....111 H6
Wills Gill GSLY LS20 ....62 B5
Willwood Av HUDW HD3 ....191 K7
Wilman Dr OSS WF5 ....174 E8
Wilman Post OSS WF5 ....174 E8
Wilmer Dr HTON BD9 ....104 C2
Wilmington Gv CHAL LS7 ....7 H3
Wilmington St CHAL LS7 ....7 J4
Wilmington Ter CHAL LS7 ....7 H4
Wilmot Rd ILK LS29 ....38 E2
Wilsden Gv DOD/DAR S75 ....260 D2
Wilsden Hill Rd WIL/AL BD15 ....102 D1
Wilsden Old Rd BGLY BD16 ....80 D5
Wilsden Rd BGLY BD16 ....80 D5
  WIL/AL BD15 ....103 C3
Wilshaw Mill Rd
  HOLM/MEL HD9 ....235 J6
Wilshaw Rd HOLM/MEL HD9 ....235 J6
Wilson Av AIRE BD20 ....35 K8
  MIRF WF14 ....194 B1
  OSS WF5 ....197 J2
  STKB/PEN S36 ....270 F4
Wilson Ct WKFDE WF1 ....176 B4
Wilson Dr WKFDE WF1 ....176 D2
Wilson Gv BSLYN/ROY S71 ....262 A2
Wilson Rd BGLY BD16 ....81 H2
  HFAX HX1 ....10 A9
  LM/WK BD12 ....148 C7
  MIRF WF14 ....194 B1
Wilson St AIRE BD20 ....56 A1
  CAS WF10 ....157 L6
  FEA/AMT WF7 ....201 L1
  GIR * BD8 ....4 B1
  PONT * WF8 ....180 F5
  WHIT OL12 ....206 B6
Wilsons Yd PDSY/CALV LS28 ....106 C7
Wilson Ter MIRF WF14 ....194 B1
Wilson Wood St BTLY WF17 ....173 K3
Wilthorpe Av DOD/DAR S75 ....260 E2
Wilthorpe Crs DOD/DAR S75 ....260 E2
Wilthorpe Farm Rd
  DOD/DAR S75 ....260 E2
Wilthorpe Gn DOD/DAR S75 ....260 E2
Wilthorpe Rd DOD/DAR S75 ....260 E2
Wilton Av HUDN HD2 ....171 G8
Wilton Gv HDGY LS6 ....87 G8
Wilton Rd ILK LS29 ....38 C3
Wilton St BRIG HD6 ....170 B3
  EARL WF12 ....173 M7
  GTHN BD7 ....4 D8
Wilton Ter CLECK BD19 ....149 M7
  WHIT OL12 ....206 A6
Wimborne Dr HWTH BD22 ....57 G6
  WIL/AL BD15 ....103 L5
Winbrooke Ter WBSY BD6 ....126 E7
Winburg Rd GTHN BD7 ....126 C1
Winchester Cl
  WKFDW/WTN WF2 ....175 M5
Winchester St WOR/ARM LS12 ....108 F7
Winchester Wy
  BSLYN/ROY S71 ....262 C7
Winden Cl HOR/CROF WF4 ....197 M8
  WKFDE WF1 ....176 E1
Winden Gv WKFDE WF1 ....176 D1
Windermere Av COL BB8 ....52 B8
  ILK LS29 ....40 C8
Windermere Cl AWLS/ASK DN6 ....249 J5
Windermere Dr AL/HA/HU LS17 ....65 H8
  GFTH/SHER LS25 ....113 H8
  KNOT WF11 ....182 A4
Windermere Rd
  BSLYN/ROY * S71 ....261 J5
  CAS WF10 ....158 F7

  EARL WF12 ....174 A3
  GTHN BD7 ....126 A3
  ROY/SHW OL2 ....228 F7
  STKB/PEN S36 ....270 F2
  WKFDW/WTN WF2 ....176 A7
Windermere Ter GTHN BD7 ....126 A3
Windgate AIRE BD20 ....36 B6
Windham Cl BSLYN/ROY S71 ....261 J7
Windham St MILN OL16 ....206 E3
Windhill Av DOD/DAR S75 ....242 C5
Windhill Cft WKFDE WF1 ....177 G6
Windhill Crs DOD/DAR S75 ....242 C5
  WKFDE WF1 ....177 G6
Windhill Dr DOD/DAR S75 ....242 C5
Windhill La DOD/DAR S75 ....242 C5
Windhill Mt DOD/DAR S75 ....242 B5
Windhill Old Rd IDLE BD10 ....83 H4
Windhill Rd WKFDE WF1 ....177 G6
Windhill Vw WKFDW/WTN WF2 ....176 F7
Winding Rd HFAX HX1 ....11 H5
Winding Wy AL/HA/HU LS17 ....87 L1
Windle Edge STKB/PEN S36 ....267 J8
Windle La AIRE BD20 ....34 C5
Windle Royd La LUD/ILL HX2 ....145 L7
Windmill Ap MID LS10 ....132 A6
Windmill Av CUD/GR S72 ....245 H6
Windmill Cha RTHW LS26 ....155 G2
Windmill Cl MID LS10 ....132 A7
  SCFT LS14 ....89 K8
Windmill Crs HIPP HX3 ....147 H4
  KBTN HD8 ....239 K5
Windmill Dr HIPP HX3 ....147 H4
Windmill Field Rd RTHW LS26 ....155 G2
Windmill Gdns MSTN/BAR LS15 ....111 M7
Windmill Gv RTHW LS26 ....155 G2
Windmill Gv CLECK BD19 ....150 D8
  TAD LS24 ....71 K4
Windmill HI PDSY/CALV LS28 ....106 E8
  WBSY BD6 ....126 C5
Windmill Hill La MILN OL16 ....217 H6
Windmill La AWLS/ASK DN6 ....227 K4
  BTLY WF17 ....151 J5
  KBTN HD8 ....255 M3
  KBTN HD8 ....256 C3
  RTHW LS26 ....155 G2
  WBSY BD6 ....126 E5
  YEA LS19 ....62 E8
Windmill Ri GFTH/SHER LS25 ....92 A8
  TAD LS24 ....71 K5
Windmill Rd BSPA/BRAM LS23 ....70 A3
  MID LS10 ....132 A6
Windmill St MILN OL16 ....206 D8
Windrose Cl NORM WF6 ....178 C2
Windsor Av AIRE BD20 ....35 M4
  DOD/DAR S75 ....241 L6
  FEA/AMT WF7 ....202 F1
  MSTN/BAR LS15 ....111 K6
  SKP/WHF BD23 ....16 C2
  STKB/PEN S36 ....270 C2
Windsor Cl EARL WF12 ....174 D3
  GFTH/SHER LS25 ....135 J4
  NORM WF6 ....178 E5
Windsor Ct AL/HA/HU LS17 ....88 A4
Windsor Crs BSLYN/ROY S71 ....261 K3
  CUD/GR S72 ....263 M7
  HWTH BD22 ....78 D4
  LUD/ILL HX2 ....146 A5
  RTHW LS26 ....133 G3
  WKFDE WF1 ....176 B5
Windsor Dr DOD/DAR * S75 ....260 B7
  HUDE HD5 ....193 J8
  KBTN HD8 ....239 K5
  KNOT WF11 ....181 K1
  LVSG WF15 ....172 C4
Windsor Gdns EARL WF12 ....174 D3
Windsor Gn GFTH/SHER LS25 ....113 K7
Windsor Gv CUL/QBY BD13 ....102 E7
  HWTH BD22 ....78 D4
Windsor Mt MSTN/BAR LS15 ....111 K6
Windsor Pl HUDN HD2 ....193 G1
Windsor Rd PONT WF8 ....202 D1
Windsor Rd BTLY WF17 ....151 J5
  EARL WF12 ....174 C4
  HBR HX7 ....143 J7
  HEM/SK/SE WF9 ....247 J4
  HUDS HD4 ....213 H3
  HWTH BD22 ....78 D4
  SHPY * BD18 ....82 D6
  TOD OL14 ....141 J8
  WKFDE WF1 ....176 B4
Windsor St BOW BD4 ....5 J9
  COL BB8 ....74 A1
  HEM/SK/SE WF9 ....247 J4
  HFAX HX1 ....11 G8
  ROCH OL11 ....228 C1
Windsor Ter MILN OL16 ....206 E7
  MILN OL16 ....207 G8
Windsor Vw EARL WF12 ....174 C4
  HBR HX7 ....143 J7
Windsor Wk WBSY BD6 ....148 C8
Windy Bank COL BB8 ....74 A1
Windy Bank La HIPP HX3 ....124 D8
  LVSG WF15 ....171 K2
Windy Gv WIL/AL BD15 ....103 L5
Windy Harbour La TOD OL14 ....141 K5
Windy Rdg CUL/QBY BD13 ....102 E7
Windyridge St HOR/CROF WF4 ....197 H5
Wine St LDS LS1 ....6 F9
Wine Tavern La
  RPDN/SBR HX6 ....166 D3
Wine Tavern Rd
  RPDN/SBR HX6 ....166 D3
Winewall La COL BB8 ....74 A1
Winfield Dr HUDW HD3 ....191 H6
Winfield Gv LDSU * LS2 ....6 F4
Winfield Pl LDSU LS2 ....6 F4
Winfield Rd BIRK/DRI BD11 ....128 A8
Winfield Ter LDSU LS2 ....6 E4
Wingate Av HWTH BD22 ....2 B7
Wingate Cft
  WKFDW/WTN WF2 ....199 G6
Wingate Gv WKFDW/WTN WF2 ....199 G6
Wingate Wy HWTH BD22 ....2 B6

Wingfield Ct BGLY BD16 ....81 J2
Wingfield Mt BFDE BD3 ....5 L3
Wingfield Rd BSLYN/ROY S71 ....243 J8
Wingfield St BFDE BD3 ....5 L4
Winnard Rw WBOW * BD5 ....127 H3
Winney Bank La
  HOLM/MEL HD9 ....254 F3
Winnipeg Pl CHAL LS7 ....87 M8
Winnow La BSPA/BRAM LS23 ....48 D7
Winrose Ap MID LS10 ....132 A7
Winrose Av MID LS10 ....131 M6
Winrose Cl LM/WK BD12 ....148 E2
Winrose Crs MID LS10 ....131 M6
Winrose Dr MID LS10 ....131 M6
Winrose Garth MID LS10 ....131 M6
Winrose Gv MID LS10 ....132 A6
Winrose HI MID LS10 ....132 A5
Winsford Dr HUDE HD5 ....193 K7
Winslow Rd IDLE BD10 ....106 A2
Winstanley Ter HDGY LS6 ....109 G3
Winston Av IDLE BD10 ....35 G7
Winston Gdns HDGY LS6 ....108 F3
Winston Mt HDGY LS6 ....108 F3
Winston Ter GTHN BD7 ....126 C5
Winter Av BSLYN/ROY S71 ....243 L1
  DOD/DAR S75 ....260 E4
Winterbourne Av MOR LS27 ....130 D8
Winterburn La LUD/ILL HX2 ....145 J8
Winterburn St KGHY * BD21 ....3 G2
Winterbutlee Gv TOD OL14 ....163 J5
Winterbutlee Rd TOD OL14 ....163 J5
Winter Ct WIL/AL BD15 ....103 J3
Winter HI HUDW * HD3 ....190 C7
Winter Rd DOD/DAR S75 ....260 E4
Wintersett La HOR/CROF WF4 ....222 C6
Winter's La HBR HX7 ....142 E4
Winter St HFAX HX1 ....10 E7
Winter Ter DOD/DAR S75 ....260 E4
Winterton Dr LM/WK BD12 ....148 E1
Winthorpe Crs
  EARD/LOFT WF3 ....153 M3
Winton Cl BSLY * S70 ....261 J7
Winton St HUD HD1 ....214 A3
  LIT OL15 ....207 K1
Wintoun St LDSU LS7 ....7 J6
Wistons La ELL HX5 ....169 J7
Witchfield Hl HIPP HX3 ....125 M8
Witham Ct DOD/DAR S75 ....260 A3
Witham Rd SHPY BD18 ....82 A6
Witham Wy GFTH/SHER LS25 ....113 J8
Withens Ct DOD/DAR S75 ....242 C5
Withens End La GTL/HWG HX4 ....189 C7
Withens Hill Cft LUD/ILL HX2 ....123 M7
Withens La GTL/HWG HX4 ....189 H6
  HBR HX7 ....165 H3
Withens New Rd HBR HX7 ....164 F4
  LUD/ILL HX2 ....123 H4
Withens Rd BTLY WF17 ....151 G4
  LUD/ILL HX2 ....123 H4
Within Flds HIPP HX3 ....169 J2
Withins Cl GTHN BD7 ....126 C4
Withyside KBTN HD8 ....239 J8
Witley Rd MILN OL16 ....206 C7
Witmore St HEM/SK/SE WF9 ....247 J3
Witton St WKFDE WF1 ....12 F1
Woburn Cl MILN OL16 ....207 L8
Woburn Dr HUDE HD5 ....193 K8
Woburn Pl DOD/DAR S75 ....260 B8
Woburn Ter CLAY BD14 ....125 K2
Wold Cl CUL/QBY BD13 ....102 F9
Wolfstones Rd
  HOLM/MEL HD9 ....235 J8
Wollaton Cl BSLYN/ROY S71 ....243 G6
Wolley Av WOR/ARM LS12 ....129 M3
Wolley Ct WOR/ARM LS12 ....129 M3
Wolley Dr WOR/ARM LS12 ....129 M3
Wolley Gdns WOR/ARM LS12 ....129 M3
Wolseley Rd BULY LS4 ....108 F5
Wolseley St CLAY BD14 ....125 L1
  MILN OL16 ....229 K2
Wolseley Ter HFAX HX1 ....10 B1
Wolsey Av PONT WF8 ....180 D6
Wolsey Cl GFTH/SHER LS25 ....116 B6
Wolsey Cft GFTH/SHER LS25 ....116 B6
Wolsey Gdns GFTH/SHER LS25 ....116 B6
Wolston Cl BOW BD4 ....128 A4
Wolvesey ROCH * OL11 ....206 A4
Wombwell La BSLY S70 ....262 B7
Womersley Pl PDSY/CALV LS28 ....106 C4
Womersley Rd KNOT WF11 ....182 C5
Womersley St HFAX HX1 ....10 B5
Wonder St WKFDE WF1 ....13 G4
Woodacre Cl AL/HA/HU LS17 ....67 L3
Woodacre Gn AL/HA/HU LS17 ....67 L2
Woodacre La AL/HA/HU LS17 ....67 L2
Wood Acres DOD/DAR S75 ....260 C2
Woodale Av HTON BD9 ....103 M3
Wood Av HECK WF16 ....172 K1
Wood Bank Rd LIT OL15 ....207 J3
Woodbine Cl IDLE BD10 ....83 K7
Woodbine Rd HUDN HD2 ....15 G1
Woodbine St BFDE BD3 ....5 J5
  HFAX HX1 ....10 C9
  MILN OL16 ....228 C1
  OSS WF5 ....174 F2
Woodbine St East MILN OL16 ....228 D1
Woodbine Ter BRAM * LS13 ....107 L3
  HDGY LS6 ....87 G8
  HFAX * HX1 ....10 C9
  IDLE BD10 ....83 K7
  TOD OL14 ....140 D5
Wood Bottom La BRIG HD6 ....170 A1
Wood Bottom Rd HUDS HD4 ....235 K1
Woodbourne Av
  AL/HA/HU LS17 ....87 L5
Woodbridge Av
  GFTH/SHER LS25 ....113 L5
Woodbridge Cl HDGY LS6 ....86 C8
  WKFDE WF1 ....13 K3
Woodbridge Crs HDGY LS6 ....86 C8
Woodbridge Fold HDGY LS6 ....108 C1
Woodbridge Garth HDGY LS6 ....108 D1
Woodbridge Gdns HDGY LS6 ....86 C8
Woodbridge Gn HDGY LS6 ....108 C1
Woodbridge Lawn HDGY LS6 ....108 C1
Woodbridge Pl HDGY LS6 ....108 C1

Woodbridge Rd HDGY LS6 ......108 C1
Woodbridge V HDGY LS6 ......108 C1
Woodbrook Av LUD/ILL HX2 ......145 L1
Woodbrook Cl LUD/ILL HX2 ......145 L1
Woodbrook Pl LUD/ILL HX2 ......145 L1
Woodbrook Rd LUD/ILL HX2 ......145 L1
Woodburn Av EARL WF12 ......196 B1
Woodbury Rd GIR BD8 ......104 D4
Woodchurch Vw
  HOLM/MEL HD9 ......236 D6
Wood Cl AIRE BD20 ......34 E1
  BAIL BD17 ......82 D4
  BHP/TINH LS16 ......86 F3
  CHAL LS7 ......L7
  HEM/SK/SE WF9 ......223 J4
  NORM WF6 ......178 A3
  RTHW LS26 ......132 F8
  SKP/WHF BD23 ......16 A1
Woodcock Cl PBR HG3 ......26 E2
Woodcock St WKFDE WF1 ......13 H6
Woodcock Wy AWLS/ASK DN6 ......249 K7
Woodcot Av BAIL BD17 ......82 F4
Wood Crs RTHW LS26 ......132 F8
  RPDN/SBR HX6 ......167 G3
Woodcroft WKFDW/WTN WF2 ......199 G5
Woodcross MOR LS27 ......130 C8
Woodcross End MOR LS27 ......130 C7
Woodcross Fold MOR LS27 ......130 C8
Woodcross Gdns MOR LS27 ......130 C8
Woodcross Garth MOR LS27 ......130 C7
Wood Dr RTHW LS26 ......132 F8
Woodedge Av HUDE HD5 ......193 J8
Wood End HUDS HD4 ......214 B3
Wood End Av STKB/PEN S36 ......270 C4
Wood End Cl HIPP HX3 ......168 D3
Woodend Cottages
  MIRF * WF14 ......194 B2
Woodend Ct WBOW BD5 ......127 H4
Woodend Crs CAS WF10 ......157 H1
Wood End Crs SHP BD18 ......82 F6
Wood End La KBTN HD8 ......237 L7
Woodend La WHIT OL12 ......184 F8
Wood End Rd HUDS HD4 ......214 A4
Woodend Rd MIRF WF14 ......194 B2
Wood Farm La
  HOLM/MEL HD9 ......236 E4
Woodfield Av BTLY WF17 ......173 J2
  GTL/HWG HX4 ......168 D7
  WHIT * OL12 ......206 A4
Woodfield Cl IDLE BD10 ......83 K6
Woodfield Cottages HIPP * HX3 ......10 E1
Woodfield Ct HUDN HD2 ......14 C3
Woodfield Dr AIRE BD20 ......34 E1
  GTL/HWG HX4 ......168 D7
Woodfield Pk
  WKFDW/WTN WF2 ......199 J8
Woodfield Rd CUL/QBY BD13 ......80 A7
  PONT WF8 ......226 D6
Woodford Av HIPP HX3 ......168 F2
  ROY/SHW OL2 ......229 M7
Woodford Cl WIL/AL BD15 ......103 J6
Woodford Dr HUDE HD5 ......193 J7
Woodgarth Ct AWLS/ASK DN6 ......227 L6
Woodgarth Gdns BOW BD4 ......128 B3
Woodgate La AL/HA/HU LS17 ......43 M2
Wood Gn CAS WF10 ......179 H1
Wood Gv OSS WF5 ......174 F6
  WOR/ARM LS12 ......107 M7
Woodhall Av BFDE BD3 ......106 A4
  KSTL LS5 ......86 A4
Woodhall Cl HOR/CROF WF4 ......196 C8
  PDSY/CALV LS28 ......106 C4
  WMB/DAR S73 ......263 J8
Woodhall Ct MSTN/BAR LS15 ......111 M8
  PDSY/CALV LS28 ......106 C1
Woodhall Cft PDSY/CALV LS28 ......106 C4
Woodhall Dr BTLY WF17 ......173 J2
  FEA/AMT WF7 ......202 B4
  KSTL LS5 ......86 A4
Woodhall Gv RTHW LS26 ......156 F3
Woodhall La AWLS/ASK DN6 ......205 J3
  PDSY/CALV LS28 ......106 C3
Woodhall Park Av
  PDSY/CALV LS28 ......106 C4
Woodhall Park Crs West
  PDSY/CALV LS28 ......106 C5
Woodhall Park Cft
  PDSY/CALV LS28 ......106 D5
Woodhall Park Dr
  PDSY/CALV LS28 ......106 C5
Woodhall Park Gv
  PDSY/CALV LS28 ......106 C5
Woodhall Park Mt
  PDSY/CALV LS28 ......106 C4
Woodhall Pl BFDE BD3 ......106 A4
Woodhall Rd BFDE BD3 ......106 A6
  PDSY/CALV LS28 ......106 A3
Woodhall Ter BFDE BD3 ......106 A6
Woodhall Vw BFDE BD3 ......106 B5
Woodhead Cl HUDN HD2 ......192 E4
Woodhead La BRIG HD6 ......171 G5
  MOR LS27 ......129 L7
Woodhead Rd BTLY WF17 ......151 K3
  GTHN BD7 ......104 D8
  HOLM/MEL HD9 ......236 C3
  HOLM/MEL HD9 ......265 M1
Woodhead St CLECK BD19 ......150 A8
  LUD/ILL HX2 ......146 A4
Wood Hey Gv WHIT OL12 ......206 B2
Wood Hey La HBR HX7 ......143 K5
Woodheys Rd LIT OL15 ......207 J4
Wood Hl RTHW LS26 ......132 F8
Wood Hill Ct BHP/TINH LS16 ......85 M2
Wood Hill Crs BHP/TINH LS16 ......85 L3
Wood Hill Gdns BHP/TINH LS16 ......85 M2
Wood Hill Ri IDLE BD10 ......84 A6
Wood Hill Rd BHP/TINH LS16 ......85 M2
Wood Hill Vw WBY LS22 ......30 A8
Woodhouse Av HUDN HD2 ......192 E4
  KGHY BD21 ......3 H9
Woodhouse Cliff HDGY LS6 ......6 C1

Woodhouse Crs NORM WF6 ......178 D6
Woodhouse Dr KGHY BD21 ......79 L2
Woodhouse Gdns BRIG HD6 ......170 E6
Woodhouse Gv HUDN HD2 ......192 D4
  KGHY BD21 ......3 G9
  TOD OL14 ......163 M1
Woodhouse Hall Rd
  HUDN HD2 ......192 E4
Woodhouse Hl HUDN HD2 ......192 E4
Woodhouse Hill Av MID * LS10 ......132 A4
Woodhouse Hill Pl MID * LS10 ......132 A4
Woodhouse Hill Rd MID LS10 ......132 A4
Woodhouse Hill Ter MID * LS10 ......132 A4
Woodhouse La BRIG HD6 ......170 E6
  DOD/DAR S75 ......242 D11
  HDGY LS6 ......6 C2
  HIPP HX3 ......168 C3
  HOLM/MEL HD9 ......253 M5
  KBTN HD8 ......218 B7
  WKFDW/WTN WF2 ......175 J3
Woodhouse Mt NORM WF6 ......178 C6
Woodhouse Rd KGHY BD21 ......79 L2
  TOD OL14 ......164 A1
  WKFDE WF1 ......13 J2
Woodhouse Sq BVRD LS3 ......6 B8
Woodhouse St HDGY LS6 ......6 C2
Woodhouse Ter WBSY BD6 ......126 F6
Woodhouse Wk KGHY BD21 ......3 H9
Woodkirk Av EARD/LOFT WF3 ......152 E6
Woodkirk Gdns EARL WF12 ......174 D1
Woodkirk Gv EARD/LOFT WF3 ......152 E6
  LM/WK BD12 ......148 C5
Woodland Av RTHW LS26 ......134 B5
  WKFDE WF1 ......177 L7
Woodland Cl HOR/CROF WF4 ......220 B4
  HTON BD9 ......103 L2
  MSTN/BAR LS15 ......111 L6
Woodland Ct BGLY BD16 ......80 F1
  RHAY LS8 ......110 B1
Woodland Crs BGLY BD16 ......103 K2
  RTHW LS26 ......132 F7
  RTHW LS26 ......134 C5
Woodland Dr BRIG HD6 ......170 B3
  BSLY S70 ......260 D6
  CHAL LS7 ......87 M7
  KBTN HD8 ......239 K6
  LUD/ILL HX2 ......167 M1
  RTHW LS26 ......134 B5
Woodland Gv CHAL LS7 ......110 A2
  DEWS WF13 ......173 H6
  FEA/AMT WF7 ......202 C5
  HTON BD9 ......103 L1
  RTHW LS26 ......134 B5
Woodland Hl MSTN/BAR LS15 ......111 K6
Woodland La CHAL LS7 ......87 M7
Woodland Meadow KBTN HD8 ......216 B7
Woodland Mt CHAL * LS7 ......110 A2
Woodland Pk ROY/SHW OL2 ......228 D8
Woodland Park Rd HDGY LS6 ......109 G1
Woodland Ri MSTN/BAR LS15 ......111 L6
  WKFDW/WTN WF2 ......197 M1
Woodlands BAIL * BD17 ......83 G2
  EARD/LOFT WF3 ......153 L7
  HOR/CROF WF4 ......197 L4
  HOR/CROF WF4 ......200 A5
  HWTH * BD22 ......78 E4
  ILK * BD29 ......38 F2
  OSS WF5 ......174 F7
  RPDN/SBR HX6 ......167 H4
Woodlands Av WCAS WF10 ......158 E6
  CLECK BD19 ......150 C5
  HIPP HX3 ......11 G1
  HOLM/MEL HD9 ......236 E6
  PDSY/CALV LS28 ......106 E5
  TAD LS24 ......71 J4
  TOD OL14 ......141 K8
Woodlands Cl EARD/LOFT WF3 ......153 L7
  GFTH/SHER LS25 ......138 A2
  HUDN HD2 ......171 J8
  IDLE BD10 ......84 B5
  ILK LS29 ......38 A2
  KBTN HD8 ......239 J8
  SCFT LS14 ......67 L6
Woodlands Ct BHP/TINH LS16 ......86 D5
Woodlands Crs CLECK BD19 ......150 C6
  HEM/SK/SE WF9 ......224 F6
Woodlands Cft
  GFTH/SHER LS25 ......135 K6
Woodlands Dr CLECK BD19 ......150 C5
  EARD/LOFT WF3 ......153 K7
  GFTH/SHER LS25 ......113 K8
  IDLE BD10 ......84 B5
  MOR LS27 ......130 B8
  SKP/WHF BD23 ......16 A1
Woodlands Fold
  BIRK/DRI BD11 ......150 D1
Woodlands Gv BAIL BD17 ......82 B4
  BGLY BD16 ......81 K7
  CUL/QBY BD13 ......125 J5
  GFTH/SHER LS25 ......135 L6
  HIPP HX3 ......11 G1
  ILK LS29 ......38 A2
  PDSY/CALV LS28 ......106 E5
Woodlands Park Rd
  PDSY/CALV LS28 ......128 V1
Woodlands Sq BRIG * HD6 ......170 E5
  WOR/ARM LS12 ......108 B6
Woodlands Ri AWLS/ASK DN6 ......227 L5
  HWTH BD22 ......78 E4
  ILK LS29 ......38 A2
Woodlands Rd BGLY BD16 ......81 L2
  BTLY WF17 ......151 J6
  CLECK BD19 ......150 C5
  CUL/QBY BD13 ......125 J5
  ELL HX5 ......169 H4

GIR * BD8 ......104 C5
  HIPP HX3 ......11 G1
  KBTN HD8 ......216 A3
  MILN OL16 ......229 G1
Woodlands Rd East KBTN HD8 ......215 J8
The Woodlands HBR HX7 ......143 J4
  PONT WF8 ......181 G8
  RTHW * WF8 ......155 L1
Woodlands St GIR BD8 ......4 B4
Woodlands Ter
  PDSY/CALV LS28 ......106 E5
  WHARF St HWTH BD22 ......54 E3
  WHIT OL12 ......206 C4
Woodlands Vw
  GFTH/SHER LS25 ......135 L6
  HIPP HX3 ......11 G2
  MILN OL16 ......206 E6
Woodlands Wk SKP/WHF BD23 ......16 A1
Woodland Ter CHAL LS7 ......87 J7
  CUD/GR S72 ......263 K1
  HEM/SK/SE * WF9 ......247 G5
  PDSY/CALV LS28 ......84 C8
  PONT WF8 ......181 G8
Woodland Vls CUD/GR * S72 ......245 K8
Wood La AL/HA/HU LS17 ......67 M3
  BRAM LS13 ......107 L2
  BRAM LS13 ......107 M6
  BSLYN/ROY S71 ......243 L5
  BSPA/BRAM LS23 ......49 G3
  CAS WF10 ......179 H1
  CHAL LS7 ......87 L7
  CUD/GR S72 ......245 J8
  DEWS WF13 ......173 L4
  DOD/DAR S75 ......243 G4
  EARL WF12 ......195 L6
  ECHL BD2 ......105 H1
  HBR HX7 ......122 D8
  HDGY LS6 ......109 G1
  HIPP HX3 ......147 K5
  HIPP HX3 ......169 M4
  HOLM/MEL HD9 ......236 C8
  HOR/CROF WF4 ......220 C3
  HORS LS18 ......85 L7
  HUDE HD5 ......193 M2
  HUDS HD4 ......214 E3
  HUDS HD4 ......237 K2
  KBTN HD8 ......239 G8
  KNOT WF11 ......161 K3
  LUD/ILL HX2 ......145 M5
  MAR/SLWT HD7 ......234 D1
  MSTN/BAR LS15 ......90 A8
  PDSY/CALV LS28 ......84 D7
  RPDN/SBR HX6 ......167 G2
  RTHW LS26 ......132 F8
  RTHW LS26 ......135 G8
  WOR/ARM LS12 ......130 B4
Wood Lane Ct HDGY LS6 ......109 G1
Woodlea BSPA/BRAM LS23 ......48 F6
Wood Lea KNOT WF11 ......159 M6
  TOD OL14 ......141 G6
  YEA LS19 ......62 B8
Woodlea Ap HDGY LS6 ......87 H5
Woodlea Av HDGY LS6 ......87 H5
  HUDW HD3 ......191 L8
Woodlea Cha HDGY LS6 ......87 H6
Woodlea Cl YEA LS19 ......84 B1
Woodlea Ct HDGY LS6 ......87 H6
Woodlea Cft HDGY LS6 ......87 H6
Woodlea Dr HDGY LS6 ......87 H5
  YEA LS19 ......84 B1
Woodlea Fold HDGY LS6 ......87 H6
Woodlea Gdns HDGY LS6 ......87 H5
Woodlea Garth HDGY LS6 ......87 H5
Woodlea Ga HDGY LS6 ......87 H5
Woodlea Gn HDGY LS6 ......87 H6
Woodlea Gv BEE/HOL * LS11 ......131 H5
  HDGY LS6 ......87 H6
  YEA LS19 ......62 B8
Woodlea Holt HDGY LS6 ......87 H5
Woodlea La HDGY LS6 ......87 H5
Woodlea Lawn HDGY LS6 ......87 H5
Woodlea Mt BEE/HOL LS11 ......131 H5
  YEA LS19 ......62 B8
Woodlea Pk HDGY LS6 ......87 H6
Woodlea Pl BEE/HOL LS11 ......131 H3
Woodlea Rd YEA LS19 ......62 B8
Woodlea Sq HDGY * LS6 ......87 H6
Woodlea St BEE/HOL LS11 ......131 H3
Woodleigh EARL * WF12 ......195 M4
Woodleigh Av
  GFTH/SHER LS25 ......113 G7
  WBOW BD5 ......126 E8
Woodleigh Crs FEA/AMT WF7 ......202 B8
Woodleigh Hall Vw YEA * LS19 ......85 G5
Woodlesford Crs LUD/ILL HX2 ......145 K4
Woodliegh Gv HUDS * HD4 ......213 L5
Woodliffe Ct CHAL LS7 ......87 L7
Woodliffe Dr CHAL LS7 ......87 L7
Woodman Av ELL HX5 ......191 H1
  HUDN HD2 ......193 H1
Woodman St WBSY BD6 ......126 A8
Woodmoor Cl HOR/CROF WF4 ......219 M2
Woodmoor Dr HOR/CROF WF4 ......219 M1
Woodmoor Ri HOR/CROF WF4 ......219 M1
Wood Moor Rd
  HEM/SK/SE WF9 ......224 B7
Woodmoor Rd
  WKFDW/WTN WF2 ......220 C1
Woodmoor St BSLYN/ROY S71 ......243 M6
Wood Mt HOR/CROF WF4 ......196 B8
  RTHW LS26 ......132 E8
Woodnook Cl BHP/TINH LS16 ......85 M4
Woodnook Dr BHP/TINH LS16 ......85 M4
Woodnook Garth
  BHP/TINH LS16 ......85 M4
Wood Nook La
  HOLM/MEL HD9 ......235 K4
  RPDN/SBR HX6 ......167 L1
Wood Nook Ter
  PDSY/CALV LS28 ......106 E5
Woodpecker Rd ILK LS29 ......39 M4
Wood Pl BEE/HOL * LS11 ......8 D9
  GIR BD8 ......4 B3

Wood Rd HTON BD9 ......104 E2
  WBOW BD5 ......127 G2
Wood Rw RTHW LS26 ......156 C3
Woodrow Dr LM/WK BD12 ......149 G1
Woodrow Crs RTHW LS26 ......156 C3
Woodroyd Av BSLYN/ROY S71 ......243 L5
  HOLM/MEL HD9 ......236 D1
  WBOW * BD5 ......127 H4
Woodroyd Cl BSLYN/ROY S71 ......243 L5
Woodroyd Dr HIPP HX3 ......146 A4
Woodroyd Gdns ILK LS29 ......39 H3
Woodroyd Ter WBOW BD5 ......127 H3
Wood Royd Hill La
  HOLM/MEL HD9 ......255 K7
Woodroyd Rd WBOW BD5 ......127 H3
Woodside CAS WF10 ......158 E6
  KBTN HD8 ......239 J8
  KGHY BD21 ......57 J5
  MILN OL16 ......229 L1
  ROY/SHW OL2 ......229 M6
  SHPY BD18 ......82 F6
  WKFDW/WTN WF2 ......176 A4
Woodside Av BGLY BD16 ......81 H7
  BULY LS4 ......108 E4
  CHAL LS7 ......87 H7
  HOR/CROF WF4 ......200 E3
  SHPY BD18 ......82 A6
  WKFDW/WTN WF2 ......176 A6
Woodside Cl MOR LS27 ......130 C8
  CUL/QBY BD13 ......79 M8
  HORS LS18 ......86 A4
Woodside Crs BGLY BD16 ......81 H7
  BTLY WF17 ......173 J2
  HIPP HX3 ......10 F2
  HOR/CROF WF4 ......200 D2
Woodside Dr BGLY BD16 ......81 H7
  MOR LS27 ......130 C7
  WKFDW/WTN WF2 ......176 A4
Woodside Gdns MOR LS27 ......130 C8
Woodside Gv CAS WF10 ......135 H8
  GTL/HWG HX4 ......168 E8
  HIPP HX3 ......11 G2
Woodside Hill Cl HORS LS18 ......85 M6
Woodside La AIRE BD20 ......34 B2
  HUDN HD2 ......192 D2
  MOR LS27 ......130 C7
Woodside Ldg HUDS HD4 ......215 K8
Woodside Ms CHAL LS7 ......87 H7
Woodside Mt HFAX HX1 ......10 F3
Woodside Park Av HORS LS18 ......85 M6
Woodside Park Dr HORS LS18 ......85 M6
Woodside Pl BULY LS4 ......108 E4
  HIPP HX3 ......10 F2
Woodside Rd AIRE BD20 ......35 L5
  BSPA/BRAM LS23 ......48 D7
  HFAX HX1 ......10 F2
  HUDS HD4 ......213 M5
  LM/WK BD12 ......148 A2
Woodside St CAS WF10 ......135 H8
Woodside Ter BULY LS4 ......108 E4
  HIPP HX3 ......10 F2
Woodside Veiw HUDS HD4 ......213 H5
Woodside Vw BGLY BD16 ......81 H7
  BULY LS4 ......108 E4
  HIPP HX3 ......11 G2
  HOLM/MEL HD9 ......253 M2
Woodsley Gn HDGY LS6 ......6 A5
Woodsley Rd BVRD LS3 ......109 G5
  HDGY LS6 ......6 A5
  IDLE BD10 ......83 J8
Woodsley Ter LDSU LS2 ......6 C6
Woodsome Av WKFDW/WTN WF14 ......172 A4
Woodsome Dr KBTN HD8 ......215 M4
  MIRF WF14 ......172 B8
Woodsome Hall La KBTN HD8 ......215 L5
Woodsome Lees La KBTN HD8 ......215 M7
Woodsome Pk KBTN HD8 ......215 M4
Woodsome Rd HUDS HD4 ......215 H7
Wood Sq HIPP HX3 ......146 D4
Wood's Rw PDSY/CALV LS28 ......107 G5
Woodstock Crs HUDW HD3 ......191 K6
Woodstock Rd DOD/DAR S75 ......260 F2
Woodstock Wk WBOW * BD5 ......127 G5
Wood St AIRE BD20 ......56 E1
  BAIL BD17 ......82 E5
  BGLY BD16 ......59 G8
  BRIG HD6 ......170 D4
  BSLY S70 ......261 H6
  BTLY WF17 ......173 L2
  CAS WF10 ......157 L6
  CLECK BD19 ......149 L7
  COL BB8 ......74 A2
  CUD/GR S72 ......223 G8
  DEWS WF13 ......173 M5
  EARD/LOFT WF3 ......153 M6
  ELL HX5 ......169 J8
  HOR/CROF WF4 ......200 D2
  HUD HD1 ......14 F6
  HUDE HD5 ......15 L7
  HUDW HD3 ......191 H8
  KBTN HD8 ......239 H4
  KBTN HD8 ......239 M5
  KGHY BD21 ......3 H7
  LIT OL15 ......207 K1
  MAR/SLWT HD7 ......212 B5
  MILN OL16 ......229 L1
  MOR LS27 ......152 B1
  OSS WF5 ......174 F7
  ROCH OL11 ......206 C8
  ROY/SHW OL2 ......229 G7
  WIL/AL BD15 ......103 L5
  WKFDE WF1 ......12 E2
Wood St North HIPP * HX3 ......146 D4
Wood Syke DOD/DAR S75 ......260 F2
Wood Ter HUDS HD4 ......214 C3
Woodthorne Cft
  AL/HA/HU LS17 ......88 B2
Woodthorpe Cl
  WKFDW/WTN WF2 ......199 G7
Woodthorpe Dr
  WKFDW/WTN WF2 ......199 G7
Woodthorpe Glades
  WKFDW/WTN WF2 ......198 F7
Woodthorpe La
  WKFDW/WTN WF2 ......198 F7

Woodthorpe Park Dr
  WKFDW/WTN WF2 ......198 F7
Woodthorpe Ter HUD HD1 ......14 C8
Wood Top BRIG HD6 ......170 A1
Wood Top Rd HBR HX7 ......143 K4
Woodvale Cl BOW BD4 ......128 A1
Woodvale Crs BGLY BD16 ......81 J1
Woodvale Gv GTHN BD7 ......126 A1
Woodvale Rd HUDE HD6 ......170 D3
Woodvale Wy CLAY BD14 ......126 A1
Woodview BIRK/DRI BD11 ......128 F7
Wood Vw HUDN HD2 ......191 M4
  HWTH * BD22 ......79 H2
  MOR LS27 ......130 E6
Wood View Av BAIL BD17 ......83 H4
Wood View Av CAS WF10 ......157 J7
Wood View Cl CAS WF10 ......157 J7
Wood View Crs LAS LS14 ......85 L4
Wood View Crs CAS WF10 ......157 H7
Wood View Dr BEE/HOL 105 L4
Woodview Gv BEE/HOL LS11 ......131 K4
Wood View Gv BEE/HOL 170 B2
Woodview La DOD/DAR S75 ......260 D3
Woodview Mt BEE/HOL LS11 ......131 K4
Woodview Rd BEE/HOL LS11 ......131 K4
  HWTH BD22 ......79 H2
Woodview St BEE/HOL LS11 ......131 K4
Woodview Ter BEE/HOL LS11 ......131 K4
Wood View Ter KGHY BD21 ......79 K2
Woodville Av HORS LS18 ......85 M6
  MAR/SLWT * HD7 ......213 G2
Woodville Ct RHAY LS8 ......88 C5
  WKFDW/WTN WF2 ......198 E4
Woodville Crs HORS LS18 ......85 M5
Woodville Gv HORS * LS18 ......85 M6
  HWTH BD22 ......79 H6
  MID * LS10 ......132 A5
Woodville Pl HORS LS18 ......86 A5
  HTON BD9 ......104 B2
  HUDN HD2 ......171 G8
Woodville Rd EARL WF12 ......173 M6
  KGHY BD21 ......2 E5
Woodville Sq MID LS10 ......132 A5
Woodville St HIPP HX3 ......10 D1
  HORS LS18 ......86 A5
  SHPY BD18 ......82 F6
Woodville Ter HORS LS18 ......85 M6
  WBOW BD5 ......127 G5
Wood Vine Rd PDSY/CALV LS28 ......106 E5
Wood Wk BSLYN/ROY S71 ......243 L1
Woodward Ct MIRF WF14 ......172 B7
Woodway BGLY BD16 ......81 H7
  HORS LS18 ......85 L7
Woodway Dr HORS LS18 ......85 L7
Woodworth Gv KGHY BD21 ......79 K3
Woolcomb Ct HTON BD9 ......104 C4
Woolcroft Dr HOLM/MEL HD9 ......236 E8
Wooldale Cliff Rd
  HOLM/MEL HD9 ......236 D8
Wooldale Rd HOLM/MEL HD9 ......236 D8
Wooler Av BEE/HOL LS11 ......131 K4
Wooler Dr BEE/HOL LS11 ......131 K4
Wooler Gv BEE/HOL LS11 ......131 K4
Wooler Pl BEE/HOL LS11 ......131 K4
Wooler Rd BEE/HOL * LS11 ......131 K4
Wooler St BEE/HOL LS11 ......131 K4
The Wool Ex BFD BD1 ......4 F6
Woolford Wy EARD/LOFT WF3 ......154 F3
Woolgreaves Av
  WKFDW/WTN WF2 ......198 E8
Woolgreaves Cl
  WKFDW/WTN WF2 ......198 F7
Woolgreaves Cft
  WKFDW/WTN WF2 ......198 F8
Woolgreaves Dr
  WKFDW/WTN WF2 ......198 F8
Woolgreaves Garth
  WKFDW/WTN WF2 ......198 F8
Wooler Rd LM/WK BD12 ......148 L5
Woolley Colliery Rd
  DOD/DAR S75 ......242 A4
Woolley Edge La
  DOD/DAR S75 ......242 K4
Woolley Low Moor La
  HOR/CROF WF4 ......219 M4
Woolley Park Gdns
  HOR/CROF WF4 ......220 C4
Woolley Vw HOR/CROF WF4 ......220 B4
Woollin Av EARD/LOFT WF3 ......175 G1
Woollin Crs EARD/LOFT WF3 ......153 G8
Woolmarket PONT WF8 ......180 F6
Woolpack's Yd WKFDE WF1 ......12 D1
Woolrow La BRIG HD6 ......148 E8
Wool Row La KBTN HD8 ......238 L5
Woolshops Sq HFAX HX1 ......11 H6
Woolstock La DOD/DAR S75 ......258 F3
Wool St HECK WF16 ......172 F3
Wootton St WBOW BD5 ......126 F2
Worcester Av EARD/LOFT WF3 ......154 B2
Worcester Dr EARD/LOFT WF3 ......154 B2
Worcester Gv HUDS HD4 ......214 D3
Worcester Pl BOW BD4 ......127 G2
Worcester St ROCH OL11 ......228 A2
Worden Gv CLAY BD14 ......126 A2
Wordsworth Ap PONT WF8 ......180 F4
Wordsworth Av
  AWLS/ASK DN6 ......227 L5
  STKB/PEN S36 ......270 E4
Wordsworth Cr RTHW LS26 ......155 L3
Wordsworth Crs LIT OL15 ......207 H4
Wordsworth Dr KNOT WF11 ......181 K1
  RTHW LS26 ......155 L3
Wordsworth Gv
  EARD/LOFT WF3 ......177 G1
Wordsworth Rd
  BSLYN/ROY S71 ......261 K2
Work Bank La STKB/PEN S36 ......270 D2
Workhouse La GTL/HWG HX4 ......168 F8
  LUD/ILL HX2 ......145 J7
Wormald Av DEWS WF13 ......7 G8
Wormald St DEWS WF13 ......173 L6
  HUDE HD5 ......215 H3
  LVSG WF15 ......172 E3
Worral Cl BSLY S70 ......261 H8
Worral Rd WKFDW/WTN WF2 ......220 C2
Worrall St MOR LS27 ......152 B3
Worsley Cl BSLY S70 ......261 K8

Worsley Pl *AWLS/ASK* DN6 ......**249** H4
　MILN OL16 ......**206** D7
　ROY/SHW OL2 ......**229** J8
Worsley St *MILN* OL16 ......**206** D7
Worsnop Buildings
　LM/WK BD12 ......**148** E2
Worsnop St *LM/WK* BD12 ......**126** F8
Worstead Rd *HWTH* BD22 ......**79** H6
Worth Av *KGHY* BD21 ......**3** M1
Worth Bridge Rd *KGHY* BD21......**3** L3
Worthing Head Cl
　LM/WK BD12 ......**148** F3
Worthing Head Rd
　LM/WK BD12 ......**148** E3
Worthing St *LM/WK* BD12 ......**148** F3
Worthington St *GIR* BD8 ......**4** B4
Worthville Cl *KGHY* BD21 ......**3** H9
Worth Wy *HWTH* BD22 ......**79** J6
　HWTH BD22 ......**100** F2
　KGHY BD21 ......**3** G7
Wortley Hts *WOR/ARM* LS12 ......**108** F8
Wortley La *WOR/ARM* LS12 ......**8** A4
Wortley Moor La
　WOR/ARM LS12 ......**108** D8
Wortley Moor Rd
　WOR/ARM LS12 ......**108** C7
Wortley Pk *WOR/ARM* LS12 ......**109** G8
Wortley Pl *HEM/SK/SE* WF9 ......**223** L7
Wortley Rd *WOR/ARM* LS12 ......**108** D7
Wortley St *BGLY* BD16 ......**81** K3
　BSLY S70 ......**261** G5
Worts Hill La *HUDW* HD3 ......**211** K2
Worts Hill Side *HUDW* HD3 ......**211** L2
Wrangbrook La
　HEM/SK/SE WF9 ......**225** L8
Wrangbrook Rd
　HEM/SK/SE WF9 ......**225** M6
Wrangthorn Av *HDGY* LS6 ......**6** A3
Wrangthorn Pl *HDGY* LS6 ......**6** A3
Wrangthorn Ter *HDGY* LS6 ......**6** A3
Wray Pl *MILN* OL16 ......**206** E8
Wrelton Cl *BSLYN/ROY* S71 ......**243** K3
Wren Av *GTHN* BD7 ......**126** A1
Wrenbeck Av *OT* LS21 ......**41** J4
Wrenbeck Cl *OT* LS21 ......**41** J4
Wrenbeck Dr *OT* LS21 ......**41** J4
Wrenbury Av *BHP/TINH* LS16 ......**85** M1
Wrenbury Crs *BHP/TINH* LS16 ......**85** M1
Wrenbury Dr *MILN* OL16 ......**228** E2
Wrenbury Gv *BHP/TINH* LS16 ......**86** A1
Wren Cft *PONT* WF8 ......**180** F3
Wren Dr *MOR* LS27 ......**152** F3
Wren Garth *WKFDW/WTN* WF2 ......**220** E1
Wren Gn *MILN* OL16 ......**206** D8
Wren Hl *BTLY* WF17 ......**151** J6
Wren Nest Rd *RPDN/SBR* HX6 ......**188** C2

Wren's Nest Av *ROY/SHW* OL2 ......**229** L6
Wren St *HUD* HD1 ......**213** M1
　KGHY BD21 ......**3** H3
Wrenthorpe La
　WKFDW/WTN WF2 ......**175** L5
Wrenthorpe Rd
　WKFDW/WTN WF2 ......**176** B5
Wrexhall Rd *EARL* WF12 ......**174** A4
Wrexham Rd *ILK* LS29 ......**39** M5
Wright Av *HWTH* BD22 ......**78** F3
Wrights La *KNOT* WF11 ......**182** F7
Wright St *AIRE* BD20 ......**55** M1
　HWTH BD22 ......**78** F4
Wrigley Av *BOW* BD4 ......**127** K5
Wrigley Hl *LUD/ILL* HX2 ......**124** A8
Wrigley Pl *LIT* OL15 ......**207** H3
Wroe Av *LM/WK* BD12 ......**148** E3
Wroe Pl *LM/WK* BD12 ......**148** E3
Wroe St *DEWS* WF13 ......**173** H5
Wroe Ter *LM/WK* BD12 ......**148** E3
Wrose Av *SHPY* BD18 ......**82** F8
Wrose Brow Rd *SHPY* BD18 ......**82** F6
Wrosecliffe Gv *SHPY* BD18 ......**83** H6
Wrose Dr *SHPY* BD18 ......**82** F8
Wrose Gv *SHPY* BD18 ......**82** F8
Wrose Hill Pl *SHPY* BD18 ......**104** F1
Wrose Mt *SHPY* BD18 ......**83** G8
Wrose Rd *SHPY* BD18 ......**82** F8
Wrose Vw *SHPY* BD18 ......**82** F8
Wuerdle Cl *MILN* OL16 ......**207** G3
Wuerdle Farm Wy *MILN* OL16 ......**207** G2
Wuerdle Pl *MILN* OL16 ......**207** G2
Wuerdle St *MILN* OL16 ......**207** G2
Wycliffe Cl *BRAM* LS13 ......**106** F1
Wycliffe Dr *AL/HA/HU* LS17 ......**87** M4
Wycliffe Gdns *SHPY* BD18 ......**82** C6
Wycliffe Rd *SHPY* BD18 ......**82** C6
Wycoller Rd *LM/WK* BD12 ......**148** E2
Wycombe Gn *BOW* BD4 ......**128** A3
Wycombe St *BSLYN/ROY* S71 ......**262** A4
Wykebeck Av *OSM* LS9 ......**110** F7
Wykebeck Crs *OSM* LS9 ......**110** F6
Wykebeck Gdns *OSM* LS9 ......**110** F6
Wykebeck Gv *OSM* LS9 ......**110** F6
Wykebeck Mt *OSM* LS9 ......**110** F6
Wykebeck Pl *OSM* LS9 ......**111** G6
Wykebeck Rd *OSM* LS9 ......**110** F6
Wykebeck Sq *OSM* LS9 ......**110** F6
Wykebeck St *OSM* LS9 ......**110** F6
Wykebeck Ter *OSM* LS9 ......**110** F6
Wykebeck Valley Rd *OSM* LS9 ......**110** F4
Wykebeck Vw *OSM* LS9 ......**110** F6
Wyke Crs *LM/WK* BD12 ......**148** F4
Wyke La *LM/WK* BD12 ......**148** F4
Wykelea Cl *LM/WK* BD12 ......**148** F4

Wyke Old La *BRIG* HD6 ......**148** D7
Wyncliffe Gdns *AL/HA/HU* LS17 ......**87** M4
Wyncroft Gv *BHP/TINH* LS16 ......**64** B4
Wyncroft Ri *SHPY* BD18 ......**104** F1
Wyndham Av *ECHL* BD2 ......**105** H3
Wynford Av *BHP/TINH* LS16 ......**86** D5
Wynford Dr *HEM/SK/SE* WF9 ......**247** J3
Wynford Gv *BHP/TINH* LS16 ......**86** D5
Wynford Mt *BHP/TINH* LS16 ......**86** C5
Wynford Ri *BHP/TINH* LS16 ......**86** C5
Wynford Ter *BHP/TINH* LS16 ......**86** C5
Wynford Wy *WBSY* BD6 ......**127** G6
Wynmore Av *BHP/TINH* LS16 ......**64** A4
Wynmore Crs *BHP/TINH* LS16 ......**64** B4
Wynmore Dr *BHP/TINH* LS16 ......**64** B4
　HUDW HD3 ......**191** H5
Wynthorpe Rd *HOR/CROF* WF4 ......**197** K5
Wynyard Dr *MOR* LS27 ......**152** B2
Wyther Av *KSTL* LS5 ......**108** C3
Wyther La *KSTL* LS5 ......**108** B3
Wyther Park Av
　WOR/ARM LS12 ......**108** B5
Wyther Park Cl
　WOR/ARM LS12 ......**108** B5
Wyther Park Crs
　WOR/ARM LS12 ......**108** B5
Wyther Park Gv
　WOR/ARM LS12 ......**108** B5
Wyther Park Hl
　WOR/ARM LS12 ......**108** B4
Wyther Park Pl
　WOR/ARM LS12 ......**108** B4
Wyther Park Rd *BRAM* LS13 ......**108** A5
Wyther Park Sq
　WOR/ARM LS12 ......**108** A4
Wyther Park St
　WOR/ARM LS12 ......**108** B5
Wyther Park Ter
　WOR/ARM LS12 ......**108** A5
Wyther Park Vw
　WOR/ARM LS12 ......**108** B4
Wyvern Av *HUDW* HD3 ......**191** L8
Wyvern Cl *BTLY* WF17 ......**151** L8
　GTHN BD7 ......**104** B8
Wyverne Rd *MAR/SLWT* HD7 ......**213** C2
Wyvern Pl *LUD/ILL* HX2 ......**146** A6
Wyvern Ter *LUD/ILL* HX2 ......**146** A6
Wyvil Crs *ILK* LS29 ......**39** G2
Wyvil Rd *ILK* LS29 ......**39** G1

Y

Yarborough Cft *HIPP* HX3 ......**147** J2
Yardley Wy *LM/WK* BD12 ......**127** G8

Yard No4 *BTLY* WF17 ......**151** H5
Yarn St *MID* LS10 ......**9** M6
Yarrow Cl *ROCH* OL11 ......**228** B1
Yarwell *WHIT* OL12 ......**206** A6
Yarwood Gv *GTHN* BD7 ......**126** A3
Yate La *HWTH* BD22 ......**100** E3
Yates Flat *SHPY* BD18 ......**82** F8
Yates La *HUDS* HD4 ......**213** J2
Yeadon Dr *HIPP* HX3 ......**169** J2
Yeadon Moor Rd *YEA* LS19 ......**63** G8
Yea Fold *MILN* OL16 ......**207** G3
Yealand Cl *AWLS/ASK* DN6 ......**249** K8
Ye Farre Cl *BRIG* HD6 ......**170** B2
Yeoman's Cl *MILN* OL16 ......**207** H7
Yewbank Cl *ILK* LS29 ......**38** C2
Yewbank Ter *ILK* LS29 ......**38** C2
Yewdall Rd *BRAM* LS13 ......**106** F1
Yewdall Wy *IDLE* BD10 ......**83** L8
Yew Green Av *HUDS* HD4 ......**214** A3
Yew Green Rd *HUDS* HD4 ......**214** A3
Yew Gv *HUDS* HD4 ......**213** H3
Yew La *GFTH/SHER* LS25 ......**113** K8
Yews Hill Rd *HUDS* HD4 ......**214** A2
Yews La *BSLY* S70 ......**261** K8
Yews Mt *HUD* HD1 ......**214** B2
Yews Pl *BSLY* S70 ......**261** K7
Yew St *HUDN* HD2 ......**14** E1
Yew Tree Av *GIR* BD8 ......**103** M5
Yew Tree Cl *AIRE* BD20 ......**16** D8
　HARS HG2 ......**26** C1
　SHPY BD18 ......**82** E8
Yew Tree Crs *GIR* BD8 ......**104** A5
Yew Tree Dr *RTHW* LS26 ......**134** A8
Yew Tree La *HOLM/MEL* HD9 ......**253** L3
　MAR/SLWT HD7 ......**212** B6
　MAR/SLWT HD7 ......**213** H3
　MSTN/BAR LS15 ......**112** A7
　WIL/AL BD15 ......**103** G6
Yew Tree Rd *HUDW* HD3 ......**191** J4
　KBTN HD8 ......**238** B5
Yew Trees Av *HIPP* HX3 ......**147** J3
Yew Trees Cft *LUD/ILL* HX2 ......**144** D5
Yew Tree St *WKFDE* WF1 ......**13** K7
Yew Tree Ter *WHIT* OL12 ......**162** A8
York Av *HUDN* HD2 ......**192** C4
York Crs *BGLY* BD16 ......**81** J4
York Dr *BTLY* WF17 ......**151** M8
　HECK WF16 ......**150** F8
York Ga *OT* LS21 ......**62** A2
　OT LS21 ......**62** B2
York Gv *BTLY* WF17 ......**151** L8
York Pl *CLECK* BD19 ......**149** M6
　FEA/AMT WF7 ......**202** D7
　LDS LS1 ......**6** E9
　TOD OL14 ......**163** K1
　WBY LS22 ......**30** A8

York Rd *BTLY* WF17 ......**151** L8
　EARL WF12 ......**174** B5
　ILK LS29 ......**40** B5
　MSTN/BAR LS15 ......**111** K3
　OSM LS9 ......**110** C6
　RYKW YO26 ......**33** K2
　SCFT LS14 ......**111** K1
　TAD LS24 ......**51** K2
　TAD LS24 ......**72** A2
　WBY LS22 ......**30** E7
　WBY LS22 ......**31** K5
Yorkshire St *MILN* OL16 ......**206** C6
Yorkshire Wy *GTHN* BD7 ......**126** D3
Yorkstone *HUDS* HD4 ......**213** K3
York St *AIRE* * BD20 ......**34** F7
　BGLY BD16 ......**81** J4
　BRIG HD6 ......**170** C5
　BSLY S70 ......**261** G5
　CAS WF10 ......**158** A6
　COL BB8 ......**74** B1
　CUD/GR S72 ......**244** C8
　CUL/QBY BD13 ......**125** C5
　GIR BD8 ......**104** A7
　HBR HX7 ......**143** J4
　HEM/SK/SE WF9 ......**246** A1
　HFAX HX1 ......**10** F7
　MILN OL16 ......**206** D8
　NORM * WF6 ......**178** B3
　OSM LS9 ......**9** K1
　TOD OL14 ......**141** M8
York Ter *HIPP* HX3 ......**10** F1
York Vls *NORM* WF6 ......**178** D4
Young's Ct *GFTH/SHER* LS25 ......**92** A3
Young St *GIR* BD8 ......**104** B7

Z

Zealand St *BOW* BD4 ......**127** M2
Zedburgh *WHIT* * OL12 ......**206** A6
Zermatt Gv *CHAL* LS7 ......**87** L8
Zermatt Mt *CHAL* * LS7 ......**87** L8
Zermatt St *CHAL* LS7 ......**87** M8
Zermatt Ter *CHAL* LS7 ......**87** M8
Zetland Pl *RHAY* LS8 ......**110** B3
Zetland St *HUD* HD1 ......**15** G8
　WKFDE WF1 ......**12** F2
Zion Cl *HUDW* HD3 ......**191** K5
Zion Dr *DOD/DAR* S75 ......**242** D5
Zion Ter *HBR* HX7 ......**144** A5
Zoar St *MOR* LS27 ......**152** C2

Index - featured places

A1 Business Park
　KNOT WF11 ......**181** L3
Abbey Grange CE High School
　BHP/TINH LS16 ......**86** B6
Abbey House Museum
　KSTL LS5 ......**108** B1
Abbey Park School
　LUD/ILL HX2 ......**123** M8
ABC Cinema
　HFAX HX1 ......**11** H7
Aberford CE Primary School
　GFTH/SHER LS25 ......**92** A7
Abraham Ormerod
　Day Hospital
　TOD OL14 ......**163** K1
Ackton Pastures
　Primary School
　CAS WF10 ......**157** K8
Ackworth Business Park
　FEA/AMT WF7 ......**202** A5
Ackworth School
　FEA/AMT WF7 ......**202** C7
Acorn Business Park
　AIRE BD20 ......**16** C7
　SCFT LS14 ......**111** G5
Acorn Park Industrial Estate
　BAIL BD17 ......**83** G4
Addingham Cricket Club
　ILK LS29 ......**19** G6
Addingham Middle School
　ILK LS29 ......**19** H5
Addingham Primary School
　ILK LS29 ......**19** G5
Adel Primary School
　BHP/TINH LS16 ......**87** J1
Adult Education Centre
　BRIG HD6 ......**170** C3
Adwalton Cricket Club
　BIRK/DRI BD11 ......**151** H1
Adwalton Moor Business Park
　BOW BD4 ......**128** D7
Agnes Stewart CE High School
　OSM LS9 ......**7** L8
Ainley Industrial Estate
　ELL HX5 ......**191** J1
Aireborough Leisure Centre
　GSLY LS20 ......**62** A5
Aire & Calder Industrial Park
　CAS WF10 ......**158** A5
The Aire & Calder
　Industrial Park
　CAS WF10 ......**157** M5
Airedale Business Centre
　AIRE BD20 ......**16** C6
Airedale Centre
　KGHY BD21 ......**3** G5
Airedale Clinic
　CAS WF10 ......**158** E7
Airedale Community
　Business Centre
　CAS WF10 ......**158** D6
Airedale Community Campus
　CAS WF10 ......**158** F7

Airedale General Hospital
　AIRE BD20 ......**35** J8
Airedale Junior School
　CAS WF10 ......**158** E7
Aireside Business Centre
　LDS LS1 ......**8** E1
Aireside Retail Park
　LDS LS1 ......**8** D1
Aire Valley Business Centre
　KGHY BD21 ......**3** G3
Aire Valley Clinic
　AIRE BD20 ......**56** E1
Aireview Business Centre
　BAIL BD17 ......**82** C6
Aire View Infant School
　AIRE BD20 ......**35** M5
Aireview Primary School
　BRAM LS13 ......**107** G2
Albion Mills Retail Park
　WKFDW/WTN WF2 ......**12** C3
The Alhambra Shopping Centre
　BSLY S70 ......**261** H5
Alhambra Theatre
　BFD BD1 ......**4** E7
Alice Ingham Primary School
　MILN OL16 ......**206** E4
Allerton Bywater
　Business Park
　CAS WF10 ......**157** M2
Allerton Bywater
　Infant School
　CAS WF10 ......**157** K2
Allerton Bywater Primary School
　CAS WF10 ......**157** K1
Allerton Clinic
　WIL/AL BD15 ......**103** K6
Allerton First & Middle School
　WIL/AL BD15 ......**103** K5
Allerton Grange High School
　AL/HA/HU LS17 ......**88** B5
Allerton High School
　AL/HA/HU LS17 ......**87** J2
All Saints CE Infant School
　OT LS21 ......**41** L7
All Saints CE Junior School
　OT LS21 ......**41** J6
All Saints CE School
　WBOW BD5 ......**126** F2
All Saints CE First School
　HIPP HX3 ......**168** E4
All Saints CE J & I School
　HIPP HX3 ......**168** E4
All Saints CE Primary School
　WHIT OL12 ......**206** C5
All Saints First School
　ILK LS29 ......**38** D2
All Saints High School
　HUDN HD2 ......**192** H1
All Saints Industrial Estate
　PONT WF8 ......**181** G5
All Saints Infant School
　PONT WF8 ......**181** G5
Alma Industrial Estate
　WHIT OL12 ......**206** B5

Almondbury High School
　HUDE HD5 ......**215** J2
Almondbury Infant School
　HUDE HD5 ......**215** G4
Almondbury Junior School
　HUDE HD5 ......**215** J2
Alston Retail Park
　BFD BD1 ......**3** K1
Altofts Middle School
　NORM WF6 ......**178** B3
Altofts Sports Club
　NORM WF6 ......**178** C1
Alwoodley Golf Club
　AL/HA/HU LS17 ......**66** A8
Alwoodley Primary School
　AL/HA/HU LS17 ......**87** J3
Amateurs FC
　ELL HX5 ......**169** K6
AMF Bowling
　LDSU LS2 ......**7** G7
Anglers Country Park
　HOR/CROF WF4 ......**222** B1
Apex Business Centre
　BEE/HOL LS11 ......**9** G5
Apex Business Park
　BEE/HOL LS11 ......**9** G5
Archbishop Cranmer
　CE Primary School
　AL/HA/HU LS17 ......**87** K3
Arlington Business Centre
　MOR LS27 ......**130** F6
Armley Clinic
　WOR/ARM LS12 ......**108** E6
Armley Link Trading Estate
　WOR/ARM LS12 ......**108** F6
Armley Primary School
　WOR/ARM LS12 ......**108** D6
Armley Sports &
　Leisure Centre
　WOR/ARM LS12 ......**108** D7
Armytage Road
　Industrial Estate
　BRIG HD6 ......**170** E4
Arndale Centre
　HDGY LS6 ......**108** F1
Arndale Shopping Centre
　SHPY BD18 ......**82** D7
A S B & S Sports Club
　FEA/AMT WF7 ......**201** L1
Ashbrow Junior School
　HUDN HD2 ......**192** D3
Ashfield Medical Centre
　MSTN/BAR LS15 ......**111** L4
Ashfield School
　IDLE BD10 ......**83** L5
Ashfield Valley Primary School
　ROCH OL11 ......**228** A2
Ashlands First School
　ILK LS29 ......**38** E2
Ashley Business Centre
　CAS WF10 ......**7** J8
Ashley Industrial Estate
　CHAL LS7 ......**7** H3
　HUDN HD2 ......**193** J2

OSS WF5 ......**175** G7
Ashmount Industrial Park
　HEM/SK/SE WF9 ......**223** L4
Ashton Road Industrial Estate
　RHAY LS8 ......**110** C3
Ashton View Medical Centre
　RHAY LS8 ......**110** B4
Ash Tree County Infant School
　LUD/ILL HX2 ......**145** L1
Ashville Medical Centre
　BSLY S70 ......**261** M6
Askwith CP School
　OT LS21 ......**40** B1
Astley Lane Industrial Estate
　RTHW LS26 ......**134** D6
Astra Business Park
　BEE/HOL LS11 ......**131** L4
Athelstan Primary School
　GFTH/SHER LS25 ......**116** A8
Athersley North
　Primary School
　BSLYN/ROY S71 ......**243** G6
Athersley South
　Primary School
　BSLYN/ROY S71 ......**243** H7
Athletic Club
　HEM/SK/SE WF9 ......**223** K3
Atlas First School
　GIR BD8 ......**4** A2
A To Z Business Park
　DOD/DAR S75 ......**242** C5
Austhorpe Primary School
　MSTN/BAR LS15 ......**112** A6
Automobilia Transport Museum
　HBR HX7 ......**143** L1
Aylesham Industrial Estate
　LM/WK BD12 ......**126** F8
Badsworth CE J & I School
　HEM/SK/SE WF9 ......**225** G4
Bagden Hall Hotel & Golf Club
　KBTN HD8 ......**239** L6
Bagshaw Museum
　BTLY WF17 ......**151** K6
Baildon CE First School
　BAIL BD17 ......**82** F2
Baildon Golf Club
　BAIL BD17 ......**82** E1
Baildon Recreation Centre
　BAIL BD17 ......**82** D5
Baileygate Industrial Estate
　PONT WF8 ......**181** G5
Bailiff Bridge Primary School
　BRIG HD6 ......**148** D7
Baillie Street Health Centre
　MILN OL16 ......**206** B6
Balderstone Community School
　ROCH OL11 ......**228** C3
Balm Road Industrial Estate
　MID LS10 ......**9** K9
Bankfield Museum
　HIPP HX3 ......**11** G2
Bankfoot First School
　WBOW BD5 ......**126** F4

Bardsey Primary School
　AL/HA/HU LS17 ......**67** L2
Barkerend First School
　BFDE BD3 ......**5** K4
Barkisland CE J & I School
　CTL/HWG HX4 ......**189** J1
Barkisland Cricket Club
　CTL/HWG HX4 ......**189** J1
Barkston Ash Catholic Primary
　TAD LS24 ......**115** M1
Barnsley Business
　Innovation Centre
　CUD/GR S72 ......**244** D7
Barnsley College
　BSLY S70 ......**261** G6
Barnsley County Court
　BSLY S70 ......**261** H4
Barnsley District
　General Hospital
　DOD/DAR S75 ......**260** E4
Barnsley FC (Oakwell Stadium)
　BSLYN/ROY S71 ......**261** J5
Barnsley Magistrates Court
　BSLY S70 ......**261** G4
Barnsley Municipal Golf Club
　DOD/DAR S75 ......**242** E4
Barnsley Private Clinic
　DOD/DAR S75 ......**260** F3
Barplas Industrial Park
　WBOW BD5 ......**127** G3
Barras Garth Industrial Estate
　WOR/ARM LS12 ......**108** D8
Barwick In Elmet
　CE Primary School
　MSTN/BAR LS15 ......**91** L3
Batley Boys High School
　BTLY WF17 ......**151** L8
Batley Business Centre
　BTLY WF17 ......**151** K8
Batley Business &
　Technology Centre
　BTLY WF17 ......**174** A2
Batley Bus Station
　BTLY WF17 ......**173** L1
Batley Grammar School
　BTLY WF17 ......**151** K7
Batley Parish CE (A)
　J I & N School
　BTLY WF17 ......**151** L8
Batley RLFC
　BTLY WF17 ......**173** L2
Batley Sports Centre
　BTLY WF17 ......**151** L8
Battyeford CE (c) J & I School
　MIRF WF14 ......**172** A4
Batty Street School
　HECK WF16 ......**172** F2
BBC North Studio
　BFD BD1 ......**4** F7
BBC North Studios
　LDSU LS2 ......**6** F1
Beacon Business Centre
　HIPP HX3 ......**11** L8

The Beaconsfield Centre
HIPP HX3 .... **11** L9
Beckett Park Athletics Centre
HDGY LS6 .... **86** C8
Beckett Park Primary School
HDGY LS6 .... **108** D1
Beckfoot Upper School
BGLY BD16 .... **81** J5
Beech County J & I School
MAR/SLWT HD7 .... **213** G1
**Beech Hill County
Primary School**
HFAX HX1 .... **10** E4
Beech House School
ROCH OL11 .... **206** A8
Beechwood Primary School
SCFT LS14 .... **111** J1
**Beeston Hill St Lukes
CE Primary School**
BEE/HOL LS11 .... **8** E7
Beeston Primary School
BEE/HOL LS11 .... **131** G4
Beeston Royds Industrial Estate
BEE/HOL LS11 .... **130** E3
Beevor Industrial Estate
BSLYN/ROY S71 .... **261** K4
Belfield Community School
MILN OL16 .... **206** E6
Belfield Trading Estate
MILN OL16 .... **206** F5
Belle Isle Medical Centre
RTHW LS26 .... **132** B6
Belle Vue Boys School
HTON BD9 .... **103** M2
Belle Vue Girls Upper School
BGLY BD16 .... **103** L1
Bell Lane Primary School
FEA/AMT WF7 .... **224** B1
Belmont Business Centre
BFD BD1 .... **5** G6
Belmont Middle School
BAIL BD17 .... **82** D3
Ben Rhydding Golf Club
ILK LS29 .... **39** H4
Ben Rhydding Sports Club
ILK LS29 .... **39** J1
Bent Ley Industrial Estate
HOLM/MEL HD9 .... **234** F5
Bentley Primary School
HDGY LS6 .... **87** H8
Benton Park School
YEA LS19 .... **84** D1
Bero Bu School
LDSU LS2 .... **7** G6
Berry Brow Infant School
HUDS HD4 .... **214** B6
Bierley CE First School
BOW BD4 .... **127** K5
Bilton Medical Centre
GIR BD8 .... **4** A4
Bingley Grammar School
BGLY BD16 .... **81** G2
Bingley Health Centre
BGLY BD16 .... **81** G3
Bingley Hospital
BGLY BD16 .... **81** J3
Bingley Little Theatre
BGLY BD16 .... **81** H3
Bingley St Ives Golf Club
BGLY BD16 .... **80** E3
Birchfield Primary School
MOR LS27 .... **129** L8
Birch Lane Medical Centre
WBOW BD5 .... **127** G3
Birdsedge First School
KBTN HD8 .... **256** C2
Birkby Infant School
HUD HD1 .... **14** D3
Birkby Junior School
HUD HD1 .... **14** F1
Birkenshaw CE F & N School
BIRK/DRI BD11 .... **128** C8
Birkenshaw Health Centre
BIRK/DRI BD11 .... **128** C8
Birkenshaw Middle School
BIRK/DRI BD11 .... **150** D2
Birksland Industrial Estate
BOW BD4 .... **5** M4
Birstall Cricket Club
BTLY WF17 .... **151** J5
Birstall J & I School
BTLY WF17 .... **151** H5
Blackburn Industrial Estate
GFTH/SHER LS25 .... **116** D6
Blackgates Infant School
EARD/LOFT WF3 .... **153** H5
Blackgates Junior School
EARD/LOFT WF3 .... **153** H6
Blakehill First School
IDLE BD10 .... **83** J8
Blenheim Primary School
LDSU LS2 .... **6** F5
BMK Industrial Estate
LVSG WF15 .... **172** D2
Bolling Hall
BOW BD4 .... **127** J3
Bolling Road First School
ILK LS29 .... **38** F2
Bolton Brow Primary School
RPDN/SBR HX6 .... **167** M2
Bolton Lane First School
ECHL BD2 .... **105** J3
**Bolton Royd College of
Further Education**
GIR BD8 .... **104** F4
Bolton Royd Primary School
PDSY/CALV LS28 .... **106** C6
Bolton Villas Cricket Club
IDLE BD10 .... **83** J8
Bolton Woods First School
SHPY BD18 .... **104** F1
Bondgate Industrial Estate
PONT WF8 .... **181** G5
Borough Market
HFAX HX1 .... **11** H6
**Boston Spa
Comprehensive School**
BSPA/BRAM LS23 .... **48** D7

Bowers Mill Industrial Estate
GTL/HWG HX4 .... **189** M1
**Bowling Community College &
Swimming Pool**
BOW BD4 .... **127** J3
Bowling Court Industrial Estate
BOW BD4 .... **127** L1
Bowling Green Primary School
GTL/HWG HX4 .... **190** B3
Bowling Park First School
WBOW BD5 .... **127** H3
Bowling Special School
BOW BD4 .... **127** K3
Bracken Edge Primary School
CHAL LS7 .... **110** A1
Brackenhill First School
GTHN BD7 .... **126** D2
Bradford & Bingley RFC
BGLY BD16 .... **81** K5
**Bradford Bulls RLFC
(Odsal Stadium)**
WBSY BD6 .... **127** G6
Bradford Business Park
BFDE BD3 .... **4** F2
**Bradford Cathedral Community
College**
BOW BD4 .... **127** K3
**Bradford City FC
(Bradford & Bingley Stadium)**
GIR BD8 .... **4** D1
Bradford Girls Grammar School
GIR BD8 .... **104** A5
Bradford Golf Club
GSLY LS20 .... **61** J7
Bradford Grammar School
HTON BD9 .... **104** E3
Bradford & Ilkley College
BFD BD1 .... **4** D7
WBOW BD5 .... **4** C9
**Bradford & Ilkley
Community College**
GTHN BD7 .... **4** B8
GTHN BD7 .... **126** D2
ILK LS29 .... **38** D3
**Bradford Industrial &
Horses at Work Museum**
ECHL BD2 .... **105** L3
Bradford Moor First School
BFDE BD3 .... **105** L6
Bradford Royal Infirmary
HTON BD9 .... **104** B4
**Bradford Royal Infirmary
Remedial Unit**
HTON BD9 .... **104** A4
Bradford Salem RFC
HTON BD9 .... **104** A2
Bradford University
PDSY/CALV LS28 .... **106** C5
Bradley Junction Industrial Estate
HUDN HD2 .... **193** H2
**Bradley Mills Cricket &
Bowling Club**
HUD HD1 .... **15** J1
Bradley Park Golf Club
HUDN HD2 .... **170** F8
Bradleys Both CP School
AIRE BD20 .... **16** E8
Bradshaw School
LUD/ILL HX2 .... **124** A6
**Braim Wood High School
For Boys**
RHAY LS8 .... **88** F7
Braithwaite Special School
HWTH BD22 .... **57** G6
Bramall Business Park
WBOW BD5 .... **127** G2
Bramham Park
BSPA/BRAM LS23 .... **69** H6
Bramham Primary School
BSPA/BRAM LS23 .... **69** M2
Bramhope Primary School
BHP/TINH LS16 .... **64** A4
Bramley Business Centre
BRAM LS13 .... **107** K5
Bramley Grange College
SCFT LS14 .... **89** L5
Bramley Health Centre
BRAM LS13 .... **107** L3
Bramley RUFC
BRAM LS13 .... **107** L3
**Bramley St Peters CE
Primary School**
BRAM LS13 .... **107** L4
Brandon Golf Club
AL/HA/HU LS17 .... **88** F1
Branshaw Golf Club
HWTH BD22 .... **78** F3
Branshaw School
HWTH BD22 .... **2** D6
Branxholme Industrial Estate
BRIG HD6 .... **148** E7
Bretton Country Park
HOR/CROF WF4 .... **219** H8
Bretton Hall College
WKFDE WF1 .... **13** H7
Bridge Court Business Park
BEE/HOL LS11 .... **8** C5
Bridge Theatre
HBR HX7 .... **121** H7
Brierley CE Primary School
CUD/GR S72 .... **245** J3
Brighouse High School
BRIG HD6 .... **170** C3
Brighouse Sports Centre
BRIG HD6 .... **170** B1
Brighouse Sports Club
BRIG HD6 .... **170** D3
Brigshaw High School
CAS WF10 .... **135** H7
**Britannia Business
Enterprise Centre**
EARL WF12 .... **174** D8
Britannia Mills Trading Estate
MAR/SLWT HD7 .... **213** H2
**The British Library
Document Supply Centre**
BSPA/BRAM LS23 .... **49** K3

Broadfield Industrial Estate
HUD HD1 .... **214** B3
Broadgate Primary School
HORS LS18 .... **85** L5
Broad Lane Business Centre
HEM/SK/SE WF9 .... **247** H5
**Broad Oak Cricket &
Athletic Club**
MAR/SLWT HD7 .... **213** G4
Brockholes CE School
HOLM/MEL HD9 .... **236** D5
Brockholes Industrial Park
HOLM/MEL HD9 .... **236** D4
Brodetsky Primary School
AL/HA/HU LS17 .... **87** L2
Bronte House School
IDLE BD10 .... **84** B4
Bronte Parsonage Museum
HWTH BD22 .... **78** D7
Bronte School
HWTH BD22 .... **79** G3
Brookfield Infant School
IDLE BD10 .... **84** A8
Brookfoot Industrial Estate
BRIG HD6 .... **170** B4
Brooklands School
SKP/WHF BD23 .... **16** B4
The Brooksbank School
ELL HX5 .... **191** G1
Brookwoods Industrial Estate
GTL/HWG HX4 .... **190** E1
Broomwood Middle School
BOW BD4 .... **127** L5
Brotherton & Byram CP School
KNOT WF11 .... **159** L6
Brownhill Infant School
BTLY WF17 .... **151** J5
Brownhill Primary School
OSM LS9 .... **110** C5
Brownhill School
WHIT OL12 .... **206** A5
Brow Quarry Industrial Estate
HIPP HX3 .... **147** M8
Brudenell Primary School
HDGY LS6 .... **109** G3
Brunswick Industrial Estate
HFAX HX1 .... **10** E8
Buckley Road Industrial Estate
WHIT OL12 .... **206** D4
Bull Royd Industrial Estate
GIR BD8 .... **104** A6
Burley FC
KSTL LS5 .... **86** B8
Burley Hill Trading Estate
BULY LS4 .... **108** E3
Burley In Wharfedale School
ILK LS29 .... **40** A5
Burley Middle School
ILK LS29 .... **40** B6
Burley Park Medical Centre
BULY LS4 .... **108** F4
**Burley St Mathias CE
Primary School**
BULY LS4 .... **108** F4
Burley Woodhead CE School
ILK LS29 .... **40** B6
Burmantofts Health Centre
OSM LS9 .... **7** M7
Burnley Road Primary School
HBR HX7 .... **143** M5
Burntwood School
HEM/SK/SE WF9 .... **246** E4
**Burntwood Sports &
Leisure Centre**
CUD/GR S72 .... **245** L4
Burton Road Business Park
BSLYN/ROY S71 .... **262** A1
Burton Road Primary School
BSLYN/ROY S71 .... **261** J3
Burton Salmon Primary School
GFTH/SHER LS25 .... **160** A2
**Business & Innovation
Barnsley Centre**
DOD/DAR S75 .... **260** D2
Butterfield Industrial Estate
BAIL BD17 .... **82** F4
Buttershaw Middle School
WBSY BD6 .... **126** B7
Buttershaw Upper School
WBSY BD6 .... **126** B6
Byram Industrial Park
KNOT WF11 .... **159** M6
Byron Primary School
BFDE BD3 .... **5** M4
Bywell CE Junior School
EARL WF12 .... **174** B4
Calderdale Business Centre
HFAX HX1 .... **10** B6
Calderdale Business Park
LUD/ILL HX2 .... **146** B3
Calderdale Industrial Museum
HFAX HX1 .... **11** J6
The Calderdale Royal Hospital
HIPP HX3 .... **168** E3
Calder High School
HBR HX7 .... **144** B5
Calder Industrial Estate
BRIG HD6 .... **148** D8
Calder Trading Estate
HUDN HD2 .... **171** J8
RPDN/SBR HX6 .... **167** L3
Calverley CE Primary School
PDSY/CALV LS28 .... **84** D7
Calverley Golf Club
PDSY/CALV LS28 .... **106** C3
Calverley Medical Centre
PDSY/CALV LS28 .... **84** C3
**Calverley Parkside
Primary School**
PDSY/CALV LS28 .... **84** C3
Calversyke Middle School
HWTH BD22 .... **2** A5
Campsmount School
AWLS/ASK DN6 .... **227** K4
Canalside Industrial Estate
MILN OL16 .... **228** D1
Cannon Hall Country Park
DOD/DAR S75 .... **258** E1

Cannon Hall Museum
DOD/DAR S75 .... **258** E1
Cape Industrial Estate
PDSY/CALV LS28 .... **107** G3
Carcroft Health Centre
AWLS/ASK DN6 .... **249** L6
Carcroft Industrial Estate
AWLS/ASK DN6 .... **249** M7
Cardigan Trading Estate
BULY LS4 .... **108** F5
**Cardinal Heenan RC
High School**
HDGY LS6 .... **87** H5
Carleton Business Park
SKP/WHF BD23 .... **16** A3
Carleton Park Primary School
PONT WF8 .... **180** F8
Carlinghow J I & N School
BTLY WF17 .... **151** J7
Carlisle Mills Business Centre
GIR BD8 .... **4** A1
**Carlton Bolling College &
Sports Centre**
BFDE BD3 .... **5** K3
Carlton Cricket Club
EARD/LOFT WF3 .... **154** F4
Carlton High School
PONT WF8 .... **203** G1
Carlton Industrial Estate
BSLYN/ROY S71 .... **243** L6
Carlton J & I School
DEWS WF13 .... **173** K4
BSLYN/ROY S71 .... **243** M6
Carlton Lanes Shopping Area
CAS WF10 .... **157** M6
Carlton Mills Trading Estate
WOR/ARM LS12 .... **108** F6
Carlton Northfield AFC
EARD/LOFT WF3 .... **154** F4
Carr Gate Hospital
WKFDW/WTN WF2 .... **176** A1
**Carr Green County
Primary School**
BRIG HD6 .... **170** B7
Carr Manor High School
AL/HA/HU LS17 .... **87** J6
Carr Manor Primary School
AL/HA/HU LS17 .... **87** J6
Carr Wood Industrial Estate
CAS WF10 .... **180** B1
Cartwright Hall Art Gallery
HTON BD9 .... **104** E3
Castlefields Industrial Estate
BGLY BD16 .... **80** F1
Castleford Health Centre
CAS WF10 .... **157** M6
Castleford High School
CAS WF10 .... **158** A6
Castleford RUFC
CAS WF10 .... **179** H1
Castleford Swimming Pool
CAS WF10 .... **157** K8
**Castleford Tigers RLFC
(The Jungle)**
CAS WF10 .... **158** B5
Castle Grove Infant School
WKFDW/WTN WF2 .... **199** G4
Castle Hall School
MIRF WF14 .... **194** D1
Castle Hill J & I School
TOD OL14 .... **141** M8
The Castle Special School
CAS WF10 .... **158** E7
Castleton Primary School
WOR/ARM LS12 .... **108** F7
**Cas Whitwood Mere
Middle School**
CAS WF10 .... **157** J6
Cathedral Retail Park
WKFDW/WTN WF2 .... **12** D5
The Cathedral School
WKFDW/WTN WF2 .... **12** A9
Cawley J & I N School
HECK WF16 .... **173** G2
Cawthorne CE Primary School
DOD/DAR S75 .... **259** G2
**Cawthorne Victoria
Jubilee Museum**
DOD/DAR S75 .... **259** G1
Central Leisure Centre
MILN OL16 .... **206** C7
**Central Library;museum &
Art Gallery**
LDS LS1 .... **6** F8
Central Street Infant School
HBR HX7 .... **143** H3
Centre 27 Business Park
BTLY WF17 .... **151** K3
Chantry Bridge Industrial Estate
WKFDE WF1 .... **12** F5
Chapel Allerton Hospital
CHAL LS7 .... **110** A1
Chapel Allerton Medical Centre
CHAL LS7 .... **87** M8
Chapel Allerton Primary School
CHAL LS7 .... **87** L8
Chapel Grange Special School
GIR BD8 .... **103** L6
Chapeltown Business Centre
CHAL LS7 .... **7** K1
Chapeltown Health Centre
CHAL LS7 .... **7** L3
Chel House Business Centre
CHAL LS7 .... **7** K4
Chellow Dene Middle School
GIR BD8 .... **103** M6
Chequerfield Infant School
PONT WF8 .... **181** H7
Chesham Building
GTHN BD7 .... **4** B8
Chesney Park Industrial Estate
MID LS10 .... **9** J7
Chevet Business Centre
KNOT WF11 .... **181** L3
Chevin Forest Park
OT LS21 .... **62** D1
Chichester Business Centre
MILN OL16 .... **206** C7

**Chickenley Community
J & I School**
EARL WF12 .... **174** C7
**Chickenley Medical Clinic &
Health Centre**
EARL WF12 .... **174** C7
Chippendale Junior School
OT LS21 .... **41** H4
Chohan Medical Centre
WBOW BD5 .... **126** F2
Christchurch CE Primary School
SKP/WHF BD23 .... **16** B3
UPML OL3 .... **230** F4
Christ Church CE School
COL BB8 .... **74** C7
Christ Church J & I School
LUD/ILL HX2 .... **145** M6
Christ Church Junior School
RPDN/SBR HX6 .... **167** L1
Christ Church Primary School
WOR/ARM LS12 .... **108** D6
**Christ Church Woodhouse
J & I School**
HUDN HD2 .... **192** F2
Christ the King RC Primary School
BRAM LS13 .... **108** A5
Church School
CUL/QBY BD13 .... **103** G8
Churwell Primary School
MOR LS27 .... **130** A4
Cineworld
BFD BD1 .... **5** G6
WKFDW/WTN WF2 .... **12** C5
City Link Industrial Park
BOW BD4 .... **106** C7
City of Leeds School
HDGY LS6 .... **109** J2
City of Wakefield Golf Club
WKFDW/WTN WF2 .... **198** A4
City Park Industrial Estate
WOR/ARM LS12 .... **130** E3
City Varieties Music Hall
LDS LS1 .... **7** G9
Clapgate Primary School
MID LS10 .... **154** B1
Claycliffe Business Park
DOD/DAR S75 .... **260** A4
Clayton CE First School
CLAY BD14 .... **125** L2
Clayton Cemetery
CLAY BD14 .... **125** M1
Clayton CE First School
CLAY BD14 .... **125** K2
Clayton Golf Club
CLAY BD14 .... **125** L3
Clayton Hospital
WKFDE WF1 .... **176** D7
Clayton Middle School
CLAY BD14 .... **125** L2
Cleckheaton & District Golf Club
CLECK BD19 .... **149** K4
Cleckheaton Sports Club
CLECK BD19 .... **149** L4
Clevedon House School
ILK LS29 .... **39** J4
Cliffe Castle Museum & Gallery
KGHY BD21 .... **2** F1
Cliffe Commercial Business Park
HUD HD1 .... **14** B7
Cliffe Hill School
HIPP HX3 .... **148** C8
Cliffe Middle School
BFDE BD3 .... **5** H1
Cliff School
WKFDE WF1 .... **176** D6
Clifton Cemetery
BRIG HD6 .... **171** G4
Clifton Forge Business Park
KNOT WF11 .... **182** A2
Clifton Infant School
HOR/CROF WF4 .... **197** H3
Clough Head J & I School
MAR/SLWT HD7 .... **212** C2
Cobblers Lane J & I School
PONT WF8 .... **181** J4
Cobden Primary School
WOR/ARM LS12 .... **130** B2
Cockburn High School
BEE/HOL LS11 .... **131** J7
Cocksford Golf Club
TAD LS24 .... **93** J2
Colden Primary School
HBR HX7 .... **142** C1
College of Art & Design
LDSU LS2 .... **6** F7
College of Technology
LDSU LS2 .... **6** F7
College of Technology (Annexe)
OSM LS9 .... **9** L2
The College
WKFDE WF1 .... **176** E7
Colne Cricket Club
COL BB8 .... **74** C1
Colne Golf Club
COL BB8 .... **52** D7
Colne Side Business Park
HUDW HD3 .... **213** H6
Colne Valley Business Park
MAR/SLWT HD7 .... **212** F5
Colne Valley High School
MAR/SLWT HD7 .... **213** G5
Colne Valley Leisure Centre
MAR/SLWT HD7 .... **212** C5
Colne Valley Museum
MAR/SLWT HD7 .... **212** G2
Colour Museum
BFD BD1 .... **4** D6
Colton Primary School
MSTN/BAR LS15 .... **112** A8
Colton Retail Park
MSTN/BAR LS15 .... **112** B7
Common Road Industrial Estate
LM/WK BD12 .... **126** F8
Concert Hall
HUD HD1 .... **14** F8
Cononley Business Park
AIRE BD20 .... **34** D4

Cononley Primary School
AIRE BD20 .... 34 C3
Conway Medical Centre
RHAY LS8 .... 110 C3
Cookridge Hall Golf &
Country Club
BHP/TINH LS16 .... 64 B8
Cookridge Hospital
BHP/TINH LS16 .... 86 A3
Cookridge Primary School
BHP/TINH LS16 .... 86 A2
Co-operative Museum
WHIT OL12 .... 206 A6
Co-operative Shopping Parade
HIPP HX3 .... 147 L6
Cooper Lane First School
WBSY BD6 .... 125 L5
Copley Hill Trading Estate
WOR/ARM LS12 .... 131 G1
Copley Primary School
HIPP HX3 .... 168 D5
Copperfields College
OSM LS9 .... 110 C8
Copthorne First School
GTHN BD7 .... 126 E1
Copwood Mental Health Clinic
BOW BD4 .... 128 A2
Cornholme J & I School
TOD OL14 .... 140 C5
Coronation Business Centre
KGHY BD21 .... 3 J1
Corpus Christi Primary School
OSM LS9 .... 110 F7
Corpus Christi RC High School
OSM LS9 .... 111 G6
Cottage Road Picture House
HDGY LS6 .... 86 E8
Cottingley Clinic
BGLY BD16 .... 81 J7
Cottingley Community
Health Centre
BEE/HOL LS11 .... 130 F5
Cottingley First School
BGLY BD16 .... 81 K7
Cottingley Hall Crematorium
BEE/HOL LS11 .... 130 F4
Cottingley Primary School
BEE/HOL LS11 .... 130 E5
The Coulthurst Craven
Sports Centre
SKP/WHF BD23 .... 16 A3
Covered Market
KGHY BD21 .... 3 G5
Cowling Primary School
HWTH BD22 .... 54 D3
Craven Clinic
SKP/WHF BD23 .... 16 C2
Craven Road Medical Centre
HDGY LS6 .... 6 F2
Crawshaw School
PDSY/CALV LS28 .... 107 H7
Crevesford Special School
BSLYN/ROY S71 .... 243 K8
Cricket Club
MIRF WF14 .... 194 E5
Crigglestone Sports Club
HOR/CROF WF4 .... 220 B2
Crofton Health Centre
HOR/CROF WF4 .... 200 B5
Crofton High School
HOR/CROF WF4 .... 200 B6
Crofton Infant School
HOR/CROF WF4 .... 200 B6
Crofton Junior School
HOR/CROF WF4 .... 200 C6
Crompton Buckstones
Primary School
ROY/SHW OL2 .... 229 M6
Crompton Cricket Club
ROY/SHW OL2 .... 229 K6
Crompton Health Centre
ROY/SHW OL2 .... 229 K8
Crompton House CE
High School
ROY/SHW OL2 .... 229 J6
Crompton Swimming Pool
ROY/SHW OL2 .... 229 K8
Crosland Heath Golf Club
HUDS HD4 .... 213 J5
Crosland Moor County
Junior School
HUDS HD4 .... 213 L3
Crosland Road
Industrial Estate
HUDS HD4 .... 235 K1
Crossflatts Cricket Club
BGLY BD16 .... 58 F8
Crossflatts First School
BGLY BD16 .... 59 G8
Cross Flatts Park Primary School
BEE/HOL LS11 .... 131 J4
Cross Gates Primary School
SCFT LS14 .... 111 J4
Crossgates Shopping Centre
MSTN/BAR LS15 .... 111 L4
Cross Green Light
Industrial Estate
OSM LS9 .... 132 C1
Cross Hall Infant School
MOR LS27 .... 152 B3
Cross Lane Business Park
LVSG WF15 .... 172 C2
Crosslane Industrial Estate
LVSG WF15 .... 172 C2
Cross Lane Primary School
ELL HX5 .... 191 G1
Crossley Hall First &
Middle School
GIR BD8 .... 104 A7
Crossley Heath School
HFAX HX1 .... 168 C2
Crossley Retail Park
HFAX HX1 .... 10 E4
Crossley Street Primary School
WBY LS22 .... 30 A8
Crowlees CE School
MIRF WF14 .... 194 C1

Crown Point Retail Park
MID LS10 .... 9 H4
Cuckoo Nest Industrial Estate
GTHN BD7 .... 4 A6
Cudworth Birkwood
Primary School
CUD/GR S72 .... 262 E1
Cudworth Churchfield
Primary School
CUD/GR S72 .... 244 D7
Cudworth Pontefract
Road Primary School
CUD/GR S72 .... 244 D6
Cullingworth First School
CUL/QBY BD13 .... 79 M8
Cullingworth Medical Centre
CUL/QBY BD13 .... 79 M8
Cumberworth CE First School
KBTN HD8 .... 238 D8
Dale Lane Industrial Estate
HEM/SK/SE WF9 .... 247 K1
Dales Bank Holiday Park
AIRE BD20 .... 35 M1
Dalton School J I &N
HUDE HD5 .... 193 H8
Dane Royd J & I School
HOR/CROF WF4 .... 220 A4
Dansk Way
ILK LS29 .... 38 E1
Darfield All Saints CE
Primary School
WMB/DAR S73 .... 263 K8
Darfield Upperwood
Primary School
WMB/DAR S73 .... 263 H8
Darrington CE J & I School
PONT WF8 .... 203 M1
Darton High School
DOD/DAR S75 .... 241 K6
Darton Kexborough
Infant School
DOD/DAR S75 .... 241 K6
Darton Primary School
DOD/DAR S75 .... 242 B6
Deanfield County
Primary School
LUD/ILL HX2 .... 146 A3
Dearne Valley Health Centre
KBTN HD8 .... 239 M5
Delf Hill Middle School
LM/WK BD12 .... 126 E8
Denby Dale Industrial Park
KBTN HD8 .... 239 H8
Denby First School
KBTN HD8 .... 257 G3
Denholme Clinic
CUL/QBY BD13 .... 101 M5
Denholme First School
CUL/QBY BD13 .... 101 M5
Dental Institute
LDSU LS2 .... 6 D7
Derby Street J & I School
ROCH OL11 .... 228 C1
Dewsbury Bus Station
EARL WF12 .... 173 L7
Dewsbury Cemetery
DEWS WF13 .... 173 J7
Dewsbury College
DEWS WF13 .... 173 K5
Dewsbury District Golf Club
MIRF WF14 .... 194 E2
Dewsbury & District Hospital
DEWS WF13 .... 173 J4
Dewsbury Moor Crematorium
DEWS WF13 .... 173 J6
Dewsbury Moor Infant &
Nursery School
DEWS WF13 .... 173 H4
Dewsbury Museum &
Art Gallery
DEWS WF13 .... 173 J7
Dewsbury Sports Centre
EARL WF12 .... 173 M6
Dimplewell Infant School
OSS WF5 .... 196 F2
District Archives Office
WKFDE WF1 .... 12 C1
Dixon Lane Medical Centre
WOR/ARM LS12 .... 130 E2
Dixons City Technology College
WBOW BD5 .... 127 G2
Dockfield Industrial Estate
BAIL BD17 .... 82 E6
Dodworth Business Park
DOD/DAR S75 .... 259 M6
Dodworth CE School
DOD/DAR S75 .... 260 A8
Dodworth Health Centre
DOD/DAR S75 .... 260 D7
Dodworth Keresforth
Road Primary School
DOD/DAR S75 .... 260 C8
Dodworth Primary School
DOD/DAR S75 .... 260 B7
Domestic Street
Industrial Estate
BEE/HOL LS11 .... 8 A4
Dominion Industrial Park
HIPP HX3 .... 147 L6
Doncaster Road Primary School
BSLYN/ROY S71 .... 261 D1
Dorothy Hyman Stadium
CUD/GR S72 .... 244 E8
Drakes Industrial Estate
LUD/ILL HX2 .... 146 C2
Drighlington Junior School
BIRK/DRI BD11 .... 129 H7
Drug Addiction Clinic
LDSU LS9 .... 6 C6
Drummond Middle School
GIR BD8 .... 4 A2
Drummond Trading Estate
GIR BD8 .... 4 C3
Dudley Hill First School
BOW BD4 .... 127 L1
Durn Street Industrial Estate
LIT OL15 .... 185 L8

Eagles Yard Business Park
WKFDE WF1 .... 12 F3
Earlsheaton High School
EARL WF12 .... 174 A6
Earlsheaton Infant School
EARL WF12 .... 174 B7
East Ardsley Health Centre
EARD/LOFT WF3 .... 153 K7
East Ardsley Infant School
EARD/LOFT WF3 .... 153 M6
East Ardsley Primary School
EARD/LOFT WF3 .... 153 M6
East Ardsley United Cricket &
Athletic Club
EARD/LOFT WF3 .... 153 L8
East Bierley CE First School
BOW BD4 .... 128 B7
East Bierley Cricket Club
BIRK/DRI BD11 .... 128 A8
East Bierley Golf Club
BOW BD4 .... 128 A7
Eastborough J I & N School
EARL WF12 .... 173 M6
Eastburn J & I School
AIRE BD20 .... 35 H8
East Crompton St Georges
CE Primary School
ROY/SHW OL2 .... 229 L7
East Crompton St James
CE Junior School
ROY/SHW OL2 .... 229 K7
East Garforth Primary School
GFTH/SHER LS25 .... 113 K6
East Leeds Clinic
OSM LS9 .... 110 D5
East Leeds Leisure Centre
MSTN/BAR LS15 .... 111 G7
Eastmoor Health Centre
WKFDE WF1 .... 177 H6
East Morton First School
AIRE BD20 .... 58 E5
Eastwood First School
KGHY BD21 .... 3 J2
Eccleshill Clinic & Health Centre
IDLE BD10 .... 83 M8
Eccleshill Cricket Club
IDLE BD10 .... 105 M1
Eccleshill North Middle School
IDLE BD10 .... 84 A8
Eccleshill School
IDLE BD10 .... 106 A1
Eccleshill United Sports Club
ECHL BD2 .... 83 H8
Edgerton Cemetery
HUD HD1 .... 14 D3
Edward Sheerien
Secondary School
BSLYN/ROY S71 .... 243 K8
Eldwick First School
BGLY BD16 .... 81 L1
Elizabeth Industrial Estate
HFAX HX1 .... 10 D3
Elland CE School
ELL HX5 .... 169 H7
Elland Old Earth School
ELL HX5 .... 169 L7
Elland Road Industrial Park
BEE/HOL LS11 .... 130 F3
Ellen Royde Health Centre
ELL HX5 .... 169 G7
Elmfield Business Park
GFTH/SHER LS25 .... 113 J6
Elmwood Health Centre
HOLM/MEL HD9 .... 236 C7
Emley First School
KBTN HD8 .... 217 M7
Emley Moor Business Park
KBTN HD8 .... 217 K8
Emmanuel Trading Estate
WOR/ARM LS12 .... 8 B3
Empire Business Centre
LUD/ILL HX2 .... 146 C1
England Lane J & I School
KNOT WF11 .... 182 C3
English Martyrs RC
Primary School
WKFDW/WTN WF2 .... 197 M1
Enterprise Park
Industrial Estate
BEE/HOL LS11 .... 131 H5
Environmental Business Centre
MOR LS27 .... 152 C2
Ermysteds Grammar School
SKP/WHF BD23 .... 16 B2
Esholt & Aire Bronians
Sports Club
BAIL BD17 .... 83 K1
Esplanade Arts &
Heritage Centre
MILN OL16 .... 206 A7
Essex Park Industrial Estate
BFDE BD3 .... 5 J8
Eureka the Museum for Children
HIPP HX3 .... 11 J7
Euroway Trading Estate
BOW BD4 .... 127 J8
The Eye Clinic
GTHN BD7 .... 4 B6
Fagley First School
ECHL BD2 .... 105 M4
Fairburn Community School
KNOT WF11 .... 159 J2
Fairburn Sports &
Recreation Centre
KNOT WF11 .... 159 J2
Fairfield Special School
HECK WF16 .... 173 G1
Fairway Industrial Estate
BTLY WF17 .... 151 H2
Fall Bank Industrial Estate
DOD/DAR S75 .... 259 M7
Farfield Primary School
PDSY/CALV LS28 .... 106 C4
Farnham First School
CHAL BD7 .... 126 D1
Farnley CE Primary School
OT LS21 .... 41 L1

Farnley Park High School
WOR/ARM LS12 .... 130 A2
Farrowdale House
Preparatory School
ROY/SHW OL2 .... 229 J8
Farrow Medical Centre
BFDE BD3 .... 5 H3
Farsley Celtic AFC
PDSY/CALV LS28 .... 107 G4
Farsley Community Clinic
PDSY/CALV LS28 .... 106 E3
Fartown Health Centre
HUDN HD2 .... 192 C5
Fartown High School
HUDN HD2 .... 192 E4
Fearnville Sports Centre
RHAY LS8 .... 110 F2
Featherbank Infant School
HORS LS18 .... 85 K6
Featherstone Cemetery
FEA/AMT WF7 .... 179 K4
Featherstone High School
FEA/AMT WF7 .... 202 B1
Featherstone Sports Centre
FEA/AMT WF7 .... 202 B2
Felnex Trading Estate
OSM LS9 .... 132 E1
Fentham Industrial Estate
BRIG HD6 .... 170 C5
Fernbank School
AWLS/ASK DN6 .... 249 L8
Ferniehurst First School
BAIL BD17 .... 82 E4
Fernley Green Industrial Estate
KNOT WF11 .... 182 D2
Ferrybridge Infant School
KNOT WF11 .... 181 L1
Feversham College
BFDE BD3 .... 5 J7
Feversham Street First School
BFDE BD3 .... 5 M6
Fieldhead Carr Primary School
SCFT LS14 .... 89 K5
Field Head Hospital
WKFDE WF1 .... 176 F4
Fieldhead J & I School
BTLY WF17 .... 151 H3
Fieldhouse Industrial Estate
WHIT OL12 .... 206 B4
Field Lane Infant School
BTLY WF17 .... 173 M2
Firbank County School
ROY/SHW OL2 .... 228 F7
Firgrove Business Park
MILN OL16 .... 206 F6
First Avenue Industrial Estate
PDSY/CALV LS28 .... 107 G6
Fir Tree Primary School
AL/HA/HU LS17 .... 87 M3
Fitzwilliam J & I School
HEM/SK/SE WF9 .... 223 K2
Fixby J & I School
HUDN HD2 .... 192 C2
Flanshaw J & I School
WKFDW/WTN WF2 .... 176 B7
Flockton CE School
HOR/CROF WF4 .... 217 L3
Flushdyke Primary School
OSS WF5 .... 175 H7
Forster Square Retail Park
BFD BD1 .... 4 E3
The Foulstone School
WMB/DAR S73 .... 263 J8
Foundry Industrial Estate
KNOT WF11 .... 181 L1
PDSY/CALV LS28 .... 107 G5
The Fountain Medical Centre
MOR LS27 .... 152 C3
Four Gates End
HBR HX7 .... 119 K8
Four Lanes Business Park
GIR BD8 .... 104 B7
Fowler Street Industrial Estate
BOW BD4 .... 127 K1
Foxhill First School
CUL/QBY BD13 .... 124 F4
Friars Industrial Estate
IDLE BD10 .... 83 K7
Frizinghall First &
Middle School
HTON BD9 .... 104 E1
Frizinghall Medical Centre
HTON BD9 .... 104 D2
The Froebelian School
HORS LS18 .... 85 K7
Frost Hill Business Park
LVSG WF15 .... 172 D2
Fulford Grange Hospital
YEA LS19 .... 84 C3
Fulneck Golf Club
PDSY/CALV LS28 .... 128 F2
Fulneck School
PDSY/CALV LS28 .... 129 G2
Garforth Clinic
GFTH/SHER LS25 .... 113 G8
Garforth Community College
GFTH/SHER LS25 .... 113 G8
Garforth Golf Club
GFTH/SHER LS25 .... 113 G3
Garforth Leisure Centre
GFTH/SHER LS25 .... 113 J7
Garforth Medical Centre
GFTH/SHER LS25 .... 113 G7
Gascoigne Wood Mine
GFTH/SHER LS25 .... 139 G2
Gateways School
AL/HA/HU LS17 .... 45 J8
Gawber J & I School
DOD/DAR S75 .... 260 C3
Gawthorpe Primary School
OSS WF5 .... 174 E5
Gelderd Trading Estate
WOR/ARM LS12 .... 131 G1
Gemini Business Park
CHAL BD7 .... 7 J3
Ghyll Royd School
ILK LS29 .... 38 B3

Gibson Lane Junior School
GFTH/SHER LS25 .... 135 K5
Gildersome Junior School
MOR LS27 .... 129 L7
Gillott Industrial Estate
BSLY S70 .... 260 F5
Gilstead Middle School
BGLY BD16 .... 81 L2
Gilthwaites First School
KBTN HD8 .... 239 J7
Girlington First School
GIR BD8 .... 104 C6
Girlington Industrial Centre
GIR BD8 .... 104 B6
Girls High School
SKP/WHF BD23 .... 16 A1
Girnhill Infant School
FEA/AMT WF7 .... 201 L2
Glasshoughton Infant School
CAS WF10 .... 158 A7
The Gleddings School
HIPP HX3 .... 168 C3
Gledholt Business Park
HUD HD1 .... 14 A8
Gledhow Primary School
RHAY LS8 .... 88 B6
Glenaire First School
BAIL BD17 .... 82 C4
Glen Cable Tramway
BAIL BD17 .... 82 B4
Glenfield Caravan Park
AL/HA/HU LS17 .... 67 H5
Glusburn CP School
AIRE BD20 .... 34 E8
Golcar J & I School
MAR/SLWT HD7 .... 212 F2
Golden Acre Park & Gardens
BHP/TINH LS16 .... 64 D6
Gomersal CE Middle School
CLECK BD19 .... 150 E5
Gomersal First School
CLECK BD19 .... 150 D5
The Good Health Centre
RHAY LS8 .... 88 C4
Gordon Street J & I School
FEA/AMT WF7 .... 179 M7
Gorrells Industrial Estate
ROCH OL11 .... 228 A3
Gotts Park Golf Club
WOR/ARM LS12 .... 108 C5
Grafton School
HDGY LS6 .... 6 F2
Grand Theatre & Opera House
LDSU LS2 .... 7 G4
Grangefield Industrial Estate
PDSY/CALV LS28 .... 107 H5
Grange Gate Junior School
BSLYN/ROY S71 .... 262 A4
Grange Lane Industrial Estate
BSLYN/ROY S71 .... 262 A6
The Grange Medical Centre
SCFT LS14 .... 111 G7
Grange Middle School
AIRE BD20 .... 58 A4
Grange Road Business Park
BTLY WF17 .... 174 A1
Grange Road Industrial Estate
BTLY WF17 .... 174 A2
Grange Upper School
WBOW BD5 .... 126 D4
Great Horton Cricket Club
GTHN BD7 .... 126 C3
Great Horton Industrial Estate
WBSY BD6 .... 125 M4
Great Horton Middle School
GTHN BD7 .... 126 C2
Great & Little Preston
CE Infants School
RTHW LS26 .... 135 G7
Great & Little Preston
Junior School
RTHW LS26 .... 135 G7
Great Northern Retail Park
HUD HD1 .... 15 H4
Greatwood Primary School
SKP/WHF BD23 .... 16 C1
Greenbank CP School
WHIT OL12 .... 206 B5
Greenfield Primary School
GFTH/SHER LS25 .... 135 J4
Greenfield School
IDLE BD10 .... 83 K5
Greengates First School
IDLE BD10 .... 84 A7
Greenhead Athletics Track
KGHY BD21 .... 57 K5
Greenhead College
HUD HD1 .... 14 C7
Greenhead Grammar School
AIRE BD20 .... 57 J4
Greenhill CP School
BRAM LS13 .... 107 M6
Greenhill Industrial Estate
HBR HX7 .... 144 A6
Greenhill Infant &
Juniors School
WKFDE WF1 .... 13 L1
Green Lane Industrial Estate
FEA/AMT WF7 .... 179 J4
Green Lane Primary School
GFTH/SHER LS25 .... 113 J6
Green Leas School
PONT WF8 .... 203 G1
Green Meadows School
GSLY LS20 .... 61 L5
Greenmount Primary School
BEE/HOL LS11 .... 8 F8
Green Mount Retail Park
HFAX HX1 .... 10 E7
Greenside Infant &
Nursery School
HUDE HD5 .... 215 H1
Greenwood Primary School
BEE/HOL LS11 .... 8 F8
Greetland Cricket &
Bowling Club
GTL/HWG HX4 .... 168 E7

Greetland J & I School
GTL/HWG HX4 .... 168 C7
Greetland Mixed School
GTL/HWG HX4 .... 168 D7
Gregory Middle School
WBOW BD5 .... 127 J5
Gresley Road Industrial Estate
KGHY BD21 .... 3 H5
Grimethorpe Hall
CUD/GR S72 .... 245 H6
Grimethorpe Ladywood
Primary School
CUD/GR S72 .... 245 K8
Grove House First School
ECHL BD2 .... 105 J2
Grove Lea J & I School
HEM/SK/SE WF9 .... 223 M7
Grove Mills Industrial Estate
ELL HX5 .... 169 J7
Grove Street J & I School
BSLYN/ROY S71 .... 261 J5
Guiseley AFC
GSLY LS20 .... 61 L5
Guiseley Cemetery
ILK LS29 .... 61 L3
Guiseley County Infant School
GSLY LS20 .... 62 A5
Guiseley School
GSLY LS20 .... 61 M6
Gulsyke Medical Centre
MSTN/BAR LS15 .... 111 J7
Gunthwaite Hall
STKB/PEN S36 .... 257 K4
Hade Edge J & I School
HOLM/MEL HD9 .... 254 C6
Haggs Business Park
PBR HC3 .... 27 M3
Haigh Hall Medical Centre
IDLE BD10 .... 83 M7
Haigh Road Infant School
RTHW LS26 .... 133 G8
Hainsworth Moor J & I School
CUL/QBY BD13 .... 124 F6
Half Acres J & I School
CAS WF10 .... 157 L7
Halfpenny Bridge
Industrial Estate
MILN OL16 .... 206 C8
Halfpenny Lane J & I School
PONT WF8 .... 180 D6
Halifax Blue Sox RLFC
(The Shay Stadium)
HFAX HX1 .... 11 H9
Halifax Bradley Hall Golf Club
GTL/HWG HX4 .... 190 C1
Halifax Building Society
HFAX HX1 .... 11 G7
Halifax Catholic High School
LUD/ILL HX2 .... 124 C8
Halifax Cricket Ground
HFAX HX1 .... 146 A7
Halifax Golf Club
LUD/ILL HX2 .... 123 L5
Halifax High School
HFAX HX1 .... 11 G8
Halifax Industrial Centre
HFAX HX1 .... 10 D4
Halifax Leisure Centre
HFAX HX1 .... 11 H7
Halifax RUFC
LUD/ILL HX2 .... 146 B2
Halifax Swimming Pool
HFAX HX1 .... 11 H8
Halifax Town FC
(The Shay Stadium)
HFAX HX1 .... 11 H9
Hall Bower Athletic Club
HUDS HD4 .... 214 D5
Hall Bower Cricket Club
HUDS HD4 .... 214 D5
Halton Building
GTHN BD7 .... 4 C7
Hambledon First School
BOW BD4 .... 127 K6
Hanging Heaton CE J & I School
BTLY WF17 .... 174 B3
Hanging Heaton Golf Club
EARL WF12 .... 174 A4
Hanson Upper School
ECHL BD2 .... 105 H2
Harden First School
BGLY BD16 .... 80 C5
Harehills Middle School
RHAY LS8 .... 110 B3
Harehills Primary School
RHAY LS8 .... 110 C3
Harewood CE Primary School
AL/HA/HU LS17 .... 45 J7
Harewood House &
Bird Garden
AL/HA/HU LS17 .... 45 G8
Hartington Middle School
HWTH BD22 .... 78 E7
Hartshead J & I School
LVSG WF15 .... 171 L4
Hatfield Hall Golf Club
EARD/LOFT WF3 .... 177 G3
Havercroft Health Centre
HOR/CROF WF4 .... 222 D6
Havercroft J & I School
HOR/CROF WF4 .... 222 D6
Hawkins Clinic
MILN OL16 .... 206 B7
Hawksworth CE School
GSLY LS20 .... 61 G6
Hawksworth Wood
Primary School
KSTL LS5 .... 86 A7
Haworth School
HWTH BD22 .... 78 E7
Haycliffe Special School
WBSY BD6 .... 126 D4
Headfield CE Junior School
EARL WF12 .... 195 L1
Headingley Golf Club
BHP/TINH LS16 .... 86 F1
Headingley Primary School
HDGY LS6 .... 108 F1

Headlands CE J & I School
LVSG WF15 .... 172 C2
Headley Golf Club
CUL/QBY BD13 .... 124 F1
Headrow Shopping Centre
LDS LS1 .... 7 G9
Headway Business Park
WKFDW/WTN WF2 .... 12 D9
Heady Fields Golf Club
HOLM/MEL HD9 .... 235 J6
Healey J & I School
BTLY WF17 .... 173 H2
Healey Primary School
WHIT OL12 .... 206 A3
Heather Grove First School
HTON BD9 .... 103 M3
Heathfield Industrial Estate
ELL HX5 .... 169 J8
Heathfield-Rishworth School
RPDN/SBR HX6 .... 188 E4
Heath View Community School
WKFDE WF1 .... 13 K1
Heaton Middle School
HTON BD9 .... 103 M2
Heaton Royds Hospital
HTON BD9 .... 103 M1
Heaton Royds Special School
SHPY BD18 .... 104 C1
Hebble Brook Business Park
LUD/ILL HX2 .... 123 L7
Hebden Bridge Cinema
HBR HX7 .... 143 J3
Hebden Bridge Golf Club
HBR HX7 .... 143 M3
Hebden Bridge Health Centre
HBR HX7 .... 143 J3
Hebden Royd Cragg Vale
County Primary School
HBR HX7 .... 165 L3
Hebden Royd Primary School
HBR HX7 .... 143 G2
Heckmondwike Grammar School
HECK WF16 .... 172 F2
Heckmondwike Sports Club
HECK WF16 .... 172 F2
Helme CE J & I School
HOLM/MEL HD9 .... 234 F2
Hemsworth High School
HEM/SK/SE WF9 .... 224 A7
Hemsworth RUFC
HEM/SK/SE WF9 .... 224 B7
Hemsworth Sports Complex
HEM/SK/SE WF9 .... 224 A8
Hendal Lane Primary School
WKFDW/WTN WF2 .... 220 D1
Henry Moore Clinic
CAS WF10 .... 157 M7
Heponstall County
Primary School
HBR HX7 .... 143 H1
Hepworth J & I School
HOLM/MEL HD9 .... 255 G5
Heybrook CP School
WHIT OL12 .... 206 C5
Highbank First School
LVSG WF15 .... 171 K1
Highburton First School
KBTN HD8 .... 216 A6
Highcliffe Industrial Estate
MOR LS27 .... 152 B1
High Crags First School
SHPY BD18 .... 82 E8
High Crompton St Marys
CE School
ROY/SHW OL2 .... 229 H6
High Fernley First School
LM/WK BD12 .... 148 E3
Highfield Middle School
KGHY BD21 .... 2 D4
Highfield Primary School
AL/HA/HU LS17 .... 88 A2
Highfield School
OSS WF5 .... 174 F5
The Highfields Medical Centre
BRAM LS13 .... 107 M4
Highfields School
HUD HD1 .... 14 D4
Highfields Special School
HUD HD1 .... 14 D4
Highlander Sports Centre
KBTN HD8 .... 216 D3
High Royds Hospital
ILK LS29 .... 61 K4
Hightown School
LVSG WF15 .... 171 L1
High Trees School
BSPA/BRAM LS23 .... 49 G8
Hillcrest Primary School
CHAL LS7 .... 7 M1
Hillside Works Industrial Estate
CLECK BD19 .... 149 M4
Hill Top CE First School
LM/WK BD12 .... 126 E8
Hill Top Infant School
EARD/LOFT WF3 .... 174 F1
Hinchliffe Mill County School
HOLM/MEL HD9 .... 253 L4
Hipperholme Clinic
HIPP HX3 .... 147 M6
Hipperholme Grammar School
HIPP HX3 .... 147 L5
Hipperholme & Lightcliffe
High School
HIPP HX3 .... 148 B7
HM Prison
BSPA/BRAM LS23 .... 49 J4
WKFDW/WTN WF2 .... 12 B2
HM Prison Service College
WKFDW/WTN WF2 .... 12 C2
HM Young Offender Institution
WBY LS22 .... 30 D7
Hockney Road Industrial Estate
GIR BD8 .... 104 D6
IDLE BD10 .... 105 K1
Holgate Secondary School
BSLY S70 .... 260 E5
Hollingwood First School
GTHN BD7 .... 126 A3

Hollingworth Lake
Caravan Park
LIT OL15 .... 207 L5
Hollingworth Lake
Country Park
LIT OL15 .... 207 L4
Hollybank Natural
Health Centre
HUDW HD3 .... 191 K5
Hollywood Bowl
BULY LS4 .... 108 F5
Holmefield First School
BOW BD4 .... 128 B2
Holme J & I School
HOLM/MEL HD9 .... 253 G5
Holme Middle School
BOW BD4 .... 127 M3
Holme Mills Industrial Estate
MAR/SLWT HD7 .... 213 H2
Holme Valley Business Park
HUDS HD4 .... 214 A6
Holme Valley Clinic
HOLM/MEL HD9 .... 236 B1
Holme Wood Health Centre
BOW BD4 .... 128 A3
Holmfield Industrial Estate
LUD/ILL HX2 .... 124 C7
Holmfirth Craft Market
HOLM/MEL HD9 .... 254 B1
Holmfirth J & I School
HOLM/MEL HD9 .... 254 C2
Holmfirth Secondary School
HOLM/MEL HD9 .... 236 E6
Holmfirth Swimming Pool
HOLM/MEL HD9 .... 236 D7
Holycroft First School
KGHY BD21 .... 2 E7
Holy Cross Deanery
CE Primary School
BSLYN/ROY S71 .... 243 K8
Holy Family Primary School
ROCH OL11 .... 228 C3
Holy Family RC Primary School
WOR/ARM LS12 .... 108 F7
Holy Family & St Michaels
RC Primary School
PONT WF8 .... 181 J5
Holy Family School
KGHY BD21 .... 2 D1
Holy Name RC Primary School
BEE/HOL LS11 .... 131 G4
Holy Rood RC Primary School
BSLY S70 .... 260 E6
Holy Rosary & St Annes
RC Primary School
CHAL LS7 .... 7 K3
Holy Trinity CE First School
BGLY BD16 .... 81 J4
Holy Trinity CE J & I School
OSS WF5 .... 174 F8
Holy Trinity CE Primary School
BHP/TINH LS16 .... 85 M1
Holy Trinity CE Senior School
LUD/ILL HX2 .... 124 B8
Holy Trinity Infant School
HFAX HX1 .... 10 E8
Holy Trinity Junior School
HFAX HX1 .... 10 E8
Holywell Green Primary School
GTL/HWG HX4 .... 190 D2
Homestead Clinic
WKFDW/WTN WF2 .... 176 B8
Honley Business Centre
HOLM/MEL HD9 .... 236 C2
Honley CE Infant School
HOLM/MEL HD9 .... 236 B2
Honley CE Junior School
HOLM/MEL HD9 .... 236 B2
Honley High School
HOLM/MEL HD9 .... 236 C1
Hopton Junior Infant &
Nursery School
MIRF WF14 .... 194 B2
Hopwood Hall College
WHIT OL12 .... 206 A7
Horbury Junction
Industrial Estate
HOR/CROF WF4 .... 197 L6
Horbury Junior School
HOR/CROF WF4 .... 197 L5
Horbury Primary School
HOR/CROF WF4 .... 197 L5
The Horsefair Centre
WBY LS22 .... 48 A1
Horsfall Stadium
WBSY BD6 .... 126 D7
Horsforth Golf Club
HORS LS18 .... 85 H3
Horsforth Hall Park Cricket Club
HORS LS18 .... 86 A6
Horsforth Newlaithes
Junior School
HORS LS18 .... 85 J3
Horsforth School
HORS LS18 .... 85 K4
Horsforth Village Museum
HORS LS18 .... 85 J6
Horsforth Woodside
CE Primary School
HORS LS18 .... 85 M5
Horton Bank Top First School
GTHN BD7 .... 126 A4
Horton Park First School
WBOW BD5 .... 126 D2
Hothfield Street Junior School
AIRE BD20 .... 35 M5
Hot Shots Ten Pin Bowl & Bar
HUD HD1 .... 14 E9
Hovingham Primary School
RHAY LS8 .... 110 C2
Howards CE J & I School
FEA/AMT WF7 .... 202 D7
Howden Clough High School
BTLY WF17 .... 151 K5
Howden Clough
Industrial Estate
BTLY WF17 .... 151 K3

Howland Centre
EARL WF12 .... 173 L6
Howley Hall Golf Club
MOR LS27 .... 152 A7
Howley Park Trading Estate
MOR LS27 .... 152 C4
Hoyers Industrial Estate
HUD HD1 .... 192 F5
Hoyle Court First School
BAIL BD17 .... 83 G3
Hoyle Head Mills
Industrial Estate
EARL WF12 .... 174 B7
Huddersfield Art Gallery
HUD HD1 .... 15 G5
Huddersfield Crematorium
HUDN HD2 .... 170 C8
Huddersfield Giants RLFC
(Alfred McAlpine Stadium)
HUDE HD5 .... 15 K3
Huddersfield Golf Club
(Fixby Hall)
HUDN HD2 .... 192 A3
Huddersfield Lawn Tennis &
Squash Club
HUD HD1 .... 14 C4
Huddersfield New College
HUDW HD3 .... 191 H6
Huddersfield Royal Infirmary
HUDW HD3 .... 191 L6
Huddersfield RUFC
HUDS HD4 .... 214 A6
Huddersfield Sports Centre
HUD HD1 .... 15 H6
Huddersfield Technical College
HOLM/MEL HD9 .... 236 C8
HUD HD1 .... 14 E6
HUDN HD2 .... 192 F4
HUDS HD4 .... 214 B4
Huddersfield Town FC
(Alfred McAlpine Stadium)
HUDE HD5 .... 15 K3
Huddersfield University
HUD HD1 .... 15 G6
Huddersfield University Annexe
HUD HD1 .... 14 D5
Hudds School of Theatre
HUDS HD4 .... 214 A6
Hugh Gaitskell Primary School
BEE/HOL LS11 .... 131 G4
Hungate Primary School
GFTH/SHER LS25 .... 116 A6
Hunningley Primary School
BSLY S70 .... 262 A7
Hunslet Business Park
MID LS10 .... 9 L6
Hunslet Carr Primary School
MID LS10 .... 132 A4
Hunslet Hall Shopping Centre
BEE/HOL LS11 .... 8 F8
Hunslet Health Centre
MID LS10 .... 9 M8
Hunslet Moor Primary School
BEE/HOL LS11 .... 9 G9
Hunslet St Josephs
RC Primary School
MID LS10 .... 9 L7
Hunslet St Marys
CE Primary School
MID LS10 .... 9 L9
Hunslet Trading Estate
MID LS10 .... 132 B3
Hutton J & I School
IDLE BD10 .... 105 L1
Hutton Middle School
ECHL BD2 .... 105 L1
Hyde Park Picture House
HDGY LS6 .... 109 G3
Hyrstmount Junior School
BTLY WF17 .... 173 L3
Ida & Robert
Arthington Hospital
BHP/TINH LS16 .... 86 A4
Idle CE School
IDLE BD10 .... 83 K5
Idle Cricket Club
IDLE BD10 .... 83 K7
Idle Medical Centre
IDLE BD10 .... 83 K6
Ilkley Golf Club
ILK LS29 .... 20 B8
Ilkley Grammar School
ILK LS29 .... 38 E3
Ilkley Health Centre
ILK LS29 .... 38 E3
Ilkley Middle School
ILK LS29 .... 39 G2
Ilkley Swimming Baths
ILK LS29 .... 38 D1
Immaculate Heart of
Mary Primary School
AL/HA/HU LS17 .... 87 L5
Industrial & Commercial Centre
LDSU LS2 .... 7 K7
Ingfield Business Centre
HUDN HD2 .... 193 G3
Inglebrook School
PONT WF8 .... 180 F5
Ingram Road Primary School
BEE/HOL LS11 .... 8 A6
Ingrow First & Infant School
HWTH BD22 .... 79 J2
Intake High School
BRAM LS13 .... 107 J3
Ireland Wood Primary School
BHP/TINH LS16 .... 86 C2
Islamia Girls High School
HUD HD1 .... 214 A2
Iveson Primary School
BHP/TINH LS16 .... 86 C4
Jacksons Estate
OSS WF5 .... 175 G7
Jawbone Industrial Estate
RTHW LS26 .... 132 D7
Jerry Clay Lane Primary School
WKFDW/WTN WF2 .... 175 M4
Joe Dean Recreation Centre
WOR/ARM LS12 .... 108 B7

John Jamieson School
RHAY LS8 .... 110 C7
John O'Gaunts Trading Estate
RTHW LS26 .... 133 G7
John Smeaton High School
MSTN/BAR LS15 .... 112 A3
John Smeaton Sports Centre
MSTN/BAR LS15 .... 112 A2
John Street Market
BFD BD1 .... 4 E5
Joseph Priestley College
MOR LS27 .... 152 D2
Junction 25 Business Park
MIRF WF14 .... 194 B7
Junction 1 Retail Park
BEE/HOL LS11 .... 130 F4
Kayes First School
KBTN HD8 .... 240 F1
Keelham First School
CUL/QBY BD13 .... 124 B1
Keighley & Worth Valley Railway
KGHY BD21 .... 3 G3
HWTH BD22 .... 78 E7
HWTH BD22 .... 79 H4
KGHY BD21 .... 79 K3
Keighley Business Centre
KGHY BD21 .... 2 F8
Keighley College
KGHY BD21 .... 3 G4
KGHY BD21 .... 3 K3
Keighley Crematorium
HWTH BD22 .... 78 C3
Keighley Cricket Club
KGHY BD21 .... 3 H1
Keighley Golf Club
AIRE BD20 .... 57 K2
Keighley Industrial Park
KGHY BD21 .... 57 L5
Keighley Leisure Centre
KGHY BD21 .... 3 J2
Keighley Retail Park
KGHY BD21 .... 3 H1
Keighley RUFC
AIRE BD20 .... 57 K3
Keighley St Andrew's
Primary School
HWTH BD22 .... 2 D5
Kelbrook Primary School
BWCK/EAR BB18 .... 52 C1
Kendray Hospital
BSLY S70 .... 261 L6
Kendray Infant School
BSLY S70 .... 261 K7
Kendray Primary School
BSLY S70 .... 261 L7
Kensington Street
Health Centre
GIR BD8 .... 104 C6
Kents Sports Club
ECHL BD2 .... 105 J4
Kerr Mackie Primary School
RHAY LS8 .... 88 C7
Kershaw Drive Health Centre
LUD/ILL HX2 .... 144 F6
Kettlethorpe High School
WKFDW/WTN WF2 .... 198 E3
Kexborough Primary School
DOD/DAR S75 .... 241 K6
Kildwick CE Primary School
AIRE BD20 .... 35 G6
Killingbeck Retail Park
SCFT LS14 .... 111 H4
Killinghall First School
BFDE BD3 .... 105 L5
Kiln Hill Industrial Estate
MAR/SLWT HD7 .... 212 C6
King James School
HUDS HD4 .... 215 J4
Kingsgate Shopping Centre
HUD HD1 .... 15 G7
Kings High School
PONT WF8 .... 180 E7
The Kingstone School
BSLY S70 .... 260 D6
Kingsway Retail Park
MILN OL16 .... 206 F2
Kingsway West Business Park
MILN OL16 .... 228 C1
Kinsley Industrial Estate
HEM/SK/SE WF9 .... 223 L5
Kippax Health Centre
GFTH/SHER LS25 .... 135 K4
Kippax Infant School
GFTH/SHER LS25 .... 135 J5
Kippax Leisure Centre
GFTH/SHER LS25 .... 135 H5
Kippax North Primary School
GFTH/SHER LS25 .... 135 H2
Kirkburton CE First School
KBTN HD8 .... 216 B8
Kirkburton Cricket Club
KBTN HD8 .... 216 B8
Kirkburton Middle School
KBTN HD8 .... 216 C7
Kirk Fenton Primary School
TAD LS24 .... 94 E7
Kirkfields Business Centre
YEA LS19 .... 62 C7
Kirkgate Business Centre
WKFDE WF1 .... 13 H5
Kirkgate Market
LDS LS1 .... 7 H9
Kirkgate Shopping
Centre & Market
BFD BD1 .... 4 E6
Kirkhamgate Primary School
WKFDW/WTN WF2 .... 175 K4
Kirkheaton Cricket &
Bowling Club
HUDE HD5 .... 193 K5
Kirkheaton Primary School
HUDE HD5 .... 193 K5
Kirklees Light Railway
KBTN HD8 .... 239 K4
Kirklees Music School
HUD HD1 .... 14 F8
Kirklees Open Market
HUD HD1 .... 14 F5

Kirkroyd Infant School
HOLM/MEL HD9 .... 236 F7
Kirk Smeaton CE Primary School
PONT WF8 .... 204 F8
Kirkstall Abbey (remains of)
KSTL LS5 .... 108 B1
Kirkstall Health Clinic
KSTL LS5 .... 108 C2
Kirkstall Industrial Park
BULY LS4 .... 108 F5
Kirkstall Leisure Centre
KSTL LS5 .... 108 C2
Kirkstall Valley Primary School
BULY LS4 .... 108 E4
Knottingley CE (C) J & I School
KNOT WF11 .... 182 C2
Knottingley Vale J & I School
KNOT WF11 .... 181 M2
Knowle Spring Industrial Estate
KGHY BD21 .... 2 F9
LA Bowl
BEE/HOL LS11 .... 8 E4
Ladderbank Middle School
BAIL BD17 .... 83 G2
Lady Anne Business Park
BTLY WF17 .... 151 M8
Lady E Hastings
CE Primary School
BSPA/BRAM LS23 .... 49 G5
Lady Elizabeth Hastings
CE Primary School
WBY LS22 .... 47 J5
Lady Lane Park School
BGLY BD16 .... 81 J1
Laisterdyke Clinic
BFDE BD3 .... 105 M7
Laisterdyke Middle School
BFDE BD3 .... 105 M7
Lakeside Industrial Estate
WOR/ARM LS12 .... 108 A7
Laneshawbridge CP School
COL BB8 .... 52 F8
Langdale Primary School
RTHW LS26 .... 133 K7
Langthwaite Grange
Industrial Estate
HEM/SK/SE WF9 .... 246 F3
Lapage Middle School
BFDE BD3 .... 105 L6
Larks Hill Primary School
PONT WF8 .... 180 D8
Lascelles Hall Cricket Club
HUDE HD5 .... 215 L1
Last of the Summer
Wine Exhibition
HOLM/MEL HD9 .... 254 B1
Latchmore Industrial Park
WOR/ARM LS12 .... 130 E3
WOR/ARM LS12 .... 131 G2
Laura Mitchell Health Centre
HFAX HX1 .... 11 G5
Lawefield First School
WKFDW/WTN WF2 .... 12 B4
Lawns Park Primary School
WOR/ARM LS12 .... 130 A1
Lawnswood Business Park
BHP/TINH LS16 .... 86 C5
Lawnswood Cemetery
BHP/TINH LS16 .... 86 D3
Lawnswood Crematorium
BHP/TINH LS16 .... 86 D3
Lawnswood School
BHP/TINH LS16 .... 86 D6
Lawrence Batley Theatre
HUD HD1 .... 15 G7
Laycock First School
HWTH BD22 .... 56 E7
Leaventhorpe Middle School
WIL/AL BD15 .... 103 K7
Lee Bridge Industrial Estate
HFAX HX1 .... 10 D3
Lee Brigg First School
NORM WF6 .... 178 A3
Leeds & Bradford
Airport Industrial Estate
YEA LS19 .... 63 G5
Leeds Bradford
International Airport
YEA LS19 .... 63 H7
The Leeds Business Centre
MOR LS27 .... 152 A2
Leeds College of Art & Design
LDSU LS2 .... 6 E4
Leeds College of Building
LDSU LS2 .... 7 J7
Leeds College of Music
OSM LS9 .... 7 K9
Leeds College of Technology
BEE/HOL LS11 .... 131 J6
Leeds Community &
Mental Health Services
PDSY/CALV LS28 .... 107 G7
Leeds Community &
Mental Health Services
Teaching NHS Trust
WOR/ARM LS12 .... 109 G8
Leeds General Infirmary
LDSU LS2 .... 6 D7
Leeds Girls High School
HDGY LS6 .... 6 A1
Leeds Golf Centre
AL/HA/HU LS17 .... 66 E5
Leeds Golf Club
RHAY LS8 .... 88 F7
Leeds Grammar Junior School
AL/HA/HU LS17 .... 66 B7
Leeds Grammar School
AL/HA/HU LS17 .... 66 B8
HDGY LS6 .... 6 B5
Leeds & Hull Business Centre
BEE/HOL LS11 .... 6 E5
Leeds 27 Industrial Estate
MOR LS27 .... 151 M2
Leeds Industrial Museum
WOR/ARM LS12 .... 108 F6
Leeds Industrial Museum at
Armley Mills
BULY LS4 .... 108 F5

Leeds International
Swimming Pool
LDS LS1 .... 6 D9
Leeds Islamia Girls School
CHAL LS7 .... 87 M8
Leeds Metropolitan University
HDGY LS6 .... 86 A9
KSTL LS5 .... 108 B2
LDSU LS2 .... 6 F6
Leeds Plaza Shopping Centre
LDS LS1 .... 9 G1
Leeds Rhinos RLFC
(Headingley Stadium)
BULY LS4 .... 108 E2
Leeds Road Hospital
BFDE BD3 .... 5 L6
Leeds Road Retail Park
HUD HD1 .... 15 L2
The Leeds Teaching
Hospitals NHS Trust
BVRD LS3 .... 6 D8
Leeds Tykes RUFC
(Headingley Stadium)
BULY LS4 .... 108 E2
Leeds United AFC
(Elland Road)
BEE/HOL LS11 .... 131 G3
Leeds University
LDSU LS2 .... 6 C5
Lee Mills Industrial Estate
HFAX HX1 .... 10 E3
HOLM/MEL HD9 .... 254 F1
Lee Mills Industrial Park
HOLM/MEL HD9 .... 254 F2
Lee Mount County
Primary School
HIPP HX3 .... 10 C2
Lees First School
HWTH BD22 .... 79 J4
Leeside J I & N School
HECK WF16 .... 151 C8
Leisure Centre
BGLY BD16 .... 80 D6
Leopold Primary School
CHAL LS7 .... 7 L1
Lepton CE J & N School
KBTN HD8 .... 215 M4
Library Headquarters
WKFDW/WTN WF2 .... 12 B1
Lidget Green First School
GTHN BD7 .... 104 B8
Lidget Green Middle School
GTHN BD7 .... 104 B8
Lightcliffe CE Primary School
HIPP HX3 .... 148 A7
Lightcliffe Golf Club
HIPP HX3 .... 148 A6
Lightcliffe Preparatory School
HIPP HX3 .... 147 M6
Light Waves Sports Centre
WKFDE WF1 .... 12 F1
Lilycroft First School
HTON BD9 .... 104 D4
Limestone Trail
BRFD/BLYE BB10 .... 118 A8
Lindley County Junior School
HUDW HD3 .... 191 K5
Linthwaite Ardron Memorial
CE Primary School
MAR/SLWT HD7 .... 213 G5
Linthwaite Business Centre
MAR/SLWT HD7 .... 212 F5
Linthwaite Clough J & I School
MAR/SLWT HD7 .... 212 E5
Littleborough CP School
LIT OL15 .... 185 K7
Littleborough Cricket Club
LIT OL15 .... 185 K8
Little London CP School
CHAL LS7 .... 7 H4
Littlemoor Primary School
YEA LS19 .... 84 E2
Littleroyd Mills Business Park
HUD HD1 .... 214 C2
Little Theatre
HBR HX7 .... 143 J3
SKP/WHF BD23 .... 16 B3
Littletown J & I School
CLECK BD19 .... 172 C1
Littleworth Lane Infant School
BSLYN/ROY S71 .... 261 M3
Liversedge Cricket Club
LVSG WF15 .... 172 B4
Lobden Golf Club
WHIT OL12 .... 184 A7
Lofthousegate J & I School
EARD/LOFT WF3 .... 154 F8
Longcar Primary School
BSLY S70 .... 260 E6
Longclose Industrial Estate
OSM LS9 .... 7 M5
Longlands Trading Estate
OSS WF5 .... 175 G4
Long Lee J & I School
KGHY BD21 .... 3 M8
Longley Park Golf Club
HUD HD1 .... 15 J9
Longley School
HUDE HD5 .... 214 E2
Longley Tennis Club
HUDE HD5 .... 214 F2
Long Marston
CE Primary School
RYKW YO26 .... 33 J3
Longroyde Junior School
BRIG HD6 .... 170 B5
Lorne First School
BOW BD4 .... 127 K2
Lotherton Hall
GFTH/SHER LS25 .... 114 E1
Lounge Cinema
HDGY LS6 .... 108 F1
Low Ash First School
SHPY BD18 .... 82 F8
Lowerfields Middle School
BOW BD4 .... 127 L4
Lower Grange Medical Centre
GIR BD8 .... 103 L7

Lowerhouses CE J & I School
HUDE HD5 .... 214 F2
Lower Place School
MILN OL16 .... 228 D2
Lower Wortley CP School
WOR/ARM LS12 .... 130 D1
Lowfields Business Park
ELL HX5 .... 169 K6
Low Laithes Golf Club
OSS WF5 .... 175 K6
Low Mills Industrial Estate
DEWS WF13 .... 194 F2
Low Moor Business Park
LM/WK BD12 .... 127 G8
Low Moor CE First School
LM/WK BD12 .... 126 F8
Low Road Primary School
MID LS10 .... 9 M8
Lowtown Primary School
PDSY/CALV LS28 .... 107 H7
Luddendenfoot J & I School
LUD/ILL HX2 .... 167 G1
Luddenden Primary School
LUD/ILL HX2 .... 144 F6
Lundwood Medical Centre
BSLYN/ROY S71 .... 261 M4
Lupset Group Medical Centre
WKFDW/WTN WF2 .... 197 M3
Lupset Hall (Club House)
WKFDW/WTN WF2 .... 198 B4
Lydgate J & I School
BTLY WF17 .... 174 B1
Lydgate Special School
HOLM/MEL HD9 .... 236 F7
Lynfield Mount Hospital
HTON BD9 .... 103 M4
M1 Industrial Estate
MID LS10 .... 9 L8
Mackie Hill J & I School
HOR/CROF WF4 .... 219 M2
Madni Muslim Girls High School
EARL WF12 .... 173 M8
Magdale Industrial Park
HUDS HD4 .... 214 B8
Magnet Sports Club
TAD LS24 .... 71 L4
Malsis School
AIRE BD20 .... 34 B8
Mandale Middle School
WBSY BD6 .... 125 M6
Manningham Baths &
Sports Centre
GIR BD8 .... 104 D5
Manningham Clinic
GIR BD8 .... 4 C1
Manningham Middle School
GIR BD8 .... 4 C2
Manorfield Infant School
BTLY WF17 .... 173 J2
Manor House Gallery & Museum
ILK LS29 .... 38 E2
Manor Leisure Centre
YEA LS19 .... 62 C7
Manor Park Industrial Estate
BIRK/DRI BD11 .... 129 G7
Manor Street Industrial Estate
CHAL LS7 .... 7 L4
Manston Primary School
MSTN/BAR LS15 .... 111 L3
Manston St James
CE Primary School
MSTN/BAR LS15 .... 111 M3
Mantra House Business Centre
KGHY BD21 .... 2 F6
Manywells Brow
Industrial Estate
CUL/QBY BD13 .... 101 M3
Maple Industrial Estate
DOD/DAR S75 .... 242 F6
Mapplewell Health Centre
DOD/DAR S75 .... 242 D6
Margaret McMillan First School
HTON BD9 .... 104 C4
Margram Business Centre
HFAX HX1 .... 10 E5
Marley Mills Industrial Estate
KGHY BD21 .... 3 G6
Marriott Hollins Hall Hotel &
Country Club
GSLY LS20 .... 61 J8
Marsden County Junior School
MAR/SLWT HD7 .... 233 J2
Marsden Health Centre
MAR/SLWT HD7 .... 233 H2
Marsden Infant School
MAR/SLWT HD7 .... 233 J2
Marshfield First School
WBOW BD5 .... 126 E3
Martin Frobisher First School
NORM WF6 .... 178 B2
Matthew Murray High School
BEE/HOL LS11 .... 8 A7
Maybrook Industrial Park
WOR/ARM LS12 .... 8 A1
Meanwood CE Primary School
HDGY LS6 .... 87 G7
Meanwood Health Centre
HDGY LS6 .... 87 H8
Meanwood Park Hospital
HDGY LS6 .... 87 G5
Meltham CE J & I School
HOLM/MEL HD9 .... 235 G5
Meltham Cricket &
Athletic Club
HOLM/MEL HD9 .... 235 G3
Meltham Golf Club
HOLM/MEL HD9 .... 235 H5
Meltham J & I School
HOLM/MEL HD9 .... 234 E3
Meltham Mills Industrial Estate
HOLM/MEL HD9 .... 235 H4
Menston Cricket Club
ILK LS29 .... 61 K1
Menston Primary School
ILK LS29 .... 61 J2
Merrion Shopping Centre
LDSU LS2 .... 7 G7

Methley Infant School
RTHW LS26 .... 156 E4
Methley Junior School
RTHW LS26 .... 157 G3
Methley Park Hospital
RTHW LS26 .... 156 C3
Methley Road Industrial Park
CAS WF10 .... 157 K7
Methodist J & I School
WKFDW/WTN WF2 .... 12 E8
Metronomesports &
Leisure Complex
BSLYN/ROY S71 .... 261 J4
Micklefield CE Primary School
GFTH/SHER LS25 .... 114 C7
Middlestown Health Centre
HOR/CROF WF4 .... 196 D7
Middlestown Primary School
HOR/CROF WF4 .... 196 D7
Middleton Park High School
MID LS10 .... 153 M2
Middleton Park Leisure Centre
MID LS10 .... 153 M1
Middleton Park
Municipal Golf Club
MID LS10 .... 153 J1
Middleton Primary School
MID LS10 .... 153 K2
Middleton Railway
MID LS10 .... 131 L5
Middleton St Marys
CE Primary School
MID LS10 .... 153 L1
Mid Point Business Park
PDSY/CALV LS28 .... 106 B6
Mid Yorkshire Golf Club
PONT WF8 .... 204 A1
Mid Yorkshire Nuffield Hospital
HORS LS18 .... 85 M6
Milefield Primary School
CUD/GR S72 .... 245 H7
Miles Hill Primary School
CHAL LS7 .... 87 J7
Milestone School
PDSY/CALV LS28 .... 107 G4
Milford RUFC
KSTL LS5 .... 108 C2
Millbridge J & I School
LVSG WF15 .... 172 D2
Mill Dam J & I School
FEA/AMT WF7 .... 224 C1
Millennium Business Park
AIRE BD20 .... 35 L8
Mill Hill Community
Health Centre
HUDE HD5 .... 193 J7
Mill Lane J & I School
BTLY WF17 .... 173 M3
Milishaw Park Trading Estate
MOR LS27 .... 131 G6
Mill Trading Estate
BSLYN/ROY S71 .... 261 K5
Milnrow Cricket Club
MILN OL16 .... 229 H1
Milnrow Crossgates School
MILN OL16 .... 207 J7
Milnrow Health Centre
MILN OL16 .... 229 H1
Minerva Industrial Estate
RTHW LS26 .... 134 A7
Minsthorpe Community College
HEM/SK/SE WF9 .... 247 H2
Minsthorpe Swimming Pool
HEM/SK/SE WF9 .... 247 J2
Mirfield Parish Cricket Club
MIRF WF14 .... 172 D8
Mixenden Clinic
LUD/ILL HX2 .... 145 M2
Mixenden County Primary School
LUD/ILL HX2 .... 123 K8
Moderna Business Park
HBR HX7 .... 144 B6
Moldgreen J & I School
HUDE HD5 .... 15 L8
Monckton Road
Industrial Estate
WKFDW/WTN WF2 .... 198 C4
Monk Bretton Health Centre
BSLYN/ROY S71 .... 261 L2
Monk Bretton Priory
BSLYN/ROY S71 .... 262 A4
Monk Fryston
CE Primary School
GFTH/SHER LS25 .... 138 D6
Moor Allerton Golf Club
AL/HA/HU LS17 .... 67 G6
Moor Allerton Hall
Primary School
AL/HA/HU LS17 .... 88 B5
Moorfield Business Park
YEA LS19 .... 62 F8
Moorfield First School
BFDE BD3 .... 105 L7
Moorfield School
ILK LS29 .... 38 E3
Moorfield Shopping Centre
HUDS HD4 .... 213 M2
Moorhouse CP School
MILN OL16 .... 207 G8
Moorlands School
BHP/TINH LS16 .... 86 F5
Moorlands Small
Business Centre
CLECK BD19 .... 149 M5
Moor Lane Trading Estate
GFTH/SHER LS25 .... 116 D7
Moor Lodge Park
AL/HA/HU LS17 .... 67 J5
Moor Park Business Centre
WKFDW/WTN WF2 .... 12 B9
Moorside School
LUD/ILL HX2 .... 146 B2
The Moors Shopping Centre
ILK LS29 .... 38 C2
Moorthorpe Primary School
HEM/SK/SE WF9 .... 247 G3
Moortown Golf Club
AL/HA/HU LS17 .... 87 M1

Moortown Primary School
AL/HA/HU LS17 .... 87 M4
Moortown RUFC
AL/HA/HU LS17 .... 87 J1
Moorview Business Park
IDLE BD10 .... 83 G5
Morley Bruntcliffe High School
MOR LS27 .... 152 A2
Morley High School
MOR LS27 .... 152 B3
Morley Leisure Centre
MOR LS27 .... 152 B2
Morley Victoria Primary School
MOR LS27 .... 152 C2
Moslem School
BTLY WF17 .... 173 L2
Moss Industrial Estate
MILN OL16 .... 228 D1
Mountjoy House School
HUD HD1 .... 14 C5
The Mount J & I School
WKFDW/WTN WF2 .... 198 B3
Mount Osborne Industrial Park
BSLYN/ROY S71 .... 261 K5
Mount Pellon J & I School
HFAX HX1 .... 10 A4
Mount St Marys High School
OSM LS9 .... 9 M2
Mount St Marys
RC Primary School
OSM LS9 .... 110 C6
Mount Vernon Hospital
BSLY S70 .... 261 H8
Municipal Baths
BRIG HD6 .... 170 D4
Muslim Girls School
WHIT OL12 .... 206 A6
Myrtle Park Primary School
BGLY BD16 .... 81 H4
Mytholmroyd Health Centre
HBR HX7 .... 144 A5
Nab Wood Cemetery
SHPY BD18 .... 81 M6
Nab Wood Grammar School
BGLY BD16 .... 81 L7
Nab Wood Middle School
BGLY BD16 .... 81 L7
Napoleon Business Park
BOW BD4 .... 127 K1
National Coal Mining
Museum for England
HOR/CROF WF4 .... 218 A1
National Film Theatre North
LDS LS1 .... 9 H2
National Museum of
Photography, Film & Television
WBOW BD5 .... 4 E8
Neil Hunt Memorial Ground &
Rugby Club
BOW BD4 .... 127 L1
Nessfield First School
HWTH BD22 .... 2 A1
Netherfield Industrial Park
DEWS WF13 .... 195 G1
Netherleigh School
HTON BD9 .... 104 D4
Netherthong J & I School
HOLM/MEL HD9 .... 236 C6
Netherton Infant School
HUDS HD4 .... 213 M7
Netherton J & I School
HOR/CROF WF4 .... 197 G8
Newbarn Infant School
ROY/SHW OL2 .... 229 J8
New Barn Junior School
ROY/SHW OL2 .... 229 J8
Newbridge Industrial Estate
KGHY BD21 .... 3 J5
Newby First School
WBOW BD5 .... 126 F3
New College
PONT WF8 .... 180 D5
New Cross Street Health Centre
WBOW BD5 .... 126 F7
Newhaven Business Park
HUDW HD3 .... 213 J1
Newhey County School
MILN OL16 .... 229 J3
New Hold Industrial Estate
GFTH/SHER LS25 .... 113 J6
Newlands County Junior School
RPDN/SBR HX6 .... 167 G3
Newlands Industrial Estate
BAIL BD17 .... 82 E6
Newlands Primary School
MOR LS27 .... 152 F2
New Line Clinic
IDLE BD10 .... 84 A7
Newmillerdam Country Park
WKFDW/WTN WF2 .... 220 E4
New Park Spring
CUD/GR S72 .... 263 K2
Newsome High School
HUDS HD4 .... 214 B5
Newsome Junior School
HUDS HD4 .... 214 C5
Newspaper Office
BFD BD1 .... 5 G6
New Street Health Centre
BSLY S70 .... 261 G6
Newton Hill Primary School
WKFDE WF1 .... 176 E4
Newton Ings
CAS WF10 .... 158 D2
Nields Primary School
MAR/SLWT HD7 .... 212 B6
Ninelands Lane Primary School
GFTH/SHER LS25 .... 113 J4
Norcroft Industrial Estate
BFD BD1 .... 4 B6
Norland CE J & I School
RPDN/SBR HX6 .... 167 M4
Normanton CE First School
NORM WF6 .... 178 D4
Normanton Common First
NORM WF6 .... 178 E2

Normanton Freeston
 High School
 NORM WF6 .... 178 D5
Normanton Health Centre
 NORM WF6 .... 178 C5
Normanton Industrial Estate
 NORM WF6 .... 178 F3
Normanton Public Baths
 NORM WF6 .... 178 D4
Normanton Town
 Middle School
 NORM WF6 .... 178 C5
Norquest Industrial Park
 BTLY WF17 .... 151 J3
Norristhorpe Primary School
 LVSC WF15 .... 172 D4
North Bridge Leisure Centre
 HFAX HX1 .... 11 H4
Northcliffe Golf Club
 SHPY BD18 .... 82 A8
North Dean Business Park
 GTL/HWG HX4 .... 168 F6
North Dean RFC
 GTL/HWG HX4 .... 168 F7
Northern Ballet Theatre
 BHP/TINH LS16 .... 86 C6
 BRAM LS13 .... 107 M2
Northern School of
 Contemporary Dance
 CHAL LS7 .... 7 J2
Northfield J I & N School
 HEM/SK/SE WF9 .... 246 E3
The North Halifax
 Grammar School
 LUD/ILL HX2 .... 124 B8
North Leeds Cricket Club
 RHAY LS8 .... 88 C6
The North of England Higher
 Secretarial College
 LDS LS1 .... 7 G9
Northowram Hall Hospital
 HIPP HX3 .... 147 J2
Northowram School
 HIPP HX3 .... 147 J3
Northside Business Park
 CHAL LS7 .... 7 J4
Northside Retail Park
 CHAL LS7 .... 87 H7
Northwest Business Park
 HDGY LS6 .... 6 F3
North York Craven Institute of
 Further Education
 SKP/WHF BD23 .... 16 B2
Norton County J I & I School
 AWLS/ASK DN6 .... 227 L3
Norton Thorpe Hall School
 HUD HD1 .... 14 E5
Nortonthorpe Hall
 Special School
 KBTN HD8 .... 239 M5
Nortonthorpe Industrial Estate
 KBTN HD8 .... 239 M5
Norwood Business Park
 LM/WK BD12 .... 148 D4
Notre Dame Sixth Form College
 LDSU LS2 .... 6 E3
Nova Scotia Medical Centre
 CAS WF10 .... 157 J1
Oakbank School
 HWTH BD22 .... 79 H2
Oakdale First School
 SHPY BD18 .... 82 F8
Oakhill Primary School
 BSLYN/ROY S71 .... 262 A6
Oaks Business Park
 BSLY S70 .... 261 M5
Oaktree Business Park
 SCFT LS14 .... 89 J7
Oak Tree School
 FEA/AMT WF7 .... 224 B2
Oaktree Special School
 FEA/AMT WF7 .... 224 B2
Oakwell Business Centre
 BSLYN/ROY S71 .... 261 K5
Oakwell Hall
 BTLY WF17 .... 150 E3
Oakwell Industrial Park
 BTLY WF17 .... 151 H2
Oakwood Primary School
 RHAY LS8 .... 110 E3
Oakworth Health Centre
 HWTH BD22 .... 78 D4
Oakworth J I & I School
 HWTH BD22 .... 78 E4
Odeon Cinema
 BFD BD1 .... 4 E7
 BFDE BD3 .... 106 B6
 BSLY S70 .... 261 H4
 LDS LS1 .... 7 G8
 ROCH OL11 .... 228 A2
Old Bank J I & N School
 MIRF WF14 .... 172 C7
Old College of Technology
 BSLY S70 .... 261 G4
Oldfield First School
 HWTH BD22 .... 77 L6
Old Mill Business Park
 MID LS10 .... 132 B2
Old Rishworthians RUFC
 HIPP HX3 .... 168 C4
Old Roundhegians RUFC
 AL/HA/HU LS17 .... 88 A4
The Open University
 LDS LS1 .... 9 G1
Optimax Eye Clinic
 LDS LS1 .... 6 E8
Orchard Business Park
 HBR HX7 .... 144 A6
Orchard Croft Medical Centre
 HOR/CROF WF4 .... 197 K5
Orchard Head Primary School
 PONT WF8 .... 181 G2
Osmondthorpe Primary School
 OSM LS9 .... 110 H4
Ossett Cricket & Athletic Club
 OSS WF5 .... 196 F2

Ossett Dimplewell
 Junior School
 OSS WF5 .... 197 G2
Ossett Health Centre
 OSS WF5 .... 196 F1
Ossett School
 OSS WF5 .... 196 F3
Otley Golf Club
 OT LS21 .... 40 E8
Otley RUFC
 OT LS21 .... 41 K6
Otley Town FC &
 Old Otliensians RUFC
 OT LS21 .... 41 L6
Oulton Health Centre
 RTHW LS26 .... 133 L8
Oulton Park Golf Course
 RTHW LS26 .... 155 K2
Oulton Primary School
 RTHW LS26 .... 133 L8
Our Lady of Lourdes CP School
 HUDN HD2 .... 192 E2
Our Lady of Victories
 RC J & I School
 HWTH BD22 .... 2 B4
Outlane Golf Club
 HUDW HD3 .... 190 C7
Outlane J & I School
 HUDW HD3 .... 190 F5
Outwood Grange School
 WKFDE WF1 .... 176 C2
Outwood Ledger Lane
 J & I School
 WKFDE WF1 .... 176 D2
Overland Industrial Estate
 MOR LS27 .... 151 L1
Overthorpe CE J & I School
 EARL WF12 .... 195 L4
The Owlcotes Centre
 PDSY/CALV LS28 .... 106 F5
Owston Park Golf Club
 AWLS/ASK DN6 .... 249 L4
Owston Skellow First School
 AWLS/ASK DN6 .... 249 K4
Oxenhope CE First School
 HWTH BD22 .... 100 D3
Oxspring Primary School
 STKB/PEN S36 .... 271 K5
Oyster Park Infant School
 CAS WF10 .... 158 F5
Oyster Park Middle School
 CAS WF10 .... 158 F6
Packhorse Shopping Centre
 HUD HD1 .... 14 F7
Paddock Cricket &
 Bowling Club
 HUDW HD3 .... 213 L1
Paddock J & I School
 HUDW HD3 .... 213 M1
Painthorpe House Golf &
 Country Club
 HOR/CROF WF4 .... 219 M2
Pannal Golf Club
 PBR HG3 .... 27 G3
Pannal Primary School
 PBR HG3 .... 26 E2
Paragon Industrial Estate
 LIT OL15 .... 207 H3
The Park CP School
 COL BB8 .... 74 B1
Park High School
 COL BB8 .... 52 B8
Parkhouse Industrial Estate
 LM/WK BD12 .... 127 G8
Parkinson Lane School
 HFAX HX1 .... 10 C8
Park Junior School
 CAS WF10 .... 158 A7
Parkland First &
 Middle School
 IDLE BD10 .... 83 M7
Parklands County
 Primary School
 SCFT LS14 .... 111 J2
Parklands Girls High School
 SCFT LS14 .... 111 K2
Park Lane College
 HORS LS18 .... 85 H7
 LDSU LS2 .... 7 H8
Park Lane College of Further
 Education
 BVRD LS3 .... 6 C8
 CHAL LS7 .... 110 A1
Park Road J I & N School
 BTLY WF17 .... 173 M1
Park Road Medical Centre
 WBOW BD5 .... 127 G1
Park Road Retail Park
 PONT WF8 .... 180 E4
Parkside Industrial Estate
 BEE/HOL LS11 .... 131 L5
Parkside Middle School
 CUL/QBY BD13 .... 80 A8
The Park Special School
 WKFDW/WTN WF2 .... 12 C5
Park Spring CP School
 BRAM LS13 .... 107 L6
Park Wood Crematorium
 ELL HX5 .... 169 H5
Parkwood First School
 KGHY BD21 .... 3 J6
Parkwood Primary School
 KGHY BD21 .... 3 J6
Parkwood Street
 Industrial Estate
 KGHY BD21 .... 3 M4
Parl Lane College
 PDSY/CALV LS28 .... 107 G6
Pavilion Business Centre
 PDSY/CALV LS28 .... 107 H4
Pavilion Business Park
 WOR/ARM LS12 .... 130 C3
Pecket Well College
 HBR HX7 .... 121 K7
Pecketwell College
 HFAX HX1 .... 10 C5
Peel Mill Business Centre
 MOR LS27 .... 152 D2

Pellon Industrial Estate
 HFAX HX1 .... 10 B4
Penistone Grammar School
 STKB/PEN S36 .... 270 E1
Penistone Hill
 HWTH BD22 .... 78 C8
Penistone St Johns
 CE Infant School
 STKB/PEN S36 .... 270 E4
Penistone St John the
 Baptist CE Junior School
 STKB/PEN S36 .... 270 E4
Penistone Sports Centre
 STKB/PEN S36 .... 270 E2
Penistone Springvale
 Primary School
 STKB/PEN S36 .... 271 H3
Penistone Thurlstone
 Primary School
 STKB/PEN S36 .... 270 B2
Pennine Industrial Estate
 WOR/ARM LS12 .... 108 D7
Pennine Industrial Park
 HBR HX7 .... 143 J2
Penny Field School
 HDGY LS6 .... 87 H5
Penraevon Industrial Estate
 CHAL LS7 .... 7 H3
Pentland Infant School
 EARL WF12 .... 195 M1
Pentland Road Clinic
 EARL WF12 .... 173 M8
Percival Whitley College of
 Education (Halifax New College)
 HFAX HX1 .... 10 D7
Peter Laycock Industrial Estate
 CHAL LS7 .... 7 H3
Phoebe Lane Industrial Estate
 HIPP HX3 .... 168 F2
Phoenix Works Estate
 HOR/CROF WF4 .... 197 G5
Pickup Business Park
 PDSY/CALV LS28 .... 107 G4
Picturedrome
 Cinema & Museum
 HOLM/MEL HD9 .... 254 B1
Picture House Cinema
 CAS WF10 .... 7 K5
 KGHY BD21 .... 3 G4
 NORM WF6 .... 178 C4
 WKFDE WF1 .... 13 G1
Pictureville Cinema
 BFD BD1 .... 4 E8
Piece Hall Art Gallery
 HFAX HX1 .... 11 J6
Pilot Theatre
 CAS WF10 .... 158 B8
Pinderfield Hospital
 WKFDE WF1 .... 176 F5
Pinderfields &
 Pontefract Hospital NHS Trust
 EARD/LOFT WF3 .... 177 H5
Pioneer Business Park
 CAS WF10 .... 179 H2
Pitt Street Business Centre
 KGHY BD21 .... 3 K5
Playhouse & Film Theatre
 BFD BD1 .... 5 H7
Playhouse Theatre
 HFAX HX1 .... 10 F6
The Point Retail Park
 MILN OL16 .... 206 C7
Police Sports Ground
 RHAY LS8 .... 88 B7
Pollard Park Health Centre
 BFDE BD3 .... 5 J3
Pollard Park Middle School
 BFDE BD3 .... 5 M4
Pontefract Castle
 PONT WF8 .... 180 F5
Pontefract Crematorium
 PONT WF8 .... 180 C8
Pontefract & District Golf Club
 PONT WF8 .... 180 A5
Pontefract General Infirmary
 PONT WF8 .... 180 F6
Pontefract Museum
 PONT WF8 .... 180 C5
Pontefract Racecourse
 PONT WF8 .... 180 C5
Pontefract RFC
 PONT WF8 .... 203 H2
Pontefract Squash &
 Leisure Centre
 PONT WF8 .... 180 E5
Pontefract Swimming Pool
 PONT WF8 .... 180 E5
Pool CE Primary School
 OT LS21 .... 42 F7
Poplars Farm First School
 ECHL BD2 .... 105 G2
Potternewton Primary School
 CHAL LS7 .... 109 K1
Powerhouse Showcase Theatre
 WKFDE WF1 .... 12 D3
Priesthorpe School
 PDSY/CALV LS28 .... 106 D4
Priestley Centre
 BFD BD1 .... 5 H6
Priestman Middle School
 WBOW BD5 .... 126 E4
Priestthorpe First School
 BGLY BD16 .... 81 J3
Priestthorpe Medical Centre
 BGLY BD16 .... 81 H2
Primrose Hill High School
 OSM LS9 .... 7 M6
Primrose Hill Primary School
 PDSY/CALV LS28 .... 106 F5
Primrose Lane Primary School
 BSPA/BRAM LS23 .... 48 F7
Prince Henrys Grammar School
 OT LS21 .... 41 J5
Prince of Wales Business Park
 BRIC HD6 .... 170 D4
Princes Mary Campus
 (Halifax New College)
 HFAX HX1 .... 10 C7

Princess Mary Stadium
 CLECK BD19 .... 172 B1
Princess Royal Health Centre
 HUD HD1 .... 14 D7
Princeville First School
 GTHN BD7 .... 104 D7
Princeville Road
 Industrial Estate
 GIR BD8 .... 104 C7
Priory Business Park
 HEM/SK/SE WF9 .... 223 K2
Prospect Business Centre
 HUD HD1 .... 14 E8
Public Baths &
 Recreation Centre
 BTLY WF17 .... 173 L1
Public Health Laboratory
 Service Seacroft Hospital
 SCFT LS14 .... 111 H4
Pudsey Business Centre
 PDSY/CALV LS28 .... 107 H7
Pudsey Grangefield School
 PDSY/CALV LS28 .... 107 G6
Pudsey Greenside J & I School
 PDSY/CALV LS28 .... 106 F8
Pudsey Leisure Centre
 PDSY/CALV LS28 .... 107 G7
Pudsey St Lawrence
 Cricket Club
 PDSY/CALV LS28 .... 106 F7
Pudsey Tyersal Primary School
 BOW BD4 .... 128 E1
Pugneys Country Park
 WKFDW/WTN WF2 .... 198 D5
Purlwell Infant School
 BTLY WF17 .... 173 K2
Python Industrial Estate
 LIT OL15 .... 185 L8
QBM Business Park
 BTLY WF17 .... 151 H4
Q F Industrial Estate
 BOW BD4 .... 127 K2
Quality Foods Industrial Park
 BOW BD4 .... 127 M1
Quarry Hill Industrial Estate
 HOR/CROF WF4 .... 197 G5
Quarry House
 OSM LS9 .... 7 K9
Quarry Mount Primary School
 HDGY LS6 .... 6 D1
Queen Elizabeth Grammar School
 WKFDE WF1 .... 176 D7
Queensbury Golf Club
 CUL/QBY BD13 .... 125 H6
Queensbury Health Centre
 CUL/QBY BD13 .... 124 F5
Queensbury School
 CUL/QBY BD13 .... 125 G6
Queensgate Market
 HUD HD1 .... 15 G3
Queens Mill Business Centre
 HUD HD1 .... 214 C2
Queens Mill Industrial Estate
 HUD HD1 .... 214 C2
Queens Road Clinic
 BSLYN/ROY S71 .... 261 K1
Queens Road School
 HFAX HX1 .... 10 A5
Queens Sports Club
 HFAX HX1 .... 10 E9
Queen Street Infant School
 MOR LS27 .... 152 C2
Queen Street J & I School
 NORM WF6 .... 178 D4
Queensway CP School
 ROCH OL11 .... 228 B3
Queensway Primary School
 GSLY LS20 .... 62 C6
Raglan Industrial Estate
 CAS WF10 .... 157 K6
Railwaymens Sports Club
 BSLYN/ROY S71 .... 244 A2
Ralph Thoresby High School
 BHP/TINH LS16 .... 86 B2
Ralph Williams Clinic
 WHIT OL12 .... 206 E3
Ramgarhia Sikh Sports Centre
 CHAL LS7 .... 7 J4
Rastrick High School
 BRIG HD6 .... 170 B5
Rastrick Squash Centre
 BRIG HD6 .... 170 C5
Ravensbridge Industrial Estate
 DEWS WF13 .... 173 H8
Ravenscliffe First School
 IDLE BD10 .... 106 A2
Ravenscliffe High School
 HIPP HX3 .... 168 D4
Ravensthorpe CE Junior School
 DEWS WF13 .... 194 F1
Ravensthorpe Infant School
 DEWS WF13 .... 172 F8
Rawdon CE Primary School
 YEA LS19 .... 84 F3
Rawdon Cricket Club
 YEA LS19 .... 84 E2
Rawdon Golf &
 Lawn Tennis Club
 YEA LS19 .... 84 C3
Rawfolds Industrial Estate
 CLECK BD19 .... 150 B8
Rawson J & I School
 HIPP HX3 .... 146 D4
Rawson Market
 BFD BD1 .... 4 D5
Rawthorpe Junior School
 HUD HD1 .... 15 M4
Raynville Primary School
 BRAM LS13 .... 108 A4
Redbrook Business Park
 DOD/DAR S75 .... 260 D1
Red Doles Industrial Estate
 HUD HD1 .... 192 E5
Redhill Infant School
 CAS WF10 .... 158 E6
Red House
 CLECK BD19 .... 150 D5

Red Ledge Business Centre
 HOLM/MEL HD9 .... 236 B5
Redledge Business Centre
 HOLM/MEL HD9 .... 236 D6
Reevy Hill Primary School
 WBSY BD6 .... 126 B5
Reinwood County J & I School
 HUDW HD3 .... 191 K7
Renji Chinese Medical Centre
 HUDN HD2 .... 192 D5
Revival Industrial Estate
 BOW BD4 .... 5 J9
Rex Cinema
 ELL HX5 .... 169 H8
Rhodesway School
 GIR BD8 .... 103 H8
Richard Dunn Sports Centre
 WBOW BD5 .... 126 F5
Richard Newman
 Primary School
 BSLYN/ROY S71 .... 243 H7
Richmond Building
 GTHN BD7 .... 4 C7
Richmond Hill Primary School
 OSM LS9 .... 110 D8
Richmond House School
 BHP/TINH LS16 .... 86 E7
Richmond Medical Centre
 OSM LS9 .... 9 M2
Riddlesden CE School
 AIRE BD20 .... 58 B4
Riddlesden Golf Club
 AIRE BD20 .... 57 K2
Riddlesden Infants School
 AIRE BD20 .... 58 B4
Ridings Business Park
 HFAX HX1 .... 10 A7
The Ridings School
 LUD/ILL HX2 .... 146 A3
Ridings Shopping Centre
 WKFDE WF1 .... 12 E5
RIFFA Business Park
 OT LS21 .... 43 H4
Rigton CE Primary School
 AL/HA/HU LS17 .... 26 A7
Ringway Industrial Estate
 HUD HD1 .... 14 E3
Ripponden J & I School
 RPDN/SBR HX6 .... 189 G1
Riverside Business Park
 BAIL BD17 .... 82 E6
 ILK LS29 .... 38 E1
 KBTN HD8 .... 239 M4
Riverside Industrial Estate
 EARL WF12 .... 173 L1
 HOR/CROF WF4 .... 197 G6
Riverside Junior School
 HBR HX7 .... 143 J4
Riverside Medical Centre
 CAS WF10 .... 157 K7
Riverside Primary School
 TAD LS24 .... 71 G2
Rochdale Curtain Theatre
 ROCH OL11 .... 206 D4
Rochdale Healthcare NHS Trust
 LIT OL15 .... 207 J1
 WHIT OL12 .... 207 G1
Rochdale Infirmary
 WHIT OL12 .... 206 A5
Rock Hill Sports Club
 CAS WF10 .... 158 C6
Rockley Mount Special School
 BSLY S70 .... 260 D7
Rodillian School
 EARD/LOFT WF3 .... 154 B4
Rodley Primary School
 BRAM LS13 .... 107 H4
The Rookeries Carleton
 J & I School
 PONT WF8 .... 181 H8
Rooks Nest Primary School
 WKFDE WF1 .... 176 E2
The Rose Hill Crematorium
 BSLYN/ROY S71 .... 262 C1
Rosemeade School
 HUDE HD5 .... 215 G1
Roseville Business Park
 RHAY LS8 .... 7 M4
Rossefield School
 HTON BD9 .... 104 C2
Rossett Business Park
 BRAM LS13 .... 107 J4
Rotherham Road Medical Centre
 BSLYN/ROY S71 .... 243 J8
Rothwell CE Primary School
 RTHW LS26 .... 133 G8
Rothwell Health Centre
 RTHW LS26 .... 155 G1
Rothwell Methley
 CP Infant School
 RTHW LS26 .... 156 E4
Rothwell Primary School
 RTHW LS26 .... 155 G2
Rothwell Sports Centre
 RTHW LS26 .... 155 G3
Rothwell West Junior School
 RTHW LS26 .... 154 F2
Roundhay Golf Club
 RHAY LS8 .... 88 E4
Roundhay Park Site
 RHAY LS8 .... 88 F7
Roundhay St Johns
 Primary School
 RHAY LS8 .... 88 E8
Roundhay School
 RHAY LS8 .... 88 C7
Roundhill Junior School
 KNOT WF11 .... 181 K1
Roundhouse Business Park
 WOR/ARM LS12 .... 8 B2
Roundwood Industrial Estate
 OSS WF5 .... 197 K1
Royal Armouries Museum
 MID LS10 .... 9 K3
Royal Halifax Infirmary
 HFAX HX1 .... 168 C1
Royal Industrial Park
 HFAX HX1 .... 10 E6

The Royal London
  Industrial Estate
  BEE/HOL LS11 .... **131** H5
Royal Park Primary School
  HDGY LS6 .... **109** G4
Royd Mill Business Park
  BRIG HD6 .... **170** D4
Royd Mount Middle School
  CUL/QBY BD13 .... **102** E8
Royds Hall High School
  HUDW HD3 .... **191** L8
Royds School
  RTHW LS26 .... **155** K4
Royston Clinic
  BSLYN/ROY S71 .... **243** L3
Royston High School
  BSLYN/ROY S71 .... **243** L2
Royston Meadstead
  Primary School
  BSLYN/ROY S71 .... **243** K3
Royston Midland J & I School
  BSLYN/ROY S71 .... **243** L2
Roystons John Baptist
  CE (A) Primary School
  BSLYN/ROY S71 .... **243** L3
Royston Summerfields
  Primary School
  BSLYN/ROY S71 .... **243** J2
Rspb Nature Reserve
  (Fairburn Ings)
  KNOT WF11 .... **158** F2
Rudgate Business Park
  RYKW YO26 .... **31** L1
Rushcroft CP School
  ROY/SHW OL2 .... **229** K6
Russell Hall First School
  CUL/QBY BD13 .... **125** G5
Rutland Industrial Estate
  WKFDE WF1 .... **13** G6
Ryan Middle School
  BOW BD4 .... **127** H3
Ryburn County
  Secondary School
  RPDN/SBR HX6 .... **167** G4
Ryburn Golf Club
  RPDN/SBR HX6 .... **167** L5
Rydings School
  WHIT OL12 .... **206** D2
Ryecroft First School
  BOW BD4 .... **128** B4
Ryecroft Primary School
  WOR/ARM LS12 .... **108** A8
Ryhill Industrial Estate
  HOR/CROF WF4 .... **222** C5
Ryhill J & I School
  HOR/CROF WF4 .... **222** C4
Ryshworth Middle School
  BGLY BD16 .... **59** G7
Sacred Heart Catholic
  Primary School
  BULY LS4 .... **108** D3
Sacred Heart
  RC Primary School
  MILN OL16 .... **206** E8
Sai Medical Centre
  GIR BD8 .... **104** E4
St Agnes PNEU School
  HDGY LS6 .... **86** B1
St Aidans CE First School
  KBTN HD8 .... **239** J5
St Andrew CE Infant School
  BRIG HD6 .... **170** C2
St Andrews CE Junior School
  BRIG HD6 .... **170** C3
St Andrews CE Primary School
  WHIT OL12 .... **207** G2
St Annes Cathedral
  LDSU LS2 .... **6** F8
St Annes RC School
  KGHY BD21 .... **2** F3
St Anthonys RC First School
  CLAY BD14 .... **125** M1
St Anthonys RC J & I School
  SHPY BD18 .... **83** H6
St Anthonys RC Primary School
  BEE/HOL LS11 .... **131** H4
St Augustines CE First School
  BFDE BD3 .... **5** J2
St Augustines
  CE Primary School
  HFAX HX1 .... **10** C4
St Augustines
  RC Primary School
  RHAY LS8 .... **110** C3
St Austins RC Primary School
  WKFDE WF1 .... **176** F7
St Barnabas CE School
  HTON BD9 .... **104** C2
St Bartholomews
  CE Primary School
  WOR/ARM LS12 .... **108** E7
St Bedes Grammar School
  HTON BD9 .... **104** C3
St Benedicts RC Primary School
  GFTH/SHER LS25 .... **113** H7
St Catherines Business Complex
  BRAM LS13 .... **107** M2
St Chads CE Primary School
  BRIG HD6 .... **170** A1
  BHP/TINH LS16 .... **86** C7
St Clares Roman
  Catholic School
  ECHL BD2 .... **105** M4
St Columbas RC Primary School
  BOW BD4 .... **127** M4
St Cuthberts & First Martyrs
  First School
  HTON BD9 .... **104** C4
St Cuthberts RC High School
  MILN OL16 .... **228** E5
St Edwards RC Primary School
  BSPA/BRAM LS23 .... **48** E6
St Francis of Assisi
  RC Primary School
  BEE/HOL LS11 .... **8** F9
St Francis RC First School
  ECHL BD2 .... **105** J2

St Francis RC Primary School
  MOR LS27 .... **152** B2
St George's Hall
  BFD BD1 .... **5** G7
St Giles CE VA Primary School
  PONT WF8 .... **180** F5
St Gregorys RC Primary School
  SCFT LS14 .... **111** M1
St Helens Junior &
  Infant School
  BSLYN/ROY S71 .... **261** M1
St Hildas School
  HOR/CROF WF4 .... **197** J4
St Ignatius RC Primary School
  OSS WF5 .... **196** F3
St James Business Park
  BFD BD1 .... **5** H7
St James CE J & I School
  HOR/CROF WF4 .... **198** A8
St James CE Primary School
  WBY LS22 .... **30** B8
  WHIT OL12 .... **184** E8
St James Market
  BFDE BD3 .... **5** J8
St James's University Hospital
  OSM LS9 .... **110** B4
St John Fisher RC High School
  DEWS WF13 .... **173** K5
St Johns Catholic School
  BSPA/BRAM LS23 .... **48** F7
St Johns CE Infant School
  DEWS WF13 .... **173** J6
St Johns CE J & I School
  WKFDE WF1 .... **176** D6
St Johns CE Primary School
  BRIG HD6 .... **171** G4
  RPDN/SBR HX6 .... **188** E5
St Johns CE First School
  BOW BD4 .... **127** M5
St Johns CE Primary School
  MAR/SLWT HD7 .... **212** F1
St Johns Health Centre
  HFAX HX1 .... **10** C1
St Johns RC Primary School
  ROCH OL11 .... **206** B8
St Johns Shopping Centre
  LDSU LS2 .... **7** G8
St Johns the Baptist
  Catholic Primary School
  NORM WF6 .... **178** D4
St John the Baptist
  CE Primary School
  BHP/TINH LS16 .... **86** E2
St John the Evangelist RC School
  WBSY BD6 .... **126** A5
St John with St Michael School
  WHIT OL12 .... **184** A1
St Josephs Catholic
  Primary School
  WBY LS22 .... **30** A8
St Josephs College
  HTON BD9 .... **104** C3
St Joseph's Primary School
  TOD OL14 .... **163** K1
St Josephs RC First School
  WBOW BD5 .... **126** F2
St Josephs RC J I & N School
  HUDE HD5 .... **193** H8
St Josephs RC Primary School
  CAS WF10 .... **158** A6
  DEWS WF13 .... **173** J4
  PDSY/CALV LS28 .... **107** H6
  PONT WF8 .... **180** E6
  TAD LS24 .... **71** L2
  TOD OL14 .... **141** J8
St Josephs RC School
  BGLY BD16 .... **81** J3
  HIPP HX3 .... **11** J3
  KGHY BD21 .... **2** E9
St Josephs RC Primary School
  BRIG HD6 .... **170** B1
St Lukes CE First School
  CLECK BD19 .... **149** K7
St Lukes Eccleshill
  CE First School
  ECHL BD2 .... **105** M2
St Lukes Hospital
  HUDS HD4 .... **213** L3
  WBOW BD5 .... **126** F2
St Malachys RC School
  LUD/ILL HX2 .... **146** A3
St Margarets CE Primary School
  HORS LS18 .... **85** K5
St Marys Catholic School
  ILK LS29 .... **38** F2
St Marys CE J & I School
  WKFDE WF1 .... **13** H3
St Marys CE Primary School
  DOD/DAR S75 .... **260** E4
  RPDN/SBR HX6 .... **166** E7
St Marys Hospital
  WOR/ARM LS12 .... **108** B6
St Marys RC Infant School
  HFAX HX1 .... **10** D7
St Marys RC J I & N School
  BTLY WF17 .... **173** K1
St Marys RC Primary School
  BFD BD1 .... **5** G5
  HORS LS18 .... **85** L5
  RTHW LS26 .... **155** H2
St Marys RC School
  ILK LS29 .... **61** J3
  LIT OL15 .... **207** J1
St Matthews
  CE Primary School
  CHAL LS7 .... **87** L7
St Matthews
  CE First School
  WBOW BD5 .... **127** G5
St Matthews Infant School
  DOD/DAR S75 .... **260** E4
St Matthews
  RC Primary School
  WIL/AL BD15 .... **103** K6
St Michael & All Angels
  CE Primary School
  COL BB8 .... **52** A6
  HIPP HX3 .... **125** M8

St Michaels CE Primary School
  HDGY LS6 .... **109** G1
St Michaels College
  BVRD LS3 .... **6** B6
St Michaels RC Secondary School
  BSLYN/ROY S71 .... **243** L7
St Nicholas RC Primary School
  OSM LS9 .... **110** F3
St Oswald's CE Primary School
  WBOW BD5 .... **126** E3
St Oswalds CE Junior School
  GSLY LS20 .... **62** A6
St Patricks RC J & I School
  HUDW HD3 .... **14** A2
St Patricks RC J & I School
  BTLY WF17 .... **151** G4
St Patricks R C Primary School
  ELL HX5 .... **168** F8
St Patricks RC Primary School
  OSM LS9 .... **110** C6
  WHIT OL12 .... **206** C3
St Paulinus RC J & I School
  DEWS WF13 .... **173** J7
St Pauls J & I CE School
  WKFDW/WTN WF2 .... **175** M6
St Pauls RC Primary School
  AL/HA/HU LS17 .... **87** J2
St Peter CE Primary School
  OSM LS9 .... **7** K8
St Peters Cathedral
  BFD BD1 .... **5** G5
St Peters CE J & I School
  BTLY WF17 .... **151** G4
St Peters CE Infant School
  RPDN/SBR HX6 .... **167** G3
St Peters CE School
  MILN OL16 .... **228** D1
St Peters RC First School
  BFDE BD3 .... **5** M6
St Philips CE First School
  WIL/AL BD15 .... **103** J4
St Philips RC Primary School
  MID LS10 .... **153** K1
St Saviours CE Junior School
  BTLY WF17 .... **151** J5
St Stephens CE Primary School
  KSTL LS5 .... **108** C2
St Stephens RC Primary School
  SKP/WHF BD23 .... **16** B2
St Stephens Special School
  WBOW BD5 .... **127** G3
St Theresas RC Primary School
  MSTN/BAR LS15 .... **111** L3
St Thomas A Beckett RC
  Comprehensive School
  WKFDW/WTN WF2 .... **199** G5
St Thomas CE Junior School
  FEA/AMT WF7 .... **201** L1
St Thomas's CE School
  MILN OL16 .... **229** K2
St Urbans RC Primary School
  HDGY LS6 .... **87** J5
St Walburgas RC First School
  SHPY BD18 .... **82** B7
St Wilfrids Catholic High
  (VA) School
  FEA/AMT WF7 .... **179** L4
St Williams RC Primary School
  GIR BD8 .... **104** C7
Salendine Nook High School
  HUDW HD3 .... **191** H7
Salford Industrial Estate
  TOD OL14 .... **163** J1
Saltaire First School
  SHPY BD18 .... **82** B6
Saltaire Medical Centre
  SHPY BD18 .... **82** B6
Salterhebble School
  HIPP HX3 .... **168** F3
Salter Lee School
  HIPP HX3 .... **147** H4
Salt Grammar School
  BAIL BD17 .... **82** B4
Sandal Castle
  WKFDW/WTN WF2 .... **198** F5
Sandal Endowed
  CE Junior School
  WKFDW/WTN WF2 .... **199** G6
Sandal First School
  BAIL BD17 .... **82** E3
Sandal Magna J & I School
  WKFDE WF1 .... **199** G6
Sandal Medical Centre
  WKFDW/WTN WF2 .... **198** E7
Sandal RUFC
  WKFDW/WTN WF2 .... **198** F7
Sandbeck Industrial Estate
  WBY LS22 .... **30** B7
Sandbeck Park
  Industrial Estate
  WBY LS22 .... **30** B7
Sandbeds Trading Estate
  OSS WF5 .... **174** F7
Sandhill Golf Club
  CUD/GR S72 .... **263** M6
Sand Moor Golf Club
  AL/HA/HU LS17 .... **65** L8
Sandylands Business Centre
  SKP/WHF BD23 .... **16** A3
Sandy Lane First School
  WIL/AL BD15 .... **103** J2
Savile Business Centre
  EARL WF12 .... **173** M7
Savile Park J & I School
  HFAX HX1 .... **168** C1
Savile Town CE Infant School
  & Nursery School
  EARL WF12 .... **173** L8
Savoy Squash Club
  KBTN HD8 .... **239** J4
Saxon Hall Leisure Centre
  MILN OL16 .... **206** E6
Saxton CE Primary School
  TAD LS24 .... **93** J8
Scaleber Park Hospital
  ILK LS29 .... **39** M6
Scammonden Sailing Club
  HUDW HD3 .... **211** H2

Scapegoat Hill Primary School
  MAR/SLWT HD7 .... **190** D8
Scarcroft Golf Club
  SCFT LS14 .... **67** K6
Scarr Hall
  BFDE BD3 .... **105** L5
Scarthingwell Golf Club
  TAD LS24 .... **94** A7
Scholemoor Cemetery
  GTHN BD7 .... **104** A8
Scholemoor Crematorium
  GTHN BD7 .... **104** A8
Scholes Cricket Club
  HOLM/MEL HD9 .... **254** F3
Scholes Elmete Junior School
  MSTN/BAR LS15 .... **90** A8
Scholes Primary School
  HOLM/MEL HD9 .... **254** F3
School Lane Health Centre
  DEWS WF13 .... **173** H5
Schreiber Business Centre
  WKFDE WF1 .... **13** H5
Scissett Middle School
  KBTN HD8 .... **239** M4
Scissett Swimming Baths
  KBTN HD8 .... **240** A4
Scotchman Middle School
  HTON BD9 .... **104** C4
Scotch Park Trading Estate
  WOR/ARM LS12 .... **108** F6
Scout Road County
  Primary School
  HBR HX7 .... **144** B6
SDH Industrial Estate
  RPDN/SBR HX6 .... **167** K3
Seacroft Clinic
  SCFT LS14 .... **111** K1
Seacroft Industrial Estate
  SCFT LS14 .... **89** K7
Seemore Shopping Centre
  OSS WF5 .... **174** F8
Selby Gas & Leisure Centre
  KNOT WF11 .... **159** L6
Seven Hills Primary School
  MOR LS27 .... **152** D2
Shade J & I School
  TOD OL14 .... **163** J3
Shadwell Medical Centre
  AL/HA/HU LS17 .... **88** A3
Shadwell Primary School
  AL/HA/HU LS17 .... **89** H2
Shafton Primary School
  CUD/GR S72 .... **244** E4
Shakespeare Primary School
  OSM LS9 .... **110** B5
Sharlston Primary School
  HOR/CROF WF4 .... **200** D2
Sharma Park Industrial Estate
  RHAY LS8 .... **7** L5
Shaw Business Park
  HUDE HD5 .... **15** K7
Shawclough CP School
  WHIT OL12 .... **206** A3
Shawcross Business Park
  EARL WF12 .... **174** B4
Shaw Cross Health Centre
  EARL WF12 .... **174** C3
Shaw Cross Infant School
  EARL WF12 .... **174** C3
Shaw House School
  HTON BD9 .... **104** C3
Shawlands Primary School
  BSLY S70 .... **260** E6
Shay Lane Infant School
  HOR/CROF WF4 .... **200** A5
Sheibarg Industrial Estate
  BOW BD4 .... **127** M2
Shelf Health Centre
  HIPP HX3 .... **125** L8
Shelley First School
  KBTN HD8 .... **238** C3
Shelley High School
  KBTN HD8 .... **239** G4
Shepley First School
  KBTN HD8 .... **238** A6
Sherburn High School
  GFTH/SHER LS25 .... **116** A8
Sherburn in Elmet Aerodrome
  GFTH/SHER LS25 .... **116** F8
Sherwood Industrial Estate
  EARD/LOFT WF3 .... **154** D3
Shibden Hall & Folk Museum
  HIPP HX3 .... **147** H6
Shibden Head First School
  CUL/QBY BD13 .... **124** E7
Shipley Baths
  SHPY BD18 .... **82** D7
Shipley CE First School
  SHPY BD18 .... **82** D8
Shipley College
  SHPY BD18 .... **82** C6
Shipley College of Education
  SHPY BD18 .... **82** B5
Shipley Golf Club
  BGLY BD16 .... **81** H5
Shipley Health Centre
  SHPY BD18 .... **82** C7
Shipley Hospital
  SHPY BD18 .... **82** C7
Shires Business Park
  GTHN BD7 .... **126** C2
Showcase Cinemas
  BTLY WF17 .... **151** K2
Sicklinghall Primary School
  WBY LS22 .... **46** D1
Siddal Infant School
  HIPP HX3 .... **169** H3
Siddal Junior School
  HIPP HX3 .... **169** G3
Sikh Leisure Centre
  HUDE HD5 .... **14** E8
Silcoates School
  WKFDW/WTN WF2 .... **176** A5
Silkstone Golf Club
  DOD/DAR S75 .... **259** L6
Silsden Cricket Club
  AIRE BD20 .... **35** M6

Silsden Golf Club
  AIRE BD20 .... **36** C5
Silsden Health Centre
  AIRE BD20 .... **35** M5
Silver Blades Ice Rink
  WBOW BD5 .... **4** C1
Silver Court Industrial Estate
  HUD HD1 .... **15** G5
Simpson Lane J & I School
  KNOT WF11 .... **181** M3
Sirdar Business Park
  WKFDW/WTN WF2 .... **176** A7
Skelmanthorpe Business Park
  KBTN HD8 .... **239** J4
Skelmanthorpe First School
  KBTN HD8 .... **239** K4
Skipton Castle
  SKP/WHF BD23 .... **16** C2
Skipton General Hospital
  SKP/WHF BD23 .... **16** B3
Skipton High School
  SKP/WHF BD23 .... **16** A1
Skipton Hospital
  SKP/WHF BD23 .... **16** A3
Skipton L M Sports Club
  SKP/WHF BD23 .... **16** B3
Skipton Parish Church School
  SKP/WHF BD23 .... **16** C3
Slaithwaite CE Primary School
  MAR/SLWT HD7 .... **212** A6
Slaithwaite Health Centre
  MAR/SLWT HD7 .... **212** C6
Slaithwaite Swimming Baths
  MAR/SLWT HD7 .... **212** C6
Smallbridge Health Centre
  WHIT OL12 .... **206** E3
Smallbridge Industrial Park
  MILN OL16 .... **206** D4
Smallbridge St Johns CE School
  WHIT OL12 .... **206** D2
Smallbridge School
  WHIT OL12 .... **206** D3
Smawthorne Infant School
  CAS WF10 .... **157** M8
Smeaton Industrial Estate
  PONT WF8 .... **227** G1
Smithy Bridge Primary School
  LIT OL15 .... **207** H3
Snapethorpe Junior School
  WKFDW/WTN WF2 .... **197** L2
Snaygill Industrial Estate
  SKP/WHF BD23 .... **16** B5
Soothill Cricket Club
  BTLY WF17 .... **174** A1
South Bradford Golf Club
  WBSY BD6 .... **127** G6
South Craven School
  AIRE BD20 .... **34** F8
South Crosland Junior School
  HUDS HD4 .... **213** M7
Southdale CE Junior School
  OSS WF5 .... **197** G4
South Elmsall Ash Grove
  J & I School
  HEM/SE WF9 .... **247** J2
South Elmsall Health Centre
  HEM/SE WF9 .... **247** H3
South Halifax High School
  HIPP HX3 .... **169** G4
South Hiendley J & I School
  CUD/GR S72 .... **222** F8
South Kirkby Common
  Road School
  HEM/SE WF9 .... **246** C2
South Leeds Business Park
  MID LS10 .... **9** J7
South Leeds Golf Club
  BEE/HOL LS11 .... **131** J7
South Leeds Sports Centre
  BEE/HOL LS11 .... **8** F6
South Leeds Stadium
  BEE/HOL LS11 .... **131** L6
Southmere First School
  GTHN BD7 .... **126** C3
South Milford Primary School
  GFTH/SHER LS25 .... **138** A3
South Ossett Infant School
  OSS WF5 .... **197** G2
South Parade Junior School
  OSS WF5 .... **197** H2
Southroyd Primary School
  PDSY/CALV LS28 .... **107** G8
South Side Aviation Centre
  YEA LS19 .... **63** G7
South View Business Centre
  GSLY LS20 .... **62** A4
Southview Business Park
  GSLY LS20 .... **62** A4
  GSLY LS20 .... **62** A7
South View Infant School
  YEA LS19 .... **62** D8
South View Junior School
  YEA LS19 .... **62** D8
South Yorkshire (Redbrook)
  Industrial Estate
  DOD/DAR S75 .... **260** C1
Sovereign Business Centre
  HUDS HD4 .... **214** B3
Sovereign Business Park
  MID LS10 .... **9** J5
Sowerby Bridge Clinic
  RPDN/SBR HX6 .... **167** J3
Sowerby Bridge CE Junior School
  RPDN/SBR HX6 .... **167** K2
Sowerby Bridge Cricket Club
  RPDN/SBR HX6 .... **167** J2
Sowerby Bridge High School
  RPDN/SBR HX6 .... **167** J1
Spa Baths
  BSPA/BRAM LS23 .... **49** H4
Spa Fields Industrial Estate
  MAR/SLWT HD7 .... **212** D5
Sparrow Hill Community School
  MILN OL16 .... **206** B7
Spenborough Industrial Estate
  LVSG WF15 .... **172** C4

Spenborough Moorend
  CE School
  CLECK BD19 .... 149 L5
Spenborough Whitcliffe Mount
  School
  CLECK BD19 .... 149 K6
Spen Trading Estate
  CLECK BD19 .... 150 B7
Spen Valley High School
  LVSG WF15 .... 172 C3
Spen Valley Industrial Park
  CLECK BD19 .... 150 A8
Spen Victoria Cricket Bowling &
  Athletic Club
  CLECK BD19 .... 150 B6
Spofforth Castle
  PBR HG3 .... 28 D3
Spofforth CE Primary School
  PBR HG3 .... 28 E4
Spring Bank Industrial Estate
  RPDN/SBR HX6 .... 167 J4
Springbank Junior School
  PDSY/CALV LS28 .... 106 F3
Spring Bank Primary School
  HDGY LS6 .... 108 F2
Spring Grove Primary School
  HUD HD1 .... 14 D8
Springhill High School
  MILN OL16 .... 228 E1
Spring Ram Business Park
  BTLY WF17 .... 151 J2
  DOD/DAR S75 .... 241 L4
Springwell Health Clinic
  WKFDW/WTN WF2 .... 199 J2
Springwood First School
  GIR BD8 .... 4 B2
Staincliffe CE Junior School
  BTLY WF17 .... 173 J3
Stairfoot Health Centre
  BSLY S70 .... 261 M7
Stairfoot Industrial Estate
  BSLY S70 .... 262 B6
Standard Industrial Estate
  ECHL BD2 .... 105 L3
Standbridge Primary School
  WKFDW/WTN WF2 .... 220 C1
Standedge Experience
  MAR/SLWT HD7 .... 232 F2
Stanley Grove J & I School
  EARD/LOFT WF3 .... 177 H3
Stanley Health Centre
  EARD/LOFT WF3 .... 177 G1
Stanley Mills Business Park
  MAR/SLWT HD7 .... 213 H2
Stanley St Peters J & I School
  EARD/LOFT WF3 .... 177 H1
Stanley Sports & Social Club
  EARD/LOFT WF3 .... 155 H8
Stanningley Industrial Centre
  PDSY/CALV LS28 .... 106 F5
Stanningley Primary School
  PDSY/CALV LS28 .... 107 H3
Stanningley RLFC
  PDSY/CALV LS28 .... 107 J4
Stansfield Hall CP School
  LIT OL15 .... 185 L6
Station Approach
  Business Estate
  ROCH OL11 .... 206 B8
Station Industrial Park
  LUD/ILL HX2 .... 144 F7
Station Road Industrial Estate
  GFTH/SHER LS25 .... 135 H7
Station Works Industrial Park
  KGHY BD21 .... 3 L4
Steed Court Business Park
  HEM/SK/SE WF9 .... 225 L6
Steeton Hallgatehouse
  GFTH/SHER LS25 .... 137 L3
Steeton Health Centre
  AIRE BD20 .... 56 C1
Steeton Junior & Infants School
  AIRE BD20 .... 56 F1
Steps Industrial Park
  HOLM/MEL HD9 .... 214 C8
Sterling Industrial Park
  CAS WF10 .... 158 B8
Stile Common Infant School
  HUDS HD4 .... 214 D3
Stile Common Junior School
  HUDS HD4 .... 214 C3
Stockingate Junior school
  HEM/SK/SE WF9 .... 246 C5
Stocks Lane First School
  CUL/QBY BD13 .... 125 K4
Stonegate School
  AL/HA/HU LS17 .... 87 J6
Stoney Lee Middle School
  BGLY BD16 .... 81 K8
Stoney Ridge Hospital
  BGLY BD16 .... 103 L1
Stoney Royd Cemetery
  HIPP HX3 .... 168 F1
Stoodley Pike Monument
  TOD OL14 .... 164 E1
The Strand Medical Centre
  ROCH OL11 .... 228 B4
Streethouse J & I School
  HOR/CROF WF4 .... 200 E1
Sues Health Centre
  BSLYN/ROY S71 .... 243 J6
Summerfield Primary School
  BRAM LS13 .... 107 H3
Sunday School
  HBR HX7 .... 121 K6
The Sunday School
  HBR HX7 .... 120 F8
Sunfield Medical Centre
  PDSY/CALV LS28 .... 106 F4
Sunny Hill House School
  WKFDW/WTN WF2 .... 176 A1
Surgery Savile Centre
  EARL WF12 .... 195 M4
Sutton County Primary School
  AIRE BD20 .... 55 L1
Sutton In Craven CP School
  AIRE BD20 .... 55 M1

Swain House Middle School
  ECHL BD2 .... 105 J2
Swillington Primary School
  RTHW LS26 .... 134 C4
Swinnow Primary School
  PDSY/CALV LS28 .... 107 J6
Swinnow Shopping Centre
  BRAM LS13 .... 107 J6
Swire Smith Middle School
  KGHY BD21 .... 3 K7
Sycamore Industrial Estate
  HECK WF16 .... 172 F4
Tadcaster Albion FC
  TAD LS24 .... 71 M3
Tadcaster Cricket Club
  TAD LS24 .... 71 L3
Tadcaster East Primary School
  TAD LS24 .... 72 A4
Tadcaster Grammar School
  TAD LS24 .... 70 F4
Tadcaster Sports &
  Leisure Centre
  TAD LS24 .... 71 L3
Tainton Park Trading Estate
  WOR/ARM LS12 .... 109 G8
Taison Industrial Park
  GTHN BD7 .... 126 B3
Takalani Dance Theatre
  RHAY LS8 .... 110 E2
Talbot Primary School
  RHAY LS8 .... 88 B5
Tandem Industrial Estate
  HUDE HD5 .... 193 M8
Tandle Hill Country Park
  ROY/SHW OL2 .... 228 C8
The Tandy Trading Estate
  BULY LS4 .... 108 E5
Tannery Business Park
  HIPP HX3 .... 147 J3
Tanshelf Industrial Estate
  PONT WF8 .... 180 C5
Tanyard Industrial Estate
  HUDW HD3 .... 213 L2
Temple Bank Special School
  HTON BD9 .... 104 A4
Temple Moor High School
  MSTN/BAR LS15 .... 111 K7
Temple Newsam
  MSTN/BAR LS15 .... 133 K1
Temple Newsam Country Park
  MSTN/BAR LS15 .... 111 K8
Temple Newsam Golf Club
  MSTN/BAR LS15 .... 111 H8
Temple Newsam Halton
  Primary School
  MSTN/BAR LS15 .... 111 J3
Tenterfields Business Park
  LUD/ILL HX2 .... 167 G1
Tetley Brewery Wharf
  MID LS10 .... 9 J2
Thackley AFC
  IDLE BD10 .... 83 J4
Thackley Cricket Club
  IDLE BD10 .... 83 K4
Thackley First School
  IDLE BD10 .... 83 K4
Thackray Medical Museum
  OSM LS9 .... 110 B4
Thomas Danby College
  CHAL LS7 .... 7 K4
Thomas Park Athletics Stadium
  WKFDW/WTN WF2 .... 12 A5
Thongsbridge Tennis Club
  HOLM/MEL HD9 .... 236 D6
Thornbury First School
  BFDE BD3 .... 105 M6
Thornbury Middle School
  BFDE BD3 .... 106 A6
Thorncliffe Park
  Industrial Estate
  GIR BD8 .... 4 D1
Thorncliffe Square
  Industrial Estate
  GIR BD8 .... 4 C1
Thornes Industrial Estate
  WKFDE WF1 .... 12 F6
Thornham St James CE Primary
  School
  ROY/SHW OL2 .... 228 F6
Thornhill High School
  EARL WF12 .... 196 A5
Thornhill J & I School
  EARL WF12 .... 195 M5
Thornhill Lees CE
  Infant School
  EARL WF12 .... 195 L2
Thorn Park School
  HTON BD9 .... 103 M2
Thornton Baths
  CUL/QBY BD13 .... 103 G8
Thornton First School
  CUL/QBY BD13 .... 102 F8
Thornton Lodge
  Health Centre
  HUD HD1 .... 214 B2
Thornton Medical Centre
  CUL/QBY BD13 .... 103 G8
Thornton Upper School
  CUL/QBY BD13 .... 103 K8
Thorp Arch Trading Estate
  BSPA/BRAM LS23 .... 49 J3
Thorpe First & Middle School
  BFDE BD10 .... 83 K6
Thorpe Primary School
  EARD/LOFT WF3 .... 154 A4
Three Lane Ends
  Business Centre
  CAS WF10 .... 157 J6
Throstle Farm J & I School
  KNOT WF11 .... 182 X4
Thrum Hall Industrial Park
  LUD/ILL HX2 .... 146 A7
Thurstonland Endowed
  Primary School
  HUDS HD4 .... 237 H4
Thwaite Mills Watermill
  OSM LS9 .... 132 D3

Tinshill Primary School
  BHP/TINH LS16 .... 86 A3
Tip Toes Complimentary
  Health Centre
  MILN OL16 .... 207 H8
Tockwith CE Primary School
  RYKW YO26 .... 32 B1
Todmorden Community College
  TOD OL14 .... 163 K1
Todmorden Cricket Club
  TOD OL14 .... 141 J8
Todmorden Golf Club
  TOD OL14 .... 141 L7
Todmorden Health Centre
  TOD OL14 .... 163 K1
Todmorden High School
  TOD OL14 .... 141 H8
Tolson Memorial Museum
  HUDE HD5 .... 193 G8
Tong Park First School
  BAIL BD17 .... 83 H2
Tong Sports Centre
  BOW BD4 .... 128 C6
Top Rank Theatre
  HFAX HX1 .... 11 G5
Towngate Primary School
  OSS WF5 .... 175 G8
Towton 1461
  TAD LS24 .... 93 K6
Tranmere Park Primary School
  GSLY LS20 .... 61 K6
Trawden CP School
  COL BB8 .... 74 E4
Treefield Industrial Estate
  MOR LS27 .... 151 M1
Trent Industrial Estate
  ROY/SHW OL2 .... 229 K6
Triangle Business Park
  BTLY WF17 .... 151 J3
Triangle CE Primary School
  RPDN/SBR HX6 .... 167 G5
Trinity Business Centre
  WKFDE WF1 .... 13 H4
Trinity Medical Centre
  WKFDE WF1 .... 12 F3
Tropical World
  RHAY LS8 .... 88 D5
Tuel Lane County
  Primary School
  RPDN/SBR HX6 .... 167 K2
Tulip Street Retail Park
  MID LS10 .... 131 M3
Tunshill Golf Club
  MILN OL16 .... 207 L8
Turnshaws Special School
  KBTN HD8 .... 216 C8
Tyersal Family Clinic
  BOW BD4 .... 106 B8
Tyersal First School
  BOW BD4 .... 127 M1
UCI Cinema
  HUDE HD5 .... 15 K3
Undercliffe Cemetery
  BFDE BD3 .... 5 K1
Undercliffe Cricket Club
  ECHL BD2 .... 105 L4
Undercliffe First School
  ECHL BD2 .... 5 L1
Union Business Centre
  ECHL BD2 .... 105 M2
University of Bradford
  GTHN BD7 .... 4 B7
University of Huddersfield
  HUD HD1 .... 15 G8
  HUDW HD3 .... 191 L5
  KBTN HD8 .... 215 L8
University of Leeds
  BHP/TINH LS16 .... 86 E5
  LDSU LS2 .... 6 C6
  LDSU LS2 .... 6 D4
  LDSU LS2 .... 6 E6
University of Leeds Trinity &
  All Saints College
  HORS LS18 .... 85 J3
University Sports Centre
  LDSU LS2 .... 6 D6
Upper Abrigg Special School
  HOLM/MEL HD9 .... 236 F8
Upperthong J & I School
  HOLM/MEL HD9 .... 254 A2
Upper Whitley J & I School
  HOR/CROF WF4 .... 217 G2
Upper Wortley Primary School
  WOR/ARM LS12 .... 108 D8
Upton ARLFC
  HEM/SK/SE WF9 .... 225 K6
Upton Clinic
  HEM/SK/SE WF9 .... 225 M6
Utley J & I School
  AIRE BD20 .... 57 K4
Valley Medical Centre
  HBR HX7 .... 143 J3
Valley Mills Industrial Estate
  IDLE BD10 .... 84 A6
Valley Road Business Park
  LVSG WF15 .... 172 C2
Vehicle Testing Centre
  BSPA/BRAM LS23 .... 49 J2
Venlo Industrial Estate
  BOW BD4 .... 127 L4
Victoria Baths
  ELL HX5 .... 169 J8
Victoria Centre
  EARL WF12 .... 173 L6
Victoria Industrial Estate
  ECHL BD2 .... 105 L2
Victoria Industrial Park
  SCFT LS14 .... 89 K6
Victoria Junior School
  RTHW LS26 .... 132 F8
Victoria Park School
  BRAM LS13 .... 108 A3
Victoria Primary School
  OSM LS9 .... 110 D6
Victoria Spring Business Park
  LVSG WF15 .... 172 B1
The Victoria Theatre
  HFAX HX1 .... 11 G6

Village Medical Centre
  LIT OL15 .... 207 K1
Vine Industrial Estate
  BRIG HD6 .... 170 B3
Vintage Railway Carriage Museum
  HWTH BD22 .... 78 E7
Wadsworth Old Town
  Primary School
  HBR HX7 .... 143 L1
Wainstalls School
  LUD/ILL HX2 .... 145 H1
Wakefield Art Gallery
  WKFDE WF1 .... 176 D7
Wakefield Cathedral
  WKFDE WF1 .... 12 F2
Wakefield City Baths
  WKFDE WF1 .... 13 G2
Wakefield City High School
  WKFDE WF1 .... 177 H7
Wakefield College
  CAS WF10 .... 157 K8
  FEA/AMT WF7 .... 201 M1
  HEM/SK/SE WF9 .... 224 A7
  WKFDE WF1 .... 12 C1
Wakefield Crematorium
  WKFDW/WTN WF2 .... 198 C8
Wakefield Girls High School
  WKFDE WF1 .... 12 D1
Wakefield Girls High
  School (Junior)
  WKFDW/WTN WF2 .... 176 C7
Wakefield Golf Club
  WKFDW/WTN WF2 .... 199 G8
Wakefield Independent
  Junior School
  HOR/CROF WF4 .... 201 H8
Wakefield Independent School
  HOR/CROF WF4 .... 201 G6
Wakefield 41 Industrial Park
  EARD/LOFT WF3 .... 176 B1
Wakefield Museum
  WKFDE WF1 .... 12 E2
Wakefield Music School
  WKFDE WF1 .... 12 D2
Wakefield RUFC
  WKFDE WF1 .... 176 E6
Wakefield Superbowl 2000
  WKFDE WF1 .... 13 L8
Wakefield Theatre Royal &
  Opera House
  WKFDW/WTN WF2 .... 12 C2
Wakefield Trinity Wildcats RLFC
  (Belle Vue)
  WKFDE WF1 .... 13 K8
Wakefield Tutorial
  Preparatory School
  MOR LS27 .... 152 C2
Walnut Business Park
  HFAX HX1 .... 10 C6
Walsden CE (e) Infant School
  TOD OL14 .... 163 K5
Walsden Cricket Club
  TOD OL14 .... 163 J6
Walsden Industrial Estate
  TOD OL14 .... 163 K7
Walsden Junior Mixed School
  TOD OL14 .... 163 J5
Walton Grove Infant School
  WKFDW/WTN WF2 .... 199 K7
Walton Junior School
  WKFDW/WTN WF2 .... 199 J7
Waltonways Cemetery
  SKP/WHF BD23 .... 16 A5
Waltonways Crematorium
  SKP/WHF BD23 .... 16 A4
Wapping First School
  BFDE BD3 .... 5 H3
Wardle High School
  WHIT OL12 .... 206 F1
Warley Road J & I School
  LUD/ILL HX2 .... 146 A8
Warley Town School
  LUD/ILL HX2 .... 145 K8
Warner Village
  BULY LS4 .... 108 E5
Warwick Road J & I School
  BTLY WF17 .... 173 L3
The Watergate Clinic
  MILN OL16 .... 206 B7
Waterloo Infant School
  PDSY/CALV LS28 .... 106 E7
Waterloo Junior School
  PDSY/CALV LS28 .... 106 E7
Waterside Industrial Estate
  COL BB8 .... 74 A2
Waterside Industrial Park
  OSM LS9 .... 132 D3
Watersports Centre
  LIT OL15 .... 207 K3
Water Street CP School
  SKP/WHF BD23 .... 16 B2
Waterton J & I School
  WKFDW/WTN WF2 .... 197 M2
Waterton Park Golf Club
  WKFDW/WTN WF2 .... 199 L8
Waverley Middle School
  GTHN BD7 .... 126 D1
Wax Museum
  BFD BD1 .... 4 D5
Weetwood Primary School
  BHP/TINH LS16 .... 86 A7
Wellgate Infant School
  DOD/DAR S75 .... 242 D5
Wellhouse J & I School
  MAR/SLWT HD7 .... 212 F3
Wellhouse Middle School
  MIRF WF14 .... 172 D7
Wellington Business Centre
  ELL HX5 .... 169 J7
Wellington First School
  ECHL BD2 .... 105 K3
Wellington Middle School
  ECHL BD2 .... 105 K3
Wellington Road
  Industrial Estate
  WOR/ARM LS12 .... 6 B9
Wellington Shopping Arcade
  BRIG HD6 .... 170 C4

Wellington Street
  Business Park
  CAS WF10 .... 157 L7
Well Lane Business Centre
  BTLY WF17 .... 173 L5
Wellwoman Clinic
  HFAX HX1 .... 11 G7
Westborough High School
  DEWS WF13 .... 173 J5
West Bowling Golf Club
  WBOW BD5 .... 127 J5
West Bradford Golf Club
  HTON BD9 .... 103 K3
West Bretton Primary School
  HOR/CROF WF4 .... 219 H6
Westbrook Lane Primary School
  HORS LS18 .... 85 J3
Westcliffe Medical Centre
  SHPY BD18 .... 82 C7
West End Golf Club (Halifax)
  LUD/ILL HX2 .... 145 L6
West End Industrial Estate
  MOR LS27 .... 151 M3
West End Middle School
  CLECK BD19 .... 149 K7
Westerton Primary School
  EARD/LOFT WF3 .... 152 F7
Westfield Industrial Estate
  YEA LS19 .... 62 C3
Westfield Medical Centre
  CHAL LS7 .... 109 H3
Westfield Primary School
  BVRD LS3 .... 6 A7
West Garforth Junior School
  GFTH/SHER LS25 .... 113 G8
Westgate Hill First School
  BOW BD4 .... 128 C7
Westgate Infant School
  OT LS21 .... 41 G7
Westgate Retail & Leisure Park
  WKFDW/WTN WF2 .... 12 C4
West Hall Special School
  EARD/LOFT WF3 .... 155 K8
West Leeds High School
  WOR/ARM LS12 .... 108 B7
Westmoor Junior School
  DEWS WF13 .... 173 H5
West Oaks School
  BSPA/BRAM LS23 .... 48 E7
West Park Bramhope RUFC
  BHP/TINH LS16 .... 64 C5
West Riding Magistrates Court
  BTLY WF17 .... 151 G5
Westroyd Infant School
  PDSY/CALV LS28 .... 106 F4
West Side Retail Park
  GSLY LS20 .... 62 B7
West Street County J & I School
  COL BB8 .... 74 A2
West Vale J & I School
  GTL/HWG HX4 .... 168 F7
Westville House
  Preparatory School
  ILK LS29 .... 20 F7
Westwood Primary School
  MID LS10 .... 153 G2
West Yorkshire College of
  Health Studies
  WKFDE WF1 .... 177 G7
West Yorkshire
  Industrial Estate
  BOW BD4 .... 127 M5
West Yorkshire Playhouse
  OSM LS9 .... 7 K9
West Yorkshire Retail Park
  BTLY WF17 .... 151 K2
West Yorks Police HQ
  WKFDE WF1 .... 12 D1
Wetherby Business Park
  WBY LS22 .... 30 B5
Wetherby Golf Club
  WBY LS22 .... 47 L2
Wetherby High School
  WBY LS22 .... 48 B1
Wetherby Leisure Centre
  WBY LS22 .... 48 A2
Wetherby Racecourse
  WBY LS22 .... 30 E8
Wharfebank Business Centre
  OT LS21 .... 41 G7
Wharfedale Business Park
  BOW BD4 .... 127 M5
Wharfedale General Hospital
  OT LS21 .... 41 H4
The Whartons Primary School
  OT LS21 .... 41 J4
Wheatsheaf Shopping Centre
  MILN OL16 .... 206 B6
Wheldon Infant School
  CAS WF10 .... 158 A6
Whetley Middle School
  GIR BD8 .... 104 C6
Whinburn Residential School
  AIRE BD20 .... 57 H4
Whingate Business Centre
  WOR/ARM LS12 .... 108 C7
Whingate Business Park
  WOR/ARM LS12 .... 108 D7
Whingate Primary School
  WOR/ARM LS12 .... 108 C7
Whitebridge Primary School
  MSTN/BAR LS15 .... 111 G7
Whitechapel Middle School
  CLECK BD19 .... 149 L5
Whitecote Primary School
  BRAM LS13 .... 107 L2
Whitehall Industrial Estate
  WOR/ARM LS12 .... 130 B2
Whitehall Trading Estate
  WOR/ARM LS12 .... 130 A2
Whitehill County Infant School
  LUD/ILL HX2 .... 124 A3
White Horse Leisure Centre
  WKFDE WF1 .... 12 D3
White Laith Primary School
  SCFT LS14 .... 89 L7

White Rose House
  WKFDE WF1 .... **12** F4
White Rose Shopping Centre
  MOR LS27 .... **131** G7
Whitkirk Medical Centre
  MSTN/BAR LS15 .... **111** M6
Whitkirk Primary School
  MSTN/BAR LS15 .... **111** K7
Whittaker Golf Club
  LIT OL15 .... **207** M2
Whitwood Business Centre
  CAS WF10 .... **157** J6
Whitwood Golf Club
  CAS WF10 .... **157** G8
Wibsey First School
  WBSY BD6 .... **126** D5
Wibsey Middle School
  WBSY BD6 .... **126** D5
Wiggan Lane Trading Estate
  HUDN HD2 .... **192** F2
Wigton Moor Primary School
  AL/HA/HU LS17 .... **88** B1
Wilberlee J & I School
  MAR/SLWT HD7 .... **211** M4
William Henry Smith School
  BRIG HD6 .... **170** A6
Willow Industrial Complex
  RPDN/SBR HX6 .... **167** K3
The Willows Medical Centre
  CUL/QBY BD13 .... **125** G5
Willow Valley Golf &
  Country Club
  BRIG HD6 .... **171** G1
Wilsden Primary School
  WIL/AL BD15 .... **102** E1
Wilthorpe Infant School
  DOD/DAR S75 .... **260** E2

Wilthorpe Junior School
  DOD/DAR S75 .... **260** E2
Windhill CE First School
  SHPY BD18 .... **82** F6
Windhill Cricket Club
  SHPY BD18 .... **82** F5
Windhill Green Medical Centre
  SHPY BD18 .... **82** E6
Windmill Primary School
  MID LS10 .... **132** A6
Windsor Medical Centre
  EARL WF12 .... **174** A6
Wira Business Park
  BHP/TINH LS16 .... **86** B5
Withinfields J & I School
  HIPP HX3 .... **169** H1
Womersley CE Primary School
  AWLS/ASK DN6 .... **205** H3
Woodbank Special School
  LUD/ILL HX2 .... **145** G6
Woodhall Hills Golf Club
  PDSY/CALV LS28 .... **106** B2
Woodhill Middle School
  SHPY BD18 .... **82** F5
Woodhouse Business Centre
  NORM WF6 .... **178** C5
Woodhouse Cricket Club
  CHAL LS7 .... **87** H8
Woodhouse First School
  NORM WF6 .... **178** C6
Woodhouse Grove School
  IDLE BD10 .... **84** B5
Woodhouse Health Centre
  HDGY LS6 .... **6** F3
Woodhouse Primary School
  BRIG HD6 .... **170** D6
Woodkirk High School
  EARD/LOFT WF3 .... **152** E5

Woodland Glade Leisure Centre
  HUDN HD2 .... **192** F1
Woodlands CE First School
  LM/WK BD12 .... **149** J1
Woodlands Cricket Club
  LM/WK BD12 .... **149** H1
Woodlands Primary School
  OSM LS9 .... **110** D3
Woodroyd Industrial Estate
  LM/WK BD12 .... **149** G1
Woodroyd Middle School
  WBOW BD5 .... **127** C3
Woodside Clinic
  WBSY BD6 .... **126** C8
Woodside First School
  WBSY BD6 .... **126** C8
Woodside Middle School
  WBSY BD6 .... **126** C8
Woodside Trading Estate
  HORS LS18 .... **86** A5
Woodsley Health Centre
  HDGY LS6 .... **6** A5
Woodsome Hall Golf Club
  KBTN HD8 .... **215** K5
Wooldale Junior School
  HOLM/MEL HD9 .... **236** F7
Woolley Hall College
  HOR/CROF WF4 .... **220** D7
Woolshops Shopping Centre
  HFAX HX1 .... **11** H6
Worsbrough Bank End
  Primary School
  BSLY S70 .... **261** L8
Worsbrough Common
  Primary School
  BSLY S70 .... **261** H8
Worthinghead First School
  LM/WK BD12 .... **148** F3

Worth Valley Middle School
  HWTH BD22 .... **79** J3
Wortley High School
  WOR/ARM LS12 .... **108** B8
Wortley Moor Lane
  Trading Estate
  WOR/ARM LS12 .... **108** D8
WRCC Clinic
  MAR/SLWT HD7 .... **212** F5
Wrenthorpe Health Centre
  WKFDW/WTN WF2 .... **176** A4
Wrenthorpe Primary School
  WKFDW/WTN WF2 .... **176** B4
Wrenthorpe Sports Club
  WKFDW/WTN WF2 .... **176** B3
Wrose Health Centre
  ECHL BD2 .... **105** H1
Wycliffe Middle School
  SHPY BD18 .... **82** C6
Wykebeck Infant School
  OSM LS9 .... **110** F4
Wykebeck Primary School
  OSM LS9 .... **110** F4
Wyke Manor Upper School
  LM/WK BD12 .... **148** F3
Wyke Middle School
  LM/WK BD12 .... **148** E3
Wyther Lane Industrial Estate
  KSTL LS5 .... **108** C3
Wyther Park Primary School
  KSTL LS5 .... **108** B3
Yarnbury RUFC
  HORS LS18 .... **85** J3
Yeadon Airport
  Industrial Estate
  YEA LS19 .... **63** G5
Yeadon Cemetery
  YEA LS19 .... **62** E6

Yeadon Cricket Club
  YEA LS19 .... **62** E7
Yeadon Health Centre
  YEA LS19 .... **62** D7
Yeadon Westfield Junior School
  YEA LS19 .... **62** B8
York Road Industrial Estate
  WBY LS22 .... **30** B8
Yorkshire Amateurs FC
  CHAL LS7 .... **88** B8
Yorkshire Bank Sports Ground
  AL/HA/HU LS17 .... **87** M4
Yorkshire CCC
  (Headingley Cricket Ground)
  HDGY LS6 .... **108** F2
Yorkshire Clinic
  BGLY BD16 .... **81** L7
Yorkshire Martyrs
  Collegiate School
  BOW BD4 .... **128** C6
Yorkshire Post Sports Club
  BHP/TINH LS16 .... **86** E7
Yorkshire Sculpture Park
  HOR/CROF WF4 .... **219** G7
Yorkshire Television Studios
  BVRD LS3 .... **109** G5
Young Street Industrial Estate
  GIR BD8 .... **104** B6
Zakaria Muslim Girls
  High School
  BTLY WF17 .... **173** M2

Notes

Notes

Notes